EXPLORATIONS IN GENERAL THEORY IN SOCIAL SCIENCE

EXPLORATIONS IN GENERAL THEORY IN SOCIAL SCIENCE

Essays in Honor of Talcott Parsons

Edited by

Jan J. Loubser

Rainer C. Baum

Andrew Effrat

Victor Meyer Lidz

VOLUME ONE

THE FREE PRESS

A Division of Macmillan Publishing Co., Inc.

NEW YORK

Collier Macmillan Publishers

LONDON

The Free Press
A Division of Macmillan Publishing Co., Inc.
866 Third Avenue, New York, N.Y. 10022

Collier Macmillan Canada, Ltd.

Library of Congress Catalog Card Number: 75–8427

Printed in the United States of America

printing number

1 2 3 4 5 6 7 8 9 10

Library of Congress Cataloging in Publication Data
Main entry under title:

Explorations in general theory in social science.

  Includes bibliographical references and index.
   1. Sociology--Methodology--Addresses, essays, lectures.
2. Parsons, Talcott, 1902-   --Addresses, essays,
lectures. I. Parsons, Talcott, 1902-   II. Loubser, Jan J.
HM24.E87   301'.01   75-8427
ISBN 0-02-919370-2 (v. 1)
ISBN 0-02-919381-8

COPYRIGHT ACKNOWLEDGMENTS

Quotations from the following titles are reprinted with the permission of The Free Press, A Division of Macmillan Publishing Co., Inc.:

Talcott Parsons, *The Structure of Social Action* (1937, 1965); Allen & Unwin, Ltd.

Talcott Parsons, *Essays in Sociological Theory* (1949, 1954)

Talcott Parsons, *The Social System* (1951)

Talcott Parsons, *Structure and Process in Modern Societies* (1960)

Talcott Parsons, *Social Structure and Personality* (1964)

Talcott Parsons, *Sociological Theory and Modern Society* (1967)

Talcott Parsons, *Politics and Social Structure* (1969)

Talcott Parsons and Robert F. Bales, *Family, Socialization and Interaction Process* (1955); Routledge & Kegan-Paul, Ltd.

Talcott Parsons, Robert F. Bales, and Edward A. Shils, *Working Papers in the Theory of Action* (1953)

Talcott Parsons and Alexander M. Henderson (trans.), *Max Weber: The Theory of Social and Economic Organization* (1954)

Talcott Parsons, Edward Shils, Kaspar D. Naegele, and Jesse R. Pitts, *Theories of Society* (1961)

Talcott Parsons and Neil J. Smelser, *Economy and Society* (1956); Routledge & Kegan-Paul, Ltd.

CONTENTS

VOLUME ONE

Preface   xi

About the Editors   xiii

About the Contributors   xv

GENERAL INTRODUCTION *Jan J. Loubser*   1

PART I: META-THEORY

Introduction *Rainer C. Baum* and *Victor Meyer Lidz*   26

Chapter 1 **On the Meaning of the Theory of Action** *Enno Schwanenberg* 35

Chapter 2 **Functional Methodology in the Theory of Action** *F. van Zyl Slabbert* 46

Chapter 3 **Methodological Dilemmas in Social Science** *Leon Mayhew*   59

Chapter 4 **The Values Problem in Social Science in Developmental Perspective** *Jan J. Loubser* 75

Chapter 5 **On the Foundations of the Theory of Action in Whitehead and Parsons** *Thomas J. Fararo* 90

PART II: GENERAL ACTION ANALYSIS

Introduction *Victor Meyer Lidz*   124

Chapter 6 **Toward a Study of Interpretation in Psychoanalysis** *Marshall Edelson* 151

Chapter 7 **Science as a Cultural System** *Thomas J. Fararo*   182

Chapter 8 **Piaget's Psychology of Intelligence and the Theory of Action** *Charles W. Lidz* and *Victor Meyer Lidz.* 195

Chapter 9 **Action and Experience** *Jan J. Loubser*   240

Chapter 10 **Expressive Symbolism** *James L. Peacock*   264

Chapter 11 **The "Emergence-Constitution Process" and the Theory of Action** *Thomas F. O'Dea* 277

Chapter 12 **The Hobbesian Problem in Marx and Parsons** *John O'Neill*   295

PART III: SOCIALIZATION

Introduction *Victor Meyer Lidz*   310

Chapter 13   **An Analysis of the Phases of Development in Self-Analytic Groups** *Thomas J. Cottle*   328

Chapter 14   **Norms and Behavior** *Francesca M. Cancian*   354

Chapter 15   **The Millenarian Movement Organization as a Socialization Agency** *Jesse R. Pitts*   367

Chapter 16   **The Hippie Movement as a Socialization Agency** *Jesse R. Pitts*   377

Chapter 17   **Toward a Psychosociological Theory of Aspirations** *Guy Rocher*   391

Chapter 18   **Inadequacy, Instrumental Activism, and the Adolescent Subculture** *Jackson Toby*   407

Chapter 19   **Family Structure and Socialization** *Terrence S. Turner*   415

Index   i

VOLUME TWO
The Companion Volume

Preface

About the Editors

About the Contributors

PART IV: GENERALIZED MEDIA IN ACTION

Introduction *Rainer C. Baum*

Chapter 20   **Systems Analysis, Macrosociology, and the Generalized Media of Social Action** *Mark Gould*

Chapter 21   **Generalized Media and the Problem of Contingency** *Niklas Luhmann*

Chapter 22   **Communication and Media** *Rainer C. Baum*

Chapter 23   **Penury and Deficit, or the Problems of Political Underutilization** *François Bourricaud*

Chapter 24   **On Societal Media Dynamics** *Rainer C. Baum*

Chapter 25   **The Mass Media, Ideology, and Community Standards** *Harry M. Johnson*

Chapter 26   **The Medium Is Not the Message** *Bliss C. Cartwright* and *R. Stephen Warner*

PART V: SOCIAL CHANGE AND DEVELOPMENT

Introduction *Andrew Effrat*

Chapter 27 **Growth, Development, and Structural Change of the Social System** *Ken'ichi Tominaga*

Chapter 28 **Societal Attributes and International Relations** *Roland Robertson*

Chapter 29 **Ideology and Modernization** *Dietrich Rueschemeyer*

Chapter 30 **Partial Modernization** *Dietrich Rueschemeyer*

Chapter 31 **Medical Evolution** *Renée C. Fox*

Chapter 32 **On Historical Continuity and Social Change in Modernization** *S. N. Eisenstadt*

PART VI: ORGANIZATIONAL ANALYSIS

Introduction *Andrew Effrat*

Chapter 33 **The Organization as a Component in the Structure of Society** *R. Jean Hills*

Chapter 34 **The Public School as a Type of Organization** *R. Jean Hills*

Chapter 35 **The Organizational Structure of Schools and School Systems** *Robert Dreeben*

Chapter 36 **Science as a Profession and Scientific Professionalism** *Joseph Ben-David*

Chapter 37 **The Structure of Professional Help** *Charles E. Bidwell*

Index

PREFACE

This tribute to Talcott Parsons has been long in coming into print. First conceived in 1968, contributions were invited in 1969 and most were completed and edited before the end of 1971. Successive appropriate target dates for publication—1972, coinciding with Parsons' seventieth birthday; 1973, when he retired from Harvard—came and passed without the end in sight. Perhaps the best *ex post facto* rationale for the date achieved is the twenty-fifth anniversary of *The Social System* or the American bicentennial! But *any* year is appropriate for a tribute to Talcott Parsons, which The Free Press, the publisher of most of his books, well realized as it met every contingency with ingenuity and efficiency.

The inspiration and object of dedication of this book is Talcott Parsons, a social scientist of rare distinction. A professed "incurable theorist," he is equally well known for some lasting empirical insights and analyses. A highly productive researcher, he is also remembered vividly as a splendid teacher by those who have had the privilege of studying with him, as have each of the editors and most of the contributors. His work, more than that of any other contemporary figure, has profoundly influenced the intellectual bases of modern social science in several disciplines. This compendium is the second to appear in his honor and is unlikely to be the last.*

This is a book by students of the theory of action, as Parsons' theoretical corpus has become known. Some of the contributors have not been students of Talcott Parsons in the personal sense but students of his work, the theory of action. These "explorations" are intended to illustrate, if not prove, the usefulness of the maps of a master "cartographer" even in territory not before charted in detail. If some of the contributions question some of the most basic aspects of the theory of action, they do so in the intellectual tradition and inquiring spirit of Talcott Parsons. As such, they are tributes to him of no less magnitude than those reflecting a more direct acceptance of his formulations. They equally demonstrate the vitality of the theory of action and the dynamics of theoretical action or action oriented to theory. The extraordinary diversity of these contributions reflects the active interest of a new generation of social scientists in sustaining a high level of discourse on and investigation of the basic issues that Talcott Parsons has articulated with greater theoretical sophistication than was possible before the theory of action.**

The usual observation that "this book would not have been possible without the help and co-operation of so and so" would sound even more pedantic in this case. But special thanks are in order: The contributors showed great patience with our editorial prescriptions and suggestions as well as with the inordinate but inevitable delays in publication. The fact that most of their contributions were completed by the end of 1971 does not in any way detract from their importance. However, the reader should be aware of this obvious explanation for the lack of references to relevant works published since 1971.

We honor the memory of Thomas O'Dea, who did not live to see the publication of the book.

At The Free Press we had the good fortune to work with James Cron in the early stages and with

---

*The first was Alex Inkeles and Bernard Barber (eds.), *Stability and Social Change* (Boston: Little, Brown, 1973).

**For the most up-to-date bibliography of Talcott Parsons, see Talcott Parsons and Charles Martel, *Dialogues with Parsons* (New York: The Free Press, forthcoming).

Charlie Smith in the final, critical stages. Both of them were most supportive in what even to them as seasoned editors was an undertaking of unusual proportions. The production editor, Bob Harrington, guided us through the various editing stages with great skill and perseverance.

Victor Meyer Lidz wishes to acknowledge the support of the Department of Sociology of the University of Chicago and especially its chairman at the time, Morris Janowitz, in arranging for time free of teaching obligations that greatly facilitated his participation in the editorial tasks.

J.J.L.
R.C.B.
A.E.
V.M.L.

ABOUT THE EDITORS

Loubser, Jan J. Born in South Africa in 1932, he is Director of the Social Science Research Council of Canada since 1974. He was Professor of Sociology, University of Cape Town, South Africa, and taught at the University of Toronto and the Ontario Institute for Studies in Education. He is a former President of the Canadian Sociology and Anthropology Association. He is author of *The Impact of Industrial Conversion and Workers' Attitudes to Change* and *The York County Board: A Study in Educational Innovation,* as well as articles on moral action, values, and social change.

Baum, Rainer C. Born in Breslau, then Germany, in 1934, he is Associate Professor of Sociology at the University of Pittsburgh, having previously been associated with the University of Toronto and the University of British Columbia. A general sociologist with interests in theory, comparative nation-building, and stratification, he is currently engaged in cross-national comparative research on modernization problems. He is the author or coauthor of articles in *Sociological Inquiry, The Indian Journal of Social Research,* and *Aging and Human Development* (1975) and in books edited by Edward Harvey, Walter Gerson, and Stanton Wheeler.

Effrat, Andrew Born in New York City in 1939, he is Associate Professor of Sociology in Education at the Ontario Institute for Studies in Education in Toronto and has also taught at Harvard and at Haverford College. He is Editor of *Sociological Inquiry* and has edited special issues of the journal on *Applications of Parsonian Theory, Perspectives in Political Sociology,* and *Critiques of Modern Culture and Consciousness.* He is also Editor of *Interchange: A Journal of Educational Studies.*

Lidz, Victor Meyer Born in Baltimore, Maryland, in 1941, he is currently Lecturer in the Department of Sociology of the University of Pennsylvania. Previously, he served as an Instructor in Sociology and the Collegiate Division of the Social Sciences at the University of Chicago. As an undergraduate and graduate student at Harvard University, he began study of the theory of action in Talcott Parsons' courses. His publications include contributions to the journal, *Sociological Inquiry,* "The Gift of Life and Its Reciprocation" (with Talcott Parsons and Renée C. Fox) in *Social Research,* and *Readings on Premodern Societies* (coeditor with Talcott Parsons).

ABOUT THE CONTRIBUTORS

Cancian, Francesca M. Born in New York City in 1937, she is Assistant Professor of Sociology at Stanford University. She has taught also at Harvard and Cornell universities. Among her publications are *What Are Norms? A Study of Beliefs and Action in a Maya Community* and articles on functional analysis and family interaction published in the *American Sociological Review* and other journals.

Cottle, Thomas J. Born in Chicago in 1937, he is affiliated with the Children's Defense Fund of the Washington Research Project. A sociologist and practicing clinical psychologist, he has taught at Harvard and M.I.T. and has been a fellow at the Center for Advanced Study at the University of Illinois. His books include *Time's Children; The Abandoners; The Prospect of Youth; The Voices of School; The Present of Things Future* (coauthor); *Out of Discontent* (coauthor); *Black Children, White Dreams; A Family Album;* and *Life Time: An Inquiry Into Perceptions of Time.*

Edelson, Marshall Born in Chicago in 1928, he is Associate Professor of Psychiatry at Yale University. He is also a graduate and member of The Western New England Institute for Psychoanalysis. He is the author of *The Termination of Intensive Psychotherapy; Ego Psychology, Group Dynamics and the Therapeutic Community, Sociotherapy and Psychotherapy; The Practice of Sociotherapy: A Case Study; The Idea of a Mental Illness; Language and Interpretation in Psychoanalysis;* and *Language and Dreams: The Interpretation of Dreams Revisited (The Psychoanalytic Study of the Child,* Vol. 27).

Fararo, Thomas J. Born in New York City in 1933, he is Professor of Sociology at the University of Pittsburgh. He is coauthor of *A Study of a Biased Friendship Net* and author of *Mathematical Sociology: An Introduction to Fundamentals.* He has contributed to formal theory appearing in *General Systems; Sociological Methodology; Sociological Theories in Progress;* and other professional publications.

Lidz, Charles W. Born in Baltimore, Maryland, in 1946, he is Assistant Professor of Psychiatry and Sociology at the University of Pittsburgh and has previously been a Research Associate in the Department of Psychiatry at Yale University. He is the author of articles on police work, heroin addiction, and other subjects and coauthor of *Connections: Notes from the Heroin World* and a forthcoming volume, *At the Public Scaffold: The Dynamics of the Drug Crisis.*

Mayhew, Leon Born in Ogden, Utah, in 1935, he is Professor of Sociology at the University of California, Davis. He was formerly with the University of Michigan and has served as visiting professor at the University of California, Berkeley. He is Editor of *The American Sociologist* and author of *Law and Equal Opportunity; Society;* and articles and essays in the sociology of law.

O'Dea, Thomas F. Born in Amesbury, Massachusetts, in 1915, he died in 1974, in Santa Barbara, where he was Professor of Sociology and Religious Studies at the University of California. He authored many publications, including *The Mormons; American Catholic Dilemma; The Sociology of Religion; Alienation, Atheism, and the Religious Crisis;* and more than forty articles in journals, encyclopedias, and anthologies. He received many honors during his career, the most recent being election to the American Academy of Arts and Sciences in 1972.

O'Neill, John Born in London, England, in 1933, he is Professor of Sociology at York University and has taught at the New School, Stanford University, and San Jose State college. He is on the editorial boards of the *International Journal of Comparative Sociology,* the *International Journal for Contemporary Social Theory, The Canadian Journal of Sociology, Philosophy of the Social Sciences,* and the *Human Context.* His more than 50 books, articles, and reviews in philosophy, sociology, and related disciplines include the books *Perception, Expression and History: The Social Phenomonology of Merleau-Ponty; Sociology as a Skin Trade: Essays towards a Reflexive Sociology; Making Sense Together, An Introduction to Wild Sociology;* and *Modes of Individualism and Collectivism.* He has translated and edited *Studies on Marx and Hegel* by John Hyppolite and several works by Maurice Merleau-Ponty: *Humanism and Terror: An Essay on the Communist Problem; Themes from the Lectures at the Collège de France, 1952– 1960; The Prose of the World;* and *Phenomenology, Language and Sociology.*

Peacock, James L. Born in Montgomery, Alabama, in 1937, he is Professor of Anthropology at the University of North Carolina, having previously taught at Princeton and the University of California at San Diego. His publications include *Rites of Modernization: Symbolic and Social Aspects of Indonesian Proletarian Drama; The Human Direction* (coauthor); *Indonesia: Anthropological Perspectives;* and *Consciousness and Change: Symbolic Anthropology in Evolutionary Perspective.*

Pitts, Jesse R. Born in East-Palestine, Ohio, in 1921, he is Professor of Sociology at Oakland University, Rochester, Michigan. He is Director of the Social Justice and Corrections Program at Oakland University and is engaged in the study of mass movements. He is coauthor of *In Search of France* and coeditor with Talcott Parsons, Edward Shils, and Kasper Naegele of *Theories of Society.*

Rocher, Guy Born in Berthierville, Quebec, Canada, in 1924, he is Professor of Sociology at the Université de Montréal, after having taught at the Université Laval. He has also been on various boards and commissions of the Canadian and Quebec governments. He is the author, among other works, of *Introduction à la sociologie générale* (which is translated in English under the title *A General Introduction to Sociology: A Theoretical Perspective); Talcott Parsons et la sociologie Américaine;* and a book of essays on Quebec and Canada: *Le Québec en mutation.* Also, he coedited *Ecole et société au Québec.*

Schwanenberg, Enno Born in Bonn, Germany, in 1938, he is Professor of Social Psychology at Johann Wolfgang Goethe-Universitat in Frankfurt/Main. He is the author of *Soziales Handeln— Die Theorie und ihr Problem* and coauthor of *Psychoanalyse als Sozialwissenschaft* and has contributed to psychological as well as sociological journals. Currently, he is working in the general area of affect relations in behavior and interaction.

Slabbert, F. Van Zyl   Born in South Africa in 1940, he is at present the Member for Rondebosch for the Progressive Party in the South African Parliament. He has a D. Phil. from the University of Stellenbosch, South Africa, and taught as Senior Lecturer at the University of Stellenbosch and the University of Cape Town and as Professor of Sociology at the University of Witwatersrand, Johannesburg. He is the author of several critical articles on aspects of South African society.

Toby, Jackson   Born in New York City in 1925, he is Professor of Sociology at Rutgers University. His recent publications include *Contemporary Society; Delinquency* (with Adam Scrupski and William Donahue); *Social Problems in America* (with Harry C. Bredemeier); and "Socialization and Control of Deviant Motivation" in Daniel Glaser (ed.), *Handbook of Criminology*. He is now working on a cross-cultural study of societies, as well as on an editorial revision of the two short volumes on societal evolution by Talcott Parsons, *Societies: Evolutionary and Comparative Perspectives* and *The System of Modern Societies*. Recently he assisted in the editing of Parsons and Platt, *The American University*.

Turner, Terrence S.   At present Associate Professor of Anthropology at the University of Chicago, he formerly taught at Cornell University, Centro Latino-Americana de Pesquisas em Ciencias Sociais, Rio de Janeiro, and the University of California, Santa Cruz, and was a fellow at the Center for Advanced Study in the Behavioral Sciences, Palo Alto. His main interests are structural analysis of myth, ritual, and other symbolic forms; kinship and social structure of tribal societies; effects of economic, strategic, and social expansion of Brazil upon indigenous societies of Amazonia; transnational corporations and their effects upon indigenous peoples; and other social elements in Third World countries. He is author of several articles and of *The Fire of the Jaguar*.

EXPLORATIONS
IN GENERAL THEORY
IN SOCIAL SCIENCE

GENERAL INTRODUCTION

Jan J. Loubser

The idea of a collection of essays in honor of Talcott Parsons needs no brief. His stature in modern sociology and other social sciences is self-evident and unparalleled. Lesser men have received similar honors. There are, of course, the particularistic as well as the universalistic reasons why we took this initiative.

As former students of Professor Parsons, we all stand in some particularistic relationship to him. We have had the privilege of studying with him, which somehow is a more apt phrase for describing Professor Parsons' relations to his students than simply "being his students." Of course, we all had other teachers, but Professor Parsons was a most unusual mentor. His genuine interest in, concern for, and taneous recognition of these admirable qualities, generosity toward his students are legendary. Spon-often rare among professors, was the constant refrain in the brief statements made by spokesmen of successive generations of students at the farewell dinner in honor of Professor Parsons arranged by the Departments of Sociology and Social Relations at Harvard in May of 1973. One always had the feeling that Parsons treats one as an intellectual equal; that he assumes that one can with equal facility scale the heights of abstraction and soar down to swoop up a relevant fact, that one is equally at home in Weber, Freud, and Durkheim; in ancient Rome, China, the Middle Ages, and early American history. While this was sometimes frustrating, especially when an interview would stay on cloud seven while one's particular intellectual problem was on cloud two and give the impression of complete imperviousness to the ordinary orbits of most mortal minds, the connections, critical insights, and fourth-order relationships would usually dawn on one some time

later. One was grateful and felt that the trust was not misplaced.

The counterpart of this in Parsons is his generosity in recognizing the insights, ideas, and other contributions of students. He usually recognized an important insight long before its author had any idea that it was anything more than an ordinary observation, and he would always give full credit in lectures and writings. Although Parsons usually does his own writing, when he doesn't his helper usually gets full recognition as co-author or otherwise; hence the long series of collaborative efforts in his bibliography.

If one doesn't know Parsons well enough, a little bit of cynicism might lead one to conclude that this willingness to collaborate is perhaps a calculated strategy for winning students over to the cause. But he has never been interested in building a school in the European tradition. He is dedicated to the task of building general social science theory; and in searching for empirical and analytical clues in this gargantuan task, he has recognized the contributions of a whole range of scholars from biologists to theologians, many of whom would hardly know his name. He conveyed to one his enthusiasm for this task and gave students very early the feeling that, whatever interests they pursued, they could contribute to the task. Hence one soon developed the capacity to separate the man Talcott Parsons from the theory of action. The theory was something quite separate on which Parsons was working, but which he treated so objectively that one felt that he would appreciate one's doing the same. The result was that students of Parsons or his assistants soon became collaborators building on something that was only indirectly connected with the man and by no means his possession or exclusive territory. No wonder then that those who could most legitimately be called Parsonians never thought of themselves as such until they were exposed to the outside observer circle of discourse, and they never thought of the theory of action as Parsonian theory.

The outline of this introduction was extensively discussed with Rainer Baum and benefited very much by it, as well as by comments from him and the other two editors. They do not necessarily agree with the viewpoints of the author.

1

Although we do not object to being called Parsonians—except to the extent that the label has acquired many extrascientific connotations and is being used as a bogey adversely to influence students and professional opinion—we strongly prefer to be seen as collaborators of Parsons or simply workers on the theory of action. This is in line with Parsons' own approach, it does not have the "school" connotation, and it helps to separate the theory from the man in the minds of people. This later aspect is rather important and one of the main reasons that we still prefer to work within the framework of the theory of action.

A theory is a set of concepts linked together by a system of interrelated propositions. It exists independently of any individual mind, even the one that originated it, or any collection of minds. As a cultural system it is subject to a whole range of actions in relation to it, ranging from ritual affirmation or denial to rigorous logical construction or destruction. The critical point is that no theory as a complex general statement about reality springs full-grown from the mind of any one man, however brilliant and however dedicated his efforts. Thus Parsons' latest general theoretical statement is an eloquent confession that, close to the end of a highly productive lifetime dedicated to this task, much remains to be done even in following through the logical implications of the main features of the general synthesis he has been able to identify.[1] Note that Parsons is optimistic and confident but that he has no delusions of grandeur or illusions about the magnitude of the remaining tasks.

In brief, then, we are working with the theory of action because we share Parsons' conviction that the development of general social science theory is a task to which some people must pay special attention. We share his conviction that the theory of action provides a framework for the development of such a theory. We also share his recognition that such a task is bigger than any one person and that only a concerted effort on the part of many to build, to test, and to consider all the evidence will develop such a theory, which soon would supersede the level reached by any one of them. Hence when we work with the theory of action, we look critically at what Talcott Parsons or any one else has to say about it or some aspect of it. We operate on the assumption that Parsons' formulations are not necessarily correct or more valid than those of any other worker, and we challenge his formulations as we challenge each other's. This is not to deny that a man of Parsons' stature has much more influence on what other people define as the theory of action than so many upstarts. Yet the nature of the scientific task requires that we maintain a rigorous scepticism with respect

to such influence and do not accept anything "just because Parsons says so." As several of the essays in this volume will show, there has been serious work deviating rather radically from Parsons' formulations. We are certain that no one will consider them more seriously than Parsons himself; and it is our sincere hope that this book, in honoring him, will stand as a landmark in the recognition of the fact that the theory of action is more than simply Parsonian theory. We are certain that we can pay him no greater tribute.

We started out with some particularistic reasons for this book. As we went along they became imperceptibly more universalistic, which is not necessarily incompatible with Parsons' insistence on the dichotomous logical structure of the pattern variables. Now we wish to deal briefly with the more universalistic reasons that we prefer to work with the theory of action, because they account for the nature of this book, not just its existence. It is part of the work on the theory of action, not an unstructured opportunity for all and sundry to pay their respects to a great man with whom they happened to be acquainted. We have asked contributors to explore some problem in the theory of action and its applications.

The following sections of this general introduction offer some considerations that attempt to account for the fact that so many people work with and on the theory of action. Some of us probably do it out of sheer inertia of past experience; others dynamically transform that experience into their own bag of tricks, their own inimitable style and approach; still others have come across it tangentially, have latched on to it, and have brought to it new perspectives. But all of us probably subject our intellectual commitments to scrutiny in terms of the standards and criteria that distinguish a community of scientific discourse from a social club or a tradition, or for that matter a "school." Hence we believe that a strong case can be made in terms of these scientific considerations for continued endeavor to develop the theory of action. Of course, we would be naive to overlook the rationalization or justification aspects of such an exercise; but then, we do confess to be ordinary mortals—symbol-using animals continuously attempting to construct meaning out of the ceaseless flow of our social existence. Let him who has managed to escape this human condition cast the first stone. . . .

ANALYTICAL REALISM

One of the major influences on Talcott Parsons and the development of the theory of action was the philosopher Alfred Whitehead.[2] Because the influence was formal rather than substantive, its importance is less often recognized than the influence of those whose substantive theories had an impact on him: Weber, Durkheim, Pareto, and Freud. Yet without the methodological insights that largely rely upon Whitehead, it is doubtful that Parsons would have achieved the synthesis of *The Structure of Social Action.*

The central achievement of that book was to isolate from four different theories, studied as empirical phenomena in themselves, the common analytical elements, namely nonrational factors in action. This was possible only because Parsons concentrated on the conceptual elements of the theories and analyzed them, instead of "letting the theories speak for themselves." Hence he could identify the common conceptual elements behind diverse terminologies that are the empirical phenomena of theories, the so-called facts. The significance Parsons could impute to the emergence of these common elements was entirely derived from his own analytical conceptual approach, the cornerstone or frame of reference of the theory of action.

Parsons called his epistemological stance "analytical realism" and justified it in terms of its ability to overcome the weaknesses of both nominalism and realism, much as his voluntaristic theory would overcome the weaknesses of both positivism and idealism. While with Whitehead he rejected the reification involved in empirical realism, he was equally dissatisfied with the relativistic "fictionalism" of nominalism. He thus rejected the common-sense descriptive concepts of both idealist and positivist empiricism as well as Weber's attempt to overcome the former by the "fictional" ideal-type methodology.[3] In his view, scientific conceptualization had to proceed by analytical abstraction, identifying essential elements of phenomena and relating them systematically to each other through logico-empirical methods, as Pareto had already seen. Such systems of analytical concepts, related to each other in logical interdependence would grasp, in Parsons' opinion, the essential features of the social reality that social scientists endeavor to understand. As Parsons emphasized, "There is no implication that the value of any one such element, or even all those included in one logically coherent system, is completely descriptive of any particular concrete thing or event."[4]

This epistemological or metatheoretical position is absolutely central to a full understanding and correct interpretation of Parsons' work and the theory of action in general. Systems of action, social systems, and the like are analytical systems consisting of analytical abstractions from concrete reality, not descriptions of any such reality. As Parsons has pointed out, following Whitehead, the greatest weakness of empiricism is the fallacy of misplaced concreteness. It will not be difficult to demonstrate that most of the criticism of the theory of action prevalent in the secondary literature stems from failure to avoid this pitfall and in some form or other is based on the fallacy of misplaced concreteness. Concern about an overemphasis on order, the so-called static bias, the incapacity of the theory to deal with conflict and change, the oversocialized concept of man, all these "problems" derive to a large extent from failure to adhere to analytical realism, judging the theory by empirical realistic standards.[5] It is, of course, not all the fault of the critics. Parsons himself has not consistently adhered to analytical realism and has fallen on occasion into the same fallacy. The same caution applies to the work of other theorists of action.

Reification is as much a problem in scientific theory as it is in religious symbolism and symbolic processes in general. The tendency to concretize symbols seems endemic in the human condition, and in scientific theory the problem of achieving proper levels of analytical abstraction seems comparable to and at least as formidable as the problem of objectivity. Yet we have far fewer effective ways of dealing with it.

Parsons' pragmatic strategy in building the theory of action steered a middle course between the Scylla of pure abstract analytical theory and the Charybdis of empirical realism.[6] Yet it resulted in the uneven and sometimes inconsistent development of the general theory and at times fell into reification, especially towards the concrete reality or empirical theory most familiar to him. The prime example is social systems theory in its heavy reliance on societies as empirical phenomena, particularly American society, and in parts on economic theory as empirical theory.

We do not have easy answers to these problems, nor do we point them out for the sake of being critical. We wish to register an awareness of problems in the development of the theory of action which have a lot to do with its critical reception. The epistemological strategy of analytical realism seems to us to be the most promising in dealing with these problems. But it needs to be specified into a set of procedures or methodological guidelines for analytic conceptualization, abstraction, classification, categorization, and operationalization. We need intersubjectively valid procedures for the development of analytical theory as well as for its application to empirical reality in order to achieve greater levels of reliability in the identification of essential analytical elements, the level at which they operate, and the appropriate empirical indices for them. Analytical realism provides only the general approach; as with other action

phenomena it needs to be translated into more specific operational standards before we will be able to
achieve cumulative, systematic development and
application of the theory of action.

THE ACTION FRAME OF REFERENCE

While the epistemological position of analytical
realism provides a safeguard against the endemic
fallacy of misplaced concreteness, the action frame
of reference provides a safeguard against the range
of reductionist fallacies that have plagued social
theory for so long.

In *Theories of Society,* Parsons claimed that there
was general consensus on the usefulness of the action
frame of reference in general theory.[7] This claim
will, of course, not go undisputed, but it is probably
justified to suggest that the burden of proof clearly
rests upon those who wish to contest it. The frame of
reference involves a number of assumptions about
the aspects of human behavior that need to be taken
into account in a general theory.[8] We do not consider it necessary to spell out all these assumptions
in detail here. Suffice it to say that the critical assumption still remains the voluntaristic postulate,
first formulated in *The Structure of Social Action.*
The empirical basis for the voluntaristic postulate
has certainly been conclusively established in that
classic analytical study of mainstream theories and,
contrary to the assertions of some critics,[9] has
remained central to the theory of action.

The assumption that, for general theoretical purposes, it is necessary to take both the actor and the
situation of action into account rejects the general
usefulness of confining analysis to either the one or
the other. This basic duality is not a static one in
which the relationship is reducible to a single mode,
such as rationality on the part of the actor. Rather,
the actor is seen as in constant tension with the situation, as striving to achieve a particular goal state vis-
à-vis the situation. This goal state cannot be assumed
to be universal for all human actors, either as being
rationally determined or as having random variations
as in the utilitarian assumption of the randomness of
wants. The voluntaristic postulate states that action
involves an effort on the part of the actor to achieve
or maintain a goal state in relation to his situation.
The goal state is defined in terms of the motivational
needs of the actor, the normative standards accepted
implicitly or explicitly as applicable in this type of
action, and the conceptions of the desirable meaning
of the object of this type of action as well as the ability of the actor to achieve the goal state. Effort is
channelled and hence action structured by the *combination* of "choices" or "decisions" the actor makes
with respect to these four components.

In making these "decisions" the actor takes into
account the situation in which he acts, in terms of the
meaning that it has for his action in relation to the
desired goal state. The critical point is that the goal
state is situation-specific, defined in relation to the
situation as defined by the actor. The action will,
therefore, be partly determined by the situation in a
variety of ways that have to be taken into account
for general theoretical purposes. First, some aspects
of the situation will constitute limiting conditions
over which the actor cannot, sees himself as unable
to, gain control for the purposes of attaining his goal
state. These aspects will condition the goal state, as
it has to be adjusted to these irreducible limiting conditions. The aspects of the situation over which the
actor can gain control for the purposes of his action
become part of his action and hence constitutive of
the goal state. Parsons defined the aspects of the
situation over which the actor has control as means,
but this seems too narrow a definition and has been
dropped in later formulations.[10]

Although situations in which there are no other
actors are conceivable and do exist empirically, they
are seen as limiting cases. The general case for
theoretical purposes is the situation in which there
are one or more other actors either physically present
or seen by the actor as part of his definition of the
situation. Action in social situations is, therefore,
the general case; and hence the theory of action is
primarily concerned with social action, that is, action
in relation to other actors. When the action of the
other actors in the situation becomes a factor in the
action of the actor, we have to do with interaction.
Again, it is assumed to be the general case that actors
must take into account the action of other actors in
their situation.

It is a fundamental assumption of the theory of
action that such a social situation is fraught with
contingencies that have to be resolved if the actors
are to attain their goal states. The Hobbesian problem
of order is only a partial statement of these contingencies. Given the voluntaristic postulate, there are
at least seven sources of conflict or a "war of all
against all." First, there is the contingency of actors
having different symbolic representations of objects;
hence there is a problem of communication or symbolic order. Second, there is the contingency of all
actors acting at the same time; hence there is a problem of temporal order. Third, there is the contingency of the actors assigning unique or conflicting
meanings to symbolic representations of objects;
hence there is a problem of meaning. Fourth, there
is the contingency that all actors would make claims
on the same aspects of the situation for the attainment of their goal states; hence there is the problem
of the scarcity of situational resources or of economic
order. Fifth, there is the contingency of the action

of each actor interfering with the attainment of the goal state of every other actor; hence there is a problem of control over the action of others or of political order. Sixth, there is the contingency of conflicting or otherwise incompatible normative standards for action among all actors; hence there is a problem of normative order. Seventh, there is the contingency that the motivational needs of the actors may be incompatible, conflicting, or mutually exclusive; hence there is a problem of motivational order.

The general theory of action is, in essence, an attempt to account for the fact that social action does occur and that actors do attain their goal states at least some of the time, in spite of all these problems or contingencies. Systems of action are seen as mechanisms of contingency reduction, not of contingency elimination.

In so far as these contingencies are irreduceable, they remain part of the human condition, the ultimate environment of all systems of action.

The action frame of reference should then be stated in contingent form: To the extent that action is symbolically mediated, is time phased, involves shared meanings of objects, involves accepted allocation of scarce resources, involves accepted control over the action of other actors, involves shared normative standards, and is compatible with the motivational needs of actors, these contingencies are reduced to manageable levels and empirical systems of action develop. Although an empirical system of action may solve these problems in a particular situation, it may not do so in another; or the introduction of a new element into the same situation which increases or creates contingencies beyond the capacity of the mechanisms of contingency reduction of the system may disrupt or destroy the system or lead to its change. Also, the existence of a plurality of empirical systems of action implies the continued existence of these contingencies *among systems* and may actually aggravate them to the extent that emergent levels of more complicated mechanisms of contingency reduction will be required. These fundamental problems or contingencies of action therefore exist not only among actors but also among systems of action.

It should be evident from the preceding that the action frame of reference avoids all forms of reductionism. In principle, action is a many-varied thing; one has to take into account both actor and situation, both values and interests, both norms and motivational needs, both rational and nonrational factors, both heredity and environment. But the analytical nature of this frame of reference must be kept clearly in mind. In practice, or in empirical theory, it does not imply that all factors are significant in contributing to the variance observed. It only forces one to

determine which factors are variables and which ones can heuristically be assumed to be constants or to vary randomly. One of the major fallacies of misplaced concreteness is the expectation that all factors in the frame of reference should feature in all empirical theory in all cases at all times. The position that either these factors are universally potent in explaining variance in all empirical cases or they are not general, as is claimed, clearly confuses analytical generality and empirical generality and as such is an example of reification.

Yet it is one of the major weaknesses of the theory of action that it has not developed replicable procedures for the translation of the analytical framework into empirical theory such as typologies of action, weighting of factors, and different models of explanation. Parsons has been aware of these problems from the start but has not seen it as one of his priorities in developing general theory. A relatively crude example would be to utilize the means-end schema, which featured so centrally in *The Structure of Social Action,* to map out a range of action types from "action oriented to ultimate means" to "action oriented to ultimate ends." One could then plot the differential amounts of variance that rational and nonrational factors respectively could be expected to explain, as in Figure I-1.

Needless to say, the development of empirical theory would be required to verify the myriad of hypotheses implied in the graph. The same kind of hypothetical graph could be drawn for action systems at various stages of development, and so on.

GENERAL ACTION SYSTEMS

Although variation in the salience of the components of action leads to heuristic assumptions about their relevance in specific empirical cases, the theory of action assumes, as we have indicated in the previous section, that action becomes organized in systems containing the components in specified relations of interdependence to each other. The concept of system is thus central to the theory of action.[11]

A system of action is the organization of the components of action into a set of relatively stable mechanisms that reduces the complexity of the contingencies impinging on the achievement of the goal-states of the actors involved. The environment of the system consists in the complex contingencies represented by a plurality of actors. The dimensions of the organization of action systems are derived from the frame of reference. The basic duality of actor and situation requires that a system of action provide mechanisms by which actors can stabilize their orientations to the situation and can relate in reliable and predictable ways to the situation. This is the

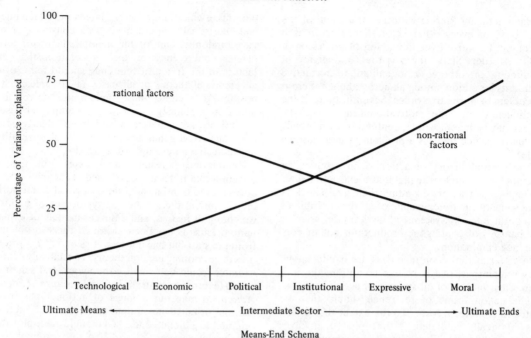

Figure I-1. Hypothetical differential contributions of rational and non-rational factors to the explanation of variance in different types of action.

internal-external dimension of the problems an action system has to solve. The voluntaristic postulate implies that there has to be a temporal order in the expenditure of effort toward solving problems instrumental to the achievement of a goal-state prior to its consummation. This is, then, the *instrumental-consummatory dimension* of system problems.

The matrix resulting from the cross-classification of these two fundamental dimensions defines the four system problems of action systems and constitutes the four-function paradigm:[12]

This paradigm involves several propositions about the relations among the components of action, the functional subsystems of action, and the action system and its environment. First, the components of action are seen as functionally specialized with functional primacies assigned as follows: Values: L; norms: I; goals: G; facilities: A.[13] Each of the functional subsystems of action in turn are seen as composed of the four components functionally

specialized according to the system problems. The functional analysis of action systems therefore requires a basic analytical model with at least two levels of functional specialization, resulting in a sixteen-fold matrix rather than the simple four-fold one.

These functional problems represent a minimal set in Parsons' view. The seven problems listed in the previous section seem to fit into this framework. First, the problem of symbolic order or communication is represented in the basic assumption that all action is symbolically mediated. In action systems the symbolic medium or media would play a special role in defining the boundaries of the system vis-à-vis its environment. The problem of temporal order relates to the voluntary postulate and the time dimension of instrumental-consummatory. The problem of meaning of objects would seem to relate most directly to the internal-external dimension where the first-order problem is to assign meanings internal to the system to objects. The four remaining problems would seem to fit the more specific four functional problems in the paradigm: the problem of scarcity of resources (A), the problem of control over others (G), the problem of normative order (I), and the problem of motivational order (L).

The concept of function implies a system that has to cope constantly with variations in its environment and is dependent on regular interchanges with the

	Instrumental	Consummatory
External	Adaptation (A)	Goal-attainment (G)
Internal	Pattern-maintenance (L)	Integration (I)

time dimension ⟶   control dimension ↑

Figure I-2. Four-function paradigm of action systems.

environment. It is thus a relatively open system that depends on the achievement and maintenance of system goal-states vis-à-vis the environment. If these goal-states could be assumed to be systemically given, the system would tend to maintain a stable equilibrium vis-à-vis the environment with disequilibrium resulting only from the time lag between changes in the environment and the operation of automatic equilibrating mechanisms. But the goal-states of action systems are not systemically given. The voluntaristic postulate implies that the goal-states are constantly redefined. The meaning of equilibrium in action systems is hence inherently dynamic, that is, it consists in the achievement of goal-states that cannot be assumed to be constant over any extended time span, certainly not over the lifespan of the system. In fact, the voluntaristic postulate implies that action systems must be seen as in an inherently dialectical relation to their environments in the sense that the achievement of a goal-state in itself leads to a change in the definition of the goal-state and hence creates a new disequilibrium with the environment. If this were not so the development or evolution of action systems would have to be seen as entirely determined by environmental changes.[14]

Parsons sees the four functional problems and the components and subsystems specializing in them as standing in hierarchical relations to each other. He postulates two hierarchies, a hierarchy of control in the LIGA direction and a hierarchy of conditions in the AGIL direction. These postulates are derived from the actor-situation duality in that action on the part of the actor requires control over aspects of the situation and aspects of the situation constitute conditions to the action of the actor to the extent that he is not able to control them. These two postulates are not simple logical corollaries: The one does not imply the other, and both are necessary to specify the relations among the functions.[15]

These postulates have led to some problems of logical inconsistency in the theory of action. The problems can probably be traced back to the fact that the voluntaristic postulate and its instrumental-consummatory derivative have not been taken consistantly into account. Two of the symptoms of these problems are the occasional reversal of A and G and the addition of a mysterious L below A.[16] Perhaps another symptom is the designation of L, which is the highest level of control, as an instrumental problem to the system which does not jibe with the voluntaristic postulate. It is not clear how these problems can be resolved. One possible solution would be to start with the voluntaristic postulate and to treat the instrumental and consummatory

aspects as orthogonal dimensions of the organization of action systems, because means-oriented action and ends-oriented action tend towards opposite poles of the means-end schema and involve fundamentally different types of action components. The actor-situation duality would then imply that each of these two dimensions would have an internal and an external aspect. In this version L-G would be the consummatory dimension and I-A the instrumental dimension. Recently Parsons has developed special theories around the L-G and I-A axes since his insight that the former represents mechanical solidarity and the latter organic solidarity in reinterpreting Durkheim.[17] The axes have also acquired special status in the treatment of the components of action, the pattern variables, and in the interchange paradigm.[18] The designation suggested here provides a more plausible basis for these developments than the one Parsons uses.

The hierarchies would remain the same except that now the ultimate control would be consummatory, as the voluntaristic postulate implies, and integration would become an instrumental problem, as the frame of reference implies. But one could also postulate the diagonals as the primary hierarchical dimensions with the control of consummatory (L-G) over instrumental (I-A) as a further implication. These must remain speculative explorations until their full implications have been worked out.[19]

The empirical implications of these analytical postulates of the hierarchical relations are by no means clear, as we shall see.[20]

Parsons has defined the four subsystems of the general action system as the cultural system (L), the social system (I), the psychological or personality system (G), and the behavioral organism (A).[21] The sense in which cultural systems and behavioral organisms are action systems has not been made very clear nor has their analysis as such been carried very far.[22] Although it is clear that all action systems have cultural, social, psychological, and behavioral organismic aspects, the sense in which these are analytical systems of action is not clear. There is a broad sense of empirical fit between these aspects of action and the four-function paradigm, and Parsons has proceeded to identify them accordingly. However, this choice has foreclosed the development of analytically derived subsystems of action according to the logic of the functional paradigm. For example, all action systems have adaptive subsystems that must be defined analytically and cannot in any meaningful way be reduced or confined to aspects of the behavioral organism. The economy as the adaptive subsystem of society is a good example of this inconsistency; the introduction of emergent overlays of action does not solve the problem. While this development is still awaited, Parsons is using the functional classification to develop the conceptualization of the general action system further by attempting to specify generalized media of interchange and input-output relations among the cultural system, the social system, the personality, and the behavioral organism.[23]

The development of the four-function paradigm and its further specification to the sixteen-fold level has been an important paradigmatic breakthrough from the earlier structural-functional analysis. It has systematized functional theory and has provided the framework for dynamic functional analysis of the structures and processes of action systems in a way that clearly overcomes some of the major weaknesses of the more diffuse popular structural-functionalism.[24]

ACTION RESOURCES AND MEDIA

The components of action, values, norms, goals, and means have to be combined in specific ways to result in action, as we have seen. Actors use these components to constitute and reconstitute the systems or situations in which they act and to redefine their roles and goal-states. The components are therefore resources for action, which have to be available at appropriate levels of specificity to be combined into action.

In action systems these resources are generated, allocated, and utilized by the four subsystems. Their

The resource table identifies seven steps in the specification of action resources, down to the activity level where implementation or action takes place. It is not altogether clear why there are seven levels of specificity or generality, but the model has been repeatedly presented and used.[26] Resource specification is seen to involve three phases: generation, allocation, and utilization. Generation and utilization are each further broken down into three steps. Generation is seen as involving primary, secondary, and tertiary processes, the latter including learning and training.[27] Resources that have been developed to the tertiary level are seen as ready to be allocated. Allocation is a single phase requiring the commitment of a still very general resource, such as motivational capacity for multiple role performance, to a specific functional market. Hence allocation can be seen as the phase in which the resources of action become functionally differentiated or differentially allocated among the four main subsystems of the general action system. Once allocated to one of the four functional subsystems, the further specification of the resource involves utilization within the subsystem to which it was allocated. The three steps of utilization are seen as further allocations of the resource to more specific uses, in the social system case first to a collectivity within the subsystem, then to a role within the collectivity, and finally to an act or activity within the role.

The seven levels of specificity of resources leading to utilization in activity within a social-system framework are given in the following resource table:

Process	Levels		Resources			
			Values	Norms	Goals	Facilities
Generation 1	1	Primary Action Resource				
Generation 2	2	General Action System				
Generation 3	3	Social System				
Allocation	4	Subsystems				
Utilization 1	5	Collectivities				
Utilization 2	6	Roles				
Utilization 3	7	Activities				

allocation among subsystems is controlled and regulated by generalized media which circulate through the system. While resources are being utilized and consumed in action, the generalized media are not; they are only acquired and spent by actors in the acquisition of action resources and thus continue to flow among actors located in the various subsystems. Parsons developed the conceptualization of these components and processes further in the resource table and the interchange paradigm.[25]

The fit of this table with the usual conceptualization of the components of the structure of the social system is not readily apparent. The components of social systems are usually listed as values, norms, collectivities, and roles.[28] In the resource table values and norms appear as resources and collectivities and roles as levels of specificity of action components. There appears therefore to be a mix-up of components and levels of structure in Parsons' conceptualization of the components of social systems, resulting in an elliptical statement which ignores two components and at least two levels of structure. The complete social system composition would thus consist of levels 3 to 6 in the resource table for all four components and can be generalized as follows:

LEVEL OF STRUCTURE	COMPONENTS			
	Values	*Norms*	*Goals*	*Facilities*
System-as-whole Subsystems Collectivities Roles				

This table makes it explicit that values are indeed specified to collectivities and roles as is sometimes stated and do not exist simply as conceptions of the system-as-whole, as they are usually defined.[29] Hence this formulation would introduce greater consistency in the conceptualization of the social system as well as the general action system.

Resources are used in action and have to be constantly renewed. Each of the subsystems of action specializes in the production of a functional resource and contributes it to the functioning of the system. But resources are not exchanged on a one-to-one barter basis in functionally differentiated systems: The complexity of the system requires that there be generalized media that can serve as mechanisms of resource allocation on a non-ascriptive basis without tying receivers and senders into particular exchanges. The generalized media and the interchange paradigm thus tie in with the resource table to provide a full conceptualization of the interdependencies among the functional subsystems. The interchange paradigm is an elaboration of the conceptualization of level 4 in the resource table, specifying the resources and media exchanged at that level in the allocation of resources among the subsystems. This does not mean that the media are not involved in the generation or utilization of resources. In fact, Parsons explicitly states that they are.[30] But the interchange paradigm does not specify the interchanges internal to each of the subsystems. We can use two subsystems, L and I, to show how the interchange paradigm relates to the resource table, as shown in Figure I-3.

This representation suggests that there must be a more analytical statement of the levels of generality of resources than we have now. Somehow "collectivities" and "roles" do not fit into the analytical statement, especially as they exist only in social

systems. Perhaps a further specification of subsystem levels is necessary, which in social systems will come very close to collectivities and roles as subsystems. The cognate analytical levels would seem to be "between sub-subsystems" and "within sub-subsystems," suggesting that further functional

specification would not seem necessary or useful. But it does suggest that the analysis of resource allocation through the generalized media and hence that the interchange paradigm has to be analyzed to the sub-system level (sixteen-fold) within any particular system of reference, confirming the conclusion reached earlier that the functional analysis of action systems has to be carried to that level.[31]

To return to the interchange paradigm, Parsons first developed an interchange paradigm for the society as a social system, specifying the media of

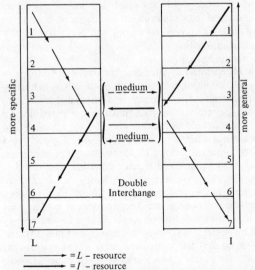

more specific *more general*

medium

medium

Double Interchange

L I

⟶ = L – resource
⟶ = I – resource

Figure I-3. L and I example of relationship of interchange paradigm to the resource table.
[NOTE: The levels of specificity are shown as "folded open." Theoretically it is possible that the specific activities of level 7 might be the process whereby level 1 resources are produced in the system. The resource table assumes interpenetration of all levels of action system differentiation.]

money, power, influence, and commitments.[32] Recently he has moved his attention to the development of an interchange paradigm at the general action system level.[33] Applying the same logic as in the societal paradigm, he sought to specify four different media, namely intelligence (A), performance capacity (G), affect (I), and definition of the situation (L), as the general action media. This formulation has raised many questions. How are these media anchored in the action frame of reference? How do they relate to the societal set? How many other sets of media need to be developed?

The development of media theory is indicative of Parsons' strategy of theory building, which is pragmatic, extremely cautious, and mindful of at least a sense of empirical fit. It is essentially an inductive strategy in its critical initiatives with deduction serving to flesh out the innovative ideas. In this sense, he is a far cry from the grand theorist who relies on deduction to build a logically closed edifice.[34] Instead we see a logical strategy following an uncanny sense of fit with empirical reality and developing theory along these fairly secure lines. It was a great insight that the logic of money as a medium could be applied to political power and then to influence and to commitments as societal media. With this paradigm fairly firmly established for the societal case, one could then venture to the heights of the general theory of action and suggest that there is a similar set of media at that level.

As a strategy this approach has much to recommend itself, especially in an atmosphere hostile, to say the least, to general theory and deductive theory construction. But it does present serious problems in attaining appropriate and consistent levels of abstraction and in shedding the more specific concrete content of special cases. Hence it is generally agreed today that money is a special case of the more general phenomenon of generalized media of exchange or communication. Yet, we have not sorted out what is special in the case of money and what is general, belonging to the class of phenomena, that is, to generalized symbolic media. The result is that we rely on economic theory to formulate societal media and on societal theory to formulate social system and general action system media. This results in high levels of concreteness in the theory where abstractness is at a premium, and it is difficult to argue that the concreteness is never misplaced.

At this point, given Parsons' pioneering work in media theory, it would be possible to proceed deductively and systematically in developing general action media theory, always mindful of course, of an inductive sense of fit with empirical systems. In such a theory money would appear to be a special case of a general action medium based in the adaptive subsystem of the general action system, or perhaps the integrative subsystem (social system). In any event, it would combine characteristics of both the adaptive medium and the integrative medium at the general level in its double specialization as the adaptive medium of the integrative subsystem. In this context the problem with Parsons' strategy can be illustrated by asking in what analytical sense money can be seen as a special case or combination of the characteristics or components of intelligence (A) and affect (I). There is controversy, for example, about affect as a medium: Is it the personality medium or the social system medium? Parsons and Lidz disagree on its location, though both see it as a general action medium.[35] Others are not quite clear about the issues involved. Perhaps this is the point at which media theory has to be rigorously and systematically developed before we end up with a collection of sets of media that do not seem to fit together or about which it would be difficult to achieve intersubjective validity of concepts and classifications.

Parsons has actually made attempts to anchor the media in the action frame of reference. One such attempt is the sanctions paradigm. Another relates the media to the pattern variables.[36] The sanctions paradigm specifies four types of sanctions derived by the cross-classification of the actor-situation duality with the consequences (positive or negative) of the sanction for the receiver of the sanction.[37] Parsons then defines the generalized media as sanction media that a sender actor (ego) uses in interaction in order to secure compliance from the receiving actor (alter) by different modes of sanction, as in Figure I-4.[38]

The lack of logical consistency with the action frame of reference is immediately apparent. Only one of the primary postulates of the frame of reference, the actor-situation duality, is used. The voluntary postulate is left out. Instead the consequence for the receiving actor is simply indicated as positive or negative. Using the instrumental-consummatory derivative of the voluntary postulate the consequence for the receiving actor can be conceptualized as of either instrumental or consummatory significance. This would provide a sanctions paradigm, derived consistently from the frame of reference and cognate

Sanction	Channel	
	Intentional	Situational
Positive Mode Medium	Persuasion Influence I	Inducement Money A
Negative Mode Medium	Activation of Commitments L	Deterrence Power G

Figure I-4. Sanction paradigm with cognate functions indicated LIGA.

with the functional paradigm without introducing the positive-negative vector as a dimension of sanction differentiation. The positive or negative consequence would be a further specification of directionality, and each sanction type could be seen as potentially having both positive and negative valence. Although money, for example, may be primarily a medium of inducement (positive) there do not seem to be sound analytical reasons to see it as only that; in fact, money, especially in pricing and hence as a cost consideration, often acts as a negative situational sanction. Obviously, this conceptualization has to be developed further before it can be proposed with confidence as a more general statement than Parsons' sanction paradigm.[39] But it does seem to provide a link in the logical chain of developing generalized media theory consistently from the action frame of reference.

The interchange paradigm provides a statement of the functional interdependencies of the four subsystems upon each other in terms of resources produced or generated by one subsystem, allocated to or exchanged with another subsystem, and utilized by that subsystem as a factor in the production or generation of its function-specific resources. In the classic economic example used by Parsons as a template for other interchanges, the L subsystem of society produces labor commitment and allocates it to the A subsystem, which utilizes it in the production of goods (and services), which in turn are allocated to L. The basic interchange between any two subsystems is therefore a single exchange of resources. The double interchange results from the introduction of a generalized medium of exchange used not as a resource but as a sanction to acquire resources and as such it facilitates the interchange of resources. In the same example, money is the medium that circulates in the exchange of resources between parties in L and A. On the one hand, such a medium when introduced reduces the complexity of matched resource exchanges by allowing several additional degrees of freedom with respect to time, place, terms, and party of an exchange. On the other hand, once introduced and institutionalized, it results in an exponential increase in complexity far beyond the limits possible before its introduction, because these degrees of freedom result in a multiplication of contingencies which can be tolerated if there is trust in the efficacy of the generalized media. Hence the state of flation of the generalized media becomes a critical problem in the analysis of the equilibrating processes of complex action systems.[40]

The resource table has been used by Smelser to develop a theory of differentiation and a theory of collective behavior.[41] It is clear that these theories could be generalized to provide a more adequate theory of social change and action change. Media theory and particularly the theory of media dynamics, dealing with processes of inflation, deflation, and conflation, would seem to be of critical importance, not only in equilibrium analysis but also in the analysis of change resulting from disequilibrating forces. For example, some of the conditions of "structural conduciveness" in Smelser's model, which is a very general category, would seem to involve media inflation or deflation or interchange disequilibrium.

THE PATTERN VARIABLES

Another aspect of the theory of action which goes back to 1939 and has proven useful across a wide range of phenomena is the pattern variables scheme.[42] In recent developments this scheme has become more firmly rooted in the action frame of reference and more closely integrated with the four-function paradigm and media theory.[43]

Parsons has identified four pattern variables, two of them specifying the orientations of the actor and two the modalities of meanings of objects in the situation. The orientation set are affectivity-affective neutrality and diffuseness-specificity. The object modality set are performance-quality and universalism-particularism.[44] Why these aspects of orientation and object meanings are of such central importance that the actor has to make these particular choices before he can act is not altogether clear, especially since these choices do not seem to define the actor's orientation and the situation that much more precisely. We will return to this problem below.

In linking the pattern variables to the functional paradigm, Parsons places the orientation of the actor in the pattern-maintenance cell (L) and the object modalities in the goal-attainment cell (G). Cross-classification of the two pairs in each of these cells provide variable categorizations of patterns of orientations and cognate object meanings, for example, affectivity-specificity categorizes "consummatory needs" which are cognate with "objects of cathexis" categorized by particularism-performance.[45] These two sets of cross-classifications (L and G) provide categorizations of the unit components of the general action system.

The relational components of the system are functionally adaptive (A, vis-à-vis or in relation to the environment of the system) and integrative (I, among units internal to the system). Parsons argues that these relations will be functional to the extent that they combine variables involved in the categorization of the unit components to be related. The adaptive set (A) is seen as media providing symbolic representation to the meanings of objects, while the integrative set (I) provides integrative standards for the orientation of the actor. Hence the symbolic medium through which the meaning of "objects of cathexis" is represented is called "expressive symbolization," and it is patterned on one component of "consummatory needs" (specificity) and one of "objects of cathexis" (particularism). Expressive symbolization is thus characterized by particularism-specificity and is located in the cognate cell (Ag) with objects of cathexis (Gg) and consummatory needs (Lg). The corresponding integrative standard for orientation is simply called "goal-attainment." It is located in the cognate cell in I (Ig) and is composed of the remaining pattern variables in "consummatory needs" (affectivity) and in "objects of cathexis" (performance); hence it is categorized by affectivity-performance.

Parsons' reasoning in choosing which variables have primarily A significance and which have I significance is complex, to say the least. But the logic is clear enough: each combination consists of one consummatory dimension variable and one external dimension variable, hence "relating" the two fundamental dimensions of action differentiation. The same logic is followed in the composition of the Al and Il relational components. The Aa, Ai and Ia, Ii components are composed by the same logic, except that the internal-external and instrumental-consummatory dimensions are reversed. For example, whereas Ag combined the *external* component of *Lg* and the *consummatory* component of *Gg*, Aa combines the *instrumental* component of *La* and the *external* component of *Ga*. Again, the reasons for this switch are not clear.

The combination of these four components involving the specified variable choices results in what Parsons calls "expressive action," as shown in Figure I-5.

The logical structure of this integration of the pattern variable schema with the action frame of reference is not very clear. Parsons starts off by using the actor-situation duality to identify two orientations of the actor pattern variables and two meanings of the situation pattern variables. He then decides not to introduce the voluntary postulate at the same level, as is the practice in deriving the functional

paradigm, to differentiate the two pairs in terms of instrumental-consummatory significance. Instead, this introduction is made at the next level down, that is *within* orientations and *within* object modalities. At this level, affective neutrality-affectivity is seen as the variable differentiating orientations on the instrumental-consummatory dimension, and universalism-particularism as having the same significance for the differentiation of object modalities. The internal-external dimension is represented by diffuseness-specificity in the differentiation of orientations and performance-quality in the differentiation of object modalities in the situation.

Parsons then places these two sets, orientations and modalities, in the larger system in the L cell, which is internal-instrumental, and the G cell, which is external-consummatory. Hence the voluntaristic postulate has slipped in by the back door, implying that the actor has to make choices only with respect to these two sets of problems, not with respect to all four of the primary action problems. Why this should be is not clear; it certainly is not consistent with the frame of reference. Certainly the actor also has to make choices with respect to facilities (external-instrumental) and norms (internal-consummatory). Parsons treats these choices as derivative in the sense that these are relational problems and hence involve combinations of the primary choices. But they can be derived only by the circuitous logic of assigning functional primacy to each of the four pattern variables at the next level down. This step is inconsistent with the derivation procedures at the general level, as there is no logical reason why it should not apply at both levels, except because of a fundamental difference in the logic of the paradigm at the two levels and between unit components and relational components. It may be necessary to postulate such a difference, but then it should be clearly identified in the frame of reference and not arbitrarily introduced in this particular excursion.

The logical inconsistency can be removed by following a more direct path in relating the pattern variables to the action frame of reference and the functional paradigm. The basic mistake Parsons

Units of Orientation to Objects (L)	Integrative Standards (I)	Symbolic Representations of External Objects (A)	Internal Meanings of Objects (G)	
Affectivity Specificity	Performance Affectivity	Specificity Particularism	Performance Particularism	Expressive Action
Consummatory Needs	Goal (attainment) Selection	Expressive Symbolization	Cathexis	

Figure 1-5. The G subsystem of the general action system. [As presented in Figure 2, p. 208, in "Pattern Variables Revisited."]

seems to have made was to identify two pattern variables as an "orientation set" and two as a "modality set." If one eliminates this step altogether the problem evaporates and one loses nothing. The obvious first step is to relate the four pattern variables directly to both major dimensions of action system differentiation, that is, both the actor-situation duality and the voluntary postulate with its instrumental-consummatory duality at the primary level. A possible step before that would be to relate each pattern variable choice to one of the four components of the unit act and then to spell out how these choices are combined in a system of action.[46] But that would take us too far afield here.

Let us start with Parsons' secondary-level classification of the four pattern variables as the first step at the primary level. The classification pairs one pattern variable from each of the two sets, the "orientation set" and the "modality set." The two pattern variables with primary significance for the internal-external dimension are diffuseness-specificity and quality-performance; the two with primary significance for the instrumental-consummatory dimension are affective neutrality-affectivity and universalism-particularism. The logic of this classification need not concern us here, although it could also be questioned.[47] The two pattern variables in each set do not have the same significance for the dimension. In the internal-external case, for example, the diffuseness choice has special significance for the internal side while performance has special significance for the external side. In the instrumental-consummatory case, affective neutrality is of special significance on the instrumental side, while particularism has special significance for the consummatory side.[48] Each one of the four functional problems of action systems represents a different set of combinations of all four choices, as in Figure I-6.

This paradigm is obviously not very helpful, which emphasizes again the need to carry analysis to the sub-subsystem level as Parsons has also done. The critical question then becomes: Which combinations of choices are functional at the sub-subsystem level? We shall now examine a method for answering this question. (Because Parsons has followed a different route in arriving at these combinations and has introduced rules based on a fundamental distinction between unit components and relational components, it is not possible to reconstruct the logical steps he followed in this respect.)

There are three simple rules for allocating the significance of choices at the sub-subsystem level. First, choices remain within the same dimension for all four sub-subsystems. That is, a choice in the instrumental-consummatory dimension does not acquire internal-external significance at this level. Spatially, this means that all vertical mapping remains vertical, and horizontal mapping horizontal. Second, the choices with *special* significance for one side of the dimension to which they apply, as seen in Figure 1-6, remain on that side at this secondary level for both the sub-subsystems to which they are relevant. This applies then to diffuseness and performance in the internal-external dimension and to affective neutrality and particularism in the instrumental-consummatory dimension. Third, the choices which do not have special significance for one side of the dimension acquire significance for the *opposite* side of the dimension at this level, *within* the side of their significance at the primary level. This rule applies to specificity and quality in the internal-external dimension and to affectivity and universalism in the instrumental-consummatory dimension. These three rules taken together maximize the probability and "purity" of functional specialization.

The application of these three rules results in the following sixteen-fold table showing pattern-variable choice patterns to the sub-subsystem level of the action system (Figure I-7).

This figure is the equivalent of Figure 2 in Parsons' "Pattern Variables Revisited" with the sub-subsystem (LIGA) components (liga) in the rows, not the columns, and without the A and G reversal in the columns.[49] A comparison of the two figures will show that they are exactly the same except for the reversal of the choice components of a and i in both the L and G subsystems.

The reason for this is also clear. Parsons, in deciding on the components of the A and I cells in Figure 1 in "Pattern Variables Revisited," has not observed our first rule. That is, he has switched the dimensions of relevance for diffuseness and affective neutrality in the L case and for specificity and affectivity

	Instrumental	Consummatory
A	*Affective neutrality* Universalism	Affectivity *Particularism* G
External Specificity *Performance*	*Affective neutrality* Universalism Specificity *Performance*	Affectivity *Particularism* Specificity *Performance*
Internal *Diffuseness* Quality	*Affective neutrality* Universalism *Diffuseness* Quality	Affectivity *Particularism* *Diffuseness* Quality
L		I

Figure I-6. Pattern variable classification by functional primacy. [NOTE: Variables in italics indicate special significance *within* dimension.]

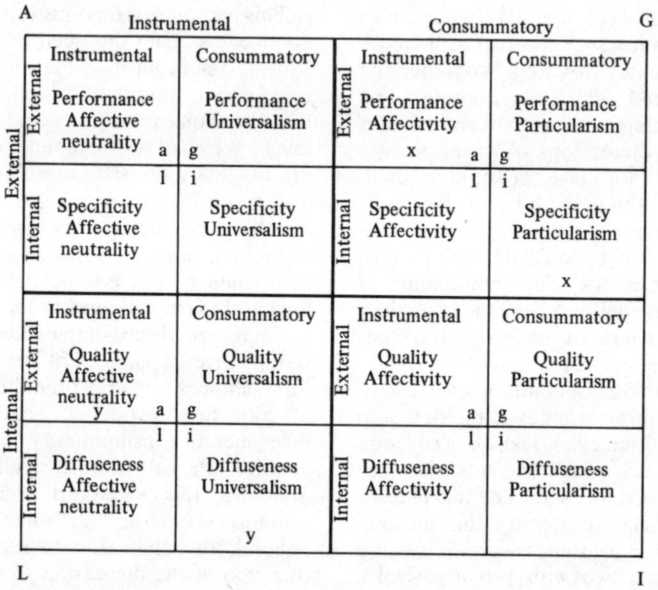
A
Instrumental
Consummatory
G
External
Internal
External
Internal
External
Internal
Instrumental
Consummatory
Performance
Affective
neutrality
Performance
Universalism
Performance
Affectivity
Performance
Particularism
Specificity
Affective
neutrality
Specificity
Universalism
Specificity
Affectivity
Specificity
Particularism
Quality
Affective
neutrality
Quality
Universalism
Quality
Affectivity
Quality
Particularism
Diffuseness
Affective
neutrality
Diffuseness
Universalism
Diffuseness
Affectivity
Diffuseness
Particularism
a g
l i
x
y
L
I

Figure I-7. Pattern-variable choice composition of the General Action System shown differentiated to the sub-sub-system level. [NOTE: x and y mark categorizations reversed from Figure 2 in "Pattern Variables Revisited." Horizontal variables are listed first, vertical ones second.]

in the G case. Why this should be necessary in these two cases and not in A and I is not clear, as we indicated.

The specific functional significance of these choice combinations at this secondary level needs, of course, to be spelled out in detail as Parsons has done. One can assume that his analysis will stand, except in the case of the four reversed categorizations, but we need not take that problem up here.

Parsons discusses the adaptive subset (A) as mediating the system's relations to its environment and refers to the components as adaptive mechanisms, as symbolic media, including language, money, and so on.[50] Hence "expressive symbolization" has the same pattern-variable composition as power as a generalized medium at the societal level. In the subsequent three essays on the societal media, power, influence, and value commitments no reference was made to this link with the pattern-variable scheme.[51]

In his most recent essay on general theory in sociology Parsons returns to the link between the pattern variables and the media.[52] In the text of this essay he uses the pattern-variable combinations of the adaptive subset in "Pattern Variables Revisited," which at the time he called symbolic media, to describe the general action media of interchange, namely, intelligence (A), performance capacity (G), affect (I), and definition of the situation (L). He sees the pattern-variable categorization as applying at both the general action and social system levels.[53] Hence we see that the same pattern component characterizes expressive symbolization, performance capacity as a general action medium, and power as a societal medium.

In the technical note to his essay Parsons places the adaptive subset of the text as one aspect of the codes of media, namely the "value principles," hence the highest level of cybernetic control in the medium. This should not in itself present a problem, but he also proceeds to indicate pattern-variable compositions for the other code element of the media, the "coordinative standards."[54] These pattern-variable combinations are the same as those of the integrative subset of the general action system in "Pattern Variables Revisited." Hence we have another common pattern element: the pattern-variable composition of the integrative standard of orientation in the general action system, the coordinative standard of performance capacity as a general action medium, and the coordinative standard of power as a societal medium.

The pattern variables thus emerge as a central core of the general theory of action, along with and integrated into the functional paradigm. It would follow that the same uniformities observed for the relational components of action systems, namely adaptive mechanisms and integrative standards, would hold for the unit components, orientations and object modalities. In our G example, the pattern-variable composition of "objects of cathexis" would be the same as that of the G aspect of personality and the same as that of political objects. These developments were anticipated as early as 1951, in *Towards a General Theory of Action*, but never pursued further. The pattern variables were seen as providing the constitutive components of normative elements in cultural, social, and personality systems, as the same patterns become institutionalized and internalized in each of these subsystems of action.[55] Recent developments have gone beyond this formulation but arose from the same premise.

There are obviously many problems of logical consistency and empirical validity to be ironed out even in these partial developments of an integrated general theory. The reversal of the cybernetic relations between A and I in the media codes is only one. But the emergence of this level of integration in the general theory is bound to increase its usefulness and the reliability with which theorists can expect to achieve intersubjective validity in their formulations. It is obvious that a more rigorous logico-deductive approach will be needed at this stage of the development of the theory. Parsons' "pragmatic" strategy has paid off well, but it has resulted in a range of inconsistencies and uneven generality, when looked at from the perspective of general theory, which indicate that the same strategy would no longer be optimal.

CHANGE AND CONFLICT

Far be it from us to revive dead issues or to flog dead horses. Although secondhand discussions of the popular critical debate of the late fifties and sixties about the inadequacies of structural-functionalism in dealing with conflict and change have markedly subsided, it is not altogether clear whether most people have seen the light or have become accustomed to the darkness. The glib phrases, stereotypes, and strawmen have lost currency; and debunking Parsons is less popular among the games sociologists play than it was a decade ago. Even attempts to redeem all of sociology from the sins of jargon by making Parsons' style a scapegoat seem to have become less essential to the identity trips of would-be saviors of the discipline. Perhaps these phenomena could be analyzed as deflationary pressures on the influence of Parsonian theory, symptomatic of its overextension and leading to equilibrating developments. Although we might be accused of explaining jargon with more jargon, the exercise might be quite useful. However, we shall not embark on it here.

It has finally become slightly old-fashioned to quote Parsons himself—when he said more than 20 years ago in *The Social System* that a theory of social change may well be impossible—to prove that social systems theory cannot explain or handle social change.[56] No one still adhering to the incredibly high standards set for such a theory in that book, which formed the basis of that pessimistic remark, would have reason for much more optimism today. Not that we have not made progress, but if we had not become less puritanical and more accommodating to the inevitable imperfection of human endeavor, especially at early stages, the progress would not have been recognized.

The development of the theories of resources, generalized media of interchange, the logic of value-adding processes, combined with the hierarchies of cybernetic control and conditioning and the return to a general action level of analysis from the earlier tendency to exclusive concern with the social system, have all opened up new possibilities for accounting for change and conflict, not to mention stability and order.

The task of developing a general theory of change out of these theoretical materials has not been carried very far. Smelser has made important beginnings.[57] The combination of the resource table with the hierarchies of control and conditioning has provided the framework for a very complex and systematic set of propositions about change.[58] These need to be carefully examined from both theoretical and empirical perspectives. The hierarchy of control logic has been applied, for example, to the different levels of specificity: The lower the level of specificity, the lower the level of control. Although this statement sounds meaningful in information theory terms, the different levels of specificity do not necessarily have different control implications. The proposition, for example, that a change at any point in the matrix will necessarily lead to changes in the sector of the matrix below and to the right of it but not above and to the left of it, is too deterministic to be acceptable even in logical terms.[59] The most we can say is that one necessary factor for such change will be present; but we have to avoid defining necessity in such a way that it implies sufficiency, or we will be back at an emanationist, idealist determinism. Part of the problem seems to be that Smelser has not taken into account the fact that there is also a hierarchy of conditioning operating in a direction opposite to that of the hierarchy of control and that the levels of specificity of resources are also levels of generality when looked at in the reverse direction. The basic logic of all four of these relational propositions is that they define ranges of variation within which changes are compatible with existing constitutions and outside of which changes imply reconstitution of components. Hence any change anywhere in the matrix that occurs outside the ranges of variation allowed by these relations among components has exactly the same logical implications in all directions in the matrix.

The important part of the theory that remains to be developed is the specification of other factors that are necessary to provide a sufficient combination of factors for change in the various directions. Smelser's theories of differentiation and collective behavior provide only two such cases. But the combination of the value-added model with the resource table provides the logical format for other types of theories of social change. So far the value-added model has been applied only to processes of action relating to the reconstitution of the components of action in the resource table. It appears that the model can also be applied to the relationships among the components in the resource table in order to overcome any deterministic implications. For example, it could be postulated that the achievement of a particular level of specificity in the structure of any one component will constitute only one factor in a combination of factors which will determine the achievement of the next level of specificity, and so on. The levels of specificity may also be seen as a statement of the order in which the values of the various factors will be added in the specification process.

Similarly the relationships among the components of action could be stated in this format. A change in norms would constitute a factor adding its value in appropriate sequence to the combination of factors causing change in the other components. The hierarchies of control and conditions and the levels of specificity and generality would then provide specifications of the order and directions in which changes in any component in the resource matrix would add its value to changes in the other components. The development of this theoretical integration would provide us with a format for systematic theories of conflict and change. Such theories would have to provide models for the analysis of both specification and generalization processes as well as for both control and conditioning processes. Smelser's theories so far have tended to deal only with specification and control. There can be no question of the empirical prevalence and analytical significance of generalization and conditioning as change processes or aspects of them. For example, the role of technological

conditioning at the one end of the scale and value generalization at the other as processes in the development of large-scale action systems, such as societies, seem to be critical in developmental or evolutionary theory.

Media theory, particularly media dynamics, is most directly relevant to equilibrium analysis, but it has clearly great potential for the analysis of other processes of change. The role of the media in resource processing and allocation, especially as measures of functional efficacy in this respect, suggests a direct link to the change processes analysed in terms of the resource table.[60] In all these respects there is emerging a level of analysis in which dynamic propositions are clearly couched at the general action level and their systematic implications explored in functional terms.[61]

These developments have made the distinction between change *of* and change *within* the system of less heuristic significance, except in the context of evolutionary theory.[62] The concept of system has become more dynamic, something seething with process and constantly changing in relation to changing environments. Change *within* seems to lead imperceptibly into change *of* the system, and it is only in longer-term diachronic analyses that stages in the change of systems can be identified. But the distinction remains important since, as Parsons has pointed out, changes *within* the system may also serve to inhibit or prevent changes *of* the system. Again, within ranges of compatible variability, the thresholds of which need to be specified, there does not seem any logical basis for postulating necessary relations among the two types of change at the analytical level.

Another aspect of these developments is the shift from the largely synchronic structural-functional theory of *The Social System* to an evolutionary, diachronic functional theory focusing on process and developmental change during the last decade.[63] This shift has revealed how changes within the system add up to changes of the system; how such processes as generalization, specification, differentiation, and the development of equilibrating mechanisms such as the generalized media often contribute to and constitute part of stages in the development of the system itself. We are also much more aware of the fact that the dynamics of change in a system may vary significantly with the stage of development of the system.[64] These developments are far from a systematic general theory of change, but they do provide a basis upon which we can confidently claim that at the moment the theory of action presents the most promising set of analytical tools for the development of such a theory.

The dynamics of conflict is never very far removed

from the dynamics of change and vice versa. It would not be very difficult to show that the developments just sketched, particularly the return to a general action level of analysis, have dispelled or should serve to dispell all the misgivings critics have had about the inadequacies of the theory for handling conflict. They have highlighted what in *The Social System* had been called "the motivational problem of order" as one of the continuing functional problems of a social system and the basis for the differentiation of an integrative subsystem specializing in the continual solution of an ever-present problem.[65] The allegation that Parsons takes order for granted and hence treats the Hobbesian problem as solved once and for all is simply unfounded.[66] If that were the case he would have long since turned his attention to the explanation of conflict as the most significant problem. This failure to understand the main thrust of the theory of action, along with the concern about the "over-socialized concept of man"[67] reflects partly a failure to keep ontological questions from interfering with the logistics of heuristic theory and partly a failure to avoid the fallacy of misplaced concreteness. Clearly analytical treatment of integration and socialization cannot be assumed to describe empirical reality, nor to answer ontological questions.[68] It is only *reification* of the analytical theory of integration and socialization that can give rise to the concerns of critics over utopianism and ontology.

However, as we have admitted in the opening section, the critics have a point to the extent that Parsons, in spite of his astounding capacity for sustained abstract thinking, has slipped into misplaced concreteness himself, hence seemingly providing empirical descriptions of concrete reality as always relatively integrated and stable. The tendency has been to assume that the theory of action would spring full-blown and completely logically consistent from Parsons' head. This assumption relieves people of the responsibility of using their own heads to explore the logical ramifications of a theoretical system fully. Our continued confidence in the usefulness of the theory of action derives from the realization that its development by any one individual will always be subject to those limitations that the action theory of knowledge would lead one to expect and that the development of a theory, if it has any potential at all for development, will require the efforts of many. Hence the lack of the development of adequate treatments of conflict and disorder is not an intrinsic weakness of the theory but a symptom of the stage of its development and the overriding concern of Parsons with an understanding of the problem of order.[69] One future task, for example, would be to spell out the multiplication of contingencies of disorder and conflict that arise out of systemic complexity or, to put it differently, how disorder or potential for disorder gets built into functionally differentiated systems with order as their raison d'être.

The analytical concept of an action system does not imply that social reality can be reduced to the workings of one empirical system of action with all its implications of relative stability and integration. In fact, concrete reality is only partially, but sufficiently for explanatory purposes, conceptualized in system terms. It is always an *empirical* question how salient systemic elements are, what their stage of development is, what their patterns are and what the boundaries of the system of reference are for the analytical purposes at hand. And it is safe to assume that there will always be multiple systems of action in any concrete situation. Even a dyad can involve several empirical action systems; and in larger, more complex empirical situations, there are many systems that may or may not form partial systems in a larger encompassing system. This multiplicity of empirical systems creates an emergent problem of order, that of order *among* systems, which cannot be resolved by the internal dynamics of separate systems. Their resolution or containment requires systemic mechanisms among systems which may require *emergent* characteristics to deal with complexities and contingencies not prevalent at the primary level. Hence the Hobbesian problem remains and becomes amplified into: Why is there not a war of all systems against all systems? And, as we have seen, although each empirical system may represent a resolution of the seven problems of contingency, these *analytically* similar mechanisms may actually *empirically* present new contingencies of the same type but a different order of magnitude, in that they may be incompatible, in competition, conflict, or contradiction.

The other set of implications that becomes clearer when one keeps analytical and empirical levels of theory distinct is that conflict is in itself a systematic mechanism of system formation and change. The postulate that no system can give primacy to all four functional problems at the same time implies at least a temporal problem of order and conflict in this respect. It further implies that these problems can be met only through phase movements which require at least cyclical primacy of each of the four functions. The empirical phenomenon that large action systems, such as societies, tend to settle into a particular primacy pattern, such as instrumental activism in the United States of America, has several theoretical implications. It implies that this primacy will be dysfunctional in the long run in terms of the adequacy of the performance of the other functions and that, given the inertia of the system and its mechanisms, it may generate major conflicts which would be functional from the system's point of reference in achieving a new primacy pattern. Much of the dynamics of the functional interdependence within systems will therefore take forms that will be classifiable as conflict in empirical classifications of types of action process.

These are only some of the ramifications of the theory of action for the development of theories of change and conflict. But they should suffice to demonstrate the invalidity of the generalization that because the theory of action so far has not proved particularly useful in these areas, a claim which itself should be challenged, therefore the theory is incapable of being useful. We believe with Parsons that the theory of action is still in its early stages of development and that there are no logical constraints inherent in the theory for these developments to take place. Furthermore, we consider it one of the areas of high priority for further development in spite of the important beginnings that have been made.[70]

CONSERVATIVE BIAS

Finally, we have to deal with the question of the alleged conservative bias in the theory of action and particularly in social systems theory. Our continued interest in the theory as a tool is by no means an acceptance of a conservative stance in relation to social issues. Quite the contrary, our interest is based on the judgment that there is no more powerful tool available for the analysis and discussion of social issues and that the alleged "conservatism" of the theory is simply a "cop-out" from mastering this tool, partly for ideological reasons and partly because of failure to avoid the fallacies of misplaced concreteness and reductionism.

The structural-functional debate of the last decade and a half with its strawmen of the juxtaposition of structural-functional theory and Marxian or conflict theory has fortunately been superceded by more sophisticated discussions.[71] But at the height of it the fact that Marx himself was a "structural-functionalist" was completely ignored and is still not fully understood. What can be more blatantly structural-functional than the proposition that one set of relationships (to the means of production) determines everything else? Neither was the voluntarist element in Marx's theory of revolution recognized in his awareness of the need to mobilize the motivation of actors in organized efforts to reconstitute the primary relationships.[72] The famous question "What is to be done?" implies the voluntaristic assumption that is at the core of the general theory of action. The crucial theoretical differences do not lie at that level but at the more specific propositions of the functional relationships and in the value position taken vis-à-vis social systems.

It has recently been emphasized that there was much continuity between Marx and Weber. Weber introduced greater complexity into Marx's social theory and thereby changed its lower-level propositions fundamentally. He did not deny the importance of economic factors, but he added to them a concern with the rationalization of organization (bureaucracy) and of force (the military).[73] Most importantly, his comparative studies of religion established the independence and central significance of that set of factors. The fundamental theoretical difference was that between Marx's acceptance of a single-factor determinism and Weber's concern with the interdependence of a wider range of factors. The most important difference was, however, ideological: Marx had a more negative evaluation of the state of affairs in the nineteenth century than Weber, and he had a more active and radical approach to its amelioration. In terms of theory, however, there can be no question that Weber had a much more sophisticated grasp of the complexities of modern industrial society.

Along the same lines, the differences between Parsons and his Marxist antagonists are first ideological and second that of level of sophistication. Parsons is certainly conservative in the sense that everything to the right of the leftist side of the political spectrum is "conservative." But any more sophisticated analysis and resistance of the labelling tendency will give the lie to this stereotype. Gouldner's elaborate ad hominem constructions have driven this sport among sociologists to its absurd extreme, thereby revealing the real nature of the beast — reductionism and reification of the most vulgar kind.[74]

In fact, it can easily be demonstrated that the theory of action has developed quite independently of ideological factors, certainly in its central frame of reference and core structure. Attempts to achieve a "synthesis" or to construct an "alternative" such as Dahrendorf's have shaken down to mild "marginal differentiations" or variations on the same theme.[75]

Social scientists today are more inclined to become engaged in the social issues of their day and to question the value-neutral stance of their disciplines of a generation ago. Some carry this further than others, but most of them wish to be able to analyse issues and to act as social critics, however mild their criticism. There are no reasons intrinsic to the general theory of action that they cannot do this, even to the extent of adopting the most radical position. In fact, the theory provides all the elements required for an independent "Archimedes point" from which to analyse or attack concrete social reality:

First, the generality of the theory would question any attempt to settle on particularistic values. It has a built-in strain towards universalism, that is, to generalization to the widest inclusive categories whether humanity or all living systems. This universalistic basis is also most compatible with concerns about value neutrality.[76]

Second, it provides a set of general categories in terms of which human values can be conceptualized and operationalized as standards against which social systems and action systems can be evaluated. We no longer need to fall back on the "noble savage" or romantic concept of the human condition that was implicit in Marx's work. We can articulate human values in comprehensive terms, from concerns with the environment to ultimate values and their symbolization of human ideals. And we can dissect societies in terms of the extent to which they realize or violate these values.

Third, we no longer need to have the secular equivalent of the devil as the source of all evil, viz: the productive system. Weber already has blazed the trail out of that monistic theory of evil. We know today that man is as much a slave of words as he is of money. The theory of action provides us with a sophisticated tool to identify the complex sources of man's alienation in modern society. The four-function paradigm applied to society alone enables us to analyse the economic, political, institutional, and latent sources of the failure of modern society to realize human values more fully and to eliminate the most flagrant violations of them, such as racism, poverty, and war. The poverty of orthodox Marxist theory in comparison stands out graphically when one tries to analyse a situation such as the South African racist society in terms of the two approaches.[77]

Fourth, the voluntaristic postulate, when kept in its central place in the theory of action, implies that people can construct, change, destroy, and rebuild the systems in which they find themselves if only they can develop appropriate situation-specific goals and mobilize the resources to achieve them. They have to be able to develop the necessary distance; they have to articulate their values, and they have to understand adequately the complex factors that have to be taken into account and controlled. The previous three points dealt with these aspects.

The demise of the new left movements in the disciplines and their failure to have any impact on modern society are indications of their poverty in theoretical tools. It is not that adequate theory is not available. But their commitments to orthodoxy and their indulgence in the distorted ideology popular in the disciplines for some time have deprived them of the most sophisticated analytical tools available to deal with the complexities of the situation in which they endeavored to play their role. If they would study the theory of action firsthand and seriously, they would discover that the "Parsonian" answer to the "Leninist" question "What is to be done?" provides a most promising strategy for the development of profoundly critical social science and social action. But they will have to make their independent contributions to the development of the theory, which will require the combination of radical insights with incisive analysis. The real challenge to modern-day radicals is not to ignore Parsons and the theory of action or to condemn him for reactionary heresy, but to master him and to make him stand on his head, if necessary, much as Marx did with Hegel in the nineteenth century. It is, however, unlikely that such a "dialectical" exercise will be necessary.

OUTLINE OF THIS BOOK

The conception of this book does not fit the conventional format of a *Festschrift* in which distinguished colleagues of a scholar pay tribute to him by writing essays essentially exemplifying the best of their own work. Rather, the purpose is to honor Parsons by making a contribution to the development of the general theory of action of which he is the main author and exponent. We selected contributors who are in one way or the other attempting to work with or from or on the theory of action as a theoretical orientation. We asked contributors to choose a topic in which they wish to deal with a critical problem in the theory of action. It was suggested that each contribution might take the form of conceptual or theoretical development of aspects of the theory that have been neglected on the whole. It could focus on specific weaknesses and inadequacies which the author considers of particular significance and seeks to eliminate by proposing new departures or developments. It could attempt to extend the theory into areas not dealt with before by any of its exponents and thus contribute to its development and the demonstration of its usefulness and generality. It could consider methodological problems in theory construction or operationalization or other research issues relevant to the theory of action. It could deal with the relations of the theory of action to other bodies of theory, seeking to identify common grounds, irre-concilable incompatibilities, possibilities of convergence, and an assessment of the special merits of the theory, if any.

We expected that these essays would provide an overview of the work currently being done with the theory of action as point of departure. They would frankly deal with the problems and weaknesses in the theory, they would assess its usefulness over a wide range of phenomena, and they would make a contribution to its development on a variety of the most critical fronts. We invited between seventy and eighty social scientists known to us to be actively engaged in work utilizing or relating to the theory of action. Undoubtedly we did not include all those who would qualify. We were particularly keen to engage the younger scholars. Many of those invited had to decline because of other commitments which made it impossible for them to meet our deadline.

The contributors whose essays are included in this volume represent fewer than half of the people originally approached. The book is therefore not comprehensive in its coverage of the work of people currently working within the theory of action. Yet it provides a good sample of the theoretical activity in this area. More importantly, the substance of the essays provides a vivid demonstration of the varie-gated nature of concerns of these scholars, the wide range of phenomena they cover, and the dynamics of a growing and developing body of theory.

The essays represent an impressive array of approaches to and uses of the theory of action. There are attempts to examine the metaphysical grounding, philosophical assumptions, and meaning of the theory of action. There are some highly original and instructive applications of aspects of the theory to a variety of social phenomena. Some essays deal with a single idea or concept and elaborate on its use in the theory. Others utilize the logic of the theory or some aspect of it to develop new conceptualizations and theoretical analyses of phenomena not hitherto treated from this perspective. There are creative revisions of aspects of the theory that were not adequately conceptualized and developed before. Some essays represent highly sophisticated developments of some of the most technical and abstract aspects of the theory. A few discuss basic problems in social science, comparing the theory of action perspective with others. In some pieces the theory of action is not much in evidence but problems that are considered of special importance in assessing the usefulness and generality of the theory are discussed. A few chapters deal with methodological issues as they impinge on the theory of action or as the latter sheds light on them. Yet, the essays do not by any means deal with all the aspects of the theory of action

that need urgent attention for testing and further development.

This general introduction has not attempted a comprehensive overview of the theory of action nor a discussion of the relevance of the contributed essays to the aspects covered. The latter aspect is the purpose of the introductions to the various parts of the book. The introduction has dealt only with a few selected aspects which in our view are critical in considering the generality, usefulness, and developmental potential of the theory of action. As such it is intended to sensitize the reader to the nature of the task of working with the theory, to the kinds of issues that are involved, and to the kinds of considerations that enter into a continued intellectual commitment to adopt this theoretical orientation. Naturally, we cannot speak for all the contributors, but as the essays clearly demonstrate there is very little evidence of slavish commitment to a given orthodoxy or even acceptance of any particular part of the theory as necessarily adequate and true. Nor is there a tendency to treat it as a given which has to be judged as either adequate or inadequate, true or false, useful or useless. In this sense the general introduction reflects probably quite adequately the orientation of most scholars who take the theory of action seriously. In this they "follow" Parsons in the challenging task of developing general theory in the social sciences by critically and constructively analysing, testing, applying, and extending those aspects of particular interest to them.

The essays are organized into six parts according to common theories or similarity in subject matter. The classification is necessarily arbitrary, as the topics were chosen by the contributors and some essays could easily be placed in any one of two or three different sections. Yet we believe that the organization provides a framework which assists the reader and is preferable to a simple list of chapters.

The introduction to each part provides a discussion of the general substantive area in which the essays fall and discuss their specific relevance and contribution to that area. As the reader will discover, in some cases it did not seem fruitful to attempt to discuss the content of the essays in detail since they represent very substantial, complex, and diverse explorations into rather technical or abstract aspects of the theory. In no case will an introduction do full justice to any or all of the essays. However, the highlights should serve to guide the reader to contributions of particular interest to him or her.

Part I contains essays dealing with metatheoretical problems such as epistemology, functional methodology, methodological dilemmas, and the problem of value neutrality.

Part II contains essays dealing with topics in the

analysis of general action or aspects of it. Three of the essays concern themselves with the relationships between the theory of action and some other theory. dealing with psychoanalysis, Piaget's theories, and Marx, with respect to symbolic process, the behavioral system, and the problem of order respectively. There is also a critical discussion of the treatment of expressive symbols in the theory of action, an attempt to conceptualize science as a cultural system, a tentative attempt to explore alternative combinations in the theory of action, and a discussion of the adequacy of the theory of action in analyzing historical processes.

Part III contains essays dealing with aspects of socialization theory as applied in small groups, the adolescent subculture, the family, millenarian movements, and the role of aspirations and norms in action.

Part IV contains essays focusing on the generalized media in the theory of action. It is perhaps not accidental that these essays are among the most technical in the book and together constitute the most concerted attempt to develop general theory. They deal with relatively recent developments in the theory of action and indicate that media theory might prove to be a crucial growth point in the further development of the theory of action with fundamental implications for the entire body of theory, particularly since information theory, linguistics, and cybernetics are at the core of the functional analyses developed here.

Part V turns to essays dealing with social change and development. The essays here are more empirical in content and explore problems in these areas with different degrees of reliance on the theory of action. The focus is on macrophenomena such as international relations, societal analysis, modernization, and medical evolution; and they demonstrate the usefulness of the theory in these areas. However, the more technical analysis of these problems as represented in the work of Smelser and Bellah is unfortunately not represented in this book.[78]

The last part, Part VI, focuses on structures, particularly organizations and roles, but also groups. Two of the essays are fairly technical applications of the theory of action to organizations in society and the public school, complemented by another focussing on organizational aspects of schools. The other two deal with critical aspects of the application of the theory to the analysis of the professions.

This very brief synopsis is intended to bring out the logical structure of the book a little more clearly. It is interesting that most of these essays are concerned with dynamic process; there is comparatively little concern with static structural analysis even in those essays that deal primarily with structure. But functional analysis is a common thread through

virtually all the essays, in line with Parsons' recent emphasis on the centrality of the concept function in the theory of action and the importance of the analysis of process in relation to it, along with structure. These essays on the whole reflect therefore the move away from the structural-functional analysis of the more popular variety and a trend towards more technical functional analysis in terms of systemic processes, rather than structures that "perform" functions.

It is our opinion that social scientists interested in general theory or in some more specialized aspect of theory will find much that is stimulating and informative in this book. It is our fond hope that in its openness, its rich variety both in range of topics and in levels of theoretical work, it will appeal to scholars and challenge them to contribute to the development of general theory in the social sciences. Obviously the major task still lies ahead. If the general theoretical framework for social science that develops eventually is something radically different from the theory of action, even to the extent of falsifying its basic assumptions and framework, and if this book has made a contribution to its development, it will still be an appropriate honor to Talcott Parsons. For that is the measure of the man, who has a lifetime commitment to the *process* of scientific discovery, rather than to a *structure* of knowledge, and who sees the *function* of his work as contributing to the evolution of a theoretical system which will be superior to earlier theories, including his own, in its capacity to reduce the complexities of social phenomena in generalized symbolic ways that meet the criteria of scientific knowledge.

NOTES

1. See Talcott Parsons, "Some Problems of General Theory in Sociology," pp. 27-68 in J.C. McKinney and E.A. Tiryakian (eds.), *Theoretical Sociology: Perspectives and Developments* (New York: Appleton-Century-Crofts, 1970).

2. See Chapters 1 and 5 in this book. Also Talcott Parsons, "An Approach to Psychological Theory in Terms of the Theory of Action," pp. 612-711 in Sigmund Koch (ed.), *Psychology: A Study of a Science*, vol. III (New York: McGraw-Hill, 1959), pp. 624-625.

3. See Talcott Parsons, *The Structure of Social Action* (Glencoe, Ill.: The Free Press, 1949), pp. 601-624, especially pp. 607 and 621; also pp. 737-742.

4. *Ibid.*, p. 730, also pp. 753-754.

5. Obviously it would take a major effort to substantiate this claim, but anyone familiar with the critical debate of the 1950's as well as with the logical structure of the theory of action should have no difficulty in detecting the pervasiveness of this problem.

6. See Talcott Parsons, "The Point of View of the Author," pp. 311-363 in Max Black (ed.), *The Social Theories of Talcott Parsons* (Englewood Cliffs, N.J.: Prentice-Hall, 1961), pp. 314-323, especially pp. 320-321. See also Chapter 3 in this book for a discussion of this and other dilemmas.

7. See Talcott Parsons, Edward Shils, Kaspar D. Naegele, and Jesse R. Pitts (eds.), *Theories of Society* (New York: The Free Press of Glencoe, Inc., 1961), pp. 30-33; also Talcott Parsons and Edward A. Shils (eds.), *Toward a General Theory of Action* (Cambridge, Mass.: Harvard University Press, 1951), pp. 47-109.

8. See *The Structure of Social Action*, pp. 732-735; "The Point of View of the Author," pp. 323-328; *Toward a General Theory of Action*, pp. 56-64.

9. See especially John F. Scott, "The Changing Foundations of the Parsonian Action Scheme," *American Sociological Review*, 28 (October, 1963), pp. 716-735.

Scott's critique seems to be based on a misunderstanding of the place of the concept "motives" in the theory of action from *The Structure of Social Action* on. See, for example *The Structure of Social Action*, pp. 719, 732, 738, 750.

10. See *The Structure of Social Action*, pp. 44-45 and *Toward a General Theory of Action*, pp. 53-54. See also "The Point of View of the Author," pp. 323-328, and "Some Problems of General Theory in Sociology," pp. 29-32.

11. See *Theories of Society*, pp. 32-36; "The Point of View of the Author", pp. 325-329; "Some Problems of General Theory in Sociology", pp. 29-36.

12. See especially *Theories of Society*, pp. 36-60; also Talcott Parsons, *The System of Modern Societies* (Englewood Cliffs, N.J.: Prentice-Hall, 1971), pp. 10-26.

13. These are shorthand terms for the components that have been conceptualized fairly consistently but indicated with a variety of terms. See *Theories of Society*, pp. 41-44.

14. For discussion of equilibrium, see *Theories of Society*, pp. 36-38, 60-70; Talcott Parsons, *The Social System* (Glencoe, Ill.: The Free Press, 1951), pp. 205-207, 272-277, 481-483, 491-492, 519-520; "The Point of View of the Author," pp. 337-339.

15. See *Theories of Society*, pp. 37-38; "Some Problems of General Theory in Sociology," pp. 33-35.

16. See Talcott Parsons, *Sociological Theory and Modern Society* (New York: The Free Press, 1967), chap. 7: "Pattern Variables Revisited," pp. 192-219, pp. 208-209 for an example of the A-G reversal and the footnote on p. 199 as an example of the lower-level L below A.

17. See *Sociological Theory and Modern Society*, chap. 1; also "Some Problems of General Theory in Sociology," pp. 45-46.

18. See "Pattern Variables Revisited;" and the media papers, chaps. 10 and 11 in *Sociological Theory and Modern Society*; and Talcott Parsons, "On the Concept of Value-Commitments," *Sociological Inquiry*, 38 (Spring 1968), pp. 135-159.

19. See Chapter 9 of this book for a tentative exploration.

20. See pp. 15-16.

21. See *Toward a General Theory of Action*, pp. 54-56; *Theories of Society*, pp. 33-34. Most of Parsons' work has focussed on the analysis of the social system. For a systematic statement see *Theories of Society*, pp. 30-79. For an analysis of the personality system in functional terms see the essay in Koch (ed.), *op. cit.*, and Talcott Parsons, *Social Structure and Personality* (New York: The Free Press, 1965).

22. *Toward a General Theory of Action* does little more than mention the behavioral organism, and the behavioral and cultural systems are not seen as action systems in the same sense as social systems and personalities, p. 55. See *Theories of Society*, pp. 964-965, for treatment of the cultural system as an action system in the sense of empirical action systems oriented to symbols, and so on. The analysis of the cultural system has been carried farthest in *Theories in Society*, pp. 963-993. See Chapter 8 of this book for an attempt to analyse the behavioral organism, and Chapter 7 for an attempt to treat science as a cultural system in the latter sense.

23. See "Some Problems of General Theory in Sociology."

24. See Chapter 2 of this book.

25. See the media papers in *Sociological Theory and Modern Society* and "On the Concept of Value Commitments." Also

Talcott Parsons and Neil Smelser, *Economy and Society* (Glencoe, Ill.: The Free Press, 1956), pp. 119-143. For the first general statement on levels of generality and specificity, see Talcott Parsons and R.F. Bales, *Family, Socialization and Interaction Process* (New York: The Free Press, 1955), chap. VII.

26. See *Family, Socialization and Interaction Process*, chap. VII; *Economy and Society*, pp. 119-143; Neil J. Smelser, *Social Change in the Industrial Revolution* (Chicago: University of Chicago Press, 1959), chaps. III and VIII; Neil J. Smelser, *Theory of Collective Behavior* (London: Routledge and Kegan Paul, 1962), chap. II. Also *Theories of Society*, pp. 62-64.

27. In *Family, Socialization and Interaction Process* these stages were identified with the oral, oedipal and latent phases in socialization, *op. cit.*

28. See especially *Theories in Society*, pp. 41-44. In the resource table, especially in Smelser's usage, collectivities and roles are sometimes collapsed into one level.

29. See particularly the discussion in *Theories in Society*, pp. 41-44 where these levels and components are interlaced and the above conceptualization comes out quite explicitly but not systematically.

30. See "Some Problems of General Theory in Sociology."

31. See p. 7 above.

32. See the media papers: chaps. 10 and 11 in *Sociological Theory and Modern Society* and "On the Concept of Value-Commitments."

33. See "Some Problems of General Theory in Sociology."

34. See Parsons' statement about his theory building strategy in "Pattern Variables Revisited," pp. 318-321.

35. See footnote in "Some Problems of General Theory in Sociology," p. 61. The disagreement also involves the nature and functional relevance of other media, e.g., "definition of the situation" and "intelligence."

36. See below pp. 12-14.

37. See *Sociological Theory and Modern Society*, pp. 361-363.

38. *Ibid.*, p. 364.

39. See Chapter 9 in this book.

40. For highly sophisticated analyses of generalized media, see Part III in this book. Chapter 9 attempts to derive media theory systematically from the interaction paradigm.

41. See especially *Social Change in the Industrial Revolution* and *Theory of Collective Behaviour*.

42. Some of the pattern variables were first formulated in an essay on "The Professions and Social Structure," published in 1939. See Talcott Parsons, *Eassys in Sociological Theory*, rev. ed. (Glencoe, Ill.: The Free Press, 1954), chap. II.

43. See *Toward a General Theory of Action*, pp. 64-69, 78-81; *The Social System*, pp. 58-67; T. Parsons, R.F. Bales and E.A. Shils, *Working Papers in the Theory of Action* (New York: The Free Press, 1953), pp. 59-62, 66-67, 97-98, 180-181; "Pattern Variables Revisited." For an account of changes in use of the pattern variables see also "The Point of View of the Author," pp. 328-338 and "Some problems of General Theory in Sociology," pp. 44-46. See *Toward a General Theory of Action*, pp. 481-496 as an example of many attempts that have been made to operationalize the pattern variables.

44. The discussion here is based on "Pattern Variables Revisited," which is the best source for the definition and organization of the pattern variables.

45. In the following discussion I shall use G as an example to try to clarify matters. It would be too elaborate to reproduce the full discussion and the accompanying figures here.

46. See as an example of such an attempt Jan J. Loubser, "The Contribution of Schools to Moral Development: A Working Paper in the Theory of Action," *Interchange*, I (April 1970), pp. 99-117. Also published in C. Beck, *et al., Moral Education* (Toronto: University of Toronto Press, 1971), chap. 5. See also Chapter 9 in this book.

47. *Ibid.*

48. While these relationships are not stated in this form by Parsons, they are implicit in his analysis of the functional significance of the patterns in "Pattern Variables Revisited," pp. 199-207.

49. *Ibid.*, p. 208.

50. *Ibid.*, p. 206; also "The Point of View of the Author," p. 330.

51. See *Sociological Theory and Modern Society*, chaps. 10 and 11; and "On the Concept of Value-Commitments."

52. See "Some Problems of General Theory in Sociology," pp. 44-48.

53. See *Ibid.*, footnote on p. 46.

54. *Ibid.*, p. 67.

55. See *Toward a General Theory of Action*, pp. 78-88.

56. See *The Social System*, pp. 480-535, especially p. 486.

57. See Neil J. Smelser, *Social Change in the Industrial Revolution, Theory of Collective Behaviour,* and *Essays in Sociological Explanation* (Englewood Cliffs, N.J.: Prentice-Hall, Inc., 1968), part II.

58. See *Social Change in the Industrial Revolution*, chaps. III and VIII and also *Theory of Collective Behaviour*, chap. II *et passim*.

59. See *Theory of Collective Behaviour*, chap. II, and Figure I-3 in this introduction.

60. See especially "On the Concept of Value-Commitments," pp. 153-159, and *Theories of Society*, pp. 70-74.

61. There was much more of this in *The Social System* than most critics were willing to admit. And *Toward a General Theory of Action* would not have been conceived without this realization. For recent statements see "Some Problems of General Theory in Sociology" and Smelser, *Essays in Sociological Explanation*, especially chap. 5.

62. See *The Social System*, pp. 481-490; *Theories of Society*, pp. 70-79.

63. This change is best reflected in the essays in *Sociological Theory and Modern Society*, but also in *Theories of Society*, pp. 70-79, and in *Societies: Evolutionary and Comparative Perspectives* (Englewood Cliffs, N.J.: Prentice-Hall, 1966) and *The System of Modern Societies*.

64. See especially *Sociological Theory and Modern Society*, chap. 15, *Societies: Evolutionary and Comparative Perspectives*, chap. 2, and "Some Problems of General Theory in Sociology," pp. 29-35. See also the introduction to Part IV of this book.

65. See *The Social System*, pp. 26-36.

66. See Chapter 12 in this book. Also, the earlier critical essays collected in N.J. Demerath III, and R.A. Petersen, *System, Change and Conflict* (New York: The Free Press, 1967); R. Dahrendorf, *Class and Class Conflict in Industrial Society* (Stanford, Calif.: Stanford University Press, 1957); and Desmond P. Ellis, "The Hobbesian Problem of Order: A Critical Appraisal of the Normative Solution," *American Sociological Review*, 36 (August 1971), pp. 692-703.

67. See D. Wrong, "The Oversocialized Concept of Man in Modern Society," *American Sociological Review*, 26 (April, 1961), pp. 183-193.

68. Parsons has tried to keep these problems separate and has insisted throughout his career that they should be. In *The Structure of Social Action* he stated: "From the scientific point of view . . . the sole question is whether this conceptual scheme 'works.' But it is not necessary for present purposes even to raise the question whether human behavior is 'really' normatively oriented. . . . the concept normative is defined only with reference to its place in a particular theoretical system, not in ontological terms" (pp. 76-77). In "Some Problems of General Theory in Sociology" he repeated: "A structure is not an ontological entity but is strictly relative to the investigatory purpose and perspective" (p. 35).

69. See "Pattern Variables Revisited," p. 350; also Black, *op. cit.*, pp. 33, 66, 89-90.

70. See especially Smelser's work, previously cited (1959, 1962, 1968). Also Chalmers Johnson, *Revolutionary Change* (Boston: Little, Brown and Company, 1966); and S.M. Lipset and S. Rokkan, *Party Systems and Voter Alignments* (New York: The Free Press, 1967), pp. 1-64.

71. See Demerath and Petersen, *op.cit.* Also Ellis, *op.cit.* and Robert R. Blain, "An Alternative to Parsons' Four-Function Paradigm as a Basis for Developing General Sociological Theory," *American Sociological Review*, 36 (August 1971), pp. 678-692.

72. See especially Louis Althusser, *For Marx,* trans. Ben Brewster (London: Allen Lane, The Penguin Press, 1969).

73. See Irving Zeitlin, "The Marx-Weber Model of Social and Historical Analysis," paper read at the 1973 meetings of the Canadian Sociology and Anthropology Association. Also Chapter 12 of this book.

74. See Alvin W. Gouldner, *The Coming Crisis of Western Sociology* (New York: Basic Books, Inc., 1970), part II.

75. It would not be difficult to show that virtually all the propositions in Dahrendorf's "conflict" model of society are logically implicit in the theory of action.

76. See Chapter 4 of this book.

77. See Jan J. Loubser, "South African Society and Human Values," Lecture delivered at the Annual General Meeting of the South African Institute of Race Relations (Cape Western Region), Cape Town, 1972.

78. See R. Bellah, *Beyond Belief* (New York: Harper and Row, 1970); and Smelser's previously cited works. Unfortunately neither of them could add another commitment to their heavy schedules during the preparation of this book.

I

META-THEORY

INTRODUCTION

Rainer C. Baum and Victor Meyer Lidz

It would certainly be a mistake to temporize scientific or philosophical knowledge with the assertion: each age has its own truth. Yet one has to realize also that the structure of human thought itself changes with historical development. Progress in science occurs not only through discovery and interpretation of new facts but also through our continuous relearning just what the term "understanding" can mean.[1]

Carl F. von Weizsäcker

All but one of the essays in this section share a location. They are expressions of men finding themselves somewhat more in the context of "discovery of science" than in the context of "justification." If the former deals with the problems of inquiry itself somewhat more than its objects and the latter presumes a sufficient level of consensus on standards evaluating knowledge, one might react with pessimism after half a century of sociological work. But whether one considers our discipline as still young or not, problems in these contexts persist. They do change in form, but as categories of puzzles they cannot be solved in the fashion that history "lays to rest" a problem such as the human consequences of the plague. Because on this point disciplines much older than ours share the same uncertainties, we selected the statement of v. Weizsäcker as an appropriate theme. Like some art and some Protestant theology, science produces statements of order radically other than commonsense constructions. In physics this has had a history. Archimedes' laws of leverage were far closer to commonsense experience than any of the "objects" a contemporary nuclear physicist concerns himself with. Sometimes histories of this sort are punctuated by revolutions in cognizing. Relativity, which destroyed the assumption that there is a universal observer in universal time-space, was one of these; the principle of indeterminacy was another. However, these do not invalidate Archimedes' laws; they only change their significance in theoretical physics.

In principle, matters are not different in the social

sciences. There may be a difference in degree. Sociology has had its own "revolutionary" emancipation from commonsense. As students of community power structure discovered, there is no universally valid scientific answer to the commonsense question: "Who runs this town?" Concept specification—how one defines power—and operationalization—how one locates power—"determine" to a very significant degree the answer found. Using a zero-sum conception and operating with a reputational procedure repeatedly yields a different answer about the structure of power than when one uses a non-zero-sum conception and operates with decision-participation classified by issue.[2] This does not invalidate Homans' universal psychological propositions about exchange, but it does change their significance in both theory and research method, aiding in the discovery among others of the logical complement to the group fallacy, viz. the individualist fallacy.[3]

What may differ between social and natural science is that the emancipation from commonsense retains a peculiar sharpness for a sociology whose business it is to explain commonsense reality constructions. Sociology became possible only after the normative and existential realms of human affairs could be legitimately regarded as distinct phenomena.[4] Once the relation between the two could be seen as problematical, the resulting tension was to become a persistent feature of social science inquiry and more so than in other sciences. The central reason for this peculiarity of inquiry into the social

26

was that its very object of knowledge, commonsense social reality constructions, is in part constituted of the normative. Keeping in mind that one deals here only with a post-Renaissance type society that has institutionalized science and not with "savages" who shared a far richer stock of interpretations of themselves and their world, perhaps one can indicate the differential impact of the normative between natural and social science rather simply. The difference focuses on the shared conception among men in general concerning the objects to be "understood." Among nonspecialists shared lore concerning the nature of rocks does not go very far; a fortiori, what rocks *ought to be like* are notions very likely even less structured than the purely cognitive conceptions of what they are. But what men are and what they should be like happen to be the kinds of conceptions that must be shared to some degree if humans are to be and act human. As all scientific activity is itself social, the difference is relative, but extant nevertheless. But the *differentia specifica* between the social and natural sciences, the observer's self-conscious membership in the observed, is only one source of difficulty in the former. It may not be the most important one. Restrictions on experiment and problems of measurement come to mind as well. Again, differences are relative but do point to greater difficulty in the social realm. As one recent commentator illustrated: sociology (when producing statements about whole societies) is like astronomy in terms of the impossibility of experiment but as yet without the benefit of measurement converging with mathematical deduction; sociology is also like geology in terms of the predominance of nondeductible diachronic and qualitative factors, but as yet without the advantage of an adequate stratigraphy or paleontology.[5] Emphasizing relative rather than absolute differences, it is in terms of experiment and measurement that the social and natural sciences converge. In the latter, too, observer and observed are in inseparable mutual contingency.

If one considers questions of meaning in general as intrinsically normatively defined in however partial a fashion, then most of the essays in this section deal with the problem of contingency between *res cogitans* and *res extensa*. Perspectives and foci vary, but the normative implications remain the common core. The role of action theory varies as well. Schwanenberg and Slabbert analyze parts of the theory itself. The former takes a genuinely gnosiological approach to search for the intrinsic meaning of the theory; the latter asks a methodological question of more restricted scope, viz., what type of explanation the theory of action proffers. Mayhew and Loubser apply the theory, the former to shed new light on persistent debates within sociology, the latter to illumine the relation between social science and society. Our concern is tracing a few common threads to arrive at a conclusion one might draw from these contributions considered as a set.

To us the most interesting aspect of Schwanenberg's effort is a result of his clearly interdisciplinary focus. He robs the most basic axiom of action theory, its conception of action, of any peculiarity. Grounding the ego-alter double contingency theorem as a special case of the more general actor-in-situation contingency, Schwanenberg invites us to view the actor scientist as "just an actor." Regardless of what he studies, the scientist is therefore inescapably bound to influence what he observes and be influenced in turn. Schwanenberg's effort to find parallels between axiomata of action theory and contemporary methodological questions in physics produces another and related insight concerning Parsons' methodological stance. This is his "analytical realism": a self-conscious location of one's position at the midpoint between nominalism and realism. By finding similarities to this in the discussions among some very renowned physicists, Schwanenberg reports two things: (1) a stance describable as analytical realism is rather widespread, and (2) there are constraining facts that make its adoption far more of a necessity and far less a matter of either heuristics or, more seriously, an axiom in the form of a nonrational belief. This comes close to changing the nature of the stance, though not quite. Presumably an axiom is a requisite not supportable by an accepted mode of proof either of a purely logical or of an empirico-logical nature. Now, it seems, the need for analytical realism is supported in part by a reproducible "fact." What used to be a relatively unproblematical axiom in action theory, Schwanenberg has linked to a "history in physics," thereby making it at once less problematical (in the sense of lowering the amount of nonrationality of the belief involved) and more problematical (in the sense of what it means to know). Let us see how.

In brief, Schwanenberg's analysis in this part moves in three steps: Step 1, Heisenberg's early answer to the Newton-Huygens controversy about the nature of light changed the nature of observation. Something "observed," in point of fact any datum, became a part of an "observation-situation," or as Piaget put it more recently: "a fact is only a relation that can be repeated."[6] Heisenberg "solved" the controversy by answering "light is what one does with it," and, raising the issue to a matter of principle, waxed emphatic in asserting that "for the first time in the history of mankind man finds himself in a situation where through all his activities he only finds himself, . . . In modern nuclear physics even the most simple geometrical and mechanical properties can no longer be said to be properties of the electron 'in itself,' they are but properties of our particular way of thinking."[7] If any fact could still be reproduced in a reproducible observation-situation, the statement could still be interpreted as allowing for reduction in the nominalist direction. But, Step 2, "relativity" destroyed the positivist assumption of the universal observer in universal time-space and thereby its peculiar assumption of an unchanging boundary between science and other modes of knowing ("where one was at" seemed to influence time-space measurements that Newton still assumed universal in terms of our commonsense scales). Result: in terms of principle, this shed doubt on the reproducibility of the observation-situation. Step 3, enter the indeterminacy principle. This shook one's faith in a datum as a *completely* reproducible relation within a defined observation-situation. Outcome in Schwanenberg's terms: "man can only find himself as man-in-nature," a conclusion he finds already implied in Parsons' basic conception of action.

This emphasis on the inescapable double-contingency between observer and observed becomes more directly visible if one realizes with Piaget[8] that the double-revolution in physics is a case of internal reciprocity. The problem of the relativity issue alerts one to the fact that the observer is influenced by what he observes; that of the "indeterminacy principle," that he influences the observed. As Piaget does not tire to assert, neither separately nor jointly do these principles pose insuperable problems concerning the question of objectivity. But they pose the question of causality anew. In the case of the indeterminacy issue the question is after all what one concludes from the "finding" that a datum is not *completely* reproducible. Traditionally one used to treat such instances as cases of imperfection in method: Something was deemed to be wrong in theory or measurement; in any case, one defined the situation as characterized by relative ignorance, thus placing the fault with the observer and not with "nature." When the protagonists for a change in the conception of causality and knowledge more broadly assert that incomplete reproducibility of a "fact" is a fact, they do something "really revolutionary." It is that they assign a "don't-know statement" the characteristic of ontological reality. They say: indeed, causal connections are no longer made in space-time between "objects" but only for observation-situations. As the "objects" of microphysics are no longer "objects out there" but only parts of observation-situations, science can be seen as describing the possible rather than the actual.[9]

Whether the impossibility of determinism has been established with the kind of acceptable proof that forces scientists to consensus is a matter beyond our ability to judge and, fortunately, beyond the purview of our intent. For all we need care, we might join Piaget and leave the issue to the future.[10] But there are two matters of import here. First, there are some facts acceptable to some as data that significantly lessen the nonrational belief aspects of analytical realism. Parsons hit on a methodological stance, seen as necessary by some students of natural phenomena, just about as far removed from social commonsense reality constructions as is conceivable. Second, just what it means to know and what it means to explain are matters intrinsically subject to change; if the debate within physics is a guide, a likely direction of change points to a conception of knowledge and explanation that incorporates these modes of action into Parsons' definition of action. To know and explain might then be as doubly-contingent as any other action.

There is furthermore a sensitive humanistic touch to Schwanenberg's analysis that might well console the peculiarly addicted *Geisteswissenschaftler* for whom man, the subject, was always an observer or creator of nature but never just a part of it. In the hands of Schwanenberg the transformation of man's subjectivity to a natural phenomenon proceeds in a fashion that does not deprive this cherished subject from dominating, or creating or whatever else traditional philosophy assigned to it. Finally, at the level of principle, Schwanenberg succeeds in laying to rest, we think conclusively, an affliction from which many in the social sciences suffered at one time or another. The reference is of course to an inferiority complex about some lesser scientific status of one's effort, sometimes allocated to the lack of experiment, sometimes to greater complexity in social phenomena, sometimes to the observer's involvement in the observed as part of himself. Surely, if there is a double contingency that binds observer and observed — and whatever one's position on the implications for understanding anything, no one seems to doubt this fact — and, surely again, if this applies to phenomena as distant from a subjective sense of self as an atom (variety radium B) of which one can never know when and in what direction it might emit an electron and thus transform itself to another atom (variety radium C), there is no need to fear that double contingency in and of itself will retard scientific maturity in the realm of human inquiry just because the observer of human affairs tended to include himself in the observed more self-consciously. On the other hand, neither the meaning of explanation nor the role of value-relevance can ever be taken for granted. That too is a lesson to be taken from the revolution in cognizing in physics. However, these are matters addressed by the remaining contributors.

There is one aspect that makes Slabbert's essay

somewhat exceptional to the description we have given the set. Examining what kind of explanation is involved in functionalism in a technical rather than a merely popular sense, Slabbert does move in the area of the context of justification. But as he traces the development of this kind of explanation historically within action theory as a "framework for explaining living systems," he also travels across the space of the context of discovery. Thus here we find a neat fusion and not a confusion of these two perspectives. That alone makes reading his chapter a pleasurable experience. Second, there is one point at which Slabbert continues where Schwanenberg left off. The point at issue is the role of the means-end schema in the history of Parsons' conception of a functional explanation. Schwanenberg traces this history to the transformation from the alter-ego double contingency to the actor-situation contingency. Here Slabbert continues and almost completes the story by emphasizing the further shift from actor-situation to system-environment as a relation also doubly contingent.

Of course, for Slabbert, with a different problem focus, it is no longer the gnosiological meaning of the schema but rather the sense of understanding involved in a functional explanation that is the issue. Though editorial commentators properly hate to clutter up what is a beautifully economic statement of the main points, some additions might deserve mention to round out the picture just a little. The first is to make explicit Slabbert's selectivity about Merton in the Merton-Parsons contrast. The second emphasizes that in our view Parsons is a diachronic functionalist, an issue that does not quite get the coverage it deserves. Lastly, as a third point we wish to lay emphasis on something that is for Slabbert but a peripheral concern. This is the relation between explanation and prediction, which does constitute a concern to this introduction.

As to Merton, Slabbert's intent is to contrast popular and technical functionalism, not to compare Merton's and Parsons' work or to characterize Merton's main use of functional analysis as such. Slabbert points this out himself, but it might well stand repetition. Perhaps the best short way to describe this contrast is that Slabbert implicitly refers to the epigones of Merton who read only his essay on the political machine. Why raise so much noise about this point? Because Merton leaves the level of popular functionalism in his generalized deviance paradigm. This is much more a technical use of functionalism that treats "society" and "personality" as interpenetrating systems which with some modifications—notably freeing from an element of culture-boundness and, more importantly, adding a more systematic treatment of social control—satisfied even Parsons.[11] But simply tracing "consequences" of some empirical

phenomenon as far as one's imagination allows throughout "society" is not functionalism in the technical sense. Two characteristics are worth emphasizing more than Slabbert cared to. First, it takes a genius of the stature of Merton to make such travel into consequence reverberations fruitful. This means one cannot institutionalize popular functionalism as a method that the less gifted can simply learn. In the hands of peasants rather than royalty, popular functionalism becomes the discovery of a few ad hoc consequences, the significance of which remain a mystery, or the tendency to pompously lable as a "latent" function anyone not obviously blatant. Second, there is the problem of tautology. Here agreement with Piaget[12] is registered. Accordingly, any intradisciplinary type of explanation is inevitably tautologous and, furthermore, the system of sciences as a whole moves in an endless spiral. This being so, one has to be especially sensitive to avoid short-circuited and therefore "offensive circularity."[13] Inventing a function *ex post facto* to make a connection between observations without heed to other extant knowledge or wider implications, a hallmark of the popular functionalist Slabbert has in mind, constitutes the central methodological trap of this approach. Finally, however, even in the hands of the master, popular functionalism could not lead to the establishment of scientific laws. If "lawfulness amounts to the assertion of nomic necessity and hypothetical force,"[14] Merton has to go beyond what he says he is doing. For lawfulness is a question of epistemic embedding of one generalization among other "laws" to which one also has commitments. It therefore goes beyond the problem of empirical evidence and involves an explicit theoretical context that is more than a mere tracing of consequences. In short, if one aims at "laws" in the sense of a fruitful imputation of nomic necessity and hypothetical force, the popular functionalist has to leave the popularity level if for no other reason than the fact that determination of a reasonable range of functional equivalences simply cannot be had on the middle-range level. Systemics is required instead.

The second issue concerns the question of Parsons' approach to the study of change. In emphasizing the distinction between "change in" and "change of" a system, an utter necessity for a technical functionalist concerned with the inherent asymmetry between maintenance of internal stability and identity in the face of environmental change, Slabbert takes in effect Parsons' 1951 position in the famous closing chapter of *The Social System* as proof of the presence of technical functionalism in action theory. For his purpose this may suffice. But it leaves unanalyzed a later addition to the theory that makes Parsons a diachronic functionalist. There is concern not only with the question of how systems maintain themselves and what parameters of environmental change they may not survive within the permissible range of their identity-specifying states, but also with the question of how they came to be what they are. Tying "process" guided by mechanisms of control to structural change in the form of differentiation (g-function) with generalization of resources (adaptive upgrading, a-function) on the one hand, and "inclusion" or normative upgrading (i-function) and "value-generalization" (l-function) on the other, Parsons *applied* the four-function schema to the study of historical genesis.[15] That Slabbert left the matter where he did is our loss. Had he carried his analysis further as indicated, another change in the categorization of basic concepts would have had to be faced. For once Parsons self-consciously turned to evolutionary problems, he had to make explicit that, like system, "function" in the notion of four-functional problems is timeless. Function is coterminous with Parsons' conception of "the problems of environment-contingent open systems," Structure and process, however, are forms, or modes of solving problems subject to change and development. Hence with the assertions that "function is prior both to structure and process" and that he is not a "structural functionalist,"[16] Parsons handed the best conceivable double proof of Slabbert's concern, namely that he thinks of himself as a systemic functionalist and that he practiced what he believed. How well the practice fared might have been a worthwhile question to examine.

Lastly, for Slabbert the logical structure of explanation is the same as that of prediction (p. 2). As this is a matter of concern in the present context, just how wide the implications of this statement are in the case of a functional explanation would be an interesting question. When we took course in methodology in the early 1960's, we learned that explanation and prediction *are* the same, period! Then, we believe, that was not an idiosyncratic view of our teachers or of student colleagues or a result of selective reading in the usual texts. If so, we have come a long way since. As Rescher showed conclusively, explanation, retrodiction, and prediction can vary independently.[17] Surely if one can both retrodict and predict, one can explain. But hypothetical system states can be drawn up in which one can retrodict and not predict or vice versa and still explain and in which one can neither predict nor retrodict. One can fix the latter state of affairs as an impossibility, which indeed signifies quite a lot of knowledge about the workings of a system, implying an explanatory grasp rather than ignorance. Recalling the revolutionaries in physics who stress that science deals increasingly with the realm of the possible among actualities, excluding possibilities when it comes to empirical assertions seems an extraordinarily powerful explanatory strategy. Further exploration in this area should advance Parsons' diachronic functionalism considerably. For it is, after all, the ability to define impossibilities that enables us to separate "change of" from "change in" systems.

Turning from a concern with some characteristics of Parsonian functionalism to its application to empirical social science issues, the remaining essays all constitute efforts of the sociology of social science. Mayhew and Loubser complement each other in the narrow sense. Applying the four-function paradigm to perennial issues of dispute and debate in social science, Mayhew presents a synchronic functional analysis. Using the same paradigm, Loubser looks at fewer but identical issues, presenting a diachronic functional analysis. They both deal with what social scientists think they ought to be doing, how they should be doing it, what they actually do and how. Also both treat such issues as a problem of the inevitable contingency between social science and "society," multiple role obligations, and role and personality contingency.

As to specifics, Mayhew presents a set of very familiar methodological issues that have been debated for a long time. He also indicates a few compromise solutions for some familiar ones. What is new and genuinely refreshing is his use of the four-function paradigm to classify them and the different perspective that results. According to Mayhew these interminable debates are interminable not by virtue of the avarice, vanity, or stupidity of those involved but because they are nearly inevitable consequences of two facts of the life of science. One, more proximal, is that there are four uses of theory, the very core of the scientific enterprise; the other and more distal fact, of which the first is but a consequence, is that science is an action system and as such subject to inherent asymmetries and tensions arising from the double-cleavage of instrumental-consummatory and external-internal functional dilemmas. As the author puts it, issues that are consequences of this kind can have no permanently satisfying solutions, as they reflect tensions inherent in social life.

In the short run, and men live in the short run, there is a zero-sum interdependency in the efficacy of solving these problems that precludes optimal solution of more than one. Hence there are six dilemmas of choice and associated tensions. Through the pen of Mayhew, our old familiar standbys become functional tensions. These are the problems of: (1) value-bias versus objectivity (G-I); (2) grand theory versus testable propositions (A-G); (3) idealism versus realism in explanation (L-A); (4) change versus stability (L-I); and the remaining dilemmas across the two diagonals in the usual four-function table, viz., (5) subjective meaning versus objective behavior as alternatives in observations (L-G); and (6) individual versus group as units of object in the subject matter of the discipline (I-A). Thus a fresh look at a set of familiar perplexities.

From Loubser we learn that there is history even in this short run. If one analyzes the emergence of the social sciences from the humanities as a process of differentiation within the sciences, an implicit law emerges: Early in the differentiation phase, any newly specialized set of organized action faces a problem of establishing its separate identity and justifying that separateness. In order to achieve genuine *sui generis* recognition and combat their own lingering insecurities, members will tend to behave as if they were part of an autarchous rather than a contingent subsystem. What is true in general applies to members of a newly differentiating discipline or sets of such as well; therefore social scientists were for a considerable time defensively heedless of others whose support they needed.

Again, one of the major foci is the problem of value-relevance. Although Mayhew locates this problem entirely on the consummatory side of the table, recognizing merely a tension between internal and external exigencies (value-neutrality serves communication *inside*; value-relevance serves to motivate investigators from the *outside*) Loubser breaks this internal-external tension into four sets of pressures by articulating it across the instrumental-consummatory axis as well. Thus "fact-finding" (instrumental) and "explanation" (consummatory) constitute the internal, and "selection of problems" (instrumental) and "application of knowledge" (consummatory) the external tensions. *Inter alia*, this results in one important conclusion. The problem of the scientist's potentially conflicting responsibilities to his discipline and "society" cannot be adequately solved by recourse to role-pluralism. One cannot just say, well, as far as application goes, the scientist simply steps into his citizen role and pursues the matter from that set of normative constraints. Such a "solution" is no solution *because* it presumes an autarchous rather than a contingent scientific subsystem of society.

More so than the other contributions, Loubser's is above all an urgent call for research into the genesis of contemporary "radical phenomena" in the social sciencies, ranging from revisionist social historians to "critical" sociologists. In short, if we could in fact establish a past tendency toward "autarchous misbehavior" on the part of the "newly enfranchised" disciplines, the presently felt crisis comes out as a more or less inevitable consequence in the form of demands for more reasonable integration among necessarily conflicting but equally necessarily contingent interests. Finding surprisingly little inherent incompatabilities between "cognitive rationality" on the one hand and "moral rationality" on the other, Loubser offers a direction in which to search for a more realistically viable solution to an apparent contemporary impasse among protagonists of the relevance debate. What the Mayhew-Loubser efforts portray jointly is this: (1) There are no permanent solutions to classic dilemmas of science, but (2) they do not press on us with equal intensity all the time, and (3) it would not be reasonable to expect that the temporary answers found should show an easily recognized cummulative pattern. Such dilemmas wax and wane in response to both the cycles of specialization and reintegration within sciences and the changes in our understanding of what it means to know.

No doubt one could be far more critical on all four chapters mentioned so far. Since our purpose is not review but introduction, highlighting a few points of underdevelopment may well suffice. In reading Mayhew, we searched in vain for the special status of those dilemmas associated with the polarities across the diagonals (L-G and I-A) which involve the double-cleavage of the instrumental-consummatory *and* the external-internal poles at the same time. Therefore at these points of juncture there should be especial tension of a degree not found elsewhere. Also, the debates polarized around issues functionally classified at these juncture points should be more conflictful than the others. Perhaps this sheds some light on the persistence and occasional acrimony of the Parsons-Homans debate which Mayhew does locate at one of these points (the I-A). Similarly, "one may have some sense" that the "verstehen vs. prediction" issue has been located at the L-G axis because, as a reflection of our changing understanding of what it means to know, this functional crossing is the most sensitive of all. But one has to do one's own projecting of implications into the material to get at this special status. Our own preference would have been to classify at these diagonals all those issues that involve the confluence of symbols from different subsystems of action. More specifically, we would have located there those issues which most blatantly involve cross-level symbol supplies, i.e., those issues which involve most clearly the contradictory demands of the social organization of science, personality needs of scientists, and non-scientific cultural elements, particularly moral commitments. Minimally such procedure would yield an opportunity to articulate ambivalence in the technical Freudian sense with conflicting institutionalized orientations. Identifying this source of disagreement with Mayhew is not an accident, as precisely this point is paralleled in Loubser's essay.

To begin with, in Loubser's essay one gains a comforting measure of assurance that a functional analysis of change is possible and indeed yields quite a number of surprises even within the short compass of an article. We learned that one can do something exciting *and* technically respectable event without doing entirely "the proper thing." In Loubser's case, the proper route would have been to functionally decompose his most important reference system, "society." Loubser treated only the scientific sub-system functionally, leaving its realm of contingency at the unpacked level of a more complex and less stable environment. Still, the results are very interesting hypotheses. This effectively allayed some of our occasional fears that to try anything Parsonian inherently demands facing up to complexities quite unmanageable for an effort confined to the space usually allotted to an article.

On the critical side, there seems to be a tremendous discontinuity between the way Max Weber approached the moral dilemma in science and the way Loubser does. As one may recall, in *Science as a Vocation* morality was in part accorded the status of the non-rational. The relation between what we must do and what we know how to do reliably and rationally was seen there as one of terrifying and unyielding tension. For Max Weber, who characterized science as intrinsically meaningless when seen from the perspective of Tolstoi's humanism, moral commitment, we believe, always contained an element of values of finality definitely beyond the individual's capacity of choice. That is of course not to be confused with society's capacity in the long run. But in the relevance debate it is individuals bound to a short-run existence that count. Also, to be sure, the non rational aspect did not apply to value commitments in total but to a nevertheless important elementary component. In that component morality was like Aristotle's paradigms, residing in heaven as given to man and beyond his manipulative grasp. In Loubser's application of the pattern-variable schema to cognitive and moral rationalities, this drama turns into a peculiarly tame affair of relative differences. Gone both pathos and irony of history, in which the unconditional devotion demanded by faith has to do battle with its very own child, science, this principal tool of the disenchantment of the world! And gone too the only and tension-laden solution: for each to find and obey "the demon who holds the fibres of his very life." We suspect that analysis would show that this results from Loubser's infusion of the formal patterns with a substantive content of values which is both historically specific and culture-bound, in effect reflecting the American mainstream of instrumental activism, which happens to be a value formula less in conflict with science.

The essay by Fararo stands off from the other contributions to this section in that it is concerned more with the context of justification than with the context of discovery. It constitutes a first attempt to bring the tools of logical and mathematical formalization to bear upon central conceptions within the theory of action. It attempts to "objectify" the relations among key elements in the theory to give greater assurance that different particular uses of the theory can indeed be regarded as applications of the same theory. It also attempts, by formalization, to render more general and more clearly fashioned statements of central hypothetical relationships in the theory, so that their logical rigor and implications may be more thoroughly examined. It should prove possible, by further work within the framework Fararo outlines, to tighten the conceptual interrelationships of hypotheses within the theory, to deduce new dimensions of hypothetical relationships from unexplicated implications of general terms in the theory, and perhaps to falsify or refashion current understandings about the groundings of specific modes of explanation within the general framework of the theory. To be sure, such operations in the justification of presumed knowledge can already be performed with interesting degrees of rigor within the theory of action. The theory of action since *The Structure of Social Action*, has exhibited a relatively constant concern with regularizing the stable "universals" of explanation within the social sciences and with deducing particular explanatory arguments from relationships obtaining among universal or totally general terms.[18] However, Fararo is proposing that we now attempt to upgrade the rigor and formal objectivity with which we carry out such operations.

Fararo's essay is thus taking up an extremely ambitious task. Although the present commentators are not very thoroughly versed in the literature on mathematical modelling of sociological theory, it appears that the measure of Fararo's ambition lies perhaps even more in the extent of his departure from previous mathematical sociology than in the extent of his reformulations of terms in theory of action. Theoretical work on mathematical models within sociology has involved, at least very predominantly, the development of formal procedures either for interpreting specific bodies of data in ways that may ground generalizations and comparisons or for explicating relationships in theories that, while abstract, are comparatively simple and applied to comparatively restricted empirical domains. There have not been substantial attempts to explicate mathematically or in terms of formal logic any theories comparable to the theory of action in complexity, grounding in analytical universals, appeal to assumptions of systematicity, or generality of empirical "coverage." We must expect, then, that Fararo's present essay will comprise only a beginning and that it may not prove entirely adequate in explicating the principal features of the theory of action, or even in establishing a framework within which future efforts may achieve such explication.

The point from which Fararo's argument departs seems to be very shrewdly chosen, especially with regard to the problem of explicating the general appeals to systematicity which have been so thoroughly incorporated in the theory of action. Fararo notes that Parsons has long acknowledged a fundamental indebtedness to Whitehead with regard to metaphysical, epistemological, and other concerns involving philosophical stance and method. Indeed, the theory of action can be regarded as a very extensive exercise in the spelling out of Whiteheadian "analytical realism" within the domain of the social sciences and with the aid of substantive materials produced by such classic figures as Durkheim and Weber. Hence, Fararo proceeds by sketching out the basic content of Whiteheadian metaphysics. Perhaps the most fundamental point in this discussion is that particular occasions or events or phenomena are to be understood as units of environing systems. The analysis of the occasion is to proceed by examination of the prehensions of other parts of the system, i.e., other occasions, within the occasion of reference. In principle, occasions are complexly composed of the prehensions of a plurality of other occasions having different locations within the system. It is appropriate, futhermore, to speak of enduring patterns within the system — in a sense quite parallel to the conception of pattern and structure within the theory of action — whenever prehensive relations with given characteristics are repeated in nexus obtaining among a series of individual occasions. One can analyze both the change and flux of the particularities of the occasions themselves and the enduring patterns of prehensions among the occasions.

Whitehead's "system theory" was in the first instance a metaphysical system in a strict sense, dealing with the analysis of occasions located in space-time geometrically. However, it was formulated with sufficient generality that its abstract form could be applied to various other domains. Whitehead did not shy from essaying its application to the understanding not only of, for example, the general form of biological evolution, but even the evolution of "reason."[19] Fararo proceeds in the fashion of this spirit. He first develops some simple formalizations of the key conceptions in Whitehead's metaphysics. He then tries to show that central formulations within the theory of action conform essentially to the requirements of these notations.

Fararo treats the actor in the social situation with a relationship to an alter as an occasion composed of prehensions with other occasions. Both orientation of the actor and the modality of the alter or of other objects in the situation may be regarded as types of prehensions. The pattern variables may then be regarded as alternative forms of prehensions which actors may choose to follow in attempting to locate themselves (or to sustain situationally given locations) within the environing system of action. The Whiteheadian framework provides strong legitimation for the procedure of abstracting from the ongoing processes of interaction stable characteristics of the standards by which actors regulate their prehensions with various features of their social situations, i.e., for focusing on the pattern variables.

Attention is then shifted to the system, rather than actor, level of analysis. Fararo starts from the assumption that the system too functions through prehensions with occasions in an environment. He then adopts the conception of inputs and outputs to describe these prehensions. The functions of adaptation and goal-attainment are ascribed the formal status of two distinct modes of the regulation of input and output prehensions. The complexity of a system implies, further, that there are many prehensions obtaining internally to the system among its various parts. Within the set of these internal relations, Fararo notes that one function — pattern maintenance — becomes specialized about sustaining the endurance of the system's fundamental patterns, while a second function — integration — is concerned with the harmony obtaining among the system's particular parts or occasions. Although this derivation of the four functions is perhaps not as rigorously developed as would be desirable, it does indicate that the four functions are apparently well grounded in conceptions of the systematicity of events as fundamental as those of Whitehead's metaphysics.

At this point in his argument, Fararo returns to the pattern-variable scheme. Here he is concerned with the very sticky theoretical issue of the relations between the pattern-variable and four-function paradigms. While at one level he is merely formalizing the particular relationships already outlined by Professor Parsons, and hence incorporating their problems within his formalization, at another level he arrives at a strong and simple statement of the relations between the two paradigms. Thus, he argues that the combinations of pattern variables associated theoretically with a given functionally defined location within an action system define the unique standards for guiding voluntaristic choices among potential lines of action that can stabilize performance at that specific location of action. This seems to be the most direct and the strongest resolution of a difficult conceptual problem that has yet been explicity articulated.

Fararo's emphasis falls on the analysis of unit actors and actions and of their relations with one another and with encompassing action systems. Action systems are treated principally as settings within which action proceeds and within which standards for action choices are established. His formalizations seem less successful in explicating the potential within the theory of action conceptions for conducting macro-level analysis. Thus, in conclusion, he notes that his treatment does not clarify the difficult conception of the "functional exigencies" confronting the operations of action systems. It may be suggested that more attention must be given to the notion of equilibrium of an action system and to the conditions theoretically necessary for sustaining equilibrium before the conception of exigencies can be handled in detailed and rigorous fashion. Until an explication of these aspects of the theory, at least, are brought into Fararo's formal treatment, we must regard his effort to capture the conceptual richness of the systematicity attributed to action phenomena within the theory of action as only partially successful. However, it should also be noted that further work on the problem of exigencies should also capture more of the dynamic qualities of the theory. Essentially, it is to the various ways in which a system may meet its functional exigencies and to their differential consequences that the action theorist refers in attempting to account for transformation or change.

At this point, it can be seen that Fararo's concern with the context of justification feeds back into the context of discovery. The portions of the theory that he has not yet succeeded in placing upon a higher level of formal justification stand out as foci for future work in two respects. First, the task of attempting their formal justification has been more sharply defined than heretofore. Second, it may be that their resistance to the present effort at justification indicates that further substantive improvement will be a precondition of the formal justification. Moreover, it is to be hoped that the conceptual work to which Fararo has brought more thorough justification can now be more generally regarded as a more viable instrument for the analysis of action.

What then can be concluded from these contributions as a set? We think there is a simple yet pregnant message. There was a time when issues of the context of discovery and the context of justification were treated in a confused fashion because the distinction was lacking at that time. That was erroneous. It was followed by a time when issues in these two contexts were treated as genuinely independent of each other.

That was erroneous too. Unless all the contributors in this section are fundamentally mistaken, these issues are interdependent; they exist in mutual contingency. As with all of men's endeavors, examining them in whatever form of splendid isolation does not promise much.

NOTES

1. Werner Heisenberg, *Der Teil und das Ganze* (München: Piper, 1969), p. 173.

2. Terry N. Clark, *Community Structure and Decision-Making: Comparative Analyses* (San Francisco: Chandler Publishing Co., 1968), pp. 72-81.

3. Erwin K. Scheuch, "Cross-National Comparisons Using Aggregate Data: Some Substantive and Methodological Problems," in R. Merritt and S. Rokkan (eds.), *Comparing Nations* (New Haven: Yale University Press, 1966); "Social Context and Individual Behavior," in D. Mattei and S. Rokkan (eds.), *Quantitative Ecological Analysis* (Cambridge: M.I.T. Press, 1969).

4. Kaspar D. Naegele, "Editorial Forward: Interaction: Roles and Collectivities," in T. Parsons et al. (eds.), *Theories of Society* (New York: The Free Press of Glencoe, 1961), p. 147.

5. Jean Piaget, "The Place of the Sciences of Man in the System of Sciences," in UNESCO, *Main Trends of Research in the Social and Human Sciences* (Paris: Mouton/UNESCO, 1970), p. 32.

6. *Ibid.*, p. 48.

7. Werner Heisenberg, "Die Einheit des naturwissenschaftlichen Denkens," in *Leipziger Universitätsreden* (1942), p. 18.

8. Piaget, *op. cit.*, p. 16.

9. Werner Heisenberg, *Der Teil und Das Ganze* (München: Piper, 1969), p. 170 fn.

10. Piage, *op. cit.*, p. 51.

11. Talcott Parsons, *The Social System* (New York: The Free Press of Glencoe, 1951), chap. VII.

12. Piaget, *op. cit.*, p. 45.

13. Hans Albert, "Probleme der Wissenschaftslehre in der Sozialforschung" in Rene König (ed.), *Handbuch der Empirischen Sozialforschung*, vol. 1 (Stuttgart: F. Enke, 1967), p. 51.

14. Nicholas Rescher, *Scientific Explanation* (New York: Free Press of Glencoe, 1970), p. 107 ff.

15. Talcott Parsons, *Societies: Evolutionary and Comparative Perspectives* (Englewood Cliffs, N.J.: Prentice-Hall, 1966); *The System of Modern Societies* (Englewood Cliffs, N.J.: Prentice-Hall, 1971).

16. Talcott Parsons, "Some Problems of General Theory in Sociology," in John C. McKinney and Edward Tiryakian (eds.), *Theoretical Sociology: Perspectives and Development* (New York: Appleton-Century-Crofts, 1969).

17. Rescher, *op. cit.*, pp. 25-75.

18. Harold J. Bershady, *Ideology and Social Knowledge* (Oxford: Basil Blackwell, 1973).

19. Alfred North Whitehead, *Process and Reality* (New York: Macmillan, 1929; Harper Torchbooks, 1960); *Modes of Thought* (New York: Macmillan, 1938; Capricorn Books, 1958); *The Function of Reason* (Princeton: Princeton University Press, 1929: Boston: Beacon Press, 1958).

1

ON THE MEANING OF THE GENERAL THEORY OF ACTION

Enno Schwanenberg

Science is made by men. . . . Natural science rests on experiments, its findings are reached through talk among the participants who consult each other concerning the interpretation of experimental results.[1]

Werner Heisenberg

If we are to believe Heisenberg in his autobiographical account, science, and expressedly natural science, is not the goddess Athena springing fully armed out of the head of Jupiter but is made just by men. If this is the basic state of affairs, the chasm between the natural and the social sciences is, as Heisenberg himself suggests (in another quotation), less than unsurmountable; and the nuclear physicist's reflections might congenially lend themselves to a considerate transfer to the state of social science. This consideration should be all the more reasonable as this is a physicist who does not urge a physicalistic standard upon social science but reminds it of its very identity founded in its genuine subject, i.e., interaction — quite in contrast to an earlier mode of social theorizing that subjected itself to the self-concept and model of classical mechanics. Social science, then, develops its theory through the discourse of the men active in its pursuit who take counsel together about the interpretation of empirical observations. As Heisenberg recalls, however, of the development of quantum theory, and as any social scientist acquainted with the problems of communication will readily expect, the discourse on interpretations, may very well be characterized by dissensus and rifts of argument. Sometimes the drivergences are basic; yet there is also the possibility, inherent in communication, that an interpretation is rejected simply because its meaning has not been grasped. The present essay has as its aim the exposure and illumination of some basic aspects of the meaning structure behind the general theory of action, to eliminate a few of those impediments of discourse that result from lack of understanding and to evaluate its interpretation more adequately.

INFERENCES FROM DEVELOPMENTS IN MODERN SCIENCE

The fact, and not an exaggeration, is that from the point of scientific discourse the interpretative endeavors by the general theory of action have met honors based rather on perplexity than on understanding. If one reviews the reviews of Parsonian theory,[2] one cannot help noticing the evasive generalities in most comments, if not an indignant tenor in quite a few of them. Typically it is said, in the case of criticism, that the terms and statements of the theory do not comply with science as understood by the critics: specifically, that the statements are not empirical. The notion of "empirical" may be self-evident for these reviewers, but it is not self-explanatory. Instead, it receives its meaning from a methodological tradition, a philosophy of science, that announced its advent in the sixteenth century and started decisively in the seventeenth century, gathering strength with the development of classical mechanics. In the nineteenth century, it was shaped into the doctrine of positivism, its twentieth-century heir and successor being that diversity of methodological orientations which Kaplan has synoptically subsumed under the name of "semantic empiricism," prominently comprising, among others, logical positivism (logical empiricism), operationalism, and pragmatism.[3] In other words: the concept and postulate of "empiricality" does not simply stand for itself but derives its claim from a specific methodological frame of reference which as such is meta-sociological, i.e., philosophical.

Such a frame of reference is, as any other, intrinsically bound up with a distinctive language, a fact which is quite obvious if we remember with Heisenberg that science proceeds through the medium of discourse. If one also remembers that the discussion on Parsonian theory is characterized by embarrassment concerning the latter's terminology, one may surmise that the difference between the two respective languages is fundamentally based on a decisive difference between frames of reference, this guess being supported by the pains Parsons undertakes in his opening work, *The Structure of Social Action,* in propounding his own frame of reference.

Before we discuss some aspects of the action frame of reference, and in order to prepare the ground for an evaluation of its distinctive properties, it will be advantageous to explore some of the premises of the empiricist frame of reference. In this we will be strongly guided by the reflections and inferences made by Heisenberg that he has clothed as dialogues with his friends from nuclear physics. The exposition of the empiricist frame of reference as it is to follow has emphatically to be understood as a pointed abstraction, i.e., as some sort of an "ideal type" for the conceptual identification of selected aspects. In actual practice, especially in a survey of the contemporary scene, empiricism comprises a broad spectrum of intellectual strands into which it has developed and differentiated from straight nineteenth-century positivism and which have incorporated modes of conceptualization that transcend the "pure type" and the classical methodological polarizations. Nevertheless, certain traditional tenets can be located on the horizon.

Modern physics began with experimental discoveries which, when they were interpreted theoretically, shook the theoretical scheme of classical physics, proving that it could claim not universal but only limited applicability. The assumption of universality was crucial, as the empiricist frame of reference was and possibly still is heavily indebted to it for its legitimation.

The theory of relativity dissolved the contention that there is a unique meaning to be given to space and a unique meaning to be given to time, i.e., that there is simultaneity concerning the times of any observers in any locations. In distinguishing, paradigmatically between the times of a resting and of a moving observer, it problematized the status of the observer which, in classical physics, had been seen for any person, in any time and space, everywhere and forever, as unchangingly the same. Quantum physics was the other revolutionary development that discarded the classical scheme. In the realm of atoms it encountered a stability of forms and a discontinuity of states of energy that could not be explained by the laws of classical mechanics. The realm could not even be described in terms of ordinary experience; it could be experienced only indirectly, intuitively. It was a world not of things but of *Wirkungen*, of abstract expressions of natural laws that are adequately described only in mathematical language.

Thanks to both the rigor and the flexibility of mathematical representation, quantum theory was able to give a totally consistent description of these atomic phenomena which at the point of translation into natural language for application in experimental settings would make a very different appearance. To speak of those phenomena in the language of the laboratory, i.e., to operationally semanticize them for discoursing about them with people other than quantum physicists meant to speak in images and analogies (waves, corpuscles, orbits) borrowed from classical mechanics and bound up with paradoxes. The results of obversations simply could not be objectified or, rather, reified as is the case in traditional physics and everyday life. Thus, as Heisenberg puts the words into the mouth of Niels Bohr, "quantum physics is a marvellous example of the fact that something can be understood in full clarity yet that at the same time one knows that one can speak of it only in images and parables."[4]

How is the atomic realm parabolically understood, in the quantum frame of reference? It can, at the outset, negatively be determined, in that it is not bound into the narrowness of an objective world running down in space and time according to a causal law. Instead there is, to a determinable degree, an indeterminacy specifically involved in the observer-observed or subject-object experiential system. Moreover, the mathematical abstractions grasp, beyond experience, a realm of the possible instead of the factual, of the inobvious instead of the obvious. It is a realm of structures, of patterns of connectedness (*Zusammenhänge*), which replaces the world of things (*Sachen*) and which underlies the *Wirkungen*. Though the systemic structures are reached by ascending to high levels of abstraction, they are nevertheless *wirklich* (which is only inadequately translated as "real," because this translation implies *res*, "things," as will be discussed further), as the simplicity of the natural laws exposed through the mathematical language demonstrates. In fact: the higher the abstraction, the simpler the structure; and the simpler the structure, the more general it is.[5]

Heisenberg recalls Einstein's inferring from the great simplicity and beauty of mathematical forms of natural law their truth in the sense of pointing at an ordered objectivity of nature, not as merely a subjective construction for enhancing a heuristic economy of thinking. Since the order of nature can be thought, Heisenberg speculates, the structures, as fundamental as they are, may be such that they are truly superordinate and encompass both the observer and the observed.

In contrast, the empiricist methodology is less oriented towards *Zusammenhänge,* especially when they are not obvious to ordinary experience and intangible for ordinary practice and cannot be determined precisely in ordinary language which, everywhere else in the world, plainly is *the* language of our affairs, practical and scientific. This is made apparent in the research strategy which Heisenberg, in the discussion with an empiricist, compares with the practical orientation of an engineer:

> Your conception of continuous progress in the sense of engineering would deprive our science of any force, or perhaps better, of any real hardness, and I would not know in what sense one could then speak of an exact science. If one does physics in this purely pragmatic fashion one would select any area just readily at hand through good experimental results, and one would try to model the observations on an empirical formula. If the model lacks precision one improves it by adding corrections. But there would be no reason left to search for the more encompassing order; and there would be little chance left to discover the really simple principles, which, for example, distinguish Newtonian physics from the astronomy of Ptolemy. In short, the most important truth criterion of our science, the finally emerging elegant simplicity of natural laws, would be lost.[6]

The formulae of the engineer are in a way a practical-phenomenological description of natural processes and certainly give the feeling that one has, more or less successfully, invented them oneself. If, however, one meets those "simple and grand patterns of connectedness (*Zusammenhänge*)" by analytical divination (*Erraten*) and subsequent reasoning which lead to a precisely formulated system of concepts and axioms, it appears as if these patterns of connectedness have always been there objectively.

There is a most intriguing perspective to this issue of formulae versus axiomatics. It may be that the respective results of the two approaches depend on the preconceptions or "beliefs" the scientist has at the outset of his research concerning the organization of nature. Heisenberg recalls Einstein saying: "First of all and only theory determines what one may observe." This is to say that observation is intrinsically linked to interpretation, but it also implies that theoretical presuppositions determine the

very methodology of inquiry. Heisenberg compares scientific research with a mountain climbing tour. A pragmatic empiricist is methodologically oriented to some particular difficulty, whereas Heisenberg understands himself as being concerned with the great whole (*Zusammenhang*). The pragmatic empiricist when undertaking difficult rock climbing will focus his attention at all times on the next three meters, thus gradually and rock by rock arriving at the summit. To focus on the whole route at once would only produce discouragement; moreover, the problems can only be conceived of when one arrives at the difficult points of the route.[7] Heisenberg himself, however, would see his method of approach as being something like starting with a decision on the whole route at once, the underlying conviction being that only if one has found the right route can the particular difficulties in climbing up to the summit be overcome. Basic to this approach is his firm belief that in nature the patterns of connectedness (*Zusammenhänge*) are, in the final analysis, simple and that nature is made in such a way that it can be understood or, rather, that reason is made in such a way that it can grasp and understand nature. This can easily be recognized as another way of saying that there are superordinate structures that encompass both the observer and the observed.

One may conclude — reminding oneself of Einstein's words that "only theory determines what one can observe" and of Heisenberg's opening statement that science is made by men — that the differences in methodologies are based on differences in preconceptions concerning nature. These suppositions materialize or take shape in frames of reference.

The empiricist preconceptions can historically be traced back to the sixteenth and especially the seventeenth centuries, when there was a general onslaught against the traditional authorities of philosophy. The old philosophical system, based on the writings of Aristotle and in scholasticism imbued with ecclesiastical rigor, did not allow for expansions of knowledge which were imperative with the advent of modern times. For overthrowing the old authorities the most effective strategy was to invoke daily experience and common sense as against "metaphysics." In those scholastic metaphysics the grand *Zusammenhänge* among God, nature, and man were of greatest concern; in opposition and contrast, early empiricism as developed by Francis Bacon rejected the idea of *Zusammenhänge* and founded the new system on the concrete experiential details. The aim and value of knowledge changed from the reverent contemplation of God's order in nature to man's own control over nature subject to his pragmatic exploits. Descartes was the second thinker to discard the superordinate *Zusammenhang* between man and his environment, adding philosophical foundations to Bacon's common sense and complementing, at least for the recipient generations to come, empiricism and pragmatism with rationalism. His philosophy began with that famous doubt which is nothing but a a doubt about the *Zusammenhang*. This doubt provides the identity for the rational subject: *Cogito, ergo sum*. The rational identity, however, that thus replaces the identity of the *Zusammenhang* is a monologous one that does not recognize itself any more in identical structures of the environment: There exists that chasm between *res cogitans* and *res extensa*. Structure is wholly and only with the rational subject. This position, of course, has most forcefully been pronounced by Kant, more than one century later, in his critique, i.e., analysis of pure reason. In science, man-the rationalist joined man-the-pragmatist to create and fuse into man-the-scientist. He experiences nature as subjugated to the law of causal determinacy and as organized into a chain of causal events, he himself being the prime factor in the causal chain. In other words: man-the-scientist — man as the rational and pragmatic empiricist— actively modifies the natural environment in order to confirm his predictions by the success of his actions. He imprints his own structures upon the *res extensa*. Alas, the rational and pragmatic determination of nature by man is not flawless: What in Heisenberg's conception of indeterminacy is an inevitable property of the observer-observed system appears in classical mechanics as an irrational event which, as there is no *Zusammenhang* between *res cogitans* and *res extensa* in which to locate it, has to be conceptualized either as randomness on the side of the environment or as error on the side of the cogitative observer.

It was mathematics in connection with, and as the language of modern relativity and quantum theory that brought the idea of *Zusammenhänge* as a non-experiential *meta-physis* back into science, as we have discussed. "The originality of mathematics consists in the fact that in mathematical science connections between things are exhibited which, apart from the agency of human reason, are extremely unobvious."[9] Mathematics, that is, transcended the subjective cognition of Descartes' observer vis-à-vis the *res extensa* and allowed for *pattern recognition* with regard to and in the environment.[10] This new awareness and conception of *Zusammenhänge* was no longer fraught with speculation as it was in scholasticism; rather, it was truly empirical, more so than Bacon's empiricism. As every one acquainted with the psychology of perception knows, in nature information is not contained in things or particles but in patterns.

It may well be that the new orientation toward pattern recognition is a way out of the dilemma posed by pragmatic empiricism. The modern crisis of civilization is possibly due to the backlash of an orientation toward the environment that is reduced to its mere manipulation. In getting aware again of the "relativity" between man and his environment, the disturbed relationship may become newly harmonized and aesthetic qualities may enter again into human life.

The first person strongly to emphasize the importance and "reality" of patterns in conjunction with the advancement of modern science and the semantic and grammatical possibilities of mathematical representation was Whitehead.[11] Whitehead's view of nature as a nature of patterns — which reads like an anticipation of Heisenberg's theoretical position — had a most decisive, though generally unnoticed, impact on the development of the theory of action:

> One of my most important intellectual impressions was derived from A. N. Whitehead's conception of science, particularly as stated in his *Science and the Modern World*. Three points stand out: first, his strong emphasis on the importance of systematic theory and the special power inherent in a well-integrated theoretical system; second, his views of the nature of abstraction involved in scientific theory, particularly as related to what he called the "fallacy of misplaced concreteness"; third, his view of the continuity of the whole empirical world including both physical and social-behavioral areas. Thus his use of the concept "society" to refer to phenomena of atomic physics seemed to me more than merely metaphorical. Certain "organic" or in some sense "antiatomistic" features of his views on all these levels have appealed to me. I have never been attracted by theories which have tried to build up behavior systems out of discrete isolated conditioned reflexes alone, or social systems out of discrete isolated "individuals" alone. The Whiteheadian views of the importance of relational interconnectedness in systems, of *organization,* have appealed to me profoundly.[12]

In the light of these inferences about certain fundamentals of traditional frames of thought, the discussion will turn immediately to an examination of Parsons' theory.

REFLECTIONS ON THE ACTION FRAME OF REFERENCE

To draw parallels between relativity and quantum theory on the one hand and action theory on the other does definitely not mean that the methodological status of the latter is identical with that of the former. It does mean that even according to theory-building in natural science, which for a long period has supplied a model and standard for social science, it is quite legitimate to analyze and transcend the obvious and to inquire into *Zusammenhänge* or patterns. To quote Whitehead: "Mathematics supplied the background of imaginative thought" and of the rise of a new — also to use Whitehead's term — "mentality" or frame of reference. This mentality, in turn, created the possibility and legitimation to try "imaginative thought" about "patterns of relationships among general abstract conditions" also in social science, though mathematical reasoning, with regard to the complex matters of the social world as contrasted to the atomic world, was not ready at hand. Parsons' mode of theorizing instead makes use, as is commonly known, of classification. As Whitehead wrote: "Classification is a halfway house between the immediate concreteness of the individual thing and the complete abstraction of mathematical notions."[13]

But in putting these classifications into "paradigms" and in attempting to establish "functional" relationships between them, Parsons moved in a sense to some kind of "functional equivalent" of mathematics, experiencing an aesthetic satisfaction similar to that of relativity and quantum theorists.[14] The intentional direction of the move is in both cases the same: a revolution of thought to overcome the mentality established by the historical revolt of the later Renaissance, which "was through and through an anti-intellectualist movement. It was the return to the contemplation of brute fact; and it was based on a recoil from the inflexible rationality of medieval thought. . . . This reaction was undoubtedly a very necessary corrective to the ʹunguarded rationalism of the Middle Ages. But reactions run to extremes."[15]

It resulted in a "fixed scientific cosmology which presupposes the ultimate fact of an irreducible brute matter, or material, spread throughout space in a flux of configurations [i.e., a *res extensa*]. In itself such a material is senseless, valueless, purposeless. It just does what it does do, following [in causal chains] a fixed routine imposed by external relations which do not spring from the nature of its being. It is this assumption that I call 'scientific materialism.'"[16]

By contrast, the new mentality has "a vehement and passionate interest in the relation of general principles to irreducible and stubborn facts." These principles aim at the "very fact of inter-related existence" and are attained in "the discovery that the totality of these general abstract conditions, which are concurrently applicable to the relationships among the entities of any concrete occasion, are themselves inter-connected in the manner of a pattern with a key to it. This pattern of relationships among general abstract conditions is imposed alike on external reality, and on our abstract representations of it. . . ."[17]

This formulation is equivalent to Heisenberg's statement that there are superordinate structures identical for both the observer and the observed; and it elucidates why Parsons takes a position between nominalism (based on the *res cogitans*) and realism (based on the *res extensa*), maintaining that the theoretically formulated analytical system basically, though not literally, corresponds to empirical systems, that is, to organization in nature. In any case, it dissolves the absolute position of the observer, making him in a way contingent upon nature — or, more correctly, cognizant at the start of an interdependence between the observer and the observed which Whitehead philosophically formulated as the aesthetic harmony between nature and reason, pictured in the "reasonable harmony of being" and conceived as the mutual correspondence of basic order in the observer and the observed.[18]

Parsons' own designation for this epistemological position which bases itself on the inter-existence of the observer and the observed and which tries to see beyond brute matter and stubborn things or facts is "analytical realism":

> As opposed to the fiction view it is maintained that at least some of the general concepts of science are not fictional but adequately "grasp" aspects of the objective external world. This is true of the concepts here called analytical elements. . . . These concepts correspond, not to concrete phenomena, but to elements in them which are analytically separable from them.[19]

Starting from this statement, the methodological specificity of the action frame of reference can in outline be unfolded as follows.[20]

In opposition to common sense and what Whitehead has termed "scientific materialism," the theory of action does not accept a description and explanation of the social world in terms of things and facts, that is, one which is plainly realistic — either in the usual meaning of the word that objectifies the *res extensa* or in that sense in which nominalism can be regarded as a "reification" of the *res cogitans*. Instead, the theory of action distinguishes again and again between the concrete and the analytical, the analytical being that mode of cognition or rather recognition by which the observer becomes aware of the order of nature and by which reason, penetrating the facts, grasps the patterns of connectedness.[21]

Specifically, what is grasped are elements; thus, analytical realism may also be called elementary realism. The elements, however, are not particles or units — though Parsons, in *The Structure of Social Action*, deals most explicitly with these in analogy to classical mechanics, considering their description and analysis, however, as representing merely a preparatory step in the direction of systematically conceiving of elements of actions through a more advanced kind of theory. The elements, are conceptualized as aspects of the systemic structure and connectedness of nature, as factors or variables in which by virtue of analytical abstraction the very essence of systemic order can be grasped. The whole evolution of action theory, from *The Structure of Social Action* onward, may be viewed as the endeavor to find out about the elements of action and to conceptualize their functional relationships. The theoretical scheme that has evolved in this endeavor and has been characterized in this chapter as some kind of a functional equivalent of mathematical conceptualization is the AGIL paradigm. It contains four elements: two elements of control or organization (L stands for the normative or value factor, and I for the systemic equilibrium factor) as against two elements representing material conditions (G for the motivational energy factor, and A for the environment (factor).

The four-fold scheme of the paradigm sketches their interplay, the hierarchy of control together with the inverse hierarchy of conditions depicting their structural organization along that continuum of nature which spans the whole range of living systems, from biological to cultural levels. A most analytical and abstract synthesis of the horizontal, systemic, or communication view and of the vertical, normative versus conditional, or control view is contained in the theory of generalized media which draws together the conceptions of communication and control.

The theory decidedly leaves the ground of common sense to push into a transphenomenal realm, making use of methodological idealization and formalization, establishing hierarchies of simultaneously independent and interdependent system levels, tracking down through the whole range of these a multitude of homologous structures and analogous processes in which aspects or analytical elements are distinguished that make for functional relationships in the total order of living systems. This seemingly complex abstractedness represents, of course, exactly the difficulty that the general theory of action has posed for discourse, namely, that the content of its interpretations, i.e., its meaning, was equally transphenomenal. But there is a content which can be expressed quite concretely in that it has social relevance. The theory of action is basically a theory of social action tinged with, or even founded on, a moral emphasis which can be communicated among humans.

The pragmatic, noncontemplative orientation of man toward his environment, inasmuch as it derived from that frame of scientific materialism which was the joint product of Baconian empiricism on the one hand and Cartesian rationalism (*res cogitans*) and

rationally conceived mechanism (*res extensa*) on the other was guided and shaped by the will and effort to establish man's mastery over physical nature to serve his material needs. To repeat, according to the empiricist-mechanistic theory of nature the environment was regarded as extended configurations of masses suited for goal-oriented manipulation by man-the-scientist, man-the-rationalist, man-the-pragmatist. As far as physical nature was concerned, this frame of mind justified itself through the pragmatic test. It worked — though in these days the test is no longer unambiguous, and civilization, confronted with the deterioration of its natural environment, is about to reflect on what had to happen when "the independence ascribed to bodily substances [*res extensa*] carried them away from the realm of values altogether. They degenerated into a mechanism entirely valueless, except as suggestive of an external ingenuity. . . . The two evils are: one, the ignoration of the true relation of each organism to its environment; and the other, the habit of ignoring the intrinsic worth of the environment. . . ."[22]

The empiricist-rationalist-pragmatist frame of mind exhibited its dangers, however, when transposed from the natural to the social environment. Again to quote Whitehead, from whom Parsons has taken over the notion of "ultimate values":

> The doctrine of minds, as independent substances [*res cogitantes*], leads directly not merely to private worlds of experience, but also to private worlds of morals. The moral institutions can be held to apply only to the strictly private world of psychological experience. Accordingly, self-respect, and the making the most of your own individual opportunities, together constituted the efficient morality of the leaders among the industrialists of that period. The western world is now suffering from the limited moral outlook of the three previous generations.[23]

To the *res cogitans* corresponded a *res extensa:*

> This misplaced emphasis [of science on *things* as opposed to *values*] coalesced with the abstractions of political economy, which are in fact the abstractions in terms of which commercial affairs are carried on. Thus all thought concerned with social organization expressed itself in terms of material things and of capital. Ultimate values were excluded. They were politely bowed to, and then handed over to the clergy to be kept for Sundays. A creed of competitive business morality was evolved, in some respects curiously high: but entirely devoid of consideration for the value of human life. The workmen were conceived as mere hands, drawn from the pool of labour. To God's question, men gave the answer of Cain—"Am I my brother's keeper?"; and they incurred Cain's guilt. This was the atmosphere in which the industrial revolution was accomplished in England, and to a large extent elsewhere.[24]

Anyone acquainted with the origin of the theory

of action, as it is documented in *The Structure of Social Action*, will at this point immediately recognize the "meaning" of it and the thrust of its argument. To relate: Parsons vehemently attacks the empiricist tradition insofar and exactly as it is linked to the utilitarian doctrine of political economy. Parsons does not hark back on Bacon but on Hobbes and Locke as those British empiricists who prepared the ground for utilitarianism in that they were the first to amalgamate empiricism and political theory, i.e., to transfer the empiricist frame of reference from the natural to the social. Paradigmatically, the problem of utilitarianism, namely, the problem of the rational pursuit of self-interest, boils down, with Hobbes, to the problem of interests, or ends, and, with Locke, to the problem of reason, Hobbes dramatized the individual interests by picturing society as a "war of all against all" which could only be prevented by a social contract motivated by the deepest of all desires, that of self-preservation, which enthroned a sovereign of supreme power to control the unbound individual desires. As Parsons criticizes, the leap from passionate desires into the rationality of the social contract is highly dubious, as is Locke's invocation of reason when playing down the problem of social order by attributing to reason the guiding role in every individual human action through insight into the equality of all men and their democratic rights; in practicing that insight, reason achieves at the same time in optimal gratification of the self-interest. Parsons declares this notion of "enlighted self-interest" to be a "metaphysical prop" and its respectively conceived utilitarian individual an empiricist "fallacy of misplaced concreteness," using Whitehead's formula and criticism meaning that a theoretical abstraction, a logical construction, had been taken for concrete phenomenal reality. Parsons adds a critique of positivism which is, in essence, nothing but a critique of that second strand of empiricist mentality: of Cartesian rationalism and specifically of the position of the observer conceived as being absolute.

"Radical rationalistic positivism," according to Parsons, cannot admit of the indeterminacy of subjective ends in relation to the situation that is still contained in the utilitarian notion of interests. Instead, it assimilates them to the conditions of the situation, to attain complete determination. There are, nevertheless, departures from the norm of rationality which the positivist — it being implicitly assumed that he has not even a concept of randomness — can only subsume under the categories of "ignorance" and "error," thus once more attributing them to "conditions," heredity and environment, that in this case attain their effects unnoticed "from behind." In this way, radical rationalistic positivism turns over into "radical anti-intellectualistic positivism" and "the utilitarian dilemma is broadened into a more inclusive form."

Parsons, besides generally discarding the pragmatic-empiricist conception of the autonomous individual as a fallacy of misplaced concreteness, starts from the critical representation of the inner contradictions of utilitarianism and positivism to specifically develop the action frame of reference. He attests that there is a means-end rationality (*Zweckrationalität*) in human action, but he contests that this is all there is to it. He criticizes fundamentally a rationalistic view and explanation of social action which interpretes action exclusively in the way of rational means-ends relationships. Action does have a means-end *sector* to which belong such important phenomena as the technical, the economic, and the political rationality; this rational sector, however, is embedded between heredity and environment (called conditions) on the one hand and a nonrational field of determination on the other. Parsons does not stop to repeat emphatically that nonrationality does not mean irrationality and ascribes to it the norms and values, including, finally, the ultimate values. Parsons' attack on empiristic utilitarianism is so passionate that he discards not only the postulate of rationalism, but also the notion of self-interest or any inborn drive in that direction. The social world is constituted in and through the minds of individal actors who are not isolated by reason and self-interest, as are the utilitarian individuals, but can unite for social action on the ground of the values which, though Parsons' analysis identifies them in the human mind (as against heredity and environment), are not private but *common* or *shared*.

Yet there lingered the problem of whether the commonness or sharedness of values could truly be founded in voluntarism. The phenomenological argument had proved their existence, but it could not explain in any way why they were common or shared. Because of these limits, it retained a "krypto-utilitarian-individualistic cast."[25]

The decisive step toward *Zusammenhänge* occurred when the actor's frame of reference was transcended by an "actor-situation" frame of reference and *interaction* became the focus of attention. Only now could the analytical elements actually be conceived as nonconcrete aspects of the systemic nature of human interconnectedness. To introduce Parsons' own summary representation of this theoretical turn:

> Perhaps the most important single result was clarification of the *relational* reference of all action theory — to actor-object relations which could not be abstracted from the relationship and ascribed to one or the other relatum apart from it. The central application was to the concept of value — as concerned with the relation of actor

and object. For example, Max Weber had placed values in the actor, as "subjective" in that sense (I had tended to follow him in this); whereas W. I. Thomas placed values in the object (as in his well-known distinction between attitudes and values). Neither view seems satisfactory. Once values are treated as relational, however, belonging neither in actor nor object, but characterizing the relation between them, then making values the focus of the *organization* of systems of action becomes immediately feasible. Along this path, a fundamental solution of the problems of the nature of internalization and institutionalization and their relations to each other was made possible.[26]

The intrinsic meaning of this brief review, however, may very probably not convey itself instantly to the reader. In fact, it is an abstraction conveying the surface of a real complexity. Specifically, what does it mean to say that "values are treated as relational?" This question, of course, restates the problem of in what sense and why values are shared or common, or the problem of *Zusammenhänge*.

In social science, the usual way of conceiving and interpreting human relationships is through the notion of social role. By this concept, an attempt is made to go beyond the concrete individual and to conceptualize the individual as a bundle of roles, roles being those sectors that are made up of multitudinous relationships into which the "in dividual" dissolves. The role may quite clearly be regarded as a focus of system interdependences but not always is. This shows itself most clearly when Parsons, in order to enter the social science discourse and to make himself understood by translating his concept of system into the current terms of the empiricist frame of reference,[27] pictures the relational reference of action theory through the ego-alter paradigm. This paradigm, however, is only another case of the empiricist "intellectual spatialization of things" (Whitehead), roles or relations being spatialized in the persons of ego and alter, introducing again the utilitarian "fallacy of misplaced concreteness." In the "complementarity of expectations" the mind versus matter, or *res cogitans* versus *res extensa*, dichotomy is retained by being duplicated: Ego views himself as mind and regards alter as manipulable matter to satisfy his needs, and alter, complementarily, does the same with regard to ego. This is certainly the view of common sense, based on a tradition of epistemological and social thought previously referred to, but with equal certainty it is not that of Parsons, who significantly qualifies the exposition of this paradigm by finishing that the "normative orientation of action" is "superadded" to the "'intrinsic' or direct behavioral reaction(s)" of ego and alter.[28]

Actually, and in accord with his early theoretical program, Parsons does not derive social relations from the rational calculus of individual actors. Rather, in his treatment of the matter, it seems as if subjective means-end rationality (*Zweckrationalität*) leads to the very isolation and immanence of the individual. His emphasis on "nonrationality" can be noticed with regard to both of the meanings he gives to the notion of "relation" by using two levels of abstraction. The first serves to concretize the abstract notion of relation; it is sent on the concrete level of phenomenological experience, "orientation." As for its modes, orientation is characterized not only by cognition, i.e., *Zweckrationalität,* but also by cathexis and evaluation. The notion of cathexis is of Freudian origin; it is a fundamental aspect of emotional transference, the phenomenon which Parsons encountered when he studied the physician-patient relationship in pursuit of the problem of utilitarianism. It seems that cathexis bridges the chasm between subject and object which cognitive mind has opened:

> Of these two modes of orientation (the cognitive and the cathectic ones), the cathectic mode is most specifically relation in the sense that we have already said the orientation itself is relational. That is, a cathexis relates an actor and an object.[29]

As for the evaluative mode of orientation, it will be discussed in due course—as the final problem.

The second meaning of "relation" is definitely not concrete but most analytical. It consists, of course, in the notion of systemic equilibrium processes derived not from common sense and/or the abstract logical construction of the ego-alter pair, but from the empirical analysis of interaction as introduced by Bales. Bales' interaction-process analysis is not couched in terms of rational social roles but analyzes the interaction of events as some kind of natural phenomenon following their own peculiar dynamics —in other words, as a natural system which establishes itself "automatically," nearly irrespective of the particular conscious minds of the participants. The dynamic laws are of an "unconscious" order; only the interaction analyst can detect them. Typically, there appears a systemic order of balances concerning expression and control of affectivity. Thus, not only on the concrete level of orientation but also on the analytical level of the equilibrium system, cathexes return as being of a crucial order. Parsons himself made this point explicit when he linked the phenomenon of cathexis to the I-cell in the AGIL-paradigm, this cell being the location of the systemic control factor—the central generator of the equilibrium processes:

> But the units of a system are . . . objects to each other in a predominantly cathectic sense. By system integration we mean the mutual cathectic adjustment of these units to each other in the perspective of the internal harmony or, as is often said for social systems, solidarity or cohe-

sion of the system. Every system then has a level of integration which is a function of the "object-relations" of its units to each other, of the adjustment of their mutual cathexes through motivational mechanisms.[30]

Nonrational affectivity, then, appears as basically related to social action. Parsons' main interest, of course, has not gone in this direction but in that of normative nonrationality; the following discussion is an extension of the explicit meaning of his theory, but his scheme and especially his concept of systemic interdependence are analytical enough to allow us to interpret recent empirical findings from subnormal strata of animal and human existence —and to come by this way to an interpretation of Parsons' own conception of the hierarchy of normative control.

Parsons' analytical concept of system which aimed at penetrating into a depth beyond everyday apprehension and at leaving the monadic phenomenology of the subjective mind for the general theory of living systems, is taken from cybernetics:

Within this dimensional framework, then, we conceive of process as occuring in a system which is treated as a point of reference. The system operates through the interaction of its member units. Every change of state of one unit . . . will affect all the other units in the system and in turn the effects on the other units will "feed back" to the original unit. We conceive here of an unbroken "circular" process of interdependence which is analyzed in terms of the concept of equilibrium.[31]

Modern research on the families of schizophrenics stunningly demonstrates the applicability of the concepts of systemic interdependence, circularity, and feedback on subrational phenomena. It is not any single individual but the family system as such in which "schizophrenia" has to be located. Certain structures in which the family processes go on are absolutely not rational but impress themselves upon the actors as "emotional roles or relationships," to use Wynne's notation. It appears that there exists a steering system of interaction beneath consciousness that is plainly affective and behavioral or "transactional," characterized, especially in pathological states when it disintegrates from the normative superstructure, by a primitive polar organization, namely, ambivalence. Here then, can most vividly be grasped that there exist *Zusammenhänge* in the human realm, interdepencies as opposed to unilinear causal chains; that they transcend the "simple locations" of individuals; and that in ordinary life they exist unnoticed by these individuals. They are simply behavioral, transactional, or "pragmatic"—in the sense in which Watzlawick, Beavin, and Jackson[32] use this term, a sense quite different from that in which it has been used as connoting the empiricist frame of reference. Again the problem of language is immanent. These affective structures and processes do have a definite pattern and follow the rules of a "pragmatic calculus," but it is very difficult to clothe it as ordinary speech. The pragmatic calculus is analogic and represents relations, the verbal calculus is digital and applies its digits to individual objects and their qualities. As Watzlawick and his fellow workers suggest—and in accord with Heisenberg's and Whitehead's general statements—the best way to represent these relations would be in mathematical language and to use the concept of function. It is this concept, though not stated in mathematical language, which action theory applies when it approaches the analysis of the patterns of relational equilibrium processes by means of the functional AGIL paradigm.

Other empirical findings on affective patterns of organization of living systems come from ethology. The steering mechanisms for interaction are, in the case of animals, clearly subrational. They exhibit most constantly a patterned circularity of actions and reactions. Also, they add an evolutionary perspective on the question of *Zusammenhänge:* as Eibl-Eibesfeldt points out, it is not the individual animal but the total communicative and reproductive *Zusammenhänge* of the species to which survival value is attached.[33]

In his own specific sociocultural evolution, man has transcended the subconscious biological and affective interconnectedness: This is the kernel of truth in the utilitarian-empiricist doctrine. The individual has become a value in itself. It allows him to be a pragmatist. Yet there are dangers inherent in loosening or giving up the sense of interconnectedness, especially with regard to the social environment. They are to be seen in individual man's considering himself as mind and considering everything else, beyond the chasm of his subjectivity, as mere matter fit for his manipulations. The meaning of Parsonian theory is exactly that in order to overcome the monologous and manipulative pragmatist-utilitarian situation another interconnectedness has to be established by means of values. This is the idea of the hierarchy of control, with the cultural system at the top embodying the values as patterns of interconnected organization. The biological-affective patterns are conceived of in the inverse hierarchy of conditions. Parsons has tended to neglect them, namely, to treat them as plastic, undifferentiated, or chaotic, asserting themselves only as "vicious circles" during illness. In this he was supported by Freud's view that the id is dominated by chaotic primary process.

One may very well think, however, of another hypothesis that the organization of the id appears to be random only in relation to of the organization of another system, i.e., the ego or the superego, and that it is unconscious just because of its analogic calculus of relationships. An additional hypothesis would be that the id may lose its pattern in a pathological development and then really become chaotic or "vicious." The "polymorphous perversity" and the Hobbesian "war of all against all" may be cases in point—and not a basic condition of humanity.

Actually, Parsons *has,* apart from explicit formalizations concerning the hierarchy of control, focussed special attention on the affective substratum; and one may even say that he has emphatically underlined it, insofar as he has stressed the importance of cathexis, identification, attachment, commitment, bindingness, trust, and affect (as a generalized medium).

One may even think of these concepts that they represent—in Parsons' thought—ultimate values. It comes to this: because of his sociocultural evolution, man is less bound into determinative, affective structures of interconnectedness. Instead, in the process of socialization, he has to learn to become interconnected according to the complex requirements of his sociocultural milieu. But in order to learn, he needs the right values, values not derived from some fallacy of misplaced concreteness, values that reflect and represent interconnectedness, values of a good society.[34]

This, then, is the last meaning of the general theory of action.

NOTES

1. Werner Heisenberg, *Der Teil und das Ganze. Gespräche im Umkreis der Atomphysik* (München: Piper, 1969), p. 9.
2. See the Introduction in Enno Schwanenberg, *Soziales Handeln — Die Theorie und ihr Problem* (Berne: Huber, 1970).
3. Abraham Kaplan, *The Conduct of Inquiry: Methodology for Behavioral Science* (San Francisco: Chandler, 1964), p. 36 ff. For a critical discussion see Jürgen Habermas, *Erkenntnis und Interesse* (Frankfurt am Main: Suhrkamp, 1968). Also see Albrecht Wellmer, *Methodologie als Erkenntnistheorie* (Frankfurt am Main: Suhrkamp, 1967).
4. Heisenberg, *op. cit.,* p. 285.
5. Cf. "Understanding nature must surely mean to really apprehend her essential relationships, to know with certainty that one has grasped the working of her inner gears. Such knowledge cannot be gained by knowing singular observed facts nor through sets of such facts even if one discerns among them a certain order but only after one has ascertained a comprehensive order among a large number of observations and has been able to reduce that order to a simple principle. Then certainty rests on such plenitude of facts. The danger of error diminishes the larger the number and the more varied the nature of observations and the more simple the common principle underlying them. The possibility of a later discovery of a yet more encompassing relational order does not contradict this." Wolfgang Pauli, as quoted by Heisenberg, *op. cit.,* p. 52.
6. Heisenberg, *op. cit.,* p. 138.
7. One may think of a plainly heuristic methodology as an extreme case in point. Marvin Minsky, in his brilliant article on "Steps Toward Artificial Intelligence" (in Edward A. Feigenbaum and Julian Feldman [eds.], *Computers and Thought* [New York: McGraw-Hill, 1963], pp. 406-456, especially 410-411), describes an analogous computer method of search which he pictures as "hill-climbing." It consists in exploring locally, i.e., in a short range about a point to find the direction of steepest ascent, "success" being defined as reaching the peak of the highest hill existing. The shortcomings of this method Minsky calls the "false-peak problem" and the problem of "finding any significant peak at all." Transformed into Heisenberg's example, this would mean the "false-route problem" and the problem of "finding any significant route at all."
8. This model openly underlies the system of psychotherapy developed by George Kelly under the name of the "psychology of personal constructs," this theoretical system being a case of a transposition of the model from man's relationship toward his natural environment to man's relationship toward his social surroundings. Cf. George A. Kelly, *The Psychology of Personal Constructs* (New York: Norton, 1955). For the problems inherent in such a transposition see the following discussion.
9. Page 19. Reprinted with permission of Macmillan Publishing Co., Inc., and the Cambridge University Press, from *Science and the Modern World* by Alfred North Whitehead. Copyright 1925 by Macmillan Publishing Co., Inc.; renewed 1953 by Evelyn Whitehead. Significantly enough, Bacon misjudged the value of mathematics for the advancement of knowledge when he construed his *Novum Organum.*
10. Minsky, *op. cit.,* opposes the methods of pattern recognition to the heuristic method of "hill-climbing" as more resourceful ways of cognitive adaptation to the environment.
11. Whitehead, *op. cit.*
12. Talcott Parsons, "An Approach to Psychological Theory in Terms of the Theory of Action," in Sigmund Koch (ed.), *Psychology: A Study of a Science,* vol. III (New York: McGraw-Hill, 1959), pp. 624-625.
13. *Science and the Modern World,* pp. 28-30.
14. "The harmony of the logical reason, which divines the complete pattern as involved in the postulates, is the most general aesthetic property arising from the mere fact of concurrent existence in the unity of occasion. Wherever there is a unity of occasion there is thereby established an aesthetic relationship between the general conditions involved in that occasion. This aesthetic relationship is that which is divined in the exercise of rationality." *Ibid.,* p. 26.
15. *Ibid.,* pp. 8-10.
16. *Ibid.,* p. 17.
17. *Ibid.,* pp. 25-26.
18. "Faith in reason is the trust that the ultimate natures of things lie together in a harmony which excludes mere arbitrariness. . . . There is no parting from your own shadow. To experience this faith is to know that in being ourselves we are more than ourselves: to know that our experience, dim and fragmentary as it is, yet sounds the utmost depths of reality: to know that detached details merely in order to be themselves demand that they should find themselves in a system of things: to know that this system includes the harmony of logical rationality, and the harmony of aesthetic achievement: to know that, while the harmony of logic lies upon the universe as an iron necessity, the aesthetic harmony stands before it as a living ideal moulding the general flux in its broken progress towards finer, subtler issues." *Ibid.,* p. 18.
19. Talcott Parsons: *The Structure of Social Action,* 3rd pr. (New York: Free Press, 1964), p. 730.
20. For a detailed description and discussion see Schwanenberg, *Soziales Handeln.*
21. "The way in which Pareto makes room for abstract analytical theory . . . is not to set theory over against fact, but *to include the element of theoretical abstraction in his concept of fact itself.*" *The Structure of Social Action,* p. 183, italics Parsons'.

Compare Whitehead: "It means that for things to be together

involves that they are reasonably together. This means that thought can penetrate into every occasion of fact, so that by comprehending its key conditions, the whole complex of its pattern of conditions lies open before it." *Science and the Modern World*, p. 26.

22. Whitehead, *op. cit.*, pp. 195-196.

23. *Loc. cit.*

24. *Ibid.*, pp. 202-203.

25. From an oral communication.

26. "An Approach to Psychological Theory in Terms of the Theory of Action," *op. cit.*, pp. 622-623. Italics and parentheses are Parsons'.

27. Note the "General Statement," in Talcott Parsons and Edward A Shils (eds.), *Toward a General Theory of Action* (Cambridge, Mass.: Harvard University Press, 1951).

28. *Ibid.*, p. 16. Parsons has himself made this point explicit in later works. See Talcott Parsons: "Social Interaction" in David L. Sills (ed.), *International Encyclopedia of the Social Sciences* (The Macmillan Company and The Free Press, 1968), vol. 7, pp. 429-441.

29. Talcott Parsons and Edward A. Shils, "Values, Motives and Systems of Action," *op. cit.*, p. 69.

30. "An Approach to Psychological Theory in Terms of the Theory of Action," *op. cit.*, p. 636.

31. Talcott Parsons, Robert F. Bales, and Edward A. Shils, *Working Papers in the Theory of Action* (Glencoe, Ill.: Free Press, 1953), p. 167.

32. Paul Watzlawick, Helmick Beavin and Don D. Jackson, *Pragmatics of Human Communication* (New York: Norton, 1967).

33. Irenäus Eibl-Eibesfeldt: *Liebe und Hass. Zur Naturgeschichte elementarer Verhaltensweisen* (München: Piper, 1970).

34. Cf. Talcott Parsons: "Some Comments on the Pattern of Religious Organization in the United States," in T. Parsons, *Structure and Process in Modern Societies* (New York: Free Press, 1960), p. 315.

2

FUNCTIONAL METHODOLOGY IN THE THEORY OF ACTION

F. van Zyl Slabbert

INTRODUCTION

Functionalism can be, and has been, approached from many different perspectives. The important point is to keep levels of analysis and points of departure distinct in any one discussion. If one wants to determine to what extent functional analysis is linked with a particular ideological position, it is well to remember that such an investigation is primarily empirical rather than logical. Similarly, if one wishes to programmatically sketch the rudiments of an eventual functional theory, then it is equally well to remember that one has not developed a set of methodological or explanatory principles.

These remarks emphasize two important preliminary points: One is that there is no predominatly important "perspective" or "approach" to functionalism; two is that whatever one's approach is, one should state it as clearly as possible.

The emphasis in this paper is first and foremost on functional methodology, i.e., the logical characteristics of a functional explanation. This emphasis should not mislead anyone into thinking that there is a clearcut and generally accepted methodological position in sociology. There is not, and those who say there is usually end up by defining other sociologists out of the field. Rather than do that, I prefer to draw the battle lines as clearly as possible by exposing my own methodological predispositions.

If the primary emphasis of this paper is on functional methodology, then the main purpose is to demonstrate how functionalism, as a methodological position, is incorporated into Parsons' theory of action. In so doing, one must keep in mind the following points of departure.

First, one must remember that the leading functionalists in sociology, Parsons and Merton, have aligned themselves with the logical empirical tradi-

tion.[1] This title should not confuse one into believing that it represents a systematic body of noncontroversial methodological principles. The pat phrases in sociological textbooks on research and theory, e.g., "Theories have to be logically tight and empirically sound," leave a host of questions begging on which widely divergent positions can be adopted. Nevertheless, there are certain general principles that are relatively noncontroversial within this position which serve to identify it. For example, that explanations of events have to be made by subsumption under general laws; that explanations and predictions have the same logical structure; that the same logical canons are applicable in the determination of the significance of formulations and explanations in any branch of science, natural or social; that the refutation or confirmation of statements are ultimately dependent on publicly observable evidence; and the like.[2] To do justice to Parson's work, one has to take into account this methodological commitment of his, to appreciate both what he has in mind with his theoretical efforts and how functionalism plays a role in it. This task has been sadly neglected by a great many critics of his work. For example, accusations concerning his verbosity, his conservative ideological bias, and his inability to explain social change are, in terms of logical empiricism, not relevant for evaluating the explanatory significance of his theoretical work or functionalism, no matter how theoretically interesting or socially urgent some of these problems may be.

Second, I am adopting the same methodological position as that of Merton and Parsons for the purpose of this paper. In terms of this position one can distinguish between a particular functional theoretical explanation and the logical structure of a functional explanation as such. For example, the theory of action would be a particular theoretical attempt at functional explanation in sociology, but as a functional explanation it displays the same logical characteristics as such an explanation in the fields of biology or linguistics. Functionalism can thus be seen as a set of methodological assumptions that can guide any theoretical inquiry. This does *not* mean that the theory of action is simply a set of methodological assumptions or a list of procedural rules in terms of which one can invariably discover good propositions. All that is implied is that the set of methodological assumptions known to be typical of functional analysis must figure in the theory of action if the latter is a functional theory.

Given these points of departure, I hope to demonstrate that Parsons' commitment to functionalism is a pervasive and consistent characteristic of his theoretical efforts and is largely responsible for the impression of continuity and unity in the development of the theory of action. Before I discuss Parsons' work, a few comments on the logical structure of functional explanations are in order. This will be followed by a brief discussion of what I call "popular functionalism," in which some attention will be paid to Merton's work.

THE LOGICAL STRUCTURE OF FUNCTIONAL EXPLANATIONS

A number of scholars have written authoritatively on the logical structure of functional explanations. Initially there were the contributions of Nagel[3] and Hempel[4] and more recently we have the works of Braithwaite[5] and Rudner[6]. In sociology, Cancian has borrowed liberally from Nagel's analysis for constructing a scheme in terms of which a functionalist study of social change could be made.[7] Rather than repeat what these philosophers of science have said about the logical structure of functional explanations, I will have to assume some familiarity with these sources on the part of the reader and state some general conclusions drawn from these analyses which are particularly relevant for the subsequent discussion.

An important and, for some, perhaps embarrassing fact revealed by these analyses is that a functional explanation is inevitably teleological. The word teleology immediately conjures up associations of the Aristotelean doctrine of final causes, but we are assured by the just-mentioned philosophers that Aristotle was concerned with only one example of a teleological explanation. The defining characteristic of a teleological statement is thus not that explanations are given in terms of final causes but that they are given in terms of a means-end scheme. Whenever an occurrence or event is

explained in terms of its contribution to or pursuance of some end or goal, we have a teleological explanation. Whether such a goal is ascribed to the behavior of a particular individual or to a mindless organism makes no difference. The fact that a goal is postulated for a particular system by the investigator and that he uses a means-end scheme to account for how this goal is achieved or maintained is, according to Braithwaite, the definitive feature of a teleological explanation.[8]

Viewed thus, teleological explanations need not be as scientifically disreputable as has commonly been accepted. In fact, Nagel, Braithwaite, and Rudner state emphatically that there are no logical grounds for banning all teleological explanations from science.[9] The problem then becomes one of distinguishing between good and bad teleology, or of making teleological assertions scientifically respectable.

One need hardly emphasize how basic the means-end nexus is to social science theorizing. In psychology it lies at the root of most volitional categories introduced for explaining individual behaviour; in sociology it is difficult to portray the relationship between normative structures and social action without it. For example, a means-end scheme is the basic framework used by Parsons in *The Structure of Social Action*. In anthropology, apart from the "functionalist school," which employs it constantly, Jarvie, for example, who rejects functionalism but wishes to retain the "commonsense core" in it,[10] does so by using the means-end nexus to accommodate Popper's "logic of the situation" approach to anthropological problems. It appears then that teleology is a problem that will have to be faced squarely by social scientists rather than one to be avoided or hastily rejected in methodological discussions. Too often we start off by agreeing that teleology is bad and then proceed to give teleological explanations.

A functional explanation however, is not just a teleological explanation. In addition to the means-end nexus the idea of a system in which interrelated variables contribute to its maintenance is fundamental. The goal-directness of functional systems emphasizes the role played by the environment in the operation of the system. In contrast to the traditional mechanist deterministic system, a functional system has to cope with changes in the relations between system variables and environmental variables, as changes in these relations influence the degree to which such a system is successful in satisfying certain needs, prerequisites, or goal states. The distinguishing feature of a functional system is then that it tends to maintain certain "preferred" states despite changes in the relations between variables in the system and between these and variables external to the system, i.e., in the environment.[11]

What are the minimum conditions that will have to be met for a successful functional explanation? At least the following information will have to be supplied:[12]

1. An identification of a functional system in terms of its components, which enables one to distinguish it analytically from its environment.
2. A description of the relations obtaining between the components in the system X and between these and the components in the environment of X.
3. A description of how the relations between all these components are responsible for maintaining certain over-all states of system X.
4. A body of well-articulated theory will have to be produced which, as the theory of system X, contains laws which serve to connect certain over-all states of X with each other and explain why they have to be maintained. Even if one is initially interested only in giving a functional explanation of some particular item Y, the same conditions will have to be met. Y will have to be brought in relation to some functional system X as one of its components, and this system will have to be explained in the same manner.

Given these conditions for functional explanations, it is easy to understand why methodologists sometimes smile indulgently on some of the efforts of functionalist theorists. However, no degree of methodological expertise can substitute for actual theorizing. On the latter level, methodologists should at least have the magnanimity to admire theorists for the quality of some of their mistakes, for many can criticize but few can think creatively. Nevertheless, as far as Parsons and Merton are concerned, these methodological assumptions are the ones to be used in evaluating their work as functional theorists. For it is in terms of the same methodological tradition that they judge their own work. I think it is for this reason that Parsons has shrugged off accusations concerning change, conflict, or ideological bias with regard to his work. He has always been much more sensitive to methodological criticism aimed at possible logical inconsistencies, empirical inadequacies, and conceptual errors in his theorizing.[13]

In this brief discussion on the logical structure and conditions of functional explanations, it must be remembered that these conditions hold for all attempts at functionalist theorizing in any branch of science. Nagel and others have drawn attention to the fact that functionalism as a methodological

approach is not limited to any particular discipline.[14] This point is easily appreciated if one keeps in mind that the philosophers of science whose works have been referred to here are only casually acquainted with the works of Parsons. They draw upon examples from biology, psychology, sociology, and anthropology, for explicating the logical structure of functional explanations. Even the relatively modern approach to cybernetics is regarded as having the same logical structure of explanation.[15]

POPULAR FUNCTIONALISM IN SOCIOLOGY

Teleological analyses, both good and bad, are a common feature of sociological interpretation. Why is this so? I think one important reason can be traced to a semantic source. Modes and figures of speech referring to the "goals," "motivations," and "purposiveness" of human behavior become accepted and attain a pseudo-explanatory power. When these volitional categories are crudely applied to such collective entities as "societies," "groups," or communities" and their use fortified by the apparent sophistication of such locutions as "the function of," "in order that," "the purpose of," and the like, then analysis moves on the level of what I call "popular functionalism." It is only when the logical structure of such "explanations" are investigated that we become aware of their inadequacies and the difference between acceptable and unacceptable functional explanations are made explicit.

Another and closely related reason for the prevalence of functional explanations in sociology could be deduced from Nagel's discussion of teleology in biology. The point that he makes is that biologists are in general concerned with a relatively specialized class of systems that receive greater attention than others.

> When a biologist ascribes a function to the kidney he tacitly assumes that it is the kidney's contribution to the maintenance of the living animal which is under discussion; and he ignores as irrelevant to his primary interest the kidney's contribution to the maintenance of any other system of which it may also be a constituent. On the other hand a physicist generally attempts to discuss the effects of solar radiation upon a wide variety of things; and he is reluctant to ascribe a "function" to the sun's radiation, because no one physical system of which the sun is part is of greater interest than is any other such system.[16]

The same seems to apply to sociologists who ascribe functions to items in the social realm. Sometimes the familiarity of the system implied is taken so much for granted that they are not even specified or distinguished from one another. For example Merton's analysis of the "functions of the political machine" is a case in point.[17] This analysis has often been praised as an excellent example of functional analysis. However, in it Merton refers to functions fulfilled for various unspecified systems ("deprived classes," "big business," "certain sub-groups in certain ecological areas," "illegitimate business"), with regard to various needs ("humanizing and personalizing all manner of assistance," "providing political privileges which entail immediate economic gain," "providing alternative channels for social mobility," and so on). It is difficult to understand how this sort of functional analysis, wherein multiple consequences are ascribed to a particular item for multiple systems "differs from the analysis of a physicist who is directed to discovering what consequences follow from, say, the radiation of energy from the sun which affects the constitution of the sun itself or of the various planets."[18]

This criticism does not mean that Merton's analysis does not produce new insights; his discussion is however no explanation in any rigorous sense of the word judged according to the prescriptions of his own paradigm, it is not even a functional explanation.[19]

If it is true that functional analysis is a common feature of sociological interpretation, then it is equally true that Merton's familiar paradigm, appearing when it did, gave some sort of systematic import to functional and teleological analysis. What for Merton was essentially a codification of the prevailing postulates of functionalism became for many an opportunity to gain some disciplinary respect for their analysis. In fact, Merton's paradigm became for many what Merton himself did not want it to become, namely, a set of rules on how to think theoretically. One prime feature of popular functionalism became institutionalized, which was to identify a social item and to trace its consequences as far as individual limitations of imagination would allow. This process has not been altogether unproductive. On the contrary, a great many provocative and challenging analyses have resulted, but these have been largely unintended consequences if we construe the intended ones to have been successful explanations that were specifically functional.

I think this has been particularly true of Merton's career as a functional theorist. To forestall any accusation that I want to add another round to the old and dreary conflict between Parsons and Merton, let me state emphatically that one does not have to be a functionalist to be a good theorist; in fact

it is not even necessary to be a good methodologist. Merton has never been as seriously committed to functionalism as the initial indications of his paradigm would imply. Since its publication in 1948, the limitations of it have been exposed competently enough; yet, as far as I am aware, Merton has never since given explicit methodological attention to functionalism in a publication or indicated in what manner he was accommodating it in his subsequent theoretical interpretations. One could legitimately have expected him to do so, considering the furor his paradigm caused and the fact that at that stage he regarded functionalism as "the most promising of contemporary orientations to problems of sociological interpretation."[20]

Another reason that I maintain that Merton has never been a serious functional theorist is related to his preoccupation with so-called middle-range theorizing. This point needs some elaboration. In discussions on the merits of middle-range as opposed to grand theorizing, three categories have been used that have contributed to a great deal of confusion. These are: "levels of abstraction," "analytical," and "degrees of generality."

In trying to untangle their meanings specifically with regard to their relevance for the debate on middle-range theory or grand theory, one important point has to be kept in mind: Two types of possible theories are being compared and evaluated—not concepts or propositions that fall within the scope of one theory. As far as the term "analytic" is concerned, we can use the well-known although not non-controversial distinction between analytic and synthetic statements. A statement is analytic if it is true regardless of empirical evidence, i.e., is true by definition. If empirical evidence is needed to establish the validity of a statement, it is synthetic. In empirical science synthetic statements can have cognitive significance only in an a posteriori way, i.e., after empirical evidence has been established for its validity. Analytic statements on the other hand refer to a priori truths. When sentences are used in a synthetically a priori fashion we have an anomaly in science, i.e., events are used as self-evident truths before their validity is established.[21] The same distinction applies to the concepts of science. The vocabulary can broadly be divided into theoretical and observational terms, the former consisting of primitive and defined terms (i.e., analytical concepts), the latter of indices that refer to the observable reality.

Given this distinction, it is clear that any scientific theory will contain both analytic and synthetic statements, or both theoretical and observational terms. Strictly speaking it is nonsense to say of two analytic statements that *A* is more analytic than *B* (a statement is either analytic or not). Consequently the term "analytic" cannot help us to decide what the differences or respective merits of middle-range and grand theories are.

With regard to the phrase "level of abstraction," a different order of problems arise. No concept or statement has a self-evident level of abstraction. Concept or statement *A* is on a higher or a lower level of abstraction *relative* to concept or statement *B*. The relativity is clearly spelled out by definitions and inferences within the analytical boundaries of a particular conceptual scheme. Thus, given a particular definition of concept *A* (for example, "social system") and definitions of concepts *B* ("group") and *C* ("society"), then concept *A* can be said to lie on a higher level of abstraction relative to concepts *B* and *C* if and only if the definitions of *B* and *C* can be logically subsumed under the definition of *A*. Thus *within this analytical scheme* all groups and societies are social systems, but "social systems" are not only either "groups" or "societies." Strictly speaking, it follows that the same words appearing in different conceptual schemes or theories do not self-evidently have the same level of abstraction, because their respective levels of abstraction are determined by the logical order of relations that obtain between the concepts and statements of their own respective conceptual schemes.

It has been suggested that theories can be compared on a "scale of abstraction-concreteness." In terms of our argument this suggestion makes no sense. On what basis can such a scale be constructed? Could it be constructed on the basis that theory *A* has literally more concepts between which deductive connections exist than theory *B*, i.e., more analytical concepts in the *numerical* sense? Or could it be constructed on the basis that within theory *A* more deductions have to be made in order to operationalize its basic propositions than within theory *B*? Even if this were possible, of what use would such a scale be and where would middle be in relation to grand?

The position adopted here is that two theoretical explanations can only be compared in terms of their respective levels of abstraction *if and only if* they share a common conceptual or analytical framework, because the process of abstraction is an analytical one, determined by the order of relations that obtain between concepts and statements within a definite theoretical framework. If two explanations can be compared in terms of level of abstraction, then they are part of such a framework. Therefore, if the terms "middle-range" and "grand" refer to different types of theories, it is doubtful whether the term "level of abstraction" can help

one to determine the order of their relation to one another in any specific sense.

With regard to "degree of generality," there are fewer problems. One theory is more general than another if the range of data to be explained and thus indicated in the one theory is greater than in the other. Thus a middle-range theory presumably would have a smaller scope than a grand theory in that sense. Although what the "size" of the scope would have to be to make a theory middle rather than grand is not clear and is best left unclear. From the preceding argument it should also be clear that a theory with a small scope can also have a great many levels of abstraction, so that the statement "the more general, the more abstract" does not necessarily follow. If this definition of generality is accepted, then the middle-range versus grand controversy becomes a bit ridiculous. Presumably a theorist is interested in a particular problem and not in limiting his analysis to a theory of a particular generality.

If we return to Merton's stated lack of commitment to functional analysis, the argument would run as follows: Given that middle-range theorizing refers to theories of a limited generality,[22] and given that functional analysis requires a description of the variables and their interrelatedness of a particular system under reference, then if the system reference is, for example, "society" (a concept which subsumes a great number of variables in its description), a functional theory of such a system can logically not be limited to a middle-range level but must be general in its import. Merton often implicitly uses "society" as his system of reference (*vide* the "functions of the political machine"), professes a predilection for constructing theories of the middle-range, and at the same time propagates functional analyses.

Consequently it would appear that there is a conflict of interests in Merton's preoccupation with functional analysis and his insistence on developing theories of the middle range. This conflict can be resolved in the following alternative ways: constructing functional theories regardless of whether they are middle-range or not; constructing middle-range functional theories at the risk of precluding analyses of more inclusive systems (for example, society) that implicate broader range of data; or constructing theories of the middle range without necessarily accommodating functional analysis. It would be interesting to determine which of these possibilities predominates in Merton's substantive sociological work. I personally believe that when he is a good theorist, he is a good middle-range theorist, period.

I have referred to Merton's work to highlight some of the aspects of what I call "popular functionalism." One is a randomness in tracing the consequences of a particular item of interest, i.e., a disregard for consistent system reference. More important, however, seen in relation to the logical demands of a functional explanation, popular functionalism displays a lack of persistent conceptual and theoretical development. To return to Merton's analysis of the "political machine," the overriding impression it gives is: "This is significant, but what makes it specifically functional?" or "If this is functional analysis then we can carry on with what we are doing anyhow, except of course for substituting the word 'function' for 'consequences' in all cases."[23]

Because of the procedural character and apparent theoretical neutrality of his paradigm on functional analysis, Merton's work as a functionalist theorist has always been less controversial than Parsons'. The point is, however, that a commitment to the methodological assumptions of functionalism does also imply a theoretical commitment of some sort — one, as has been pointed out, in which the idea of a self-maintaining system in interchange with an environment plays a fundamental role. What the empirical characteristics of such a system are assumed to be can differ from theorist to theorist, but Merton himself has indicated at least what the methodological properties of a functional system are.

Parsons' work, on the contrary, has always been controversial. It is easier to attack than to defend Parsons simply because there is such a great amount of work that can be exposed to criticism. Furthermore, the idea seems to persist that if one aspect of Parsons' work is subjected to criticism the whole lot is involved, because every bit seems to be part of the "whole thing." This is of course not true. Parsons' interests have ranged widely, and his levels of analysis have shifted constantly; even the basic "framework of action" has undergone reformulation. Nevertheless the impression of apparent unity and coherence in Parsons' work is sustained. *This, I believe, is so because of his commitment to functionalism and the manner in which he has accommodated these methodological assumptions into his theorizing.*

FUNCTIONAL METHODOLOGY IN THE THEORY OF ACTION

In tracing functional methodology in Parsons' work the following qualifications will have to be kept in mind: First, I have to assume some familiarity with Parsons' conceptual scheme on the part of the reader. Second, I am not concerned with a conceptual analysis of his definitional scheme nor with determining the logical integration of the analytical schemata developed from it. Third, most of the references to Parsons' work are confined to the "social system level of analysis," as most of his attention has been devoted to the problems of "social systems." Finally, and most important, this paper is not concerned with judging, complementing, modifying, or even explicating the level of *theoretical* development in the theory of action. *I am only interested in determining to what extent a set of methodological assumptions known as functionalism form an important part of the theory of action.* In other words, I want to determine to what extent the theory of action can be regarded as a *functional* theory rather than any other kind of theory. References to theoretical data will illustrate the use of these methodological assumptions rather than validate or justify their utility as theoretical insights.

Means-Ends Logic and the Theory of Action

In 1937 Parsons formulated the "framework of action," which consisted of an agent or actor oriented to attaining some end(s) in an environment in which there are (1) conditions which can be manipulated as means for attaining ends and (2) conditions which do not change but are given. Because of this voluntaristic bias in the framework Parsons maintained that "the scheme of action was inherently teleological."[24]

This is a somewhat narrower conception of teleology than that I am using. According to my argument, the "framework" is teleological because it uses a means-end scheme of analysis, not because this scheme is employed in a voluntaristic or futuristic manner. Whether a means-end construct is imputed to the behavior of an individual actor or used as a principle of analysis by an observer in understanding a complex system of interrelated parts does not change the basic logic of the eventual explanation, i.e., a goal is postulated and "facilities," "processes," "mechanisms," "structures," "actions," and so on are "employed to" or "contribute to" or "facilitate" the "maintenance" or "achievement" of this goal. When this means-end scheme is linked with the idea of a self-maintaining system in interchange with an environment, we have a fundamental methodological assumption of functional analysis. In one of his most recent papers Parsons agrees that this proposition is "the focus of the accusation of functional teleology."[25] Once again, it seems, his conception of teleology refers to the possibility that a non-psychological system, for example an organism, can be interpreted in a personalistic fashion. Similarly, with regard to a social system problems arise as to who sets the goals, how does the system know that these goals have to be pursued, and the like.

Parsons tries to argue these problems away by stating that it is a *fact* that human organisms maintain constant body temperatures despite variations in the environment and that to ask *how* this pattern is maintained is not a teleological question. This is an erroneous argument and does not rid us of the problem of teleology. Facts do not just "present" themselves; they become relevant because of certain questions we ask and observations that we make, and these occur in terms of certain theoretical interests that we have. Let us assume that by random good fortune we happen to discover that human organisms maintain constant body temperatures in varying environmental conditions. If we answer the question as to *how* this is possible by postulating that the organism is a system with a definite set of goalstates that are maintained by an intricate interplay of processes within the organism, and between them and the environment, then we are right back to questions that we have tried to avoid, namely: Who sets the goals, and how does the organism know that it must pursue them?

The point is of course that these questions are irrelevant. They are irrelevant in precisely the same way as the favorite distinction of "popular functionalism" viz. "manifest and latent functions" is irrelevant.[26] If the subjective disposition of an individual is relevant for explicating an aspect of his behavior, then one can formally introduce such a variable into one's explanation. If "subjective disposition" or "point of view of the actor" is not relevant then it makes no difference to our analysis of a functional system whether the item in question is "manifestly" or "latently" functional. Similarly, with regard to the example of constant body temperature, it makes no sense to introduce "subjective disposition" as a variable in explicating this problem; if one insists that it does, one is on the level of metaphysical teleology proper. However, it does make sense to postulate goalstates for the organism and to try to explain how it maintains them, and furthermore, there is no reason why this cannot be done in a scientifically respectable way. I reiterate, if one accepts, as I do, that the defining characteristic of a teleological explanation is the use of a means-end scheme, then the problem is to distinguish between scientifically acceptable and unacceptable teleology. A voluntaristic use of the means-end scheme is but one way in which it can be employed.[27]

Let us return to the means-end nexus in the theory of action. With the publication of *The Social System* Parsons maintained that all his work up to that stage had been couched within the framework of action.[28] In the meantime, he admitted, "the framework" had undergone some modification:[29]

The structure of social systems cannot be derived directly from the actor-situation frame of reference. It requires functional analysis of the complications introduced by the interaction of a plurality of actors.

This is an important modification, one that does present definite terminological problems.[30] Basically what has happened is that the words "actor," orientation," "means," and "ends (goals)" in the framework are no longer employed in only a voluntaristic manner but metaphorically refer to the organismic, social, psychological and cultural systems as being "actors" and pursuing "goals,"[31] that is simply another way of saying that, for example, as regards the "social system," the *voluntaristic* means-end nexus of the original framework is no longer adequate as a principle of analysis. A new explanation of the means-end relation is asked for; one in which more than just volitional categories will have to be taken into consideration. To me it is particularly significant that for this new type of explanation Parsons introduces functional analysis, which for him works with the idea of a goal-directed system maintaining a distinctive pattern despite variations in the environment.[32] It is fair to say that the four-functions scheme forms the deductive core of Parsons' theorizing. This scheme has also proved to be the most important *theoretical* principle in terms of which Parsons has applied functional analysis. In his most recent statement on general theory in sociology, the intimate link between a means-ends logic and functional analysis is succinctly portrayed:[33]

The logical outcome of dichotomizing on both of the two primary cross-cutting axes of differentiation is a four-fold classification of function. In terms of previously established usage, the four functions are referred to as pattern maintenance (internal means), integration (internal ends), goal attainment (external ends), and adaptation (external means).

To recap the argument thus far: The first formulation of the framework of action had the actor-situation dichotomy as the most important elements. This framework was later extended from an actor-situation to a system-environment relationship. In both instances we have a means-ends logic of analysis; in the first in a voluntaristic sense only, and in the latter in a nonvoluntaristic sense as well. This shift in the formulation of the framework of action coincided with the introduction of functional analysis into Parsons' theorizing.

Since then Parsons has repeatedly commented on the characteristic postulates that distinguish functional systems from, for example, mechanistic systems.[34] Ideas such as "self" and "boundary maintenance," "equilibrium" or "homeostasis," "exchange processes" between system and environment, internal "control mechanisms," and so on all attest to what Parsons claims is the basic "asymmetry" between functional systems and their environment, i.e., on the one hand a tendency toward stability, on the other (environment) a tendency to change.

> This basic asymmetry is the main ground of the teleological character of *living systems*, and of the *theory of living systems*. It is reflected in the reversal of the direction of explanation characteristic of functional analysis. A functional explanation begins with a postulated state of affairs, and refers back to the necessary antecedent of underlying conditions. Such teleology must of course be conditional, couched in the form that if certain patterns are to be maintained, or certain goals achieved, certain conditions must be fulfilled.[35]

Quite apart from Parsons awareness of the teleological character of a functional explanation, as displayed in this quotation, the interesting point is his reference to living systems. The implication is quite clear that functional analysis, and hence the conception of a functional system, is a mode of analysis not peculiar to sociology, but for Parsons appropriate wherever *any* aspects of "living systems" are being analyzed, in biology or linguistics as well as in sociology and psychology.[36] Such a position not only displays Parsons' own commitment to functional analysis but also indicates that the theory of action should be judged in terms of the methodological prerequisites for functional explanation referred to earlier. To me this point needs to be stressed. The theory of action can be evaluated as a functional theory because the postulates of functionalism appear in it consistently and play a definitive role in the explanations offered by it. Quite apart from any substantive theorizing, then, the consistent use of functionalist assumptions can lend a considerable degree of coherence and continuity to the work of a theorist. For Parsons these assumptions have provided him with a general methodological framework in terms of which he could concentrate on more specific theoretical problems.

These different theoretical problems are all related to the general problem of interpreting social behaviour in terms of the conception of a functional system. Like Merton, one can briefly devise a "paradigm" of problems to which Parsons has addressed himself. This is also about the closest one can get to spelling out how Parsons goes about implementing functional analysis.

Parsons' Paradigm

The following list of problems, compiled from various publications, will necessarily be incomplete, though it is adequate to indicate that Parsons has a systematic approach to the problem of analyzing functional systems. This presentation should not be construed as representing a chronological procedure to be followed when applying functional analysis. Nor need it reflect any priority of interest in Parsons' theoretical preoccupations. The underlying logic is that of the interrelated problems of functional systems that have to be subjected to theoretical interpretation.

1. What are the most important elements of the conceptual scheme? In distinction from Merton, Parsons has always stressed the importance of a conceptual scheme that makes "genuine theoretical development possible."[37] In terms of such a conceptual scheme the components of a functional system can be identified and their interrelatedness with other functional systems and/or its own environment spelled out.

When Parsons states that "the four-function scheme is grounded in the essential nature of living systems at all levels of organization and evolutionary development, from the unicellular organism to the highest human civilization"[38] one can appreciate the tremendous — almost fantastic — scope implied in the conceptual scheme of the theory of action. At the same time it is also clear that it cannot be the task of one particular theorist to give a complete elaboration of such a conceptual scheme. Parsons has concentrated mainly on the concepts necessary for interpreting the social system, as one analytically distinct functional system, in the theory of action.[39] In his more recent work he has been occupied with spelling out the relation between the social system, as a subsystem of action, to other subsystems of action and thus giving a more articulate framework for the theoretical development of action theory.[40]

What is most significant at this conceptual level is that development does not take place in an arbitrary way. It is not simply a case of: "Here we have an interesting problem. What would be interesting concepts?" Parsons employs explicit "principles of classification" in developing and elaborating his conceptual scheme. These principles themselves are also not come upon in an arbitrary fashion. For example, the four-function scheme, the most familiar principle of classification of the problems of action systems in the theory of action, is derived from the methodological assumption that the variables of a functional system have to perform certain functions so that the system can meet certain basic requirements. Once this is grasped then the underlying logic of a great number of conceptual distinctions can be understood, even if not accepted.

2. What are the functional requirements or goals or needs of the system? As early as 1951, with the publication of *The Social System*, Parsons has indicated that in answering this question one must guard

against "inventing ad hoc generalizations about these prerequisites which allegedly explain certain classes of *concrete* social phenomena."[41] From this it is clear that one cannot expect a checklist of simple empirical circumstances that would be an indication of the exigencies that any one social system would have to meet.

What the needs of any functional system are can be understood only in terms of the *system-environment* relationship. To the extent that the social system is analytically defined vis-à-vis its own environment which, in terms of the theory of action, refers to analytically defined cultural, psychological, organismic, and other social systems, the needs of that social system will have to be derived from the analytically conceived relation between system and environment.[42] Thus, if society happens to be the social system under discussion, one would have to calculate the concrete goalstates of any one particular society in the following manner:

> With this understanding, the criterion of self-sufficiency can be divided into five sub criteria, each relating to one of the five environments of social systems — Ultimate Reality, Cultural Systems, Personality Systems, Behavioural Organisms, the Physical-Organic Environment. The self-sufficiency of a society is a function of the balanced combination of its controls over its relations with these five environments and of its own state of internal integration. [43]

From this it should be evident that the idea of a social system is a very general one and that society is only slightly more specific (i.e., society is an example of a social system), but equally analytical (for example, "A society is a type of social system, in any universe of social systems, which attains the highest level of self-sufficiency as a system in relation to its environment.").[44] For the latter Parsons has given general directives as to what exigencies are[45] as well as indicated what more or less the "evolutionary universals" (structures and processes) are within society that enhance its "adaptive capacity."[46]

Logically more central to Parsons' conception of a functional system than the spelling out of the particular exigencies of any one system is the well-known four-function scheme. This scheme is derived from his conception of function as applied to the concept system:

> I wish to argue that the concept function is central to the understanding of all living systems. Indeed it is simply the corollary of the concept living system, delineating certain features in the first instance of the system-environment relation, and in the second, of the internal differentiation of the system itself.[47]

Earlier, mention was made of the "axes of differentiation" in classifying the four functions. These axes refer to two basic assumptions concerning the nature of functional systems. One is that there is a process of interchange between system and environment; the other is that the system must somehow survive as a distinctive pattern.[48] These are relatively simple assumptions, but their simplicity is a reflection of their intended level of generality, for in terms of such a conception of a relatively simple system Parsons hopes to deal with "complexity beyond the capacities of a single empirical reference of the simple theoretical system by treating the empirical phenomena — with adequate empirical justification of course — as resultants of the involvement of a plurality of systems which are variants of the generalized system."[49]

Whether and to what extent he has been successful in the task he has set himself is not at issue now, although I do believe that his claim that the four-function scheme permits of genuine deductive development in the theory of action can be substantiated.[50] For the present purposes it is more significant that another characteristic assumption of functional methodology forms one of the main theoretical points of departure for the development of the theory of action.

3. Is there a consistent system reference? This question is of course closely linked to the previous one and needs only brief exposition here. However, it needs separate emphasis simply because the failure to ask it has been a regular source of confusion in functional analysis.

For the theory of action, with its myriad analytical distinctions of system-subsystem relations, this question is particularly relevant, for there is an immediate loss of analytical focus if system references are diffused or obscured. It implies that the system reference has to be consistent for any given unit of analysis. However, in a complex analysis involving interaction between a number of systems and subsystems, more than one reference can be applied. This presupposes, of course, that the analytical boundaries of the systems involved are explicit so that the change of reference in the analysis can be accounted for. This point was made by Parsons as early as 1953[51] and is the most important procedural rule underlying his analyses of system-environment interchange.[52]

The point we are emphasizing here is logically the same as that of distinguishing between dependent, independent, intervening, and residual variables explicated by Smelser[53] and is a procedural rule to cope with the problem of not being able to explain everything at once. At the same time, if this rule is adhered to, it imposes on one the necessity of being theoretically explicit. Such an imposition can, with regard to the intended scope of the theory of action, place severe demands on the powers of concentration of any reader of Parsons' work!

4. How are the interrelated structures and processes of a system controlled? The problem of control arises because of the open character of functional systems, i.e., the system is not closed or independent of the variations in its own environment. Consequently the system must have a certain degree of structural variability in order to accommodate the fluctuations in its own environment. Because, however, the system maintains a distinctive pattern, i.e., is that particular system, its own structures cannot have an unlimited variability in relation to the environment. This raises the problem of controlling the ranges of variability of structures and processes of the system.

Parsons uses the following two distinctions to accommodate this problem within the theory of action:[54] First, he distinguishes the problem of how "resources" from the environment come into the system, are "processed" in the functioning of the system, and then "put out" to the environment again. The classification here is in terms of the "input-output" categories. The second distinction is concerned with the problem of how "mechanisms" control the processes of "resource generation and utilization." These "mechanisms" would then be responsible for keeping the structures and processes within definite "ranges of variability" so that the system maintains a distinctive pattern relative to its own environment.

Given these distinctions, then the most important principle in terms of which classifications of input-output categories and mechanisms of control are made is what Parsons has called the "principle of cybernetic priority."[55] This states that systems high in information and low in energy control systems low in information and high in energy. Thus, for the whole action system we have an ordering of subsystems of action in terms of both the four-function scheme and the principle of cybernetic priority. This ordering is also done with regard to the *mechanisms* which control the interchange and internal processes of the various subsystems of action.[56]

During the last few years Parsons has devoted considerable attention to the problem of control with regard to social systems. The results of his labours were published in his "Media Papers."[57] For those who are acquainted with Parsons' work it is clear that these "mechanisms of the social system," namely value commitments, influence, power, and money, are related to one another in terms of the logic of the four-function scheme and cybernetic control. For those who are not so well acquainted with Parsons' work it is best to consult these papers,

as limitations of space prevent me from spelling out these relations. In any event it is not necessary for the purpose at hand.

It should by now be quite clear to the reader to what extent the postulates of functional methodology are involved in the theory of action. Two central principles of analysis of this theory, namely the four-function scheme and self-regulation have been directly developed from the postulates concerning the nature of functional systems, namely the necessity of the system to meet certain needs in order to survive, and the fact that at the same time the system is an open relationship to its environment.

5. How does the system change its structure? This question has been included in the paradigm because it has been a popular point of attack not only on Parsons' work but on functional analysis generally. To my mind the debate concerning the necessity and importance of studying social change is clouded with spurious and ideologically toned arguments primarily because methodological justification of what change is supposed to imply is often absent.[58]

The answer to the question is of course closely linked to the answer to the question to the previous one. In terms of the logic of functional system its over-all state will change when the ranges of variability of its structures are exceeded. It logically becomes a new system. Parsons has made a distinction between "processes which maintain the stability of a system internally through both structure and process, and in interchange with its environment" and "processes by which this balance between structure and more 'elementary' process is altered in such a way as to lead to a new and different 'state' of the system, a 'state' which must be described in terms of the alteration of its previous structure."[59] Thus with regard to the social system one could logically expect a change of its structure only when the mechanism of control is no longer capable of regulating resource utilization within the system or sufficient resources cannot be generated for the system's functioning. How this is spelled out in the theory of action and whether such an exposition is testable are problems quite apart from the fact that it is in principle (i.e., logically) possible to account for the problem of social change.

Summary

The aim has been to demonstrate to what extent and in what manner Parsons has accommodated the methodological assumptions of functionalism in his theoretical work. The evidence that this approach provides the basic methodological frame of reference of his work is conclusive. Back of every attempt of his to describe the characteristics of a social system—its structure, the processes which maintain it and change it, and the presumed laws which govern it—is the conception of a functional system.

Contrary to the exponents of popular functionalism, Parsons has consistently been sensitive to the technical prerequisites for functional explanations. His conceptual framework, encompassing as it is, is primarily concerned with identifying functional action systems, describing the properties of these systems and their internal relations, defining their analytical boundaries, and describing the relations between system variables and environmental variables. On a number of occasions Parsons has emphasized that the conceptual scheme must make genuine theoretical development possible and that this can be achieved only if the ideal is to make it ". . . methodically impossible to overlook anything important, and thus explicitly to describe all essential structural elements and relations of the system."[60]

Even on this level of analysis there is a clear distinction from popular functionalism. However, as was indicated earlier, description of the properties and their interrelations within and among functional systems are only preliminary prerequisites for adequate functional explanations. In addition there have to be descriptions of how the relations between all these components are responsible for maintaining certain over-all states in a functional system as well as a body of theory and laws which connects over-all states of a system with each other and explain why they have to be maintained.

For the present purposes it is not important whether Parsons has succeeded in conforming to these demands. That he is aware of their import for his own theoretical work cannot be doubted. His preoccupation with problems such as "functional prerequisites for the system," "ranges of variability of structure of the system," and "mechanisms of control" as well as tentative attempts to formulate statements on the "generalized conditions of equilibrium of action systems"[61] attests to this.

Because of Parsons' awareness of these technical conditions for functional explanations one can, through the methodological extrapolation of the logical structure of such systems, derive some idea of what the theory of action could possibly be like as an explanatory system. This is one level, and a very necessary one, on which the theory of action has to be evaluated, for an attempt at constructing a functional theory, as is evident, poses its own methodological problems.

Furthermore, the more encompassing the reference of a system (for example, "society" as compared to a "small group"), the more difficult these problems are to accommodate. Hempel has emphasized the importance of giving operational testability to the presumed needs or prerequisites of such a system.[62]

Rudner warns that one should not draw too much comfort from the fact that it is logically possible to construct functional theories, for the practical difficulties involved in doing so are immense.[63] Braithwaite argues that even though functional theories may not have much predictive power their utility lies in the organization of a great deal of valuable information and that, as theories, they may eventually be subsumed under more general and perhaps successful theories.[64]

For many sociological theorists these issues may seem remote in terms of the immediate theoretical problems which concern them. Parsons is however, seriously concerned with them in his theorizing. What commands respect is that he is aware of most of the methodological problems involved in constructing functional theories and yet has not despaired. For evaluating the theory of action as a functional theory is necessary but not sufficient. In addition, other equally important levels of evaluation are necessary, for example, the operational specification of propositions[65] and conceptual and terminological inadequacies.[66] Such attempts at evaluation are hampered by two general conditions: The one is that the theory of action, generally speaking, has not developed past the programmatic stage, which raises the problem of developing criteria for evaluating partial theoretical formulations. The second general condition is that Parsons has not been greatly concerned about the lack of logical integration in his theoretical scheme. In preference to developing a "logico-deductive system" he has followed a "pragmatic approach" which amounts to paying attention to "a whole series of restricted problems dealing with aspects of the more general scheme, and to work on them with the double reference to their logical and theoretical structure and the available empirical evidence."[67]

Because of these conditions I believe that any level of evaluation and criticism of the theory of action are seen in better perspective when they are assessed within Parsons' general methodological framework. The idea of a functional system and the problems related to it does lend an identifiable degree of coherence to the design of the theory of action.

CONCLUSION

Perhaps it is appropriate to conclude with a few comments on functionalism in general. Like any commitment or set of assumptions, it falls within what methodologists have called "the context of discovery of science."[68] This context is concerned with the process of inquiry itself: the way in which scientists develop certain insights, come upon hypotheses, discover new problems to be studied, and suggest programmes for their analysis. This content is distinguished from the "context of justification," wherein questions are directed at the way in which a theory or explanation is formulated, the logical consistency of a pattern of explanation, the degree of confirmation for generalizations, and so on. The decisive difference between these areas is that the latter — the context of justification — consists of relatively fixed standards for the evaluation of scientific work, that is, comprises the full range of methodological expertise at any particular moment in the history of a science. The other — the context of discovery — has in contrast no such systematic prescriptions for the attainment of well-constructed theories and explanations.

Now such convenient methodological distinctions are confounded by practical problems in a young discipline such as sociology. One such problem is that most of the activity going on in sociology falls within the context of discovery. Because of this, theoretical commitments are not made cheaply. There is a desperate need to organize our field, to discipline our inquiry into problems and our search for knowledge. When leading sociologists decide to do so in terms of "functionalism," "middle-range theory," "grand theory." "the classical tradition," "empiricism," "operationism," or "conflict theory," they are not just casually committing themselves to interesting possibilities. For them their approach is the "most promising of contemporary orientations"[69] or "the most likely and suitable to play a dominant role in sociological theory,"[70] meaning a deployment of their intellectual energies which could, and often does, occupy the major part of their careers.

As we have seen, functionalism can be a very expensive commitment, especially if applied to a general theory level. What is encouraging and deserves our respect is when such a theorist still remains aware of the conditional nature of his commitment:

> But we can never know whether a research idea of a theoretical scheme is of the first importance until it has been fully worked out and tested in innumerable ways. With all due tentativeness this requires heuristic acceptance of it for purposes of exploration, development and testing, and, if preliminary results are not too drastically negative, it requires acceptance at this level over long periods.[71]

During this "period of acceptance" and the efforts related to it, Parsons hopes that a distinction will be kept between competent understanding of what he has done, which to him is "the indispensable basis for good criticism, positive or negative," and "commitment to doctrines".[72] Such a position, with the attitudes it implies, seems entirely reasonable and in keeping with the quest of science.

NOTES

1. See R.K. Merton, *On Theoretical Sociology*, chap. IV and V (New York: The Free Press, 1967), and T. Parsons, "The Present Position and Prospects of Systematic Theory in Sociology," in G. Gurvitch and W.A. Moore, *Twentieth Century Sociology* (New York: Philosophical Library, 1945).

2. These principles have been explicated by philosophers of science such as G. Bergman, *Philosophy of Science* (Madison: The University of Wisconsin Press, 1966); R.B. Braithwaite, *Scientific Explanation* (Cambridge: Cambridge University Press, 1964); C.G. Hempel, *Aspects of Scientific Explanation* (New York: The Free Press, 1965); E. Nagel, *The Structure of Science* (London: Routledge & Kegan Paul, 1961), and R. Rudner, *Philosophy of Social Science* (Englewood Cliffs. N.J.: Prentice-Hall, Inc., 1966).

3. E. Nagel, "A Formalization of Functionalism" in *Logic Without Metaphysics* (New York: The Free Press, 1956).

4. C.G. Hempel, "The Logic of Functionalism," *op. cit.,* chap. 10.

5. R.B. Braithwaite, *op. cit.,* chap. 10.

6. R. Rudner, *op. cit.,* chap. 5.

7. F. Cancian, "Functional Analysis of Change," *American Sociological Review,* 24 (December 1960), pp. 818-827.

8. See in this regard especially Braithwaite's exposition, *op. cit.,* p. 323.

9. E. Nagel, "Types of Causal Explanation in Science," in D. Lerner, *Cause and Effect* (New York: The Free Press, 1965), pp. 11-33; Braithwaite, *op. cit.,* chap. 10; Rudner, *op. cit.,* chap. 5.

10. I. Jarvie, *The Revolution in Anthropology* (London: Routledge & Kegan Paul, 1964); K. Popper, *The Poverty of Historicism* (London: Routledge & Kegan Paul, 1957).

11. R. Rudner, *op. cit.,* chap. 5.

12. *Ibid.,* pp. 108-109.

13. Note for example the points on which he replied in "The Point of View of the Author," in M. Black, *The Social Theories of Talcott Parsons* (Englewood Cliffs, N.J.: Prentice-Hall, Inc., 1961).

14. E. Nagel, "The Structure of Teleological Explanations," in *The Structure of Science,* pp. 401-428; D. Martindale, *Functionalism in the Social Sciences,* The American Academy of Political and Social Science, 1965.

15. E. Nagel, *The Structure of Science,* p. 411.

16. *Ibid.,* p. 408.

17. R.K. Merton, *Social Theory and Social Structure* (Glencoe, Ill.: The Free Press, 1957), pp. 72-82.

18. *Ibid.,* p. 525.

19. Under point 3 of his paradigm he says: "Functions are those observed consequences which make for the adaptation of a given system." *Ibid.,* p. 51.

20. *Ibid.,* p. 19.

21. G. Bergman, *op. cit.,* p. 26, gives a lucid explanation of the analytic-synthetic distinction.

22. R.K. Merton, *On Theoretical Sociology,* p. 39.

23. It is this: "We are all functionalists anyhow" attitude which pervades K. Davis' controversial paper, "The Myth of Functional Analysis," *American Sociological Review,* 24 (December 1959), pp. 757-772.

24. T. Parsons, *The Structure of Social Action* (Glencoe, New York: reprinted by The Free Press, 1949), p. 44.

25. T. Parsons, "Some Problems of General Theory in Sociology," in J.C. McKinny and E.A. Tiryakian, *Theoretical Sociology* (New York: Appleton-Century-Crofts, 1970), p. 32.

26. See for example E. Nagel, *Logic Without Metaphysics,* p. 271, and Rudner, *op. cit.,* p. 111.

27. Parsons appears to be aware of this for in *The Structure of Social Action* he formulated it as follows: "It is true that the biological level of analysis involves teleological elements. The concept of organism itself implies them. But these are teleological elements of a character which do not imply a subjective reference, though they do involve the conception of an organism as in some degree an active entity which does more than merely reflect the conditions of existence" (note D, p. 85).

28. T. Parsons, *The Social System* (Glencoe, Ill.: The Free Press, 1951), p. 6.

29. T. Parsons, "The Present Position and Prospects of Systematic Theory in Sociology" in Gurvitch and Moore, *op. cit.,* p. 45.

30. T. Parsons, "The Point of View of the Author," in *op. cit.,* p. 333.

31. On the similarities between the "various subsystems of action," see: T. Parsons et al. (eds.), *Theories of Society,* vol. II (Glencoe, Ill.: The Free Press, 1961), p. 964, and "Pattern Variables Revisited," in *American Sociological Review,* 25 (August 1960), p. 60.

32. T. Parsons, "Cause and Effect in Sociology," in D. Lerner (ed.), *Cause and Effect* (New York: The Free Press, 1965), p. 60.

33. T. Parsons, "Some Problems in General Theory," in *op. cit.,* p. 32.

34. See for example T. Parsons and E. Shils, *Toward a General Theory of Action* (Cambridge, Mass.: Harvard University Press, 1951), p. 107; *The Social System,* p. 482; T. Parsons and R.F. Bales, *Working Papers on the Theory of Action* (New York: The Free Press, 1953), p. 92; M. Black, *op. cit.,* pp. 338, 340.

35. T. Parsons, "Some Problems of General Theory in Sociology," in *op. cit.,* p. 32.

36. *Ibid.,* p. 35.

37. *The Social System,* p. 20.

38. "Some Problems of General Theory in Sociology," in *op. cit.,* p. 35.

39. See especially *The Social System* and "An Outline of the Social System," in *Theories of Society,* pp. 30-79.

40. "Some Problems of General Theory in Sociology," in *op. cit.,* pp. 37-59.

41. *The Social System,* p. 29 (my emphasis).

42. "The Concept of Society," in *Politics and Social Structure* (New York: The Free Press, 1969), p. 9.

43. *Ibid.,* p. 10.

44. *Loc. cit.*

45. T. Parsons, *Societies: Evolutionary and Comparative Perspectives* (Englewood Cliffs, N.J.: Prentice-Hall, Inc., 1966), pp. 17-18.

46. "Evolutionary Universals in Society," in *Sociological Theory and Modern Society* (New York: The Free Press, 1967), pp. 490-520.

47. "Some Problems of General Theory in Sociology," in *op. cit.,* p. 31.

48. *Ibid.,* pp. 29-32.

49. *Ibid.,* p. 48.

50. See for example the technical note appended to his paper "On the Concept of Political Power," in *Politics and Social Structure,* pp. 397-404.

51. *Working Papers in the Theory of Action,* p. 95.

52. See for example T. Parsons and N. J. Smelser, *Economy and Society* (New York: The Free Press, 1956).

53. N.J. Smelser, *Essays in Sociological Explanation* (Englewood Cliffs, N.J.: Prentice-Hall, Inc., 1968), chap. 1.

54. *Theories of Society,* p. 60.

55. *Ibid.,* p. 38.

56. See appendix to the paper on "Some Problems of General Theory in Sociology," in *op. cit.,* pp. 64-67.

57. "On the Concept of Political Power," "On the Concept of Influence," in *Politics and Social Structure* and "On the Concept of Value-Commitments," *Sociological Inquiry,* 38 (Spring 1968), pp. 135-159.

58. One of the few lucid discussions on "social change" in which this point was stressed is that of K. Rudner, "Logical Foundations on the Theory of Social Change," in *Sociology and Social Research,* 51 (April 1967), pp. 287-301.

59. "Some Considerations on the Theory of Social Change," in *Rural Sociology,* 26 (September 1961), p. 222.

60. "The Present Position and Prospects of Systematic Theory in Sociology," in *op. cit.,* p. 49. *See* also *The Social System,* p. 20.

61. "The Dimensions of Action Space," in *Working Papers in the Theory of Action,* pp. 102-103. See also "Pattern Variables Revisited," *op. cit.,* pp. 481-482.

62. Hempel, *op. cit.,* pp. 308-314.

63. Rudner, *op. cit.,* p. 108.

64. Braithwaite, *op. cit.,* p. 345.

65. For example R. Dubin, "Parsons' Actor: Continuities in Social Theory," *American Sociological Review,* 25 (August 1960), pp. 457-466.

66. M. Black, "Some Questions About Parsons," *op. cit.* pp. 268-288.

67. "The Point of View of the Author," *op. cit.,* p. 317.

68. R. Rudner, *op. cit.,* p. 6.

69. Merton's position.

70. Parsons' position.

71. T. Parsons, "Comment on Llewellyn Gross: Preface to a Meta-theoretical Framework for Sociology," in *American Sociological Review,* 26 (1961), p. 139.

72. "The Point of View of the Author," *op. cit.,* p. 349.

3

METHODOLOGICAL DILEMMAS IN SOCIAL SCIENCE

Leon Mayhew

A large part of the energies of students of social science is invested in controversy over the appropriate methodological stance for students of group life. Is it true that sociological analysis cannot escape the ideological perspectives of particular groups or interests? Or can social science be universalistic and free from bias? Should analysis be limited to the solution of concrete empirical problems, or should social scientists seek to develop generalized encompassing theories? Should social science study "subjective" meaning or "objective" behavior? Which are more potent in social life, "ideal" or "real" forces? Should sociological analysis start with the individual, or should sociology study the group as a reality in its own right? Should sociologists attempt to explain the persistence of stable orders, or is it more important to study the forces of change?

Perhaps it is unwarranted to refer to the time expended on these questions as "investment," for the problems are perennial. Science is often defined as a cumulative enterprise, especially in elementary texts in sociology, but whatever knowledge may have accumulated as a consequence of the efforts of social scientists there is no emergent consensus on first methodological premises.

The seemingly eternal quality of the methodological disputes in social science is a consequence of the source of the issues: What appear to be resolveable philosophical issues actually reflect inescapable tensions in the character of social life itself. It is the thesis of this paper that the ideas of Talcott Parsons suggest new ways of looking at these issues, ways that understand and exploit parallels between theoretical disputes and tensions in social organization.

This essay does not pretend to be a strict application of Parsonian theory. No attempt is made to guess what Parsons himself might believe or say about the problems or to follow in a strict way the complex terminologies, classifications, and models that he has proposed for social analysis. On the other hand, this paper does constitute an attempt to take seriously and to consider the implications of two Parsonian postulates:

1. The basic categories of structural and functional analysis are applicable to all action systems, including not only cultural systems in general but science and knowledge in particular.[1]

2. The functional requisites of social organization are inherently in tension with one another in the sense that no system of social organization can maximize the effectiveness of its performance of all of its functions at the same time.[2] (For example, to cite a well-known example from functional research on small groups, in maximizing productivity, a group places strains on its internal cohesion.)[3]

These two premises suggest an extremely interesting possibility: *The fundamental and pervasive issues in the methodology of the social sciences reflect tensions inherent in the nature of social life itself.* Moreover, it should be possible to analyse these issues with the same tools available for the analysis of the functional problems of organizations.

BASIC PREMISES

This analysis is founded on a number of basic premises that have become quite commonplace in the philosphy of science. A brief presentation of these premises in outline form will facilitate later exposition of the more novel aspects of my position:

1. Science consists of a set of interrelated symbolic *statements*. To speak of "facts" and "theories," "data" and "assumptions," is not to speak directly of the real world but of a set of descriptions of and propositions about the world.

2. The interrelations between scientific statements are logical in character, and one of the most important forms of logical relation is the relation of the general to the specific. There is, in other words, a ladder of

abstraction with determinate logical relations, both deductive and inductive, between relatively concrete descriptive levels and relatively abstract theoretical levels of statement.

3. Scientific statement is inherently selective. The observable world is so rich in detail, so multifaceted, and so complex in its interrelations, and the bases of our interest in that world are so varied, that it is impossible to describe or explain even the smallest sector of "reality" in exhaustive detail.

4. The problem of selectivity also applies to the first premises of scientific argument. Such premises are not empirical generalizations about the supposed real state of the empirical world. Rather they are strategic assumptions, chosen for their promise or potential as organizers of the logic and coherence of large numbers of statements about the world. Thus, to anticipate a later argument, the scientific adequacy of such statements as "everything is always changing" is not judged according to whether they do or do not appear to describe truly the character of some possible ultimate reality. Rather, such statements are evaluated according to whether they direct our attention to means of constructing the edifice of interrelated statement that we call science.

5. Science is not distinguished from other forms of discourse by its symbolic character, its logical structure, or its selectivity. These it shares with other types of bodies of human statement. Its distinguishing feature is its scrupulous attention to the verification of statement by means of communicable observations. First-order statements of the form "x is a fact" must contain clear directions as to how others could make similar observations that would lead them to agree that x is indeed a fact. Higher-order statements of the form "x is a consequence of y" must be susceptible to test. A scientific test of a statement is possible if it is possible to specify what facts we would observe if the statement were true, with the proviso that the requisite facts be themselves subject to communicable observation.

In sum, "science" is not another name for rational truth. It is a mode of discourse that proceeds to construct an integrated body of statements about the world according to a set of distinctive rules.

THE FUNCTIONAL REQUISITES OF SCIENTIFIC CULTURE

To refer to science as a mode of symbolic discourse is to insist that it is a form of human conduct involving human actors with motives and dispositions, actors who must communicate with each other. The participants in scientific enterprise collectively produce the symbolic product we call science by adhering to the norms of scientific investigation, communication and cooperation. If science is a set of symbolic statements, produced by a group of actors who are constrained by a set of special standards and norms, then it is appropriate to speak of science as a cultural system. As a type of cultural system, it is subject to the exigencies of action systems in general and cultural systems in particular; it has resources and tasks, norms and values; it is subject to the exigencies of change; it competes with other modes and purposes of statement. Among the exigencies of action systems are the requisites of successful functioning. Action systems, including cultural systems, involve processes of obtaining and expending resources, maintaining structures over time, and coordinating diverse elements.

Parsons has suggested that the functional problems of action systems can be reduced to four: *adaptation* or securing generalized resources for use in achieving the varied output goals of the system, *goal attainment* or providing for the effective expenditure of resources in the pursuit of particular goals, *integration* or providing for the coordination of the diverse elements and units within the system, and *pattern maintenance* or maintaining the stability of the over-all structural reference points and boundaries that define the system. This paradigm for defining the functional requisites of systems is treated elsewhere in this volume and need not be elaborated in detail here. However, given the variety of interpretations of the four-function system it is appropriate to note that I will stress the analytical version that derives the four functional requisites from the intersection of two general dimensions of the problems confronting systems, the so-called internal-external and instrumental-consummatory axes.[4] In this analytical context "goal attainment" connotes the pursuit of immediate goals, and "adaptation" the development of generalized resources to permit "economizing." Similarly, "integration" connotes the solution of concrete coordinative problems, while (in the case of social systems) "pattern maintenance" implies the development of the generalized values and commitments that define the underlying structure of the system. These resources can be drawn upon whenever specific integrative problems arise.

This scheme is intended to apply to all types of action systems, including cultural systems such as science and other scholarly endeavors. All have functional problems: There is the purely logical problem of achieving internal consistency in sets of scientific statements, and there are also a number of more realistic or worldly problems. The varied contributions of a diverse set of participants must be integrated. The enterprise must be efficiently organized to achieve its defined tasks, and so forth.

These problems may be defined and classified analytically using an application of the four-function scheme especially adapted for the analysis of cultural systems of the scientific variety:

Pattern Maintenance: *Legitimacy.* Any cultural system must be meaningful in the sense of intelligible and "worthy." These qualities are provided by the inclusion within the cultural system of basic structural premises and categories and by relating the system to relevant grounds of meaning such as values, cultural premises, theodocies, or philosophical ontologies. Science is not exempt from this requirement.

Integration: *Orderly Framework.* A usable cultural system requires a communicable frame of reference that provides theoretically useful definitions of its objects of reference and depicts the character of the relations between these objects. Moreover, there must be modes of communication that transcend the particular vantage points and time perspectives of various investigators. At the same time a communicable frame of reference allows investigators who do operate from specialized vantage points to make a determinate translation of their work to a more general level of discourse. Without such an orderly framework there can be no collective cultural enterprise.

Goal Attainment: *Empirical Problem Relevance.* An effective cultural system of the scientific type can cope with and solve particular empirical problems.

Adaptation: *Economical Application.* One of the first premises of the conception of science just outlined is that the world is too rich to be captured in a limited framework of statements. "Reality" and our interests in it are too diverse to be depicted fully in any limited set of propositions. Hence, science is analytical; we economize by making statements about *aspects* of things. In consequence we can handle a great variety of materials within a limited symbolic framework. An adequate science economizes theoretical statement without denying the multifaceted variety of the world.

This four-fold scheme stresses the cultural or symbolic component of scientific activity or, broadly speaking, its *theoretical* component. It may be briefly summarized as a paradigm that locates four functions or "uses" of theory. Theory permits us to locate our thoughts in relation to stable and meaningful cultural reference points, to articulate our particular contributions with those of others working from alternative perspectives on related problems, to solve particular problems, and to economize our mental efforts.

TENSIONS AMONG THE FUNCTIONS

In a general sense the conflicts among the functions are implied by their analytical definitions. The dimensions that generate the four problems are defined by polar opposites, *inside* versus *outside,* and *creation* versus *use.* Potential incompatibilities between the functions are suggested by two old adages: "You cannot be in two places at once," and "You cannot have your cake and eat it too." More specifically, as the subsequent sections of this paper will argue in more detail, the scientific investigator may often face hard choices between such dilemmas as satisfying but idiosyncratic approaches to problems versus detached but communicable approaches, between short-run success and long-run economy, between meaningful and effective methods, and between competing strategic postulates about the nature of the world of scientific objects. The choices are hard because it is not always possible to satisfy multiple criteria at the same time. The solution to one side of a problem intensifies the other side. We face such dilemmas in our everyday life and also in our scientific activity. They are present in both contexts because both contexts are subject to the incompatibility between obtaining and expending resources and between solving external problems and maintaining internal stability.

If the solution of each functional problem competes with the solution of every other functional problem (in the sense that the solution of one is gotten at the expense of neglecting or intensifying the others), then there are six types of functional tension in every action system. (There are six combinations of two items from among a set of four.) I will argue that extreme methodological stances in social science represent attempts to place exclusive emphasis upon one of the functional requisites of social science considered as an action system and that for each of the six functional tensions of social life there is a corresponding methodological dilemma in social science.

The character of these tensions and dilemmas can best be understood by considering each pair of functional requisites in turn, specifying the incompatibility of each pair, and examining the corresponding metatheoretical problem in social science.

The Problem of Values and Bias: Goal Attainment versus Integration

The problem of the role of values in social science is the most controversial of all metatheoretical issues, especially in this day of pressing and critical social problems. Published rhetoric on the issue even extends to the claim that colleagues' opinions on the subject fill one with nausea.[5] Unfortunately, much of the rhetoric on the subject is correspondingly mindless and curiously ill-grounded in philosophy. Opponents of the separation of factual and evaluative analysis write as if Gerald Moore had not written on the naturalistic fallacy and thus presented a formidable (if not necessarily impossible) task of philosophical rebuttal.[6] Proponents of scientific neutrality often rely on a casual and facile reading of Max Weber and make their argument by merely bowing to the authority of that revered master.[7]

Weber's position was not so clear and so unequivocally accepting of neutrality as it is sometimes thought to be. Weber recognized that there is a value bias, explicit or implicit, in all thought because of the inescapable selectivity of human statement. His famous separation of value relevance and value freedom along the dimension of selection and investigation of problems cannot be construed as a defense of the possibility of value-free inquiry. It is equally an insistence on the inescapability of values in scientific study. Secondary critics sometimes make Weber's position more antiseptic by pretending that Weber said that values are necessary only in selecting a topic for study. Thus, values might make one select race relations as a topic of study because of the value relevance of the subject. But once race relations has been chosen as a field of study, investigation can proceed without value bias — or so the simplified interpretation of Weber would have us believe.

Weber's analysis was more profound. He recognized that values are criteria for deciding what it is about a topic that is relevant. They determine not just broad areas of investigation but the very hypotheses that we choose to test.[8] Values need not determine the answers to our questions, but they determine the questions we ask. Hence, values permeate scientific investigation: The principle of value relevance means that a completed scientific edifice, considered as a structure of interrelated and tested statements, constitutes only a picture of a subject matter from a given perspective. The topic can be reexamined from other perspectives to reveal new facets, new meanings, and new relationships. In this sense social scientists can remain value free only by refusing to formulate any soluble problems.

An appreciation of the intimate connection between values and perspectives is the key to understanding the problem of value neutrality as a special case of a functional tension. Variations in perspectives come about because we approach reality with different interests and goals. Our criteria of selection are derived from our interests. As we cannot characterize objects in every possible way, we edit our characterizations according to the principle of value relevance. Total neutrality is impossible because total neutrality would imply total description and bar selectivity. The conflict between committed and neutral stances in social science is more usefully

seen as a conflict between narrow and wide perspectives.

In this light the conflict can be seen as parallel to a similar tension in social life itself, for both relatively neutral and relatively colored perspectives are functional requisites of organized group activity. The conflict in social science over how neutral we should be or can be reflects a tension deeply rooted in the dilemmas involved in orienting ourselves to objects in socially relevant ways.

The tension stems from the contrary imperatives of goal attainment and integration. The effective pursuit of goals pushes actors to the characterization of objects in immediate, goal-relevant ways. When we see a chair we need not be aware of all its features. It is enough to see it in the how-can-I-sit-in-it frame of reference. Or perhaps it might be viewed in an aesthetic frame, as an object of color and form. But if we want someone else to fetch the chair for us, we must describe the chair and its location in terms that he can understand. He may not share our standards and purposes. "Bring me the comfortable one" or "bring me the pretty one" will not do. This is one of the principal differences between the pursuit of immediate goals and organizing for concerted activity. Where the former function dominates, then very limited and selective frameworks are efficient and effective. For the latter function it is necessary to suspend immediate purposes in order to successfully communicate with a set of alters who have diverse purposes. Organization implies communication, and communication requires transcending narrow perspectives derived from immediate purpose. To communicate we must enter into a shared perspective founded upon a broader and more common meeting ground.

This argument has application beyond our initial example of the conflict between individual and group perspectives. The wider the range of groups, interests, and purposes involved in a cultural enterprise the more necessary is a general perspective for characterizing objects in terms that transcend the particular perspectives of constituent persons and groups. Without a common perspective it is impossible to integrate diverse contributions into a unified cultural system. To return to our earlier terms, it is necessary to balance *problem relevance* and *orderly framework*.

This need for perspective suggests a possible reformulation of Weber's classic solution to the problem of values. Rather than arguing for one side or the other we can synthesize the issue. Each perspective has a determinate function in the investigative process. Value relevance refers to the selective aspect of all characterization and thus to an insistence on the relevance of social science to human purpose. Value neutrality refers to the imperative of creating communicable knowledge of social reality, knowledge with, as it were, *scientific* relevance independent of the goals of any particular group. The latter is achieved by adopting canons of investigation that are shared by the widest possible community of observers, namely the canons of science. But this does not mean that social science is value *free* in its content. The problem of reconciling the tensions inherent in the choice of a perspective remains. Hence there is a second element in the reconciliation. It remains necessary to mediate between the value *relativity* implicit in the need to formulate problems in a goal-relevant manner and the *universalism* implied by neutrality within a scientific community. Judging from Weber's own substantive research and the guiding values that he utilized, it appears that his own resolution of this inherent conflict was to formulate problems from the widest possible value perspective, the over-arching values of Western civilization. The interests and goals of given factions or even given nation-states are too narrow. Great themes from the Western tradition, such themes as rationality, make a more appropriate starting place for social science. In this way we can avoid the tension that would develop in any science that tried to integrate an extremely narrow and partisan political focus with the universalism of scientific objectivity. Whatever inherent bias is involved in formulating the problematic in value-relevant terms does not interfere with science as a collective enterprise (and the level of communication such enterprise implies), *if truly broad perspectives are used*, perspectives that encompass the entire intellectual community.

From this point of view two approaches are inadequate to the development of social science as a cultural system. One is the narrow cameralist idea that Weber opposed, the notion that social science should serve the state or, for that matter, any other established institution. The other is the idea that social science should be the handmaiden of any preconceived ideologies or strategies of change. Either of these views might be desirable for the solution of given politically defined intellectual problems, but in either case *science* as the development of communicable knowledge suffers, and our depiction of social reality is truncated, partial, and time-bound. When broad values rather than immediate political goals govern inquiry, any established or partisan orthodoxy is exposed as dependent on one value position from among many possible options, and the implicit value choices of specific programs of social change or resistance to change are placed in perspective.

Even then, we must recognize that "exposing" is only placing in a broader perspective, and even broad perspectives are relative. Hence social science has an open quality; it is always possible to construct an alternate picture of the social world, one that emphasizes different facets and relationships, one that takes as variable, or potentially variable, what previous analysis assumed to be constant. In consequence what once were viewed as hard inescapable exigencies come to be seen as contingent, dependent on conditions that are subject to change. This is the crucial thrust of the critics of neutral social science. What they rightly object to is the tendency of the "neutral" social scientist to take background conditions for granted and hence to defend unnecessarily conservative positions as eternal scientific truth.

This account of the reconciliation of value relevance and value neutrality has proceeded on the assumption that the solution of the problem is cognate with the resolution of the generic problem of conflicts between goal attainment and integration as it appears in many facets of social life. Premature emphasis on obtaining immediate goals prevents the instrumental delay that is requisite to mustering collective power in the pursuit of goals. The integration of collective effort requires attention to building languages, channels of communication, common perspectives, and shared assumptions.

It is not surprising that impatience with value-neutral modes of inquiry is heightened during periods when there is a strong collective sense of urgent and rapidly worsening group problems. Science is oriented to its own standards and to the development of generalized resources for solving intellectual problems. Ideology is oriented to the world and its crushing problems. Thus, the two endeavors are opposed along both of the axes that differentiate functional problems, and conflict between them is inevitable. And yet the cognate problem is handled continuously in social life. Actors inhibit their impulse to view objects entirely in relation to immediate needs. Objects are reperceived from the perspective of a larger community. In the terms of G. H. Mead, actors "take the role of the generalized other" in order to communicate because through communication collective efforts can be organized.

The Problem of Level of Abstraction: Goal Attainment versus Adaptation

The contribution of social science to the solution of social problems represents an output from science to other social systems and is in this sense a "goal" of science but, considering science as a cultural system, this is a relatively derivative goal. The first-order goal of science is the production of scientific knowledge. Science, like other action systems, confronts a dilemma as to the allocation of resources to generalized facilities or to immediate output. In general functional terms this is the problem of the tension between adaptation and goal attainment. Should resources be committed to the solution of immediate and specific problems, or should they be invested in generalized facilities that may, in the long run, prove useful in a wide variety of contexts? Generalized facilities have the advantage of being uncommitted to specific uses in advance; hence they become obsolescent more slowly. It is possible to come to terms with new problems without starting over *ab initio*.

For science, considered as a cultural system, the tension is between concrete problem relevance and economy. Economy is a product of the generalization of theory. Generalized statement is, by definition, applicable to a wide variety of particular scientific problems. And yet, in a sense, the goal of science is the solution of scientific problems: A general theory is accounted useless if, despite elegance, internal consistency, and plausibility, it cannot be specified to account for a range of problematic phenomena. An adequate science contains statements at a variety of levels on the ladder of abstraction and provides the necessary logical connections between low-level factual assertions and high-level theoretical explanation. Despite this general presumption of potential unity of logical structure in science there are a number of practical problems at the level of social action. At which level of the hierarchy should investigators begin? Should they invest resources in facilities or in more immediate problems of explanation?

In social science this antinomy is often expressed in the old chestnut about the relative priorities of theory and research. In a sense this "problem" was solved in sociology when it was recognized that there is no necessary logical opposition between theory and research. Indeed, they complement each other and, together, they *constitute* science. The rapprochement was accomplished in the classic articles of Robert Merton.[9]

Merton's articles were very influential and certainly dampened further discussion about whether theory and research were inherently opposed or could be carried on as totally separate enterprises. At the same time, the fundamental issue is not so easily resolved, and several symptoms indicate an underlying possibility that perhaps Merton solved the problem in principle but not in fact: It is generally agreed that theory guides research, suggests problems, makes us see facts in a different perspective, and avoids prediction by mere extrapolation of past trends to the future. It is also agreed that research tests theory and forces us to redefine and differentiate our theoretical concepts. But there is lingering doubt that theory is really useful; we do not seem to be confident about what social science theory would look like if there was such a thing. Highly abstract or "grand" theory, such as the abstract theory of the social system, is criticized as too far removed from real problems of social science.[10] Moreover, all general theories are usually severely criticized if it is not immediately clear how their terms would be "operationalized." Indeed, this is usually the first and most easily acquired piece of abstract sociological acumen proudly displayed by budding sociologists. The prevalence of this attitude, as well as the solution that is now commonly proposed for the problem are both elucidated by referring again to the generic problem of the conflict between adaptive and goal attainment functions.

In ordinary life this tension is resolved by developing channels for rather easy movement from the general to the specific. For example, suppose a group within a business firm advocated investing time and funds in general facilities, say, a large electronic computer. Management would probably insist "You may have your computer, but we must be provided with manuals that tell us how to use the computer, training courses for our employees, packages of easily usable computer programs, and so forth." And so it is elsewhere in action systems. What might be called "secondary adaptive resources" develop in the form of organization devoted to specifying or channeling investments in generalized facilities into specific uses. Whether it be a university placement service facilitating the movement of graduates into jobs, or even the index in a reference book, we see the same function performed: Facilities are provided to aid the translation of generalized investment to specific use. Perhaps the generic prototype of this phenomenon in human interaction is the role of grammar in communication. In a sense language is a huge batch of words but, as Suzanne Langer has pointed out, one can memorize the dictionary of a language and still be unable to speak the language.[11] In order to produce utterances one must know the rules of grammar, the rules of ordering and combining words to form meaningful propositions. Similarly anyone who possesses a body of resources requires a grammar of use if the resources are to be put to effective and purposeful use.

Current concern with the logic of theory construction is, in effect, an attempt to ensure that sociological theory has a grammar. Criticisms of a theory as "overly abstract" are more properly stated as complaints that the theory lacks a grammar, i.e., lacks a set of rules of combination and inference that would produce meaningful testable propositions. There is nothing undesirable about abstraction *per se* any more than there is something undesirable about any other investment in generalized resources. Such investment is unproductive only when its generality cannot be specified for want of a grammar of use.

Those who work on problems of theory building or theory construction are sometimes criticized for avoiding problems of substantive sociological concern. They are said, to quote my own previous phrase, to worry about "what social science theory would look like if there were such a thing." According to the present analysis this worry is quite legitimate. It represents a concern for the construction of theory with built-in links to observable data, established ties to other bodies of scientific knowledge, and clear internal relations among its own propositions. It represents a concern for constructing a theory with a grammar and is cognate with any other desire to link the creation of resources with their use.

The Problem of Subjectivity: Goal Attainment versus Pattern Maintenance

A third historic issue in metatheory divides those who insist that the subject matter of social science is the tangible physical behavior of human beings and those who say that social science must go behind external behavior to the inner intentions or states of mind of the actor. The latter position is variously termed subjectivism, a phenomenological approach, or the action frame of reference. Those who affirm this position usually insist on substituting such terms as "action" or "conduct" for "behavior" because the contrary position, emphasizing the external, directly observable aspects of activity, usually employs the latter term. Unfortunately several other issues have been superimposed on this one, debates between scientific and humanistic approaches and debates between specific schools of psychology. Here we will try to focus on the specific issue of whether social science must go beyond external acts to the subjective meanings of the actor.

All social systems exhibit symptoms of one or another form of the problem of whether one must look only at behavior or should look at the motives behind conduct. Legal theory, for example, must ask whether only the external act should be regulated by law or whether law should look at motivation. Sometimes the law takes one position and sometimes the other. It is intent, a state of mind, that makes a homicide a murder. Throughout the law there is general recognition that social policy requires looking at behavior and its actual consequences. "I didn't mean to" does not help the victim of an accident or

an illegal act. And yet no legal system refuses to look at intention. Somehow, the defense, "I didn't mean to," alters our moral response to an act.

The legal example is a good one because it leads us directly to the divergent social implications of actors viewing each others' acts only externally or viewing their acts as manifestations of states of inner consciousness. On the one hand, as a practical matter, no social system can afford to ignore the actual external acts of persons and the consequences of those acts. Social systems cannot reach goals without extracting useful contributory performances from participants. On the other hand, it is difficult to maintain the legitimacy of a social system that fails to make activity meaningful to participants, that fails to relate the demands of the system to a meaningful moral order. When such legitimation is a component of the order, then it is difficult to exclude reference to meaning and intention in assessing the responsibility of participants.

To return to the language of the functional requisites, the conflict between pattern maintenance and goal attainment stems from tension between the need to motivate activity (by attaching demands for specific behavior to stable systems of meaning and value), and the unreliability of mere motivation as a guarantee of performance. The achievement of concrete goals requires concrete behavior, not mere intention. To some extent, all social systems justify their demands on participants on the grounds of necessity and sanction performance independent of intention. Yet, it is also important to maintain the integrity of systems of meaning, which involves taking the actor's intentions into account. Hence, in all interaction there is a functional dilemma as to whether to orient oneself to the actor's concrete behavior or to his meaningful intentions.

If we move to the level of science, this generic tension is manifest as a conflict between appreciative and manipulative modes of understanding. Do we wish to "understand" conduct in the subjective sense of *verstehen*, that is to subjectively appreciate the actor's situation and motives? Or do we want to "understand" in the sense of having the capacity to manipulate and predict behavior? On the one hand the *empirical problem relevance* of science requires objective observation; verification requires reference to something empirically observable. It is impossible to test the scientific adequacy of our solutions to concrete empirical problems without referring to visible events as indices of our concepts. Hence, in the last analysis an adequate scientific theory must contain propositions that describe and predict the observable external events of conduct. States of mind must necessarily be observed indirectly and inferentially from observations, predictions, and manipulations of observable behavior.

On the other hand we may properly question whether manipulative understanding is the main motive for endeavor in social science. The *legitimacy* of social science is also founded on aspirations for understanding in an appreciative mode. Some positivistic philosophies of science to the contrary notwithstanding, most social scientists are dissatisfied by accounts of human conduct that provide no understanding in the appreciative sense. I would venture to suppose that many who abhor behavioristic social science do so on the basis of value premises. It is not simply a matter of doubting the scientific adequacy of a given school of thought; it is a matter of being dissatisfied with explanations that fail to convey a sense of the relation between human action and human purpose. It is not surprising to discover this conflict in the values of social science for it is cognate with the pervasive conflict between getting the job done, in this case the job of developing a verifiable social science, and maintaining the "correct" motivation for getting the job done, whether the method is effective or not.

Returning to the level of the social system, the main theory that has been applied to the tension between goal attainment and pattern maintenance is the theory of socialization. Through socialization people are made to want to do what they must do, thereby linking the motivation of the individual to the behavioral requirements of the system. In this way the structure of the society is said to be incorporated into the personality of the actor. Social structure is incorporated in the form of learned values that legitimize the demands of the social system and implant in the actor a generalized store of commitment to conform to the concrete demands of the system, whatever they might be.

However, the over-socialized conception of man has been rightly criticized.[12] Actors are not infinitely plastic to the molding of the social system. Values cannot justify all the varied, contradictory, painful, absurd, and unexpected demands that systems place upon actors. Actors are commonly asked to march in step in the face of what they take to be different and more legitimate rhythms from distant drummers. Good intentions are often ignored or even punished because of the demands of expediency.

A more adequate concept of socialization would take internalized social controls to be only one component of personality. Internalized norms constitute a component at a fairly high level in the hierarchy of behavioral control. Values (and their associated commitments in the actor) guide conduct into one general course or another. Without them conduct would be an unstructured sequence of purposeless

adjustments. But effective action is always subject to the demands of a reality principle. The realistic requirements of successful concrete performance enter into action as modifications of socially defined procedures even in the most well-socialized individuals. And so it must be, or social systems would wallow in an excess of demands and quests for absolute virtue.

Returning to social science, there is a similar hierarchy of ends and conditions. As long as its practitioners are motivated by a desire to appreciate conduct and to understand the implications of human action for human purposes, it is bootless to create conceptual schemes that are not relevant to the ends of human activity as men perceive them. Accordingly, we must recognize the goal directed character of human activity and allow some inferred subjective categories to enter into the research process as guiding concepts. These categories include motives, desires, goals, values, and cultural definitions and premises, concepts that direct our attention to those aspects of observable conduct that bear upon human aspiration, either as successful implementations or as frustrating conditions. Such concepts guide in the sense that they select, delimit, and define the range of relevant observable conduct. They render statements about physical behavior intelligible to the scientist who insists upon humanistic relevance in explanatory schemes.

At the same time, science requires validating as well as controlling perspectives. A validating perspective moves outside of the experience of the actor and depicts his actual behavior in objective terms. We try to develop strategic concepts cognate to the concepts of the actor in order to capture the active selection and goal direction involved in the human act. But we must insist on behavioral referents for concepts for two reasons. First, science must deal with verifiable phenomenal data. Second, a realistic social science must record the realistic press of the actor's social and natural environment as it impinges upon him.

This position is in some respects similar to that of George Herbert Mead who, as some of his students persistently insist, called our attention to the self-directed character of human conduct.[13] Nevertheless, Mead designated his thought as social *behaviorism*[14] because he accepted the notion that an adequate social psychology must have behavioral referents for its concepts. This is why students as far apart as Herbert Blumer[15] and George Lundberg[16] can both claim Mead as spiritual forefather. It is a matter of which side of Mead's resolution of the dilemma one chooses to pursue. But Mead was not trying to choose a side. He was trying to transcend the issue by creating a behavioral social psychology that could capture the creative, constructed, goal-directed, that is, *human* character of conduct. Hence for him there can be no issue between humanistic and scientific approaches to the study of interaction.

This discussion leads us back to a familiar cart-and-horse problem. I have asserted that the *guiding* perspectives cognate with the categories of the actors who are being studied are at a higher level in the control hierarchy than *validating* perspectives adopted by the scientist. It should be asserted as a corollary that methods of investigation should not control the development of science. The purpose of validating instruments is to introduce a testing procedure, not to determine which problems are scientifically strategic. There is nothing in the scientific commitment to strict testing procedure which commits him on principle to a theoretical scheme that presupposes in advance the appropriateness of a given theory of human behavior on the grounds that it is easily testable. Nothing in the scientific commitment precludes a conceptual scheme because it contains terms such as value, meaning, or intention, even though such terms are more easily used as components of inferential arguments than as the terms of specific testable theorems.

The Ideal and the Real: Pattern Maintenance versus Adaptation

In many systems of thought the problem of subjectivity is closely bound up with the problem of the influence of ideal factors in social life. Those who assert that motives and intentions must be taken into account are easily led to the position that values, ideals, meanings, and norms shape the social order. Those who assert that only objective behavior can be studied find it difficult to acknowledge the importance of concepts with such elusive referents. Nevertheless the issues are somewhat different. There is a closer relationship between subjectivists and idealists than between behaviorists and materialists. Both subjectivists and idealists stress, in effect, the importance of pattern maintenance in social systems. Social systems require motivated actors, and motives are closely connected to the ideals, values, and concepts that define meaning for the actor. But the behavioral and materialist positions are less closely related because they represent different types of functional conflict with pattern maintenance. As we have seen, behaviorism is closely related to problems of goal attainment. Materialism is closely related to problems of adaptation. Let us first deal with the tension between pattern maintenance and adaptation at the level of the social system and then return to this preliminary "identification" of materialism and adaptation.

Social systems can be viewed in an ecological perspective as systems of organization relating populations to an environment. Without social organization, adaptation to the environment would fail. Social organization in turn requires stable reference points, e.g., values, institutions, and definitions, that permit actors to anticipate each other's reactions and mutually adjust their conduct. Yet the environment and its demands are constantly changing, and adaptive flexibility to change may well require alteration of the stable references of interaction. If normative systems cannot completely control the activities of the participants in social systems, even less can they control or stabilize the flux in the environment. Hence, pattern maintenance, or the requirement of a constant store of reference points for dealing with integrative problems, is in constant conflict with adaptation, or the need to adjust to the flux in the environment. Both are necessary. Marx, with his stress on progressive adaptation to reality, that is, the inevitability of social reorganization to meet the possibilities inherent in new technologies, stresses the adaptive side. The economic determinist insists that people will seek economic advantage in the most efficient way. They will not, in the long run, sacrifice economic interests because of the imperatives of norms, values, or systems of ideas; they will adjust to environmental opportunities. Such a position is termed "realistic" because it affirms that people adjust to reality rather than express ideas.

The idealist counters by questioning the concept of reality. He insists that the actor lays his meanings and categories on to reality. The goals he seeks and his conceptions of the environment are affected by the stable and culturally relative systems of meaning that he brings to situations. As systems of meaning intervene between reality (if there is such a thing) and the adjustive response (if, indeed, this is a meaningful phrase), there is no cause for viewing either individual action or human history as a process of seeking material interests in whatever manner is dictated by an ever changing and obdurate world.

The problem of the relation between the stable orders created by human beings and the variable and changing demands of the real world remained insoluble as long as it was viewed in the positivist framework that saw no intermediate layers of orders between the intentions of man and the demands of the world.[17] In some nineteenth-century social thought, man was seen as related to the environment through his needs. The sociological revolution in thought was, in effect, the discovery that organized social and cultural systems intervene between the physical environment and men as mere need-bearing, information-gathering organisms. In the first place, the flow of raw sense experience and physical want is organized into systematic goal-directed activity. In the second place, goal-directed activity is institutionally organized to interrelate the goals of different persons and groups. Finally, institutional organization is legitimated and imbued with value because of its articulation with bodies of cultural definition and meaning. In other words, cultural organization and the flux of material reality are at opposite ends of a hierarchy of control with institutional organization and organized goal-seeking in between. Pure idealism and pure material-ism arise as alternatives for thinkers whose conceptual apparatus short-circuits the hierarchy of control and assumes the direct confrontation of ideals and reality. Once this short circuit has occurred it is easy to fall either into the extreme positivist position that ideals are just names for adjustments to reality or the extreme idealistic position that reality is just a projection of ideals. Extreme positions reflect the difficulty of coping with the relation between ideals and reality as an *interaction* if we lack concepts for dealing with the organization of that interaction. Once the inter-vening organization is recognized then the relation between cultural stability and the flow of the material world can be understood. New perceptions, motives, and interests no longer merely confront established structures; they are viewed, expressed, and demanded in terms derived from the very structures that they challenge.

For the sociologist the main intervening systems are institutional The conflict between pattern main-tenance and adaptation is resolved in the context of institutional order. Institutions are systems of established legitimate norms. One foundation of the stability of any society is that the participants do not express their needs and demands nakedly but clothe them, consciously or unconsciously, in normative modes and vocabularies. Moreover, their needs are not given by biology or random wants but are shaped by commitments derived from the institutional order. This provides a measure of predictability to diverse human activity and allows for the normative ordering of conduct.

Some institutions specifically provide for diversity of motive and interest by incorporating procedural norms. Languages, systems of legal procedure, and enabling institutions such as the legal forms of con-tracts, trusts, incorporation, municipality, and the rules of order in deliberative assemblies serve to regularize activity and incorporate it within establish-ed systems of normative control. But these institutions are procedural in the sense that they specify how to achieve variable and changing instrumental goals within a given normative framework rather than defining the goals that are to be achieved. Language, considered as a normative system does not tell us what to say; it permits us to say things. The laws of contract do not dictate the terms and goals of con-tracts; they allow us (within broad limits) to choose

contract partners and to adjust the terms of the contract to the exigencies of situation and moment. Procedural institutions provide flexible forms for incorporating variable instrumental content and at the same time avoid the chaos that would be implied by leaving actors "free" to create framework *de novo* at each contact. This of course is the point of the famous central chapter of Durkheim's *Division of Labor*. From the perspective of the arguments being presented in this paper this fame is well deserved, for it rests on an understanding of one of the inherent conflicts of organized social life and a profound appreciation of how society manages to straddle this conflict.

However, procedural institutions are not necessari-ly purely instrumental, Insofar as they maintain a high level of legitimacy, procedural institutions are suf-fused with value and reflect dominant cultural themes; they are grounded on the most stable cultural reference points in the system. Hence the interest-driven activity that is animated by institutional com-mitments and couched in institutional vocabularies is similarly inbued with value.[18]

Turning to the cultural system of social science, the tension between pattern maintenance and adapta-tion comes to focus when the social scientist attempts to *define his object of study*. At this point it is neces-sary to note that the six methodological dilemmas treated in this paper fall into two groups. The first three methodological dilemmas involve problems of scientific orientation. Should the scientist's perspec-tive be determined by his values, or should it be neu-tral? Should he be oriented to high-level abstractions or the solution of specific problems? Should he be ori-ented to the external properties of events or to their meanings? The second set of dilemmas involve the first premises of our conceptions of the objects of study in social science. For this reason there is a more direct link between understanding how the dilemma may be treated in social science and understanding how the corresponding tension is reconciled in the social world that provides social science its objects of study.

The first problem of this second set, the problem of the ideal and the real, may be stated as a dilemma between characterizing social reality as a body of cultural definitions, regulatory norms, and systems of thought or as a complex of needs, interests, and demands. Idealism, by positing ideas as "eternal" objects that become embodied in social reality, finds an extreme solution to the problem of defining a set of stable objects of study for social science. On the other hand, the purest materialism, which reduces all human activity to the impact of environmental forces, destroys the integrity of the object of study. Society is reduced to the play of environmental forces, and sociology becomes, in effect, a branch of natural science; its boundary is destroyed, and it therefore does not exist as an entity for intelligible study in its own right.[19]

To view the social realm as a hierarchy of layers of organization quite transcends the problem. We have an object of study, but that object is constituted by a set of functions or relationships between firmly grounded institutions and the flow of ongoing, adjustive activity. To repeat the argument in the language of functional components of social science, we have found a compromise between two possible extremes: One extreme view would attempt to provide *legitimacy* for a specifically scientific study of social life by asserting timeless fixed structures as stable objects of study, arguing that exclusive attention to the play of real needs and interests is essentially historicist. As against this view the extreme realist would argue that to treat cultural phenomena as the objects of social science is to divorce analysis from the concrete play of interest-driven activity, in all its variety and flux, The order of the social world is a direct product of whatever orderly realistic conditions exist in the world to which human beings must adjust themselves. The idealist, of course, responds that the materialist has now deprived social science of any *sui generis,* legitimate object of study. The intermediate position proposed here is that the institutional organization of activity provides a *legitimate* and *economical* object of study that incorporates the variable interests and demands involved in social life without falling into the trap of asserting that "all is flux."

The Problem of Change: Pattern Maintenance versus Integration

The foregoing treatment of the problem of idealism represents one way of looking at the problem of change. Stable reference points were viewed as in tension with the change implied by adaptive flexibility. The problem of change in the structure of social systems is encountered less obliquely when we consider the tension between stable reference points and flexibility in meeting *internal* problems within the social system.

Most students of functional theory, especially its critics, have failed to see any conflict between pattern maintenance and integration. On the contrary, many students seem to virtually equate the two concepts. Integration is said to occur because there are stable reference points in the system in the form of norms and values. Integration flows from the commitment of participants to these values. Such a view uses the word integration in a loose, general sense, not in the sense implied by the position of

integration in the four-fold scheme of functional requisites. Pattern maintenance and integration are on opposite sides of the dimension defined by the polarity between instrumental and consummatory needs. It is true that some conflict can be resolved by merely applying stable integrative resources, i.e., values, norms, and commitments. An authority may decide a question of law, and the parties, though unhappy, may be satisfied that the law has spoken; or a straying and disruptive group member may be reintegrated by reminding him of his underlying commitments. But many other integrative problems can be solved only by *changing* stable structures. Stability requires that problems be solved in the context of stable structures. But real social integration requires that integrative solutions be responsive to the actual needs and demands of various sub-units and groups *even* if this requires modification of established arrangements. Social-system theory would have the utopian flavor it is sometimes alleged to have[20] only if it posited that social systems always possess the integrative resources to respond to strains without structural modification. But social-system theory makes no such claim; on the contrary it asserts that systems sometimes achieve integration *through* change.

In short, we can speak of the tension between *stability* of structure and the *validity* of integrative solutions. The theory of the social system goes on to posit a mechanism for transcending this dilemma. That mechanism is referred to as the hierarchy of control.[21] According to the theory of the hierarchy of control the normative structures that constitute the stable reference points in social systems are arranged in a hierarchy of specificity. At the top are the most general shared social values and at the bottom the most particularized obligations of specific individuals in specific roles. Higher levels are then said to "control" lower levels in the sense that changes at lower levels occur within the context of stability at higher levels; indeed the change at the lower level affirms rather than destroys the higher levels in the structure. For example, some racial conflicts are resolved by structural changes in the rules governing eligibility for employment and advancement. But these normative changes have the effect of reaffirming the higher-level stable social value of equality of opportunity.

According to this theory problems of integration are ordinarily solved by the application of norms at relatively low levels, but where the application of norms at low levels fails to produce valid solutions, new integrative norms must develop. However, these new norms are not developed *de novo*; actors draw upon (and thus reaffirm) a higher-level institutional framework as they seek new normative solutions. Hence, neither change nor stability is primary. Structural change is a constant feature of the way in which social orders continually reconstitute themselves; but, at the same time, change occurs within and is influenced by constraining structures.

A parallel tension is manifest at the cultural level when social scientists argue about strategies for coping with the fact of change. An adequate social science would contain within its conceptual apparatus means of dealing with new forms of social organization. The discussion of this problem should begin by returning to a point stressed earlier in this paper. Social science is often accused of an inherent conservatism because of the tendency to assume implicitly that the established structure of the society is a given. This or that action program is labelled impractical and this or that proposed theorem is said to be false because that analyst implicitly assumes that the underlying structure of the society is a given and could not itself be changed to make new programs possible and new statements true. It is not that the analyst cannot account for change; he cannot even conceive of it. Recognition of this possibility leads us to understand that social science itself changes in the sense that its object of study, society, changes. When a society is reorganized, old systems of relationships between the variables of social science change. Old theories, especially theories at a low level of abstractions, are no longer true in that they were true only given the stability of parameters that have now changed. In this sense the internal integration of the logical structure of the science is modified, not only because new external facts about society have been discovered, but because the entity itself has been reorganized.

Some writers who recognize that social life has this quality of being a "multipossibility"[22] thing then move on to assert that social science must therefore take ceaseless flux as its first premise. Such authors fail to understand that ontological questions are not at issue here. Science is not concerned with essences and ultimates but with the adequacy of an explanatory framework. An adequate explanatory framework must not only recognize the changing character of the relationships between variables, it must also have stable reference points in order to have something to talk about. The problem is one of strategy, and the strategy must cope with the requisite of continuity of discourse. The matter has been well stated by Parsons:

> The statement that everything empirical is subject to change may be metaphysically correct; but this is often translated into the scientifically untenable doctrine condemning as invalid a heuristic assumption that any reference point is structurally given, on the grounds

that such an assumption would commit the investigator to deny the fluidity of ultimate reality. Science is not a photographic reproduction of reality, but is a highly selective mode of organizing man's orientation to reality — however philosophers define the latter. The scientifically specific component of this organization depends on ability to establish reference-points structurally stable enough to justify the simplification of dynamic problems prerequisite to logically manageable analysis.[23]

What would constitute an adequate strategy? To repeat again the argument of this paper, we must look for guidance to the mechanisms found in social systems for transcending the functional tension at that level. In this case the mechanism for mediating between pattern maintenance and integration is the hierarchy of control wherein integration problems at any given level are solved within the framework of stability at higher levels.

At the level of theory the analogue is the hierarchy of stability within the propositional structure and variable systems of a well-constructed theory. We implicitly refer to this hierarchy when we use the phrase *ceteris paribus*, "other things being equal." But of course, as everyone knows, other things are not equal. An adequate general theory would, in effect, specify the structure of *ceteris paribus*. It would specify what other things must be equal, what happens when they are not equal, and arrange these various paramenters in a hierarchy of stability. Then, we could approach a given problem knowing what could be taken as constants within the specified time span of analysis. By the same token, if we understood our own procedures we would appreciate that our results will not necessarily be valid if longer time spans are considered. Whether the hierarchy or *ceteris paribus* should be interpreted, as Parsons' work implies, as a hierarchy of normative specificity remains to be seen. Whatever the ultimate fate of this particular solution of the problem, it is important to understand that it is a species of the genus under discussion, namely, attempts to specify the structure of *ceteris paribus*. When the hierarchy of *ceteris paribus* is adequately specified we need not make a forced choice between positing the eternality of given social structures, on the one hand, or, on the other hand, adopting the equally unsatisfactory alternative of assuming that every alteration in social structure requires a complete reworking of sociological theory.

Defining a hierarchy of *ceteris paribus* is another aspect of the problem of orderly framework in science. Part of the orderly framework of theory is a scheme for specifying the level of generality of findings and locating any given relationship in a network of larger relationships. When a map of this sort is available it is possible for the findings of investigators working on different problems at various levels of generality and specificity to locate their contribution with respect to the contributions of others. In the absence of such a map, investigators are prone to assume that superficial contradictions are fundamental contradictions and that each new finding overthrows previous work, leaving the corpus of investigation an unintelligible hodgepodge without cumulative import, a corpus without scientific legitimacy.[24]

The Reality of the Group: Integration versus Adaptation

Should social science see groups as the sum of their individual members, or are groups *sui generis*, a reality in their own right? This is an old and very vexed question and one that is heavily overlaid with the special concerns of sociologists, anxious as they are to protect the autonomy of their discipline.

To what do the theoretical propositions of sociology refer? Do they refer to the conduct of individuals or to some superindividual constructs, whether conceived as group minds, structural properties, rate of behavior, relations, or interactions? One frequently used premise in arguments for the reality of the group is that the units of groups, organizations, or social systems are not individuals at all but some other analytical components such as roles and statuses.[25] The concept of an "individual" or "person" is just as analytical or abstract as the concept of a group. We see or construct an individual by laying our categories on to the actual bits and pieces of behavior that we observe.

Whatever the ontological or epistimological validity of abstract arguments of this sort, they cannot sweep under the rug the practical and apparent, indeed proverbial, conflict between the individual and the group. The problem is inescapable not just because we feel a subjective tension between personal proclivities and group demands or because we experience a continuous stream of testimony from others who feel such tensions. The tension is founded on an inherent tension between two functional requisite of group life, in this case the tension between integration and adaptation.

The relation between social control of the individual and integration of the group is such a commonplace idea that it requires no further elaboration. The relation between adaptation and individual autonomy is less frequently noted. No open system could achieve adaptation to fluctuating reality without permitting some autonomy, that is, freedom from preprogrammed response, to the units of the system, whether these units be defined as individuals or as persons-in-role. Imagine the members of a hunting and gathering society attempting to subject the hunting and gathering process to detailed and complete normative and authoritative regulation. The norm "Every third day of the week at the third hour of the day walk forty-four paces from the first tree on your left and shoot a rabbit" is ludicrous for obvious reasons. Hunting requires autonomous search behavior, initiative, and freedom to adjust to external exigency without inflexible prior constraint. Units that have this degree of capacity for autonomous action must themselves be well-bounded, well-organized systems. Roles, statuses, and similar purely structural units of organizations do not have these properties; people do. The autonomy of the individual is directly related to the adaptive function of unit autonomy within social systems.

On the other hand, unlimited unit autonomy disorganizes the system. Hence, there are sets of relations between units that organize the system and limit autonomy of units. These relations can be examined as objects of study, and for this reason the sociologistic position has a measure of validity. But there is a tension between the integration of relational systems of control and the need to allow freedom for units to come to terms with the variety and complexity of the external world. Autonomy can be put either to adaptive or to destructive uses. In society innovation and control are reconciled in the context of the procedural institution as just described. But for the general theory of social science the need for reconciliation emerges as a problem in social psychology: How shall we characterize the social person? How can the units of social interaction and of social systems be conceived as persons that are both innovative and yet subject to social control? The most powerful solution is that proposed by the American symbolic interactionists, especially George Herbert Mead.[26] The solution is founded on the isomorphism of the concept of role, which can be simultaneously treated as a component of personality, of society, and of ongoing interaction. A central organizing component of personality, the self, is formed in the process of playing roles. The actor draws on the responses of others to him in order to define his own self. But other's responses to him are derived from the social roles that he plays. Accordingly, it is not difficult to understand social control; there is a direct link between the actor's conception of himself and the requirements of his social roles.

This theory has become a commonplace entry in elementary textbooks. Less well appreciated is the other side of the coin, the impact of the self-directed person on the emergence of new systems of roles or, alternatively stated, the social incorporation of the innovative acts of individuals. This subject is beautifully treated in the relatively unrecognized sections of Mead's *Mind, Self and Society* dealing with sympathy, cooperation, and the individual's contribution to the society.[27] The conduct of a social person is not mere automatic external expression of a socially formed self. The self-guided person is capable of adapting his conduct to situational exigency. Moreover, because of the human capacity for taking the role of the other in the imagination, the person's co-actors can sympathetically appreciate the innovator's adaptive, original acts and incorporate new patterns of social activity into their repertory of roles. Once one understands the self to be a process of role-taking and self-definition rather than a fixed entity it is possible to understand that the members of groups can reconstruct their group life by reconstructing their selves.

In other words, Mead attempted to work out the implications of he idea that mind, self, and society are all symbolically regulated processes. The group can achieve integrated organization because of the possibility of *symbolic* social control; the group can be responsive to the adaptive innovations of individuals because of the possibility of symbolic incorpration of innovative acts.

At the cultural level within systems of social science the problem of integration versus adaptation is manifest in another problem in characterizing the object of social science. Is that object an integrated irreducible entity? If it is, then the task of producing an integrated social science with a perfectly orderly framework would seem to be relatively easy. Sociology would be the only social science. It would be an independent science with no problem of relating one level of reality to another. If the units are mere expressions of group demands or needs then a single logically unified system of theoretical propositions *about groups* could explain all observed conduct. But if societies have units whose conduct is in part free of social constraint then it would seem unlikely that all conduct could be explained by propositions deducible from theorems about groups.

I contend that the latter view is correct. A social science that comprehends and is responsive to the actual variety of conduct in the world, in other words an adaptive social science, must come to terms with the autonomy of the units of social systems.[28]

Mead, because he understood the relation between society and the social self, understood how social science must define its object of study. The object of study is neither society nor people, it is symbolic interaction. Symbolic interaction has social and individual aspects, and the perspective of the social

interactionist points the way to the development of an integrated social science that comes to grips with autonomous self-directed activity.

CONCLUSION

Six metatheoretical problems have commanded the attention of social scientists since the emergence of the field. Three concern the appropriate orientation of the social scientist to his materials. Should he attempt to implement values, or should he be neutral? Should he be concerned with broad general theories or with the solution of specific problems? Should he be interested in concrete behavior or in subjective intentions? The other three problems concern the appropriate scientific strategy for defining the object of study. Is society an embodiment of cultural values, or is it a response to the press of realistic conditions? Is it stable or constantly changing? Is it a reality in its own right or a sum of the acts of individuals?

The conclusion of this paper is paradoxical. On the one hand, in each instance I have stated that the conflicting positions are irreconcilable when stated in their usual form. Moreover, both sides of each argument are sound in the sense that they reflect an appreciation of real and inescapable problems in the organization of social life. On the other hand, I have also suggested that each of the issues is resolvable if properly stated. The notion that each is resolvable is founded on the fact that social life goes on. Somehow the tensions inherent in social organization do not bring social life to a grinding halt. A series of arguments have been presented suggesting that an understanding of how, in our ordinary social life, compromises are found to the dilemmas inherent in defining social objects and in orienting ourselves to objects helps us to understand how social science can deal with its cognate problems.

One implication of this line of argument is that basic methodological disputes are endemic and permanent in the sense that no one-sided resolution is possible, for in the long run any such resolution must be unresponsive to a given functional requisite of social science considered as a system of cultural action. This point provides an effective paradigm for reviewing the themes of this paper. Let us recall each of the functional components of social science and then, for each of these, list the three extreme methodological positions that are unstable because of the requisites of that function.

1. *Legitimacy.* The legitimacy of a scientific discipline can be maintained only if it can be provided with

a stably bounded, independent, and meaningful subject matter. Hence, extreme positions of positivist materialism, behaviorism, and historical relativism undermine the legitimacy of social science — materialism by collapsing the distinction between the physical world and the world of human action, behaviorism by divorcing social science from problems of human meaning and intention, and historical relativism by denying the stability of any laws of social life.

2. *Orderly Framework.* The integration of diverse findings, propositions, and contributions from the multiple participants in scientific study requires an agreed framework for locating the diverse perspectives, levels of abstraction, and components of social action that are involved in inquiry in the social sciences. Extremely value-laden positions, static approaches, and reductionist approaches undermine the orderly framework of social science. Politicized social science impedes communication. Static social science prevents the articulation of long-run and short-run propositions and diverts attention from the parameters that define and locate the framework of contingencies that can reconcile apparently contradictory findings. Reductionism makes it impossible to relate layers of order to each other without denying the reality of one or another layer; hence, reductionism integrates at the expense of denying the autonomy of some of the participants in scientific enterprise. All three positions lead to conflict among participants rather than reconciliation between apparently diverse view points and findings.

3. *Empirical problem relevance.* Social science must be validated by success in solving particular problems. Extreme subjectivism cuts social science off from empirical data, as does exclusive attention to theory at a high level of abstraction. So, indeed, does the attempt to maintain a completely value-free posture, for such an attempt could be sustained only by refusing to formulate any particular problems for study.

4. *Economical application.* Science must be economical in its coverage of the diversity and flux of the world, but it must not do so at the expense of ignoring diversity and change. Extreme empiricism is not economical, and idealism is not responsive to the flux of events. Finally, sociologism ignores the necessary diversity of self-regulated human conduct.

Perhaps none of these arguments were presented in sufficient detail to be persuasive. Perhaps the four-fold scheme of functional prerequisites has been misused, or perhaps the scheme itself is not adequate to the task at hand. Nevertheless, the arguments do suggest a distinctive and fresh approach to some very old problems.

NOTES

1. Talcott Parsons, *Societies* (Englewood Cliffs, N.J.: Prentice-Hall, Inc., 1966), p. 7.
2. Gideon Sjoberg in "Contradictory Functional Requirements and Social Systems," *Conflict Resolution,* 4 (1960), pp. 198-208, takes the position that recognition of the contradictory requirements of social systems would constitute a "modification" of structural-functional theory. On the contrary, I would suggest that this has always been a feature of Parsonian macrofunctional analysis, central to the notion that structural differentiation frees resources from ascription to the contradictory requirements involved in a multipurpose structure.
3. See Robert F. Bales, "The Equilibrium Problem in Small Groups," in A. Paul Hare *et al., Small Groups: Studies in Social Interaction* (New York: Alfred A. Knopf, 1955), pp. 424-456.
4. Talcott Parsons, "General Theory in Sociology," in Robert K. Merton *et al.* (eds.), *Sociology Today* (New York: Basic Books, 1959), pp. 3-38, at pp. 4-8.
5. Henry Etzkowitz and Ferald M. Schaflander, "A Manifesto for Sociologists: Institution-Formation — A New Sociology," *Social Problems,* 15 (1968), pp. 399-408, at p. 399.
6. G. E. Moore, *Principia Ethica* (Cambridge, England: Cambridge University Press, 1903).
7. Max Weber, *The Methodology of the Social Sciences,* trans. Edward A. Shils and Henry A. Finch (Glencoe, Ill.: The Free Press, 1949).
8. See, for example, Weber's discussion of value relevance as it relates to the selection of hypotheses in the sociology of music for an illustration of how values determine the specific content of sociological queries, *Ibid.,* p. 30.
9. Robert K. Merton, "The Bearing of Sociological Theory on Empirical Research" and "The Bearing of Empirical Research on Sociological Theory" in *Social Theory and Social Structure* (Glencoe, Ill.: The Free Press, 1957), pp. 85-117.
10. C. Wright Mills, *The Sociological Imagination* (New York: Oxford University Press, 1959), pp. 25-48.
11. Susanne K. Langer, *Philosophy in a New Key* (Cambridge, Mass.: Harvard University Press, 1942).
12. Dennis H. Wrong, "The Oversocialized Conception of Man in Modern Sociology," *American Sociological Review,* 26 (April 1961), pp. 183-193.
13. Herbert Blumer, "Sociological Implication of the Thought of George Herbert Mead," *American Journal of Sociology,* 71 (1969), pp. 535-544.
14. George Herbert Mead, *Mind, Self and Society,* Charles W. Morris (ed.) (Chicago, Ill.: University of Chicago Press, 1934), pp. 1-41.
15. Blumer, "Sociological Implications," *op. cit.*
16. George Lundberg, *Foundations of Sociology* (New York: McGraw-Hill, 1939).
17. This, of course, is one of the principal arguments of *The Structure of Social Action* (New York: McGraw-Hill, 1937).
18. The Parsonian analyst would ordinarily view the procedural institutions depicted by Durkheim as mediating between I and A rather than between L and A. That is, the two diagonals of the four-fold table are termed mechanical and organic solidarity, L-G or mechanical solidarity being the primordial regulation of motivation by values, and I-A or organic solidarity being the institutional regulation of diverse differentiated interests. Strictly speaking, L-A is neither of these solidarities; and the relationship between L and A is not mediated by procedural institutions *per se* but by the articulation of the evaluative component of institutions with commitment to performance in institutional roles on the part of actors. Nevertheless, it is important to remember that institutions have a dual aspect. Within this conceptual framework the functions of integration (a *consummatory* component) should not be seen as

corresponding to the structural category "institution" but to the *process* of institutional integration. The *structural* components of institutions are always problematic in relation to the concrete diversity and flux of human interests. Such diversity is controlled to the extent that it is encapsulated in normative modes of expression. See Talcott Parsons, "Durkheim's Contribution to the Theory of Integration of Social Systems," in Parsons, *Sociological Theory in Modern Society* (New York: The Free Press, 1967).

19. Footnote 17 bears repeating at this point.

20. Ralf Dahrendorf, "Out of Utopia: Toward a Reorientation of Sociological Analysis," *American Journal of Sociology*, 64 (1968), pp. 115-127.

21. Talcott Parsons, "An Outline of the Social System," in Parsons *et al.* (eds.), *Theories of Society* (New York: The Free Press of Glencoe, Ill., 1961), pp. 30-79 at pp. 37-38.

22. Ernest Cassirer, *An Essay on Man* (New Haven, Conn.: Yale University Press, 1944), pp. 56-62.

23. Parsons, "Outline of the Social System," *op. cit.,* p. 70.

24. The point may be illustrated by a familiar problem in the realm of physics. Those who are drawn to revolutionary images of change are fond of speaking of quantum mechanics as "overturning" the classical Newtonian physics. An integrative approach would insist that quantum theory showed that the classical model held only for bodies that are large in relation to Planck's constant.

25. Charles K. Warriher, "Groups Are Real: A Reaffirmation," *American Sociological Review,* 21 (1956), pp. 549-554.

26. Mead, *Mind, Self and Society.*

27. *Ibid.,* pp. 260-310.

28. It may be reification to term those units "individuals." Strictly speaking, they are those components or aspects of the social person that are not subject to detailed social control.

4

THE VALUES PROBLEM IN SOCIAL SCIENCE IN DEVELOPMENTAL PERSPECTIVE

Jan J. Loubser

There is currently great concern in the profession about the status and role of sociology in society. It is reflected in a number of fringe movements such as that of the "radical" sociologists as well as in some major efforts by sociologists of stature such as Gouldner and Etzioni, among others. But it is also widespread in the profession itself, as is evidenced in the concern of several national associations and the international association with the professional ethics of sociologists and their role in the contemporary world. In June 1971, the *American Sociologist* published a special issue dealing with "Sociological Research and Public Policy," in which current concerns about the role of sociology in society are reflected.

In this issue, Duncan MacRae, Jr. discusses what he calls a dilemma of sociology, namely science versus policy.[1] He reviews problems in the relations between pure and applied research in the natural sciences and comes to the conclusion that the same analysis applies to the social sciences, with the additional complication, familiar to us all, that social scientists have a peculiar involvement with their subjects. He then reviews six different attempts by sociologists to move from the "is" to the "ought," which need not concern us here. MacRae adds his own solution, namely, to foster a concern with social philosophy, perhaps as a subfield of sociology as a vehicle for the discussion and communication of valuative and ethical questions. Out of this, he hopes a greater awareness of the "ought" dimension of their professional role will emerge among sociologists.

In the same issue, Elbridge Sibley asks whether scientific sociology is at bay, points out that in 1970 sociologists were in turmoil, and asks the pointed question: Will objective sociology survive?[2] The prospect he holds forth is for sociologists to expose themselves in depth to cultures different from their own and through this experience rid themselves of their ethnocentrism.

These two responses to the problems of professional sociology are typical of the mainline response to attacks from all sides. They confirm a commitment to scientific value-free sociology and at best advocate strategies for achieving greater awareness of the problems which they themselves cannot deny.

When we turn to the radical sociologists and their attack on the establishment of the profession, we find a similar situation. The substance of their position is too well-known to dwell on at length: their total rejection of value-free sociology, their onslaught on the profession as completely corrupted by its allegiance to and compromises with the status quo and powers-that-be, and their espousal of a radically activist sociology, critical of every aspect of the existing social structure and actively revolutionary in their participation.[3] "Anti-minotaur"[4] is still one of the basic texts along with C. W. Mills' *Sociological Imagination,*[5] even though Gouldner has since announced his abhorrence of the breed spawned by that classic piece[6] and Mills was spared embarrassment by an early death. Apart from a sporadic avowal of a commitment to scientific values and weak attempts to indicate the relevant social values, this movement is basically, with a few exceptions, anti-intellectual, antiscience, and agnostic with respect to social values.

The Achilles heel of mainline sociology is, of course, its attempt to model itself on the natural sciences and to insist on the standards of objectivity and value freedom in doing so. This has often added up to a naïve denial of value relevance, a total disregard of one part of Weber while embracing the other.[7] After all, Weber's methodological position cannot be fully understood and appreciated without remembering his emphasis on both value relevance and value freedom. His espousal of the standard of objectivity was tempered by a very sophisticated sensitivity for the almost insurmountable obstacles in achieving it.

The current debate on the role of values in sociology and social science in general so far has failed to grasp this Weberian position and to introduce the necessary distinctions to cope with the complexity of the problem.

In this essay, I shall discuss some of the issues by introducing a conceptualization of the scientific process, of the development of social science in relation to society, of value commitment and patterns, and of universal human values. The central argument of the essay is that social science as an action system cannot be exclusively committed to scientific values but has to develop a commitment to universal human values. The implications of such a position are discussed in the final section.

THE SCIENTIFIC PROCESS

Discussion of the values problem in social science requires specification of the processes involved in social scientific action at a sufficient level of generality to allow consideration of types rather than particular processes. At this level, I would suggest that it is useful to distinguish four types of processes, two of them internal to the scientific action system itself, namely fact finding and the explanation of findings, and two external, i.e., having to do with the relations of the scientific action system to its environment, namely the selection of significant problems and the application of scientific knowledge. I shall discuss them in the sequence in which they tend to occur in the scientific action system:

The Selection of Significant Problems

The selection of a specific problem to which scientific action is to be oriented is, of course, the first step in the production of scientific knowledge. There are various ways of selecting problems, depending on who makes the selection and what the criteria of selection are. It is generally agreed that when the purpose is intrinsically scientific, that is, when the primary concern is the advancement of scientific knowledge, the selection is best done by the scientist himself, as an expert in the relevant universe of knowledge. The appropriateness of the selection is then evaluated and sanctioned mainly by fellow scientists. When the main concern is with

the production of knowledge about some practical extrascientific matter, the selection is often dictated from the outside by an agency whose main interest lies in the practical significance of the knowledge rather than its scientific importance. These two types of selection of problems often characterize the difference between basic and applied research, respectively.

In applied science, or the selection of problems on nonscientific criteria, there is no question about the fact that values are relevant to the selection of problems; it is almost true by definition. With respect to the selection of problems for basically scientific purposes, Max Weber has convincingly argued the case for the relevance of values, recognizing particularly that the scientists' personal values and interests color his perception and selection of problems. In the more exact sciences the appropriateness of problem selection can be subjected to fairly rigorous scientific criteria. In the social sciences it is much less easy to apply such criteria in the selection of significant problems.

The social sciences are not characterized to the same extent as the hard sciences by the emergence of basic paradigms on which all specialists agree.[8] Hence paradigmatic criteria for research priorities and problem selection have been much less prominent. As a result, the range of problems is much wider and the role of values much more pronounced and critical.

Another reason why values have played a greater role in social science has to do with its subject matter. It is much more difficult to divest interaction with social objects (or objects with social meanings) of value imbeddedness than it is in the case of nonsocial objects that do not have special social meanings.

The relevance of nonscientific values in the selection of the problems to which scientific activity is directed is, therefore, generally conceded. The issues arise around the question: which values? The tendency has been to opt for either scientific values or a particular social value commitment; the former choice has been justified in terms of value freedom and neutrality in a misplaced application to this aspect of the scientific process; the latter, in terms of the complete impossibility of the attainment of value freedom and neutrality. From both the philosophy of science and the sociology of knowledge perspectives these tendencies are ultimately indefensible and provide no adequate resolution to the problem of value relevance with respect to problem selection. Once the relevance of values in the selection of problems is conceded, there is no way of avoiding the question: Which values? At least not in the long run, and there is no simple solution.

Fact Finding

There are a whole range of processes involved in fact finding or the establishment of facts through observation and related processes. One could call this type of process quite legitimately "the selection of facts," to make more explicit the extent to which observation and other processes under this rubric involve selectivity in terms of conceptualization and measurement. The successful determination of facts is, of course, indispensible in the production of reliable valid empirical knowledge. This type of process is internal to the scientific action system and is governed and supported by an elaborate arsenal of rules and prescriptions, depending partly on the type of phenomenon investigated.

With respect to fact finding, objectivity has been widely accepted as the standard to which all processes should conform. Objectivity implies that facts can be established only to the extent that the scientist can apply methods and techniques of observation, discrimination, analysis, and generalization that can be repeated by other scientists with the same results. Factual knowledge should be intersubjectively transmittable and hence should not contain elements dependent on the subjectivity of any particular scientist. In this sense objectivity is the scientist's way of "telling it as it is," ironically making the special meaning this phrase has acquired stand on its head.

Objectivity, Max Weber warned us, is existentially unattainable, and all we can do is strive for it. Claims of objectivity of most social science knowledge often ignore the difficulties in substantiating such a claim. On the other hand, the basic ambiguity involved has often proven too much for the tolerance of some people, with the result that they discard all concern with objectivity as illegitimate and fruitless. Whatever one's ultimate epistemological position, at the operational level of the processes of fact finding, objectivity seems to be a necessary principle of scientific action. As in other types of action, the normative should, however, not be confused with the actual state of knowledge.

The Explanation of Facts

Facts are observations in terms of some conceptual scheme, not raw data that somehow speak for themselves. Empirical generalizations are statements of fact also in terms of a conceptual scheme, which determines to a large extent the directions of generalization within a given frame of reference. In spite of this, factual knowledge as such has a very low information yield. Facts do not speak for themselves; they have to be interpreted and explained within a generalized conceptual and theoretical framework before their scientific significance can be determined. This requires a framework that gives priority to cognitive standards, that enables the scientist to examine the relationships among facts independently of the evaluation of these relationships from the vantage point of other evaluative standards such as moral considerations. It also requires a theoretical system of logically interrelated propositions from which explanations can be derived. In other words, the determination of the scientific significance of findings can best be achieved if scientists consider the meaning of facts in terms of a scientifically derived theoretical framework, without regard to the question whether the facts are good or bad from any particular value position. Hence, theoretical propositions and empirical generalizations are ideally couched in terms that do not automatically imply that the relationships among variables are by definition good or bad. A theory with a bias in the direction of integration that implies that equilibrium is a good thing is usually judged as of limited usefulness in the analysis of conflict and disruption. In this sense a value or ideological bias tends to restrict the generality of a theory and to reduce its usefulness.

Weber's famous discussion of value neutrality or value freedom applies most directly to this set of processes. In theory building as in research methodology, scientific action requires a tension in the direction of freedom from the infringement of noncognitive standards on the relevant processes. Again, it does not follow from the recognition of the standard that theories are, in fact, value neutral; far from it.

The Application of Scientific Knowledge

While fact finding and the explanation of facts can be seen as primarily internal to the scientific action system, the application of knowledge is, like the selection of problems, a type of process with primarily external reference. Although the selection of problems is usually recognized as part of the scientific process, the application of knowledge is most often considered to be beyond the pale of the responsibility of the scientist qua scientist and in this sense not part of the scientific action system. It is seen as part of the expectation of other roles of the scientist, e.g., his citizen role, to be concerned with the application of knowledge. This conception of the nature of scientific action and the role of the scientist does not acknowledge sufficiently the interdependence of the scientific system with other action systems. It implies that the scientific system is relatively closed, not interdependent and interrelated with its action system environment. Obviously, such a conception is quite inadequate.

The issue is not whether all scientists have an obligation to specify all possible applications of knowledge being produced, to evaluate these applications from a given value position, and to participate in or promote the desirable applications. Some will be doing just this, while others will be less directly involved. One major aspect of the problem is the differential status implications of such involvement and the extent to which recognition for achievement in these processes are on a par with the rewards for achievement in the internal processes of fact finding and theoretical interpretation. Without recognition of this type of process as an essential part of scientific action, those members of the community primarily concerned with application will always have low prestige and status—as they tend to have in North America, in contrast with such countries as Italy and Holland.

The critical issue is one of identifying an ultimate reference point for a stable solution to the problem of "Knowledge for what?" Within science the solution of knowledge for the sake of knowledge has been an attractive one. Yet it has proved inadequate and for obvious reasons unstable; it is vulnerable to displacements by other theories of the uses of knowledge generated outside the scientific system with at least the possibility of arbitrary imposition. Therefore, an intrinsically scientific solution is needed that has extrascientific validity. Hence the question of the value of scientific knowledge is inescapable, and the various processes involving the application of knowledge cannot be ruled out-of-court in science.

Values are as relevant to the application of scientific knowledge as they are to the selection of problems. Yet these two types of processes are not reducible to one but are clearly distinct. Again, the same question has ultimately to be faced: Which values? There is no escape into assumptions of randomness, denial of the problem, or espousal of a social value commitment to the extent of eliminating a commitment to scientific values. So far, the question of which values should be served has largely been ignored or neglected, with unfortunate results for both science and society.

In summary, then, in processes at the boundary between scientific action and other systems of human action, the relevance of nonscientific values in science is clearly demonstrable if not generally recognized. The other two types of processes, which are more clearly internal to scientific action, namely, fact finding and interpretation of findings, are governed by the principles of objectivity and value neutrality. Values should not interfere with these processes, hence the standard of value freedom. In other words, an adequate understanding of the nature of scientific action and its relation to other human action systems requires the distinction of these four types of processes, and the recognition of both the role of the principle of *value relevance* and that of *value freedom*. To recognize only one of these as legitimate, either denies the possibility of science, in the first case, or sees it as a closed system, in the latter case. Both positions are clearly untenable.

The relative emphases that the social science system has given historically to these different sets of principles can best be understood in the context of its development in modern society. For simplicity's sake, I shall discuss only two major stages in this development to demonstrate the kind of interpretation that seems plausible.

THE DIFFERENTIATION OF SOCIAL SCIENCE

The institutionalization of science in the universities belongs to the history of the nineteenth century. By the end of the century science, natural science in particular, was institutionalized in the universities in most advanced societies of the period. The scientific community became professionalized and was recognized as such by society. Its ideology of professionalism emphasized the freedom and autonomy of the professional scientist as an expert who should be trusted by society to regulate his action in terms of principles conducive to the advancement of science and the welfare of society. This ideology served to buttress the newly differentiated and specialized subsystem against the intrusion of extraneous pressures from society.

The social sciences went through essentially the same stage somewhat later, mainly in the first half of the twentieth century. The differentiation of the social sciences from the two cultures of humanities and the hard sciences was substantially completed by 1950, having received a final booster from World War II. The shifting emphases of this period resemble vaguely an oedipal crisis in which the social sciences were characterized by a love-hate relationship with father science (in which overidentification predominated) and a compulsive concern with declaring its essential nature, different and independent from mother humanities. The recognition of the social sciences as the legitimate offspring of the two and as a fully grown third culture is still rather tenuous.

The early stages of the development of social science have roots far deeper in history. The first stage was largely protoscientific, characterized more by fusion of social values and concerns and scientific values. Sociology in particular thrived on ameliorative concerns with specific social problems. Sociological knowledge was seen as necessary for the solution of pressing social problems caused by urbanization, industrialization, and immigration; fact finding was unsystematic, dictated by non-scientific concerns rather than scientific values and not controlled by rigorous scientific standards. This early pre- or incipient-differentiation stage was, therefore, one in which dependence on social value commitments was clearly evident. Scientific values and standards to the extent that they were articulated were subordinate to the social. This was perhaps more clearly the case in the United States, where sociology developed early from bases other than the more classical scholarly fields of philosophy, law, and history typical of European sociology.

The differentiation of the social sciences that followed this early stage of fusion represents a marked shift in commitments and interests. It is typical for differentiating systems to be preoccupied with the working out of identity problems, the specification and establishment of appropriate codes and standards, the consolidation of the new structures, and the affirmation of their essential nature.

During this stage the social sciences concerned themselves with the distinguishing characteristics of their methodology and developed the doctrines of objectivity and value neutrality and freedom. Apart from Weber's recognition of the principle of value relevance and Lynd's question of "Knowledge for what?" they were predominantly concerned with the internal standards of the scientific system and gave relatively less attention to boundary problems with other action systems.[9] This is particularly true for the period between 1930 and 1950, although it started earlier. The initial fused state lasted into this period and in some respects continued in pockets and provided fertile soil for some of the more recent protest movements against the excesses of the differentiation phase, the Chicago school being the most notable example.

Much of the historical significance of the social scientist's commitment to objectivity and value neutrality lies in the extent to which it facilitated the rapid growth and institutionalization of the social sciences in modern society during this century. This facilitation was largely the result of an overcommitment to these principles and their misapplication to the boundary processes between the social science system and society. On the one hand, modelling themselves on the natural sciences, social scientists claimed that, because they are required to be objective and neutral in their scientific action, they should be in a position as scientists to select their problems on the basis of what they considered to be significant from a purely scientific point of view. On the other

hand, they showed little concern with the application of social science knowledge in socially valued directions, also on the basis of the primacy of their commitment to scientific values.

It was argued that sociology as a discipline could achieve scientific status only by being "value free," by strictly separating questions of value from questions of fact and being concerned primarily with the latter. The tendency was to answer the question "Knowledge for what?" with statements ultimately reducible to knowledge for its own sake. In the professional community rewards were structured against involvement in the application of social science knowledge, particularly to conventionally defined social problems. The highest prestige went to the individuals and institutions who achieved excellence in the internal processes of the social science system, namely, fact finding and explanation or interpretation, while those involved in application had low prestige. In the case of sociology in particular there was the image of the "social worker" to destroy before the professional social scientist could become accepted. Except in the former capacity, the social scientist therefore lacked an adequate influence base in society. The "social engineer," which represented a higher status than the "social worker," did not provide a better base for the recognition of the social science profession since, in contrast to the social worker, that role was regarded with distrust by society and was accorded the same low prestige in the social science community.

In effect, commitment to the standards and principles applicable to the internal problems of the scientific system was used to withdraw commitment to the principles of value relevance and to deny their full application on the boundaries of the system. As a result, the system turned in on itself, compulsively independent from its action environment, over-conforming to its internal standards, and unconcerned with the exigencies of its environment. The selection of problems was increasingly recognized as the prerogative of the individual scientist or scientific agency. It was felt that it would be to the disadvantage of the advancement of science if the problems to which it should address itself were determined by any other considerations than those derived from the values and goals of the scientific action system. The professional scientist was primarily concerned with his autonomy and academic freedom to pursue his scientific interests to the best of his ability. Hence the ideology of professionalism was used to justify this overcommitment to scientific values in order to cope with the strains of the differentiation process.

This development has had two major effects on the selection of scientific problems. It individualized the selection process, giving a very large role to the esoteric interests, individual concerns, and personal values of scientists of every description. In addition, it was influenced by the social scientists whose interests converged on such problem areas as social mobility and race relations and also by those of institutions and granting agencies. The professional community as such, however, did not give attention to the indentification of the most significant problems for research or with the establishment of priorities. As a result, problem selection remained random and atomistic, only partially and arbitrarily structured by fluctuating group interests and fad movements. Although this probably broadened the range of problems investigated, it also diffused effort and inhibited cumulative development of social science knowledge. The only sense in which the professional community influenced the selection process in a collective way was in recognizing scientific values as the only relevant collective standards for the selection of significant problems.

On the positive side, these developments have served to insulate social science considerably from the pressures of parochial social values and immediate social concerns which might have dictated the directions of its growth and development during a period of rapid modernization, industrialization, growth of bureaucracy, and development of technology in particular during which the social science system was extremely vulnerable. One could argue that they were a necessary condition without which the development of social science would not have been possible, at least not on the same scale.

At the same time, however, the costs have been high in terms of negative effects. With some notable exceptions, such as population and modernization, much of social science literature has little bearing on the problems of the second half of the twentieth century. The social sciences have contributed relatively little to the development of a global social conscience and solutions to major social problems. There was evidence during this period of a serious lack of systematic concern with social planning based on social science findings. To the extent that the relevance of social values was recognized, it was a function of the demands and requirements of governmental, industrial, and other granting agencies, which are highly selectively biased toward the status quo and vested interests in society, defining social problems from these vantage points. The social value commitments of social scientists have played a role mainly in so far as they were part of these strata in society.

In sum, then, the development of social science in the first half of the twentieth century was characterized by concerns which related to the process of differentiation of the system. Commitment to objectivity and value neutrality was given primacy to the neglect and even denial of value relevance. These commitments became firmly internalized and institutionalized with evidence of overcommitment and its social and cultural costs, particularly in terms of a serious lack of integration of the social science system in the larger society. To these problems we now turn.

THE INTEGRATION OF SOCIAL SCIENCE IN SOCIETY

The application of the standards of objectivity and value neutrality to the boundary relationships of the social science system with other social action systems has had the effect of hardening these boundaries, lowering capacities to adapt to these environments. It has tended to specify things the social scientist should *not* do and focus concern on the autonomy and academic freedom of the scientist. The scientific community was seen as entitled to self-regulation in conducting its own affairs without prescription or interference. The general assumption was that, if scientists are allowed to pursue their own interests in selecting their problems and priorities on the basis of scientific values, somehow society and culture in general will benefit in a serendipitous way from the development of science. No articulated positive conception of the inputs that the social science system should make into its social environments has been developed.

These emphases were perhaps necessary in the early processes of differentiation of a relatively radically new role in modern society, that of the professional social scientist. But newly differentiated roles and structures always require a new level of integration in the system in which they develop. They usually involve new types of patterns of action and higher degrees of specialization for which the earlier integrative framework is inadequate. The need for a new level of integration also results from the tendency of a differentiating system to develop hard boundaries, to be preoccupied with identity and goal setting problems, and develop a rationale for its own further development. Without subsequent development of mechanisms integrating it with other differentiated subsystems of the larger system, the newly differentiated system cannot be institutionalized on a stable basis.

Differentiation, because it always involves the introduction of new categories of structure, requires the generalization of values, integrative standards, and related norms. The degree of generalization required depends largely on the nature of the newly differentiated unit and how different it is from the previous categories of structure.

If social science in the first half of the twentieth

century was preoccupied with differentiation, it is evident that the first two decades of the second half have witnessed an increasing concern with the integration of the social science system in society and the integrative standards that would facilitate this process. There can be no question that the system is in dire need of a higher level of integration with the rest of society at this point in its development. This integration may require a quite radical reorientation or shift in emphasis on the part of social scientists, a fuller recognition of the standard of value relevance with respect to both the selection of problems and the application of knowledge, and explicit attention to the types of social values compatible with the value primacies of the social science system itself.

The symptoms of the need for a new level of integration are evident on many fronts. Social scientists of every description are dissatisfied with the splendid isolation of the disciplines from the major contemporary social problems. The "new sociologists" and the "radical sociologists" have made "relevance" their rallying cry. But there is also evidence of much greater involvement of social scientists in applied fields and a notable upsurge of interest in social planning and development. Only recently the BASS reports have recommended the establishment of five graduate schools of applied social science in the United States. There is an increase in the demands of government and other agencies for the services of social scientists in research, consultation, and advisory capacities. Professional associations at recent meetings have addressed themselves to social policy issues and have developed or are in the process of developing codes of professional ethics. The crises in higher education in the sixties everywhere involved the issues of relevance and the responsibility of the scientific community to the larger society.[10]

The issue of relevance is often phrased in terms of the significance of social science findings for major contemporary social problems. The underlying values in terms of which problems are defined as problems are seldom articulated. But the logical outcome of this demand is an insistence on the recognition of a set of social values as relevant to the selection of scientific problems and the application of knowledge. In this sense there is normative strain in the direction of discovering and articulating, in addition to the personal values and interests of the individual scientists and scientific values as such, a set of generalized social values that could be brought to bear on the boundary processes between the social science system and society. Protagonists of value relevance, particularly the "new" and "radical" sociologists, on the whole fail to articulate this set of values.[11] Their position often boils down to an assertion of the legitimacy and relevance of their own set of parochial social values or ideology to the boundary relations between social science and society. This egocentric solution to the problem is clearly regressive to the primitive fused relations between the two systems.

One of the foci of the integrative crisis is the role of public and private funding agencies, particularly government, in the selection of research problems. The objectives and policies of these agencies have not always been based on the primacy of scientific values or recognition of the interests and personal values of the individual scientist. The advancement of science has not been the primary goal. Instead, they represent the introduction of social values as standards of selection of problems and application of scientific knowledge from extraneous sources often not at all mindful of the integrity of the social scientific system. The extent to which social science, and science in general, has become coopted by corporate capitalism and socialism through funding agencies of government and industry is a clear indication of the serious problems on this front. The allegation that this type of research often serves the social values of the establishment and reinforces the status quo and the powers that be is hard to refute entirely.

There is, of course, no simple solution. With all these pressures from the social environment the social science system requires a set of commitments in addition to commitment to scientific values and the personal commitments of individual scientists. The assumption of the randomness of social values implied in the refusal to be systematically concerned with them is clearly no longer valid, if it ever was.[12] The recognition of the relevance of social values to scientific action requires a systematic effort to institutionalize the appropriate values in the social science system itself. Only when social scientists are committed to a set of social values consistent and compatible with scientific values can they cope with the critical problems of value relevance. Such a set of values will function to minimize the chances that the scientist will select on the basis of his personal values and interests entirely esoteric research problems or, on the other hand, that he will be vulnerable to selecting research problems on the basis of social values dictated by funding agencies in all likelihood serving extraneous vested interests. A commitment to such set of social values will sensitize social scientists to identify social problems in terms of these values and to the importance of doing research relevant to the fuller implementation of these values in the social environment, regardless of whether they are shared by the powers that be.

Essentially, the same considerations hold for the application of knowledge. Commitment to such a set of social values does not imply that scientists should devote more of their time to the application of knowledge to the fuller implementation of these values. They will still be able to do research that could be applied to either the implementation or violation of these values. It does imply, however, that the social science community has a collective responsibility to evaluate the application of knowledge in terms of this set of values, to discourage the misuse of knowledge, and to advise on social policy that would be sound application for the implementation of these values. It also has to establish mechanisms for the development of commitment to these values and effective sanctions for their implementation by individual scientists. It will require fundamental changes in the reward structure so that the commitment of the community to these social values is reflected in its status system. In short, the social science community will have to develop a sense of responsibility for the value implications of the application of social science knowledge on a universal basis; the individual social scientist will not be concerned only or primarily with the applications of his own research, but also with this broader responsibility.

The sum of this analysis is that the social science system in modern society is faced with a crisis of integration with its social environment. It has become clearly differentiated. It has established a fairly firm institutional basis in society and has developed scientific values that are essential for its continued growth and development. But it faces increasing demands for relevance and higher yields of practical knowledge in the interest of a whole range of social values. It is in danger of becoming a tool of other differentiated, highly specialized, and rationalized agencies in society, being coopted into elitist and establishment values. There is clearly a need for generalized social values consistent with scientific values and the objectives of the advancement of universally valid knowledge. The development of such a system of values and the establishment of adequate mechanisms to develop commitment to these values among social scientists and to sanction their implimentation are among the most critical problems facing the social science community.

VALUE COMMITMENTS AND VALUE INNOVATION

This integrative crisis on the boundary between social science and society may be further elucidated by analysing it in terms of the dynamics of value commitments.[13] As we are dealing with the role of values in social science, this theoretical perspective is particularly useful. The foregoing analysis of the differentiation and integration of the social science system could be seen as involving processes of value commitment inflation and deflation as well

as attempts at value innovation and accommodation of innovations in the system.

It is necessary to treat value commitments to science and value commitments to society as distinct systems subject to independent fluctuations in the flow processes. Hence it is possible to see the same movement, for example, the new sociology, as involving both *deflation* of *scientific* value commitments and *inflation* of *social* value commitments.

The traditional value-free position can thus be seen as involving the opposite combination, namely a deflation of social value commitments combined with inflation of scientific value commitments. The extreme position is that the scientist has a commitment only to scientific values and that by giving primacy to them his social responsibility is fulfilled and society will benefit automatically from the advancement of science. It is the knowledge for its own sake or science as an end in itself position. As such it is a form of scientific fundamentalism, a deflationary pressure on the social value commitment system, insisting that the "soundness" of scientific knowledge depends solely on value neutrality and objectivity to the exclusion and degrading of all other commitment bases.

The "new" sociologists or radicals have, on the whole, represented the polar opposite of this position. They represent a deflationary pressure on the scientific value commitment system as well as on the influence of the scientific community. They are essentially saying that science is possible without a commitment to scientific values, that "sound" knowledge can as well be achieved on the basis of a commitment to a particular substantive social value commitment. Their claims and demands for instant relevance and commonsense application of knowledge are inflationary pressures on the scientific system and involves a deflation of scientific value commitments to standards of validity, reliability and consistency. Hence they deny the primacy and in extreme cases even the relevancy of scientific values. It is in this sense that the first movement in social science is associated with the differentiation phase, tending to close the boundaries of the system, being exclusively concerned with internal problems. On the other hand, the "new sociology" movement of the fifties and after is associated with the integration phase, tending to abolish the boundaries, to de-differentiate the two systems, and to regress to a diffuse fusion of social science and societal values. This, of course, leads to reactions that polarizes the issues and state them in terms of the scientistic fundamentalist position of the earlier phase.

These movements also constitute different modes of accommodating and reacting to value innovation and change. In the context of the developmental perspective of this paper, the argument is that there are pressures and demands for value change and innovation that would provide a new level of integration to the social science system in society. These pressures give rise to several modes of accommodation according to the relevant evaluation of the direction of the pressure. We may distinguish four modes of accommodation, namely, regression to a more primitive level, countervailance, institutionalization, and value generalization.[14]

There is clearly a sense in which both extremes of the "radical" and "conservative" positions are confined to the first two modes of accommodation to the pressures. Both represent regressions to more primitive stages of the development of the system, with the radicals perhaps being more regressive than the conservatives. That is, they regress to a more primitive level, that of the diffuse fusion of social and scientific concerns, to the virtual elimination of the latter. The conservatives, on the other hand, regress to the early differentiation stage, repeating its shibboleths of value freedom, to the denial of the importance of social value relevance, thus closing off the boundaries of the social science system with society.

These two forms of regression are polarized to the extent that they both have become countervailing forces, hence reinforcing each other in a vicious circle. Regression and countervailance are likely to have this tendency to vicious polarization.

At the same time, there is evidence of relatively broad levels of fairly smooth institutionalization of social value commitments alongside scientific value commitments in such areas as urban sociology, race relations, education, health services, population, social welfare, and development. These have been without major revolutionary effects on societies and already have added some value to social development within the confines of particular societal value systems. We have seen some evidence of this in our preceding analysis of the integration stage. This mode of accommodation steers a middle course between the extremes of value commitment in either direction, social or scientific.[15]

The tendency is to see commitment issues as unproblematical and to assume compatibility and complementarity of social and scientific commitment. Because of this lack of concern, this mode of accommodation is unlikely to lead to value generalization. There is little tension in that direction because given social values are accepted as relevant and at least adequate value-orientation points.

Partly for this reason, the fourth mode of accommodation, value generalization, has been much less in evidence. It was also inhibited by the other two modes and the broader deflationary and inflationary pressures on the commitment systems of which these were extreme manifestations. Hence strain towards generalization of social values was deflected by the intensity of commitment to value freedom and objectivity, and the associated inflation of the scientific value commitments evidenced in the insistence that their implementation contributes indirectly in and of itself to social value implementation. The concomitant deflation of the relevance of social value commitments to scientific action has deflected all concern with the integration of social and scientific values and hence with value generalization.

Yet, as I have argued, there is a clear need for this type of value innovation and accommodation in social science and science in general. For such innovation to take place it is necessary to identify a clear object of reference and orientation to which generalization should proceed. Without such a clear empirical system reference, value generalization is likely to be fragmentary disjunctive, and partial; the integration of social and scientific values on a higher level is likely to be unstable over a longer period of time.

VALUE PATTERN INTEGRITY OF COGNITIVE RATIONALITY

I have argued above that the integrative crisis of social science in society can be met by the development of commitment to an appropriate set of general social values that could serve as standards of relevance. The basic problem, of course, is that raised with respect to the principle of value relevance at the outset, namely, which values?

It is my contention that as social scientists we have to be committted, not only to a set of *scientific* values but also to a set of universal *social* values, which ultimately have to be human values. Several arguments can be offered in favor of this position:

First, as social scientists we study all aspects of man's social life. We therefore see the whole man in all his roles. We study human communities and relations among them and have as such a very special opportunity to discover universal human characteristics and reactions to social arrangements.

Second, we are in the position to discover and study the universal community of man. Human thought is saturated with awareness of humanity as an object of thought. But as an object of identification, as a concrete community of reference, the human community is not much in evidence. There are incipient developments on Spaceship Earth with its modern communication and transportation technologies. However embryonic this community might be, I think we can announce its discovery and begin to study it.

Third, one of the first questions we might ask as good social scientists is: What are the values of this community? Are there common values that men hold everywhere despite the wide range of variation of their parochial value systems? Is it possible to conceptualize such values in terms of what we know about the universals of the human condition, human needs, and human communities? Hence some general social values, universally applicable to man everywhere, might result. Although these values may yet not be much in evidence, the social science community has a particularly pivotal role in identifying and developing them.

Fourth, as social scientists we pride ourselves in being members of a supranational, supra-ethnic community clearly integrated on the basis of common scientific values, despite the dissent we hear on the fringes. But this community cannot stand on scientific values alone. In fact, despite shared commitments to these values, the community is still divided by parochial social values, as we all know. It has become increasingly clear that the real binding factor is a sense of shared social values as a global community that has developed a global social consciousness and conscience.

Fifth, the espousal of universal human values has several advantages relevant to the values-problem in social science:

1. These values, being universal, will in and of themselves introduce less of a bias than any other more parochial values would, and the bias will operate more uniformly.
2. These values will provide a standard for the detection of parochial value biases that will still be operating. There is thus a double protection against ethnocentrism: in the scientific values *and* in the human values.

In this sense the universal social values provide a functional alternative to the unattainable complete value freedom, *and* assists attainment of freedom from parochial values.

This idea that as social scientists we need a commitment to human values is, of course, not new. Some would say: Do we really have to return to August Comte? The humanism of the early Marx is well known. But a recent international anthology on *Socialist Humanism,* edited by Erich Fromm, is a sad commentary on how humanism has fizzled out in that tradition of thought. There is no sociologically sophisticated conception of humanism as a value system, and many of the authors are critical of the extent to which state communism and revolutionary strategies have violated human values.

C. Wright Mills was fairly explicit about the need

for a commitment to man as such. Gouldner undergirds his freefloating reflexive sociology with a profession of humanism but does not develop its application, especially not in his criticism of other theorists.[16] Etzioni is not much more explicit than a brief recognition of the need for human values, and it is difficult to figure out how one can ensure that the *Active Society* is also a humane society. However, his emphasis on universal human needs and his discussions of responsiveness and authenticity are indications that the direction in which he would see the Active Society develop is towards greater humanity.[17] Szymanski is one of the few radical sociologists who seems to be aware of the humanistic basis required to escape the parochialism of far left ideologies.[18]

But one should object strongly to this monopolization of humanism as the exclusive domain of "radical" sociologists. Unfortunately, it is not true that all radical sociologists are committed to human values, and fortunately all humanists are not "radical." The radicals are doing the disciplines a great disservice by cloaking their tactics in humanistic garb. It is very important to recognize the fact that a commitment to universal human values does not co-vary with radical strategies. This unjustified claim can only serve to hamper the development of this commitment in social science in general.

But all these earlier signs of awareness of the need for a commitment to human values appear as little more than after-the-fact rationalizations of something that has dawned upon them in a serendipitous way. Nowhere do we find an attempt to justify such a commitment, nowhere an attempt to conceptualize and specify such values. And yet it is clear that this is an unavoidable task without which there can be no hope for eventual consensus and effective implementation.

The critical question is whether commitment to such universal social values is compatible with commitment to scientific values as far as the internal processes of fact finding and explanation are concerned. One might argue that it might be harder to achieve objectivity and neutrality in the face of commitments to such universal values. This might be the case, but even in such a case it would seem unlikely that such commitments would substantively interfere or conflict with the scientific values. Instead, there generality is likely to reinforce the scientific standards by sensitizing the scientist to parochial values. just as they do in the boundary processes.

Perhaps the issue will become somewhat clearer if we approach it in terms of the value pattern of science, which is cognitive rationality in the pursuit of knowledge. The value pattern of such a set of universal human values, I have argued elsewhere, is moral rationality.[19] A comparison of the pattern elements of these two value patterns is very helpful in this connection. The pattern-variable values involved in cognitive rationality are specificity, universalism, neutrality, and performance, listed in the order as they primarily apply to the four types of processes (i.e., problem selection-specificity; fact finding-universalism; explanation-neutrality; application-performance). For the scientific system one of the major problems is the maintenance of the *integrity* and *consistency* of this pattern. In one sense, any substantive value rationality (*Wertrationalität* in Weber's sense) is incompatible with the integrity of the congnitive rationality value pattern. The degree of such incompatibility will, of course, be determined by the characteristic elements of the pattern in question. The most critical pair are the internal ones, universalism and neutrality. The external pair, specificity and performance, allow wider ranges of variability in compatibility.

Hence the real issue is the compatibility of the value pattern of moral rationality with cognitive rationality. The elements of the former have been identified as diffuseness, universalism, neutrality, and quality.[20] First, we note that moral rationality involves elements opposite to the two external elements of cognitive rationality, specificity and performance—namely, diffuseness and quality. One could argue that diffuse moral criteria are indeed incompatible with the selection of scientific problems. Specificity applies to the standards for selection of problems in the sense that scientific action must be oriented to the solution of a specific cognitive problem: One cannot solve problems in general. It does not require specificity in orientation to the objects involved in the selection and solution of the problem. On the other hand, the element of diffuseness in moral rationality refers to the scope of orientation to objects in the situation, not to the specific purpose of the action. The incompatibility between the two horns of the pattern-variable dilemma is therefore reduced, in that they do not apply to the same aspects of the action system. Diffuseness in this context may simply generate a wider range of specific problems, from which the scientist can choose. But it will also limit the range in the sense that problems requiring that social objects be treated only in terms of their specific meaning and usefulness in the scientific problem solving process would be ruled out. Certain aspects of professional ethics of research having to do with respect for the privacy and autonomy of subjects in human experimentation are examples of the application of this element.

In the application of knowledge the relevant criterion in evaluating knowledge is: Does it work? Does it apply? Does it produce social-problem solutions? These are performance standards. The relevant moral rationality element is the opposite of performance, namely, quality, which requires that objects be evaluated on the basis of their quality rather than their performance. Here again, the potential incompatibility is reduced in that the two elements apply to different aspects of the action system. The relevant question deriving from the quality element of moral rationality (combined with universalism) is: is it human? Hence, does the performance, the application (the usefulness) of knowledge contribute to human values, the quality of human life? Again, the moral rationality element applies most directly to the selection of problems to be solved and the applications sought, without inhibiting the performance standard for knowledge selection. But it does inhibit knowledge for its own sake and application for its own sake or for any old reason. It sets a standard for technological development and other developments based on cognitive rationality and subjects them, as Ashby and others have suggested they should be subjected, to human values derived from the pattern element of quality. The performance of science should be regulated in this way to contribute to the implementation of human values, regardless of the performance of the recipients of the benefits, i.e., regardless of whether they "deserve" it or not.

The other two elements of cognitive and moral rationality are the same, namely universalism and neutrality. Although they do not apply to the same aspects of the action system either, it should follow from the preceding analysis that the simultaneous application of the two rationalities in scientific action would not be likely to give rise to problems of value-pattern integrity and consistency. Problems will, of course, arise in establishing priority of human values over scientific values, but these are inevitable and have to be resolved by the order of priority. This order is already evident in formulations of professional ethics, and it is unlikely that this trend will be reversed. Moral rationality will always take precedence over cognitive rationality, but the specification of what such precedence implies in typical scientific action situations is a difficult one. Even more difficult, if not impossible, is the specification of such implications for particular situations, such as, for example, the decision to develop the atom bomb. In such cases, there is no emanating moral rationality that is self evident. Specific solutions to such dilemmas can only be arrived at by processes of moral reasoning, taking fully into account the parameters of the particular situation. There is no room for moral absolutism; rather, moral rationality implies moral freedom and autonomy institutionalized within a framework of human moral universalism.

UNIVERSAL HUMAN VALUES

So far we have been concerned only with the value pattern of universal human values and its compatibility with cognitive rationality as the patterns of scientific values. Substantive human values derived from the application of the pattern to the human condition are much more difficult to specify at a level where their relevance to scientific action can be easily demonstrated. At the most general level, they are relatively contentless; and there are many steps of specification before their import for scientific action would become apparent. Nevertheless, in line with the argument that value generalization will not proceed systematically without a stable reference point being identified, I believe that this general level of human value articulation is necessary and fruitful, as long as it is clearly understood that we can take only a first step on a long road. These values can at best act as orientation points sensitizing the scientists to the dimensions of value relevance and possible issues that might have to be resolved. But one has to begin somewhere in conceptualizing these human values, i.e., conceptions of the desirable human condition. Because the strain is toward value generalization, I am inclined to believe that these values have first to be conceptualized and ordered at the general human level and then specified down to the various aspects of the role of the social scientist in the scientific action system. One clearly needs a conceptual scheme that comprehends the significant aspects of the human condition and provides systematic lines of specification. In my opinion, the theory of action of Talcott Parsons provides such an apparatus.[21] In attempting such a conceptualization, I shall confine myself to the general human action level and not attempt further specifications.

Human values may be conceptualized as desirable states of: the human organism in relation to its environment, human personality, human society, and human culture.

With respect to the organism in relation to its environment, such values as life, health, freedom from hunger, suffering, fear of death, poverty, and safety might be specified. The relevant value principle seems to be the *optimization of human adaptive capacity*. Minimally human survival is valued; optimally, human prosperity. The universal reference point is the human species as an open system in relation to its environment, which is itself a closed system, i.e., it is for all practical purposes seen as not dependent on some other environment. This conception implies that the resources of the human environment are finite, that deficits resulting from human use and waste are not recoverable. The human system has a fundamental responsibility in the interest of its own survival and prosperity to preserve the environment, to maintain the vital resources of human existence for an indefinite future as shown in current concern about the population explosion, nuclear escalation, poverty, and the destruction of the environment.

With respect to human personality, such values as human dignity, mental health, self-respect, identity, integrity, autonomy, freedom, self-determination, and actualization or fulfilment come to mind. Here the value principle is *optimization of human self-realization capacity*. Minimally human freedom is valued, optimally, self-fulfilment. Social alienation, self-estrangement, and degradation are negatively valued.

The values of human society would include justice, equality, peace, and basic human rights and freedoms. The value principle is *optimization of human integrative capacity*. Minimally peace is valued; optimally, solidarity or love. Here the negative evaluation of war, oppression, exploitation, discrimination, and the use of violence that do not serve higher human values are critical issues.

With respect to human culture such values as cultural identity, continuity, language rights, religious freedom, meaningfulness, expression, truth, beauty, and education, come to mind. The value principle is *optimization of human meaning creation capacity*. Minimally, continuity is valued; maximally, cultural development. The concerns with education, cultural development, and the expressive media are relevant here. Commercialization, repression, persecution, indoctrination, and the intrusion of technology are negatively valued.

Human culture and human personality require the valuation of diversity, while the human organism-environment and human society require values stressing the commonness of problems and universality. The basic value principle in all four cases is the desirability of *optimal conditions for human development and realization of human potentials*. With respect to each, there is a base line of concern with the maintenance of minimal conditions of human existence and a search for optimal conditions for the enhancement of human potentials and the enrichment of human life.

IMPLICATIONS FOR SOCIOLOGY

A concern with universal human values does not imply that all sociologists have to do the same thing, no more than adherence to scientific values has this implication. Certainly it does not imply that all of us have to become radicals, although we might find that in most societies this label will even more readily be hung around our necks.

As I see it, a humanistic sociology would have the following priorities, advantages, and possibilities:

1. It would establish clearly the priority of human values over scientific values as the ethical base of the discipline. We have already seen a development in this direction in the adoption of codes of ethics by the profession in several countries, and the I.S.A. is working on the same problem. It is a sad commentary, however, that these codes are almost exclusively confined to recognition of the rights of individuals to privacy, anonymity, and protection from ill effects of research. The recent widespread concern about norms for human experimentation are also focussed mainly on the individual. The social conscience of the sociologist should also reflect the rights of groups. It should cover problems of the application of sociological knowledge and appropriate expectations for sociologists in consultant and contract research roles. Here the concern has focussed on classified research, research for the military or counterinsurgency research.

2. Humanistic sociology should give specialized attention to the sociology of the human community. This could involve a wider range of activities. We would require, for example, consensus on the assumptions we make about basic human needs. Etzioni's work in this respect, among others', is an important beginning.[22] His insights into the importance of such a reference point are very helpful. He says, for example, "Basic human needs are universal. All men are expected to have them and any theory which is not open to this possibility is open to racist ("superiority") interpretations."[23] From this reference point, then, we can construct models of the ideal institutions, communities, and society in which these human needs and values would be optimally realized. This element of utopianism should be clearly recognized as such and not confused with empirical descriptive models. But as we begin to develop a sociology of the future, it becomes increasingly clear that it is sterile prognostics to simply extrapolate current trends to the end of the century. Human values will give us a reference point for futurist sociology, especially as the human community becomes increasingly aware of itself and develops a consciousness.

3. Such a model will also provide us with a reference point for the critical analysis of existing institutions, communities and societies. For example, recent critics of formal educational systems have come to the conclusion that these systems are poor breeding grounds of fully developed human beings. Kohlberg's research on moral development has shown that the development of moral judgement is related to intelligence and is in a comparable way influenced by socioeconomic factors, which on the whole act as in inhibitors of full development.[24]

Jacques Ellul's *Technological Society* and Herbert Marcuse's *One-Dimensional Man* are examples of critical analysis of the human implications of industrial-technocratic society, relying mostly on rather intuitive and implicit humanistic sentiments and perspectives. Our analysis of these problems can be much more penetrating and trenchant if we are explicitly committed to a fully conceptualized set of human values.

4. Students of development and modernization have become increasingly aware of the inadequacy of western institutional and societal models in both studying and assisting these new societies. In the advanced industrial societies we only now begin to realize some of the undesirable consequences for humanity of unrestrained development, particularly of technology. Although it may be virtually impossible to rectify this state of affairs in advanced societies, their consequences may be anticipated in developing societies by subjecting the forces of the technological, industrial, and communications revolutions to the standards of human values. For example, serious doubts have been raised recently with respect to the advisability of instituting western-style mass formal education as a priority rather than exploring alternatives which may be more compatible with the priorities of these societies in economic, political, and other fields. The implications for developing societies of Ivan Illich's case for the *Deschooling of Society* are only now beginning to be considered. The models of optimally human institutions, communities, and societies which a humanistic sociology will have to construct, will be particularly useful in the developing world.

5. When we look at the global human community we are confronted with some of the most staggering problems that mankind has ever faced. There are the problems of international relations, escalation of nuclear armaments, communication barriers on a shrinking globe and the growing rift between haves and have-nots. Then there are the three perennial P's of the contemporary human condition, population explosion, poverty, and pollution, all three of which can be most fruitfully and adequate-

ly approached from a universal human point of reference.

6. Mainline sociologists could continue the essential tasks of the discipline, but they would be better able to assess the practical and policy implications of their work. The human values will provide them with the necessary reference point from which they can assess whether they are inadvertently supporting an undesirable status quo or are being exploited by either state capitalism or state communism and establishments of various descriptions. Their value freedom from the parochial values and vested interests of the powers-that-be will be more apparent to themselves and to others as they subject these values to the scrutiny of universal social values and make their commitments explicit.

7. Such a commitment to human values will provide a more adequate basis for active involvement in social change and intervention. The work of anthropologists such as Sol Tax in a midwest Indian community and Allan Holmberg in Vicos, Peru, provide examples of interventive participation in community life that can contribute to better realization of human potentials. And Etzkowitz and Schaflander's experience in institution-building in the Community Cooperative Center in Bedford Stuyvesant provides another strategy for action in implementing human values in the face of inhumane institutions.[25] These action projects often provide much better opportunities for research into institutional and social dynamics than conventional methodology.

8. Even the radical sociologists will benefit from such a commitment. So far their movement has had no firm theoretical and philosophical grounding in spite of the occasional avowal of a humanistic perspective and the romantic model of man often implicit in their statements. For those who find this strategy congenial a humanistic sociology will provide both a set of very necessary constraints and a basis for a more constructive program. Some of them will still want to man the trenches and others will continue to shout the shibboleths of radical revolutionary rhetoric. In doing so, they will contribute mainly to the public defamation of sociology as a radical, deviant science and put sometimes insurmountable obstacles in the way of those of us who endeavor to establish it as a normative humanistic social science.

9. Social scientists working in Southern Africa and under other oppressive regimes are probably keenly aware of the problem of racial division, domination, exploitation, and racism, especially to the extent that this division coincides with that between the haves and the have-nots. Commitment to universal human values will help them to see more clearly not only the injustice but also the inhumanity of apartheid and its concommitment forms of exploitation and suppression in South Africa and its functional equivalents in other societies. Even those who wish to work from within racist institutions and a racist society will have a sharper awareness of the issues involved. In such situations human values are of particular importance because the onslaught on them is so direct and immediate and it is so easy to become coopted into the pervasive and subtle intrigues and moral binds which the legitimation and rationalization of such inhumane systems require. For those who are committed to participate in action to change such situations, a commitment to human values will provide some protection against the pitfalls of forms of action that may be equally questionable and reprehensible from a human perspective. They will also do well to study the sociology of totalitarianism and fascism, especially as they relate to racism.

We see thus that there are many ways to skin the human cat sociologically. There is no single way from a commitment to general human values to action strategies. Whether we choose to be reflexive sociologists in Gouldner's sense, active sociologists in Etzioni's sense, radical sociologists in the sense of the New Left, of aloof in the mainline so-called value-free sense, a commitment to human values will result in a more relevant, more objective, more free-from-parochial-biases sociology than we have at the moment. The alternative to value-freedom is not value relativism but a humane sociology which will provide a firm basis for whatever role individual sociologists wish to choose in society. The probability that sociology will have some contribution to make to the tremendous social problems of contemporary humanity will be considerably enhanced.

These are problems that would not have been engaged by social scientists during earlier stages of the development of the system, at least not in this general form and not with the same normative orientation. The values problem in social science is not an insurmountable one in the integrative stage of the development of the social science system in modern society. Yet most of the solutions proffered today are rather simplistic—almost unrealistic flights of the imagination. Theoretically, we have to accept both value freedom and value relevance; we have to recognize the need for value generalization and innovation. Practically, we have to conceptualize and specify values down to norms for specific role expectations in the various aspects of the scientist's role. And we have to determine and institutionalize mechanisms for the implementation of these values. This essay is obviously a *very* preliminary step; it is inconclusive, suggestive rather than definitive, proposing a general framework within which a sociological theory of values in social science can be developed as a cognitive underpinning to a committed humanistic sociology.

NOTES

1. See Duncan MacRae, Jr., "A Dilemma of Sociology: Science versus Policy," *The American Sociologist*, 6 (June 1971), pp. 2-7.

2. See Elbridge Sibley, "Scientific Sociology at Bay?" *The American Sociologist*, 6 (June 1971), pp. 13-17.

3. See "Some Radical Perspectives in Sociology," *Sociological Inquiry*, 40 (Winter 1970); Steven E. Deutsch and John Howard (eds.) *Where It's At: Radical Perspective in Sociology* (New York: Harper & Row Publishers, 1970).

4. Alvin W. Gouldner, "Anti-minotaur: the Myth of a Value-free Sociology," *Social Problems*, 9 (Winter 1962), pp. 199-213.

5. C. Wright Mills, *The Sociological Imagination* (London: Oxford University Press, 1959).

6. Alvin W. Gouldner, "The Sociologist as Partisan: Sociology and the Welfare State," *The American Sociologist*, 3 (May 1968), pp. 103-116.

7. Max Weber, *The Methodology of the Social Sciences*. Trans. and ed. by Edward A. Shils and Henry A. Finch (Glencoe, III.: The Free Press, 1949).

8. See Thomas Kuhn, *The Structure of Scientific Revolutions* (Chicago: University of Chicago Press, 1962).

9. See Robert S. Lynd, *Knowledge for What?* (Princeton, N.J.: Princeton University Press, 1939).

10. For some of these developments see Deutsch and Howard, *op. cit.*; *Sociological Inquiry*, 40 (Winter 1970); *The American Sociologist*. 1, Supplementary issue on "Sociological Research and Public Policy," June 1971, and *The Behavioral and Social Sciences: Outlook and Needs*: A Report by The Behavioral and Social Sciences Survey Committee (Englewood Cliffs, N.J.: Prentice-Hall, Inc., 1969).

11. Erich Fromm (ed.), *Socialist Humanism: An International Symposium* (Garden City, N.Y.: Anchor Books, Doubleday & Co. Inc., 1966); see also Albert Szymanski, "Toward a Radical Sociology," *Sociological Inquiry*, 40 (Winter 1970), pp. 3-13.

12. There is a certain similarity between the naive value—involved stance in social science and the utilitarian assumption of the randomness of wants. In one sense the value—freedom stance is a radical rationalistic solution to the problem, insisting that it is possible to eliminate or minimize error by a commitment to rationality, cognitive rationality. The solution here advanced is a voluntaristic one. See Talcott Parsons, *The Structure of Social Action* (New York: McGraw-Hill, 1937). Reprinted by The Free Press, New York, 1949.

13. See Talcott Parsons, "On the Concept of Value-Commitments," *Sociological Inquiry*, 38 (Spring 1968), pp. 135-159.

14. *Ibid.*, pp. 157-159.

15. Much of recent concern with policy research and the "uses of sociology" reflects this accommodation. See Paul F. Lazarsfeld, et al. (eds.), *The Uses of Sociology* (New York: Basic Books, Inc., 1967).

16. See Alvin W. Gouldner, *The Coming Crisis of Western Sociology* (New York: Basic Books, Inc., 1970).

17. See Amitai Etzioni, *The Active Society: A Theory of Societal and Political Processes* (New York: The Free Press, 1968); "Basic Human Needs Alienation and Inauthenticity," *American Sociological Review*, 33 (1968), pp. 870-885. Commenting on the problem of relativism, Etzioni remarks: "The only systematic escape from such relativisim and latent ideological commitments is to rely on the one foundation all social scientists, whatever their affiliations, can share and measure—values whose community is all men" (*The Active Society*, p. 608).

18. See Albert Szymanski, *op. cit.*

19. See Jan J. Loubser, "The Contribution of Schools to Moral Development: A Working Paper on the Theory of Action," *Interchange*, 1 (April 1970), pp. 99-117. Also in C.M. Beck et al., *Moral Education*. (Toronto: University of Toronto Press, 1971), pp. 147-179.

20. *Ibid.*, pp. 103-107.

21. See T. Parsons and E.A. Shils (eds.), *Toward a General Theory of Action* (Cambridge, Mass: Harvard University Press, 1951)

22. Etzioni, Amitai, *The Active Society* and "Basic Human Needs, Alienation and Inauthenticity", *op. cit.*

23. Etzioni, Amitai, *The Active Society*, p. 632.

24. See Lawrence Kohlberg, "Stages of Moral Development as a Basis for Moral Education," in C.M. Beck, et al., *op. cit.*, pp. 23-92; J.J. Loubser. *op. cit.*

25. See Deutsch and Howard, *op. cit.*

5

ON THE FOUNDATIONS OF THE THEORY OF ACTION IN WHITEHEAD AND PARSONS

Thomas J. Fararo

PRELUDE

How could a person interested in the mathematical formulation of sociological theory come to take an interest in the work of Talcott Parsons? By way of indicating the background for my work in this paper, I will try to describe the path that led to it. Work in applying net models to sociometric situations persuaded me that the modern abstract mathematical systems were the key to the formulation of sociological theory on a proper basis. Following an interlude of study of pure mathematics, I examined the work of the Stanford group,[1] looking at it from the standpoint of abstract mathematics.[2]

In looking at this work, I was naturally led to write down the primitive notions and to seek the axiomatic structure connecting these primitives. As simple as the idea may seem to sociologists (because of its informal everyday usage in sociological analysis) it seems that the key ideas in this theoretical work could be framed relative to a type of mapping which I denoted:

$$c: A \to C, \quad \text{(or, } A \xrightarrow{c} C\text{)},$$

and which associates to each actor α in A a property or state x in set C, so that $c(\alpha) = x$ is the characterization of α. C itself is termed a characteristic.

Several obvious questions arise in this type of mapping. Most importantly, is c to be interpreted as the mapping by the sociologist, independent of the conceptual activity of members of A? Or is c to be interpreted as a representation of a mapping made by some member of A? By indexing c with the name of its author, generically α, we allow all possible interpretations:

$$c_\alpha: A \to C.$$

If α is in A, then $c_\alpha(\beta)$ is the characterization of β, by α, as β varies in A. Thus we have $c_\alpha(\alpha)$ as the self-characterization. If α is not in A. then the mapping is

"exterior" in its standpoint, authored by an actor in a wider set of actors including A and α together. As α and β vary in A, we generate all interior characterizations of the form $c_\alpha(\beta)$.

A natural question to ask is if these characterizations agree in several senses: are the same categories (in C) used? Are identical states assigned to a given actor by the various mapping actors? (For example, if $c_\alpha(\beta) = x$, does $c\gamma(\beta) = x$, where γ is a third actor in A?) Then since states are evaluated (also represented in additional formalism) the same questions arise in regard to evaluations.

Expectations may be thought of as tacit assignments of behaviors to states: If someone is characterized as in a certain state or having a certain property, then a certain mode of behavior follows (from the point of view of the characterizing actor). But this simple idea, which has the mapping form

$$e_\alpha: C \to B,$$

where B is a set of possible behaviors, already assumes that the fact that some particular actor in A is assigned to state x in C does not affect the expectation. Surely this is a special form of expectation and not the general case. More generally, e_α takes as its point of departure not merely the state in C, but the particular actor assigned that state. Thus the characterization mapping potentially enters into the determination of the expectation for behavior.

Then instead of the idea

$$e_\alpha(x) = b$$

(behavior b expected by α of someone assigned by him to state x), we have the form

$$e_\alpha(\beta, c_\alpha(\beta)) = b,$$

which says: Behavior b is expected by α of β when α characterizes β in terms of state $c_\alpha(\beta)$ in C. If now, as β varies in A, it is the case that this expectation depends only upon the second component of its domain (i.e., upon the state assigned), then the expectation e_α may be termed *universalistic*. Otherwise it may be termed *particularistic*. Thus, underlying the innocent idea of "a certain behavior expected of someone in a certain position or state" is the assumption that the expectation involved is of the universalistic type.

Another and even more fundamental distinction apparent in the formalism added interest to looking at the Parsons scheme for general theory. The two characterization mappings,

$$c_\alpha: A \to C,$$
$$c_\beta: A \to C,$$

where α and β are actors in A, provide two distinct standpoints toward the typical actor, say α. First, there is α as the subject, he who characterizes and expects, as in:

$$c_\alpha(\beta).$$

Second, there is α as object, as one of those entities mapped, say by β:

$$c_\beta(\alpha).$$

Of course, the decision to represent the action patterns of actors in A in terms of representing how *they* map each other is the crucial first step that then determines the *dual standpoint* toward any *one* actor in A. Reiterating, each actor in A, say α, is both a subject and an object. Moreover, the self-characterization $c_\alpha(\alpha)$ shows that every actor is object to himself.

Thus, the general term

$$c_\alpha(\beta) \qquad (\alpha, \beta \text{ in } A)$$

defines (1) α as subject and (2) β as object. Exchanging α and β leads to the treatment of β as subject, α as object. This is what Parsons calls the *fundamental duality* of the action framework. From my point of view, if one tries to write down formally what sociology is dealing with, this duality arises as soon as one admits the existence of mapping activity by the entities under analysis. But the fact that actors characterize each other is the primordial basis of all sociology; for example, no researcher would claim that race is in some absolute sense significant. Race is an important distinction for sociologists studying certain social systems because the actors in those systems characterize each other in terms of skin color. For the same reason, eye color is of little interest to the sociologist.

The next point to notice is that actual behavior may not agree with the expected behavior, however it is defined by the actor, so that the diagram for the universalistic case:

may not be "commutative." This means that the dotted line representing the map of actual behavior may not agree with the expected behavior. For instance, β does b_1 but $e_\alpha(c_\alpha(\beta)) = b_2 \neq b_1$.

In one sense, the problem of integration of these actors involves the question of the commutative diagram. If all actors agree in the universalistic expectation,

$$e_\alpha = e_\beta$$

and if whenever $c_\alpha(\beta) = x$, then $c_\beta(\beta) = x$, it will follow that the behavior that β expects of himself is identical with the behavior that α expects of him. In such a case, the basis for actual behavior is non-coercive, residing in the properties of the actors themselves. The prior history of action may show that β may have been "exploited" to adopt a self-characterization in agreement with the state to which α assigns him. But in the present state of the system, the commonality of expectation and characterization provides a basis for actual behavior being defined as "natural," "proper," and so forth, by both parties.

The point of this discussion is that although not *all* states and not *all* expectations may be uniform in A, *some* uniformity appears to be a strong empirical property of existent sets of actors we describe as "groups," "societies," and the like. These higher-order entities may be racked by conflict, but as long as they exist some basis of order exists among the set of actors; in other words, the order is not merely externally imposed by an investigator who says, "let this be a group, because I want to analyze it." The basic point of a collection of actors being more than mere multiplicity grouped by an external observer is that the actors themselves determine a formal structure of relationships for recognition by the observer amid the flux of behavior and of conflict within the system and in the system's relation to its environment. This invariant pattern is what the entity "is," as long as it exists. The pattern has two aspects. In the physical side of things, it is regularity in the sense of physical science: the factual order, for instance, of people working, eating, sleeping, in regularized ways. This is the regularity of the "dotted line" of our diagram.

The second part of the invariant pattern, however, is the order in conceptual activity that results from the fact that the entities exhibiting regularities are just ourselves, so to speak, the mappers of their worlds. As they act in accordance with their maps, regularity of actual behavior presupposes coordination and uniformity in mapping. This is the normative order. Without this order, we could still describe the actors as mappers, but relative to each other's expectations there would be chaos. A system of action with regularity in its factual order but without a corresponding normative order is in an unstable state. Either (1) the actors modify expectations and characterizations to suit the behavior, (2) the behavior is modified, or (3) the actors "explode" into isolates incapable of characterizing each other at all.

But how do the actors represent to themselves "behavior?" Formally, what distinguishes B from C? Surely actual behavior is just another basis for characterization, is it not? Yet, as an empirical fact, actors employs the scheme: If such-and-such a property, then such-and-such behavior. For example, "If a person is a professor, then he teaches and does research." This scheme appears to be based upon a cognition of the object-actor (the actor β in the characterization $c_\alpha(\beta)$) as comprised of an entity with two orders of dynamics: short-term instabilities and longer-term stabilities. The former constitutes behavior and the latter some basis for behavior, what the object-actor "is" for the subject-actor. In general, one part of the characterization is a stable base for the other part: one is the state of the object-system and the other is the response or output of the object-system. That is, the actor α maps as a scientist maps: identify the system (β), provide a state-description ($c_\alpha(\beta)$), and observe and explain outputs (actual behavior of β) in terms of the expectations ($e_\alpha(x)$) associated with the state-description (in the universalistic case). This is only to say that scientists are actors and that actors are "generalized scientists."

According to the preceding paragraph, then, each actor is able to discriminate two dynamic patterns in any object-actor: the first ("state") is what Parsons calls *quality*, and the second (output, "response") is what Parsons calls *performance*. Hence, intrinsic to characterization is the presence of two maps of the object-actor: one defines the state, and the other defines the response or behavior. As the state can be modified by the behavior, quality is not static in any absolute sense.

So far, I have tried to show how some of the most basic distinctions in Parsons' action scheme arise naturally when one writes down a formal object to represent some aspect of action and asks some simple questions about it. In this way, universalism-particularism, quality-performance, and the fundamental duality idea strike me as sound foundations for social theory. With respect to the other pattern variables (affectivity-neutrality and diffuseness-specificity) I am somewhat more uncertain. I have not been able to find a natural interpretation of these two variables in my own formal work, which may reflect a selection of only some components of action from the fuller array outlined by Parsons. In any case, my point has been to give a partly autobiographical account of how, starting from an interest in setting up the formal basis for sociological theories, one is led to take a more than casual interest in the action scheme of Talcott Parsons.

It is much more difficult to explain why metaphysics is needed in foundational work. I will try to indicate briefly how metaphysics becomes of interest. The focus of a sound theoretical science is ordinarily some class of dynamic systems. A dynamic system is described in terms of equations referent to the law of transition, in-the-small, of the state of the system. Deductive work aims to deduce the trajectory of the system, over time, given the initial and boundary conditions and the law for transition in-the-small. If such a system is described, in all generality without reference to one particular such system, the following components are noted: (1) a generic enduring object, such as an arbitrary vibrating string, an arbitrary planetary system, an arbitrary clock, an arbitrary post office queue, an arbitrary small group, and so forth; (2) a set of associated aspects of this enduring object, properties in numerical or non-numerical form which collectively form a "space" for state-description of the object; (3) a time domain and a class of functions which map the points in the time domain into the state space for the particular enduring object; and (4) a set of conditions on the class of time-functions which generates a *definite* time-function in the class of time-functions, interpreted as that time-function realized by the object under the conditions. The conditions divide into those peculiar to the one enduring object in its circumstances (initial conditions, boundary conditions) and those said to be valid for an entire class of similar enduring objects (the laws).

This entire structure, in the case of an exact theory, defines a complex mathematical pattern, which we may think of as specified by the predicate, "is a dynamic system of type X," say. If E is an enduring object, then the proposition "E is a dynamic system of type X" is true just in the case that E is defined in part by its realization of a type X dynamic system. For instance, a particular violin would be something else if it did not realize a dynamic system for vibrating strings when played in particular circumstances. Thus, if the proposition is true, then the dynamic system in all generality is instantiated to a particular realization that is a component of the enduring object making the proposition true. In this sense, for instance, it is true to say that the violin *is* a dynamic system or a planet *is* a dynamic system. But it is "the fallacy of misplaced concreteness"[3] to then assert that a type *Y* dynamic system is not *also* ingredient in the very same enduring object. For example, a rocket is much more than a realization of a spatial trajectory: The general equations of motion are specified to the rocket's conditions and a particular solution describes a pattern ingredient in what the rocket *is*. For if *that* rocket did not undergo *that* trajectory it would be a different entity. In general, then, the various dynamic systems of interest to us describe ingredient components of enduring objects.

If *E* is an enduring object then the set

$$\{D: E \text{ is a type-}D \text{ system}\}$$

is the set of dynamic systems inherent in *E*, or (to use Whitehead's terminology) "ingredient" in *E*. Yet *E* is not *identical* to this set, for *E* is the actual togetherness of these systems and not a mere class of dynamic systems. The idea that the rocket is what it is, and then "in addition" realizes a particular trajectory to the moon is valid in the following sense: The various systems *D* ingredient in *E* are of vastly different "dynamic orders." For example, the state for one component dynamic system changes on the average of once per minute and in another it changes at the rate of once per millisecond, while in a third dynamic system no change takes place for years. The entity *E* is incessantly changing because of the variety of dynamic systems, and yet in some respects it remains time-invariant over suitable time domains. Some of these invariances serve to define it for us, although they do not tell the whole story about it.

Consider now the spatial trajectory. When this trajectory is realized, the space itself is invariant in regard to its dimensions, among other properties. Ordinarily we think of three dimensions as fixed. But the dynamic system standpoint encourages one to think of a dynamic system whose state includes the dimension of space. Our particular cosmic epoch is realizing a dynamic system of such a totally different dynamical order than most other systems we experience that the number of dimensions of space is constant. If the number of dimensions is a part of the state-description of our cosmic epoch — an enduring object we can grasp as an entity only with difficulty — then even deeper properties may exist that are invariant in an epoch in which the number of dimensions has increased to five, say. That is, the cosmos changes state in regard to spatial dimension, but other cosmic properties remain invariant. The question then arises as to whether any absolute invariants exist. For instance, is time an absolute invariant? That is, is the structure of reality such that every enduring object must realize a system of serially ordered durations? Clearly, this question is fundamental, for the dynamic systems all have the common property of *some* time domain. Clearly, the question cannot be resolved in isolation by pretending that time may not exist but enduring objects will exist. Only a theoretical system which treats space, time, and enduring objects as *problematic* and explicates how they require each other in realization can avoid paradoxes and nonsense.

In Whitehead's cosmology[4] to endure means to sustain a pattern. Take "pattern" as primitive. What does "sustain" mean? Some things, otherwise in flux, exhibit some invariance, which is the pattern. Call these things *occasions*. Then an enduring object is a series of occasions in each of which a certain pattern is repeated. When a pattern is realized, it defines a quantum of actuality in an extensive continuum. This quantum is then repeated if we have an enduring object. The repetitions define the temporalization of the successive quanta, whose common pattern realisation defines the space of the enduring object. Thus if the occasions in the world exhibit any stability of pattern then each such exhibition of endurance defines space and time, although not necessarily with uniformity as between different enduring objects.

If this discussion is applied to action theory, the enduring objects which are people and groups and the things in their environment are much more problematic than a commonsense standpoint encourages us to think. Wherever there is enduring pattern, there might not have been. If this point of view is taken, then all patterns are theoretically problematic. If a group has ten members it might have had nine; if it has strong loyalty to its standards it might not have such loyalty tomorrow; if everyone speaks English in this generation, they might not in the next; whatever endures does so under the potentiality of alternatives as yet unrealized but relevant to each occasion. Thus the analysis of the foundations of action must give its attention to patterns that endure and to their problematic character. Thus it must investigate forms of process and the stability of patterns realized in process.

All this implies at least an abstract language for making clear the different entities under discussion: enduring objects, patterns partially definitive of them by virtue of realization in them, such patterns as dynamic systems, and so forth. In addition, the whole idea of duality in the action scheme may be "grounded" from a metaphysical standpoint. This means we ask if duality is present in the theoretical system which takes space, time, and enduring objects as problematic. We ask if the description of occasions as a community in which time, space, and endurance are realized also exhibits this duality as a created aspect, as endurance, or if, on the other hand, it lies even more deeply in the nature of the community of occasions. In the latter case, the duality of subject and object is a greater invariant than the dimension of space or than the existence of any of the great types of endurance we witness in our lives. Put another way, every occasion in the community of occasions is then both something for itself — an actuality with its associated world — and something for other occasions, an object for other actualities. From this point of view all the classic dualisms of philosophy are treated as natural phenomena, as it were, as cravings after unique solutions to problems that admit two solutions. For example, is final cause or efficient cause the true description of the world? Materialism: efficient cause. Vitalism: final cause. Dual solution: efficient and final. Each occasion is both controlled by an aim and conditioned by its past. Thus each occasion is a *cybernetic* complex system: The aim establishes a final cause toward which process is directed, but in turn the actual world introduces a massive set of conditions.

In the last few paragraphs I have tried to show how an interest in looking at the world and at action in terms of dynamic systems leads to a metaphysical point of view which can be taken to be the general conceptual foundation of the action framework. I will pursue this topic in certain selected respects in the body of the paper.

One final and important remark will conclude this prelude to the paper. It cannot be emphasized too strongly that the paper is a *working paper:* Nothing in it is final, and it is offered as an effort whose purpose will be accomplished if a better paper of the same kind emerges from it, no matter who authors it.

To give the reader some idea of the topics to be covered in this working paper—although they are not yet sufficiently integrated—the following may be noted about the paper's four sections: In the first section, I treat a topic that leads into Whitehead's metaphysics, namely, the relations of endurance to time and space. The important concept here is that of pattern. In the second section, I provide a sketch of some important parts of Whitehead's system, especially as they illuminate the concepts I think are important for the foundations of action theory. In the third section, I begin with a bridge from Whitehead to Parsons and then attempt to specify in formal terms the abstract structure of that category of dynamic systems called action systems. Finally, in the last section, I offer a series of brief interpretative essays.

PATTERNS IN SPACETIME

The Extensive Continuum

The contemporary world for a percipient is displayed to the percipient as a connected region with potentially infinite divisibility into subregions, connected with each other. In other words, perception of the world as a contemporary entity displays that world as an *extensive continuum.*

Let *R, S,* . . . be regions within the world. Relations among regions exist. For example, the region of my book is connected with the region of my pencil, although there is no overlap. A particular page of a copy of this book is occupying a subregion or part of the book region, connected in a special mode to the region of the book. The patch of the page I can arbitrarily demarcate is also a part of the page and so a part of the book: but the arbitrary number of patches that one can so define are merely potential regions of objects of experience rather than actual objects of experience. This is part of the meaning of the idea of continuum: What is in fact undivided (e.g., a page) is perceived as potentially divisible.

These remarks may be systematized by some proper definitions and axioms, providing for present purposes only a fragment of the theory described in Whitehead's *Science and the Modern World* and in more detail in his *Process and Reality.* The main function of this material in this context is, on the one hand, to provide a lead-in to Whitehead's mature metaphysics by way of his own path into metaphysics, starting from the nature of spacetime, and, on the other hand, to show the great significance of *patterns* in the foundations of the differentiation of time from space.

The relation of *inclusion* may be taken as a primitive, undefined idea that makes intuitive sense for regions as a relation between pairs of regions. These intuitions can be the basis for systematic meaning postulates for the inclusion relation that relates regions. The following axioms are so construed.

Axiom 1. Inclusion is transitive: If *R* includes *S* and *S* includes *T,* then *R* includes *T.*

Axiom 2. Inclusion is antisymmetric: If *R* includes *S* and *S* includes *R,* then *R* and *S* are the same region, *R=S.*

Axiom 3. Every region includes itself.

If *R* includes *S,* we also say that *S* is a *part of R.*

In mathematics, these three axioms are said to define a *partially ordered set,* often abbreviated as *poset.* Thus the regions form a poset. They cannot be ordered in a single series, however, because there are regions that are not related by inclusion. The extensive continuum is the multidimensional space of regions which, in its order properties, forms a poset. A poset is familiar to sociologists in its realization in some formal organizations as the "tree of authority." Instead of regions there are positions and instead of inclusion there is the superordinate-subordinate relation connecting positions. However, the extensive continuum is more than a poset, just as an organization is more than its authority structure. Moreover, the extensive continuum is not a finite entity, as is the organization chart. Thus, there is a family resemblance because of the poset aspect, but this must be contrasted with the differences in the specific posets.

The major difference is the continuity of the extensive continuum. For any collection of regions there is the region that includes each of the regions in the collection, but it includes no other regions. We term this region the *union* of the given regions. Also, for any finite collection of regions there is a unique region included in each of these regions and such as to be included in no other region which is also included in each given region. This is termed the *intersection* of the regions. Thus, the intersection of the set of regions is the largest region—in terms of inclusion—which is a part of each of the given regions. Regions which do not have an intersection are called *disjoint;* technically, their intersection is "the null region." (There are no "points" because in fundamental spacetime theory points are abstract constructions based on regions.)

The space of all regions, with the two operations of union and intersection, satisfies two distinct sets of axioms: (1) the axioms for a topological space, the basis for concepts depending upon continuity, and (2) the axioms for a poset.

Axiom 4. There does not exist a pair of non-null regions R and S whose union is the whole space and whose intersection is the null region.

This is the axiom of nonseparability of space: If such a pair of distinct regions existed space would be separable into two subregions that with respect to each do *not* intersect. But then intuition would immediately fill "the gap" with a third region, thus nullifying the potential separability of space. Another way of labelling Axiom 4 is that it is the axiom of *connectedness* of space: there is a rejection of the pure possibility of separability of space and so an acceptance of the impossibility of the separability of space: This is the meaning of connectedness.

We note that if we consider any *given* region in the space, its parts satisfy: (1) the inclusion axioms, thereby forming a poset; (2) the region of course includes all its parts and so the region is the union of all its parts. If the region also satisfies Axiom 4 it is called a *connected subspace.*

For an illustration of this notion, consider the region given by a man's body, assuming him stationary. This region is connected. Contrast the region that is the union of two such regions, one for each man, so that the two regions are disjoint. Then the union region is not a connected subspace.

Patterns in Events: Endurance

At this point, a certain oversimplification in the treatment of regions must be noted: No temporal aspect was explicitly introduced. With the ideas already developed, we now may simply drop any tacit assumption that "region" means "spatial region," and wherever the term "space" was used we replace it with "spacetime." Then spacetime forms a poset, a topological space, and satisfies Axiom 4 in that it is connected. This partially characterizes spacetime as an extensive continuum, but it does not provide a basis for distinguishing time from space. This basis is provided in the extensive continuum of the world by *patterns exemplified in events.* Our next objective, then, is to show how time becomes analytically distinguishable from space by the nature of patterns in events.

We introduce patterns, undefined for the present, but with partial meaning provided by an embedding into the system of concepts. For instance, "event" and "pattern" are related.

Axiom 5. Any event is associated with a unique pattern.

This axiom is to receive elucidation gradually. For the present, we note the "association" of a pattern to an event. Thus, we write:

$$E \rightarrow p_E$$

where p_E is the pattern of event E. We say that the pattern is *ingredient* in E. We write p to signify the pattern p_E in abstraction from the event E. This raises the question as to exactly what *is E* and exactly what *is* p_E? We know intuitively that patterns exhibit relationships to each other. For example, several patterns of three dots may be located within the following pattern of four dots:

Is the pattern of four dots on the page p_E or p? In other words, how do we specify the distinction between events-with-patterns and patterns? In your copy of this book, there is p_E and in my copy $p_{E'}$ with p the same. The distinction arises in the regions of spacetime.

Axiom 6. Any event is associated with a unique region of spacetime. We write,

$$E \rightarrow R_E$$

In Axiom 5, the association of a pattern with an event is *not* a one-to-one correspondence: Distinct events may display the same pattern. If events E and F have the same associated pattern, we say that E and F have a common pattern. This can be the case even though $R_E \neq R_F$. Assume that E has an associated region of spacetime R_E and that F has an associated region of spacetime R_F.

Definition 1. Suppose that pattern p is ingredient in event E. We say that p *endures* from E to F if and only if (1) p is ingredient in F and (2) R_E is included in R_F.

For example, the dot pattern endures in your copy of this book. But it does not endure from your copy to my copy, as the associated regions are disjoint and the one is not included in the other.

The relation of *endurance* so defined relates a pattern to a pair of events. For a fixed pattern, the relation is transitive:

Consequence (transitivity of endurance). If p endures from E to F and from F to G, then p endures from E to G.

The reasoning here is as follows. If p endures from E to F, then R_E is included in R_F, and if p endures from F to G, then R_F is included in R_G. As the relation of inclusion among regions in the extensive continuum is transitive (Axiom 1), then R_E is included in R_G. Also if p endures from E to F, it is ingredient in F. Hence, if p endures from F to G, it is ingredient in G. Thus, p is ingredient in G and R_E is included in R_G. Therefore, p endures from E to G.

We note also that every pattern endures from E to E if it is ingredient in E.

Suppose that p endures from E to F and from F to E. Then R_E is included in and includes R_F, so by Axiom 2, $R_E = R_F$. The question then arises: Are we really dealing with two events? We have to recall that the pattern of an event is its "full" pattern in the sense that Axiom 5 associates one pattern to the event (and we have not yet discussed any subpatterns in detail). Thus with mutual endurance we have (1) identity of spacetime region and (2) common pattern. This seems a necessary and sufficient condition for event identity.

Definition 2. Event $E =$ Event F if and only if (1) pattern p_E and pattern p_F are identical, that is, the one pattern p is ingredient in both E and F, and (2) $R_E = R_F$.

It is an immediate consequence that "two" events are identical if and only they have a common pattern which endures from each to the other. (Technically, the endurance relation is antisymmetric.) For illustration, consider the event E which is the pattern of dots in my copy of this book, with region R_E, and contrast it with any other pattern also in R_E. Then by virtue of this contrast, a distinct event is being specified, for otherwise we would have (1) $E = F$, (2) $R_E = R_F$, and (3) $p_E \neq p_F$, which contradicts Definition 2. Thus patterns in regions of spacetime are definitive of events.

The event E with ingredient pattern p_E might be such that p has endured from some event, say E', to E. Then there may exist an E'' such that p endured from E'' to E', and thence to E. Proceeding in this manner we "filter" down in spacetime by "reverse" endurance. At some region, then, there is the absence of such an antecedent event realizing p. Hence, if this limit to the reversal be accepted, we have a region of spacetime such that it is associated with an event with p for its ingredient pattern and no part of this region has an associated event with this same pattern. This may be thought of as a "quantum" of spacetime for realization of the pattern, call it R_p.

Then under certain conditions that will not be given here, if R_E is the region of an event E with p as its associated pattern, we can represent R_E as a union of a certain number of regions of the form R_p, i.e., R_E is a "sum" of so-many quanta of realizations of pattern p,

$$R_E = R_p + R_p + \ldots + R_p \qquad (t \text{ terms}).$$

Hence, E may be assigned a number t based on the number of quanta of realizations of its pattern. (Here " $+$ " means union of regions.)

In summary, starting with the idea of patterns ingredient in events associated with regions of spacetime, we find that by virtue of endurance, the region of spacetime of an event is differentiable into a *space aspect*, based on the particular pattern, and a *time aspect* based on pattern repetition. When a region R_p is not merely the potential space for realizable p but actually is the region of an event realizing p, this event may be termed an occasion. Thus, an event in the wider sense—as an E with associated region R_E and pattern p_E—is conceived as an ordered series of occasions in which p is realized.

The relativistic character of these results is to be noted: each endurance—of a molecule, of a man, of an explosion—is a basis for a particular differentiation of spacetime into time and space in the extensive continuum. However, it also follows that if a pattern can be ingredient in many events—starting from distinct initial realizations—then many chains of endurance may sustain this pattern: Thus the universe has the potential for *analogous enduring objects*. Each one of the analogous enduring objects defined by its own successive endurance of the pattern common to them all, will differentiate spacetime in a similar manner. Note that with a constant pattern, successively realized, the space of an enduring object is constant. Thus, each enduring object is "at rest" in its own version of the differentiation process.

Occasions: Prelude to Metaphysics

The preceding discussion makes clear that the world's work is done in the occasions of pattern realization and that time emerges from reiteration of pattern realization in occasions.

Thus, an occasion is a pulse of pattern realization in the extensive continuum. Yet patterns cannot be "automatically" realized either in origination in the first of a series of occasions or in inheritance in some later occasion in the series realizing a common pattern. Whatever is realized might not be realized. The past history of realizations of patterns in the continuum does not "force" any particular form upon a fresh occasion. This is true if for no other reason than the enormous variety of patterns already realized and the fact that patterns may mutually exclude each other for joint realization. Thus the new occasion must synthesize its past but the past alone does not provide the mode of synthesis. It follows that realization in the extensive continuum—the advance of occasions—is a continuous transition into novelty. The initial data for the immediacy of pattern realization in an occasion are the givens for the process of the universe in that regional standpoint, but the multiplicity of the givens requires synthesis to achieve the pattern definitive of an occasion.

Yet, what is a pattern? If the spacetime analysis is applied to each of an entire system of events, each event with its corresponding pattern, in each case we filter "down" in extent to the occasions for each pattern. Then each event is a series of occasions with a common pattern. Also, the events included *in* any one occasion are thereby seen to be various series of occasions. Thus the "interior" of any one occasion consists in *other* occasions. Hence *the pattern of the occasion is its manner of composition of other occasions*. This is "realized" pattern. Under conceptual activity, this pattern may be abstracted from the actual occasions present in the one occasion in composition: Then there is a form of composition in abstraction from the particularities of the occasions synthesized in that occasion.

Under this idea of pattern, to say that each occasion is a pulse of pattern realization in the extensive continuum means: Each occasion is a creative synthesis of the universe of existent occasions. What becomes is one more occasion. The many occasions become one, in synthesis, and the many are increased by one: This is Whitehead's fundamental "formula" for metaphysics.

The preceding exposition is based upon Whitehead's discussion of these topics in *Science and the Modern World*. They provide a background for the treatment of cosmology in the metaphysical treatise Whitehead produced several years later, *Process and Reality*. In the next section, the focus is changed to the analysis of the actual occasion.

The following methodological remarks may help the reader to orient himself to the subsequent discussion. The term "actual occasion" or "occasion" is analogous to the term "point" in geometry, in two senses: (1) A point is an element of an abstract set of entities postulated to satisfy a set of mutually binding conditions, the axioms of a geometrical system; analogously, an occasion is an element of an abstract set of entities postulated to satisfy a set of mutually binding conditions, the axioms of a cosmological or metaphysical system; and (2) such a system, whether geometrical or metaphysical, is applied to the actual world by a process of exemplification indicated by identifications of the abstract entities in the theory with observed things in the world. To the extent that such exemplifications are persuasive of the system's adequacy in the interpretation of experience, one may be led to believe that the world realizes the pattern described by the axioms of the system. Thus, one may believe that space is Euclidean or that the universe is Whiteheadian. The major difficulty is to get a grasp of the whole system, because the claim is that the elementary things of the system — the points, the occasions — make no sense in isolation from their community (of points, of occasions). Unfortunately, Whitehead did not produce a definite set of axioms for his metaphysical system, nor any clear correspondence rules. Any attempt to describe the system is then, in some subtle way, if not wrong then at least an individual interpretation of the Whiteheadian system. In any case, because of the massiveness of the system, the description has to be selective.

Another aspect of the metaphysical system is worth noting. If there were a definite set of axioms descriptive of an abstract pattern, and if this pattern were indeed the realized pattern of the universe, then it would be the widest possible pattern. That is, its realization would not entail the realization of any other particular patterns, but all particular patterns other than itself would entail its realization.

Thus, if p is a pattern, and if W is the Whiteheadian system, then

$$\text{if } p, \text{ then } W$$

expresses the idea that when p is realized so is W, for any p. Thus, W formulates the system of necessary conditions for pattern realization — which is the flow of events. In this way, the metaphysical pattern is the underlying stable base for the universe. This means not just this cosmic epoch, but any cosmic epoch. Thus that some definite geometrical system is realized in a given epoch entails the order of W, but the order of W does not entail any of the usual special geometries of space. Again, time is realized in the pattern invariance in realizations, so that if time is exemplified in the world, so is W. However, W does not entail that special uniform mode of order by which spacetime separates into time and space in the analogous occasions of our epoch.

In a sense, then, a metaphysical system has very little to say. What it must do is provide us with the generic form of process in the universe, set out in a language that does not betray a loss of generality to some special epoch or standpoint. To accomplish this, ordinary language is often "stretched" so that words function as parameters do in mathematical formulas. For example, the formula $y = ax + b$ is such that when $a = 0$ then $y = b$, and y is independent of x. Yet we say that the formula expresses y as a function of x. The case $y = b$ is allowed to be subsumed under the formula as a special case in which certain potentialities ($a \neq 0$) are simply not realized. Similarly, in metaphysics, one might say that every occasion exhibits mentality which includes the special case where the mentality is "trivial," so that the occasion involves mere causal transmission with no introduction of novelty. The "highest" occasions of experience provide the paradigm for *all* occasions, as the "lower" are captured as special cases.

Finally, the "height" of the occasion is left open to possibilities as yet unrealized. Clearly none of this generality is possible without using ordinary words in meanings stretched into novel technical usage. Above all, the concepts "actual occasion" and "feeling" are technical terms for elements in the metaphysical pattern as described by Whitehead. (To avoid confusion, I have dropped the term "eternal objects," used by Whitehead in the 1920's, in favor of "pattern," his term in the 1930's.)

PROCESS METAPHYSICS

Modes of Analysis

According to the prior section, there is a continuous advance of the universe into novel occasions, each of which is a synthesis of other occasions. We can think of this as a mapping of the many "initial data" for the occasion into the unity which *is* the occasion (say α):

$$\text{many-for-}\alpha \rightarrow \alpha.$$

This dynamic synthesis of many into one we call *concrescence*. Hence any occasion is a concrescence. The following two assumptions are suggested by the idea that the concrescence is a transformation; they are based on our earlier discussion.

First, for any two distinct occasions α and β, the many-for-α is distinct from the many-for-β.

Second, in any concrescence, the occasion α is not a member of the many-for-α.

This is the assumption of novelty as a fundamental property of the ever-repeated concrescence but with each occasion in some way distinct from what exists in the many data for that occasion.

There are two modes of *analysis* of an occasion, say α. The first mode involves the analysis of its concrescence. Here we say that we are analyzing the *formal constitution* of the occasion. This is the occasion in full pattern realization in its own right:

relative to this pattern the occasion is a "pulse" which does not have any internal time measure.

The second mode of analysis of an occasion involves the analysis of the way that the occasion, say α, is involved in any concrescence other than its own. In this mode of analysis we call α an *object*. When α is *in* another occasion, it is there objectively but not formally: There is loss of the immediacy, the pulse of its own actuality, achieved in its formal constitution.

There are objects other than occasions. The basic criterion for being an object is: to be a potential element in a concrescence. Thus each member of the many-for-α is an object in the analysis of the formal constitution of α. But if β is such an occasion, then in its own right β has its own concrescence. Also, the various patterns are objects, because they are possible modes in which the other actual occasions enter into the formal constitution of a concrescent occasion as subpatterns of the formal constitution. In addition, in an occasion viewed as an act of experience there may be a feeling of a pattern not realized in the many for that occasion. This feeling of something missing is an essential element in the concrescence: It involves ideals. Thus a pattern may be exemplified in an occasion in distinct modes.

If x is any object in the many-for-α, then this preliminary classification of objects shows that either (1) x is an actual occasion, functioning as an object for α, or (2) x is a pattern, functioning as a potential for exemplification in α in some mode.

Suppose that we focus on an arbitrary occasion α in terms of its own concrescence. Then the object of analysis, called the formal constitution, is α itself. This is α as *process*, namely concrescence. The outline in the first section of the nature of the relationship of time to space through endurance should have prepared the reader to see that concrescence is not just another temporal process; it is the ground for the creation of time by the community of occasions. "Becoming" is not *in* time; time becomes. Time, it will be recalled, is defined by endurance of patterns *across* occasions; and this is a condition for many of the special modes of order in the universe. The system W (of actual occasions) must be necessary for time rather than time's being necessary for the system. Hence, the immediacy of an actual occasion is analyzable as "passage" but not passage *in* time.

In this concrescence of α, each occasion and each pattern in the many-for-α passes from the status of object — in which it is a potential for partial determination of α — to the status of *inclusion* or *exclusion* from the formal constitution. Thus, we can say that each of the objects in the many for that occasion is mapped into α in some determinate manner to achieve a definite concrete "location" in the formal constitution of α. This passage to definite concrete relationship is termed *prehension*. One says: in concrescence, for any object in the many-for-α there exists a prehension of that object by α. The occasion α is a "prehensive unification" of the many occasions in existence.

The prehensive unification of the many-for-α can be regarded as a passage into definite objective pattern for α and definite subjective form of this pattern. Every object is felt, under some elimination from the formal constitutions of the actual occasions in the world, and felt in some way. There is a self-consistent objective pattern to α and a harmony of subjective feelings of the objects. By this is meant: How any one object, say x, is felt depends upon the entire objective content as required to form a self-consistent pattern. Moreover, each occasion has a subjective aim which controls the concrescence: The occasion is "cybernetic." (In special cases, the subjective aim is trivial.)

It is clear that to provide an *analysis* of a prehension we need to consider a series beginning with the object x and terminating in some component of α. This series may be thought of as an integrative progression of feelings beginning with simple physical feelings of other occasions and conceptual feelings of patterns.

In this analysis it must be recalled that we assume that an occasion *is* a concrescence. Hence when an occasion functions as an object, its own complex unity of prehensions is drawn upon to establish the new prehension. In other words, there is elimination of components from the formal constitution of the object, if that object is an actual occasion.

One picture that may help the reader to obtain an intuitive grasp of the Whiteheadian system of thought is to take seriously the dictum that appears in *Process and Reality* more than once, namely "a feeling is a vector." In this case, the notation

$$x \rightarrow \alpha$$

is the "vector feeling" or x by α. Here x is among the many-for-α. The occasion is the complex of vector-feelings and so is a vector "space" (at least intuitively, if not by axiomatic construction). This suggests the following illustration.

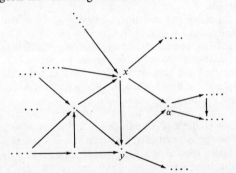

The nodes represent the occasions: Those pictured

to the left of α (the concrescent occasion) are representing objects for the α occasion. They are among the many-for-α which are felt by α, directly or indirectly. The actual world is a *medium*, so that x is felt also through y, and a remote occasion is one which is felt only through very many intermediaries. Occasions shown to the right of α are those in which α functions objectively: having become, attained definiteness in concrescence, it is available for feeling and is felt. At the "node" α we have an immediacy of *combined* vector feelings, achieving a complex pattern of the universe of occasions in its world. As actuality, α is a brief nodal pulse of attainment of individuality through synthesis: Its becoming is its perishing. For beyond itself only the vector components and not the nodal attainment are felt. Although the nature of reality is such that there is no object that is not locatable in a vector feeling, so that a mere x is nothing — what is required is some vector feeling of x — there is the pulse of actuality in the attainment of unity of many vector feelings in one complex integrated feeling which is the subject as creature of the process, perishing in subjectivity as its feelings become mere objects for creativity beyond itself. The vector space of feelings exhibits the actual occasion as abrupt, immediate, and perishing, the universe halting momentarily in the process of realization. The reality is before the occasion and beyond the occasion; the actuality is the immediacy of unification of what is before the occasion into something, an object, for that which lies beyond the occasion in novel concrescences of the world.

Feelings: Physical and Conceptual

Let β be an actual occasion in the many-for-α, where we are in the mode of analysis of the formal constitution of α. Then β has its own concrescence,

$$\text{many-for-}\beta \rightarrow \beta,$$

with its vector feelings,

$$y \rightarrow \beta,$$

where y is any object in the many-for-β.

The prehension of β by α begins with elimination of all but some components of the formal constitution of β. Only some of the vector feelings that constitute β are felt by α: This is a consequence of the world as a medium. The many feelings of β by occasions felt by α impose a task of elimination of "perspectives" inconsistent with each other. Thus, β is felt only "abstractly."

Let us write β^* for the felt components of β in the concrescence of α. Then the transformation,

$$\beta^* \rightarrow f(\beta^*)$$

is termed a *physical feeling*, with *initial datum* β, *objective datum* β^*, and *subjective form* $f(\beta^*)$. The concrescent occasion α is called the *subject* of the feeling.

In abstraction from the subject, the subjective form is a mere abstract form of feeling, expressed by words like "warm" or "hard." The wide, indeed unlimited, range of possibilities of these forms of feeling and the medium aspect, such that β might be quite remote, means that β might be felt in what amounts to an extremely "trivial" way. (Recall the physical hypothesis that *every* pair of bodies in the universe "attract each other" and that the rule of attraction generates a fading into triviality under certain conditions.)

The objective datum β^* is the *objectification* of β for α. The feeling of β is mediated by the pattern of β^*, itself a complex contrast of vector feelings in the world that are focussed about the feeling of β by other occasions, including the concrescent occasion. Thus the pattern of β^* is a form of synthesis, of composition, in which actualities are relegated to their role as elements in the composite pattern.

Patterns can function in α in diverse ways. For instance, there are the patterns of the objective data of feelings. There are the patterns of subjective forms of feeling. Later, when we discuss integration of feelings, there will arise patterns of integral data and integral subjective forms. The main distinction is between patterns of the objective data and patterns in the subjective forms. Both are forms of synthesis of feelings. But the objective patterns, those exemplified in the formation of β^* as the objectification of actual occasion β, are created by virtue of the many occasions feeling β. It is the complex contrast of the many feelings of β by *other* occasions which is *what* α feels that produces the public character of the pattern. Thus, that same pattern can be felt by other occasions. For example, shape is such a pattern. But with respect to the subjective forms the unified vector feelings are unified by α in novel synthesis, in which the subjective form of the feeling of β is but a subsidiary element in one balanced subjective feeling of the world. There is privacy in the feeling by one of the many, even as those many are objectified by virtue of their feelings of each other. For instance, "warm" is a pattern of this type. Both "shape" and "warm" are forms of synthesis of vector feelings, but one is public and the other private.

But, apart from all this, patterns also function as *data*. They are felt as possibilities quite apart from realization. They are lures for activity. An occasion is driven forward, so to speak, by the way in which a certain *possibility* is felt, a form that process *might* take. Thus, patterns also function as felt possibilities, which is not the same as saying that such possibilities are *consciously* felt. It is in the occasions in the life

histories of human beings, of course, that such patterns perform their widest role as felt possibilities. The whole basis of science, art, religion, and daily life is the challenge to mere *realized* pattern, to *fact,* presented by felt possibility, consciously or tacitly contrasted with fact.

So far it has been argued that patterns may function in "physical" realization and in "conceptual" realization. By conceptual realization in α one means that the occasion α feels the pattern itself as a possibility. This is the pattern as datum of a feeling. For instance, it is the dot pattern p rather than the occasions of the event E realizing p in a region R_E.

In this connection, we can note that the endurance of a pattern over a series of occasions—the earlier language referent to a pattern p of event E in region $R_E = R_p + R_p \ldots + R_p$—means in the simplest cases that the pattern of β^* is inherited in a following occasion by virtue of feelings of the component of the concrescent occasion α which includes the feeling of β^*. Thus, the realized pattern (of β^*) is "born" in α by a synthesis of the feelings of β in α's world; then when α is felt by α', say, this feeling of β is felt by α', thus reproducing the realized pattern in β^* in α'. The "region" idea is an abstraction from the synthesis to the possibility of the synthesis. In other words, space-time, or the extensive continuum, is the field of possibility for pattern realization, which is the same as saying that regions are placeholders for possible syntheses of vector feelings (origination) and for possible feelings of those syntheses (reiteration).

Our next problem is classification of various *modes of ingression* of patterns in an occasion. Three bases of classification exist. First, a pattern p which is exemplified in any way in the objective data will be termed *public* in α. A geometric form is an example. Thus, an arbitrary pattern p is either public or not in α.

Consider, now, the subjective forms of feelings. A pattern which is exemplified in any way in the subjective forms of feelings in that occasion is termed *private* in α. Hence, an arbitrary pattern is either private or not in α. For example, anger is such a pattern.

Consider the question of conceptual realization. Here the point is that the pattern becomes a *datum* of feeling, per se. Arbitrary pattern p which is taken as a datum is said to be *conceptually realized* in α. For brevity, I will also say that p is *ideal* in α if p is conceptually realized. Thus, arbitrary pattern p is either ideal in α or not.

Combining these three dichotomous possibilities yields eight possible paths or cells for classifying the modes of ingression of a pattern in an occasion.

There is an assumption that relates public to ideal realization; namely, each physical feeling gives rise

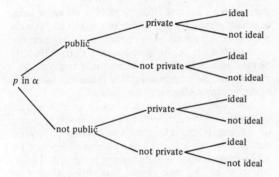

to a conceptual feeling of the pattern exemplified in the objective datum of the physical feeling.

This assumption amounts to saying that there is no such thing as an object, *as felt,* without its felt pattern. For instance, in feeling the particular exemplified dot pattern in your copy of this book you also are feeling the dot pattern in abstraction from its physical realization in the successive occasions of your reading. A remark by Whitehead is relevant at this point.[5] "Owing to the disastrous confusion, more especially by Hume, of conceptual with perceptual feelings, the truism that we can only *conceive* in terms of universals has been stretched to mean that we can only *feel* in terms of universals. This is untrue. Our perceptual feelings feel particular existents...." Here "perceptual feeling" is a type of physical feeling, that is, the initial data of the feeling are other actual occasions. But the initial data of the conceptual feelings are patterns in abstraction from their physical realization in those occasions. Moreover, of course, such patterns can be conceptually felt without the direct physical feeling of their exemplification in the occasion.

There may not be consciousness of the "pure" pattern as such, but there is always the feeling of the pattern which objectifies the initial datum by the synthesis previously described. Hence such a pattern has both a public and a conceptual mode of ingression in the occasion. To say that an entity in some occasion could not feel the pattern of β^* would be to imply that some other objectification of β would exist, if β is in the actual world of this occasion.

Note that the eight modes of ingression for a particular pair, a pattern and an occasion, are mutually exclusive: Each occasion in concrescence has each pattern ingredient in it in a single one of these modes of ingression, one of which is the special case "complete nonrealization." (Recall from the discussion of occasions the mention of the use of language to include special cases, i.e., the word as parameter.) Another important mode is *purely ideal realization* (*not* public, *not* private, but ideal). For example, one may think of a form of data analysis and only later, in another occasion, physically realize that pattern.

Nexus and Transmutation

Enduring objects are not actual occasions but complex series of occasions with some endurance of pattern amid the wealth of patterns exemplified in the data, the forms of feeling and the ideal ingressions, or ideas. In the metaphysical system that we are discussing these enduring objects are one type of nexus. A *nexus* is a real fact of togetherness of actual occasions in the actual world of a concrescent occasion. This fact is constituted by the feelings that the occasions have of each other. To see this vividly one can examine the following vector-feeling representation of a concrescence of α:

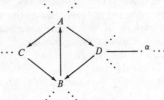

An example of a nexus in the world of α is given by occasions A and B. There is a vector feeling of B by A, and B in turn feels C and D, which feel A. Thus A and B form a nexus by virtue of their prehensions of each other, in one case direct and in the other mediated by other occasions. Also, A and B thereby feel each other in some particular objectifications reflecting how each is felt by the whole community of occasions. When α feels D, the actual world of α includes the A-B nexus. This nexus is part of the prevalent *order* in the world *given* for α. It may be seen from this picture that "boundaries" for nexus are only defined by elimination from the totality of vector feeling connectedness. Thus the whole actual world of α is a nexus with many subordinate nexus. The occasion does not create these nexus. They are stubborn facts for it. Higher-order occasions achieve depth of subjectivity by eliminations from the many data to focus on dominant modes of order in the actual world. Such an occasion is itself a "moment" in the life-history of some nexus with enduring pattern.

The next assumption relates nexus to our feeling that the world consists of things with properties. Let N be a nexus of actual occasions in the actual world of a concrescent occasion α. Then if the conceptual feeling of the pattern of each of several occasions in N is the same, the subject of the feelings may *transmute* this datum to make it a form of the nexus. Then the nexus is felt as "one thing," with that pattern as its form.

For example, suppose that N is the nexus of occasions A and B just described and that A and B are felt by α, via D and other occasions:

$$A^* \to f(A^*)$$
$$B^* \to f(B^*)$$

Then, by earlier assumption, each such physical feeling is accompanied by a conceptual feeling of the pattern of the respective objective datum, say, p in A^* and q in B^*. Now if $p = q$, the new assumption says that this p may be attached to the nexus, as such. Then the nexus is felt as a unity, with form p.

Thus, with respect to a nexus in the actual world we have to distinguish (1) the nexus itself, with its reality as an object established by the prehensive connectedness to each other of the members of the nexus, (2) the way in which such a nexus may be felt as a unity in some concrescent occasion. The nexus itself may illustrate a variety of patterns, woven together into the fabric of the nexus, so to speak. As felt by different subjects, then, the nexus may exhibit a variety of the forms mentioned in the preceding new assumption, because of the diverse membership of the nexus and the diverse physical feelings of the subjects.

To review briefly, we have concrescence,

$$\text{many-for-}\alpha \rightarrow \alpha,$$

analyzable into prehensions

$$x \rightarrow \alpha,$$

where x is in the many-for-α. Then an example of such a prehension was a physical feeling, in which x is an actual occasion, say β. We wrote,

$$\beta^* \rightarrow f(\beta^*)$$

to mean that β is objectified for the concrescent occasion by β^* and felt under the subjective form $f(\beta^*)$. The associated derived conceptual feeling may be denoted

$$p \rightarrow v(p),$$

where p is the pattern exemplified in β^*. As β^* is the objectified version of β it has a definite form which is p, and the existence of β^* for α physically means that α is also feeling the pattern itself.

The notation $v(p)$ for the subjective form of the conceptual feeling of p is chosen because this subjective form is called a *valuation*. A valuation is the subjective form with which a pattern is felt.

Passing to nexus, with N a nexus in the actual world of α, a transmutation of N as the datum of the many derived conceptual feelings may be denoted,

$$N^* \rightarrow f(N^*)$$

where N^* signifies that nexus N is felt as a unity with a form, say p. Since p is felt as $v(p)$, we also have a valuation $v(p)$ associated with the feeling of the nexus.

We note that a nexus may be such that there exists a pattern p exemplified in *each* member of the nexus. This alone would only mean that an occasion may feel the nexus as a unity. But there is a stronger sense in which p may be ingredient in the nexus. Namely, p may be inherited or reproduced throughout the nexus because of the prehensions that define the nexus. This is the notion of an enduring object: It means that the common form is sustained by reason of the occasions forming the nexus.

In any case, it is clear that we can regard these nexus as the *concrete systems* from which science takes its starting point. They are the bodies in physics: pendulums, vibrating strings, planets. They are the actors in sociology: human beings, groups, and larger collectivities. Science, then, starts with enduring objects, strands of occasions felt as unities with form; and theoretical ideas are developed around various analytical systems that may be descriptive or explanatory of patterns exemplified amid this endurance.

One final point is necessary which relates to derived conceptual feelings. When p is derived from a felt exemplification and becomes the datum of a conceptual feeling, it is possible that the pattern derived involves what Whitehead calls *reversion*. This means that new patterns can enter process without direct derivation from a physical feeling, so that purely ideal realization is involved. These patterns may be only slight perturbations of the exemplified patterns in the data, or they may involve wider divergence. In any case, we assume in the following notation that p may be the result of some reversion. The reversion depends upon the subjective aim controlling the concrescence.

Propositions in Process

An *integral feeling* is a "binary operation" on feelings: It combines a pair of feelings in one new feeling, just as addition takes a pair of numbers into a number. Any finite number of feelings may be integrated.

The basic integral feelings we want to consider as a foundation for the subsequent work concern propositions. Propositions enter into process by becoming *data* for feelings. The role of propositions in process can only be described appropriately by *not* focussing on the issue of truth-value. This truth-value interest is a special aspect of the subjective form in some occasions. In general, propositions will play a role in process as "lures for feeling."

A proposition cannot be felt by an actual occasion unless it is in the actual world for that occasion. For instance, Aristotle could not feel the proposition that Kennedy was assassinated. The metaphysical problem is make clear in what sense propositions are in the actual world at all, for a given subject. The theory is elaborate, and it relies on the background of the *Principia Mathematica,* while not being drawn into the narrowness of a purely logical or linguistic point of view. For our purposes, it is only necessary to note that propositions are differentially located in the actual worlds of occasions, with the basic requirement being that there be actual occasions in the actual world such that they can function as logical subjects ("elements" of a predicative pattern) for the particular proposition. The multiplicity of all actual worlds such that such requisite occasions exist is called the *locus* of the proposition. The proposition is itself an object, i.e., in the technical sense a potential for role in process, if it is in the actual world of an occasion. However, it may not be felt. Thus, a proposition is the potentiality of a certain *predication* occurring in process: namely, that certain specified objects in the actual world satisfy a specified pattern, which functions as that which is predicated of the objects.

Thus, any proposition in abstraction from its role in concrescence can be considered as a *hybrid entity* involving (1) actual occasions as objects potential for being logical subjects in the proposition and (2) a pattern as a potential for predication involving those logical subjects. Strictly speaking, there are different kinds of propositions as to generality, but for explication let us deal with the simplest type: so-called singular propositions. For example, that Kennedy was assassinated is a singular proposition present in the actual world of any occasion subsequent to the event which was the assassination. The nexus which constituted Kennedy, as a route of occasions, will function in the proposition only in a "logical" role as logical subject. A logical subject is an occassion or a nexus divested of its full actuality with retention of its identification as that to which the pattern applies. Thus, whenever a proposition does enter process some sort of feeling of the actual world must occur which transforms selected occasions or nexüs into logical subjects of a proposition. Also, the pattern must be ingredient in the process in some mode of ingression which involves realization. Thus a singular proposition enters process by integration of a feeling of a nexus that transforms it into the set of logical subjects in a pattern itself ingredient in the occasion. The proposition is then the integral datum of the integral feeling.

To continue this drastic simplification of the theory of propositions presented by Whitehead, I will describe one basic species of *propositional feelings,* defined as follows: A feeling in this class is an integral feeling based upon (1) a feeling called "indicative," which identifies the particulars of the predicative pattern; (2) a feeling called "physical recognition," which is a physical feeling basis for the predicative pattern; and (3) a feeling termed "predicative," which has the predicative pattern as datum arrived at by abstraction (with possible reversion) from the

physical recognition. Feelings (1) and (2) are physical in that their data are in the actual world, while (3) is conceptual. The propositional feeling is integral with respect to these three feelings.

Let N be the nexus of occasions to become the logical subjects. Let M be the nexus which is the datum for physical recognition, so that it provides the basis for the pattern, say p.

These propositional feelings may now be readily classified as to their component structure. The tree shown in the diagram will help fix ideas.

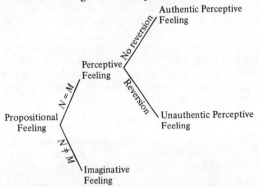

In the tree, we show the major possibilities for systematic classification. If the nexus of logical subjects is not the physical feeling basis for the predicative pattern we term the propositional feeling "imaginative," otherwise we call it "perceptive." Then, there is the important question as to whether the subject exhibits reversion with respect to the derived conceptual feeling, based on physical recognition. If so, then the perceptive feeling is called "unauthentic." If no reversion occurs the predicative pattern is a physically recognized pattern in abstraction from its exemplification in $M,$ as felt, and we term the perceptive feeling "authentic."

At this point it is necessary to introduce two cautionary notes by way of anticipation of higher-order integrations. First, language is not a necessary condition for these propositional feelings. A dog can feel a proposition. What is required is that a certain contrast be felt in the process, namely the contrast with two components: (1) physical feeling of some actualities (the logical subjects) and (2) the predicative pattern. But the latter does not require a verbal predicate. This introduces the second caution. Consciousness is treated as a very high-order contrast in a subjective form of an integral feeling. The implications of this should be clear: In concrescence there *may arise* consciousness. But concrescence is not dependent upon the existence of consciousness in that or any preceding occasion. Also, what is felt consciously is only a portion of the feelings integrated to constitute the formal constitution of the given occasion. This corresponds to our intuitive judgments about the nature of consciousness and to the character of any "realistic" action theory.

We may symbolize an integral feeling which combines a simple physical feeling and a conceptual feeling as follows:

$$(\beta^*, p) \rightarrow (f(\beta^*), v(p)),$$

where the component integrated feelings are the simple physical feeling of β in terms of its objectification β^* and subjective form $f(\beta^*)$, and the conceptual feeling of the pattern of β^*, say p, with valuation $v(p)$. In a propositional feeling of the type just discussed, the datum is more complex: N is felt, M is felt, and a pattern is derived or originated from the M-feeling. Thus the bare proposition is the datum (N,p) of the feeling. The subjective form involves how that subject feels that proposition. By analogy with the previous notation, we may write,

$$(N,p) \rightarrow (f(N), v(p)).$$

To symbolize the higher-order integration of the physical feeling of the nexus N and the propositional feeling referent to the nexus, let us first define the notation.

$$V(N,p) = (f(N), v(p))$$

for the subjective form of the proposition. Then an *intellectual feeling* based on the proposition is given by the integral feeling of the form,

$$(N, (N,p)) \rightarrow (f(N), V(N,p))$$

whose subjective form involves consciousness: a contrast between the way the nexus is felt and the complex valuation of the proposition expressing a potential for pattern in that nexus.

To illustrate some of these concepts, I will apply them to the context of an act of measurement. For this purpose, we need to introduce a certain type of intellectual feeling. Depending upon which of the three types of propositional feelings is integrated in the intellectual feeling, we note one of two types of intellectual feelings. If the intellectual feeling is based on a propositional feeling of the type termed authentic or unauthentic perception, it is termed *conscious perception*. If the propositional feeling is imaginative, then the intellectual feeling is termed an *intuitive judgment*.

These intuitive judgments are the bedrock of science, in which a proposition derived imaginatively (i.e., not by any physical recognition involving the logical subjects) is contrasted as a potential for pattern of some nexus with the way that nexus is felt. Clear agreement or negation are two special cases; just as important is the case in which the judgment takes a "suspense" form. In this form, the

nexus has a felt pattern not excluding the predicative pattern of the imaginative propositional feeling, but on the other hand the two patterns are not identical. The subject is conscious of what could *also* be the case in the nexus.

For the example, consider an act of physical measurement. At some point, such measurement always involves a direct intuitive judgment of congruence or equivalence of distinct items. A unit is selected: this is some nexus labelled, say, "inch." Any nexus "congruent" with the inch, in a specific conceptual meaning of this term, is also called an inch. And a measured nexus is said to be so many inches, meaning: The measured nexus is congruent with so many inches.

In practice, a single nexus (a ruler) is compared with the measured nexus. In terms of the above distinctions, there is an imaginative propositional feeling based on the ruler (M) while the conscious feeling has as its datum the contrast $(N, (N,p))$ between the measured nexus N and the proposition about N having the predicative pattern p derived from the ruler: "so many inches long." The intuitive judgment is the feeling of this contrast. Without such a basis in many intuitive judgments the hardest of sciences would be impossible. Every act of measurement resolves itself into an intuitive judgment in an actual occasion involving a concrescent subject in an actual world. In turn, such occasions are controlled by the subjective aim at affirmation or negation of a potential contrast between some felt nexus and some propositions referent to the nexus. In other words, the occasion in arising from its past is dominated by the urge to realize an intellectual feeling of a certain type: the intuitive judgment consequently reached in concrescence. In terms of ancient philosophical distinctions, the subjective aim at the intuitive judgment is the final cause which animates the process.

THE ABSTRACT ACTION SYSTEM

Introduction

Process metaphysics provides a basis for discriminating various types of abstraction. For present purposes, it provides part of the conceptual background for action theory. In particular, it helps to introduce coherence into discourse about "systems" of the analytical type as compared with "concrete systems." Of course, according to the metaphysics, abstraction is exemplified in every occasion because "to abstract" means "to eliminate something." Each occasion involves other occasions objectively, in abstraction from their formal constitutions. Thus every concrescence exemplifies abstraction in some degree. But in action theory the concern is with a domain of entities—primarily "actors"—whose occasions are "high-grade." This means that they take cognizance of the enduring objects in their actual worlds and of the patterns exemplified in such objects.

The enduring objects recognized by human beings, such as stones, trees, mountains, and living beings, are the "particulars" of their experience. A mountain may not have a name, but its insistent particularity is what the human being feels: *its* realized pattern, reiterated in process. This pattern recognition is accompanied, on many occasions, with the entertainment of propositions referent to the enduring object. These propositions relate to patterns in which the object functions as one among a possible multiplicity of logical subjects. For example, the proposition may have a predicative pattern involving the mountain and the stream. These two complex enduring objects, embedded in the actual world of occasions, are felt, say, to be related. This feeling of relatedness may be expressed by a verbal statement, "The stream is near the mountain." The logical subjects of this proposition comprise a complex nexus in the actual world, inclusive of the two subordinate nexus which are the mountain and the stream. For the subject all this complexity is transmuted into three entities: the mountain, the stream, and the relatedness of "being near to," with the words symbolic of these entities. The relatedness is the deepest truth about the actual world, but in the verbal formula based on transmutations, the relatedness almost appears abstract. For the subject, however, in an actual occasion, there is likely to be little hesitation about relatedness. For process metaphysics, relations are patterns realized in nexüs in the actual world. A binary relation is a very special type of pattern, felt by abstraction from the multiple relations that constitute the richer patterns ingredient in the actual world. Nevertheless, for action theory at least, such simplifications are part of the data about subjects: The actor is a great simplifier.

At the level of a community of human beings, then, we are likely to find an evolving series of modes of transmutation that form a communal world of (1) enduring objects felt under transmutation as things with properties and (2) observable relations among such objects. Whereas metaphysics would say that what is concrete is the formal constitution of the actual occasion, discourse in theoretical science names the enduring entities in the communal world "concrete." Thus a man is concrete, and a man striking a dog is a concrete relationship involving two concrete things. Upon this communal world, science builds its world-picture as an evolving conceptual system for relating the entities in this communal

world to a "deeper" view which penetrates to the composition of enduring objects and to the multiple relatedness of occasions of the actual world. The postulation of entities such as fields of force and radiation belts accompanies the effort to represent the details of experience of the actual world, such details having been eliminated in the accommodation of humanity to the more obvious modes of order in the environment. Thus, abstract modes of composition are conceived scientifically that restore details, but such details comprehended in terms of abstract pattern exemplification. For instance, the sun may be treated as a continuum of particles and a man as a system of roles.

It will be recalled that an enduring object is a special kind of nexus, one which exhibits pattern repetition in a series of actual occasions and in which this pattern is derived from the prehensions of other members of the nexus. It is useful to add that an enduring object may be "corpuscular" in the sense that its component occasions form subordinate strands of enduring objects. Indeed, a physical object is such a nexus with such strands of endurance, for example, as its molecular composition. Unless otherwise specified, "enduring object" means such a corpuscular nexus. Further, to make contact with language outside of Whitehead's system, I shall say that by a *concrete system* I mean such a corpuscular enduring object. Some examples are: physical bodies, plants, animals, machines, persons, groups, societies.

Such concrete systems must be contrasted with abstract and applied analytical systems. Whereas the "members" of a concrete system are actual occasions in interwoven strands of endurance, the "members" of an analytical system are propositions with a domain of unspecified actual occasions—usually treated in terms of a set of unspecified concrete systems—and a pattern involving the potential relatedness of the occasions. The multiplicity of unspecified entities in the analytical system may be termed its *primitive entities*. An *analytical element* is a mapping over the domain of primitive entities into some abstract space of "values," in the sense of qualitative or quantitative elements. The structure of the analytical system is the manner in which these analytical elements form a pattern. For example, they may form an abstract dynamic system whose properties are the subject of analytical study and, in the more precise and coherent cases, mathematical analysis.

By an *identification* of such an analytical system one means a mapping relating the domain of primitive entities to some domain of concrete systems. For instance, in a system of two particles the mapping may identify one particle as the sun and the other as the earth. In a continuum-of-particles system the mapping may be such as to identify the continuum with the entire sun, so that the image of the entire continuous space of primitive entities is the one concrete system. Such flexibility is inherent in the nature of an analytical system. It means that such a system has no definite "strings" which tie it down descriptively to particular concrete systems. Rather, it has the potential for diverse identifications even with respect to one concrete system in the same circumstances. It cannot be emphasized too strongly that the entire structure of the action scheme is predicated upon the construction of a framework such that its analytical systems have this flexibility.

Identification also includes identifying a sufficient number of the analytical elements—the mappings with domain the primitive entities, such as their properties and relations—to provide a determinate model of the entire set of relevant properties and relations of the identified entities. With sufficient degrees of freedom, some of these remaining properties stand as "computed" and predicted vis-a-vis their actual values in the concrete system. If these predictions are sufficiently accurate, we may say that the concrete system exemplifies the analytical pattern as one of its aspects. In anticipation of this finding, one could say that the aim of the theoretical model was to describe *an analytically distinct subsystem* of concrete system. In this sense, every *fitting* model testifies to the probable existence of such a subsystem.

In Parsons' theoretical work, there is aim at high generality as well as at analytical system formulation. In the following I reproduce some of his most general work in the abstract analytical system form. It is still not all coherent, but it may be useful in passage to a more coherent statement of the nature of the general system. Because of the generality of this system—in theory, if not in fact—it is not possible to appeal to special interpretations that would make the theory less general but more comprehensible. For example, a claim is made as to "duality" that makes some psychological sense if the actors are human beings, but if the actors are collectivities this argument does not apply. Thus in writing down some of these notions I admit to their lack of intuitive meaningfulness at all levels, at least so far as I can see. But one reason for being formal is to reveal the *need* for interpretation. Here "interpretation" means a rule of correspondence to a class of concrete systems such that purely formal notions receive meanings that allow a decision to be made about the adequacy of the theoretical analysis. In other words, interpretation is *general* identification. I think this is the aspect of the work to follow that is weakest. My concentration has been on the questions: What are the abstract entities under discussion? What formal assumptions apply to them? The answers are not complete, but I have made a start at framing them.

My primary reference for the following work is Parsons "Pattern Variables Revisited" article.[6]

Basic Notions

Let

$pv_1 = \{D, \bar{D}\}$	(diffuseness-specificity)
$pv_2 = \{A, \bar{A}\}$	(affectivity-neutrality)
$pv_3 = \{P, \bar{P}\}$	(particularism-universalism)
$pv_4 = \{Q, \bar{Q}\}$	(quality-performance)

These are the four dichotomous pattern variables of Parsons and his co-workers.

Also, there exists a nonempty set, denote it Q, termed *the system*. Any u in Q will be termed a *unit*.

There is a relation on Q, denote it 0, called *orientation,* and another relation on Q, denote it M, called *modality.*

Definition P1. An *actor* in Q is any unit in Q such that (u, u) is in the orientation relation 0, and we denote an actor, generically, by $\alpha, \beta, \ldots$ Any unit which is not an actor will be termed a *non-actor.*

If (α, u) is in 0 we say that α has an orientation toward u. If (α, u) are in M we say that u has a modality for α. The relatedness of (α, u) in 0 is called their orientation relationship: it is a specific exemplification of 0 in the system Q, for this pair.

Assumption P1. Let (α, u) be in the 0 relation. Then there is a unique value of pv_1 and a unique value of pv_2 such that these two patterns are realized in the orientation relationship.

In other words, if we let

$$pv_1 \times pv_2 = \{DA, D\bar{A}, \bar{D}A, \bar{D}\bar{A}\},$$

then by Assumption P1, for any orientation relationship in Q there is a unique value in $pv_1 \times pv_2$ exemplified in the relatedness of (α, u).

Assumption P2. Let (α, u) be in the M relation. Then there is a unique value of pv_3 and a unique value of pv_4 such that these two patterns are realized in the modality relationship.

In other words, if we let

$$pv_3 \times pv_4 = \{PQ, P\bar{Q}, \bar{P}Q, \bar{P}\bar{Q}\},$$

then by Assumption P2, for any modality relationship in Q, there is a unique value in $pv_3 \times pv_4$ exemplified in the relatedness of (α, u).

Assumption P3. If x is a non-actor, then there is no pair (x, u) in the orientation relation 0, for any u in Q.

If u is in Q, then either u is an actor (α-notation) or a non-actor, by Definition P1. Only actors "have orientations," i.e., stand in the relation O as first members.

Assumption P4. A pair (x, u) is in the O relation if and only if it is in the $\mathcal{M}$ relation.

From Assumption P4 and Definition P1, it follows that an actor always stands in the modality relationship to itself, because if α is an actor, then (α, α) is in O and so, by Assumption P4, we have (α, α) in $\mathcal{M}$.

Also, suppose x is a non-actor. Then x has no modality for itself, for if it did then we would have (x, x) in O, a contradiction.

Further, if x is a non-actor, then no object has a modality for x. For if x is a non-actor, then by Assumption P3, no pair of the form (x, u) is in O, and so by Assumption P4, no pair of the form (x, u) is in

Definition P2. A couple of units, denoted αu, is said to form an *elementary dynamic component* of system $\mathcal{Q}$ if and only if:

(i) α is an actor, i.e., (α, α) in O; and,
(ii) (α, u) is in O, and if u is an actor, then also (u, α) is in O.

If, also, u is an actor we term the component of *interactive* type, and then we write $\alpha\beta$.

Then, by Assumption P4, it follows that if $\alpha\beta$ is of the interactive type, then both (α, β) and (β, α) are in the $\mathcal{M}$ relation.

Definition P3. If αu is an elementary dynamic component, we term u a *situational object* for α.

Note that if u is an actor, then u is also a situational object for α as well as an actor. Also, every pair $\alpha\alpha$ is an interactive elementary component, since (α, α) in O. Hence every actor is a situational object for itself. Also, there are no situational objects apart from orientations, because we require (α, u) in O.

Let αu be an elementary dynamic component. Then by Assumption P1, we can map αu into $pv_1 \times pv_2$ by attending to the O relationship of α to u.

We write this as,

$$\alpha u \overset{O}{\to} pv_1 \times pv_2.$$

For instance, the form

$$O(\alpha u) = \text{DA}$$

means: the orientation relationship of actor α to unit u exemplifies the pattern DA (diffuseness and affectivity).

Similarly, by Assumption P2 we can map αu into $pv_3 \times pv_4$ by attending to the modality of u for α. We write,

$$\alpha u \overset{\mathcal{M}}{\to} pv_3 \times pv_4$$

For instance,

$$\mathcal{M}(\alpha u) = \text{PQ}$$

means: the modality of u for α exemplifies the patterns of particularism and quality. In the above, " O' and "$\mathcal{M}$" do double duty to symbolize, first, relations and then corresponding maps. This avoids cluttering the notation.

Let αu be an elementary component of the non-interactive type. Then, by joint mapping under O and $\mathcal{M}$,

$$\alpha u \to [\ O(\alpha u),\ \ \mathcal{M}(\alpha u)\ ],$$
$$\alpha\alpha \to [\ O(\alpha\alpha),\ \ \mathcal{M}(\alpha\alpha)\ ],$$

may be said to carry αu into its *state*. There are $4^4 = 256$ possible states.

Suppose that αu is an interactive elementary component, and write $u = \beta$. Then we introduce *four* joint mappings, namely,

$$\alpha\beta \to [\ O(\alpha\beta),\ \mathcal{M}(\alpha\beta)\ ]$$
$$\beta\alpha \to [\ O(\beta\alpha),\ \mathcal{M}(\beta\alpha)\ ]$$
$$\alpha\alpha \to [\ O(\alpha\alpha),\ \mathcal{M}(\alpha\alpha)\ ]$$
$$\beta\beta \to [\ O(\beta\beta),\ \mathcal{M}(\beta\beta)\ ]$$

The configuration on the right is called the *state* of the interactive component. One may picture it graphically as shown in Figure 5-1.

There are four possible patterns in each part of the interactive component. Hence, a priori — i.e., before theory restricts these possibilities — we have $4^8 = 2^{16}$ possibilities. This number is 65,536.

Note that from the definition of the state of an interactive component the state of $\beta\alpha$ is given by mapping $\beta\alpha$ under O and $\mathcal{M}$:

$$[O(\beta\alpha), \mathcal{M}(\beta\alpha)]$$
$$[O(\alpha\beta), \mathcal{M}(\alpha\beta)]$$
$$[O(\beta\beta), \mathcal{M}(\beta\beta)]$$
$$[O(\alpha\alpha), \mathcal{M}(\alpha\alpha)].$$

By interchanging various lines of this array, we see that this is the identical set of patterns characterizing $\alpha\beta$. Hence, the state of an elementary dynamic component of the interactive type $\alpha\beta$ is the same as the state of $\beta\alpha$: an interactive pair has a single state description.

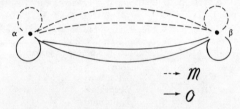

Figure 5-1. The state of the interactive component.

The question immediately arises if all possible states are exemplified in $\mathcal{U}$ by the elementary components αu, as we let α and u vary. While each may be realized in *some* pair in *some* time span, the scientific question involving the dynamics of state has several aspects: (1) What is the time-trajectory, starting from some initial condition in some specified component? (2) Is there an equilibrium state such that if αu starts in that state then it stays there? (3) If an equilibrium exists, is it unique? Does it possess stability? The last question means that if the initial state is, say, for a dynamic noninteractive component at $t = 0$:

$$[\, \mathcal{Q}_0(\alpha u), \; \mathcal{M}_0(\alpha u) \,]$$

then as $t \rightarrow \infty$, the component approaches the equilibrium state. Finally, (4) How does the stable state, or set of states, if it exists, depend on the parametric conditions?

An analysis which is such as to assume stable states exist and which proceeds to characterize or stipulate them may be called *comparative statics* if it nevertheless specifies stable states as functions of the varying conditions of the system. It seems that Parsons' work falls in this category.

The range of values that can be taken by the state of a dynamic process is called the *state-space*. Thus αu has a state-space of 256 elements if u is a non-actor. But if u is an actor, the elementary dynamic interactive component has over 65,000 states.

Duality

Let $\alpha\beta$ be an elementary dynamic interactive component. Then the state is given by

$$[\, \mathcal{O}(\alpha\beta), \mathcal{M}(\alpha\beta)]$$
$$[\, \mathcal{O}(\beta\alpha), \mathcal{M}(\beta\alpha)]$$
$$[\, \mathcal{O}(\alpha\alpha), \mathcal{M}(\alpha\alpha)]$$
$$[\, \mathcal{O}(\beta\beta), \mathcal{M}(\beta\beta)].$$

The following is a metaphysical account of the action scheme's *duality*. Regard $\mathcal{O}(\alpha\beta)$ and $\mathcal{M}(\beta\alpha)$ as the same pattern in two-way functioning: $\mathcal{O}(\alpha\beta)$ is the subjective form under which this pattern is realized, while $\mathcal{M}(\beta\alpha)$ is the objective type of realization. For example, what is affectivity for the subjective form (of orientation of α to β) is performance (in the

modality of α for β). Thus, concretely, an exhibited responsive action by α to β is taken to realize a pattern (say "active") under two exemplifications: affectivity and performance. The latter is the exterior mapping of the activity, the former is its subjective form. This is essentially the argument given in the *Working Papers*:

> ...making all due allowances for peculiarities of terminology which reflect the special paths by which the conceptions have developed, we may say that affectivity is directly linked with performance in that, *as distinguished from neutrality,* on the motivational side of the conceptual scheme it signifies the *release* of an impulse into actual overt behavior. Performance on the other hand is the corresponding behavior seen from an observer's point of view: that is to say, it is *the same thing as affectivity* [italics in original] with "actor" seen as *object* rather than as an agent of action. This relation between affectivity and performance provides the prototype for treating all of the pattern variable components in terms of their relationships *across* the motivational-situational axis of the system rather than as confined to one or the other side of it.[7]

There are, however, some difficulties of interpretation in trying to carry out this strategy in all cases. For the present I will assume it can be done and defer discussion to the last part of this paper.

Thus the scheme of two-way pattern functioning creates a duality in the state space. We equate pattern variable values under the rubrics "interior form" and "exterior map," using "interior" instead of "subjective" for greater connotative generality. Also, "underlying" patterns isomorphically exemplified in the interior form and exterior map are denoted in a content-free manner by: Π_1 and Π_2. Their "opposites" are denoted $\bar{\Pi}_1$ and $\bar{\Pi}_2$, respectively, with the precise idea of "opposite" gradually unfolding as we proceed.

Table 5-1 provides these basic duality correspondences.

The next assumption effects the state-space reduction.

Assumption P5. (1) For any elementary dynamic interactive component, either Π_1 is realized or $\bar{\Pi}_1$ is realized. (2) For any elementary dynamic component, either Π_2 is realized or $\bar{\Pi}_2$ is realized. Also, the pair Π_1-$\bar{\Pi}_1$ cannot be jointly realized and the pair Π_2-$\bar{\Pi}_2$ cannot be jointly realized.

Table 5-1. DUALITY CORRESPONDENCES

	INTERIOR FORM		EXTERIOR MAP		
	Name	*Symbol*	*Symbol*	*Name*	
(Π_1)	Affectivity	$\underline{A}$	$\bar{Q}$	Performance	(Π_1)
$(\bar{\Pi}_1)$	Neutrality	A	Q	Quality	$(\bar{\Pi}_1)$
(Π_2)	Diffuseness	$\underline{D}$	P	Particularism	(Π_2)
$(\bar{\Pi}_2)$	Specificity	D	$\bar{P}$	Universalism	$(\bar{\Pi}_2)$

Using this assumption, a tree diagram provides the four possible paths of realized $\Pi_i (i = 1, 2)$ together with corresponding interior form and exterior map based on Table 5-1. For reference later, we call the tree "T," as shown on the left in the following illustration.

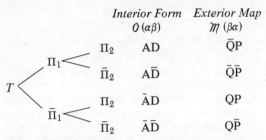

		Interior Form $O(\alpha\beta)$	Exterior Map $\mathcal{M}(\beta\alpha)$
Π_1	Π_2	AD	$\bar{Q}P$
	$\bar{\Pi}_2$	$A\bar{D}$	$\bar{Q}\bar{P}$
$\bar{\Pi}_1$	Π_2	$\bar{A}D$	QP
	$\bar{\Pi}_2$	$\bar{A}\bar{D}$	$Q\bar{P}$

The column of interior forms $O(\alpha\beta)$ contains what Parsons calls "elementary orientation patterns" or, in other contexts, "value patterns." The column of exterior maps $\mathcal{M}(\beta\alpha)$ contains what he calls "elementary modality patterns" or, in other contexts, "cognitive patterns." A "pattern" in this sense is any element of pv_i or of $pv_i \times pv_j$ ($i, j = 1, 2, 3, 4, i \neq j$). Thus there are other possible patterns, in this sense, to appear shortly as normative and adaptive patterns.

In the type of "boxing" used in Parsons' "Pattern Variables Revisited," we represent the tree T by Figure 5-2.

The particular ordering of patterns in the cells of Figure 5-2 is chosen for reasons that will become clear later in the analysis.

We recall that the state space for an elementary interactive component had 2^{16} possible values of orientation-modality patterns. The preceding assumptions reduce this space considerably. From

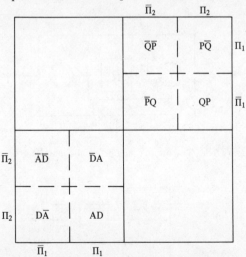

Figure 5-2. Parsons' representation of the tree T.

Figure 5-3.

$O(\alpha\beta)$ we know $\mathcal{M}(\beta\alpha)$ and from $\mathcal{M}(\alpha\beta)$ we know $O(\beta\alpha)$, by interchanging α and β in tree T. Similarly, $O(\alpha\alpha)$ yields $\mathcal{M}(\alpha\alpha)$ and $\mathcal{M}(\beta\beta)$ yields $O(\beta\beta)$.

Thus, the number of possible states is reduced from $4^8 = 2^{16} = 65,536$ to $4^4 = 2^8 = 256$. The graphical image is now shown in Figure 5-3.

If we know (1) the self-orientation of α, (2) the orientation of α to β, (3) the modality of β for α, and (4) the modality of β for β, then we know the state of the component, for the remaining parts are calculated from the givens. (Other combinations of "givens" versus "calculated" parts of the total state are possible, of course.)

The result just given is based on the duality of the pattern-variable scheme. The next question that arises is the character of the dynamics and of the stable states, with reference to the whole system in which a given pair is imbedded.

Dynamics

The system $\mathcal{Q}$ is conceptualized in terms of modern systems theory as a feedback system in steady interaction with an environment. The only way to see the behavior properly is by the tools engineers have invented for coherent discourse about systems.[8]

The picture of $\mathcal{Q}$ is shown in Figure 5-4. Although we label the middle block by "$\mathcal{Q}$," this is only one part of the system, as is clear from the entire diagram. The description of the system in symbolic terms is:

(1) $\Delta X = f(X, i, e) \cdot \Delta t$

(2) $r = g(X, i)$

The explanation of all this is as follows. $\mathcal{Q}$ is a system with state-description (more or less complex set of variables) given by X, as a function of time. Process involves moving $\mathcal{Q}$ along a state-space of values of X, as time varies. Equation (1) says: In-the-small from time t to time $t + \Delta t$ the *change of state* ΔX depends on (1) the current state X; (2) the current input i from the environment; (3) the most recent response-feedback (also denoted by r, the response itself), all acting through a time Δt. For example, if there were no input and no separate response term, one exemplification of equation (1) might be:

$$\Delta X = 2X \cdot \Delta t,$$

which describes exponential growth of the state variable. Equation (2) says: the current output to the environment, called response, is a function of the current state and the input.

We can eliminate from particular aspects of the

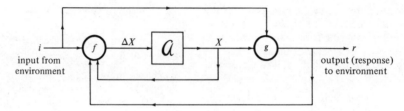

Figure 5-4.   The system $\mathcal{A}$.

process to see certain crucial distinctions. Thus, Figures 5-5 shows the $\mathcal{A}$-system as having both an *internal* and an *external* dynamics.

These are analytically separable, as seen by the still greater elimination to the black-box standpoint shown in Figure 5-6.

In the black-box representation, only external dynamics appear to exist. The internal-external distinction is essentially the state versus the response, or inner versus outer. As such it is a distinction of central significance in the modern state-space approach in systems theory.[9]

But *within* this first external-internal distinction, there is an *inner* distinction of external-internal (involving the functions f and g in the symbolism). That is, f and g locate two processes by which the entire system is related to its environment: one on the receptive or input side, the other on the output side. Thus (recalling environmental inputs to both the f and g operators), we have the *analytically distinct subsystems*:

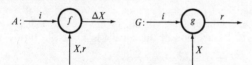

These have been labelled by the Parsons' symbolism. The *adaptive (A) subsystem* of $\mathcal{A}$ maps the input from the environment into a "change of state message" which is incorporated into the system by a transition to a new state. The *goal-attainment (G) subsystem* of $\mathcal{A}$ maps the input into an output by reference to the current state, itself modified by the very input it carries into an output.

Relative to the internal dynamics, the inside of the black box in the first internal-external distinction, then, we have two subprocesses of the over-all process of system $\mathcal{A}$ which relate   to its environment. Let E and $\bar{E}$ be the external and the internal aspects of the dynamics of any system. Then we are now analyzing $\bar{E}$ of $\mathcal{A}$. We have found two analytically distinct inner aspects of $\bar{E}$ itself referent to inputs and to outputs to the environment, respectively: A and G. Thus the following important statement results: A and G are both *external* aspects *of* the internal dynamics, where "external" preserves its meaning of

relating $\mathcal{A}$ to its environment on the input or on the output side as in Figure 5-7. Here E designates the external subprocesses of the internal dynamics.

Turning now to the "inner" feature of the dynamics shown in Figure 5-5, we have Figure 5-8.

This is undifferentiated process: X is simply changing, with all previous distinctions combined to create the transition magnitude ΔX of the state. Nevertheless, even this simple picture makes sense only if $\mathcal{A}$ is preserved in its defining characteristic as X changes. Thus a pattern of nexus $\mathcal{A}$ must be assumed, as a feature of *theoretical* dynamic analysis, as repeated in process while its state alters. Yet this very pattern is threatened with extinction in every successive operation of process. Thus, there is no real or empirical guarantee of $\mathcal{A}$ existing at $t + \Delta t$ if the change of state "message" ΔX is outside certain bounds.

Now $\mathcal{A}$ is a system, treated in the present section as a unitary entity exhibiting process but not analyzed as to its unit-composition. It is precisely these units which are the subordinate nexus whose composition realizes or fails to realize the defining characteristic of $\mathcal{A}$ under process. Hence for a deeper look at $\mathcal{A}$, the diagram of Figure 5-8 should be altered to show its typical elementary dynamic component, as in Figure 5-9.

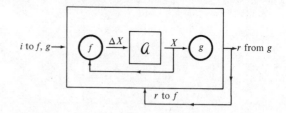

Figure 5-5.   The internal and external dynamics of $\mathcal{A}$.

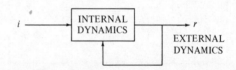

Figure 5-6.   The "black-box" representation of the dynamics of $\mathcal{A}$.

Figure 5-7. External aspects of the internal dynamics.

Figure 5-8. Internal aspect of the internal dynamics.

From Figure 5-9 it is clear that there are two aspects of the inner or *internal* aspect of the internal dynamics of $\mathcal{a}$:

1. On their own level, units α, β, . . . are themselves exemplifying dynamic system behavior; hence, their *own* repetitions in their own defining characteristics are problematic.
2. The *interactive* stability of $\alpha\beta$ and other such components is problematic, as time passes.

We term the first process, in which the units themselves have defining properties which may or may not be stable, the *latent process* (*L*). The latent process involves the maintenance or alteration of the units in regard to their defining characteristics.

The second process, in which dynamic components $\alpha\beta$ are involved, is termed the *interaction process* (*I*). If we assume, analytically, a *given* system $\mathcal{a}$, then it is necessarily the case that the pattern defining the system, which is unit composition in realization, is assumed as reproduced: The latent and the interaction processes are "working" in a stable mode.

However, what relationship exists between the patterns definitive of units — such patterns invariantly reproduced if the latent process is stable — and the patterns of stable interaction? This question is answered in the following discussion of internal stability. For the moment we diagram the internal processes of the internal dynamics of $\mathcal{a}$ as in Figure 5-10.

This figure shows that the internal (E) processes of the internal dynamics of system $\mathcal{a}$ involve two processes, *L* and *I*. Putting the entire internal dynamics together, by combining Figures 5-7 and 5-10 we obtain Figure 5-11.

Now putting together the internal *and external* dynamics of $\mathcal{a}$, using the diagrams given in Figures 5-4, 5-6, and 5-11, we obtain Figure 5-12.

It should be clear from this study of $\mathcal{a}$ in what sense we can say (1) the *concrete units* of $\mathcal{a}$ are α, β, . . . , u, . . . , whose own patterns are in process in *L*, while (2) the processes *A, G, I* and *L* are all *analytically*

Figure 5-9. The two aspects of the internal aspect of the internal dynamics of $\mathcal{a}$.

Figure 5-10. Internal aspects of internal dynamics of $\mathcal{a}$.

distinct dynamic subsystems of the system $\mathcal{a}$ in its interaction with its environment.

Internal Stability

Let us recall that the pattern variables define orientation-modality states of elementary components of the form $\alpha\beta$ or αu. The Parsons' pattern-variable theory goes beyond the duality noted earlier.

The theory of the internal stability of the system $\mathcal{a}$ is based on the assumption that an elementary dynamic component is to be analyzed relative to the system $\mathcal{a}$. Thus, it is thought of as caught up in some aspect of $\mathcal{a}$-dynamics, at any time. Hence, as it is internal to $\mathcal{a}$, such a component is caught up in one or more of the exigencies of *A, G, I* and *L*. (The *I* and *L* exigencies refer to the processes involving the component and its units *per se,* of course, but with reference to the consequences for the system.) In a small enough time interval—or under functional specialization—the component may be located in a unique functional context of $\mathcal{a}$. This idea of "location" is described in connection with "phase movements" in the *Working Papers*.[10] In discussing the problems of relating the action unit to the system of reference, the authors write:

If the level is not kept clear, each concept will have multiple referents, the descriptions given of a single referent or piece of behavior will conflict with each other, and intolerable confusion will result. For example, a single concrete act of a given individual may be said to have a *goal-attainment* emphasis, as a piece of neurotic acting-out (when the personality of the individual is taken as the system point of reference), an *integrative* emphasis as an act of compromise (when the interaction process of a small group is taken as the system point of reference), and an *adaptive-instrumental* emphasis as an item in a factual report handed to a staff superior (when the larger organization is taken as the system point of reference). This is simply another way of saying that our way of describing behavior in this conceptual scheme is in *relational* terms — that is, in relation to some system taken as the point of reference.

Figure 5-11. Internal dynamics of a.

The system point in reference here is the abstract system a, and the behavior involved is represented in terms of the orientation-modality state of the dynamic component au at a particular time.

The theory bases the internal stability conditions for the system on the intuitive analysis of the characteristics of each functional context. We state the assumption in compact form, referring the reader to Parsons for detailed justification.[11]

Assumption P6 (internal stability).

Necessary Conditions for Stability of a:

Exigency	$O(au)$	$M(au)$
A	$\bar{D}$	$\bar{P}$
G	A	$\bar{Q}$
I	D	P
L	$\bar{A}$	Q

For example, if au is located in an adaptive exigency for a, then for the internal stability of the system it is necessary that actor α orient towards unit u in a *specific* manner and that u have a *universalistic* modality for α. If the focus for au is an integrative exigency *per se,* however, it is necessary that α orient to u in *diffuse* manner and that u have a *particularistic* modality for α. If the *latent* process is the focus, then it is necessary that α orient in a neutral manner towards u and that it have a quality modality. It seems that in this case we should consider $u = \alpha$ as the intended scope: for in this case, the unit *itself* is the focus and so we should treat a component of the form $\alpha\alpha$. With respect to the internal stability of a, if α should focus on itself then the focus must be neutral, as opposed to affective. If A held for $O(\alpha\alpha)$ this would be an active self-orientation, detrimental to *system* integration.

It is clear from Assumption P6 that the two arrays together form the *patterns of internal stability* of a. For instance, a component au in an A exigency has to exemplify in its state-description, namely,

$$au \to (O(au), M(au))$$

the pattern $D\bar{P}$ as a part of the over-all system stability. Then, the state-description

$$au \to (\bar{D}A, Q\bar{P})$$

exemplifies this pattern, where it is clear that $\bar{D}\bar{P}$ is exemplified via $\bar{D}$ in $O(au)$ and $\bar{P}$ in $M(au)$. However, in the case of

$$au \to (DA, Q\bar{P})$$

the stability condition is violated if au is in A.

The patterns necessary for internal stability of a, namely,

$$\{\bar{D}\bar{P},\ A\bar{Q},\ DP,\ \bar{A}Q\}$$

are abstract *norms* or *normative patterns*. Note that each is associated with a functional exigency of a and that each allows variant exemplifications: These norms are abstract and so an indefinite multiplicity of concrete realizations, differing markedly among themselves, are inherent. Note that by basic conceptualization a norm is a necessary condition for system *existence*—the referent is a amid flux in actual state—referent to the integration of the system units. For if a does not have norms, then a is not a well-defined system: There are only the units in some random interacts.

Examining these norms in the light of Table 5-1, in which the orientation and modality patterns were displayed relative to abstract patterns Π_1, Π_2 and their opposites, it is seen that the normative patterns $D\bar{P}$, associated with A, realizes Π_2 in $\bar{D}$ and Π_2 in $\bar{P}$. Analyzing the remaining norms, we have:

A: $\bar{D}\bar{P}$ realizes $\bar{\Pi}_2$ uniformly
G: $A\bar{Q}$ realizes Π_1 uniformly
I: DP realizes Π_2 uniformly
L: $\bar{A}Q$ realizes $\bar{\Pi}_1$ uniformly

Here we have appealed to the associated interior forms and exterior maps shown in Table 5-1. This result is a generalization of tree T, where the orientation of α to β was the interior form and the modality of α for β was the exterior map. Now the exterior map is the modality of β for α. In other words, α's interior form of orientation to β agrees with α's exterior map of β.

Returning to the picture of system dynamics shown in Figure 5-12, we have just given the pattern-variable characterization of the internal stability conditions. Namely, in each location a component displays an orientation-modality state conformable with the normative patterns of Assumption P6. Thus, we can alter that diagram to that of Figure 5-13 to show this stable pattern of interaction.

It should be noted that the L process deals with properties of *units* entering into the *components*

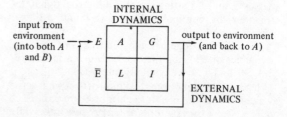

Figure 5-12. Dynamics of a.

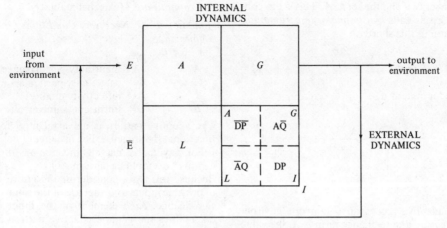

Figure 5-13. The stable interaction pattern of $\mathcal{U}$.

of $\mathcal{U}$ in internal stability under Assumption P6. The question arises whether if the components can be stably related, the units are not themselves stable as to pattern. For example, αu cannot realize $\overline{\text{DP}}$ if α does not realize D in 0 (αu). Thus, a *necessary condition for internal stability is stability of the L process with respect to those orientations required in the particular exigency.* We say that $\mathcal{U}$ possesses *normative order* if its internal process is stable. We see that necessary conditions for normative order exist in terms of the orientations of actors. Moreover, the orientation of α in αu must be $\overline{\text{D}}$ in the context of the adaptive subsystem *for any u* in the system. This universality makes the orientation pattern a *property* of α. The property has four parts:

1. If αu in *A*, then for any u, 0 $(\alpha u) = \overline{\text{D}}$.
2. If αu in *G*, then for any u, 0 $(\alpha u) = \text{A}$.
3. If αu in *I*, then for any u, 0 $(\alpha u) = \text{D}$.
4. If αu in *L*, then for any u, 0 $(\alpha u) = \overline{\text{A}}$.

Thus an *orientation base* or *pattern-maintenance* for every actor in $\mathcal{U}$ is a necessary condition of normative order and so of total system existence. Put another way: no orientation-base, no system. Also, if we recall that conditions (1)-(4) care not at all about α as such— they tacitly begin, "for any α in $\mathcal{U}$"—it follows that the orientation base must be *common*. Thus every α has an intrinsic feature, built into the constitutive system of α as such, to the effect of the mapping:

$$A \to \overline{\text{D}}$$
$$G \to \text{A}$$
$$I \to \text{D}$$
$$L \to \text{A}.$$

This *is* the orientation base of $\mathcal{U}$.

Similarly, on the modality side, we reason to the conclusion that any actor must have an *associated modality mapping:*

$$A \to \overline{\text{P}}$$
$$G \to \overline{\text{Q}}$$
$$I \to \text{P}$$
$$L \to \text{Q}$$

This is also a stable base of the system, but it is referent to the modalities *of objects* in the system, i.e., of units in their capacity as objects *of* orientation. But it is the actors "holding" this mapping that is constitutive of part of the stable base. For any α, $\mathcal{M}$ $(\alpha u) = \overline{\text{P}}$ when α is in A with u, for any u, for any α. The meanings are *shared* or *common*.

If we compare these results to the idea of interior form and exterior map associated with Table 5-1, we see that the abstract patterns Π_1, $\overline{\Pi}_1$, Π_2, $\overline{\Pi}_2$ are associated with processes as shown in Table 5-2.

Table 5-2. THE LATENT BASES FOR SYSTEM $\mathcal{U}$

ORIENTATION BASE	MODALITY BASE
$A \to \overline{\text{D}}$ $(\overline{\Pi}_2)$	$A \to \overline{\text{P}}$ $(\overline{\Pi}_2)$
$G \to \text{A}$ (Π_1)	$G \to \overline{\text{Q}}$ (Π_1)
$I \to \text{D}$ (Π_2)	$I \to \text{P}$ (Π_2)
$L \to \overline{\text{A}}$ $(\overline{\Pi}_1)$	$L \to \text{Q}$ $(\overline{\Pi}_1)$

We also note that

$$G \longleftrightarrow \Pi_1, \qquad L \longleftrightarrow \overline{\Pi}_1,$$
$$I \longleftrightarrow \Pi_2, \qquad A \longleftrightarrow \overline{\Pi}_2,$$

when a stable base exists. Thus we can interpret the Π_1, $\overline{\Pi}_1$ as *forms of action process,* functioning in interior form and exterior mapping. We introduced $\overline{\Pi}_1$ as "opposite" to Π_1, $\overline{\Pi}_2$ as opposite to Π_2. This opposition appears now to be grounded in *contrast* between the set *G, I* and the set *L, A*. This is the contrast that Parsons calls *consummatory-instrumental.* We will return to this shortly.

External Stability

Recall that, for system $\mathcal{A}$,

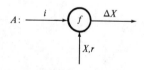

so that the adaptive process in $\mathcal{A}$ converts environmental input *i* into a state-change term ΔX, the value of which depends on its current state *X*. To get from *raw* input *i* to *coded* message ΔX is the *adaptive problem* of system $\mathcal{A}$.

The analysis of the process has the same character as the analysis of any process, with a prominent question being: what are the *conditions* of adaptive or external stability of $\mathcal{A}$? Such conditions must refer to *capacities* of $\mathcal{A}$ to code inputs, over wide ranges of environmental input and states. We have to analyze the entity *f:* the coding process.

On grounds based on symmetry[12] or on the basis of an analysis of symbolism[13] a rather complex argument may be given to show that the stable patterns of adaptive functioning "cross" orientation-modality sets of patterns in a manner analogous to that of normative patterns. For each possible "functional significance" of input *i,* there exists a representation *in* the system $\mathcal{A}$, the coded *i,* say *i*.* In analogy to the normative patterns for internal stability, the patterns for external stability are listed below and termed *adaptive patterns.*

Assumption P7 (external stability).

Functional Significance of *i* for $\mathcal{A}$	Necessary Conditions for Stability of $\mathcal{A}$
A	$\bar{A}\bar{Q}$ (neutrality-performance)
G	$\bar{D}P$ (specificity-particularism)
I	$A\bar{Q}$ (affectivity-quality)
L	$D\bar{P}$ (diffuseness-universalism)

The adaptive pattern is universal in $\mathcal{A}$ for a given functional significance. For instance:

For any *i,* if *i* has significance *A,* then coding into *i** exemplifies pattern $\bar{A}\bar{Q}$.

Because this is so, considering the entire collection of possible inputs to $\mathcal{A}$ that are of the same functional significance, *each* element of the input collection exemplifies the generic adaptive pattern in coding. Also any combination of them, input to $\mathcal{A}$ with the same functional significance, enjoys the same coded pattern. The pattern in the case of *G*-significance, for instance, is specificity-particularism; that for *A*-significance is neutrality-performance. Figure 5-14 expands Figure 5-13 to include the adaptive patterns.

To say that the coding exemplifies a certain pattern can be interpreted as follows. The orientation to the actual entity *i* is such as to match the modality of the representation *i** in the system. That is, $\bar{A}\bar{Q}$ stands for,

$$O\,(\alpha i) = \bar{A},$$
$$\mathcal{m}(\alpha i^*) = \bar{Q},$$

so that the *meaning* of *i in* the system—which is the modality of its representation—is constrained to fit the orientation to *i.*

Steady State

In analogy with Table 5-2, the patterns of Assumption P7 may be written:

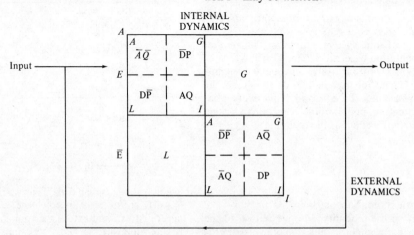

Figure 5-14.   Patterns of internal and external stability of $\mathcal{A}$.

For symbols i^*:

Orientation Base	Modality Base
$A \to \bar{A}$ $(\bar{\Pi}_1)$	$A \to \bar{Q}$ (Π_1)
$G \to \bar{D}$ $(\bar{\Pi}_2)$	$G \to P$ (Π_2)
$I \to A$ (Π_1)	$I \to Q$ $(\bar{\Pi}_1)$
$L \to D$ (Π_2)	$L \to \bar{P}$ $(\bar{\Pi}_2)$

We note that in each row the "underlying form" occurs in opposite form on the modality side, if we define the opposite of $\bar{\pi}_i$ to be π_i. As we shall see below, this is a result coherent with the original duality formulation in tree T that led to Figure 5-2. These are mappings, held by actors in $\mathcal{Q}$, as a condition for *adaptive* or external stability. Combining the two orientation bases and the two modality bases, we write,

Combined Orientation Base	Combined Modality Base
$A \to \bar{A}\bar{D}$ $(\bar{\Pi}_1, \bar{\Pi}_2)$	$A \to \bar{Q}\bar{P}$ $(\Pi_1, \bar{\Pi}_2)$
$G \to \bar{D}A$ $(\bar{\Pi}_2, \Pi_1)$	$G \to P\bar{Q}$ $(\Pi_2, \bar{\Pi}_1)$
$I \to AD$ $(\Pi_1, \bar{\Pi}_2)$	$I \to Q\bar{P}$ $(\bar{\Pi}_1, \bar{\Pi}_2)$
$L \to D\bar{A}$ $(\Pi_2, \bar{\Pi}_1)$	$L \to \bar{P}Q$ $(\bar{\Pi}_2, \bar{\Pi}_1)$

We note that these are precisely the patterns matched in the duality argument leading to Figure 5-2; except that we now associate them, by pairs, with system process. Figure 5-15 sums up the total pattern-variable correspondence with processes in the system. It is obtained from the above correspondence and from Figure 5-14. It *is* Figure 1 of Parsons' "Pattern Variables Revisited."

To gain some intuitive sense of the meaning of Figure 5-15, suppose we consider a system in an integrative exigency. Then consider input i, and the problem is: Find the meaning of the input in an integrative exigency. We proceed as follows: the relevant cells are those labelled I. The assumption is made that $\mathcal{Q}$ is both internally and externally stable. Then

$$I \to AQ, \quad I \to DP$$

are the two normative orientation-modality patterns. The first yields,

$$O(\alpha i) = A, \quad \mathcal{M}(\alpha i^*) = Q,$$

and the second yields,

$$O(\alpha i^*) = D, \quad \mathcal{M}(\alpha i^*) = P,$$

whereby we conclude,

$$\mathcal{M}(\alpha i^*) = QP$$

as shown in the goal-attainment box in cell I. Thus, with a meaning of QP, the response of the system would be a function of this meaning—but no response rules are given in conjunction with Figure 5-15. Strictly speaking, it carries us to the point of response without revealing the response. This raises a difficulty from the standpoint of testing action models (see the final part of this chapter for related discussion).

Analogous computations apply to each exigency for determination of the meaning categorization of an input.

To summarize the nature of Figure 5-15, we note the following:

1. The whole system, $\mathcal{Q}$, is in interaction with an environment (external dynamics).
2. The system is assumed to have a stable base as to its units' orientations (cell L), both in regard to the requirements for normative order in internal interaction and in regard to "cultural order" in orientation to symbols of environmental inputs and systems.
3. Similarly, the system is assumed to have a stable base as to modalities and meanings in the sense that both units and symbols are objects for which modalities exist that are necessary for, on the one

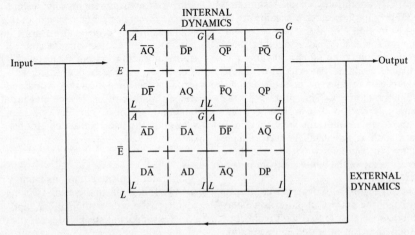

Figure 5-15. The total pattern-variable correspondence with system processes.

hand, normative order in the interaction of units and, on the other hand, cultural order in the meanings given to symbols.

4. The process A transforms raw input to coded form, and this code (by orientation-modality bases) is common and "understood" by units in $\mathcal{Q}$.

5. The process G transforms coded states or messages into outputs to the environment, using the entire "apparatus" of cultural and normative order.

6. In interpreting this diagram it should be noted that: (a) cells of A contain not units or components, but four generic types of mappings; (b) cells of I contain not units or components, but mappings in the sense of the prior remark, except that the referent objects are internal; (c) the cells of L contain patterns realized in the orientations of every unit of $\mathcal{Q}$, indexed in that unit by the "appropriate" contexts for display of such patterns; and (d) cells of G contain images under mappings held by actors, and applicable to all units and symbols, in $\mathcal{Q}$, and as such they form a stable base of forms of objects, realized in the conceptual activity of the actors in $\mathcal{Q}$.

We ask at this point: Exactly what *is* the state of the system? This is X of our earlier block diagrams. Parsons' scheme seems to assume that the state is a set of meanings. In the preceding notation, the typical meaning is $\mathcal{M}(\alpha i^*)$. It means, then, that while the *external* dynamics are all *decoded* in form, where the term "code" means any one of the codes used in the A process, the *internal* dynamics are all *in* code. The response or output is a transformation of $\mathcal{M}(\alpha i^*)$ into decoded form.

As a logical point it appears that the stability argument associated with Figure 5-15 is: if $\mathcal{Q}$ is the type of system of interest then $\mathcal{Q}$ has a stable adaptive mode of behavior and a normative order. That is, such a system has a steady state defined by the internal and external stability conditions. From Assumption P7, adaptive stability implies certain conditions on L and G. By Assumption P6, normative order implies conditions on L and G. Taken together these conditions specify uniquely the (abstract) value patterns and (abstract) modality patterns of $\mathcal{Q}$. These are presumably the mappings in terms of which all objects are characterized. The process is the time-varying characterization. The word "abstract" was inserted above to remind the reader that a modality pattern such as universalism-performance can be exemplified in countless ways, so that there is no rigid determination of the *concrete* from purely formal considerations.

Another aspect of Figure 5-15 deserves comment. Its pattern content — the pattern of patterns we may as well call *structure* — is a *potential* with respect to process in $\mathcal{Q}$ such that the intended interpretation

is: (1) if at any time the structure is realized in $\mathcal{Q}$ process then the system exhibits a stable mode of abstract transformations of inputs to outputs, i.e., with respect to external dynamics forms a nexus with an enduring, time-invariant structure; and (2) if at any time the structure fails to be realized in $\mathcal{Q}$-process, the concept of stability implies that the processes will gravitate toward this structure. Under the latter point of view, we can regard $\mathcal{Q}$ as incessantly "perturbed" by processes to which it is not linked (as a unit) in any enduring concrete system. Also, as patterns may be exemplified in diverse concrete modes, there is a process of continuous re-exemplification in concretely *realized* diversity which nevertheless exemplifies the generic patterns of Figure 5-15. (In this sense, it is never quite clear in pattern-variable theory what is under discussion — and the roots of this problem lie in the failure to provide an associated empirical methodology.)

INTERPRETATIONS

Action Process

The two operators f and g both relate the system to its environment. But from an external standpoint what is observable is the operation of the g mechanism: response to input. For example, in a learning experiment x is the subject's state of knowledge, i is the stimulus input, and r is the response. The experimenter is the relevant environmental object who returns a feedback stimulus to the subject following a response. The theory of learning deals with how such successive episodes of process create successive changes of state X even though such states and such changes are not directly observable.[14] This coordinates well with Parsons' claim that the goal-attainment subsystem is the locus of interchange with the environment in any system of action. To pursue the analogy, regard the operator g as G. Thus, goal-attainment process transforms inputs into outputs by reference to current state. This would be true in any action system at any level. Then, as noted, the f operator can be identified with the other external process in action theory, namely, the adaptive transformation of environmental inputs into coded (meaningful) form. Thus let operator f be A. Then we obtain the two abstract equations,

$$\Delta X = A(X, i, r)\,\Delta t$$
$$r = G(X, i)$$

The fact that the equations cannot possibly show the two functions, in the usual Parsons sense, related to internal matters (namely, L and I) makes the correspondence plausible. Just as the deep structure of the subject in a learning experiment is not at

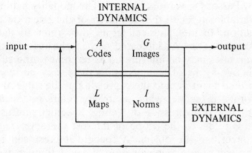

Figure 5-16. Process interpretation of the action scheme.

issue in the context of the process of learning, so in any action system during a process throughout which it persists there is a deeper time-invariant structure. Parsons identifies "learning process" with change in (what I am calling) deeper structure. I suggest instead that one identify adaptation as the generic concept of which learning is a special case. Then a change in deeper structure, from the point of view of the idea of steady state amid process, might be simply called "system change." This would be specialized to "personality change," "economic change," and "social change," among other instantiations to special cases.

In reference to these two equations, the functional exigency in regard to G is to *do* something based on current states of orientation-modality and the input. With reference to A the functional exigency is to *re*define and *re*orient (thus creating a shift in orientation-modality state) in the face of the input and the current state.

Some additional insight into the process interpretation of the action scheme may be gained by examining Figure 5-16. Internal dynamics, the generating structure and process for the observable external response processes, are shown to consist in a time-invariant structure of maps (the orientation maps), norms (the normative patterns for internal stability), and codes (the adaptive pattern for external stability). Also, in G there are "images." I think of this as the distinction between the map and the image of the map. Action process is mapping, using maps, resulting in images of things mapped. The modalities of situational objects are the images under mappings by actors who hold the basic structure of map, norm, and code. You code a stimulus; the map links the norm and the code to elicit an image. Finally, that image, in the state of the system built around a multidimensional array of such images, yields an operation upon the environment, the output. For an observing action system in the environment, attending to the focal action system in terms of performance, this output is "response." It is meaningful response if the observing system

can put it into the code of the action system emitting it. Essentially this is the requirement of a super-system in which both observer and observed are imbedded and share representations of the environment beyond.

I omit any discussion of "cybernetic hierarchy." It seems that there has never been a detailed justification of this idea in the work of Parsons. Apparently, that a particular ordering is induced on the analytical subsystems is not problematic for him. Indeed, "Figure 2" of "Pattern Variables Revisited" literally comes about by rearranging the prior figure in that article, but why this rearrangement should be a revelation of "hierarchy" is not made clear. However, if we assume this notion, there is the interesting concept of "ultimate reality" worth exploring — which I will treat briefly a little later.

Whitehead, Parsons, and the Pattern Variables

More than one type of correspondence between the ideas of Whitehead and the concepts of the action scheme can be made. It is of interest to look first at the most generic types of distinctions made in Parsons' scheme in terms of Whitehead's metaphysics.

Recall that a fundamental property of the action scheme is the actor-object duality and the "subjective point of view." Also, the theoretically most microscopic unit of analysis is the unit-act, associated with some actor. A plurality of unit-acts of a given actor form an action system of the simplest type, and it is an "actor-situation relational system." In this system, there is an orientation standpoint and a modality of objects for the actor. The more recent cybernetic hierarchy idea, when applied to a simple unit-act, implies some governing aim, and when applied to an action system some continuing body of aims. This suggests a few interesting correspondences in which Parsons' concepts appear as special cases of Whitehead's:

Whitehead	Parsons
Actual occasion	Unit-act
Enduring object	Action system
Concrescence	Subjective point of view
Actual world	Situation of action
Objectified entity	Modalities of objects
Subjective form	Orientations
Subjective aims	Cybernetic relation
World as medium	Symbolic media

Just as an actual occasion is a process of concrescence, with a subject feeling its actual world, so the unit-act is a process involving an actor in a situation of action. Action theory abstracts from the formal constitution of the actual occasion in the interest of studying action systems, which are a species of enduring objects. The form of endurance here involves invariance in the subjective forms of feeling of occasions, of transmuted nexus, and of patterns *per se*. In each actual occasion, the actor — construed as a life-history of actual occasions — has an associated actual world. This world is objectified for the actor in the first instance by the presence of order, of nexus in the world, which are transmuted into things. These things, however, are always very definitely particular things. Modality refers to the manner in which these felt nexus and occasions are classed into higher-order entities. In addition, if the actor takes the point of view toward the object which is a subjective point of view, i.e., he treats the object as controlled by subjective aims and as a succession of occasions in which the world is felt subjectively, then the actor is defining the object as an actor, in the sense that the flux of occasions which form the enduring object is interpreted by the actor in terms of imputed subjective aims held by the object.

We can interpret Parsons' modality pattern variables in these terms. In a definite occasion in the life-history of α as an enduring object, in an actual world containing an enduring object β felt by α in this occasion, the actor α may define β as a feeling subject of its (β's) own occasions or not. In the former alternative, α has defined β in terms of *performance*; in the latter case, he has defined β in terms of *quality*.

The investigator begins by defining α as an actor, then the actor α defines other enduring objects in his actual world as actors or not, using the same definition as the investigator, namely, whether or not the subjective point of view seems to be appropriate.

Given the performance-quality decision — which does not involve consciousness necessarily but determinateness of viewpoint — then the two classificatory possibilities are relevant. If α defines β in terms of performance then this performance may be classed with other such performances in the endurance of the object or it may be classed with other such performances without regard to this object, so that the performance is treated in abstraction from the particular other actor. In the first case we have a particularistic criterion, in the latter case a universalistic criterion. Similarly, if β is defined in terms of quality, then a particularistic criterion is employed if this quality is classed with qualities of the object, and β is classified universalistically if the quality is grouped with other qualities independently of the enduring object.

This discussion has dealt with the way in which the process metaphysics provides one interpretation of the modality pattern variables, performance-quality and particularism-universalism. By and large, the interpretation seems consistent with that given by Parsons in various writings. The modality pattern variables refer to the definition of the situation of action. In metaphysical terms, they refer to data for the actor. As indicated earlier, the orientation variables may be interpreted as referent to the subjective forms of feelings. Affectivity may be interpreted as referent to the expression of the subjective forms of feeling, while neutrality refers to the inhibition of expression of feeling. Specificity-diffuseness refers to the scope of interest the actor feels concerning the object. A specific interest can be thought of as a high valuation of one definite aspect in the full pattern recognized in the endurance of object β, with other elements providing only background. A diffuse interest can be thought of as a uniform valuation of the full pattern recognized in the endurance of the object.

It may be seen that these two pattern-variables are somewhat more difficult to interpret than the modality variables. A genuine dichotomy does not seem to be involved. For example, interest appears to be a continuous variable, and expression need not be all-or-none.

However, some sense of the dichotomy emerges if we consider the definition of the situation once again. If β exhibits the affective side of the pattern variable, then this means β is releasing into expression the forms of feeling he has vis-à-vis the actor. Essentially this is the basis for the actor, in turn, defining β as another actor. This is the pattern Π_1 of Table 5-1. On the other hand, if β exhibits no such release — because of inhibition or because β develops only a trivially low level of subjectivity in concrescence — then α will be led to define β as a non-actor. This is pattern $\overline{\Pi}_1$. The "two-way functioning" is a consequence of the fact that one occasion feels components of the other. There is a sense in which the decision by α in regard to β defines a local threshold for affectivity-neutrality. Over a series of occasions, the threshold could "flicker," just as in our own analysis of occasions we could (in imagination) switch from the concrescence analysis of a given occasion to the analysis of it as objectified in other occasions, and then back again. The actor may be said to have his attention forced into the concrescent or subjective point of view when the object exhibits "sufficient expression of feeling," and otherwise the definition of the object lapses into the object standpoint.

Diffuseness relates to particularism in a somewhat different way. To relate diffuseness to particularism we seem to need to fix the actor and consider the objective datum (particularistically defined by α) and its corresponding form of feeling in α (diffuse interest). This relates the orientation of α toward β to the modality of β for α. In the case of affectivity matching performance, however, we considered affectivity the orientation of β toward α and performance in the modality of β for α. Thus in the first case we have $O(\alpha\beta)$ and $\widetilde{m}(\alpha\beta)$, while in the second case $O(\beta\alpha)$ and $\mathcal{M}(\alpha\beta)$. What was said for diffuseness in relation to particularism applies immediately to relate specificity to universalism. For example, a scientific interest involves high valuation of some aspects of enduring objects rather than their full pattern, and the objects play a subsidiary role as mere examples of a class of objects with such aspects. Once again the relation matches an orientation of α toward β and a modality of β for α.

Hence, by this method the patterns Π_2 and $\overline{\Pi}_2$ of Table 5-1 cannot be given a uniform metaphysical interpretation with the patterns Π_1 and $\overline{\Pi}_1$, not even a uniform action theory interpretation. A second interpretation of Π_1, the matching of affectivity with particularism, can be made in the interest of symmetry of interpretation of the matching. Namely, if α defines β as an acting subject, then α will express feelings toward β, which relates performance (in the definition of β by α) to affectivity (in the orientation of α toward β). Similarly, if α defines β as a non-actor, this can be related to α's not expressing feeling toward β. These interpretations are rather forced, but some such interpretation seems to be needed to give a meaning to Table 5-1. Note that the second interpretation is consistent with Figure 5-15. In general, I am certain much better *general* interpretations of the pattern variables are needed.

The Cultural System

The system $\mathcal{Q}$ is abstract. It has received many action interpretations at the hands of Parsons. To give some idea of the structure of such interpretations, let us consider the cultural system.[15]

The strategy is to start from a given abstract action system $\mathcal{Q}$ and to define its cultural system such that the latter is an action system: then it too is subjected to the steady-state pattern analysis.

The first step is to define the cultural system of $\mathcal{Q}$ to be comprised of the actors of $\mathcal{Q}$ together with those units that are symbols of environmental objects. Then the typical dynamic component of the system has the form αu^*, where u^* is the representation of u (where u is in the environment). The O relation is restricted to the pairs of the form (α, u^*) so that no pair (α, β) of actors is in O. This means that the "interaction process" is restricted to the integrative aspects in regard to orientations toward and modalities of symbols. A modality of a symbol may be termed a *meaning*. Hence the typical orientation-modality mapping becomes a typical orientation — meaning mapping.

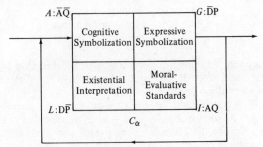

Figure 5-17. The cultural system application.

Call this system $C\alpha$. Internal stability of $C\alpha$ is in reference to matching of these orientations (to symbols) and meanings. External stability is referent to the environment of the system $C\alpha$, namely the environment of $\mathcal{Q}$ itself.

Finally, the conditions for internal stability of $C\alpha$ are given by the pattern $\overline{AQ}$ associated with exigency A in the adaptive process of $\mathcal{Q}$ itself.

To give this some concreteness, we use the Parsons' terminology:

Adaptive Pattern	*Interpretation*
$A: \overline{AQ}$	Cognitive symbolization
$G: \overline{DP}$	Expressive symbolization
$I: AQ$	Moral-evaluative standards
$L: DP$	Existential interpretation

Then we have just said that for the $C\alpha$ steady state the relevant pattern for internal stability is the category of moral-evaluative standards and for external stability the category of congnitive symbolization.

This yields a two-step application of Figure 5-15 to $C\alpha$. In the first step, the cell A becomes the whole figure. That is, we have the system shown in Figure 5-17.

To analyze the external stability conditions — the adaptive patterns of $C\alpha$— means applying the earlier results but interpreting them in terms of cognitive symbolization. Thus, Parsons' interpretation is:

Adaptive Pattern of $C\alpha$	*Interpretation*
$A: \overline{AQ}$	Data
$G: \overline{DP}$	Problems
$I: AQ$	Theories
$L: DP$	Frameworks

For internal stability his interpretation is:

Normative Pattern of $C\alpha$	*Interpretation Standards*
$A: \overline{DP}$	Costs

G : A$\overline{Q}$ Evaluation of goals
I : $\underline{DP}$ Moral principles
L : $\overline{AQ}$ Interpretation of meanings

In each case standards are required because this is the breakdown of the system of normative standards of the cultural system $C\alpha$ of α.

The process of $C\alpha$ seems to involve shifting *meanings of* external objects (i.e., $\mathcal{M}$ (αu*) modality terms are involved). Thus in keeping with this and with the above two sets of stability conditions, the content of the orientation-base and the space of categories of symbols is constructed. We have, for the orientation-base of $C\alpha$,

Orientation (Value) Pattern of $C\alpha$	Interpretation
A : $\overline{AD}$	O re: meaning of performance
G : $\overline{D}A$	O re: meaning of spheres of activity
I : $A\underline{D}$	O re: concepts of order
L : $D\overline{A}$	O re: meanings of ultimate reality

Consistently, the modalities are interpreted as forms of meaning because the objects are all symbols:

Meaning Patterns in $C\alpha$	Interpretation
A : $\overline{QP}$	Symbols of utility
G : $P\overline{Q}$	Symbols of cathexis
I : $\underline{QP}$	Symbols of identification
L : $\overline{P}Q$	Symbols of respect

There is good consistency of interpretation here. The basic weakness is the role of the abstract patterns: Just what function do they play in the interpretative process? Surely, if they are abstractly meaningful they should both inform and yet constrain the structure of the interpretation. For example, what is the relationship in the last array between the abstract P$\overline{Q}$ for G and the idea that we have to interpret this part of the system in terms of cathexis? The abstract patterns seem not to play a major role here, for Parsons relies upon the "axes": internal-external and instrumental-consummatory. But if the patterns *must* be associated with the system $C\alpha$ as in Figure 5-15, then they *should* play a role in the special $C\alpha$ interpretation. An interesting point to note is the presence of patterns as parameters in Figure 5-17. Surely here is a place for further work in clarifying the structure of action models.

Ultimate Reality

In recent work Parsons[16] has seen any human grouping as embedded in two "non-action" environ-

ments: the physical-organic and "ultimate reality." They are distinguished in terms of the cybernetic hierarchy idea: ultimate reality controls the full-human action system, which in turn controls the physical-organic basis.[17] In this section, I will give an interpretation of "ultimate reality" in terms of Whitehead's metaphysics — in the spirit of intellectual experimentation and not of dogma. The ideas of the second part of this chapter, "Process Metaphysics," now play a heavy *technical* role.

Consider the typical concrescence,

$$\text{many-for-}\alpha \rightarrow \alpha,$$

and demand by an "ontological principle" that whatever exists in any sense at all be located in some actuality. The actualities are the actual occasions. Now the typical concrescence has not been so located: It *is* the typical actual occasion, but as it is felt only under elimination because of limitations inherent in the world as a medium of transmission of feelings, this typical concrescence exists without location *in* an actuality. Also, consider a pattern not felt in any actual occasion up to a given set of contemporary concrescences: then this pattern is not located. To believe that such patterns do *not* exist is to rob the evolving world of unrealized potentialities. Thus all potentialities must *be* somewhere, where "somewhere" means in the community of actual occasions.

Introduce, following Whitehead, a special actual occasion into the definition of the metaphysical system specified by Whitehead. This special actual occasion will be one among the others, but distinct from them in its structural role in the system. Thus this occasion is like an identity element in an abstract algebra. Call the occasion the G-occasion. My proposal is that the G-occasion is a concept of "ultimate reality," as this idea appears in Parsons. The theory of the G-occasion is an application of the general metaphysical theory to a structurally distinct occasion.

The concrescence of G has the form,

$$\text{many-for-}G \rightarrow G,$$

and the special postulate is that G differs from all other actual occasions in that its concrescence starts with conceptual feeling. It has a conceptual prehension of the multiplicity of *all* patterns. Thus G is not limited by starting from physical feelings. But G's feeling of the patterns only defines them as possibilities for realization in other actual occasions — i.e., this is purely ideal realization of every pattern in the formal constitution of G.

The concrescence also involves physical feeling of the actual world,

$$\text{many-for-}\alpha \rightarrow \alpha$$

The "many-for-α" is the *initial datum* of G's physical feeling, α is the *objectification* of the actual world for G, and then there is a subjective form of α, say $f(\alpha)$, in G: the way that G feels the actual world in a given occasion α. Next G has a conceptual feeling of the *pattern* of α which is nothing but the concrescence with loss of the actuality of complete feeling that is α as fully actual: Call the concrescence c. The immediacy of α is lost: the form is preserved and this is c.

Then the conceptual feeling is,

$$c \rightarrow v(c),$$

and the *reason* that G can feel the entire formal content of the concrescence of α is that this c is a potentiality in the original conceptual feeling of *all* patterns. G feels c and then its realization, which is α.

Integration of the feeling of the actual world and its concrescence yields the propositional feeling in G,

$$(\alpha,c) \rightarrow V(\alpha,c)$$

The left side is the proposition that α exhibits the particular pattern of concrescence. The right side is how G feels this proposition.

Next there is the emergent contrast of the proposition with *what* is felt, an intellectual feeling of the form,

$$(\alpha, (\alpha,c)) \rightarrow (f(\alpha), V(\alpha,c))$$

The left side is the contrast of the given occasion of the world with the proposition of the concrescence exhibiting form c. The right side is G's consciousness of this contrast. (The notation used here was explained on page 104 in reference to propositional and intellectual feelings.)

G does not reach completion because of the term "many-for-G". Each occasion renews it and provides new data for the G concrescence based on many-for-G. Hence, G is ever in concrescence, hence never perishes, hence never becomes temporal, hence is not an enduring object, hence is not a person. G is the occasion that always is in the making, never concrete, always becoming. G feels the world and unifies it, but the unification is the continuing *process* and not the outcome.

As G is an actual occasion, it is available for feeling and so there is a component of G felt. But the limitation induced by the many feelings of G in the world means that the novel occasion receives an objectification of G (itself an initial datum for feeling) that establishes what *can* be accomplished by creativity, by concrescence, in *that* actual world *there*. Thus, the actual occasion is controlled by its subjective aim, arising from that element in the universe which expresses the fullness of all potentialities in the creative process of the universe. The passage of the occasion is cybernetic in its "development" toward the initial subjective aim at what *can* be.

Thus the theoretical model is complete, but the universe is not. The idea of the G-occasion expresses the need to *rationally represent* what men have striven to express in religious doctrines with their particularistic tribal limitations: the feeling of one universal process. Thus, G is always present, never past, the "companion" in every occasion. For this reason, Whitehead uses the term "God" in reference to what I have called "the G-occasion." For Parsons, it corresponds to "ultimate reality."

Concluding Remarks

In this paper, I have treated the action scheme "from above," focussing on the metaphysical and formal aspects that might help others to join in the task of elucidating the structure of the concepts and to criticize the assumptions that can be located. Above all, the difficult process remains of connecting the scheme to *definite* concrete systems in such a way as to subject the constructed action models to possible rejection.

This paper was written on the premise that the action scheme is important: it is rooted in the classics, in the many independent and convergent streams of modern thought about man and society, in an appreciation of dynamics and of the problem of stability, and in a commitment to understanding of human interaction phenomena at a general level.

As an "uncomfortable" aspect of the action scheme, however, one must note the difficulty in *retaining* the dynamic viewpoint once one is immersed in the system. It is no wonder that so many sociologists think of the system as a set of "static pigeonholes." The irony of this view is that there can be no doubt at all that the action system is intended by Parsons as a dynamic feedback system and that he recognizes that a first and foremost theoretical problem in the study of dynamic systems has to do with stability. Yet the strongest feeling that I have in concluding this admittedly incomplete and inadequate formal treatment of the system is that there is a real discontinuity between the initial setting-up of the ideas, relevant to a dynamic system, and the subsequent categorizing and relating of categories at various levels. This discontinuity arises, perhaps, from the lack of firm understanding on my part as to what the *state* of an action system is supposed to be.

There are many entities involved that are not observationally identifiable: for instance, "exigencies." But then only definite model rules permitting a calculation of response outputs of the internal dynamics can make these various entities do a job for social science, conceived as requiring an empirical basis. One possibility is to investigate relatively simple small-group experiments, with a response axiom that does not have the complexity of the Bales' coding scheme. Then the states of the action system can be treated as an underlying Markov chain with a response function defined over the state space.[18] The phase structure proposed in the earlier work with Bales suggests an ergodic chain. The parameters are transition probabilities between states, as phases of group process. But such an effort is not worthwhile without continued investigation of the formal and conceptual properties of the system in all generality.[19] Above all, it would seem that attendance to feedback diagrams with at least some attempt to specify the state of the system in terms of the theoretical ideas would be beneficial. It was to induce this dynamic emphasis that led me to write the dynamics portions of the third part, "The Abstract Action System," as I did, even though I am convinced the treatment given there is far from adequate.

In all of this, the fundamental problem is to bring the action scheme under the guided control of rigorous norms as to theoretical procedure in science and as to empirical verification. One *concrete* and immediately applicable technique for doing so has been suggested: a strongly self-conscious sense of the *method* of theoretical analysis. The system must be "mentioned" as well as "used." The *craft* of application must develop, and its development should be accompanied by formalization of rules and guidelines for building action models.[20]

The whole question of parameters needs some discussion. In dynamic mathematical models, parameters play a large role. Generality of the abstract system exists not only in the unspecified character of the units. It resides also in the continuum of potential conditions denoted by a parametric variable. My work on the abstract action system was hampered by an inability to see exactly how the pattern variables related to parameters and to the presumed range of values of parameters for which the system is stable. Thus, not only does the state of the system need more precise specification, but also the concepts that are playing a qualitative role analogous to parameters in quantitative models should be carefully specified. (In the last part of the paper, we noted the appearance of patterns in a parametric role in Figure 5-17. Having realized this late in the writing, I have had no chance to exploit it.)

It is possible that for lack of appreciation of what is involved in the action system at the level corresponding to system parameters, some failure of correspondence with the usual scheme has resulted. One cannot be sure that the scheme outlined in this paper's third part is, in detail, the same scheme used in standard works. Certainly, the intention was both to

capture the given standard thinking and to imbed it in a formal dynamic system logic, but the latter aim helped shape the conceptualization. Perhaps it is even the case that some small clarification of the action scheme has resulted from attending to the dynamic system model more closely.

NOTES

1.   See, for instance, J. Berger, B.P. Cohen and M. Zelditch, Jr., "Status Characteristics and Expectation States," in J. Berger, M. Zelditch, Jr. and B. Anderson (eds.), *Sociological Theories in Progress*, vol. 1 (Boston: Houghton — Mifflin, 1966).

2.   See T.J. Fararo, "Theoretical Studies in Status and Stratification", *General Systems*, 15 (1970), pp. 71-101.

3.   See A. N. Whitehead, *Science and the Modern World* (New York: The Macmillan Co., 1925), reprinted by The Free Press, New York, 1967.

4.   A. N. Whitehead, *Process and Reality* (New York: The Macmillan Co., 1929), reprinted by Harper Torchbooks, New York, 1960.

5.   *Ibid.*, p. 351.

6.   T. Parsons, "Pattern Variables Revisited: A Response to Professor Dubin's Stimulus," *American Sociological Review,* 25 (August 1960), pp. 467-483.

7.   T. Parsons, R. F. Bales and E. A. Shils, *Working Papers in the Theory of Action* (New York: The Free Press, 1953), p. 82, italics in original.

8.   See, for instance, R. Bellman, *Adaptive Control Processes: A Guided Tour* (Princeton: Princeton University Press, 1961; M.D. Mesarovic, O Macko, and Y. Takahara, *Theory of Hierarchical Multilevel Systems* (New York: Academic Press, 1970); and R. J. Swartz and B. Friedland, *Linear Systems* (New York: McGraw-Hill Co., 1965). These tools are used here in a purely heuristic way. They help to make clear that the focus is on a dynamic system.

9.   See, for example, L. A. Zadeh and C. A. Desoer, *Linear System Theory: The State Space Approach* (New York: McGraw-Hill Co., 1963).

10.   T. Parsons *et al.*, *Working Papers in the Theory of Action*, p. 176.

11.   See T. Parsons, "Pattern Variables Revisited."

12.   *Ibid.*

13.   T. Parsons *et al.*, *Working Papers in the Theory of Action.*

14.   For a good example of the methodology of the mathematical model with two levels, state and response process, see R. C. Atkinson, G. H. Bower and E. J. Crothers, *An Introduction to Mathematical Learning Theory* (New York: J. Wiley & Sons, Inc., 1965), chap. 2.

15.   See T. Parsons, "Introduction to Part Four: Culture and the Social System," in T. Parsons, E. Shils, K. Naegele and J. Pitts (eds.), *Theories of Society* (New York: The Free Press, 1961), vol. II.

16.   See T. Parsons, *Politics and Social Structure* (New York: The Free Press, 1969).

17.   For a critique of this idea, see G. Müller, Review of *Societies* by T. Parsons in *History and Theory*, 13 (1970), pp. 145-156.

18.   For examples, see Atkinson, *et al, op. cit.* and J. Berger, B. P. Cohen, T. L. Connor and M. Zelditch, Jr., "Status Characteristics and Expectation States: A Process Model," in J. Berger, M. Zelditch, Jr. and B. Anderson (eds.), *op. cit.*

19.   For an example, see L. Brownstein, "A Formal Account of Talcott Parsons' Action Scheme" Ph. D. Thesis, University of Pittsburgh, Pittsburgh, Pa., 1974.

20.   See chap. 7 in this book for an effort prior to this essay.

II

GENERAL ACTION
ANALYSIS

INTRODUCTION

Victor Meyer Lidz

Sociology and many of its neighboring disciplines in the social sciences have long been troubled by baffling problems concerning the scope of their frames of reference. Many recent discussions have included the idea that sociology and certain other social sciences should concentrate upon the analysis of social systems.[1] This formulation has had an important but at crucial points qualified place within the theory of action. In this formulation, the conception of a social or interactive system has been put forward as a central concept delimiting the core of the social scientific frame of reference. The concerns of sociology, political science, economics, social anthropology, and certain other disciplines have been expected to revolve about social systems or about analytically defined aspects of social systems. At least since the publication of *Toward A General Theory of Action*,[2] however, it has been recognized that for some important purposes the social sciences must concern themselves with matters that fall beyond the bounds of social systems.

Classically, problems grouped under such headings as "culture and personality," "character and social structure," "national character," the social psychology of group membership and of group processes or dynamics, and the cultural sources of values have most clearly led social scientists beyond the social system frame of reference. Within sociology, such subdisciplines as the study of deviance and social control, the study of religion, political sociology, and economic sociology — to cite some prominent cases — have routinely come to take various psychological factors into their frames of reference. In the study of processes of socialization, a very deep-seated intermingling of social and psychological factors has become a prominent feature of practically all recent theoretical work.[3] In such areas of sociological endeavor as the study of religion and of law, comparative work has made powerfully evident the need for taking cultural factors into

theoretical account.[4] Thus, it has become apparent that the social sciences must treat social systems as fundamentally "open" at their boundaries and as often deeply affected by psychological and cultural factors.[5] Although the matter has not often been addressed directly, it should also be apparent that general theory of the relations between social systems and nonsocial factors entering into the determination of processes of social action must comprise an important part of any systematic codification of social scientific theory. Until such theory is developed, it will not be possible to know whether substantial bodies of work in a number of areas of specialization can be rendered mutually consistent in parsimonious fashion. Social scientific theory can be only very partially systematized in the absence of a strong version of what we will be calling "general action" theory.[6]

The essays included within the present section of this collection have been grouped together because, in the eyes of the editors, their most significant contributions concern theory of the relations obtaining between social systems and nonsocial factors of action. Broadly, the nature of these contributions may be divided into two types. Essays of the first type proceed analytically, departing from the division of action systems into distinct subsystems, including the social system, and then discussing structural or processual relationships between subsystems. Essays of the second type proceed more phenomenologically. They treat characteristics of observable social action as entities constructed through the volitional strivings of human actors, documenting and providing contextual grounds for interpreting meanings of actions. Although they tend to avoid the parsing of processes of action into analytical constituents or factors, they do broaden the frame of reference of social system analysis in calling attention to the contextual, meaningful, and motivationally creative qualities of routine forms of action. If essays of the first type seem to be more thoroughly grounded in the analytical thrust of the theory of action, it must yet be noted that, ever since *The Structure of Social Action*, Parsons has insisted upon the crucial importance of interpretive methodology for the social sciences and has sustained a rather Germanic neo-Idealist component in his works.[7] A major task of the present introductory essay, then, will be to explore some possibilities for bringing about convergence between these two approaches to understanding the openness of social action to determination by factors outside social systems.

The contributions developed by essays of both types take on their significance against the background of theoretical work that has been very central to recent theory of action. Perhaps the single most important conception has been that of a general action system, which establishes a much more inclusive frame of reference for social scientific analysis than that of the social system itself. As a matter of definition, all components of "meaning" — here, Weber's classic reference characteristic for action is still invoked — are included within this frame of reference, whether such components are psychological, social, or cultural. Theory concerning this frame of reference has attempted, albeit still in a rather preliminary fashion, to render a formally codified account of the structural organization and processual combinations that may obtain among all the "meaningful" factors that enter into action. Such theory, now usually called "general action" theory because it generalizes beyond all the more particular and specialized frames of reference concerning human action and indeed logically subordinates them, provides the general theoretical resource for a social scientific treatment of the problems of the "openness" of social systems just noted.[8]

The present essay will attempt both to draw upon and to contribute to the general action level of theory in order to provide the theoretical background necessary for a critical understanding of the other contributions to this section. Certain special foci within the vast theoretical territory covered by general action theory will be adopted as appropriate to this task. In building upon Parsons' recent treatments of general action theory, more attention will be given to the dynamic mechanisms operating at the most general or inclusive level of the organization of action than to structural arrangements *per se*. An effort will also be made to show how important exigencies of linkage with the specifically general action level mechanisms affect characteristics of dynamic mechanisms having narrower specializations within action systems, e.g., within particular subsystems of action systems. Finally, a principal concern will be to develop a more adequate and refined analysis of the "openness" of social systems and, especially, of the nature of social system contributions to the ongoing processes of the construction of social action. In this context, a groundwork will be presented for a more satisfactory integration between the theory of action and the symbolic interactionist and social phenomenological perspectives on social science. At the same time, however, a selective emphasis will necessarily be imparted to the treatment of the general action system, in that discussion will center on the social factors in action processes and attend only somewhat secondarily to cultural and psychological factors. Nevertheless, the theoretical advantages of treating social processes "openly" in the context of general action dynamics that include cultural and psychological aspects should become apparent.

Theory of action analyses of the most inclusive frame of reference of social action have departed from two distinct starting points. The first involves the attempt to specify the essential, irreducible constituents of the elementary relationships of meaningful action. Its key terms have been the conceptions of actor, alter or social object of action, orientation of the actor, and modality of the object for the oriented actor.[9] Action is interpreted as an emergent mode of relation among these fundamental entities. The characteristics of more complex systems are treated principally as arising from the more complicated relationships that emerge whenever exemplars of these basic entities become empirically interdependent in large numbers. The crystallization of differentiated and autonomous cultural, social, and psychological systems may then be regarded as the means by which complex action systems stabilize very complicated relationships among their parts. As the fundamental entities of action systems are thus treated as necessarily penetrating into the structural forms of all areas of action systems, the focusing of central analytical categories upon them places an action theory upon a general foundation.[10] In brief, this theoretical argument comprised the basis for the claims about the very general status of the "pattern variables" as an analytical scheme. It is an argument to which we will recur, not in the context of pattern variable theory, but in considering certain major characteristics of the most inclusive dynamic mechanisms of action systems.

At present, our point of theoretical departure will be the second foundation for generalization that Parsons has propounded. This point is not inconsistent with — indeed, is complementary to — the first; but it encompasses a somewhat different strategy for attaining theoretical generality. It first emerged with the four-function schema and has moved toward the center of the theory of action along with that theoretical device.[11] Its focus falls not upon the elementary relationships of action but upon the conception of an action *system* directly. The four-function paradigm is utilized to analyze the conception of system itself, so that, wherever empirically interdependent entities may legitimately be said to comprise a system, logically parallel or similar theoretical categories may be deployed for their analysis.[12] Here, a general status — logically, a universal status—is attained by a definitional device, i.e., by the definition of each of the four-function categories directly in terms of its relationship to the master category of system.

Our substantive starting point, then, will be the four-function analysis of the action frame of reference itself. The same functional paradigm that has been used most familiarly for analyzing societal systems into the component subsystems of economy, polity, societal community, and the fiduciary (or cultural-institutional) system may, on a more comprehensive level of analysis, be used to distinguish subsystems of the entire action system.[13] The resulting schema of action subsystems is theoretically important because it does not consist simply in a list of parts or components but incorporates certain general functional relationships among the specialized parts of systems that have become known through four-function analyses of other systems. For example, the knowledge that a cybernetic hierarchy of control obtains among systems serving, respectively, the pattern maintenance, the integrative, the goal attainment, and finally the adaptive functions can be applied to the relationships among the subsystems assigned those functional specializations within action systems. In such ways, the four-function paradigm provides a very general ordering among components of a system from which the analyst may theoretically generate a number of more specific hypotheses.

The application of the four-function paradigm to the system of action as a whole serves to define the following set of subsystems:

1. The pattern maintenance function is performed by cultural systems.[14] In this usage, culture is defined more narrowly than has been common in much anthropological literature, where it has encompassed all symbolically mediated products of human behavior that cannot be attributed to the human genetic inheritance or individual psychological factors. In the action theory usage, culture consists of the systems of stable beliefs, whether cognitive, expressively symbolic, moral, or existential, that impart enduring patterns to the meanings that may be generated in action process. The constituent beliefs of a culture, while variously specialized to make meaningful different dimensions of human realities, in-

teract and interlock with one another so as mutually to sustain common patterns for action. Cultural beliefs, then, are not thoughts or attitudes casually engendered in processes of action, but constraining "objects of respect" (in Durkheim's phrase) that embody the enduring modes of solving the difficult problems of human social life. The cultural dimension of human action thusly concerns itself with abstracting from the flow of events what Geertz, in speaking of religious culture, has called "models of and for" proper living.[15] No culture can accomplish this abstracting function along the many dimensions of meaning upon which human society requires enduring models or patterns without coming to incorporate many apparent or latent conflicts. Consequently, all cultures continually undergo processes of the generation of new beliefs, the adjustment of discrepant beliefs to one another, and the discarding of some older elements of belief. Cultural beliefs must also adapt themselves to changing conditions in their "environments," as constituted principally by the other action subsystems, especially perhaps social milieux. Nevertheless, the cultural dimension of action involves an effort to stabilize in the realm of beliefs some grounds of action to which there can be general and common adherence by all actors concerned with the salient sphere of action. In this sense, culture is intrinsically *common* culture in its essential *form*, even though the scope of the commonality may apply to only very limited references (as in highly specialized sciences or art forms) or may be challenged by alternative beliefs.

The theoretical linkage between culture and the performance of the pattern maintenance function lies at the very center of the cybernetic intent of the theory of action. As the unity of the action frame of reference is demarcated fundamentally by the "meaningful" nature of all units or entities within all subsystems of action, the cybernetically controlling or highest-order subsystem must be comprised of a form of "pure meaning." What we are here calling cultural beliefs—in part, to avoid the ambiguities associated with the common formula that culture consists of "symbol systems"—may be regarded as a category of "pure meaning," i.e., meanings that have been abstracted as generally stabilizable from the embodiments of meaning in psychological or interactional substances and systemic exigencies. Elements of cultural systems are thus interrelated, within the culture, sheerly in terms of their meaningful implications upon one another. Particular beliefs assume their degrees and types of functional importance within a culture on grounds of their meaningful prehensions with other beliefs—e.g., of generalization, specification, typification, consistency, and congruency. Change within a cultural system will involve some alteration or adjustment in such meaningful relationships among beliefs. Cultural elements may, however, besides sustaining relationships with other beliefs, become embodied in social and psychological systems. The theory of action has devoted considerable attention to the processes by which cultural content becomes structurally incorporated in the noncultural subsystems of action, processes termed institutionalization for the case of social systems and internalization for the case of psychological systems.[16] These processes of incorporation make possible, on the one hand, the effective engagement of cultural content in the routine processes of action systems and, on the other hand, the relatively consistent meaningful patterning of the characteristic substances of social and psychological systems. In brief, they bring about the cybernetic control of social and psychological processes on the part of the institutionalized and internalized cultural content.[17] The functional significance of these cybernetically hierarchical linkages can be better appreciated when an additional characteristic is also considered: Particular cultural elements may, in varying combinations with other beliefs, become institutionalized and internalized in a large number of specific structural complexes of social and psychological systems. A change in the nature or systemic position of a particular cultural element may consequently ramify through many situations in which social interaction is routinely generated. Conversely, the stabilization of a patterned relationship among certain cultural beliefs may, where there is also stable institutionalization and internalization, serve to regularize a very diverse set of processes of interaction. The very ramified effects of both continuities and changes in such basic cultural themes as that of "equality," taken as a major constituent of contemporary culture, exemplify the diverse impacts that cultural beliefs may control in many areas of an action system. The identification between the performance of pattern maintenance function within the general action system and cultural systems refers to the characteristic capacities of complexes of belief to set limits of meaning upon not only the products of action processes but also the structures regulating the processes of all sectors of action systems. Given the fact that the most general unity of the diverse constituents of action revolves about their meaningfulness, it seems that only in the realm of belief can the maintenance and development of fundamental patterning be effected.

The essay by Thomas J. Fararo in this part comprises a very ambitious effort to bring the conception of a cultural system to bear upon the analysis of the functioning of science. In that it utilizes four-function theory to delimit the operative sphere of science and then to define both subsystems and sub-subsystems within science, it proceeds upon a very technical level of discussion. Its treatment of the relations obtaining among sixteen major components of scientific systems in a theoretically ordered fashion must be regarded as a powerful demonstration of the synthetic potentials of the theory of action procedures as well as a substantial contribution to the general understanding of the functioning of science.

From the point of view developed in the present essay, however, there are some difficulties—interesting ones—in the way in which Fararo articulates his analysis of science into the cultural frame of reference. Science should probably be treated as a system that gains its coherence at the general action level from the convergence of components that are cultural, social, personal, and behavioral.[18] As a sociologist, then, Fararo would presumably be concerned principally with its cultural and social components. However, he attempts to include the range of sociologically most salient components of science within the context of the cultural system alone, treating the identification of science with a primary subsystem of culture as a feature of the functional differentiation of action systems.[19] Fararo is very much aware that a problem arises from this procedure. One might say that the effort to analyze science so very generally within the cultural frame of reference stimulates a certain "return" of the "repressed" social system components. Hence, the rounding out of the general analysis brings certain social system factors to the fore and, as Fararo notes, comes at some points to focus upon institutions which are "cultural" only in the sense of being social relationships that are specialized about the maintenance, protection, and development of cultural content or beliefs. After having begun his analysis within a cultural frame of reference in terms very close to those we have just outlined, especially in locating scientific knowledge within the adaptive subsystem of culture after a model outlined by Parsons, Fararo finds himself breaking out of it to include institutional factors within his discussion. The ultimate unworkability of such mixing of cultural and social frames of reference is perhaps best indicated in the dilemma that then faces the input-output processual analysis. The interchanges between the scientific system and its principal environments, all cultural, must be accomplished on the cultural level. Yet, Fararo's analysis indicates that the interchanging structures within science are in some instances social or institutional in nature. We must conclude that this theoretical situation is in part anomalous. Fararo's effort to carry out an important analysis within cultural terms, despite its synthetic achievements, has not been entirely successful. A principal problem for future theoretical work is to sharpen the conceptualization of cultural process, so that the analysis of process within cultural systems need not revert to the social frame of reference and interactive processes.

Because Fararo's inclusion of social system elements within his schema of the components of science results in a "rounded-out" four-function table, we may presume that an analysis which segregated social components from cultural components would require the identification of some additional elements to complete a cultural analysis. His discussion of the integrative system of science especially seems to focus upon social elements rather predominantly, e.g., in the conception of scientific community. Thus, an effort to extend and improve his valuable analysis might well adopt the task of identifying integrative components that operate upon the cultural level in the strict sense as its point of departure.

2. Social systems perform the integrative function within the system of action as a whole.[20] In the theory of action, social systems have been defined as consisting not of pluralities of individuals or members, but of the interactive relationships among persons. To be sure, all concrete action is in an important sense performed directly by individual persons; yet, in Durkheim's sense, individuals act within a field of constraints imposed by their social relationships.[21] Social system analysis abstracts beyond the individual characteristics of the personal agents of action to focus upon the ways in which constraining social relationships may operate to determine courses of action. The psychological systems of the individuals are thus defined as external to social systems—as to cultural systems—and as separate subsystems of action. The generation, organization, and evolution of interrelationships among the agents of action, then, comprise the concern of our integrative frame of reference.

Within the social system frame of reference, the scope of analysis may vary quite considerably. For some purposes, the analyst may attend to the details of the creation and adjustment of relationships among interactors with respect to some very specific performances. The analytic concern may fall principally upon the procedures or strategies which the interactors may adopt in attempting to manipulate or adjust to the social constraints affecting the interactive situation.[22] A complementary concern may be given to the alternative "fates" that may befall certain constraints as they enter into different specific situations or become subject to different types of interactive manipulation. However, the interests of the analyst often extend beyond specific situations or categories of situations toward broader social matrices that constrain the possibilities for action within situations. Attention may then be given to various modes of organizing relatively stable environments for situations or relatively stable relationships among discrete situations, e.g., to various types of bureaucracy, community, social stratification, or markets. The very complexity of the processes encompassed by such organizations may require the analyst to forego attending to many of the details of the interactions they entail if he is to develop an understanding of the full range of their effects upon diverse situations. Studies of the more complex mechanisms of organization tend to fall back upon the empirical "shorthands" of indices representing aggregates of interactions which cannot all be examined individually and of "structural" descriptions which attempt to outline the stable constraints that regulate *classes* of situations or aspects of them. Although these empirical methods may fairly be criticized as elliptical in their inattention to concrete interaction, they do make possible the synthesis of variegated information into empirical foundations for macroscopic analysis. They enable the analyst to view particular complex socially organized entities as parts of a field characterized by dynamics of a systemic sort, dynamics which may compactly produce important effects on very diverse situations. Theoretically, it is then possible to develop constructs of whole systems of social relationships and to examine the conditions of stability and change across the systems or across analytically defined sectors of them. Much recent work in the theory of action has proceeded at the macroscopic level, often taking whole societies, major subsystems of societies, or, at times, international systems composed of politically organized societies, as principal empirical reference points.[23] The four functional categories have been used to generate hypotheses concerning the requisites of the maintenance, change, and evolution of such large and extensive, often abstractly defined entities. At present, it is important to understand that studies carried out at this macroscopic level are just as thoroughly controlled by the conception that social interaction comprises the reference characteristic for the integrative subsystem of action (i.e,, for social systems) as are studies of the more concrete details of interaction. They fall within the same basic frame of reference, but are simply executed upon more highly aggretated data.

It should be apparent from the foregoing remarks that the understanding of the fundamental and enduring features of any substantial social system or of the location of specific interactive transactions within more stable social relationships—including understanding of openness to change or transformation—requires an acute conception of social structure. The theory of action has focused its treatment of social structure, following Weber and especially Durkheim, very sharply upon normative entities. Since the very early phases of the development of the theory, the discussion of structure has departed from consideration of the Hobbesian "problem of order."[24] If individual actors within a social system were in a radical sense truly free to pursue the satisfaction of their own wants or interests in whatever way they found expedient, social life would be profoundly chaotic. Efforts to explain why societies, though often conflictful, tend not to approach the pure type of the war of all against all have classically emphasized such "structural" factors as the imposed power of the sovereign, the authority of the law, the "invisible hand" of the free market, diffuse deference to the interests of the elite, or even the failure, through alienation, of the masses to pursue self-interests. The Durkheimean and Weberian solution to the problem of order need not deny that such factors may contribute substantially to the structured orders of many societies, yet stresses a more fundamental element without which none of these could be effective. Durkheim—and, somewhat less directly, Weber—argued that the most radical source of order involved the presence in a social system of moral constraints upon the ways in which actors might or should act. Such constraints rested on their general acceptance throughout the "community" of the society, such that actors would tend to enforce them upon one another to a degree that they could not effectively be avoided as grounds of action.[25] Yet, their organization into a moral system made them seem desirable, so that they became the objects of the moral commitments of actors. Hence, they became effective through their own "moral authority" rather than sheerly by the imposition of a sovereign power. Indeed, it has been stressed that what the sovereign can impose, what the market may permit, what the elites may presume to control can become structurally stabilized only where they have substantial legitimation within the normative order of the society.[26] More recent work in the theory of action has striven to show, further, that all "structural" descrepancies or discriminations in allocations of resources, including authority, and of rights to act rest on normative factors. A broad theoretical position has been developed that social structure in general can be treated as comprised of *institutionalized normative culture,* i.e., of normative culture effectively established as constraining for actors in the social systems of reference. Efforts to distinguish different kinds of structure, e.g., Parsons'

well-known paradigm of values, norms, collectivities, and roles,[27] involve the discrimination within institutionalized normative culture of components serving different functions in the constraining of actors' choices for action.

We are now in a position to review the theoretical basis upon which social system functioning is claimed to be integrative for action systems. The institutionalization of normative culture within social relationships enables actors to live with one another with some degree of order, perhaps even concert. It makes possible the pursuit of particular endeavors by some actors, perhaps in coordination with one another, with a degree of confidence that their legitimate activities will not be countered by the illegitimate designs of others. Further, a system of stable social constraints provides fixed reference points whereby actors may engage mutually in rational calculations about how they may expect to coordinate their present and future activities with one another. Indeed, an individual would not be able to coordinate the activities involved in his *own* disparate pursuits if he lacked relatively stable constraints as reference points, as Durkheim demonstrated in his discussion of the limitless expansibility of sheer wants.[28] Thus, the integrative status of social systems involves theoretically not only the coordination of activities among individuals but also the sheer possibility of sustaining positive interdependence among discrete pursuits by human endeavor. The organization and structuring of social systems provides the unique basis of integrated action, i.e., *inter*action, in the most profound sense.

John O'Neill's essay presents a penetrating reexamination of the theory of action position with regard to the problem of order and to the sense of what is problematic for sociological theory that has been established along with the solution of the problem of order. With regard to the abstract, analytical framework of concepts that has been grounded in the solution to the problem of order at the most general level of conceptual work, O'Neill seems not to be attempting to breach the structure of theory within which work upon the theory of action has proceeded. Yet, he develops quite strong criticisms of certain consequences which he attributes, to some degree along with other critics, to Parsons' strategic use of the solution to the problem of order in further specifying social system theory, especially at the macrosocial level.

O'Neill's line of criticism departs from a very original conjoining of the theories of Durkheim, Weber, and Marx. He admits that Marx himself did not develop an adequate treatment of the problem of order, yet maintains that Marx's senses of the problematic in modern society may importantly enrich the implications of more solid solutions of the problem of order. He then discusses Durkheim's and Weber's contributions to the solution of the problem of order, showing that, in different ways, both addressed themselves to issues that had already been articulated by Marx. Thus, Durkheim's treatment of order focused upon the issue of the dynamic interrelations between the rational and the sentimental grounds of attachment to normative constituents of society. It took as deeply problematic the tendencies toward alienation and anomie within modern society, with their consequences especially for the possibilities for a humane moral and sentimental wholeness of the individual. Weber's analysis of order focused upon the evaluative grounds of the legitimation of institutions in modern societies. It was profoundly colored by a deep-seated anxiety about the consequences of the modern commitment to thorough-going rationalization of the bases of order. Weber feared that Western rationalism was perhaps destroying not only importantly supportive traditional orders but even its own nonrational foundations. In brief, O'Neill fears that the formal rationality of current theory of action is perhaps destroying its fruitful rooting in such evaluative concerns with the nature of modern society as those which seem to have motivated Durkheim's and Weber's conceptual efforts. He proposes that the theory of action return more assiduously to treating these problems and suggests that careful study of the ways in which they have been handled in Marx's sociology might prove to be strongly reinvigorating.

3. Performance of the goal attainment function on behalf of systems of action is provided by personality systems.[29] A personality is a psychological system of an individual which organizes, both over time and across different spheres of activity, human motivations to engage in specific lines of action. The theory of action has drawn principally from psychoanalytic thought, including the more recent ego psychology as well as the classically Freudian formulations, in its treatments of personality.[30] From a theory of action standpoint, perhaps the key psychoanalytic conception has been the notion that human motivation is structured by attachments of the libido. By emphasizing the importance of attachments to social objects, including the self as object, Parsons has developed a conception of the personality system in which object-cathexes provide the major constitutive elements. Thus, the motivational dispositions of the individual can be treated as, in general, controlled by the internalized and cathected representations of social alters and of ideals and symbolic patterns absorbed through relations with alters. A central concern of the analysis of a personality must be the

mechanisms, e.g., those which psychoanalysts have called "mechanisms of defense," with which an individual organizes his various complexes of object-cathexes into a relatively coherent system permitting him to act in motivated ways with some degree of consistency. Yet, unless the personality system is to be rather rigid, these mechanisms must allow the individual to make flexible adjustments of his motivational dispositions to various new or changing conditions or realities of the specific situations in which he may become engaged.

Within the social system frame of reference, "the actor" is comprised technically of just those motivations and abilities involved in the performance of the normatively structured role that designates his mode of participation in the situation(s) under study. Especially insofar as one is analyzing not the details of specific sequences of interaction but just the normative organization of the role, one abstracts beyond the characteristics of given individual actors and examines only the structurally standardized requirements upon any actor taking the role.[31] Analysis of personalities also involves the concept of role in important respects, but in a different perspective. Basically, it is through role relationships with alters that a personality comes to internalize representations of cathected social objects. Thus, following Mead's treatment of the construction of the self through the internalization of roles,[32] Parsons has come to treat the structural foundation of the personality as being established through the cathecting of social objects within organized role relationships. Roles, as cathected to take the form of desired potentialities for individual action, comprise a structural level within the personality. A framework of motivational capacities for acting is established by the manifold role relationships that the personality has internalized and cathected through its individual experiences. Each individual personality is, of course, characterized by a unique combination of internalized roles. No one else will have experienced socialization to the same concrete role relationships at the same time in history or the development of the social systems in question. In this respect, each individual personality may be regarded as a unique variation of (or location within) the role-structured potentialities for action permissible within his society—much in the sense that genetically he is also a unique variant of the human gene pool. It follows from our understanding of how particular complexes of cathexis are affected by their dynamic involvements in larger motivational systems, then, that each individual will have rather unique ways of relating motivationally to particular socially structured roles. One may not be able to understand how an individual will behave within even a highly standardized role—and why—without giving consideration to quite a broad range of factors in his personal life experiences. Thus, within the personality system frame of reference, one must attend to the motivationally dynamic relationships that operate both synchronically and over time in a life history among the cathectic complexes of the individual's internalized roles.

The importance of the internalization of roles within personality systems requires that normative culture in general be extensively internalized by individuals, for the structural significance of roles is inherently ambiguous except in the context of collectivity structures, norms, and values. That internalized object-cathexes and role constructs require the support of controlling moral standards is a proposition broadly in line with Freud's and especially the ego-psychologists' treatments of the superego. Theorists of action are apt to place even greater stress on the importance of superego functioning for the personality as a whole than do most psychoanalysts.[33] However, they are also apt to emphasize, perhaps even more than the ego-psychologists, that the superego, although necessarily authoritative within the personality, need not be inflexible or blindly domineering. The theory of action tends to accent the need of the mature, autonomous adult for a superego that can maintain a balance among stable cathectic attachments to many elements of a complex moral system so that the individual can sustain the freedom to select or synthesize appropriate normative standards to regulate action in situations that present difficult moral problems and ambiguities. Individuals saddled with superegos lacking these qualities of flexibility would be ill-equipped to participate in social interaction in situations requiring the creation of new normative grounds of cooperation or, broadly, under conditions of social change. They would be motivationally blocked from exercising the moral creativity essential for participating in cooperative action under such conditions.

Despite the importance of the internalization of normative culture within the personality, it is expressive culture that apparently plays the most strategic role in the organization of personality and in the linkages between culture and personality systems.[34] Expressive culture may be regarded as composed of beliefs and complex symbols which have become functionally specialized about the control of motivational appeal. Since Freud's early work on dreams, which may be regarded as the principal source of contemporary theory concerning expressive meaning, it has been understood that personalities process symbolic meanings largely in terms of their motivational significance.[35] Representations or symbols

may be conjoined or disjoined, projected, displaced, or repressed in ways that yield up symbolic constructs that are affectively satisfying to the individual, given the motivational organization of a personality. The extremely important contribution to this volume by Marshall Edelson explores the possibilities of advancing our knowledge of these expressive processes of the personality by subjecting them to analysis in the technical terms of recent work in transformational linguistics and in the philosophy of symbolism. He demonstrates that the expressive symbolizations of the personality, encompassing the different perspectives upon meaning associated with the various subsystems of the personality as well as both primary and secondary process, can be viewed as the products of the use of recursive transformations upon basic, stable symbolic complexes cathected by the personality in a structural fashion. The transformational processes enable the personality selectively to activate and combine elements of its stable cathectic structures into new symbolizations motivationally appropriate to the requirements of current situations of action. The multiplicity of dimensions of meaning commonly incorporated in expressive symbolization, then, indicates the variety of ways in which a motivational project may be rooted in the structure of the personality. Edelson shows that attention to the systematic mechanisms by which multiple meanings become compacted into symbolizations can reduce the apparent arbitrariness which the psychoanalytic (or action theoretic) interpreter employs in attempting to understand symbolic products. His conclusions in this regard appear to carry methodological import for the whole array of disciplines for which the hermeneutics of expressive symbolism pose substantial problems. Moreover, his theoretical treatment seems to demonstrate that the transformational processes of symbolization and the utilization of symbols comprises the principal mechanism of affective functioning within the personality. That is, it comprises the major means by which affect is communicated among the various constituent cathectic complexes of the personality, hence in which the various parts of the personality can, to some degree in concert with one another, adjust to the emergent problems of motivating action under continually changing conditions.

The essay by James Peacock addresses substantially different, but importantly interrelated, issues associated with expressive symbolism. Peacock argues that the very depth of the penetration of expressive symbolism into the functioning of personality systems requires, if coordination between individual personalities and their sociocultural controls are to be effective, that cultural and social systems must also be prominently involved with expressive symbolism. Expressive beliefs within a culture may thusly be treated as means by which the culture attracts the motivational energies of individuals to its own basic patterns. Indeed, insofar as cultural beliefs become expressively internalized within personalities as templates for the active symbolizations of individuals, the culture may be said thereby to be molding motivations appropriate for gaining implementation of its constituent patterns. To this point, Peacock is putting forward a very strong and general version of a fairly straightforward theory of action interpretation of psychoanalytic discussions of myth, art, and other expressive productions. However, he then argues very originally that a crucial feature of expressive symbolism is the effectiveness it may exert when deployed in processes of social control. By indicating to members of society how their motivational interests may be involved in various collective processes, expressive beliefs comprise forceful persuaders in many types of social interaction. Not least among these is discussion of public matters within the political arena, where the expressive dimensions of political leadership assume a prominent position in the collective process. More generally, Peacock advocates that social scientists attend more seriously to the study of expressive *form* in social interaction, as form seems to be an index of the presence of subtle control over highly charged motivational stakes in a situation of action.

It seems that all primary sectors of an action system must adapt to the fact that action requires motivation. Social and cultural systems are apt to alienate individuals from taking up the tasks of implementing patterns and performing roles unless they adjust to the motivational requirements of their members. Yet, it is personality systems alone that consist structurally of stable motivational dispositions and function to generate the positive motives that lead individuals into active participation in projects of action. The goal attainment status of personality systems within the general action system revolves about their motivational specialization. Cultural and social systems function respectively to define enduring models for action and to establish constraints upon the possibilities for action. Neither functions to mobilize the energies of individuals toward the implementation of specific lines of action under specific conditions. Personalities serve to select among the many desirable potentialities for action just those projects which may fulfill the needs and desires of individuals. They must be comprised of highly complex, differentiated, and ramified systems because individuals must be able to sustain many distinct types of desires and must find motivation to fulfill many different kinds of roles. It is in developing and ordering motivated choices to pursue ends that are quite finitely selective among the infinite possibilities for action, then, that personality systems contribute to goal attainment functioning.

4. The subsystem of action serving the adaptive function has been termed by Parsons the behavioral organism.[36] With this conception, Parsons has attempted to define a framework for abstracting from the full concreteness of human organisms just those aspects which contribute relatively directly to the capacities to act. The central nervous system occupies the primary position in the functioning of the behavioral organism, with its abilities to process symbolic materials constituting its most important characteristic. The responsivity of the central nervous system to the visceral needs of the organism, to such drives as sex, hunger, and thirst, or to the excitations of fear, aggression, and anxiety, often in relation to symbolic communication with others, also comprises a major factor in the functioning of the behavioral organism. Parsons has also stressed the degree to which the interrelations between the libido and the central nervous system make it possible, despite the senses in which the libido specially serves sexual and other particular drive structures, for individuals to find some "reward"—often in a very symbolic fashion—in many kinds of acts which do not directly satisfy biological needs. The resulting "plasticity" of behavior, i.e., its openness to organization on bases other than the physiological or instinctual, constitutes a major foundation of all action. Besides these respects in which the organization of the central nervous system itself structures the behavioral organism, a number of more peripheral factors have substantial conditioning effects. Thus, the opposable thumb and the manual skills it facilitates, the erect posture and its effects on mobility, the physiology of binocular vision and its consequences both for seeing and imaginatively envisioning, and other such factors comprise significant constituents of the behavioral organism.

The paper by Charles W. Lidz and Victor Meyer Lidz proposes an alternative conceptualization of the adaptive subsystem of action. They argue that the concept of the behavioral organism violates the action frame of reference in placing physiological rather than meaningful entities in so central a position in a primary subsystem of action. Consequently, they attempt a reformulation of the adaptive subsystem under the heading of "behavioral system," using Piaget's psychology of intelligence as their principal theoretical base. The elementary units of a behavioral system are Piaget's "schemas," the mental constructs that directly control behavioral performances more complex than simple reflexes.

The organization of a behavioral system is comprised largely of means of coordinating schemas with one another in ways that allow complex projects of behavior to be developed. The ontogenesis of behavioral systems moves, as Piaget has demonstrated, from direct sensory and motor coordination among schemas to their coordination through significant or symbolic representation and then through the performance of operations upon the representations. Piaget has argued that full adult intelligence is attained only when the coordinative operations themselves become abstract and formalized. Intelligence in this usage constitutes the characteristically human generalized resource for implementing lines of action in ways that can cope with or even master environing conditions.

Lidz and Lidz devote much of their paper to analysis of the internal differentiation of the behavioral system. They identify, through four-function analysis, distinct subsystems, each specialized about the control of a different dimension of the use of intelligence. They argue that the differences among the behavioral subsystems may best be understood as concomitants of differential articulations with the other primary subsystems of action. Sociologically, they stress that the detailed examination of processes of interaction may be appreciably advanced by Piagetian analyses of the specialized intelligent understandings and operations involved in the behavioral capacity to engage in the dynamics of social relationships.

The conceptualizations of the adaptive subsystem of action advanced respectively by Parsons and by Lidz and Lidz converge in focusing upon categories of characteristically human resources for gaining control over the environments of action systems. In this respect, they are both guided by the same notion of what constitutes adaptive functioning. They differ principally over where the line should be drawn between the action system proper and its conditioning environment. Parsons attempts to include within the action system, through the analytical distinction between the behavioral and the merely "vegetative" organism, all elements that routinely function in the production of concrete behavior. Lidz and Lidz prefer to exclude from the action system those factors of behavior which do not seem to fall directly within the frame of reference of the "sciences of meaning," although they do not dispute the empirical importance of the physiological resources in the generation of human behavior. They do argue, however, that the Piagetian psychology of intelligence should be regarded as treating primary complexes of action, which must be included within the action system and which should not be handled as a sector of personality. In an essay attempting to outline

current thinking on the whole action system and emphasizing certain elements of interdependence among diverse parts of action systems, it seems appropriate to note, finally, that Lidz and Lidz claim to be facilitating certain aspects of cultural and especially social analysis through their reconceptualization of the adaptive subsystem.

The essay by Thomas F. O'Dea raises problems concerning the general adequacy with which the theory of action formulations manage to cover their entire frame of reference with analytically fruitful concepts. Although O'Dea addresses most of his doubts and questions to social system matters specifically, it seems that the most productive reading of his essay would generalize his concerns to the level of the general action system as a whole. O'Dea develops his critical stance from his own involvements with theory in the sociology of religion, with the methodological issues raised by German historicism and by *Verstehende* procedures in social science, and with the phenomenological critiques of structuralist theory in sociology. He contends that the theory of action has placed a disproportionate emphasis upon a model which defines the actor as a task-fulfiller, one who adopts certain discrete means to attain certain chosen ends. He suggests that greater emphasis should be placed upon analysis of the processes by which actors create, construct, form, express, act out, or evolve systems or complexes of meaning. As it is systems of meaning that provide context for the normative structures that regulate the pursuit of goals, an analytical framework focused upon the construction of meaning would seem to provide access to a more fundamental aspect of human action. A phenomenologically adequate theory within this framework will have to confront directly the senses in which man, himself, through his multiply interpretable symbols and beliefs, is an ambiguous being.

In order to capture the open-ended, continually reconstructing nature of man as creator of meanings, O'Dea proposes that we conceive the actor, far more inclusively than as a task-performer or a rational thinker, as a responder. Such an actor would state the scope of his actuality by paraphrasing Descartes in the words, "*Respondeo, ergo sum.*" On such a conception of the actor, O'Dea suggests that the four-function analysis of action be "opened up" by placing it in the context of a dialectical, responsive interaction with certain enduring features of the human condition. He puts forward a schema, termed the BASE model, with which he proposes to capture the essentials of the human condition generally — its relation to the Beyond or transcendent reality, its fulfillment of the requisites of human Association, its involvement in the Structure of the human being, and its location in a challenging Environment. Perhaps the principal problem associated with O'Dea's proposal is that the relations between the four-function analysis of the action frame of reference and the BASE model are certainly very complex, especially in that the latter is not simply environmental or external to the action frame of reference but at many points penetrates into it. Nevertheless, if this new formulation draws more attention to the dynamics involved in the relations between the action system and its plurality of environments, it may serve as a fruitful complement to the theory of action.

The contribution by Jan J. Loubser is the essay in this section developed at the highest level of generality and which deals with the broadest array of elements within action systems in a technical fashion. It amounts to a very general review of the organization of the analytical categories that have figured most prominently in recent developments within the theory of action. Loubser intends it as a preliminary exploration of some alternative formulations of basic theoretical relations, but not yet as a thoroughly justified conceptual scheme in itself. I believe that it is best read as a stimulating theoretical exercise, raising a host of questions about, and new possibilities for, the articulation of a parsimonious general theory of action.

From the present point of view, perhaps the most interesting characteristic of Loubser's discussion is its broad strategy for the development of theory at the general action level. In a sense, it covers much of the same material included in the present introductory essay but builds the theory from a rather different starting point. The reader will therefore find a number of differences in emphasis and in formulation despite the fact that the two essays attempt to work within the same general theory.

Loubser's theoretical strategy, in a fashion following Parsons' early focus upon the "unit act," makes consideration of the very simplest system of action the starting point for construction of a theory that should apply to all action systems. Thus, Loubser begins by listing four elements that seem to be essential to the very definition of the action which can be accomplished by an actor involved in a situation of minimal complexity. He then treats these four elements as the primitive variables of the general theory, the central terms with which all others are to be associated as the theory gains elaboration. The foundation for elaborating a very inclusive, internally differentiated, and technically articulated theory is developed by linking both the four-function paradigm and the pattern-variable scheme to these master terms. In this process, some major revisions in the articulations between the four function and pattern-

variable formulae are proposed. The revised comprehensive paradigm is then used to define four basic types of action and to characterize them in terms of functional specialization and in terms of the sequences of pattern variable choices through which they are realized. With the resulting conceptual corpus, Loubser has new theoretical means for addressing problems of the characteristics of action systems that emerge with larger scales and with complexity.

Loubser takes up the problems of complexity by introducing not only the emergent contingencies of interaction between an ego and an alter, but also, following Luhmann (in this book), the distinction between the effects of an actor's conduct upon the situation, termed "action" in a special, narrower sense, and the effects of processes in the situation upon the actor, termed "experience." Informally, Loubser is explicating the consequences of complexity upon each of four cells in a two-by-two table, attending to the action and the experience of both ego and alter. In doing so, he comes to focus upon the sanctioning processes that link an ego's conduct to an alter's experience or vice versa. In this theoretical context, the interplay of sanctions in on-going systems of interaction is portrayed as a crucial form of exchange among actors. The kinds of sanctions entering interaction are grouped according to their associations with the four general types of action, so that their characteristics can be analyzed in pattern-variable terms and their differential bearing upon specialized sectors of social systems can be analyzed in four-function terms. Loubser then treats the generalized media of interchange, which consist in circulable symbolic representations of sanctioning capacities of specialized kinds, as, on the one hand, reducing the complexities of multiple contingent sanctioning processes and, on the other hand, imparting flexibility and open-endedness to interaction.

Loubser's discussion of the generalized media and the dynamic qualities they bring to interaction holds for the most part quite closely to the format of considering exchanges of sanctions between an ego and an alter. Thus, double interchanges are considered as arising from an interplay of a sanction and a sanctioned action on the part of both ego and alter. A figure is developed to indicate all the logical possibilities for the exchange of holdings of different media between an ego and an alter. Consideration is given to the possibility that an ego and an alter may exchange resources or media that have been generated at processes located at different "levels" in the organization of the whole system of action. Reference is made to problems of aggregates primarily in discussing the effects of decisions to save, spend, hoard, or invest holdings of media upon the dynamics of larger systems. From the present point of view, however, more emphasis should be placed on markets and their institutional regulation and on problems of aggregation in all aspects of the treatment of media of social interaction. For example, double interchanges occur only exceptionally between particular egos and alters. Their principal functional significance is that they permit the more or less orderly movement of resources among very large numbers of actors playing very different kinds of roles in an encompassing system. Moreover, the sense in which they emerge at the boundaries of sectors of a system can be understood only in relation to the needs for resources — needs of units as well as systems, to be sure — that are determined by aggregate conditions due to differentiations among sectors. Finally, only by considering the nature of the structure of a market, e.g., the types of contractual exchange permitted by salient norms and the terms of competition, scale of resource circulation, and degree of concentration, can one provide very accurate analyses of the interchanges between particular egos and alters occurring in that market.

In a final section, Loubser addresses a problem which has concerned a great many commentators on the theory of action, namely, what the paths may be from the abstract corpus of the theory to focused treatment of particular empirical systems. He proposes that a crucial part in the operationalization of the theory must be played by variables falling outside the scope of the functional categories of the formal theory itself. What he terms "state variables" are intended to "capture the non-functional ranges of variation in social action." In the analysis of empirical systems, the proposed state variables, of which Loubser lists fourteen, are to be given values prior to the bringing of the functional categories to bear upon the phenomena at hand. The state variables are then to serve as parameters for guiding the processes by which variables internal to the theory are assigned empirical values. The implication seems to be that determinate relations cannot be drawn among variables internal to the theory until some parametric quantities have been established.

For some kinds of variables, e.g., Loubser's fourteenth, the space-time parameters of social action, this point is quite unexceptionable. We can all agree that human action does not occur outside of certain parameters of space, time, temperature, nuclear radiation, chemical composition of the environment, and so on. Moreover, it is not idle to treat such factors as parameters of the action system, for they deeply condition its internal organization. What would action be like if men could reverse time or, in a physically objective sense, change its

pace during their interaction? Action does change when the temperature changes, when the earth shakes, when night comes, as the seasons pass. However, Loubser wants to treat many variables that actually fall within the action frame of reference as parametric in a comparable sense, e.g., the integration, stability, pluralization, and differentiation of the system.

While I do not doubt that this proposal has its heuristic attractions for more rapid development of the capacity to analyze many systems in approximate ways, I do not think that such advantages should be confused with theoretical desirability on a general level. The theoretical strategy of the theory of action has long been to attempt to build systematically into the hypothetical corpus all important variables that fall within the action frame of reference. To be sure, the contents of Loubser's state variables are not built directly into the abstract categories of the four-function paradigm. But then *no* categories of empirical variables are built directly into the paradigm. The paradigm itself constitutes only an abstract ordering of abstract categories that make no direct empirical references. Only as the theory is contexted to particular empirical systems or classes of them can empirical variables be aligned with the functional categories. Loubser presents no reason for us to expect that his state variables can in principle not be accommodated through the general analytical process of contexting abstract categories — or of "filling the boxes," in Smelser's phrase — that has been followed in previous studies. Thus, it seems preferable to uphold the theoretical ideal that the state variables too can in principle be treated as context-specific instances of aspects of and relations among the general categories of the theory. To treat empirically important and theoretically significant variables falling within the action frame of reference in any fundamentally different fashion would be seriously to undermine the conceptual integrity of the theory. In the longer run, the heuristic benefits gained by following Loubser's method would, unless other work continued following a method attempting a tighter theoretical integration of all variables, come at the cost of a considerable debasement of the dynamic potential of the four-function scheme itself.

Finally, a critical comment must be ventured on the changes that Loubser introduces in the articulations between the four-function paradigm and the pattern variables. If these changes are conceptually valid, they bear very fundamental consequences for the general ordering of the theory. The logical format of the four-function paradigm as a cross-classification of dichotomous variables would be undermined. The cybernetic ordering among the functional categories would be rendered quite problematic, or at least quite substantially changed. Also, as Loubser emphasizes, the nature of the pattern-variable choices associated with specialization about performance of certain of the functions would be altered.

I believe that the difficulties in Loubser's presentation of the theoretical categories stem from the nature of the action system which he uses as a baseline in defining his primitive terms. By focusing upon *an* actor in relation to a situation, he has abstracted beyond at least much of the social organization of a simple action system. In defining the primitive terms, then, the pattern maintenance aspect of the system is treated as "motivational," since the basic stabilizing patterns of an individual only seemed essential to consider. However, as generalization to a multi-actor system should make clear, "motivational" is too restrictive and reductive a category. A more appropriate master term would have been "orientational," I believe, as it would have shown that the commonality of orientation and motivation of a plurality of actors is crucially problematic for a social system. By the time Loubser considers such problems, it is in the section addressing the complexities emergent with interaction. But by that point, he has already developed his general conceptual apparatus using "motivational" as the key pattern maintenance term.

Stressing the characteristics of motivation, Loubser links the category of pattern maintenance with the consummatory dimension of action, rather than with the instrumental dimension as has been customary. He then suggests that the regulatory import of normative structures should be regarded as instrumental, and hence that the function of integration should be aligned with the instrumental dimension. A reversal of the instrumental/consummatory linkages of the pattern maintenance and integrative functions has thus been proposed. Loubser follows this proposal through in a logically consistent manner by maintaining the alignments between the pattern-variable choices and the instrumental and consummatory dimensions, thereby altering the pattern-variable choices that cluster about the pattern maintenance and integrative functions. It is the resulting integral paradigm articulating the four functions with the pattern variables that becomes the foundation of much of the rest of the essay, as I have outlined above.

As the term "orientational" would have made clearer, the pattern maintenance function is properly associated with the instrumental dimension of action systems. The systemic significance of pattern maintenance functioning is to establish principles and standards for evaluating the conduct of units in the system and to generate commitments to such principles and standards. Functioning of this type is not consummatory in a direct fashion, especially not for the system involved. To be sure, there may be

consummatory involvements for certain units within the system — e.g., in the tension management aspects of the functioning internal to the units. Nevertheless, the direct significance of the action is on the system level preparatory or preliminary to any possibility of consummation, and hence is instrumental. For example, setting and inculcating standards by which an actor can judge whether some line of conduct should be regarded as enjoyable or not does not amount to the enjoyment itself. It is a process instrumental to subsequent events of enjoyment.

The consummatory status of the integrative function seems to me to be equally straightforward. The detailed normative regulation that comprises the core of integrative functioning in social systems assures that the outcomes of the various processes in which various units engage will be consistent with a state of internal solidarity. It comes to focus upon the relations obtaining among the units of the system taken as an endpoint of particular action processes. The solidarity of the system is a state of at least temporary consummation, albeit a state of consummation concerned with internal conditions of the system rather than its achievement of goals in relation to environmental conditions.

It follows from these considerations, I believe, that the basic paradigmatic changes proposed by Loubser are unfounded. Of course, the reader is entitled to his own judgment, and may find Loubser's account more persuasive than I have indicated it to be. What we can certainly agree upon, though, is that it is precisely through challenges to very fundamental formulations in the theory, such as those Loubser has mounted, that the fruitful grain and the chaff in the theory can be separated. Moreover, skepticism about particular proposals should not distract one from attending to the virtues of Loubser's broad synthesis of perspectives and levels of analysis in the theory of action.

We have to this point concentrated our discussion upon reviewing the basic conceptualization within the theory of action of the four primary subsystems of action and of their respective functional specializations. The notion of an integral system of action, however, implies that these distinct types of system can, despite their important differences, engage in coordinated processes with one another. Hence, we now turn to the question: How is it possible for the distinct subsystems of action to communicate and coordinate processes with one another? The answer to this question will require our giving attention to what appears to be the most general and inclusive of the generalized symbolic mechanisms of action.

It may be helpful first to refine our orienting question somewhat. It may seem that our sense of problem here is sheerly an artifact of the analytical perspective of the theory of action. To be sure, if we did not distinguish four subsystems of action by abstraction from action in the concrete, we would have no problem of accounting for communication among subsystems of action. However, it would still be a legitimate and important matter to ascertain how the meaningful processes of action can be sustained on bases that permit prehensions among elements of action to extend over substantial spans of time simultaneously in dimensions that, analytically, we identify as cultural, social, personal, and behavioral. That is, although the conceptualizations of subsystems may be artifacts of theory, the ingression of diverse dimensions of organization in specific projects of action appears to be fact substantially independent of the present theoretical perspective. Thus, we may, starting from a more concrete or phenomenological perspective, identify an obverse aspect of our problem: How is it possible for particular projects of action to stand simultaneously in relationships to cultural, social, personal, and behavioral dimensions of actuality?

Our answer will focus upon the generalized symbolic medium of language. The theory of action has now had a fairly long-standing interest in the mechanisms of language. From his first discussions of the conceptual category of "generalized symbolic medium of interchange," Parsons has introduced the Jacobson-Halle distinction between code and message into the general model of a medium.[37] Language has often been discussed as a prototypical instance of the media. Indeed, it has stood second only to money in being treated as a prototypical medium. Yet, no convincing analysis has been put forward of the precise functional location within action systems that should be attributed to language.[38] It has remained something of a "free-floating" medium, therefore, and the value of holding it up as a prototypical medium has perhaps been considerably reduced on that account. Here, a functional location for language will be proposed, and it will be maintained, moreover, that this functional location makes clear why language should be given high theoretical priority as a model for the treatment of other media.

Language will be discussed as comprising the core of the generalized mechanism of the whole system of action. It stands "over" the media which have been treated as specialized about regulation of the combinatorial and interchange processes of each of the four primary subsystems of action.[39] Thus, it provides the basis in common meaning by which the processes generated by the respective action subsystem media may be coordinated with one another. Moreover, the use of language seems to require the convergence under specific conditions of processes

identifiable as cultural, social, personal, and behavioral. It is for this reason that the study of language penetrates into such a broad range of humanistic, sociological, psychological, and even physiological disciplines.[40]

As a medium, language imparts a certain validity and mobility to messages of meaning. Action organized in terms of the grammar of a language gains a certain breadth of *currency* which cannot be guaranteed to symbolic meanings lacking that formal discipline. Action so organized may be characterized by a stability at the level of meaning — what linguists operationalize in terms of at least relative freedom from ambiguity[41] — that enables it to be communicated with comparatively little entropy upon (or decay of) meaning to other "locations" within systems of action. The locations to which a linguistically well-formed action can be communicated may differ from its location of origin in any of the basic dimensions of the organization of action systems, or any plurality of them. Locations of generation and of destination may differ as regards specialization of the behavioral schemas, of the motivational complexes, of the institutional situations, and of the cultural constructs involved. Communication may be contained within any of the primary subsystems of action, for example, within the behavioral or personality systems of a given individual, within a specific interactive situation, or within a specialized complex of culture (e.g., a science). Or, communication may extend indefinitely far from its original source — for example, as have the words of Aristotle when they become incorporated within a modern philosophical work, which involves vastly different schemas, motivations, social milieux, and cultural contexts. Language, by lending a formal "validity" to action, makes possible both the codification and indefinite storage of meaning *and* the indefinitely wide transfer of symbolic meaning of extraordinary import. The potential for storage and transfer of meaning becomes bounded only by the condition that the grammar of the language must be understood and that ambiguities and failures of communication will be introduced as the grammar changes.

It is not necessary to maintain that language provides the only medium for such indefinite transfer of meaning. There seem to be a large number of other forms of symbolic communication that, especially within various types of specialized contexts, also provide quite generalized validation of meaning: e.g., mathematical notation, representational drawing, or gestural signs. It seems that any symbolic mechanism containing a systematic "code" of signs having arbitrarily established meanings (and hence approximating Saussure's famous characterization of language)[42] may stabilize meaning adequately for extensive storage and transfer. Thus, it may be best to speak of signification, including linguistic signification, as comprising the full generalized medium of the general action system. For present purposes, however, this formulation is a technicality. Language clearly constitutes overwhelmingly the most widely employed means of signification. It is itself highly differentiated internally, for example, in the differences between spoken and written language, formal and colloquial usage, specialized technical terminologies and everyday speech, or between expressive, poetic, or ritual uses and profane usage. Yet, language generally manages to contain such internal differentiation within a fremework that sustains a very broad currency of meaning for standard, commonly employed usages and that restricts specialized usages to relatively simple variations of the ordinary grammar. By focusing sharply upon language within the field of signification, we are probably best assured of gaining understanding of the methods by which meanings gain such vast combinatorial flexibility and breadth of currency within action systems.

A bit of digression is necessary at this point to provide background for our analysis of how language can accomplish its mediating functions throughout the realm of action. The digression concerns the background of the first of the two approaches just noted through which the theory of action has attempted to gain theoretical generality in its analysis of the action frame of reference. This model—that of actor, alter, orientation of actor, and modality of object—shares a Cartesian background with the current linguistic formulations of the transformational grammarians. It will provide the basis upon which we can draw some key linkages between recent linguistic generalizations about the universal nature of human languages and the action frame of reference.

The Cartesian paradigm[43] of the observer who comes to "know" objects in his environment has provided a foundation for important analytical systems in a variety of modern intellectual disciplines. It has established the principal terms for most modern speculation on epistemological problems, especially in contexts in which evidentiary standards have been set up for intellectual disciplines. In the social sciences, it has framed various efforts to establish clear standards concerning the types of objects (or events) and the means of coming to "know" them that should guide the disciplined observer.

Durkheim's conception of a realm of "social facts" which are made known to the social scientist by their characteristics of "externality" and "constraint" is clearly a specification of the Cartesian framework.[44]

Durkheim also employed the Cartesian paradigm in a more substantive way, however. Thus, he treated the processes of social action basically as relations obtaining between an actor and the social objects in his milieu. That is, Durkheim developed a general "model" of action which was fundamentally a generalization of the Cartesian model of knowledge. Although he restricted the realm of objects with which he was concerned to the social, he expanded the modes of relation between subject and the realm of objects from simply that of "knowing" to all forms of "acting."[45]

G. H. Mead arrived at the same general post-Cartesian position. Moreover, he stressed specially that social relationships always involve actors who are at the same time the objects of the actions or behavior of other actors and even of their own action.[46] Mead also focused specifically upon the ways in which language made possible precise and effective communication between actors and their objects. Here, he placed emphasis upon the respect in which the individual's interactively constructed "self" involved the embodiment of a reflexive relationship—the category "reflexive" being originally a grammatical one. More generally, he held language, with its socially and objectively given meanings, to be a crucial means for transforming the consciousness of the self and its experiences from the subjective to the objective form.[47] Of course, the reciprocal transformation, by which external or objective events could be made subjectively meaningful, would also comprise a principal component of a system of signification. Thus, for Mead, significant behavior could not conceivably be sustained in a system of interaction without the presence of language and its capabilities for mediating between the subjective and objective components of human experience.

Against this background, certain recent findings in linguistic research seem to be very striking. It should be emphasized that these findings have emerged from extensive efforts to outline what is called "universal grammar," i.e., a theoretical account of some central generalizations that apply to the ways in which all human languages are organized grammatically.[48] These efforts have been grounded in the theoretical expectation that, insofar as elements of a universal grammar can be identified, they should pertain to some very fundamental characteristics of human nature.

A key generalization—which apparently has the support of structuralists[49] as well as of the transformationalists who have been most involved in the project to discover a universal grammar—is that a core element of the grammar of every known human language involves the categorization of parts of sentences into subjects, objects, verbs, and modifiers.

Languages do not require each sentence to contain at least one instance of each of these grammatical categories. Moreover, languages differ markedly in the ways in which they permit these types of sentential parts (or phrases) to be combined with one another and ordered within sentences. Yet, all do include the distinctions among the categories as crucial elements of the syntactical structures which all individuals must understand in order to communicate linguistically. Thus, an element of grammar that is *universal* among human languages (and therefore human action) is the susceptibility of sentences to parsing in terms of the phrase categories of subject, object, verb, and modifier.

We can see that the categories of sentential parts in universal grammar correspond directly to the central categories which Parsons has proposed for analysis of the action frame of reference. Both consist of subject, object, mode of subject's relation to object (verb, orientation), and qualities of the object, actor, or relation (modifier, modality). The well-formed sentence in any natural language must contain elements—though some will lack objects or modifiers—which are exemplars of the crucial, irreducible elements of action, as schematized by Durkheim, Mead, and theorists of action. In the present formal terms, sentences will differ principally in the degree of complexity with which they combine exemplars of these central categories. Perhaps the syntactical structure of a sentence should be regarded as a basic instance and model of the "unit act" in essentially the meaning given that term in *The Structure of Social Action.*[50] What seems most important for current concerns, however, is that the categorial structure of well-formed sentences permits them to mediate among the primary subsystems of action. Given that this structure corresponds to that of action at the most general level, it may be said to be shared among the primary subsystems of action. The cultural, social, personal, and behavioral dimensions of action all consist in ways of operating upon some or all of the basic categories of action.[51] Language, which also incorporates the same categorial structure, then comprises the mechanism by which these separate systems may communicate with one another and in terms of which projects of action can become composed of "contributions" from the several action subsystems simultaneously. The universal syntactic structure of human languages thus appears to constitute the key functional characteristic which, theoretically, one would have to attribute to the symbolic medium of the general action system.

The parallel we have just noted between the "Cartesian" categories for analyzing the action frame of reference and the syntactic categories now regarded as linguistic universals should stimulate an interest on the part of theorists of action in the recent return of linguistic theory to a Cartesian foundation. The transformationalists of the Chomsky school have rejected the scientistic and behavioristic standards of most earlier modern linguistics, which tended to limit the empirical concerns of the linguist to directly observable features of concrete speech acts. Instead, they have departed from a Cartesian conception of "mind," i.e., of the organization and operations that the Cartesian school attributed to the observer or subject of knowledge in order to account for his capacity to cognize objects.[52] Within the domain of linguistics, they have taken grammatical sentences of the natural language as the field of objects which speakers of the language "know" in the sense of being able to interpret. The "mind" that can know this field of objects requires some special attributes, however, because the number of potential objects is infinite in the sense that sentences with new and original structures are continually being created. It must be able to analyze sentences into the abstract grammatical categories in terms of which their parts are organized and then perform transformational operations upon these abstract categories. It is through the application of the finite set of transformational rules to the syntactic categories in variable combinations that the language speaker gains his mastery of an infinite number of sentence structures.[53] Chomsky has referred to this capacity of the syntactical mechanism as "generativity," i.e., the ability freely to create newly organized linguistic entities. He has argued, largely within a psychological frame of reference, that the implications of the capacity of generativity extend beyond linguistics and that it reveals very fundamental characteristics of the human mind, perhaps human nature generally. Sociologists such as Habermas,[54] Cicourel,[55] and Garfinkel and Sacks[56] have recently been toying with a conception of a more diffuse communicative generativity that, while entailing linguistic generativity, enters into human interaction in ways other than the linguistic. The theorist of action may recognize in the discussions of generativity many themes from the older discussions of "voluntarism."[57] Attention to the analysis of generativity in the linguistic case seems warranted for the light it may shed on how mechanisms of action sustain their voluntaristic freedom while remaining ordered.

Transformational theory has developed a relatively narrow, well-focused frame of reference for analyzing language. It has not attempted to cover the full range of factors which bear upon the determination of who says what, when, and why. Rather, it has concentrated upon the properties of sentences (or other language products) which validate them as grammatical. Its principal source of data has consisted in the judgments of "native speakers" about whether or not particular productions are grammatical and about why they are or are not grammatical.[58] It has tried to construct for each language — or part of a language — subjected to study a grammar that provides the most parsimonious account of what the judgments of native speakers will prove to be with regard to any particular linguistic product.

More technically, syntactic theory concerns itself in the first instance with the grammaticality of what is termed "surface structure." Surface structure refers to the linear ordering and syntactic marking of the constituents of a sentence into a form appropriate for phonological interpretation, i.e., for conversion into sounds. Surface structures must be contrasted with "deep structures," which are comprised sheerly of the meanings that are to be brought into the salient sentences. Deep structures may not be ordered in a fashion that can be recognized as grammatical or that can be given a direct phonological interpretation. It is the work of the transformational rules of the grammar to convert deep structures into surface structures that may be directly realized in speech or, obversely, to permit the surface structure obtained by a phonological analysis of a spoken or written sentence to be converted into a deep structure from which a meaning can be apprehended.[59] A matter of current theoretical debate is whether semantic rules are to be included in the component of the grammar that converts deep structures into surface structures, and vice versa, or whether semantic rules can be assigned the exclusive function of rendering deep structures meaningful. The resolution of this debate is not strategically important to present considerations, however. What we are concerned with is the conception that deep structures which embody meaning in an abstract form that is either syntactically simple or perhaps syntactically disordered may be converted by undergoing a series of rule-ordered transformations into an indefinite number of different, individual grammatical surface structures.[60] The detailed understanding of the generativity of a grammar must focus, then, on the ways in which transformational rules — and not simply single rules but often ordered sets of rules — reorganize the syntactical materials of sentences. If we are to examine the voluntaristic generativity of action mechanisms other than language itself, we might be advised to search out sets of transformational processes that convert "deep" forms into "surface" forms that have added functional capacities yet ascertainable relations to the "deep" forms they represent.

The crucial matter of generativity may perhaps be clarified somewhat further by brief consideration of a convergent dimension of Levi-Strauss's work on the analysis of myth. Leach's recent account of Levi-Strauss's structuralism emphasizes that there are two senses in which a mythical product may appear to be structured.[61] The first, considered under the term metonymy, concerns the organized relations of conjunction between a symbol or sign and the others with which it is used in a particular product. Linguistically, the syntactical structure of a sentence is an instance of metonymical relationships, whether at the level of deep structure, surface structure, or intermediate products of transformations. Structure in the second sense, which Leach calls metaphor, consists in the common meanings or patterns which underlie all particular metonymical usages. Thus, a Freudian analysis of the Oedipal meanings of various events in various myths would comprise analysis of metaphorical structure. So would the effort to develop a "dictionary" giving the stable meanings of words incorporated in different sentences generated by the grammar of a language. Leach makes clear that metonymical structure consists in the conjunction with one another of items selected for appropriateness in the immediate situation of their stable metaphorical meanings.

We may now see that the relation between metaphor and metonymy is none other than that which the theory of action has long treated under the heading of code and message.[62] This relation is not equivalent to that between deep structure and surface structure, for both of the latter are instances of metonymy. Yet, transformational grammar does clarify the relation between metaphor and metonymy by making clear how, in ordered ways, metonymical structures can assume so vastly various forms even when based on common metaphorical structures. Most broadly, it is the relation between metaphor and metonymy that is generative. We will now proceed to explore some of the ways in which generativity is characteristic of mechanisms of the general action system other that language itself.

Language should probably be regarded as the most powerfully generative of the mechanisms of action. By identifying it as the "master" mechanism of the general action system most inclusively, we are claiming that language exercises its generativity over the broadest range of analytically distinct elements of action systems, i.e., over elements of all four primary subsystems of action. It also appears to be the mechanism that routinely produces the greatest number and substantively most diverse metonymical entities. Yet, we do not claim that language is the medium of all action, but only symbolically generalized action that has substantial *currency* throughout action systems. Action is composed within the medium of language —

or, more generally, signification—only insofar as it is symbolically generalized action. However, it is the symbolically generalized action, i.e., significantly meaningful action, that comprises the matter of central interest to a theory of action.

The critical part of language in the production of symbolically generalized action certainly constitutes important grounds for placing it in the theoretical position of an analytically prototypical medium. However, an additional, though related, reason may also be put forward. The processual outputs of the primary subsystems of action, in forms mediated by their respective generalized symbolic media, must feed into the processes by which action becomes composed within the medium of language. For this to occur relatively successfully, it is necessary for the mediated outputs of the primary subsystems of action to have a form upon which linguistic processes can operate. We may hypothesize that the outputs in fact take on this type of form because the processual mechanisms through which they are produced have themselves evolved, at least in certain respects, in a language-like fashion. That is, the operative constraint that they produce outputs having broadly linguistic qualities may be hypothesized to have shaped their own evolutionary development. In this essay, we will attempt to demonstrate that at least certain characteristics of the media of the primary subsystems of action may fruitfully be analyzed in terms of a linguistic model. We would expect that media anchored at lower levels of the action system, e.g., the media operating in the four subsystems of society, being further removed from the operations of language in the composition of action, would be less likely to exhibit language-like qualities to such an important degree.

Taking language as a prototypical medium, we may summarize from the foregoing discussion some key elements of a theoretical model of media or of symbolically mediated processes. First, it should be possible to parse or analyze grammatically the processual outputs in terms of the universal categories of syntax and of the components of the action frame of reference. Second, particular outputs, with their syntactic organization, should stand as generated metonymical constructions which take on their meanings by reference to a metaphorical code. Third, it should be possible to identify the valid products of the mediated processes as constituting the outcomes of specific transformations. The generativity of the processual mechanism should demonstrably be the result of the application of transformations. Fourth, the transformations should accomplish the work of moving produced entities from a "deep," relatively unformed or situationally unadapted, level to a "surface" level suitable for use in the situation of

action. For the media of the primary subsystems of action, the "surface" level would seem to correspond to the "deep" level of linguistic process. Within a given situation, the four general action media regulate the transformation of products of their respective systems into entities that can become "deep structures" for the activities of language. As products of the respective primary subsystems are taken up as entities of deep structure by linguistic processes, become selectively interrelated with one another, and undergo linguistic transformation into ordered sentences appropriate for action, we may speak of action as being composed. By analogy, it seems that, for the primary action subsystems, the "deep" level should designate the point at which the outputs of *their* subsystems are gathered together. The transformational work of their media involves the selective conjoining and adjusting to situational requirements of products of their internal subsystemic processes.

Among the papers included in this section of our collection, Edelson's is by far the most adequate in treating the mediated processes of an action subsystem in terms close to the linguistic model. He departs from the fact that the imagery of deep and surface levels of meaning has perhaps as important a part in psychodynamic theory as in linguistic theory. What has often been called "depth psychology" has maintained the necessity of searching out the full meanings of surface acts within the various stable, specialized root complexes of the personality. Yet, the surface or manifest meanings of dreams or other symbolic products of the personality appear in great, often bewildering, variations of intricately convoluted expressive intents. Edelson notes that, as compared with manifest content, it has generally been understood that the deeper, latent content consists in relatively simple and direct, if intense, wishes. The production of manifest from latent content, then, may be understood as a process of the conjoining and defensive transformation of finite material into an indefinitely large quantity of dreams, feelings, hopes, fears, symptoms, and so on, adapted to various situations of action. The deep elements consist in the enduring needs and dispositions of the personality, embodied variously in drives, moral imperatives, senses of identity, and attachments to others, which may not be easily reconciled with each other or with situational requirements. Processes of transformation may bring to the surface combinations of these elements, often suitably disguised so that they do not offend one another, that the individual can "face" and "own up to" within the context of his action.

Edelson suggests that the transformational medium in terms of which these processes occur is comprised of object-representations. As a means of symbolization, what object-representations stand for are the cathectic-affective involvements of the personality (or self) with internalized objects. It should be noted that such involvements clearly include various symbolizations of the subjectivity of the self, of orientations toward objects, and of qualities of objects as well as the objects themselves in a narrow sense. Thus, object-representations as medium can be understood to operate upon exemplars of the basic categories of syntax and of the action frame of reference. Indeed, as Edelson demonstrates, the affective transformations of the personality seem to act principally upon such exemplars—e.g., in substituting objects, changing "orientations" from active to passive or from love to hate, or altering modalities from strong to weak or from rewarding to punitive.

In bringing his general theoretical materials to bear upon the problem of interpretation, Edelson indicates that the "material" produced by the patient must be regarded by the psychoanalyst as presenting a symbolic, conceptual reality. The psychoanalyst can penetrate this reality only by following the repertoire of transformations through which the patient has constructed it. In our present terms, we may say that, by employing the transformations that enable him to apprehend the deep structures underlying the patient's productions, the psychoanalyst can reach the empirical basis for attempting to reconstruct the patient's metaphorical code. Insofar as his examination of a very diverse set of the patient's metonymical symbolic constructions enables him to deduce consistently a relatively restricted set of metaphorical meanings, he may be said to have prehended the structure of the patient's personality.

Besides exemplifying the analysis of a medium in terms of a language-like model, Edelson takes up some important issues that indicate the congruence of this approach with more conventional analyses of media. Thus, he insists that object-representations comprise the medium which regulates the interchange of resources among subsystems of the personality, with their respective transformational repertoires. His treatment also makes clear that interchange processes between the personality and the other subsystems of action must require mediation in terms of object-representations. Furthermore, he outlines a very general analysis of the ways in which inflation and deflation of the object-representations medium may affect the functioning of the personality. The respect in which object representations must be conceived as a generalized resource of the personality, as well as its medium of communication and of the composition of its products, is thus quite fully essayed.

Edelson's analysis strikes the present author as sufficiently convincing to justify a parallel effort to apply the language-like model of media to the case of the generalized medium of the social system. As with Edelson's discussion, the point of departure recurs to some very fundamental issues and to some classical conceptions at the same time that it leads toward an effort to resolve some current sociological controversies. Thus, we will be concerned again with the problem of order, with the notion of definition of the situation, and with the differences between analytical and phenomenological perspectives.

We have noted, following O'Dea, that social system theory must treat the problem of social order in a dynamic fashion, attending especially to what he terms the processes of emergence and constitution. Even a theory that could adequately account for the dialectical processes whereby normative orders are continually being constituted, de-institutionalized, and reconstituted on somewhat different terms, however, would not exhaust the problem of order. There would remain what we might term the processual or interactive problem of order. By this phrase, we intend to indicate that, given an institutionalized normative order, which is always an order of very great internal complexity, there remain critical problems for analysis concerning the ways in which elements of the order come actually to regulate specific interactive situations.[63] For example, specific elements of the normative order cannot bind a situation until the situation itself has been normatively categorized and typified in ways indicating *which* elements of the whole normative order should be binding. Such categorization and typification must be the accomplishment of interactors; and interaction may be unregulated, loosely regulated, or ambiguously regulated, at least in certain aspects, until the situation has become adequately characterized in normative terms. Further, many kinds of situations may legitimately be brought under the regulation of a plurality of alternative normative elements of a more specific nature. Yet, unless certain clear choices are made about which of the alternative norms will be regarded by interactors as regulatory, even though such choices may be quite arbitrary, it remains impossible for interactors effectively to rationalize their actions. Finally, it is often the case that actors must accept the concomitant regulation of normative standards which are sharply differentiated from one another and which cannot easily be brought into a stable or general relationship with one another by any simple rational calculus. Unless certain situational priorities are indicated as guidelines for interactors, they may then find their activities immobilized by normative—often profoundly moral—dilemmas. Indeed, problems such as these concerning the deployment of a normative order for the regulation of given situations seem to be so pervasive and to carry so much potential for immobilizingly deep penetration into the normative order that they are probably not soluble on general and enduring grounds. It appears that they must be resolved with reference to the particular practical problems that emerge within interaction and that specific resolutions must have a somewhat provisional standing—even if certain components of them may prove highly stable.

With his conception of "definition of the situation,"[64] W. I. Thomas seems to have provided an account of the interactive mechanism that provides mediation for resolutions of the processual problem of order as manifested in specific situations. Because his famous aphorism, "If men define situations as real, they are real in their consequences," has so often been quoted out of the broader context of his treatment of definition of the situation, Thomas's theoretical intent has generally been misapprehended. Generally, the aphorism has been assimilated to a cultural relativist perspective emphasizing that what are very strange beliefs to us can be taken very seriously by some other peoples. However, within the context of "Chicago School" interactionist theory, Thomas used the concept of definition of the situation with a more sharply focused intent. Thus, in *The Unadjusted Girl,* he emphasized that the effort to define the situation comprises a preliminary phase of all planned and coordinated social behavior. Here, the term phase must be stressed in an analytical sense, since it becomes apparent that processes of interaction can become stalled in ways that force them back to the definition of the situation phase even after they have previously completed it. Thomas indicated that this phase is preliminary in the sense that actors can calculate what activities will comprise appropriate contributions to social action and what wishes or motivations may be pursued in interaction only on the basis of a prior definition of the situation. Thus, only insofar as a shared definition of the situation has been established as binding the interactors together in a cooperative venture, can orderly interaction proceed. Without definition of the situation, the interactors are apt to be unable to rationalize their activities and are prone to damage from the discrepant actions of their others.

Although some specific definitions of the situation may derive fairly directly from normative beliefs general in the culture, Thomas emphasized that they are nevertheless emergent in and through particular lines of interaction. Particular actors must put definitions of the situation forward under specific conditions of interaction and gain their acceptance by the other parties to the situation. As definitions of the situation are intrinsically fragile, their binding effects may be escaped by some actors or undermined by changing conditions. They must then be reasserted and resecured, perhaps in somewhat altered terms that adapt to the deviance or the newly emerged or newly salient conditions. The reassertion of definitions of

the situation in order to control deviance often consists in the stigmatizing—now generally called "labelling"—of the deviant: Thomas emphasized that terms such as "traitor," "scab," "whore," or "coward" may be invoked to secure definitions of the situation.

Thomas stressed the importance of *agency* and *resource* in defining situations. There are asymmetries within social settings about who can define the situation and to what degree. Privileged and prestigeful actors have resources beyond others in gaining acceptance throughout the situation for their attempts to define it. Social agency may have both a collective and an individual aspect. Thus, collective contexts such as family, school, court, and local community provide settings for the establishment of definitions of the situation. Individuals in such roles as parent, teacher, judge, or political leader have both responsibilities and generally accepted advantages for defining situations within these milieux. Thomas indicated, further, that resources such as wealth, power, and influence may comprise means of gaining acceptance for definitions of the situation.

For Thomas' theory, "social organization" (in the old Chicago School sense) is crucial to the capacity of a collective setting to sustain orderly definitions of the situation. Such failures to ensure well-defined situations as the occurrence of deviance appear, then, to index "social disorganization." Disorganized milieux are also apt to be characterized by the encumbering of the processes of the development of definitions of the situation by the emergence of much argument, bargaining, negotiating, compromising, trading, and the like. Cooperative activities will tend to be stalled while these disorderly processes of arriving at definitions of the situation consume energies—i.e., the interaction tends not to move out of its preliminary phase. Both collective and personal demoralization may result if a social setting remains long unable to define situations.

The definition of the situation within one milieu operates independently, yet interdependently, with definitions in other settings. Thomas regarded it as something of a functional necessity that each operating social setting be able to produce its own definitions of the situation. However, he also recognized that, where collective milieux must operate interdependently, they must hold mutual respect for the definitions of the situation in terms of which their activities might impinge on one another. Thus, it is demoralizing for the pupil if his family and his school fail to respect one another's definitions of the situation that affect his activities. Further, Thomas noted that collectivities that prove incapable of defining their situations and hence become embroiled in disorganizing internal conflict tend to have their problems resolved by appeal to some outside setting. For example, the problems of a "disorganized" family may be appealed to relatives or to the community at large through the means of gossip, or the staging of a dramatic dispute may bring referal to the police, social workers, or a court.

Finally, Thomas emphasized that "social situations never spontaneously repeat themselves; every situation is more or less new, for every one includes new human activities differently combined."[65] Here, he seems clearly to recognize the generativity of social action. However, his treatment of definition of the situation in this regard seems to fall a bit short. He attempted to set definition of the situation off against the tendency toward a constant originality of action. He treated definition of the situation as serving to schematize similarities within the on-going creativity of action in terms of old and established ways of organizing action. He held that moral, legal, customary, or normative codes developed simply as means of schematizing situations in general terms and of gaining stability among situations. To be sure, this does state an important aspect of the functioning of codes. However, Thomas's conception of normative codes fails fully to incorporate what, in terms of our linguistic model, is a key point: Situations may be new and original not only in their practical or interactive details, but also in the meanings with which they are symbolically defined. We must re-examine the relation between definition of the situation and normative order in terms of our general distinction between metonymical and metaphorical structures.

We are proposing that definitions of the situation comprise metonymical entities or messages while institutionalized normative structures constitute metaphorical codes. An instance of definition of the situation "circulates" among the interactors within a milieu in the sense that it must prove acceptable to them, albeit perhaps under considerable constraint, as a binding basis of the coordination of their activities. A well-formed definition of the situation is relatively unambiguous in providing the normative grounds for the rationalization of action. But it can attain a high degree of freedom from ambiguity only through incorporation of specific references to many features of a given situation. In this sense, its duration is always as limited as the stability of the conditions of interaction within the situation. As important features of the situation change, the definition of the situation is apt to become permuted also. The permutation of definitions of the situation is an essential characteristic of the capacity of human social action to sustain adaptation to changing conditions.

Normative structures, though certainly capable of undergoing change, are characterized by a substantial degree of insulation against changes in practical conditions of action within stable milieux. They also differ from definitions of the situation in maintaining stability across practical conditions of interaction that vary from one situation to another of the same general type. In brief, normative structures are *institutionalized* as stable, enduring grounds of action, whereas definitions of the situation are intrinsically too evanescent and situation-bound to become institutionalized. However, it is only by reference to the stable metaphorical codes of institutional structures that actors can ascertain and agree upon the normative significance of definitions of the situation.

Definitions of the situation may vary considerably in their complexity as messages or metonymical structures. Some are very simple injunctions or "labels." Others are comprised of fairly complex hierarchies of a number of independently important terms. Some stand as systematic conclusions to extensive discussions in the preliminary phase of interaction. Some are merely small addenda or adjustments to prior definitions, produced during brief and partial regressions to a preliminary phase. Most definitions of the situation leave much information implicit or unspecified, so that flexible adjustment may be made subsequently in the light of the particular problems of the regulation of interaction that arise in the course of subsequent activities. Implicitly or explicitly, definitions of the situation tend to make references to the agents and objects of the projected action, to the central obligations obtaining among parties to the situation, to the ends or purposes of planned activities, to the boundaries and limits of involvements in the situation, and to resources that are allocable to projects developed in the situation. Moreover, definitions of the situation tend to include references to a plurality of independently specialized normative structures that have a categorical salience to the given situation. For example, definitions of appropriate contributions to discussion in a university classroom are apt to draw upon standards of decorum, fair competition, the limitation of erotic interests, perhaps concern with certain public events, chauvinism of the particular university, and status-related symbolizations of life-style, as well as upon standards of intellectual judgment associated with the particular discipline in question and academia in general. It is necessarily the case, then, that references to normative structures included, implicitly or explicitly, within specific definitions of the situation will be complicated in nature. It should be clear that situations can be defined in ways adequate to the normative regulation of interaction only if the mechanism of definition of the situation is fully generative in its creativity. The preliminary phase of interaction must have the capacity to generate from selected exemplars of the categories of social structure an indefinite number of situationally adapted normative projects for subsequent action.

In the abstract, a very large number of elements of a normative order bear categorically upon almost any given situation. Lacking situationally specific guidelines for orienting himself to just those elements that are crucial to the shaping of interaction under the immediate conditions at hand, the actor may be said to be confronted by a problem of order regardless of how well-institutionalized the general social structure may be. Indeed, one might argue that the more thorough the institutionalization of a full range of the components of a complete social structure, the more deeply conflicted the actor may be. He will not be able to ignore any of the potentially salient categories of normative structure with freedom from constraint. Thus, definitions of the situation may be said—here, again, we invoke linguistic terminology—to provide normative *disambiguation* for interactors. Faced with some very general moral-normative dilemmas, actors gain specific guidance about the choice of normative guidelines from their shared definitions of the situation. The definition of the situation must, then, be unambiguous in the sense of providing normative orientation that is consistent for practical purposes. The consistency may exist *merely* in terms of practical purposes, i.e., not be evident when the definition of the situation is subjected to more principled examination. Yet, it is only when conflicting normative projects begin to emerge from an initial definition of the situation that interactors are drawn into disorder. If definitional conflicts can be prevented from arising in subsequent interaction, practical consistency may be sustained regardless of any inconsistencies in theory or principle.

The deep structure of definition of the situation is comprised of simple selective combinations of exemplars of categories of normative social structure. They may cover the range of normative issues categorically salient to regulation of the situation. Thus, at the deep level, definitions of the situation contain the normative information necessary for the proper regulation of interaction, whatever specific developments may emerge within the situation. However, only quite selective elements of the deep structures are combined into the metonymical entities that are brought to the surface level. Careful choice in the selection of elements for inclusion at the surface level is requisite for assuring that definitions of the situation will be able to provide practically focused normative guidance. Flexibility in adapting to changing conditions within a situation or variable conditions within categorically similar situations we attribute primarily to the operation of transformational procedures.

Empirical studies of interaction seem to provide many examples of transformational properties of definition of the situation. The policeman who elicits information from a suspect by adopting the manner of a "friend" and then redefines his obligations so that the suspect cannot protect himself by appealing to standards of friendship has exercised a simple transformation. The gang delinquent may use (or, better, misuse) a transformation in attempting to neutralize laws against interpersonal violence by claiming the privilege of "self-defense" when he is attempting to defend his "tough" reputation.[66] The parent may invoke a transformation of special politeness to change the conduct of children in the presence of honored guests. Each of these examples should, we believe, be treated as a transformation because it serves to alter or reorder a series of elements included within a definition of the situation. Although in each case a definite reordering takes place, the precise effects upon the regulation of interaction cannot be deduced from the transformation itself without more detailed examination of other elements involved in the deep structure and of other ways in which they are transformed in being brought to the surface under particular interactive conditions.

We may give a bit closer attention to the grounds for imputing the presence of a transformation by examining some evidence reported by Gerald Suttles in his *Social Order of the Slum*.[67] Suttles indicates that definitions of the situation in public places, expecially "on the street" but also in stores, on playgrounds, and the like, within his slum community often operated on the basis of making very little moral demand upon others. Many people within the community were rather generally stigmatized in terms of their moral characters due to public knowledge of serious normative infractions in their pasts. Consequently, expectations of them tended to depart from the standards generally acknowledged to be "right" or desirable in order to adapt to their stigmatized statuses. It seems that this process affected a very great amount of interaction within the community and was readily understood by participants in the many specific situations involved. The imputation of a "demoralized conditions" transformation to explain why many people were not expected to act very morally under many conditions offers a parsimonious account of what, empirically, comprised quite different events on different occasions. It also permits a stronger explanation than Suttles offers of why members of the community continued to insist that they did honor firm standards of proper conduct in public: These standards were represented in the "deep structures" of the definitions of the situation, but were simply deleted when carrying them to the surface would have left some actors relatively unprotected against the strong possibility that immoral conduct would occur.

Matza's analysis of states of drift[68] indicates that definitions of the situation have certain syntactic properties. Drift emerges in situations that are improperly defined, so that certain actors, at least, are able to escape the binding effects of the definition of the situation. The drift may be due to the failure of certain responsible actors to assert the applicability of essential sanctions, in which case the definition of the situation might be the analogue of an incomplete sentence. Or, it may result from illegitimate or inappropriate appeal to neutralizing considerations, as in much of what Matza calls "subterranean convergence" whereby elements of "respectable culture" seem to allay the applicability or bindingness of institutionalized norms. Perhaps such definitions of the situation are analogous to sentences that are ungrammatical by virtue of an improper combination of transformations.

In brief, it seems that transformations must be included in the explanation of the generation of definitions of the situation as metonymical entities for reasons of parsimony. If we are to understand in detail how situations come to be defined, we must realize that they continually emerge in new variety. They exist in infinitely different forms, yet they emerge in ordered fashion because they derive their meanings from a stable and finite normative code. If they did not refer back to stable institutions, their meanings could not be apprehended and shared by parties to situated interaction. The generative relation between metaphorical normative structure and metonymical definitions of the situation can be understood finitely and voluntaristically only in transformational terms. Unless a transformational generativity assumes a prominent place in our theories of social interaction, our understanding must vacillate between rigid overemphasis on structure that fails to acknowledge the variety of definitions of the situation, on the one hand, and sheer description of unique situations that cannot synthesize a finite sense of social structure, on the other hand.

Without attempting even an outline of a systematic statement, we may round out the treatment of the generalized media of the primary subsystems of action by offering some remarks on the media of the behavioral and cultural systems. The appendix to the paper by Lidz and Lidz discusses the generalized medium of the behavioral system under the heading of "intelligence," in a sense derived from Piaget's usage. The discussion approaches the present language-like model at a few points without conforming to it very closely. It makes clear that generalized intelligence functions through what Piaget calls operations, a conception that shares important features with the present notion of transformations. Intelligence does operate in a generative fashion: From the stable schematic structures of the behavioral system, it must generate infinitely variable means of coordinating behavior adapted to the needs of the moment. Given the importance of generating behavior in relation to expectations of others and, especially, in terms of schemas developed out of the activities of the self, it seems probable that the syntactical categories of the action frame of reference comprise the principal entities upon which intelligence as a medium operates also.

It may be suggested that Durkheim's term "collective representations" adequately denotes the cultural medium. Collective representations gain their meaning by reference to the stable belief structures of the culture. They mediate into the composition of social action a foundation in what the phenomenologists call intersubjectivity for the patterning of orientations. That is, they bring representations of "objects of respect" into the definition of the orientation of action. From the deference given to the objects of respect, collective representations create common, shared foci of action adapted to the orientational problems posed within the immediate context of action. As metonymical entities, not themselves stable structures of belief, they can bring unique combinations of respectworthy elements to bear upon the stabilization of orientations. Transformational processes are needed to regulate the selection, combination, and ordering of just those collective representations concerned with orientations of a general class that are directly salient to the orientational problems arising in a given action context. Thus, we find in religion or civil religion that on different occasions the culture's general patterns of belief tend to be invoked through different combinations of collective representations. Even stable sets of collective representations such as prayers tend to take on somewhat different meanings when they are placed, as units, within different larger metonymical patterns.

CONCLUSION

The present essay has attempted to outline for the reader the knowledge of the general action system essential to understanding and evaluating the contributions included in this section of our volumes. Beyond that, it has tried to indicate some of the principal ways in which work within the action frame of reference at the most general level has affected sociological analysis. Here, the major theme, developed principally in the latter parts of the essay, has been that the theory of action can in fact accommodate major critical points that have been developed from the interactionist and especially the phenomenological perspectives in recent years. Analysis of the generalized media and their contributions to the voluntaristic, generative qualities of action systems has been the primary vehicle of enriching the theory of action in the phenomenological direction. However, it should also be emphasized that the theory of action has long been committed to a predominantly *Verstehende* methodology of empirical investigation and has long drawn extensively from ethnological studies. The phenomenological "openness" which is currently being demonstrated within the theory, therefore, has substantial historical roots. At the same time, the theory of action account of the "constructed" nature of social action remains importantly different from the analyses that have been put forward by symbolic interactionists, phenomenologists, and ethnomethodologists. The theory of action continues to emphasize systemic functioning and operations of mechanisms that have structural foundations within systems. It is expected, of course, that these emphases will continue to be controversial.

At several places, the foregoing account of specific elements within the theory differs somewhat from prior accounts given by Parsons. It may, then, be fitting to conclude with a brief review of these differences and with some remarks on their apparent significance.

In the discussion of the primary differentiation of the action system, the chief departure from previous accounts concerns the adaptive subsystem. Here, the major emphasis was given to the Lidz and Lidz account of a Piagetian psychological system, which they term the behavioral system. The principal concern was to build the frame of reference within which Piaget has developed his psychology of intelligence into the theory of action on a basis independent of personality theory. No claim was put forward that the matters which have previously been treated under the heading behavioral organism are unimportant in the determination of concrete behavior. The analysis of these matters remains a task of the first order within the larger theory of behavior. In the present conception of the action frame of reference, however, it is a task for the principal boundary discipline of the theory of action, not an integral part of the theory itself.

A second departure, probably not so important, involves the substitution of the term "belief systems" for the more widely used "symbol systems" in specifying the entities, especially the structural entities, which comprise cultural systems. The purpose of this change was to avoid certain ambiguities associated with the term symbol. Historically, it appears that the categorization, "symbol systems", derived from certain usages in cultural anthropology, where a more diffuse conception of culture was intended. At any rate, symbols, symbolic mechanisms, and symbol systems seem to be involved — according to usages essential at many points in the theory of action and much stressed in the present essay — in all primary sectors of action systems. Consequently, substantial ambiguity was involved in the effort to characterize cultural systems as uniquely specialized about symbols. Moreover, the analysis of the symbolic mechanisms involved in the general action system seemed to make possible a further focusing of the conception of culture — e.g., in the way that language came to be treated as a general action rather than specifically as a cultural mechanism. The term "belief systems," then, appeared to be one means of expressing a sharpened focus for the analysis of culture. Yet, the term clearly has its drawbacks too. For example, many would regard the provisional, skeptical quality of respecting conceptions within scientific culture as poorly expressed by the term belief. Many would also question whether the forms of conceptions or representations involved in certain areas of expressive culture comprise beliefs. Perhaps, further rationalization of terminology is still required in this field.

A larger number of substantial changes are involved in the discussion of the generalized symbolic media of the general action system. The assignment of a theoretically specific category of function — though an extremely general and diffuse function — to language as a medium stands at the center of these changes. It is hoped that the theory of action will, upon this new foundation, be able to contribute more to the study of language generally and to sociolinguistics and psycholinguistics. What is perhaps of greater significance for the theory itself, however, is that a new basis has been established for treating language as a prototypical generalized medium. While the code-message distinction has long been central to treatments of the media, the present essay has attempted to set up a more general and systematic model for analysis of the language-like properties of the media. In the author's view, exploration of some of the possibilities of this model constitutes the most important theoretical innovation of this paper. It must be acknowledged, however, that innovation in this context has been — to say the least — strongly foreshadowed by Edelson's application of transformational ideas to the analysis of personality process.

It should be emphasized that the language-like model for the analysis of media is not intended to supplant, but just to complement, the already established money-like model. A more complete analysis of the general action media would have entered into the question of interchanges, categories of input and output, the mediation of equilibria, inflation and deflation, and so on. Theoretically, the dimensions of functioning captured in the two models seem to be orthogonal. Here, emphasis has been placed on the language-like model in part to explore the possibilities of this line of analysis, in part because the proximity of all the general action media to language apparently accentuates its importance for this level of the organization of action, and in part because Parsons has already discussed the general action media in terms of the money-like model.[69]

Given the orthogonal relation between the frames of reference of the present discussion of the general action media and Parsons' prior discussions, direct comparisons between the treatments of the various individual media is theoretically difficult. Yet, certain limited comments may prove valuable in guiding further discussion. Both treatments term the medium of the behavioral system "intelligence," and there is broad agreement on the nature of its functioning. Whereas Edelson discusses the personality medium as object-representations, Parsons has used the term performance capacity. The object-representations conceptualization seems to have two clear advantages. First, it indicates much more clearly the relation between the personality medium and the emotional or cathectic structures of the personality system. Second, it seems to stand more neutrally among the subsystems of the personality, so that its role in regulating the internal combinatorial and generative processes of the personality can be better understood. By contrast, performance capacity seems overly to accentuate ego functioning. It might be argued that the performance capacity conception better indicates the goal-attainment nature of the medium's functioning on behalf of the whole general action system. However, this advantage is perhaps offset by the deeper penetration of the object-representations conception into the general theory of the motivation of action.

The present treatment of the social system medium as definition of the situation contrasts, apparently, quite sharply with Parsons' discussion of affect as the social system medium. The principal defect of Parsons' analysis from the present perspective is that it does not provide a systematic treatment of what we have termed the processual problem of order. Further, it seems not to exploit the openness of the theory of action toward handling the theoretical problems raised by the social phenomenologists when the focus of analysis is shifted from the intrasocial to the general action level. The advantage of Parsons' treatment is the direct linkage it provides for explicating what Durkheim called the "sentimental" attachments of individuals to society, interactive milieux,

and the normative order. Moreover, it is an attractive idea that solidarity may be analyzable on the general action level in terms of the circulation of quantities of affect among participants in interaction. It is possible, however, that the theoretical dilemmas are more apparent than substantial. It is certainly the case that flows of affect are controlled by understandings of the normative status of solidary relations involved in the interactive situation. Thus, it may be that definition of the situation comprises not directly the medium but the form of processual mechanism controlling the medium and that affect can be consistently treated as the medium itself. What we propose here is that perhaps a line of distinction and of determinant interrelation between definition of the situation and affect can be developed somewhat after the pattern of the relationship between market mechanisms and money in the economic prototype.

The cultural medium has been termed definition of the situation in Parsons' account and collective representations in the foregoing account. Two orders of objection may be raised to the utilization of definition of the situation in this theoretical context. First, as emphasized here, Thomas' more complete discussion of definition of the situation emphasized strongly its embeddedness within interactive processes and its functioning as a direct means of control of interaction. This has provided the basis of our treatment of definition of the situation as the social system medium. Second, definition of the situation seems to place too strong and too exclusive an emphasis upon the normative dimensions of culture, whereas the most general cultural medium must have the functional scope to regulate combinatorial processes in all sectors of the cultural system. Perhaps, the principal countervailing consideration is that the Durkheimean term collective representations has usually been treated as designating entities that are structural to culture. Some adaptation of past usage will be needed if collective representations are to be regarded as comprising a processual medium.

NOTES

1. Talcott Parsons, *The Social System* (Glencoe: The Free Press, 1951), and "An Outline of the Social System" in *Theories of Society*, Talcott Parsons, Edward Shils, Kaspar D. Naegele, and Jesse R. Pitts (eds.) (New York: The Free Press, 1961).

2. Talcott Parsons and Edward Shils (eds.), *Toward A General Theory of Action* (Cambridge: Harvard University Press, 1951).

3. See, for example, the essays in Talcott Parsons, *Social Structure and Personality* (New York: The Free Press, 1964).

4. See Talcott Parsons, *Societies: Evolutionary and Comparative Perspectives* (Englewood Cliffs: Prentice-Hall, 1966).

5. See Talcott Parsons, *Politics and Social Structure* (New York: The Free Press, 1969), Chapters 1 and 2.

6. A general overview of general action theory is presented in Talcott Parsons, "Some Problems of General Theory in Sociology," in *Theoretical Sociology: Perspectives and Developments*, John C. McKinney and Edward A. Tiryakian, (eds.) (New York; Appleton-Century-Crofts 1970). This essay is in certain respects the most important source for the present discussion.

7. See the discussions of Weber's methodology in Talcott Parsons, *The Structure of Social Action* (New York: McGraw-Hill, 1937), and "Evaluation and Objectivity in the Social Sciences: An Interpretation of Max Weber's Contributions" in his *Sociological Theory and Modern Society* (New York: The Free Press, 1967).

8. Talcott Parsons, "Some Problems of General Theory in Sociology," *op. cit.;* also, see the theoretical materials in Talcott Parsons and Gerald M. Platt. *The American University* (Cambridge: Harvard University Press, 1973).

9. Talcott Parsons and Edward Shils: "Values, Motives, and Systems of Action" in *Toward A General Theory of Action*, and *The Social System*, Chapters 1 and 2.

10. *Ibid.*

11. The four-function paradigm was introduced in Talcott Parsons, Robert F. Bales, and Edward A. Shils, *Working Papers in the Theory of Action* (New York: The Free Press, 1953). A major advance in its application to macrosocial analysis was developed in Talcott Parsons and Neil J. Smelser, *Economy and Society* (New York: The Free Press, 1956). "An Outline of the Social System," *op. cit.*, presents a general overview of the social system level applications of the four functions that probably remains the best introduction.

12. See Victor Lidz, "On the Construction of Objective Theory," *Sociological Inquiry*, 42 (Winter, 1972), pp. 51-64.

13. "An Outline of the Social System," *op. cit;* "Some Problems of General Theory in Sociology," *op. cit.*

14. Talcott Parsons, "Introduction to Part Four — Culture and the Social System," in *Theories of Society*, vol. II, pp. 963-993.

15. Clifford Geertz, "Religion as a Cultural System," in Michael Banton (ed.), *Anthropological Approaches to the Study of Religion* (London: Tavistock, 1966).

16. "An Outline of the Social System," *op. cit.*

17. *Ibid.*; also, Robert N. Bellah, *Beyond Belief* (New York: Harper and Row, 1970), especially the introductory chapter.

18. See Talcott Parsons and Gerald M. Platt, *The American University*.

19. At this point Fararo is following Parsons' account in "Introduction to Part Four — Culture and the Social System," *op. cit.* However, in defining subsystems of science, Fararo does not follow the suggestion which Parsons outlined in "Unity and Diversity in the Modern Intellectual Disciplines," in *Sociological Theory and Modern Society*.

20. See Talcott Parsons, "An Outline of the Social System," *op. cit.*, "Some Problems of General Theory in Sociology," *op. cit.*, and Chapters 1 and 2 of *Politics and Social Structure*.

21. Emile Durkheim, *Rules of Sociological Method* (Chicago: University of Chicago Press, 1938).

22. For example, see Talcott Parsons, *The Social System*, Chapters VI and VII.

23. For example, Talcott Parsons, *The System of Modern Societies* (Englewood Cliffs: Prentice-Hall, 1969); Neil J. Smelser, *The Theory of Collective Behavior* (New York: The Free Press, 1963); Robert N. Bellah, "Epilogue," in Robert N. Bellah (ed.), *Religion and Progress in Modern Asia* (New York: The Free Press, 1965).

24. Talcott Parsons, *The Structure of Social Action*.

25. See Emile Durkheim's discussion in *The Division of Labor in Society* (Glencoe: The Free Press, 1949), Book I, Chapter II.

26. Max Weber established all these points in his analysis of the religious and ethical foundations of classical Chinese civilization in *The Religion of China* (Glencoe: The Free Press, 1951).

27. Talcott Parsons, "General Theory in Sociology," in Robert K. Merton, Leonard Broom, and Leonard S. Cottrell. Jr. (eds.). *Sociology Today* (New York: Basic Books, 1958).

28. See Emile Durkheim, *The Division of Labor in Society*, Book II, Chapter I.

29. Talcott Parsons, "An Approach to Psychological Theory in Terms of the Theory of Action" in Sigmund Koch (ed.), *Psychology: A Study of a Science* (New York: McGraw-Hill, 1959); *Social Structure and Personality*, especially Chapters 1 and 4; Talcott Parsons and Robert F. Bales; *Family, Socialization and Interaction Process* (Glencoe: The Free Press, 1955), especially Chapters Three and Four.

30. See references cited in *ibid*.

31. On the concept of role, see Talcott Parsons, "General Theory in Sociology," *op. cit.*

32. G.H. Mead: *Mind, Self, and Society* (Chicago: University of Chicago Press, 1934), especially the section on the Self.

33. Talcott Parsons, "The Superego and the Theory of Social Systems," Chapter 1 in *Social Structure and Personality*.

34. See the chapters on expressive symbolism in *The Social System* and in *Working Papers in the Theory of Action*.

35. Sigmund Freud, *The Interpretation of Dreams*, included in *Basic Writings of Sigmund Freud* (New York: Modern Library, 1938).

36. Talcott Parsons, "An Approach to Psychological Theory in Terms of the Theory of Action," *op. cit.*, and "Some Problems of General Theory in Sociology," *op. cit.*

37. Talcott Parsons, "On the Concept of Political Power," Chapter 14 in *Politics and Social Structure:* "Introduction to Part Four — Culture and the Social System," *op. cit;* "Some Problems of General Theory in Sociology," *op. cit.*

38. A somewhat tortured attempt is made in "Introduction to Part Four — Culture and the Social System," *op. cit.* However, formally, the location assigned to language within action systems violates the requirements of the general media paradigm. Moreover, it would provide no clear basis for attending to the "psycholinguistic" aspects of language.

39. That is, we are positing that language operates at a higher level of generality than the four general action media identified in "Some Problems of General Theory in Sociology," *op. cit.*

40. See Eric H. Lenneberg, *Biological Foundations of Language* (New York: Wiley, 1967).

41. Jerrold J. Katz and Paul M. Postal, *An Integrated Theory of Linguistic Descriptions* (Cambridge: M.I.T. Press, 1964).

42. Ferdinand de Saussure, *Course in General Linguistics* (London: Peter Owen, 1959).

43. Rene Descartes, *Discourse on Method* (Chicago: Open Court, 1899).

44. Emile Durkheim, *Rules of Sociological Method*; Talcott Parsons, "Unity and Diversity in the Modern Intellectual Disciplines" (*op. cit.*).

45. *Ibid.*

46. G. H. Mead, *Mind, Self, and Society*. In his *Movements of Thought in the Nineteenth Century* (Chicago: University of Chicago Press, 1939), Mead makes clear that the sources of his conception of the self lay more directly in the works of such German Romantics as Fichte than in the work of Descartes himself. However, there is certainly an important and appropriate sense in which Fichte and his cohorts were themselves Cartesian.

47. G. H. Mead, *Mind, Self, and Society*, section on Self.

48. See Noam Chomsky, *Language and Mind* (New York: Harcourt, Brace and Janovitch, 1968); also, Emmon Bach and Robert T. Harms (eds.), *Universals in Linguistic Theory* (New York: Holt, Rhinehart, and Winston, 1968).

49. Joseph H. Greenberg, *Universals of Language* (Cambridge: M.I.T. Press, 1963), especially Greenberg's own contributions.

50. Talcott Parsons, *The Structure of Social Action,* Chapters II and XIX.

51. Note that we have now arrived by quite a different route at basically the same generalization that we made concerning the scope of applicability of the frame of reference categories near the outset of this essay.

52. Noam Chomsky, *Cartesian Linguistics* (New York: Harper and Row, 1966).

53. This generalization has provided the foundation for the "generative grammar" paradigm in linguistics ever since Noam Chomsky published his *Syntactic Structures* (The Hague: Mouton, 1957).

54. Jurgen Habermas, "Toward a Theory of Communicative Competence," in Peter Dreitzel (ed.), *Recent Sociology II* (New York: Macmillan, 1970).

55. Aaron Cicourel: "Basic and Normative Rules in the Negotiation of Role and Status," in Peter Dreitzel (ed.), *Recent Sociology II.*

56. Harold Garfinkel and Harvey Sacks, "On Formal Structures of Practical Actions," in John C. McKinney and Edward A. Tiryakian, (eds.), *Theoretical Sociology: Perspectives and Developments.*

57. Cf. Talcott Parsons, *The Structure of Social Action.*

58. Noam Chomsky, *Language and Mind* ; Jerrold J. Katz and Paul M. Postal: *An Integrated Theory of Linguistic Descriptions.*

59. *Ibid.*

60. Compare Noam Chomsky, *Aspects of the Theory of Syntax* (Cambridge: M.I.T. Press, 1965) with James D. McCawley, "The Role of Semantics in a Grammar," in Emmon Bach and Robert T. Harms (eds.), *Universals in Linguistic Theory.*

61. Edmund Leach, *Claude Levi-Strauss* (New York: Vintage Press, 1970), especially Chapters III-V.

62. For example, see Talcott Parsons, "On the Concept of Political Power," *op. cit.*

63. Harold Garfinkel has probably played the most important role in dramatizing for contemporary sociology the very fundamental implications of what we are calling the processual problem of order. See his *Studies in Ethnomethodology* (Englewood Cliffs: Prentice-Hall, 1967). Aaron Cicourel's analysis in his *Social Organization of Juvenile Justice* (New York: Wiley, 1968) has also been outstandingly important in this regard.

64. The basic source of the following discussion of definition of the situation is W. I. Thomas, *The Unadjusted Girl* (New York: Harper Torchbooks, 1967), especially the chapter entitled "The Regulation of the Wishes."

65. W. I. Thomas, *On Social Organization and Social Personality,* Morris Janowitz (ed.) (Chicago: University of Chicago Press, 1966), p. 27. The quoted passage originally appeared in W. I. Thomas and Florian Znaniecki, *The Polish Peasant in Europe and America* (New York: Dover, 1958).

66. David Matza, *Delinquency and Drift* (New York: Wiley, 1964).

67. Gerald D. Suttles, *The Social Order of the Slum* (Chicago: University of Chicago Press, 1968).

68. David Matza, *Delinquency and Drift.*

69. Talcott Parsons, "Some Problems of General Theory in Sociology," *op. cit.*

6

TOWARD A STUDY OF INTERPRETATION IN PSYCHOANALYSIS

Marshall Edelson

INTRODUCTION

The therapeutic action of psychoanalysis is an effect of interpretation. Psychoanalysis as a technique of investigation relies upon examination of the effects of interpretation. Psychoanalysis as a theory of mental processes is an elaboration and integration of interpretations.

Yet I am not satisfied that we have an adequate theory of either the psychoanalyst's act of understanding the analysand or the psychoanalyst's act of giving an interpretation. What do we mean by "the psychoanalyst understands the analysand—the utterances, the actions, the dreams, the symptoms of the analysand"? What is the act of interpretation in which the psychoanalyst conveys his "understanding" to the analysand? What part of that "understanding" does he convey? In what form? When? Why that part, that form, at that particular time? And what is it that can be identified as the effect of an act of interpretation? How is it identified as such? What form does such an effect assume? Why that particular effect, that form, at that particular time?[1]

This essay on symbolic process in psychoanalysis and Parsons' theory of action was submitted for publication in this volume in December, 1970. It has since then become one-third of a triptych, each part of which is dominated by one of those who have been, as these pages make clear, major influences: Talcott Parsons, Sigmund Freud, and Wallace Stevens. Since submitting it, I have written another paper and a book: "Language and Dreams: *The Interpretation of Dreams* Revisited" *(The Psychoanalytic Study of the Child,* 27: 203-282, 1972); and *Language and Interpretation in Psychoanalysis* (Yale University Press, 1975), which has at its center a detailed examination of a poem by Wallace Stevens. I have not revised this essay to conform with terminologies, conceptual strategies, formulations, and conclusions in these works that followed and continued it. Instead I have decided to let this essay stand as it was submitted; it represents an important aspect (not elsewhere duplicated)—as well as an important stage in the development—of my thinking about these problems.

I am not sure which is prior to which, my concern with such questions or my interest in the symbolic function, in symbolic systems, and in the actualization of such symbolic systems in personality and social systems of action. I am, however, convinced that progress in formulating answers to questions about interpretation in psychoanalysis depends upon some integration of the insights of those in diverse realms—art, philosophy, linguistics, the social sciences, psychoanalysis—who have given priority to the study of the symbolic function and symbolic systems. This paper adumbrates one form such an integration might take.

This attempt to understand interpretation, thereby, may contribute something of value to another effort, that of amplifying and clarifying certain aspects of those theories for which the symbolic function and symbolic systems are crucial, namely, psychoanalytic theory and the general theory of action.

The preeminence of psychoanalysis as a theory of personality in my judgment is in large part a consequence of its origins in the attempt to understand symbolic phenomena and to cope with such phenomena with exclusively symbolic means and of its continued preoccupation with the symbolic function and symbolic systems. Like transformational-generative approaches to language, psychoanalysis at least tries to account for, and so far seems best able to account for, the salient characteristic of personality (and also of language): creativity, the capacity to generate with finite means an infinite set of novel forms. That personality shares this characteristic with language may suggest to some how useful it might be to regard a personality system as essentially an organization of symbolic processes.

Parsons with increasing explicitness has emphasized the importance of the symbolic function and symbolic systems for the general theory of action.

For example, in a recent article[2], he makes the following statements:

> In the relevant sense action is . . . specifically human, and concerns those aspects of human *behavior* which are involved in and controlled by culturally structured *symbolic codes*; language is an obvious prototype. "Acts" in this sense are behaviors to which their authors and those who significantly interact with them attribute, in Weber's phrase, a "subjective," which is to say cultural or symbolic, meaning.[3]
>
> The eminent biologist, Alfred Emerson, has spoken of the functional equivalence of gene and "symbol," by which he meant that for culture-level systems of behavior, which we here call action systems, symbolic systems have the same *order* of functional significance that genetic systems have at the organic level.[4]
>
> It follows from our conception of action that the most important structural components of *any* action system are the symbolic codes by the use of which detailed adaptive activities take place.[5]
>
> Money, then, not only resembles a language, but *is* a very specialized language through which intentions and conditional consequences of action are communicated. If this is true, then a whole range of considerations about the nature and operation of symbolic media should apply to money.
>
> Power is defined as the capacity of a unit to mobilize obligations of the unit-members of a collective system in such a way as to make decisions binding on the collectivity and ensure their implementation through the performance of those obligations. The mobilization of such obligations, the promulgation of relevant decisions, and explication of their consequences for performance of obligations, all occur through ordinary processes of *linguistic* communication.[6]

We may recall, here, that Wallace Stevens, the poet, wrote: "Money is a kind of poetry."[7]

I shall indicate here what influences in particular press upon and surround me as I write this essay, as, no doubt, these presences shall continue to hover over these words long after I have delivered myself from the writing of them. I might epitomize these influences—risking the grotesquery that may arise from drastic truncation—in the form of three books: *The Interpretation of Dreams* by Sigmund Freud,[8] *The Structure of Social Action* by Talcott Parsons,[9] and *The Collected Poems of Wallace Stevens.*[10]

However, none of these investigators ever made a final statement. Each one turned his attention now to one facet, then to another, made one kind of emphasis or choice here, another there, refused any simplistic formulation that offered a pseudo-peace by denying some necessary term in a continuous, imaginative struggle to grasp conceptually the reality to be understood. Stevens represented a sensuous apprehension of the way these three thought in these words: "Three times the concentred self takes hold, three times / The thrice concentred self, having possessed / The object, grips it in savage scrutiny, / Once to make captive, once to subjugate / Or yield to subjugation, once to proclaim / The meaning of the capture, this hard prize, / Fully made, fully apparent, fully found."[11] In the sense in which Stevens regarded his collected poems as one poem, each of these men is entitled to be represented by the entire corpus of his work.[12]

With respect to the clarification of philosophical issues, I have found especially helpful works by Kenneth Burke,[13] Ernst Cassirer,[14] Susanne Langer,[15] and Jean Piaget;[16] and, for additional clarification of issues in the study of language in particular, works by Roger Brown, C. K. Ogden and I. A. Richards, Edward Sapir, Claude Lévi-Strauss, and Benjamin Lee Whorf.[17]

I would choose for particular mention as extraordinarily illuminating Susanne Langer's explication of the forms of art as nondiscursive, presentational symbols, which immediately present their meaning in illusions, semblances, or virtual appearances that symbolize through homologous morphology qualities of subjective experience. The following paragraph, which just precedes her discussion of the relation of Freud's description of "the dream work" to a theory of art, should be sufficient to indicate the relevance of her insights for this essay.

> The laws of combination, or "logic," of purely aesthetic forms—be they forms of visible space, audible time, living forces, or experience itself—are the fundamental laws of imagination. They were recognized long ago by poets, who praised them as the wisdom of the heart (much superior to that of the head), and by mystics who believed them to be the laws of "reality." But, like the laws of literal language, they are really just canons of symbolization; and the systematic study of them was first undertaken by Freud.[18]

As must be clear from allusions already made, I have been much impressed by what I can gather about the main outlines of transformational-generative approaches to language.[19] However, that many of the details are tentatively offered, in the process of development, or yet to be developed, and that many of the more technical expositions appear to be at the border of, or beyond, my present competence to master, leave me somewhat diffident about my grasp of the implications of these approaches for the problems in which I am interested and somewhat dubious about the analogies that crowd pell-mell into my susceptible mind. For example, I am perhaps momentarily overenthusiastic about the apparent resemblance between the following statements. Members of the finite set of deep structures of syntax—abstract "kernel sentences," all in present, active, declarative form—are changed and combined in various ways by transformational operations into an infinite set of surface structures. Members of a finite set of wishes (latent content) are transformed by the dream work into an infinite set of dreams (manifest content). Members of a finite set of impulses that constitute the id, a system in which there is no past or future or any negative, are transformed by ego and superego operations into an infinite set of surface structures—actions, subjective events, symptoms, character structures. The similarity of these statements may follow not from any shared intrinsic connection with symbolic function, but from the effort of theorists to view a large number of facts as exemplifications of a small number of propositions.

With regard to the problems with which I am concerned in this paper, I have certainly felt the impact of the climate of inquiry and diverse interests created by the faculty of the Western New England Institute for Psychoanalysis, to a greater degree than can be reflected in references to the writings of Hans Loewald, William Pious, and Roy Schafer that bear most directly upon the theoretical problems considered here.[20] There are reminiscences in this essay of discussions with Albert Solnit and Samuel Ritvo on the nature of the transference neurosis and on the importance of a steady focus upon psychic reality in psychoanalytic work even when, as in work with children, the pressure of the vicissitudes of current external reality upon the psychoanalytic situation is great; of discussions with Seymour Lustman on research models in psychoanalysis and, in particular, on the use of "dream samples" in *The Interpretation of Dreams* and on standards for the theoretical essay; and of a first, exciting, scholarly reading of *The Interpretation of Dreams* with Richard Newman. The relation between Wallace Stevens' conception of reality and that of Freud was first discussed with Henry Wexler. Stanley Leavy's essay on Keats supplies one precedent for my attitude toward Stevens:

> I am therefore quite deliberately using Keats's ideas as if they were themselves, so to speak, "psychoanalytic interpretations" of the data of experience. I am making almost no attempt to "analyze" Keats by uncovering the unconscious intentions of his ideas; if anything the thrust is in the opposite direction, to determine what the poet's experience as *he* understood it may do for psychoanalysis.[21]

The climate created by this faculty includes a special awareness of conceptual advances in ego psychology, in the work, for example, of Anna Freud, Heinz Hartmann, Ernst Kris, Rudolf Loewenstein, and David Rapaport,[22] the distinction between self-representation and object-representation, and its implications, in Hartmann's work and that of Edith Jacobson;[23] and Leo Stone's sensitive analysis of the psychoanalytic situation.[24]

Heinz Hartmann's work, exemplifying as it does a notable attempt on a conceptual level to bridge gaps between psychoanalysis and the biological and social sciences, has been an important model, although I do not share his special interest in energic concepts or his apparent conviction that psychoanalytic theory may be amended without damage or limit to become a general psychology. Hartmann from psychoanalysis, in mastery, intent, and intellectual background—note, for example, his references to Max Weber, his interest in action, and his essays on values and on rational and irrational action[25]—is the counterpart of Parsons, who builds the same bridge from the opposite shore.

I have been engaged on two different occasions by two very different clinicians, William Pious and Lars Borje Lofgren, in the imaginative study of an individual interpretation and its immediate context (as the empirical unit). These experiences provided impetus for an investigation of interpretation in psychoanalysis, on the path to which this essay is another step.

In two previous books, *Sociotherapy and Psychotherapy*[26] and *The Practice of Sociotherapy: A Case Study*,[27] I have been concerned with the relation between psychoanalysis and the theory of action. In those books, a consideration of the question of the interarticulation of personality and social systems was crucial for an attempt at formulating a theory of groups and a theoretical model of psychiatric hospital organization and at exploring the implications of such theory for the concept of therapeutic community and for the practice of sociotherapy and psychotherapy in a therapeutic community.

My interest in the relation between psychoanalysis and the theory of action continued as I turned my attention to problems of providing a conceptual foundation for a medical school curriculum in *Training Tomorrow's Psychiatrist*.[28] The cornerstone of that foundation was the convergence of psychoanalysis and the theory of action in a view of man as the symbolizing animal.

In *The Idea of a Mental Illness*,[29] I made a first extended exploration of symbolic process. I started with the convergence of psychoanalysis and the theory of action in a view of man as the symbolizing animal and went on from there to consider the implications of this view of man for the idea of a mental illness. The principal hypotheses in that work concerned the relation between the achievement of higher levels of symbolic process and the achievement of higher levels of consciousness. These hypotheses were applied to the problems of the treatment of a mental illness, schizophrenia providing the primary example.[30]

SYMBOL, SIGN, SIGNAL

A symbol is an entity that stands for, represents, or presents a meaning. The meaning, insofar as the entity is a symbol, is always an abstraction.

A conception is any abstraction, whether this abstraction be the isolation of an indivisible, and perhaps even nongeneralized essence, quality, or value from a particular experience; an imaged configuration or pattern; or a class, category, or set, defined by criteria for membership that may specify a quality or combination of qualities, a pattern or combination of patterns, or a relation or combination of relations.

An exemplar is any particular event (object or occurrence) that may be said to be an example of, to exemplify, or to illustrate an abstraction, or to qualify as a member of a class, category, or set.

A symbol connotes a conception; the relation between symbol and conception is connotation. A conception may denote or refer to an exemplar; the relation between conception and exemplar is denotation. A symbol insofar as it is a symbol never denotes or refers to an exemplar, never stands for or represents a particular concrete object or occurrence. The relation between symbol and exemplar is always mediated by a conception or abstraction.

A symbol is to be distinguished from a sign or signal. Either sign or signal is a part of the particular event it signifies. Either sign or signal elicits automatic reaction, not contemplation. A sign—what Piaget called an index[31]—is an intrinsic part of the existential event it announces or indicates. Sign and event are related as follows: if (sign), then (event). It would be just as true to say: if (event), then (sign). No abstraction mediates the relation between sign and event. A footprint, a ring around the moon, a scream of pain or snarl of anger are signs.

Signs that express states of affairs are to be distinguished from symbols that represent conceptions of states of affairs. A manifestation of affect, therefore, may be either sign or symbol. For this reason, Parsons' term "expressive symbolization" may be considered ambiguous.[32] In psychoanalysis, a similar ambiguity arises when affect such as guilt or anxiety is said to act as a "signal"—what I would call a symbol, insofar as its efficacy results from its function in representing a conception of a possible inimical state of affairs. There is a significant difference between signal-affect that functions as a symbol and affect that functions as a sign that, for example, a behavioral organism is reacting to an existent state of affairs or that a psychological system is in fact disorganized by an existent state of affairs.[33]

A signal is similar to sign in every respect except that the relation between signal and event is extrinsic rather than intrinsic. A signal and an event, therefore, may be connected by conditioning. A dinner bell may function as a signal. This definition of signal is also followed by Piaget.[34]

The many different terminologies in this realm create endless opportunities for confusion. Langer in *Philosophy in a New Key*[35] distinguished between sign and symbol as I have here, although she did not make the distinction between sign and signal that I have made. In *Feeling and Form*, however, she decided to follow Charles W. Morris, using signal where before she used sign, and using sign to include both signal and symbol. Piaget[36] uses sign for the symbol that is assigned by rule, convention, or social agreement to represent its meaning (a usage common among contemporary linguists)—what Langer has called a discursive symbol[37] and I have called a rational symbolic form.[38] Piaget confines the term symbol to those symbols that are not fully differentiated from the meanings they represent (such symbols are related to the conceptions they represent by resemblance rather than by rule and are, therefore, in part at least, also exemplars of the conception they represent)—what Langer has called a presentational, nondiscursive symbol[39] and I have called an apparitional symbolic form.[40] Piaget encompasses with "symbolic function" both what he called symbol and sign. I have not followed Piaget here because his terminology suggests a profound discontinuity between symbols of rule and symbols of resemblance, both of which are manifestations of a symbolic function that is uniquely human; the profound discontinuity exists, I believe, between the realm of what I have called sign and signal—which man shares with other species—and the realm of symbolic function, and it is that discontinuity I wish my terminology to reflect.

Parsons in early discussions in his work[41] seems to use sign for the most part as Langer, following Morris, does, to include both what she calls signal and symbol. Therefore, perhaps, he tends to use a model for the development of signs that emphasizes stimulus-response conditioning and some sort of principle of analogic extension as the process by which meaning is developed and also as the process by which signifier is connected to what is signified (these two processes not being clearly distinguished). This emphasis—which may follow from his interest in communication (signs and signals may, of course, enter into communicative processes) rather than the representation of conceptions—is not, I believe, congruent with the general position he has taken with respect either to the inadequacy of positivistic approaches to human behavior or to the importance of subjective components of action. Although conditioning is important in the realm of what I have called signals, there is no reason to believe—as Piaget in one way[42] and Chomsky in another,[43] for example, have also argued—that it is important or adequate in accounting for the symbolic function. Parsons in later work[44] has been primarily interested, when discussing symbolic media such as money and power, for example, in language as a model for the symbolic function; language as a system of symbols of rule or convention (Parsons refers to the code-components of a symbolic medium) is generally considered the most completely developed manifestation of the symbolic function.

Psychoanalysis, on the other hand, has been preoccupied with symbols of resemblance, and, as Piaget has done, has confined the term symbol to representing this kind of symbol. It is almost impossible to use symbol in discourse with a psychoanalytic audience to connote anything else, including language as just described, although language in general is a manifestation of the symbolic function that should claim a major portion of the practical and theoretical interest of psychoanalysts. Furthermore, because Freud depended in part (unnecessarily, I believe) upon an associationistic psychology, involving fortuitous, extrinsic connections such as those that characterize the relation between signal and event, psychoanalytic theory is susceptible to formulations that, violating its central import, portray the behavioral organism as automatically reacting to a signal connected in a fixed one-to-one relation to an event it inevitably indicates and, therefore, to reformulations in a stimulus-response conditioning frame of reference.[45]

EXTERNAL REALITY AND PSYCHIC REALITY

At the center of Freud's inveterate dualism is the distinction between psychic reality and external reality. This distinction is paralleled by Parsons' insistence that the theory of action is built upon the distinction between actor and object. Similarly, Piaget seeks to understand mental life in general, and the symbolic function in particular, in terms of departures from and returns to an equilibrium between processes of accommodation to external reality and processes of assimilation of reality to internal schema.

Wallace Stevens represents the same view in a symbolic form different from that used by scientist or philosopher. His work is a "variations on a theme" of surrender to the pressure of the world of things-as-they-are—a sun too immediate to manage with myth, a rock too bare to yield to adjective—and the imagination's sometimes triumphant, sometimes impotent struggle to resist mere surrender by creating a world of necessary fictions. "From this the poem springs: that we live in a place / That is not our own and, much more, not ourselves / And hard it is in spite of blazoned days."[46]

Freud's discovery of psychic reality, described reluctantly in relatively few passages throughout his writings, yet the foundation of all his major achievements, is one of the great intellectual adventures. Rarely has any discovery been made so contrary to the intentions and predilections of its discoverer. In fact, it was in the *Project for a Scientific Psychology*, in the midst of his earliest efforts to ground explanation in psychology in an external, empirically observable neurophysiology, that Freud indicated he had already made the distinction between thought-reality and external reality (importantly enough, in the context of this essay, in a sentence referring to symbolic activity): "Indications of discharge through speech are also in a a certain sense indications of reality—but of thought-reality not of external reality. . . ."[47]

Subsequently, Freud wrote to Fliess "the great secret" that he no longer believed in the traumatic theory of neuroses, the expected "feeling of shame" mitigated by the "feeling of a victory" in the recognition that "honest and forcible intellectual work" had led him not only to criticize his previous assumptions about the role of experience in the etiology of the neuroses but to realize, however tentatively, that the world of phantasies has a force, a causal efficacy, akin to that of external reality.[48] In *Totem and Taboo,* he wrote confidently: "What lie behind the sense of guilt of neurotics are always *psychical* realities and never *factual* ones." He added, however, in a tone that suggests a depreciation of psychical reality: "What characterizes neurotics is that they prefer psychical to factual reality and react just as seriously to thoughts as normal people do to realities."[49] Later, he added the following sentence to *The Interpretation of Dreams* (does its syntax suggest that he is still not altogether easy about this concept but feels compelled to accept it?): "If we look at unconscious wishes reduced to their most fundamental and truest shape, we shall have to conclude, no doubt, that *psychical* reality is a particular form of existence not to be confused with *material* reality."[50]

It was not until *On the History of the Psychoanalytic Movement* that Freud finally made explicit the despair and recovery that accompanied his discovery of psychical reality:

> The firm ground of reality was gone. At that time I would gladly have given up the whole work, just as my esteemed predecessor, Breuer, had done when he made his unwelcome discovery. . . . At last came the reflection that, after all, one had no right to despair because one has been deceived in one's expectations; one must revise those expectations. If hysterical subjects trace back their symptoms to traumas that are fictitious, then the new fact which emerges is precisely that they create such scenes in *phantasy,* and this psychical reality requires to be taken into account alongside practical reality.[51]

Freud's despair and even antipathy were not simply a rejection of the sexual content of psychical reality (the seduction by parents of children), although it may be noted in that connection that he deferred until late in his life the revelation that not only the father but also the mother was the parent in these phantasies.[52] His anguish is that of the utilitarian rationalist who, wishing the cause of psychopathology to be "out there," is confronted by the obdurately nonrational and subjective. In his account in *Introductory Lectures on Psychoanalysis,* he wrote somewhat plaintively:

> If the infantile experiences brought to light by analysis were invariably real, we should feel that we were standing on firm ground; if they were regularly falsified and revealed as inventions, as phantasies of the patient, we should be obliged to abandon this shaky ground and look for salvation elsewhere. But neither of these things is the case: the position can be shown to be that the childhood experiences constructed or remembered in analysis are sometimes indisputably false and sometimes equally certainly correct, and in most cases compounded of truth and falsehood. Sometimes . . . symptoms represent phantasies of the patient's *which are not, of course, suited to playing an aetiological role.*[53]

In a vivid passage, he went on to depict the dilemmas of thought and technique which the distinction between psychical reality and external reality continued to present.

> After a little reflection we shall easily understand what it is about this state of things that perplexes us so much. It is the low valuation of reality, the neglect of the distinction between it and phantasy. We are tempted to feel offended at the patient's having taken up our time with invented stories. Reality seems to us something worlds apart from invention, and we set a very different value on it. Moreover the patient, too, looks at things in this light in his normal thinking. When he brings up the material which leads from behind his symptoms to the wishful situations modelled on his infantile experiences, we are in doubt to begin with whether we are dealing with reality or phantasies. Later, we are enabled by certain indications to come to a decision and we are faced by the task of conveying it to the patient. This,

however, invariably gives rise to difficulties. If we begin by telling him straight away that he is now engaged in bringing to light the phantasies with which he has disguised the history of his childhood (just as every nation disguises its forgotten prehistory by constructing legends), we observe that his interest in pursuing the subject further suddenly diminishes in an undesirable fashion. He too wants to experience realities and despises everything that is merely "imaginary". If, however, we leave him, till this piece of work is finished, in the belief that we are occupied in investigating the real events of his childhood, we run the risk of his later on accusing us of being mistaken and laughing at us for our apparent credulity. It will be a long time before he can take in our proposal that we should equate phantasy and reality and not bother to begin with whether the childhood experiences under examination are the one or the other. Yet this is clearly the only correct attitude to adopt towards these mental productions. They too possess a reality of a sort. It remains a fact that the patient has created these phantasies for himself and this fact is of scarcely less importance for his neurosis than if he had really experienced what the phantasies contain. The phantasies possess *psychical* as contrasted with *material* reality, and we gradually learn to understand that *in the world of the neuroses it is psychical reality which is the decisive kind.*[54]

Starting with the phrase "created . . . for himself," Freud represented dramatically the nature of his attempted resolution of his ambivalence toward his own conceptual offspring, which is further adumbrated in a passage on "the origin and significance of the mental activity which is described as 'phantasy' [or 'imagination']," where, in a tone that more than verges on the appreciative, he refers to the necessity for "auxiliary constructions" and to psychical reality as a natural reserve.

> . . . Thus in the activity of phantasy human beings continue to enjoy the freedom from external compulsion which they have long since renounced in reality. They have contrived to alternate between remaining an animal of pleasure and being once more a creature of reason. Indeed, they cannot subsist on the scanty satisfaction which they can extort from reality. "We cannot do without auxiliary constructions", as Theodor Fontane once said. The creation of the mental realm of phantasy finds a perfect parallel in the establishment of "reservations" or "nature reserves" in places where the requirements of agriculture, communications and industry threaten to bring about changes in the original face of the earth which will quickly make it unrecognizable. A nature reserve preserves its original state which everywhere else has to our regret been sacrificed to necessity. Everything, including what is useless and even what is noxious, can grow and proliferate there as it pleases. The mental realm of phantasy is just such a reservation withdrawn from the reality principle.[55]

In his last works, Freud still manifested traces of

his complex attitude toward psychical reality. In *Moses and Monotheism,* he attributed the "compulsive quality" of such phenomena as symptoms, ego-restrictions, and stable character-changes to their "great psychical intensity" and their "far-reaching independence of the organization of the other mental processes, which are adjusted to the demands of the real external world and obey the laws of logical thinking." Such phenomena were said to constitute "a State within a State, an inaccessible party, with which co-operation is impossible, but which may succeed in overcoming what is known as the normal party and forcing it into its service." He warned that "the domination by an internal psychical reality over the reality of the external world" opens the path to psychosis.[56]

At the same time, he sought to redeem psychical reality by ascribing some truth-value to its manifestations, which were seen as not merely distorting but conserving traces of some past reality. Having made, in a number of his writings, a distinction between material truth and historical truth in reference both to religious belief and psychotic delusions, he declared in *Constructions in Analysis:* "...there is not only *method* in madness, as the poet has already perceived, but also a fragment of *historical truth....*"[57] In a final *Postscript* to *An Autobiographical Study,* he recanted *The Future of an Illusion's* "essentially negative valuation of religion": "Later I found a formula which did better justice to it: while granting that its power lies in the truth which it contains, I showed that the truth was not a material but a historical truth."[58]

MATERIAL REALITY AND PSYCHIC REALITY

It was not only "psychic reality" that was troublesome. Judging from the variety of adjectives preceding "reality"—external, factual, material, practical —we may conclude that the conceptual status of "external reality" offered as much difficulty. Freud avoided philosophical questions as much as possible in his work in the interest of creating an empirical science, but here an ontological specter seems impossible to evade. In his distinction between a material and a psychical reality, was Freud merely contrasting a naively accepted "real" reality with an unreal, spiritual, psychical reality? There seems to be good reason to think not.

He had certainly thought about such questions. That he knew and admired the work of Kant and was aware that our knowledge of external reality was shaped by the character of our minds is evident from Jones' biography[59] and from the passages in which Freud refers to Kant, especially the following:

> The psycho-analytic assumption of unconscious mental activity appears to us, on the one hand, as a further expansion of the primitive animism which caused us to see copies of our own consciousness all around us, and on the other hand, as an extension of the corrections undertaken by Kant of our views on external perception. Just as Kant warned us not to overlook the fact that our perceptions are subjectively conditioned and must not be regarded as identical with what is perceived though unknowable, so psycho-analysis warns us not to equate perceptions by means of consciousness with the unconscious mental processes which are their object. Like the physical, the psychical is not necessarily in reality what it appears to us to be.

He concludes, perhaps somewhat surprisingly: "We shall be glad to learn, however, that the correction of internal perception will turn out not to offer such great difficulties as the correction of external perception—that internal objects are less unknowable than the external world."[60]

Men have thought about reality in ways one may regard as essentially romantic, i.e., illusory. (One would not consider it likely that Freud, the brusque stoic, would be found in their company.) Men have comforted themselves with illusions about reality, not only in their pantheistic attribution of spirit to nature, but also in their assumption of a scientifically knowable, intrinsically lawful, empirical reality about which ideas were either true or false and which, it was expected, would eventually be adequately and exclusively encompassed by one set of propositions that had proved to be both most general and most valid.

William James, however, suggested another view of reality when he wrote:

> Is not the sum of your actual experience taken at this moment and impartially added together an utter chaos? ... [The] real order of the world ... is an order with which we have nothing to do but to get away from it as fast as possible.... [We] break it: we break it into histories, and we break it into arts, and we break it into sciences; and then we begin to feel at home.[61]

Similarly, Alfred N. Whitehead:

> The most obvious aspect of this field of actual experience is its disorderly character.... This fact is concealed by the influence of language, moulded by science, which foists on us exact concepts as though they represented the immediate deliverances of experience. The result is, that we imagine that we have immediate experience of a world of perfectly defined objects implicated in perfectly defined events.... My contention is, that this world is a world of ideas, and that its internal relations are relations between abstract concepts....[62]

The whole poem that Stevens wrote amounts to a stringent rejection of what I have suggested are two romantic myths about reality (although, paradoxically, Stevens is regarded by most who read him to be a romantic poet). So he wrote in *The Idea of Order at Key West* of the singer who sings "among / The meaningless plungings of water and the wind," "Then we, / As we beheld her striding there alone, / Knew that there never was a world for her / Except the one she sang and, singing, made."[63] Parsons has documented his own refutation of these myths about reality in *The Structure of Social Action*. His repudiation of them has its clearest expression in his rejection of positivism and of exaggerated claims for empiricism, his "conviction of the independent significance of theory," his allegiance to Henderson's definition of a fact as a statement in terms of a conceptual scheme, and his emphasis on the distinction between the normative and nonnormative aspects of action.[64]

About his own speculations, Freud could declare as emphatically as the most radical of empiricists, ". . . these ideas are not the foundation of science, upon which everything rests: that foundation is observation alone."[65] Eschewing philosophical questions, especially when these touched on the conceptual equipment he more or less had to accept if he were to make his journeys into the unknown from any stable starting point at all, he did not bother to emphasize or make explicit that the apparently objective reality of the rational ego—created according to the reality principle—is as much a result of an act of the mind as the inner world of psychic reality he so brilliantly revealed: the phantasmagoria created according to the pleasure principle. So, Wallace Stevens, in defense of imagination as a necessary agent (in interaction with the brute, bare, essentially unknowable "rock" of reality) for the creation of any reality apprehendable and comprehensible by man, is able to make the following bitter comments, paradoxically enough, about Freud, the discoverer of psychic reality, the archeologist of the imagination at work in the creation of reality:

Boileau's remark that Descartes had cut poetry's throat is a remark that could have been made respecting a great many people during the last hundred years, and of no one more aptly than of Freud, who, as it happens, was familiar with it and repeats it in his *Future of an Illusion*. The object of that essay was to suggest a surrender to reality. His premise was that it is the unmistakable character of the present situation not that the promises of religion have become smaller but that they appear less credible to people. He notes the decline of religious belief and disagrees with the argument that man cannot in general do without consolation of what he calls the religious illusion and that without it he would not endure the cruelty of reality. His conclusion is that man must venture at last into the hostile world and that this may be called education to reality. There is much more in that essay inimical to poetry and not least the observation in one of the final pages that "The voice of the intellect is a soft one, but it does not rest until it has gained a hearing." This, I fear, is intended to be the voice of the realist.[66]

However, it is clear from the following passage that Freud was not a naive empiricist. He did not suppose the scientist simply extracts his ideas from a close observation of "real" phenomena. He was aware that theory or ideas about reality and phenomenal reality are independent, that observations are always made in a conceptual frame of reference, that ideas determine what indeed is observed as "real" phenomena. Ideas are conventions, which happen to fit, which order experience; there can be no one-to-one correspondence between a "real" reality independent of the activity of the mind and the one true description of it radical empiricists believe they are seeking.

The true beginning of scientific activity consists . . . . in describing phenomena and then in proceeding to group, classify and correlate them. Even at the stage of description it is not possible to avoid applying certain abstract ideas to the material in hand, ideas derived from somewhere or other but certainly not from the new observations alone. Such ideas . . . must at first necessarily possess some degree of indefiniteness; there can be no question of any clear delimitation of their content. So long as they remain in this condition, we come to an understanding about their meaning by making repeated references to the material of observation from which they appear to have been derived, but upon which, in fact, they have been imposed. Thus, strictly speaking, they are in the nature of conventions—although everything depends on their not being arbitrarily chosen but determined by their having significant relations to the empirical material, relations that we seem to sense before we can clearly recognize and demonstrate them.[67]

Freud wrote that the "human ego is . . . slowly educated by the pressure of external necessity to appreciate reality and obey the reality principle. . .,"[68] and Piaget wrote that for adapted thought there must be accommodation to reality. In these passages, "reality" in part should be understood to represent an imaginative conception: of a something "out there" that exists independently of the subjective activity of the mind that knows it, a something that is in and of itself indifferent to the wishes, desires, intentions, anticipations or orientations to future end-states, attitudes, preferences or values, and interests constituting such activity. I write "an imaginative conception" in the same way that Stevens, writing of the "plain sense of things"—the "blank cold" for which it "is difficult even to choose the adjective"—remarks: "Yet the absence of the imagination had / Itself to be imagined."[69]

External reality in an ontological sense is a fiction, an irresistible inference perhaps, but a fiction nevertheless. That reality is not directly knowable, even by the heroic effort of abstinence from anthropomorphizing exerted by Stevens' snow man with his "mind of winter," who is "not to think / Of any misery in the sound of the wind," but who "listens in the snow, / And, nothing himself, beholds / Nothing that is not there and the nothing that is."[70]

"Material reality" as an ontological concept is a representation of the chaotic and meaningless, of the experience of a resistance—located "out there"—to man's "rage for order." It is the pressure of that unknowable reality which, so man imagines, threatens to defeat him, oppresses him, and, finally overwhelms him, as the activity of his mind fails. Any reality that is apprehended or comprehended by man is in this ontological sense a "psychic reality" —reality as constructed by the activity of the mind; there is no other reality that man can know.

An understanding of psychic reality in this ontological sense may have contributed to the development of a predominantly id psychology, which will consistently tend to interpret any kind of representation of experience—waking or sleeping, rational or nonrational, realistic or unrealistic—as essentially symbolic representation of mental activity, especially unconscious impulses. I suppose such a tendency has been most often attributed to the work of Melanie Klein and her adherents.[71]

The evidence cited suggests, however, that Freud had something other than ontology in mind when he distinguished between material and psychic reality as "forms of existence." It is likely that he came to take for granted that any kind of reality is a construction of the mind. In any event, the logic of his work leads me to believe that, in referring to psychic and material reality as "forms of existence," he was distinguishing between forms: I would call these "symbolic forms."

A symbolic form constitutes psychic reality: fantasy, an apparition, a virtual appearance, an illusion, which, like Langer's nondiscursive, presentational symbols, presents in compelling immediacy a kind of meaning—the qualities of subjective experience, subjective activity, that it symbolizes. Fantasy possesses psychic reality, as Freud put it, because as a symbolic form it symbolizes meaning; because as an apparitional symbolic form it presents that meaning as a virtual appearance, as do, similarly, the dream and the work of art; and because as a symbolic form functioning to symbolize meaning and to communicate that meaning in intrapsychic exchanges (if we may conceive communicative processes

occurring among subsystems of the personality), it possesses symbolic rather than intrinsic efficacy (as Parsons put it, in discussing such "symbolic media" as money and power, it possesses value in exchange rather than value in use).

In contrast to fantasy are discursive or rational symbolic forms, exemplified by the language of rational discourse and by cognitive perception, which conform to the canons of the reality principle, submit successfully to reality testing, and possess their efficacy by virtue of the meanings they represent—for example, adaptive exigencies.

As the realization has grown that the distinction between material and psychic reality is a distinction between meaningful symbolic forms, so the distinction between id and ego, primary process and secondary process, has become less pejorative and has involved a keener appreciation of the interdependence and interpenetration of these two systems or processes—for example, in the work of Kris on creativity and in the writings of other ego psychologists.

Hartmann has repeatedly challenged the assumption of any intrinsic connection between fantasy and illness, on the one hand, and reality and health, on the other. From Freud's discovery that patients suffer from reminiscences, that is, from symbolizations of the past, which are not true representations of the past but fantasy, the conclusion tends to be drawn that illness is equivalent to subjugation to fantasy, to the nonrational, while health is equivalent to recognition of brute reality. This in effect equates health with primacy of one mode of symbolization or construction of reality, the cognitive or rational, and denies any but dysfunctional effects to any other. Confrontation with reality becomes the antidote to fantasy; the often unwitting assumption is that there is one true reality and that it is possible to know it directly independently of any imaginative apprehension of it or valuation of it.

However, all knowledge of reality is symbolically mediated; external reality is a symbolic creation in the same sense that fantasy is a symbolic creation. The relation between fantasy and illness is a complex one. Fantasy as a symbolic form may present a reality that conforms to conceptions of the desirable; these conceptions vary widely in content. The gift of creation, of symbolization, of life in a world of symbolic constructions has functional and dysfunctional effects. With such a gift, one may create a reality in which men may feel at home or one in which men suffer, a reality in which men will love or must hate, will communicate with or must destroy each other. Among psychoanalysts, Hartmann, especially, has emphasized that rationality and health cannot be equated and that rational action is not the only nor at all times the best means to optimal adaptation.[72]

In the theory of action, the recognition of distinctive symbolic forms implied by the distinction between psychic reality and material reality has found another expression in Parsons' definition of the adaptation component of any subsystem of a system of action as a mode of representation or symbolization of adaptive exigencies, that is, as a mode of representation or symbolization of the situation.[73] The character of the representation of the situation changes, depending on the aim of the subsystem. All types of aims are regarded without prejudice as potentially functional—as meeting some requirement of the entire system.

So, for example, the situation is represented in the adaptation subsystem by cognitive symbolization. Such cognitive symbolization constitutes the adaptation component of the adaptation subsystem and is required if the aims of the adaptation subsystem are to be achieved. The situation is represented in the goal-attainment subsystem by expressive symbolization. Such expressive symbolization constitutes the adaptation component of the goal-attainment subsystem and is required if the aims of the goal-attainment subsystem are to be achieved. The situation is represented in the integration subsystem by moral evaluation. Such moral evaluation constitutes the adaptation component of the integration subsystem and is required if the aims of the integration subsystem are to be achieved. The situation is represented in the pattern-maintenance subsystem by existential interpretation, which symbolizes "the significance of 'sources of normative authority.'" Such existential interpretation constitutes the adaptation component of the pattern-maintenance subsystem and is required if the aims of the pattern-maintenance subsystem are to be achieved.

Each of these modes of symbolization requires a particular combination of a kind of categorization of objects and a kind of cathectic attitude or orientation toward objects. These kinds of categorization and cathectic orientation are defined by Parsons' pattern variables.

Each subsystem (adaptation, goal-attainment, integration, or pattern-maintenance) of a system of action has four components: (1) an adaptation component, which is a kind of representation of adaptive exigencies; (2) a goal-attainment component, which is a kind of meaning an object may come to have— e.g., object of utility, object of cathexis, object of identification, object of respect—as an end of a process of action; (3) an integration component, which is a kind of canon or standard, according to which choices are made by the subsystem; and (4) a

pattern-maintenance component, which is a kind of orientation to objects (interest in instrumental utilization, consummatory needs, needs for affiliation, needs for commitment) characteristic of, or "motivating," the subsystem.

There is, clearly, some analogy between the adaptation subsystem with its four components (cognitive symbolization, goal-object of utility, cognitive standards, interest in instrumental utilization) and the ego subsystem of personality in psychoanalytic theory; between the goal-attainment subsystem with its four components (expressive symbolization, goal-object of cathexis, aesthetic or appreciative standards, consummatory needs) and the id subsystem of personality in psychoanalytic theory; between the integration subsystem with its four components (moral evaluation, goal-object of identification, evaluative standards, needs for affiliation) and the superego subsystem of personality in psychoanalytic theory; and between the pattern-maintenance subsystem with its four components (existential interpretation, goal-object of respect, ground-of-meaning anchorage, needs for commitment) and the ego-ideal subsystem of personality in psychoanalytic theory.

Parsons, emphasizing the aspect of meaning of id that has to do with energic resources deriving from the organism rather than the aspect of meaning that has to do with the priority of gratification as an end and expressive symbolization as a response to adaptive exigencies, has tended to discuss the id as belonging to the behavioral organism and, therefore, as a source of resources or facilities mobilized by the adaptation subsystem of the personality system. Similarly, emphasizing the aspect of meaning of ego that has to do with control rather than the aspect of its meaning that has to do with the priority of adaptation as an end and cognitive symbolization as a response to adaptive exigencies, he has tended to discuss the ego as the goal-attainment subsystem of personality.[74] In general, if one starts from his papers on symbolism and pattern variables, e.g., in *Working Papers* and "Pattern Variables Revisited," one seems to be led to different conclusions from those one reaches by starting from his work on interchanges among subsystems and symbolic media, e.g., *Economy and Society,* in *Sociological Theory and Modern Society,* and "On the Concept of Value-Commitments." Why this should be so, I cannot tell.

Without stretching the analogy too far, on the basis of it one may ask some questions about psychoanalytic theory. For example, does it not seem as if sometimes ego, id, and superego are defined in terms of aggregates of similar components (the ego is constituted by all adaptation components and, therefore, by all processes of symbolization or representation, the id by all motivational components, the superego by all evaluative components)? Sometimes, though, ego, id, and superego are defined in terms of the aim of the subsystem (adaptation or mastery, goal-attainment or gratification, integration), in which case any one of these aims is served by a particular *organization* of all three kinds of components—a kind of mode of symbolization, a kind of motivational component, and a kind of evaluative component.

Schur, apparently, had something like these different bases for definition in mind when he argued against viewing the id as a bubbling cauldron of chaotic impulses and for viewing the id rather as a particular kind of organization of "structural" components such as cathected memories of gratification.[75] Memory, of course, has usually been given by ego psychology the status of an ego apparatus. But is memory an ego-function? What, then, of memory as an indispensable aspect of the wish, which is par excellence an element constitutive of the id? Does judgment, an evaluative component, belong to the ego or superego?[76]

To some extent such questions arise because of the tendency to reify ego, id, superego, and ego-ideal rather than to regard these as concepts to be defined—necessarily arbitrarily—in the terms of a conceptual frame of reference. However, such questions may also arise because of a confusion between: (1) sets or classes of components of subsystems of personality, the members of any one such set serving in different forms every subsystem; and (2) the subsystems of personality, which are defined in terms of the particular aims or goals of the personality system each such subsystem is differentiated to serve in its own way. Function as in ego function or superego function sometimes refers to a resource or component activity such as memory, perception, judgment, thought, affect, wish—each of which could be conceived to contribute in some form to a number of different subsystems. Function sometimes refers to the overall function of ego, superego, or id served by—the particular requirement of the personality system met by—some distinctive organization of these resources or component activities.

This line of thinking may suggest that some caution should be observed concerning the assignment of facilities such as memory, perception, and so on, to one subsystem such as the ego. The logic of Parsons' distinction between organism and personality, which is paralleled by the distinction between the psychological system and the neurophysiological system Freud actually followed in his work (as in his distinction between physiological processes and their psychic representatives), would suggest the assignment of such facilities or, as they are called in ego psychology, "apparatuses" to the organism rather than the psychological system. Similarly, caution should be observed concerning the assignment of component psychological processes or the products of such processes, such as remembering or memory images, to one subsystem such as the ego.

The advisability of such caution is in addition supported by the recognition that subsystems of personality are processes in time—each involving a variety of resources and component processes—not structures in space, as Loewald has discussed in his paper, "Superego and Time."[77] Parsons, similarly, has pointed out that action is a process in time; space is a condition of action but not part of it.

Should superego and ego-ideal be regarded as differentiated subsystems of personality? The tendency in psychoanalytic theory has been to regard the ego-ideal as an aspect of the superego subsystem.[78] However, the superego and ego-ideal appear to have a different genesis; in psychoanalytic theory, the superego is conceived to involve especially vicissitudes of aggression and object-libido, and the ego-ideal especially vicissitudes of narcissistic libido.[79] The superego and ego-ideal appear to achieve full functional differentiation in different developmental epochs, the former following the resolution of the Oedipus complex during latency and the latter during adolescence. The superego is primarily concerned with internalized norms, injunctions to act or refrain from acting in certain ways in relation to objects, while the ego-ideal is primarily concerned with the commitment of effort to actualize ultimate, most general, internalized values — including, but not only, moral values —and with the organization of a hierarchy of such values.[80] The internal sanction regulating superego processes is guilt; that regulating ego-ideal processes loss of self-esteem or shame.

Does it follow from our understanding so far of the distinction between external (i.e., material) reality and psychic reality that it is possible, that it might be useful, to think of ego, id, superego, and ego-ideal as subsystems of symbolic process, each subsystem dominated by different conceptions of goal objects, motivation (i.e., the nature of the relation with objects sought), adaptive exigencies, and integrative exigencies; by different modes of symbolization of such conceptions (e.g., primary and secondary process are different modes of symbolization); and by different modes of regulation of symbolization processes (e.g., pleasure and reality principles are different bases for choice—prescribe different standards for selecting—among alternative symbolizations)? Such conceptions, modes of symbolization, and modes of regulation might compete with each other for the allocation of priority or resources; conflict with each other in serving different ends; exclude each other as bases of abstraction; or contribute in varying degrees to "multiply-determined" compromise-formations—e.g., complex symbols such as symptoms or acts having many meanings.[81]

PRACTICAL REALITY AND PSYCHIC REALITY

Even if we accept that all that we know of reality is mediated by symbolic processes, it is still possible to distinguish analytically (i.e., conceptually—such distinctions are not "out there" but a way we create order out of chaos) between a subject aspect of symbolic process and an object aspect of symbolic process. The subject is distinguished by activity—for example, wishes, impulses, or desires; intentions and intentional acts; choice, preferences, or values; attitudes; or interests. The states the subject seeks to attain or maintain are desirable in and of themselves; i.e., there is no reference to their status as means to other ends. There is no incentive to cease such activity, only to maintain or repeat it. A crucial characteristic of such activity is that, as it is interfered with, it comes to involve evocation of the future: It comes to be organized by anticipation of, or orientation to, the future. Evocation, of course, is a sine qua non of symbolic processes.

We may imagine that if such activity were perpetually pursued without interruption or interference, no conception of reality would be necessary.[82] The object world or external (i.e., practical) reality is distinguished by its interference with the subject's activity.

An aspect of experience that interrupts or interferes with activity is classified as an obstacle, by virtue of its presence or absence, to the maintenance of activity and, once activity has been interrupted or interfered with, to its renewal. If the object's *presence* is an obstacle, to the extent it is unalterable, the interfering practical reality is considered—as in Parsons' conceptual frame of reference—a condition of activity. If the object's *presence* can be made to serve the subject's activity, to the extent its resistance to the subject's activity can be overcome, the interfering practical reality is considered—as in Parsons' conceptual frame of reference—a means-object. If the object's *absence* is an obstacle, to the extent it comes to be regarded as a necessary constituent for maintaining a subject's activity, the interfering or interrupting practical reality has the status of goal-object. In the latter case, end states of affairs sought

come to have a subjective and an objective aspect: the subject's activity and the relation with a goal-object that is viewed as a constituent, essential element of such activity.

In Freud's instinct theory, the subject's activity tends to be conceived as independent of the external object world (in which Freud did not apparently—in any systematic way—include the subject's body) and as an end in itself; reality is a condition or means. In Freud's conception of instinct as including a source (reference appears to be to the neurophysiological organism as a system), an aim (subject activity), and an object (external or practical reality), it is the aim that is the end sought. The object is a means. That objects are interchangeable with respect to the gratification of an instinctual aim means that any one of a variety of objects may be a means to the realization of a particular instinctual aim. In other words, no object is committed a priori to the gratification of one and only one instinctual aim.

Parsons, however, conceives the end state of affairs to involve, always, a *relation* between subject and object. His position parallels that of those who like Fairbairn[83] would modify psychoanalytic theory so that object relations rather than subject activity is the central characteristic of the ends sought by the subject. Parsons differentiates between means-objects (including conditions)—that is, the situation—and goal-objects. For him, external reality as practical reality is the situation. For Freud, external reality as practical reality encompasses both what Parsons means by means-objects and what he means by goal-objects; Freud conceives both to be means-objects.

This difference has some bearing on the interesting question (for those who would compare psychoanalytic theory and the theory of action): what is the analogue in psychoanalytic theory to Parsons' concept of the generalized symbolic medium?

Parsons does not use "symbolic medium" to mean a resource out of which a symbol is made. As Parsons uses the term "generalized symbolic medium," it means that a symbolic entity qua symbol is a resource or means to an end.[84] To the extent such a symbolic medium is generalized, it is not committed a priori to the attainment of one end, or to use in particular contexts on particular occasions, but is potentially usable in the attainment of a variety of unspecified ends. This property would follow from the intrinsic multi-functionality characteristic of symbols.

Instinct in psychoanalytic theory has a similar property. An instinct is not committed a priori to the attainment of a predetermined end—i.e., an instinctual object is not committed a priori to the gratification of a particular instinctual aim, but represents rather a potentiality for the gratification of a variety of instinctual aims. Probably aggression and libido in the entirety of their meaning should not be regarded as analogous to generalized symbolic media; in psychoanalytic instinct theory, only one aspect of instinct may be considered to have the conceptual properties just enumerated. The instinct considered from the viewpoint of source does not have these properties; it might be conceived as capacity, but it is also regarded as intrinsically efficacious (that is, its efficacy derives from the neurophysiological organism, which is logically, if not always regarded as such in the psychoanalytic literature, a situational object) rather than as symbolically efficacious. The instinct considered from the viewpoint of aim does not have these properties; it is not a means to an end, but the end itself. Only the instinct considered from the point of view of object might have these properties. The object is a generalized means, as it is not committed a priori to the gratification of one instinctual aim but may potentially serve in the gratification of a variety of such aims, depending upon the significance with respect to instinctual gratification that is attributed to it.

Because objects can be known only through symbolic representations of them, and it is their significance as symbolized that confers upon them their potential efficacy, may we conclude that symbolic representations of the meanings of objects (i.e., symbolic representations of conceptions of the significance of objects with respect to gratification of instinctual aims)—in other words, in psychoanalytic terminology, object-representations—are the analogues to Parsons' generalized symbolic media? Instinctual objects or, more exactly, object-representations, might then be considered to be media; to circulate in different forms as means to the attainment of different ends (the gratification of instinctual aims or their derivatives) among the subsystems of the personality system; and to have properties similar to those Parsons attributes to money, power, influence, and value commitments, which are symbolic media circulating in different forms as means to the attainment of ends among the subsystems of the social system.

The adaptation components in Parsons' theory are types of symbolization. The goal-attainment components in Parsons' theory are the meanings or significance of goal-objects: here, I put it, the meanings or significance (with respect to the gratification of instinctual aims) of the object that is symbolized. We, therefore, have as components both symbol and the conception the symbol represents. Such object-representations—symbolizations of the meanings of objects—may be regarded as symbolic media

circulating in different forms (types of symbolization) among the subsystems of personality.

There are different ways of symbolizing a particular conception or abstraction. This characteristic of symbolic process is reflected in the following formulations.

Parsons conceives money, power, influence, and value commitments to represent generalized symbolic capacities having different forms. These different forms ultimately are organizations of social acts or sanctions in an interactional system. Forms of money, for example, include: wage income; consumers' demands for commodities as in the use of money to purchase such commodities; control over a share of productivity; and control over fluid resources such as budgeted funds. Forms of power include: policy decisions; political support; employment, representing a commitment of services; capital, representing an opportunity for effectiveness. Forms of influence include: interest-demands; the assumption of leadership responsibility; justifications for allocations of loyalties; value-based claims to loyalty. Forms of value commitments include: labor capacity; commitments to produce or fulfill expectations for goods; commitments to valued associations; commitments to shared values.

These forms symbolize, according to Parsons, conceptions of possible alterations in the situation (essentially, in the relation between a social object and its object-situation) or in a social object (essentially, in terms of psychoanalytic theory, in the relation between one subsystem of the personality such as the ego and another subsystem of the personality such as the superego). These alterations are contingent, i.e., depend upon the response to the possible state of affairs represented by the symbol.

When a symbol represents a possible advantageous alteration in a social object's situation, such a symbol is an inducement and as such a means to the attainment of ends requiring certain actions of social objects. Money is a generalized symbolic medium of inducement. When a symbol represents a possible disadvantageous alteration in a social object's situation, such a symbol is an invocation of obligations and as such a means to the attainment of ends requiring certain actions of social objects. Power is a generalized symbolic medium of obligation-invocation. When a symbol represents a possible advantageous alteration within a social object, such a symbol is a persuasion and as such a means to the attainment of ends requiring certain actions of social objects. Influence is a generalized medium of persuasion, justifying courses of action by symbolizing the "reasons" for them. When a symbol represents a possible disadvantageous alteration within a social object, such a symbol is an activation of value commitments, motivating fulfillment of value commitments without reference to situational sanctions, and as such a means to the attainment of ends requiring certain actions of social objects. The generalization of value commitments is a generalized medium of commitment-activation. In the language of the theory of action, such symbols possess their efficacy through representing possible negative or positive sanctions.

If, in the personality system, we regard the image or memory image as a prototype of one kind of symbolic representation, thought in language as another, and affect or feeling as the prototype of still another kind of symbolic representation, then we may come to the following formulation. Such symbols may represent conceptions of a relation with a potentially inimical situational object (external danger) or a relation with a situational object that may provide an occasion for gratification of instinctual aims (temptation). Such object-representations may take the form of memory or anticipatory images, thought in language or pleasurable or painful feelings, or a combination of these. Symbols also may represent conceptions of a potential deterioration in the relation between subsystems of the personality (internal danger or conflict) or a potential enhancement or improvement in the relation between subsystems of the personality. These self-representations may also take the form of images (personality subsystems are imagined in the form of images of internalized objects, i.e., modelled after the images of situational objects), thought in language, or feelings (anxiety, guilt, shame, self-esteem).

Pursuing the analogy, for what it may be worth, we shall say that symbolic object-representation of conceptions of objects as potential occasions or opportunities for gratification of instinctual aims resembles money, that symbolic object-representation of conceptions of objects as potentially inimical resembles power, that symbolic self-representation of conceptions of potential deterioration in the relation between subsystems of the personality resembles value commitments, and that symbolic self-representation of conceptions of potential enhancement or improvement in the relation among subsystems of the personality resembles influence.

The distinction between practical reality and psychic reality is the distinction between the object world and the subject's instinctual aims: In the broadest terms, it is the distinction between the object-situation of the subject and the subject's aims and activities. However, the distinction between object-representation and self-representation is not a translation of any one of these other distinctions, although it is related to them.

It is not usual, but it would be useful, to distinguish between conception of self or object, and the symbolic representation of such conceptions, reserving the terms "self-representation" and "object-representation" for the symbolic representations of conceptions of self and object.

The self, as the term is commonly used, includes all that has the feeling of "me," and all that is located inside rather than outside "me." The body may be felt to be part of the self. One's capacities and one's aims may equally be felt to be part of the self. However, there is a useful distinction to be made between conceptions of the self as situational object—as the locus of obstacles to, means that may be used to realize, or occasions for the gratification of the subject's activity or aims—and the self as the locus of such activities or aims. The self-representation ordinarily symbolizes the self, including aspects of the body and the personality system, as possessing or failing to possess in one degree or another capacities by virtue of past achievement, capacities for present achievement, or qualities that interfere with, facilitate, or afford opportunities for the gratification of, the subject's activities or aims. The nature of the symbolic representation, if any, of these activities and aims—i.e., of the subject as subject or agent (not object or agency), in process (not in retrospect as capacities or qualities)—is a theoretical problem, to which Hartmann alludes when he distinguishes between the cathexis of an object-representation (also presumably the self-representation in the way that I have defined it) and the cathexis of an object-directed ego function. This allusion occurs, for example, in a discussion that begins with the distinction made by the child between his activity and the object toward which this activity is directed.[85]

We may, of course, distinguish between conceptions of motivational activity and conceptions of self or object as situational objects (as Parsons has distinguished between cathectic and cognitive classifications in his sets of pattern variables). We may wonder then if there is any necessary difference in the form of the symbolic representation of conceptions of motivational activity from the form of the symbolic representation of conceptions of situational objects. Langer seems to have concluded that art forms or what she calls presentational symbols as distinguished from discursive symbols are the form par excellence for the symbolic representation of feelings or motivational states or activity.[86] I have chosen, however, tentatively to regard feelings as interiorised (in subjective experience) or exteriorised (in expressive action) symbols of conceptions of the state of the personality system. There seems to be little question, in any event, that from Freud's statements about psychic reality we may infer that fantasy is held by him to be the symbolic representation of the subject's conceptions ("ideas" is Freud's term) of his own instinctual aims or instinctual activity. Such a formulation may prove to be a useful amplification of Freud's view of the instinct as a psychic (this must mean, I would say, symbolic) representation: ". . . an instinct appears to us . . . as the psychical representative of the stimuli originating from within the organism and reaching the mind. . . ."[87]

In the theory of action, if the actor actually alters the situation of a social object or some state of a social object itself irrespective of its situation in a way that is advantageous or disadvantageous from the point of view of the social object, such that the social object has no choice but to respond as desired by the actor, symbolic process is not necessarily involved. There are many degrees of freedom for a social object between the option to respond as an actor desires and the compulsion to respond. A gift alters a situation advantageously; it is a positive sanction. Ordinarily, a gift is not an inducement, because there is little choice for the object concerning the acceptance or rejection of the offer. Force alters a situation disadvantageously; it is a negative sanction. Ordinarily, force is not an invocation of obligations, because there is little choice for a social object concerning whether or not he will perform as desired. Giving information is ordinarily not persuasion, if the information is so compelling that the object cannot choose but to act in terms of it; persuasion implies the giving of "reasons" that will be accepted because of the prestige of the actor or the evaluative beliefs of the object even in the absence of complete cognitively verifiable information. A demonstration that to act otherwise than is desired is unthinkable in view of the values of the object is ordinarily not activation of commitments; activation of commitments implies that the object has a choice whether or not to fulfill his commitments, but the failure to do so will result, for example, in a negative sanction from within such as loss of self-esteem or shame.

A generalized symbolic medium, then, is one that makes possible an enhanced capacity to induce, invoke obligations, persuade, or activate commitments because such a medium involves abstraction, which frees it from attachment to specific concrete circumstances. Therefore, such a medium does not bind its possessor to use it in the service of any particular end, at any particular place or time, or in relation to any particular object. The possessor of such a medium has maximum freedom in deciding how, when, where, and for what he shall employ it — thus, the term generalized. On the other hand, because

such a means to the attainment of ends is symbolic, its effect and, therefore, its effectiveness as a means are not unequivocally determined, absolutely predictable, or in any way guaranteeable.

For possible illustrations of these propositions we may look in psychoanalytic theory at the distinction between anxiety or guilt as a signal — that is, a *symbol* of a conception of a possible state of affairs — and the anxiety or guilt that overwhelms the personality system. In the latter case, affect does not symbolize but acts as a sign or index of an existent, pressing state of affairs, for the conception of which the personality has insufficient resources, including time, and to which the organism with minimal symbolic mediation merely reacts.[88]

Another possible illustration in psychoanalytic theory is to be found in the consequences of the representation of false or inappropriate conceptions (that is, conceptions which have failed to conform to such standards as the reality principle) of a potential state of affairs. When action is guided by such a representation, dysfunctional effects accrue to the personality system. Confidence in its symbolic media suffer, in a way that resembles the loss of confidence in an inflated medium such as money in a social system. In these terms, psychosis and neurosis might be characterized by inflation of symbolic media (and character constriction by deflation of symbolic media).

Parsons has pointed out that there are two bases of security in the use of a symbolic medium in a system. One, it is backed by intrinsically valuable entities of utility, effectiveness, solidarity, or integrity, such as gold or force. Two, in its most generalized, symbolic aspects, its use depends upon confidence or trust in the functioning of the system. However, there are always risks in using a generalized symbolic medium. One may find that one is left with the symbol and nothing else, that expectations of consequence of its use are disappointed. Only within a range of optimal system functioning can such a medium be counted upon to mean what it "says." A continuous choice, therefore, must be made between the degrees of freedom afforded by use of a generalized symbolic medium — the use of which involves acceptance of risks and requires trust or confidence in the functioning of the system — and the security that results from sticking to intrinsically valuable media, which, however, must be used for the attainment of a narrow range of given or prescribed ends, only in certain ways in relation to only certain objects, in particular times and places, about none of which may there be much choice.

A symbolic medium may serve more than one function at the same time, only if its users are willing to forego immediate pay-offs and to wait the time required—for example, for recombinations of factors as in organizational changes—for such pay-offs, and only if there is confirmation of the expectation that there will not be a demand for pay-offs from a variety of sources at the same time or over too short a time. As long as confidence or trust in the functioning of the system exists, and the medium is used symbolically, the amount of the medium circulating in the system is not a constant; instead, the amount of the medium used within the system may be, in essence, expanded. In such a case, an addition of the capacity represented by the medium somewhere in the system does not necessarily mean a loss of the capacity represented by the medium elsewhere in the system.

If there is an insistence upon immediate pay-offs in the form of intrinsically valuable entities or immediate results, then the system acts as if it were a "closed" rather than "open" system. An addition of capacity somewhere in the system is likely to mean a loss of capacity elsewhere in the system. The value of the symbolic medium is contracted, restricted, or narrowed. Such a state of affairs is analogous to deflation and may be termed deflation of the medium. If a symbolic medium is overextended in its uses such that it increasingly fails to achieve desired effects, then the value of the symbolic medium is inflated. Such a state of affairs may be termed inflation of the medium.

Similarly, any language may perform a variety of functions at once. For example, in verbal language, the same proposition may serve both cognitive and cathectic functions, or the same word both denotative and connotative functions; ambiguities of meaning in language are well known. The multifunctionality of language is the basis of its extraordinary usefulness but also renders it vulnerable to certain impairments. An inflated language is one that pretends to more meaning than it has, that attempts more than it can accomplish, given the state of the system of relations determining its resources or capacities. It cannot fulfill the expectations it arouses, thereby becoming increasingly depreciated, but as the rate of demand upon it to fulfill expectations is (from the point of view of its devaluation) too low, it continues increasingly to become overextended. A deflated language has such high demands upon it to fulfill certain expectations that its functioning becomes increasingly contracted. For example, an insistence on maximum denotation in language may result in a restriction of freedom to explore in directions requiring connotation as well as denotation.

Inflation and deflation are, then, impairments of symbolic process inherently risked in the use of any generalized symbolic medium.

In psychoanalytic theory, the assumption is sometimes made that libido and aggression are constant quantities and that, therefore, if some quantity appears or increases in one part of the personality system, it must disappear or decrease in another part of the personality system. This assumption is usually regarded as a heuristic axiomatic postulate. Critics point out that personality is not in fact a closed system and that its input of energy from the physiological organism cannot be regarded as constant. They are answered that libido and aggression are not forms of "real energy" but rather hypothetical quantities endowed with quality that are assumed to take different forms and to decrease at some point in the system when there is an increase elsewhere in the system. Such assumptions, it is thought, are helpful in accounting for the quantitative aspects of psychological phenomena.

It is possible that this argument does not simply involve the question of what is heuristic and economical in theory, but rather reflects whether or not sufficient account is taken of the fact that the personality system is constituted by symbolic processes. In the language of psychoanalytic theory, object-representations or self-representations, which are the objects of libidinal or aggressive instinctual aims, have the properties of symbolic media. Then, the efficacy of a quantity of aggression or libido may depend upon the state of the personality system—for example, the level of confidence in its symbolic media, the level of trust that the use of such media will in fact lead to the realization of valued ends. We may expect that in a state of inflation, there may be such an overextension of the uses of such symbolic media to attain such a variety of ends that increasingly use of such media fail to achieve desired effects. If, then, there is a panicky insistence that symbolic resources in the personality system be fully backed by, if not abandoned for, intrinsically efficacious resources, such as immediate action, or that there be immediate gratifications, symbolic media may be said to be deflated. The incapacity to delay discharge may be, in some sense, one manifestation of a personality system suffering from deflation of its symbolic resources. In a state of such deflation, the value of the symbolic medium is contracted, restricted, or narrowed. The personality system will act as if it were a closed rather than open system. An addition of capacity somewhere in the personality system (investment in a particular object- or self-representation) is likely to result in a loss of capacity elsewhere in the system. This characteristic of system "closedness" becomes, then, an indication of pathology—of symbolic impairment: inflation or deflation of symbolic resources.

What Hartmann describes as instinctualization of a psychological function may be regarded in these terms as a manifestation of the contraction of the value of a symbolic medium. De-instinctualization, neutralization, or the achievement of relative autonomy of a psychological function from dominance by the requirement to fulfill direct, immediate instinctual aims may represent increasing use of symbolic media to attain ends, and increasing confidence in their capacity to lead to gratification. Neutralized libido or aggression may, then, serve a variety of ends, just as money as a symbolic medium—while it is in the form of savings — may also be used for investment.

The significance of such formulations, which no doubt seem somewhat strained, is that they focus attention upon the role of symbolization in processes of interest to the psychoanalyst, in preference to letting the explanation of these depend upon analogy to nonsymbolic physical systems (e.g., the troublesome hypothesis of forms of psychic energy—an energy that not only is quantitative, but is conserved in quantity and is endowed also with qualities apparently determining a priori the nature of the ends sought by the personality).

FACTUAL REALITY AND PSYCHIC REALITY

The transference neurosis is one of Freud's greatest scientific discoveries. Here is a phenomenon that is, to judge by complaints about the behavioral sciences, rare indeed in their realm! It is unexpected. It is of critical theoretical significance. It is replicable, under carefully controlled conditions.

The carefully controlled conditions are comprised by the psychoanalytic situation, which includes a patient capable of prolonged commitment to attempts at free association and a psychoanalyst whose participation is rigorously disciplined. The patient is willing and able to devote himself to make verbal productions in a situation designed to minimize *external* excitants, guidance, or interference that might evoke, shape, or obstruct these productions. Furthermore, he agrees himself to try to refrain from preventing in any way—as a result, for example, of deliberate efforts to order, select, or judge material— the utterance in verbal form of whatever comes to his mind. The psychoanalyst's aims in relation to the patient's verbal productions are limited to the interpretation of their meaning and the communication of such interpretations in a way that increases the likelihood that they will be meaningful to the patient: All the psychoanalyst's skills are exercised to these ends alone. The psychoanalyst, ideally, will not be moved or persuaded to respond to the patient's verbal productions in any way other than interpretation of their meaning.

What happens under these circumstances is truly remarkable. Typically, after an initial, apparently relatively uninhibited period of expression, the patient's symptoms may suddenly disappear, gradually subside in severity, or increasingly cease to concern or preoccupy him. Concomitantly, he finds free association increasingly difficult. Regularly, it is to ever more persistent thoughts and intense feelings about the psychoanalyst that he is reluctant to give verbal expression, despite the injunction to free association.

The disappearance or mitigation of the patient's symptoms, as well as the relative disappearance from his verbal productions of concern with past or current relationships outside the psychoanalysis and the obstruction of free association, are all related to his increasing preoccupation with his (to him usually unacceptable) conceptions of the psychoanalyst and the psychoanalyst's attitudes toward, feelings about, or intentions in relation to, himself; with his own (to him usually unacceptable) attitudes toward, feelings about, or intentions in relation to, the psychoanalyst as so conceived; and with his own efforts to verify his conceptions of the psychoanalyst and to realize his aims or bring about some state of affairs in relation to the psychoanalyst.

It may be, moreover, that, given the conditions described above, these preoccupations of the patient will hold sway over him only or mainly for the period of the psychoanalytic hour. Astonishingly enough, after an hour of hesitation, strain, hints of passion, or explicit torment, muteness, imprecations, or beseechings, the patient may rise calmly from his recumbent position, perhaps indicate, however fleetingly, his recognition of the psychoanalyst as psychoanalyst, and go about his business, relatively untroubled, only to immerse himself once again in his *creation* the next hour. For the impression is irresistible that the patient creates something, something circumscribed in space and time, something out of the materials of the psychoanalysis. He makes, according to a process of creation—using methods— determined or made possible by the constraints of the psychoanalysis, something with form, however strange, the shape of which at first is dim, vague, as if seen always from afar through a mist, there, lost, recovered, and lost again through many hours, but in time looming closer, increasingly precise in outline and rich in detail and design.

Freud did not ignore this phenomenon, damn it as a nuisance, or exploit it to noninterpretive ends. His astonishing feat, of course, was instead to discover that this impediment to the psychoanalysis, this obstacle to the patient's participation in the psychoanalytic situation as defined, was, in fact, a representation of the patient's conception of his inner world (a psychic reality), of the conflicts between imagined entities (of which his illness, his symptom, was still another apparitional symbolic representation) now quintessentially in the form of the transference neurosis. As such, this representation called for interpretation no less than the patient's free association verbal productions.

A fantasy is a symbol of conceptions of inner reality in the form of time past, time present, or time future. Because a fantasy is an apparitional symbol, it is not only a representation of psychic reality but an exemplar of it, i.e., such a symbol in part creates the reality, conceptions of which it also represents. The transference neurosis, similarly, which is not a revival of earlier events or relationships but of the patient's earlier, perduring conceptions of events and relationships, is an apparitional symbol of these conceptions.

Psychoanalysis, despite its preoccupation with a genetic or developmental frame of reference, despite the historicism of many of its theoretical formulations, is not a science of history but a science of the symbolizing activity of the mind. Psychoanalysis cannot be concerned with the recovery—as a method it is not suitable for the study—of actual events. The patient may refer to what is apparently the same event at different times in different contexts during a psychoanalysis. At these different times the presentations of the event and its elements are likely to differ from each other: Details, emphases, conceptions of the event, and the attitudes and feelings aroused by or associated with such conceptions differ. The very history of the patient seems to change as he reconstructs it during different periods of the psychoanalysis. For during these various periods what the event and its elements mean, what the patient made and makes of them, changes. If a history is revived, it is the history of the acts of the patient's mind, creating symbols to represent his conceptions of reality.

We may or may not infer an actual event at that imaginary point where the patient's various representations of an event intersect, but that actual event as an entity is not knowable through, nor can it be investigated by, the method of psychoanalysis. The pathogens exorcised by psychoanalysis are not physiological processes nor historical situations but transformations, symbolic representations of conceptions or "ideas," of these: mental shades, memories, fantasies. Not reality but representations of reality. Not organism but representations of body and self. Not object-relations but conceptions of object-relations. Between stimulus and response, between event and behavior, falls the act of the mind. It is the creation of the symbol, the "poem of the act of the mind,"[89] that is the object of study in psychoanalysis.

Freud had been disturbed to discover that the patient's reported memories were fictions. Evaluated according to standards of empirical validity and instrumental logic which are applied to discursive symbolization, the memories were not factual or true, although they were clearly meaningful. These vivid mnemic events, however potent as symbolic representations of the patient's conceptions of reality in governing his life, were illusions.

Kris has, for example, demonstrated that even apparently factual memories must inevitably represent abstractions from the immeasurably varied, chaotic flux of experience, must inevitably to some extent be personal myths, which are nodes of condensation of multiple conceptions of innumerable experienced realities.[90] A memory is, also, quintessentially, a virtual event in the same sense that Langer has described a work of art to be a virtual event.[91]

The conviction commanded by a memory is similar to the conviction commanded by a work of art. Both are virtual happenings, semblances, a seeming to be and to transpire. Both command conviction through the creation of an illusion, embodied and presented in the form of an apparitional symbol. (Representations of "real" events are one kind of material used in the creation of such an illusion.) The symbolic efficacy of such an illusion derives from its function as a symbolization of a conception in a form which (unlike that of discursive or rational symbols) also exemplifies the conception it presents.

Wallace Stevens, quite suggestively in the present context, proposes that Freud "might have said that in a civilization based on science there could be a science of illusions. . . . "[92]

> Then, too, before going on, we must somehow cleanse the imagination of the romantic. We feel without being particularly intelligent about it, that the imagination as metaphysics will survive logical positivism unscathed. At the same time, we feel, and with the sharpest possible intelligence, that it is not worthy to survive if it is to be identified with the romantic. The imagination is one of the great human powers. The romantic belittles it. The imagination is the liberty of the mind. The romantic is a failure to make use of that liberty. It is to the imagination what sentimentality is to feeling. It is a failure of the imagination precisely as sentimentality is a failure of feeling. The imagination is the only genius. It is intrepid and eager and the extreme of its achievement lies in abstraction. The achievement of the romantic, on the contrary, lies in minor wish-fulfillments and it is incapable of abstraction. In any case and without continuing to contrast the two things, one wants to elicit a sense of the imagination as something vital. In that sense one must deal with it as metaphysics.
>
> If we escape destruction at the hands of the logical positivists and if we cleanse the imagination of the taint of the romantic, we still face Freud. What would he have said of the imagination as the clue to reality and of a culture based on the imagination? Before jumping to

the conclusion that at last there is no escape, is it not possible that he might have said that in a civilization based on science there could be a science of illusions? He does in fact say that "So long as a man's early years are influenced by the religious thought-inhibition . . . as well as by the sexual one, we cannot really say what he is actually like." If when the primacy of the intelligence has been achieved, one can really say what a man is actually like, what could be more natural than a science of illusions? Moreover, if the imagination is not quite the clue to reality now, might it not become so then? As for the present, what have we, if we do not have science, except the imagination? And who is to say of its deliberate fictions arising out of the contemporary mind that they are not the forerunners of some such science? There is more than the romantic in the statement that the true work of art, whatever it may be, is not the work of the individual artist. It is time and it is place, as these perfect themselves.[93]

So, then, here the distinction between factual reality and psychic reality becomes a distinction between factual reality and virtual reality, which is to say a distinction between two different kinds of symbols or ways of symbolizing conceptions of reality, i.e., between two symbolic forms, the apparitional and rational or, as Langer has termed them, the presentational and discursive, with the emphasis placed by the term "factual" on the difference between the standards according to which these two kinds of symbols are evaluated.

An evaluative standard provides a basis for selection or rejection—for choosing between one conception and another, or one symbol and another of the same kind, or for choosing between symbols of one kind and those of another kind. Such choice may be made in the interest of the integration of a cultural system — a system of symbolic entities — or in the interest of the integration of an interactive (social) or a personality system and the achievement of the ends to which such action systems are oriented.

In the context of Parsons' theory of action, these criteria are likely to be formulated as value standards: (1) truth or cognitive validity, according to the canons of empirical science; (2) beauty or appreciative standards, involving considerations of appropriateness, taste, and aesthetic preference; (3) harmony or moral standards, involving considerations of the integration of a system and, therefore, questions of right and wrong; and (4) ultimate grounds of meaningfulness.

The first value standard prescribes that choice be made to maximize the aims of instrumental action: adaptation to, or mastery of, a situation (means and conditions), according to a cognitive understanding of verifiable means-end relations. The second value standard prescribes that choice be made to maximize the aims of expressive action: gratification or attainment of ends desirable in and of themselves without regard to their status as means to other ends. The third value standard prescribes that choice be made to maximize the aims of responsible action: integration of the elements of a system or integration of a system with a supraordinate system that includes the former as subsystem. The ultimate grounds of meaningfulness provide a basis for choosing between values or for establishing a hierarchy of value priorities.

In the context of psychoanalytic theory, these criteria are likely to be formulated as regulatory principles, such as the reality principle and pleasure principle, and the mechanisms implementing such principles through the effects of dysphoric or euphoric affects, such as anxiety, gratification, guilt, and shame.

Freud's reality and pleasure principles seem to correspond significantly to Parsons' first and second value standards. There is no statement in psychoanalytic theory of two principles that might correspond to Parsons' third and fourth value standards, although Freud does detail the functions of guilt and shame in maintaining, respectively, the integration of the personality system through conformity to internalized norms (superego) and the integrity of the pattern of ideals against which a self-representation is judged (ego-ideal).

Freud's ultimate contribution to the understanding of symbolic forms, however, was to evaluate them in terms of the criterion of meaningfulness. The questions "Is the symbolic form meaningful?" "In terms of what assumed operations of symbolic function may it be understood as meaningful rather than rejected as meaningless?" replace the questions "Is it true? Is it beautiful? Is it moral?" If the symbolic representation of a conception does not conform to cognitive standards (canons of "reality testing"), it does not represent factual reality. To the extent it represents a conception according to other canons, it may, however, be meaningful.

Freud's distinction between factual reality and psychic reality bears a significant resemblance to the distinction Parsons makes between factual order and normative order.

Man's rage for order is manifested in two ways: discovery of factual order, of "natural law," of existential order; and devotion to achieved or normative order. Factual order arises from an interaction between the invention of theory; the observation of facts guided by a conceptual framework (no matter how little or how much explicit or precisely formulated); and the discovery that theoretical formulations fit facts (observable aspects of empirical reality). The implications of such formulations are verifiable according to the canons of science. The cognitive comprehension or explanation of empirical reality in this sense is the cognitive comprehension of factual order. The element of creation here is in the invention of theory that fits. Symbolization enters into the representation of factual order. However, although symbolization through processes of abstraction, for example, may impose order upon a chaos of phenomena, symbolization is not necessarily a constituent of that which is conceived to have such order. Factual order is order in the natural world of things.

Parsons' preoccupation with normative order (i.e., achieved order) is his tribute to its problematic status. Achieved order arises from a commitment — a felt obligation — to make an effort to act in accordance with a conception of the desirable (a value-conception) and in so doing to overcome the obstacles to its actualization. To compose reality and to maintain such a composition in conformance with a conception of the desirable, in the presence of obstacles opposing — and implacable conditions limiting — the possibility of such a realization, is to achieve order. Libido theory in psychoanalysis may be regarded as a theory of the origin, relation, and symbolization of different conceptions of the desirable, and the ways in which these conceptions are realized in action[94]

Action, in this sense, is the attempt to create and maintain achieved or normative order. Depending on the conception of the desirable, the order achieved may be hellish or heavenly. Depending upon available means or resources, including the strength of commitment or effort exerted, relative to the strength of obstacles and limiting conditions, it is always possible that an attempt to create and maintain achieved or normative order may fail. One cannot say of a factual order that it may succumb to forces opposing it. The influence of such forces are simply included as part of the factual order. An achieved normative order, however, is a tentative, vulnerable, precarious, never an ultimate, order; a pattern of change may be part of such an order, but also change may occur to disrupt it.

Symbolization is a necessary constituent of achieved, normative order, a part of that which is conceived to have such order. Achieved, normative order is order in the world of action; it is an emergent characteristic of the human world, the world of person, society, and culture. Achieved, normative order is dependent upon the existence and activation of capacities to orient to the future; to create conceptions of the desirable as against the merely actual; to appreciate possible as against merely present alternatives; and to choose between such alternatives according to criteria or standards derived from or implied by conceptions of the desirable. Achieved, normative order in a social system requires the existence of supraindividual symbolic entities; individual members share a commitment or obligation to act in conformance with these.

As many conceptions of the desirable are possible, many kinds of achieved, normative order are possible. Each achieved, normative order is a reality. Many kinds of reality or interpretations of reality are possible. An actor may look at reality in different ways; he may value reality for different reasons; he may see reality by the light of different values. The apprehension of reality is imaginative and not merely sensate; that is, the apprehension of reality confers value upon reality. The value conferred is determined by what particular conception of the desirable dominates an achieved order, implying criteria or standards for selecting between alternative representations of reality (i.e., for selecting what aspect of reality is relevant, what kinds of relation to reality are relevant).

Note that a chaotic structure or process from the point of view of the creation or maintenance of an achieved, normative order may still have a factual order. On the other hand, value-conceptions may be, but are certainly not always, part of a factual order — that is, they may be a "variable" or "factor" in a theory or explanation of empirical reality.

Parsons' distinction between behavior and action is implicit in Freud's distinction between psychic reality and factual reality. Behavior results from the "physicality" of man and the effect of physical forces upon him (as in "falling down a hill") as well as from the "animality" of man and the effects of physiological processes unmediated by symbolic process. It is a fallacy to attribute consequences of symbolicity (which are, for example, implied by Freud's "primary process," "psychic representatives," "id," "instinct") to physicality or animality. Behavior may be part of factual but not of achieved, normative order; only action by definition may be part of achieved, normative order as well as factual order.

In an achieved order, action is constrained primarily by normative elements internalized within the actor, ultimate values he holds in common with other men, with which he is identified, and which enter into the constitution of his ends and the means by which he pursues them. Far from passively recognizing and adapting to such normative elements as external facts, as aspects of his situation, the actor feels a moral obligation to make an effort in opposition to obstacles to actualize these values; upon such actualization, he feels his self-fulfillment depends. Psychoanalysis embodies these conclusions by including the "superego" and "ego-ideal" as indispensable structures of personality.

Thus, "happiness" does not depend upon the gratification of impulse or the fulfillment of desire, but is the state of an individual whose values and actions are integrated with a system of values shared with others—even though these others may constitute a group outside of in time or place the concrete society in which he lives. Such a view of happiness challenges any psychology that regards pleasure-seeking or the reduction of physical tension as logically prior to all motivation and all ends sought as states of satiety determined by conditions—physical states—rather than by normative, i.e., symbolic, elements. Instead, with respect to any desire, 'satiety—what is "enough?"—which may be defined by conditions, by physical states, by the exhaustion of physical resources or means, by the assertion of competing claims or the accrual of consequences of ignoring such claims, may, perhaps, primarily, be defined by normative, symbolic elements such as values. The formulation that satiety may be defined normatively goes far toward resolving the old dilemma for psychoanalytic theory concerning the existence of tension-increasing action when men are supposedly actuated primarily by a desire to reduce tension.

Conceptions of the desirable command commitment in part because of the nature of the thought process or type of abstraction involved in their generation; see, for example, Freud's description of primary process and Cassirer's description of mythic thought. Such conceptions probably derive their power to compel devotion not simply from what they include of the vicissitudes of social experience, certainly not merely from some supposed status as generalizations of past experience, but perhaps primarily from the very nature of the symbolic process that creates them.

SYMBOLIC SYSTEM

A symbolic system is a distinctive organization of elements that are symbols or capable, in combination with each other, of functioning as symbols. A morpheme is an example of a minimal functional element of a symbolic system.

A particular symbolic system is characterized by: (1) the nature of its functional elements—morphemes as well as expressive (in Langer's sense of the word) lines, shapes, rhythms, movements, and perhaps constant "symbols" in dreams, are examples; (2) the obligatory canons of symbolization according to which these elements are combined into a finite set of most simple patterns—obligatory rules of syntax for simple or "kernel" sentences, and perhaps the requirement of representability in the formation of dreams, are examples; and (3) the recursive devices (optional canons of symbolization, for example, may operate repeatedly) according to which a finite set of such elements and/or their basic combinations may be transformed into an infinite set of symbolic forms—optional rules of transformation in syntax, and perhaps the operation of condensation and displacement in the formation of dreams, are examples.

A symbolic form is the distinctive product of the recursive devices or transformational canons of a symbolic system. Embodied or objectified in a sensuous medium, a symbolic form is potentially apprehensible and comprehensible; that is, as a component of a process of action, it may be apprehended and comprehended by an actor. Although a symbolic form may be said to be generated by a symbolic system, it is an actor in a process of action that in actuality creates symbolic forms.

At the human level, a behavioral organism possesses the requisite capacities to function in terms of or to "obey" the canons of a symbolic system. A personality system makes use of these capacities, and determines to what ends they should be used; a personality system creates a very large subset of an infinite set of novel symbolic forms as ends in themselves and as means to the attainment of a wide range of ends. A particular personality system is characterized by the particular nature of the very large subset of an infinite set of novel symbolic forms it does create or, by extension, is conceived to have a tendency to create; that is, a particular personality system is characterized by the recursive devices (for example, defense mechanisms) which typically operate to create its symbolic forms. The creation, the apprehension, and the comprehension of novel symbolic forms are the distinctive functions of the personality system as a system of action.

A generalized symbolic medium in Parsons' sense is a resource that is symbolically rather than intrinsically efficacious and that may be used to attain a wide variety of ends. ("Medium" is used here to mean "resource," not "sensuous vehicle through the use of which a symbol is objectified or embodied.") The recursive devices or transformational canons of any symbolic system, which make it possible to generate an infinite set of novel symbolic forms belonging to that system, might be regarded as the prototypical generalized symbolic medium of the personality system; different recursive devices or transformational canons, perhaps of different symbolic systems, might be regarded as generalized symbolic media of different subsystems of the personality system. The id, ego, and superego might be conceived, for example, to attain different ends through the use of different recursive devices or transformational canons. The effects of any subsystem of the personality, then, would depend upon the potency with which it is able to impose its characteristic recursive devices or transformational canons upon the creation of symbolic forms.

Suppose the ego imposes certain recursive devices or transformational canons in the interest of defense and adaptation. Freud's formulation of certain mechanisms of symptom-formation suggests that this conception of the ego's operations is not perhaps so far-fetched. For example: (1) "I (a man) love him" becomes "I do not love him — I hate him" which, in turn, becomes "He hates (persecutes) me, which will justify me in hating him"; or (2) "I (a man) love him" becomes "I do not love him — I love her" which, in turn, becomes "I do not love him — I love her, because she loves me"; or (3) "I (a man) love him" becomes "It is not I who love the man — she loves him"; or (4) "I (a man) love him" becomes "I do not love at all — I do not love any one," perhaps resulting inevitably in "I love only myself." The transformational canon imposes contradiction or negation upon the verb, in the first case; upon the object, in the second case; upon the subject, in the third case; upon the entire proposition in the fourth case. It is in just these linguistic terms that Freud discussed delusions of persecution, erotomania, jealousy, and megalomania.[95]

The id, then, might be conceived to impose other transformational canons in the interest of gratification. The id creates apparitional symbolic forms (in Langer's terms, presentational symbols), for example, hallucinatory images of gratification — in the waking infant (supposedly, a precursor of thought), in psychosis, and in the dream according to the dream work, which encompasses such transformational canons as are suggested by concepts like "condensation" and "displacement." Similarly, the superego, in the interest of integration, imposes transformational canons to create symbolic forms in the imperative mood. Each subsystem of the personality system might be said, then, to contribute to the creation of certain kinds of symbolic forms, serving, thereby, different requirements of the personality system as a whole.

This analysis, however, does not parallel Parsons' discussion of generalized symbolic media with respect to his emphasis upon the exchange of forms of such media across the boundaries of subsystems. Perhaps, this difference follows from the emphasis here and in psychoanalytic theory upon the representation

function of the symbol: in Parsons' work, the emphasis is on the communication function, the communication of symbolic sanctions. How fundamental this difference in emphasis is, I am not at this time able to judge.

It is possible that all symbolic systems include deep and surface components.

Deep components include: (1) unit functional elements; (2) deep structures; (3) obligatory structural canons of symbolization; and (perhaps in some symbolic systems — those that might be termed "languages" — and not in others) (4) devices of elemental signification or disambiguation.

Unit functional elements are symbols, classes of symbols, or entities capable, if combined, of functioning as symbols. Morphemes or classes of morphemes in language are examples of unit functional elements.

A finite set or limited number of basic, most simple, or nuclear patterns — organizations, combinations, or arrangements of unit functional elements — constitute the deep structures of a symbolic system. The number and kind of deep structures is probably characteristic of a particular kind of symbolic system. Any symbolic forms generated by a symbolic system may be reduced by analysis to deep structures — that is, result from the transformation (including the combination) of deep structures. But such nuclear patterns are not, themselves, reducible to simpler meaningful patterns of unit functional elements.

Such nuclear patterns — for example, elemental configurations or relations between classes of symbols — organize the way in which conceptions can be represented in a particular symbolic system. For example, in some sense, we are bound to think in terms of the relations between subjects and predicates, if our conception is represented by linguistic symbolic forms; and perhaps, if Langer's analysis holds,[96] in terms of tensions and the resolution of tensions, if our conception is presented in musical symbolic forms. To the extent that conception anticipates the morphology of its representation, nuclear patterns are a constraint upon what can be conceived and what shape conception takes. The morphology of nuclear patterns is always homologous to the morphology of conception; therefore, part of the meaning represented by a symbolic form is represented by the structure or morphology of the symbolic form, and not simply by its (for example, semantic) content. This is always true, not simply so in the case of presentational symbols or apparitional forms such as art forms, dreams, images. However, it may be true, as Langer claims, that some (she says, all) apparitional symbolic forms present a conception solely by means of their morphology; that is, semantic content is nonexistent or only apparent; if it seems to be present, as in poetry, it does not function semantically or imitatively, but rather as mere material pressed into service to create the illusion, semblance, or apparition that actually functions to present a conception.

If symbolic process, that process by which symbolic forms are generated, is conceived to be a process of action, then the deep structures or nuclear patterns correspond to pattern-maintenance components of a symbolic system, in Parsons' terminology. In psychoanalytic theory, the deep structures of interest are "wishes." As Schur has pointed out, the "wish" is a structural component in personality.[97] A wish is a hypercathected memory-image — a symbol of a conception of past gratification.

Nuclear patterns are formed according to, obey the laws of, or conform to the obligatory structural canons of symbolization characteristic of a particular symbolic system. "Obligatory" means that patterns violating these structural canons (e.g., boy the yellow house grieves) are incapable of representing any conception in this symbolic system, that is, are to whatever extent evaluated as meaningless. That a sentence must combine a noun phrase and a verb phrase is an example of an obligatory structural canon belonging to a linguistic system.[98]

A particular nuclear pattern may represent a conception through means other than its morphology. Devices of elemental signification or disambiguation (for example, semantic rules, a lexical device such as a dictionary) make it possible to assign with a certain level of precision (noun, human noun, man, father) what conception is represented by a unit functional element in a nuclear pattern. Therefore, a device of elemental signification or disambiguation may function, also, to distinguish between or disambiguate these nuclear patterns (the boy is happy, the girl is sad) which, while similar in pattern, represent different conceptions, or those nuclear patterns (the man looked hard=the man looked tough — hard is an adjective; the man looked hard=the man looked intensely — hard is an adverb) which appear to be similar both in form and content, but are not, and, in fact, by differing in both form and content represent different conceptions.

Such a device of elemental signification or disambiguation may select what subset of members or even what particular member of a class of symbols actually does operate: noun, human noun, man, father. It is clear then that (if a hierarchy of subsets is involved) we may speak of degrees of ambiguity or the levels to which disambiguation is carried. "Noun phrase-verb phrase" is ambiguous, in the sense that it may represent an infinite set of conceptions. "Noun-be-adjective" is less ambiguous, in the sense that the set of conceptions it may represent has been considerably reduced. "Human noun-be-state of mind" is even less ambiguous; "young person-present tense-be-state of mind" still less; and "the boy is happy" quite easy, but only at this level of disambiguation, to distinguish from, for example, "the girl is sad." The progressive narrowing of the range of possibly operative members is a process of disambiguation; in this sense, a device of disambiguation is a constraint upon what conception may be represented.

Symbolic systems differ in the degree to which disambiguation in this sense is possible. Discursive symbolization (involving what I have called rational symbolic forms) and presentational symbolization (involving what I have called apparitional symbolic forms) differ, of course, with respect to the level of disambiguation possible. Langer claims that presentational symbols such as art forms, in fact, do not involve any devices of elemental signification or disambiguation; therefore, while a presentational symbol or art form may represent the morphology of feeling in general, it is incapable of distinguishing between qualitatively different feelings such as happiness and sadness because as feelings these are likely to share the same morphology. There is no device, she believes, by which music, for example, can be made to present a particular feeling unambiguously; in fact, such ambiguity is deemed by her to be an essential characteristic of the life of feeling and, therefore, of the symbolic form that presents it. I am not sure I follow her strictures here. For example, it seems to me possible that the limited violation of obligatory structural canons of symbolization, as in the semigrammatical utterances of poetry, may itself be a device of disambiguation, for example, emphasizing through distortion one possible reading of a poem over another.[99] But it would not make sense to speak of alternative or possible readings of a poem or of its ambiguities, if in fact no devices of elemental signification or disambiguation existed to apply.

Nevertheless, it is possible that the effect of a psychoanalytic interpretation, which replaces an apparitional symbolic form such as a dream or symptom with a discursive symbolic form — the linguistic representation of latent thought or unconscious conflict — may be related to changes in the level of disambiguation such translation makes possible. That such translations are possible, that poems may be paraphrased and one paraphrase justified as superior to another, suggest that devices of elemental signification or disambiguation do operate to some extent in the creation of symbolic forms other than those of linguistic discourse; perhaps such devices operate to disambiguate to different levels in different symbolic systems or perhaps the devices themselves are different in kind in different symbolic systems. Devices, for example, may operate to exploit or to restrict ambiguity; to minimize or to maximize (in the service of deautomatization or the attraction of attention-cathexis as well as disguise) deviation from, or violation of, canons of symbolization; to give priority to explicitness, declaration, and clarity, or to implicitness, concealment, allusiveness, so that meaning is suggested by the way in which a medium is used, through form rather than content or through patterns of contrast and convergence or the disruption of such patterns. The intrinsic qualities of a symbolic medium or vehicle may be exploited in representing a conception, or such intrinsic qualities may be subordinated to an extent or be so independent of the representation of specific conceptions that we may speak — as I have in *The Idea of a Mental Illness* — of a transparent medium, which can be used to create a symbolic form that represents a conception without calling attention to the intrinsic qualities of the medium used.

The acceptance of a symbolic form as meaningful or its rejection as meaningless, its selection as a bona fide member of the symbolic system generating it or its rejection as at best a member of some other symbolic system, depend upon obligatory structural canons of symbolization and devices of elemental signification or disambiguation. These canons and devices correspond to integration components of a symbolic system, in Parsons' terminology.

A symbolic form may be judged — in the frame of reference of the symbolic system itself — to be capable or incapable of representing meaning in that system. We may ask: is it meaningful? but not: is it true? is it beautiful? is it moral? These latter questions involve an evaluation of the suasive effect or symbolic efficacy of a symbolic form as it participates in a personality or social system of action, and as it does so becomes subject to the standards of the various subsystems of those systems of action. It is important to separate a consideration of symbolic process as itself a process of action, of the symbolic system that provides a frame of reference for investigating problems of symbolic process, from a consideration of the functions that a symbolic form may serve as it enters into a process of action in a social or personality system. In a personality or social system of action, a symbolic form is suasive or exerts effects by virtue of symbolic rather than intrinsic efficacy, by virtue of the meaning it represents. The contribution it makes thereby to the attainment of various sought ends are subject to evaluation according to the various standards appropriate to such ends.

A principal distinction between the structural and topographic points of view in psychoanalysis may be expressed as follows. The former point of view is concerned with that difference between symbolic forms which has to do with differences in their suasive effects, differences in the direction of their symbolic efficacy as they contribute to the attainment of the different kinds of ends which we associate with the terms "ego," "id," "superego," "ego-ideal" sought in a process of action. The topographic point of view focuses rather on the level of symbolization[100] and ultimately is concerned with the nature of the symbolic system to which a symbolic form belongs — the operations, devices, and canons according to which a symbolic form has been created and in terms of which it may be judged to be meaningful.

Deep components of a symbolic system — its pattern-maintenance and integration components — may be regarded as in some sense latent. The deep structures of a linguistic system, for example, are inferred abstractions, which do not appear or are not performed: "he + past + shall + have + en (past participle) + write + the + paper" is an example of a deep structure, which requires transformation by surface components to become: "He should have written the paper." The manifest symbolic form, in other words, is a derivative of surface components. Surface components include: (1) a surface structure, formed by recursive devices or obligatory and especially optional transformational canons of symbolization operating to alter, combine, delete from, add to, and rearrange deep structures; and (2) a performative translation of surface structure into a sensible medium.

Obligatory structural canons transform "past + shall" and "en + write" into "shall + past" and "write + en," but a performative translation is required to write or say "shall + past" as "should" and "write + en" as "written," and a recursive device or an optional transformational canon of symbolization, is required to arrive at the symbolic forms: "should he have written the paper?" and "should he have written *what* paper?" Similarly, a performative translation is required to sing or play notes as music. In linguistic systems, questions, emphasis, possession, passive constructions, negation, nominalization. and compound and complex sentences are all achieved through the action of canons of transformation upon deep structures. In music, if scales, chords, and intervals are deep structures, then the generation of musical forms by harmonic, melodic, and rhythmic processes occurs according to transformational canons acting upon such deep structures. As we have noted, defense mechanisms have what is probably a fundamental similarity to linguistic transformational canons; and Freud's discovery of primary process and of the difference between primary and secondary process seems essentially a discovery that different symbolic systems have different transformational canons.

The transformational canons of symbolization are, in reverse, also devices of analytic disambiguation. That is, ambiguities of surface structure may be resolved to the extent that surface structure may be analyzed back into the deep structures that were transformed to form the surface structure. For example, "important decision-making council" is ambiguous; to disambiguate it, one would need to know whether its history involves a transformation of "the council is important, the council makes decisions" or "the council makes decisions, the decisions are important."

Again, the analogy to the psychoanalytic investigation of such symbolic forms as symptoms, which involves seeking the deep structures and the transformations acting upon them throughout personal history, may not involve mere superficial resemblance but rather may arise because psychoanalysis in fact investigates symbolic phenomena. The psychoanalyst, moreover, tends to evaluate changes arising from psychoanalysis as therapy in terms of content and structure. A chance from miserliness to extravagance (from "I retain money" to "I expel money"), essentially a change in semantic content but not in structure, is considered less fundamental than a change from either of these to: "I neither retain nor expel money, but do find it useful," which involves not only changes in semantic content but results from the operation of transformational canons, creating a new surface structure from deep structures.

It is probable that the degree of independence or dependence of components of a symbolic system determine important characteristics of the symbolic forms generated by that system. For example, in discursive symbolization, canons of symbolization (for example, rules of syntax), devices of elemental disambiguation (for example, rules of semantics), and performative translation into a sensible medium (for example, rules of phonology) are relatively independent. It is possible that some of the characteristics of presentational, nondiscursive symbolic forms may result from a relative dependence of such components upon each other or a relative nondifferentiation of such components from each other.

The generation of symbolic forms is the end of a symbolic system; therefore, performative translations of surface structure into sensible medium, i.e., into manifest symbolic forms, may be regarded as the goal-attainment components of a symbolic system.

As recursive devices or transformational canons are also standards for judging meaningfulness, one might suppose that such devices or canons belong among integration components. However, there is a crucial difference between recursive devices or transformational canons and obligatory structural canons. Recursive devices or transformational canons are a generalized facility, in Parsons' sense, by virtue of their recursiveness; such devices or canons alone are the finite but generalized means by which an infinite set — rather than a finite set — of symbolic forms (ends) may be generated or attained. Therefore, I would, tentatively, at least consider such devices or canons to correspond to adaptation components, in the terms of Parsons' analysis of systems of action.

In this discussion of symbolic systems, I have assumed — tentatively, at this point — that the transformational-generative approach Chomsky and others have taken to language may be, in some respects at least, generalizable to all languages, and perhaps to all symbolic systems — that is, then, to any system that is a manifestation of symbolic function. If so, such an approach is relevant to understanding mental processes in general, to the extent that mental processes may be said to be equivalent to symbolic processes. The appropriateness of such an assumption would certainly be rejected by those who are inclined, as I am not, to include nonsymbolic events as aspects of *mental* life. I have as a corollary to this assumption questioned that there is any radical difference in kind between what I have called rational symbolic forms or symbols of rule and apparitional symbolic forms or symbols of resemblance, between what Langer has called discursive symbols and presentational symbols, between what Piaget has called symbols and signs. In psychoanalytic terminology, I have assumed that primary process may be regarded as a different form of the same kind of thing as secondary process; that is, both involve canons of symbolization, both may involve a logic, but different kinds of canons and a different kind of logic.

INTERPRETATION IN PSYCHOANALYSIS [101]

A vulgar notion of psychoanalysis pictures the patient reacting to what he out of error or ignorance regards as *signs* of danger, and the psychoanalyst — like a keen-eared, sharp-eyed Holmes — reacting to the patient's verbalizations, appearances, and acts as *signs* of the patient's immediate feelings or dispositions. The psychoanalyst's interventions are presumed to be based on his recognition of signs of the patient's state in the psychoanalysis as well as his recognition that the patient is interpreting signs ignorantly or erroneously. The psychoanalyst's interpretations, then, are supposed to rectify the patient's error and ignorance.

An alternate notion of psychoanalysis would have the patient *making a symbol* such as the transference neurosis to represent his conceptions of his inner reality, so that in the contemplation of such an objectification of his conceptions of inner reality he and the psychoanalyst may come to understand these conceptions.

The notion that psychoanalysis is primarily a process of interpreting signs to mitigate a pathology of signs is similar to the notion that a work of art may best be understood as a sign of the feelings and dispositions within the artist when he created the work. The processes of producing art or emitting verbalizations in the psychoanalysis are deemed essentially to involve unwitting expression, ejaculation, or discharge of feelings and impulses; such expressions are then the signs of such feelings and impulses. This view of psychoanalysis must disregard Freud's continued use of the term "ideas" when referring, for example, to that which is repressed, and his emphasis that "psychic representatives," not physical processes or situations, are the objects of study in psychoanalysis and the subject matter with which psychoanalytic theory (including conceptions such as "id" and "instinct") is concerned. As there is an alternate notion of psychoanalysis, so there is another one of art, which holds that the symbolic forms of art represent the artist's *conceptions* (his "ideas," in Freud's sense of the word) of attitudes, feelings, or inner reality, rather than express (as signs of) his attitudes, feelings, or inner reality.

Interpretation in psychoanalysis probably does not, at least for the most part, involve the development and transmission of propositions asserting cause-and-effect relations. The assumption that the psychoanalyst is generating cause-effect explanations of psychological phenomena and communicating these to the patient, if not true, may lead, if held, to some misunderstanding of the therapeutic action of psychoanalysis. Furthermore, such an assumption, since the theory of psychoanalysis derives in large part from interpretations of psychoanalysts, may lead, if held, to some misunderstanding of the logical status, as well as the fundamental subject matter, of many propositions of psychoanalytic theory.

Interpretation in psychoanalysis probably does, for the most part, involve the development and transmission of propositions asserting the *meaning* of psychological phenomena. I do not mean anything mystical, philosophically abstruse, or "existential" by the word meaning. The implication of the use of the word meaning is that the relevant phenomena or the phenomena of interest to the psychoanalyst are symbolic forms — symbols of conceptions — and that to understand such a phenomenon is not to identify the cause of which it is an effect, but rather is to identify the conception or conceptions that it (as a discursive or rational symbolic form) represents or that it (as a nondiscursive, presentational, or apparitional form) presents. Multiple determination in psychoanalysis is, probably, largely a consequence of the fact that a symbol may and often does represent or present, i.e., connote, a number of conceptions simultaneously, and, therefore, of the fact that the disambiguation of a symbolic form is a problem — the determination of which conception or conceptions is or are to be given priority, i.e., the determination of a hierarchy of conceptions, in any attempt in particular circumstances to understand or respond to a symbolic form, is a problem. This view of interpretation is, I believe, essentially, the one Freud held in his masterwork, *The Interpretation of Dreams.* [102]

It follows from the relation I have tried to demonstrate exists between the theory of action and psychoanalysis that the theory of action, similarly, is probably in large part concerned, in the sense just stated, with the meaning of psychological, social, and cultural phenomena, rather than with their explanation in terms of cause-effect relations.

We may identify two kinds of processes of interpretation in psychoanalysis.

One is a process of elemental signification or disambiguation, which functions, through the procedure of free association, to develop and use a lexical device — a personal lexicon, if you will. Experience may be regarded as an array of materials out of which symbols may be constructed. Any element of experience may be used to create a symbol of a conception of any other element of experience. The experiential materials that have been used by the analysand to create symbols of his conceptions — to create his psychic reality — are identified by the psychoanalyst, who detects (through careful attention to the contexts in which symbolic forms recur) contrasts, convergence, patterns, and, crucially, patterns of disruption of pattern, in the apparently chaotic stream of free association.

For a particular patient, for example, the smell and taste of a cake have come in apparitional form to symbolize, and therefore, to evoke conceptions of aspects of his past. Actually, this symbol evokes another apparitional symbolic form, a mnemic image, which comes to be perceived as a "semantic" equivalent of the symbol that evoked it, and, therefore, to symbolize similar conceptions of aspects of his past.

From cake to memory, actually, from one mnemic image to another, we have a translation from one symbolic form to another in the same symbolic system — a system of apparitional symbolic forms. Such a translation is, essentially, what Pious has called translation at the same level.[103]

One may establish a hierarchy of such symbolic forms, according to such criteria as vagueness or explicitness, inclusiveness or exclusiveness, such that replacing one with another results in a progressive narrowing of the range of connotations or the size of a set of conceptions, or a progressive reduction in the degree of ambiguity. As has been previously suggested, translation from a symbolic form (e.g., an apparitional symbolic form) in one symbolic system to a symbolic form (e.g., a discursive or rational symbolic form) in another symbolic system — as in the translation of the manifest imagery of the dream into the discursive symbolic form representing the latent thought of the dream, or the translation of apparitional manifestations of the transference neurosis into the discursive symbolic form of the psychoanalyst's statements or "interpretations" — may have as an essential consequence a change in the level of possible disambiguation, i.e., a change in the extent to which disambiguation may be carried out. This kind of translation is, essentially, what Pious has called translation from one level to another.[104]

It may be useful to refer to interpretations that translate — (1) from one apparitional symbolic form to another, or (2) from one rational symbolic form to another, or (3) from an apparitional symbolic form to a rational symbolic form, or (4) from a rational symbolic form to an apparitional symbolic form — as translative interpretations.

An example of the first kind of translation: the psychoanalyst relates a feeling to a mnemic image. An example of the second: the psychoanalyst relates an interpretation stating the latent thoughts of the dream to an interpretation stating the wishes that lie behind action "in the transference." Examples of the third: the psychoanalyst relates the manifest dream images to a statement of the latent dream throughts, or relates manifestations of the transference neurosis to a statement describing conflicting motives. An example of the fourth: the psychoanalyst presents in feeling or in action the conception he believes the analysand is representing discursively, perhaps as a device to focus more sharply the analysand's attention upon this conception.

The second process leading to interpretation in psychoanalysis is a process of analytical disambiguation, identifying the recursive operations (e.g., defenses) transforming deep structures such as nuclear patterns (e.g., wishes) into surface structures (e.g., symptoms, character-traits) and one surface

structure into another, and identifying also the sequence in which such transformations have taken and do take place.[105] Analytic disambiguation seeks to discover, for example: (1) the nature of the deep structures of a particular personality; (2) the nature of the recursive operations that have acted upon these deep structures throughout personal history and into the present, transforming these deep structures into many surface structures (including various self-representations and object-representations) and these surface structures into still others; and (3) the sequence in which such recursive operations, typically, have been and are applied.

The present repeats the past because the system of recursive operations (which function as transformational canons), including the order in which these are applied, is a relatively stable characteristic of a particular personality system.[106]

Many interpretations from the so-called genetic point of view in psychoanalysis may belong in the category of analytical disambiguation. It may be useful to refer to interpretations of analytical disambiguation as transformative interpretations.

Does this approach hint at possible hypotheses, in addition to or supporting those already in the psychoanalytic literature, concerning the therapeutic action of psychoanalysis?

First, consider the effect upon the analysand of becoming aware as he participates in the psychoanalytic process of himself as a human animal, the *animal symbolicum,* living in a psychic reality of his own creation, which in itself is a change in conception of self from "creature" merely reacting to or determined by its situation — by nonsubjective factors such as heredity and environment — to "man."

The analysand begins with a conception of himself as compelled — his self-representation is often a machine-variant — rather than creative. The analysand conceives, "This is done to me; this happens to me; my action, my dream, my self is the effect of a cause," rather than, "I do this; I make this happen; I create symbolic representations (which become me and the reality in which I live) of my own conceptions, which I can then retain, contemplate, and so even change." A focus in psychoanalysis upon symbolic process makes possible the analysand's realization that he may regard himself as, to some extent at least, free.[107]

This hypothesis, of course, implies a limit upon the therapeutic action of psychoanalysis. When misery is, as Freud said, normal misery rather than neurotic misery — i.e., to the extent that the analysand's suffering is caused by his situation rather than created by his own symbolic activity — then and to that extent psychoanalysis may have no specific therapeutic action.

Second, consider the effects upon the analysand

of what follows. He overcomes obstacles to the exercise of capacities for freely translating from one symbolic system to another, for freely creating both apparitional and rational symbolic forms. He himself forges new symbolic forms, including self-representation and object-representations: he cannot simply be told what he does not know by the psychoanalyst; he must himself discover what he apparently does not know in the effort to construct the symbolic forms that will adequately represent his knowledge. In so doing, he achieves higher levels of consciousness.[108]

This achievement, this becoming conscious, Freud, from the beginning, considered the "foundation of psychoanalytic therapy." Wallace Stevens, also, alludes to this achievement, this becoming conscious, in the quiet, tentative, contemplative, yet triumphant, final line of the final and great poem of awakening in his *Collected Poems*: "It was like / A new knowledge of reality."[109]

NOTES

1. See, for example, Otto Fenichel, "Concerning the Theory of Psychoanalytic Technique," in Louis Paul (ed.), *Psychoanalytic Clinical Interpretation* (New York: The Free Press, 1963), pp. 42-64; Sigmund Freud, *The Interpretation of Dreams* in *The Standard Edition of the Complete Psychological Works of Sigmund Freud* Vols. 4 and 5, James Strachey (ed.) (London: The Hogarth Press, 1953, first published 1900), pp. 1-621; *Papers on Technique* in *The Standard Edition* 12 (1958, first published 1914), pp. 83-173. "Introductory Lectures on Psychoanalysis." *The Standard Edition* 16 (1963, first published 1916-17), pp. 431-63; *Constructions in Analysis* in *The Standard Edition* 23 (1964, first published in 1937) pp. 255-69; Edward Glover, "The Therapeutic Effect of Inexact Interpretation," *International Journal of Psychoanalysis*, 12 (1931), pp. 397-411; Ernst Kris, "Criteria for Interpretation," *International Journal of Psychoanalysis*, 20 (1939), pp. 148-60; "Ego Psychology and Interpretation in Psychoanalytic Therapy," *Psychoanalytic Quarterly*, 20 (1951), pp. 15-30; "On Some Vicissitudes of Insight in Psychoanalysis," *International Journal of Psychoanalysis*, 37 (1956), pp. 445-55; "The Recovery of Childhood Memories in Psychoanalysis," in *The Psychoanalytic Study of the Child*, Vol. 11 (New York: International Universities Press, 1956), pp. 54-88; Rudolph M. Loewenstein, "Ego Development and Psychoanalytic Technique," *American Journal of Psychiatry*, 107 (1951), pp. 617-22; "The Problem of Interpretation," *Psychoanalytic Quarterly*, 20 (1951), pp. 1-14; "Remarks on the Role of Speech in Psychoanalytic Technique," *International Journal of Psychoanalysis*, 37 (1956), pp. 460-68; "Some Thoughts on Interpretation in the Theory and Practice of Psychoanalysis," in Louis Paul (ed.), *op. cit.*, pp. 162-88; Louis Paul (ed.), *op. cit.*; James Strachey, "The Nature of the Therapeutic Action of Psychoanalysis," in Louis Paul (ed.), *op. cit.*, pp. 1-41.

2. T. Parsons, "Some Problems of General Theory in Sociology," in John C. McKinney and Edward A. Tiryakian (eds.), *Theoretical Sociology* (New York: Appleton-Century-Crofts, 1970), pp. 27-68.

3. *Ibid.*, p. 29.

4. *Ibid.*, p. 34.

5. *Ibid.*, p. 36.

6. *Ibid.*, p. 40, italics mine.

7. See Wallace Stevens, *Opus Posthumous* (New York: Alfred A. Knopf, 1966), p. 165.

8. *Op. cit.*

9. First published 1937 by McGraw Hill, New York. Reprinted by The Free Press, New York, 1949.

10. New York: Alfred A. Knopf, 1961.

11. *Ibid.*, p. 376. Acknowledgment is extended to Alfred A. Knopf, Inc. for permission to quote from the copyrighted poetry of Wallace Stevens.

12. Let me note here, at least, the writings of each especially relevant to one preoccupied with symbolic process: Sigmund Freud, *The Standard Edition*: "Project for a Scientific Psychology," 1 (1966), pp. 283-397; "Extracts from the Fliess Papers," 1 (1966), pp. 175-280; "The Interpretation of Dreams," 4 and 5 (1953), pp. 1-621; "The Psychopathology of Everyday Life," 6 (1960), pp. 1-279; "Three Essays on the Theory of Sexuality," 7 (1953), pp. 123-245; "Character and Anal Erotism," 9 (1959), pp. 167-75; "Psychoanalytic Notes on an Autobiographical Account of a Case of Paranoia (Dementia Paranoides)," 12 (1958), pp. 3-82; "Papers on Technique," 12 (1958), pp. 83-173; "Formulations on the Two Principles of Mental Functioning," 12 (1958), pp. 213-26; "Types of Onset of Neurosis," 12 (1958), pp. 227-38; "Totem and Taboo," 13 (1955), pp. 1-161; "On the History of the Psychoanalytic Movement," 14 (1957), pp. 3-66; "On Narcissism: An Introduction," 14 (1957), pp. 67-102; "Instincts and Their Vicissitudes," 14 (1957), pp. 109-40; "Repression," 14 (1957), pp. 141-58; "The Unconscious," 14 (1957), pp. 159-215; "A Metapsychological Supplement to the Theory of Dreams " 14 (1957), pp. 217-35; "Mourning and Melancholia," 14 (1957), pp. 237-60; "Introductory Lectures on Psychoanalysis," 16 (1963), pp. 243-463; "Beyond the Pleasure Principle," 18 (1955), pp. 3-64; "Group Psychology and the Analysis of the Ego," 18 (1955), pp. 67-143; "The Ego and the Id," 19 (1961), pp. 3-66; "Neurosis and Psychosis," 19 (1961), pp. 147-53; "The Loss of Reality in Neurosis and Psychosis," 19 (1961), pp. 181-87; "An Autobiographical Study," 20 (1959), pp. 7-74; "Inhibitions, Symptoms and Anxiety," 20 (1959), pp. 77-175; "The Future of an Illusion," 21 (1961), pp. 3-56; "Female Sexuality," 21 (1961), pp. 225-43; "Analysis Terminable and Interminable," 23 (1964), pp. 209-53; "Constructions in Analysis," 23 (1964), pp. 255-69; "Moses and Monotheism," 23 (1964), pp. 7-137; "Splitting of the Ego in the Process of Defence," 23 (1964), pp. 271-78; *On Aphasia* (New York: International Universities Press, 1953).

Talcott Parsons, *The Structure of Social Action*; *The Social System* (New York: The Free Press, 1951), especially Ch. 8, "Belief Systems and the Social System: The Problem of the 'Role of Ideas,'" pp. 326-83, and Ch. 9, "Expressive Symbols and the Social System: The Communication of Affect," pp. 384-427; "Values, Motives, and Systems of Action" (with Edward Shils), in *Toward a General Theory of Action* (New York: Harper and Row, Torchbook edition, 1962), pp. 47-275; *Working Papers in the Theory of Action* (with Robert Bales and Edward Shils) (Glencoe: The Free Press, 1953), especially Ch. 2, "The Theory of Symbolism in Relation to Action," pp. 31-62; *Economy and Society* (with Neil Smelser) (New York: The Free Press, 1956); "An Approach to Psychological Theory in Terms of the Theory of Action," in Sigmund Koch (ed.), *Psychology: A Study of a Science*, Vol. 3, (New York: McGraw-Hill, 1959), pp. 612-711; *Social Structure and Personality* (New York: The Free Press, 1964), especially Part One, "Theoretical Perspectives," pp. 17-126; *Sociological Theory and Modern Society* (New York: The Free Press, 1967), especially Ch. 7, "Pattern Variables Revisited: A Response to Robert Dubin," pp. 192-219; Ch. 9, "Some Reflections on the Place of Force in Social Process," pp. 264-96; Ch. 10, "On the Concept of Political Power," pp. 297-354; and Ch. 11, "On the Concept of Influence," pp. 355-82; "On the Concept of Value-Commitments," *Sociological Inquiry*, 38 (Spring 1968), pp. 135-60; "Some Problems of General Theory in Sociology" (*op. cit.*).

Wallace Stevens. *The Necessary Angel* (New York: Vintage Books, 1951); *The Collected Poems of Wallace Stevens* (New York: Alfred A. Knopf, 1961); *Opus Posthumous* (New York: Alfred A. Knopf, 1966).

13. See especially Kenneth Burke, *Permanence and Change* (New York: The Bobbs-Merrill Company, 1965); *Language as Symbolic Action* (Berkeley: University of California Press, 1968); *A Grammar of Motives* (Berkeley: University of California Press, 1969); *A Rhetoric of Motives* (Berkeley: University of California Press, 1969).

14. See especially Ernst Cassirer, *An Essay on Man* (New Haven: Yale University Press, 1944); *Language and Myth* (New York: Dover Publications Inc., 1946); *The Philosophy of Symbolic Forms* (New Haven: Yale University Press, 1953).

15. See especially Susanne K. Langer, *Philosophy in a New Key* (New York: Penguin Books, 1948); *Feeling and Form* (New York: Charles Scribner's Sons, 1953); *Problems of Art* (New York: Charles Scribner's Sons, 1957); *Mind: An Essay on Human Feeling* (Baltimore: The Johns Hopkins Press, 1967).

16. See especially Jean Piaget, *Play, Dreams and Imitation in Childhood* (New York: W. W. Norton and Co., Inc., 1962); *Six Psychological Studies* (New York: Vintage Books, 1968).

17. See especially Roger Brown, *Words and Things* (New York: The Free Press, 1958); C. Ogden and I. Richards, *The Meaning of Meaning* (New York: Harcourt, Brace and World, 1923); Edward Sapir, *Culture, Language and Personality* (Berkeley: University of California Press, 1966); Claude Levi-Strauss, *Structural Anthropology* (New York: Basic Books, 1963); *Totemism* (Boston: Beacon Press, 1963); *The Savage Mind* (Chicago: University of Chicago Press, 1966); Benjamin Lee Whorf, *Language, Thought, and Reality* (Cambridge: The M.I.T. Press, 1956).

18. Langer, *Feeling and Form,* p. 241.

19. See especially Emmon Bach, *An Introduction to Transformational Grammars* (New York: Holt, Rinehart and Winston, Inc., 1964); Seymour Chatman and Samuel R. Levin, *Essays on the Language of Literature* (Boston: Houghton Mifflin Company, 1967); Noam Chomsky, *Cartesian Linguistics* (New York: Harper and Row, 1966) and *Syntactic Structures* (The Hague: Mouton and Co., 1969); Jerry A. Fodor and Jerrold J. Katz (eds.), *The Structure of Language* (Englewood Cliffs: Prentice-Hall, Inc., 1964); H. A. Gleason, Jr. *Linguistics and English Grammar* (New York: Holt, Rinehart and Winston, Inc., 1965); Jerrold J. Katz and Paul M. Postal, *An Integrated Theory of Linguistic Descriptions* (Cambridge, Mass.: M.I.T. Press, 1964); Samuel R. Levin, *Linguistic Structures in Poetry* (The Hague: Mouton and Co., 1964); Paul Roberts, *English Syntax* (alternate edition) (New York: Harcourt, Brace and World, Inc., 1964).

20. See especially Hans Loewald, "Internalization, Separation, Mourning, and the Superego," *Psychoanalytic Quarterly,* 31 (1962), pp. 483-504; "The Superego and the Ego-Ideal: II. Superego and Time," *International Journal of Psychoanalysis,* 43 (1962), pp. 264-68; William Pious, "Obsessive-Compulsive Symptoms in an Incipient Schizophrenia," *Psychoanalytic Quarterly,* 19 (1950), pp. 327-51; "A Hypothesis About the Nature of Schizophrenic Behavior," in Arthur Burton (ed.), *Psychotherapy of the Psychoses* (New York: Basic Books, 1961), pp. 43-68; Roy Schafer, "The Loving and Beloved Superego in Freud's Structural Theory," in *The Psychoanalytic Study of the Child,* Vol. 15 (New York: International Universities Press, 1960), pp. 163-88; "Ideals, the Ego Ideal and the Ideal Self," in Robert Holt (ed.), *Motives and Thought* (New York: International Universities Press, 1967), pp. 129-74; *Aspects of Internalization* (New York: International Universities Press, 1968); "The Mechanisms of Defence," *International Journal of Psychoanalysis,* 49 (1968), pp. 49-62.

21. Stanley A. Leavy, "John Keats's Psychology of Creative Imagination," *Psychoanalytic Quarterly,* 39 (1970), pp. 173-97, at p. 176.

22. See especially Anna Freud, *The Ego and the Mechanisms of Defence* (New York: International Universities Press, 1946); *Normality and Pathology in Childhood* (New York: International Universities Press, 1965); Heinz Hartmann, *Ego Psychology and the Problem of Adaptation* (New York: International Universities Press, 1958); *Psychoanalysis and Moral Values* (New York: International Universities Press, 1960); *Essays on Ego Psychology* (New York: International Universities Press, 1964); Heinz Hartmann, Ernst Kris; and Rudolph Loewenstein, *Papers on Psychoanalytic Psychology,* Psychological Issues, Monograph 14, Vol. 4, No. 2 (New York: International Universities Press, 1964); Ernst Kris, "Criteria for Interpretation," *International Journal of Psychoanalysis,* 20 (1939), pp. 148-60, and works listed in note 1. See also works of Rudolph Loewenstein listed in note 1 and Merton Gill (ed.), *The Collected Papers of David Rapaport* (New York: Basic Books, Inc., 1967).

23. See Edith Jacobson, *The Self and the Object World* (New York: International Universities Press, 1964).

24. See Leo Stone, *The Psychoanalytic Situation* (New York: International Universities Press, 1961).

25. See his *Psychoanalysis and Moral Values* for values and *Essays on Ego Psychology* for rational and irrational action.

26. Chicago: University of Chicago Press, 1970.

27. New Haven: Yale University Press, 1970.

28. See my essay "The Integration of the Behavioral Sciences and Clinical Experience in Teaching Medical Students," in Theodore Lidz and Marshall Edelson (eds.), *Training Tomorrow's Psychiatrist* (New Haven: Yale University Press, 1970); pp. 17-44.

29. New Haven: Yale University Press, 1971.

30. This essay and *The Idea of a Mental Illness* are in many ways offshoots of the same intellectual impulse and have been in a sense written side-by-side. Necessarily some passages from that book are woven, in most cases in somewhat different form, into this essay, and are reprinted here with the kind permission of the Yale University Press.

31. See Piaget, *Play, Dreams and Imitation in Childhood.*

32. See Parsons, *The Social System.*

33. See M. Edelson, *The Idea of a Mental Illness,* and Sigmund Freud, "Inhibitions, Symptoms and Anxiety," *op. cit.*

34. See Piaget, *Play, Dreams and Imitation in Childhood.*

35. See K. Langer, *Philosophy in a New Key.*

36. See Piaget, *Play, Dreams and Imitation in Childhood.*

37. See Langer, *Philosophy in a New Key* and *Feeling and Form.*

38. See Edelson, *The Idea of a Mental Illness.*

39. See Langer, *Philosophy in a New Key* and *Feeling and Form.*

40. See Edelson, *The Idea of a Mental Illness.*

41. See Parsons, *et al., Working Papers in the Theory of Action,* especially Chapter 2, "The Theory of Symbolism in Relation to Action", pp. 31-62.

42. See Piaget, *Play, Dreams and Imitation in Childhood.*

43. In Jerry A. Fodor and Jerrold J. Katz (eds.), *op. cit.,* pp. 547-78.

44. See Parsons, *Sociological Theory and Modern Society,* especially Chapters 9, 10 and 11. See also Parsons, "On the Concept of Value-Commitments," *op. cit.* and "Some Problems of General Theory in Sociology," *op. cit.*

45. See John Dollard and Neal Miller, *Personality and Psychotherapy* (New York: McGraw-Hill Books Co., Inc., 1950).

46. Stevens, *The Collected Poems of Wallace Stevens,* p. 383.

47. Freud, "Project for a Scientific Psychology," *op. cit.,* p. 373.

48. Freud, "Extracts from the Fliess Papers," *op. cit.,* pp. 259-60.

49. Freud, "Totem and Taboo," *op. cit.,* p. 159.

50. Freud, "The Interpretation of Dreams," *op. cit.,* p. 620.

51. Freud, "On the History of the Psychoanalytic Movement," *The Standard Edition of the Complete Psychological Works of Sigmund Freud,* 14 (1957), James Strachey (ed.) (London: The Hogarth Press), pp. 17-18. Quoted with the permission of the Hogarth Press. Also from *Collected Papers of Sigmund Freud,* Volume I, edited by Ernest Jones, M.D.. authorized translation under the supervision of Joan Riviere, published by Basic Books, Inc., by arrangement with The Hogarth Press Ltd. and The Institute of Psycho-Analysis, London, and quoted with the permission of Basic Books.

52. Freud, "Female Sexuality," *op. cit.*

53. Freud, "Introductory Lectures on Psychoanalysis." *The Standard Edition of the Complete Psychological Works of Sigmund Freud,* 16 (1963), James Strachey (ed.) (London: The Hogarth Press), p. 367, italics mine. Quoted with the permission of George Allen and Unwin Ltd., England, and Liveright Publishing Corp., U.S.A.

54. *Ibid.,* pp. 367-68.

55. *Ibid.,* p. 372.

56. Freud, "Moses and Monotheism," *op. cit.,* p. 76.

57. Freud, "Constructions in Analysis," *op. cit.,* p. 267.

58. Freud, "An Autobiographical Study," *op. cit.,* p. 72.

59. Ernest Jones, *The Life and Work of Sigmund Freud* (New York: Basic Books, 1953, 1955, 1957); Volume 1, p. 367; Volume 2, p. 415; Volume 3, p. 466.

60. Freud "The Unconscious," *The Standard Edition of the Complete Psychological Works of Sigmund Freud,* 14 (1957), James Strachey (ed.) (London: The Hogarth Press), p. 171. Quoted with the permission of the Hogarth Press. Also from *Collected Papers of Sigmund Freud,* Volume IV (Chapter VI), edited by Ernest Jones, M.D., authorized translation under the supervision of Joan Riviere, published by Basic Books, Inc., by arrangement with the Hogarth Press Ltd. and the Institute of Psycho-Analysis, London, and quoted with the permission of Basic Books.

61. William James, "Reflex Action and Theism," in Walker Gibson (ed.), *The Limits of Language* (New York: Hill and Wang, 1962), pp. 3-9, at pp. 8-9.

62. A. N. Whitehead, "The Organization of Thought," in *ibid.,* pp. 10-14, at p. 12.

63. Stevens, *The Collected Poems of Wallace Stevens,* pp. 129-30.

64. Parsons, "An Approach to Psychological Theory in Terms of the Theory of Action," *op. cit.,* p. 626

65. Freud, "On Narcissism: An Introduction," *op. cit.,* p. 77.

66. Stevens, *The Necessary Angel,* pp. 14-15. Copyright by Wallace Stevens. Quoted with the permission of Alfred A. Knopf, Inc.

67. Freud. "Instincts and Their Vicissitudes," *The Standard Edition of the Complete Psychological Works of Sigmund Freud,* 14 (1957), James Strachey (ed.) (London: The Hogarth Press), p. 117. Quoted with the permission of the Hogarth Press. Also from *Collected Papers of Sigmund Freud,* Volume IV (Chapter IV), edited by Ernest Jones, M.D. authorized translation under the supervision of Joan Riviere, published by Basic Books, Inc., by arrangement with The Hogarth Press Ltd. and The Institute of Psycho-Analysis, London, and quoted with the permission of Basic Books.

68. Freud, "Introductory Lectures on Psychoanalysis," *op. cit.,* p. 371.

69. Stevens, *The Collected Poems of Wallace Stevens,* pp. 502-3.

70. *Ibid.,* pp. 9-10.

71. See especially Susan Isaacs, "The Nature and Function of Phantasy" in Melanie Klein *et at.* (eds.), *Developments in Psychoanalysis* (London: The Hogarth Press, 1952), pp. 67-121; Melanie Klein, *Contributions to Psychoanalysis* 1921-

1949. (London: The Hogarth Press, 1948); and *The Psychoanalysis of Children* (London: The Hogarth Press, 1949).

72. See especially his *Ego Psychology and the Problem of Adaptation* and *Essays on Ego Psychology.*

73. See Parsons, "Pattern Variables Revisited: A Response to Robert Dubin," *op cit.,* pp. 192-219.

74. See Parsons, "An Approach to Psychological Theory in Terms of the Theory of Action," *op. cit.,* and *Social Structure and Personality.*

75. See Max Schur, *The Id and the Regulatory Principles of Mental Functioning* (New York: International Universities Press, 1966).

76. See M. Stein, "Self Observation, Reality, and the Superego," in R. Loewenstein *et. al.* (eds.), *Psychoanalysis—a General Psychology* (New York: International Universities Press, 1966), pp. 275-97.

77. Hans Loewald, "The Superego and the Ego-Ideal: II. The Superego and Time," *op. cit.,* pp. 264-68.

78. *Ibid.,* and Roy Schafer, "Ideals, the Ego-Ideal and the Ideal Self," *op. cit.*

79. Narcissistic libido encompasses the idea of focus of attitudes, motivations, intentions, or affects upon the self-representation rather than an external object-representation.

80. Schafer has discussed the necessity to distinguish other ideals from moral ones in *ibid.*

81. Multiple determination, having its origin as a concept in a positivistic frame of reference, may be a misnomer; in a system characterized by symbolic process, that phenomena seem to have multiple "causes" is in part at least a consequence of the fact that a symbol may represent at the same time a variety of conceptions or meanings.

82. I do not mean here to reiterate a psychoanalytic conception of the origin in ontogeny of the recognition of reality, secondary process, or the operation of the reality principle—only to indicate the basis for the following theoretical distinction.

83. See W. R. D. Fairbairn, *Psychoanalytic Studies of the Personality* (London: Tavistock Publications, 1952).

84. See Parsons, *Sociological Theory and Modern Society* Chapters 9, 10, and 11, and "On the Concept of Value-Commitments," *op. cit.*

85. Hartmann, *Essays on Ego Psychology,* pp. 187-8.

86. See especially, Langer, *Feeling and Form* and *Mind: An Essay on Human Feeling.*

87. Freud, "Instincts and Their Vicissitudes," *op. cit.,* p. 122.

88. "Sign" is Langer's term in *Philosophy in a New Key* and "index" is Piaget's term in *Play, Dreams and Imitation in Childhood.*

89. Stevens, *The Collected Poems of Wallace Stevens,* pp. 239-40.

90. See Ernst Kris, "The Recovery of Childhood Memories in Psychoanalysis," *op. cit.* A memory may also serve as a disguised screen, behind which stand other memories; what we might say in the context of this essay is that a memory may represent a transformation of other memories, according to certain canons of a symbolic system to which all such memories belong as symbolic entities of a particular kind.

91. See Langer, *Feeling and Form* and *Problems of Art.* Similarly, Piaget has described a disturbance of the equilibrium of cognitive structures as a virtual intrusion—an imagining or anticipation of instrusion—which he distinguishes from actual, external intrusion, i.e., real and actual modifications of the environment; also, then, compensatory activity in response to disequilibrating intrusion may involve virtual transformations rather than real, actual transformations. See Piaget, *Six Psychological Studies,* p. 113.

92. Stevens, *The Necessary Angel,* p. 139.

93. *Ibid.,* pp. 138-40.

94. Psychoanalysis in its theory of libidinal phases, fixation, and regression, essentially describes ways in which one kind of

conception of the desirable may dominate or have primacy in phases of development or come to have primacy over other kinds of conceptions of the desirable in determining the nature of the reality in which a person lives and acts—the nature of his object-representations and self-representation. Oral, anal, and phallic represent classes of conceptions concerning preferred means (part of oneself or part of the object-world), preferred aims or desirable ends, functional interests and relationships, and modes of integration and types of ideals. The significant resemblance is to, classification is based upon, what is abstracted is, a prototype relationship with a body-part and with others around an interest in, and the functioning of, that body-part. Means, ends, functional interests and relationships, and modes of integration and types of ideals all have forms, characteristics, or attributes of—or similarities to—abstracted aspects of that model prototype relationship. Genitality represents, in addition, a higher-order conception of the desirable, to which these other conceptions contribute as subclasses. That is, genitality involves a conception of a class of aims defined in such a way that other classes of aims, no one of which is any longer dominant, are conceived to be subordinate.

95. Freud, "Psychoanalytic Notes on an Autobiographical Account of a Case of Paranoia (Dementia Paranoides)," *op. cit.*, pp. 63-65.

96. See Langer, *Feeling and Form.*

97. See Schur, *op. cit.*

98. Freud, of course, discovered that an apparently accidental, meaningless pattern in one symbolic system—boy the yellow house grieves—may in fact be discovered to be quite meaningful according to the canons of another symbolic system.

99. See Fodor and Katz (eds.), *op. cit.*, pp. 384-416; also Chatman and Levin, *op. cit.*, pp. 224-30.

100. See Edelson, *The Idea of a Mental Illness,* for a discussion of the relation between the level of symbolization and consciousness.

101. This section will merely suggest a few directions in which thinking, related to the frame of reference outlined in this essay, about interpretation in psychoanalysis might proceed. Limitations of space confine this presentation to a series of bare assertions, which will, therefore, sound more dogmatic than intended. Especially so, as I am not able to review here fundamental discussions of interpretation in psychoanalysis such as Otto Fenichel, "Concerning the Theory cf Psychoanalytic Technique"; S. Freud, "The Interpretation of Dreams," "Papers on Technique," "Introductory Lectures on Psychoanalysis," pp. 431-63, "Constructions in Analysis"; Edward Glover, "The Therapeutic Effect of Inexact Interpretation";

Ernst Kris, "Criteria for Interpretation". "Ego Psychology and Interpretation in Psychoanalytic Therapy," "On Some Vicissitudes of Insight in Psychoanalysis," and "The Recovery of Childhood Memories in Psychoanalysis"; Rudolph M. Loewenstein, "Ego Development and Psychoanalytic Technique," "The Problem of Interpretation," "Remarks on the Role of Speech in Psychoanalytic Technique," and "Some Thoughts on Interpretation in the Theory and Practice of Psychoanalysis"; Louis Paul (ed.), *op. cit.,* and James Strachey, "The Nature of the Therapeutic Action of Psychoanalysis," *op. cit.* The intention of my comments should be assumed to be, unless otherwise indicated, to supplement these discussions or to illuminate or highlight aspects of them, perhaps by merely restating these in a different language, from the perspective of interest in this essay—and not to contradict them.

102. Kris has an excellent discussion of ambiguity in a psychoanalytic frame of reference in *Psychoanalytic Explorations in Art.* pp. 243-64, which is consistent with the focus here upon multiple connotations and the importance of attention to emphasis and reliance upon context, and the like, as resources used in disambiguation.

103. See William Pious, "A Hypothesis about the Nature of Schizophrenic Behavior," *op. cit.,* pp . 43-68.

104. *Ibid.*

105. Defenses are fantasies, not "mechanisms", and as fantasies involve transformations of symbolic self-representations and object-representations and, therefore, of the conceptions of the inner reality these symbolic forms present. See Marshall Edelson, *The Idea of a Mental Illness;* Susan Isaacs, "The Nature and Function of Phantasy" in Melanie Klein *et al.* (eds.), *op cit.,* pp. 67-121; and Roy Schafer, *Aspects of Internalization* and "The Mechanisms of Defense," *op. cit.*

106. These systems of recursive operations, which may operate in the interest of defense or adaptation, i.e., in the interest of the attainment of a variety of unspecified ends, and the efficacy of which is completely symbolic in nature, are, I would at present suggest, the generalized symbolic media of the personality system, which the theory of action requires to treat the personality system and its relation to other systems. But I have not thought through the difficulties consequent upon acceptance of such a suggestion.

107. It is not unimportant, in this connection, to note that Parsons called the theory of action "the voluntaristic theory of action" to distinguish it from positivistic and idealistic variants.

108. See Edelson, *The Idea of a Mental Illness.*

109. *Op. cit.,* p. 534.

7

SCIENCE AS A CULTURAL SYSTEM

Thomas J. Fararo

Some time in the late 1950's, the concept of *cultural system* in the analytical framework of Talcott Parsons underwent a transformation. In earlier formulations,[1] cultural systems associated with a social system consisted of "eternal objects," in the sense of Whitehead,[2] as explicitly pointed out in Parsons' early work.[3] That is, a cultural system consisted of patterns not actually located in time but possessing potentiality for "ingression" in actual occasions.[4]

This kind of formulation is systematically clarified and formalized in a paper by Anderson and Moore.[5] In their logical formulation, culture consists of the "learnables" associated with a system of action. For Parsons, in the earlier work, the learning process implies that a system of culture (in this sense) can be transmitted, while in contradistinction a social system is not a transmissible entity.[6]

Beginning with the paper "Pattern Variables Revisited,"[7] however, a different concept of a cultural system is employed. In the subsequent work, *Theories of Society*, this new usage was remarked upon by Parsons as follows:

> A great deal of the treatment of culture has emphasized the element of *pattern* as such, considering culture as a system of "eternal objects." Culture conceived exclusively in these terms, however important its part in the determination of action might be, would be deprived of the status of being a *system* of action in the same sense that behavioral organisms, personalities, and social systems are action systems. . . . From the general premises of action theory it follows that, if the functions of culture are as essential as they seem to be, the important patterns of culture, i.e., complexes of meaning, could not be created and/or maintained as available resources for action in the other systems of action unless there were processes of action primarily oriented to their creation and/or maintenance. These processes may be part of a "society," just as the life of an individual as personality

may be; but analytically, the subsystem of action focussed in this way should be distinguished from the social system as focussed on interaction relationships. The maintenance of a religious orientation through the functioning of a church would be considered as a case of interpenetration of cultural and social system; but a church as such would be regarded as a collectivity with cultural primacy, i.e., as first, a cultural "system of action," and second, a social system. Similarly, the organization of scientific research is, in the first instance, cultural in focus, and secondarily social, because it must meet exigencies of interaction.

Cultural patterns as such will be considered as forming the focus of organization for a set of subsystems in the action system. The primacy of this focus distinguishes a cultural system from a social system, a personality system, or a behavioral organism.[8]

Given this prelude, it is possible to state the purpose of the present chapter, which is to present a preliminary conceptualization of science as a subsystem of the cultural system of a society, using the preceding concept of the cultural system and employing somewhat the same technique as that used by Parsons and Smelser in their analysis of the economy.[9] But this somewhat overstates the case; instead, one should emphasize that the point of the paper is to present the beginnings of such an analysis, letting a full-scale analysis on the same level of detail as that given to the economy await a critical consideration of the present approach. In particular, in this paper less emphasis is placed on the content of the input-output interchanges then would be desirable in a more detailed treatment. Instead, there is an elaboration of the "nest" of systems and subsystems that form the entities which engage in the interchanges.

The present formulation is not beyond criticism; far from it, for it abounds in the oversimplifications that haunt this kind of "boxing" of phenomena. Yet, the sociology of science is in need of a conceptualization that is linked to general sociological theory. Put another way, the development of the sociology of science has followed closely the typical middle-range propositions of Merton's "desire for

The research reported here was conducted with the support of a research grant from the National Science Foundation (GS-2538). I am grateful to Roland Robertson for his comments on an earlier draft.

recognition" model,[10] as may be seen in both empirical work[11] and purely theoretical work,[12] as well as in the comprehensive analysis made by Hagstrom.[13] Typical of this middle-range approach is the abandonment of any attempt to "locate" the system of interest in a scheme which sees science as a *sub*system of culture, systematically articulated with its "neighboring" cultural subsystems. Roughly speaking, the sociology of science has been developing the verbal equivalent to an economic dynamics in the classical sense, and the present paper aims to look at this dynamics in a way which is analogous to the way in which Parsons and Smelser look at economic dynamics: namely, by locating the economy (the system whose dynamics are studied by economics) as a subsystem of a societal system. This means that one accepts rather than repudiates these efforts toward a "dynamics of science," but one attempts to fit the results into a more systematic treatment of the place of science in human culture. The groundwork is already present in the work of Parsons.[14]

In this chapter, I will draw freely upon this work, but this is not an essay reviewing the position of Parsons; rather, it is a piece of systematic conceptualization to be evaluated in terms of the usual logical and scientific canons rather than in terms of fidelity to Parsons' own *application* of his abstract scheme.

However, the attempt to work out the model of science by strict adherence to the abstract system, along the lines of the economic application, runs into certain difficulties. Chief among these is the difficulty in keeping track of the types of objects under discussion. Which are purely cultural and which are social? Is science a social system with a cultural emphasis? Or is it a cultural system with a social aspect? Indeed, does it make any difference as to which of these two viewpoints we take? In this chapter, the initial viewpoint is that described earlier: science is a cultural system, with a social aspect. But, as the reader will see, this viewpoint more and more gives way to science as a social system, with a cultural focus. The reader may judge for himself where the source of this difficulty lies, having been forewarned that it will appear.[15]

This treatment of science begins in the first section of the chapter with a very brief review of the basic logic of the AGIL analytical system as applied to the cultural system; this takes us to the point of "locating" science. In the second section, the subsystems of science are considered: this is the first "mesh" placed upon science. In the third section, each cell of this first mesh is partitioned once again, as it were, and we are looking at the subsystems of the subsystems of science, itself construed as a subsystem of the cultural system. In the fourth section, some additional ideas and problems related to the interchange relationships between science and the other subsystems of the cultural system are discussed. Finally, in the last section, there are some concluding remarks about this work.

SCIENCE AND THE ADAPTIVE CULTURAL SYSTEM

The starting point of this analysis of science is the cultural system interpretation of the general action system model outlined by Parsons.[16] Central to this model are two underlying ideas. First, an action system is an example of that type of system termed "teleological" by cybernetic theorists.[17] This means that the system possesses goals and that its behavior is continuously guided by a feedback which depends upon the difference between the actual state of affairs and the goal. This feedback aspect, in turn, implies the existence of various devices for sensing deviations and communicating the "desired" change in behavior.

This takes us to the second major idea that underlies the notion of an action system: it is a system which maps its environment into some internal image. In sufficiently complex action systems this mapping activity itself takes on a teleological aspect. That is, among the purposes of complex action systems are those dedicated to the controlled development of mapping systems, in the broadest possible sense of *systems of meanings*.

Corresponding to the types of problems confronted by such an action system vis-à-vis its environment, there will be differentiated systems of purposive activity vis-a-vis the development of systems of meanings. Such a system will be termed a cultural system. Thus a cultural system is not itself a system of meanings. However, as its behavior is feedback controlled by purposes bearing upon the creation of certain types of mappings it will *produce* systems of meanings. It is exactly in this sense that "science" means both a system of *action* of a very complex character and also a system of knowledge, i.e., a controlled *product* of a certain action system.

The AGIL or four-function scheme, when applied to the cultural system associated with a society, permits a relatively systematic way of portraying the structure of an otherwise bewilderingly complex action system. We can introduce the four-function scheme of analysis in this context in the following way. We imagine that in the course of creating mappings related to a variety of purposes, a society faces the following four generic types of questions, labelled for subsequent discussion:

A: "What is out there?"
G: "What does it mean in terms of our present purposes?"

I: "On what grounds do we evaluate its meaning?"
L: "What does it *all* mean?"

The A-question is a specification of the system problem of naming, classifying, and relating things in the object-world of the system. It is the *adaptive* problem. The G-question specifies the problem of orientation to the object-world in terms of the current interests of the system, i.e., its goals. This is the *goal-attainment* problem, in its cultural system interpretation. The I-question specifies the problem of developing and applying standards of evaluation in relation to decisions related to system interests: cost, welfare, moral standards, for example, may be relevant. This is the problem of *integration* for the cultural system. Finally, the L-question specifies the "ultimate" problem of what the world, in the light of the system's fluctuating interests and its standards "means" in a more interpretative and overarching sense than that given by the cognitive coding in response to the adaptive problem. This is the *pattern-maintenance* problem for the cultural system.

The analytical subsystems of the cultural system that exist as processes addressed to these functional problems have been designated by Parsons as follows:[18]

A: Cognitive symbolization
G: Expressive symbolization
I: Moral-evaluative standards
L: Existential interpretation

This nomenclature is a naming of the *functional subsystems* of the cultural system. As in the case of the analysis of the social system, when we analyze the cultural system we regard various concrete activities and social units as having a "weighting" in the various functional subsystems. One says that in a highly differentiated system, activities and units exist with strong weighting within certain of the functional systems and low weighting in others. Thus, the economy is a functional subsystem in which firms weight very strongly, while these firms play a more negligible role with regard to pattern-maintenance. Similarly, in the cultural system of an "advanced" society, one may locate elements that weight more heavily in certain functional systems than others. A reasonable assignment of "bundles" of such elements, carrying certain global nomenclature, is as follows:

A: Science
G: Arts
I: Ethics, Law
L: Religion, Metaphysics, Cosmology

On the structural level, in an advanced society, science will be a bundle of structures and processes organized around the adaptive function of the cultural system: cognitive symbolization of the object-world. For the sake of simplicity in this first analysis, a more definite analytical viewpoint will be taken: We will regard science, in its action system sense, as *the* adaptive subsystem of the cultural system of a societal system. This makes science strictly parallel to the economy: Science is to culture as economy is to society.

The abstract four-function model utilized by Parsons and Smelser[19] for the analysis of the economy will be applied to science. It can be compactly shown as a series of ever-finer "meshes" in which a given subsystem is further analyzed "down" into subsystems. We will present a three-level analysis: (1) science as the adaptive sector of the cultural system of a society; (2) science as a system with four functional subsystems; and (3) each such subsystem of science as a system with four functional subsystems.

The abstract diagram for a three-level analysis can be abstracted from *Economy and Society*[20] and is shown in Figure 7-1.

A brief explication of this diagram will make its structure evident. The outer subsystems, labelled in italic letters, are those of the cultural system. The second level down is that of the subsystems of A. This corresponds to a first breakdown of science; the subsystem labelling is of the form A_L, A_I, A_G, A_A, for each of the four subsystems. The third level down is that of the subsystems of each such subsystem, which is denoted by lower-case letters. A typical such subsystem is say, $A_I\alpha$, which is the adaptive (a) subsystem of the pattern-maintenance (L) subsystem of the cultural system's adaptive system (A).

Table 7-1. Boundary-interchange rules

SYSTEM PAIR		LOCATION OF INTERCHANGE*
A	G	A
A	I	I
A	L	G
G	I	G
G	L	I
I	L	A
A_A	A_G	a
A_A	A_I	i
A_A	A_L	g
A_G	A_I	g
A_G	A_L	i
A_I	A_L	a

*In the appropriate subsystem identification. Thus A in the first row stands for the A of A and A of G, which are denoted A_A and G_A respectively, in Figure 7-1. Similarly, in the seventh line, a signifies the a of A_A and the a of A_G which are denoted A_{Aa} and A_{Ga} respectively, in Figure 7-1.

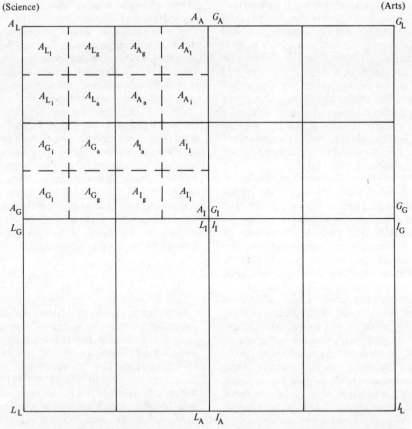

Figure 7-1. The abstract subsystems configuration of the cultural system.

The arrangement of the cells in Figure 7-1 is not arbitrary. We obtain this figure by successive application of six rules, one for each couple of subsystems at any given four-system level (see Table 7-1). Each rule prescribes the subsystem location at which an interchange takes place. For example, the rule with regard to the adaptive and goal-attainment systems is: The interchange is across their respective adaptive subsystems. At the outermost level in Figure 7-1 we show this interchange location by juxtaposing A_A and G_A. At the next level down, the two systems A_A and A_G must interchange across *their* adaptive subsystems, and so we juxtapose the two cells A_{Aa} and A_{Ga}. The final arrangement must take into account the mutual constraints of all six rules at each level.

THE FUNCTIONAL SUBSYSTEMS OF SCIENCE

The logic of constructing the actual content of these abstract subsystems for the analysis of the cognitive symbolization subsystem, interpreted as science, is that of first specifying the G-function in terms of the role of the system in the larger system. Thus, since cognitive symbolization constitutes the *function* of science in the cultural system it follows that the primary *goal* of science is given by activities directly related to cognitive symbolization as such. That is, if science performs the adaptive function for the cultural system, it follows that the main goal of science is the codification of the object-world in terms of naming, classifying, and relating. We will call this subsystem of science, which is A_G, the *research subsystem*.

Given this goal of science, it follows that science in the pursuit of its goal must adapt itself to an environment whose interchanges with science will be across certain boundaries. First, each of the other three subsystems of the cultural system has an interchange relation with science. Second, science construed as the adaptive subsystem of the cultural system will have a direct interchange with the adaptive subsystem of the society (by applying the rules of Table 7-1, with a new identification in which *I* means the society and

L means its associated cultural system). It follows that the action environment of science is given by (1) the arts, (2) religion and metaphysics, (3) ethics, law, and related norm-producing systems, and (4) the economy of the given society (see Figure 7-7). The subsystem of science which consists of structures and processes developed in adaptation to the action environment will be termed the *scientific support subsystem*. Its primary function is to assure adequate resources, in the widest sense, for the accomplishment of the goal of science, within a structured economic and cultural environment. This subsystem is that which is abstractly given by A_A.

We turn now to the integrative problem of science, the problem that arises from the interaction of the various structures and processes developed in "the pursuit of knowledge" and in adaptation to the environment of science. The basic problem may be thought of as coordination. In a finer analysis of the *units* participating in the research process (human individuals and groups construed as multifunctional systems), one would form an analytical model of a plurality of goal-oriented units. These units face inputs from the environment of science, while yet pursuing science ("research") for its own sake. These actors organize around these adaptive and research problems and in this process generate "social" problems of science. The result is a collection of structures and processes analyzable around the problem of social integration of these units. This functional subsystem of science, which is abstractly given as A_I, will be termed *the scientific community*.

This discussion provides an interpretation of the three functional problems of science related to adaptation, goal-attainment, and integration. The last functional problem of science is that of certain *commitments to science* within the social and cultural system as a whole. That is, if there is to be a research process at all, with resources supplied by a scientific-support system and organized around a community of scientists, there is a prerequisite normative pattern required for these dynamic elements. This prerequisite pattern is like the commitment to work in relation to the economic processes within the economy. Without some minimal commitment to certain values, there could be no scientific process. Put another way, if a cultural system is to develop an "advanced system of cognitive symbolization" — namely, modern science — it must possess certain kinds of values as fundamental, if tacit, commitments. This is the normative basis of science described by Merton and others.[21] Here we follow the parallel of the analysis of the economy and say that these form the cultural system's fundamental value commitments to science. Thus, the abstract subsystem A_L will be termed "Scientific Value Commitments." These are "pattern" elements

in the system of science analyzed at this level. Like the grammar of a given language, they are relatively time-invariant while other processes presupposing them (like message sending and receiving, i.e., communicative discourse) are undergoing a faster dynamics. The A_L system will consist of mechanisms and structures whose latent function is to preserve these pattern elements amid the dynamics of science.

Let us summarize what has been constructed this far with a diagram (see Figure 7-2) showing the first level of systems analysis (A, G, I, L) and the second level for the A system, using the concrete nomenclature just introduced. (The reader should compare Figure 7-2 with Figure 7-1 to see "where" we are at this point.)

Our next task involves a functional analysis of the four subsystems of science, or rather, defining and naming the nature of the functional problems confronted by each such subsystem.

THE ANALYSIS OF THE SUBSYSTEMS

First, let us specify the functional aspects of the scientific commitment system. These are to be four basic types of value commitments, regarded as elements whose maintenance is necessary for the dynamics of science. The "basic norms" of science as described by Merton and others fit well into this scheme. To indicate this fit, we show that each of the four functional problems of science poses a value issue, such that a commitment is necessary — must be maintained — for the dynamics of science to be pursued.

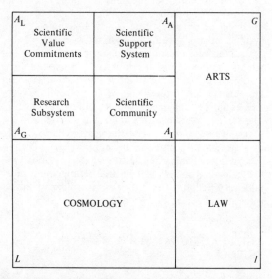

Figure 7-2. The subsystems of science.

In the adaptive subsystem of science, involving what we termed the scientific-support system, there is a value issue in regard to the possible confounding of the goal of science with the goals of the support system itself or of external systems providing inputs to the support system. Money, for example, may "pollute" the system of science.[22] National loyalties present a similar problem, since science is bounded by a societal environment which is multinational. In short, all kinds of environmental systems threaten to create a deflection in the direction of interests other than the accumulation of knowledge. Impure interests threaten pure interests. It is clear from the sociological description of the norms of science, that Merton's norm of *disinterestedness* is the value commitment which, given it is maintained in the system, provides a pattern element (a normative time-invariant aspect) which "resolves" the value issue in the adaptive sector of science "in favor of" the goal of science itself.

When we turn to the goal attainment problem of science itself, i.e., to its research system, we find that a value issue arises in the evaluation of claims to knowledge. That is, the actors in the system of science confront an issue in which the goal of individual actors vis-a-vis cognitive symbolization may confound the system goal vis-a-vis cognitive symbolization. The issue arises in evaluating *private* claims as to the coding of the object-world as over against the goal of *system* coding, i.e., in some sense *public* mapping of the object-world. Thus the goal of science is threatened by the fact that its component units, at their own level of adjustment to the object-world, develop their own cognitive mappings of that world. Merton's norm of *organized scepticism* is the value commitment that, when it is maintained, guarantees a protection of the system goal from its "pollution" by private codes. This value commitment orients the scientist who has internalized it in the direction of intersubjective validation of knowledge claims, with a scepticism toward all claims that fail the test of "verifiability."

Turning now to the integrative problem of science, which we see as the focus of the scientific community, the value issue raised here is the coordinative issue of how individual symbolic products are to become public, system codes. That is, granted a commitment to the *public* character of the symbolizing activity, the integrative issue involves the problem of transmission to the "public" of science what is, in its origins, a particular *unit's* symbolic activity. The Mertonian norm that applies here is *communality*. This value commitment, when held by a scientist, orients him to "contributing to science," i.e., to place his private product in the public domain. This raises the question as to what orients the scientist to create the product in the first place, a point central to the sociological theory of science provided by Storer.

We shall return later to the contribution of Storer.

To review our treatment of the system of scientific value commitments to this point, what has been described is the content of three particular functional problems within this system (see Figure 7-3). The result has been a conceptual location of three of Merton's norms of science: disinterestedness appears as the content of the pattern element maintained in A_{La}; organized scepticism appears under A_{Lg}; and communality appears in A_{Li}. The fourth functional problem for a system of value commitments must relate to the pattern-maintenance aspect itself. The value issue in question must arise in the pattern element of science itself. One way of conceptualizing this value issue is to note that as the research subsystem undergoes its process of developing knowledge, utilizing resources provided by the support system, the scientific community tends to a finer and finer differentiation of specialized units, corresponding to which there are specialized symbolic products. Therefore, the question that arises is: In what sense can the resulting system provide a single scheme of coding the object-world? Will it not produce a whole host of fragmentary and disconnected symbolic systems, especially developed around certain specialized roles? Indeed, in one aspect, this is exactly what contemporary science does look like.[23] Apart from a pattern (time-invariant, normative) element that oriented the actors in science to seeing science as *one* system, it would appear that the cultural system of science would generate a collection of independent sciences. Each science would have its own version of

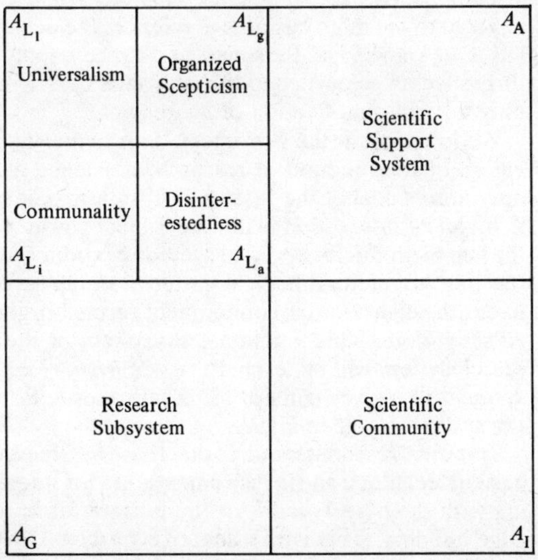

Figure 7-3. The subsystems of the scientific value-commitment system.

the scientific value commitments; among other things it might include a specification of the disinterestedness norm to the "protection" of that particular science from *other* sciences. Indeed, something like this has happened historically, but its potentially discordant and disorganizing aspects have been dampened by an image and an idiom, within the scientific community, of science as a single entity.

At the highest level, then, this value issue is one of disciplinary particularism versus scientific universalism. The choice may occasionally arise: "What matters most, *this field* of mine or 'science'?" The existence of a value commitment to science, in this overarching sense, as opposed to only or primarily this *field* of science is what helps sustain the imagery and the social-systemic reality of a single cultural system: science. This is the functional interpretation we give to Merton's norm of *universalism* in the system of science. It is a higher-order value commitment, not to some particular aspect of the dynamics of science but to "science." (In turn, it is likely to be a specification to science of a higher-order cultural value commitment of the universalistic type.) Note we are not saying that the answer to the primacy question (involving particularistic scientific groupings versus "science") *necessarily* involves an answer in favor of universalism. The argument is that if the cultural system is to sustain a *single* system of science, at some nontrivial sense of "wholeness," then a pattern element valuing science in and of itself must be maintained. This concludes our treatment of the value-commitment subsystem of the system of science, examined in terms of the four-function paradigm.

The *research subsystem* is the subsystem of science devoted to the main business of science: the accumulation of knowledge. Parsons[24] has already analyzed this aspect of science, and the approach here will be only a slight modification of his results.

We look first at the g-problem. This is the specification of the function of research in science as an *operational* goal of the research subsystem. Clearly, it involves interaction with the object-world with the aim of producing codified symbolic products conforming to methodological criteria which evolve under the higher-order commitment termed organized scepticism. This functional subsystem of the research system will be termed the *empirical research system*. This gives content to the abstract notion of the system A_{Gg}. (See Figure 7-4.)

Empirical research requires that there be a facilities basis in technique and in instrumentation for interacting with the object-world for the purpose of knowledge-building. This is the adaptive problem of the research system of science that may be thought of as being "solved" by the development of measuring

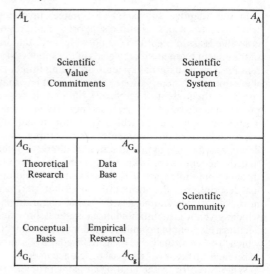

Figure 7-4. The subsystems of the research system.

instruments, laboratory devices, and other such facilities. We may say that it involves the *data base* of science. Thus, the system A_{Ga} will be termed the *data-base subsystem*.

Empirical research, utilizing a given data base, generates information in the form of facts and generalizations about the object-world. The integrative problem of the research system is one of investigating the manner in which these facts and generalizations may be organized and coordinated at a somewhat higher level of analysis. This higher level of analysis is precisely that of developing symbolic methods for bridging the otherwise unconnected results of different empirical investigations culminating in distinct facts and generalizations. If the main business of the research system of science is *empirical* research, it is nevertheless true that this research is such as to produce an integrative problem answered by a *theoretical research* subsystem. The activities of this subsystem are not those of interaction with the object-world; instead, the activities involve the manipulation of the coding or mapping schemes *as such*, with the function of producing unifying symbolic products. In role terms, when specialization occurs along this distinction, we have the experimentalist on the one hand and the theoretician on the other. For example, we have "experimental physicists" and "mathematical physicists."

Thus far, in our analysis of the research system of science, we have talked about the data-base (adaptive) system, the empirical research (goal-attainment) system, and the theoretical research (integrative) system. Finally, we arrive at the pattern-maintenance subsystem within the research system. As always, this involves the maintenance of the pattern (normative, time-invariant) element that is presupposed in the dynamics of the other three subsystems. For research, this involves fundamental conceptualization, changes in which define "scientific revolutions," in the sense of Kuhn.[25] This subsystem will be termed the *conceptual basis* of the research system. As Parsons points out,[26] this system maintains the *paradigm* employed in the science. The integrative function, by contrast, involves the dynamic functioning of time-varying theories *within* such a paradigm. In this sense, a change in a theory is "normal," to use Kuhn's word.

This concludes our four-function breakdown of the research subsystem of science, and we turn now to the integrative subsystem.

The integrative subsystem of science we gave the name *scientific community*. A four-function analysis of the scientific community, then, begins by a specification of its goal-attainment problem in the light of its function: namely, the coordination of scientific research for optimal utilization of the resources provided by the support system of science. This is the function performed by *scientific collectivities*. such as research institutes and some university departments.

The basic facilities which collectivities of this type can employ involve categories of "scientific labor." Adaptively, the scientific community responds to the dynamics of the research and support systems by developing specialized *roles* to be deployed in organizational contexts.

The existence of organizations and roles implies that normative solutions exist to typical problems arising in the course of interaction within such contexts. These normative solutions form the content of the integrative subsystem of the scientific community; they involve *norms* at a lower level than the four value-commitment categories described earlier. These are norms guiding the interaction of scientists with each other as they specialize in various aspects of the enterprise of science. For example, when a scientist "writes up" his experimental results a description of the experimental scene is required which is governed by the value commitment to organized scepticism: The description must be such as to inform other scientists as to how they could replicate the experiment should they decide to do so. Norms regulating the interaction of experimentalists and theoreticians involve an orientation to mutual relevance. The experimentalist must begin by "locating" his problem in a more general context; the norm that specifies this orientation urges the experimentalist to seek out problems raised by theoreticians. Similarly. theoreticians internalize norms that stress that at

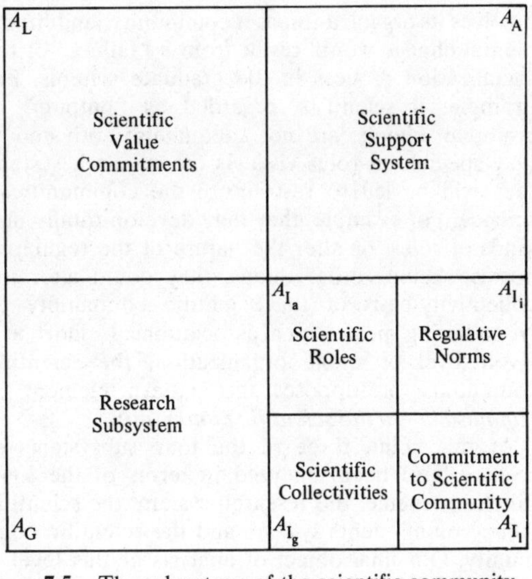

Figure 7-5. The subsystems of the scientific community.

certain crucial junctures there exists a primacy of empirical facts over deductions.

Note that when scientists in various roles interact, they are guided by more than these kinds of norms, but this is only to say that the concrete scientist is more than a scientist and that concrete interactions always involve an overlap of analytically distinct types of social systems. Therefore, norms of the kind that regulate interaction within *any* formal organization do not logically fall in the integrative system of the scientific community, as its norms specifically regulate interactions in collectivities organized around scientific research.

To review briefly our treatment of the scientific community to this point: The adaptive function involves scientific roles, the goal-attainment function involves scientific collectivities, and the integrative function involves norms regulative of the interaction of scientists in various scientific roles. (See Figure 7-5.) Finally, the pattern element presupposed in these dynamics must be discussed. Clearly, this involves the problem of *socialization* to science. Concrete collectivities connected with the modern university play a central role here. The point is that if scientific collectivities organized around certain roles and norms are to produce an integration of science at a certain level, it must be the case that new entrants to science internalize these norms and are prepared to play these roles. This is not to say that patterns cannot change (any more than one says that paradigms cannot change), but a change at this pattern level is a fundamental change vis-à-vis a certain state of science. In this case, the relevant state of science involves its organization as a community, and fundamental change would result from a "failure" of the socialization process in the graduate schools. For example, if scientists, regarded as "outputs" of graduate schools, are not adequately motivated to play specialized roles vis-à-vis the research system, they will be led to restructure the community of science. For example, they may develop totally new kinds of roles, or alter the nature of the regulative norms. Among other things, they could alter the collectivity-basis of the scientific community by "repudiating" professional associations. In short, at a given level of stable organization, the scientific community presupposes the pattern element of *commitment to the scientific community.*

At this point, three of the four subsystems of science have been analyzed in terms of the four-function scheme: the research system, the scientific value-commitments system, and the scientific community. Our final object of analysis at this level is the support system of science, the system fulfilling the adaptive function in the system of science. Figure 7-6 gives the results of the analysis to be presented.

To arrive at a coherent view of the subsystems of the support system of science, we have to analyze the nature of the environment of science. There are four systems which directly bound the adaptive subsystem of the cultural system: each of the other three subsystems of the cultural system and, in addition, the adaptive subsystem of the society. To see that this is a correct analysis, we should "move up" one level to present a diagram of the general

societal system comprising organism, personality, cultural system, and society. (See Figure 7-7.)

This figure is constructed by following the rules of Table 7-1, except that A, G, I, and L, are replaced by α, γ, ι, and λ; and, in addition, A, G, I, and L are replaced by A, G, I, and L. This is an "embedding" of the cultural system in its larger system context. To say that science is construed as the adaptive subsystem of the cultural system means that it figures as the content of λ_A, while to say that the economy is construed as the adaptive subsystem of society means that it figures as the content of ι_A. Figure 7-7 makes it clear that science will engage in direct interchanges with three cultural subsystems and, in its role as the cultural system bounding the society, it will have a direct interchange system with the economy.

In the next section, these interchange systems will be discussed, but for the present the task is to outline the character of the subsystems of the support system of science. The preceding analysis of the action environment of science makes it clear that the support system will reflect the need to adapt to the productive capacity of the society (economy), to the modes of expressive interests in the societal system (the arts), to the formalized normative-evaluative order (ethics, law), and to the existing religious doctrines.

One way of thinking about this support system is that it plays the role of a kind of economy *of* science. This means that just as the goal of the economy of the society is the production of things ("utilities") that satisfy *given* wants, so the goal of the support

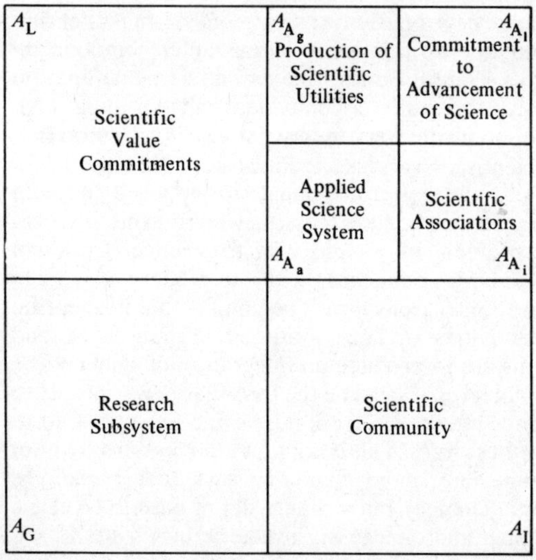

Figure 7-6. The subsystems of the scientific support system.

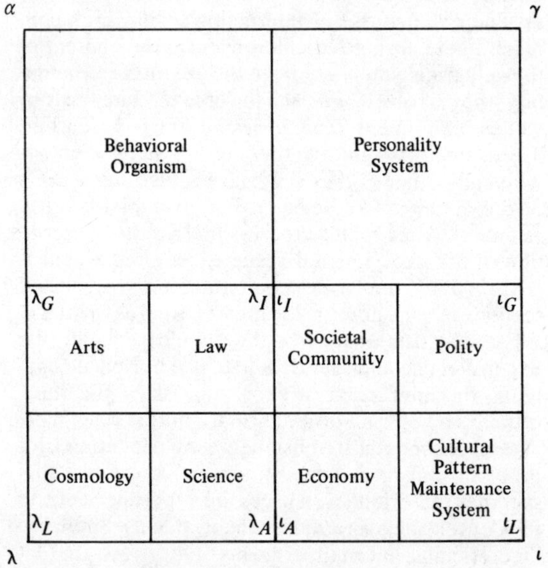

Figure 7-7. The general societal system.

system of science is the production of "things" that satisfy *given* scientific wants. The word "production" means: processing external materials to a set of forms that satisfy wants. Thus we shall say that the goal of the support system is the *production of scientific utilities*. These "wants" are determined within the goal-attainment system of science: the research system. Thus, by and large, the support system supplies "things" which are instrumentally important for the current state of scientific research. Manpower and hardware are two obvious types of objects of scientific utility, the acquisition of which forms part of the concrete action basis in this sector. A different, but important, category of object of scientific utility is a *cognitive problem*. Cognitive problems arise, of course, within the research system as well; but relative to a *generalized* resource for science what is required is an environment in which a series of felt problems are expressed as problems for cognitive inquiry. In this sense a cultural milieu can be highly favorable or very unfavorable for science. Thus, an important aspect of the goal-attainment sector of the support system is its "translation" of exogenous problems into definite scientific problems. Put another way, one function of this "economy" of science is to convert cognitive raw materials from the cultural environment into cognitive problems for science; and the cultural milieu can be more or less rich in its provision of raw materials.

The adaptive subsystem of the support system must play a kind of "investment system" role vis-à-vis the goal-attainment subsystem. This investment role seems to be played by *the system of applied science*, for its ongoing involvement in the external social environment of science guarantees a continuous flow of new problems, as well as a "plant" in which scientific problems can arise and be solved. It is customary, especially in discourse concerning the funding of science,[27] to emphasize that pure science is a kind of investment for future utilities, with applied science put in the consummatory role. This inverts the functional roles of applied science and pure science for science. Applied science functions for science by assuring objects of scientific utility in the future: manpower, hardware, and problems for scientific research. From an external standpoint, from the vantage point of the economy, the instrumental role of science appears primary. Within science, however, what is instrumental for the total cultural system has become a consummatory goal aspect of science. From this vantage point, applied science is instrumental for "more fundamental" aspects of science.

The role of "the entrepreneur" in the support system of science is played by *scientific associations* (for example, The American Association for the Advancement of Science). These associations perform the integrative function of combining the "investments" in the applied science sector with the internal needs of science vis-à-vis its research system. In contrast to scientific collectivities, such as research institutes, they are not organized to do research but to encourage the growth and maintenance of a favorable environment for research.

Finally, the dynamics of scientific support at a given level presuppose the maintenance of a certain kind of normative pattern, a degree of commitment to the *advancement* of science. This pattern aspect of the support system will depend strongly upon the cultural subsystems surrounding science, as well as on the level of development of the economy. Optimal commitment to the advancement of science exists when there is a highly advanced economy, a religious system supportive of investigative processes, a normative-evaluative code encouraging purely cognitive interests, and an expressive symbolism emphasizing an active interest in nature.

This analysis of the support system concludes our breakdown of science into four functional subsystems. In Figure 7-8 the results of the various analyses shown in Figures 7-3, 7-4, 7-5, and 7-6 are combined into one diagram.

Our next task will be to indicate a direction of conceptualization of the input-output interchanges between science and its cultural environment.

SCIENCE AND ITS CULTURAL ENVIRONMENT

According to the present model, the interchange between the adaptive subsystem (science) and the goal-attainment subsystem (arts) of the cultural system is across the A-border. That is, an output occurs from the adaptive subsystem of science into the adaptive subsystem of the arts and conversely. (We omit any treatment of possible double interchanges.) From the philosophical and historical treatment of the rise of modern science provided by Whitehead,[28] what is suggested is that the output to the arts is an *image of nature* and what is received from the arts is an *interest in nature*. From Whitehead's discussion of nineteenth-century literature one can see that the image of nature provided by science made a strong impression on the romantic poets: "the romantic reaction" is a reaction to an input from science. Similarly, Whitehead notes that at an earlier time the increased interest in nature among the educated men of Renaissance Europe provided part of the foundation for the rise of modern science; this is the category of output from the arts

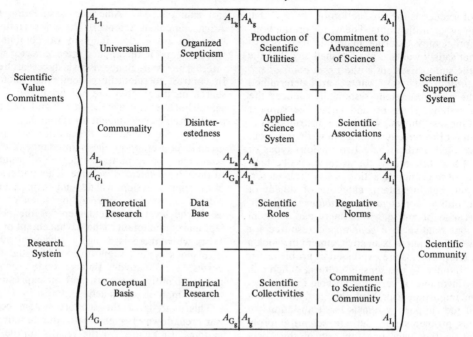

Figure 7-8. The subsystems of science.

to science in the form "interest in nature." At a concrete level, it involves a willingness "to get one's hands dirty."[29]

The interchange between the adaptive system (science) and the moral-evaluative system ("ethics") is across the integrative boundary. One can think of this as an output from science in the form of an *image of man* and an input from ethics in the form of a *code of conduct.* Just as the arts may be thought of as providing a motivational-imaginative milieu of science, so one may think of the ethical sector of the cultural system as providing a codified moral basis for science.

Finally, the interchange between science and cosmology (construing the latter as part of the content of the pattern maintenance subsystem of the cultural system) is across the goal-attainment boundary. One can think of this as an output from science in the form of an *image of ultimate reality* with a return input from the cosmological subsystem in the form of some degree of a *sense of order.* This latter input is categorized by Whitehead as the primary necessary cultural condition for science. Indeed, his phrasing — "an instinctive sense of order" — is exactly what is implied by the idea that the input is from the pattern-maintenance sector of the cultural system. We may think of the cosmological subsystem as providing the conceptual foundations of science; indeed, the research system of science is the sector of science directly receiving the input from the cosmological system.

The diagram shown in Figure 7-9 summarizes these brief remarks concerning the input-output interchanges between science and the other cultural subsystems.

These inputs to science may be related in a "cybernetic hierarchy," to use Parsons' phrase, in the order L-I-G-A wherein the inputs may be construed as:

from L: instinctive sense of order
from I: order in human relations
from G: order in concrete content of individual experience

These inputs combine to produce, in conjunction with the operation of intrinsic scientific factors and the inputs from the economy,

A: order in concepts related to experience,

which is the scientific synthesis of the "order" elements of culture.

CONCLUDING REMARKS

To summarize briefly the main theme of this paper we may say that science may be regarded as a set of structures and processes highly specialized in the adaptive function of the cultural system. For a first model, it is assumed that science *is* the adaptive cultural system. This point of reference is further specified by a functional subsystems analysis of science, followed by a similar analysis of each of

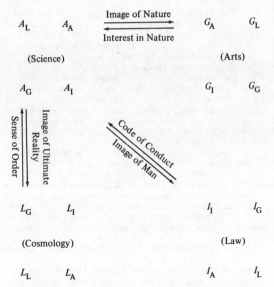

A_L A_A Image of Nature $\longrightarrow$ G_A G_L
              Interest in Nature $\longleftarrow$

(Science)   (Arts)

A_G A_I G_I G_G

Image of Ultimate Reality / Sense of Order

Code of Conduct / Image of Man

L_G L_I I_I I_G

(Cosmology)   (Law)

L_L L_A I_A I_L

Figure 7-9. Input-output relations between science and other cultural subsystems.

these subsystems. As a result one obtains a conceptual "sketch" which is built upon one of the major paradigms of contemporary sociological theory.

Some major aspects of this model are incomplete, and these define problems for future work.

First, one must define the nature of the interchanges among the subsystems of science.

Second, one must locate various institutions of science. A parallel to the treatment of economic institutions by Parsons and Smelser[30] would be a good starting point for a four-function analysis of scientific institutions.

Third, we must try to follow up the lead of Storer[31] as to the existence of a special symbolic medium in science, parallel to the role of money for the economy, power for the polity, commitment for the cultural pattern-maintenance system, and influence for the societal community. According to Storer, this medium is *competent response.* The formula is: the creative product is exchanged for competent response. To place Storer's insight into the context of this chapter we should try to look for various entities that play the role of codes, messages, value principles, and coordination standards.[32] It would appear that the value principle is *knowledge* and the coordination standard is *verifiability*. These correspond to utility and solvency, respectively, in the economy. The symbolic medium itself, parallel to money, would appear to be *publication,* as the symbol of knowledge is the published object. This is an important point in the original argument of Merton concerning recognition.[33] What of competent response? From this point of view, competent res-

ponse is a sanction, sent in accordance with the code (knowledge, verifiability) governing the use of the medium (publication). This emphasis on the role of publications in science would tie in nicely with a considerable amount of empirical work in the sociology of science which relates to publication phenomena.[34]

These are only a few of the substantive theoretical problems one can frame within this framework for the analysis of science.

Another type of problem exists, however, if we question the methodology of model-construction under this framework. In Table 7-1 and related figures, an attempt has been made to spell out some of the formal rules. Much more needs to be done in this direction. To take one example, when we drop down to the analysis of a subsystem of a given system, what rules govern what we may say or may not say about its functional problems? One rule followed in this chapter in the analysis of the sybsystems A_G, A_I, and A_A is to analyze a given functional system S, then proceed in the order: S_G, S_A, S_I, and S_L and let S_G be defined by the function of S. In this way, we postulated the goal of a given system to be an operational realization of the system's function in a higher-order system. Then its adaptive problem was one of provision of generalized facilities for this goal-attainment sector, while its integrative problem involved some coordinative system with respect to these two lower levels. Then, having decided these three subsystem aspects, in the given order, we asked what kinds of normative patterns needed to remain time-invariant in order that the dynamics could proceed at an analytically given level. Then the pattern-maintenance problem is given by the assumption that this normative order itself is stable only under certain conditions.

These remarks suggest another problem in the methodology of this framework: the need to make the control systems hierarchy (LIGA) link directly to the heuristic and formal tools used by engineers to study control systems. An important beginning toward this linkage can be made by noting that any four-function system is actually a *hierarchical multi-level* control system, in the sense of Mesarovic, Macko, and Takahara.[35] The mathematical work in this area, an important part of general systems theory, is just beginning. If this work can be related to the "cybernetic hierarchy" notion of Parsons, it is possible that an important advance can be made in the coherence of the four-function approach.[36]

A final reminder: the actual content of the analysis of science given here is intended to be very tentative. It is subject to extensive correction with advancements in the methodology of four-function analysis, as well as correction as to substantive content.

NOTES

1. See, for example, T. Parsons and E. Shils, "Values, Motives and Systems of Action," in T. Parsons and E. Shils (eds.), *Toward a General Theory of Action* (Cambridge: Harvard University Press, 1951).

2. A. N. Whitehead, *Science and the Modern World* (New York: Macmillan, 1925, reprinted by The Free Press, New York, 1967).

3. Parsons, *The Structure of Social Action* (New York: McGraw-Hill, 1937, reprinted by The Free Press, New York, 1949).

4. The terminology is that of Whitehead, *op. cit.*, and in *Process and Reality* (New York: Macmillan, 1929).

5. A. R. Anderson and O. K. Moore, "Toward a Formal Analysis of Cultural Objects," *Synthese*, 14 (1962), pp. 144-170.

6. However, certain concepts of social system—say, concepts of desirable types of social systems as used by Parsons in *Societies* (Englewood Cliffs: Prentice-Hall, 1966)—are transmissible and so part of culture.

7. Parsons, "Pattern Variables Revisited: A Response to Robert Dubin," *American Sociological Review,* 25 (August 1960), pp. 467-483.

8. Parsons, "Culture and the Social System," Introduction to Part Four of T. Parsons, E. Shils, K. Naegele, and J. Pitts (eds.), *Theories of Society* (2 vols.) (New York: The Free Press, 1961), p. 964.

9. Parsons and N. Smelser, *Economy and Society* (New York: The Free Press, 1956).

10. See R. Merton, "Priorities in Scientific Discovery: A Chapter in the Sociology of Science," *American Sociological Review,* 22 (1957), pp. 635-659.

11. See, for example, B. G. Glaser, *Organizational Scientists: Their Professional Careers* (Indianapolis: Bobbs-Merrill, 1964).

12. See, for example, N. W. Storer, *The Social System of Science* (New York: Holt, Rinehart and Winston, 1966).

13. W. Hagstrom, *The Scientific Community* (New York: Basic Books, 1965).

14. See especially Parsons, *The Social System* (New York: The Free Press, 1951); "An Approach to the Sociology of Knowledge," *Proceedings,* Fourth World Congress of Sociology at Milan, Italy, Volume IV (1959), and "Culture and the Social System," *op. cit.*

15. A companion foundations paper, Chapter Five in this volume, attempts to define the notion of a cultural system in closer adherence to the original sense that it is some kind of symbolic system. It may be mentioned that the foundations paper was written after the present paper was completed.

16. See especially Parsons, "Pattern Variables Revisited," *op. cit.,* and "Culture and the Social System," *op. cit.*

17. See A. Rosenblueth, N. Wiener, and J. Bigelow, "Be-havior, Purpose and Teleology," in W. Buckley (ed.), *Modern Systems Research and the Behavioral Scientists* (Chicago: Aldine, 1968).

18. See Parsons, "Pattern Variables Revisited," *op. cit.*

19. See Parsons and N. Smelser, *op. cit.*

20. *Ibid.*, especially pp. 68 and 208.

21. See Merton, *op. cit.*, and "Studies in the Sociology of Science", Part IV of *Social Theory and Social Structure* (New York: The Free Press, 1957) (revised). Also, B. Barber, *Science and the Social Order* (New York: The Free Press, 1952); Glaser, *op. cit.*; Storer, *op. cit.*; and E. Shils (ed.), *Criteria for Scientific Development: Public Policy and National Goals* (Cambridge: The M.I.T. Press, 1968).

22. This, and related points interpreted in terms of an exchange theory, are discussed at greater length in Storer, *op. cit.*

23. For a cogent analysis of this development, see K. Boulding, "General Systems Theory—The Skeleton of Science," in W. Buckley (ed.), *op. cit.*

24. See Parsons, "Culture and the Social System," *op. cit.*

25. T. S. Kuhn, *The Structure of Scientific Revolutions,* second enlarged edition (Chicago: University of Chicago Press, 1970).

26. See Parsons, "Culture and the Social System," *op. cit.*

27. See Shils (ed.), *op. cit.*

28. See Whitehead, *Science and the Modern World.*

29. For an analysis of this attitude toward the empirical world as a factor in the history of Science, see S. F. Mason, *Main Currents of Scientific Thought* (New York: Abelard-Schuman, 1956).

30. In *Economy and Society*.

31. In *The Social System of Science*.

32. As developed by Parsons, especially in "Theory and the Polity," Part IV of *Politics and Social Structure* (New York: The Free Press, 1969).

33. See Merton, "Priorities in Scientific Discovering," *op. cit.*

34. See, for example, the bibliographies in B. Barber and W. Hirsch (eds.), *The Sociology of Science* (New York: The Free Press, 1962), and N. Kaplan, "Sociology of Science," in R.E.L. Faris (ed.), *Handbook of Modern Sociology* (Chicago: Rand McNally, 1964). For more recent work, see D. Crane, "Social Structure in a Group of Scientists: A Test of the 'Invisible College' Hypothesis," *American Sociological Review,* 34 (1969), pp. 335-352.

35. M. D. Mesarovic, D. Macko, and Y. Takahara, *Theory of Hierarchical Multilevel Systems* (New York: Academic Press, 1970).

36. From the standpoint of the companion foundations working paper (Chapter Five in this book), the notion of *coupling* action systems will arise. In this way, the input-output interchanges are represented. Then not only the hierarchy notion but also the media notions need treatment in the extended foundations.

8

PIAGET'S PSYCHOLOGY OF INTELLIGENCE AND THE THEORY OF ACTION

Charles W. Lidz and Victor Meyer Lidz

The conceptualization of the adaptive subsystem of action has long stood as the most poorly articulated segment of the theory of action standing at a comparable level of generality and importance in the body of theory as a whole. In brief passages in essays devoted principally to other subjects, Professor Parsons has designated this system as the *behavioral organism* and has indicated very briefly and tentatively some of its major characteristics.[1] Not all of these brief treatments have been consistent with each other, however, even on some very basic issues. Thus, some accounts draw the boundary between the behavioral organism and the personality system in terms of the *learned* nature of the constituents of the latter, whereas others speak of the generalized medium of the behavioral organism as *intelligence* in a way that clearly includes learned elements.[2] The relationships between the behavioral organism and the extra-action physiological organism have also been formulated somewhat differently in different essays.[3] Beyond the problems of such discrepancies, much of the basic work in conceptualizing a system of action has not yet been specified for the behavioral organism: its structural components have not been characterized in terms distinguishing them from components of other action subsystems, its subsystems have not been distinguished and characterized, its interchange relations with other action subsystems have been explored in only the most preliminary fashion, and the nature of its developmental processes have not been discussed in a way which clearly distinguishes them from personality-level processes.

The present essay comprises a preliminary effort to develop a consistent set of concepts for the analysis in general terms of the adaptive subsystem of action. Attention will be given first to clarifying the basic frame of reference of this subsystem of action, and then to some principal characteristics of its

structures, internal processes, structural relations with the other primary subsystems of action, and functional differentiation into subsystems. The discussion will emphasize the senses in which conceptualization at this psychological level carries important significance at the sociological and general action levels as well.

The particular stimulus for this conceptual work has been a careful reading and critical consideration of a number of Piaget's major books and essays.[4] Piaget's principal contribution to general psychology seems to be the systematic examination of a dimension of the organization of action which has not heretofore received explicit attention within the theory of action but has been substantially overlooked. Moreover, Piaget's general theoretical perspectives seem to be congruent with those of the theory of action in some very fundamental respects.

Our starting point will be consideration of some of the more important theoretical and methodological convergences between Piaget's work and that of Parsons. Our discussion will then turn to an effort to characterize the frame of reference within which Piaget has conducted the bulk of his research concerned with matters other than purely perceptual processes. Here our aim will be to develop a basis for "locating" Piaget's findings and formulations within the more general schemes of the theory of action. We will then attempt to outline certain of the central substantive concerns of Piaget's theory of "cognitive" development. Although limitations of space will make our account regrettably selective and broad, it has seemed important to include some empirical discussion, for Piaget's theoretical work has been very closely tied to experimentation—especially by comparison to theoretical work on social or cultural systems or on personality development. Later sections of our paper will then be concerned with utilizing Piaget's researches as resources for formulating a conceptual scheme within the theory of action for analysis of the functioning of the adaptive subsystem of action. The concluding discussion and a theoretical appendix will concern certain respects in which our analysis impinges upon the sociological understanding of the nature of interaction and its normative regulation in social systems.

THEORETICAL AND METHODOLOGICAL CONVERGENCES

Both admirers and critics of the theory of action have often prefaced their judgments by noting that much of the conceptual apparatus of its functionalism has been borrowed from the biological sciences. Parsons has often acknowledged that his emphasis on theoretical principles such as the "functional" interrelations of the components of systems and contributions of components to the systems in which they operate or the homeostatic nature of system processes in the aggregate stems in considerable part from his early education and continued interest in biology.[5] Piaget, too, has adapted important elements of biological thought for use in the study of systems that fall within the realm of action. His earliest scientific work concerned a specialized area of evolutionary biology. When his interests turned to the study of the development of intelligence in humans, he came to interpret intelligence as a principal means by which individuals of the species could maximize their adaptation to their environments.[6] He treated the intelligent structures of the mind as entities that emerged through enhancement of the organism's adaptation to its particular environment and through complex processes of adaptation to one another in the functioning of the mind.[7] The structures of intelligence were conceptualized as dynamically interacting elements within an encompassing system that sustained a moving, evolving equilibrium under constant stimulation from a complex environment.[8] Thus, from points early in their respective careers, both Parsons and Piaget have been profoundly concerned with devising systems concepts which are functional, evolutionary, dynamic, and highly pluralistic in the sense of allowing for the interaction of a great many autonomous units. Given the substantial divergence in their respective subject matters and in the intellectual traditions in terms of which they have otherwise been oriented, this basic methodological convergence seems very striking.

Within the confines of this general methodological convergence, Parsons and Piaget have also converged in some more particular respects which are also remarkable. Both have come in their more recent works to stress the continuities between the principles of cybernetics and the general study of complex, self-regulating systems, on the one hand, and basic patterns in the organization of systems of action, on the other hand.[9] Here, both have come to focus their analyses upon the problem of identifying a characteristic mechanism of process by which highly complicated systems can sustain order while they are engaged in carrying out extremely diverse, functionally differentiated, and largely autonomous subprocesses, i.e., in Parsons' conception of combinatorial processes and interchanges facilitated by generalized media and in Piaget's conception of the organization of intelligent processes through formal operations.[10] Moreover, both have emphasized the functional importance of mechanisms of representations or symbols or conventionally coded signs in mediating and facilitating the exercize of the cybernetic controls that operate to order complex action systems.

Piaget and Parsons have also both complemented their empirical interests in this theme of order in complexity with what may be termed a structuralist or formalist approach to the construction and ordering of empirical and theoretical propositions. In Piaget's work, the structuralist focus has fallen upon the effort to develop mathematicized paradigms which compactly summarize the intelligent capacities of individuals at the various stages of development.[11] The behavioral capacity of an individual at a given stage of development is conceived to be a function of the sets of interrelations among mental schemata—or mental representations of objects, events, or acts developed through experience[12]— which the individual can organize and utilize in a controlled fashion. The capacity of the individual's behavioral system, then, can be summarized by a logical-mathematical formula which represents the structural relations obtaining among the schemata as units either of the entire system or of some particular domain within it. The formula provides a concise statement of the ability of the individual to bring discrete schemata into determinate, flexible, and stable states of mutual implication in his efforts to understand or plan processes of action. Different levels of capacity that emerge within different stages in the development of intelligent behavioral systems can be represented by different formulae, varying, for example, in the degrees of hierarchization and substantive specialization of schemata which they include.[13] The developmental process itself can be analyzed in terms of the succession from simpler to more complex structures as specified by the stage-linked structures.

Here, we wish to call attention to two principal claims which are made for the formulae (or the set of them) and various propositions that can be derived from them by virtue of their structuralist status. First, the formulae are regarded as summarizing not simply some particular experimental results on individuals tested at various stages of development, but as models of universal capacities to act which are intrinsic to human adaptation in its most general sense. In this respect, their status is at least very close to that of a grammar in transformational linguistics, where a grammar represents the ability of the competent speaker to create sentences under any conditions. It is expected that understanding *any* phenomenon of intelligent behavior requires analysis of the organization imparted to its controlling schemata by the underlying systemic structures through reference to the appropriate stage-specific formula or formulae. Perhaps most importantly, it is claimed that the model of formal operations provides universal access to the understanding of the type of capacity for intelligent thought and behavior characteristic of the human adult.[14] Second, the formulae are said to summarize in a powerful and determinate fashion the relations between the system of reference and its various theoretically salient components. Piaget specifies that a structural analysis should represent the wholeness of the system as a set of transformations in a self-regulated equilibrium.[15] Paradigms which are structural in this sense, then, should enable the analyst to project by theoretical manipulation diverse operations that are possible within the stated parameters of the system and to distinguish them from "impossible" conditions beyond the system parameters. Thus, a given transformational representation of basic characteristics of a system should generate a plurality—indefinite in number for a complex system—of models of relatively concrete, observable *system* states. Here, the "possibility" of any particular states is theoretically recognized by their status as instances of selective combinations of system universals (cf. the Whiteheadian terminology of specific ingressions of eternal objects).[16] At the same time, the parameters of the system can be specified as "impossibilities" which fall outside the theoretically permissible combinations of the stated universals. A virtue of Piaget's formalizations is that they permit these theoretical operations to be performed in quite clear and determinate ways which greatly restrict any interference or error stemming from the biases of the analyst or other ad hoc factors. That is, they make possible quite detailed and specific particularizations of system states while giving substantial assurance of the objectivity of the analysis. It is our judgment, at least, that they realize these structuralist ideals more fully than any other body of knowledge within the action sphere having a comparable generality, with the possible exception of economic theory.

Piaget has criticized Parsons' work as insufficiently structuralist in the foregoing sense.[17] He notes that Parsons has treated structure in social systems in the empiricist fashion as simply observable, stable dispositions of elements of social relationships. He finds the treatment of values more interesting, especially in regard to the way in which values are claimed to establish both the pattern of functioning and the long-range direction of development for a social system. However, he does not detect any systematic effort to set forth a structuralist, transformational analysis of the detailed mechanisms of self-regulation in social systems.

Even though Parsons has not formally ordered his theoretical discussions in transformational terms, it is our view that recent developments in the theory of action have paralleled structuralist analysis in some striking ways which Piaget has simply overlooked.[18] Perhaps we can briefly indicate the scope of this convergence by commenting upon two of the most prominent notions in current work in the theory of action, namely, the conception of generalized media of interchange and the four-function paradigm.

The theory of generalized, symbolic media grows out of the effort to extend the economists' conception of processes of value-addition in economic relationships toward a conceptual foundation for analyzing all types of action processes. The media are understood to be symbolic mechanisms which serve, in highly differentiated systems, to rationalize functionally specific lines of action.[19] By providing both standards of value and circulating symbolic claims to the use of resources which are functionally specific, they assist actors in rationalizing choices among alternative paths of action. Insofar as particular lines of action "consume" resources, both real and in the form of symbolic media, and can be sustained only if they "earn" the return of fresh resources, the theory of the media becomes centrally concerned with questions of feedback and contingent controls upon action. As sustained and differentiated processes of value-addition require the flow or interchange of resources among interactors, and as resources are inherently entities which are scarce in their aggregates, resource allocation and use must be treated as having at least aspects which comprise systemic phenomena. Consequently, media theory is much concerned with analyzing particular processes as states of encompassing systems and as bound up with mechanisms of self-regulation operating within and between functionally specialized systems. Moreover, in moving beyond the identification of mechanisms analogous to money for subsystems of society other than the economy and toward discussion of common factors in the operations of diverse media, the theory has become directly involved in issues of formal universals in the processual functioning of all action systems. Thus, it converges in quite fundamental ways with the Piagetian notion of a structuralism that addresses the most general questions of the nature of self-regulation in systems of action.

The four-function paradigm derives its structuralist status from its formal relations with the conception of system. It is not simply an open-ended list of generalizations about components or structures which have been observed in systems of a given class, but an analysis or definitional subdivision of the very concept of system. Hence, it establishes analytically an invariant set of categories that can be used as universally as the concept of system itself within the domain of human action.[20] Each of the functions takes on a formal meaning that is given entirely through its relations with the other functions and through the relations of the set of functions with the master concept of system. The theoretical grounds of explanation follow from the proposition that a system can maintain any given or hypothetical state of equilibrium only if each of the functions is fulfilled in a certain degree and in a certain way—and that breakdown or change must occur insofar as these equilibrium conditions are not satisfied. To be sure, empirical specification of the nature of such "requisite" conditions can be presented only after the salient systems have been studied empirically. However, the categories of the four-function paradigm enable the analyst to frame his discussion in universal terms, and in ones which encourage formal theorizing about basic modes of interdependence among the principal dimensions of the organization of action systems. All empirical systems can be treated, in the Whiteheadian terminology, as variant ingressions of the same eternal objects—that is, of the four functions. The systematicity of very diverse phenomena may, then, be studied in ways which are not only formally comparable but which, further, permit the accumulation of theoretical knowledge that can be transferred and adapted by formal operations from one type of system to another. For example, ideas concerning the cybernetic hierarchy of control, formalized as a set of restraints upon the interrelationships of elements fulfilling different functions and subfunctions, may be applied to cultural and psychological systems even though first developed in studies of social systems. Further development of four-function theory holds out a promise that analytical operations of such general theoretical significance might be performed with a logico-mathematical rigor comparable to that of Piaget's treatments of structures in the development of intelligence. At present, four-function theory already is comparably structuralist in its focus on the analysis of systematicity or wholeness, in its pursuit of generality or universality, in its emphasis on deductive integrity and formalization as a foundation for analysis, and, though latently, in its operational or transformational organization.

Finally, we wish to note a more substantive convergence between Piaget's work and the theory of action. Parsons has long set his work off from more "behavioristic" social science by emphasizing certain qualities of the "action frame of reference."[21] While some behaviorists have announced the intention of restricting the field of scientific interest to the physical movements of behaving organisms and various indices of them, Parsons has specifically included the meaningful and the symbolic within the field of hard facticity to which social science must attend. In one crucial formulation, much influenced by the prior definitions of Max Weber and others writing at least partly within the intellectual traditions of German Idealism, action is defined as "subjectively meaningful behavior."[22] Thus, the theory of action has been strongly committed to the study of the cultural, the meaningful, the symbolic, the intentional, the goal-directed—all that has comprised the subjectivity of the human actor in the idealistic tradition except for any assumption of ineffable, unanalyzable individuality. Piaget also has rejected any attempt to discover laws founded empirically only upon the external qualities of human behavior. His work shares the assumption that behavior must be studied at the level of systems of meanings and of goal-directed adaptations to complex environments.[23] It has thus striven to analyze the processes of *mind* underlying behavior in much the sense of modern philosophy since Descartes. It has been deeply involved—within its special frame of reference—with constructing models of the meaningful subjectivity of the actor taken as a system of capacities for behavior. Here, it converges importantly with the principal descriptive ends which have been set forth by all schools of *verstehende* social science, notably including phenomenological sociology and ethnomethodology as well as the theory of action, if the problem is defined very broadly. Piaget's success in developing parsimonious and precise formal models of at least aspects of an actor's psychological subjectivity carries, it seems to us, profound implications for all *verstehende* schools of social research.

THE PSYCHOLOGY OF INTELLIGENCE

The foregoing remarks indicate that Piaget's psychology of intelligence falls squarely within the action frame of reference. There can be no doubt, therefore, about its direct salience for the theory of action, even if questions of convergence on a "structuralist" methodology are set aside. We now wish to discuss the special nature and coherence of the subject matter of Piaget's psychology of intelligence and its theoretical status within the broader domain of action.

Although Piaget's work has generally been assimilated to the field of "cognitive psychology," he himself set out to develop what he calls a "genetic epistemology."[24] Genetic epistemology was conceived as an effort to solve many of the classic philosophical problems of epistemology through empirical investigation. Man's knowledge and his capacity for knowledge were to be studied through examination of how individuals actually gain knowledge. Thus, Piaget became concerned with the *development* of the ways in which the baby, the child, the adolescent, and the adult come to know the world that surrounds them in its many salient dimensions.

Piaget's special interest in knowledge was soon complemented by the empirical realization that the processes by which knowledge is gained are entailed within some much broader processes of psychological development. He found knowledge to develop through coordination of the schemas which were the stable, general mental constructs set up through the interactions of the individual with his environment.[25] Consequently, the path toward a general and coherent genetic epistemology seemed to lead through thickets of problems concerned with the development of capacities to coordinate schemas and with the establishment of schemas and relationships among them through the active engagement of the environment. In struggling with these problems, Piaget worked out the frame of reference which we will call the psychology of intelligence. Although Piaget has also made important contributions to a variety of other related fields—genetic epistemology itself, perception, and affective psychology being perhaps the principal ones—our present effort to develop linkages with the theory of action will be concerned mainly with the psychology of intelligence.[26]

The concern with knowledge had become a very general concern with the developing individual's active interrelation with his environment. With his early background in biology, Piaget formulated his enlarged problem area as one of the individual's adaptation to his environment. Mental life and its qualities of intelligence were treated as a form of the organism's adaptation.[27] Mental activity was interpreted as an evolutionary emergent which, compared with physicochemical life, provided effective adaptation over greater distances, more complicated problems, and more diverse contingencies. Intelligence became the capacity to equilibrate behavioral interaction with the environment through the use of various operations.

In treating intelligence as a capacity for organization which extends the functional adaptation of the organism, Piaget also took over from biology a theoretical basis for distinguishing levels or degrees of intelligence. An individual's behavior could be said to be more intelligent as the set of operations by which it attained equilibrium in its active relations with its environment became more complex.[28] In this sense, greater intelligence would provide a larger manifold of alternative actions for attaining more diverse goals under a broader range of conditions without upsetting the internal organization of the behavioral system. In general, the schematic and operational complexity of the behavioral system would seem to be the major determinant of intelligence or adaptive capacity at the level of action.

While quite consistently maintaining the coherence of his frame of reference by deriving more specific conceptions from the foregoing general notions, Piaget has experimented with extremely diverse and ramified subjects related to the development of intelligence. The major thrust of his investigations has been to demonstrate that there are distinct stages in the ontogenesis of intelligence and that the developmental sequence through the stages is invariant, i.e., universal.[29] Establishing this very general point has required myriads of experiments that test sequences of developmental change with respect to particular domains of behavior and then examine similarities in the sequences across different domains. Thus, Piaget's works have concerned the evolution of children's conceptions of objects, motion, changes of form (as in the famous conservation experiments), words and symbols, numbers, moral rules and judgments, and many other matters. Moreover, the same concrete matters have often been explored at different levels of structuring—for example, not only the development of a child's ability to understand, follow, or sanction according to particular rules is studied but also his ability to integrate systems of rules in ways that provide a generalized justice or fairness. The basic frame of reference has been filled out by an extremely complicated mosaic of empirical studies covering a wide range of particular topics and a variety of levels of theoretical analysis. The sociologist must admire not only the way in which theoretical argument is expounded, clarified, and demonstrated through reference to a wide variety of empirical examples but also the way in which such extremely diverse material is tied together by such tightly synthesized theory. Methodologically, we tend to attribute these qualities of Piaget's work to the clarity and coherence with which his focus on intelligence defines a principal frame of reference directly subordinate to that of action itself.

If the foregoing judgments about the generality and integrity of Piaget's frame of reference are correct, they raise a fundamental problem of how the vast body of work accomplished by Piaget and his associates should be related to the four-function analysis of action. Our solution to this problem rests in part upon our views concerning the differences between Piagetian psychology of intelligence, on the one hand, and certain key reference points in the psychological theories that have previously been included within the general theory of action synthesis, on the other hand, notably Freudian personality theory, the Dollard-Miller version of learning theory, and the theory of the behavioral organism.

Initially, it may seem tempting to argue that the psychology of intelligence, of cognition, or of learning should be treated as a subfield of personality psychology. During the fifties and perhaps into the sixties, it seems to us, the major efforts to synthesize a general psychology out of various materials from the traditions of post-Freudian personality theory and of academic learning theory tried some variant of this approach. In Parsons' treatments, selected hypotheses from the Dollard-Miller type of learning theory were used to explain the mechanisms by which internalized structures of object-relations are established and interrelated within the personality system.[30] A crucial supporting link in this synthesis—the importance of which in many contexts we would not wish to challenge—was the dynamic relationship that was developed between the sociologically central concept of sanction as a support of equilibrium in interaction and the psychologically central concept of reward as a support of motivational equilibrium. In some respects, however, this theoretical synthesis adopted a sharply reductionistic stand vis-à-vis matters of intelligent operations of the actor. Thus, there was little appreciation of the extreme complexity of the operations of intelligence which are necessary conditions for the functioning of personality or of the need for explaining the ontogenesis of these capacities in the individual in detailed, yet systematic ways. To some degree, intelligent operations and their development were said to follow the contingencies of reward in ways which would not seem to allow for their autonomous organization in a systematic fashion and which have been shown by Piaget not to account for the general structures of intelligence,[31] even if they account for the use of certain intelligent capacities upon certain occasions. Finally, little attention was given to a broad range of problematic intelligent abilities which must be at the disposition of the

actor in human society, e.g., knowledge of language and its use, of motion of objects, and of logical constructs in the culture. To us, this reductionism foreclosed analysis of a broad range of problematic phenomena of action, and we are inclined to believe this foreclosure inherent in any effort to link intelligence and learning too closely to personality. We have therefore been very impressed by the degree to which the history of psychology in the past decade or so has shown a growing split between "cognitive" and personality psychologies. Indeed, the split seems to be growing just as the older reductionistic, positivistic, associationalist psychologies have been losing ground.

We propose, then, to accede to the tendency for the fields of "cognitive" and personality psychology to move somewhat apart in order to prevent the subject matter of either from becoming somewhat *reduced* to that of the other. We regard this conceptual differentiation as having a status somewhat akin to the differentiation between social and cultural systems within sociological theory. An earlier, more crudely developed theory could adequately speak of sociocultural systems, but current theory must insist upon some basic distinctions between social and cultural systems with regard both to their organizational principles and characteristics of their dynamics.[32] Neither social nor cultural systems can be reduced to the other without substantially impoverishing analysis of a very broad range of issues. We intend to make the same type of claim for the relationships between the psychological systems of intelligent operations and of motivation and affect. Of course, we do not deny that there are dynamic relationships between these two classes of psychological system such that states in one system may be in important part responses to states in a system of the other type. Rather, we affirm that dynamics of this nature comprise matters of the first order of importance for the general organization of systems of action. They should be analyzed at the general action level, where recognition of the functional autonomy of both personality systems and systems of intelligent behavior can be made a major theoretical premise and where relationships with the cultural and social systems must also be treated as problematic.

We may gain some perspective upon the relations between Piaget's frame of reference and that of post-Freudian personality theory by considering briefly some of Piaget's discussions of Freud and of the affective capacities of individuals. Piaget's critique of Freud's work on dreams, symbolism, and the unconscious may comprise our most important source.[33] Piaget begins by noting his acceptance of much in the general framework of Freud's treatment of dreams, fantasy, and symbolic products such as art. Thus, he agrees that only a surface meaning is given in the manifest content and that an underlying latent content tells the true significance of the dream or other symbolic product. He also approves of Freud's analysis of the various ways in which latent content is transformed into manifest content, such that it remains satisfying of certain wishes yet avoids bringing the threatening nature of the wishes and satisfactions into consciousness. Finally, Piaget agrees that the issues and themes of wishes, satisfactions, threats, and defenses revealed in the dream work are structured by very fundamental components of the psychological system as developed through the individual's life experiences. Piaget's criticisms of Freud concern principally the apparent assumption that the symbolic processes of the personality operate through practically limitless intelligent capacities. For example, it is assumed that any experiences which cannot be remembered, even experiences of early childhood, have been repressed. Piaget argues that memory must be treated strictly in developmental terms, with no more capacity for memory being attributed to an individual than could have characterized his ability to schematize experiences at the time of the events in question.[34] On this basis, the recollection of even crucial childhood experiences can be expected to show indications of selectivity, low levels of generality, poor articulation with other schemas, egocentrism, and the like in subsequent memory, quite aside from questions of censorship and repression. Broadly, the same point about limitations on intelligent capacities can also be made with respect to the process of symbolization itself. Long developmental processes stand behind an adult's ability to form symbolic products which are rich in their significant references and subtle and complex in their transformational structures. Children, and adults recollecting childhood thoughts, must be expected to produce simpler types of symbolization. Moreover, it is important not to attribute the fuller range of adult symbolic meanings to constructs recollected from childhood—e.g., the symbolic meaning of relations with parents is very much simpler in early childhood than later, and later meanings should not be read back into the early relationships.[35] Piaget would argue that Freud committed the error of attributing later meanings to earlier symbolizations in his discussions of the nature of the Oedipal-stage boy's attachments to his mother. The foregoing criticisms, Piaget claims, may provide the basis of substantial change in the theory of repression and censorship in general. Here, we may leave such matters moot. We agree, however, that Piaget has shown that the Freudian theory of symbolic process must be used with much greater qualification and caution than has been common in psychoanalysis. The basis of his critique seems to us to have con-

siderable theoretical specificity, namely, that he treats the intelligent capacities which must become engaged in any process of symbolization as theoretically problematic in a way that entirely escaped Freud's frame of reference. His criticisms seem to be taken less against Freud than besides or in addition to Freud's analysis, and we suggest that they seem to leave the central dynamics about which Freud theorized quite intact. Freud's and Piaget's discussions of dreams and symbolization appear on the whole to be quite complementary, simply treating different aspects of the general subject matter. This complementary relation seems to be the consequence of a more general complementarity between the frames of reference of their respective theoretical systems.

Further evidence of the theoretical validity of a basic complementarity between personality psychology and the psychology of intelligence is perhaps provided indirectly by the treatment of affective development in a recent work by Piaget and Inhelder.[36] They do not treat the emergent affective complexes as a system autonomous from that of intelligent operations, but simply as a special field within it. While they distinguish affective from cognitive development, they argue that affective development can be understood only as intrinsically a part of a broader developmental process organized mainly in terms of the enhancement of intelligence. Thus, the first emergence of object-relations is treated as simply part of the more general process of decentering, but with affective implications. A new stage of affective development emerges when egocentrism is overcome at a representational level, so that some understanding of social relationships can occur in an operational form and the child can engage in social exchanges which are genuinely cooperative. This development is closely bound up with the first construction at an operational level of representations of the rules regulating social relationships. Later, the structures of affectivity and of moral understanding gain much more openness and flexibility as organizations of the possibilities for the individual's projected activities when they become truly transformational in nature. Again, the developmental advance in affective organization is explained as a part of a restructuring of the inclusive system of intelligence. It is our interpretation, therefore, that Piaget and Inhelder attempt to reduce the field of personality development to that of the ontogenesis of intelligence. We agree that developments in intelligence play a very important part conditional to personality development, focusing especially on capacities to form socialized and rule-regulated expectations of others in cooperative social relationships. However, we do not see how Piaget and Inhelder can assimilate the full range of issues concerning the organization of an actor's motivational resources, as treated in post-Freudian personality theory, to their framework. Thus, they do not seem to allow adequately for a conception of an "economy" of cathexis or affect binding the individual to the pursuit of the marginally most satisfying goals through the ongoing course of his projected activities.[37] Their account of the enhancement of decentering through the formation of object-relations seems to fall considerably short of treating fully the ways in which the cathectic complexes established through the Oedipal experiences serve to structure the maturing personality and its stable tendencies to act in motivated patterns.[38] Their analysis of the development of capacities to orient toward normative rules and moral standards seems to overlook the motivational dimension emphasized in the Freudian theory of the superego, i.e., questions of whether the individual will utilize his moral understandings in ways that are self-punitive, manipulative of others, highly principled, pragmatically flexible, and so on. Considerations such as these lead us to conclude that the Piagetian psychology of intelligence must be complemented within the context of a general theory of action by an independent psychology of motivation. There must be a theoretical framework for analyzing individuals' decision-making in systematic terms not only as an intelligent deployment of capacities to perform actions but also as a motivated selection of potentially satisfying pursuits.

The present conception of a system of intelligence diverges considerably from Parsons' conception of the behavioral organism, which has long been treated as the adaptive subsystem of action. In order to establish the theoretical position of the system of intelligence as the adaptive subsystem of action, therefore, we are obliged to criticize Parsons' earlier formulations. As we noted at the outset, a principal problem with these formulations has been their lack of specificity and detail. A clear picture of a primary subsystem of action and its internal complexity and principles of organization has not been presented. Even the accounts of the interchanges between the behavioral organism and the other subsystems of action have not made the basic conception of the system itself very clear.[39] As the boundary between the personality and the behavioral organism has not consistently been conceived to follow the distinction between the learned and the innately maturing, the principal formulation concerning the nature of the behavioral organism has been the conceptualization of its boundary vis-à-vis the remainder of the organism. Here, the emphasis has been upon the highly analytic nature of the conception of the behavioral organism, which has been treated as the part or element or aspect of the organism which becomes involved in the implementation of social behavior.

A contrast is made with the merely "vegetative" aspects of the organism's functioning, i.e., with the aspects which are less directly linked with the distinctively human capacities for meaningful behavior and voluntaristic choice of ends and means.[40] Stress is placed upon the genetically determined "plasticity" of the human organism, i.e., its capacity to become quite variously organized depending on certain characteristics of early formative, socializing experiences. The functioning of the human brain, especially, but also the hand with the opposable thumb and highly detailed nerve controls, bipedal locomotion, and the complex of organs implementive of speech are bound up with the unique behavioral capacities of the human species.[41] Thus, the conception of the behavioral organism has come to include certain organ systems and some physiological processes, especially those involved in brain functioning, within its major categories of structure and organization. Parsons' references to intelligence as the generalized medium of interchange centered in the functioning of the behavioral organism have tended to emphasize more sharply than the more nearly Piagetian usage we will develop that intelligence is a measure of the individual's physiologically organized ability to utilize cognitive ideas. The principal problem we find with this conceptualization of the behavioral organism is that it includes too much within the master concept of "action," or is insufficiently controlled by a sharp formulation of the concept of "action." In Weber's definition of action as "subjectively meaningful behavior" the critical term at present is "meaningful." Only what is organized on a basis of meaningfulness should be included within the action frame of reference directly. Thus, however important the organ systems and physiological processes constituent of human plasticity may be as conditions of the implementation of action, it seems very dubious that they should be treated as directly constitutive of a primary subsystem of action. They are not themselves structured in terms of meaning, as are complexes of motivation or cathexis in the personality, institutions in social systems, or belief structures in cultural systems, and therefore are not functionally coordinate with the categories of structure in the other primary subsystems of action. Piaget's conceptions of schemas and intelligent operations, however, do provide categories of meaning which can be taken as structural to the adaptive subsystem of action.

The possibility of treating schemas and larger complexes of them as the structures of the adaptive subsystem of action suggests, then, that the bulk of the problems heretofore treated as matters of the behavioral organism should be handled as problems of the conditional boundaries of action. The conception of the behavioral organism seems to cut too "low" in the total hierarchy of control and conditions obtaining among all elements that are determinative of concrete behavior. Piaget's formulations suggest that we raise somewhat the level in the hierarchy at which the boundaries of the action system are set, thereby gaining greater consistency in the conceptualization of the action system. We will try to show that this conceptual change can considerably enrich the senses in which sociological matters must be seen as strongly contingent upon interdependencies between social systems and adaptive systems of intelligence.

To be sure, the substantive matters which have been addressed through the conception of the behavioral organism remain important to the theory of behavior at the most general level. The processes of action systems are definitely conditioned upon and implemented through the functioning of human organisms. Our point is simply that the organism as a system should be treated as environmental to action rather than as directly a component of action. As we shall see, this approach makes the "lower" or adaptive boundary of the action system interestingly problematic, for it is necessary to give considerable theoretical attention to the relations between the system of intelligent operations and the environing biological organism. Perhaps, the most important problem at this boundary concerns the structuring of drives within the organism, on the one hand, and the awareness within the system of intelligence of these crucial states of its immediate environment, on the other hand.

We face something of a quandary in selecting a name for the present conception of the adaptive subsystem of action. Parsons' term, the behavioral organism, seems inappropriate given our argument that the "organism" aspect cannot properly be included within the action frame of reference. Our citation of the growing independence of the cognitive and personality frames of reference in contemporary academic psychology might suggest that we should call the adaptive subsystem the "cognitive system". However, this usage would also raise some difficulties of a potentially serious nature. The system which Piaget has subjected to study comes into play with regard to aspects of action which most psychologists would not treat under the heading of cognition. Thus, we have noted that Piaget shows how processes of intelligence become involved in dreaming, in fantasy, in various sorts of symbolization, and in the generation of wishes and expectations.[42] Indeed, we will argue that intelligent operations become involved in the coordination of the meaningful psychological resources for the implementation of all types of action. That is, many types of action can be implement-

ed only through the intelligent coordination of schemas even though neither the activities nor the schemas are "cognitive" in the usual sense. To label the adaptive subsystem "cognitive", therefore, might give rise to important misunderstandings and might seem to accede to the narrowing of Piaget's frame of reference toward what has been regarded as cognitive in American academic psychology, a tendency which has already proceeded too far. It might, then, seem more directly in line with Piaget's own terminology to continue to speak of a system of intelligence or of intelligent operations, as we have done. In places we will, as a matter of convenience, do this. However, our wish to treat intelligence as the generalized medium of interchange anchored in the adaptive subsystem brings this into conflict with the theory of action conventions in terminology — for example, the economy is not formally identified with the monetary system or the system of monetary transactions nor is the polity called the system of power. The theoretical reason behind the terminological convention is that a generalized medium must circulate in systems other than that in which it is centered or functionally anchored. We propose, therefore, to call the adaptive subsystem of action the "behavioral system." This choice has the advantage of providing some continuity with Parsons' terminology. It also emphasizes that the practical problems confronting this system concern the development and articulation of the capacities to implement and coordinate behavior, especially complex projects of behavior in relation to complex environmental contingencies. We wish to cut free of the many reductionistic, atomistic implications that have often been bound up with the use of the term behavior in several disciplines in the field of action. We mean to follow Piaget in attending both to the organization of capacities to coordinate behavior into complex individual systems and to the common, species-related, pan-human characteristics of such complex systems.

In brief, we suggest that the system composed of the meaningful schemas and operations that provide intelligent coordination of behavior should be treated as the adaptive subsystem of action. The very meaningfulness of its principles of organization necessitates its inclusion within the system of action generally. It is distinguished from the personality system, which performs the goal-attainment function for the inclusive action system, in ways that roughly parallel the classic distinctions between thought and feeling, reason and emotion, intelligence and affectivity. The personality system is concerned with the organization of the individual's motivational predispositions, with their cathectic structuring, and with their affective realizations and combinations — in short, with the motivated selection of goals of action. The behavioral system is concerned with the intelligent coordination of the human means of action, the schematic structuring of such coordinative capacity, and the transformational operations by which actions are projected. Thus, the behavioral system organizes the generalized capacity of the acting individual to deal with his environment. The further development of an individual's behavioral system enhances his ability to make intelligent decisions about some class or classes of situation. In socially cooperative action, the behavioral capacities of a plurality of individuals may be aggregated and perhaps enhanced by processes of differentiation and specialization, communication, and mutual exploitation. In this context, the genetic epistemology of human capacities to share the benefits of intelligent operations becomes an important subject matter for sociology.

EMPIRICAL STUDIES OF THE DEVELOPMENT OF INTELLIGENCE

Before embarking upon discussions of the formal analysis of the functioning of the behavioral system, it seems important to provide some empirical embodiment of Piaget's developmental studies. As we have noted, the development of intelligence has comprised the principal topic of Piaget's work. Piaget has been extremely painstaking to ensure that practically every theoretical proposition — and certainly every one of substantial importance — is accompanied by a plethora of empirical evidence. Much of this evidence has been gained through truly brilliant experimental procedures. Indeed, much of the importance of Piaget's work is recognized by some psychologists to derive from his experimental methodology. We would be prepared to argue that sociologists, too, may have much to learn from his empirical methods, although this is a topic which cannot be addressed here. Unfortunately, we can give only a very brief outline of findings of Piaget's developmental research. We cannot even suggest the wealth of experimental materials it encompasses, but can only outline the principal stages of development and give some indication of the sorts of experimental data which have justified the stage concepts. We hope, however, that this brief discussion will clarify somewhat the foregoing remarks on the Piagetian frame of reference as well as provide a basis for a more analytical treatment of the explanation of development in the behavioral system.

The problem of exactly how many stages Piaget has discriminated has been confused by some terminol-

ogical shifts which Piaget made in mid-career and which, we believe, have sometimes been misinterpreted. John Flavell, for example, has argued that there are really only three stages of development. He treats what we are discriminating as the first two stages as two substages of the same stage. This is a consequence of Piaget's statements to the effect that there are only three major stages in the development of intelligence. In a strict sense, this is the case, because intelligence does not emerge until the beginning of what we are calling the second stage. It then can be argued that our first stage is not an autonomous stage in the development of intelligence, but a sort of preparatory aspect of the stage in which intelligence first develops. However, the development of the behavioral system in our present sense clearly has four different stages; and the first stage, even though technically pre-intelligent, plays a very fundamental part in the epigenesis.

At the most general level, setting aside consideration of many substages, Piaget has analyzed the development of intelligent capacities into four primary stages. These stages are: (1) sensori-motor behavior, (2) pre-operational intelligence, (3) concrete operational intelligence, and (4) formal operational intelligence.[43]

Sensori-motor behavior begins at birth and ends roughly with the first acquisition of significant amounts of language sometime around the end of the second year. Probably more theoretical and empirical work has gone into studying this stage than any other.[44] The child is born almost completely disorganized from the viewpoint of functioning at what we are treating as the behavioral level of action. He has a series of instinctual responses such as smiling, sucking, and grasping, and he has a set of primary perceptual mechanisms that can activate the responses in some simple and mechanical ways. Examples of this process would be the way in which the perception of hunger or of some other pain activates a crying reflex or stimulation of the cheek or lips may activate a sucking reflex. These inborn capacities, both reflexive or instinctual and perceptual, provide the primary bases for the development of schemas controlling behavior.

The schemata first emerge as simply capabilities to act or perceive in specific manners. The child's system of schemata is poorly coordinated, providing a very limited range of responses to events. Almost from the moment of birth he begins the effort of extending the capabilities of each of his various schemata. In the beginning each schema seems to operate relatively independently. There is reason to believe that at first he does not see what he grasps or make any effort to grasp what he sees. It is only after some months that any coordination beyond the instinctual level develops between independent schemata. At first he is totally unable to distinguish the environment from himself. He is, to use Piaget's phrase, "egocentric."

There are six substages of development within the sensori-motor period.[45] The first stage, corresponding roughly to the first month of life, is one in which the child is essentially simply testing his reflexes. He will suck whatever object presents itself to his mouth, grasp whatever he can get into his hands, and look at whatever can be focused on. While he will reject those things that produce negative experiences, he does not learn much from them. After a brief period of time, he will repeat the acts which previously produced negative results. While even during the first substage he shows some minor modifications of reflex behavior, it is only in the second month through the end of the fourth month that there is systematic accommodation of any sort. During this period the first coordinations between schemata occur. Also, worthy of note is what Piaget calls a "primary circular reaction." In this, for the first time, the infant shows some awareness of his own behavior, even though in a primitive way. He will make efforts to repeat actions which produced interesting results earlier. He will repeat the same action almost mechanically in a rhythmic manner. In the next stage there are further elaborations of this procedure. The infant seems capable of minor reactions of the behaviors that produced ,nteresting results if such modification becomes necessary in order to reproduce the result. He also shows some eagerness to explore the effect of his behavior on the environment.

Between eight months and the end of the first year, true intentionality of behavior begins to develop. There is much more developed sense of relationship between means and ends in behavior. Thus, for example, when the experimenter hides something which the child wants behind another object, the child can at this point begin to learn to push away the intervening object in order to get the object which he really wants. In the fifth stage the child begins to develop what Piaget calls "means schemata" in which he actively explores the means of attaining something for their own sake. Finally, in the sixth stage, the child begins to work into the pre-operational system of intelligence with the use of symbolic procedures. At this point he is beginning to *represent* the relations between his actions and the external world. Clearly these substages are not distinctly divided from one another. They flow into one another and the distinctions between them are not always clear. Although there seem to be more or less clear

ways of distinguishing the four main stages of cognitive development, one cannot help but feel that the substages are simply heuristic devices for explaining development within stages.

A principal consequence of developments during the sensori-motor stage is that the perceptual mechanisms of the individual, i.e., the linkages between structured schemas and the conditioning, extra-behavioral, physiological processes of perception, assume their basic structural form.[46] While the behavioral abilities to represent, conceptualize, operate on conceptions, and organize patterns structural to the behavioral system continue to evolve, no basic changes in the perceptual mechanisms themselves develop after the sensori-motor period. There is a vast expansion of the things that can be perceived and the ways in which they can be perceived as the child's system of intelligence develops, but this is due not to fundamental change in the pattern of perceptual processes themselves but to the more complex ways in which perceptions can become entailed within schematic operations.[47]

During the sensori-motor period the child often operates on the basis of various cues or indices in the environment. Some indices take on meaning through some interesting interpretations on the part of the child. For example, the child may come to expect dinner — and the satisfaction of his rising hunger — by interpreting the indices involved in the mother's spending time in the kitchen, setting the table, and so on. The sound of running bathwater may stimulate impatience for being allowed to climb upstairs to the bath and to climb into the tub. However, it is not until very late in the sensori-motor period that the child becomes able to symbolize anything. In large part this is due to the lack of an ability to differentiate between the symbol and what is being symbolized, i.e., to understand the meaningful relation of representation. This inability is one aspect of egocentrism, the failure to distinguish at a schematic level what is the child's understanding and what meanings may be externally given. In the sixth stage of the sensori-motor period, the capacity to overcome this form of egocentrism emerges and with it begins the transition to pre-operational intelligence.

The critical capacity of pre-operational intelligence is the ability to represent. The most important development during this period is the initial crystallization of an autonomous system of schemas for generating symbolic representations.[48] This development departs from a diffuse egocentrism, just as sensori-motor development does, and also works toward a more generalized and objectivized understanding of the environment. However, at this stage, it is not simply sensori-motor interactions with objects that comprise the reality to be schematized but representational or symbolic relations among actions and/or objects. Egocentrism of representational perspectives gradually gives way to a capacity to relativize perspectives through the use of representation. An example of pre-operational egocentrism is given in the following experiment:

When Piaget places a child in front of a dollhouse and asks him to depict, with an identical set of figures and furniture, what it would look like were he standing on the side of the dollhouse, the most common response from a young child is to create a view identical with his own. While he can represent the dollhouse, he is incapable of creating a representation in a perspective different from his own.[49] It is worth noting that even here a major change has taken place between sensori-motor and pre-operational intelligence. During the sensori-motor period the child's primitive efforts at representation were entirely expressed in his own motor activity. For the first time, in pre-operational intelligence, the child is clearly representing something internally and then expressing it in his behavior. We seem to have crossed the line between simple intuitive reactions to situations and the primitive use of intelligence.

Another important development here is the ability to operate across time periods much more than was possible during the sensori-motor period. The child no longer lives exclusively in the present. However, it is a primitive type of approach to time. The child considers two separate states of time and simply compares their differences. He is not able to conceive dynamically of the way in which one is transformed into another. It is in this sense that pre-operational thought is static. The child's understanding of causality, which Piaget has tested extensively with experiments on essentially physical processes, is similarly based on static comparisons.[50]

It is very important for purposes of social analysis that the child is unable to represent his own thoughts until late in the pre-operational stage. In part, this is based on a property which Piaget calls the irreversibility of pre-operational intelligence. Intelligent processes are considered reversible by Piaget when, after following a pattern of thought, the child is able to reverse his direction and return logically to the starting point of the thought processes. When reversibility is attained, a large step toward the objectification of thought has been completed because the thoughts can be removed from the very particular contexts in which they were initially embedded and can even be reexamined.[51] Representation of one's own thoughts greatly facilitates the flexible, nonegocentric examination of the thoughts, but can be carried very far only after a reversible understanding

of thought-process has been attained. Where the understanding of one's thoughts is not very fully reversible and objectified, severe limitations are placed upon the qualities of communications with others. One cannot understand in any profound way how one's own thoughts and actions must appear to others. Nor can one fully understand how others view their own thoughts and actions. The extreme degree to which the lack of capacities for objectification may affect interaction has been demonstrated by Piaget's studies of how young (pre-operational) children play with one another. While they may play in the same place and with the same toys quite happily, they do not enter one another's subjective definitions of the situation at all effectively. As they play together, the meaning of the play may be quite different for each child. Each may even explain to the others what is occurring in his play, but the others are not likely to be deflected from their own understandings of the play by such explanations.[52] Thus, the situation of play lacks a common definition in the sense of the organized games of older children or adults. It lacks such a common definition because the participants lack the intelligent capacities to sustain one. Here, Piaget has succeeded in specifying in much greater detail the psychological prerequisites of the ability to "take the role of the other" or to partake in some aspects of the "generalized other" that G. H. Mead stressed so strongly in his social psychological works.

The emergence of representation in the pre-operational period, however, also involves aspects that set the most basic conditions for much more complete objectification of thought and action later in the developmental process. The child's representational schemas soon come to incorporate what Piaget, following Saussure, calls signs, namely representations that have conventionally established meanings. Signs, representing conventional meanings, are distinguished, in Piaget's terminology, both from indices, which can be interpreted but do not stand for meanings, and from symbols, which carry meanings besides or in addition to conventional meanings and are not sheerly arbitrary in meaning (as are signs) but must be metaphorically appropriate to their meanings.[53] Language comprises the principal system of signs which the child comes to internalize. However, he learns to use it in ways that are very flexibly interwoven with symbolic forms of meaning. For example, at the same time that he may learn the sign "doll," he may learn to play with the doll as its "Daddy," thereby invoking the relations in size between himself and the doll as a metaphorical symbol of the more diffuse relations between his father and himself. At a deeper level, such play may involve early processes in the understanding of the emerging "Oedipal" relation from a broader range of perspectives, e.g., that of a "Daddy." Gradually, incorporation of culturally structured beliefs having related symbolic meanings is attained, e.g., in the parental symbolism involved in orientations toward God, teachers, policemen, the President, and so on.[54] At the pre-operational stage, the schemas developed about such signs and symbols are relatively simple. Moreover, the types of relationships which may be generated among such schemas are comparatively simple and inflexible. Recent researches into the acquisition of syntax by young children has shown, for example, that the grammars by which they conjoin linguistic signs are much simpler and cruder than the grammars of adults. From a Piagetian perspective, it is most interesting that the grammars of young children are not just simpler *versions* of adult grammar, i.e., the same grammar with perhaps some of the more complex rules omitted, but substantially simpler grammars that cannot generate quite such complex and variable relations among the constituents of sentences.[55] The differences between adult and child grammars may be quite direct indications of the respects in which pre-operational children have a less penetrating and less objective understanding of the linguistic signs they command —both of the meanings and of the relationships which may be generated among them. Nevertheless, the conventional meanings given with signs do provide children with tools for penetrating to some degree into the subjective outlooks of others in a rather detailed way. As words carry conventional, objective meanings, they can be relied upon to make possible thinking and acting which is intersubjective in at least some dimensions of its significance. Even very complex and ideosyncratic symbolization may be communicable in substantial part through linguistic signs. While the achievements of the pre-operational child in penetrating the intersubjective world are certainly quite limited, he does show a fascination with learning words and with trying to bring them into new combinations with one another.[56] As he becomes able to operate on more abstract and generalized levels of intelligence, his capacity for more profoundly social communication increases with the gains in objectivity and flexibility of his representational schemas.

During concrete and formal operations, the ability to integrate and develop a coherent abstract pattern for a particular schema is created. In the meantime, these functions are performed quite primitively. The process of maintaining stability within the behavioral system, prior to the advent of operations, must be done with the perceptual and representational mechanisms that are at hand. As Piaget says of this type of thinking:

> This type of thinking is Pre-operational, i.e., pre-logical and it differs from concrete operational thought on three points: 1) when the child considers static situations, he is more likely to explain them in terms of the characteristics of their configurations at a given moment and in terms of the changes leading from one situation to another; 2) When he does consider transformation he assimilates them to his own actions and not as yet to reversible operations. We can reduce these two differences to one by saying that at the level of Pre-operational thought the static states of a given system and its modifications do not yet form a single system, whereas at the level of concrete operations the static states will be conceived as resulting from transformations in the same way as the results of various operations are also subordinated to the operations. 3) Nevertheless, even at this level we can find tendencies toward the organization of integrated systems. And we can discern them in the orientation toward certain forms of equilibrium. However, the only instruments available to the subject for the organization of such systems are perceptual or representational regulations, in contrast to actual operations.[57]

The emergence of formal operations also serves the general functioning of the behavioral system by enabling intelligent schemas to adapt to broader ranges of events or actions without having to alter their structural relations with other schemas. The schemas involved in a set of formal operations derive their characteristic stability from a new concern with the lawfulness of events and actions. Occurrences come to be viewed as interrelated in law-like ways. Variations are understood in a systematic fashion through the invoking of various combinations of generalized laws. In this sense, the flux of experience becomes organized schematically into a set of general and stable conceptions. Where a set of formal operations has been fully articulated, any new events or actions within its domain can be understood sheerly by application of the established schemas of laws or generalizations without any ad hoc adjustments.[58]

The schematic stability gained through developments in the periods of concrete and formal operations contrasts sharply with the understanding of occurrences in the pre-operational child. Even though the pre-operational child lacks orientation toward the law-like properties of events, he nevertheless seeks answers to questions of basic causes. Typically, his responses will be personalistic, egocentric, projective, and motivational in nature. Thus, for example, the pre-operational child will claim that the sun moves across the sky because God pushes it, that a piece of wood stays on top of the water because it swims, and so on.[59] The pre-operational orientation to social norms is similarly primitive: In games, rules are learned and used as imitations of older children or adults, and they are not understood to be systematized but are casually invoked as they may help to give meaning to the egocentric play of the child.[60] In neither the understanding of causation nor the orientation to rules can there be an underlying, general stability among the schemas on the abstract plane. The ideas that God pushes the sun or that a specific rule should be used at a particular time are not the products of abstract constructions of the general implications of the concepts of God and of the rule in question. Thus, the intelligent functioning of the pre-operational child is quite severely limited, however great the advances over the sensori-motor period made possible by the onset of representation.

The enhancement of the structural stability of the system of intelligence requires the construction of more abstract, hierarchically superordinate elements of intelligence. This process begins with what Piaget calls the stage of concrete operations. The period of the development of concrete operations begins at approximately age 7 and is frequently completed by about age 11. This stage is important in developing the capacities in the child's thought which provide some stability and coherence among the various elements of a schema. It is fair to say that it is at this point that the child first begins to sound consistently reasonable to adults who listen to him. There are a number of problems which he is not capable of solving, but he does not show the manifest inconsistencies that are apparent in earlier childhood. Unlike the pre-operational child who is concerned only with finding a means to achieve an end, the concrete operational child begins to become very concerned with answering the problem of why something occurs in *generally* satisfactory ways.[61] He becomes concerned with how to establish a consistent pattern of general control over his environment, rather than simply how to manipulate an individual situation for a specific end.

Perhaps the distinction between pre-operational and concrete operational intelligence can best be understood with the aid of some of Piaget's transcripts from his experiments. In one experiment he asked children of various ages and developmental levels to place various objects in a pan of water and explain why they float or sink. Thus, one subject aged 5 years nine months (pre-operational):

> BEZ explains the floating by the weight: *"Why do these things* (previously classified) *go to the bottom?"* — "They are little things" — *"Why do the little ones go to the bottom?"* — "Because they aren't heavy, they don't swim

on top because it's too light." — *"And these?"* (class of floating objects). — "Because they are heavy, they swim on the water." We go to the experiment: The key sinks, "Because it's too heavy to stay on top." Whereas the cover sinks, "because it's light". Comparing two keys: The larger one does not stay above the water, "because it's light" — *"And the little one?"* — "It will go to the bottom too." — *"Why"* — Because it's too light." [62]

The subject here clearly has the idea that the weight of the object has something to do with whether or not it floats, but he has no general or stable basis for tying one representation in with the other. In concrete operations, the child develops a much more organized picture of the reason some things float and some things sink. However, the concept of specific gravity, necessary to explain the property of sinking or floating of any object, eludes him. His thought is grounded in the specifics of the situation, in the "concrete" empirical world. Thus, a child successively tries such factors as weight, composition of the object, and form of the object in an effort to explain, but he fails because he cannot sufficiently abstract from the situation. Thus:

> BAR (7 years, 11 months) first classifies the bodies into three categories: Those which float because they are light (wood, matches, paper, and the alluminium cover); those which sink because they are heavy (large and small keys, pebbles of all sizes, ring clamps, needles and nails, metal cylinder, eraser); and those which remain suspended at a mid-way point (fish). *"The needle"* — "It goes down because it's iron". — *"And the key?"* — "It sinks too." — *"And the small things?"* (nails, rings, clamps). — "They are iron too." — *"And this little pebble?"* — "It is heavy because it is stone." — *"And the little nail?"* — "It's just a little heavy." — *"And the cover, why does it stay up?"* — "It has edges and sinks if it is filled with water." — *"Why?"* — "Because it's iron." [63]

Here the child is capable of making the general categories and makes a clear effort to resolve the contradictions which he finds empirically. However, in an effort to resolve these contradictions, he goes back and forth between talking about the specific gravity of types of objects (this is what he is saying when he says something goes down because it is iron), and talking about the weight of the object. Even if he can find an empirical solution, the child is unable to formulate in lawful terms the concepts necessary to solve the problem. This is the concrete operational child's most consistent failing.

Critical among the new capacities that develop during the concrete operational period is the reversibility of cognitive processes. Simply stated, the child can now trace his own thought patterns and reverse them. A complete understanding of this concept necessitates the understanding of the logical properties of what Piaget calls "groupings" and the logical organization of concrete operations in general. There is not sufficient space to go into these in any detail. Piaget maintains that the properties of the logical system which he calls the grouping closely approximate the organization of the child's cognitive processes during concrete operations.[64] In other words, the grouping is an ideal type or model of concrete operational thinking. Logically, it is derivative from two systems of mathematical models, groups and the lattices. From the logician's point of view, the most obvious property of the grouping is its sloppiness and uneconomical structure. The assumptions are partly contradictory and necessitate a series of qualifications in order to eliminate contradictions. From a psychologist's point of view, the most interesting property of concrete operations is probably their concreteness. That is, groupings do not *generate* categories that are not present in the immediate reality except in the most limited way. The two major types of logic involved are what are called class inclusion and serial ordering logic. As Ann Parsons has put it, class inclusion operations

> relate to the child's ability to manipulate part-whole relationships within a set of categories. In order to define the operations in the class inclusion, logicians use the terms addition, subtraction and multiplication. . . Two classes can be added up so that they are included in a larger one: boys plus girls equal children; children plus adults equal people—i.e. $A + A_1 = B$. By the same token, a part can be subtracted from the whole: people minus adults equal children. When the child can do this systematically, reversibility is present in that when the child needs to generalize or discriminate he can pass from a part to the whole and back again.[65]

Serial ordering operations concern such things as the recognition that if *A* is greater than *B* and *B* is greater than *C* then *A* is greater than *C*. It allows the child to arrange objects systematically along any quantitative continuum. It must be emphasized, however, that these are structures for ordering present reality, not structures for generating possibilities. These develop only in the next stage, that of formal operations.

If we believe Piaget, around the age of 12 and continuing until at least the age 16, the child begins to develop the most broadly equilibrated set of cognitive structures, known as formal operations. While concrete operations are concerned with the manipulation of empirical data in order to solve problems, formal operations develop the logical possibilities inherent in any data. Formal operations are essentially hypothetical and deductive. Reality is seen as the empirically present aspect of possibility.[66] It is particularly important to remember when considering formal operations that Piaget is not saying that all thinking from adolescence on goes on under

a formal operational model. He is saying that at this point the individual develops the *capacity* to think in a formal manner. He develops the capacity to think in a way which we usually loosely call "logical." He is capable for the first time of delimiting a universe of possibilities, setting up a series of hypotheses about which of these possibilities actually exist, and establishing criteria and tests for empirically ascertaining which exist. This is not to say that in reality most of the time the individual's thinking closely approximates this ideal-typical model. To make such a suggestion would certainly be to oversimplify the complex realities involved, and to overidealize the nature of most practical thought and behavior. Research currently being conducted by Charles Lidz indicates that indeed most discussion and interaction conducted among even highly educated people does not conform very fully to the model of formal operations. Most of Piaget's studies have been concerned with an individual's efforts to solve rather clearly delineated problems of physics, geometry, or chemistry rather than moral, philosophic, or social problems. Many domains of thought, however, may lack the clarity and closure of abstract constructs which seem to comprise prerequisites of full systematization of thought upon the level of formal operations. The projection of the capacity for thinking in terms of formal operations into these domains may, therefore, fail to achieve the same type of equilibrated complex of operations that can be attained in domains such as geometry or algebra or physics. Piaget's discussion of the ways in which adolescent thinking on moral or ideological issues tends to become romantically idealistic or cynically pragmatic, i.e., lacking in balance in its efforts to accommodate both principled orientation and concern with practical issues, may be regarded as one demonstration of this possibility.[67] We would suggest that the difficulties of obtaining a formal operational understanding of complex social and moral issues continue to be formidable even for well-educated adults. Nonetheless, it remains perhaps the premier characteristic of the intelligent capacities of at least many individuals past their adolescence that they are able to think in formal operational terms across some domains and will attempt to develop a formal operational understanding in others. Here, the conception of formal operations, like that of concrete operations discussed earlier, is defined by an ideal typical mathematical model. In this case, the model is based on the logical concepts of lattice structure.[68]

We cannot here explore the many important characteristics and dimensions of formal operations in the strict mathematicized sense. Perhaps we can, however, suggest the senses in which the individual's intellectual quest for necessity and lawfulness is critical to the stability of the operational system and, indeed, the structuring of thought in general. Probably the best illustration of the construction of formal operations and the role therein of the ideas of necessity and lawfulness is given in Piaget's experiments with billiard balls.[69] The child is given a billiard cue-like instrument which is fixed in its place on one of the cushions of a billiard table but which can be rotated to form any horizontal angle desired. The child is then given a ball and told to bounce it off the adjacent cushion to hit something on the same side of the table as the billiard cue. To solve successfully the problem of how to hit things at various points on the side of the table opposite the cushion, the child must understand that the line which the ball makes going from the billiard cue to the cushion produces an angle with the cushion identical to the angle created when the ball goes from the cushion to the object aimed at. The pre-operational child cannot solve this problem, although he may occasionally manage to hit the target object by acting on a more or less intuitive basis. The concrete operational child does learn how to solve the problem. He figures out that he must aim so as to make the angles equal. He is not, however, capable of understanding that these angles are of necessity equal. It is only during the stage of formal operations that the individual becomes capable of making a law-like statement to the effect that the angles will be equal. Only then does he understand that the law has the kind of reality which transcends the specific situation.

It should be noted that experiments such as this one seem to indicate that a formal operational understanding of occurrences within a specific field of empirical phenomena can generally be gained only through — or at the least is very greatly facilitated by — careful observation and experimentation. It would therefore seem all the more difficult to gain formal operational understandings of domains which most directly interest the sociologist, in which the nebulousness of the "ideological" issues and the lack of clear boundaries to the matters at issue make it hard for the individual to conduct clearcut thought experiments. The well-structured domain of mathematics, although abstract in a way not very different perhaps from the domain of expectations, normative understandings, and ideological beliefs, permits many more clearcut determinations to be made upon the hypothetical or theoretical plane and thereby provides much stronger support for efforts to gain a formal operational understanding. Only where quite special institutional supports operate, as in the procedures for appeal within the court system,[70] can the sociologist make a strong presumption that

normative orientations are being utilized in a formal operational manner with a high degree of closure and determinacy.

BASIC CONVERGENCES

Against the backgrounds of the previous sections of this paper, concerning formal similarities between Piaget's work and the theory of action as well as the function of intelligent operations within action systems and Piaget's researches on the development of intelligence, we may now consider some basic convergences between the two theories with respect to the nature of explanation. Here we will focus upon the ways in which the development or evolution of changing systems is explained. Our central point will be that there is a very important convergence on a special sort of functionalism, which establishes some remarkable parallels in the theoretical structures of explanation despite many differences in terminology and theoretical content.

We have already noted that the four-function paradigm of the theory of action is based upon a special grounding of the conception of function in a formal analysis of the idea of system. It is the direct relation between system and function that enables the theory to employ its functional concepts in formally similar or parallel ways whenever it is legitimate to invoke the concept of system. Although Piaget's scheme of functions or "functional invariates" is not quite so refined or carefully formalized, it, too, consists in an analysis of systematic relationships rather than an ad hoc list of functions.[71] Consequently, Piaget is also able to apply his basic functional categories across a great many fields of distinct content or material. The mode of theoretical generalization directly parallels that of the theory of action, resting on the derivation of universal categories of function from the concept of system in a way employed by no third body of theory within the action domain, so far as we know. Given this very fundamental convergence on the treatment of function, it should prove fruitful to search for some underlying common elements among more specific formulations that may appear on first examination to be quite divergent.

In Piaget's formulations, a system operating in an environment is characterized by two functional invariates, "organization" and "adaptation." These may be regarded as two independent aspects or dimensions of the interrelations of components of any system. The equilibrium of the system requires that both organization and adaptation be adequately served through the modes of interrelation of system components.[72] In a way strikingly parallel to Parsons' treatment of one parameter of the four-fold table of his functional paradigm, Piaget designates organization as the internal function—having to do with the stable relations of components strictly within the system—and adaptation as the external function—having to do with relations between system components and environmental factors.[73] Adaptation can then be broken down into two parts, which Piaget terms assimilation and accommodation. Assimilation is the process by which "all the given data of experience" become incorporated within the schematic complexes of the system. Accommodation is the obverse process by which the system or components within it become adapted to the data of experience. Empirically, action involves variable mixtures of these two adaptive processes in a dynamic equilibrium.[74] Over the long run, a system must equilibrate both its processes of adaptation with its environment and the two processual aspects of adaptation with each other. Only in the limiting cases of fantasy, which is interpreted as pure assimilation without admixture of accommodation, and imitation, which is regarded as pure accommodation without admixture of assimilation, does intelligent functioning become dominated by one aspect of adaptation or the other.[75]

It may initially seem attractive to work out some direct correspondences between Piaget's functional invariates and the four-function paradigm. Thus, accommodation might be identified with adaptation in that it seems to be the essential process for developing resources which can be practically effective within the environment of the system. Assimilation might be identified with goal attainment in that both are concerned with how the system can benefit from specific states or conditions present in its environment. Organization might then be treated as a more diffuse formulation of the functions of integration and pattern maintenance. However, such correspondences can be drawn only at the cost of much distortion in the meaning of the technical terms involved. For example, realistic accommodation would seem to be an essential characteristic of the means and procedures for selecting, ordering, and implementing goals if goal attainment functioning is to be effective. Similarly, adaptation must involve the assimilation of resources or potential resources available in the relatively immediate environment to the priority operations of the system or it will certainly be very costly and inefficient functioning.

A better starting point for drawing correspondences between the two functional theories would seem to be reconsideration of Piaget's distinction between the external and internal functions. It seems necessary to us to qualify Piaget's formulation that adaptation is the external function and organization the internal function. Although this is certainly true if each complex of schemata and operations is considered independently, it may not always be the case for an entire system of behavioral or intelligent functioning. Thus, one of Piaget's subcategories of assimilation (which is, of course, an "external" function) is "reciprocal assimilation." This is the process whereby two schemata or subsystems composed of any number of schemata assimilate to each other by the construction of various new connections between them.[76] Thereby, a reorganization takes place such that previously uncoordinated schemata become coordinated with each other. For example, in the first few months of a child's life, he is unable to coordinate the use of his hands and eyes. After a certain point, the child gradually develops the ability to locate the things he manipulates in his visual field and to manipulate the things he sees. Clearly, an assimilatory development of this type is not "external" with reference to the entire system of intelligent operations. With respect to that system, an internal reorganization has occurred. The development is external only with respect to each of the original, uncoordinated schematic complexes or in the sense that all intelligent functioning is "external" in its contributions to the general action system. The point we are making here about reciprocal assimilation could, through further detailed discussion, be extended to what Piaget calls "generalizing assimilation" and to some accommodatory processes. Thus, it does not seem that the common designation of some functions as internal or external provides a basis of correspondence between the two functional schemes.

An alternative approach would be to identify Piaget's contrast between the internal and external functions with the theory of action distinction between structure and process or dynamics. Piaget has come very close to this formulation himself, for example, in saying that "assimilation is hence the functioning of the system of which organization is the structural aspect."[77] Moreover, it is clear that his theory does not permit the notion of organizational processes, and it may be claimed that assimilation and accommodation, though certainly structured, properly consist in dynamic relations among structures and in the emergence of structures, but not in structures themselves, for with pure structure a state of the system passes into the organizational aspect. The occasional references to assimilatory or accommodatory structures would seem to comprise an ellipsis that falls somewhat short of technically precise usage.

If assimilation and accommodation are treated as the central categories of process in a system, they may be seen in a new perspective, though one suggested very much by Piaget's own emphasis upon cybernetic theory.[78] We wish to suggest that the concepts of assimilation and accommodation constitute within Piaget's dynamic perspective on the development of systems a striking parallel to the concepts of "control" and "conditions" which Parsons has developed to emphasize the cybernetically ordered nature of action and which Smelser, without emphasizing the terms, has employed so effectively in his study of collective behavior.[79] To be sure, there have been somewhat different thrusts to the directions in which Parsons and Piaget have taken their respective conceptual pairs. Parsons—and with him Smelser and, less formally, Bellah[80]—has developed the notion of counterbalanced hierarchies of control and conditions that emphasizes the cybernetic importance of the relations obtaining among the structures of a system. Parsons has used these cybernetic concepts most effectively, perhaps, in analyzing major trends of change in social systems which evolve over long periods of time.[81] Smelser has shown that the same structural cybernetics can be useful in gaining a finer-grained understanding of at least some diverse types of shorter-run change. However, he, too, employs the cybernetic concepts principally in structural analysis and moves toward "value-added" conceptions in developing the processual aspects of his argument. Bellah, whose emphasis has perhaps been the closest to the Piagetian one, has stressed the diversity and importance of the functional problems associated with establishing and maintaining the structural nature of the cybernetic controls in systems of action. Piaget's emphasis has been less on the problems of the structuring of control than on the system's need for dynamic equilibration between the two processes of assimilation and accommodation. Consequently, he provides a strong basis for understanding the impact of cybernetic exigencies upon the details of short-run dynamics of a system, though perhaps less adequate grounding than have the theorists of action for analysing the importance of cybernetic principles in determining the long-run patterns of stability in a system. The basic complementarity of these two approaches, one structural and one processual, seems to derive from their common concern with bringing cybernetic concepts to bear upon problems of the development or evolution of action systems.

Piaget's use of the term adaptation derives from the very general usage of evolutionary biology. The central proposition of his theory of adaptation, namely, that a strong adaptation to the environment can be combined with firm integrity of the system only if the processes of assimilation and accom-

modation are in equilibrium, specifies theory of the highest order of theoretical generality. We may regard this very high level of generality as a first similarity to Parsons' concepts of control and conditions. A second similarity is that both pairs of concepts are intended to deal with problems of a system's capacity for, openness to, or resistance against change.[82] Processes of control and assimilation are parallel in that both are "determined" from—or set the analytical perspective upon—the inside elements of the system, especially the very core of it, as it comes to engage aspects of the environment. Thus, when we speak of the assimilation of certain activities to some established schema, we become concerned with the ways in which the schema extends the area of its control to new types of action. The initial reference is the established control of the already existing schema, and analysis moves toward understanding of the increased scope of control. Both control and assimilation stand, in the cybernetic senses, high on pattern and information and low on flux and energy.

By contrast, processes of conditioning and accommodation are parallel in that both are "determined" from or call analytical attention to factors external to the system, or at least external to the sector of the system exercising control, and the ways in which they may have an impact upon the system and its pattern of control. The accommodation of a system or pattern to factors or conditions in its environment involves the ways in which adjustments are made to environmental realities or, conversely, the ways in which the environment penetrates the system and its core patterns of organization. The processes of accommodation and conditioning are both low on pattern or information and high on flux or energy. Thus, a third parallel between the Piagetian and Parsonian conceptual pairs concerns their correspondences in cybernetic theory of informational and energic elements of systems. A fourth parallel involves a certain asymmetry which is built into both pairs of concepts. Just as theorists of action, especially in discussing the long-run evolution of a system, have placed greater emphasis on the hierarchy of controls than on the hierarchy of conditions, Piaget has given a certain priority to the processes of assimilation. Assimilation and control both have a more central foundation in the system and its core patterns than their conceptual partners and therefore must be given the larger part when analysis focuses upon explication of how the particular system functions within its environment. Accommodation and conditioning might be given the priority if analysis were to focus, as sometimes it should, on the characteristics of the set of systems which might emerge out of conditions present within the environment of reference. Taken as a group, these four parallels seem to us to comprise strong evidence that Piaget's concepts of assimilation and accommodation constitute another theoretical scheme for analyzing the same cybernetic realities, but perhaps somewhat different aspects of them, which are the objects of Parsons' hierarchies of control and conditions.

Despite these rather fundamental theoretical parallels, the similarities between the two conceptual schemes may not seem very clear. Perhaps this is to be expected, given the very different substantive materials which Piaget and the theory of action sociologists have subjected to analysis and Piaget's use of a much more experimental, empirically detailed methodology. Yet, it is exactly because the detailed propositions developed out of the two theories have been so different that recognition of their fundamentally similar theoretical groundings should prove useful. The analytical approaches already fruitfully articulated within each may perhaps also prove fruitful in the other. Thus, we might suggest that the theory of action should treat more carefully the dynamic interrelations between the hierarchies of control and of conditions as principal determinants of short-run states of equilibrium, thereby following the analytical path suggested by Piaget's treatments of the interdependencies between assimilation and accommodation. Piagetian theory might similarly gain a broader grasp on certain aspects of system functioning were it to attend more carefully to the cybernetic hierarchies which emerge among diverse types of structures within systems of intelligence. Both the experimental technique and the theoretical emphasis on dynamic formulations which have characterized Piaget's research appear to have obscured some aspects of the organization of systems which might become more evident if a macrostructural perspective were also adopted. In the next section of this paper we will develop some preliminary formulations within a macroanalytical approach to the functioning of the behavioral system.

Piaget's functionalism provides the theoretical basis for his explanation of the development of intelligence. No specific "cause" of development is hypothesized. On the contrary, Piaget recognizes that innumerable specific factors may serve as stimuli to advances in intelligent or behavioral capacities. Moreover, there may be considerable variation among the factors that seem to play the critical parts for different individuals or under different circumstances. Thus, various exigencies of the actor's environment, innate human species characteristics, individual giftedness, elements of internalized culture, practical requirements for specific abilities, and many other factors may be admitted as causative in

some degree. Piaget does not admit, however, that reference to particular factors operating under particular conditions can explain the very general phenomena of development. Rather, he focuses upon analysis of the general characteristics of the dynamics by which the various particular factors gain the capacity to contribute to further development of the system of intelligent operations.[83] In question are not particular causes, but the systemic mechanisms which make developmental change, rather than some other response of the system, possible. Piaget's functionalism is thus associated with a characteristic sense about what is most profoundly problematic and in need of explanation in the field of behavioral development.

In one of its several interrelated theoretical senses, intelligence is defined by Piaget as the form of equilibrium of all the intellectual functions of the individual.[84] This is to say that the point of equilibrium of the intellectual operations of the mind provides the "intelligent" solution to the behavioral problem confronting the actor, i.e., the solution which is the best that the behavioral system can devise with its limited resources. The point of equilibrium is also a state of stability of the behavioral system in its efforts to cope with the changing conditions and exigencies of the environment of action. Piaget contends that the intelligent faculties have emerged by evolutionary processes because they provide individuals and society with greater capacity to deal with a broader range of behavioral problems than can mechanisms operating entirely on the biological or physiological rather than the action level.[85] The development of intelligence on the part of the individual is fundamentally an instance of ontogenesis repeating phylogenesis in the pursuit of higher degrees of adaptation. The growth of the individual's intellectual capacity is the consequence of his search for more effective and stable adaptation within his personal life-environment. Thus, each step in general development of intelligence represents an increase in capacity to provide stable solutions to broader ranges of problems imposed by the meaningfully immediate conditions of action. In order to achieve this, there must be an expansion of the scope of elements brought into the equilibrating mechanisms of the behavioral system. Here, Piaget analyzes the expansion of the intelligence mechanisms in terms of his dynamic theory of assimilation and accommodation. On the one hand, intelligence is enhanced when a larger number of categories of fruitful actions can be assimilated to the behavioral system. On the other hand, the enhancement of intelligence requires that the behavioral system accommodate itself to a broader manifold of the practical exigencies which confront action. It is the capacity to expand the equilibrium of the behavioral system in at least one of these two senses which determines the establishment of a new type or pattern or project of action within the behavioral system. Regardless of what may be the immediate "causes" of an action, developmental analysis must focus upon the specific respects in which its relations with other components of the behavioral system serve to broaden the stabilizing capacities of the basic equilibrating mechanisms of assimilation and accommodation.[86]

Although Piaget's ultimate explanation of development appeals simply and parsimoniously to the effects of a search for greater stability and adaptedness, he is able to specify this general explanation into a much more detailed paradigm for interpreting the results of experiments. The analytic rigor of this paradigm comprises a major source of Piaget's ability to devise strong theoretical generalizations from his experimental data. The core of the theoretical derivation of the paradigm stems from an abstract analysis of the concepts of assimilation and accommodation. Thus, the paradigm consists of a set of dimensions of assimilation and accommodation along which the experimenter can detect comparatively detailed "steps" of development toward greater adaptation. The sociologist will note that there is in the logic of such a paradigm a strong convergence with the current neo-evolutionary approaches to the study of societal development. Both attempt to derive, from functionalist principles, some theoretically general dimensions of development while at the same time allowing for a large number of specific lines or areas of development or evolution that may become realized within the possibilities prescribed by the general dimensions.[87] The categorizations of stages of development or evolution in the two theories also have the same theoretical status, for both describe an epigenetic sequence of major steps in systemic transformation toward increased adaptation. Given these essential similarities between sociological theories of evolution and the theory of the development of intelligence, it might prove fruitful for students of social evolution to examine the Piagetian literature, with its greater refinement in empirical application, for transferable theoretical insights.

Piaget's subcategories of assimilation constitute perhaps the most successful effort to specify dimensions criterial of development from his general functional concepts. These categories are interesting in the present context also because they seem to correspond very closely to Parsons' paradigm of four processes of evolutionary change. Given the difficulties of reviewing all of Piaget's developmental categories within brief compass, perhaps we can best illustrate the potential fruitfulness of interchange between the two theories by outlining the four types of assimilation[88] and their apparent correspondences in the theory of action.[89]

The first type of assimilation is called "repetitive assimilation". A good empirical example is the young child who, upon discovering that a certain action produces a certain response from his environment, will repeat the same action over and over again. Repetitive assimilation is performed solely to strengthen the capacity of the schema or complex of schemas involved to function, and consequently is sometimes called "functional assimilation." It develops the behavioral component as a resource for action and strengthens its place within the total system of intelligent operations. In four-function terms, it seems to involve enhancement of adaptive functioning. Thus, it corresponds quite closely to the developmental process which Parsons has termed "adaptive upgrading" by which resources gain the capacities to meet the more stringent and diverse needs of systems becoming increasingly complicated in internal organization.

A second type of assimilation is what Piaget calls "recognitory assimilation." This process involves the splitting of a schematic complex into two or more functionally different parts so that each differentiated part develops a better fit with a distinct aspect of the environmental realities. A change of this type would seem to enhance goal-attainment functioning most directly and is very close to the process of differentiation, which Parsons' writings on social evolution have stressed so strongly.

A third type of assimilation is called "generalizing assimilation," but it corresponds less closely to Parsons' evolutionary process of generalization than to that of inclusion. Piaget uses the term generalizing assimilation for instances in which the range of events, objects, or actions included in a schematic complex has become extended in the sense that stable orientation is provided toward a greater number or more types, even though there is no other basic change in the structures of the schemas involved. A young child who learns that the game of stacking objects can be applied not only to toy blocks but also to small boxes, tin cans, and old magazines has taken a step in generalizing assimilation. As with Parsons' similar process of inclusion, the advance seems to fall within the integrative dimension of the four-function paradigm, especially in that new modes of interrelation are achieved among actions that formerly were intrinsically diverse in the salient respect, i.e., formerly could not be assimilated to the same schemata.

Piaget's fourth type of assimilation is termed "reciprocal assimilation." This is the process by which formerly independent schemata assimilate each other and determinate connections are constructed between them. This process may seem to be largely integrative and parallel to inclusion in Parsons' paradigms. However, Piaget tends to stress that reciprocal assimilation must involve the generation of new coordinating principles that bring the schemata under a higher level of unity and coherence. Thus, despite some difference in emphasis, reciprocal assimilation seems most fundamentally to coincide with Parsons' conception of the process of generalization. In four-function terms, both processes emphasize the establishment of more general, abstract, and pluralistically open components of pattern maintenance for the salient system.

Finally, it should be noted that the analytical interrelations of the four types of assimilation and the four aspects of evolutionary change are basically the same. Both claim to analyze parts or aspects of major steps of developmental transformation of a system. From one state of equilibrium, through a process of evolutionary transformation, to a new point of equilibrium, all four of the processes schematized in each of the paradigms must occur. Insofar as one or more of the subprocesses have not occurred, the process of change remains in a state of disequilibrium, with its attendant strains and instabilities. Perhaps the major source of dissimilarity between the two developmental paradigms concerns some consistent differences regarding references to the system and the unit levels of analysis — differences which are also evident at other points in the encompassing theories, of course. Piaget tends to focus upon the relations among units within a system, while Parsons tends to emphasize characteristics of the system as exhibited through the actions of its units. As both theories have formalized their treatments of the relations between systems and units of systems, however, it is often easy to transform abstract theoretical statements from one theory to the other, as we have attempted at several points in this section.

Throughout this section, we have been comparing the explanatory structures of Piaget's theory of the development of intelligence and the theory of action, especially the parts of the latter concerned with societal development or evolution. We have noted a number of substantial differences between the theories, even setting aside those due to different empirical methodologies. Perhaps the most important divergence has concerned the emphases of the "functionalist" components of the theories. Thus, Piaget's theory seems to contain no major component analyzing the division of labor and functional specialization emergent among the major constituents of the system, while such analysis is the principal concern of Parsons' four-function paradigm. Piaget's functionalism seems to converge most importantly with Parsons' notion of the cybernetic hierarchies of control and conditions which, however, do articulate with the four-function categories. Despite these dif-

ferences, we have also noted some very important points of convergence, e.g., about a functionalism based on a closed set of functions derived from the very conception of system, about cybernetic concepts of equilibrium in a system, about the derivation of developmental or evolutionary dimensions from the basic functional concepts, about the theoretical status of categories of developmental or evolutionary stages, and about the very content of certain concepts for analyzing changes that enhance a system's level of adaptation to its environment. The scope of these convergent conceptions seems quite remarkable indeed, considering both that the theories have grown almost entirely without direct dependence on each other and that they have been concerned primarily with substantially different aspects of action systems. For us, the convergence seems so massive as to warrant the suggestion that the two theories comprise in fact two components of the same general theory. If there be some exaggeration in this claim, certainly the bases for building the theories into one another — i.e., developing a reciprocal assimilation between the two — must be readily clear. In the final two sections of this paper, we will take up two tasks within this enterprise of reciprocal assimilation. We will apply the four-function paradigm to the macro-analysis of the functioning of the behavioral system. Then we will conclude by briefly indicating some respects in which the Piagetian conception of intelligence and intelligent operations may help to clarify understanding of the interactive processes of social action. Piaget's analysis of behavioral processes seems to us to carry important implications for the analysis of practically all sectors of the action system.

THE BEHAVIORAL SYSTEM AND ITS PRIMARY SUBSYSTEMS

In certain respects, Piaget has contributed a great deal to the understanding of the dynamic relationships obtaining among various specialized sectors or domains within the behavioral system. His researches have demonstrated that a large number of specialized complexes of intelligent operations evolve through the same developmental stages, from sensori-motor origins through concrete or formal operations. Moreover, he has shown that a certain progressive strain to consistency operates in relations among differentiated schematic complexes such that, when a more advanced stage of intelligence is attained within one specialized complex, there arises a tendency to reorganize other sectors of the behavioral system on the basis of the more advanced form of functioning.[90] The system tends to extend its gains in adaptive or functional capacity from sector to sector in ways that make clear that the gains become characteristics of the system, not just of individual sectors. After a certain point has been achieved in the consolidation of the operational forms of a new stage, the enhanced capacities can be deployed in whatever domains of intelligence the older forms of understanding or behavior come under substantial stress. In having established these general points, Piaget has certainly demonstrated a striking functional unity of all intelligent operations, and one with many dynamic implications. Indeed, it is perhaps this functional unity which provides the most powerful justification for our present conception of an integral behavioral system.

Nevertheless, Piaget has not directly posed the question of what functional categories of intelligent operations, and of the organization of intelligent operations, may be treated as generally composing a behavioral system. He seems implicitly to recognize that there are constraints operating upon the functional differentiatedness and specialization of any behavioral system. Thus, he seems to acknowledge that any individual must have certain general categories of abilities, e.g., of entering into social communication about expectations on alters and their normative groundings, of generating realistic orientations to various practical features of the surrounding physical environment, of utilizing a variety of common sign systems, especially language and the like, as behavioral requisites of participation in a general action system.

However, Piaget seems to take the importance of such systemic constraints somewhat for granted. For the most part, his researches have been restricted to considering the specialized domains of the behavioral system independently of one another and outside of the context of membership in an encompassing system, except with regard to problems concerning their structural similarities. Piaget has not taken the possibility of subjecting the systemic constraints to a unified theoretical examination as a point of departure for a general analysis of the functioning of the behavioral system. Yet, from the theory of action standpoint of using the four-function paradigm to analyze all types of action systems into functionally distinct subsystems, theoretical discussion of the nature of systemic constraints affecting the operation of specialized sectors of the behavioral system appears to be a first-priority task. The ensuing discussion is intended to analyze our basic conception of the behavioral system in a way that leads to an initial functional mapping-out of the principal categories of structures and operations that comprise its primary subsystems. This task can be accomplished only through a good deal of reconceptualization of and addition to what Piaget has written himself. It is necessary to emphasize, there-

fore, that our present formulations are in the true sense preliminary: They have not been tested by the type of experimentation which Piaget has established as the standard in this field. However, these formulations do seem to us to offer not only proximate solutions to some general theoretical problems but also some different lines of thought for guiding future experimentation.

Four-function analysis of the general organization of the behavioral system must depart from the postulate, which we have just defended, that the behavioral system functions as one of several types of action subsystem. More specifically, we are treating the behavioral system as the adaptive subsystem of the general system of action. Formally, we may derive from this proposition the consequence that the behavioral system must be viewed as operating within or in relation to four independent categories of environment, namely, the extra-action environment of the physical and biological conditions of action and the intra-action environments of personality, social, and cultural systems. Following recent paradigms in Parsons' works on social evolution, we will treat, as a major aspect of the functional differentiation and specialization among sectors of the behavioral system, each of its primary subsystems as being to a degree specialized about the organization of the boundary relations with one of the four principal environments.[91] The adaptive sector is importantly specialized about controlling relations with the physical and biological conditions of action, including importantly the biological organism of the individual actor in its ecological setting, while the goal attainment, integrative, and pattern maintenance sectors sustain special organizational relations with, respectively, the personality, social, and cultural subsystems of action. Only by bringing together specialized capacities to act in relation to each of these different types of environment is a behavioral system able to function in an integral way over the long run. In discussing each of the subsystems of the behavioral system, therefore, we will attend to what seem to us to be its most important capacities for regulating relationships with the category of environment with which it is most closely involved. Perhaps it is the more sharply defined theoretical conception of an action system operating in a plurality of action environments while maintaining a functional integrity based on the *interdependence* of the constituent specialized capacities that most crucially distinguishes our present notion of a behavioral system from Piaget's concept of a system of intelligence.

We will call the adaptive subsystem of the behavioral system the perceptual sector. By this, we mean to designate something much broader than what psychologists have usually included under the category of perceptual structures and processes. Especially, we mean to focus not merely upon specific perceptions of the immediate surroundings, but upon the entire complex of schemas and operations which provide the individual with his understanding of his natural environment in all its salient aspects. While in the young child all elements of this adaptive complex of intelligence will be closely tied to particular physiological mechanisms of perception, the processes of development involve the construction of more autonomous and more generally stable schemas and operations that provide an abstractly integrated understanding of states of the environment. The functioning of adaptive intelligence then continues to be conditioned upon the operations of the major organs of the senses, most critically the eyes and ears. But in turn the functioning of these organs comes to be regulated at an intelligent level, so that perceptual energies are allocated and perceptual "findings" are interpreted through controlling schemas and operations. At the intra-action, meaningful level adaptive perception is constituted not by particular percepts of the sense organs but by the structural schemas and operative mechanisms that provide intelligent bases of understanding and coordinating percepts.[92] A perceptual subsystem is necessarily comprised of a great many specialized complexes of schemas and operations, e.g., for understanding motion, mass, volume, and shapes of objects, or differences among various species of plants and animals, or means of using tools and mechanical equipment encountered in daily life; and these constituents may be interrelated in a number of different ways. Thus, schematized representations of particular percepts may become: either coordinated with or dissociated from other perceptions; examined cursorily as simple examples of routinely familiar phenomena or carefully studied as anomalies understandable only through a reorganization of schemas; regarded directly in terms of a limited schematic complex or analyzed in terms of a number of independent complexes concerning different aspects of the phenomena or giving different understandings of the same aspect; incorporated into a pre-operational or concretely operational understanding or more fully integrated into a formal analysis; acted upon in an entirely practical way attending only to immediate consequences or taken as the object of reflection through a hierarchy of more abstract considerations. Process in the perceptual sector serves to construct about the sensory percepts more general, inclusive, and penetrating intelligent understandings of the conditions environing projected lines of action.

Among the environments of which the perceptual sector must provide adaptive understandings, one of central theoretical import is the internal physio-

logical environment of the individual. The physiological equilibrium of the individual organism is fundamentally dependent upon certain coordinated processes at the action level, often involving various alters as well as the actor of reference. For example, sufficient food and drink must be supplied through action to sustain the organism's energy, and care must be taken that organ systems are not seriously damaged in the course of the individual's behavior. Through what have been called drive mechanisms, indexes are provided by physiological processes of the degrees of the organism's various needs at a given time. Thus, such feelings as hunger, thirst, sexual need, and pain are sensory percepts of states of physiological disequilibrium requiring some behavioral remedy.[93] These percepts provide conditional bases about which behavioral schemas of response to physiological needs are constructed with the development of intelligence. The baby cries reflexively when he senses hunger or thirst, leaving it to others to provide means of satisfying the needs. With the onset of representation, the child learns to interpret the sensations and cooperatively to ask others for assistance in fulfilling his needs. In the operational stages of development, the ability is gained not only to anticipate bodily needs and to plan for their satisfaction, but also to interrelate the means for satisfying various needs with one another and with other factors determining projected behavior.[94] Thus, although the processes may be largely preconscious, behavioral attention to the fulfillment of drives depends fundamentally upon intelligent capacities to organize very complex schematic representations of need sensations. Moreover, these id-related capacities are necessarily quite continuous and interdependent with various other capacities involved in the selective planning or projecting of behavior in scarce time and space and in relation to scarce means.

We are thus insisting that certain "cognitive" intelligent capacities play a crucial role in the general processes of the motivation of action. We treat the principal complexes of emotion and affect organized upon a meaningful symbolic level and serving directly in the choosing and ordering of action goals as constituents of the personality system. Following Parsons, we conceive the id in comparatively narrow, functionally specific terms as the sector of the personality, comprised of affective elements, involved in organizing goal-attainment so as to ensure that projected lines of action will serve, "actually" or symbolically, to reestablish situations which have proven emotionally satisfying in the individual's developmental past.[95] Constituents of the id, then, will operate to establish as goals opportunities to act in ways that satisfy, for example, dependency needs or strivings for achievement or rebellious tendencies. Yet, this sector of the personality must function in some coordination with the extra-action processes generating the physiological needs of the organism. Otherwise, the affective or emotional and physiological needs of the individual would tend to "drive" the processes of concrete behavior in severely conflicting directions. A crucial function in coordinating the satisfaction of physiological needs with the affective-emotional operations of the id is served by the perceptual sector of the behavioral system. This system in a sense incorporates physiological need within the action system by developing representations of internal states of the organism at the meaningful, schematic level where operative processes can link them into the goal-planning of the personality, especially of the id. Only if organismic needs are represented within intelligent operations can patterns of action be planned and coordinated in ways that blend the satisfaction of drives with the attainment of such other goals as the enjoyment of a desired style of life, occupational attainments, marital and parental relationships, and so on. Although there are certainly a number of important differences between the adult id and the id of a child, a principal one is that the adult id relates to its immediate physiological environment through a perceptual system organized on the operational levels of intelligence.

We are thus distinguishing three different systems within the broad area of functioning which has generally been designated "id": the physiological system of needs and drives, the behavioral or intelligent system of the schematic representation and organization of needs, and the sector of the personality motivated toward the recapturing of emotionally satisfying situations. All three become intimately linked with one another in the ongoing processes of the motivation of action. Here, we are emphasizing the importance of the intelligent capacities to involve problems of drive satisfaction in the projecting of action which can attain goals that are diverse and "overdetermined" in the sense of being organized at many motivational levels. Freud, of course, understood at least something of the importance of such intelligent capacities. Thus, he emphasized the difficulties of bringing the needs associated with the various erogenous zones coherently together so that a unified motivational pattern could operate without too severe repression of any of the basic sets of drives.[96] At times, he seems also to have realized that sublimation of drives, essential to the orderly fulfillment of needs and the avoidance of the domination of wide ranges of action by particular drives, could present difficulties of an intellectual as well as an affective-cathectic type. What is perhaps new about our present proposals, aside from simply greater stress upon the intelligent factors,

is the suggestion that the intelligent perception and organization of drives at the action level is accomplished by schematic and operational complexes within the behavioral system concerned with the understanding of the conditional environment in general. We are perhaps also being somewhat unorthodox in insisting that the basic means by which needs and drives gain entry to the action system should be treated simply under the category of perception and as complexly interdigitated with other perceptual processes. We do not take this position in order to deemphasize the importance of physiological needs as conditional determinants of action, however. On the contrary, we believe that only an analytical approach which treats the awareness of drives and the planning of ways to satisfy them as embedded in intelligent operations having very considerable openness and flexibility of combination with a broad range of other types of behavioral controls can approach theoretical adequacy in accounting for the diverse and subtle ways in which needs may penetrate into processes of action.

It may be objected that the parts of the perceptual sector involved in the schematic representation of the bodily needs seem not to become so fully engaged in the "adult" mechanisms of formal operations as do other of its major constituents, hence that they should not be treated as fully parts of the same system. Here, it would seem helpful to attend to what may be a parallel case at the social system level, namely gift exchange.[97] In modern societies, gift exchange is certainly a much less generalized procedure of both the circulation of resources and the reinforcement of solidary ties than the major market and influence mechanisms. Nevertheless, the circulation of gifts continues to have substantial economic and integrative significance in the society. Moreover, its importance can be understood only through analysis of the ways in which the buying and giving of gifts articulates with the economic markets and especially with the structuring of solidary ties. Most gifts are bought over economic markets and consist of goods which are made available only through the diversified productivity of a modern economy. Gifts are generally exchanged within *gemeinschaftlich* relationships which, even in modern societies, remain quite central not only to the entire structure of solidary ties but especially to the loyalties of the individual. We would suggest that some strikingly parallel considerations apply to the ways in which schematized representations of bodily needs become articulated into the larger perceptual sector of the behavioral system. Although often not so highly generalized in themselves, such representations become effective in the determination of specific lines of action predominantly through their linkages with more generalized mechanisms in the perceptual sector.

Very generalized understandings about the nature of the entire conditional environment may be involved in the perceptual construction of manifold possible lines of action for satisfying needs. That is, the more general the understanding of the environment and of the effects of various different activities within it, the more diverse may be the perceptions of ways in which needs may gain satisfaction. Thus, the practical consequences of given perceptions of drives or need states for the planning and projecting of action are determined importantly through linkages with highly generalized parts of the perceptual sector. At the same time, there are crucial functional consequences of the less generalized, somewhat egocentric nature of the individual's perceptions of his own bodily needs. First, the awareness that certain regularizable patterns of behavior can provide comparatively secure assurance that needs will be satisfied serves to crystallize routines and habits that reduce the perceptual complexities involved in planning everyday action. Second, more fundamentally, the continual input of need or drive representations into the perceptual sector, through their at least partially egocentric form, serves to "locate" the individual actor within his environment, so that he cannot long remain disinterested as to *whose* needs are being served by projects of action. Despite the formally decentered nature of the more generalized understandings within the perceptual sector, then, there remains an essentially egocentric perspective for the calculation of the consequences of action grounded within perception of needs. Some such element of egocentricity is obviously a critical guard to the protection of the individual's capacities to act. Formally, we may regard this egocentricity as strictly parallel to the particularistic structuring of loyalties within ramified networks of solidarity by *gemeinschaftlich* ties.

The goal-attainment subsystem of the behavioral system may be called the interpretive sector. The fundamental type of intelligent ability operating within the interpretive sector involves the coordination of the various resources of the behavioral system into organized projects for action. Projects for action in this sense carry the significance not only of being articulated plans for future action but also of comprising the manifold of alternatives for action from which motivated choices must be made. In both respects, the functioning of the interpretive sector must be "realistic" in a special sense: It must engage within its operations "truthful" representations of the diverse factors that affect, more fundamentally than just how available means may be used to lead to certain goals, how various possible ends, when articulated into practical projects, sustain their status as desirable goals of action. In short, it must keep action within bounds where it is realistic

not only in relation to the environment world but also in relation to the inner world where practical and meaningful satisfactions must be produced.

The controlling dimension with respect to which the interpretive sector must function realistically is the intra-action one. The composition of projects for action involves the arrangement of intricate patterns and hierarchies in which diverse means and goals are brought into flexible articulations with one another. Complicated projections of alternative means of attaining satisfaction and of the ways in which satisfaction may be hindered, compromised, or foreclosed by particular efforts must be weighed. Operations of this type must in essence be based upon an imaginative form of intelligence, for the root problems in the determination of projects rest upon understandings about the expressive significances of various projected states of action.[98] The generalized constituents of the interpretive sector must be concerned with the comprehension of depictions of various realities from the standpoint of facets of motivational interest in them. Thus, we are here concerned principally with the schemas and operations that organize the use, understanding, and creative generation of expressive symbolization, metaphor, and imagery.[99] These elements of the behavioral system serve to interpret to the actor the expressive significance of his actual or potential engagements in particular lines of action, individual or collective.

We have already noted that the goal attainment sector of the behavioral system is importantly specialized about adaptation to the personality system as a primary environment of behavioral functioning. The nature of this adaptation is quite complex. A principal factor is that the expressively symbolic qualities of the main constituents of the interpretive sector may be understood to derive from the need of the behavioral system to understand and communicate with an environment that is motivationally and affectively organized. The personality system functions to set the goals of action processes at the most general level, so the behavioral subsystem concerned with the intelligent composition of projects of action must have penetrating means of understanding the nature of goals. In this sense, the interpretive sector functions as a system of self-understanding that serves to assure that patterns of behavior are coordinated in ways that will prove satisfying to the expressively structured cathectic elements of the personality system. Within the hierarchy of control obtaining among all elements of the action system in general, however, the intelligent capacities of the interpretive sector comprise the central category of means that condition the functioning of the personality system. That is, expressive patterning can be given cathectic structuring within the personality system only insofar as, at the behavioral level, there operate intelligent capacities for discerning, utilizing, and generating symbolic relationships. The ability of the interpretive sector to sustain equilibria among multiple symbolic interpretations of the expressive realities implicated in a projected line of action — which is the form of intelligence fostered by the development of operations in this subsystem — determines the manifold of opportunities for cathectic attachment to goals at the personality level.[100] Thus, the complexity and richness of personality organization within any given stage or phase of development is delimited by the schematic and operational capacities of the interpretive sector.

It should be noted that the adaptation of the interpretive sector to its personality environment — analytically, an instance of the interpenetration of constituents of two systems — is importantly affected by relations with two somewhat more distant intra-action environments. First, processes of goal attainment are generally not simply individual, intrapersonal phenomena, but have collective aspects. The personality-level processes involved in the determination of goals are embedded in constraints associated with the establishment of goals at the collective level. Consequently, the behavioral processes of the composition of projects must coordinate with the collective as well as the intrapersonal determinants of the establishment of goals. Priorities among potential goal states must be understood not simply with reference to directly motivational implications but also in relation to the collective exigencies on the utilization of symbolic patterns and standards. Practically, activities must be planned with regard to the ways in which the pursuit of individual goals may be coordinated with collective ends and with collectively organized undertakings. Even where action is not embedded in actively mobilized collective undertakings, however, the projection of activities must be sensitive to collective reactions to expressively meaningful dimensions of the planned activity. Thus, action must be designed to avoid imputations that it is "disreputable" or "disloyal" by the collective standards of symbolic sensitivity or to assure that it will be regarded as "democratic" or "sincere" or "charitable," to cite some simple symbolic constraints. Second, underlying both the intrapersonal and the collective levels of organization of symbolism is the environment of expressive culture. The cultural patterning of expressive symbolism establishes the general framework of meanings within which or in terms of which collective, personal, and behavioral processes can create particular expressively meaningful acts under specific conditions. For the interpretive sector, understanding

of the general expressive culture makes available a basic code through which projected actions or the symbolic acts of others can be assigned motivational meaning.[101] Knowledge of expressive culture does not obviate the need for behavioral engagement in the collective and personal environments. The selective organization of specific, circumstantially appropriate patterns of the use of encoded symbolism crystallizes at these levels of functioning, and the behavioral system could not contribute to specific processes of consummatory action without engagement in them. However, the availability of interpretable expressive culture makes it possible for the behavioral system to have determinate means for comprehending the expressive meanings of diverse acts in its field of concern. Its scope of understanding is not limited to processes in which it becomes directly engaged but can extend to all expressive action undertaken in the terms of the same culture. Hence, involvement with expressive culture may vastly enrich the expressive "world" or system of "realities" with respect to which action may be projected.[102] Moreover, it may also make possible a coordination of motivationally salient meanings, through the terms established in the expressive culture, with actors in other respects operating under extremely different practical conditions. In these respects, behavioral involvement in expressive culture is indispensable to the projection of action which is consummatorily involved with distant rather than immediately practical "realities."

For a functioning interpretive sector, the motivational processes of the personality system, the constraints of collective goal attainment, and cultural codes of expressive symbolism comprise three crucial environments to which strong adaptation must be sustained. Hence, the interpretive sector must include, among its principal constituents, representations of the symbolic "realities" in each of these environments. Moreover, in order to be able to compose projects of action, it must be able to develop determinate ways of interrelating the distinct, if interdependent, modes of affecting the projection of action found in each environment. Such constructed interrelationships, then, stand as the particular, circumstantially appropriate products of equilibrating mechanisms that operate upon the schematic representations of each of the major intra-action environments of interpretive functioning. Given the subtlety, scope, and complexity of the schematized considerations which must enter into the equilibrating processes, it appears that an interpretive sector can stably integrate a general equilibrium only on a basis of formal operational capacities. A preoperational or concrete operational basis of general equilibrium would prove to be too literalistic and inflexible in its interpretations of expressively symbolic patterns and too egocentric in its tendency to focus upon particular expressive elements while excluding others from consideration in the projection of action, hence severely narrowing the scope and stability or consistency of the combinatorial processes of projection.

Piaget's account of the ontogenesis of representational activities,[103] although concerned with a type of intelligent capacity that is deployed in various ways throughout the behavioral system, provides important indications about the nature of the development of the interpretive sector. At all levels of development, Piaget focuses upon a dynamic involved in representational activity in which an adapted or equilibrated form of intelligence mediates between tendencies toward primacy of dream, fantasy, or play and tendencies toward primacy of the imitation of externally given realities—that is, between a disequilibrating emphasis on representative assimilation and a disequilibrating emphasis on representational accommodation. Each developmental stage brings forth new possibilities of depth and richness at both the fantasy and the imitation poles as well as at the point of adapted equilibrium. There may be profound and developmentally positive reasons for the individual to behave in ways that emphasize fantasy or imitation rather than adapted representation under many circumstances. Yet, only the capacity to equilibrate an adapted mode of representation can provide the basis for an effective general equilibrium for all types of representative activity taken in the aggregate. Thus, in a brief sketch, we may emphasize the conditions of adapted representation and their development.

Piaget shows that the diffuse matrix from which later representative abilities differentiate consists of what we would term primitive motor projections of action. The adapted form here involves the capacity to utilize a motor schema without abandoning either its assimilative grounding as an enjoyable behavior or its accommodational potential as an effective activity. With the initial onset of representational thinking, schemas must develop the capacity for equilibration not only with respect to the conditions of use and implementation but also with respect to the signifier-signified relation. Thus, there must emerge equilibrated linkages between the meanings of specific signs and symbols and the meanings of the objects, events, or phenomena they represent, i.e., linkages which are not necessarily distorted either towards fantasy or towards reification.[104] With the fuller crystallization of pre-operational thought, the child becomes capable of "intuitional" representational activity. He can then construct complex configurations of meanings, drawing diversely upon the relations of signifier to signified, so that important extensions and decentrations of representational relationships can be achieved under particular circumstances. However, a static, non-reversible quality pervades all intuitional configurations, and relationships derivable from them are lost once the configuration is decomposed.[105] With the emergence of the stage of concrete operations, representational configurations take on a dynamic and reversible nature. When specific configurations are decomposed, the decomposition has a certain analytical quality whereby the constituent relations of the configurations may be retained and operated upon. Indeed, configurations can be transformed into new ones—or interrelated with others—through the use of representational operations. Specific configurations tend to become embedded in more inclusive meaningful projects of action—for example, the child can explain that his drawing and various elements within it should be understood as having significance within some general efforts or programs to interpret features of his life-world in personal terms.[106] The stage of formal operations crystallizes about the intelligent capacity to order operations on the basis of abstract principle. In the representational sphere, this involves the ability systematically to embue specific constructed configurations with abstractly conceived expressive themes and patterns so that they become disciplined, controlled expressions of definite symbolic "points of view." The symbolic product may be "multiplex" in terms of the varieties of references to diverse "realities" incorporated within its configuration, but it is symbolically coherent in the sense of integrating about a construction of a new reality, a new but disciplined statement of the significance of some phenomenal field. Of perhaps more pervasive importance in everyday life is the obverse ability, namely, that symbolic products or configurations can be understood as statements about expressive principles in their bearing upon specific elements of the human condition. The individual attending in formally operational ways to representational configurations of different kinds can "see" in them a variety of expressive principles for interpreting facets of his life world and can abstractly order these principles into an expressive world of his own.

The integrative subsystem of the behavioral system may be called the expectational sector. It serves to integrate behavioral capacities by ordering, selecting, and combining potentialities of action in order to produce situationally specified expectations. It functions to provide specific expectations within a defined situational context. An important standard of reference for the generation of expectations is provided by the generalized normative structures of the social system. It is important here to understand that we are using the term "normative" to mean standards of right and wrong, correctness and incorrectness. Despite the emphasis on the rule-like form of normative structures in the literature, other natural forms of moral structures exist. Perhaps most important are stories and "life histories." The expectational sector in particular involves the interpretation of the various normative structures for use in practical activities. But only situationally specific prescriptions can readily be combined with the products of other sectors of the behavioral system in order to form capacities which are well adapted for implementing particular specialized lines of action. More general prescriptions are apt not to be clearly and appropriately determinative within the given situation, hence not sufficiently precise in providing a standard for judging the appropriateness of alternative ways of implementing action. Indeed, it seems best to speak of expectations only in the case where the actor is able not simply to determine quite specific prescriptions but even, through taking the roles of the others with whom he is involved, to understand how the prescriptions will be regarded and treated under the practical circumstances of the situation. Put somewhat differently, the generation of expectations is an integral part of the development of a clear definition of the situation and is dependent for its stability on its integration into a specific interactive situation.

We have noted that the integrative sector of the behavioral system provides the adaptation to its social environment. Theoretically, it seems that behavioral integration can be sustained only where there is positive adaptation to the higher-level integration of the general action system, which is provided by the maintenance of coordinated interaction in the social system. The basis of this hypothesis is actually quite simple: Practically all behavior is in some significant degree cooperative, i.e., involving the coordinated efforts of a plurality of individuals. An individual's efforts to plan and organize his own behavior must therefore be fundamentally dependent upon the similar efforts of others. His understandings about how others will act must become major factors in the determination of his own behavioral planning. Expectations become in an important sense an inter-individual category, for an individual's internally operating expectations are very substantially consequences of expectations communicated from others.[107] Clarification of expectations which can effectively enter into behavioral processes of the planning of action may comprise an important communicative aspect of social process. Yet, the possibility of successful social communication about expectations is importantly conditioned by the presence of intelligent abilities to understand and

use expectations on the part of the interactors, i.e., rests on certain behavioral capacities. An important ramification of the dependence of interaction on behavioral capacities is that the structure of social systems in general and normative systems in particular is not simply mechanically expressed in interaction but is, to use Harold Garfinkel's phrase, "artfully produced" by the actor. We are maintaining that this artful production of expectations is critically dependent on generalized intelligent capacities of the actor.

The normative structures that are institutionalized within particular social systems provide an important set of entities for the common orientation and understanding of individuals engaged within the same social milieux. Normative entities comprise basic points of orientation to which the behaving individual may make constant reference in generating expectations that can prove to be socially viable within his immediate interactive environment. Because they also orient his alters in stable situations, the normative structures stand as the common grounds for calculating how expectational statements will be received by others and for negotiating stable situated expectations.[108] The central phenomenon of the expectational sector's adaptation to and interpenetration with the social system lies in the importance of institutionalized normative patterns as foci of orientation in the development of mutually acceptable expectations.

Two more distant intra-action environments provide important, if secondary, contexts to which the expectional sector must sustain positive adaptation. The first is the superego system of the personality. The superego is comprised of cathectic attachments to moral principles and standards.[109] It serves to regulate the moral quality of the goal-directed choices of paths of action made within the personality system. Cathectic energies bound up with the components of identification in the structuring of the personality are deployed by the superego, largely through mechanisms of guilt, in order to assure that moral precepts are observed in the selection of paths of action. Within the processual integration of the whole action system, the superego occupies a position in the cybernetic hierarchy superordinate to the expectational sector. The supergo may be said to establish the moral parameters within which the intelligent generation of expectations is pursued by the individual actor. At the same time, superego functioning is importantly conditioned by the behavioral capacities of the expectational sector. The greater the intelligent capacities which are brought to bear on normative structures, the greater are the abilities of the actor to employ moral reasoning in the structuring of his activities. This makes possible greater refinement of the moral regulation of the personality, but it also provides greater intelligent capabilities to subvert such moral regulation. The extreme example of the latter case is the ideal typical "sociopath" who uses his high intelligence to manipulate expectations relatively unconstrained by his superego.

The moral-evaluative subsystem of culture comprises the second of the more distant and specialized environments to which the expectational sector must maintain strong adaptation.[110] The moral-evaluative system provides foundations for normative orientations that are more generalized, more directly derived from abstract principle, and more tightly integrated on a theoretical or hypothetical level than are the normative institutions structuring particular milieux within the social system. Understanding of the components of the moral-evaluative system can provide the actor with intellectual means of developing expectations about its obligations, rights, responsibilities, and so on, as well as those of its alters, from grounds that transcend its practical modes of engagement in specific situations. Some crucial elements of flexibility may thereby be gained for the expectational sector, allowing the actor to reformulate and renegotiate aspects of the expectations in the given situation. A moral basis of resolving gaps, conflicts, and uncertainties in expectations developed with reference to situationally salient institutional structures is also acquired. More importantly, standards may be developed on a general foundation, but with salience to individual circumstances, for regulating the allocation of behavioral energies — including the capacities needed to generate new sets of situationally appropriate expectations — among morally or normatively problematic situations. The expectational sector is thus provided with categorical means of preventing itself from becoming egocentrically engaged in specific situations to a degree which would inhibit its capacities to generate expectations across a morally appropriate manifold of activities. Finally, understanding of moral principles and standards in general terms gives the expectational sector grounds for the critical discounting of expectations that may prove socially viable and acceptable despite being morally dubious or illegitimate. This is not to say, of course, that this capacity for discounting morally dubious expectations is always employed. The practical attractions of developing, sharing, and sanctioning morally dubious expectations often produce substantial debasing of the normative quality of action, individual and collective. However, if actors were systematically lacking in the moral capacity to orient themselves on the basis of culturally intersubjective standards transcending specific situations and institutions, the generation of morally dubious expectations would build up into a moral entropy through which the normative qualities of social action would gradually be run down.

Thus, the functioning of the expectational sector requires a capacity to adapt to the normative components of the social system, the superego system, and the moral-evaluative system and to sustain an equilibrium with each of them and among all of them. The diversity of these three environments of expectational operations imposes substantial difficulties upon efforts to equilibrate the expectational sector, not only with respect to immediate circumstances but over some "long-run" planning of action. The intelligent operations of generating expectations must interrelate in viable fashion schematic representations of institutional, cathectic, and cultural entities without sacrificing the adaptation of each type of representation to its specific environment. Developing a structure for a system of this sort which can maintain general equilibrium in the face of the variant conditions and control which are environmental to it is an intellectual task of some magnitude. Even given that such systems rarely have the range and depth that require them to deal with all situations in a completely unified manner, such an equilibrium cannot be reliably sustained except on the basis of formal operational functioning.

Although constructed about a somewhat narrower range of considerations than the present conception of an expectational sector, Piaget's writings on the development of "moral judgment" have established basic information about major structures within the expectational sector.[111] The fundamental direction of ontogenesis of moral judgment involves an increase in the comprehensiveness with which normative constructs can be understood, and hence in the specificity and flexibility with which they may be used to regulate the formation of expectations. The later stages of moral development come to be concerned with phenomena of the integration of specific normative constructs into broader complexes of the just and principled regulation of interaction — that is, with underlying frameworks for the combinatorial invocation of moral principles rather than with the direct content of particular rules.

During the first phases of intellectual development, the child shows no consciousness of the normative qualities of the coordination of action in a strict sense. As sensori-motor development becomes subordinated to the emergence of representation, the child will organize some of his behavior into established habits and even make coordinations with the habits of others, e.g., parents and siblings. However, there is initially no awareness of moral constraint or obligation, so that habits are organized sheerly out of interests in the symbolic patterns and practical conveniences which they may embody.[112] Later in the pre-operational period, though, an intuitive consciousness of normative phenomena emerges. The child's understanding focuses sharply about the particular prescriptions and proscriptions of a given rule, failing to interrelate it with other rules, with standards of justice, and with criteria of reasonable interpretation. Only by coming to focus on another rule in an equally egocentric fashion can he avoid absolutizing the terms of the rule.[113] Norms are regarded as absolutely imposed by morally superior agencies, generally adults and sometimes older children. They are regarded as timelessly fixed and unchangeable, any efforts to change them not being distinguishable from simple deviance. Conduct that seems to break a rule is judged according to what Piaget has termed "objective responsibility." That is, the severity of the contravention is judged according to the severity of the practical consequences without regard to the intentions of the actor. For example, a child who breaks fifteen pieces of crockery accidentally is thought to have behaved more naughtily than one who breaks just a few very deliberately.[114] The consequence of such limited development of moral judgment is that the children are capable of only shallow coordination of their activities with others, especially when they are not directly supervised by adults. Their play tends to be egocentric, characterized by little competition to "win" over others through mutually accepted procedures and, indeed, by selective, *ad hoc* application of rules that would make such competition almost meaningless.

With the onset of concrete operations, the child's understanding of normative constructions becomes very fundamentally transformed.[115] Rules gradually lose their absolute or sacred and unchangeable qualities and come to be acknowledged on the basis of their mutual acceptance by the salient interactors. The practical function of norms in sustaining cooperative relations is recognized and hence norms come to be regarded as subject to improvement and refinement. The child begins to codify normative constructs, so that he can ascertain their interdependencies and the limitations upon the scope of application of any given rules. When obligations are normatively established, detailed and generally known procedures for their fulfillment may also be specified, so that the boundaries of obligation can be known to all operational participants in a collective process. In these respects, the normative elements regulating specific social milieux come to be understood as constituting a unified corpus comprised of definite and operationally interpretable interdependencies. The child then begins to show considerable interest in questions about the nature and structure of the system of rules and other normative structures—e.g., in a game or regulating a classroom—and about the fair and just application of rules and supportive sanctions. In contrast to the pre-operational child, who tends to judge more severe punishments as better because they seem to punish the wrongdoer more strongly, the operational child understands that sanctions must be proportioned to the importance of the wrong. He regards sanctions that are disproportionately severe as unjust, in part because they raise difficulties for a moral demonstration of the importance of more fundamental issues of good and evil. Thus, his judgment about the propriety of alternative sanctions is determined to a considerable degree by his systematic understanding of a moral order. Moral judgments having this level of intelligent articulation can function to generate expectations that are vastly more stable, more flexible, and more thoroughly socialized (that is, less egocentric) and hence socially circulatable than the expectations of a pre-operational child.

We have noted that the concrete operational child begins to show concern for issues of the general organization of a rule complex and of the just use of rules. Increasingly as the child matures, this concern comes to focus upon principles and general standards of moral right and justice. At a certain point, it may become transformed from an interest in how justice may be achieved within specific milieux into an abstract interest in how the possibilities for just social arrangements may be maximized in general. A concern of the latter type can be developed only through a system of formal operations. Not only must there be a comprehensive formulation of the basic features of a normative order, including hierarchical organization, dimensions of internal differentiation, and the morally problematic aspects of the situations it regulates, but there must also be a capacity to formulate how the content of particular normative elements would be changed if different emphases were placed upon different principles and standards or if different aspects of situations were taken to be morally problematic. That is, this sort of moral thinking must be understood as the outcome of a series of transformations whereby hypothetically general premises and standards become interrelated in ways designed specifically to provide just resolutions of the moral issues viewed as problematic within given situations. It can then be understood that variation in the nature of the transformations interrelating premises and standards and adapting them to features of situations can produce different forms and degrees of justice, and that abstract conscientious selection among transformations, i.e., establishing the validity of invoking specific transformations to regulate the allocations of rights and obligations within *categories* of situations, lies implicitly at the heart of the ways in which an actor operationalizes normative structures.

Piaget has emphasized the intellectual difficulties involved in the development of a formal operational understanding of moral issues.[116] Typically, the adolescent in the early stages of developing a formal operational capacity in the domain of moral judgment cannot equilibrate a system of transformations. His judgment tends to become highly "idealistic" in the sense of attempting to resolve all moral issues on the basis of ultimate principles while overlooking many of the practical considerations and details of dilemmas which must be taken into account in order to arrive at stable resolutions.[117] At the same time, there may be an egocentric focusing on specific principles or standards of justice in a way that prevents attention from being given to the complete manifold of problems at issue even at the most abstract level. Piaget attributes the adolescent susceptibility to engagement in "ideological" movements largely to such properties of the early development of moral judgment based on formal operations.

Generalizing considerably beyond the important qualifications which Piaget has made himself, Kohlberg has recently questioned whether individuals in all societies and cultures actually attain mastery of the general understandings which emerge in the later, operational stages of moral development.[118] Indeed, he tends to argue that only within select social circles of modern societies do many individuals advance beyond the early phases of the concrete operational stage. There can certainly be little doubt that even in sophisticated circles of modern societies adults typically fail to control their expectational behavior on a formal operational basis in many, probably most or maybe all, situations. Indeed, even those who have firm command of formal operational capacities probably lack a formal operational understanding of the normative considerations entering into most of the social milieux in which they routinely act. Moreover, there are obviously many independent aspects and degrees of attainment of formal operational understandings, so that partial attainment of formal operational bases of developing expectations, which would be less than fully equilibrated, is probably a common phenomenon. It does not follow, therefore, that individuals who show operational incapacities within specific contexts of moral judgment are necessarily incapable of utilizing operational (concrete or formal) understandings in other interactive situations or that they are incapable of accepting expectations developed by others on a formal operational basis and thereby gaining added flexibility in the organization of their own behavior. Often, we suspect, there are personality or social level factors which prevent the utilization of operational, especially formal operational, capacities.

Thus, formal operational understandings may be prevented from entering interaction by controlling cathectic attachments that compel the superego to give diffuse, seemingly egocentric support to particular normative content or particular partisan interests within a dispute. Similarly, insufficient trust within a social situation may lead an individual to judge that his interests lack the security requisite for venturing to gain the cooperation of others on a basis of expectations generated through so abstract a mechanism as formal operations. Whatever the form of the underlying moral judgment, then, it may often seem inappropriate to interact on the basis of formal operationally generated expectations. Thus, we concur with Piaget and Kohlberg that a formal operational regulation of moral judgment is so complex an attainment as to be quite problematic for many individuals to manage across any ramified set of interactive milieux or, for some, at all; and yet we do not believe their evidence supports the general claim that whole societies or major subsystems of societies can function without the important resource provided by the existence of formal operational understandings of normative matters. Recent anthropological evidence on the legal institutions and procedures of even quite primitive societies, for example, indicates that they would be quite unable to resolve the more serious and complex disputes or to maintain a common normative framework for resolving diverse disputes unless at least the leading legal experts were operating on an intellectual plane that seems to require a formal operational intelligence.[119] Thus, we would suggest that the adaptive advantages of formal operational understandings are so important for the maintenance of the normative integration of any highly complicated action system that they probably comprise an intrinsic component of the "evolutionary universal" that all human societies are normatively regulated. All societies must have substantial access to formal operational capacities for generating expectations, even if not all situations require them and not all members of society can provide them.

We may discuss the pattern maintenance subsystem of the behavioral system itself, which we will call the formal-categorial sector, more briefly than the others. It will become apparent that we have already outlined its general content and line of ontogenesis at some length in other contexts. Here we need to focus primarily on questions of the nature and importance of its functional contributions to the broader behavioral system and especially of its adaptation to the cultural environment of behavioral functioning.

Recent studies of the evolutionary origins of the human species, hence of the origins of human action, have suggested that the construction of a meaningful, culturally patterned "internal" environment for human behavior came in turn to constitute a major factor in the emergence of the unique characteristics of pan-human capabilities. Whereas it has long been understood that humans are unique among all species in their capacity to use symbolically meaningful culture, and indeed organize their societies on a cultural basis, more recently it has been shown that the massive specialization of the human organism about this capacity evolved as an adaptation to culture.[120] Archeological indications of capacity to symbolize and of some primitive types of simple culture have been found in association with species having only rudimentary specialization about the symbolic-cultural capacities. The very rapid evolution of these capacities among the various humanoid species can be explained only in terms of the overwhelming selective advantages gained by the emergence of the capacities to utilize culture intelligently and creatively. It is in terms of the advantages gained by a thorough exploitation of the intra-action cultural environment, then, that the vast human specialization about *intelligence* of behavior—more technically, about the organism's capacities for developing intelligence—can be explained in the most general fashion.

Some important bodies of research have begun to make clear, moreover, that it is not simply high levels of intelligence that should be explained by reference to an adaptation to culture but also some specific forms of intelligence. The understanding and flexibly generative use of culture, including especially its abstract and hypothetical components, as well as orientation in terms of the cultural-symbolic elements institutionalized in social systems and internalized in personality systems, seem to set some fairly specific requirements regarding informational form upon the nature of behavioral process. We suggest that the fundamental significance of the specific forms involved in intelligent operations, concrete and formal, is precisely that they enable individuals to make generative use of culture and consequently enable human groups to be enculturated with regard to the patterning of action. Substantial generalization of the behavioral system's adaptation to its cultural environment requires that its constituent processes not only be intelligent but adhere to some version of the forms of concrete or formal operations.

The plausibility of this general hypothesis may be indicated by noting some recent research on a general action mechanism, namely language, which operates on a different level from, but definitely articulates with, the intrabehavioral processes we have been discussing. The work of the transformational grammarians has shown that there are very probably some quite definite and specific universals to be found in the grammars of all languages.[121] Such universals include certain parts of speech and the abstract grammatical relationships among them, the generation of sentences from underlying "deep" orderings of meaning toward a "surface" composed of exemplars of parts of speech placed in serial order according to general grammatical rules, and the transformational nature of the rules which can regulate the generative movement from deep to surface structures. Much recent psycholinguistic research has been concerned with the nature of the competence involved in the generative use of language by individuals.[122] The central notion has been that the universals of grammar should be complemented by some universal elements of the psychological competences involved in using language. Thus, all speakers of languages must have the abilities to analyze sentences into parts of speech and to treat the exemplars of different parts of speech in different ways, to apprehend the grammatical ordering and meaning of "deep structures" on the basis of surface constituents, and to transform the elements of sentences in accordance with the transformational rules of a grammar.[123] Given the apparent universality of such general linguistic capacities among "normal" human individuals, and their apparent absence except perhaps in rather marginal degrees among individuals of other species, it has been argued that they should be treated as "innate" to human beings.[124] Some theoretically serious ambiguities have been attached to claims of this nature. For example, whatever their foundation in the physiological organization of the human organism, such universals are certainly activated not simply through physiological maturation but also through requisite experiential constructions of specific types of behavioral schemas and operations. The use of language requires that the innate capacities be *realized* through the development of certain specific types of intelligent abilities.[125] In the cases of many individuals, fundamental linguistic competence may be impoverished—temporarily or even permanently—by a lack of appropriate experience even though they are fully endowed with the innate elements of linguistic competence. The presence of the innate elements of linguistic abilities serves only to make the general mastery of language a relatively secure achievement of individuals in their efforts to adapt to the intra-action environments of their behavior. A completely secure mechanism has not evolved and would probably restrict the degree to which socioculturally important new meanings could be flexibly generated were it to appear.

We suggest that the intelligent ability to perform concrete and formal operations should be treated as an innate human ability in much the same sense as linguistic competence may legitimately be treated as innate. It seems to be a universal of the normal human central nervous system that an individual possesses the physiological apparatus necessary for the development of intelligent operations. Yet, this normal capacity comprises only a condition for the intra-action ontogenesis of intelligence. Intelligence cannot attain operational form except through the development of certain types of schemas and processual relationships among schemas. However the innate components of operational intelligence may be structured physiologically, they do serve to provide some security that behavioral abilities will develop broadly along certain lines of intelligence.

Comparative studies in sociology and anthropology, perhaps especially within a tradition established by Durkheim and currently exemplified by Levi-Strauss[126] and his followers, have given considerable attention to questions of form within systems of collective representations, symbols, categories, beliefs, hypotheses—that is, within culture. While it is difficult to draw clearcut, widely accepted generalizations from these studies, some tentative conclusions may be ventured within the present context. All cultures seem to require quite generalized abstractions in order to set their most basic, constitutive frameworks. Where autonomous modes of establishing specialized types of discourse have become differentiated from the primordial, diffuse "religious" cultural framework, they too require abstract grounding.[127] The culture will then contain perhaps artistic, ethical, and cognitive frameworks that are distinct from the religious at highly abstract levels.[128] All cultural frameworks, regardless of their relative diffuseness or specificity, are integrated in hypothetical ways. Only if general theoretical relationships are drawn among abstract terms or representations, so that inferences can be made from general principles, can cultural complexes adapt flexibly to significant and substantial variation in the practical needs for cultural orientation. In this sense, a complex of totemic categories requires theoretical integration in order to provide grounds of inference about the "religious" commitments of members of the tribe for much the same reasons that a modern science needs hypotheses to integrate the specific findings of particular researches into bases for understanding conditions of a general type.[129] Finally, the key terms of a cultural complex must be ordered in some definite ways. Nesting hierarchies containing a plurality of independent dimensions, so that they prescribe an inverted "tree" structure, seem to be extremely common if not universal.[130] Considerations such as these at least indicate that the search for some formal universals of culture, as undertaken most energetically by Levi-Strauss, may be entering some very fruitful problem areas in which, if more specificity can be gained, much of theoretical import may be learned.

In the present context, it suffices to point out that there appears to be much convergence between the posited universals of cultural form and Piaget's conceptions of concrete and formal operations. Piaget has stressed that the conception of formal operations converges importantly with the understanding of basic logico-mathematical structure which has emerged within the modern disciplines of logic, mathematics, and scientific methodology.[131] Our concern is that types of culture as varied as the totemism of primitive societies and the ethical-legal thought of modern societies seem definitely to share in this cultural form. To be sure, any logico-mathematical form underlying a primitive belief system does so in a way substantially different from its direct and explicit ingression within modern science. To emphasize its presence in other types of culture need not involve underestimating the methodological achievements of modern science. The possible universality of the basic logico-mathematical form, with its definite relations to formal operations at the behavioral level, seems important to emphasize specifically because of its bearing upon questions of the mutual adaptations between cultural and behavioral systems.

We wish to stress that the adaptations between culture and intelligent behavior, though having certain universal characteristics, are nevertheless also achieved through evolutionary processes. Processes of cultural evolution may substantially enhance the cultural deployment of intelligent capacities, so that specific behavioral operations become more tightly determined or controlled by salient cultural standards. Behavior may then become oriented in determinate fashion by more complex cultural constructions requiring the coordinated use of more complicated intelligent operations. Assuming the cultural complexes to be appropriately adapted to the salient aspects of the human condition, more difficult and baffling problems can be solved in the course of behavioral operations.

A variety of types of cultural change may be involved in the production of positive evolutionary consequences of this sort. A prominent type is certainly cultural differentiation, which enhances the functional specificity with which cultural complexes control behavioral processes. Thus, intelligent understanding of problems in organic chemistry, for example, is enhanced when cognitive knowledge is differentiated from other cultural spheres, chemistry is differentiated from other sciences, and organic chemistry comprises a specialized sector within the area of chemical knowledge. In terms of the present theoretical concerns, however, a more interesting aspect of cultural evolution pertains to changes that may occur in the formal patterning of culture. We have interpreted the available, albeit scant, evidence as indicating that culture seems universally to be organized in patterns that approximate the "logico-mathematical structure" in general form. If this is so, it must certainly be true in a highly generalized fashion that includes many variations of more specific forms. Presumably, the ingression of logico-mathematical form into various specific cultural complexes has been greater in the Western traditions affected by the concerns with *logos* first generated in Greek culture than in other traditions.[132] The mark of such greater ingression has been the methodological strain in Western thought—that is, the effort to generate explicit rational standards against which the validity of substantive thought is to be systematically judged. However, form has also varied by domain of cultural specialization. The methodical rationalization of cultural form has carried the furthest in the sphere of cognitive knowledge and especially cognitive methodology. Normative culture—ethical, moral, and legal—has been rationalized in some similar ways, especially in regard to explicit acknowledgement of the importance of standards of logic and rational deduction and proof.[133] However, within this sector of culture, standards have not been articulated with the same specificity — e.g., proofs in legal discourse are not established through mathematical demonstration, as they generally must be in modern physics. Matters of artistic style and criticism or of religious or theological discourse, although subject to certain standards of formal rationality,[134] tend to be less objectively or explicitly rationalized than matters of normative culture. Yet, examination of evolutionary changes in artistic and religious culture make clear how importantly content in these domains may be shaped by a formal articulation of abstract premises.[135] For example, the vast differences on many specifics between early Lutheran theology and the Catholic theology which it claimed to "reform" can probably be explicated in terms of the systematic working out of a small number of changes in fundamental abstract premises. Similarly, the stylistic unity of an artistic school such as Impressionism seems to derive from the sharing of some abstract principles about the nature of expressive perception and depiction of shape, color, emotion, and human circumstance.

The foregoing considerations indicate that the individual having an operational understanding of his general cultural environment must come to terms with a variety of types of abstract forms. Cultural complexes of practically all types may share the characteristic of being comprehensively understandable only on an operational, especially formal operational, basis. However, within the category of operations, concrete and formal, there appear to be significantly different types of intelligence that

are required to gain understanding of different forms of culture. Although all may lie within the realm of operations, the kinds of intelligence involved in the understanding of science, morals, art, and theology seems to be very significantly different from each other. Our discussion of the formal-categorial sector and its functions will proceed also with a view towards explicating some consequences of this generalization.

The formal-categorial sector serves to regulate the development and stabilization of appropriate schematic and operational forms throughout the various sectors of the behavioral system. A consequence of its functioning is that, as noted in our preceding discussions, the adaptive, goal attainment, and integrative sectors of the behavioral system all develop through stages which are *formally* the same despite the vast differences in their substantive contents. It cannot be argued that the formal correspondences among these sectors derive from a condition in which identical intelligent capacities are directed toward different specialized uses at the same time. In fact, the various sectors do not actually function in terms of the same form or level of intelligent organization during many phases of development. The intellectual problems which must be resolved in order for development to proceed differ substantially among the sectors. The very starting points of *autonomous* ontogenesis consequently differ among the sectors. Thus, the goal attainment sector does not become autonomous of the adaptive sector until the representative capacities emerge, and the integrative sector first gains independence of the goal attainment sector only with the onset of the later, "intuitive" phases of the pre-operational stage. Throughout subsequent development, there appear to be systematic lags whereby development in the goal attainment sector follows that in the adaptive sector and development in the integrative sector follows that in the goal attainment sector. Of course, the convergence of the various specialized sectors upon formally similar types of organization is importantly conditioned by the exigencies of increasing complexity which each confronts in its ontogenesis. However, just as computer and human intelligences differ in form, it must be acknowledged that the convergence about formal operations is not fully determined by exigencies of complexity alone. The adherence of the diversely specialized intelligent complexes of the behavioral system to a common succession of formal patterns through the independent courses of their respective ontogeneses can be understood only by reference to a particular regulatory mechanism. The "autoregulation" of the behavioral system whereby formal convergences and complementarities among its various components are sustained so that information may circulate coherently throughout the system comprises the pattern maintenance dimension of its functioning.[136]

The formal-categorial sector performs its autoregulative function by exercising a cybernetic control over the other sectors of the behavioral system. Its own internal ontogenesis consists in the progression from the abstract form of the simple coordination of sensori-motor schemata, to that of representational coordinations at the pre-operational level, to those of first concrete and then formal operations. At any given point, its functioning may be said to involve the abstraction of the most parsimonious forms of organization of schemata from the various sectors of behavioral activity and then the generalizing projection of such forms into whatever sectors seem less parsimoniously organized. In this way, the formal-categorial sector, while in a certain sense remaining latently removed or abstracted from any specific area of behavioral activity or particular contents of any given types of behavior, exerts a constant pressure throughout ontogenesis towards a more parsimonious — more intelligent — organization of all behavior. It is through the latent involvement specifically of formal-categorial functioning in the development of the whole behavioral system, then, that the general forms of the respective stages, culminating in formal operations, are cybernetically impressed upon the various differentiated sectors and subsectors of behavior.

The foregoing analysis may seem to account for the emergence of a common general *order* among the various sectors of a particular individual's behavirol system, whereby possibilities for continued communication among the differentiated sectors can be assured at the same time that each becomes increasingly specialized about the performance of its own characteristic tasks. However, especially in discussing the expectational sector, we have emphasized that no human system of intelligent behavior is an island unto itself. Structurally, behavioral systems must incorporate means of communication and exchange with other behavioral systems. Thus, it is essential that the very processes through which the formal-categorial sector takes on its own structural forms, with their general impact upon the subsequent organization of the entire behavioral system, also be processes which secure the viability of communication with others.

The common availability of cultural categories and the abstract relationships among them to members of a society comprises the principal source of order among behavioral systems. We have noted that the formal nature of the relationships among cultural entities appears to parallel that among schemata within a behavioral system that has attained operational levels of organization. Consequently, internalization of complexes of culturally structured meaning offer one means for a behavioral system to obtain resolution of the problems it must face in attempting to create parsimonious formal structures for its own functioning. Given both the limitations on the creative intelligence of most individuals and the scarcity of behavioral energies that can be allocated to the performance of the formal-categorial functions, there are strong constraints favoring a tendency to adopt the formal structurings offered within the sets of available cultural categories. At the same time, of course, adoption of formal orderings given in the culture provides some substantial assurance that behavioral operations may proceed upon terms that allow for flexible communication with other members of the society. Thus, we may conclude that, broadly, the construction of general order within the formal-categorial sector corresponds with the process of acculturation of the behavioral system. Of course, we are not here overlooking the extent to which important acculturation may occur within the other sectors of a behavioral system. Rather, we are emphasizing that precisely with respect to the aspect of behavioral functioning concerned most deeply with matters of general order, the exigencies favoring reliance upon the structural patterns of the culture seem to be the strongest.

Finally, we may note that, secondary to its massive interpenetration with cultural structure, the formal-categorial sector interpenetrates with the fiduciary subsystem of society and the identity subsystem of the personality. The fiduciary system is comprised largely of social relationships specialized about the generation of commitments to components of or complexes within the culture. Its internal differentiation apparently revolves about the adaptation of its various constituent milieux to the exigencies of fostering commitments to specific types of culture.[137] For example, the differences between churches and colleges or universities may be regarded as deriving from the different social conditions necessary for acculturating individuals to religious and intellectually disciplined culture respectively. It is through engagement in specific roles within the fiduciary system, then, that the general socialization of individual behavioral systems to specific complexes of "higher" culture ordinarily takes place in modern societies. The specific fiduciary roles in which an individual gains the opportunity to participate will largely determine the types of cultural categories he may internalize as constitutive of his formal-categorial system. Given the highly pluralistic nature of participation in a modern fiduciary sector, it is to be expected that particular persons are apt to construct highly individualized combinations of the various cultural materials available within the society. The social patterns of communication with respect to the more highly specialized cultural complexes will be determined not only by processes of the behavioral internalization of the culture but also by the social structuring of the "division of labor of knowledge" within the fiduciary system. The distribution of intelligent operational capacities to use specific types of culture will be determined mainly by the allocation of socializing resources within the fiduciary system. The principal category of such resources, however, consists in the culturally qualified operational intelligence of individuals who may serve as socializing agents. In this respect, fiduciary relations seem to be more critically than any other type of social relationship conditioned by formal-categorial intelligence.

The identity subsystem of the personality may be regarded as intervening within the special relationship between the fiduciary system and the formal-categorial sector. The extensive commitment to a particular complex of "higher" culture involved in developing a formal operational understanding of it cannot be implemented without very substantial motivational attachment to the cultural complex. Indeed, the behavioral effects of the incorporation of a cultural complex within the formal-categorial sector are commonly so general and diffuse as to be "senseless" except insofar as guided by a motivational identification with the cultural content. In this respect, the acculturating operations of the formal-categorial system may be regarded as implementive of elements of personal identity.[138] It should be noted, however, that only identity elements which make broadly realistic demands upon the prior intelligent capacities of the individual can gain such implementation — we do not all command the specialized intelligences involved in forming large areas of our behavioral systems about the understanding of theoretical physics, the appreciation of Romanesque art, or existential involvement with Thomist religious philosophy.

CONCLUSION

In this chapter, we have tried to begin the long and complex process of integrating the extremely rich and important work of Jean Piaget into the more general framework of the theory of action. This has involved the demonstration of several different, though interrelated, points. Our point of departure has been the contention that Piaget's conceptions of behavior and of the proper modes of theorizing about behavior are substantially similar to the conceptions developed by Parsons and other theorists of action.

Indeed, we believe that we have shown that many of the formal analytical constructs in the two theories comprise essentially parallel attempts to analyze similar phenomena located at different positions within action systems.

Given the degree to which the treatment of psychological phenomena within the theory of action has long depended heavily upon psychoanalytic thought, the task of integrating Piagetian psychology into the theory of action has necessarily involved consideration of its relations to Freudian theory. Our reading in Piaget's work has resulted in the impression that it treats not a subcategory of psychoanalytic personality theory but a parallel dimension of psychological phenomena of equal generality. When they discuss the same types of concrete behavior, Freud and Piaget seem not to be disagreeing with one another so much as they are addressing themselves to independent aspects of the phenomena in question. Along with certain other considerations reviewed in this chapter, this conclusion has led us to reformulate the conception of the adaptive subsystem of action. We are proposing that it be treated as a Piagetian system in the same sense that the goal attainment subsystem of action has long been treated as, roughly, a Freudian system. Further, we have attempted to specify in some detail how the primary functional subsystems of the behavioral system — i.e., the adaptive subsystem of action — may be conceptualized. We must emphasize that these are preliminary formulations based on research that covers the range of salient problems quite unevenly and on four-function conceptions that yet require much further systematization. We expect that serious problems in our formulations will be revealed by future investigations. Yet, we feel that our examination of Piagetian materials and of the alternatives for their four-function analysis has been sufficiently general and thorough that our formulations should provide a fairly sound point of departure for further work, within the theory of action framework, upon the adaptive problems of action systems.

We have pursued the integration of Piagetian psychology into the theory of action in large part because of the specifically sociological ramifications that we have seen in this task. To be sure, a major change in the rounding out of the four-function analysis of the action frame of reference carries importance in itself. Yet, we believe that the ramifications for sociology of the systematic understanding of the behavioral system extend far beyond simply enhancement of knowledge about one environment of social systems. We hold that systemic properties of the behavioral environment of social system functioning penetrate deeply into the nature of that functioning itself. Thus, the intelligent capacities of the behavioral system comprise absolutely indispensible resources for the accomplishment of interaction within social systems. Interaction cannot be deeply and fully comprehended without understanding of behavioral intelligence and its functional operations.

Social system structures do not actualize themselves in interaction. With respect to the importance of the motivational characteristics of individuals and their formative effects on specific projects of interaction, sociologists have long been sensitized to this principle by psychoanalytic thought and by such social psychological notions as W. I. Thomas's "wishes."[139] However, the same principle holds with respect to the part played by intelligent operations in the development of interactive processes. To the extent that states of action systems are generated and maintained by the orientation of actors to various sorts of normative standards, intelligent capacities must be employed to actualize normative judgments. As Garfinkel has so clearly pointed out,[140] no list of normative rules, however long, could provide an actor with totally adequate normative guidance for even the simplest of practical, everyday tasks. All such lists must, in Garfinkel's words, "end in an et cetera." That is to say, intelligent operations comprise a requisite part of the process of obeying normative prescriptions, and normative regulation is probably intrinsically ambiguous and indeterminate unless selectively reduced into practical definition of the situation in part by intelligent operations. More generally, we believe that, in theory of action terms, an important part—but by no means do we intend to imply all—of the ethnomethodological critique of structuralist sociology amounts to an insistence upon the role of an intelligent behavioral system in the processes of social action. At the most inclusive level of the treatment of social action, we believe, only a general theory of the engagement of the capacities of the behavioral system in interaction can break down the barriers that have separated structural analysis from process-oriented analysis within sociology.

We would like also to suggest that analyses of interaction may benefit substantially from consideration of the different levels and forms of intelligence discriminated within Piaget's developmental theory. Even for the well-educated adult, it is not to be taken for granted that the logical organization of his belief systems and specifically the ways in which he formulates social situations are functioning at the level of formal operations. A closer study of the procedures involved in organizing moral, ideological, or normative beliefs or representations defining situations and managing organizations may indicate that major problems in our theories have stemmed from erroneous implicit assumptions about the nature of intelligent behavioral functioning. Our own preliminary

observations in several empirical fields have convinced us of both the necessity for social action to have access to formal operational capacities and at the same time the pervasive importance assumed by less developed forms of intelligence in everyday interaction.

The potential ramifications for sociological theory of systematic explorations into the interrelations between the behavioral and social systems are enormous. We hope that this paper will stimulate others to join us in the study of this dynamic sector of systems of social action.

APPENDIX: INTELLIGENCE AND SOCIAL ACTION*

Most of the body of the present essay has been devoted first to theoretical justification of the effort to build Piagetian psychology into the theory of action and then to a general outline of a systematic proposal for doing so. It has seemed necessary to address both of these problems, perhaps especially the latter, in order to give evidence of the feasibility of a fruitful discharge of the task we have taken up. There have been some unfortunate consequences of the ways in which we have concentrated our efforts, however. Foremost among these, I feel, is that we have not had space to essay with any thoroughness some of the basic theoretical consequences of our reconceptualization of the adaptive subsystem of action. The ensuing remarks, then, are intended as preliminary indications of theoretical speculations and arguments which may be set forth rather more systematically in the future. They are included here primarily to highlight some of the specifically sociological relevances of the foregoing formulations.

Professor Parsons has recently developed the proposal that "intelligence" can be treated as the generalized symbolic medium of interchange regulating the internal combinatorial processes of the adaptive subsystem of action as well as its boundary processes of input and output in relation to the other primary subsystems of action.[141] I feel that our reconceptualization of the adaptive subsystem of action makes possible a still richer treatment of intelligence as a generalized medium. Here I will only indicate a few chief features of such a treatment, focusing mainly

---

*The author of this Appendix is Victor Meyer Lidz. Charles W. Lidz has added this note: "Although there is certainly merit to the concept, I find the notion of generalized medium still insufficiently clear to warrant its use, particularly at the general action level. Furthermore, Piaget's research and theorizing do not seem to me to warrant this type of conceptualization of intelligence."

upon the relationships between intelligence as a medium and behavioral functioning and then upon the contributions of intelligence to the processes of interaction.

Intelligence has been a very prominent term throughout our essay, in two principal senses. First, we have spoken of the ontogenetic emergence of different forms of intelligence at the various stages of behavioral development. Second, we have spoken of behavior organized in the forms of the more advanced stages as being more intelligent than behavior embedded in the forms of the earlier developmental stages. A developmental perspective imbues both usages in a way that is strongly congruent with the evolutionary perspective that has been a principal feature of the discussion of generalized media within the theory of action.[142] Just as money emerges in its more generalized forms, e.g., bank deposits, checks, stock certificates, marketable bonds, only in rather highly developed economies, so intelligence in its more formal operational or systematically rationalized sense emerges only in highly developed behavioral systems. Much as a highly developed monetary system imparts a wide range of flexibilities or "degrees of freedom" to a system of economic markets,[143] formal operational intelligence adds vastly to a behavioral system's capacities to interrelate its schematic components and to adapt creatively to new exigencies.

Nevertheless, we have generally followed Piaget in treating intelligence simply as an important quality of either a developed system of behavior or the behavioral outputs of such a system. Now I wish to treat intelligence more technically as a mode of the representation of behavioral capacities. Much as money stands for the productivity of the economy, intelligence, as a medium, may be said to stand for a capacity to perform behavioral operations. Intelligence may be deemed generalized insofar as it stands for capacities to perform whole types or categories of behavioral operations rather than the repetition of particular routines or the attaining of particular outcomes. Thus, the generalization of intelligence encompasses the emergence of abilities to *generate* new and original behavioral adjustments on the basis of categorial rather than particularized or concrete understandings of given situational features. The generativity of human language may be regarded in past as a prototypical form of both human intelligence in general and the intelligence of particular human individuals.[144] Linguistic generativity involves highly generalized capacities to form or interpret symbolic communications.

Intelligence takes on a quantitative aspect—again much as money in its relation to the productivity of the economy—when it refers to shares of behavioral capacities, either those of a given individual or those of the membership of groups. A certain amount of intelligence, then, may control the allocation of a specific share of a system of behavioral abilities to the completion of one task or another. In this sense, some tasks require the allocation of greater amounts of intelligence than others. A behavioral system may be said to "economize" its allocations of intelligence, so that the more important and more difficult tasks will receive greater quantities and more generalized forms of intelligence. The functioning of a behavioral system or indeed a collectivity of behavioral systems is-importantly conditioned by such economization of intelligence, for otherwise the greater abilities might be deployed toward accomplishing the simple or trivial tasks. Behavior must always be rationalized in light of the scarcity of both behavioral capacities and intelligence as a generalized means of controlling them.

Intelligence as a medium circulates both within an individual behavioral system and across the personal, social, and cultural boundaries of a behavioral system. Within a behavioral system, the control of a quantity of intelligence holds out the possibility of mobilizing behavioral operations of a corresponding "value" into the performance of a complexly coordinated task. We have noted above a variety of profound structural interdependencies among the various functionally specialized sectors of behavioral systems. A processual counterpart of such structural interdependence is that well-adapted behavior can in general be developed within any functionally specific mechanism only with the benefit of contributions from other sectors of the encompassing behavioral system. The routine generation of expectations, for example, requires information about the situation and consequences of action from the perceptual, interpretive, and formal-categorial sectors. In general, the greater the intelligence of the expectational process in itself, the greater are the needs for complementary orientation from the other specialized sectors. However, it also appears that the more intelligent performances within the expectational sector are apt to have greater reciprocal impact upon the other sectors of the behavioral system—i.e., to concern more important problems or to develop more reliable results from the standpoint of the functional needs of the other sectors. Theoretically, we may unite these rather reciprocal hypotheses into a more general proposition about the circulation of intelligence: The intelligence controlled by a specific behavioral mechanism is, on the one hand, a function of its ability to meet operative needs of diverse other mechanisms within the system and, on the other hand, the generalized resource by which it attracts other mechanisms to undertake operations that can meet its own needs for heterogenous information.

More specifically, I conceive a behavioral mechanism as gaining incomes of intelligence from the ways in which it manages to satisfy the informational needs of other specialized mechanisms. Such incomes of intelligence represent shares of the total behavioral capacity of the system—and, under certain circumstances, of other individuals' behavioral systems integrated into the same interactive "division of labor." The mechanism's income of intelligence may then be expended in order to gain control of the diversely specialized information which is necessary for it to sustain its own operations. A positive balance of intelligence represents the mechanism's capacity to call up the behavioral resources which can maintain its future viability within the larger system.

Two features of this formulation of intelligence as a circulating medium should be noted. First, intelligence is conceptualized as lacking "value in use" and resting upon "value in exchange."[145] The level of intelligence ascribed to any particular behavioral mechanism depends upon the "market value" of its informational products as set by the requirements of other mechanisms. Given the scarcity of behavioral resources, one may assume such requirements to become effective in competitive terms—i.e., through competition for gaining control of behavioral operations and the information they produce. Unlike the energies engaged in all behavior, or the particular processes of behavioral operation themselves, intelligence is not "consumed" in actual behavior. Rather, it is merely circulated among the specialized behavioral mechanisms involved in exchanges. Once circulated, a given quantity of intelligence enters the "funds" of a new behavioral mechanism and comprises a part of its resources for gaining necessary information. Second, the present conception of intelligence may be said to bridge theoretically between two common senses of the word. On the one hand stands the sense in which intelligence represents a capacity of intellect or understanding. On the other hand stands a reference to a quality of information, i.e., intelligence as information, especially reliable information, about some situation of interest. In the aggregate, good or valuable intelligence is apt to be that which has been produced through the utilization of highly intelligent behavioral operations. It is basically trust in the intelligence of any given behavioral processes that provides the grounds of the acceptance of their informational products in other spheres of the behavioral system.

Parsons' recent treatments of intelligence as a medium have focused upon the interchange between the behavioral system (the behavioral organism in his terminology) and the cultural system.[146] He has emphasized that intelligence comprises a crucial category of generalized resource for cultural functioning. The processual utilization of culture requires that the individuals involved have intelligent understandings of the cultural content. Moreover, they must make their intelligence available to cultural functioning on a generalized basis in that the specific nature of the associated behavioral operations must then be determined by the nature of the cultural issues. A generalized intelligent understanding of a cultural complex may be utilized in many different ways under various circumstances, and insofar as the process is intracultural the uses will be controlled by functional problems confronting the organization of the cultural materials. The cultural exploitation of intelligence—which can be interpreted as a cultural investment of intelligence—may under certain circumstances result in actual "growth" within the cultural system. That is, through intelligent "work" upon issues defined within the culture, specific cultural complexes may become transformed in ways that enhance their capacities to provide intersubjective orientation of a given type. The example of such cultural growth which Parsons has emphasized is the advancement of the scientific qualities of intellectual disciplines through intelligent research.[147] However, artistic creation, the construction of more developed moral or ethical orientations, or the origination of more profoundly "constitutive" religious symbolism would seem to involve broadly comparable investments of intelligence, albeit in different mixtures with nonbehavioral resources. In all of these cases, however, a common outcome of the processes of the investment of intelligence and the creation of new components of culture is the enhancement of cultural "knowledge." There is an addition to what is "known" culturally, whatever the functional modality of the knowledge. For our present concerns, a crucial further consequence is that the intelligent operations of the behavioral system may become reoriented by the new knowledge. Insofar as the cultural development is a productive one, all the behavioral systems engaged in the relevant cultural complex have access to means for enhancing the intelligence of certain of their component operations. By mastering the new culture, a large number of individuals may increase the quantities of their intelligence. In this sense, the original investment of intelligence may result in important advances in intelligence throughout many interconnected behavioral systems. In such dramatic cases as Einstein's discoveries in the theory of relativity with their subsequent impact upon many areas of knowledge and a vast number of scientists, the growth of intelligence may have massive and diverse impacts upon the encompassing systems of action.

Although the foregoing account of the growth of knowledge and intelligence would, if formalized, differ from Parsons' own account in certain theoretical details, I regard it as quite strong confirmation of his account of the behavioral-cultural interchange that an independent inquiry should arrive at an analysis so close to his after departing from a substantially different conception of the adaptive subsystem of action. In this context, nevertheless, we do find some substantial advantages offered by our treatment of the behavioral system. Its more fundamental articulation with the general frame of reference of action enables it to deal better with the ranges of common meaning that pervade both the cultural and the behavioral systems. In the present treatment, intelligent operations are conceived to be acculturated in quite fundamental respects. The impact upon intelligent capacities of changes in cultural complexes then becomes rather more directly understandable. Conversely, detailed empirical studies should be able to illuminate more thoroughly how the investment, mediated through generalized intelligence, of specific operational capacities may result in cultural innovation following particular cultural paths. The "intelligence" which Einstein brought to bear upon general issues in theoretical physics with such great fruitfulness probably consisted much less of his intrinsic, physiologically grounded abilities, which were certainly matched by many of his contemporaries, both physicists and nonphysicists, than in his specific operational outlooks and sensitivities about what were the most fundamentally problematic issues in the physical theory of his era, which were quite uniquely his own.

Sociologically, the interchange between the behavioral and social systems comprises the most important context of the circulation of intelligence as a generalized medium. Although a formal account of the categories of resources involved in this interchange seems to me somewhat premature, I would like to conclude with some general observations about how the present conception of intelligence may affect the sociological understanding of social interaction.

Our discussion of the expectational sector emphasized broadly that behavioral systems must adapt intelligently to their social environments, and in ways that permit realistic participations of individuals in the details of specific interactive processes. Here I wish to address the obverse proposition, namely that the functioning of systems of interaction requires that social activities be implemented, coordinated, and adapted to conditioning factors in intelligent ways. It seems to me that only the most reductionist treatments of the intersections between psychological and social systems can fail to acknowledge matters of the level and form of the intelligence with which interaction is carried out to be theoretically problematic. Yet, very little systematic atten-

tion has been devoted in the sociological literature to problems of this sort.

Interaction cannot be implemented within a stably structured milieu — i.e., a milieu that is, in Durkheim's phrase, "well determined" by structural complexes of values, norms, collectivities, and roles — without being positively adapted to features of the practical conditions of action present in the particular situation. The stable constituents of the milieu do not in themselves entirely determine the processes of interaction. Variable features of particular situations may importantly condition the ways in which structural elements of the milieu constrain interactive sequences. A given sequence of interaction must become positively situated in the sense of adapted to variables such as time pressures, the skills of the individual actors, the motivational propensities and moods of the interactors, scarcities of resources, and so on.[148] Analytically, one cannot build the variation involved in such situational adaptations into conceptions of social structure without sacrificing the understanding of what stabilizes milieux across the differences among the particular conditions of the implementation of action. It seems more parsimonious to draw a distinction between the stably structured milieu — keeping in mind that not all milieux are *very* well determined by their structural elements — and the conditionally variable situation. It then becomes apparent that the generation of particular sequences of interaction within the milieu requires *intelligent* adaptation to features of the situation.

Thus, the interactors must employ their intelligent capacities to understand and communicate about features of the conditioning situation in order to coordinate their activities. Certain characteristics of such involvement of intelligence in the generation of interaction are of interest. In one perspective, one may say that the interactors must produce and share "intelligence" about the situation of their interaction. For some types of milieux, especially rather undifferentiated ones, such intelligence may consist largely of references to features indexed in commonsensical terms directly understood by all interactors.[149] Other milieux may require that highly technical and refined types of intelligence be provided by actors differentiated into a number of specialized roles. The interactors may have to act upon the implications of the intelligence provided by others while having little technical understanding of it themselves. Such "competence gaps," as Parsons has termed such differences in the understanding of intelligent contributions to interactive processes in his analyses of professional roles,[150] can be stably bridged only by the institutionalization of trust in intelligence as a medium within the salient social systems. The interactors must be willing to accept the intelligence which they circulate to one another in their efforts to gain common understanding of the contingencies imposed by features of the situation upon their interaction. Ultimately, the value of such circulating intelligence, although supported by institutionalized trust on the social system side of the interchange, is "backed" fundamentally by the qualities of the behavioral operations involved in the skills and understandings of the interactors. Intelligence provided by formal operations commands greater capacity to stabilize its trustworthiness across a more diverse set of situations than intelligence which is less generalized.[151]

Thus, many milieux, especially highly differentiated ones, depend upon interdependent uses of a variety of specialized applications of intelligence in order to gain situational adaptation. The particular uses of intelligence may involve all spheres of the behavioral systems of the interactors, given the many modalities of situations that may be problematic for a sequence of interaction. Indeed, the diversity of respects in which intelligence may be required in order to situate interaction certainly comprises a major functional exigency favoring the coordination of information on the basis of *generalized* intelligence. Only if intelligence of a variety of functional types is widely and rather freely trusted and accepted by the interactors can they manage to coordinate activities in which at least some play highly specialized roles. In this sense, it may be seen that forms of the "competence gap" are practically universal to interaction, not limited to professional or highly technical role relationships. It also appears that intelligence as a medium has pervasively important social dimensions. A given individual's behavioral system cannot in itself comprise a very extensive or socially productive source of intelligence. Rather, his intelligence must be coordinated with the intelligent capacities of others. His products of intelligence must, broadly, be acceptable in circulation to various classes of alters. He must be willing to accept the intelligent reports of others in attempting to coordinate his own behavioral activities. Intelligence that lacks coordination within a system of interactive relationships must be in danger of losing its generalization and must certainly be restricted in the flexibility of its deployment to work upon practical problems.

Although all sectors of the behavioral systems of the interactors may become involved in the situating of action, a predominant or focal part is played by the expectational sector. Action cannot become situated without an intelligent understanding of the structural features of the milieu. Part of the situating of interaction concerns the selective invocation of normative constituents of the milieu applying specifically to the situational features determined to be present as constraining for the emergent process of interaction. In this sense, the constraining normative order for the particular situation must—in the symbolic interactionist sense—be selectively and generatively constructed out of the stable structures of the milieu. The stability of the milieu derives in considerable part from its inclusion of elements which can be flexibly and diversely combined so as to make possible realistic normative adaptations to a range of different situational conditions. Perhaps one may take the generativity of the normative rules of a grammar, constituents of a vast preponderance of human social mileux, as prototypical of this quality of the structuring of interaction. If so, the diversity of situational specifications that can be generated from a limited set of stable structures, i.e., the flexibility which the constructive processes derive from their regulation by general normative entities, becomes a very prominent characteristic of interaction generally. In the present context, I wish only to emphasize that some very interesting operational characteristics of expectational intelligence must be shared by interactors if they are able to coordinate the normative construction of situations. I believe that our account of the expectational sector and its functioning may make understandable how in general terms individuals acquire these operational capacities. However, it remains to examine their actual deployment in processes of social interaction where quite specific intelligent understandings of features of milieux must become shared by the participants.

Finally, I wish simply to note that the present analysis of the involvement of intelligence in the normatively constructive processes of interaction may carry implications for the conceptualization of social structure. The theory of action has long insisted that social scientists must employ their capacities for abstraction in order to prehend the structural elements embedded in the flux of interaction.[152] Here, I have been insisting that actors must be hypothesized to be using their abstract abilities in the processes of intelligently providing normative regulation of their social action. Further, I am suggesting that, by attending to the nature of the informational operations which actors must perform upon normative representations if they are to situate their interaction, it may be possible to learn more about the constraints delimiting the informational nature of elements of social structure. Constituents of social structure may not take on just any form if they are to regulate interaction only upon the basis of intelligent communication of expectations developed through concrete or formal operations. Rather,

they must conform to some definite formal characteristics, e.g., abstraction, logical cohesion, hierarchical ordering, pertinence to general principles,
and order of application. I suspect that in some ways
matters of this sort have long been studied in more
intuitive fashion by scholars of jurisprudence concerned with the general nature of good and just
law.[153] Piaget's studies of games of marbles played
by children at different stages in the development of
intelligence provide us with a classic illustration of
the importance of formal qualities of normative
orders, even though this was not the perspective on
his material that he stressed.[154] We suggest that
such formal analysis of structure may prove a fruitful
area of research and that, if attention is given to the
intelligent capacities that can operate upon structural entities, it may prove a less chaotic area than
some of the ethnomethodological and phenomenological studies have implied.[155]

NOTES

1. See Talcott Parsons, *Social Structure and Personality*
(New York: The Free Press, 1964), Chapters 4 and 5; "An Ap-
proach to Psychological Theory in Terms of the Theory of
Action," in Sigmund Koch (ed.), *Psychology: A Study of a
Science* (New York: McGraw-Hill, 1959), pp. 612-711; "Some
Problems of General Theory in Sociology," in John C. McKin-
ney and Edward A. Tiryakian (eds.), *Theoretical Sociology:
Perspectives and Developments* (New York: Appleton-
Century-Crofts, 1970), pp. 27-68.

2. Parsons, "An Approach to Psychological Theory in
Terms of the Theory of Action," *op. cit.;* "Some Problems of
General Theory in Sociology," *op. cit.;* also, Parsons and Gerald
M. Platt, *The American University* (Cambridge: Harvard
University Press, 1973). The first essay draws the boundary on
the criterion of learning, while the latter two seem to imply that
some learned elements are crucial to the behavioral organism.

3. Parsons, "An Approach to Psychological Theory in
Terms of the Theory of Action," *op. cit.; Social Structure and
Personality,* Chapters 1, 4, 5; "Some Problems of General
Theory in Sociology," *op. cit.*

4. A thorough general review of Piaget's psychological
researches is presented in John H. Flavell, *The Developmental
Psychology of Jean Piaget* (Princeton: Van Nostrand, 1963).
A shorter and simpler account is given in Jean Piaget and Barbel Inhelder, *The Psychology of the Child* (New York: Basic
Books, 1969), although it treats the relationship between the
psychology of intelligence and affective psychology rather
differently than we propose to in this essay. Jean Piaget, *Six
Psychological Studies* (New York: Random House, 1967)
covers a good range of important materials quite succinctly.
Jean Piaget, *The Psychology of Intelligence* (Totowa, N. J.:
Littlefield, Adams, 1966) is an older work but remains a classically fine statement of Piaget's fundamental theoretical outlook
and of some key researches.

5. See Parsons: "On Building Social System Theory: A
Personal History," *Daedalus* (Fall, 1970), pp. 826-881.

6. Piaget, *The Psychology of Intelligence,* Chapter 1.

7. Perhaps this position is developed most clearly in Piaget,
The Origins of Intelligence in Children (New York: Norton,
1963).

8. Flavell, *op. cit.,* Chapters 1 and 2.

9. Piaget, *Structuralism* (New York: Basic Books, 1970);
Parsons, "An Outline of the Social System" in Talcott Parsons,

Edward Shils, Kaspar D. Naegele, and Jesse R. Pitts (eds.),
Theories of Society (New York: The Free Press, 1961), Vol. 1,
pp. 30-79; Talcott Parsons, *Politics and Social Structure* (New
York: The Free Press, 1969), Part IV, including essays on the
generalized media of interchange, power, influence, and value
commitments.

10. A technical account of formal operations is presented
in Flavell, *op. cit.,* Chapter 6; also, along with much illustrative
experimental material, in Barbel Inhelder and Jean Piaget,
*The Growth of Logical Thinking from Childhood to Adoles-
cence* (New York: Basic Books, 1958). A nontechnical account
is presented in Piaget and Inhelder, *op. cit.,* Chapter 5.

11. Flavell, *op. cit.;* Inhelder and Piaget, *op. cit.*

12. Although this is a very fundamental point, it perhaps
emerges especially clearly in Piaget, *The Origins of Intelligence
in Children.*

13. Flavell, *op. cit.*

14. *Ibid.,* Chapter 6; Piaget and Inhelder, *op. cit.,* Chapter 5.

15. Piaget, *Structuralism.* This is a fundamental and recurrent theme in the book.

16. See Alfred North Whitehead, *Process and Reality* (New
York: Harper Torchbooks, 1960; originally published in 1929).

17. Piaget, *Structuralism,* Chapter VI.

18. It is the account in *ibid.* that seems inadequate in this
regard. See also Victor Lidz, "On the Construction of Objective
Theory," *Sociological Inquiry* (Winter, 1972).

19. Parsons, *Politics and Social Structure,* Chapters 14,
15, 16.

20. Victor Lidz, *op. cit.*

21. Talcott Parsons and Edward Shils, "Values, Motives, and
Systems of Action," in Parsons and Shils (eds.), *Toward A
General Theory of Action* (Cambridge: Harvard University
Press, 1951).

22. The sociologically commonplace phrase "subjectively
meaningful behavior" has not been invoked directly by Parsons
in theoretically crucial contexts. However, the categories of
subjectivity and meaningfulness have been treated as central to·
the action frame of reference. See "An Outline of the Social
System," *op. cit.,* pp. 32-33. See also his discussion of Weber's
methodology and its background, especially in German Idealism, in *The Structure of Social Action* (New York: McGraw-
Hill, 1937). The treatment in "Some Problems of General Theory
in Sociology," *op. cit.,* places meaning in the position of a very
general reference category for action.

23. See especially Piaget, *Genetic Epistemology* (New York:
Columbia University Press, 1970).

24. *Ibid;* note also the account of Piaget's general interests
and theoretical intents in Flavell, *op. cit.,* Chapter 1.

25. Piaget, *Genetic Epistemology* and *The Psychology
of Intelligence,* and Piaget and Inhelder, *The Psychology of
the Child.*

26. Piaget, *The Psychology of Intelligence* presents perhaps
the clearest of the very general accounts of this framework but
is less technical than more recent statements. Flavell, *op. cit.,*
adheres quite closely to this frame of reference and provides
more technical formulations and an overview of more recent
research.

27. Piaget, *The Psychology of Intelligence,* especially Chapter 1, and *Biology and Knowledge* (Chicago: The University of
Chicago Press, 1971), *passim.*

28. Piaget, *The Origins of Intelligence in Children.*

29. Flavell, *op. cit.;* Piaget and Inhelder, *The Psychology
of the Child* perhaps provide the most general accounts.

30. Parsons, *The Social System* (Glencoe: The Free Press,
1951), especially Chapter VI; "An Approach to Psychological
Theory in Terms of the Theory of Action," *op. cit.; Social
Structure and Personality,* Chapter 4.

31. Note the critique in *The Origins of Intelligence in Children, passim,* but especially in the introduction and in the section
on conclusions.

32. See Parsons, "An Outline of the Social System" and

"Introduction to Part Four — Culture and the Social System" in *Theories of Society*.

33. Piaget, *Play, Dreams, and Imitation in Childhood* (New York: Norton, 1962), Chapter 7.

34. *Ibid.*

35. *Ibid.*

36. Piaget and Inhelder: *The Psychology of the Child*.

37. Sigmund Freud: *The Ego and the Id* (New York: Norton, 1962); "Mourning and Melancholia" in *General Psychological Theory*, Philip Rieff (ed.) (New York: Collier Books, 1963), and *Group Psychology and the Analysis of the Ego* (New York: Bantam Books, 1960); also, Parsons, "Some Problems of General Theory in Sociology," *op. cit.*

38. See the treatment of the Oedipus complex and its changing part in the functioning of the personality as the latter matures in Theodore Lidz, *The Person: His Development Throughout the Life Cycle* (New York: Basic Books, (1968).

39. Parsons, "Some Problems of General Theory in Sociology," *op. cit.*

40. Parsons, "An Approach to Psychological Theory in Terms of the Theory of Action," *op. cit.*, and "Some Reflections on the Problem of Psychosomatic Relationships in Health and Illness" in *Social Structure and Personality*.

41. See Parsons, *Societies: Evolutionary and Comparative Perspectives* (Englewood Cliffs: Prentice-Hall, 1966), Chapter 2.

42. See especially Piaget, *Play, Dreams, and Imitation in Childhood*.

43. Early formulations of the stages in the development of intelligence are presented in Piaget, *The Psychology of Intelligence* and *Judgment and Reasoning in the Child* (Totowa, N.J.: Littlefield, Adams, 1968). Inhelder and Piaget, *The Growth of Logical Thinking from Childhood to Adolescence*, and, in less technical form, Piaget and Inhelder, *The Psychology of the Child* present the more recent formulations. Flavell, *op. cit.*, provides a very general account of the nature of the stage formulations and of the scope of evidence that can be adduced in support of them.

44. Piaget, *The Origins of Intelligence in Children*, is the most general source on this stage of development.

45. Here, we are simply following the analysis of Piaget in *ibid.*

46. See the discussion of perception in Flavell, *op. cit.*

47. *Ibid.*

48. *Ibid*; Piaget, *Play, Dreams, and Imitation in Childhood*.

49. Inhelder and Piaget: *The Growth of Logical Thinking From Childhood to Adolescence*.

50. *Ibid.*

51. Flavell, *op. cit.*, presents a strong discussion of reversibility in his chapter on "Concrete Operations."

52. Piaget, *The Language and Thought of the Child* (Cleveland: Meridian Books, 1955), Chapters 1 and 2.

53. For definitions of Piaget's terms in this complicated area, see his *Play, Dreams, and Imitation in Childhood*, especially p. 67ff.

54. Parsons: "The Father Symbol: An Appraisal in the Light of Psychoanalytic and Sociological Theory," in *Social Structure and Personality*; also, Robert N. Bellah, "Father and Son in Christianity and Confucianism," in his *Beyond Belief* (New York: Harper and Row, 1970).

55. For example, see the contributions to Frank Smith and George A. Miller, *The Genesis of Language* (Cambridge: M.I.T. Press, 1966).

56. See Ruth Weir, *Language in the Crib* (The Hague: Mouton, 1962).

57. Inhelder and Piaget, *The Growth of Logical Thinking From Childhood to Adolescence*, p. 246.

58. *Ibid*; Flavell, *op. cit.*, Chapter 6.

59. Piaget, *Judgment and Reasoning in the Child*, pp. 152-153 especially, but *passim*.

60. Piaget, *The Moral Judgment of the Child* (New York: The Free Press, 1965), Chapter 1.

61. See Piaget and Inhelder, *The Psychology of the Child*. Chapter 4.

62. Inhelder and Piaget, *The Growth of Logical Thinking From Childhood to Adolescence*, pp. 26-27.

63. *Ibid*, p. 29.

64. Flavell, *op. cit.*, Chapter 5.

65. Ann Parsons, "Translator's Introduction," in Inhelder and Piaget: *The Growth of Logical Thinking From Childhood to Adolescence*.

66. Flavell, *op. cit.*, Chapter 6; Piaget and Inhelder, *The Psychology of the Child*, Chapter 5.

67. Inhelder and Piaget, *The Growth of Logical Thinking From Childhood to Adolescence*, final chapter.

68. Ann Parsons, *op. cit.*

69. Inhelder and Piaget, *The Growth of Logical Thinking from Childhood to Adolescence*, Chapter 1; Flavell, *op. cit.*, p. 347.

70. See Lon L. Fuller: *The Anatomy of the Law* (New York: Praeger, 1968) and *The Morality of Law* (New Haven: Yale University Press, 1964) for discussion of the science-like properties of the law and of formal legal procedure.

71. See Piaget, *The Psychology of Intelligence* and *The Origins of Intelligence in Children* for general accounts; also, Flavell, *op. cit.*, Chapters 1 and 2.

72. *Ibid*; Piaget, *Play, Dreams, and Imitation in Childhood* presents perhaps especially interesting analyses of psychological change developed in terms of equilibrium theory.

73. Piaget, *Origins of Intelligence in Children*.

74. This theme is perhaps most subtly developed in Piaget, *Play, Dreams, and Imitation in Childhood*.

75. *Ibid.*

76. Piaget, *The Origins of Intelligence in Children*, e.g., p. 236ff.

77. Flavell; *op. cit.*, quotes this on p. 48. It is from *Origins*, p. 410.

78. See Piaget, *Structuralism*.

79. See Parsons, "An Outline of the Social System," *op. cit.*, *Societies: Evolutionary and Comparative Perspectives*, and Neil J. Smelser, *Theory of Collective Behavior* (New York: The Free Press, 1963).

80. See Robert N. Bellah, *Beyond Belief*, especially the introductory chapter, and "Epilogue" in Bellah (ed.), *Religion and Progress in Modern Asia* (New York: The Free Press, 1965).

81. See Parsons, *Societies: Evolutionary and Comparative Perspectives*.

82. See Piaget, *Biology and Knowledge*.

83. This methodological position is developed in Piaget, *Structuralism*.

84. Piaget, *The Psychology of Intelligence*, Chapter 1.

85. *Ibid*; also, *The Origins of Intelligence in Children* and, especially, *Biology and Knowledge* for more recent and extensive discussions.

86. See, for example, Piaget, *Origins of Intelligence in Children* and *Play, Dreams, and Imitation in Childhood*.

87. See Marshall D. Sahlins and Elman R. Service, *Evolution and Culture* (Ann Arbor: University of Michigan Press, 1960); Robert N. Bellah, "Religious Evolution," in his *Beyond Belief*; Parsons, *Societies: Evolutionary and Comparative Perspectives*.

88. See Flavell, *op. cit.*, Chapter 2; and Piaget: *The Origins of Intelligence in Children*, especially Chapter III and IV.

89. Parsons, "Some Considerations on the Theory ot Social Change," *Rural Sociology* (September, 1961).

90. See Flavell's discussion in *op. cit.* of Piaget's notion of horizontal *decalages*, pp. 20-24.

91. See Parsons, *Societies: Evolutionary and Comparative Perspectives*, pp. 28-29, for schemas outlining the relevant relations among system components and their environments.

92. See Flavell, *op. cit.*, especially Chapters 3, 6, and 10, for

discussion of the relations between Piaget's work on perception and his work within the frameworks of the psychology of intelligence and of genetic epistemology.

93. See Sigmund Freud, "Instincts and their Vicissitudes," in *General Psychological Theory;* also Erik H. Erikson: *Childhood and Society* (New York: Norton, 1950 — revised and enlarged edition, 1963).

94. See Theodore Lidz, *The Person*, especially Chapters 4-8.

95. Parsons, "An Approach to Psychological Theory in Terms of the Theory of Action" and *Social Structure and Personality,* Chapter 4.

98. See Parsons, *The Social System,* Chapter IX, "Expressive Symbols and the Social System; The Communication of Affect," and "The Theory of Symbolism in Relation to Action" in Talcott Parsons, Robert F. Bales, and Edward Shils, *Working Papers in the Theory of Action* (Glencoe: The Free Press, 1953).

99. Piaget, *Play, Dreams, and Imitation in Childhood.*

100. *Ibid;* cf. Sigmund Freud, *The Interpretation of Dreams* in *Basic Writings of Sigmund Freud* (New York: Modern Library, 1938).

101. Parsons, "Introduction to Part Four — Culture and the Social System," in *Theories of Society*; see also, Parsons, "The Father Symbol: An Appraisal in the Light of Psychoanalytic and Sociological Theory," in *Social Structure and Personality*, and Robert N. Bellah, "Father and Son in Christianity and Confucianism," in *Beyond Belief.*

102. Ernst Kris, *Psychoanalytic Explorations in Art* (New York: Schocken Books, 1964); Walter Abell: *The Collective Dream in Art* (New York: Schocken Books, 1966); John Dewey, *Art and Experience* (New York: Putnam, 1934).

103. Piaget, *Play, Dreams, and Imitation in Childhood.*

104. *Ibid,* Chapters VII, IX, X.

105. *Ibid,* Chapters IX, X.

106. *Ibid.*

107. The term "expectations" is used by Parsons in *The Social System* with an emphasis on its interindividual status that is very close to our own emphasis, even though it is not given systematic status within a theory of the behavioral system.

108. Our understanding of these processes of expectational calculation has been much influenced by Aaron Cicourel's analysis in *The Social Organization of Juvenile Justice* (New York: Wiley, 1968), even though he places less emphasis than we do upon stable normative structures.

109. Freud, *The Ego and the Id;* Parsons, "The Superego and the Theory of Social Systems," in *Social Structure and Personality.*

110. Parsons, "Introduction to Part Four — Culture and the Social System," in *Theories of Society.*

111. Piaget, *The Moral Judgment of the Child*, and Inhelder and Piaget, *The Growth of Logical Thinking from Childhood to Adolescence,* final chapter.

112. Piaget, *The Moral Judgment of the Child*, Chapter I.

113. *Ibid,* Chapters 1 and 2.

114. *Ibid,* pp. 128-130.

115. Our account here follows that of Piaget quite closely. See *ibid.,* Chapters 1.3.

116. See Inhelder and Piaget, *The Growth of Logical Thinking From Childhood to Adolescence,* final chapter.

117. Piaget's discussion in *ibid,* should be compared with Erik Erikson's in *Identity and the Life Cycle* (New York: International Universities Press, Psychological Issues, no. 1, 1959), which in the notion of identity diffusion seems to refer to the personality aspect of the individual's instabilities in confronting moral dilemmas during the adolescent phases of development.

118. Lawrence Kohlberg, "Moral Development," in D. Sills (ed.), *The International Encyclopedia of the Social Sciences* (New York: Macmillan, 1968).

119. For example, see Max-Gluckman: *The Judicial Process Among The Barotse* (Manchester: Manchester University Press, 1955) and *The Ideas in Barotse Jurisprudence* (New Haven: Yale University Press, 1965).

120. A. Irving Hallowell: "The Protocultural Foundations of Human Adaptation" in Victor Lidz and Talcott Parsons (eds.), *Readings on Premodern Societies* (Englewood Cliffs: Prentice-Hall, 1972); J. N. Spuhler, editor: *The Evolution of Man's Capacity for Culture* (Detroit: Wayne State University Press, 1959); Sherwood L. Washburn: "Behavior and Human Evolution" in Washburn (ed.), *Classification and Human Evolution* (Chicago: Aldine, 1963).

121. Noam Chomsky, *Language and Mind*, enlarged edition (New York: Harcourt, Brace, and Janovitch, 1972); Eric H. Lenneberg, *Biological Foundations of Language* (New York: Wiley, 1967).

122. *Ibid;* Frank Smith and George A. Miller, *The Genesis of Language* (Cambridge: M.I.T. Press, 1966).

123. Noam Chomsky, *Language and Mind.*

124. *Ibid.*

125. Piaget and Inhelder, *The Psychology of the Child*, Chapter 3, especially section VI.

126. Claude Levi-Strauss, *The Savage Mind* (Chicago: The University of Chicago Press, 1966); *The Raw and the Cooked* (New York: Harper, 1969).

127. Emile Durkheim, *The Elementary Forms of the Religious Life* (London: Allen and Unwin, 1915), especially the Conclusion.

128. Parsons, "Introduction to Part Four — Culture and the Social System," in *Theories of Society.*

129. Claude Levi-Strauss, *Totemism* (Boston: Beacon Press, 1963).

130. See Claude Levi-Strauss, *The Savage Mind,* Chapters 1 and 2.

131. Piaget, *Structuralism.*

132. See Max Weber's discussion of the effects of the absence of logical standards upon classical Chinese culture in his *Religion of China* (Glencoe: The Free Press, 1951).

133. See Lon L. Fuller, *The Anatomy of the Law.*

134. See Max Weber, *The Rational and Social Foundations of Music* (Carbondale: Southern Illinois University Press, 1958); Albert C. Barnes, *The Art in Painting* (New York: Harcourt, Brace and Company, 1925).

135. For example, see E. H. Gombrich, *Art and Illusion* (New York: Bollingen Foundation, 1961); and Werner Jaeger, *Early Christianity and Greek Paideia* (Cambridge: Harvard University Press, 1961).

136. See Piaget, *Biology and Knowledge* for a more general emphasis upon the importance for systems of autoregulation in the present sense, though one that does not touch directly on the pattern-maintenance problem of interest here.

137. See Parsons and Gerald M. Platt, *The American University, passim.*

138. Here we intend specifically to draw upon Erik Erikson's notion of personal identity. See *Identity and the Life Cycle*; also *Young Man Luther* (New York: Norton, 1958) for more emphasis on the intertwining of identity and sociocultural dynamics.

139. W. I. Thomas, *The Unadjusted Girl* (New York: Harper Torchbooks, 1967), Chapters 1 and 2.

140. Harold Garfinkel, *Studies in Ethnomethodology* (Englewood Cliffs: Prentice-Hall, 1967).

141. Parsons, "Some Problems of General Theory in Sociology," *op. cit.*; Parsons and Gerald M. Platt, *The American University*. I am indebted to Parsons and Platt for the opportunity to see crucial portions of their treatment of intelligence in manuscript prior to publication. My remarks refer to the general schematization of that treatment included in the first few chapters of the book, but not to some of the more detailed and empirical discussion of later chapters, which I did not see until some months after the present analysis was completed. I do not find in

these latter materials grounds for substantial change in the present formulations, although there are interesting leads toward further refinement.

142. Parsons, *Politics and Social Structure*, Chapters 1 and 2 and Part IV.

143. See the discussion of the media in Parsons, "An Outline of the Social System," *op. cit.*

144. The concepts of generation and generativity of concern here are discussed in Noam Chomsky, *op. cit.*, and Eric H. Lenneberg, *op. cit.*

145. This has been a basic characteristic of all the media. See Parsons, *Politics and Social Structure*, Part IV.

146. Parsons, "Some Problems of General Theory in Sociology," *op. cit.*, and Parsons and Platt: *The American University,* especially Chapter 2.

147. *Ibid.*

148. See Garfinkel, *Studies in Ethnomethodology*; Cicourel, *Social Organization of Juvenile Justice*; Gerald D. Suttles, *The Social Order of the Slum* (Chicago: University of Chicago Press, 1968).

149. Cicourel, *op. cit.*

150. See Parsons, *The Social System*, Chapter X; "The Field of Medical Sociology" in *Social Structure and Personality*; "On the Concept of Influence," in *Politics and Social Structure.*

151. Parsons has tended to treat the bridging of competence gaps as a problem to be overcome by the generalized medium of influence. Here, without denying that influence also plays an important part, I am trying to indicate that paying attention to the involvement of generalized intelligence and its circulation may substantially enhance our understanding of how competence gaps are successfully bridged. This may be an instance in which a mode of linkage between different media other than that of interchange will prove to be theoretically important.

152. Parsons, *The Structure of Social Action*, especially the discussions of Weber's methodology, and "Evaluation and Objectivity in the Social Sciences: An Interpretation of Max Weber's Contributions," in *Sociological Theory and Modern Society* (New York: The Free Press, 1967).

153. See Fuller, *The Anatomy of the Law and The Morality of Law,* for the kind of treatment I have found most useful.

154. Piaget, *The Moral Judgment of the Child.*

155. For example, Alfred Schutz, *The Phenomenology of the Social World* (Evanston: Northwestern University Press, 1967), and Garfinkel: *Studies in Ethnomethodology*. However, Garfinkel and Harvey Sacks seem to be exploring a line of interest in formal qualities of social structures and the modes of their use that may prove to be convergent with the present interest in the paper, "On Formal Structures and Practical Actions," in John C. McKinney and Edward A. Tiryakian (eds.), *op. cit.*

9

ACTION AND EXPERIENCE

Jan J. Loubser

This essay is a very tentative excursion into alternative combinations in the theory of action. I considered the title "Taking an Action Theory Trip or Games Parsonians Play" but decided that it would be passé before it was current. Yet it would reflect more accurately my intellectual attitude to and in this essay. There is the element of a logical game in it, following a logical path, wherever it may lead. This is extremely high-risk action for someone committed to orthodoxy in the theory of action (which I am not), as it opens up a Pandora's box of possibilities. There are many components in the theory of action, which could be combined in combinations equalling their square. Once we open the door to the consideration of different combinations than the ones currently accepted as viable, the variations are virtually limitless.

Yet we cannot afford to be committed to orthodoxy in scientific theory; we cannot be Parsonians in the sense of accepting as doctrine the combinations Parsons has proposed; and certainly Parsons has never expected such a commitment from anyone. If the frame of reference is valid and the component analytical concepts reflect the crucial aspects of empirical reality, it is imperative that we use both logical and empirical methods in identifying the combinations that reflect most adequately the combinations or systemic aspects of empirical reality. By considering the whole population of possible logical combinations and selecting from them different models of further combinations in building theoretical systems, we will have different models to test out simultaneously. The two processes taken together should then enable us to identify the most useful model in understanding empirical systems of action.

Of course, one has to proceed with great caution and bring all one's accumulated empirical knowledge and sensitivities to bear on the task. Not all of us will master that art as well as Parsons has. But the logical task is the first priority and is in itself a formidable undertaking. On what basis does one propose the reversal of combinations or classifications with which Parsons has been satisfied for a lifetime of concentrated effort? Empirical research would be one basis if one would be able to test the theory at that level of generality. But this would be another lifetime task. The logical alternative is no less imposing and requires no less concentrated effort.

By these standards this essay should quietly be placed in a drawer while its various aspects are developed further and considered experimentally against logical alternatives and empirical evidence and published twenty years from now, if at all, in the form in which it survives all this scientific action. That would be the deadly serious, committed way of doing it. But that approach would elevate science too much to the level of religion, the serious way of life, to be palatable in the post-Heisenbergian world as the only valid approach. We have today a healthy cynicism with respect to all forms of truth claims and reification of symbols. We are aware of the finiteness of our most serious efforts. We are beginning to realize that our elaborate arsenal of methods and techniques to precision-engineer our knowledge are subject to the same scepticism which they were supposed to implement and eliminate.

All of this may drive us to deep alienation and withdrawal. Or it may give us a new sense of freedom and daring in playful exploration of the here and now as a finite point in an infinite, evolving universe of meaning which is an all-possibility thing.

This essay then is a tentative excursion to which the author would not want the reader to take a religious attitude. It is a serious effort because games are ways of acting to discover meaning. It is an experiment in the consideration of alternative combinations to open the theory of action up as a more-than-one-possibility thing. But I am not prepared to present it as *my* version of the theory of action as an alternative to Parsons' and on which I am going to spend a lifetime of scholarship to prove that it is more "true" or "useful" than his. To reflect fully my personal assessment of it, as outlined here, I have stripped it of all the trimmings with which we ritualistically adorn our scientific offerings, such as footnotes, references, lengthy qualifications, and textual analysis of the corpus of writings within which it explores one possible logical path. Yet it is not a frivolous permutation of the paraphernalia of Parsonian theory. If there were not a strong sense of potential usefulness in clarifying some of the issues I see in the theory of action there would be very little sense in including it in this volume.

ACTION AND ACTION SYSTEMS

The epistemological position of analytical realism, the frame of reference, and the assumptions of the theory of action are not in question for the purposes of this essay.

These assumptions require that action be abstracted from the phenomena of concrete human behavior. Action does not include all forms of human behavior. It is concerned only with those components and aspects that are considered most useful in the explanation of the regularities and variations in patterned human behavior. This usefulness has of course, to be proven in empirical research and in the development of empirical theory. Although the general theory approach recognizes the limited status of analytical theory and conceptual schemes, it is assumed that it provides the most economical and fruitful strategy for building systematic empirical theory, which remains the ultimate goal of scientific endeavor. This essay is confined to analytical theory.

Action is defined as that symbolically mediated behavior emitted by an actor in a situation in which the actor

1. seeks gratification of motivational needs
2. through the attainment of specific goal states
3. by the application of available means under given conditions
4. subject to the control of normative standards.

Action always involves an actor exerting effort to gratify his symbolically mediated needs in a situation. For the purposes of the analysis of most action the process of symbolic encoding is treated as given, except when this process itself is the object of study. Similarly, the existence of needs is taken as given, except when the focus is on the explanation of their genesis. The conceptualization and analysis of all action otherwise assumes the existence of these two types of components which form the base lines on which the structure of action is built.

Within the framework of an actor in a situation we have to conceptualize action in terms of the minimum number of concepts sufficient to the explanation of social phenomena involving action in one form or another. These concepts have to be systematically related to each other in terms of a minimum number of logical principles. Action is assumed to be systemic even at the level of the single unit act. Action systems are open systems consisting of four interdependent types of components, existing in highly variable environments on which they are dependent and with which they are in constant interchange. The environments of action systems are not seen as dependent on action systems to the same extent; hence the same order of interdependence and systematic patterning of relationships that exist among the components of the system do not exist between the system and its environment. Being goal-oriented in satisfying needs, action systems constantly attempt to control and transform their environments to attain goal states. But systems are also constantly conditioned by their environments, have to adapt to variations in these environments, and have to secure resources from these environments for their functioning as systems.

This analysis of action systems will start with an analysis of the unit act which constitutes the smallest unit of action as defined. The emission of a unit act on the part of an actor in a situation involves the following analytically separable components as implied in the definition:

1. the activation of a motivational need in the actor, the gratification of which is given priority in this unit act;
2. the selection by the actor of normative standards of appropriateness of means, goal states, and optimal gratification levels;
3. the setting of the goal of the act or the assignment of gratification significance or meaning to an object or aspects of an object in the situation, which becomes the goal object of the unit act, over which the actor has to gain control;
4. the facilitation of the act in terms of the actor's ability to select and apply means and the limiting conditions beyond his ability.

The unit act consists in the combination of these four components to emit the act, which can take place only after these components have been combined. The consummation of the act is not simply the combination of these four components but a separate event involving the expenditure of motivational energy to attain the goal state of gratification given the available facilitation and normative controls.

The order in which these components are listed represents the sequence in which the actor has to choose them, conceived as a value-adding process.

Although as components they may exist or appear in any order, their choice and combination as factors or components of the unit act follow the sequence of need activation, normative standard, setting of goal state, and facilitation. The unit act results at the completion of the sequence *as a separate event;* the sequence is a prerequisite for the emission of the unit act, not the act itself.

This conception of the unit act is voluntaristic in the sense that it involves choices and effort on the part of the actor. The voluntaristic postulate implies that there are certain universal dimensions represented in the composition of the unit act and of action in general. The fundamental dimension may be called the consummatory, having to do with the consummation of the act. The need component and the goal state components are obviously specifications of this dimension, the first internal to the actor and the second external in the sense of specifying the aspects in the situation over which the actor has to gain control for gratification of the need. The second dimension represents the instrumental problems which have to be overcome. The facilitation and normative standard components are specifications of this dimension, with the problem of facilitation constituting the external aspect and the selection of normative standards the internal problem.

These two dimensions are seen as orthogonal and hence as axes of action differentiation, each with an internal and an external pole, the actor being the point of reference. The consummatory axis has primacy over the instrumental axis in that it gives rise to instrumental problems. Within each axis the internal poles have primacy over the external poles in that the actor is seen as defining the goal state and facilitation problems in terms of internal problems. Relative to each other, the internal poles have high information significance in action while the external poles have high energy significance. The expenditure of energy in action takes place not with respect to need activation and normative standards but in the attainment of goal states through the application of means.

The activation of the motivational need of the actor is a control mechanism in the sense that it "turns on" the energy flow and sets the sequence in motion. The satisfaction of the need through the act may be seen as "turning off" the energy flow. This component thus defines the desirable consummatory state of the actor. The normative standard serves a different control function; it channels energy rather than turning it on and off. In this sense it is instrumental to both the setting of the goal of the act and the selection of means. The setting of the goal in turn acts as a triggering mechanism in relation to the facilitation of the act. It turns energy expenditure on facilitation

on and off, the latter being the case when the instrumental problem of facilitation has been solved. Hence it defines and controls the goal state of the actor vis-à-vis the situation, which may not be one of full satisfaction of the internal consummatory state. The facilitation component represents a further channeling of energy within the instrumental axis in terms of specific expenditure in the facilitation of the act.

These components of action therefore present a set of controls through which an actor uses his energy to achieve states of gratification. Energy is used in action but is not part of action. Action is the turning on and off of energy and channeling it into the appropriate channels to achieve the goal state of the action. These controls operate in a value-adding sequence leading to the consummation of the act. The rationale for this sequence is based on the nature of the components as control mechanisms and the relations among them on the major dimensions of action space-time represented by the instrumental and consummatory axes and their internal and external poles. These relations are implied in the preceding analysis: Consummatory states have to be defined prior to instrumental questions about how to achieve them; instrumental problems have to be solved before consummatory states can be achieved. The controls are therefore coupled across the consummatory-instrumental axes in order to result in the consummation of the action in the sequence shown in Figure 9-1.

Unit acts do not occur in isolation, and the preceding analysis of a unit act in abstraction from a population of unit acts provides only the primitive terms of the theory of action. One implication of this analysis is that the unit act is not the smallest unit of

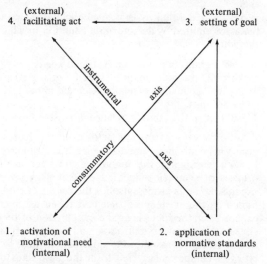

Figure 9-1.   The value-added sequence of the unit act.

analysis of interest to the social scientist; we have to conceptualize the internal structuring and process of the unit act itself. But we also have to be able to analyse aggregates of unit acts and the relationships among them. We have treated the unit act as a system; the relations among a population of unit acts are also patterned in systematic ways. A system of action consists in the relations of ordered interdependence among a population of unit acts. Systems of action, as we have seen, are open systems dependent on inputs from their environments and emitting outputs to their environments, which may include other action systems. Action systems, like unit acts, are emitted by actors in situations; and their environments also include actors and situations.

Action systems are patterned along the same axes as the unit act but the plurality of unit acts gives rise to exigencies that require emergent patterns in action systems of larger scale. These emergent patterns crystallize in analytically differentiated sub-systems of the system of action along the consummatory and instrumental axes and at the internal and external poles of these.

The internal pole of the consummatory axis becomes the focus of the differentiation of the *pattern maintenance and tension management subsystem* (L). The main functional problem from the point of reference of the action system as a whole becomes the stability of the supply of motivational energy for the gratification of the needs of the system as well as the activation of new motivational needs requisite for new unit acts or action-chains in the system. This involves the assignment of priority to certain needs in the system, the maintenance of this priority pattern, and the management of tensions resulting from the inherent frustrations and deprivations resulting from it. The subsystem retains its internal consummatory significance in that it seeks the optimization of the gratification of patterned motivational needs.

The external pole of the consummatory axis becomes the focus of the differentiation of the *goal-attainment* subsystem (G). The main functional problem from the point of reference of the system as a whole is the setting of goal states in the particular situation on the basis of the priority patterns of motivational needs of the system and to mobilize motivation and other resources for their attainment. This involves mobilization of agents or actors into goal-attainment action in the interest of the system regardless of their own motivational needs. Hence a critical functional problem for this subsystem is that of control over action and the stabilization of this control.

The external pole of the instrumental axis becomes the focus of the differentiation of the *adaptive* subsystem of the action system (A). The main functional problem from the point of reference of the system as a whole is that of generalized access to the environment to acquire the facilities required by the system and the appropriate encoding of objects in the environment in terms of their general significance and usefulness for the system. It involves several steps of transformation of environmental inputs, depending on the specific use and level of facilitation that is required by the system. This subsystem also manages the adaptation of the system to conditions in the environment beyond the control of the system which set limits to the range of facilities available.

The internal pole of the instrumental axis of action becomes the focus of the differentiation of the *integrative* subsystem of the system of action (I). The main problem from the point of reference of the system as a whole is that of the stabilization of generalized normative regulation governing the action process in terms of normative standards for the appropriateness of levels of gratification, facilitation, and goal-attainment for a plurality of unit acts or actors. Stabilization of generalized normative regulation in the system serves to optimize acceptance of the normative standards of the system, which can by no means be taken for granted. The functionally differentiated system of action is presented in Figure 9-2.

It should be noted that this model of the action system does not necessarily imply a plurality of actors but only a plurality of unit acts, which may involve only one actor in a situation. The emergent functional

A	G
Ultrastability of generalized facilities (external-instrumental)	Ultrastability of control over performance (external-consummatory)
Ultrastability of motivation (internal-consummatory)	Ultrastability of normative regulation (internal-instrumental)
L	I

Figure 9-2. Functionally differentiated action system.
L = Pattern Maintenance and Tension Management Subsystem
I = Integrative Subsystem
G = Goal Attainment Subsystem
A = Adaptive Subsystem
[NOTE: Ultrastability is here used in the general systems sense of continual adjustment of an open system to variations in its environment.]

problems all derive from the plurality of unit acts and the need to pattern interdependent relations among them. With a plurality of actors, still further problems arise, as we shall see.

THE PATTERN-VARIABLES OF ACTION

Although the components of action have specific functional significance within the unit act with respect to the instrumental-consummatory axes and their external and internal poles, these dimensions of action also present dilemmas of choice to the actor in selecting each of the components. These dilemmas of choice must be specified because they become the bases for the patterning of the components of unit acts and of different types of unit acts through the combination of patterns. These dilemmas are seen as four logically dichotomous choices which the actor has to make before he can emit the unit act. He has to make one choice with respect to each component of the unit act, and these choices have to be combined in specified ways in the determination of different types of unit act. These combinations can be seen as a secondary series of choices.

With respect to the motivational need, the actor has to decide whether this particular unit act requires the gratification of a consummatory need or an instrumental need. The actor must be seen as having at any one time a variety of needs that may be activated at the same time. The gratification of one type of need necessarily implies the delay of gratification of another. Hence this is a question of setting of priority between needs with respect to the unit act. The primary dilemma is that of *affectivity*, which means giving priority to a consummatory need, and *affective-neutrality*, which means giving priority to instrumental needs. This choice variable is therefore of primary significance for establishing, *within* the need component of the unit act, a consummatory or an instrumental pattern. It is the principal focus for the differentiation of the instrumental and the consummatory axes. Given the voluntary postulate and the gratification-seeking tendency of action, the critical problem and contingency at this point is the establishment of instrumental primacy, that is, choosing affective-neutrality. The strongest tendency is the obverse, to give primacy to consummatory needs.

With respect to the goal state the actor has to choose between the internal or external primacy of the significance of goal objects, within the consummatory dimension. If the goal state has primarily internal significance, it will be a matter of the *quality* of the goal object. If the goal state has primarily external significance, that is, if it requires the achievement of control over a goal object, it will be a matter of interest in the *performance* of the object. Because this choice is located at the external pole of the consummatory axis, the performance choice is particularly critical in establishing patterns of external goal attainment. With the basic consummatory focus at the internal pole there is a tendency to establish internal primacy in goal attainment, which requires lower levels of control over objects.

With respect to the facilitation component, the primary focus is instrumental and the basic dilemma one of choosing between the instrumental and consummatory significance of objects. The instrumental choice involves choosing a means object on the basis of its general usefulness, its belonging to a class of means objects. The consummatory choice involves choosing a means object on the basis of its particular usefulness for this particular unit act, regardless of its general usefulness. This choice between general facilitating capacity and particular facilitation is conceptualized in the pattern-variable of *universalism-particularism*. This pattern variable then has primary significance for the determination of the instrumental or consummatory significance of the facilitation component. Again, it is important to keep in mind that this is differentiation of objects *within* the instrumental axis. Hence the tendency here is toward universalism, an interest in generalized facilitation capacity; and the critical problem is to establish particularistic primacy with respect to means objects for particular consummatory purposes.

At the internal pole of the instrumental axis, the locus of the normative standard component, the basic problem is again one of internal-external significance determination, as in the case of the external pole of the consummatory axis. Within the instrumental axis the primary pole is the external one, and with the tendency toward universalization there is a tendency to externalization, that is, to assign primary external significance to objects. This is represented by a specific interest in the object, confined to the context of its usefulness. The main problem at the internal-instrumental pole is, therefore, to establish a choice of internal-instrumental significance. This is represented by a diffuse interest in the object, regardless of its specific usefulness in external terms. The master pattern-variable here is thus *specificity-diffuseness,* with specificity being the dominant tendency and the critical problem being one of establishing internal primacy or diffuseness.

The logic of these special relationships of the pattern-variables to the axes of action differentiation derives from the intrinsic opposite tendencies of the two axes. Not only do they involve opposite choices themselves, but they represent opposite polar tendencies, with the consummatory axis having a centripetal or internalizing tendency and the instrumental axis a centrifugal or externalizing tendency. Therefore, the critical problems or contingencies of action are those *opposing* the opposite tendencies and thereby establishing interdependence or systemic integration.

The four pattern variables are therefore exhaustive of the choices an actor has to make with respect to establishing *primacy* for each type of component before he can act. Figure 9-3 shows the master pattern variables for each component, with the critical choice variable opposing the primary tendency at each pole in italics.

These four master pattern variables provide the basis on which we can derive a typology of unit acts. Given the propositions we have presented, there are two basic polar types of unit act, the instrumental and the consummatory. The instrumental gives primacy to instrumental tendencies in the choice of all four components. This involves the affective-neutrality choice of motivational need and the universalism choice in the facility component. Further, because of the external polar tendency of this axis, it involves the external choices in the setting of the goal state and the normative standard, that is performance and specificity respectively. By the same logic the consummatory polar opposite involves the choices of affectivity, particularism, quality, and diffuseness.

The other two types are not polar in the same sense as the first two but are structured to counteract or balance the polar tendencies of the two axes. They are therefore external-consummatory and internal-instrumental unit acts. The first, external-consummatory, combines consummatory choices on the two axes with the critical choices at the two external poles, in the latter respect therefore opposing the internalizing tendency of pure consummatory action. The choices are affectivity, particularism, performance, and specificity. Internal-instrumental action is the exact opposite, presenting instrumental choices combined with internal ones: affective neutrality,

universalism, quality, and diffuseness. Given the basic tendencies of the consummatory and instrumental axes to internalize and externalize respectively, these two types of unit act obviously counteract these tendencies by providing *external* primacy in consummatory action and *internal* primacy in instrumental action.

These four types of unit act are ideal types, representing opposites. If the logically possible matrix of sixteen types of unit acts is generated by applying the value-adding sequence in the unit act analysed earlier, these four types fall on the extreme corners of the matrix, which one would expect of ideal types. The same result can be obtained by classifying the two variables with primacy for instrumental-consummatory axes differentiation (affective neutrality-affectivity, universalism-particularism) with the remaining two with internal-external differentiation primacy.

These four ideal types of unit act form the basis for a typology of action types, as in Figure 9-4.

As can be seen in Figure 9-4, summarizing the preceding discussion, each type of unit act has two components patterned on the same choices as two components of one of the other three. Within each of the two sets of types, the instrumental and consummatory, the choices are the same at the internal-consummatory and external-instrumental poles, the two poles of primary significance for determining the basic type of action. Between types, however, the

External-Instrumental	External-Consummatory
facilitation of act	setting of goal state
Particularism-Universalism	Quality-*Performance*
Internal-Consummatory	Internal-Instrumental
motivational need	acceptance of normative standard
Affectivity-*Affective-Neutrality*	*Diffuseness*-Specificity

Figure 9-3. Position of master pattern-variables in unit act with variables relating to critical choices in italics.

Instrumental Act		External-Consummatory Act	
Facilitation	Goal State	Facilitation	Goal State
Universalism	Performance	Particularism	Performance
Motivational Need	Normative Standard	Motivational Need	Normative Standard
Affective neutrality	Specificity	Affectivity	Specificity
Consummatory Act		Internal-Instrumental Act	
Facilitation	Goal State	Facilitation	Goal State
Particularism	Quality	Universalism	Quality
Motivational Need	Normative Standard	Motivational Need	Normative Standard
Affectivity	Diffuseness	Affective neutrality	Diffuseness

Figure 9-4. The four basic types of unit acts.

choices are the same at the external-consummatory and internal-instrumental poles, establishing external-internal differentiation across types.

Before all the components of these four types of unit act can be defined by unique patterns, the patterned choices have to be combined in a specific way which is the same for all four types and leads to a complete differentiation of the types with each component of each type characterized by a unique combination of two pattern choices.

We have already postulated the value-added sequence for the combination of the components of the unit act (see Figure 9-1). The sequence of choices of the primary pattern of each of these components is the same. In fact, it is the same sequence specified further with respect to choice of the primary pattern of each component. The sequence of combination of components is, however, *not* the same. The sequence must be such that

1. the consummatory axis of the type of action, whether instrumental or consummatory, contain the critical variable in determining the primacy of that type of action at *both* internal and external poles;

2. the same situation should be true of the instrumental axis of each type of action;

3. *each* component of the type of action should combine a variable critical for consummatory-instrumental differentiation with one critical for internal-external differentiation;

4. the sequence should be compatible with the sequence of combination of components of the unit act with its provision for coupling of types of controls of energy flow.

The sequence is the same for all four types of acts. Figure 9-5 shows the sequence of combination of patterns for the consummatory unit act.

This sequence meets all four requirements. *It is the only sequence that meets them all.* It is necessary to note how each step in the sequence adds its value to the establishment and stability of the patterns of the components:

1. Affectivity is the choice variable of both types of consummatory acts, internal and external. The first problem is to establish the need pattern for an internal consummatory act. This is achieved by combining affectivity with the critical variable for *internal* stability, diffuseness.

2. Quality is the critical goal state variable for both internal-consummatory and internal-instrumental acts. The critical problem is to establish the goal state pattern for the internal consummatory act, that is, to establish consummatory primacy. This is achieved by combining quality with the primary pattern for *consummatory* stability, affectivity.

3. Particularism is the critical primary pattern of the facility component of both internal and external

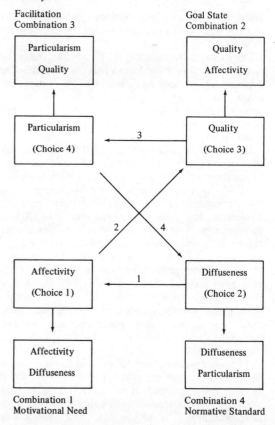

Figure 9-5. Sequence of combination of primary variables in producing patterned components of the consummatory unit act.

consummatory acts. The problem is to establish internal primacy in the combination. This is achieved by combining particularism with the critical variable for *internal* stability at the external pole of consummatory action, quality.

4. Diffuseness is the primary variable of the normative standard for both internal-instrumental and internal-consummatory acts. The critical problem is therefore to establish the pattern for consummatory primacy. This is achieved by combining diffuseness with the critical variable for establishing *consummatory* primacy and stability at the external pole of the instrumental axis, particularism.

This sequence also crossties and couples the two types of control mechanisms and maintains the hierarchial relationship among them, once the sequence is completed. In the case of the triggering controls (needs and goal states) the coupling and crosstying are achieved by building the primary pattern of the higher component into the lower (steps 2 and 3). In the case of the channelling controls (normative standards and facilitation) coupling and crosstying is achieved by building the primary pattern of the lower component into the higher (steps 1 and 4).

The application of the sequential model to the other three basic types of action renders the complete patterning of the components of all types as evident in Figure 9-6.

Note in Figure 9-6 that affectivity emerges as the master choice variable along the consummatory axis for the consummatory types and universalism as the master choice variable along the instrumental axis for the instrumental types. Their opposites define the opposite axis *within* each opposite type, as one would expect from the special significance they have in this respect. Hence particularism defines the *instrumental* axis of both types of consummatory action and affective neutrality the *consummatory* axis of both types of instrumental action.

The correspondence of the four basic types of action with the functional paradigm derives of course from the fact that the same logic was followed in the construction of both. It follows that if we have a system of action consisting of a population of unit acts and differentiated along functional lines, the subsystems of this action system will be structured on the patterns indicated by this correspondence with the basic types of action, and will consist of the cognate unit acts. For example, the adaptive subsystem of action will be patterned on the same pattern variable values as instrumental action and will consist primarily of instrumental unit acts and emergent structural concretions of the same patterns of the components. Given the functional correspondence the four types of action may be called adaptive (A—) action, goal attainment (G—) action, integrative (I—) action and pattern maintenance (L—) action. These are then seen as characterizing the respective subsystems of a system of action.

Although the subsystems of action are interdependent as parts of the system, they obviously represent opposite forces within the system. This is inherent in the logic of the pattern variables as dilemmas of choice, and their combinations in patterning types of action of functional significance to the system of action represent structured opposing forces in action. The patterning and externalizing tendency of external-instrumental action is, for example, directly opposite to the internalizing tendency and patterning of (internal) consummatory action. The first might be seen as the force of rationalization in action, and the latter as the inertia of tradition analytically defined. The phase movements of action systems have therefore a distinctive dialectical character; it is not just a matter of the system not being able to maximize functional sufficiency in all four functions at the same time, but even more a matter of the inherent tendency of these subsystems to pursue their own consummatory imperatives rather than those of the system as a whole. Parsons' discussion, in reinterpreting Durkheim, of the differences between the L-G axis and the I-A axis in the integration of social systems is relevant in this context. They are two distinct bases of system integration. But in this analysis they also emerge as the axes of countervailing forces within the system that pull in opposite directions, contributing to the functioning of the system, yet following their own determining requirements. It is impossible to pursue this logic fully here, except to indicate that these axes are also critical in the evolution of action systems and experience systems with the development of the G and I subsystems as differentiated controlling and countervailing forces being crucial stages in the process.

Adaptation (A)		Goal Attainment (G)	
External-Instrumental Act		External-Consummatory Act	
Universalism	Performance	Particularism	Performance
Performance	Affective neutrality	Performance	Affectivity
Affective neutrality	Specificity	Affectivity	Specificity
Specificity	Universalism	Specificity	Particularism
Internal-Consummatory Act		Internal-Instrumental Act	
Particularism	Quality	Universalism	Quality
Quality	Affectivity	Quality	Affective neutrality
Affectivity	Diffuseness	Affective neutrality	Diffuseness
Diffuseness	Particularism	Diffuseness	Universalism
Pattern Maintenance (L)		Integration (I)	

Figure 9-6. Unique combinations of component patterns of the four basic types of unit act, with functional correspondence indicated.

ACTION AND EXPERIENCE

The construction of these ideal types of action is based on functional logic from the vantage point of the individual actor. It does not deal with the case of a collective actor, in which case "motivational needs" has to be translated into a collective equivalent such as values. It also does not take into account the factors both in the actor and in the situation which influence the probability of the actor emitting a certain type of action. Both actors and situations are structured through past experience and action; and as the functional problems of action are seen as inherent in the human condition, past experience and action tend to be structured along the same axes and involve the same patterns, conditioned by the "givens" of the physical environment, genetic constitution, and other constitutive inherited elements.

It is important to draw an analytical distinction between action and experience. Action is what the actor does in and to the situation in which he acts. Experience is what the situation does to the actor, including the action of other actors. In social action or interaction, action means being on the sending end; experience means being on the receiving end, including receiving feedback on what was sent. In the present context, the important point is that the behavioral system and personality of an individual actor are to a large extent experience structures; they are shaped by his experience through primary, secondary, and tertiary socialization processes and consist of internalized experiences in addition to genetic constitution. Similarly, the social system and cultural system of collective actors are experience structures shaped by collective experience through processes of institutionalization, patterning, and acculturation. These systems are therefore experience structures constituent of actors and situations and the major factors defining the parameters of action systems. The patterns established in these experience systems determine to a large extent the patterning of action regardless of the immediate functional exigencies. To the extent that these experience systems become patterned along the functional dimensions of action they will facilitate action appropriate to the immediate functional problem the actor is facing.

Both individual actors and collective actors act in situations containing all four types of experience systems. The degrees of similarity, continuity, consistency, and compatibility among the experience systems of the actor and the situation are major variables in the analysis of action. They determine to a large extent the availability of the appropriate components or resources of action.

Experience systems as such are not analytically seen as functionally specialized with respect to any one of the four functional problems of action. Cultural systems, for example, or elements of them enter into the patterning of all four components of action; and all four subsystems of action have cultural elements and aspects. In fact, action is defined as symbolically mediated behavior. And the behavioral system is involved in pattern-maintenance action as well as in adaptive action; dead men can't act. But experience systems do become functionally differentiated as they increasingly provide appropriate patterns for components or resources of action in situations posing differentiated functional problems. An actor's capacity, either individual or collective, to emit functionally specialized action, such as adaptive action, depends, therefore, on the functional differentiation of his constitutive experience systems—in the individual case, the behavioral organism and personality and in the collective case, the social system and cultural system. The individual systems are, of course, apart from the genetic constitution, constituted to a large extent by the experience or the action of both individual and collective actors and hence are partly shaped by social and cultural systems. Social and cultural systems are more enduring than behavioral organisms and personality systems, the latter being subject to phases of the life cycle of the individual organism and its limited life span. These two experience systems transcending generations of individual actors are, therefore, of much greater significance in the development of action systems; their own stages of development determine the stages of development of action within them.

Another aspect of the distinction between individual and collective actors is the possible combination of the two. Action by an individual may simply be action that is emitted on behalf of the actor himself, with the choice of type of action initiated by the actor without regard for its consequences for a collective system of action. Action on behalf of a collective actor, while still emitted by an individual, is role action or collectivity-oriented action. Collective actors, such as organizations, can, just as individual actors, act on behalf of themselves or in the interest of some larger collective actor. Action systems consist of both types of action, and both individual and collective action have functional significance for the larger system. But the distinction is important, because it postulates that all action emitted in an action system is not on behalf of the system, hence determined by the functional requirements of the system. Depending on the position of the role of an individual actor, his action on behalf of the collective actor can be of major significance in a collective action system. The role of collective actors in action systems is on the whole of greater significance in the analysis of action than that of individual actors. The role of states and larger corporations, especially multinational giants in recent history, are good examples, especially since they act in situations where their actions are not primarily oriented to larger collective actors.

From this perspective there are two approaches to

the analysis of social systems that are not exclusive of each other. Social systems can be analysed as actors; the focus here would be on the action that they emit at various levels and the systemic features in terms of function, structure, and process of this action. They can also be analyzed as experience systems within which action takes place, focussing on the way they structure action along with other experience systems, and are changed by action. The analysis of social systems as action systems has tended to fall between these two stools, although elements of both have been present to varying degrees. The analysis of social action systems is concerned with individual and collective action within social and cultural experience systems, and as such it will draw heavily on the conceptual framework of social system analysis. But the analysis of the functioning of experience systems, although important in the analysis of social action, cannot capture the dynamics of action, of different types of general action or functionally specialized action, especially not in complex concrete situations involving a large variety of action systems.

With respect to the behavioral organism, for example, a major factor is the generalized abilities and specific abilities which the actor commands. His action at any one point in time is conditioned by his innate and acquired abilities or the abilities available in the situation to facilitate action. In social action systems involving large populations of actors, action is also conditioned by the aggregate of abilities. Hence the importance of literacy rates, level of education, innate intelligence (most often taken as a constant), language skills, labour skills, and participation skills in various markets in the analysis of the probability and frequency of the emission of certain types of action. The acquisition of abilities is, of course, in turn influenced by such factors as innate ability, opportunity structures, and motivational, social, and cultural factors.

The importance of treating abilities as a variable varies from problem to problem. In the explanation and prediction of such action as completion of college education and achievement in college it is obviously a variable, as it is in such action as economic growth. In other cases such as changes in birth rate, divorce rate, ritual action, and even voting behavior, abilities may often be treated as constants for explanatory and predictive purposes.

Similar considerations can be spelled out for the main factors derived from the social system, cultural system, and personality as experience systems. The analysis of social action systems is thus seen as involving all these factors and treating them as either constants or variables, depending on the problem being investigated. Social action system analysis should therefore not be equated with social system analysis, as the latter represents only one set of factors in the former.

INTERACTION ANALYSIS

When two actors meet, not only are the contingencies that require an actor in a situation to make certain choices multiplied by two but also many others are added. Whether or not they will interact depends on many factors. Each brings to the situation not only the patterned components of his own action but also experience systems that may vary from the other's in many ways and may enter as factors in the interaction. A further element that tends to multiply all these contingencies is the fact that interaction is basically dependent on the response of the one actor to the other and that each actor acts not only on the basis of the response of the other but also on his own expectations of what that response will be, based on past experience in interaction.

It is useful in this context to retain the analytical difference between action and experience. Experience in the interaction context is an actor's subjective perception, interpretation, and evaluation of the action of the other actor. This experience may vary quite significantly from the actual action as it may be seen by the sending actor or by an observer. Hence alter's experience of ego's action becomes a partially independent set of factors to be taken into account as adding to the contingencies of interaction. It is not just a matter of double contingency of expectations, but a whole set of double contingencies which may best be conceptualized by analytically separating the experience aspects from the action aspects in interaction analysis.

This multiplication of contingencies makes even a dyad of actors a very complex world of possibilities. The one limiting case is, of course, that of a perfect match on all factors between the two actors, resulting in an interaction system characterized by mutuality, complementarity, cooperation, harmony, and intersubjective validity of experience. The other limiting case is a complete mismatch, resulting in the failure of an interaction system to emerge as a viable process. In between lie many possible interaction systems marked by varying degrees of integration and conflict and various degrees of development depending on the extent to which the actors are able progressively to reduce the complexity of the situation by matching modes of action and experience in dealing with the various contingencies.

In addition to the independence of the patterning of the action and experience systems of the two actors, there are some further factors that have to be taken into account which do not necessarily derive from the patterning factors. These factors may be shaped by the experience systems but are not simply the result of the matching or nonmatching of them.

The first factor is the positive-negative polarity of basic orientations. An actor enters an interaction situation with either a positive or negative assessment of the other actor and the potentials for interaction. The possibility of neutrality does, of course, exist. This factor may be related to the pattern factors mainly through the affectivity-affective neutrality need-orientation variable. It adds, however, a further specification of the affective orientation by indicating whether it is positive or negative. Especially through the experience systems of an actor this may result in a basic negative or positive orientation to action situations, quite regardless of the real potentials of these situations. Hence, whether or not the two actors are matched on the positive-negative polarity introduces another set of contingencies into the interaction situation.

A second factor has to do with the activity-passivity orientation of the actors. To refrain from action is a mode of action, as is a disposition to act all the time. This factor is also influenced by the experience systems of the actor and relates most directly to the pattern factors through the quality-performance variable. Whether an actor is inclined to be active or passive is to a large extent influenced by the primacy of the performance or quality patterns respectively in his experience systems. The matching of the two actors in an interaction situation on the activity-passivity factor adds another set of contingencies.

A third factor is the relative status of the two actors. This factor again is largely determined by their respective experience systems but is not simply an epiphenomenon of these structures. Action inherently involves evaluation of actors on various dimensions including those of action differentiation, and actors establish a pecking order in relation to other actors as superior, equal, or inferior. The criteria on the basis of which this status structure is established derive most directly from the pattern variables and the patterning of experience systems. But the specific choices, for example, on the quality-performance variables, do not necessarily have status implications; status can be assigned on either quality or performance criteria. Certain quality criteria such as age, sex, and race have a very general tendency to enter into interaction situations as status criteria. Whether or not the two actors can match their status allocations and expectations is another contingency in the interaction situation.

A fourth factor is the sanctions which the actors can apply to each other to secure compliance from each other in the interaction situation. The choice of appropriate or inappropriate sanctions adds a whole new set of contingencies to the situation.

In attempting to get the other actor to emit a desired unit act, the actor can apply a sanction to one or all of the components of the unit act, depending on his assessment of the probability that a certain type of sanction or combination of sanctions would be successful. He has to choose, therefore, one or more of the four basic types of sanctions; and he has to choose whether to apply the sanction in a positive or a negative direction.

Figure 9-7 presents the four basic sanction types derived from the functional paradigm and indicates some positive and negative forms of each.

The way alter will respond or react to ego's sanction will depend on:

1. The extent to which they share experience systems.
2. The extent to which they share the patterned components of action, or the extent to which these are complementary or compatible.

External-Instrumental		External-Consummatory	
Exchange		Control	
Positive:	gain, induce, inform, enrich, enable, share, bribe	Positive:	empower, permit, liberate, instruct, direct, enfranchise, submit
Negative:	lose, deprive, keep ignorant, exploit, disable, withhold, blackmail	Negative:	coerce, constrain, restrict, prohibit, oppress, oppose, threaten, dominate, resist, revolt
Activation		Persuasion	
Positive:	arouse, implore, realize, fulfill, approach, appeal, praise, encourage, engage, accept	Positive:	agree, approve, comply, support, assent, conform, recognize, appease
Negative:	deny, block, frustrate, deplore, blame, withdraw, discourage, alienate, reject	Negative:	disagree, disapprove, protest, dissent, deviate, ignore, enrage
Internal-Consummatory		Internal-Instrumental	

Figure 9-7. Sanctions paradigm: forms of action in securing desired reaction in interaction with tentative examples of positive and negative forms.

3. The extent of intersubjective validity of action and experience.
4. Alter's action dispositions in relation to ego, whether they are positive or negative, active or passive.
5. The extent to which the status structure between them is accepted by alter.
6. The extent to which he accepts or reacts to the appropriateness of the sanction.
7. The cost to alter of compliance with ego's wishes.
8. Alter's ability to apply effective sanctions to ego.

On ego's choice of sanctions and alter's reaction to them will depend the nature of the interaction relationship, its duration and growth or developmental potential, whether it will be marked by conflict or cooperation, change or stagnation.

From this paradigm, we can develop such propositions as:

1. The more frequently ego frustrates or alienates the need-orientations of alter, the more likely that the relationship will be marked by conflict and will eventually break down.
2. The more frequently ego has to secure alter's compliance by coercion, the more likely that the relationship will be conflictful and eventually break down.
3. The more frequently ego exploits or deprives alter, the more likely that conflict will ensue and that alter will terminate the relationship.
4. The more frequently ego disapproves of alter's action, the more likely that the relationship will become characterized by conflict and will eventually be terminated by alter.

The master proposition underlying all four of these is, of course, that the more frequently ego applies negative sanctions the more likely is conflict and breakdown, depending, of course, on the values of the other variables just listed. These propositions are obviously not exhaustive of the possibilities, but only examples. An opposite set of propositions to the ones given are needed for positive sanctions, although they do not simply follow by implication. Encompassing both negative and positive sanctions one could suggest an even more general proposition: The more frequently ego uses a sanction in relation to alter, the more likely that the sanction will decline in value and lose its efficacy.

Propositions relating to the other factors such as the experience systems, status, the orientation (positive-negative, active-passive) and type of action systems will have to form part of an empirical interaction theory.

Interaction also takes place as part of the action of collective actors. Hence the two actors may interact on behalf of different actors and in different capacities. In this context the structure of the collective actor and the roles and positions of the interacting parties present further contingencies, which may be reduced by the larger actors by matching or otherwise controlling the interaction situation in advance. Negotiations, deals, representations, and coordination among collective actors are usually governed by sets of rules, sometimes involving elaborate protocol. And the sanctions appropriate in such structured interaction situations are usually determined in advance with respect to type, direction, and quantity. Interaction in personal or private capacity is, therefore, subject to fewer constraints than action in representative or public capacity on behalf of some collective actor.

GENERALIZED MEDIA OF SOCIAL ACTION

From the analysis of interaction just given, it should be clear that even the dyad is a very complex system of social action. With every additional actor it becomes exponentially more complex depending on the degree of variance each actor brings with him in experience systems, action systems, and other factors. Complexity means increased contingency and unpredictability of outcome. The more complex the system the greater the problem of reducing contingency to a practical level where choices can be made and action can proceed with some predictability.

It is also clear from the above that social action and interaction in particular is a process of action and reaction, of stimulus and response, mediated through current experience and experience systems. Ego's sanction is chosen on the expectation of a reaction from alter; it is the stimulus to which alter's reaction is the response. In this sense, social action is fundamentally responsive and involves communication of messages. Both action and reaction are structured and affected by the experience systems of the actors as outlined above. Social action is shaped by these sanction processes of action and experience as "surface structures" or processes of action systems, and the experience systems provide the "deep structures" that pattern both stimulus and response, both action and reaction. The greater the degree of sharedness, complementarity, or compatibility of the deep structures of actors, the smaller the degree of complexity in the system and the fewer the practical contingencies, as distinguished from those that theoretically exist.

The sanction paradigm forms the basis of the development of a set of deep structures through experience in complex systems that reduce the complexities and contingencies of the sanctioning process even further. There develop generalized media of sanctioning and reacting for each of the four types of sanctions. These generalized media enable each actor to reduce the immediate contingencies involved in emitting a unit act as a sanction or a reaction. Thus, in accepting information as true, the actor reduces the contingencies involved in the unknown in the parameters of his action. In accepting money in exchange for something else he reduces the complexity of the exigencies of his action because it is in general demand in the system.

Corresponding to the four sanction types there are thus four basic types of generalized media that serve to reduce the contingencies involved in sanctioning action and reaction in complex systems:

1. Generalized media of exchange, for example, abilities, money, knowledge.
2. Generalized media of control, for example, power, laws, threats, rules.
3. Generalized media of persuasion, for example, influence, interpretation, suggestions, opinion.
4. Generalized media of activation, for example, value needs, value commitments, faith, ideology, love.

All these generalized media are media of communication and share basic characteristics with language. In a sense they are types of language, distinguished from it and from each other by the *differentia specifica* on which the typology is based. They all involve the transfer of messages that have meaning to sender and receiver in terms of shared symbolic codes.

The function of the generalized media in action systems is such that differentiated and specialized subsystems develop at least one medium to facilitate the acquisition of the inputs, both *factors* and *products,* from other specialized action systems. In functional terms, a medium is, therefore, of strictly *instrumental* significance to the system and is in effect patterned on the instrumental components of the system or subsystem that generates it. It represents generalizations of these components for the purpose of the most general usefulness in exchange. A medium, therefore, has only two patterned or code components, the one being a generalized facility component (external-instrumental) and the other a generalized normative standard (internal-instrumental). Each medium of each subsystem is thus patterned on the instrumental axis of the subsystem that generates it.

The control relationships among these two components remain the same with I being the more general control and A the more specific, both being of the channeling type, rather than the cybernetic (on-off) type. Figure 9-8 shows the components of

Code components of media

Generalized media of	Normative (Coordinating) Standard I	Facilitation Code A
Activation: L (commitments)	Diffuseness Particularism Loyalty	Particularism Quality Identity
Persuasion: I (influence)	Diffuseness Universalism Integrity	Universalism Quality Authenticity
Control: G (power)	Specificity Particularism Authority	Particularism Performance Competence
Exchange: A (money)	Specificity Universalism Utility	Universalism Performance Liquidity

Figure 9-8. Code components of the generalized media of action systems. [NOTE:The labels represent lower levels of analycity and are hence even more tentative.]

the functionally specialized media. These are the same patterns as those on the instrumental axes of the four types of action in Figure 9-6.

The development of generalized media depends on the degree of internalization and institutionalization of these patterns in the experience systems of the actors and their situations. This establishment of the patterns in the experience systems provides the basis for shared trust and confidence among the actors in the system that the value of the media in interchanges will be recognized by all actors and that they will be useful as sanctions in interaction to acquire the factors and products for action and consumption. The level of trust in the media varies in systems according to the stability of their components in both experience systems and action systems and among action systems. When this trust breaks down in crisis situations, a generalized medium loses its efficacy and actors tend to fall back on what may be called the security base of the medium. Hence they opt out of the institutionalized channels of sanctioning through the generalized medium of the system in question and "take matters into their own hands." In the case of the societal media that Parsons has developed, for example, actors fall back on gold or land (money), force or violence (power), order or solidarity (influence), and primordial values (value commitments).

There is a variety of possibilities in what an actor can do with a medium, depending on his supply of the medium. He may have a surplus or a deficit of a particular medium in terms of his regular requirements for it, which he sets himself in his particular situation. If he has a surplus of a medium:

1. He may simply keep it in his own possession and control it without using it. This can be called *hoarding,* as in keeping money under the mattress. This is a withdrawal of holdings of the medium from circulation. If the actor is concerned about the value of his hoardings in crisis situations, he will hold it in the form of the security base of the medium.

2. He may develop new requirements over and above his regular level and spend the surplus on new items that have value in use. If his supply resulting in surplus is regular, he may raise his regular level of *spending* accordingly.

3. He may save the medium by depositing it with another actor on the condition that he retain possession of it, relinquish control over it, but reserve the right to draw on it at any time or specified times. *Saving* may involve a further increase in the surplus of the medium in the form of interest on it or it may not, as in the case of deposits in a normal bank account where no interest is paid but services are rendered that facilitate the use of the medium on a current basis.

4. He may *invest* the medium in another actor who uses it and agrees to have the actor share in the profits, both in the form of increased value of invested shares and in dividends.

In the event of scarcity of the medium or a deficit for the actor he may do any of the opposites of these four alternatives: he may use his hoardings, curb his spending, draw on his savings, or unload his investments.

Under normal circumstances, that is, with neither surplus nor deficit conditions existing, the actor may exercise any of these options in his regular pattern of use of the medium, with consequences, of course, for the other options. For example, without experiencing a deficit in his normal supply of the medium he may decide to curb his spending of the medium, tighten his belt so to speak, and exercise some of the other options instead, such as hoarding, saving, or investment.

In any complex system these options are exercised by the actors within the framework of the patterning and control of the media by that system and such parameters as the total strength of the media in the system. But these parameters and controls do not operate automatically on actors in the system. The way they exercise their options may lead to conditions in which existing controls are no longer adequate because aggregate results of options exercised by actors within the system are not realistic in relation to the parameters within which the system as a whole has to operate.

These aggregate results also relate to the rate of activity in the subsystem for which the particular medium has primacy, whether it expands, grows, retracts or declines or remains stagnant. The problem from the perspective of the system as a whole is how to stimulate the right types of choices that will attain the goal states set by the system, each of its subsystems, and actors in the system. These system-level actions always have to be taken into account as critical parameters in the analysis of action rates, intensity, direction, and changes.

Although from a functional point of view the media have instrumental significance, actors tend to develop goal-state values with respect to them and to rank each other in terms of the quantity of the medium in possession. Hence they compete for these media and their relative success determines their status in the ranking system according to these values. Thus wealth, power, prestige, respect, or honor determine status among actors in a system quite apart from their contribution to the functioning of the system. In fact, these pursuits and rankings may be highly dysfunctional from the system's point of view. This does not contradict the fact that the media also serve as measures of value of contributions to the functioning of the system and that the system places different values on different contributions from this point of view. The extent to which the stratification system of actors in an action system reflects their contributions to the functioning of the system may therefore empirically vary widely. This is one context in which the dialectics of the opposing forces in action systems needs to be analysed in much more depth.

Apart from the problems of the maintenance of state variables and the attainment of goal states, the system has to deal with fluctuations in the values of the generalized media that are partly consequences of the state variables but often also of the perceptions of these by large proportions of actors in the system. Particularly the spread of perceptions of the state of a subsystem may send its medium into an upward or downward spiral affecting its value. The system then has to apply control measures to maintain the state of the medium.

We can refer to these fluctuations as processes which consist mainly in assessments and choices on the part of actors in the system that are unrealistic in relation to the parameters of the system or one of its subsystems.

The upward spiral or inflation of the medium consists in the actors making increasingly unrealistic assessments of the amount of the medium available and making choices to spend which create an artificial demand for the "outputs" they acquire and stimulate artificial growth and a level or rate of activity out of proportion with the total amount of the medium that can be made available in the system. This unrealistic activity level actually has the effect of lowering the value of the unit of the medium and can lead to a crash and a panic if not properly controlled. The spiral here moves away in an upward direction from the backing the medium has in the level of output of the type of action that generates it. A condition of flation is seen as a relatively stable state of the value of the medium measured in terms of its relation to or distance from the level of output of the relevant subsystem.

Deflation is a spiral in the opposite direction, forcing the medium downwards closer to the actual level of output of its type of action. It is characterized by the spread of an unrealistic assessment of the amount of the medium available and of choices other than spending or investment in growth activities. The belief is that there is a deficit in the medium, that its value is in question, and that it is necessary to move closer to the level of output. The aggregate of these choices affect the rate and nature of activity in the subsystem and can lead to a general depression of activity in the subsystem. These two spirals are represented in Figure 9-9.

The main problem from the perspective of the system is to keep the media in a flationary state in relation to the level of output of its relevant subsystems. This state in itself involves upward and downward movements within a range of variation considered as tolerable limits. There is, of course, no universal rule that the distance between the medium and level of related output is the same for all systems or for all subsystems. Systems vary in the distance at which they peg their media in relation to these bases. The lower a system pegs its media, the more "conservative" the system; the higher the media are pegged, the more "liberal"

the system. A system may be quite "liberal" in its control of some media and "conservative" in others. Systems also vary in the range of variation in the flation of the media they permit from the pegged distance and consider as normal or tolerable. Some undulation within these limits is unavoidable simply because of the time lag between the application or release of controls and the effects of these measures.

The dynamics of inflation and deflation of the media can be derived from the propositions about the functioning of sanctions, which would be variations on the laws of supply and demand. One could, for example, suggest that: The more frequently actors use a medium, the more likely it will be to decline in value and become less efficacious, leading to inflationary trends. One would also want to spell out the system conditions under which this is likely to occur.

Generalized media are thus subject to equilibrium problems just as action systems, and their own state of equilibrium relates directly to the equilibrium of the system and more directly to the subsystem within which they function. But they also serve as media and means for the opposing tendencies and forces in the system. Money and power, for example, become major means of the instrumental, externalizing forces in the system as consummatory concerns of actors, particularly collective actors, specializing in these functions.

The final aspect of the media that has to be taken into account is the problem of the relation between the amount of a medium held by the actors in the system in the aggregate and the total amount available in the system and the implications for the distribution of the medium in the system. At one level it is possible to say that the total amount of a medium available in the system is the simple sum of the holdings of actors in the system. The implication then is that one actor's gain is some other actor's loss. This is the zero-sum concept of a medium, assuming that the distribution always has to equal zero, representing the sum of the holdings of actors. This condition can be said to pertain "in the last analysis" and represents a view of the medium that assumes a very close relation to or short distance from its action base. In other words, it insists on a deflated conception of the medium. But the zero-sum concept does not hold at the flation level of media where it is set at a realistic distance from the action base, the distance depending largely on the level of institutionalized trust in the system but also on other factors.

The phenomena of banking, investment, and credit creation introduce conditions raising the flation level of a medium away from its security base and have a multiplication effect rather than addition effect on the availability of a medium for use. They

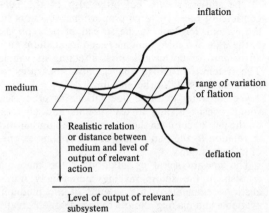

inflation

medium

range of variation
of flation

Realistic relation
or distance between
medium and level of
output of relevant
action

deflation

Level of output of relevant
subsystem

Figure 9-9. Processes of flation, inflation, and deflation of a generalized medium.

separate possession from use and hence make the analysis of the operation of a medium more complex than the zero-sum concept would suggest. The distribution of the medium in use is no longer a simple function of its distribution in possession. The effect of this is that possession becomes less important in the analysis of media dynamics, which tend to depend more on patterns and rates of use. But as we have seen, the relationship between these means for extending the use of the media and the total amount available for possession in the system cannot become too far extended without inflationary consequences. Also, the distribution of the medium in use among actors does not vary in a very wide range from the distribution in possession, which determines credit standing. Therefore, the zero-sum problem cannot be eliminated altogether and has to be taken into account in the analysis of media dynamics and distribution, as well as in the general dynamics of social action systems. The problem is also different for the different media, and the preceding analysis applies more directly and clearly to money and to a lesser extent to power and to the other two societal media. The tendency of actors to develop goal states with respect to media and the resulting ranking affect the distribution of possession; hence the zero-sum concept has most direct applicability in the analysis of the consequences of these tendencies for the distribution of the media among actors within the system, but also remains applicable at the system level.

THE INTERCHANGE PARADIGM

Any complex social action system develops many generalized media for interchange processes between specialized activities of a great variety. We have identified four basic types of generalized media, but there are several media of each type in any complex system. Actors in such a system command differential holdings of these media depending on their position both in the status structure of the system and in its functional structure. The possession and use of these media are governed by patterned norms embedded in the experience structures of the system. Each actor in the system has a role set consisting of several roles specialized around the four functional subsystems of action. The same actor may have several roles in which instrumental action is primary, several in which consummatory action is primary, and so on. The use of the generalized media becomes structured along the same lines, with the positions of ego and alter(s) in the system being main determinants of the choice of media and their functional efficacy in specific interchanges.

If we take for the moment ego and alter in the abstract and assume that each of them has command over holdings of all four types of media to use in relation to each other, then it is logically possible that ego can use each of the types of media in exchange for any of the types alter is holding. The logical possibilities are given in Figure 9-10.

In any complex social action system of a plurality of actors there is of course a constant flow of media among the actors and these logical possibilities lead to a great variety of types of interchanges. Many of them are prohibited or prescribed or otherwise normatively regulated by the system so that their occurrence is less frequent. Other types are not functional and are eliminated or regulated by experience systems. Out of this labyrinthine complexity of possibilities emerges a pattern of functional specialization of the major media interchanges in complex social action systems that can be derived from the logic of functional specialization itself.

Within a functionally differentiated system each

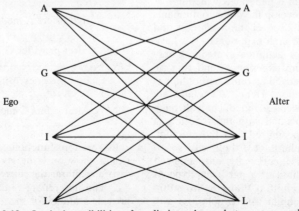

Figure 9-10. Logical possibilities of media interchange between ego and alter.

subsystem consists of actors that emit primarily unit acts of the basic type that serves that functional problem best, for example, instrumental action in the adaptive subsystem. But within each of these subsystems action and actors-in-roles become further specialized with respect to the four functional problems which the *subsystem* as a system of action faces. In other words, in analyzing complex action systems it is necessary to proceed at least to the sub-subsystem or sixteen-fold level of the functional paradigm.

The logic of the interchange paradigm of a social action system differentiated to the sub-subsystem level can best be understood by starting with actors assumed not to be functionally specialized and to analyze their action in relation to each other, proceeding to at least the doubly specialized sub-subsystems of action.

In the absence of any generalized medium the interaction between ego and alter is on a barter basis, tit for tat, or scratch each other's back. This is the case of the use of particular sanctions to receive particular reactions by both ego and alter.

Ego-sanction to secure Alter-action

⟶

Alter-action in response to Ego-sanction

Ego ⟵   Alter

Ego-action in response to Alter-sanction

⟶

Alter-sanction to secure Ego-action

⟵

If the two particular sanction categories are equivalent to the response categories there is, of course, only one interchange between the two, but this conceptualization seeks to emphasize the limits of particular sanctions.

In a situation in which a generalized medium of sanction exists, actors develop the code components through experience and discover the usefulness and value of the medium through experience. We have to assume that an actor acquires a medium only through action, not from experience, and that he is unable to use a generalized medium before he has acquired it through action. Hence he would acquire the functionally specialized media only through the type of action associated with the function in which the medium is specialized. For the moment, we can exclude gifts, inheritance, theft, and so on from consideration. A functionally unspecialized actor acquires the medium of a particular type of action or subsystem by emitting that type of action in exchange for the medium. AGIL notations will be used for actors, action, and media.

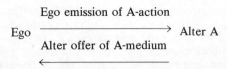

Ego emission of A-action

Ego ⟶ Alter A

Alter offer of A-medium

⟵

The more ego emits a type of action in response to offers of the medium, the more he becomes competent and specialized in that type of action and the more holdings he acquires in that medium. He is then able to use the medium in any of the ways we have noted, to spend, save, hoard or invest. Of these four uses only hoarding does not imply an interchange with a functionally specialized alter. Once he has acquired one medium he can use it in acquiring

1. any of the four types of action or components of action or other objects he may need as *intrinsic satisfiers,* which he consumes;
2. the same categories as in 1, which he may need as components or *factors* in any of the specialized types of action systems in which he is engaged;
3. any of the other three types of generalized media, in general or further specialized form depending on the level of specialization he needs in types of action;
4. more of the same medium through saving or investment.

Two-dimensional space obviously has serious limitations in the construction of a model of ego reflecting these various uses. Let us deal with them briefly *seriatim* and discuss their implications for the interchanges in action systems and especially for the functional interchange paradigm:

1. An interchange in which ego secures from the same alter, specialized in a different function, an intrinsic satisfier he needs by using a medium, looks as follows (with alter's counterpart it becomes a double interchange):

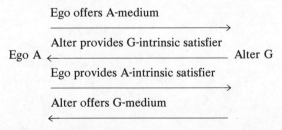

Ego offers A-medium

⟶

Alter provides G-intrinsic satisfier

Ego A ⟵ Alter G

Ego provides A-intrinsic satisfier

⟶

Alter offers G-medium

⟵

In the four-functional model such a paradigm would show only the six interchanges for intrinsic satisfiers among the subsystems.

2. The interchange and paradigm that would provide a model for the acquisition of the three different functional factors which each subsystem

requires for its specialized action, would have the same format, with the generalized media again serving only as media of exchange and assuming, as in the case of intrinsic satisfiers, that a medium acquired does not provide a factor or component of action.

3. Here we have to drop the assumption that the media do not serve as factors of action. By definition the media are instrumental and have no value in use, if by use is meant consumption. But an actor can use the media as factors in his action. The following interchanges are implied in this assumption:

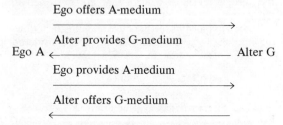

Ego A — Alter G

    Ego offers A-medium
    ——————————————→
    Alter provides G-medium
    ←——————————————
    Ego provides A-medium
    ——————————————→
    Alter offers G-medium
    ←——————————————

Obviously, no double interchange is necessary for the same pair of actors, but with more than one alter it becomes necessary. However, as a general statement of subsystem interchanges it would be redundant unless we assume that two different categories or specifications of the two media are involved. This is in fact the case in Parsons' paradigms for the societal and general action media, wherein he postulates hierarchical relations for the media among interchanges and within interchanges. He also defines one case of each medium a factor and the other a product. If by product is meant intrinsic satisfier, his paradigms violate one of the basic assumptions of media theory. From the context it is clear that products are equated with intrinsic satisfiers. It is possible to interpret Parsons' paradigm as not defining categories of the media at all but simply specifying the two factor and intrinsic satisfier exchanges that are controlled by the media. The media would then appear in his paradigms *only* in the notations of C,I,P, and M to indicate which products and intrinsic satisfiers they control. But this is inconsistent with the central place of the Keynesian model in his conceptualization of the interchanges. If this were the case his paradigm would represent a combination of interchanges 1 and 2, but with the media indicated only by notations instead of as the fourfold or six-fold interchanges implied.

There has to be a different rationale for the different categories of the media involved in such an interchange. One such rationale would be the involvement of each medium at two different system levels. For example, a subsystem can be seen as requiring a specification of the generalized medium to the sub-

system level as a medium of interchange *within* the subsystem. Or, to return to the actor, ego may require a more specific form of power for a specialized type of action in his system of action.

This introduces the question of different levels of specificity of the generalized media. Although at first thought such a notion would seem inconsistent with the concept *generalized* medium, this is not the case. Generalized means having universalistic meaning and value for all users in the system. But there are different levels of actors and experience structures in any system of action, and the resources of action or components have to be specified through these levels for the system to function. Figure I-3 in the General Introduction to this volume shows the relation of the interchange paradigm to the resource table in the theory of action. It is clear from that figure, as it is from the content of Parsons' conceptualization of the media, that the interchange paradigm applies at the subsystem level of society.

It is clearly necessary to develop the conceptualization of the media beyond this level. One clear indication of that is that they do serve as factors in action — and hence as such would need to be specified through the same levels as other factors or resources. To illustrate how this could proceed, let us carry the interchange above through at least three levels, that of the system as a whole (S), the subsystem (SS^1), and the sub-subsystem (SS^2). This interchange would only make sense if we indicate differences of levels in it:

Ego A — Alter G

    Ego offers A-medium (S)
    ——————————————→
    Alter provides G_A-medium (SS^1)
    ←——————————————
    Ego provides A_G-medium (SS^1)
    ——————————————→
    Alter offers G-medium (S)
    ←——————————————

This is in fact, in my view, the proper format of the interchange paradigm at the subsystem level for the interchange of the media with the subsystem-specified (SS^1) media categories serving their cognate functions in circulation *within* each subsystem (SS^2).

This still leaves out the factor and intrinsic satisfier interchanges at the subsystem level. To provide for them, two more interchanges have to be added at each boundary, resulting in quadruple interchanges, if these interchanges in fact take place over these boundaries. It is clearly necessary to examine interchanges at the other system levels. Before we proceed it is necessary to indicate that there are several interchanges possible between actors on nonadjacent levels of structure. Figure 9-11 shows that with actors at four levels of structure there are six interchanges possible, three of them between non-adjacent levels.

So far the interchange paradigm in the theory of action has been developed only between subsystems at the same level, with the assumption that isomorphic interchange paradigms have to be developed among subsystems at the next level down or up, and so on. Hence Parsons' attempt to develop a set of general action media, modelled on the societal interchange paradigm's logic. This I suggest is a mistaken procedure that will inhibit seriously the development of media theory.

Instead, we need to pursue the effort to develop a truly analytic and abstract conceptualization of the media of action and analyze their function in interchanges among systems, among system levels, among subsystems at each level, as well as among actors outside the functional context. One solution to the problem of the size of the fully conceptualized interchanges between two subsystems may be to look at boundaries above and below as logical possibilities for the location of some of them. Gould's chapter in this book suggests, for example, that the product interchanges in Parsons' paradigm are located at the subsystem level and the factor interchanges are located at the sub-subsystem level, not between sub-subsystems within the same subsystem but between subsystems. He still keeps the boundaries over which each of these interchanges takes place at the same system level.

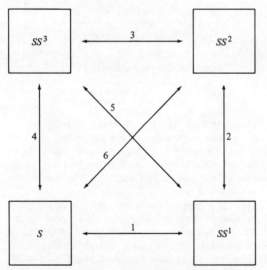

Figure 9-11. Possible interchanges among actors at four different levels in the system. [NOTE: Interchanges 4, 5, and 6 are nonadjacent.]

It may, for example, be suggested that the interchange considered earlier between Ego A and Alter G, involving four different categories of media at two different system levels, actually involves an interchange *between system levels* as well as one between subsystems, namely, that between the system as a whole (S) and the subsystems (SS^1). It could be portrayed as in Figure 9-12.

The need for this is particularly clear when we deal with such actors as the government relating to the economy in its various ways and at various levels. It would also provide a better conceptualization of the various levels of control that are exercised in the system.

We can pursue this further by examining the following interchange, which may at first be considered at the *within* subsystem ($SS^2 - SS^2$) level:

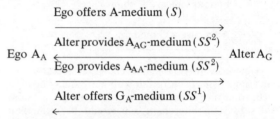

If we break out of that mould, we see that one side involves an interlevel interchange between Ego A_A (SS^2) and Alter A_G (S) and the other side one between Ego A_A (SS^2) and Alter A_G (SS^1). These notations might be confusing if one did not keep in mind that highly specialized subfunctions are performed at the system-as-a-whole level. An actor functionally located in A_A (SS^2) may still act on behalf of the system-as-a-whole (S) in terms of responsibility of office, hence making a direct input into the system-as-a-whole and an output on behalf of it to other levels. This interchange therefore takes the

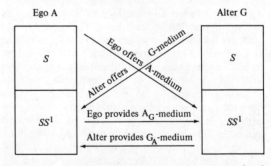

Figure 9-12. Possible intersystem and intrasystem level double interchange between functionally specialized actors. [NOTE: S (system) and SS^1 (subsystem) may represent system positions of different actors or different system level roles of the same actor.]

specification of one category of one medium one level down, while one category of the other medium stays at the system level, as in Figure 9-13.

If we pursue the flow of the four types of generalized media in the system, it appears that their specification follows roughly the same steps as the resources or components of action. But there appears to be an inverse relationship between the generality of the medium generated by the subsystem and the level of specificity of the resources that are combined as factors in the specialized type of action to which the medium relates. The type of medium is generated at the most general level by the action of its subsystem and is used in interchange at more and more specific levels in the other three subsystems. Obviously much further work will be needed in this area. A tentative paradigm carrying interchange analysis to the sub-subsystem level suggests that the doubly specialized sub-subsystems (SS^2) are the sources of the generalized medium related to the functional subsystem (SS^1). They specialize in the generation of the medium, in maintaining its liquidity, and in its allocation to uses within the subsystem for further specification to other subsystems, as well as in the interchanges of the system with its various environments. Thus the boundary of the system is defined and maintained by the generalized media it generates and controls. Over each of the four boundaries the most important environmental problems arise from relations with other social action systems, their cognate specialized sub-subsystems, and the cognate generalized media they generate and control. This boundary maintenance function of the doubly specialized sub-

subsystems and the generalized media is an important problem at the between-systems level or system-environment level of analysis. Assumptions of isomorphism should be critically examined and allowance made for emergent phenomena. These interchanges involve environmental inputs and system outputs seeking to maximize the system's capacity in all four functional areas — adaptive capacity, goal attainment capacity, integrative capacity, and pattern maintenance capacity.

4. Finally, we have to consider how the actor uses a medium to acquire more of the same medium through saving or investment. This will to a large extent depend on his location in the system, whether he is primarily an A-actor, and in which subfunction he specializes. The three uses of a medium, spending, saving and investment, represent different levels of control over the medium, listed from the lowest to the highest level of control and use. While spending may be seen as primarily related to the acquisition of intrinsic satisfiers, saving signifies an extension of possession of the medium for later use, and investment relates to the acquisition of factors of the specialized type of action that will have long-term significance for the acquisition of more holdings of the medium. These different levels of control and use of the media form the basis for the assignment of a hierarchical order to each medium among the three interchanges in which it is involved. The order is different for each type of medium according to its primary subsystem location. The diagonal interchanges (L-G, I-A) represent the highest level of control for all four types of media. This special significance of the diagonal interchanges relates to their being the primary axes of action differentiation and the main vectors of system tendencies. For the same reasons they are also the most important for the stability of the media, the level of trust in the efficacy of the media, and the equilibrium problems considered briefly in the previous section.

This attempt to build an interchange paradigm for the generalized media of social action has stopped short of presenting the actual tentative paradigm on which this tentative analysis is based. A paradigm that carries the interchanges of the same set of media to the sub-subsystem level and also attempts to separate levels of structure is too complex a model to present here. It was built up from interaction analysis combined with system function analysis. Although this approach may have weaknesses that will only appear when one tackles high-level system problems, it does seem to provide a central position for the actor and the analysis of the functioning of his action systems and their functional significance in larger systems. The generality of this approach,

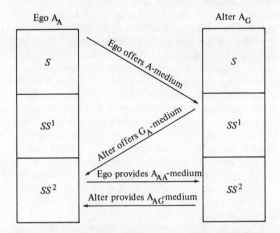

Figure 9-13. Possible intersystem and intrasystem level double interchange between two doubly functionally specialized actors. [NOTE: *S*, *SS*¹, and *SS*² may represent system level positions of different actors or different system level roles of the same actor.]

confined to general types of media, makes it difficult to place Parsons' paradigms in the context of it. All the questions raised here will need to be carefully considered, especially attempting to reduce the tremendous complexity implied in any systematic attempt to develop media theory.

The tentative paradigm built up from the interaction paradigm had two critical elements of agreement with Gould's analysis in this book, which is much more technical than this exercise in logical analysis. First, the boundary interchanges among the subsystems are the same as the ones that he proposes, namely, over adjacent boundaries signifying closest functional interdependence, for example, L_A-A_L, L_I-I_L, which also indicates agreement on abandoning the special status of L, at least at the subsystem level, although I am probably willing to go further than Gould on this. Second, he also recognizes the special significance of the doubly specialized sub-subsystems with respect to the media. In addition, he sees them as directly involved in interchanges among subsystems in the acquisition of factors of production. This fits with the concerns developed above about analysis of media interchange not only at different levels but also between them. That we came to more or less the same conclusions, or at least identified the same problems, from such very different vantage points as macroeconomics and interaction analysis, probably indicates some intersubjective validity.

PATHS TO EMPIRICAL THEORY

So far this essay has been mainly concerned with analytical functional theory. The relationship of the theory of social action to empirical reality has been left in the status of an assumption, the assumption of analytical realism, namely, that the analytical concepts and relations among them do capture aspects necessary for the explanation of empirical social action. This assumption has definitive implications for the application of the theory in the explanation of empirical social action. It implies, first, that the theory does not *describe* empirical social action or systems of social action: To ignore this implication is to fall into the fallacy of misplaced concreteness. Second, it also implies that the theory does not *explain* fully the empirical reality of social action: To ignore this implication would be to fall into reductionism, albeit of a more general kind.

To avoid both these pitfalls we have to develop the conceptual framework to include variables in addition to those primarily of functional significance. These additional variables should capture the non-

functional ranges of variation in social action systems which relate to the functional variables in such ways that taken together they account for more of the variance. The size of a social action system is a good example; we may conceptualize variations in size from microsystems to macrosystems, and we need to specify at which points size becomes critical for the emergence of new functional elements or how size otherwise influences system functions.

These state variables and parameters apply to the basic elements of the frame of reference: actor and situation, system and environment, action and experience. They abstract those dimensions of the variable states of these components of the frame of reference which do not derive from the functional dimensions, vary independently of them, and relate to them in specifiable interdependent ways. As such they are indispensable components of analytical theory; and the propositions linking them with functional variables are indispensable in the translation of analytical theory into empirical theory, as they force the theorist to relate functions to states and to parameters.

The introduction of these two classes of variables into analytical social action theory forecloses the most prevalent shortcircuits to empirical theory, namely, to *reduce* the description of empirical systems to functional terms and to *reify* functional categories in empirical systems. Instead, the theorist is forced to identify the state of the system of reference and its environment in terms of both state variables and parameters in advance, before relating these to the functional propositions as specified in the analytical theory. Hence it is the determination of the empirical values of the state variables and parameters that will provide the student with some indication of the applicability of the analytical functional model to the empirical system, including an indication whether he can expect to find an empirical *system* at all.

For these reasons analytical action theory has to specify the relationships among functional concepts, state variables, and parameters of action in terms of implicit if not explicit contingent propositions. Analytical models can be translated into stochastic models only if the former specify the relations among variables in terms of different values of these variables and if these values are quantifiable in measurable terms. The development of empirical theory then becomes a problem of operationalization, measurement, testing, replication, and so on.

The following list of some state variables and parameters is neither exhaustive nor systematic, but it should provide some indication of the types of variables which have to be introduced into the analytical theory and be taken into account in the analysis of empirical social action prior to as well as in the course of the application of functional analysis:

Degree of Integration

Analytically, social action systems have integrative problems; their actual state of integration is variable, with a lower threshold where it does not make sense to speak of a system any more. The degree of integration, the degrees and types of conflict accommodated or contained within it, are system states that have to be determined empirically. The model of social action developed in this chapter implies systemic forces that operate towards both system integration and disintegration. Hence equilibrium in differentiated systems is seen as a precarious balance between opposing forces of types of action and action subsystems. In this conceptualization the Hobbesian problem of order takes on a systemic character, rather than an atomistic war of all against all.

Degree of Stability

Social action systems contain forces that make for both system change and stability along the fundamental axes of action differentiation. Their equilibrium is by definition a moving equilibrium constantly seeking new goal states in relation to the environment using externalizing instrumental forces, yet subject to the inertia of internalizing tendencies to maintain consummatory states. The relative strength of these forces and the resultant rates of change or degree of stability have to be assessed empirically.

Degree of Differentiation

The analytical model allows for the functional specialization and structural differentiation of actors in a social action system to the sub-subsystem level. Empirically social action systems differ widely on the degree of specialization by function and structural differentiation of actors in the system. The application of the model therefore calls for careful consideration of the empirical data on the system to determine its degree of structural differentiation.

The processes of functional specialization of actors and the consequent structural differentiation of actors in a system are central to a theory of social change. The opposite processes, de-differentiation and consequent fusion of functions, also occur under certain conditions where differentiation becomes untenable.

The specialization-differentiation processes involve a sequence of processes, the first of which is dissatisfaction of the actors involved with some aspect of their situation, which may derive from higher aspirations on their part or from changes in the situation. Sequential models of change processes applying the value-adding logic of the constitution of unit acts and types of action need to be developed, along the lines of Smelser's work.

Degree of Pluralism

Social action systems are influenced by the degree of pluralism in their experience systems. This relates to segmentation at the collective level, that is, the existence of a plurality of collective units with the same function such as families, communities, organizations. Pluralism involves the existence of segmental units that differ significantly with respect to the structuring of experience systems, particularly of culture and social system. The most common bases for pluralism are religion and ethnicity, but pluralism in the political and economic spheres is also variable. Pluralism introduces an element of diversity and heterogeneity of structure that must be taken into account in the explanation and prediction of social action. The relative independence and autonomy of the plural units are also important factors. Pluralism may involve conflicting or crosscutting but complementary solidarity patterns, affecting the solidarity of the system as a whole.

Degree of Centralization

A social action system has a center and a periphery, the relations between which are of importance in analysis. The degree of centralization is an important variable in this connection. The basis of centralization, e.g., whether it is based on consensus or coercion, must be taken into account. Centralization may be uneven, with a greater degree of centralization in different spheres. There may be a high degree of political centralization combined with a decentralized, pluralistic cultural system or economic system. There may be a clearly identifiable center of the system as a whole and yet a low degree of centralization of subsystem functions. The relations among actors in the system and social action are influenced by the location of actors in the center or on the periphery of the system.

Variation in Hierarchical Structure

All social action systems are influenced by the hierarchical structure of the experience systems of the actors. Stratification factors must be taken into account in the explanation and prediction of social action. The openness of classes, the distance between classes, the number of classes, the bases of class distinctions, the mobility rates among classes, and the strength and composition of elites are all important aspects. The stratification system has particularly important implications for the opportunity structure of actors in the system, for their experience systems, their access to markets and the media, and their role in the reconstitution of the components of social action.

Complexity of Organizational Structure

Social action is influenced by the complexity of group and organization structure, particularly at the secondary level. The formation of collective actors is partly determined by the scope, facilitation, and rate of social action in the system. Not only are there more collective actors in complex systems, but they are also more complex in their internal structure and external relations and hence shape social action in significant ways. The degree of functional specialization and structural differentiation of the system, the degree of segmentation and pluralism and the size of the population of actors relate to the collective actor structure and the way in which they influence social action.

Scope of Social Action

Experience structures vary in the scope they leave for social action, from oppressive and restrictive extremes to free and permissive, leaving large scope for action. An important aspect is the distinction between public and private spheres of action. Experience systems differ in the types of social action they classify in the public domain or the private domain. It is, for example, a critical variable whether religious action is regarded as public or private. The scope of social action permitted to a large extent determines whether a society is active or passive, responsive or submissive and this in turn influences rates and types of social action in the system.

Degree of Openness

Analytically, social action systems are defined as open systems characterized by ultrastability. Empirically the degree of openness is clearly variable. Some systems are more closed in relation to their environment than others, and this closedness calls for explanation. The conditions under which closedness is probable must be specified or, alternatively, the conditions under which social action systems will maintain maximum openness must be specified. This variable is particularly important for assessing the

system's ultrastability in all four functional spheres. The four major aspects of this openness to the environments of the system are adaptive capacity, goal attainment capacity, integrative capacity, and pattern maintenance capacity. Optimal conditions for each of these constitute an important dimension for identifying the evolutionary universals of a social action system.

Degree of Environmental Complexity and Variability

Social action systems vary in the complexity and variability of the environments with which they have to cope. All the variables listed above constitute aspects of complexity and variability when they pertain to social action systems and experience systems in the environment of the system being analyzed. It is important to realize that the most significant environments of empirical social action systems are experience systems and other social action systems. Complex and variable environments call for a more complex and flexible range of social action on the part of the system than do simple, stable environments, and relate to the degree of openness of the system.

Stage of Development

Many of the structural variables just listed relate to the state of development of the social action system, particularly its experience systems. Pluralism, complexity, openness, differentiation, activeness— all relate to higher stages of development, to name a few. In comparing systems of social action, the developmental stage is an important variable. A sequential stage model is an essential conceptual tool in the analysis of the evolution of social action systems.

Type of Value Primacy

The predominant value pattern of the experience systems of a social action system will provide a basis for the prediction of the types of social action likely to be emitted by actors in the system. But predominance has to be specified in terms of the preceding structural variables. If the value pattern is predominant at the center but not at the periphery of the system, the social action patterns will be different from those where it is also predominant at the periphery. The typology of social action developed above from the pattern-variables would provide a basis for comparison. This does not obviate subsystem analysis; on the contrary, it has determinate implications for subsystem differentiation.

Scarcity and Distribution of Resources

Scarcity or plenitude of resources for social action influences the rate and also the type of social action in the system. The distribution of resources is not simply an epiphenomenon of the stratification system but is also influenced by other structural variables, including the effectiveness of control of access and allocation by the center(s). Conditions of scarcity and plenitude (or perceptions of such) should be taken into account in the explanation and prediction of social action. If both conditions pertain in the same system for different classes of actors, it will lead to specifiable types of social action, such as conflict, competition, or revolution.

Space-time Parameters of Social Action

The space-time parameters of a social action system need to be taken into account as significant aspects of its environment. Such aspects as duration, age, stage, size, composition, density, isolation, concentration, territory, resource base, climate, ecological and diachronic patterns, and time and space limits on communication and transportation are conditions impinging particularly on the adaptive capacity of a social action system and are often given for a particular system at its level of technological development. But in comparative studies these conditions are obviously variable and should be taken into account in so far as they relate to the problems under investigation.

This list of variables may appear to the reader as little more than basic textbook material. The significance of their inclusion in an analytical essay has been stressed in the opening paragraphs of this section and needs to be reemphasized here. They constitute an essential checklist, albeit incomplete, of the states and parameters to be taken into account in applying analytical functional theory to empirical social phenomena and serve to sensitize the analyst or researcher to the perennial pitfalls of reification and reductionism.

CONCLUSION

This essay has ranged widely and yet stayed close to the core of the theory of action as a general theory. Looking back over it, one sees obvious major problems of logical inconsistency and perhaps some plain wrong-headedness. The reversal of the instrumental-consummatory significance of L and I alone could not have been adequately dealt with in an essay of this length. But I hope it does show in some respects that the theory of action is alive and well and hovering somewhere between empirical reality and analytical veracity. If I flew too many kites too high, maybe it is because the winds of theoretical change in sociology are blowing so strongly. This exercise will be fully rewarded, apart from its intrinsic satisfaction, even if only one of its excursions contributes to the development of social action theory.

10

EXPRESSIVE SYMBOLISM

James L. Peacock

Talcott Parsons asserted in 1951, and again in 1961, that the sphere of expressive symbolism is one of the least developed within the theory of action.[1] Yet, in company with Shils and Olds, he has also stated that "there is probably no problem in the analysis of action systems which would not be greatly clarified by a better understanding of symbolism."[2] If Parsons' own assessment is correct, a critical review of what has been and could be formulated in the realm of expressive symbolism is clearly needed at this stage in the development of action theory. Because of the underdeveloped character of the symbolic facets of that theory, I shall not hesitate to indulge in some exploration and speculation that would be out of place for a more developed topic.

This essay will attempt, first, to summarize central points in the Parsonian conception of expressive symbolism; second, to criticize and elaborate that conception; third, to suggest some directions for substantive generalization. The thrust, then, is toward substantive generalization derived from the action framework.

EXPRESSIVE SYMBOLS IN RELATION TO THE SOCIAL SYSTEM

The most complete Parsonian statement on this subject appears in the chapter in *The Social System* entitled "Expressive Symbols and the Social System: The Communication of Affect." The following summary is largely based on that chapter but by no means covers all of its points.

I wish to express my gratitude to the editors and to Mr. William Schneider and Dr. Joseph Tamney for their helpful comments. As this paper was written in the midst of anthropological field work in Southeast Asia made possible by grants from the National Science Foundation and the American Council of Learned Societies, I am happy to express my thanks to these bodies for financing a suitably exotic creative milieu.

Parsons begins his discussion with the familiar paradigm of an interacting ego and alter. For these, expressive symbols (1) aid in communication of cathectic meanings, (2) regulate the interaction by imposing standards, such as of taste, and (3) serve directly as objects to gratify the needs of the actors. The basic expressive symbol is the symbolic act itself. An act becomes symbolic insofar as it acquires meaning apart from its instrumental uses. Thus, the mother's response to her child's cry not only relieves the child's distress but also symbolizes motherliness. The meaning of "motherliness" denoted by the mother's actions generalizes to associated objects, and complexes of symbolism emerge. Explicating their character, Parsons goes beyond the Freudians in noting that not only may derivative objects symbolize the primary one, but also vice versa: For the child, the breast could in time symbolize the bottle as well as the bottle the breast.

Symbolic complexes become institutionalized, which is to say, stabilized in accord with established rules and expectations. With institutionalization, evaluative attitudes surround the expressive symbols. Thus, in kinship and courtship the rules for where, when, and how to do symbolic acts and manipulate symbolic objects are usually quite strict and moralistic.

Evaluative culture (which may be defined as a system of moral conceptions embodied in decrees, doctrines, ethics, laws, sermons, and other symbolic forms) becomes important whenever the survival and integration of society is at stake. Evaluative culture provides legitimacy and meaning to social values, which guide and control the social system. Expressive culture (which may be defined as a system of symbolic forms regarded more for their formal qualities, their sensuous surfaces, than for any moral or cognitive conceptions they happen to express) is not so important for the social system but is important in expressing the need-dispositions of the personality. To perform its functions, evaluative culture must be institutionalized in the social system. To perform *its* functions, expressive culture must be internalized in the personality.[3]

Carrying forward his general notion that expressive symbols are less closely connected to the social system than are evaluative symbols, Parsons' analysis of the artist — key wielder and creator of expressive symbols — accentuates the loose connection between art and the wider social system. The appreciative standards that artist and audience share are, according to Parsons, "institutionalized only in 'acceptance' terms. As we ordinarily put it, we are 'pleased' or 'moved' by a work of art or its performance. But this attitude does not have specifically binding implications for our actions beyond this specific context."[4] Attendance at a performance or exhibition is usually voluntary in the first place, and sanctions of the theater or gallery apply only when one is there. They do not ramify into the participants' behavior in the wider society.

The exception to this is where coteries or schools emerge whose primary rationale is a set of artistic standards to which members must conform. Here participants in an artistic performance are part of an organization which enforces principles of the art in ramified spheres of the participants' lives. But Parsons emphasizes that these artistic principles could become dominant only in the lives and social organization of a specialized clique. They could never become the basis for organization of the total society.[5] Parsons does observe that in some societies, such as the communist ones, artistic standards become crucial *parts* of values and ideologies controlling the wider society. Insofar as this occurs, the standards stop being merely expressive and become strongly evaluative. Rules forcing conformity to them become severe. Communist rules controlling artistic portrayal of private emotions illustrate the point.

Criticism and Elaboration

A recurrent theme in Parsons' paradigm is that where concerns of society as a whole come into play, evaluative rather than expressive orientations tend to dominate. Regarded as an empirical hypothesis, what does this principle imply? Only that a typical human reaction is to assume a moralistic attitude when the integration and survival of the society as a whole is at stake. The question remains, is this reaction actually functional to the integration and survival of the society? One is tempted to answer yes on the grounds that matters important to the integration and survival of society as a whole must be controlled by the no-nonsense mechanisms of evaluative culture — decrees, laws, and the like. The assumption is that important realms of behavior must be controlled by the most powerful devices society can muster and that these are devices of evaluative culture.

One can at least entertain another argument that if expressive culture could be demonstrated to be a more efficient mechanism of control of behavior than is evaluative culture, then emphasis of expressive culture would be a functional response when society is at stake. One can ask whether the frivolous weapons of expressive culture — forms with power to thrill, move, and amuse — do not possess advantages. Because the sanctions, sermons, and decrees are often pompous, obvious, and rude, they put people on their guard and arouse their resistance. The subtle and undercover techniques of expressive culture, which do not so obviously aim to control, may seduce people into letting their guard down. Thus, expressive culture has at least one type of control potential that evaluative culture does not. Furthermore, in this day of reaction against moralistic postures and their supernatural base, the traditional control power of evaluative culture is weakened. What this type of argument implies is that if leaders of society think rationally and insightfully, they will see that the complex of prescriptions and prohibitions which in the past has served well socially to control critical affairs must give way to more subtle devices exploiting expressive orientations. And if they proceed to emphasize expressive culture in matters vital to the welfare of society as a whole, analysts of society as a whole must give more attention to expressive culture than they have been doing.

Speculative as this argument may be, perhaps it can set in motion discussion of whether Parsonian theory is improperly biased in its emphasis of the social importance of evaluative as opposed to expressive culture. Is Parsons correct in emphasizing that evaluative culture is institutionalized in society, expressive culture merely internalized in the personality? Is he correct in believing that where society is at stake evaluative rather than expressive culture necessarily comes to the fore? These traditional Parsonian emphases encourage the analyst of society to focus more on evaluative than on expressive culture, and most do. A more pro-expressive view would encourage more sociological attention to expressive culture.

Parsons' analysis of artist, audience, and the absence of binding ramifications of the artistic performance reinforces his theme that expressive culture is comparatively irrelevant to wider social concerns. His analysis here seems largely true except, of course, where the performance or exhibition is part of some ramified religious or political organization which controls numerous facets of the lives of those who happen to attend the performance or exhibition. What might be emphasized to balance the

Parsonian emphasis is that precisely because the artist's performance is not binding on daily behaviors, he is freed to concentrate on the purely expressive enterprise of evoking emotional response from his audience. The result is sometimes a depth of human portrayal which is lost when the art becomes more tightly integrated into a wider religiopolitical network, in which case it becomes either mythology or propaganda. And the human portrayal may more deeply affect the society than the socially directed mythology or propaganda.[6]

EXPRESSIVE SYMBOLS AS PART OF CULTURE

Whereas *The Social System* viewed expressive symbols as elements in a network of social interactions, later Parsonian writings, notably his "Introduction to Part IV" of *Theories of Society*[7] have attempted to treat the symbols as part of systems that bestow meaning, that render human action and existence meaningful. That analytically distinguishable system of categories and orientations (values, beliefs, ideas, and symbols) which renders human action meaningful may be called "culture."

According to Parsons, cultural systems bestow essentially four types of meaning: cognitive, cathectic, evaluative, and (my label) "existential." Each type of meaning is bestowed at four levels of generality. Thus, cognitive systems (scientific schemes being prototypal) delineate conceptual elements ranging from the most specific to the most general, i.e., facts, problems, theories, and underlying premises. Evaluative systems (ethical philosophies being prototypal) delineate categories for evaluating means, goals, scales for ranking means and goals, and finally, all evaluations. Existential systems formulate frames (e.g., the Calvinist notion of Calling) that provide meaning to performances (e.g., work), spheres of performance (e.g., the economy), the essential order of the universe and, finally, all phenomena, including the various elements of culture.

The fourth subsystem of culture, the cathectic, is composed of expressive symbols. Like the other cultural elements, expressive symbols may be ranked along a gradient of generality. The least general symbols codify utilitarian attitudes toward objects which are typically physical and organic. The next level codifies emotions of love or reciprocity toward personalities. The next codifies feelings of identification with collectivities. The most general level of symbolism codifies attitudes of worship or generalized respect toward cultural objects (e.g., God). As respective examples of such symbols, one might

name a hammer, a painting of the Madonna and Child, a national flag, and a rosary. I believe it is correct to say that Parsons views all these symbols as objectifying, codifying, conceptualizing — in a word symbolizing — the various raw emotions, thereby rendering them more meaningful than if they were simply left raw. Elsewhere Parsons defines expressive symbols as "culturally codified generalizations about emotional experience."[8]

Criticism and Elaboration

A major gap in Parsons' exposition is that he fails to explain how expressive symbols bestow meaning. Yet he classifies these as part of culture, which is defined or envisioned as a system oriented primarily around bestowing meaning. Clearly Parsons does not regard expressive symbols as conferring meaning in the manner of cognitive, evaluative, or existential culture — through the classifying of acts and objects in cognitive, evaluative, or existential schemes, such as scientific theories, moral doctrines, or religious theologies. A trial formulation of the senses in which expressive symbols confer meaning will help fill the Parsonian gap.

First and most important, expressive symbols codify emotional experience by transforming it into sensuous (visible, audible, tactile) form.[9] Thus the muddle of raw experience is objectified and ordered. A good example is the narrative plot which transforms directionless conflict of real life into orderly progression toward climax and resolution. Conversion of experience into form renders experience orderly, hence meaningful.

In addition to formulating experience as form, symbols may subsume experience under a cognitive framework. The philosopher Ernst Cassirer emphasized this process.[10] A painting of the Madonna unites the image of the female, embodied in the canvas and embodying experiences derived from real females, with the concept of womanhood or motherhood defined by the relevant religio-aesthetic tradition. Experience is rendered cognitively meaningful. In Parsons' terms, should this cognitive function become primary for a symbol, the symbol is cognitive instead of expressive.

Expressive symbols may subsume experience under an evaluative framework. The anthropologist Victor Turner[11] emphasizes this process when he analyzes the Ndembu *mudyi* tree as a symbol which expresses via such sensuous images as tree sap (likened to mother's milk) the moral principle of matriliny, which is the *grundlage* of Ndembu social life. The sensuous form is ennobled by the moral principle, and the moral principle is rendered palatable by the sensuous form. In Parsons' terms, should this evaluative function become primary for a symbol, the symbol is evaluative instead of expressive.

By the logic of Parsons' formulation, expressive symbols are distinct from cognitive or evaluative ones in that they do not serve primarily to classify acts or objects in an evaluative or cognitive framework. Their primary function is the codification of experience into form. But such codification is possible only insofar as the forms themselves are classified in and defined by aesthetic schemas (rules of style, definitions of genre, and the like). These schemas orient to the expressive endeavor itself rather than to social or physical reality. It is their relation to this type of schema, rather than their lack of relation to any schema, that distinguishes expressive symbols and their method of bestowing meaning as part of culture.[12]

EXPRESSIVE SYMBOLS IN RELATION TO THE PERSONALITY SYSTEM: THE ROOTS OF EXPRESSIVENESS

Moving "below" the level of the cultural and social systems to seek the elemental personal motives and life experiences that engender and sustain expressive symbols, we encounter three interconnected themes in Parsons' writings: (1) as a psychological orientation (which of course supports and is supported by institutional and cultural patterns), the expressive urge is toward direct gratification; (2) this type of gratification is commonly provided in particularistic contexts; and (3) particularistic and expressive modes of behavior are learned first and most importantly through relations with the mother.

According to Parsons, expressive symbols

In the "purest" form . . . constitute the cultural patterning of action of the expressive type where the interest in immediate gratifications is primary and neither instrumental nor evaluative considerations have primacy. It should immediately be pointed out that this does not in the least imply that such expressive interests are in any sense crudely "hedonistic." They consist in the primacy of the interest in immediate gratification of *whatever* need-dispositions are relevant in the action context in question. These may be need-dispositions to care for others, or to "create" highly abstract ideas or cultural forms. The essential point is the primacy of "acting out" the need-disposition itself rather than subordinating gratification to a goal outside the immediate situation or to a restrictive norm. The "quality" of the need-disposition is not at issue.[13]

I would suggest, though, that the *pattern* of gratifying the need-disposition is at issue. One may argue that the essence of art is that through emphasis on

sensuous form it sustains a delicate balance between gratifying and deflecting basic needs. Because this issue is fundamental, it is best to confront it before proceeding with the other themes in Parsons' expressive psychology.

Art (as opposed to pornography) shies from portraying those physiological organs which most directly gratify the sexual drive. The Freudian insight that it is rarely the genitals themselves but rather the secondary parts such as breasts, legs, mouth, and hair that are considered beautiful seems largely correct. Why this concentration of art on the secondary parts? Perhaps because it can thus best deflect attention from direct gratification of the sex drive and concentrate attention on the form — the sensuous surface — of its symbolization of sex. Artists would be merely pimps were they to prompt their audiences to abandon the contemplative posture, leave their seats, and gratify their needs by means of unadorned genitals situated on the stage.

George Devereux[14] considers that by emphasizing the form of his art, the artist can deny interest in its content, thereby gaining the right secretly to express through that content illicit sexual needs. A youth who declares his love for a girl in a poem can repudiate the poem's content if it becomes embarrassing by claiming, "It was just a poem, not a declaration of love." Similarly, a lady who wants to hear a dirty joke can agree to listen, "if it is really a good one." Again, by denying interest in the content and emphasizing the form, artist and audience may jointly express illicit content. But in so doing they are entrapped in contemplation of the form.

An interesting example of this process is provided by the Javanese drama, *ludruk*, which features as one of its strongest fascinations male transvestites, whose impersonation of females is deemed by Javanese the essence of *ludruk* as art.

The transvestite represents various illicit drives[15] which focus around regressive and pre-genital needs, such as sucking of breasts and escaping from adult familial responsibilities by enjoying sex without procreation, which the transvestite, being unable to give birth, is particularly good at providing. As *ludruk's* repository of illicitness, the transvestite finds it necessary to adorn himself with the most elaborate and refined (*alus*) symbolism that *ludruk* can provide. Only under the cloak of this symbolism can the illicit needs be expressed. While claiming to contemplate refined artistic form, singer and listener enjoy images of regressive and illicit sex, including the promise of homosexual relations backstage after the show. But this is not all. The transvestite even in his most direct representation symbolizes partial (as opposed to full) gratification of sexual needs. After all, he is a man, hence he cannot provide true coitus for his male partners. The audience may only contemplate the transvestite's *illusion* of womanliness, projected by rouge, padding, and long tresses. Tales are rife of the man who attempts to penetrate beyond this facade to the organic reality underneath and is disillusioned.

At several levels, the transvestite epitomizes the process of deflecting sexual drive toward the surface of the art form itself and away from sources of direct gratification, while at the same time alluding to that gratification. It is therefore revealing that certain Javanese consider the transvestite the essence of *ludruk* as art (*seni*).

What this analysis implies is that Parsons' portrayal of the expressive orientation is too simple. We may agree that instrumental orientations are toward future goals, evaluative orientations toward conformity with restrictive norms, and expressive orientations toward gratifying the needs of individual actors. But the patterning of gratifications organized by expressive symbols is more complicated than this formulation implies. The deflection of a need, by diverting attention to a form, may be as crucial as its immediate gratification.[16]

In Parsons' thought, expressive orientations are most likely activated within particularistic social relationships. Instrumental orientations are most likely activated within universalistic social relationships.[17] This follows directly from Parsons' conception of the expressive orientation as focussed toward immediate gratification. To orient instrumentally or universalistically to persons is not to enjoy them immediately as objects of gratification but to use them as means toward some goal or ideal that transcends one's particular relationship to them. Thus, a man orients instrumentally or universalistically to a woman when he judges her according to her usefulness for some goal transcending their relationship, such as civic solvency or national prosperity. To orient particularistically toward the woman would be to enjoy her for herself—to treat her as an object of immediate gratification—and thus to relate to her in terms of one's relationship to her, rather than in terms of some transcendent goal or ideal.

The ability to relate to persons particularistically is, in Parsons' thought, acquired during early association with the mother. Put differently, the ability to orient *expressively* is learned through such experiences. The mother rewards the child with erotic pleasure (fondling, cuddling, and the like). In return the child loves the mother. A diffuse and expressive reward greets a diffuse and expressive commitment. From this the child learns trust. He does not treat the mother as merely a means toward an end that transcends their particular relationship.

She is not merely a tool to fill the stomach. The mother-child relationship is gratificatory in itself, not merely a means toward gratification, and it becomes stabilized as worthy of commitment for its own sake.

Following Parsons' argument, we might ask if this ex-primeval experience with particularism is the root of the ability to orient expressively. If the mother-child relationship becomes less particularistic, does the child become less able to orient expressively? For instance, what happens when mothers follow the conditional love pattern supposedly characteristic of middle-class America? American mothers relate universalistically—rewarding the child by affection when he achieves a goal defined by sources external to the mother-child bond, punishing him when he fails to achieve such a goal. According to the logic of Parsons' theory, in this way mothers deprive the child of a chance to learn to orient expressively. Pushing the theory to its empirical limits, one might propose—as a hypothesis worthy of testing—that such universalistically reared children will be more productive of expressive symbols, including art forms, than children raised more particularistically.

In light of the earlier criticism of Parsons' conception of the expressive orientation—more concretely, the aesthetic urge, the artistic impulse—this hypothesis is problematical. True, a broad similarity may be seen between the orientation of child to mother and artist to symbol. Neither mother nor symbol is treated instrumentally (and therefore may in Parsons' terms, be treated expressively). But if it is accepted that the expressive urge as focussed toward art forms is organized as a complicated pattern of deflection/gratification, we should ask whether the child's drives as focussed toward the mother are organized in a similar way. This question is beyond the scope of this paper, depending, as it does, on empirical investigations in child psychology. What is clear is that Parsons' basic variables such as "expressive orientation" and "particularism" interrelate in interesting ways and can generate empirical hypotheses and that such hypotheses will stand investigation to the extent that their basic terms, e.g., "expressive orientation," accurately denote the real-life phenomena, e.g., orientation of artist to symbol, that they are supposed to denote.

IMPLICATIONS

Thus far, this essay has striven to lay bare the base points in Parsons' conception of expressive symbolism, to criticize whatever weaknesses could be discerned in the conception, and to modify and elaborate where necessary. From this endeavor emerge the following themes:

By comparison with evaluative culture, expressive culture is less directly institutionalized in the wider society, less binding in a legal sense on its participants' ramified spheres of life. This situation does not necessarily mean that expressive culture is less important for the wider society or that it has less control over behavior. It does imply that expressive culture must influence social patterning through the medium of the personality, by subtle psychological routes, rather than through the direct sanctions employed by evaluative culture. One implication of this notion, to be elaborated hereafter, is that though knowledge of the social implications of expressive culture may be increasingly important for understanding the wider society, such knowledge may be more difficult to acquire than in the case of evaluative culture.

Unlike evaluative or cognitive culture, expressive culture bestows meaning not by classification of acts and objects in evaluative-cognitive schemes but through codification of raw experience into forms whose qualities conform to such expressive standards as rules of style. An implication of this notion is that any theory of expressive symbolism must move away from the cognitive or evaluative content expressed by the symbolic forms and confront the features of the forms themselves.

Basic variables of the theory of action such as particularism, mother-child socialization, and personality need-dispositions compose the psychological complex associated with expressive symbols and expressive orientations. Because of the tendency of art to deflect as well as gratify needs through emphasis on form, some refinement seems necessary in Parsons' conception of the expressive orientation as applied to symbolic, especially artistic, contexts. This criticism also raises questions about the degree to which the so-called expressive orientation as expressed in art is psychologically similar to the expressive orientation expressed in the mother-child relation and other particularistic contexts. Nevertheless, the similarity is suggestive enough to inspire various empirical hypotheses, such as some to be proposed here.

Keeping in mind these themes and Parsons' conception—in both its pristine and its elaborated forms—as a frame of reference, we turn to the question of empirical generalization.

Some Difficulties and Directions in Generalizing about Expressive Symbolism

Before generalizing, it is good to analyze cases. Even the analysis of cases is fraught with difficulty when the aim is to show behavioral correlates of expressive symbolism. The difficulties are probably greater with respect to expressive symbolism than with evaluative or cognitive culture. Thus, it seems easier to show convincingly that Muslim laws shape the form of Muslim families than to demonstrate that Muslim music works a determinate and regular influence on any Muslim institution except the musical.

The relative ease of making the first analysis convincing doubtless derives in part from biases and conventions of contemporary social science, and these should not remain unchallenged. More basic reasons, however, can be cited. To begin, it is generally easier to arrive at an unambiguous verbal statement of what is said or even what is meant by a written or informal law than to state what an art form says or means. This is due to the richness and variety of meanings connoted by any expressive form.

A step in tracing the social implications of the expressive form is to analyze the myriad emotional and mental responses to it. On the basis of introspection and intuition, the investigator may suspect that Muslim listeners harbor deep and profound feelings about Muslim music. To record these feelings is difficult. The listener rarely shouts his innermost emotions, and even if he is made to lie on the psychiatrist's couch, only a portion of his emotional reactions come to light.

The reader may protest that it is just as difficult to record inner feelings concerning the Muslim laws. But much of the influence of the laws may be demonstrated merely by recording the family patterning that they directly enforce. Because the musical forms cannot directly enforce any particular pattern of social organization, only through a tortuous psychosocial analysis can their influence be displayed. One must somehow dissect the subjective experience derived from participation in the musical performance, then trace the effects of this experience on participants' behavior in daily life. Especially in complex society such analysis is difficult because the daily contexts—economic, political, familial—are differentiated from aesthetic contexts, and the connections between the two are not binding. The social ramifications of the music may be great, but it is empirically a staggering task to trace them.

In the example just envisioned, one would construct empirical generalization by laboriously analyzing the patterning of empirical cases, then stating similarities among the different patterns. What might be deemed the strategy of functional generalization pursues a more abstract procedure. The analyst abstracts from reality analytical systems, such as cultural, social, and personal, then defines functions that one system must serve for another.

He states that if cultural systems do not properly supply meaning and legitimacy to social systems, social systems cannot maintain their patterns, motivate their members to produce, integrate their units, and flourish, survive, modernize, or whatnot. If "proper supply of meaning and legitimacy" could be operationally defined, then societies that successfully solve this problem could be compared to those that do not, and conclusions could be drawn as to the social consequences of failing to solve it.

A similar procedure could be followed regarding variables less general than "culture." The analyst could assert that a society must possess certain expressive forms (e.g., dramatic performances) in order to sustain a certain pattern (e.g., the habit of systematically working toward a climactic goal). Comparative analysis could then test the assertion. Someone could check to see if societies lacking drama had notably fewer members with the goal-climax habit than do societies with drama. Unfortunately, it would probably turn out that even where drama is not present, other expressive forms serve the function in question. The function is more general than the form. A very specific function, such as mobilization of actors on stage to portray a narrative, would correlate well with presence and absence of dramatic form, as it virtually defines dramatic form, but the correlation is trivial. The challenge is to formulate a function sufficiently different from the form so that the correlation between the two is not trivial, yet not so different that the two are not correlated. The challenge may be especially great for the student of expressive forms. Any form can serve multiple functions, and any function can be filled by multiple forms, but from a sociological standpoint expressive forms are particularly prone to functional ambiguity. It is more difficult to predict the social functions of expressive forms than of legal forms because legal forms directly enforce particular social patterns, but expressive forms influence social patterning only through the tortuous and ramified psychological routes discussed earlier.

To be sure, not everyone agrees that expressive forms are functionally ambiguous. Marshall McLuhan[18] strongly asserts that they are functionally determinate. Each form or medium carries its own distinctive message and has its own distinctive psychosocial functions. Print, for example, always and everywhere brings about a linear, analytical mode of thought and a bureaucratic, specialized, industrial style of social organization. Television works just the reverse effect. Television encourages a configurational, participational type of emotionality that gives rise to everything from tiny, cozy automobiles to renewed appreciation of body odor and the decline of bureaucratic, specialized society. Print, television, or any other form works its distinctive effect and function regardless of its context.

Owing to his determinist stance, McLuhan is customarily termed a technological determinist. The label "symbolic determinist" is more accurate. McLuhan argues that media work their effects on society not by permitting distinctive opportunities for exploiting the environment, but by expressing and evoking distinctive sensory-emotional orientations which eventuate in distinctive sociocultural patterns. McLuhan is doubtless deficient in that his variables—print, television, radio, newspapers—are too concrete. A refinement would be to abstract the relevant aspects of these variables—those that do consistently correlate with social variables—and to work these into a coherent theory. Such an endeavor might usefully contribute to the theory of action, which has made virtually no attempt to define analytical variables that systematically take account of the distinctive qualities of the *forms* of expressive life. Where in Parsons' work are social variables systematically related to the differences between oral and visual media, or drama, myth, and poetry? Some effort at such generalization is woven into the analysis to follow.

SOME ILLUSTRATIVE GENERALIZATIONS: THE ROLE OF EXPRESSIVE SYMBOLS IN SOCIOCULTURAL EVOLUTION

The generalizations to be proposed are not intended as empirical hypotheses ready for testing. They are merely to illustrate some of the paths of substantive generalization suggested by the logic of the theory of action especially in one area recently emerging into prominence — the study of sociocultural evolution.

In the following are outlined some correlations between types of expressive performance and Bellah's stages of socioreligious evolution, grouped here as primitive, archaic-historic, and collectivist/individualist early modern.[19]

Primitive

Characteristic expressive performances in primitive society are what Gluckman[20] has named "rites of social relations." Such rites are distinguished, among other things, by the extremely diffuse bond uniting the ritual participants. Not only are they co-ritualists, but they are also neighbors, co-landholders, and kinsmen, and they share other roles. Their empathy with one another during the rite is therefore along a wide band, tapping a number of social relationships. This kind of empathy is lost at later stages of sociocultural evolution when audience and actors share only a very specific social relationship, such as paying audience and paid actor, and so empathize with one another along a much narrower band. Owing to the diffuseness of the bond uniting primitive ritual participants, the ritual ordering of this bond is perceived by primitives as affecting a wide range of phenomena—not only the community but nature and the cosmos. Participants believe that performing the rite is itself sufficient to effect desired change in these spheres — e.g., to help the witchetty grub flourish, in the case of the Australian aborigine. The relevant contrast is with modern participants in drama, who relate to one another along narrow and specific bands and who do not believe that manipulating their social relations on the stage will automatically affect society, nature, or cosmos. Because moderns do not attribute power to the performance itself, they are encouraged to believe that after the performance is over, it is up to the individual to struggle to change the world in accordance with ideals dramatized on the stage. According to this idea, dramatic form of all types, regardless of content, tends to evoke a more innovative and activistic attitude than does the ritual of social relations found in primitive society.

Archaic-historic

Characteristic performances in archaic-historic societies (e.g., medieval Southeast Asian kingdoms, such as Java, Malaya, and Thailand, and some medieval European kingdoms) are the comedy 'of manners and the legend of royalty, often combined into a single performance which features a hero-king endowed with supernatural powers and a clown who lampoons the hero-king. In the larger society, the characteristic social relationship is diffuse but hierarchical. Father-son, master-servant, and king-subject exemplify such a relationship. Because the relationship is diffuse, disturbance of it would ramify deeply and widely into the lives of the community members. To avoid such disturbance, to harmonize and preserve the relationships, elaborate manners are developed. To sanctify and to satirize these manners, comedies of manners are interwoven with the legends of royalty, both of which are staged as dramas, e.g., the *wajang wong* and *wajang kulit* of Java. In such comedies, plot line counts less than periodic jokes or maudlin episodes. The jokes satirize kings and aristocrats. The episodes depict a helpless creature, pregnant woman or orphan child, suffering passively at the hands of a cruel aristocrat or king. Because plot line is not crucial, such performances often run for hours, perhaps all night, with frequent recesses for the audience to eat, sleep, excrete, and socialize. As custom, beginning with child-rearing, teaches not identification with superiors' personalities but imitation of their manners, performances (at least those by proletarians) feature little psychological analysis of the heroes but rather imitation of their manners and mien by clowns. The dance, which is markedly developed in the Southeast Asian archaic-historic societies, also imitates refined manners and mien of superiors.

Early Modern Collectivist Variant

Characteristic performances in early modern collectivist societies (e.g., Nazi Germany and certain new nations) are the nationalist film, play, or ceremony which depicts individuals as relentlessly (but enthusiastically) swept along by forces of history toward a collective goal. Horror tales wherein individuals are moved by dark spiritual forces and destinies may also be popular.[21] Heroes are charismatic and superior to onlookers but lack the supernatural powers of archaic-historic kings. Nationalist forms are moralistic and didactic to teach nationalist and revolutionary ideals. Unlike in archaic-historic kingdoms, a youth culture is prominent and oriented around nationalism. Both the ultra-refined dancers and the ultra-crude clowns of archaic-historic drama decline in importance with the early modern de-emphasis on manners and hierarchy. With the declining importance of joke and dance interludes and the increasing spirit of nationalist thrust toward goals, dramatic performances become shorter and more tightly directed toward a climax.

Early Modern Individualistic Variant

Characteristic performances in early modern individualistic society (e.g., pre-war America) are films depicting success or Hollywood romance. Such films are neither didactic nor moralistic, as they accentuate doing for the sake of doing rather than loyalty to an abstract collective ideal. Fast-moving, light plots with much hustle and pep are the rule. Unlike collectivist, nationalist stories, such plots feature heterosexual romance instead of homosexual comradeship. Comradeship may aid collective military-nationalist struggle, but it can be distracting to the individual striver after success. For him, romance leading to a mobile nuclear family unit that climbs the social ladder with him is more relevant. Early modern individualistic performances tend to be even shorter than collectivist performances, partly to keep the action moving, partly in order clearly and compactly to depict the link between characters' initial ambition and final success, and partly so as not to take too much time from the job. Youth is geared into the art of early

modern individualistic society but not into its eco-
nomic-political system. As a result, the art often
becomes silly and trivial.

What about the dynamics that incite societies
to shift from one evolutionary type to the next?
In Parsons' and Bellah's formulations, a key dynamic
is provided by discrepancy between cognitive-
evaluative (religious) culture and daily society. To
match society with the cultural ideals, men reform
the society, thus modernizing it. One may ask
whether a similar dynamic derives from discrepancy
between expressive culture and daily society. This
question brings us back to psychological matters
basic to the action framework — the association
between expressive symbolism, emotions, personality, particularism, others, childhood, and, of course,
the expressive as opposed to instrumental orientation. From these associations derive the following
notions:

1. Childhood experiences tend to be organized
according to principles of magical thinking, aesthetic
fit, and convention, rather than rationality, utility,
and efficiency. Especially is this true in early modern
society where childhood and adulthood are sharply
differentiated. In early modern society, adult jobs
specialize in rationality and efficiency, but children's
lives are more oriented around fantasy, custom,
parentally imposed codes of morality, and aesthetic
rules for organizing play.

2. Similar considerations to those of childhood
(e.g., conventions of style that call forth connections
between symbols and referents which are, from a
utilitarian standpoint, arbitrary)[22] guide artistic
and expressive endeavors. That is, certain formal
similarities link expressive symbolism to childhood
experience. Because of those similarities, any expressive form, regardless of its story, moral, or message, will tend to evoke regressive fantasies and
emotions derived from childhood.

3. If expressive symbols evoke childhood memories and fantasies from adult beholders, the emotions
elicited by discrepancy between expressive culture
and daily society may differ from those elicited by
discrepancy between evaluative culture and daily
society. Discrepancy between evaluative culture
and daily society frequently incites a relentless drive
toward reform (e.g., note the Calvinist response to
his perception of mis-mesh between the Kingdom of
God and the Kingdom of Man). Discrepancy between
expressive culture and daily society frequently
evokes nostalgia, a sense of loss, and a reluctance to
leave the world of fantasy (note the emotions
experienced by many persons upon leaving the
cinema or finishing a novel and then confronting a social reality different from the fantasy
just experienced). These emotions are perhaps

engendered by the similarity between the expressive symbols, the fantasies they evoke, and the
remembered childhood experience. The removal
of the fantasy world reenacts loss of childhood and
evokes a nostalgic "remembrance of things past."

4. Such nostalgia is perhaps less likely to result
in action and reform than is the militant feeling
incited by discrepancy between social reality and
evaluative culture. At the same time, the sense of
nostalgia and loss doubtless encourages a creative
drive which is more exploratory than that of the
reformer.[23] The artist is more likely to encourage
evolutionary advance by exploring the limits of
imagination and emotion than by militant reform.
If his art always tends to evoke nostalgia and a remembrance of things past, it will always support
custom and tradition as well as exploratory innovation, whereas the militant reformer is single-
minded in his rejection of tradition.

Thus, discrepancy between expressive culture
and society would seem to produce an evolutionary
dynamic different from that produced by discrepancy
between evaluative culture and society.

Arguing from different premises, Talcott Parsons
reaches a similar conclusion. Parsons observes that
expressive symbols do not evolve in a clearly cumulative line as cognitive systems (e.g., scientific theory)
or evaluative systems (e.g., ethical-theological formulations) supposedly do. The reason, Parsons suggests, is that of all the "essential relations" (cognitive,
cathectic, evaluative), "the cathectic relation to situational objects is the most particularized."[24] Expressive
symbols generalize, therefore, through "the patterning of symbols rather than the symbolization of patterns."[25] What this last statement apparently means
is that expressive symbols formulate general notions
and dispositons not by defining abstract formulae,
but through a Hemingway-like combining of concrete images. Because of their concreteness, such
images mirror the flux and flow of reality rather than
evolving in their own determined stream. Failing to
stand above particular relationships and situations
and define premises and forms applicable to all,
expressive culture cannot be a strong force for
change. Culture is a force for change only when it
formulates a systematic and independent set of orientations and symbols in terms of which society can be
judged and, if found wanting, changed.

On these grounds, Parsons views expressive symbolism as reinforcing traditionalism and social
stasis. He remarks that the Tao, Yang, and Ying of
ancient China were expressive symbols, rather than
cognitive categories, and that this expressive orientation "fits with the particularism, traditionalism, and
'ritualism' of traditional Chinese society."[26] Similarly, he characterizes Spanish America as having

both a strongly "traditionalist" and a strongly "expressive" focus.[27] He asserts that in general, because of its association with particularism, expressive symbolism embodies "a whole complex of factors making for stabilization through traditionalization, which did not operate so strongly in the case of beliefs."[28]

I argued before that especially in modern society expressive culture tends to evoke an orientation toward the past and tradition associated with nostalgia and fantasy. Parsons is proposing that especially in archaic-historic society (Chinese and Spanish-American) expressive culture tends to evoke an orientation toward the past associated with ritualism and particularism. The two arguments thus converge, but I have also emphasized the exploratory aspect of expressive culture in modern society, and similar observations could be made regarding archaic-historic society. Granted, the systematic rationalization of cognitive and evaluative culture, possible only through culture's independence from particular social relational complexes, is a strong lever for change. But another source of change in archaic-historic society is surely the scattered and periodic comedy. Analysts of literature tend toward a view precisely opposite to that of Parsons in accentuating the traditionalism of moral culture and the creativity of disorganized expressive culture such as comedy, which lampoons old views and fantasizes new views that only many generations later are incorporated into the organized moral systems.[29] Parsons does not explicitly deny this viewpoint, but had he taken it into account he would perhaps not so consistently identify expressive symbolism with traditionalism.[30]

A REVIEW OF BASIC PREMISES

Though engaging in criticism and elaboration of the theory of action, I have attempted to stay within its basic premises. Are the premises themselves acceptable? Are they the only ones available? Starting from new premises, might we develop a new perspective that serves better to make sense out of expressive phenomena? As a start toward answering these questions, let us consider what is probably the most basic available criticism of Parsons' treatment of expressive symbolism, a critique launched by Hugh D. Duncan.

The Duncanian Critique

Duncan claims to have written his *Symbols in Society* specifically to oppose and refute the "mechanistic" treatment of the subject by Parsons and his associates.[31] For Duncan, Parsons is one of the "American sociologists who thinks of communications as a 'map,' a pattern, or a net,"[32] that is, who thinks mechanistically about communications and symbols. Duncan admits that Parsons has preached the importance of the study of symbolic expression. Nevertheless, in Duncan's opinion, Parsons has contributed little to that study, and has even confused and vulgarized it by his distasteful models that mix the mechanical with the symbolic. The resulting "mechanical monsters almost rival the chimeras of antiquity: firebreathing monsters, with a lion's head, a goat's body, and a serpent's tail, have been matched by grotesques with mechanical heads and symbolic bodies."[33] The basic difficulty is that for the theorist of action symbols are only "epiphenomena which exist on the surface of a social system whose 'gearing' and 'meshing' (in modern mechanistic parlance) really determines human motivation."[34] The result is a fundamental misunderstanding and underestimation of the role of symbolic form — as form, not merely as vehicle for social content — in human action. The analysis of form as form is subordinated to the analysis of the social (and moral) machinery that form presumably reflects.

In his earlier book, *Communication and Social Order*, Duncan presses essentially the same argument, but with different materials and emphases.[35] Here too mechanists such as Parsons are villains and scapegoats, but they are overshadowed by European social theorists with whom they (especially Parsons) are strongly allied. Durkheim, Weber, and Malinowski err, in Duncan's opinion, by treating religion as key for society and art as a mere vehicle for basic religious sentiments. Their error is to underestimate the role and power of form itself: "The point is not that Giotto painted on his knees, or that Bach worshiped through music, but that they give religious experience new forms and new realities which would not have been possible without such forms."[36]

As an alternative to the mechanist model, Duncan proposes in *Symbols in Society* a "dramatistic" one inspired by Kenneth Burke as well as by members of the Chicago symbolic interaction school. Duncan's formal definition of his dramatistic model is vague and in any case resembles the model of social action defined by his opponent, Parsons. More important than the formal definition are the images of society as drama that emerge from Duncan's potpourri of insight, harangue, and analysis. These images are two, the tragic and the comic.

Society as tragic is hierarchical, emphasizing relations between superiors and inferiors. Guilt is the constant product of hierarchies because inferiors repeatedly fail superiors, and they feel guilty about it. To purge that guilt from society, scapegoats shoulder it, and are then ostracized. Balancing this negative movement toward purge is a positive movement toward sanctification. Through association with symbols of dignity and radiance, the highest principles of social order are glorified. Into these heights of glory are continuously thrust the elite, even as the damned are shoved into the depths of pollution.

Society as comedy is egalitarian, emphasizing relations among equals. The thrust is neither upward nor downward, neither toward the gods nor the devils, but horizontal — within the bounds of normal society. In comic society, "We talk to *each* other, not to our gods, about the social ills that beset us." The comic victim is the clown, and he is never totally banished from society but remains instead with his audience. Conversing with them, he objectifies their doubts and frustrations. Clowns and comedy encourage rationality through discussion among equals.

As examples of the two forms of society, Duncan proposes communism and democracy: "Communism is essentially a tragic victimage in which enemies within the state are killed in solemn and awful rites called purge trials...democracy is more a comic drama of argument, bickering, disputation, insult, beseechment, and prayer."[37] The world today turns around the struggle, before mass audiences, of these two dramatic forms.

Implications: Toward Dramatism

Duncan's model of human action clearly differs in tone, emphasis, and imagery from that of Parsons and most other sociologists (as well as anthropologists and other social scientists).[38] To regard society as drama *is* different from perceiving it as a system of role clusters, economic exchanges, ritual mechanisms, and cybernetic hierarchies. With the difference in imagery and metaphor comes a difference in language. Duncan's perspective naturally encourages a dramatic language, Parsons' perspective a mechanistic and idealistic terminology. But beyond this, what does Duncan's model imply?

The clearest proof of substantive (as opposed to merely stylistic) difference between the Parsonian and Duncanian models would be a demonstration that different predictions and conclusions derive from the different models. As neither model is formulated with sufficient rigor to permit this type of test, a less empirical question must be asked. Parsons has formalized his perspective to the point of explicitly defining categories, variables, and functions. Were the Duncanian perspective to be incorporated into the Parsonian scheme, would it substantively modify

these elements? To push the Duncanian position as far as it can go, and doubtless further than Duncan himself intended, I would suggest one possibility. Duncan calls for a view of society itself as a dramatic form. Society viewed in this way might be seen not merely as oriented around the familiar four functional problems defined by Parsons (adaptation [generation of resources], goal-attainment [mobilization of resources], integration [coordination of units], and pattern maintenance [delineation of controlling values]) but also as solving the basic problem of drama: the mounting of a performance that arouses and fulfills expectations of an audience. That is, we might derive from Duncan's perspective a fifth functional exigency — the dramatic. Parsons could doubtless subsume this exigency under one of his four, such as pattern maintenance, but I believe that analysis of society as oriented around the dramatic problem would produce insights and generalizations that have not resulted from analysis of society as oriented around the four exigencies as they are commonly conceived.

Consider first that some societies do seem to orient strongly toward the dramatic function, at times to the detriment of the other functions. Thus, native and foreign observers alike were moved to characterize Sukarnoist Indonesia as if it were a Javanese shadow drama playing to audiences at home and abroad rather than a society striving seriously to solve basic economic and political problems. Sukarno himself frequently depicted Indonesia through the imagery of the shadow drama (*wajang kulit*) and characterized his role as that of the puppeteer (*dalang*). At least one political scientist[39] struggling to make sense of Indonesia has been inspired to write a scholarly monograph on the *wajang*. Perhaps a Parsonian prepared to believe that societies orient around dramatic as well as the other exigencies could go further toward understanding a society such as Indonesia than a Parsonian who thought merely in terms of the tradtional four exigencies.

One may even hazard generalizations about the principles that a society should follow in order satisfactorily to fulfill the dramatic function, just as one may formulate principles such as "supply and demand" or "reciprocity" that a society must follow in solving its economic and social problems. Thus, according to the rule of classical theater, a society should organize its public events to sustain unity of time and place. Or maybe it should simply "leave 'em laughing," or produce a scapegoat on whose shoulders guilt can be placed, after which — according to Kenneth Burke's iron law of dramatic climax — the scapegoat must be eliminated to complete the purge. Generalizations of this type help formulate the dynamics of certain societies, especially those which, like Indonesia, accentuate the dramatic. Analysis of society as though it were drama should at the least be a stimulating exercise. Through applying laws of drama formulated by philosophers and critics of literature new insights into the workings of society might well be achieved. And Parsons' language would be freshened by a dash of dramatic imagery.

With Duncan, we may observe that sociologists in general, Parsons in particular, fail to treat aesthetic form adequately. Though Parsons does take some account of expressive form in the abstract, his substantive analyses consistently fail to treat form as a significant variable. His discussion of father and mother images, for example, pay no heed to the literary or other forms that express such images. As I have tried to demonstrate in several places[40], such omission is typical of social science, yet it may engender faulty interpretation of social action. Note that this is a different issue from that of whether it is useful to treat society as itself an aesthetic form, e.g., as drama. The question here is merely whether aesthetic form is treated as a significant variable within society, and if it is not, what are the consequences for social analysis.

Closer attention to expressive form might stimulate some entirely new directions of generalization and analysis. For example, consider the well-established correlations between technology and society. The orthodox interpretation of such correlations is functional and technical: "Why are plows found in sedentary villages?" "Because the plow permits special ways of exploiting the environment, thereby increasing crop yield to the point that dense populations can stay in one place." But suppose it should be discovered that plows, as physical and aesthetic forms, universally elicit certain perceptual and emotional sets because of the sensuous surface they present to the plowmen and that these sets encourage the dense patterns of community settlement? The old correlation could be interpreted in a new way. Evolutionary theory would gain a new dimension, for its established correlations could now be seen as due not only to functional-technical chains or requirements and opportunities but also to the power of physical forms to influence patterns of perception, behavior, and, ultimately, social life. Given relationships could be explained as due to symbolic determinism as well as technological determinism. Granted, this is a highly speculative argument and, like most that turn on psychological processes, would be more difficult to substantiate than the conventional technological one. All that is claimed is that fresh perspectives flow from treating expressive form as a significant variable in social action.

CONCLUSION: DIRECTIONS OF FUTURE DEVELOPMENT IN THE THEORY OF EXPRESSIVE SYMBOLISM

Clearly the study of expressive symbolism as a category within the theory of action covers a wider scope and has greater potential than any of the traditional fields focussing on expressive form — sociology of art, sociology of literature, folklore studies, the anthropology of myth and ritual, and the humanities. Yet all of these disciplines possess the advantage of centering firmly on qualities of expressive form itself. The absence of this focus is a glaring deficiency in the theory of action. Attention to expressive form as a significant variable in social life in the course of formulating substantive generalizations would seem an expedient direction for future development of the theory of expressive symbolism within the theory of action. The theory of action already provides a solid and seminal foundation for such developments.

NOTES

1. *The Social System* (New York: The Free Press, 1951), p. 384, and T. Parsons, E. A. Shils, K. D. Naegele, and J. R. Pitts (eds.), *Theories of Society* (New York: The Free Press, 1961), p. 1165.

2. Parsons and E. A. Shils (eds.), *Toward a General Theory of Action* (Cambridge: Harvard University Press, 1951), p. 242.

3. See Parsons *et al.*, *op. cit.*, as well as Parsons, *op. cit.*

4. Parsons, *op. cit.*, p. 411.

5. *Ibid.*, p. 412.

6. Even in societies wherein the integrated network obtains, religious and political controls need not override the elemental response of artist to audience. A study of Indonesian proletarian drama (J. L. Peacock, *Rites of Modernization: Symbolic and Social Aspects of Indonesian Proletarian Drama* (Chicago: University of Chicago Press, 1968), p. 45) revealed that in socialist Indonesia of 1963, plots varied independently of political sponsorship of troupes but correlated neatly with dispositions and needs of varied audiences. For a general discussion of the importance of the audience response as an inspiration to the artist, see Kenneth Burke, *Counter-Statement* (Los Altos, Cal.: Hermes Publications, 1953), especially p. 31.

7. Parsons *et al.*, *op. cit.*

8. *Ibid.*, p. 1166.

9. A further step is to convert one sensuous form into another. This occurs in synaesthesia, a sensory state in which one sensory medium is perceived in terms of another: "The light is braying like an ass" (W. Empson, *Seven Types of Ambiguity* [London: Chatto and Windus, 1949], p. 12). Satire furnishes another example, as in Joyce's *Ulysses*, where maudlin form is satirically converted into savvy form.

10. See E. Cassirer, *The Philosophy of Symbolic Forms* (3 Vols.), Ralph Manheim (tr.) (New Haven: Yale University Press, 1953-7).

11. See V. W. Turner, "Three Symbols of Passage in Ndembu Circumcision Ritual" in Max Gluckman (ed.), *Essays on the Ritual of Social Relations* (Manchester: Manchester University Press, 1962).

12. In the extreme case, expressive symbols may accomplish little more than stating the schemas that guide symbolic expression. This poem states little more than the rule that a composition should both begin and end:

> I'll tell you a story of Jack O'Norey
> And now my story's begun.
> I'll tell you another about his brother.
> And now my story is done.

Nonrepresentational paintings may be regarded as functioning similarly, if one agrees with Levi-Strauss that they "represent the manner in which (the painter) would execute his pictures if by chance he were to paint any." C. Levi-Strauss, *The Savage Mind* (Chicago: University of Chicago Press, 1966), p. 30.

13. Parsons, *op. cit.*, p. 384.

14. See G. Devereux, "Art and Mythology; a General Theory," in Bert Kaplan (ed.), *Studying Personality Cross-culturally* (Evanston, Ill.: Row, Peterson, 1961).

15. For detailed description of these, see Peacock, *op. cit.*, p. 203-4.

16. Parsons' formulation can be salvaged by including within the definition of aesthetic need the gratification-deflection pattern. One could then say that art immediately gratifies this aesthetic need. But this formulation conceals interesting psychological processes distinctive of expressive symbolism.

17. Parsons, *op. cit.*, pp. 83, 500; and Parsons and Shils (eds.), *op. cit.*, p. 86.

18. See M. McLuhan, *Understanding Media; The Extensions of Man* (New York: McGraw-Hill, 1965).

19. For details on the socio-cultural features of these evolutionary stages, see R. N. Bellah, "Religious Evolution," *American Sociological Review*, 29, (June 1964), pp. 358-374, and J. L. Peacock and A. T. Kirsch, *The Human Direction: An Evolutionary Approach to Social and Cultural Anthropology* (New York: Appleton-Century-Crofts, 1970).

20. See M. Gluckman, "Les Rites de Passage," in Max Gluckman (ed.), *op. cit.*

21. See S. Kracauer, *From Caligari to Hitler* (New York: Noonday Press, 1959).

22. To a degree the artist's techniques are, of course, guided by utility as well as convention. He will quite rationally choose a given image or medium to achieve a given effect. At the same time, as the vagaries of aesthetic criticism show, it is difficult in art, probably more difficult than in business or engineering, to demonstrate that one technique is more effective than another. For that reason, the artist often falls back on intuition governed by convention. And even if the artist is rational in his creation, the audience is certainly not in its response. Certainly most audience reactions flow from feelings guided by convention rather than from rational analysis of whether this or that technique effectively achieves its end.

23. One example of this phenomenon has emerged in field research. I am presently completing a study concerning education and innovation in Muslim society. One group of innovators is of the classical reformer type. Devout Muslims, they perceive grave discrepancy between today's Malayo-Indonesian society and the moral ideals of Mohammed, so they strive to reform society. The other group is not keen on Muslim morality, and they concentrate on art rather than reform. In narrating life histories, a consistent difference between the two groups is apparent. The artists virtually without exception speak spontaneously of literary imagery of romantic love and narrate at length their nostalgic remembrances of youthful romances that conform to the romantic imagery. The reformers never spontaneously mention either the imagery or the nostalgia. Instead, they preach rather than narrate, presenting their lives as a militant thrust toward carrying out the will of God.

24. Parsons *et al.*, *op. cit.*, p. 987.

25. *Loc. cit.*

26. Parsons, *op. cit.*, p. 414.

27. *Ibid.*, p. 198-199.

28. *Ibid.*, p. 500.

29. John Dewey, *Art as Experience* (New York: Minton, Balch, 1934), p. 375; and J. Feibleman, *In Praise of Comedy: A Study in its Theory and Practice* (New York. Russell and Russell, 1962); and N. Frye, *Anatomy of Criticism* (Princeton: Princeton University Press, 1957).

30. Another line of criticism of Parsons' position would question his assumption that cognitive and evaluative culture evolves cumulatively and in a determinate direction, whereas expressive culture does not. Thomas Kuhn, *The Structure of Scientific Revolutions* (Chicago: University of Chicago Press, 1962) provocatively argues that science does not evolve cumulatively. Northrop Frye, *op. cit.*, suggestively argues that literature does evolve cumulatively. Frye's "theory of modes" portrays literary forms as evolving from *myth*, whose heroes are gods, superior in kind to men, to *romance*, whose heroes are human but with supernatural powers, to *low mimetic*, whose heroes are simply like us. Though somewhat arbitrary, Frye's scheme orders a rich array of correlations which highlight the systematics at work in the evolution of literary form. His materials emphasize that expressive culture does, to a degree, evolve in a determinate stream independent of the whims of society. Expressive culture, therefore, can stand above society and serve as a systematic base from which to criticize society. It is not simply embedded in the myriad particularistic complexes that sustain tradition.

31. See H. D. Duncan, *Symbols in Society* (New York: Oxford University Press, 1968).

32. *Ibid.*, p. 15.

33. *Ibid.*, p. 17.

34. *Ibid.*, p. 6.

35. See H. D. Duncan, *Communication and Social Order* (New York: Bedminister Press, 1962).

36. *Ibid.*, p. 36.

37. Duncan, *Symbols in Society*, p. 25.

38. See J. L. Peacock, "Religion, Communications, and Modernization: A Weberian Critique of Some Recent Views," in *Human Organization*, 28 (1969), and "Society as Narrative" in *Proceedings of the 1969 Annual Spring Meeting, American Ethnological Society*, Victor W. Turner (ed.) (1970).

39. See B.R.O.G. Anderson, *Mythology and the Tolerance of the Javanese* (Ithaca: Cornell University, Modern Indonesia Project, 1965).

40. See Peacock, *Rites of Modernization*, "Religion, Communications and Modernization", *op. cit.*, and "Society as Narrative," *op. cit.*

11

THE "EMERGENCE-CONSTITUTION PROCESS" AND THE THEORY OF ACTION

Thomas F. O'Dea

The scholarly study of religion from the point of view of sociology raises a number of fundamental questions which concern both the study of religion and sociology itself. It leads us to a consideration of the basic presuppositions undergirding our theoretical formulations concerning the significant dimensions of man's social existence. The reason for this first becomes apparent in relation to the basic dilemma of religious life as pointed out in the works of a host of scholars. Two formulations of this dilemma shall serve as the starting point of this presentation. There is first of all the distinction between the "sacred" and the "profane," which characterizes the religious attitude as one specifically different from that of the ordinary workaday world, a condition of heightened mental alertness and emotional intensity characterized by a "curious harmony of contrasts" in which are mingled attraction and joy with fear and dread.[1] In this state of mind which is seen as central to the religious experience and lying at the origin of the institutionalized forms of religious life, many of which serve as the occasion for its symbolic recall, the person is related to a beyond. He is brought to a "breaking point" beyond the mundane, the ordinary, the workaday, the routine.[2] A second form in which it has become customary for sociologists to speak of the religious experience is in the formulation of Paul Tillich. Here the distinction is between ultimacy as contrasted with the less-than-ultimate world of the everyday. Faith "is understood as the state of being ultimately concerned." Tillich declares: "The criterion of every faith is the ultimacy of the ultimate which it tries to express. The self-criticism of every faith is the insight into the relative validity of the concrete symbols in which it appears."[3] What these two formulations have in common is that they each portray man as oriented to an aspect of his situation which transcends the here and now of the everyday world. In fact it might be suggested that the second formulation is a "demythologization" of the first.

This aspect of man's life was first seen by sociologists as "illusory," an attitude on their part which assumed a rather naive "commonsense" view of what is "really real." But these "illusions" were recognized to be performing a valuable function in human societies. Religion provided consensus on values, sanctified them, and thereby contributed to social control — gave it its basic undergirding; it produced high morale by its reassurance that man's interests are not without significance in the larger picture of things. In short religion made life seem livable and supported social order at those breaking points of impossibility and uncertainty which threatened the world men had collectively made. It did this by relating them to its own breaking point in relation to a sacred beyond. Thus the functional view of religion presupposed that man was doing something more serious and more real than religion itself but in doing it he encountered difficulties which made it necessary to have recourse to religion to aid in maintaining psychological composure and social stability.[4] Here is raised implicitly the most fundamental question with which social theory is concerned — what is man really doing? It may be asked within the context of sociology by inquiring which are the dimensions of man's social existence which must receive explicit formulation in any adequate statement of sociological theory. The first reply of functional theory was that man was surviving, but it was recognized that in order to survive he had at the same time to create something like an "imagined world" which he considered tremendously important and which though unreal in the opinion of sociologists was recognized as making a real contribution to survival itself. Thus was it recognized that men "needed" a beyond or somehow "felt themselves related to" a beyond and that their

277

empirical mundane survival depended in part on such a nonempirical nonmundane element.

The better minds in the social sciences long saw the inadequacy of the so-called "functional" approach to religion when taken in that somewhat simplistic form, and in their writings may be found a broader implicit frame of reference. It was this which Parsons endeavored to make explicit in *The Structure of Social Action,* first published in 1937, and in his essay on the sociology of religion, first published in 1944 and republished in his *Essays in Sociological Theory* in 1949 and 1954. In the former work he examined the writings of Durkheim, Pareto, Weber, and Marshall, concluding that each of these men had used a frame of reference which defined human action as meaningful and purposeful and saw it affected both by the canons of empirical knowledge and by ethical considerations. Parsons concluded that deviation from empirical norms in human conduct was not simply the consequence of "ignorance and error" but was also and most significantly a result of "normative orientations" consensually accepted in a given society. Parsons saw in the work of these four men a major shift in the frame of reference of social science, a shift from a utilitarian positivism to a recognition of action as end-oriented, of ends as ultimately derived from world-views, some significant parts of which were "supra-empirical," and of the primary significance of norms.[5] This frame of reference was palpably more adequate than a more simplistic functionalism, and at the same time it did not abandon the insights of an authentic functional theory that society is in a real sense "causally integrated" and that consequently human action often has hidden and unintended consequences. For the sociology of religion what was most important was the recognition of empirical ends as ultimately derived from and systematically related to the ultimate ends which are part and parcel of the society's and culture's answer to what Weber called the "problem of meaning."[6] "Following up the same general line of analysis which provides one of the major themes of Pareto's and Malinowski's work, Weber made clear above all that there is a fundamental distinction between the significance for human action of problems of empirical causation and what, on the other hand, he called the 'problem of meaning.'" Parsons states that Weber attempted to show that problems "concerning the discrepancy between normal human interest and expectations in any situation or society and what actually happens are inherent in the nature of human existence. They always pose problems of the order which on the most generalized line have come to be known as the problem of evil, of the meaning of suffering and the like." Both Weber and Parsons point out that different definitions of the human situation arise in the historical experience of various societies and cultures and that they provide the background against which "the rational solution of these problems may be sought."[7]

This "action frame of reference" offers us a more adequate theoretical context for the sociological study of religion than has generally been the case with its sociological forerunners. But it also presents us with an ambiguity which has been little explored and which eminently deserves such exploration. Indeed it may prove to be one of those "creative ambiguities" of which commentators on science have often spoken.[8] It raises for us as well the most significant question of what is rounded adequacy in such a frame of reference.

The action frame of reference begins with an actor in a situation oriented to the achievement of certain ends. The situation is characterized by two categories of elements. There are "means and conditions"—elements which can be manipulated or adjusted to by the actor; and there are "normative orientations" which are internalized by the actor and are an integral element of his particular culture. Thus it would appear that what is primary in human behavior is end-oriented action and that such norms are significant primarily in defining the means permitted or prescribed in such action. Here Parsons follows Weber with his great emphasis upon *"Zweck und Mittel."*[9] It appears that what man is really doing is end-oriented activity; that his most basic activity is the pursuit of goals; and that normative orientations, though strategic in the scheme, impinge upon a human consciousness which passively receives them—with respect to norms man being "patient" rather than "agent." Man is largely task-oriented and the identification and definition of tasks is largely a straightforward cognitive operation rather self-evident in character about which the social scientist need not be concerned.

This is not really the whole picture, although it is too often taken implicitly to be so by many of Parsons' interpreters. In his earlier work Parsons stressed the significance of "effort." Norms do not merely constrain, they enter into the formation of goals and interests and thereby elicit effort from individuals. They become "ideals," and men are actively related to them by "effort." This is what Parsons called "the creative or voluntaristic side of it."[10] Moreover, in his theoretical treatment of the sociology of religion, he accepts wholly and integrates into his own view as central to it Weber's position that ideas play a creative role in history, and this is true not only of scientifically verified ideas but of the "non-empirical cognitive patterns" associated with religion as well.[11] It is from such complexes of "non-empirical cognitive patterns" that final ends are derived, and according to Parsons from such final ends the less-than-ultimate ends of everyday action are themselves derived. "Within the context of a given system of ultimate ends, the *immediate* ends of acts within the sector *are* given as facts to the actor, in much the same sense as means and conditions are. . . . within the framework of an ultimate end system these immediate ends are 'given' in the sense that the postulate of rationality involves the pursuit of them."[12] Hence, for Parsons the task is not just given for man but is relative to a culture and a value system. Moreover, in his treatment of Marshall he recognizes that activity is self-rewarding, although he makes no great use of this insight. "Social good lies mainly in that healthful exercise and development of faculties which yields happiness without pall."[13]

At this point an interesting ambiguity reveals itself. Looked at from one angle, end-oriented action is primary and norms though important are secondary. Looked at from another angle, however, all ends are derived from or integrated into and sanctioned by the system of ultimate ends which is part of the definition of the human situation accepted in the culture, a definition in which "non-empirical cognitive patterns" are important—in which religion answers the "problem of meaning." From one point of view the action frame of reference represents man as a task-oriented animal; he is a "problem-solver" in the sense primarily of practical problems as understood by the contemporary problem-solving mentality of Western secularized culture. But from another point of view men are primarily the creators of over-all conceptions of reality which always go beyond what is scientifically verifiable—of at least partly "imagined worlds"—which become the context for their definitions of themselves, their situations, and their very tasks. Although the over-all meaning system with its system of ultimate ends is basic to this conception, the process of the evolution of this system or of the social system are not made the point of Parsons' focus. Both in his earlier and later work the major emphasis has been on evolved structure rather than the process of emergence. Yet such emergence is part of the total picture of the action frame of reference.[14]

Parsons is aware of the importance of symbolism in the meaning systems which men develop. Men develop symbols, and Parsons is concerned with the kinds of possibilities open to them in this evolution.[15] Yet the background process of the evolution of symbols and systems of meaning remained largely hidden and is only fleetingly revealed in his work. How men create symbolic forms in acting out their relationship to their world is not presented as a central problem for sociology, although it is a social process. Men act out a relationship to their situation. It is a relationship which is evolved, formed, expressed, understood, and acted out. All of these are overlapping processes, as in the human drama man in part inherits plot, lines, roles, and stage from the past and in part develops them as he goes along. Man creates his meanings, his

tasks, and his norms out of the insights granted to him in the forward movement of human life. The ambiguity which we have seen in the action frame of reference cannot be explored and understood unless we concern ourselves with this great over-all social process precisely as process. What is suggested here is that the greatest significance of Parsons' theory-building endeavor, many aspects of which are significant, may indeed be that it brings us to the major challenge of theoretical reformulation. What Parsons has accomplished in broadening and deepening of the frame of reference in which sociology studies human societies calls for a most thorough reformulation of that frame of reference involving a major shift of perspective. We have indicated one strand in Parsons' thinking which brings us up against this theoretical breaking-point. Let us briefly indicate a second.

THE AMBIGUITY OF SOCIAL KNOWLEDGE

Certainly in his translation of Max Weber and in his own theory construction Talcott Parsons has tried and to some extent succeeded in the tremendously difficult job of constructing theory that reflects the self-conscious and self-critical attitude of its constructors and users concerning its undergirding presuppositions and its originating perspectives. This is especially to be seen in his following of Weber with respect to the use of generalized categories of sociological analysis. Parsons' formulation of this significant problem takes its start with Weber's relation to historicism and what in Germany were called the *Geisteswissenschaften,* the disciplines devoted to the study of the human spirit and its cultural objectifications, or translated somewhat inaccurately into American academic jargon, the humanistic disciplines. Weber tried to take a middle ground between a nineteenth-century natural science view of social science and the view of the humanistic and historical disciplines in Germany which, highly influenced by German idealism, stressed the intellectual apprehension and sympathetic intuition of the symbolic structures and meanings comprising cultural entities. Here of course the work of Dilthey was strategic.

Perhaps we can see the problem involved here most dramatically in relation to the sociology of religion and in the work of Weber's friend and colleague, Ernst Troeltsch. Troeltsch, who came from theology to history and sociology, encountered historicism as a sharp challenge to his entire spiritual stance—to his mode of facing reality and living in the world, as well as to his perspective as a scholar. In his book *Der Historismus und seine Probleme* in which he developed the implications of his years of scholarship and thought, he examined, in his own words, the "relation of individual historical facts to the standards of value within the entire domain of history" across a wide spectrum of the types of human experience and found in every realm a deep and profound relativity. Indeed, "even the validity of science and logic seemed to exhibit, under different skies and upon different soil, strong individual differences present even in their deepest and innermost rudiments."[16] All cultures and all systems of value he came to see as exhibiting a "permanent dependence upon the natural basis and the temporary and special historic position of that basis" and the only thing he felt could be said to be "independent of time and universally valid" was the "stimulus and obligation to create a system of culture."[17] This radical historicism represents one strategic factor which has affected all modern thinking and raises philosophical and general cultural problems which remain beyond the scope of the present article, although they are not without subtle and obvious significance for the issues of sociological theory with which we are concerned.

Troeltsch sought for a transhistorical or extra-historical stance or element to give himself both a philosophical and a methodological position within the flux of history and the relativity of cultures. Such a philosophical position would involve a relation to some transcendent which although not removing man from his concrete embeddedness in his time and place, would give him a view in which he could handle all relativities including his own because of his involvement with some transcendent mode of being or relationship. Later the phenomenological movement with Husserl would point to a methodological possibility, but for Troeltsch this problem appeared to have received only the anguished and uncertain answer he found in religious faith. Here, however, we are concerned with the methodological problem and for the discussion of that we turn to Weber.

Weber accepted the basic contribution of historicism which held that social existence consisted in unique specific historical configurations and that these could be understood basically only as Dilthey had declared — through the understanding of their meaning and quality, that is through *Verstehen*. He also felt it possible, however, to develop generalized categories for analysis on a comparative crosscultural and transhistorical basis. Weber devoted his energies to this task and did generate a number of categories which have proven to be of general use — action, economically oriented action, economic action, rationalization, types of authority, the elements of bureaucracy, traditionalism, and so on.[18] Parsons accepted this combination of internal empathetic understanding and the use of general categories as the basic method of sociology. Whereas Weber had most often used these conceptions as ideal types, rationally

and artificially constructed from historical experience, Parsons sought to render them truly analytic elements. Weber sought to compare real social phenomena to the ideal types, for example, to compare a case of traditional authority to the ideal type and thereby both to see its inner structure and its deviation from the ideal construction and to study the reasons for such deviation. Parsons saw the cumbersomeness of this procedure and sought to apply his categories to an analysis of existing structures — to delineate and examine the relationships among the elements of an authority structure in terms of the pattern variables, for example, or in terms of role strain encumbent upon office holders. Both Weber and Parsons emphasized the undoubted significance of crosscultural or transhistorical studies as enabling the investigator to isolate and "control" strategic variables by comparative analysis. As a strategic person in bringing the consequences of this aspect of German thinking into American sociology, Parsons finds an entire discipline in his debt. Although the conflict between the *Geisteswissenschaften* and the *Naturwissenschaften* out of which Weber's methodological solution developed was not quite isomorphic in issue and structure with comparable intellectual conflicts in the English-speaking world, the issues raised do appear to possess a certain universality.

In the opening of this chapter we examined one strand in Parsons' thought which led us to two interesting and significant ambiguities. We saw the question "what is man doing?" answered in terms of "task" and "ethics" and an ambiguity as to which answer was basic and primary. We also noted that the situation of task and ethics was actually part of a larger situation which involved a system of meaning — an at least partly "imagined world" — from which both the goals to be sought in problem-solving and task-performance and the norms which prescribe, permit, and proscribe suitable behavior are derived to a significant degree. Now we find the interesting and significant ambiguity involved in the use of causal-functional categories which rest ultimately upon meaningful experience or, to use Parsons' terms, the ambiguity involved in the use of categories constructed from the point of view of the observer which are derived from and rest upon experience experienced from the point of view of the actor. It is as himself a participant in society — as enmeshed in the complex of human communication — that man knows how to construct the causal-functional concepts of the observer's point of view. Indeed the concepts of natural science began with similar subjective and projective content derived from human experience. But natural science has followed a path of reducing this element to a minimum as it has proceeded to change the perspective of scientific knowledge from considering the relation of the things observed to the observer to considering their relations to each other. The obvious example of a basic concept beginning with considerable subjective and projective content is that of *cause,* which has such a long and subtle history.

In social science, however, there seems little to be gained in developing disciplines which are denuded so far as possible of anthropomorphic content, for while man can deepen his understanding of himself by analogy with other phenomena — a general theory of systems, for example, reveals significant general systemic elements and relations with which students of social systems must be concerned — yet in the final analysis it is as man that he must achieve self-understanding. Thus it seems that the basic thrust of development in the sciences of man cannot be the elimination of an anthropomorphic perspective but rather a more self-conscious and critical awareness of its character. The central dilemma of the religious experience — that man lives in a kind of boundary situation, that human experience involves an experience of a beyond — and one aspect of the ambiguities we have found in Parsons and Weber — that men generate universalistic categories from the subjective and projective content of the point of view of the participant and can then use these concepts to achieve a degree of intellectual transcendence over experience — suggest that man himself is an ambiguous phenomenon. If in modern times, as Cassirer suggested, man has become problematic to himself, it is because the conditions of modernity have revealed a structurally inherent ambiguity of the human condition in a more striking and urgent way than had happened previously. Man appears to be immersed in culture but also able to go to breaking-points in his experience which go beyond the established meanings of his culture. The existentialists have attempted to formulate what is involved here by describing man as "project" or as *Dasein,* and the like. Husserl saw in the "transcendental reduction" which he proposed as a philosophical method a way of consciously anchoring the sciences in that potential of man which he found in an important way transcendent to time and cultures.

It is out of this potential that men constitute their selves, their identities, their social structures, and their symbolic meanings. They do this in relation to a world which they in part produce. This human world is evolved in interaction with fellows within situations which are themselves "recognized" and evolved as consisting of tasks, demands, and symbolic relations. The identities that man evolves together with the social and cultural forms in which he objectifies both relationship and meaning by making them shared intersubjective or intermental realities are finite and transient. They are man's self-expressions,

objectified in the quasi-objective realities of social structure and shared ideas and values, conditioned and deeply affected by the circumstances of their development. But men always reveal a capacity to go beyond them. In religion this takes the form of doubt, which exhibits such an intimate yet contradictory relationship to faith. Doubt is the shadow side of faith; it expresses man's ability to go beyond; it testifies to that which is transcendent in him.[19] As Tillich put it, "Existential doubt and faith are poles of the same reality, the state of ultimate concern."[20] When not combined with aggression or despair, doubt can issue in a more profound attitude of faith. Similarly breakthroughs in knowledge and ethics express and reveal man's potential for both transcending his own social and cultural objectifications and for constituting new forms. Breakthrough is a significant element of the constituting process, and it is in his concern with breakthrough that the work of Weber comes closest to that of the phenomenologists.[21] The ambiguities of theory reflect real ambiguities of the human condition. However, here we are primarily concerned with the methodological aspects of the matter.

First of all we would stress with Weber the chief justification of sociological analysis, for although it should be obvious it is often lost from sight. The purpose of sociological analysis is to enable us better to understand concrete historical human existence. There is always a danger of confusing pattern and meaning, as Marx was the first to do. Social life reveals a host of patterned regularities; when conceptualized as empirical generalizations they become tools for analysis. But their usefulness consists in the fact that they enable us more profoundly to understand detailed and unique configurations of social existence. The general categories of sociological analysis — both conceptual definitions and empirical generalizations — are intended to contribute to our understanding of particular events and configurations of events in terms of their human meaning. They are not meant to warrant the suppression of the specifically individual meaningful content of the event by substituting for analysis a generalized description of process denuded of its unique and proper meaningful characteristics. Weber states this clearly in his discussion of the use to be made of general formulations of "recurrent causal sequences" in sociology. "Wherever the causal explanation of a cultural phenomenon — an 'historical individual' — is under consideration, the knowledge of causal *laws* is not the *end* of the investigation but only a *means.* It facilitates and renders possible the causal imputation to their concrete causes of those components of a phenomenon the individuality of which is culturally significant. So far and only so far as it achieves this, is it valuable for our knowledge of concrete relationships."[22] A misguided though understandable desire to imitate physics has at times obscured the understanding of this issue among sociologists.

However, with this in mind let us address ourselves to the problem stated at the outset, to wit: Which dimensions of man's social existence must receive explicit statement in any adequate formulation of sociological theory? What we have said so far suggests that our most advanced and explicit formulations are only partial and contain significant ambiguities. This conclusion could be reinforced from much of the theoretical literature but it would involve a considerable lengthening of our presentation. Let us also concern ourselves with the perspective from which sociological theory can most self-critically and efficaciously be formulated. What we mean by this will become apparent in the course of the discussion.

Reality and Relativity in Social Knowledge

So far we have approached the problem of a reformulation of sociological theory from a rather narrow point of view — from that of the problems revealed and the contributions made by four significant social scientists, especially as reflected in Parsons study of them and those raised by his own original work. But sociological study, like all other study, is part of the experience of the men of a specific time and place, a particular culture, and a given historical experience; and sociological theory like all formulations of human meaning will reflect the experience of those who formulate it and their historical and cultural setting. Weber observed that in science and scholarship the "guiding 'point of view' is of great importance for the *construction* of the conceptual scheme which will be used in the investigation." This he felt was an abiding condition of social science, but at the same time he affirmed that valid studies could be done from several different perspectives. He would have agreed with Mannheim's later insight that such perspectival approaches are amenable to a synthesis of perspectives and a consequently wider and more overarching point of view. But he felt that there was no one correct or orthodox point of view and that with different backgrounds and different periods of history new points of view would become relevant. In this respect he commented on "the meaninglessness of the idea which prevails occasionally even among historians, namely, that the goal of the cultural sciences, however far it may be from realization, is to construct a closed system of concepts, in which reality is synthesized in some sort of *permanently* and *universally* valid classification and from which it can again be deduced."[23]

Weber saw a social science capable of finding truth

"*valid* for all who *seek* the truth" but determined "in the choice of the object of investigation and the extent or depth to which investigation attempts to penetrate in the infinite causal web" by what he calls the "evaluative ideas which dominate the investigator and his age."[24] In other words he saw social scientists achieving *genuine* but at the same time *partial* truth whose very partialness is a consequence of their historical relativity. Nor is this simply a matter of quantitative partialness, for the definition of problems — the kinds of questions asked — impart certain emphases to the formulation of research plans and findings and hence in terms of over-all structure our findings are affected profoundly by the historical specificity and cultural relativity of our position. Parsons has here attempted to go beyond Weber in a way which again appears ambiguous but highly instructive. Parsons holds that in the development of explicit theory a science develops an internal logic which indicates theoretically significant problems with a degree of relative independence from the concrete and specific conditioning of one's own time and circumstances. Yet the fact remains that such theory receives and derives its major paradigms from the thinking of an age and culture. Indeed in the history of natural science we see this clearly as we witness old paradigms being abandoned and new ones being adopted in ways which cannot be explained simply in terms of the continuities inherent in the body of theory and the logic of the accepted conceptual scheme leading to the selection of the new question and formulation. Rather, we often see shifts of emphasis with a new generation or the passage of time. Kuhn has made the significant point that historians of science often try to attribute much more continuity than actually exists and to prefer to emphasize the continuities while slighting significant discontinuities.[25]

Yet Parsons' idea of a body of theory which is also effective in designating selection of problems and influencing what deserves emphasis in the formulation of findings has genuine merit and deserves careful evaluation. The present writer is inclined to accept it as one important element designating significant questions and influencing the perspectives of scholars. He would suggest two qualifications. Such theory must be the work of several generations and several cultures and subcultures to insure a growing synthesis of perspectives and a genuine reflection of a broad spectrum of historical experience. Moreover, it must remain a vocabulary of analytical concepts and a growing set of empirical generalizations which can never become a closed system. As against Parsons' predilection for a closed system the writer would agree with Weber that the "points of departure of the cultural sciences remain changeable throughout the limitless future as long as a Chinese ossification of intellectual life does not render mankind incapable of setting new questions to the eternally inexhaustible flow of life."[26]

All this means that social science knowledge is genuine knowledge of realities outside the heads of the investigators, although it is also affected by interpretation which is in part a creation of the investigation. Although it is not isomorphic in all significant details with the extra-mental reality, it does characterize elements of that extra-mental reality with a variable degree of accuracy, though it does not "describe" them in the sense of reproducing seeing. Since Einstein and Heisenberg such a characterization of knowledge in physics has become commonplace. No one today could say with Galileo that we are "reading the language in which God wrote the creation." Knowledge is neither simple seeing as Aristotle at times seemed to assume nor the proper reading of nature's text whose notations are mathematical characteristics more primary in ontological character than what is actually experienced. It is a combination of observation with empirically verified inferences and constructions.

In the light of this we may say that sociology can claim to designate in its theoretical formulations typical structures and processes characteristic of the life of men in mutual relationship and association with one another. But it must concede the culturally and historically relative character of all attempts at systematic formulation or indeed of all formulation. Consequently such formulations contain two elements closely intertwined and not easily disentangled — real reflection of social reality and a necessarily culturally and historically slanted hermeneutic. This is a subtle affair, and the problems of interpretation involved tend to come out chiefly in conflicts over methodology. All perspectival and value problems in social science get projected into that realm, not altogether inappropriately, and there too frequently become obscured. At the present time we see some younger sociologists projecting these problems into politics where they feel they find a more adequate or at least a more dramatic and satisfying expression. Yet sociology and social science can claim to participate with various degrees of realization in those characteristics of scientific knowledge of which natural science with its successful space exploration has given incontrovertible evidence — that our knowledge does reflect with some considerable accuracy certain real structures and processes but that it is also the product of construction in which inference is involved and in which the creative imagination is a significant element.

As Weber said, history and social change alter the focus of investigation and study. In our day two sets of phenomena have focussed our attention on human construction — the process of human constitution or emergence — of cultural realities. Since the end of World War I we have seen the passing away of empires and states of long duration and the coming to be of a variety of new social entities. The cultural quality of life has been radically altered. The history of our times has confronted us anew with the fragility and transcience of social and cultural structures and their character as human constitutions or creations. Second, scholarship, science, and the philosophy of knowledge have reflected this edge of the modern experience in their concern with the evolution and relativity of institutions, cultures, and all social, intellectual, and scientific forms and with the character and function of language. The study of religious life in history and biblical scholarship has long been an important locus of this experience of fragility and transcience and of the fact that men elaborate a partly "imagined world" in which they live, as we have already indicated with the examples of Ernst Troeltsch and Max Weber.

THE EMERGENCE-CONSTITUTION PROCESS

From within the context of academic sociology, the question has been raised of how to understand the significance of two intriguing ambiguities whose character one might have thought would long ago have elicited comment. There is first of all the situation of action seen as composed of ends, means, and conditions, and normative orientations. Seen from one point of view man's basically significant activity is end-oriented action. Seen from another, however, it is seen that both the goals pursued and the normative orientations which often dictate deviation from the canons of task efficiency are derived from a cultural universe of meaning which men have evolved, much of which consists of ideas that are not empirically verifiable. Here man would seem to be primarily the evolver or constitutor of systems of meanings. This circularity is not the "fault" of the author in whose works we found it, but rather, it is suggested here, reflects a genuine circularity characteristic of human life. Man does pursue goals, and he does evolve systems of meaning — and the two are closely related. But how are they related? And are these two things alone adequate to characterize what he is doing?

The second ambiguity is that involved in the use of relatively objective causal and functional concepts which are useful for the analysis of a social system from the point of view of the observer but which are themselves derived from experience with social life that was originally undergone from the point of view of the participant. These concepts represent a certain kind of objectification of experience which was originally experienced from the point of view not of an analyst but of an actor or participant. Here man as social analyst is seen to rest upon man as social being and the former to be evolved from the latter by a process of constitution or construction. Moreover, if the social scientist makes use of both the *Verstehen* and the analytic approach, and if the latter finally derives from the former, then the additional question arises whether the experience which enables the social scientist to convert *Verstehen* into objectified categories covers a sufficiently wide range of human experience or does it arbitrarily (or influenced by cultural values and implicit frames of reference) restrict the dimensions of social existence that find formulation in theory in such a way as to exclude some that are of great importance?

These ambiguities and questions point to the need of reexamination of theory and its presuppositions and assumptions. But they also suggest what may indeed be the fruitful point of approach for such examination. Behind the ambiguities we have examined we see man's form-creating activity, his constitution of a social and cultural world, the emergence of social structure and culture, and even of individual selfhood. This process is one in which men create objectified or relatively objectified social and cultural entities out of their activity and interaction. They create them in situations which condition the results. There is both an active and passive side to this process — man is creator of his history and of its products; he is also the creature of his experience. It is man as creator-creature of history and cultural products that lies behind the ambiguities and circularities we have examined; it is this man that we must represent adequately in the dimensions of our theory. It is this combined "emergence-constitution process" whose elements we must become able to delineate.

What we have discovered as a fruitful problem raised by the implications of theory itself (as Parsons has maintained to be a significant function of theory), we also find projected into the center of our awareness by the intellectual, spiritual, and political experience of our time (as Weber said would be the way in which fruitful shifts in the focus of scientific attention would come about). The critical study of religion and philosophy, the challenge of our urgent domestic and international problems, the nation-building efforts of peoples trying to develop their resources and societies, so full of problems and uncertainties, all point to the double relativity of the creator-creature role of man and its subtle and often involuted implications and the similarly reciprocal emergence-constitution

character of social process as the central phenomena to be understood in a reexamination of the undergirding presuppositions of sociological theory and method. What both theory and experience indicate is the necessity of being able to grasp and articulate the significant dimensions of man's mode of being in the world which enter into and effect his constitutive activities and their objectified products and by becoming objectified in these products become strategically important elements in society and culture. It is the very process of constitution — of both societies and cultures, and of scientific theory and method — about which social scientists must become more self-conscious.

This implies first of all the necessity to discover the core experiences and core responses which constitute the experiential basis upon which men elaborate and standardize forms of meaning and social relationships. The world of men — what Husserl called their "life-world" (*Lebenswelt*) — is a world they have elaborated and standardized out of interaction and experience. It is an intersubjective, an intermental phenomenon. It arises in human communication, intending the term communication in the broadest sense of a "tacit dialogue" involving cooperation and conflict, adaptation and adjustment, within the setting of and in relation to an environment to which men respond in terms of their own developing definition of it. What is given first of all, and this nobody ever denies, is a world outside consciousness and a human potential for experiencing that world and responding to it — an external world and an "intentional" consciousness. From that relationship of world and human potential, men develop *their* world. Different cultures and civilizations develop worlds in significant ways different from each other. From that basic life-world of their culture men develop specialized subworlds such as those segmented universes of discourse which make up the scientific disciplines. How are we to get at the core experiences and responses of men on the basis of which they evolve their worlds? It is indeed such an operation which our proposed reconsideration of theory and method demands. The problem is made extremely difficult by the undeniable fact that men always experience these core experiences within the developed meaning systems and frames of reference of their culture — as part of their life-world. Yet it is such an operation which the "deinstitutionalization and reinstitutionalization" of our age — the passing away and coming to be of social forms — and the critical intellectual studies of the past century make imperative for genuine understanding of the human situation and the achievement of more adequate intellectual modes of studying it.

One way of getting at such core experiences lies in the comparative study of cultures in which we can by abstraction reach a certain common denominator with reference to experience found in various societies and cultures. As Parsons has indicated, Max Weber's comparative study of religion in East and West assumes a certain frame of reference whose elements are common to both. The elements of that frame of reference if examined should reveal themselves as such abstract common denominators which designate experiences in some sense common. It is similarly the case with crosscultural studies in anthropology and with respect to the religious symbolism found in the work of historians of religions such as Mircea Eliade. In the latter we see how a great variety of archaic religious symbolism reveals itself as repeating a set of themes which may be stated in common denominator form. Two of great significance are concerned with sacred space and sacred time. In the "recurring symbolism of the center" we find a series of elaborations upon what must be a common or parallel experience. Also in the conception of mythic time — of a pure and ritually available present in which the votary can be brought to participate, the "*in illo tempore*" as Eliade puts it — we see an elaboration of meaning around a core experience.[27] In an anthropological study of North American Indian religion, Hartley Burr Alexander pointed to the importance of the "Middle Place." He pointed out moreover that such a concern with the center is based upon the very structure of human experience.

> The quarternity of the cardinal directions and the trinity of heaven, earth, and hell belong to many lands and peoples. It is a mathematical construction, but it is one developed not from chance but from a reason universal to mankind, and that reason is to be found in the human skeleton itself. Man is upright, erect, in his active habit, and he is four-square in his frame, and these two facts give him his image of a physical world circumscribing his bodily life. . . . Man in his abode, his mid-earth station, arises from that night which is his symbol of chaos and negation to greet the first rays of the morning sun. This is the hour of his day's creation, and the hour also of *cosmos*, of order in his life. He looks to the east and names it the before or the arising; and having established this, the first radius of his universe, from his station and his own upright posture, he gives to his awakening world its orientation, its eastering, and perceives it as a field of action . . . . The Old World, of course, knows the same ancient adoration, for it springs from our essential habit as creatures of the day. *Fiat lux* is, in a more universal sense than the writer of Genesis could have guessed, the law of our world's creation. . . . There are many rites and myths in Indian lore elucidating this fundamental metaphor, which lies at the root of so much of man's philosophy and reflects perhaps most of the greatness of his understanding.[28]

Here we see a most instructive attempt to discuss the origin of a host of conceptions central to a great variety of mythologies — the Center, the Quarternity,

the three-levelled universe, the creation of cosmos from chaos, the dialectic of light and darkness. Again Eliade has shown how the Center appears as a key symbol in a great variety of cultures; it is the place where man is in touch with the beyond and where he can participate in the recreation of the world — the primordial bringing of order out of chaos *in illo tempore* or *in principio*. He generalizes from his studies by saying:

> To take in all the facts in a single broad view, one may say that the symbolism in question expresses itself in three connected and complementary things —
> 1. The "sacred mountain," where heaven and earth meet, stands at the centre of the world;
> 2. Every temple or palace, and by extension every sacred town and royal residence, is assimilated to a "sacred mountain" and thus becomes a "centre";
> 3. The temple or sacred city, in turn, as the place through which the Axis Mundi passes, is held to be a point of junction between heaven, earth and hell.[29]

Thus we see how such crosscultural archetypal symbols point to a common denominator of experience and that the meanings formulated are congruent with the basic experience of man as having a body as well as with a certain psychic unity of the human race.[30]

Phenomenological studies of how men do experience time and space, when they are more or less successful in suspending ("bracketing") the habitual frames of apperception of their cultures, point to an experience of the center and of an ever-present now. "Thus as a rule the space lived by men arranges itself around a determined center which is conditioned by his place of residence." In this lived experience "there is both a distinct coordinating zero point which depends upon the place of the living man in space, and a distinct axis system which is connected with the human body."[31] Like Merleau-Ponty's work, these quotations show the importance of the human body as the basic mode and foundation of man's experience, but not simply the body as an entity abstracted from the total human experiencer as studied by biological science, but the body as lived. Gaston Berger has suggested that time is "a construction of man." As for the core experience he states: "the transcendental experience gives us nothing which resembles what the common notion of time suggests. After the reduction, there is no time; there is the present."[32] In the phenomenological reduction one experiences two interrelated poles in the experience of time. There is the "now" of the experiencer — his experience of a present and of his own entity in that present; there is also the coming to be and passing away of the phenomenal pole. The experiencer thus both experiences a present and a kind of heightened being there for himself in that present and the impermanence of the object pole which suggests chaos and threat. This does bear a most suggestive resemblance to mythic time in which men ritually escape from the flux and impermanence of profane time and experience a present now and their own heightened reality in relation to a sacred beyond. It would seem that the ground for experiencing both transcendence and diffusion, both cosmos and chaos, both sustenance and threat are to be found in their rudimental form in the phenomenological experience of time.

Thus we see a second way of getting near the "core experiences." Not only can we find common denominators by abstraction which we believe isomorphic with such core experiences in significant ways, but we can find in phenomenological method a way of trying to get as close as possible to the core experiences themselves. There are of course differences in phenomenological interpretation such as Merleau-Ponty's emphasis upon perception and the body and Husserl's emphasis upon the trancendental ego. Such differences are not simply either/or problems but point to significant subtleties. Moreover, men cannot by any reduction escape from their embeddedness in time and space, but they can achieve a relative transcendence with respect to them. In other words, core experiences are not purely had, they are approached. They point to the experiential foundations upon which men elaborate their worlds — their partly "imagined worlds" or more accurately their partly constituted worlds. This process of constitution, of elaboration and standardization, is a social process, and "worlds" are social products. That is to say, they are evolved in interaction and communication.

Let us recapitulate in the words of Husserl and Schütz:

> The world and its property, "in and of itself," exists as it exists, whether I, or we, happen or not, to be conscious of it. But let once this general world make its "appearance" in consciousness as "the" world, it is thenceforth related to the subjective, and all its existence and the manner of it, assumes a new dimension, becoming "incompletely intelligible," "questionable." Here, then is the transcendental problem: this "making its appearance," this "being for us" of the world, which can only gain its significance "subjectively," what is it? . . . The problem also touches every "ideal" world, the world of pure number, for example, and the world of "truths in themselves." And no existence, or manner of existence, is less wholly intelligible than ourselves. Each by himself, and in society, we, in whose consciousness the world is valid, being men, belong ourselves to that world . . . . We, . . . are, therefore, "appearances" unto ourselves, parcel of what "we" have constituted, pieces of the significance "we" have made.

We create a world in experience and interaction of which we are a part. It is a constituted world — or more accurately a world that is the consequence of a process which involves both "constitution" and "emergence" as man is both agent and patient in the process. Yet man is potentially always more than his social and cultural products. "The 'I' and 'we', which we apprehend, presuppose a hidden 'I' and 'we' to whom they are present." That is, behind the 'me' and 'them' observed are the 'I' and 'we' observing. Man as subject is always more than his productions. That is why Weber was right in pointing to the impossibility of closed systems in sociological theory. Yet without the ambience of those productions and stable association with his fellows, man's potentials would not be realized at all. Husserl emphasizes the importance of this social setting too. He comments that the psychological concept of "internal experience" reaches its full extent as an "inter-subjective" phenomenon — "a 'society' of 'persons,' who share a conscious life."[33]

Schütz has shown that "this world, as has been shown by Husserl, is from the outset experienced in the prescientific thinking of everyday life in the mode of typicality. The unique objects and events given to us in a unique aspect are unique within the horizon of typical familiarity and preacquaintanceship." Moreover, "the world of everyday life is from the outset also a social-cultural world in which I am interrelated in manifold ways of interaction with fellow men known to me in varying degrees of intimacy and anonymity. To a certain extent, sufficient for many practical purposes, I understand their behavior, if I understand their motives, goals, choices and plans originating in *their* biographically determined circumstances. Yet only in particular situations, and then only fragmentarily, can I experience the others' motives, goals, etc. — briefly, the subjective meanings they bestow upon their actions, in their uniqueness. I can, however, experience them in their typicality." Schütz comments that we have here in "the common-sense thinking of everyday life" a kind of core experience (to use our term) which is "the origin of so-called 'constructive' or 'ideal types'. . . as a tool in the social sciences." In life we understand each other in terms of shared and collectively evolved implicit "ideal type" categories; in social science we perform a similar constitution of categories but presumably more self-consciously and critically.

Indeed what Weber suggested refining and self-consciously using as a sociological method, the method of *Verstehen* proposed as basic by Dilthey, is based upon what Schütz called "the peculiar experiential form in which common-sense thinking takes cognizance of the social-cultural world." This form of communication is what makes society and culture possible. It is a process of intermental or intersubjective communication whose forms of expression are both implicit and explicit. It is a process in which the potentials of relationship become realized as forms of interaction and communication. It is a process in which social and cultural forms and selves become constituted out of these potentials. In short, it is a many-sided "tacit dialogue" in which new social forms are precipitated in human interaction. How does this communication work? This is a many-sided question, because it concerns a many-sided process. There are all the forms of human interaction and the potentials in which they are grounded. They are the object of our study, and we cannot presuppose definitive knowledge of them. In fact the most fundamental question in this regard — how do we have knowledge of other persons?—has never been handled well in philosophy. Indeed, as Kant said, it is a scandal for philosophy. This is obvious in classical philosophy. It is a severe problem which Aquinas failed to handle well. Following the Greeks he saw intellectual knowledge as abstract, but as a Christian he had to give knowledge of persons great significance. For him the problem remained unsolved. He spoke of a deeper kind of knowledge — a knowledge by "connaturality" based upon a common human nature, but the way this knowing process works remains obscure. Schütz states that "so far the problem of our knowledge of other minds and, in connection therewith, of the intersubjectivity of our experience of the natural as well as the social-cultural world, has not found a satisfactory solution and that, until rather recent times, this problem has even escaped the attention of philosophers."[34] The problem is always taken for granted in our everyday life, and all our most sophisticated scientific ventures rest upon the basis of common human communicability little understood. When this form of communication is refined into social science method, the philosophical problematic of how it functions remains as little understood as in everyday communication. It too often leads to methodological conflict where it becomes entwined with value positions and in which a subtle use of authority — albeit the authority of the professor or the methodological clique — "settles" the issues involved. What is necessary is to develop alongside the sociological study of the general emergence-constitution process, a similar study of the concept formation process in sociology itself. This set of problems attracts a small but increasing number of sociologists today. They represent a new stage in the intellectual maturation of the field and its emancipation from the implicit unexamined foundations of the past.

MAN AS MEANINGFUL RESPONDER

Let us finally return briefly to our second question — which dimensions of social reality must be delineated and identified in any adequate formulation of sociological theory? Here we shall have to confine ourselves to brief indications. We have already seen man as manipulator, as the performer of tasks, the pursuer of goals, and man as ethically oriented with respect to normative orientations. We have further seen him as the constitutor of meaning and elaborator of meaning systems from which he ultimately in part derives and in which he ultimately in part integrates the ends and norms of his daily life. We have seen, moreover, that the emergence-constitution process is a many-sided one deriving from a number of sides or aspects of man.

What is implied in this whole discussion is that man is a meaningful responder to situations who constitutes himself and his cultural products in his responses — evolving needs, interests, ideals, ends, relationships and institutions, ideas and values. Heinemann has said:

> Man could be defined as the responsive animal, καт εξοχην, i.e., as that being in which the responsiveness of organic beings reaches its highest peak and its widest application. He possesses the whole range of responses, from automatic, instinctive, unconscious, involuntary, to conditioned, ideo-motor, voluntary and unit responses. He beats the animals by being able to alter the modes of his response, i.e., by learning, by responding to signs, and with their help to absent or non-existent objects, and by formulating his conscious responses in answers, i.e., by speech.[35]

Heinemann suggests that the *cogito, ergo sum* of Descartes be replaced by the more general *respondeo, ergo sum*, which both broadens the basis of man's relationship to the world and leaves open for empirical investigation the many-sided facets of that relationship. In this he parallels important implications of our own presentation. Man's consciousness is a "consciousness of"; his basic activity a "response to." Moreover, such response to does not simply take the form of doing things to achieve ends; it is neither simply nor necessarily always primarily task activity. It is relational, and out of it stabilized institutionalized relations evolve.[36] Moreover his responses are meaningful, and out of them evolve ideas and values. Indeed man not only experiences the products of his responses as worthwhile, he finds response itself rewarding and at times fulfilling. Besides entering into relationships and pursuing ends, men also express themselves and find gratification and realization in such expressive actions. Man's sexuality indicates how profoundly built-in to his very structure is his relational character. The ubiquity of ritual, ceremony, protocol, propriety, style and bodily adornment testify to the significance to men of their mode of presence; they testify to both the aesthetic and the dramatic character of human interaction.

As in the animal, so also in man, there exist the exigencies of underlying materials, and the pattern of experience has to meet these exigencies by granting them psychic representation and conscious integration. [Man's life is *dramatic*.] It is in the presence of others, and the others too are also actors in the primordial drama that the theatre only imitates. If aesthetic values, realized in one's own living, yield one the satisfaction of good performance, still it is well to have the objectivity of that satisfaction confirmed by the admiration of others . . . . The characters in this drama of living are moulded by the drama itself.[37]

In these words Lonergan sums several points which follow from our own discussion.

Hannah Arendt has in several of her works paid especial attention to this dramatic element. She has traced the consciousness of this back to classical times, showing how the Greeks in the development of the polis created a "public space" for acting in the presence of others. She has emphasized how the Greeks saw this action essentially as dramatic and made this dramatic aspect of human action central to their definition of man as the political animal. The Greeks began in the archaic period seeing man as warrior; it was out of the warrior ethic, which stressed dramatic action in war and athletics and the immortalization of the hero in poetry, that the dramatic value of citizenship so central to the polis evolved.[38] With the end of the polis and eventually of political life properly so called in the ancient period and with the concomitant triumph of philosophy, Plato and Aristotle transmuted the intrinsic rewards of dramatic action into the contemplative pleasures of philosophy. The citizen was replaced by the philosopher as the ideal man. Thus intellectual fulfillment became the central value of the literate strata, and with the triumph of Christianity this was transformed into religious and indeed monastic contemplation.[39] For centuries Christianity maintained "the enormous superiority of contemplation over activity of any kind."[40] Yet this high evaluation of contemplation represents the recognition as central to man's nature of precisely that characteristic by which he is removed from activity. At the same time there took place in the apolitical conditions of life after the end of the polis a changed understanding of the active life. Political action, the "acting and speaking" in which "men show who they are, reveal actively their unique personal identities and thus make their appearance in a human world,"[41] lost its high place in the hierarchy of values and that place was taken by work, which became the most accepted form of the active life. At that point man was seen primarily as *homo faber,* as fabricator with "his instrumentalization of the world, his confidence in tools and in the productivity of the maker of artificial objects; his trust in the all-comprehensive range of the means-

end category, his conviction that every issue can be solved and every human motivation reduced to the principle of utility. . . ."[42] Thus the fact of the dramatic character of human action was lost from sight, and philosophy first in England and then in France made utility the central conception necessary to answering the question of what man is doing, thereby severely limiting what aspects of social existence it was felt necessary to recognize in analysis of the character of society.

Human life remained essentially dramatic, although a conscious conceptualization of it as such was long lost. It remained true in the words of Hartley Burr Alexander, whom we quoted earlier, that

A true view of the world must be cast in the particular — i.e., the dramatic mode. Our understanding of experience must be historical and dramatic rather than abstract and mathematical. This is why Plato was a wiser man than Aristotle. Plato never built his house in a static sense. He used the myth to present a dramatic interpretation. To Aristotle the world was something which could be represented by an intellectual photograph, by an architect's drawing. Hence there was always a contradiction in Aristotle's metaphysics. Today too, philosophers like Russell write as if experience were all finished — as if all we had to do was to catch it as it is and describe it. No such abstract and mathematical models will suffice because of constant flux. Only drama "catches things as they really are."[43]

Hannah Arendt has shown how this original "political" element, this recognition of the dramatic character of action and attribution of high value to it, made its appearance in the French and American revolutions. At that time revolutionary leadership found that dramatic satisfaction in action of which the ancients were aware, the happiness of participating in the drama of public life — what in France was called "public freedom" and in America "public happiness."

For the absence of political freedom under the rule of the enlightened absolutism of the eighteenth century did not consist so much in the denial of specific personal liberties, certainly not for the members of the upper classes, as in the fact "that the world of public affairs was not only hardly known to them but was invisible" [quoted from De Tocqueville.] What the *hommes de lettres* shared with the poor, quite apart from, and also prior to, any compassion with their suffering, was precisely obscurity, namely, that the public realm was invisible to them and that they lacked the public space where they themselves could become visible and be of significance.[44]

In America the importance of the dramatic public life was recognized as fact, not simply as longing:

What was a passion and a "taste" in France was clearly an experience in America . . . the Americans knew that public freedom consisted in having a share in public business, and that the activities connected with this business by no means constituted a burden but gave those who discharged them in public a feeling of happiness they could acquire nowhere else. They knew very well, and John Adams was bold enough to formulate this knowledge again and again, that the people went to the town assemblies, as their representatives later were to go to the famous Conventions, neither exclusively because of duty, nor, and even less, to serve their own interests but most of all because they enjoyed the discussions, the deliberations, and the making of decisions. What brought them together was "the world and the public interest of liberty" (Harrington), and what moved them was "the passion for distinction" which John Adams held to be "more essentially remarkable" than any other human faculty. . .[45]

RECAPITULATION

In this essay we have attempted to identify and explore the present challenge to sociological theory — that of producing a more rounded frame of reference for the description and analysis of human social existence which will do justice to the many-sided potentiality of men as made evident in the vast range and variety of human behavior and experience available for study by modern scholarship and social science. We have taken for our starting point the sociological study of religion and have tried to show how the challenge arises both in that area and within sociological theory generally. We have also noted the significant fact that the same kind of problem arises out of experience typical of the human condition in our epoch. We have been especially concerned with the theory of action as the locus of certain ambiguities in which the import of the challenge becomes visible. Against this background we have suggested what seem to us significant directions of thought and study for the exploration of the fundamental question — *Which are the dimensions of man's social existence that must find explicit formulation in delineating the basic frame of reference of sociological theory?*

A consideration of the more naive forms of functional theory often employed in the sociological study of religion revealed both their inadequacy and their peculiarly formulated and oddly understood recognition of the fact that human life involves responses and attitudes at certain breaking-points of contingency and powerlessness which involve aspects of the human situation largely ignored within the usual functionalist purview. The theory of action was next considered and seen to be a larger, more adequate, and intellectually more comfortable frame of reference which made it possible for the sociologist to consider aspects of the human situation central to the study of religion in relation to man's social life. Most interesting was the significance of the ambiguities there uncovered, ambiguities which derived fundamentally not from improprieties of theoretical formulation but rather from a profound rootedness in the character of the human condition itself. Man was seen to be both the *creator* of his history and its products, social institutions, culture patterns, and personal identities and at the same time the *creature* of his social setting of which these very products constituted the principal elements. It was seen that the theory of action could be utilized with two possible emphases, depending upon the preference and perspective of the user. One could emphasize the already formed stabilities of the society-culture-personality triad and give salience to the fact that men are formed by the internalization of the "already there." Or, contrariwise, one could emphasize the evolving, emerging process which continually produces and reproduces such stabilities and gives salience to the fact that man is an externalizer and objectifier of the products of his activity and interaction — a constitutor of stable relationships and meanings. It was suggested that Parsons and many of his interpreters tend to the former emphasis, but that the possibility of the second was authentically present within the theory of action itself. It was further suggested that the second, the dynamic, emphasis did more justice to social realities and implied a more open-ended interpretation of terms like system and others describing the functional-meaningful interconnectedness of the components of social order. The first emphasis was seen to tend towards rigidity — a certain woodenness in the use of otherwise useful categories of description and analysis. A consideration of category-formation in sociology revealed another derivative version of this ambiguity and again suggested the significance of understanding process as primary and avoiding tendencies to reification. In all this, a shift in emphasis from the object pole of the stable, established, externalized social order to the subject, emergence-constitution pole of social interaction is to be seen. Moreover, these implications of theory are seen to be supported by a hermeneutical commentary on the historical experience of our time. Thus the character of a first shift in emphasis in the formulation of the theory of action is to be seen.

The recognition of man as primarily a constitutor of meaning raises a set of problems concerning the meaning of action itself. Parsons is seen to have greatly modified the rationalistic positivistic frame of reference drawing creatively upon the work of four prominent predecessors, Durkheim, Pareto, Weber, and Marshall, yet following the emphasis of Weber to give a certain strategic analytical primacy to seeing human conduct primarily oriented in terms of means and ends. That is to say despite a vastly enlarged scope that makes room for meaning and purpose, task activity remains central. Yet the question arises in this context as to where the task comes from. It is related, of course, to an environmental challenge, a situational exigency, but such a challenge or exigency is reacted to as it is perceived, understood, and formulated in terms of the cultural systems of meanings which men evolve. If man is a doer of tasks; if tasks derive from meaning systems as much as from the environment; if meaning systems are evolved by men; and if meaning systems contain as essential elements supraempirical components unrelated by utility or function to tasks — all of which is part of the suppositions of the theory of action — then two things follow. First man does not simply evolve meaning systems out of task activity or the task aspects of activity in general, but also out of supraempirically oriented and nonutilitarian activity. Hence the centrality of task in human activity needs to be reconsidered in relation to other possible components of man's existential dynamic — his activity in the most general sense. Second, task is itself relative to a culture, to an over-all meaning system, to an at least partly "imagined world." The definition of tasks as a social process takes place within the context of an over-all relational configuration of a cognitive-affective character. Hence the implication of the theory of action itself renders problematic the centrality of task activity with its means-end action in the variegated and changing configurations of human behavior. Thus a second shift in emphasis in the reformulation of theory is suggested: from the primacy of task to the possibly equal emphasis upon the other modes of man's being in the world.

This recapitulation and summary introduces the need for a third consideration vital to an improved theoretical reformulation. Man is both creature and creator of society and culture; he is both active agent and acted-upon patient. He evolves externalized products of his activity and lives within the context of an experienced world of which they constitute major dimensions. They affect his further action and constituting activity. Thus we see a kind of hen-and-egg relationship of "creature-creator-creature-creator...." These sequences reveal to us moments of an ongoing dialectical process. Such moments are to be recognized as interpenetrating in a significant way. Men evolve new forms within the context of the old. They do so under various conditions, and the character of the conditions affect the character of the process and its products. For example, there are both abrupt breakthroughs as one kind of change and gradual evolution as another kind; there is also a variety of combinations of the two.

Berger and Luckmann speak of the "paradox that man is capable of producing a world that he then experiences as something other than a human product.... [I]t is important to emphasize that the relationship between man, the producer and the social world, his product, is a dialectical one.... The product acts back upon the producer." They sum this up by saying, "Externalization and objectivation are moments in a continuing dialectical process. The third moment in this process ... is internalization (by which the objectivated social world is retrojected into consciousness in the course of socialization).... *Society is a human product. Society is an objective reality. Man is a social product.*"[46]

Thus we have not only removed our central emphasis from task activity freeing ourselves from the nineteenth-century partiality of Max Weber (an emancipation implicit in much of the work of both Parsons and Weber) and shifted our emphasis from established structure to ongoing process, but we have also introduced the dialectical view of this process, enabling us to take into account both its ongoing character and the way in which its moments are both successive and simultaneous, that is, their reciprocal interpenetration.

Next arises the question: What do we put alongside or perhaps in place of task as the central type of human activity? In answer to that it was suggested that the less precise, more protean notion of response might offer a fruitful substitute. We may summarize what is meant by that as follows: Descartes affected the starting place of Western thinking about man and the human condition for the last four centuries by making cognition the central activity characteristic of man's significant mode of being in the world. *Cogito, ergo sum.* I think, therefore, I am. The theory of action has recognized that cognition and thought are significant, but it has also recognized that much more needs to be added to characterize the human condition. It has said, *Ago, ergo sum.* But it was in effect argued above that it tended to understand *Ago, ergo sum* fundamentally as *Facio, ergo sum*; to understand "I act" chiefly as "I make." It understood *agere* largely as *facere.* Here it followed the confusion which Plato introduced into the issue after the decline of the *polis* and the eclipse of dramatic political interaction as central to the Greek notion of *arete.* We have suggested that it is necessary to reintroduce the notion of *agere* as the dramatic acting out and externalization of human potentialities in interaction as central to action itself.[47] Moreover, it was further suggested that knowing, acting, and making must all be seen as particular aspects and specifications of a more general mode of being in the world characteristic of man. Furthermore, in Martin Buber's now overworked words, men meet their worlds — what is there — in both a technical (I-it) and a relational (I-Thou) mode. Men relate to each other; they identify themselves with collectivities. This form of relating is especially significant for the evolution of systems of meaning. Culture is not a mode of doing, although it contains various modes of doing various things; it is a historically conditioned, humanly constituted, relational mode of being in the world. It is the object pole — the stable, established, produced side — of a dynamic process involving human subjects. We have designated that latter dynamic process by the term "response." Response is the active dynamic protean mode of man's being in the world out of which the other forms — knowing, acting, making, relating — are differentiated and specified. Such differentiation is possible because what is made specific in it is implicitly present to one degree or another in all response. Hence most fundamentally descriptive of the human condition is the statement, *Respondeo, ergo sum.* Man realizes aspects of himself and objectifies his social products in response. Task itself is subsidiary to response. This indeed would seem to be involved in Parsons' statement that tasks are ultimately derived from ends which are ultimate.

THE *BASE* PARADIGM

These three fundamental shifts of emphasis open up before us the prospect of a reformulation of the theory of action in a manner conducive to giving a more adequate answer to the fundamental theoretical question we have raised — What are the dimensions of the human situation that must be explicitly taken into account and receive explicit categorization in any adequate statement of sociological theory? We cannot proceed to such a reformulation here. Indeed the task is beyond the capacity of the single individual sociologist and requires the scholarly dialogue of the sociological community. It is indeed not to be accomplished by one generation and within one culture if it is to be done in depth. A variety of perspectives need to be brought to bear upon it. To avoid anticlimax in our presentation, however, it may prove worthwhile to suggest some partial adumbration. In what follows we emphasize the tentative and exemplary character (in the nonnormative sense of "example") of what follows.

Let us introduce first a brief statement of Parsons' now well known AGIL formulation. In developing this formulation Parsons has designated what may most properly be called two phases of action and two fundamental conditions constitutive of the situation in which action takes place. Action possesses two basic moments. There is first of all a "working" moment of manipulation and adjustment, what Parsons early called "adaptive instrumental object

manipulation." Second, there is a consummatory moment, the arrival of the end of the action, the moment of achievement or accomplishment, what Parsons has called in his earlier treatment "goal attainment or gratification." Such action being meaningful and involving interaction takes place in a situation which is seen to possess two chief integrative dimensions. There is the relational social context and its related over-all meaning system, that is, an "integrative" context in terms of social and cultural setting. There is also the maintenance of internal personal integration, the maintenance of meaning for the individual that involves the sustaining of his internalization of cultural meanings, and the management of psychological tensions that inevitably are built up in action and interaction, what Parsons early had designated as "latent-receptive meaning integration and energy regulation" including "tension build-up and drain off." These four have been called adaptation, goal attainment, integration, and latent pattern maintenance and tension management.[48] In short, A and G refer to action, I and L to the context of action — to social and personal integration as the context of action. What we have suggested in our shifts of emphasis would involve a more explicit recognition of this distinction and the granting of a certain primacy to I and L. It would also involve not interpreting L in a manner that gives an unwarranted centrality to goal attainment and adaptation, as is done in Parsons' later work.[49] Moreover, what we have been saying means that I and L as conditions of action evolve not simply out of action alone (understood as means-end oriented activity) but also and indeed primarily out of responses which are dominantly relational rather than manipulative in character. Social ties are stabilizations of reciprocal responses largely of a relational rather than an adaptive or instrumental character. They are internalized together with their value implications and become social structure. To this characterization there must, of course, be added the dialectical conception presented in this chapter.

If response is central to the emergence process, then the question arises: What are the significant aspects of the situation to which men respond? By significant we understand here not necessarily significance in terms of an ontological characterization of the human condition, but simply significance with respect to the evolution of social order, culture and selfhood. The two are of course related, but here our interest in the former is dictated by our sociological interests. In those terms we would suggest four aspects of the human situation significant as foci for human response.

There is first of all the environment seen as an external situation challenging or demanding the performance of tasks. However, it must be recognized that the environment is also responded to in a relational manner as can clearly be seen in the ubiquity of natural phenomena and human events as the foci for the emergence of religious symbolism. Let us designate this aspect by the initial letter of "environment," E. Next men respond to the exigencies of human association. They respond to the problems that arise out of the interaction process itself and its required integrative and communication aspects. Here both a manipulative and a relational kind of response are possible. Here both kinds of response are clearly to be observed, yet perhaps the manipulative one becomes the dominant one. This however may not be the case in so-called primitive and archaic societies. We may designate this focus of response by the initial letter of "association," A. The existence of other human beings and the basic characteristics of human beings and their life trajectories provide a third focus of response. This is to be seen in the emergence of age and sex roles, as well as in other established forms of social relations based upon expressive realization. This aspect may be designated by the initial letter of "structure," S. Finally, as we saw in our consideration of the sociology of religion, men respond to a Beyond experienced as possessing a sacral and ultimate character—to a supraempirical transcendent or immanent reality eliciting a relational response. This focus of response is basic to the evolution and maintenance of social order since from it and from the belief systems generated out of response to it are derived and rooted the basic undergirding legitimation of human societies. Let us designate this aspect of the over-all human situation by the initial letter of "beyond," B. Let us now arrange this presentation in paradigmatic form for purposes of clarity. We formulate it as BASE to suggest that these aspects of the human situation are basic to the responses out of which social structure and culture, as well as selfhood, are evolved in the emergence-constitution process.

If these represent the foci which elicit and receive responses out of which social structure evolves, then a second question arises: What is it that is externalized and objectified to become established as culture and social structure? The four foci represent the object pole of response; what is expressed, externalized, objectivized, and established

as social reality from the subject pole? This is a difficult and indeed profound question. We know man from his works and creations, that is from his expressions, externalizations, and objectifications. To answer the question of what potentialities are realized in these products we must infer backwards from the object to the subject pole. The forms men evolve and constitute bear the imprint of the external foci upon the human-potential-in-the-act-of-expression. The sides of men elicited by the foci reveal a series of resonances or affinities between man and situation. These resonances suggest a typology of realms of experience, some of which we have designated already. Let us deal only in a summary fashion here with what deserves extended treatment and speak of such realms of human experience as relational experience, aesthetic experience, ethical experience, the experience of coping and conflict, the making experience, the cognitive experience, and the religious experience.[50] As Georg Simmel has observed, these realms of experience represent a later differentiation and specification of human capacities which in everyday life operate together in implicit combinations.[51] The fine arts become possible because men are capable of experiencing an aesthetic dimension resonant with a corresponding aesthetic human sensitivity, but in everyday life this realm is experienced not in pure form but as part of a total complex response which often involves utility, relationship, religion, and other factors. Out of such prereflective experiential totalities there evolve differentiated and specialized spheres of experience and their institutions—art, religion, science, and the like. Out of this everyday totality there also differentiates a task area and the specific tasks composing it and an area which we may designate as the dramatic, that of realization through acting-out which is a part of all undifferentiated everyday action. Obviously all of these nontask areas are vaster and more profound than task itself, but equally obviously all of them involve and specify tasks. Religious ritual is fundamentally expressive, but it is performed and must be performed properly: It presents tasks. Artistic expression is creative expression in relation to certain situational resonances between the subject and his situation, but it is a highly sophisticated matter and involves highly developed skills: It presents tasks.

Beyond—supraempirical transcendent or immanent aspects responded to as *sacred*—related to "legitimacy"	Requisites of Human *A*ssociation —necessities of order, communication, and the like
*S*tructure of the Human Being, especially age and sex, but also characteristics of the life cycle—helplessness in extreme youth and age, for example	*E*nvironment—external situation seen as challenge or demanding performance of *tasks*—responded to as understood—as situation

Primary are relation, expression, dramatic act, but they all give rise to tasks. The former are primarily "gesture" in the grand sense, and out of such gesture, tasks arise. Moreover, within certain kinds of gesture, there is a basic utilitarian element out of which environmental tasks arise. In terms of the elements of the BASE paradigm men respond to the situation and to each other as part of the situation. From this interaction (or "tacit dialogue") the emergence-constitution process proceeds, and there are evolved those precedents which tend to become consensually validated and commonly shared. These latter become the stuff of institutions: They externalize and objectify the particular configurations of the responses involved and may give dominance to any of the various aspects of experience which we have indicated.

It now becomes apparent that the AGIL paradigm is related to the BASE paradigm in an interesting way. A and G are most clearly related to the responses we found dominant with respect to E and A. Yet A and G also become involved in relation to other foci, as tasks derive from gestural responses. I and L, which provide the context of action (for A and G), are largely evolved from responses to B and S. Yet because in the performance of tasks men also relate and as order is possible only with relationship, I and L elements also evolve around E and A. Moreover it will be noted that we used the term "related to" when speaking of A and G (that is of "Action") and the foci E and A, but we used the term "evolved from" to express relationship of I and L to their foci B and S. All of this indicates what we have called the primacy of gesture in characterizing man's mode of being in the world.

It is against this background that our discussion of lived experience and core experiences may best be considered. A vocabulary of analysis is based upon what Parsons has called invariant points of reference. We have suggested in this article that an important service which phenomenology can render to sociological theory is in offering another and more self-conscious method of identifying the invariant points of reference characteristic of man's being in the world. It can enable us to identify the core experiences characteristic of man's mode of being in the world which would indicate which aspects of human experience must find formulation in theory and at the same time provide the strategic invariant points of reference for description and analysis. What we see in various cultures (so it seems from our whole endeavor here) is such core experiences elaborated upon and standardized in particular historical, geographical, social structural, and psychological situations. These core experiences can be classified in terms of types of experiences as we have suggested in our tentative typology of experience, and in terms of combinations of them in the specific configurations which they assume in everyday life. There are for example core religious experiences from which evolve archetypal religious symbolism that is formulated differently in various cultures.

The tentative character of this final presentation must be emphasized. Yet it is forthrightly proposed that the kind of changes suggested here in this rough sketch will help to realize the hidden potential of the theory of action and to bring it into contact and confrontation with other tendencies in theory formation in a truly fruitful and creative encounter. Again let it be emphasized that such creative confrontation is the task of the entire community engaged in the sociological enterprise.

NOTES

1. See for example Rudolf Otto, *The Idea of the Holy*, J. W. Harvey (tr.) (London: Oxford University Press, 1950); Emile Durkheim, *The Elementary Forms of Religious Life*, Joseph Ward Swain (tr.) (Glencoe, Ill.: The Free Press, 1954); G. Van der Leeuw, *Religion in Essence and Manifestation*, Vols. I and II, J.E. Turner (tr.) (New York: Harper Torchbooks, 1963); Mircea Eliade, *The Sacred and the Profane,* W.R. Trask (tr.) (New York: Harper Torchbooks, 1961); and *Patterns in Comparative Religion*. Rosemary Sheed (tr.) (New York: Sheed and Ward, 1958).

The phrase is from Gustav Mesching, *Die Religion* (Stuttgart: C. E. Schwab, 1959). Louis Schneider (tr.), in his *Religion, Culture and Society* (New York: John Wiley and Sons, 1964), p. 36.

2. See Chapters One and Two of Thomas F. O'Dea, *The Sociology of Religion* (Englewood Cliffs: Prentice-Hall, 1966).

3. Paul Tillich, *Dynamics of Faith* (New York: Harper Torchbook, 1957).

4. See O'Dea, *op. cit.*, pp. 13-16; pp. 100-104.

5. It is interesting here to note that Parsons deliberately and explicitly took what he called a rationalist positivist frame of reference as his starting point and, basing himself on the four writers he had chosen, reformed it. Yet all reformed entities bear some relation to the perspective of their origin. "The starting point, both historical and logical, is the conception of intrinsical rationality of action . . . . Historically, this concept of rationality of action, not always clearly and unambiguously, has played the central role in what has been called the utilitarian branch of the positivistic tradition." *The Structure of Social Action* (Glencoe, Ill.: The Free Press, 1949), pp. 698-699. What will be suggested here is that times arrive in the development of thought when it becomes necessary to shift perspectives.

6. *Ibid.*, pp. 257ff.

7. Talcott Parsons, *Essays in Sociological Theory,* rev. ed. (Glencoe, Ill.: The Free Press, 1954), pp. 208-209.

8. The term is Einstein's.

9. For example, "All serious reflection about the ultimate elements of meaningful human conduct is oriented primarily in terms of the categories 'end' and 'means.'" (Max Weber, *The Methodology of the Social Sciences*, Edward A. Shils and Henry A. Finch (trs.) (Glencoe, Ill.: The Free Press, 1949), pp. 52. Modern scholarship of a great variety of cultures and epochs would lead to challenging that exclusivity of emphasis upon task-performance aspects of human activity.

10. Parsons, *The Structure of Social Action*, p. 396. See also his discussion of Pareto and effort, p. 298; Durkheim and effort, p. 440.

11. Parsons, *Essays in Sociological Theory*, p. 211.

12. Parsons, *The Structure of Social Action*, pp. 262-263.

13. *Ibid.*, p. 141. The quote is from Alfred Marshall.

14. See especially his late work, eg., *Societies: Evolutionary and Comparative Perspectives* (Englewood Cliffs: Prentice Hall, 1966).

15. For example, see *The Structure of Social Action*, pp. 422-423.

16. Ernst Troeltsch, *Die Historismus und Seine Probleme* (Tübingin: Mohr, 1922). The quote is from Ernst Troeltsch, *Christian Thought: Its History and Application* (New York: Meridian, 1957), pp. 52-53.

17. *Ibid.*, p. 53.

18. Max Weber, *The Theory of Social and Economic Organization*, A.M. Henderson and Talcott Parsons (trs.) (New York: Oxford University Press, 1947).

19. See O'Dea, *op. cit.*, pp. 116-117, and Tillich, *op. cit.*, pp. 16-22.

20. Tillich, *op. cit.*, p. 22.

21. See especially Max Weber, *Ancient Judaism,* Hans H. Gerth and Don Martindale (trs.) (Glencoe, Ill.: The Free Press, 1952). For a very interesting study of knowing and knowledge as built upon the structure of insight see Bernard J.F. Lonergan, *Insight: A Study of Human Understanding*, rev. ed., (New York and London: Philosophical Library and Logmans, 1958), especially Chapters Five and Six on common sense, which are quite pertinent to sociology.

22. Max Weber, *The Methodology of the Social Sciences*, Edward A. Shils and Henry A. Finch (trs.) (Glencoe, Ill.: The Free Press, 1949), p. 79. Italics in original.

23. *Ibid.*, p. 84. Italics in original. Mannheim's treatment of a synthesis of perspectives may be found in Karl Mannheim, *Ideology and Utopia* (New York: Harcourt, Brace and Company, 1949).

24. Weber, *The Methodology of the Social Sciences*, p. 85. The italics in these quotes are in the original.

25. See Thomas S. Kuhn, *The Structure of Scientific Revolutions*, rev. ed. (Chicago: University of Chicago Press, 1970).

26. *Ibid.*, p. 84.

27. See Eliade, *Patterns in Comparative Religion* (tr.).

28. Hertley Burr Alexander, *The World's Rim: Great Mysteries of the North American Indians* (Lincoln: University of Nebraska Press, 1967), pp. 12-13.

29. Eliade, *Patterns in Comparative Religion*, p. 375.

30. The quote from Alexander's book, which was prepared for publication as early as 1935 but did not appear until 1953, is remarkable as an anticipation of Merleau-Ponty. See Maurice Merleau-Ponty, *The Phenomenology of Perception*, Colin Smith (tr.) (London: Routledge and Kegan Paul, 1962); and Remy C. Kwart, *The Phenomenological Philosophy of Merleau-Ponty* (Pittsburgh: Duquesne University Press, 1963).

31. O. F. Bollnow, "Lived Space," in *Readings in Existential Phenomenology*, Nathaniel Lawrence and Daniel O'Connor (eds.) (Englewood Cliffs: Prentice Hall, 1967), pp. 179-180.

32. Gaston Berger, "A Phenomenological Approach to the Problem of Time," in Lawrence and O'Connor, *op. cit.,* pp. 192 and 195.

33. Edmund Husserl, "Phenomenology," *Encyclopedia Britannica*, Vol. XVII, pp. 699ff (appeared first in 1929).

34. Alfred Schütz, "Concept and Theory Formation in the Social Sciences," in Lawrence and O'Connor, *op. cit.*, pp. 382-383.

35. F. H. Heinemann, *Existentialism and the Modern Predicament* (New York: Harper Torchbooks, 1958), p. 193.

36. Cf. Martin Buber, *I and Thou*, 2nd ed. Ronald Gregor Smith (tr.) (New York: Scribner's, 1958); Henri Frankfort, Mrs. Henri Frankfort, John A. Wilson and Thorkild Jacobsen, *Before Philosophy* (Harmondsworth, Middlesex: Penguin Books, 1949).

37. Lonergan, *op. cit.*, pp. 187-88.

38. See for example Werner Jaeger, *Paideia: The Ideals of Greek Culture*, Vol. I., Gilbert Highet (tr.) (New York: Oxford University Press, 1945).

39. *Ibid.*, Vol. II.

40. Hannah Arendt, *The Human Condition* (Garden City: Doubleday Anchor Books, 1959), p. 15.

41. *Ibid.*, p. 159.

42. *Ibid.*, p. 279.

43. Alexander, *op. cit.*, p. vi. Quoted "from rough notes" by Clyde Kluckhohn in his Foreword.

44. Hannah Arendt, *On Revolution* (New York: Viking Press, 1965), p. 121.

45. *Ibid.*, pp. 115-116.

46. Peter L. Berger and Thomas Luckmann, *The Social Construction of Reality: A Treatise in the Sociology of Knowledge* (Garden City: Doubleday, 1966), p. 61.

47. For a more historical treatment of the sociological significance of the dramatic — of action as *agere* — see "'Acting Out' — Man Makes Himself?" in Thomas F. O'Dea, *Sociology and the Study of Religion: Theory, Research, Interpretation* (New York; Basic Books, Inc., 1970), pp. 271-293.

48. Talcott Parsons, *Essays in Sociological Theory*, rev. ed. Glencoe, Ill.: The Free Press, 1954), pp. 412-415. These four "dimensions" or "phases" remain important in Parsonian theory and represent a genuine contribution to a sophisticated analytical treatment of social groups of all kinds, including and particularly the macroanalysis of societies. In his later work Parsons makes varied use of them, often to good effect. See, for example, *Societies: Evolutionary and Comparative Perspectives*, pp. 28-29, where they are characterized—both as "functions of general action systems" and of "intra-societal systems." It will be noted that in this article we have given particular attention to the earlier work of Parsons. This is because we wished to get back to the original thinking and formulation in which the ambiguities and their possible one-sided interpretation were to be found. The original perspective and emphasis of a theoretical idea always remains strategic. Indeed Parsons has been a consistent thinker, and what is to be seen in his early works with respect to basic perspective remains true of his later work as well. One implication of what we are saying here is that it would have been more auspicious for the development of Action Theory had Parsons not begun with the reform of the "rationalistic-positivistic frame of reference." But under the historical circumstances it was inevitable that he should in fact begin there. Therefore, his insights can best be made available now in the kind of reformulation we are suggesting. There comes a qualitative point in the development of thought when qualification leads to and must give rise to such reformulation.

49. See, for example, *Societies: Evolutionary and Comparative Perspectives*, p. 7.

50. I shall deal with the realms of experience and their implications for sociology in greater detail in a forthcoming book on sociological theory soon to be published by Basic Books, Inc.

51. Georg Simmel, "A Contribution to the Sociology of Religion," W.W. Elwang (tr.) *American Journal of Sociology* 60 (May 1955), pp. 2-14.

12

THE HOBBESIAN PROBLEM IN MARX AND PARSONS

John O'Neill

The problem of order is as much a question about the human nature of social reality as an inquiry into the nature of moral and political order. The consideration of the structure and logic of social order involves us in the imputation of some concept of human nature and truth. The legitimation of any state implies a notion of some repository of truth and the conditions of access to it. In turn, any conception of the nature and scope of true human knowledge has direct consequences for the nature of social action and participation. Political action involves the coordination of means towards the goals of life as determined by the needs and values of a given social structure. But the conditions of political action are never merely factual givens, just as their realization is never a simple end in itself. The conditions of political action are always immanent to the principles of legitimation which arch the goals of social life. Thus it may be argued what has been called the Hobbesian problem of order is also tied to the nature of the ultimate legitimacy of the formal and substantive modes of rationality and action, or the *Weberian problem*, as well as the institutional relations between the sentimental and rational bases of social order, which constitute the *Durkheimian problem*. The metatheoretical concerns of Hobbes, Marx, Durkheim, and Weber are so finely interwoven with their analytic concepts and empirical generalizations that extreme care should be exercised in trying to separate their theories of human nature from their conceptions of sociological and political analysis. The pattern of these concerns cannot be discerned in purely analytical terms. It also requires an historical approach to the sociological tradition itself as an emergent feature of industrial

optimism and its subversive and disenchanted alternations.

What is unique in the work of Parsons is the profundity of his grasp of the whole intellectual tradition in which the Hobbesian problem of order arises. For this reason, I am inclined to regard *The Structure of Social Action* as in many ways the greatest of Talcott Parsons' works. For it is both a major work of social and political philosophy in the great tradition of utilitarianism with which it struggles and the embryo of the general analytic theory of action to which we owe the major theoretical and empirical synthesis of the social science. I am not myself a Parsonian. This itself may be painfully obvious to those who are Parsonians from the kind of emphasis I have chosen to put on *The Structure of Social Action*. All the same, there it is, I regard Parsons as one of the great social philosophers in the sentimental tradition[1] of Adam Smith, Burke, McLuhan, and Goffman.

Parsons is so much at home in the western intellectual tradition from Hobbes to Freud, that even when he attempts a fresh theoretical synthesis or brings some further empirical domain within the Parsonian framework it is always with a sense of the whole intellectual tradition from which sociology emerges and claims its "analytical" autonomy. For this very reason, it is necessary to recognize that Parsons' conception of sociology, particularly the sublimity of that conception, rests very much on the way Parsons reads the classics from which he constructed *The Structure of Social Action* and the general theory of action. As much has already been said to one side and another about Parsons' views on the social system and its subsystems of action,[2] along with the contributions in the present volume, perhaps I may be permitted an exercise of a somewhat different nature. I cannot claim any greater

This essay has benefited from the attempt to deal with editorial comments as well as from several discussions with my colleague H. T. Wilson.

295

merit for my approach and, indeed, its only value may be to call attention to considerations that others will articulate more clearly. I am going to examine the Hobbesian problem in some detail and, with a look at Hegel and Marx, consider what Parsons calls the Durkheimian and Weberian problems.[3] However, instead of regarding these problems solely as stages in the development of the general analytic theory of action, I am going to treat them in the framework of a historical-philosophical essay on the problem of rationality.[4] The perspective I am adopting is to be found, I believe, in Marx, Durkheim, and Weber in their concern with the *meaning* or value of Western rationality, which seems to them to undermine its own presuppositions in the sentimental or precontractual order of human relations and patterns of motivation, raising questions about the relative value of formal and substantive rationality.[5] This is, then, as Parsons would say, an essay in residual categories, or the points where the theory of rational action becomes conscious of its limitations.

RATIONALITY AND THE PROBLEM OF ORDER

The problem of the relationship between the nature of Western rationality and the social order is a question with which historicism is deeply concerned. However, Parsons restricts his discussions of historicism to its methodological features: the institutional critique of generalizations and the holistic arguments against methodological individualism within historicism itself.[6] But this account ignores the historicist phenomenology of knowledge and rationality which is the very foundation of the method of *Verstehen*. It seems to me that the problem of the relation between the physical and social sciences when discussed solely in terms of the unity of scientific method, an important theme in *The Structure of Social Action,* rests upon an abstract or inadequately historical concept of rationality. It is this observation which I consider to be at the heart of the phenomenology of Hegel, Marx, Durkheim, and Weber.

Parsons' own methodology invites us to weave together the historical and empirical contexts in which the theoretical problem of rationality arises. It is this existential connection between theory and practice which underlies the ideal-type method which Parsons adopts from Weber and Marx. The method of ideal-type understanding represents, of course, a radical break with the common assumption of rationalists and empiricists on the identity of actor and observer points of view on social conduct. The assumption of this identity was basic to the positivist

conception of scientific research and the utilitarian ethic which adopted the paradigm of rationality as a code for moral as well as scientific conduct.

The significance of Marx and Weber is that between them they raised the idealist question — if you will, Nietzsche's question — of the intrinsic meaning of accumulation and rationalization apart from its purely practical and technical significance.

> Consequently, "will to truth" does *not* mean "I will not let myself be deceived" but — there is no choice — "I will not deceive, not even myself:" *and with this we are on the ground of morality.* For one should ask oneself carefully: "Why don't you want to deceive?" especially if it should appear — and it certainly does appear — that life depends on appearance; I mean, on error, simulation, deception, self-deception; and when life has, as a matter of fact, always shown itself to be on the side of the most unscrupulous *polytropoi.* Such an intent, charitably interpreted, could perhaps be a quixotism, a little enthusiastic impudence; but it could also be something worse, namely, a destructive principle, hostile to life. 'Will to truth' — that might be a concealed will to death.
>
> Thus the question "Why science?" leads back to the moral problem, "For what end any morality at all" if life, nature, and history are "not moral?" . . . But one will have gathered what I am driving at, namely, that it always remains a *metaphysical faith* upon which our faith in science rests — that even we devotees of knowledge today, we godless ones and antimetaphysicians, still take *our* fire from the flame which a faith thousands of years old has kindled: that Christian faith, which was also Plato's faith, that God is truth, that truth is divine. . . .[7]

How shall we understand the pursuit of cultural and economic values in the absence of any self-imposed or socially imposed limit which would make the acquisition of these values a meaningful end rather than a self-expanding and socially alienating process? This is the crux of the Durkheimian and Weberian problems. German idealism and historicism were just as much concerned with the ordered disorder or anomie of industrial society as with the nature of historical "laws." This is the intuitive focus of their comparative studies of Western philosophy, social sciences, and social structure; and it is from that standpoint that we can best understand the Marxian and Weberian ideal-type conceptions of capitalism. The model of economic rationality is not simply a construction of the social scientist's understanding. It also reflects the shift from a social structure in which power was based on status to a social structure in which all statuses are ascribed on the basis of economic power. In short, the ideal-type of capitalism is, as Hegel might put it, the truth of subjectivity as it experiences itself under the conditions of liberal society in which the bonds of traditional sentimentality are broken in favor of a vast machinery of individual rights, exchange, and private property. In the Marxian and Weberian use of the ideal-type there is never any question of the reduction of social facts to technological factors. The latter are only introduced as middle principles whose meta-economic meaning is the self-transvaluation of human experience through the market as a Faustian generator of wants and needs and the problem of death. This is the context of the Weberian problem to which we shall return.

The idealist critique of positivist methodology and its conception of physical and social reality may be seen as a response to a reversal within the positivist theory of action itself. As Parsons sketches it, the positivist theory of action is internally unstable and results in a switch from a "radical rationalist" positivism to a "radical anti-intellectualistic" positivism.[8] I believe this oscillation is a constant in the whole tradition of thought with which Parsons is dealing, from Hobbes to Freud, and that it even affects the theory of action.[9] The early potimism of seventeenth- and eighteenth-century rationalism which inspired the positivism of classical utilitarianism had gradually turned by the late nineteenth-century to the fatalisms of heredity and environment as rationalizations of a social order threatened by the specter of its own violence in the opposing rhetorics of class struggle, Superman, and the mythology of Oedipal revolt.

Positivist methodology is predisposed to the notion of social reality as an external constraint of the same sort as physical reality. But the assumption of the externality of social reality prejudices the question of the relation between individual action and social order, despite the mediations of internalization or socialization processes, in the direction of constraint in terms of the social system values of functional hierarchy, technical rationality, and pattern maintenance. Parsons approaches the structure of the positivist theory of action primarily as a problem in the conceptual analysis of the social act. The result is that although he is not unaware of the historical crisis which is the empirical context of the problem of the subjective meaning of order and rationality, in the end he settles for a "rational optimism,"[10] This perspective seriously affects Parsons' reading of the intellectual tradition to which Hobbes, Marx, Durkheim, Weber, and Freud all belong, for they were all concerned with the subjective meaning of action as a problem of meaningful freedom and order not to be settled as a derivative of the values of technical rationality.

But it is not my purpose here to quarrel with Parsons' conceptual or behavioralist analysis of the unit social act. I am interested in tracing the historical and philosophical background to Parsons' conception of the normative orientation of social

action,[11] which I think offers a more substantial basis to the ideological controversies around Parsons' assumptions of rational optimism and consensus and the place accorded to conflict and strain.

I want now to take a close look at the problem of order as Hobbes confronted it, paying particular attention to the problematic nature of the Hobbesian concept of knowledge and rationality. Medieval ontology was profoundly individualist and may be regarded as the ultimate source of the natural rights and social contractarian principles which established the double standard of equality before God and equality in hope which underlay the secular doctrines of liberty, authority, and obligation.[12] The seventeenth-century discussion of the nature of social and political conduct represents a fusion of a *normative* law of nature with a deterministic theory of the *conditions* of action based upon the model of mechanical physics.[13] It is assumed that the ends of action are essentially random and that rationality consists solely in the efficient pursuit of whatever ends man proposes to himself. As Hobbes saw it, the basic problem of rational egoism is to command the services and recognition of other men. Where men are so equal in nature that they can entertain "equality of hope," there is nothing to prevent them from resorting to fraud and violence in the pursuit of their ends. In short, Hobbes raised very clearly the question of the need to set limits to violence in a social order predicated upon the principle of rational egoism.

The fiction of a social contract fails to save the question raised by Hobbes because, as Marx later pointed out, the costs of keeping promises can be shifted onto a class which lacks the freedom to contract and thus Hobbes's "state of war" comes to rest upon a "class war." Thus the problem of order is ultimately a problem of power which could not be solved within the liberal utilitarian tradition. But, as Parsons remarks, theoretical difficulties are often patched in practice, and in this case Locke's postulate of the natural identity of interests matched the early experience of liberal individualism better perhaps than Hobbes's more consistent fears. Thus the problem of recognition came to rest in the doctrine of the natural identity of interests until Marx demonstrated that the system of social exchange and division of labor under capitalist conditions produces a class which recognizes itself only in the conditions of its own dehumanization.

The Hobbesian problem should also be considered in the context of the challenge to knowledge raised by the collapse of the feudal community. The question raised for political knowledge by the loss of a natural basis for community was whether it was possible to construct a community out of the principles of individualism and rational egoism. It had always appeared from the standpoint of medieval community that chaos could be the only result of slipping the divine anchor and leaving the passions to a free play. Indeed, this was the fearful prospect of Renaissance and Reformation freedom, especially once it had found in the market an infinite field for the expansion of desire and the accumulation of power. At the same time, this sudden and terrible expansion of moral and political freedom was being translated into an orderly system of economic exchanges, which in turn rested upon the growth of mathematical and physical knowledge and its applications to technology and commerce. But there is a subtle and profound change between the ancient and medieval conception of order and the Hobbesian concept of order. It is a change which stems from the shift in concept of truth and knowledge which occurs between ancient and modern philosophy.[14]

Modern rationality and its institutional organization rests upon the axiological assumption of man's domination of nature, which radicalizes the subject-object split and propels knowledge towards quantification and the creation of a moral and political arithmetic. It is natural that the scientific aspirations of sociology should lead to similar assumptions. But prior to the question of whether sociological laws have the same kind of universality as physical laws and thereby guarantee the scientific status of sociology is the phenomenon of the ambiguity in the moral and physical senses of the concept of law upon which the drama of western civilization is founded. Socrates, it will be remembered, turned away from the study of physical nature in favor of the study of human nature. In this manner Socrates raised the question of the unity of human knowledge as a *praxis* whose values are revealed in the effects upon the soul of the kinds of knowledge pursued in a given social order. With the Renaissance discovery of the experimental method the dramatic affinity of Western knowledge for power was unleashed, unfettered by the moral universals of the ancient and medieval world. Yet to Erasmus the Baconian equation of knowledge and power appeared to be a pagan reversal rather than the intensification of the inherent logic and axiology of Western knowledge. "Never forget," he remarked, "that 'dominion,' 'imperial authority,' 'kingdom,' 'majesty,' 'power,' are all pagan terms not Christian. The ruling power of a Christian state consists only of administration, kindness and protection."[15] Erasmus's comment is a reflection of the crisis of community to be found in the political and religious controversies of the late sixteenth and early seventeenth centuries. In the face of the collapse of church unity and the rise of individual conscience the normative grounds of community could no longer

be presumed upon; and yet it became clear that any particular covenant or contract was nothing more than, in Milton's words, "the forced and outward union of cold, and neutral, and inwardly divided minds." Hobbes's concept of philosophy as the pursuit of clear and precise discourse on the model of geometry dictates his aim of bringing peace and order into civil life by a set of political definitions founded on sovereign authority which would put an end to the anarchy of values and opinions. "For I doubt not, but if it had been a thing contrary to any man's right of dominion, or to the interest of men that have dominion, *that the three angles of a triangle, should be equal to two angles of a square;* that doctrine should have been, if not disputed, yet by the burning of all books of geometry, suppressed, as far as he whom it concerned was able."[16]

Henceforth rationality is never a substantive concept based on the "nature of things." The task of reason is confined to providing conclusions "about the names of things." Ultimately, it is Hobbes's conception of philosophical knowledge and science which governs his treatment of the problem of order. What has happened is that the standard of rationality furnished by Hobbes's science of politics is totally divorced from the traditional sentiments and usages of reason. "This dilemma faced by Hobbes was partly owing to a failure to realize what other apostles of 'scientific' politics have not yet seen, that one of the basic reasons for the unsurpassed progress of science was that scientific discourse, unlike political discourse, had rejected not only the common vocabulary of everyday life, but also the modes of thought familiar to the common understanding."[17] In the end Hobbes failed to solve the problem of order in anything but an external fashion. Hobbes's citizens live in a mutual and common fear which corrodes their private lives and leaves society dependent upon the sovereign whose power can never be anything but the exercise of fiat because the civil order itself lacks any sense of community or constituency.

Hobbes's positivist concept of law and his doctrine of the state as *causa sui* is the strict derivation of his empiricist rejection of the rationalist conception of law as the embodiment of a rational principle open to speculative reason, such as we find in Hegel's *Philosophy of Right*. The rule of *auctoritas, non veritas facit legem* means that only sovereign sanction can impose truth and rationality upon the political community. The Hegelian position is that the appeal of law is based upon its a priori rationality grounded in the nature of being itself. To this Marx adds that the rational foundations of law and order can only be grounded in a rational society in which submission to law is an act of freedom and not just a means to material rights and property. This argument is essential to Marx's conception of the nature of organic solidarity and should not be overlooked in the discussion of the Durkheimian problem to which we now turn.

THE RATIONAL AND SENTIMENTAL BASES OF ORDER: MARX AND THE DURKHEIMIAN PROBLEM

Hobbes's doctrine of political sovereignty raised in its sharpest form the problem of the relation between utilitarian rationality and the sentimental or nonrational bases of political community. However, an intellectual tradition does not live by logic alone. Hobbes's fearful Erastianism did not suit the liberal temper, which settled for the more sentimental metaphysics of the natural identity of interests. In this case, Parsons remarks that the development of the theory of social action was better served by Locke's utilitarianism than Hobbes's logic, even if less respectably.

> For, in so far as the basic action schema is employed for analytical purposes, the fact that economic action is actually empirically important must inevitably raise the question of the adequacy of the utilitarian version of the theory of action, if the contention is right that it cannot without extraneous assumptions, account for the element of order in social relationships necessary to make this possible. Indeed, the central problem may be stated thus: How is it possible, still making use of the general action schema, to solve the Hobbesian problem of order and yet not make use of such an objectionable metaphysical prop as the doctrine of the natural identity of interests?[18]

The utilitarian theory of action oscillates between two conceptions of the rational pursuit of means to given ends. To the extent that rationality is conceived as a social exchange process coinciding with the identity of interests of the partners to it, it is necessary to assume a social order in which violence and fraud are restrained. On the other hand, where rationality is conceived as a process of satisfying intrinsically conflicting interests, some measure of consensus or rules of the game have to be assumed if anarchy is to be avoided. This is what Parsons calls the Durkheimian problem. Now I think that this problem involves a conflict between the patterns of "substantive" rationality and "formal" or technical rationality and is not simply a question of the analytic differentiation of the normative and nonnormative elements in the general theory of action. I also think this view is closer than Parsons' interpretation of Durkheim and Marx. Parsons sees clearly enough that the reason why the utilitarian theory of action is socially and politically indeterminate is that it cannot solve the problems of *class* interests. In the context

of the increasing inequality of property and power the postulate of the natural identity of individual interests becomes a sheer illusion. Now this is not simply a Marxist reduction of the relation between economy and politics,[19] as in any case such a move at least presupposes an awareness of the analytic distinction between polity and economy. Parsons argues nevertheless that Marx failed to make the distinction between economic and political interests because his theory of class interests and its rhetoric of class polarization and revolution required the identification of these two levels of action.

> The Durkheimian problem raised the question of the long-standing ambiguity in Marxian theory about the status of normative order, notably at the legal level, with respect to the distinction between "material" base and the superstructure. Marx's inclination to work at a rather low level of analytical abstraction, reinforced by his historicism, tended to locate this element of normative order in the "relations of production," which constitute the core of the interest structure of capitalism itself. Durkheim's analysis, however, showed that the crucial institution of contract, as he called it, was analytically distinct from the interests of contracting parties and varied independently of them.[20]

I think it can be shown that Marx was quite aware of the analytic distinction between the institution of contract, or the rule of property, as he would call it, and the class interests which it serves. Indeed, Marx, no less than Durkheim or Weber, pointed out that the universality or normative status of the rule of property is essential to the transition from feudal to bourgeois society. However, this does not require the rule of property or contract to vary independently of the general social structure in which it functions. What Durkheim and Marx, as well as Weber,[21] were concerned to argue was that the normative system of technical rationality, expressed in the doctrines of rights, property and contract, itself generates counternorms of substantive rationality based on the values of participation, self-expression and the common ownership of property.

Parsons' own reduction of the Durkheimian problem to the analytic distinctions between economy, law, and polity misses the central concern in Durkheim, Marx, and Weber over the historically specific contexts of the interaction of law and economy. In particular, it avoids the problem of the way in which legal rationality undermines the traditional, sentimental bonds of association in favor of market "freedoms" or property rights, and, ultimately, the heartless laws or the meaningless ways of bureaucracy. Again, the Durkheimian and Weberian problems cannot be kept separate if we are to understand the relationships between the ultimate principles of legitimacy or political authority, the state, the class and property systems, and the problem of the subjective meaning of individual action within these contexts. Marx and Durkheim criticized the utilitarian theory of action, not merely to elaborate the argument for the analytic levels of individual and societal action but as part of a metatheoretical concern with the meaningfulness of individual behavior in different kinds of society, that is to say, with the substantive bases of the legitimacy of social and political order.[22]

It is the tension between these historical patterns of rationality which underlies the ideal-typical contrarieties of mechanical and organic solidarity or *Gemeinschaft* and *Gesellschaft*. The latter are not, properly speaking, societal polarities so much as pattern alternatives of value orientation in any society and consequently expressive of the problem of integration rather than contrary solutions to it. Understood in this way, the ideal-type contrast between substantive and technical rationality represents a tension within the self-understanding of Western rationality which cuts across the resort either to optimism or despair.

Parsons "dehumanizes"[23] the Durkheimian problem by treating it as a question of the analytic distinction between the state and economy, whereas it is part of the larger problem of anomie and alienation. Durkheim was concerned with the way in which organic solidarity is predisposed to anomie because the relationship between law and economy in modern society is such that the state can hardly hope to contain the social forces which make for the infinitude of wants, class conflict, and the anomic division of labor. Durkheim attacked these problems in terms of the need to ground social solidarity in a transcendental bond which would provide a sense of meaning deeper than the regulative norms of mechanical and organic solidarity. Marx's notion of alienation furnishes a criterion in individual expression and social relations of an ultimate but immanent principle of social solidarity. His conception of the basis of a just social order differs from Durkheim's because Durkheim's failure to propose any scheme for the reform of the economic system left him with an ultimately Hobbesian concept of human nature faced with an external political constraint.

An adequate discussion of the issues here involves some consideration of the idealist critique of utilitarianism contained in Hegel's *Phenomenology of Mind* and the *Philosophy of Right*. Parsons' treatment of idealism deals only with the historicist and methodological arguments against utilitarian atomism and empiricism. But the Hegelian discussion is essential for the critique of the utilitarian conception of rationality and randomness of ends which are the complementary assumptions of utilitarian atomism and empiricism. There is further reason for considering Hegel because Marx was thoroughly familiar with the Hegelian critique of the utilitarian conception of civil society and the state and adopted it as the model of his own theory of the relation between state and society.[24]

Hegel regarded history as a process which unfolds through a number of living ideologies, such as the Enlightenment, Utilitarianism, and the Absolute Liberty of the French Revolution. Each of these ideologies is correlated with a definite cultural and social reality through which the nature of human rationality and freedom is progressively revealed. Once the Enlightenment had won its struggle with religious superstition, the question arose as to the nature of the philosophical truth which the Enlightenment was to set in its place. The truth of the Enlightenment is utilitarianism, which makes everything subject to its usefulness for man but is unable to solve the dilemma of man's utility to other men, which raises the problem of exploitation which could not be solved within the utilitarian tradition.[25] Marx seizes upon this dilemma in utilitarianism in a passage characteristic of his own development of Hegelian insights:

> Hegel has already proved in his *Phänomenologie* how this theory of mutual exploitation, which Bentham expounded *ad nauseam*, could already at the beginning of the present century have been considered a phase of the previous one. Look at his chapter on "The Struggle of Enlightenment with Superstition," where the theory of usefulness is depicted as the final result of enlightenment. The apparent stupidity of merging all the manifold relationships of people in the *one* relation of usefulness, this apparently metaphysical abstraction arises from the fact that, in modern bourgeois society, all relations are subordinated in practice to the one abstract monetary-commercial relation. This theory came to the fore with Hobbes and Locke, at the same time as the first and second revolutions, those first battles by which the bourgeoisie won political power.[26]

Once the Physiocrats had demonstrated the nature of the economic process as a circular flow, all that remained to complete classical political economy was to give an account of individual attitudes and motivations within that economic framework. This was Bentham's contribution, although, as Marx observes, the theory of utility could not have the generality it claimed because it ignored its own institutional assumptions. For a time, the utilitarian theory of the natural identity of interests had some empirical basis in the facts of the social division of labor and exchange. It was not until Marx adapted Locke's labor theory of value to demonstrate that it contained the working principles of the exploitation of formally free labor that the sociological framework of classical economics was shattered. The point here is that utility is subject to appropriation in the form of capital, which is then able to command the services of others to their disadvantage whatever the circumstances of a formally free contract. Hence the attempt to base the social and political order upon the postulate of the natural identity of interests is broken once and for all.

Marx's labor theory of value expresses both the quantitative and the qualitative features of the laws determining the distribution of productive effort in a commodity-producing society.[27] In its quantitative or economic aspect, the labor theory of value is essentially a general equilibrium theory which summarizes the forces integrating (1) the exchange ratios between commodities, (2) the quantity of each produced, and (3) the allocation of the labor force to the various branches of production. Qualitatively, the labor theory of value expresses the exchange relationships between commodities as a social relationship based upon the historical phenomena of the existence of (1) a developed social division of labor and (2) private production. Marx argues that it is not possible to express the workings of the law of value apart from the specification of a set of sociological middle principles. The procedure in *Capital* is to construct a model of simple commodity production, that is, an economy of independent producers each owning his own means of production. The labor theory of value expresses the general equilibrium conditions for this special case.[28] Marx then varies the institutional features of his model of simple commodity production. The ownership of the means of production is concentrated into the hands of a class of capitalists, and labor itself becomes a commodity subject to the laws of exchange value.

Between them Hegel and Marx developed a thorough critique of the social and political foundations of utilitarian economics. Classical liberalism depended upon the protection of a sphere in which the values of personal integrity, property, and contract could be realized as the expression of market society. But, as Hegel showed in the *Philosophy of Right*, in a society conceived solely as a field for market behavior, economic laws cannot provide the only framework of law, if personality, property, and contract are to be preserved as anything more than instruments of market freedom. The political principles of liberal utilitarianism can only be preserved by a system of civil laws based on the principle of rational understanding which differentiates them from the laws of the market.[29] In other words,

Hegel argues that the utilitarian concept of society based upon economic laws presupposes a rational concept of law, which is the basis of civil society (*bürgerliche Gesellschaft*). The laws of economic society and civil society are in turn distinct from the State, which is the highest stage of the realization of the ethical will.

Marx's critique of the liberal bourgeois concept of the state, society, and individual rights is substantially the same as Hegel's. The difference is that Marx's argument also proceeds in terms of a destructive critique of Hegel's own concept of the state and its bureaucratic rationality which in many ways anticipates Max Weber.[30]

> If power is taken as the basis of right, as Hobbes, etc. do, then right, law, etc. are merely the symptom, the expression of *other* relations upon which State power rests. The material life of individuals which by no means depends merely on their "will," their mode of production and form of intercourse, which mutually determine each other—this is the real basis of the State and remains so at all stages at which division of labour and private property are still necessary, quite independently of the *will* of individuals. These actual relations are in no way created by the state power; on the contrary they are the power creating it. The individuals who rule in these conditions, besides having to constitute their power in the form of the *State*, have to give their will, which is determined by these definite conditions, a universal expression as the will of the State, as law—an expression whose content is always determined by the relations of this class, as the civil and criminal law demonstrates in the clearest way.[31]

Marx's argument concerning the relation between state and society is not primarily a reductionist theory of politics so much as an argument over the nature of society. The utilitarian conception of society, i.e., of civil society (*bürgerliche Gesellschaft*), is characterized by a separation of the state and society which reduces the enforcement of law to the preservation of property and the personal rights in its acquisition and alienation.[32] The utilitarian conception of society enforces a radical dualism between private and public man which is the basis for all other forms of individual and social alienation.

"Political man is only the abstract, artificial individual, the individual as an allegorical, moral person .... All emancipation leads back to the human world, to human relationships, to men themselves. Political emancipation is the reduction of man, on the one side, to the egoistic, independent individual, on the other side to the citizen, to the moral person."[33] Marx's distinction between political and human emancipation turns upon the difference between the utilitarian conception of civil society and Marx's rationalist conception of society whose laws would not appear to the individual as an external constraint simply, not merely as the framework of his own appetites. "Not until the real, individual man is identical with the citizen, and has become a generic being in his empirical life, in his individual work, in his individual relationships, not until man has recognized and organized his own capacities as social capacities so that the social energies are no longer divided by the political power, not until then will human emancipation be achieved."[34] By shifting the emphasis from political to human emancipation Marx's theory of the state goes beyond Hegel's political realism and its conception of personality as the subject of civil rights and economy. In Hegel's view it is only in the context of civil society that man feels he has rights as a person and is insofar prepared to assert his equality. "In [abstract] right, what we had before us was the person; in the sphere of morality, the subject; in the family, the family-member; in civil society as a whole, the burgher or *bourgeois*. Here at the standpoint of needs what we have before us is the composite idea which we call *man*. Thus this is the first time, and indeed properly the only time, to speak of *man* in this sense."[35] Marx argues that Hegel's definition of man as the subject of material needs and rights is a reflection of the spiritual division between man's public and private morality in bourgeois civil society. It is important to understand that Marx did not question the brilliance of Hegel's conception of bourgeois civil society but only his presentation of it as an essential structure of state-society relations.[36]

It is not the recognition of the Durkheimian problem which divides Marx and Durkheim so much as their different responses to it. The critical analysis of utilitarianism undertaken by Hegel, Marx, and Durkheim all pointed to the problem of discovering a basis for the legitimation of the norms which liberal economic freedom presupposed but continuously undermined short of an arbitrary appeal to coercion or the metaphysical postulate of a natural identity of interests. Marx concluded that this contradiction or instability in the utilitarian pattern of means/end rationality was the critical basis for an attack upon it by the social forces working towards the institutionalization of a pattern of substantive rationality, based upon participation and the abolition of private property. Durkheim's vision of the consequences of the instability of the normative pattern of organic solidarity was not different from Marx's, but his response was more like Hegel's divinization of the rational state as the highest realization of ultimate common values. Durkheim's solution has also to be understood, as I have argued throughout, in terms of the theory of knowledge with which he and others opposed the individualistic conception of rationality developed in the classical epistemologies of Locke,

Kant, Mill, and Spencer. Durkheim's critique of utilitarianism involved a reassertion of the sacred origins of truth and social institutions which it had been the task of individualist nominalism, utilitarianism, and secularization progressively to deny. The clincher in Durkheim's argument is his demonstration that modern individualism, so far from creating industrial society, presupposes its differentiation of the sociopsychic space which creates the concepts of personality and autonomy. By the same token, Durkheim was aware that he had not changed the nature of his problem: he had only described its "field." The Durkheimian or Hobbesian problem of the integration of knowledge, moral authority, and personality still remained to be solved under the conditions of organic solidarity. More precisely, Durkheim leaves it unclear whether religion is the idealization of society as it is to be found with both what is good and evil in it or whether religion is the vehicle solely of the idealism which social life may inspire in individuals. Here Marx's views on the relation between religion and social life are too well known to need more than a mention.

I remarked earlier that Parsons dehumanizes the Durkheimian problem by reducing it to a question of the analytic status of the polity and economy rather than taking the problem in the broad sense of the meaning of life in a modern industrial society. Now that is not entirely the case, and I should now consider how Parsons in fact treats the larger question. Parsons also discusses the Durkheimian problem as a problem of the structural location of the motivational aspects of social commitment. A modern industrial economy can only function provided "A positive obligation to enter into the general allocative system"[37] is institutionalized in the existence of a market, money, and mobile, alienable factors of production, including labor. "The division of labor brings freedom from ascriptive ties regarding the utilization of consumable goods and services and the factors of production themselves. The structural location of organic solidarity thus concerns the dual problem of how the processes by which the potentially conflicting interests that have been generated can be reconciled without disruptive conflict (this leads, of course, into the Hobbesian problem), and of how the societal interest in efficient production can be protected and promoted."[38]

The commitment to the "generalization" of resources and factors of production through their release from ascriptive and kinship ties is a commitment to the values of technical effectiveness and legal-rationality which rests upon nonrational values. In the context of a modern industrial economy based upon technological and legal rationality the Hobbesian problem becomes a cybernetic problem of the interchange of generalized symbolic media of money and value-commitments.[39] The task of the polity is to translate the generalized commitment which it receives from the value-system into "effectiveness," i.e., collective action in the public interest. The "factor" interchange between the polity and the value-system raises the question of the nature of the ultimate legitimacy principles, that is to say, not just their congruent or conflicting tendencies but also the relations between the component of rational and nonrational values which determines political commitment or alienation. The problem of the ultimate legitimacy of the social and political order is a question of meaningful values which is broader than the pattern-variable subordination of expressive values to technical-rational organization.

Parsons is well aware that Durkheim's argument is that *anomie* is not the experience of an alien institutional order. It is a problem of the meaningfulness of the actor's goals and situational chances which under conditions of institutionalized scarcity leads to nonnormative but subjectively meaningful responses of revolt, ritualization, and alienation. From Hobbes to Durkheim the problem of order and solidarity has not changed except for the escalation-effect of the shift to civil society, under the conditions of the capitalist property system, upon the psychology of individual wants and desires. As the nineteenth century wore on, the attack on economic rationalism from the standpoint of its consequences for social solidarity was joined by romantic conservatives, utopian socialists, Marxists, and even Fascists. It is also the background of Freud's work in social and political anthropology.

In *Group Psychology and the Analysis of the Ego*, Freud adumbrated the distinction between two archetypes of social psychology: the individual psychology which in the primal horde belonged to the father alone, and the group psychology of the sons, or brothers. Fatherhood and brotherhood are the archetypes brooding in the background of such sociological abstractions as Durkheim's mechanical and organic solidarity, or Gierke's *Herrschaft* and *Genossenschaft*, the imperial and fraternal principles, which dialectically combine to weave the changing fabric of Western social corporate bodies. It is the specific gift of psychoanalysis to see behind these sociological abstractions the human face; and their name is "fatherhood and brotherhood."[40]

Regarded in this way, the principle of the identity of interests must be seen as furnishing a counternorm of substantive rationality variously grounded in the family, fraternity, class, or utopian community, depending upon the context chosen for the abolition of property and the subordination of sentimental to technical rationality.

These are ideological thickets which Parsons is

always anxious to avoid. Yet he chooses an extremely vulnerable strategy in his attempt to "generalize" the problems involved. As Parsons sees it, the "fashionable" concern with alienation and the problem of identity is a problem of locating oneself in the social system. This problem has cognitive and affective dimensions which it is the task of the theory of social control or commitment to understand. I do not wish to quarrel with Parsons' account of identity as a precipitate of subsystem social interaction processes linked with codes of generalization at the social system level. In this he has made a significant theoretical integration of Durkheim and Freud. But at the same time he has sacrificed the founders' concern with the problems of instability, conflict, and alienation involved in these processes. Parsons regards instability as a "reasonable" feature of the modern social system and its model personality type. He classifies critical responses to its risks in terms of two types of "irrational" responses (1) a security "demand" which minimizes risk at the expense of creativity, and (2) a "utopian" orientation which ignores the constraints on creative success for the sake of blind commitment.[41]

In essence, this represents the Mertonian version of Durkheim's conception of anomie. Durkheim's argument, unlike that of Merton and Parsons, does not leave unquestioned the nature of the ultimate values of the society which result in a range of anomic responses on the part of the individuals. His point is precisely that it is because individuals are committed to the norm of institutionalized discontent as well as to norms of equality and justice that there exists an endemic strain towards social disorganization and class struggle. "Just as ancient peoples needed, above all, a common faith to live by, so we need justice, and we can be sure that this need will become ever more exacting if, as every fact presages, the conditions dominating social evolution remain the same."[42]

Parsons is quite aware that the value-system, like other media, is subject to hot and cold alternations, or, as he prefers, to the inflation and deflation of commitments.[43] Thus the norm of institutionalized discontent is the source of an inflationary tendency in the value-system of the capitalist social order (complex society) which attempts to cool itself through a variety of deflationary commitments ranging from fundamentalism to socialism and yippie love cults. The "liquidity" problem of the modern value system arises not only because of its own tendency to undermine depositor's trust but because moral innovators threaten to cause "runs" on its "commitment banking" system. These are basically neo-Keynesian metaphors which reflect the way in which Parsons responds to the moral challenge that faces the American social and economic order. Their effect is to lose the sense of squalor that infects, for example, Galbraith's concerns for the quality as well as the "effectiveness" of affluence. A proper discussion of this context of the Hobbesian problem would require an analysis of the way in which the relative disposition of the public and private sectors of the capitalist economy shapes the contours of the generalized pattern of social values, and leaves life "nasty, brutish and short" even today in America's own cities and countryside, not to speak of her colonies.[44] It might then be possible to relate these structural features of the social and economic order to the levels of surplus repression and repressive desublimation through which the "commitment banking" system seeks to control the psychic economy of its card-carrying creditors. We need only refer to Marcuse's development of the Marxian and Freudian interpretations of the mechanism of civilized discontents.

This aside, it might be observed that once again Parsons' attempt to achieve generality through high levels of abstraction results only in a sublimation of the problem, in this case by means of a money metaphor which enables him to speak in apparently value-free terms about the phenomena of value conflict, moral innovation and alienation. Alternatively, in the face of these questions Parsons settles his analytical conscience by passing the torch to the "theory of cultural systems," inasmuch as shifts in value patterns fall to the anthropologist's care. This move, as well as Parsons' return to the use of economic conceptualizations of the problem of order and legitimacy, seems to me to contradict his own sense of the autonomy of sociological abstraction in favor of his old desire for a general theory of action.[45] Here I think Weber is a better guide. What we can understand from Weber is that the *sociological ethic* requires of us the study of the problems of power and authority without any hope for a "scientific" politics beyond what reasonable men may hope for in the conflict of values.[46]

RATIONALITY AND MEANING: MARX AND THE WEBERIAN PROBLEM

At several points in the discussion we have suggested that the problem of order has to be seen in the context of the nature of Western rationality and its tendency to destroy the nonrational foundations upon which it rests. Thus Hobbes's science of politics divorces itself from commonsense opinion, which is the traditional fabric of political experience. Hobbes's nominalist precision only introduces order into opinion by veiling its own inability to deal with the problem of recognition and mutuality in the doctrine or fiat of an ultimately divine sovereignty. The tendency of scientistic rationality to undermine the nonrational bases of trust and recognition is the focus of what Parsons calls the Durkheimian and Weberian problems. Parsons, however, frames the problem solely in terms of the analytic differentiation of the normative and institutional conditions of social action. I have argued that in this way Parsons gives us rather special readings of Durkheim, Marx, and, as I believe, of Weber's conception of rationality. Indeed, Parsons' viewpoint by and large misses the subjective context in which the Hobbesian problem of order arises.

Classical utilitarian thought from the time of Hobbes, through Locke, Marx, and Durkheim, cannot be understood apart from the sense of constitutional, class and industrial crises in which the doctrine of the natural identity of interests, however logically objectionable, provided a metaphysical prop without which the drama of modern individualism and market rationality might not have been staged. As the framework of market society, class, and property gradually evolved, the shift from the sentimental ties of kinship to the rational social division of labor figures as the articulation of modern self-consciousness.

The problem of order is an historical as well as a sociological problem. It is the problem of the origins and teleology of civilization. It is important not to overlook that this is the way the question of order appeared to Marx, Durkheim, and Weber and, of course, to Freud. The other line through which this question comes into modern consciousness is Nietzsche, Dilthey, Burckhardt, and Husserl.[47] In this aspect the problem of order is the riddle of history, namely, the problem of man's estrangement through civilization lay in the need to set restraints to the infinitude of wants. Durkheim attempted to draw a distinction between individuality and personality in order to cope with the ways in which society at once aggravates and ennobles individual aspirations. Moreover, Durkheim was aware that these problems were wider than the limits of law and the bonds of solidarity. He sensed that they had their origins in the ambivalence of modern knowledge, including perhaps sociology, despite his hopes of it as a social remedy.[48] Marx argued that the forces which divide man against himself derive from the class division of property which is prior to the problems of specialization and division of labor. But the deep question is what is the meaning of the surplus repression or value set upon value-accumulation which provides the driving force, the glory, and the misery of modern civilization.

I have tried earlier in this essay to sketch the history of Western knowledge and its affinity for power.

Admittedly, this is a rough sketch and lacks an adequate consideration of the theological, political, and historical-psychoanalytic features of the problem.[49] Since not everything can be attempted at once, I shall have to confine myself to expanding the earlier discussion in terms of a treatment of the ascetic bases of modern rationalism first brought to attention by Weber, but also, as I shall show, a feature of Marx's understanding of the problem.

The understanding of Western rationality demands a structural analysis of the dialectic between man's fundamental historical and social nature and the alternations of freedom and determinism. It is necessary to start from the institutional matrix in which specific norms of action shaped and were in turn shaped by a particular conception of human nature. With the rise of capitalism man's rational nature was increasingly understood in terms of an instrumental orientation toward the domination of physical nature. At the same time, this instrumental orientation toward nature involved an expressive as well as cognitive reorientation toward the perception of self, society, and the elements of nature. The essence of this shift is grasped by Hegel and Marx in their conception of human freedom as "man making himself." Between Hegel's *Phenomenology of Mind* and Marx's *Communist Manifesto* the "world" has become the immanent term of human thought and activity which sustains the alternation of freedom and determinism. The significance of Marx's critique of the ideological relations of philosophical thought is to bring human ideas into a permanently efficacious present, shaped by and giving shape to the processes through which a society endures and changes. Thus the weight of the past, articulated in the social division of labor and the ideological superstructure of past religions and philosophies, is not just the residue of historicism or relativism. It is the phenomenological reality of truth as the product of social life and the creation of *homo faber*.[50]

With the benefit of Hegel, Marx grasped the internal logic of knowledge and action in modern society. Furthermore, with the advantage of a more detailed knowledge of the nature of capitalist institutions, Marx was able to show that the logical connection between man's technological domination of nature and the complete integration of man's individual and social experience lay outside of the conception of utilitarian rationality. Marx's analysis of capitalist society is directed primarily at the connections between social norms and economic systems. Marx, no less than Weber, makes very clear the ascetic basis of capitalist rationality and its conditioned motivation to the accumulation of value. Parsons, however, holds to the criticism that Marx failed to go beyond the utilitarian assumption of the given-ness of wants and their essentially materialistic bias. "The crucial point is that Weber's analysis, the core of which is the Protestant ethic thesis, bridged the theoretical gap between 'want' in the economic-psychological sense and 'cultural patterns' in the idealistic senses. To put it simply and radically, Weber's solution was that, once cultural patterns of meaning have been internalized in the personality of an individual, they define the situation for the structuring of motives."[51]

In drawing attention to Marx's argument my intention is not simply to question whether Marx understood the Weberian problem. It is ultimately to argue with Parsons' view of the orientation toward increasing rationality,[52] which I think overlooks Weber's own questions about the meaning of rationality and the concern with alienation which brings him closer to Marx.[53] In a remarkable passage from the *Economic and Philosophical Manuscripts*, Marx explains how political economy develops against the background of the alienation of labor and property from their anchorages in use-values. The emancipation of labor is the precondition of the substitution of exchange values for use-values which leads to the subordination of all fixed forms of life and property to the accumulation and expansion of wealth. In their endlessly reproducible forms, as the prices of capital and labor-power, private property and labor alienate human needs in favor of market wants. Marx concludes that modern individualism acquires its impulse through the subjectivisation of the bases of feudal community which simultaneously supplies the motivational orientation toward market behavior. The Physiocrats identified all wealth with land and cultivation, leaving feudal property intact but shifting the essential definition of land to its economic function and thereby exposing feudal property to the later attacks on ground-rent. The objective nature of wealth was also in part shifted to its subjective basis in labor, inasmuch as agriculture was regarded as the source of the productivity of land. Finally, industrial labor emerged as the most general principle of productivity, the factors of production, land, labor and capital, being nothing else than moments in the dialectic of labor's self-alienation.

Thus, from the viewpoint of this enlightened political economy which has discovered the *subjective* essence of wealth within the framework of private property, the partisans of the monetary system and the mercantilist system, who consider private property as a *purely objective* being for man, are *fetishists* and *Catholics*. Engels is right, therefore, in calling Adam Smith the *Luther of political economy*. Just as Luther recognized religion and *faith* as the essence of the real *world*, and for that reason took up a position against Catholic paganism; just as he annulled *external* religiosity while making religiosity the *inner* essence of man; just as he negated the distinction between priest and layman because he transferred the priest into the heart of the layman; so wealth external to man and independent of him (and thus only to be acquired and conserved from outside) is annulled. That is to say, its *external* and *mindless* objectivity is annulled by the fact that private property is incorporated in man himself, and man himself is recognized as its essence. But as a result, man himself is brought into the sphere of private property, just as, with Luther, he is brought into the sphere of religion. Under the guise of recognizing man, political economy, whose principle is labour, carries to its logical conclusion the denial of man. Man himself is no longer in a condition of external tension with the external substance of private property; he has himself become the tension-ridden being of private property. What was previously a phenomenon of *being external to oneself*, a real external manifestation of man, has now become the act of objectification, of alienation. This political economy seems at first, therefore, to recognize man with his independence, his personal activity, etc. It incorporates private property in the very essence of man, and it is no longer, therefore, conditioned by the local or national *characteristics of private property* regarded as existing outside itself. It manifests a cosmopolitan, universal activity which is destructive of every limit and every bond, and substitutes itself as the *only* policy, the *only* universality, the *only* limit and the *only* bond.[54]

Marx and Weber raised a common question. They asked what is the human value of a specific mode of social organization, namely capitalism: what is its *raison d'être*; what is the sense in its universality. Admittedly, Weber may have gone further in the comparative study of the conditions of the emergence of the normative and institutional bases of capitalism. But each took the same view with regard to the major task of understanding the historically unique phenomenon of the rational domination of nature and the accumulation of values in the determination of conduct or action in capitalist society. We need to understand the "vocation" of Western science and rationality. Modern science is chained to progress through invention and discovery. Every scientific finding asks to be surpassed in the light of accumulated knowledge. Each scientist resigns himself to making only a partial and fleeting contribution to a task that is conceived as limitless. "And with this we come to inquire into the meaning of science. For, after all, it is not self-evident that something subordinate to such a law is sensible and meaningful in itself. Why does one engage in doing something that in reality never comes, and never can come to an end?"[55]

Weber compares the question of the meaning of science which he himself raises to Tolstoi's question about the meaning of death in modern civilization.[56] Civilized man has broken with nature. Cultural values have replaced use-values and the cycle of life familiar to the peasant and feudal lord has exploded into a self-infinitizing progression in the accumulation of cultural values. The peasant could encounter the totality of meaning ordained for him in the feudal order and die at peace with his station in life because his daily life was congruent with the whole of his life. But modern man, in virtue of being pitted against an ever-expanding universe of ideas, problems, and values, though he can be weary of life always encounters death as meaningless; for death robs him of infinity. "And because death is meaningless, civilized life as such is meaningless; by its very 'progressiveness' it gives death the imprint of meaninglessness."[57] For want of a science of ends which might illuminate the ideal of Western rationality and its affinity for power and accumulation Weber turned to the notions of the "calling" and the "ethic of responsibility." It is implicit in the Weberian use of the ideal-type method that the growth of rationality in science, politics, and economics is only a meaningful way of representing Western experience so long as we choose to understand it *in its own terms* (*verstehen*). But as soon as we consider Western rationality from the standpoint of comparative history it loses its self-evidence. That is to say, the increasing rationality of modern technology and of the sciences developed on the model of functional rationality remains a self-styled enigma. For this reason Weber's pessimism is surely no worse than Parsons' optimistic generalization of the "law of increasing rationality."[58]

Although Parsons is aware that Weber's conception of the process of rationality involved judgments about its substantive meaningfulness and its potential for alienation, he nevertheless relegates these considerations to factors which affect merely the *rate* of the process of rationalization but hardly its direction. Again, Parsons presumes that the question of the value relevance (*Wertbeziehung*) of rationality is merely a question about the integrative function of the cultural norm of functional rationality with respect to the adaptive subsystems of empirical knowledge and thus raises no other questions outside those of the "strains" in the institutionalization and differentiation of the sciences.[59]

The pattern of rationality (the subordination of particularistic-ascriptive values to the values of universalism and achievement) characterizes the major institutions, businesses, schools, factories, and hospitals of modern society. Weber reminds us that rationality becomes an "iron cage" as soon as it segregates itself from nonrational values and behavior. Weber had a sense of the volatile and vital forces of history which make it possible for the human spirit to go underground or to come out of the desert, the jungle, or the mountains to wage war in the arid lands of bureaucracy and rationality. "No one knows who will live in this cage in the future, or whether at the end of this tremendous development entirely new prophets will arise, or there will be a great rebirth of old ideas and ideals, or, if neither, mechanized petrification, embellished with a sort of convulsive importance. For of the last stage of this cultural development, it might well be truly said: 'Specialists without spirit, sensualists without heart; this nullity imagines that it has attained a level of civilization never before attained.'"[60] Whether because of its own electric technology or to the inherent primitivism of Left pot and politics, the urban industrial landscape is now ablaze with tribal costumes, wigs, dance, and music. Weber's prophets have forsaken the cage, and the birds of paradise are on the wing in New York City, Chicago, Los Angeles, Liverpool — and in Canada they flock in strawberry fields.

The confrontation of reason with its own non-rational sources is a necessary exercise which forces upon us the justification of the limits of reason and nonreason which brings the artist to the edge of his own sanity and sets the scientist on the margins of his own culture. The Hobbesian problem demands nothing less. In Marx, Durkheim, and Weber sociology has been fortunate in the rare combination of a poetic and scientific sense of the limits of the reality we inhabit. Today the Hobbesian problem is as much as ever a motive to creative sociologies of action, talk, death, revolt, accommodation, and numerous other parcticalities. Meantime Parsons' structural-functionalism strains to accommodate conflict, change, and more radical empiricism. Yet there are few who would want to forsake the theoretical legacy which Parsons has preserved and consolidated for sociology. There is enough of the artist in Parsons that he had to shape the sociological tradition in his own style, with magnificent insights here and blindnesses there — but never without vision. Nowadays it is said that Parsons has no followers. That is a conceit of critics.

NOTES

1. By "sentimental tradition" I refer to the concern with the relation between the rational and sentimental bases of social order raised by the market reorientation of motivation, for example, in Adam Smith's *Theory of Moral Sentiments*, as well as the political contractarian interpretation of motives, for example, in Edmund Burke's *Reflections on the French Revolution*. McLuhan and Goffman extrapolate these concerns into the cool media of bureaucracy, electric technology, and their motory and sensorial codes.

2. Max Black (ed.), *The Social Theories of Talcott Parsons* (Englewood Cliffs: Prentice-Hall, Inc., 1961).

3. *Sociological Theory and Modern Society* (New York: The Free Press, 1967), pp. 117-118. For the statement of the reasons why Parsons regards Marx and Tocqueville as outsiders with respect to the core development of sociological theory see his Introduction to the paperback edition, *The Structure of Social Action*, Vol. I (New York: The Free Press, 1968, first

published by McGraw-Hill, New York, 1937).

4. Edmund Husserl, "Philosophy and the Crisis of European Man," in *Phenomenology and the Crisis of Philosophy*, translated with notes and an introduction by Quentin Lauer (New York: Harper Torchbooks, 1965). For an approach to the problem of rationality in terms of a constitutive phenomenology of routine social structures, see Alfred Schutz, "The Problem of Rationality in the Social World," *Collected Papers II: Studies in Social Theory*, ed. Arvid Broderson (The Hague: Martinus Nijhoff, 1964); and the contributions to a social phenomenology of practical reasoning in Harold Garfinkel, *Studies in Ethnomethodology* (Englewood Cliffs: Prentice-Hall, 1967); as well as Alan F. Blum, "The Corpus of Knowledge as a Normative Order: Intellectual Critiques of the Social Order of Knowledge and the Commonsense Features of Bodies of Knowledge," *Theoretical Sociology, Perspectives and Developments*, John C. McKinney and Edward A. Tiryakian (eds.) (New York: Appleton-Century-Crofts, 1970), pp. 319-336.

5. Karl Mannheim, *Man and Society in an Age of Reconstruction* (London: Routledge and Kegan Paul Limited, 1966). p. 58.

6. For a discussion of the Marxian position, as I understand it, on the issues of holism and individualism, see John O'Neill, "The Concept of Estrangement in the Early and Late Writings of Karl Marx", *Philosophy and Phenomenological Research*, XXV (September 1964), pp. 64-84.

7. *The Gay Science:* Book V, *The Portable Nietzsche*, selected and translated, with an introduction, prefaces and notes by Walter Kaufmann (New York: The Viking Press, 1954), pp. 449-450.

8. Parsons, *The Structure of Social Action*, Chap. II.

9. John Finley Scott, "The Changing Foundations of the Parsonian Action Scheme," *American Sociological Review,* 28 (October 1963), pp. 716-735.

10. Edward A. Tiryakian, "Existential Phenomenology and the Sociological Tradition," *American Sociological Review*, 30 (October 1965), p. 684.

11. Harold Kaplan, "The Parsonian Image of Social Structure and its Relevance for Political Science," *The Journal of Politics*, 30 (October 1965), p. 684.

12. Otto Von Gierke, *The Development of Political Theory,* Bernard Freyd (tr.) (New York: Howard Fertig, 1966).

13. The tendency to deduce normative propositions from factual propositions is not just an instance of the naturalistic fallacy, as might be argued nowadays. It can be understood in the light of certain sociological preconceptions assumed in Hobbes's analysis. C. B. Macpherson, *The Political Theory of Possessive Individualism, Hobbes to Locke* (Oxford: Clarendon Press, 1962).

14. Michael Oakeshott, Introduction to *Leviathan* (Oxford: Basil Blackwell, 1946).

15. Quoted by Erich Hula in his Comment on Hans Jonas, "The Practical Uses of Theory," in Maurice Natanson (ed.), *Philosophy of the Social Sciences: A Reader* (New York: Random House, 1963), p. 151.

16. *Leviathan*, Part I, Ch. 11, p. 68.

17. Sheldon S. Wolin, *Politics and Vision* (Boston: Little, Brown and Company, 1960), p. 261.

18. *The Structure of Social Action*, p. 102.

19. For an exhaustive documentation of Marx's views on the relation between the state, law and economy, which should make it quite clear that Marx's position is not reductionist see, Stanley W. Moore, *The Critique of Capitalist Democracy* (New York: Paine-Whitman Publishers, 1957).

20. *Sociological Theory and Modern Society*, p. 115.

21. "If it is nevertheless said that the economic and the legal order are intimately related to one another, the latter is understood, not in the legal, but in the sociological sense, i.e., as being *empirically* valid. In this context 'legal order' thus assumes a totally different meaning. It refers, not to a set of norms of logically demonstrable correctness, but rather

to a complex of actual determinants (*Bestimmungsgrunde*) of actual human conduct." *Max Weber on Law in Economy and Society*, Max Rheinstein and Edward Shils (trs.) (Cambridge: Harvard University Press, 1966), p. 12.

22. For an attempt to relate the principle of authority to the substantive values of the organic, sensible, and libidinal levels of the polity, see John O'Neill, "Authority, Knowledge and the Body-Politic", *Southern Journal of Philosophy*, VIII (Summer and Fall, 1970), pp. 255-264.

23. John Horton, "The Dehumanization of Anomie and Alienation: A Problem in the Ideology of Sociology", *The British Journal of Sociology*, XV (December 1964), pp. 283-300.

24. Jean Hyppolite, *Studies on Marx and Hegel*, translated with an introduction, notes, and bibliography by John O'Neill (New York: Basic Books, Inc., 1969).

25. "As everything is useful for man, man is likewise useful too, and his characteristic function consists in making himself a member of the human herd, of use for the common good, and serviceable to all. The extent to which he looks after his own interests is the measure with which he must also serve the purposes of others, and so far as he serves their turn, he is taking care of himself: the one hand washes the other. But wherever he finds himself there he is in his right place: he makes use of others and is himself made use of." G. W. F. Hegel, *The Phenomenology of Mind*, translated with an introduction and notes by Sir James Baillie (London: George Allen and Unwin, 1910), pp. 579-580.

26. Karl Marx and Friedrich Engels, *The German Ideology* (Moscow: Progress Publishers, 1964), pp. 448-449.

27. P. M. Sweezy, *The Theory of Capitalist Development* (New York: Monthly Review Press, 1956), Chaps. II and III; K. Marx, *Capital* (Chicago: C.H. Kerr, 1906), Vol. III, Chap. II.

28. O. Lange, "Marxian Economics and Modern Economic Theory," *Review of Economic Studies*, II (1934-35), pp. 189-201.

29. Hegel's *Philosophy of Right*, translated with notes by T. M. Knox, (Oxford: Clarendon Press, 1942), Third Part, Sub-Section 2.

30. Henri Lefebvre, *The Sociology of Marx*, Norbert Guterman (tr.) (New York: Pantheon Books, 1968), Ch. 5.

31. *The German Ideology*, p. 357.

32. Mitchell Franklin, "On Hegel's Theory of Alienation and Its Historic Force," *Tulane Studies in Philosophy*, IX (1960), pp. 50-100.

33. Henri Lefebvre, *op. cit.*, p. 133.

34. *Ibid.*

35. Hegel, *Philosophy of Right*, para. 190.

36. For the problems underlying Marx's final aesthetic or ethical conception of the relations between men in society, see Eugene Kamenka, *The Ethical Foundations of Marxism* (New York: Frederick A. Praeger, 1962), Pt. I, 4 and Part III, 2.

37. "Durkheim's Contribution to the Theory of Integration of Social Systems," *Sociological Theory and Modern Society*, p. 16.

38. *Ibid.*, pp. 14-15.

39. Talcott Parsons, *Politics and Social Structure* (New York: The Free Press, 1969), Chapter 16, "On the Concept of Value-Commitments".

40. Norman O. Brown, *Love's Body* (New York: Random House, 1966), p. 9.

41. Talcott Parsons, "The Problem of Identity in the General Theory of Action," *The Self in Social Interaction*, Chad Gordon and Kenneth J. Gergen (eds.) (New York: John Wiley and Sons, Inc., 1968), pp. 11-23.

42. *The Division of Labor in Society* (New York: The Free Press, 1949), p. 388.

43. *Politics and Social Structure*, pp. 463-467.

44. John O'Neill, "Public and Private Space," *Agenda* 1970: *Proposals for a Creative Politics*, T. Lloyd and J. McLeod (eds.), (University of Toronto Press, 1968), pp. 74-93; Paul A. Baran

and Paul M. Sweezy, *Monopoly Capital* (New York and London: Monthly Review Press, 1966).

45. "Problems of order, as distinguished from those of the categories of 'interests' that define the primary subject-matter of economics and political science, thus constitute the core of sociological concern; normative order also forms the basis of sociology's intimate interdependence with the theory of cultural systems." Talcott Parsons, "Max Weber 1864-1964," *American Sociological Review*, 30 (April 1965), p. 174.

46. Guenther Roth, "Political Critiques of Max Weber," *American Sociological Review*, 30 (April 1965), pp. 213-223; but especially Maurice Merleau-Ponty's essay on Weber's ethic, "The Crisis of the Understanding," *The Primacy of Perception*, James M. Edie (ed.) (Evanston: Northwestern University Press, 1964).

47. Reinhard Bendix, "Max Weber and Jacob Burckhardt," *American Sociological Review*, 30 (April 1965), pp. 176-184.

48. Reinhard Bendix, "The Age of Ideology: Persistent and Changing," *Ideology and Discontent*, David E. Apter (ed.) (New York: The Free Press of Glencoe, 1966), Ch. viii.

49. *The Protestant Ethic and Modernization*, S. N. Eisenstadt (ed.) (New York: Basic Books, 1968), provides considerable historical and comparative materials but makes no mention of the psychoanalytic interpretations in Herbert Marcuse, *Eros and Civilization* (Boston: Beacon Press, 1955); Norman O. Brown, *Life Against Death* (New York: Vintage Books, 1959).

50. Hannah Arendt, *The Human Condition* (Chicago: University of Chicago Press, 1958); Kurt H. Wolff, "On the Significance of Hannah Arendt's *The Human Condition* for Sociology," *Inquiry*, 4 (Summer 1951), pp. 67-106.

51. *Sociological Theory and Modern Society*, p. 184.

52. *The Structure of Social Action*, p. 752.

53. Strictly speaking, Parsons does note these concerns of Weber, as in the following passage, but in my opinion he has not drawn upon them in the same way that he developed the analytical and comparative aspects of Weber's work. "Weber takes the fundamental position that, *regardless of the particular content of the normative order*, a major element of discrepancy is inevitable. And the more highly rationalized an order, the greater the tension, the greater the exposure of major elements of a population to experiences which are frustrating in the very specific sense, not merely in the sense that things happen and contravene their 'interests', but that things happen which are 'meaningless' in the sense that they *ought* not to happen." Max Weber, *The Sociology of Religion*, trans. by Ephraim Fischoff, Introduction by Talcott Parsons (Boston: Beacon Press, 1963), p. xlvii. But see the Review Article of this work by Benjamin Nelson, *American Sociological Review*, 30 (August 1965), pp. 595-599.

54. Karl Marx, *Early Writings*, Translated and edited by T. B. Bottomore (London: C. A. Watts and Company, Limited, 1963), pp. 147-148.

55. "Science as a Vocation," *From Max Weber: Essays in Sociology*, translated, edited, and with an introduction by H. Gerth and C. Wright Mills (New York: Oxford University Press, 1958), p. 138.

56. Leo Tolstoi, *The Death of Ivan Ilyich* (Letchworth, Herts.: Bradda Books Ltd., 1966); Barney G. Glaser and Anselm L. Strauss, *Time for Dying* (Chicago: Aldine Publishing Company, 1968); David Sudnow, *Passing On* (Englewood Cliffs: Prentice-Hall, 1967).

57. *From Max Weber*, p. 140.

58. *The Structure of Social Action*, p. 752.

59. "An Approach to the Sociology of Knowledge," in *Sociological Theory and Modern Society*, pp. 139-165.

60. Max Weber, *The Protestant Ethic and the Spirit of Capitalism*, trans. by Talcott Parsons (New York: Charles Scribner's Sons, 1958), p. 182.

III

SOCIALIZATION

INTRODUCTION

Victor Meyer Lidz

The term socialization is generally understood in the social sciences to refer to the processes whereby individual personalities gain essential preparation for their subsequent performances in social interaction. The topic is a theoretically difficult one in large part because it requires treatment of articulations between at least two distinct orders of system, personality and social systems. Moreover, any general treatment of socialization must delve into an area that, within contemporary Western culture, is fraught with ideological sensitivities. At least implicitly, it must deal with the questions of the interdependence of "individual" and "society": How independent is the individual of his social matrix? To what degree is he, in his individuality, something more than just the agent of his society? Does society, with its constraints, stifle the creativity of the individual? Do we demean the individual, existentially, in highlighting the extent to which he is the creature of his society? It seems that there is much potential for inner conflict when the sociologist, as analyst of social systems and their effects, must take up the topic of socialization within the context of our strongly individualistic culture.

The conditions under which socialization has been addressed within the theory of action seem perhaps to amplify these potentials for tension. Before taking up that topic Parsons had committed his theoretical position to giving the highest theoretical priority to analysis of the "causes" of social order.[1] Inevitably, the matter of socialization was taken up in part as an effort to analyze with greater refinement the question of how social order is continually produced, or, better, reproduced.[2] Given the earlier analysis of the voluntaristic generation of social order, the interest in socialization was perhaps bound to gravitate toward a concentration upon the processes by which commitments to the general values and norms of society are instilled within the individual. Unless

he could develop a convincing analysis of how social actors come to be characterized by broadly "socialized" patterns of commitment to the normative orders of their societies, Parsons would have been confronted with a very serious theoretical impasse.

Certain critics, noting Parsons' apparent concern to avoid this impasse, have charged that his most general theoretical predilections required him to develop what has been called an oversocialized model of the social actor.[3] This is a charge worthy of careful evaluation, for it touches directly upon the question of what kind of analysis of processes of socialization can be integrated into a general theory of action or human conduct. Moreover, we can be certain that an "oversocialized" account of the actor will be inadequate to deal with the facts of the relations between man and his society in so individualistic a setting as American society.[4]

During the period in which he concentrated most heavily upon problems of socialization, Parsons also developed a profound involvement with psychoanalysis. Certain of his key essays[5] must be regarded as deeply bound up with issues in the psychoanalytic literature, perhaps as deeply as with the sociological treatments of socialization. In this respect, his essay on "The Superego and the Theory of Social Systems," with its effort to integrate the theories of Freud and Durkheim, may be taken as symbolic of his entire treatment of socialization.[6] Its intent is to demonstrate that there need be no inconsistency between a treatment of the requirements of social integration and order, on the one hand, and concern with the individuality and autonomy of the personality, on the other hand.

While arguing that there is a fundamental correspondence between the notions of the institutionalized collective conscience and of the internalized superego, and thus that there are systematic societal sources of the superegos of individuals, Parsons does not deny the dynamic autonomy of the intrapersonal superego from social system processes. The superego is understood to be an individualized version of the moral culture of the society, one which will in many respects reflect the unique conditions of the socialization of the individual personality and which will express the unique moral outlooks of the individual. Indeed, a superego could not provide effective detailed moral regulation of the motivation and conduct of the individual personality unless it were in many respects adapted realistically to the specific characteristics of the individual. Moreover, Parsons follows psychoanalytic treatments rather closely in describing the dynamic nature of the superego's control over other sectors of the personality system. Such control operates principally through the mechanism of repression, which rests upon a respect for and fear of internalized representations of parental authority. This account of the superego's basic effectiveness focuses, even more sharply than the account of its normative content, upon intrapersonal factors which may be expected to vary quite substantially among individuals in a society differentiated by religion, class, region, ethnicity, style of life, and so on. Thus, the theoretical linkage which Parsons has developed between the superego and the normative institutions of society should not be interpreted as a reduction of the superego to social system conditions or characteristics.[7]

Yet, the linkage between superego and normative order has provided the main focus for the theory of action discussions of the aggregate, macroscopic interpenetration between personality and social systems. The subsystems of the personality other than the superego have generally been treated as still more fully independent of structural features of the social system than the superego. To be sure, Parsons has tended to treat even the id as having a somewhat socialized aspect: presumably, an attachment to modes of action or features of social relationships that have proven satisfying in the past does not develop easily when confronted by severe social sanctions.[8] The ego functions importantly to enable the individual to pursue interests and attain gratifications within social situations and often in cooperative relations with others. In most individuals, the identity or ego-ideal subsystem is comprised of complexes of aspirations and personal ideals that are positively valued within the encompassing sociocultural environment. However, for each of these subsystems of the personality, the socialized dimension of their functioning operates within a manifold of other, more deeply personal factors. The id functions to assure that the individual's action will be motivated in ways that, given the structural dispositions of the personality, will prove gratifying. The ego operates to organize the emotional structures of the personality into dispositions that are susceptible to effective discharge or satisfaction under the given circumstances of action. The identity system acts to synthesize an enduring emotional sense of the self in ideal terms, setting the stable parameters of valued dispositions for the entire personality.[9]

In these respects, as well as in regard to the superego's actual exercise of dynamic normative control over motivation and conduct, Parsons follows psychoanalytic theory closely in emphasizing the importance of emotional structures and intrapersonal dynamics. Consequently, the concrete processes of social action are treated as in very large part not directly "socialized," but the product of such factors as the "mechanisms of defense" with their intensely personal modes of operation. To be sure, the incorporation of the socially institutionalized normative order within the structures of the personalities of members of the social system is treated as a crucial requisite of the stability of a system of social action. However, many independent factors are regarded as intervening between the "socialized" normative structuring of personalities and the modes of practical conduct adopted by individuals under given conditions of action. The incorporation of so much of psychoanalytic theory, with its individualistic concerns and emphases upon the unconscious, fantasy and private symbolism, and the mechanisms of defense, would seem to protect the theory of action from an "oversocialized" conception of the actor in any general and gross sense, to say the least.

A second factor affecting the degree to which the theory of action has been protected from "oversocialized" conceptions of the actor concerns certain elements in Parsons' understanding of modern American society, which has been the predominant empirical focus of his analyses of socialization. Two interrelated characteristics of American society have sensitized him to the importance of avoiding sweeping generalizations about the extent to which individual members of a society will be uniformly socialized to a common normative order. First, American society has been integrated in a highly organic and pluralistic fashion. Socialization toward capacities to make valued contributions to the functioning of American society must involve the generation of strong commitments to specialized lines of activity and to regional, ethnic, religious, status-related, and occupational variants of the normative order, as well as to a more general common framework.[10] Second, as American society has, precisely in its moral culture, placed much emphasis upon individualism, its members are often socialized with considerable strength of feeling to the conviction that they should exercize individual responsibility on matters of the normative bases of social action. The normative order, then, tends not to be accepted in a passive manner but to be subjected to active efforts to develop conscientious improvements. Individuals are apt to put forward and defend their own formulations concerning elements of the normative order that impinge importantly upon their own life circumstances. Thus, the very processes of socialization to the normatively engendered pattern of individualism are apt to produce a certain conscientious autonomy of individuals from particular terms of the normative order. In this situation, we may note, the "oversocialized" actor is apt to appear to be a compulsive individualist who tends to reject all normative regulation to which he cannot give his own personal rational consent.

The foregoing considerations appear to comprise a *prima facie* case that the theory of action treatment of socialization proceeds on sufficiently complex foundations that no simple "oversocialized" account could be satisfactorily accommodated within it. This would seem to be the case with regard to both the personality psychology level and the social system level of theoretical treatment. Yet, it remains true that the crux of the theory of action analysis of socialization processes has turned on the effort to treat, within one framework, both the personality and the social system aspects of the relevant phenomena. We will return to the issue of the alleged "oversocialized" model once we have attended in more detail to the general structure of the theory of action discussions of socialization processes.

SOCIALIZING ROLE-RELATIONSHIPS

The central, integrating conception in Parsons' analyses of various socialization processes has been that of the socializing role-relationship.[11] It is a conception that has been developed to a high level of generality, so that it may be applied to parent-child relations, teacher-student relations, relations of "secondary" socialization "on the job" in employing organizations, and to many other contexts. Indeed, the effort has been to characterize it at such a high level of generality that it may be invoked for analysis of any relationship that carries socializing effects. At the same time, an effort has been made to demonstrate functional linkages between its principal features and a socializing outcome of interaction, i.e., to show that socialization requires interaction

to have these specific characteristics. In this respect, socializing relationships may be systematically compared with a number of other generic types, e.g., economic, political, communal, religious, though in some cases they may also be interdependent with each of these latter types. Attention has also been given to the systematic analysis of differences among various kinds of socializing relationships. Here, the general strategy has been to show that certain features of the generic type of socializing relationship can be treated as variables which will assume different "values" or forms under different specific socializing conditions. Further, it has been possible to utilize this strategy to demonstrate that the "full" socialization of the individual in a complex society will require that he become involved, at different ages and in different circumstances, in a fairly wide range of specific subtypes of socializing relationships.

As noted, Parsons accomplished his most fundamental work on socialization during a period in which he was especially involved in working out the interrelations between sociological and psychoanalytic theory. Against the most "purely" sociological theories that might consider all concern with the motivations of individuals somewhat reductionistic, he insisted that a general theory of action had to attend to the respects in which lines of action would be implemented only insofar as actors were motivated to pursue them. Thus, for all social systems, the motivation to pursue even positively valued and legitimated paths of action must be regarded as problematic. Moreover, the limitation of the motivations of individuals to lines of action that are institutionally legitimate must also be regarded as a problematic aspect of social control.[12] Against the "purely" psychoanalytic understanding of the nature of human motivation that might consider all concern with the normative constraints of social institutions as somewhat epiphenomenal, however, Parsons insisted on what he called the institutional integration of motivation.[13] In general, he argued, actors can gain satisfaction in terms of their personal motives only if their actions are not frustrated by the actions of others. Actors can gain some assurance that their alters will not frustrate their motivated actions only if they share frameworks of the normative regulation of action with the alters. Consequently, the core motivational investments of the personality must, in general, have the authorization or legitimation of a normative order shared by the significant alters. These fundamental, if in some senses quite preliminary, considerations dictated that a comprehensive theory of interaction proceed simultaneously upon the two levels of concern with personal motivation and social interaction.

Later efforts to develop a general theory of action have emphasized that four levels of concern must be treated as problematic, the cultural and behavioral as well as the social and personal. Work during the period in question did not emphasize the behavioral factors as a source of independent variation. While they did emphasize that both personal and social systems must be treated as culturally patterned, they did not treat cultural elements as comprising a fully independent set of processually contingent factors.

At present, the understanding of the processes of socialization has not yet been reconstructed in terms of theory that would treat all four of the primary subsystems of action as fully contingent and problematic. Such theory would require a systematic exploration of the differences between socialization and enculturation, the latter presumably emphasizing, in its moral dimension especially, the realm of legitimating ideals as independent of institutionalized normative standards. It would also require a systematic distinction between internalization within the personality and internalization within the behavioral system, the former focusing upon motivational exigencies and the later upon sheer skill or capacity to coordinate processes of action. Of course, it would have been ideal for the present essay to have reconsidered the theory of socialization in terms that ascribed full independence to all four complexes of factors. Such an effort certainly should rank high among the projects of theorists of action. However, it is simply too demanding a task to undertake in the present format. I have chosen, rather, to attempt a fairly general exploration of the concomitant independence and interdependence of the social and personal factors, though perhaps stressing the importance of the social factors more strongly, in terms which may later be translated into a scheme allowing for the independent variation of states of all four subsystems of action.

Parsons' effort to develop a sociopersonal theory of interaction drew upon three principal theoretical resources. At the personality level, it departed from the psychoanalytic theory of object relations, which provided grounds for emphasizing the degree to which the structure of the personality resulted from the introjection of qualities of social objects to which the individual had become cathectically attached. At the social system level, it departed from the analysis of social order developed in *The Structure of Social Action* by critical treatment of the grounds of convergence among the works of Marshall, Pareto, Durkheim, and Weber. Among these classical figures, however, Durkheim was perhaps the most important for the task of developing a broader synthesis, as his work emphasized the sentimental or emotional attachment to the various elements of the normative order of society. Finally, the social psychological work of George Herbert Mead provided a set of mediating concepts focusing upon the ways in which the structure of the self or personality is actively constructed by the individual through his internalization of socially organized role-relationships.

A socializing role-relationship is in the first instance a role-relationship. We may best understand it by first reviewing the principal features which Parsons has ascribed to all role-relationships.[14] A role-relationship involves the interaction of two or more actors. (For present purposes, we may follow the convenient simplification of taking the dyadic case as prototypical.) Thus, it is implied that, whatever the asymmetries incorporated in the relationship with respect to control of resources of one type or another, each actor has at least some capacity to act upon the other. Even the slave may have some effect upon his master, the private citizen upon the political leader, the child upon the parent, however much stronger the reciprocal effects may be. As each actor can be effective within the role-relationship and can have his own life-circumstances to some degree affected by the reciprocal acts of his alter, his own motivations will become involved in the processes of interaction. At least, it is a limiting case when an actor becomes engaged in a role-relationship involving some stability of interaction yet withholds all affective attachment from the social process. Generally, each actor will come to cathect his alter, his own role in the relationship, the collectivity that he comprises along with his alter, the normative order binding both actors, and perhaps various of the achievements or products of past interaction. Given, minimally, the affective attachments of each actor to various features of the role-relationship and, usually, the concomitant involvement of other "investments", e.g., material resources, power, prestige, there is enough contingently "at stake" in the interaction processes that both actors require protection of their interests.

Ultimately, secure protection must involve complexes of mutual expectations that enable each actor to calculate the ranges of alternative actions open to himself and his alter reciprocally. The expectation complexes may be differentiated in the kinds of action which are permitted to each of the actors. Indeed, insofar as the interactors occupy different roles, the expectations will be so differentiated. Yet, the understandings about what actions are permitted each party to the interaction must, in general, be shared if the role-relationship is to remain stably ordered, for otherwise at least one of the actors would be unable to calculate the interactive consequences of either his own or his alter's conduct. Hence, the standards of mutuality and reciprocity of expectations do not imply a uniformity of the regulations affecting each participant, but rather a common understanding of the different expectations impinging upon each of the differentiated roles involved in the interaction. Only in the limiting case will there be a complete uniformity among the expectations impinging upon all actors.

The expectations must be substantially normative in nature. To be sure, they have a sheerly "practical" or predictive aspect in that they allow the actors to calculate one another's alternative lines of action and the consequences of each. However, they must also set up certain boundaries around the possible lines of action and certain standards for judging the relative degrees of appropriateness of all alternative actions. Such boundaries and standards, which may certainly be infracted, are inherently moral and evaluative, for they rest upon judgments of the desirability of different kinds of action and interaction. The mark of the pervasiveness with which the normativity of expectations regulates interaction consists in the degree to which the actors' capacities to affect one another's circumstances become transformed into sanctions, i.e., rewards or punishments for furthering or frustrating expectations that are contingent upon the performances of the alter. Expectations cannot stably regulate interaction unless they are supported by sanctions, for otherwise it would make no practical difference to the alter whether or not he acted within the terms of ego's expectations.[15]

A socializing role-relationship is one which has a structural form adapted specifically to conveying normative expectations from one actor to another. The latter becomes socialized in the sense of coming to internalize the mutual expectation complexes characteristic of the role-relationship. Consequently, a socializing relationship differs from other types precisely in that full mutuality of expectations is not present at the outset but is gradually approached in the course of interaction.[16] The absence of full mutuality of expectations has, of course, very substantial impact upon the nature of the interactive processes. Interaction—the case of parents with very small children may be taken as prototypical—is apt to be rather unstable, with cooperative activities becoming frequently frustrated, the imposition of sanctions, positive rewards as well as negative punishments, being frequently required, and the expressions of affective attachments tending to be somewhat labile and unsteady. Analytically, there is thus a partial anomie in socializing relationships

which requires very special controls. Moreover, there is an inherent asymmetry with regard to potential for effective action in the relation between the socializee and the socializer, with only the latter being fully familiar with the very terms of the interactive framework. Hence, the party undergoing socialization is in an especially dependent and exposed situation—the more so, the more fundamental the nature of the socialization process in question. The fundamental asymmetry with regard to command of the expectational complexes may or may not be complemented by high degrees of asymmetry in control of resources, power, influence, and so on. But it is inherent in socialization that one party cannot, entirely from his own capacities, fully manage his own pursuit of self-interest. Along with professional relationships,[17] the socializing role-relationship comprises an analytical category of social situations which it is hard to conceive being well analyzed within the utilitarian theoretical framework.

Given the interactive vulnerability of individuals undergoing socialization, it is essential that socializing role-relationships incorporate some special protections for their personal interests. It is in this respect that socializing relationships fall under the category of what Parsons has recently been calling fiduciary institutions.[18] The individual or agency assuming responsibility for the socialization process takes on a fiduciary obligation to protect the needs and interests of the socializee. Moreover, the socializing agent is expected to meet certain cultural standards of adequacy and fairness in the process of transforming the expectational complexes of the individual undergoing socialization.[19] Prototypically, the parent does not relate to the child in a manner regulated by the pursuit of self-interest but in a manner that promotes the long-run interests of the child. Further, the parent must assume certain responsibilities in determining, under quite a broad range of circumstances, what the interests of the child may be. The young child, at least, is presumptively incapable of adequately determining and pursuing his own interests and hence requires fiduciary assistance. Of course, as the child matures, the extent of the fiduciary responsibility of the parent becomes attenuated, and the child gradually assumes the burden of fiduciary judgment for himself. Within certain limits, though, the parent holds the right to set the pace of the transfer of such responsibility and judgment. Yet, the parent is required, usually in informal ways but on occasions even legally, to exercize fiduciary judgment according to standards of the broader societal culture and to be socializing the child not simply to the intrafamilial field of interaction but to a normative foundation for widespread participation in the society at large.[20]

An important condition of the fulfillment of the fiduciary responsibility in the socializing role-relation is that the interactive system be characterized by a strongly positive valuation of the role of the fiduciary or socializing agent. As the actor undergoing socialization gains familiarity with the expectational complexes involved in the interaction, he will come to share this positive valuation. He can then himself gain higher status within the role-relationship by attempting to realize the same set of values in his own actions. In the psychological or motivational dimension of his involvement in the role-relationship, this effort to reorganize the self on the model of the fiduciary agent comprises identification.[21] As Freud demonstrated, identification is an especially fundamental and powerful mode of cathectic involvement of the personality with social objects. It assumes not only a high level of attachment to the salient social objects but also a basic propensity to undergo transformation of the personality in order to make it more like the positively valued features of the social objects. When the mechanism of identification has been activated, the personality is especially likely to become fundamentally changed by the acceptance of the expectational complexes of the interactive system.

An individual's involvement in processes of identification is apt to unsettle the pre-existing states of equilibrium in his personality system. Certain new modes of action are coming to be regarded as desirable while others may be rather abruptly downgraded in evaluative terms. Often massive adjustments in motivational pattern must be made in order firmly to establish the new personal values. Within the personality system, one may therefore expect to find a broad range of defense mechanisms activated in support of the new identification, e.g., repression of older likes and dislikes and projection of formerly valued but now disvalued characteristics upon those outside the interactive system.[22] On the level of social interaction, it seems important that sanctions become especially firmly supportive of the expectational complexes bound up with the new identification.[23] At the points in time in which the actor undergoing socialization is very likely to be highly ambivalent and perhaps quite confused about the nature and implications of crucial expectational complexes, it is essential that the structure of rewards and punishments support the progression to the interactively valued identification. The dredging up of regressive ambivalences on the part of the socializing agent in ways that interfere with his capacities to impose well-rationalized sanctions may, at these times,

severely disturb the effectiveness of the socialization process.

Within this theoretical perspective, briefly, socialization involves the reorganization of the personality to incorporate new expectational complexes. The core of such reorganization consists in the internalization of elements of a normative order. However, a wide range of the instrumentalities of the use of, and of the appropriate affective attachments to, normative expectations must also be mastered and developed. Insofar as these processes occur within interactive experience of discrete role-relationships, they may be legitimately summarized, following G.H. Mead, as the internalization of a series of reciprocal roles and of the normatively integrating relationships among roles. At one structural level, the personality may be regarded as a normatively organized manifold of internalized roles. However, we would have an oversocialized view of the actor if we regarded the entire personality as functioning upon this level. Actually, it must be realized that the integration of attachments to various discrete roles with one another must be accomplished in an affectively or emotionally dynamic fashion. Deeply intrapersonal and individual processes of "defense" are necessarily involved. Personalities can sustain their unity in the face of the historical discontinuities among their successive role-involvements and the synchronic conflicts among the demands and obligations of their manifold contemporaneous role-involvements only through repression, regression, projection, displacement, denial, and the like. Socialization itself cannot proceed without becoming embedded in the profoundly *unsocialized* aspects of personality functioning.

The Developing Personality and Socializing Role-Relationships

Parsons has suggested that stages in the socialization process may be discriminated by analysis of the complexity of the manifolds of internalized role-relationships that structure the personality at different points in development.[24] Thus, a primary stage involves the internalization of the single role-relation between child and mother. A second stage starts when the child begins to relate to the father in terms of systematically different expectations, hence a different role-relation. Soon afterwards, the child must begin to define his role within the family taken as a whole independently of his roles with each particular parent and sibling. In this type of analysis, new stages will then become defined when the child successively develops significant social relationships with such categories of alters as peers or playmates, grandparents and other kin, schoolteachers, class-mates, and other members of the broader com-munity.[25] At each point in development, the structure of the personality will become more highly differenti-ated in terms of the number of role-relationships in which it can master participation. Of course, the adjustive mechanisms of the personality will also have to function with respect to a larger complex of elements, e.g., cathectic attachments, identifica-tions, values, and motivational needs. It should be clear that the discrimination of stages in this approach rests upon judgments about the complexity and functional differentiatedness of the personality as determined by a comparative morphology focusing upon the manifolds of internalized roles, not upon suppositions about any universal sequence of partic-ular role-relations through which the personality must develop. We may presume that cross-culturally there may be considerable variation in the sequences in which individuals become engaged with various categories of significant alters.

As the personality progresses through stages in its socialization it becomes transformed in at least two fundamental respects. First, it gains the capacity to engage with relative stability in interaction in an increasingly broad set of social milieux. Thus, the child who can at first interact comfortably only in a dependent relation to a parental figure within the family gradually learns to act differentially in relation to two parents, siblings, peers, extended kin, school-teachers and schoolmates, and various figures in the community. Of course, along with each new relation with a different category of alter, the child must also learn new modalities of his own behavior. He cannot be the dependent child of his playmates or his teachers, but must act quite differently with such alters than with his parents. Broadly, learning to act with greater independence and autonomy comprises a principal aspect of the development of new relationships outside the family.

Second, the integration of the personality through the operation of its dynamic, adjustive mechanisms becomes increasingly refined as it must integrate broader ranges of role-involvements, and this re-finement tends to be generalized to all spheres of conduct. For example, the personality gains in capacity to repress inappropriate impulses, to delay gratification to appropriate opportunities, to mobilize motivational energies for concentration upon highly valued tasks, and to sustain attachment to valued objects and ends. Such advances in integrative capaci-ties, although they may originate within certain specific role-relationships, tend to become general characteristics of the whole personality, so that they can become deployed across a range of interactive

involvements.[26] Hence, a developmental dynamic operates throughout the personality rather generally and will encompass even the sectors of the personality structured about the oldest, most firmly established role-relationships. The motivational discipline which a child learns most directly in his role as a pupil in school may affect his relationship with his mother, for example, by enabling him to act more independent-ly in relation to her. As socialization progresses by the learning of new roles, then, conduct in all roles structured within the personality may become affect-ed. Yet, the effects will not be the same in all roles, for a crucial aspect of the enhancement of socializa-tion is comprised of the ability to sustain different patterns of conduct within different categories of social situations. Though certain dimensions of activism and independence may become generalized to practically all role-relationships, the child will learn to act under standards of universalism, specifici-ty, neutrality, and performance in school and later in occupational contexts while continuing to act under primary standards of particularism, diffuse-ness, affectivity, and ascription in the home.

The requisites of effective socialization obviously change considerably as the child progresses through the stages of personality development. The young baby is necessarily dependent upon the parent in a highly general and diffuse fashion. Socialization cannot be successfully sustained except insofar as it caters quite directly to the diffuse needs of the baby. Although there must be genuine interaction between child and parents, only a very limited application of contingent sanctions can produce socializing effects upon the child. Certainly, little responsibility can be imposed upon the child. By comparison, continued socialization of the grade-school child necessitates that he be required to take substantial responsibility for his own conduct and its consequences and that a broad range of sanctions be imposed contingently upon him. If he were treated as permissively as the young baby, he would not internalize the more con-straining expectations that must operate within the classroom if its public order is to be protected. More-over, the structure of interaction in the classroom must frustrate his tendencies to relate to the teacher in a way that would directly transfer the diffuse de-pendency needs involved in his prior relationship with his parents.[27] While a considerable element of transference is undoubtedly involved in a successful relationship between teacher and primary school pupil, if it were to operate too diffusely and particularistically it would be destructive of the general relationship between the teacher and the whole class, hence of socialization to conduct in more formal collectivities and of the focused task-involvement of school work. Similarly, effective progression of the socialization process for secondary school students will require that, to degrees that would be quite unmanageable for students in the lower grades, autonomy and independence be encouraged with regard to responsibility for "original" school work, for maintenance of orderly relationships with classmates, for appropriate conduct in relation to the teachers themselves, and for acceptance of certain standards of general citizenship in the community at large.

Here, we have considered only a few select examples of socializing relationships that impinge upon different stages of the larger socialization process. By generalization from these brief considerations, however, we can see that the crucial components of socializing relationships necessarily assume different forms or values in order to contribute effectively to different stages of socialization. A systematic analysis of the nature of the transformations of the various components of socializing relationships would comprise a very difficult task, and cannot be taken up in the present context. However, we may indicate just a few of the general propensities.

The scope of the active fiduciary responsibility of the socializing agent or agency tends to become increasingly specialized as the socializing relationship impinges upon more developed personalities. Relationships which run counter to this general propensity, for example, the broad socializing responsibility which military agencies adopt over new recruits undergoing basic training, tend to require exceptionally strong and diffuse complexes of sanctions. More generally, the narrowed fiduciary responsibility interacts with a presumption of a wider capacity of the socializee to conduct himself in a responsible fashion that requires only selective and specialized socializing supervision.

In a comparable way, the motivational investments in the socialization process tend to become more sharply focused. Relatively advanced socialization relationships operate upon a presumption that the socializee has a relatively adequately functioning basic character structure and can be relied upon to manage his own generalized motivational dispositions appropriately. It should be noted, though, that this is not to claim, along with some of the earlier Freudian discussions, that basic character structure becomes so firmly established in the early phases of socialization that it is not itself susceptible to change through subsequent socializing relationships. Indeed, subsequent relationships produce motivational effects that may, given relatively delicate states of equilibrium in the personality, produce highly generalized impacts upon character structure. The identity crises induced by college or graduate education, for example, may crystallize broad motivational reorganizations of quite a dramatic nature.[28] However, it is the case that socialization cannot operate past the primary phases unless the individual can manage fairly autonomously the basic motivational dispositions that we summarize term character structure. If the socialization processes were to intrude too deeply into the motivational structures of the individual undergoing relatively advanced socialization on a routine basis, they would tend to precipitate degrees of regression that would undermine their own effectiveness. Of course, there are exceptions to this generalization, e.g., in the motivationally reconstructive work of psychotherapy, but these specialized socialization processes then require unusual or atypical safeguards against the effects of regression, including substantial indulgence of them.

The expectational complexes conveyed through socializing relationships tend also to become increasingly narrowed and specialized as the individual progresses through the stages of development. In the primary socialization relationships, the individual learns some of the fundamental and highly generalized features of expectational complexes—their mutuality and reciprocity, their relations to contingent sanctions, their effects in limiting wants and desires, the discipline of conducting oneself in accordance with them. Similarly, the content tends to focus upon highly generalized standards for regulating conduct, with the normative meaning of attachment and love, of basic fairness in reciprocal interaction, of respect for other individuals, of honesty, and so forth, comprising the chief emphases. Later socialization is apt to be concerned with, first, how such general normative or expectational themes and modalities of their use apply to specific contexts of interaction and, second, the standards that apply only within specialized situations.[29] Thus, much of school socialization is concerned with the development of expectational complexes appropriate for the regulation of relationships among citizens in the sphere of public activities. Another component of school socialization, which undergoes a number of levels of refinement from the primary grades through advanced education, focuses upon the standards of intellectual activity. Socialization to a job in an employing organization may, while facilitating the individual's participation in a strategically important category of role-relationship, touch in a rather shallow fashion upon only a thin layer of specialized expectations concerning the specific work situation over and above the kinds of expectations that normally regulate the interactions of autonomous adults.

The sanctions applied in socializing relationships tend to become more refined in their support of expectational complexes as the individual advances through the stages of socialization. They become contingent on increasingly detailed and sophisticated qualities of the performances of the actor undergoing socialization. The sanctions imposed within socializing situations tend to become less drastic in their impact upon the very conditions of the behavior of the socializee. The grosser forms of misconduct that require sanctioning come, with the maturity of the actor, to be handled in the normatively distinct context of social control, not within socializing role-relationships. Relations of social control do not have the fiduciary structure of socializing relationships, so that the individual is held responsible for his own action and may be "punished" or "treated" in a fashion that does not make sense for actors presumed not yet to know how to conduct themselves properly. The distinction is, of course, analytical and may be clouded by such mixed types as psychotherapy. But it is important to recognize that the misconduct of those undergoing socialization — whether small children misbehaving or advanced students who make an "unprofessional" mistake — falls normatively in a different category from the misconduct of the presumptively responsible criminal or even juvenile delinquent. This is not to deny that there may be many cases on the boundaries between the two types which the frustrated agents of socialization and the publicly accountable agents of social control find difficult to classify.

The young child is generally sanctioned in negative ways only for conduct that disturbs the social situation in fairly substantial respects. But, then, even within quite "liberal" families, the child may quickly be subjected to sanctions of compulsion, e.g., by being picked up and removed from the scene or otherwise dramatically convinced of parental disapproval. Comparably severe sanctions cannot be invoked in the socializing relations of higher education, for example, without severely disrupting the relationship and thwarting all socializing effects. They may be employed only where a "social control" definition of the situation can be justified and where socializing intent must be renounced. Similarly, the positive sanctions of the expression of affective attachment tend to be much more effusive and massive in relations of primary socialization. The schoolteacher cannot provide the child with emotionally rewarding sanctions of the sort essential to the maintenance of early parent-child relationships without upsetting the expectational framework of the classroom and of the focus upon schoolwork. It should be clear that my point is not that primary socializing relationships rest on intrinsically more effective sanctions than the later, more specialized relationships. Rather, it is that the expectations involved in the primary relationships cannot be supported among young children by very subtle sanctions, while the invocation of rather gross sanctions are apt to upset the relatively subtle expectations involved in the more advanced socializing relationships.

The foregoing considerations should be adequate to indicate that, while various socializing relationships differ in rather systematic respects, the manifold of variations in basic combinations of their characteristics is exceedingly complex. The general type of social structure which we term the socializing relationship can be transformed into an immense number of different specific forms adapted to different requirements for socializing actors.

Socialization may be concentrated in the early stages of life, but it continues throughout the life cycle. The adult is apt to undergo new, though generally rather focused and specialized, socialization processes whenever he enters upon new domains of social activity. Parsons has recently suggested that some types of the autonomous activity of adults — the example he discusses in some detail being the research work of academic professionals[30] — may be treated as a form of self-socialization. In such activities, the individual may develop importantly new sets of specialized expectations while playing the fiduciary role on his own behalf. Perhaps, a rather wide range of creative adult experiences, e.g., in responsibly and autonomously participating in complex political affairs of a type that can enrich the individual participant or in developing original patterns of conduct through a unique career of economic entrepreneurship, can fruitfully be analyzed in these terms.

Another type of adult socialization, also in part a form of self-socialization, arises from the performance of the fiduciary role in the socialization of others. Insofar as such socialization involves the communication of expectations, it necessarily activates the internalized expectational complexes of the fiduciary agent. The very process of putting the expectations in a conveyable form, that is, a form that can be communicated to one who has not yet been fully socialized, would seem to involve a propensity toward regression in the sense of a reactivation or reexperiencing of the fiduciary agent's own comparable socialization processes. The conduct and responses to socializing expectations of the individual undergoing socialization may specifically trigger the regressive experiences of the fiduciary agent.

However, a self-socializing aspect may also emerge out of a determination to reshape the meaning of the experiences to which the regression brings a motivational recurrence, perhaps out of intent to become an improved model for identification but often also for the purpose of enhancing personal freedom from deeply rooted anxieties and compulsions. Elements of such resocialization are probably quite intrinsic to parenthood and have been best analyzed in the context of parent-child relationships.[31] However, they also comprise an important part of the experience of teaching, and perhaps of a considerable range of other socialization processes. Both the special satisfactions and the special stresses and discontents of teaching must be understood in the light of this type of impact of the socialization processes upon the teacher as fiduciary agent. The different kinds of satisfactions and discontents experienced by teachers of different age-groups may be analyzed with reference to the specific parts or levels of the expectational complexes that become problematic for fiduciary agents in having to re-experience different stages of socialization.

Individuals continue to undergo socializing experiences throughout the life-cycle. For many, the ultimate major process of socialization concerns preparation to die and perhaps to membership in the category of people treated by others as dying, terminally ill, or in a final stage of life.[32] Before reaching these situations, most adults will experience a great many, perhaps hundreds, of interactive processes in which social preparation for the assumption of a new status is involved. Nevertheless, there are important limitations upon the socialization of adults. The vast preponderance of their socializing experiences are markedly of the type usually considered "secondary," i.e., assuming socialization to generalized capacities for undertaking valued kinds of action, the specific processes focus upon inculcating expectations and motivation differentially important for social action in specific organizations, communities, role-relationships, or activities. The psychological interpretation of this general fact has usually stressed the fixity of character structure to which the adult has become socialized. However this may be — and it is certainly an important factor in many individual cases, perhaps most — there are also fundamental sociological factors. Thus, it seems to be quite basically inconsistent with the adult role in society for the individual to become subordinated to a socializing fiduciary agent in a very diffuse role that renders problematic his capabilities or motivation to regulate his own *general* conduct. The amount of infantilizing, or at least radically regressive, dependency involved in socializing relations of a primary or fundamental nature is simply too intolerably destructive of adult status. The notable exceptions, e.g., intensive psychotherapy and, perhaps, "thought reform" in the early phases of the Communist revolution in China, have concentrated upon people who have been stigmatized as performing adult roles inadequately, e.g., because of mental illness or ideological turpitude.[33] It seems that only in the context of highly charismatic social movements are substantial portions of the aggregate adult populations of societies subjected to quite fundamental processes of socialization.

PRESENT CONTRIBUTIONS TO SOCIALIZATION THEORY

A principal theme in Parsons' writings on socialization has emphasized the functional adaptation of certain institutions in society, especially modern society, to the socialization of individuals. Perhaps the major focus of analysis in this theoretical context has been the institutional complex known as the nuclear family. Parsons has been closely identified with two strongly contested generalizations about the nature of the nuclear family.[34] The first concerns the adaptation of family organization in the context of specifically modern society. It has been argued that given, on the one hand, the strong evaluative emphasis placed on the development of an autonomous career for the individual adult male and, on the other hand, the very high levels of social mobility, both vertical and horizontal, the kinship system has tended to concentrate its core loyalties of solidarity about the comparatively small nuclear family.[35] In this situation, strong family solidarity does not become inconsistent with the needs to make adjustments in terms of residence, status, and style of life to the specific career line of the head of the household. The autonomy of the nuclear family from the careers, statuses, and concerns of parents, siblings, and affines tends to insulate its members from becoming cross-pressured between the pursuit of its own career interests and loyalties to other kin. Referring to these characteristics of the modern nuclear family system, Parsons has termed it "isolated."[36] The term has been intended in a comparative sense, i.e., to emphasize the distinctive qualities of the modern system as compared with the "extended" systems of most primitive societies and of many peasant and feudal societies. It refers specifically to the rather sharply bounded membership of the nuclear family as a household unit, to its autonomy from more extended kin groups as a solidary and budgetary unit, and to the parents' near monopoly of the fiduciary role in socialization of their children. Parsons has not argued that members of an "isolated" nuclear family do not maintain meaningful and even strong relationships with other relatives, but only that such relationships are institutionally regarded as beyond the bounds of the principal focus of kinship solidarity. Further, it has been acknowledged that within some ethnic and perhaps social class sub-groupings of modern societies this pattern may be partially attenuated. Hence, the several empirical studies which have claimed to refute the hypothesis of the isolated nuclear family by documenting the extent of attachment between family members and relations outside of the family have simply misconstrued the argument under consideration.

The second strongly contested generalization about the nuclear family touches rather more directly on problems of socialization. It is the hypotheses of the universality of the nuclear family. Broadly, Parsons' argument has been that the nuclear family is so very well adapted to performance of the most fundamental primary socialization processes that it may well comprise a universal feature of institutional adaptation to the human condition. Although societies may differ over the degree to which nuclear families are embedded within or isolated from more extended kinship groupings, all should contain structured nuclear families for their facilitation of the socializing processes. Here, reference is made to several principal features of the nuclear family.[37] As it is relatively small, at least in the number of differentiated role-types, it places the child in a comparatively simple environment. The child may thus benefit from greater clarity of expectations and from a set boundary around the sources of impinging expectations, during his early experiences of social interaction. In having parents of both sexes present within this small social circle, the child has the advantage of learning the basic expectational complexes bound up with sex identity through reciprocal interaction with a member of each sex. The major differentiation of roles within the nuclear family between the two generations provides a firm structural foundation for the asymmetries involved in the fiduciary relationship. The intensity of affective and cathectic ties within the family, including their rather direct relations to erotic matters, places socialization in an interactive context that almost necessarily activates very fundamental motivational complexes. Hence, the transformation of the motivational structure of the personality is much facilitated for the socializing aspects of intrafamilial interaction.

The essay by Terrence S. Turner included in the present part of this collection develops a critique of and then a substitute formulation for Parsons' discussions of the universality of the nuclear family.

A principal starting point of Turner's discussion is simply the recognition that empirically the nuclear family has been shown not to be universal. Turner does, however, find Parsons' sense of problem — the need for identifying and analyzing the universal institutional foundations for socialization at the most general and primary level — to be meaningful and important. Building upon Parsons' notion that the structure of the personality, at least for certain strata within the organization of personality, can be analyzed in terms of the manifolds of internalized roles, Turner pursues the problem of developing a formal analysis of the isomorphism between social structure and personality. One departure from Parsons' treatment is that Turner emphasizes the anthropological notion of the "developmental cycle of the domestic group." He points out that socialization involves not simply the interactive engagement of a socializee in particular roles but also the communication of means for mastering transformations from one role to another. Thus, the development of the child toward maturity is accompanied by and bound up with systematic transformations in the child's role-relationships with others in the family, especially the parents. Turner points out that these socializing changes in role-relationships comprise, within a different perspective, the same processes of change in family organization that anthropologists have been analyzing under the heading of the developmental cycle of the domestic group.

Turner argues that the universal social framework of the initial stage of socialization consists in the collectivity of mother and child or children. Only later, when the child must gain a distinct jural status in the society and when he begins to participate in extrafamilial contexts of interaction, does a more inclusive family grouping enter into socialization in all societies. He treats the child's passage into the more inclusive family grouping, which is also hierarchically superordinate to the primary socialization grouping of mother and children, as the most fundamental of the socializing transformations. He notes that this passage also comprises a step in the developmental cycle of the family, because of the substantial reorganization of roles which it entails. A parallel analysis is presented for certain subsequent transformational steps in the development of socialized child and of family grouping.

Turner is then in a position to make two claims of very major theoretical importance. The first is that, by substituting a more complex analysis of the dimensions or parameters of family organization, i.e., sex, generation, affinity, and hierarchical inclusion, and of their possible transformational combinations, for the older argument about the universality of the nuclear family, he is able to synthesize a treatment of the general institutional foundations of socialization that seems empirically to be on universal ground. Second, it seems that one can match the universal points of transformation in socialization and in the domestic group with very general stages in the development of personality systems. Drawing upon Piaget to amplify the latter point, Turner links his generalizations about the universal social bases of socialization processes to recent theory about psychological universals of the human individual. Thus, he concludes on a note of emphasis upon human universals even exceeding that of Parsons' original formulations, especially upon the psychological side. His transformational notions have also placed the analysis of the relations among the different solidary groupings within a kinship system and of the development from birth into a primary socialization group to performance of fiduciary roles in a family of procreation upon a far firmer and more unitary foundation. The new theory is both substantially more comprehensive and more tenable empirically.

Three of the essays in this section are concerned with a specific phase of socialization that has been a special focus of a number of Parsons' writings, namely that of direct transition between the status of childhood dependency and the formally autonomous status of adulthood. Parsons has emphasized that the crucial transition which must be accomplished during this phase if serious adaptive problems are to be avoided in adulthood places very great stress upon the personality system.[38] He has essayed especially the ways in which the stress is structured in contemporary American society. The individual must develop a sense of his own individuated personal identity as a guide for his adult aspirations. He must develop a motivationally profound commitment to the terms of his identity. He must gain a sense of personal freedom and autonomy through his new identity in order for it to seem valid in our individualistic normative culture. At the same time, the identity and the prospects for its realization must satisfy a sense of self-worth that may be deeply stressed by the intensity of the emphasis upon achievement in our society. The individual must feel that his aspirations are fully worthy of his personal potential. Yet, he must also have some confidence that he is not committing himself to a life of failure to attain ambitions. Parsons has emphasized that the intermixing of stresses potentially so severe in nature may result in substantial reactions of an irrational sort, both individual and collective. He has analyzed certain characteristics of the so-called youth culture in terms of the non-

rational and irrational, as well as rational, support that they provide to individuals in the throes of this stressful transition.[39]

Jackson Toby's essay contributes specifically to this line of analysis. He is discussing the personal discontent among high school students that is associated with the effort to realize the American value-pattern of instrumental activism, as Parsons has termed it,[40] in their maturing domains of action. Toby argues that there is bound to be much ambivalence tied up with the commitment to achievement. For most students, faced continually with comparative evaluations of their role-performances in many contexts, there is apt to be considerable unhappy experience with the judgment that performance has been inadequate. Males especially are susceptible to rather pervasive anxiety that they are in general inadequate relative to the expectations being placed upon them. Toby then suggests that many of the themes and preoccupations of the youth culture must be understood as defensive against the potentially overwhelming anxieties about inadequacy. More specifically, he interprets in this light data about the extent to which high school students report that they are more meaningfully involved in matters of sports and popularity among peers than in academic achievement. Given the obvious degree to which future potential for career achievement seems for most students to rest most heavily upon academic success, these data have puzzled many analysts. Toby emphasizes their compulsive nature as defenses against the serious threats posed by any inadequacies in the academic realm. In a sense the vehemence with which high school students often produce such data indexes also the intensity of their underlying commitments to achievement standards, but in a context of anxieties about inadequacy. Finally, in a close reexamination of the available data, Toby shows that the students, in their genuine ambivalence, in fact do not single-mindedly reject the importance of academic concerns and achievements but make clear a substantial commitment to academic performance.

Thomas J. Cottle's essay is concerned with the behavior of members of self-analytic (Bales') groups conducted as a course in Harvard College and with the development of that behavior through the life-cycles of the groups. Members of these groups are engaged in a different phase of the larger stage of youth than the high school students discussed by Toby. One aspect of a college education comprises a continuation of the socialization gained in high school and may be pointed rather directly toward advancing mastery of instrumental techniques and social expectations necessary for success in adult careers. However, another aspect involves a certain remove from a direct progression toward particular adult roles. Here, there is an opportunity for at least elements of what Erikson has termed the psychosocial moratorium, a period in which alternative commitments are constructed and tested rather than one in which specific commitments are furthered.[41] Especially in the more elite colleges, students are given considerable freedom to pursue intellectual and motivational interests in tentative and experimental ways. Considerable risk of vagueness, confusion, and regression may be tolerated in order to enhance the possibility that later senses of identity will prove more mature, more original, and more creative. It should be understood, though, that this pattern does not comprise a simple indulgence of adolescent sensitivities but an often very trying arrangement for encouraging the construction of identities that will serve both the individual and various sectors of society more valuably. Thus, the moratorium aspects of college life are not simply tolerated but in many respects positively promoted by general institutional arrangements.

One major frame of reference within which Cottle discusses the self-analytic groups concerns the four-function analysis of the development of structure within groups. Modifying the early four-function analyses of self-analytic groups,[42] Cottle proposes that the groups crystallize differentiated structures for the performance of relatively specific functions in the sequence of pattern maintenance, integration, goal attainment, and adaptation. The pattern-maintenance phase concentrates about the development of a collective conscience for the group, such that it gains a common sense of its collective identity and a set of shared values for guiding activities within the group. The integrative phase involves an enriching of the affective involvements of the students in the groups and hence a motivational deepening of their collective solidarity. More differentiated relationships of interdependence among members and categories of members (e.g., the sex categories) are introduced into the functioning of the group. In the goal-attainment phase, the group crystallizes a more differentiated and stable hierarchy of power and establishes a new level of rational procedure in its collective deliberations. Members become constrained to make more definite commitments to performance of collective work. Finally, in the adaptive phase, the group takes up its task of self-analysis with a new refinement and seriousness of deliberation. The members of the group are able to display a new level of independence, self-confidence, and sense of competence in their contributions to group process. They seem to be making more effective identifica-

tions with the leaders/instructors of the group. Cottle's four-function analysis of the developmental processes in self-analytic groups can be fully appreciated only if compared with the original formulations by Parsons, Bales, and Shils in which they first developed the four-function categories in the analysis of similar groups. Cottle manages to organize a substantially richer array of variables and to trace their transformations through the various phases of group development in more systematic terms.

Cottle argues that many of the characteristics of self-analytic groups observed in the Harvard College setting seem to derive less from the processes of group development than from qualities of their student members. He argues that matters of authority and of intimacy seem to comprise the focal developmental problems for the students, who are testing out their capacities as effective adults and as adult men and women. The concerns about authority and intimacy, then, become projected into each stage of group development. Adequate group functioning in each stage requires that these core motivational problems receive some fresh resolution through the group processes, so that attachment to the group on the part of the members can be sustained. Much of the richness of Cottle's analysis derives from his attention to the different ways in which the matters of authority and intimacy become problematic at the collective level during the various phases of group development. For example, he shows that the group is often driven into a collective regression to a prior phase by its inability to synthesize new ways of handling the core motivational problems in line with the developmental thrust of an emergent phase while meeting the members' needs for emotional security. In exploring the several transformations upon the ways in which the problems of authority and intimacy condition group functioning, Cottle both demonstrates the importance of these concerns in the socialization of college students and the rich variety of respects in which creative resolutions of enduring motivational problems may be the outcomes of collective processes.

Jesse R. Pitts' contribution, "The Millenarian Movement as a Socialization Agency," presents a generalized treatment of the motivational/socialization problems of the millenarian movement organization. Here, he articulates his analysis with socialization theory by emphasizing, not the motivational discontents of a specific stage in the life-cycle, as in his essay on the hippies, but the general malleability of adult deviant motivation into commitments toward radical social movements. The millenarian movement organization must socialize deviant motivation into a positive and firm commitment to withdrawal from many of the institutional frameworks of the larger society in favor of commitment to a total institution. Here, some form of "regressive idealistic commitment" plays an important part, for it legitimates a downgrading of ordinary roles in society in the interest of working toward a morally "higher" betterment of society. Yet, its oversimplified hold on social reality and its tendency to emphasize direct unification with the ultimate source of the good and desirable presents great difficulties for efforts to institutionalize routine commitments within the movement.

The stabilization of commitments to the movement is consequently profoundly problematic, and is apt to become a principal focus of the movement's practical concerns. Pitts, then, views membership in millenarian movement organizations as an inherently dynamic and unstable phenomenon. He proceeds to analyze it in terms of stages in membership careers. At any of his four stages, the organization may fail to sustain the commitment of the individual member and the member may then leave the movement. At a given point in time, the organization may have to cope with the practical problems raised by members' having different motivational interests in the group, hence different types of personal propensities to withdraw, and being in different stages of socialization to the movement, hence having different forms of specific attachment to it. Pitts' first stage consists in a radical motivational regression on the part of the member, often stimulated by a powerful conversion experience. During this stage, the movement comes to represent for the member an omnipotent parental figure that can be the source of all that is good and perhaps all that is immediately or personally effective. The second stage involves the transfer of these intense emotions to the ideology of the movement, so that membership and its obligations become fully justified. The risk arises that the extremity of the doctrine or the frailties of the organization and its other members will shock the neophyte back to a more critical outlook. However, there is also the possibility that the neophyte member will come to feel a new self-realization out of the deeper engagement in the movement and in its ideological perspectives. In the third stage, the member comes gradually to make more realistic judgments about the nature of the movement, the possibilities for its success, the capabilities of co-members, and the functional needs of the organization. There is a strong tendency for the onset of this newer realism to be accompanied by depression. In the fourth stage, this element of depression may be countered by more routinized and regularized involvement in organizational activities.

At a high level of generalization, we can see that the pattern of development through these stages converges rather closely with that which Cottle found in self-analytic groups. Moreover, both seem to parallel the path of development in the course of the life-cycle, namely, from a first crystallization of very fundamentally but rudely articulated elements of self-awareness and collective-awareness, to a broadening of the dimensions of concern and activity included within the system, to a more realistic construction of a framework for effective action, to, finally, routinization of the performance of valued tasks. The scope of these convergences and parallels may indicate that a very generalized model of some aspects of socialization is emerging within a four-function framework in a way similar to, but now empirically much richer than, that envisioned by the authors of *Working Papers in the Theory of Action*. An important future task will be to explore more exactly the limits or boundaries of these aspects, so that we will know better just what facets of socialization require a different mode of conceptualization.[43]

In his other contribution, "The Hippie Movement as a Socialization Agency," Pitts also focuses upon the motivational concerns of approximately college-age youth. True hippies have, much more than students meeting their obligations in college settings, become engrossed in psychosocial moratoria. They act upon a quite substantial alienation from the routine role-expectations ordinarily impinging upon individuals of their age-status. Pitts terms the evaluative patterning of their conduct "regressive idealistic commitment" because of its rather sweepingly utopian but egocentric impetus. In many respects, the hippie values must be interpreted as symbolic counter-positions to the principal practical components of the generalized American value pattern of instrumental activism. Thus, Andrew Effrat has suggested that the hippie value system be called "consummatory passivism."[44] The Hippies commit themselves to a pattern of withdrawal from all stable ego-involvement in the positively valued collectivities of the larger society. Hence, careers are renounced in favor of minimal engagement in whatever jobs permit self-support while requiring little positive commitment. Family ties and older friendships, community activities and associational memberships will be sustained in only passive fashion, if at all. The ideal is a permissiveness that allows each to "do his own thing" quite independently of explicitly co-ordinated collective obligations. Within the hippie communities, friendships and group memberships ideally take on a floating quality of minimal reciprocal obligation and of permissiveness toward bizarre conduct.

Pitts argues that the hippies' self-conceptions of sheer individualism and permissiveness do not capture important qualities of their social organization. Thus, hippie communities themselves exercise strong social control at certain points, e.g., in the prevention of violence or extreme acts of deviance, in warning members against the dangers of "ego-trips," and sometimes in forestalling the return of a member to more conventional social circles. There are often substantially effective structures of leadership within hippie communities, even ones that may impose rather authoritarian limitations of certain sorts upon much of the followership. Further, the hippies tend to share a rather millenialistic hope, perhaps expectation, that they will manage to convert their own generation and, ultimately, society to their own passivistic values. Pitts demonstrates that, indeed, the organizational structures within the hippie social movement correspond quite closely to the general sociological type of the "millenarian movement organization"—even down to the revivalism which he finds in the staging of "love-ins." From this perspective, he is able to essay the careers of individuals within the hippie movements in terms of the motivational problems of the maintenance of socialized commitment to the hippie value complex.

Two essays address quite directly a principal concern discussed earlier in this essay, but from a different perspective that will, in a sense, bring our considerations full circle. This concern is the problem of whether or not the theory of action has incorporated an oversocialized conception of the actor. Guy Rocher implicitly contributes much to our understanding of this problem in discussing the general theory of aspirations, with their personal and collective aspects, within the theory of action framework. Francesca Cancian addresses the difficult matter of the relations between norms and behavior, drawing especially upon social psychological research in attempting to define a general position that is both empirically sound and theoretically comfortable for theorists of action.

Aspirations, in Rocher's formulation, comprise symbolic and hopeful expressions of needs, both psychological and social. They are dispositions to undertake lines of action, sometimes quite specific, sometimes quite general. However, they always involve substantial tension between realities and dreams. On the one hand, they must be oriented with a degree of realism toward actual conditions of action, however unsatisfactory and constraining, and toward the possibilities that these conditions may yield to active transformation. On the other hand, they are guided by dreams, visions, ideals, and utopias of conditions that would prove more satisfactory in evaluative terms. Rocher comes to argue that they inherently involve conceptions of future states of action systems, both social or collective and individual or personal, that, as constructs, differ importantly from the contemporaneously given states. He stresses especially that the theory of action should heighten its sensitivities to the ways in which processes of action are constrained by actors' senses of future conditions of action as well as their contemporary institutionalized structures.

Rocher subjects to analysis the functional dynamics by which aspirations are composed and become effective in action. In four-function terms, he locates the core processes of the formation of aspirations within the goal-attainment subsystem (the ego) of the personality system, which comprises the goal-attainment sector of the action system as a whole. This part of the personality functions to direct and coordinate the motivational dispositions of the individual into the pursuit of discrete and organized goal-states. Rocher's point is that this ego function can be performed in large part only through aspiration, i.e., through future-directed hopes that the relation between the actor and his environment can be improved. Rocher then indicates that the other subsystems of the personality also become involved in the formation of aspirations by contributing important elements from which aspirations are constructed. Similarly, the cultural and social subsystems of action provide very important environments within which aspirations are developed. Thus, various cultural standards, values, ideologies, and underlying patterns will shape the personal senses of hopefulness and dream that enter into the aspirations of particular individuals. Socially institutionalized norms may provide effectively constraining channels for the crystallization of aspirations, as when an occupational system fosters aspirations for a glorious career, or may frustrate personal motivations in ways that generate aspirations for radical social change.

To counter the respect in which most studies of aspirations have focused upon jobs and careers within societies that emphasize economic and occupational institutions, Rocher presents a general typology of attitudes toward society that may influence aspirations. He focuses upon the generalized attitudes of indifference toward the social order, acceptance of the social order, and belief in social change, but indicates several subtypes in each case. He then cross-classifies this typology with a typology of basic kinds of orientation of personal motivational systems. The resulting table unifies the personal and social dimensions of aspirations, showing that any general type of aspiration has both personal and social aspects embedded within itself. Presumably, a still more complex and generally adequate table could be constructed if cultural variables were also given independent treatment.

Rocher's essay demonstrates that a general theory of action must treat the aspirational dimension of human behavior. Whether or not one accepts the specific consequences for formal theory that Rocher hypothetically delineates, it is clear that action systems must be conceived as "open" toward the future in the time dimension, and often as "open" in a hopeful fashion. However limited by social constraints in the here and now, human actors have a strong propensity—though one which must be set off theoretically against propensities for inhibition and repression—to hope to transform their social conditions in the future. However socialized they may be, their projects for future action encompass substantial elements of hopefulness that transcend the particular institutional frameworks to which they have become socialized. Rocher finds the general conceptual resources for analyzing this aspirational dimension of action best articulated in the theory of action, with its purposefully developed voluntaristic notions. It would have been surpassingly strange for a social scientist of Rocher's concerns to have chosen a theoretical framework seriously encumbered by "oversocialized" conceptions of actors.

Francesca Cancian's paper is developed as a theoretical and empirical critique of the "theory of the socialized actor". This theory is said to be constituted by the conjunction of three generalizations: that norms become internalized as part of the personality, that norms crucial to the social order are learned early in life, and that such early normative learning is not easily changed in subsequent experience. Cancian presents substantial evidence that empirical research, especially survey and experimental research, has disconfirmed the effort to conjoin these generalizations. There can be no doubt that she has severely undermined any simple theory of the socialized actor—what we have been calling the conception of the oversocialized actor. Yet, we may doubt that, in theory of action terms, this conception of socialization would have been taken as theoretically adequate in the first place. We will conclude, then, by indicating some very fundamental grounds on which, theoretically, we are inclined to reject the oversocialized conception.

The theory of action does hold that social situations and, by aggregation of social situations, social systems are structurally integrated by institutionalized norms. Moreover, it also holds that individual actors must internalize normative orders if they are to be able to orient themselves and coordinate actions with

one another in the course of social interaction. However, two important qualifications must be made with regard to the relationship between norms as institutionalized in social milieux and norms as internalized in personalities. First, it has been maintained that norms must be institutionalized in the sense of having direct support from an array of sanctions in order for them effectively to regulate social situations. Hence, it has long been maintained that neither the simple moral authority of norms nor the internalization of norms within the personalities of the participants in a situation is adequate to stabilize a process of interaction. In this sense, it has been denied on general theoretical grounds—the same grounds which, in the era of *The Social System,* set Parsons off from the culture and personality school, which did not insist on the independent importance of institutionalization at so high a level of theoretical generality—that norms as institutionalized and norms as internalized simply constitute the same entities. Second, norms comprise only one of several categories of structure within both social and personality systems. Social systems are treated as consisting, structurally, in values, norms, collectivities, and roles. Out of contexts of values, collectivities, and roles, norms do not regulate situations in what Durkheim called a "well-determined" way. Rather, they will be quite ambiguous, and hence they may be susceptible to much disagreement about what they imply or require in the way of conduct from particular actors. Similarly, in personality systems, internalized norms function in a dynamic mixture with various categories of needs, cathexes, dispositions, and so on. The ways in which they will actually regulate the motivation of action must be treated as varying with the contents of other components of personality. It is in large part for this reason that even actors who have internalized a normative structure may not act directly in line with its institutionalized form unless constrained to do so by effective sanctions.

The foregoing considerations should make quite clear that one cannot accept, on theoretical grounds, a direct investigation of individuals' attitudes as providing measures of the presence of institutionalized norms. We should not be surprised that Cancian's investigation demonstrates the substantial divergence between individual attitudes concerning normative issues and institutionalized norms. That is, the conception of the socialized (oversocialized) actor has no firm theoretical status in the theory of action.

However, we do not mean to conclude that there are no interesting relationships between the normative attitudes of individuals and the normative components of social structure. Rather, we mean to imply that some more subtle modes of relation must be sought in future research. Perhaps this research should be, rather than experimental or survey-oriented in nature, comprised of a mixture of probing and testing with naturalistic observation. It might well eschew a search for generalized attitudes in favor of probing for conditional sanctioning responses that would be deemed appropriate by actors as actual interactive situations evolve in one fashion or another. It may be that only once we have a broad range of such precise normative data bearing on specific situations will we learn to prehend the form and content of the norms which they express and in terms of which they are unified. We might remember that in a dimension of behavior which may be regarded as apparently prototypical in the thoroughness and detail with which it is regulated by general norms, i.e., language, people are often quite unable to state the content of the norms which they use habitually, freely, and automatically, i.e., rules of grammar. Linguists must generalize from substantial arrays of diverse data in order to state the often simple content of grammatical rules. The form in which grammatical rules should be stated in order best to reflect their regulation of linguistic behavior is proving to be a difficult and controversial problem. There seems no reason to believe that sociologists will have an easier task in handling this problem than the linguists. Indeed, the balance of evidence would seem to indicate that our problem ranges away from the linguistic one in a direction of greater difficulty. Yet, sociologists are not yet discussing the issue of the relations between norms and behavior at the level of complexity that is now assumed in linguistic research. When we manage to conceptualize norms and their regulation of normative sanctioning in a more adequate fashion, it may be that we will then be able to identify the realms of interindividual agreement and of the intervening effects of interactive sanctions more clearly.

NOTES

1. Talcott Parsons, *The Structure of Social Action* (New York: McGraw-Hill, 1937).

2. Talcott Parsons, *The Social System* (Glencoe: The Free Press, 1951), especially Chapter VI.

3. Dennis Wrong, "The Oversocialized Conception of Man in Modern Sociology," in *American Sociological Review,* 26 (1961), pp. 183-193.

4. See Talcott Parsons and Winston White: "The Link Between Character and Society," in Talcott Parsons, *Social Structure and Personality* (New York: The Free Press, 1964).

5. See *Social Structure and Personality,* Chs. 1-4.

6. *Ibid.,* Ch. 1.

7. For this account, refer to *ibid.,* Chs. 1 and 4, and to Talcott Parsons: "An Approach to Psychological Theory in Terms of the Theory of Action" in Sigmund Koch (ed.), *Psychology: A Study of a Science,* Vol. 111 (New York: McGraw-Hill, 1959).

8. See *ibid.*

9. See *ibid.,* for the most general discussion of the differentiation of the personality into subsystems. What is here called the identity system was formerly called the ego-ideal, following Freud rather than Erikson.

10. See the discussion of American society in Talcott Parsons, *The System of Modern Societies* (Englewood Cliffs, N.J.: Prentice-Hall, 1970).

11. See *The Social System,* Ch. VI.

12. *Ibid.,* Ch. VII.

13. *Ibid., passim.*

14. *Ibid.,* Ch. VI.

15. See "An Approach to Psychological Theory in Terms of the Theory of Action," *op. cit.*

16. *The Social System,* Ch. VI; *Social Structure and Personality,* Ch. IV; and Talcott Parsons and Robert F. Bales, *Family, Socialization, and Interaction Process* (Glencoe: The Free Press, 1955), especially Ch. II.

17. *The Social System,* Ch. X.

18. Talcott Parsons and Gerald M. Platt, *The American University* (Cambridge: Harvard University Press, 1973).

19. *Family, Socialization and Interaction Process.*

20. *Ibid.,* Ch. 1.

21. *Ibid.,* Ch. II; and *The Social System,* Ch. VI.

22. "An Approach to Psychological Theory in Terms of the Theory of Action," *op. cit.*

23. *The Social System,* Ch. VI.

24. *Family, Socialization and Interaction Process,* Chs. 11 and III.

25. Talcott Parsons, "The School Class as a Social System," in *Social Structure and Personality.*

26. See "An Approach to Psychological Theory in Terms of the Theory of Action," *op. cit.*

27. "The School Class as a Social System," *op. cit.*

28. See Erik Erikson, *Identity and the Life-Cycle* (Psychological Issues, number 1; New York: International Universities Press, 1959).

29. *Family, Socialization, and Interaction Process,* Chs. 11 and III.

30. *The American University.*

31. See the discussion of parenthood in Theodore Lidz, *The Person* (New York: Basic Books, 1969).

32. See Talcott Parsons, Renee C. Fox, and Victor Lidz, "The Gift of Life and Its Reciprocation," in *Social Research,* XXXIX (Autumn 1972), pp. 367-415.

33. See Robert J. Lifton, *Thought Reform and the Psychology of Totalism* (New York: Norton, 1961).

34. *Family, Socialization, and Interaction Process.*

35. Talcott Parsons, "An Analytical Approach to the Theory of Social Stratification," in Talcott Parsons, *Essays in Sociological Theory* (New York: Free Press, 1954).

36. Talcott Parsons, "Age and Sex in the Social Structure of the United States" in *Essays in Sociological Theory.*

37. *Family, Socialization, and Interaction Process.*

38. Talcott Parsons: "Youth in the Context of American Society," in *Social Structure and Personality;* also, *The American University.*

39. *Ibid.*

40. "The Link Between Character and Society," *op. cit.*

41. Erik Erikson, *Identity and the Life-Cycle.*

42. Talcott Parsons, Robert F. Bales, and Edward A. Shils, *Working Papers in the Theory of Action* (Glencoe: The Free Press, 1953).

43. For example, certain aspects of development should perhaps be analyzed in terms of a simultaneous countervailing cycle running from adaptation to goal attainment to integration to pattern maintenance; or, a model of differentiation of a goal attainment system from a basic diffuse pattern-maintenance system, and then of adaptive and integrative

systems from aspects of both of the prior goal attainment and pattern-maintenance systems, might be appropriate to still other facets of socialization. The specifics of the empirical application of these models are not in question here, but just the notion that there are formal resources within the theory of action for accommodating some processes rather different from those we have discussed. The summation in a formally grounded model does not in this case imply that even the general framework of our discussion is exhaustive of empirical possibilities. Indeed, we suspect that the contrary is the case.

44. Private communication in a discussion among the editors of an earlier draft of Pitts' essay.

13

AN ANALYSIS OF THE PHASES OF DEVELOPMENT IN SELF-ANALYTIC GROUPS

Thomas J. Cottle

In this chapter, I attempt to utilize a series of notions fundamental to Parsons' theories of social structure and social action in order to explain performance in self-analytic groups.[1] It is important to keep in mind throughout this analysis, first, that one must be somewhat selective in the materials he chooses from the theoretical literature, although the emphasis here clearly is on the AGIL paradigm, and second, that we are applying theory of action notions in order to explain phenomena about which Parsons himself has never written. As Parsons gives us only minimal guidance in this enterprise, the problem of the relationship between or fit of theory and data again arises. In recontextualizing the theory of action in self-analytic groups, one must wonder about the degree to which theory is indeed explaining the data of the groups or whether, by merely "juxtaposing" theory and data, we have simply altered one to coincide with the other in more suitable ways than they might naturally fit.

Although selection of materials from self-analytic groups has been accomplished with a built-in bias, this does not imply that only the minor or insignificant bits of group data have been reported. Indeed, our intention is to report primarily the most significant conceptual issues of groups, issues which in one form or another appear to be universal phenomena of self-analytic groups when they are conducted in accordance with the style and structure described later on.

As a final introductory note, it should be stressed that the descriptions and analyses we are about to examine are essentially sociological in nature. The purpose of this chapter, therefore, is not to explore or explain idiosyncratic functions of individual group members or leaders or to linger on the psychological or, more exactly, personality dimensions of group members. To be sure, as Parsons[2] himself has written, the interaction of social and personality systems is an undeniable fact of human existence; but for the present analysis, our task is to examine systematically the structure of action as it evolves over time in a self-analytic group. Accordingly, in the following analysis, the concepts of structure and time assume important roles, for we must conceive of group formation first in terms of the differentiation of roles of actors and second in terms of the development of action over time—over a time, moreover, collectively shared by all actors.

This last is a subtle but important point, one holding true most typically for dyadic relationships. In a self-analytic group, however, it should be recalled that all actors, members, and leaders perform their roles and actions in the same circumscribed time. As in the case of the groups we will consider, the members' collective life history is comprised of three hours a week for an entire academic year. The group literally exists only at these times, and at no other times. As part of the structure of their contract, such as it is, members are discouraged from meeting in other ways or at other times beside the prescribed three hours per week.

In this and other ways, the self-analytic group deviates greatly from the institution of family with which it frequently is compared. All members are potentially present at all sessions, hence all action, even interpersonal interaction between two members, always is played out in front of the audience of remaining members. Whereas in a family, a father and son, say, may be together quite a bit apart from the mother and other children in ways that deeply affect subsequent interaction in the total family, in the self-analytic group, all symbolic father-son relationships are made public to the other members and are thereby incorporated collectively into the group's shared history. If group and family processes are in any ways similar, to a great extent the similarities are based on dinner-table conversations of families when all family members are present. But for the most part, the action of a self-analytic group is better understood without making too many references to family structure.

THE NATURE OF SELF-ANALYTIC GROUPS

As practiced at Harvard University, self-analytic groups are first and foremost designed as a course in an academic department.[3] They are neither extracurricular nor advertised as therapy. Group members are university students, male and female, usually from 18 to 22 years old. Infrequently there may be older persons in the groups. This fact must be stressed, for in this era of burgeoning group experimentation and practice, enormous variations in style and procedure have emerged, with so many practitioners claiming success and productivity. What is often left unreported, however, along with accurate studies of just what transpires in those groups and conceptual descriptions of what is supposed to transpire, is a simple statement of who undertakes these various types of group experiences and how their backgrounds may be affected by and affect the experience.[4] The groups we are describing here have been constructed for young adults in a university setting. The data coming out of these groups therefore reflect the age of the members. Most particularly, issues of authority and intimacy, which we will have occasion to speak about later, remain most salient not necessarily to all people, nor even to all people who seek out group experiences of any sort, but to people of this age group who find themselves in protective institutions like universities where, among other things, dependencies are nurtured.

The leaders of the self-analytic groups about which we are speaking are male and female instructors from the university faculty or graduate students. Each group, consisting of from twenty to twenty-five students, is led by one male and one female instructor who, in the way it has been practiced, sit together at the head of an oval table, usually in the same seats. The groups are observed by graduate students and professional group workers from behind a one-way mirror. Group members know about these observers and indeed see them, as the course requires students to observe their own group from behind the mirror from time to time.

The point here is that built into the visible structure of these groups are the figures of authority. No announcements of equality or symmetry in roles are made in introducing students to the course. Reading lists, paper and examination assignments all represent the fact that two people in each of five groups are in charge. The fact that leaders sit in the same chairs and grade papers serves as a constant reminder of the so-called authority issue.

As justification of this stress on authority, the purpose of the self-analytic group is described to members as being the study of psychological and sociological processes of group development. In the presence of trained faculty leaders, students are to generate their own data vis-à-vis the structure of the group as it has been established by the "course," namely, two leaders, three hours a week. Members are told that individuals seeking personal therapy should not enter these groups, as the expression of personal materials, especially those of a psychopathological nature, is not going to be encouraged. Instead, people are meant to come together to form a group, express their feelings about what is happening, and then seek to understand these feelings and their impressions and to learn about the processes that unravel about them.

This essentially is what the self-analytic group is all about. Twenty or so students, having heard about the group experience from those who have previously been in the course, make application to the instructors. Schedules are arranged, and at the first meeting instructors offer information about the course. They describe the reading list, which includes studies of groups as well as psychological, sociological, and anthropological literature that might elucidate for the students some of the issues they will be speaking about. The reading list and the course paper assignments, which include analysis of dreams and early memories, interpretations of the literature or of a particular theme emerging in the group, or even a discussion of friendship patterns, become major guiding features of the group experience. That is, what is happening in the group is, to a certain extent, oriented to issues on the reading list, which itself follows a pattern of course development.

This is not to say that group members are not spontaneous. It is also not to imply that group behavior is totally predictable. Obviously it is not. What is true, however, is that in all groups any number of topics or issues arise, and leaders see their role as facilitating personal expression and interpreting behavior. In this role they must necessarily pick and choose when they will speak, and about what issues they will speak. Thus, their theoretical orientations will guide them in selecting out certain material, or their own personal preferences and interests will guide them. Either way, all issues cannot be examined, and in the case of the self-analytic group, leaders believe that certain issues are more important than others and hence they tend to emphasize them. In this regard, it is easy to see why leaders might discourage the expression of personal problems if these expressions prevent the group from working on issues that the staff feels it must cover in the course of the academic year.

What some of these issues are will become clear in the body of the chapter. The point to be stressed now is that essentially, the spontaneous reaction of group members to the somewhat circumscribed nature of the course structure in part constitutes the work of the group. In simplistic terms, members are trying to get to know one another, establish a viable network of relationships or social structure, express their feelings about the proceedings, and learn how to understand what is taking place. But they must also wonder about the course, what it is that they are supposed to be learning, and how well they are performing this partly discrete, partly ambiguous task.

To some, therefore, that a self-analytic group provides a medium in which pure social behavior merely evolves is incorrect. Closer to the truth is the idea that students attempt to make sense of this new (group) situation and learn not only group process, but the directions in which their action is meant to proceed by dint of leader observations and interpretations as well as by the course outline and reading lists.

In one sense, the purpose of so-called learning groups (by which term we hope to differentiate them from sensitivity or personal growth groups), is modeled after the early phases of classical psychoanalysis, the phases describing the transference neurosis. For as one comes to perceive it, much of the group's year is spent reacting to the materials that arise not wholly spontaneously from "out of the blue," but rather from the group's structure. In particular, reactions to one's relationship to authority, to other group members, and to the tasks of personal expression and analysis become most salient for all the members. These two dimensions of group work are of course inherent in the very structure of the course and more than merely safeguarded by group leaders. They are at the center of learning experience, and students will be taught ways of dealing with them.

It has been said that essentially what learning groups do is to make for their members a series of problems which must then be resolved so that the members develop an impression that they are "making progress," doing work, or learning about the realities and subtleties of their group. Maintenance or self-regulation therefore become the task of a learning group. However, this is not exactly what self-analytic groups purport to do. As simple-minded as it may seem, I think even year-long self-analytic groups spend much of their time dealing with the personal as well as sociological problems provided by the natural reaction to this unique social setting. It is not only the case that individuals coming from similar backgrounds will experience different responses to authority, or to the constrained intimacy offered in these groups. Equally true is that eighteen, nineteen, and twenty year old men and women will, because of their age or sex, react systematically to these issues of authority and intimacy or to the tasks of expression and analysis.

It is this latter empirically demonstrable fact, namely the similarity of action across groups of similar structure and purpose, that allows researchers to discern universals in different populations, and, even more, that gives us confidence in our belief in a constancy of social structures even when these structures are examined over a period of time as long as one year. Again, in overly simple terms, the sociological constancy provides evidence that the idiosyncratic nature of an individual's psychology is in some way affected, even shaped, by a structure that has been determined literally years before the individual's arrival in this one particular social setting. It is this constancy and coherence of social structure that makes the adaptation of the theory of action, or any theory for that matter which has been derived from the observation of action outside a self-analytic group, appropriate for describing such an enterprise.

Perhaps what I am saying is that I have been so frequently struck by the fact that people of such different backgrounds and personalities, living in such different social worlds, who carry such discrepant impressions of what a group experience will be like, enter self-analytic groups and enact the exact same problems and tasks using almost the exact same language and imagery at almost the exact same point in their respective histories. I am not concluding from this that self-analytic groups brainwash people, nor that leaders of these groups tend to think of all the members, past and present, as being identical, and not at all unique. To the contrary. What I am pointing to is a fact of social existence, namely, that processes of socialization and adaptation bring people to a stage of development where notions of society or social structure become viable constructs not just for social scientific research but for all people as they organize existence. It is in self-analytic groups that individuals learn the power of the collective and the force of conformity laid on them by the very same persons who scream individuality and uniqueness. It is in these groups too, that people learn just how much constraint they seek and require in their quest for absolute freedom, and just how much love for and dependency on authority they nurture in their overt demands for its total annihilation.[5]

The point to be underscored here is represented by the members' expression of a tension between personal growth or individuation, or what they often call a quest for "rolelessness," on the one hand, and their seemingly paradoxical desire to entertain crystal-clear roles which might help them to define their identities and personal development, on the other. The tension becomes one of conceiving of a certain discrepancy between psychological and sociological action. To assume a role, the students might say, is to forfeit authenticity and will. Yet to be unburdened from what they consider to be the vestiges of a role causes them anxiety and leads them, time and again, to a fear that in the absence of structure and consensual social definitions of roles and expectations, they may go crazy. One of the major problems of learning groups in contrast to therapy groups, is that in the absence of a therapeutic contract promising treatment, individuals are obliged to confront the social or public ramifications of their own feelings, fears, fantasies, anxieties, or whatever and obliged moreover to analyze these ramifications in the course of the group's development over time. One of the main features of sociology that members come to learn is, again, the systematic nature of social action and social evolution which originally appear to them as idio-syncratic, unpredictable, or, as we might say, motivated "merely" by the psyche of a single member.[6] Let us elaborate a bit on this point because it serves to introduce the application of the theory of action to self-analytic groups.

There comes a time early in a group's history when the majority of members are conflicted by their desires, as they say, to "get closer" to one another. They are now beginning to recognize that the structure of the group, some of which they have contributed to, is holding them back from something, perhaps preventing intimacy or in some other way inhibiting their behavior. Logically, they seek an alteration, a change, an adjustment, crude or refined, something that might mollify the experienced tension. While it is evident that projective material is uttered in their grievances and rationales for change, there is, nonetheless, a systematic differentiation in the forms of proposals that emerge. First, there is a suggestion to alter, substantially or minimally, the physical and normative nature of the group. Longer sessions, sessions with fewer people, after-session or before-session sessions, marathon sessions and sessions without leaders are proposed. Counterproposals are offered, intimating that various members, while manifestly supporting the desire for change, are perhaps frightened by the concrete measures being advanced.

A second category of change is predicated on keeping the group as it is, but adding a party or an informal get-together which is to be construed as an "extra-curricular approach" to easing tensions and en-

couraging closeness without tampering with the essential structure of the group. This proposal too, is met with all sorts of enthusiasm as well as fear, agreement as well as protest. In some cases parties are held, sometimes with the leaders but usually without the leaders.

While there are many differences between these two proposed styles for change, one for example being the party's unique problem of whether spouses and dates should be allowed to attend, one systematic feature emerges in these proposals which in a way launches us into a discussion of the AGIL paradigm analysis of self-analytic groups. This feature is simply that the alteration of group structure characteristically is proposed by males, whereas the party idea characteristically comes from females. Although it is true that sexually characteristic behavior reflects greater social realities and differentiations, the structure of the group itself is also contributing to the determination of action which ultimately will be differentiated by sex and sex-role appropriate demeanor.[7]

ANALYSIS OF THE ORGANIZATION OF THE GROUP

Keeping this last example in mind, for it will become a crucial one later on, let us turn to the application of the AGIL paradigm to the study of self-analytic groups. As space does not permit a complete exposition, the task at hand becomes one of listing the variables and processes that one might examine in attempting to analyse group content over time with the use of this guiding scheme.

Let us keep in mind throughout the following discussion the difficulty of determining whether acts should be called instrumental or expressive. In this regard, we might suggest that a person may see his or her own act as being either instrumental or expressive, but one of the purposes of this chapter is to suggest that the phases of group development theoretically determine the character of action and how this action is accounted for in the group. But one point should be made clear. Merely expressing a feeling or an attitude that can be interpreted by the group is not enough to call that action or utterance instrumental. Instrumentality, in this theoretical perspective, is organized around phase movements and the central tasks of the group characteristic of that phase. Thus, at one point in the group's development an action may seem to be instrumental, but at another time a similar action may seem expressive. Time and function, among other factors, determine the characteristic of the action. This point should not seem unfamiliar, for in therapy, as an example, the expression of certain material can be viewed very differently as a function of when in time the therapy has progressed and how a particular expression will be interpreted.

Thinking now of the AGIL paradigm recontextualized for self-analytic groups, we start with two obvious differentiating features of the groups, authority or age, and sex. Present is an older man, an older woman, younger men, and younger women. In fact an important qualification must already be raised, for in the early stages of group development, periods exist when age alone becomes the prominent differentiating variable and sex or sex-role differentiation practically disappears from the imagery of members' utterances. Boys become girls, girls become boys, members become children, fathers become mothers, mothers fathers, and older people, irrespective of their sex, remain plain old parents or adults.[8] Toward the end of the group, when as Philip Slater[9] has beautifully documented, religious imagery becomes salient in the rituals and fantasies connected with termination, age differentiations which have previously been so significant tend to dissipate, and sex re-emerges as a dominant differentiating variable. Then, and not surprisingly, age is replaced by a subtle and rather evanescent quality which may best be described as a differentiation between the sacred and the profane.[10] More about this later.

Simplifying the AGIL functions, let us again conceive of them in the classical four-fold representation as follows: The A and G or adaptation and goal-attainment systems now represent the male and female leaders respectively, the adults, the systems of authority or high power, and the predisposition to the sacred. The I and L systems, integration and latency, represent low power, the position of the younger members, or respectively of the girls and the boys. We have then, as Parsons and Bales suggested in their studies of the family, functions more or less of father, mother, daughter, and son. The major vertical differentiation of A-L as opposed to G-I may be described as male versus female or more conveniently, masculine versus feminine. Although the word "versus" is rather strong and possibly misleading, let us suggest that sexual differentiations become of paramount significance for the following reasons.[11]

To begin with, it must be recalled that the self-analytic group consists of two major functions which in turn comprise its learning task. They are expression and interpretation or analysis. Members must be encouraged to undertake both tasks so that ideally, by the end of the group experience, they are able to perform both tasks practically simultaneously with a feeling of competence. In a sense, the tasks may be conceived of as ego functions. In psychoanalytic

theory, it has been written that the ego's function must be "split" into expressing and analysing modes.[12] Because analysis has a good many social-control features about it, we describe it as an instrumental task, the end product, as it were, of the means-oriented expression. Thus, it may be alleged that the act of analysis places the ego conceptually closer to the superego, whereas expression depends upon the ego "becoming in touch" with components of the id. In the case of the group, analysis is associated with the A and L systems which now may be characterized as masculine, instrumental, analytic or interpretive, and social-controlling. Expression in contrast, is associated with the G and I systems and hence with femininity, expressiveness, personal and interpersonal enhancement, and what might be called, for want of a better term, "existential freedom."

In more pragmatic terms, we are suggesting that given, first, the leader's actions, his natural dispositions perhaps, and training, second, the structure of the group, and third, the members' responses, learned or spontaneous, to these structures, dispositions, and training, men emphasize understanding and control of emotion or rationality, whereas women emphasize expression of emotion, although not necessarily irrationality. Said differently, and presumably this phrase would make sense to people who have undergone group experiences, men evidence a concern to know where the group is going, where it has been, and why, not only in a particular session, but in the entire course of a group's history. In addition, they assume an agential function in directing the outcome of events and for that matter, whole sessions.[13] This would be the instrumental modality. Women, in contrast, seem less concerned with how events fit together, particularly in the historical context, but more involved with making something happen for a present instant. This would be the expressive modality. It is essentially to explain these features that we have put forth the phrase, "existential freedom."

The vertical differentiation of the AGIL system also involves the distinction between the masculine cerebral or cognitive and the feminine affective, by which we mean control of knowing versus reinforcement of emotion. Still another distinction, although one of a more metaphorical nature, is a male concern with the form of group content and the female concern with the color or mood of this content. Kant's distinction of the intellectual or rational versus the sensuous is relevant here,[14] and though the terms are slightly different, they describe well many of the problems faced by men and women during the group's evolution.

As we have mentioned, the age disparity causes a major differentiation for group members at the very start. More accurately, the connection of adulthood with power makes the superordinate-subordinate arrangements or the authority issue the essential problem of the group's first phases. Members must learn how to deal with it, define and control it. But with the issue of identification with authority or opposition to it arises as well the group's internalization of authority functions which ultimately means the establishment of a normative order, or a social contract for the group.[15] Even with the instructions contained in the original course contract, the so-called ground rules as set down by adult authority, members themselves must reconstruct this contract and necessarily confront its unwritten clauses and its specific applications for themselves. Initially, men assume this role, a role we now might label "appropriateness advisor." In the early stages of the group, this role characterizes the primary functions associated with the latency system. The task of interpreting, codifying, and implementing the leaders' instructions and ideals for the group falls to the group sons. Contracts and "laws" must be rewritten, agreed upon and eventually sanctified by the father figure, but in the beginning the sons believe it is they who have somehow conceived of the moral order that will bind the group together.[16]

Among the earliest roles established in the group, therefore, are the roles of politician/lawyer/policeman, or more precisely, the boys who wish to play politician/lawyer/policeman. All three of these related roles, moreover, are predicated on the maintenance of collective coherence and law obeyance. People must be present and accounted for, and things and events must make sense. And all must be controllable or somehow calculable. It is not uncommon in these early hours for groups to try out governmental routines. Potential leaders then are elected in some simple fashion or someone will be designated to come in each time with a topic for discussion. But whether it is a young lawyer arguing for cognitive coherence and rationality and thereby social control, or a young policeman employing his physical strength in order to keep people in line, the earliest task is one of establishing a normative order sufficiently durable to withstand the expression of impulses and feelings. Nothing must damage the coherence and cohesion that this order purportedly is meant to protect.

In summary, the instrumental task characteristically performed by male members in their position of low power is initially a task of arranging or preparing for organized collective action. In superego terms, the inhibition or control of impulses and keeping people from breaking the law become paramount concerns. For a while in these early hours, the authority of the group, the father and mother figures as it were, is honored and obeyed, and even cherished.[17]

So that the terms we are employing and borrowing from Parsons will not be confused, it should be stress-

ed that the emphasis in this first group phase is one of predictability of behavior and social coherence. Social integration in the early phases remains more characteristic of women's demands, as we now will observe.[18]

The function of the integrative system in the early stages of group development is consonant with the expressive-feminine mode. Women emphasize the urge to express impulses, particularly impulses of sexuality and intimacy. For the moment it is inconsequential whether one chooses to call the expression of erotic material at this point in the group's history "pre-Oedipal" eroticism or "mature" eroticism. The point is that the stress on integration comes about as women insist on cohesion based on a sexualized intimacy. In this regard, coherence is transposed slightly to mean interpersonal coherence which in effect presages the notion of a series of marriages, serial monogamy, rather than the depersonalized collective egalitarianism advanced at about the same time by the group's men. It is not surprising to find some women suggesting that everyone pair off and let the various fragmented partners keep the diffuse concept of a group alive as best they can. What one finds then, in this the early "stage of daughters," is a tendency to legitimate impulse expression and to discover a profane communion by dividing the group into a series of partnerships, friends, or mates.[19]

Whereas men seek a coherence to be used for control, women argue for expression of emotion which they hope will lead to individual personal acceptance and a generalized public communion.[20] Both sexes, therefore, announce their ideal plans for group development and in so doing express the most difficult problems they face in confronting the transcendent structure of the group.

If one recognizes that authority and intimacy are powerful issues in such learning groups, male members are at a strict disadvantage if only because they can neither advance to the position of group father nor use eroticism or seduction as women might, as means of attaining even a precarious psychic equality with either of the adults present. Accordingly, a profound differentiation in purpose results as men in the group band together in the form of the proverbial horde, in an effort to stop the male leader from owning all the women in the group and to keep the women from seducing the male leader away from them. Even though the men recognize the fantasy components and justifications of their budding union, they nonetheless attempt to work it out. But their task is not easily completed, for they also must deal with their need to keep the male and female leaders united because a split at this higher level might make both leaders sexually "available" to group members. In addition, the men must somehow resolve what emerges as a frightening need to kill not only the male leader (in somewhat of a replication of the Oedipal myth) as the only way to deal with his (imagined) force, but the women too, perhaps because of their imagined sexual potency, and one another as well, for each represents a potential threat to the integrity of the horde.[21]

Working backward a bit, we note that the males' drive for predictibility, rationality, coherence, and what amounts to "law and order" has been generated precisely by their very own drives to kill and make lawlessness and disorder. In these early phases, the impulses to agress and destroy have been neutralized somewhat and then socialized in part by a superego demanding control and sanity. In a word, the men have worked to keep the women together and simultaneously apart from the male leader. Because of this, a rather rigorous system of taboos must be instituted if only to make certain that no man in the group, old or young, will develop a special ("outside") involvement with any woman, and vice versa. In what we might call a primitive modality, the men implicitly agree that should there be a violation of this rather elaborate fantasied taboo arrangement, the guilty woman will be singled out and punished, while the implicated man will be exonerated.[22]

Conversely, in the integrative system, women select a very different philosophy to govern their work. Emerging rather early is not the desire to silence through death, but a pattern of possessing or incorporating through intimacy, sexuality, or social communion or pairing off. In contrast to the male strategy, the female tactic implies that women in no way desire collective unity or equality, at this time anyway. Quite the opposite. Be it conscious or unconscious, their strategy is to demonstrate to the men their availability and individuality. To be "really in the group," they must somehow lessen any bonds that hold them to outside persons and objects. In this way they communicate to the male authority that they are attached to no group member, male or female, and certainly free from a collective loyalty which might make them less attractive or less committed. Not surprisingly, the ensuing competition among women shocks and frightens some of the men who, in the beginning, have agreed to keep themselves in line and compete together as a team, gang, or horde. Ironically, the concept of individuality now seems to be more consonant with the feminine role than with the masculine role, as seduction and eroticism become a woman's essential weapons.

It is every woman on her own and may the best woman win. Men are not on their own, but instead find themselves busily at work strengthening the male-male bonds that Freud, Durkheim, and more recently Lionel Tiger allege provide them solidarity and life support. Everyone seems to know that, if finally agreed upon, sexual activity between the male leader and the female members would destroy the group's social and psychological coherence in the same way as might an assassination of the male authority. Everyone also seems to realize that the Oedipal configurations of father and daughter, on the one hand, and mother and son, on the other, are not symmetrical. For whatever reasons, the former is a more legitimate possibility for group members than the latter, although both possibilities clearly exist in the fantasies of members.

PHASES IN GROUP DEVELOPMENT: L AND I

The foregoing discussion has revealed at least two theoretical propositions. First is the differentiation of characteristically masculine and feminine behavior, and second is the allegation that groups confront a series of maintenance problems over time and must, at some level, resolve these problems one by one, presumably, in some manageable order. As the order corresponds to the sexual differentiations, men deal first with the problems of predictability, preparation, normative order, and social control, and thereby initiate practically all of the group's action by honoring, if we may say it this way, the primacy of latency functions. For the moment, women must wait their turn; hence, when the development of the group moves counterclockwise into the "modalities" of the integrative system, different behavior and a truly distinct form of social order prevails, an order which often enough men cannot fully comprehend.

The logical extension of this argument would be that group development proceeds, still counterclockwise, through a stage of goal attainment or gratification functions and concludes by pursuing those functions described by the adaptive system. It is precisely this extension in our argument that we will advance in a moment.[23] Before reaching that point, however, several preparatory issues must be outlined.

If there are tasks which characterize the early phases, the L-phase and I-phase of a self-analytic group, they are de-differentiation from the world outside the group, and then the resolution of the exclusion-inclusion or membership definition problem. As with so many group phenomena, the analogous structures outside the group in the larger society will begin to seem rather obvious. Initially the task of de-differentiation is handled by men particularly, presumably because of their overriding orientation to what Parsons calls instrumental activism.[24] During both the early and later phases of the group (that is, during the L- and A-phases) male members work to relate in-group activity to outside-group activity or vice versa. For some men this means hunting for the utilitarian values of the group. How, they ask, may group experiences be used elsewhere? What can be taken away and applied to external action? What from the outside may be successfully employed in here?

In social psychological terms, de-differentiation falls to men partly because it threatens or contributes to the normative order they have established. What existed in the outside must be immediately transplanted to the inside. At least this is their first position. This means that status hierarchies will be established around some agreed-upon dimensions like potency, intelligence, analytic skill, sexual attractiveness, even physical size and strength, or maybe age or university status. Freshmen after all, cannot lead seniors. But the major point in this context is that at the outset, the males need to initiate agential activity to believe that action is occurring. Accordingly they attempt a replication of an external social and moral order within the group. At this time, they evidence their concern for making action and events happen. Things will just not evolve on their own; they must be directed to some created end states of ideals.

Inherent in this initial confusion over the differentiation process of the external and internal characteristic of the L-phase are the inchoate strands of what later on will emerge as exchange: what to include from the outside and what to transport from the inside (as soon as one can) to the outside. We mention this here because early group development is often characterized by members' attempts to turn many of their outside friendships into group-like activities. Any gathering is almost immediately transformed into a pretend self-analytic group, despite the leaders' previous admonishments to refrain from doing this. Theoretically, this spreading of its work is an indication that the group has not yet fully differentiated either its membership or its functions and tasks from the realities external to it. Members are transporting group material to the outside. Later on, they will seek the reverse when they bid to allow outsiders to attend a group session. Both of these occurrences symbolize the unsettled resolutions of de-differentiation, as well as the complexity of arranging for a viable social order in the group. Importantly, they also symbolize forms of *resistance* to group work, something we will say more about later on. For the present, let us keep in mind the proposition that much of the action of the I- and L-phases in fact turns out to reveal qualities of a resistant nature, resistant, that is, to the tasks of expression of feeling and analysis.

At the psychological level, a significant preparation is underway during the latency phase. Related to de-differentiation, this preparation has to do with members' recognition that eventually group activity will employ fantasy and feeling as the essential media of exchange, indeed as the essential media of affective exchange. Unlike the outside world of money, work and performance, the expression of fantasy and feeling will assume a primary value for these men in this new and strange context. Unhappily, there is little they now find that can be brought in from the outside that might help them to transcend their early fears and anxieties about this novel and rather frightening prospect. It is not surprising, therefore, that in the latency phase men attempt to establish a viable, even permanent order of social relationships which they hope might sustain them through the crises that must inevitably occur when affect and fantasy supplant instrumental activism and cognitive rationality as the main parameters of social existence and exchange.

In summary, the de-differentiation process involves a resolution of the external-internal problem, as well as a delineation of the boundary lines between the pattern variable of affectivity versus affective neutrality.[25] In fact, one might argue that all four pattern variables of action shift emphasis during group development as persons learn to leave behind some of their prior expectations about groups, as well as some of the strategies they had been accustomed to using in "regular" or more routine interactions. More precisely, what men in particular will have to reconcile is that action occurring in the goal attainment and integrative phases will be characterized by the pattern variable options of affectivity, individual orientation, particularism, and diffuseness. In the latency phase, the alternative options, affective neutrality, collective orientation, universalism, and specificity are more appropriate as they will be again months later when the group concludes in the adaptive phase. In the meantime, men have begun to recognize that the pattern variables governing their forms of action will have to be altered at some point, then altered again.

The second early task, the resolution of the exclusion-inclusion process, is handled a bit differently by men and women. Pursuing our temporal suggestions, it appears in slightly different forms in the L- and I-phases. In the L-phase, the issue to be settled is one of sociological inclusion, or one man, one vote. No one must have more or less power, more or less say. No one's voice must be louder than the others. The purpose of the social structure desired at this time is to hold people in check. Without doubt, men in particular begin to feel a tension stemming from the ambivalence about leading the group.

While they might like to take over, they soon learn that it is best to conform and remain innocuous, at least in the beginning. Later on they will learn that what in part is causing this ambivalence is the fact that criteria for leadership performance cannot be derived from the world outside the group but must come from within the group. Members will not learn of these criteria, however, until the group as a whole moves into the goal attainment phase of its development.

While the members make certain that all are present, accounted for, and of roughly equal status, a task which implies that males and females would be best lumped together simply as people, or group members, there suddenly emerges a new form, a later form perhaps, of social inclusion. This form revolves around the problem of silent members, those persons who, after even a short period in the group, are accused by members of not participating at the yet unstated but still agreed upon level of appropriate contribution. In a word, it is felt that silent members are not "pulling their load" and therefore do not deserve equal status or, more severely, the right to be included. The urging of silent persons to speak is typically an action taken by group members who seek leadership positions, however slight. Without the knowledge of how they are performing in the eyes of certain (silent) members, they cannot know whether they have won those members' votes of confidence and approval.

There are in addition religious as well as sexual aspects to the impressions of and projections onto silent members. Without going into detail, it may be suggested that silence is associated simultaneously with purity and prudery. Silent members, therefore, lead what in the early phases of the group appear to be ascetic roles which, for one reason or another, cannot be tolerated by the majority of members. Interestingly, the resistance to group work which in part determines the silence, is rarely commented upon at this time. Yet, this could be explained by the fact that members generally do not begin to appreciate the meanings and forms of resistance until much later on. For the moment, silence is necessarily treated in the context of differentiation, inclusion, and leadership, and as an obstruction to an agreed upon social order. But it is even more complex.

To understand the problems of inclusion and the coercing of silent members to speak, it must be recalled that nothing happens in the way of social action that may be shared by all and given proper status in the group's history until someone speaks aloud. Speaking, therefore, is the medium of social cohesion, action, dissolution, and progress. It is in a sense, life itself. Not to speak is death; it is nonbeing,

anti-existence. Silence is to be stilled and paralyzed; it is the feeling of being unable to come untracked. At no time is this more in evidence than at the beginning of the group when, after all administrative items have been attended to and the leaders suggest it is time to begin, the group sits in silence for a period of time that seems to them centuries, hoping that someone will speak and thereby launch them and their lives together. Although they inevitably resent the first speaker, the first voice, they also remain thankful to him throughout the course of the group's history.

To withold thoughts or feelings, not to speak, to sit in silence, therefore, means many things to the various members. But in a sociological sense it implies exclusion, an action the group cannot condone. Silence violates the ethic of equality and equal sharing in responsibility, danger, and health. It means failure to obey the law and use one's right to vote. Moreover, for some reason, the silent member looms larger than life and in a way he becomes more important than all the remaining members.[26] He is the devil himself, for in his refusal to speak, his silence augurs the death of the group. As the devil, the silent member becomes the polar opposite of the person who has spoken first, for this member becomes the Son of God, the one whose voice was heard first upon the earth.

Regressive Phenomena and Group Change

Earlier we spoke of a differentiation along the horizontal axis of the AGIL system and suggested that the L- and I-systems, the systems of the "children," were also the systems of the profane. The A- and G-systems, conversely, were given the status of adult and predisposition to sacredness. The L- and I-systems, the first two phases of the group, now may also be seen as phases of what we might call "talk-acting." By this term we mean that while spoken language remains the essential method of communication, there is, both in the imagery of language as well as in the physical actions of members, a method of acting out the problems confronting the group in these early phases. Later on, the group will learn to talk everything out rather than talk-act, but at the outset, social movement and action seem to be congenial methods for approaching issues. Until the group reaches G- and eventually A-phase functions, it does not really have a codified sense of the problems it has been facing in maintaining its own miniature system of social interactions. Earlier, it acts and speaks its way through the problems it encounters.

This is a key point, one that relates to the notions

of de-differentiation of the external and internal, the change over from cognitive rationality to fantasy, and the problem of member inclusion.[27] In the first two phases of the group's development, members are not yet able to articulate what in fact it is that they are doing, for what reasons and for what consequences and value. Not surprisingly, they feel tension, confusion, and perhaps even a fear that they may be going crazy. Never before perhaps has social reality been so flexible, ambiguous and, importantly, so crammed full of fantasy materials that individuals can barely begin to recognize much less comprehend or reincorporate as part of their behavior. The acting out of fantasies like climbing on tables, crawling under chairs, wearing unusual clothing, or bringing all sorts of strange objects into the room reveal the bewilderment and fright associated with living in a context predicated on undeciphered fantasies and uncodified expressions.

These actions, moreover, are symbolic of and serve as an indication that regression in this new social reality has begun to take place. We might even argue, as many have, that regression, the belief that social order is breaking down and that subsequently people may go crazy, is a fundamental requirement for the group. People must regress somewhat as the phenomenon of regression is associated with the constant expression of fantasies and feelings, the letting down of social defenses, and a de-emphasizing of cognitive skills. At the same time it is a vital component and consequent of a social order built around the values of expressing feelings, some of which are poorly understood. The act of regression and the type of language and processes of exchange which ensue during regressive periods allow the group to move through its early phases relatively unencumbered by adult, coherent, logical, and rational constraints. As best as they can, leaders have asked members to let their feelings come out and to temporarily suspend the consequences of these feelings, or at best, their fears of constraint and punition, for this is a time and a place (though not a microsociety) where (almost) anything goes. It is more a period of id expression than of superego control, and not yet the time of assumption of the ego's executive functions. A certain degree of regression, therefore, is required in order to produce the energy and the materials, that is, the substance and the limitations of the group's developing history.

As it plays such an important role in the group, the act of regression must be clarified somewhat. In the main, group regression occurs as a result of the leaders' encouragement to permit the free expression of feelings despite the degree to which members might believe they are acting in an *infantile* fashion. In one respect therefore, adult sanctions and generalized rules governing actions are suspended or weakened so that expressions rarely heard or understood may emerge. To a good measure, the energy of regression is narcissism,[28] and here narcissism refers to self love as well as love of one's group: I am important; the group is important. Even more, the image of this "infantile self" is now reflected in the pool that is the group.

As regression implies the reduction of normal rules and rituals of interaction, it is expected that regulations and rules of language will also begin to relax. Indeed, in self-analytic groups where regression only infrequently implies the frenetic acting out of emotion usually associated with behavior of deeply disturbed persons, the best indicator of regression along with the content of materials, is the breakdown of linearity in speech. A single member's sentences may not follow one another, and conversation seems to lose coherence as one person's utterance has little to do with the utterances of the person who has spoken previously. Although the content of regressive material is affected by the particular phase of group development, it is the breakdown of linearity in speech that offers the clue that regressive activity is underway. Suprisingly, the mood of a group may seem sanguine and sane even though language is becoming less intelligible or comprehensible.

There is an important theoretical point about regression that should be noted. The nature of the self-analytic group structure coupled with members' anticipations of what might happen, or indeed their knowledge of what has happened to fellow students in groups of this sort, greatly complicates the issue of regression. For one thing, it is possible that term-paper assignments and books in the reading list throw people backward and forward in time, in terms of how they conceive of the group. For another thing, the so-called sociological phase in which the group is presently located can and does affect the type of personal material that a person might wish to speak about. Then too, it may be, as Parsons has suggested in other contexts, that each phase will itself show sub-phases, reflections, perhaps, of all four phases. Thus, for example, in the goal attainment phase of the group, one may see behavior characteristic of the prior phases, the tendency we are calling regression, as well as behavior anticipating the adaptive phase. This too, is part of the so-called regressive phenomenon, namely, that in realizing that the group's tasks and orientations are changing, some members may suddenly appear to be acting in ways more characteristic of a later phase. It is not uncommon, therefore, in these phase-shifting regressive periods, for leaders to remind certain members that termination is still way off in the distance.

There is another source of evidence for this notion

of subphases within a particular phase. It is not atypical of self-analytic groups to reveal subcultures, small groups of students whose population may indeed shift from time to time. Clusters of friendships, naturally, grow up in every group, but one also sees these clusters being affected by the task confronting the group or by the phase of its development. Thus, what we are calling regressive behavior may very well be instigated or perpetuated by certain group members who for some reason attempt to keep the group at a particular phase.

Regression, however, like so many other group actions, contains qualities of resistance as well. Building social structures, having sexual relationships, and regressing are not the goals of a self-analytic group. They probably are the situations and contents which the group must work with in order to achieve its goals of relatively free expression without the corresponding action and analysis, but in this sense, they are all but means to an end. Consequently, leaders speak to the resistance component of any of these activities when they feel that members are indulging in them. In other words, it is the excessive indulgence in a mood, fantasy or activity that indicates that the constraining or controlling elements have been suspended or done away with for too long a time. Said differently, from sociological and psychological points of view, groups can deal with a particular problem, crisis, or phase for only so long. At some point, they must move on. This is especially true of regression.

But regression is also embarrassing to group members. To a certain extent, it is found to be degrading and surprising, if not mortifying. Members confess amazement that they would be participating in such a "ridiculous activity" or weaving such foolish fantasies together, but of course there are also pleasures connected with it. Yet, what stays with the members and becomes a central maintenance problem is precisely this temporary impression of the degradation associated with regression. It would be all right if everyone regressed together. But if silent members refuse to participate and assume the role of observer, then the silent members have slipped out of the level of the profane (and no one presumably, can be more profane than regressed people) and have moved into either of two other projected levels, the sacred or the subhuman.

Group members, however, will not permit their silent colleagues to raise themselves to the level of the sacred, for this would be to acknowledge the silent members' alliance with the group leaders, who, in these early phases, are viewed as being omnipotent, immortal, and in many ways, sacred. No, the silent members must not be allowed to sit with these God-like people; they must not be seen as being above it

all. That means they must be relegated to the level of the subhuman, which in turn implies that they are either too ignorant, too poorly "equipped" to participate or that they are sexually inadequate or perhaps overly adequate and therefore freaks of nature. These notions incidentally are not speculative; they are derived from the actual speech of group members.

The inclusion of silent members therefore, is associated with the regulation of the group's social order, the differentiation of fantasy and cognitive rationality, and with the emerging styles of members' relation to authority. Let us touch briefly upon this last point.

The Development of Sex Roles

We noted earlier that male bonds are drawn fairly tightly together in order to produce a protective horde which might fend off the projected power of the male leader as well as maintain the integrity of all male-female relationships in the group. We noted also that women appear less ready to establish comparable bonds, or at least bonds of similar intensity. For women, remaining sexually available to men in the group, especially at first to the male leader, meant that they must compete among themselves in order to establish what amounts to a hierarchy of not only sexual attractiveness, but of inferred sexual experience or maturity. Whether they are aware of it or not, women may "line up" in a group according to age, marital status, motherhood, or unstated sexual maturity. To be fully included, some women make it clear that they have had many sexual encounters and are prepared thereby to become a good and seasoned wife or "group woman." Other women feel excluded by token of the fact that in "real life" they are engaged or married. For some group members this fact makes them even more appealing, as sexual fantasies now may develop free of the inhibitions and sanctions imposed by social reality. Other women opt for the role of innocent little girl or "group baby." Forfeiting the possibility of heterosexuality altogether, they communicate in their way that when all group marriages have taken place and that when all the fantasied orgies and adultery are committed they will be happy to join any new family of adults that might have formed.

Male potency and attractiveness, among other qualities, produce similar effects among men, although in the beginning of the group, this hierarchy is greatly submerged by the features of the latency phase of which we have spoken previously.

All of these arrangements are fine and seem to work out adequately, given the stage of the group's development. That is, all goes well until the silent member emerges as a threat to or violation of the status quo the males have sought to erect. The silent one is often accused by the men of knowing too much about them and of using this knowledge to hurt them in some fashion. This type of projection thereby elevates the silent member to a plane of transhuman status or sacredness and clearly represents the male association of silent members with group leaders who also are relatively silent in these early phases and who also could render damage with the information they too seem to be gathering.

In conceptual terms, during the L-phase of development, a silent male threatens the exclusion-inclusion resolution and weakens the possibility that when regression commences, individual impulses may be collectivized and brought safely to the level of social structure. Silence violates the part of the contract demanding that freedom of expression means that everyone must talk. It becomes the job of these young "appropriateness advisors" to urge the silent member, especially a male member, to participate, to join the horde, the club, the gang, and thereby become identical in status and role to all other group members. Notice here that we say identical to all other group members, not just identical to the other men. The important function of the latency phase in the fantasies of these politician/lawyer/police figures is to render everyone alike, men and women, and everyone responsible to the same degree to the same laws and rituals. There must be no exceptions, no exclusions. Indeed, in a later phase of development, the integrative phase, men will insist that leaders too become exactly like them, do like them, and speak like them. But that time has not yet arrived.

The corner stones underlying the primacy of the L-phase's stress on collectivization and social control, therefore, are the thrust of conformity and conventionalism, in this growing childlike world: If one speaks, all must speak; if one regresses, all must regress; if one goes crazy, all must go crazy, and if one fails to understand, all must fail to understand. Coherence, cohesion, collectivized action all add up to the crystallization of roles, the temporary inhibition of individuality, and a resulting identicality of the members. And all of this is accomplished as preparation for a later differentiation which will insure a tolerance of human differences and the growth of individuation and autonomy. The silent members had better obey or get out. And here, "getting out" would be the punishment meted out by members themselves as a way of dealing with individuals who seek a special status of any sort. The punishment and the poorly formed "theory" behind it serve to keep the mechanisms of social control in the ruling hands of the members and hence out of the hands of leaders. This procedure differs somewhat from the mechanism we are about to examine, the mechanism of inclusion that occurs among women and characterizes action in the integrative phase.

The resolution of the inclusion-exclusion problem among women, which for the moment prevents group development, is tied to the notion of intimacy in the integrative phase and symbolized by the crisis presented by the silent member. To understand the process we are about to describe, it is essential that two earlier notions of Parsons' AGIL paradigm be recalled, particularly as the paradigm has been employed for study of family interaction. Those notions suggest, first, that a series of relationships emerge between the functions of the various system-phases. More specifically, daughters relate in characteristic fashion to fathers, mothers, and brothers. Second, within each phase, action occurs which will be subsumed by the primacy of that phase, as for example, the stress on collective coherence in the latency phase, but which, in addition, will anticipate or recall for the group the action and behavior of later and prior phases. Thus, one finds in the integrative phase remnants of material that "properly" could be designated as latency material. Indeed, one often hears members saying to one another, "oh, come on, we've been through that already," or "don't hang us up on that again." Usually, the reversion of action to a prior phase is colored by the primacy of the phase in which the action presently is taking place. In other words, when there is a reversion from say, the I-phase to the L-phase, I-phase action does not evolve in the same way it did when the group in fact was in the L-phase.

There are then, two features relevant to our analysis of temporal phases of self-analytic group development, first, the relationship between people representing the various phases or primacies and, second, the incorporation of A, G, I, and L components in each of the four phases.

We return to the female resolution of the exclusion-inclusion problem, which we now recognize to be a problem common to both the L-phase and the I-phase, although one treated distinctly in each. During the I-phase, women usually reveal for the first time their relationship with or attitudes toward authority, that is, they express their conceptual relationship with the adaptive and goal attainment primacies and figures by handling the inclusion problem in the following symbolic form.

To begin, they establish the sexual hierarchy to which we have previously alluded. It is a hierarchy predicated on sexuality but as the psychosocial development of the group has not yet reached a point transcending the level of regression characteristic of the two early phases, sexuality now must be considered "at most" Oedipal sexuality. Said differently, while the women might insist that the love they have begun to express for the male leader is real, honest, mature, and "like all other love," it is evident later on in the goal attainment phase that the sexuality is in fact that expressed by daughters for their fathers and mothers.

But how can it be that if the young women are lined up along these sexual criteria and characteristics that they could fail to differentiate between fathers and mothers? As we noted before, in the two earliest phases, there comes to be a blurring of the L-phase and the I-phase, on the one hand, and the A-phase and the G-phase, on the other. We suggested that this blurring results in part from the regressive action necessary in these early phases. Thus, there is a time in the group's history, a time which follows the events we are about to describe, when it actually does seem as though men and women are identical, except perhaps for differences in their ages. Nonetheless, at one level, a sexual hierarchy is retained which ostensibly excludes the males. This exclusion is attested to by the infrequency of male utterances during this period of the I-phase.

When the hierarchy is formed in its loose way, the silent female, should there be one, is then approached, this time by the women, and especially by the potential female leaders of the group. It becomes their special task to pull the silent one "into line." But the hierarchy, recall, is a sexual one, predicated on the projection of perceived purity and prudery. Here then is the key to this significant action of the integrative phase, and here too is the demonstration of a paradigmatic relationship between the primacy figures of the various stages. For the action taken by these young female leaders may be interpreted as an insistence that initiation, that is, inclusion into the group, requires that no one be free of sexual experience. It requires that no one be pure, no one be puritanical, no one be a virgin, no one be at an age preceding menstruation. Throughout the formative weeks of the group, such as they are, many references are made to drawing first blood, pricking the skin, and the like. Surely these references may be connected to the acts of circumcision, menstruation, childbirth, and other sources of blood flow that make people whole, mature, official members of a group or simply the incumbents of an established status as, for example, "blood brothers."[29]

But action in the integrative phase possesses, in addition, components that Freud described in his paper on "The Taboo of Virginity."[30] The women, it would seem, cannot tolerate a woman in the group either so young that she has not yet been reminded of her sexual capabilities through the onset of menstruation or, more likely, one so inexperienced that she has not yet known sexual intercourse. If in fact she has remained pure, it would happen that she would become the prime and ideal sexual object of the male

leader. For in his early capacity as protector and father, it would be he who would have to perform the defloration, ultimately allowing this silent woman to become an honorable member of the group. (Notice here, in these first two phases of membership stability, that individuals must pass through ceremonies which allow them to become full-fledged "neuter" members as well as full-fledged group males or females.) This primitive conceptualization by group members seems to take on a powerful significance in the integrative or what we have referred to as the impulse-expressive phase of a self-analytic group.

Standing in contrast to the controlling components of latency phase styles of inclusion, the initiation ceremony of the I-phase represents the relationship of I-phase actions to A-phase and G-phase actions. Specifically, in the L-phase, the inclusion of silent members by males typifies a masculine method of obeying the directive of group integrity handed down by authority. Women perform the inclusion-virginity ceremony by employing a method that depicts their style of obeying what they interpret to be a demand by the leaders. Neither sex permits the most silent or for that matter, the most vociferous group members to attain a status above them, which in this case means a position closer to the leaders. Thus, whereas the masculine procedure is to have all obey the law, the feminine response is to insist that all reveal a willingness to "play the game" on an equal basis, with the game now involving sexual overtures in part because of the women's own stress on intimacy.

This last point should be underscored, for in a small way it answers the question, from what sources do group members develop the fantasy that the male leader wishes to possess all of the group's women? We now see that one source is the women themselves, who have hurled sexuality into the group during the integrative phase just when the men had presumably prevented such a "disruption" through the contracts of social order and constraint which they had negotiated in the latency phase.[31] Yet it should not be forgotten that the daughter-father role dominates this female intimacy just as the son-father role determines the fantasy that fathers possess all women. As it happens, the erotic attachment generally between members, as Slater[32] has pointed out, is mediated in these first two stages through the group leaders. It is for this reason that we argue for the Oedipal or even pre-Oedipal nature of the love expressed during the integrative phase.[33] It is only natural then that seduction would be a style of action considered, if not finally accepted, by the group's women but strongly resisted by its men. More importantly, seduction, rape, and even sadistic action become the natural projections of members onto leaders in the I-phase, for they represent action based on the very impulses that have to be socially controlled by the social contracts previously negotiated. The impulses, therefore, undergo two transformations. First, they are controlled through the structure of social order, and, second, the residues are projected on to the leaders whose initially superior status makes it appear that their actions will neither be governed nor controlled by the contracts. This in turn implies, as some members confess, that the fantasies expressed in these first two phases may just come true.

Overview of the First Two Phases

Let us now take a moment to recapitulate not the content of these theoretical notions but, more generally, some of the notions we have advanced thus far.

First, the phases of a self-analytic group follow a counterclockwise motion through, respectively, L, I, G, and A system functions. Second, each phase possesses components of the other three phases, hence, various developmental sequences may be delineated at any point in time of the group's history.[34] These components, moreover, anticipate or recall for the group movements in its history. Third, each phase presents its own characteristic maintenance problems or crises which are attacked by the group according to the primacy of action inherent in a particular phase. Fourth, each phase is affected, as it were, by the phases immediately in touch with it in this counterclockwise model. The work of the latency phase for example, carries out the "orders," such as they are, of the adaptive phase, but it is also affected by the action appropriate to the integrative phase. Said differently, in one respect, sons have more in common with their fathers than do their sisters, while in another respect, children of either sex have more in common with one another than they do with either of their parents.

The work of the latency and integrative phases is essentially preparative in nature. As we noted in the earlier discussion of resistance, arranging for a socially coherent order in which impulses may be expressed is not the end state of the self-analytic group; it is one foundation. This foundation, furthermore, is comprised of characteristically masculine and feminine features which are themselves somewhat coincident with group phases. Although expression and analysis remain the group tasks, authority and intimacy remain the fundamental social psychological issues. The vertical and horizontal axes of the AGIL system, therefore, retain their prominence throughout the group's life. The notion of phases clarifies the content of the changing ways in which fundamentally authority and intimacy are managed, or, as we say, "worked through." The interrelationship of phases and of the primary figures in the phases over time and the presence of components from the other three phases within any particular phase help to clarify, above all, this "working through" of authority and intimacy issues.

The social structure which men in particular seek to establish in the latency phase serves several functions. Among them are group cohesion, the development of trust, a stress on coherence and control which are themselves related to the preparation for and recognition of later expression of impulses and fantasies, and the honoring of authority in terms of respect and obedience. At the group's inception, leaders are accepted as part of the fabric; their instructions and authority remain unquestioned. Men's first work is to carry out the directives handed down from above as best as they can interpret them. This does not mean, however, that members are not a bit frightened by what they imagine will soon come to pass. Their fantasies reveal this fright as well as the contents of it.

During the integrative phase, women in particular bring to the group a sense of inclusion rather than coherence and collectivity, essentially through their emphasis on impulse expression. Impulse expression becomes the proposed method for integrating members. Whereas men, in their way, tend to neutralize sexual attractions in the earliest phase, women transform attractions into infatuations which for a while seems to be the result of their involvement with authority. Desiring and being desired are characteristic themes of the integrative phase, with both terms suggesting a sense of incompleteness, inadequacy, or lack. In what amounts to almost a play on words, men bind impulses, socialize them to bring about group cohesion. Women, however, bind themselves to people, especially authority, through the expression of their desires and impulses of intimacy. It is for this reason that pairing off becomes a major form of integration in this phase rather than total group love which will emerge in the goal attainment phase. It is also because of this binding capacity of sexual impulses and the ensuing infatuation that we have attributed an Oedipal or pre-Oedipal character to the infatuations developing at this time.[35]

To be sure, the binding of people together that results first from the construction of a social order and then from the expression of sexual impulses, Oedipal or otherwise, brings the group one step closer to the state of interpersonal trust and gratification discovered in the G-phase. But the expression of impulses, infatuation, desire, and this binding process which could be construed as an object cathexis alters the relationship of the men in the group vis-à-vis authority. Where earlier the male authority in particular was trustworthy and respected, he now is invested with sexual powers, desires, and impulses that if used would destroy the group. Suddenly, his very presence must be questioned and his intentions made public and unequivocal. And all of this must happen before he "answers" the women's invitation.

In summary, one result of the integrative phase is to place the father and the sons in a highly competitive situation from which women are excluded and about which women seem confused. At this point, the manifest content of impulse expression and infatuation is heterosexual in nature. Later on, the latent homosexual content will emerge. It is during the integrative phase of the group that the power of impulses, infatuations, and fantasies becomes so strong and overriding that the only way to handle it seems to be through denial. We will say more about this further on in a discussion of phase-specific defenses. For the moment, let us note how group development not only brings new content and new recognitions, but constantly demands a reordering of relationships between members and authority figures. The forms and feelings associated with intimacy and authority, it seems, refuse to stand still even for an instant.

PHASES IN GROUP DEVELOPMENT: G AND A

Holding these notions in mind, let us examine what occurs in the goal attainment and adaptive phases and then touch upon the notions of temporary regression and resistance, as the Parsonian model offers a rather important guide to these actions as well.

The goal attainment or goal gratification phase of the group represents the first of the two phases of rational action, sacred status and high power. It also marks the first period of what we will call socialization to group work, namely, the emphases on impulse management, "tellability," and mutual support in an atmosphere of growing sex role differentiation. We might spell out these issues just a bit.

The movement of the group into the G-phase implies that external-internal differentiation problems, themselves associated with reality-fantasy differentiation problems, have been resolved, however minimally. Membership or the exclusion-inclusion crisis has also been successfully passed to the point where members can tolerate infrequent absences from sessions on the part of their colleagues. Like all phases, the G-phase too is highlighted by the group's identification with the family figure who symbolizes the primacy of the phase, in this case the mother. But the G-phase also means that the period wherein action is taken against the male leader in an effort to disarm or remove him or neutralize his strength has passed. This common theme of a group revolt is made possible by the union of forces developing in the first stages, namely, collectivization of impulses. It results, too, from the recognition of the inequality in power between members and leaders. Now, however, during the goal attainment phase, it is not unusual for the group to recognize how foolish they were in investing so much strength in the male leader, and how absurd was their quest for his demise. In a way, they have begun to resolve some of the so-called hardened authority problems, if only because they have worked their way to a position of perceived power for themselves. The whole group, in other words, has become equalitarian. As a result, the male leader now is the object of kindness and love, which means that the group males must confront the cultural, sociological, and psychological definitions and problems associated with feelings of homosexuality.

In their identification with the group's mother, men and women together now may attempt to split the two leaders in order to continue diminishing their power while making them more available to the needs and desires of the members. The attempt to split the "parental figures," however, should also be seen as an indication that the group no longer prefers a lack of sex role differentiation. The group too, has moved beyond the two stages where their own sexual differentiations were minimized, if not neutralized. Males and females now are truly distinct; and post-Oedipal intimacy, love if you will, begins to be a reality.

The stress of the G-phase is on the simultaneous actions of individual expression, though no longer merely in terms of integrative intimacy, and mutual or collective support. Intragenerational competition now assumes precedence, and intergenerational expression is laden with support. The horde has receded somewhat, the forms of sexuality are maturing, and although members encourage one another to "open up" and let their "guts spill out," the sexual attractions between members become more realistic and in their way more reasonable or feasible. Infatuation is beginning to give way to love. Just being in the group rather than forming it or creating some special brand of freedom, what we called existential freedom, seems to have taken over in the G-phase. If impulses are not actually better controlled than they were in the previous two phases, then at least members are better able to differentiate between fantasy and reality, impulse binding and impulsive intimacy, and better able to speak about events and feelings, rather than "talk-act" them out. Never before and never again perhaps in the group's history will a stress be placed more heavily on the here-and-now, for until this phase, a mood of integrative anticipation and latency preparation dominated what might be called the temporal orientations of the various phases.

The period of goal attainment, then, is marked by the group's first task, open expression, and the controlled display of immediate affect rather than the exposure of naked impulses in which magical beliefs are invested. The period offers the first glance at an incipient ego control of id impulses. Merely telling about feelings and fantasies now constitutes sufficient gratification for group members who by this point have come to fear less the efflux of their own feelings, and who have correspondingly developed a genuine trust in one another. Expression of desires and being desired grows into discussions of what would be socially and psychologically desirable.[36] The social contracts of the L-phase seem less salient, although the prevailing trust the group now experiences is predicated upon the work completed in the first two phases. Especially important have been the social control and intimacy exercises performed by the group.[37]

Because of the primacy of expression of feelings and the identification with at least one legitimate authority, the mother, and the trust placed in her, it is common for group members in the G-phase to speak a great deal of their dreams. Partly this is because dreams are in their way codified representations of the interior and of fantasies. To share a dream is to offer a gift of feelings and ideas which have come deep from within one's soul and about which one can truly say he is not certain of their meaning. The gift, then, has qualities of a secret and a puzzle as well as a message for the group; hence the dream for a self-analytic group is often felt to be the most valuable item one might express about himself. It is the stuff of group work, until it becomes, as it very well may, a dodge or a resistance.

In one sense, the G-phase is the least difficult for members. Many confess to receiving gratifications from their expressions merely because the need for support which they require now is offered by leaders as well as remaining members. Individual competition revolving around the leaders has slackened. The G-phase also introduces actions which ultimately lead to the development of an interpersonal morality coupled with personality differentiation. Members respond positively now to the fact that even though they are different from one another, they are still accepted, loved, and valued by their colleagues. This is quite a change from the L-phase's demand for conformity and conventionalism. More importantly, G-phase action gives birth to the seeds of identity or, more exactly, social identity[38] and dissipates the drive toward member identicality. Members begin to dig for demographic data about their friends. Home town, fields of interest, educational back-grounds, and the like are explored for the first time even though the group might have been in existence for over four months. But whatever it is, the style of support in the G-phase allows for greater individuality than the group has previously known or, for that matter, previously has confessed they desired, even during the integrative phase.

But the move toward individuation, individual differences, and social identity do not produce true individuation. Rather, the drive toward it is coupled with the prior stress on social coherence and the new-found freedoms of personal preference and desirability to produce the complicating and stressful issue of group fractionalization or simply subgrouping. Like so many processes, subgrouping reflects a combination of socialized responses to the old problems of authority and intimacy. Although persons admit to their preferences for certain members, there is always a tinge of competition between groups for proximity to and ownership of leaders. Who for example, do the leaders feel is the favored, more intelligent, more attractive group. Who really is leading the group? Who is getting most from it? Who is doing most of the work? Who deserves a sacred status with the leaders and above the others?

Interestingly, the transition through the phases has brought to the G-phase a new form of horde, a heterosexual one, but a horde not primarily interested in overthrowing the leader. To the contrary. The hordes now may be arising in response to the splitting of the two leaders and hence to a desire to incorporate at least one leader in their subgroup. Zeus and Hera are meant to war.[39] A choice between the Apollonian and the Dionysian is to be made, and in a strange way, whereas one subgroup usually anticipates the group's final phase, the other subgroup often seeks to construct a friendship and selective solidarity of such intensity that it might prevent the group from moving on and hence from terminating. For this group, the stoppage of time might be their greatest wish. But one last transition remains.

Transformation of the Leader's Role

The transition from the goal attainment to the adaptive phase means, among other things, the first intellectual head-on confrontation with the male leader, his role as "interpretive specialist," and his stance as an authority articulated to some degree with an external system of authority which legitimates his presence and action in the group. This last issue now becomes a paramount problem for the members, as they had all but convinced themselves that autonomy meant a collective solidarity internal to the group, free of the constraints derived from external realities and social structures. Again in the adaptive phase, as group development moves to complete its cycle, the external-internal differentiation is raised, and with it, the problems of membership and the differentiation of fantasy and reality return in a new and distinct cloak.

Oversimplifying these complex issues, the movement of the group from the G-phase to the A-phase means that the group's father, the model, the ego-ideal and consequently the personification of its superego, now will assume a unique form of dominance.[40] No longer the seducer of women, nor the teacher-ogre asserting his authority over the students, no longer even the problematic object of homosexual love and attraction, the male leader pushes for a cerebral, cognitive, or intellectual prominence. He does this through his stance of being half in the group and half out of it and by his insistence that the controlled expressions that found their way to the conversational surface during the G-phase must now be analyzed. The task of analysis and what Parsons calls the denial of reciprocity[41] on the part of the male leader together produce the last important obstacle for the termination of the group. A word now about these two prime actions, analysis and the denial of reciprocity.

By analysis, the group learns that action is not considered complete until it is understood, scrutinized from the points of view of anthropology, sociology, and psychology. Personal support has receded somewhat in the A-phase, and efforts are directed at comprehending the myriad levels of meaning of a simple utterance which months before would have been dismissed as "small talk." Almost as a scanner, the leader puts aside all claims to authority except for his expertise in teaching this limited analytic procedure. In so doing he again looms important. His status above the group is reinstituted to become more God-like, perhaps, just when members (in the G-phase) had convinced themselves that they had "shut him up for good" and "cut him down" to their size. Where they are wrong is in their belief that G-phase expression and the support and solidarity to which almost everyone, including the male leader, has contributed represents the final task of the self-analytic group. More work remains to be done.

Coupled with the emphasis on analysis is the male leader's stance of denial of reciprocity which, while prevalent throughout the group's history, is never more salient than during the adaptive phase. In developing this term from Bibring's work, Parsons suggests that actions demanded by ego of alter may be met with a refusal to respond in kind by ego himself. Ego, in this example the male leader, announces to the group, I will not participate fully in the actions which I demand that you perform. I will not do as you do, and hence I will serve as a constant reminder to you that another world, another social order, exists, an order to which you must return at the completion of each session and at the termination of the group.

The coupling of analysis with denial of reciprocity produces many ramifications. Importantly, members are meant to feel safe with the knowledge that should a social order break down, causing people to feel that they are going crazy, the leaders, and especially the male leader representing the A-phase, will not go crazy with them and thereby will serve as an anchor of stability and health. His refusal totally to play the group game will allow him to remain clinically astute and able to pull the group back if it should move in dangerous directions. He has, as it were, just enough of a footing in the world external to the group to provide a perspective of "proper" reality and health.

In his instrumental-interpretive role, the leader differentiates for members not only reality from fantasy but the various sorts and levels of reality and fantasy. Moreover, he articulates private fantasies with the most public (external to the group) social order in order to articulate, in an adaptive sense, the group as an institution with its corresponding institutions on the outside. He is, in other words, a link between institutions, a link between the group's family and the society from which it has taken life and form.[42] Accordingly, in this capacity, a capacity gained to a great extent through his denial of reciprocity, the group concludes its history articulating its own themes of life' and death, birth and rebirth, with external religious institutions and ceremonies.[43]

The male leader of the group has himself progressed through various stages of seducer, supporter, father, president, and finally priest. The very nature of his role moves him to a position of keeper of the flock, and in a sense causes the group to terminate with his becoming unattainable for different reasons than existed at the group's beginning. This last phase of the unattainable must not be overlooked, for it reminds us that in Parsons' analysis, the development of a self-analytic group does not come full circle. Members and leaders do not end up where they began. If anything, the model is helical.

Development of Autonomy in Members' Roles

More precisely, the group has moved respectively through the L, I, G, and A systems or phases. This movement implies that the autonomy felt by individual members at the commencement of the group experience, should have been transformed by the experiences of the G- and A-phases. After relinquishing their insistence on a strangulating conformity and what turns out ironically to be an equally constraining period of integration through intimacy, members have learned to tolerate differences in the G-phase. Now in the A-phase they learn to use analysis and ratiocinative processes generally, not as defenses as they were used in earlier phases, but as the means by which persons come to be genuinely autonomous. Not only should members express their feelings, attitudes, and values more freely, they now should learn to analyze some of these feelings without wholly depending upon the interpersonal support which characterizes so much of the G-phase and which contributes to the many gratifying experiences contained in it. In the A-phase, group members learn that a man must stand on his own, expressing his feelings, to be sure, but not indulging in these feelings or fantasies to the extent that he cannot employ them as data to be analyzed for his own well being. Cognitive rationality and the inclusion of fantasy material for personal growth become the goals of the final stage. There are other features to it as well, and we must mention a few of them.

Notably, A-phase action includes an emphasis on independence, competence in expression, analysis, and social interaction and identification with adult roles, all of which in their way prepare the group for its culmination.[44] Analysis, especially, has a way of communicating a sense of mastery over materials, such that the past is integrated with the present, and the future made more logical, rational, and less mysterious if not actually predictable. The notion of independence carries with it familiar meanings, but one special feature of independence in the group is worth mentioning. This would involve the redefinitions of social exchange occurring in the four phases.

During latency, the conception of exchange begins to form as members recognize that sooner or later they will have to give and take from the group, not merely from certain members of it, just as they presently attempt to exchange "group commodities" with external systems. In the integrative phase, the stress on impulse expression and social equality causes members to exchange object for object. One gives something to the group and expects to be given an identical "thing" of identical value in return: "I told you what *I* thought of Bill, now you tell me what *you* think of Bill;" or, "I told you how *I* feel about *you*, now you tell me how *you* feel about *me*."

The concept of exchange changes again during the goal attainment phase. As a result of trust, support, and management of impulses, members learn to expect something in exchange for their expressions and gifts, but no longer demand a return in kind. Thus, announcement of a dream may be a call for support or love but not necessarily the confession of a dream from anyone else. G-phase exchange represents an important development, for it means that primitive eye-for-an-eye forms of exchange are no longer required.

The dissipation of a need for exchange during the adaptive phase marks the most crucial transition of all. Now, as practically a test of personal efficacy and independence, a member's expression or interpretation stands on its own, free of any expectation that something is due in return. By itself an action becomes autonomous and self-contained. When this form of interactional exchange emerges, individuals find themselves independent and able to express their feelings and thoughts in what may be a less supportive environment than they are used to. Furthermore, expecting little in return, they are able to care for fellow members in a nonpatronizing gesture that implies neither sexual attraction nor intense love.

Transference and Resistance

If there is, perhaps, a residual desire for exchange, the commodity during the A-phase most probably is *approval*. In the end, when the hostilities and attractions have subsided, authority becomes the agent of legitimate evaluation.[45] Now the leader not only says that a member or the entire group is good, he indicates that they are good at performing certain tasks. This form of evaluation almost always causes certain group members to wonder just how significant their group is for their leaders. Are they his all-time favorites? Is the pride they feel in their efforts justified and able to be documented? How do they stack up with other groups, even the ones about which they have read?

Brief mention might be made of the concept of transference. To be sure, this notion is losing favor among group practitioners advocating more and more leader participation. In the traditionally run self-analytic group, leaders are more silent and hence more likely to receive the so-called projections of members. Even then, these projections, to the extent that they exist, are shaped by the phase of the group and the tasks inherent in that phase.

Reaction to authority, naturally, is a vital part of the transference phenomenon, as is the notion of closeness to the leader or intimacy. Ambivalence toward authority characteristic of the latency phase gives way to open animosity, usually demonstrated in the goal attainment phase. During the integrative phase, leaders are invested with more erotic qualities which in some ways resemble the magical feelings shown them in later phases.

It is also true that as the group develops, closeness to and distance from leaders become salient variables. Indeed, the formation of a group identity, ideology, and sense of fidelity constantly require a re-examination of the relationships established between members and leaders. But as we observed earlier, each phase reveals subphases just as each group will have its subcultures which themselves are characterized by phase specific activity. Once again, these subcultures may very well be organized consciously or unconsciously about the issue of transference. There is, for example, the group that comes to be seen as the leaders' little helpers. There is also a group that forms around the issue of opposition to the leaders' styles or ideology. Thus, transference-type behavior, while shifting with the flow of the group's development, is also responsible in part for the substructural organization necessary in the emergence of subphases and subgroups.

Let us now reiterate some earlier propositions in the hope of clarifying them somewhat, and then return to our discussion of group resistance.

The movement of the group in its counterclockwise direction produces a series of crises which have been preceded by resistances and which result in the temporary adaptation of what we now call social psychological styles or moods of action. In the beginning, the directions laid down by the leaders produce in men an emphasis on law and order and collective coherence. They initiate as well a resistance that emerges in the psychological forms of avoidance and intellectualization. Expression of feelings and analysis, the major tasks of the group, are avoided. But as is true with so much of resistant action, the avoidance and intellectualization are not brought fully to a (group) conscious level. Indeed, in the first two phases, the phases of so-called irrational and regressive action, a good deal of group material never reaches the stage of total conscious awareness, much less of understanding. It remains, as it were, uncodified. One result of these two forms of resistance, therefore, is what we call the social psychological style or mood of alienation. Simply, a lack of fit exists between self-conceptions and the roles that one must undertake in this proposed group "business." Furthermore, what has "worked" before in terms of social action and efficacy now seems inappropriate.

Although we cannot dwell upon the sources of the resistances we will enumerate, it might be pointed out that, in each phase, resistances derive much of their form from the primacy of action in that phase, as well as from the identifications made with the phase's prime figure. Thus, from the son's identification with the father figure, representing analysis and "all-knowing," comes intellectualization which reveals the son's somewhat distorted but yet logical comprehension of his own future task, as well as his fear of the sexuality he associates with the women and the father figure in the group. Intellectualization tends to neutralize the threat of sexuality.[46]

Theoretically, the exclusion-inclusion problems and the emphasis on intimacy which reach their high point in the I-phase lead to a resistance of denial and the social psychological mood of isolation. In one sense, I-phase isolation represents a more personalistic side of L-phase alienation. By denial, we mean both the denial that feelings are coming out and, as group members will often say, the denial that anything of any consequence ever happens in the group. Whereas alienation involves the feeling of being powerless to effect action, denial is characterized by the more passive sentiment that the group is not progressing and that the emotions being expressed have little or no value. The resulting mood of the I-phase is isolation, the fear that in fact the group might run on without me, leaving me behind, rejected, incapable of understanding what has transpired, and never able to "catch up."

Another source of alienation and isolation bears heavily upon our original application of the theory of action paradigm to self-analytic groups. We recall that the I- and L-phases are characterized by so-called irrational action, regression, and profane status. When these features are combined with the leaders' original statements guaranteeing that special brand of group freedom, men and women respond with distinctly different impulses which they then attempt to socialize or otherwise insert into the ongoing culture of the group. The male impulse of aggression and the female one of sexuality or intimacy now may be regarded as rather logical responses to an absence of moral restraints, or at least a lessening of these restraints. A better term than profane, perhaps, is amoral, for members soon learn that control of impulses is not highly valued in these early phases. Ironically, the moods of alienation and isolation may be unintended by-products of the lessening of moral constraints, by-products which in fact members later discover are neither comfortable nor comforting.

Not until the goal attainment phase is a codified morality, such as it is, instituted in the group. This morality is based on trust and support and the important discovery that even without "classical" moral restraints, impulses to kill or aggress or have sex have not been consummated. Impulses have remained impulses. Just as in psycho-therapy, members now come to experience the relief generated by the fundamental recognition that thought and action are two very distinct phenomena. The wish to kill and the desire for sex may lead somewhere, but left as thoughts and wishes will not engender overt action.

This does not mean, however, that the G-phase is without its characteristic patterns of resistance and its corresponding mood. Although repression and displacement are common in this phase, more relevant to group progress, expression itself often serves as its own defense. Although valued as the primary action of the phase, the expression of feelings may be used as a method of filibustering and thereby become a resistance to actual and impending analysis. Group members at this time may believe that as long as they speak about feelings, they need not work toward the pure expression of feelings, much less attempt to comprehend them. Consequently, in the presence of a supportive mother figure and supportive group colleagues, none of whom would dare curtail such discussions, emotional *dependency* looms as the social psychological mood of the phase.

Part of the dependency is a reaction to the mutual support now offered and the group's budding morality. Part of it is the trust and the recognition by each member of just how much he needs these other people as an audience for his feelings and beliefs. But part of it, too, is in reaction to the group's termination. Although the fact of termination hangs in the air above almost every group session (as each session too, contains its own termination), and certainly plays a role in the shaping of each phase, it assumes special significance in the G-phase. Suddenly, after all this time, life seems so good and so blissful it seems a shame it all must end. The themes of a conclusion to infantile omnipotence and the end of adolescent innocence frequently are heard in the G-phase as members sadly admit to the glory that was the relative peace and perfection of this loving, trusting period of their group life.

In similar fashion, finally, the adaptive phase concludes the group, with analysis serving as its own resistance, this time to expression. Silence, too, may now be used by the group as a resistance to analysis, just as in the latency phase it was used by a few members as a resistance to the entire group experience. One function of A-phase silence is simply to cease the flow of data. If nothing is presented, nothing can be analyzed. Consequently, leaders now insist upon the fact that the group's final goal be the incorporation of expression and analysis, not the substitution of one for the other, not the evasion of either one.

The mood of the A-phase is deeply complicated; but among the many sentiments the virtue of identification and the "liabilities" associated with evaluation and rejection become salient. The leaders seem to be included somewhat in the life styles of the members, and the models of behavior and action which they have been now are internalized as models of group behavior. This process in turn contributes to the hoped-for sense of individual autonomy. Yet, the termination and the encouragement of individuation and autonomy started in the goal-attainment phase only naturally lead to a sense of desertion, rejection, and betrayal. "How do you like that," the

members sigh. "After taking us all this way, they (the leaders) now leave us only to form another group. We've just been guinea pigs all along." At this juncture the denial of reciprocity stance aids the leaders in reminding members of that other world outside, and hence the termination is made more palatable. Leaders, in other words, now "pull" the members out of their fantasies of termination and ultimately out of the group experience altogether.

A slight variation to the theme of rejection is worth brief mention, for it says something about the religious imagery connected with termination as well as about the strangely new status of the male leader. This variation has to do with the group's insistence that the leader himself has been led by some higher-order power such as the "course," the "syllabus," the head of the course, the chairman of the department, or the dean. While everyone recognizes the grains of truth in these allegations, for who, after all, need not answer to a higher station, the allegations serve both to lower the leader to the level of the members, and at the same time to lift him up again above them, in the symbolic form of the Son of God. Thus he too has undergone a transformation during the group's history, which in a way reveals, or should reveal, his own identifications with the group members and with that higher-status person or ideal, as well as his own sense of feeling rejected by the group and by this other "person." Fathers, then, are seen to be human, but still special in the status they will forever hold, no matter how old we, the children, become. In the end, the "moral" of the adaptive phase, and really the moral of the group's entire history with authority, is captured by these words of Brecht: "The only way to overcome authority is to outlive it."

The mood of rejection in the final phase is most difficult to transcend, especially because commitment to the group, which has reached its zenith in the G-phase, now, with time rapidly running out, must be dissipated so that preparations for the end may be undertaken. The transformation from the G-phase to the A-phase will be met with resistance, resentment, and a third "R" as well, regression.

Temporal Parameters of Group Process

As a final note on regression, it should be suggested that the temporal components of action in a group is perhaps the most complex element confronting the members. Each session, as well as the entire group experience, is circumscribed by time. So, theoretically, are the phases, but these temporal parameters are objective and linear. That is, time continues to run out, history accumulates, and the group's future continuously shrinks. But just as time runs out, some members may be saved by a session's or a group's concluding bell. Group practitioners know well the cases of members who speak only as a session ends or when the group itself approaches its last hours.

A similar notion involving the time-circumscribing group activity suggests that some people cannot speak freely until the group has worked its way into a particular phase. So for example, a member may wait for others to "push" the group into the G-phase, at which point, feeling comfortable in this new ambience of support and trust, he becomes more vocal. Some group members actually believe, although they would hardly articulate it this way, that their work is completed when they have successfully carried the group through a particular crisis. Other members may treat them accordingly by continuing to honor them for past deeds. For many reasons, some members may remain preoccupied by the work or action of certain phases and hence cause leaders to feel that upon termination they have not evolved into the adaptive phase. These people are literally "hung-up" in time.

Being hung-up in time has an important ramification, namely the development of phase-specific role specialists. This notion would suggest that certain talents cannot be operative until the group progresses to a certain phase. In the mean time, although participating as best they can, some members, in a sense, must bide their time until the group recognizes a need for their type of personality or special capabilities. In fact one might wish to generalize this notion to say that analogously, certain roles useful for a society cannot be "invented" or "perfected" until that society reaches an accommodating point in its history. Until that time, these roles exist only as unsocialized talents or perhaps as unthinkable fantasies.

A useful metaphor for thinking about a temporal progression or lack of progression among group members is a line of people moving through a somewhat dangerous, always changing environment. At one point in time, because of their reactions to this "environment," some inevitably will lead, others will follow closely behind, and still others, the stragglers, will wander on even farther back. Later, the order and the shape of this distribution of people will change, so that at times all may move together, or the men may move in advance of the women, or five new leaders and six new stragglers may appear and just as quickly disappear.

Throughout this movement, leaders too are guided by temporality and must, therefore, adjust their performance and styles. Sometimes they will take command, sometimes they will recede, but always they will abide by the action·primacy of the phase. Thus, leaders stress manipulation of rewards in the L-phase in an effort to initiate group movement; permissiveness or indulgence of impulses in the I-phase; support of expression in the G-phase; and the denial of reciprocity and special respect in the A-phase.[47]

But there is also a subjective, nonlinear, or spatial aspect to the time of groups, because "forward" progress carries with it the propensity for regression. The concept of nonlinear time is but another key to understanding group behavior, for, in one respect, leaders ask members first to move forward and backward over this new environment and second to bring the time of the past and the time of the future back in upon themselves into a time we now call an extended present.[48] It is not enough to recall or anticipate. What members must do is churn the time of their experiences about them such that history, on the one hand, and intentions or fears, on the other, are brought together into the swirling tides of the present instant. Needless to say, members quickly discover that their respective times cannot be perfectly synchronized and that the resulting collective time is not easily comprehended or, for that matter, easily reconciled. Furthermore, as the material being expressed is liable to transport any or all members into a totally new temporal orientation, it is almost impossible to know where in psychological time different individuals are located during a particular session. Some seem more impulsive, others more reflective; some are involved with a recalled childhood, others seek to carve a future ten years hence. Some mix regrets with hopes, others appear unwilling to extricate themselves psychologically from the exact present moment.[49]

Given this complexity, it seems almost laughable to think that a leader's interpretation could be "properly timed." However, what in part guide the timing and, for that matter, make sense of much of what occurs are the theoretical and actual contents of the various phases and the progressions and regressions they imply. What to a good measure determines an "appropriate" or "well-timed" interpretation is where in a sociological phase the group is located. For example, leaders may do better speaking to the nonverbal action or emotions or even the ambience of the group during the L- and I-phases, whereas in the A- and G-phases, actual utterances and then ideas may be more easily and appropriately interpreted. If the interpretation can somehow be fitted into the "space" of what people have been speaking about, and then connected to the conceptual issues characteristic of the developmental phase, the self-analytic group may experience the rewards of cognitive learning and experiential progress or growth.[50]

What complicates group action and the subsequent analyses of it, is the idiosyncratic nature of the temporal phenomena ultimately shaping the content of the group's history. With some people located here and some there on a "psychotemporal" distribution, it seems almost foolish to suggest that a systematic development of a group or systematic resolutions of its problems can be traced. Yet, it has been a fundamental argument of this chapter that just such tracings may be made.

At the conceptual level, as part of this tracing, temporal orientations need not be considered idiosyncratic. Like many of the other processes we have described, temporal orientations may be examined in our phase specific paradigm. Briefly, taking only one aspect of temporal orientations, the latency phase is characterized by what seems to be an oscillation of the past and future. As a feeling of reaching backward and forward prevails, an almost "transpresent" orientation emerges. More concretely, the relationship of the past, present, and future is so minimal or at best ambiguous, we call the orientation of the L-phase "temporal atomicity."[51] By atomicity we mean a sense of an unrelatedness among the past, present, and future.

The integrative phase is characterized by a shifting of interest from the past and future to the present. The emerging "impulsive present" contains all time, personal and historical, and gives to the member involved in the expression of impulses a sense of timelessness. In addition, the future is conceptualized as little more than repetition of the past and present. Accordingly, as all time seems to be contained within the present, we call the orientation temporal projection in order to suggest the image of each time zone being contained in the other zones.

Time appears to "spread out" somewhat during the goal attainment phase. The past is treated as a period governed by its own integrity, whereas the future comes to be seen as a period that now must evolve from the present and past but not merely as a replication of them. The result is an "extended present," fitting snugly between the past and future in such a way that a sense of temporal continuity prevails. The continuity, moreover, contributes to a belief in the possibility that over time an individual can change some aspects of self while holding other aspects constant. Thus, temporal continuity represents the first stage, the social stage perhaps, of a growing sense of identity.

Finally, in the adaptive phase, the future is perceived as being more manageable than ever before, as the feelings of independence and competence, and the acts of analysis and planning gain prominence. In addition, the recognition that one can overcome portions of his past while shaping portions of his present and future leads to the belief that over time an individual simultaneously changes some aspects of self while holding other aspects constant. The simultaneity of change and sameness is what produces the second stage, the personal stage perhaps, of identity.[52] Furthermore, the simultaneity factor, the knowledge that the past, present, and future share portions of their temporal mass with one another and yet keep other portions unique and uncontaminated by the remaining zones, produces the orientation we call "temporal integration."

So much for the conceptual level. At the empirical level, the issue of time is best examined perhaps by the action of regression.

It is a well-known fact that members of self-analytic groups seek and find different planes of emotional expression and content which they deem important for their learning and well-being at various times in their history. Certain planes are felt to be regressive, and often some aspects of individual regression seem almost perfectly idiosyncratic. Yet it is also true that just as a theoretically systematic series of phases may be drawn, so too, may a systematic series of regressions be detailed. More precisely, we would argue that each major group progression from one phase to the next is met with a corresponding regression which recapitulates prior progressions. Importantly, the regression supplies an energy that ultimately drives the group into its next phase. In no way should this "natural regression" resulting from progression be conceived of as retrogressive or destructive.[53] It is rather, a necessary part of group evolution, and to a certain extent its components are somewhat predictable, given the parameters of the AGIL paradigm.

The content of the regression recapitulates the materials characteristic not merely of the immediately prior phase but of the combination of prominent characteristics of the previous phases. Movement from integration to goal attainment, for example, typically is preceded by a regression to materials and action characteristic of the I- and L-phases. Alienation and isolation momentarily return, along with an "acting out" of the child's (low power) amoral role. The lack of sex-role differentiation reappears, nonverbal information again becomes important, and the inclusion-exclusion, external-internal crises are, in different ways, re-experienced. Absent or tardy members now may be severely chastised by the group. Similarly, the passage from goal attainment to adaptation causes a regression constituted of materials of the L-, I-, and G-phases. It is not uncommon now for the female leader, in what some might call countertransference, to regress along with the group and seek in some way to prevent the male leader from pulling the members into the last phase. The quality of the regression becomes clear as many early themes are repeated, even though, as we have said, individual members reveal highly idiosyncratic and personal reactions.

Regression at the A-G juncture is probably related in some way to the fact that some women may not progress with the men to the A-phase, but rather will remain as guardians of the goal attainment system. This performance would seem appropriate in light of the proposition that "maturity" for women means moving into the maternal role. Thus, the reluctance of the female leader to progress to the adaptive phase may not be countertransference as much as an acknowledgement that her work in the group is completed. Men, however, having passed through the phases of the daughter and mother, have one additional step to take, a step which assumes their final identification with male authority (father figure) and then sanctifies the ultimate sex role and age differentiations which ultimately characterize the final resolutions of the self-analytic group.

An interesting question now arises: Given this theoretical orientation of regression as a counter-force to progression, what then is the source of the igniting regression, that is, the regression that launches the group to its first phase? Part of the answer is that personal anxieties and projections onto the group contribute to the regression. It is also true that a good portion of the regressive content derives from the impression brought in by each member of what a group is supposed to do or be, or what they fear or hope it will do or be. We have alluded to this previously. However, we have not before spoken of the *mythology* of a group, the information that has been passed on about group experiences which, when combined with private impulses and reactions to this information, as well as with the emotional anticipations of what is about to transpire, produces a mythology which in part generates the regression launching the group. Stretching this point somewhat, the mythology is constructed from the reputations, tactics, and impressions of the leaders as well as from the projections onto them; in a way, the regression of the L-phase is built upon materials of imagined A- and G-phases. We should recognize that this same mythology holds an important place for members as they begin to differentiate their own private internal group from the external and public world from which they have sculpted this mythology.[54]

THE PROGRESSION OF THE FOUR PHASES

Let us now conclude our overly swift trip through self-analytic group development by summarizing Parsons' descriptions of the functions of the four systems as they have been applied to the phases of a self-analytic group.

The first phase, latency, represents in most general terms, the resolution of the group's *orga-nizational* or *sociological crises.* Latency is characterized by the maintaining, expressing, and reviewing of motivational and cultural patterns, patterns to be integrated into the ongoing system; the suspension of interaction; and a somewhat qualified universalistic orientation. Importantly, latency is a phase of rising and falling tension, tension to be used for action and as a safety valve as well. Furthermore, according to Parsons, it is a self-contained qualitative state.

Integration, the second phase, represents the period in which the group generally must confront the motivational or so-called psychological crises anticipated or reviewed during latency. Integration is characterized by particularism and affectivity; an emphasis on distinguishing between members and nonmembers, possessions and nonpossessions; and the commencement of durable affective attachments, although in self-analytic groups this second phase implies a primacy of Oedipal attachments.

Phase three, goal attainment or goal gratification, is the period in which social psychological or interactional crises begun earlier are resolved. Goal attainment is characterized by gratifying activity generally; the culmination of preparatory action; and an emphasis on particularism, affectivity, and enjoyment. Note that particularism and affectivity, in contrast to universalism and affective neutrality, are, theoretically, associated with femininity and expression.

The last phase, adaptation, describes the period in which sociological legislation combines with motivational and interactional components to become the time for resolving the group's cultural (and probably religious) crises. Adaptation is characterized by the following theoretical phenomena, all of which might now be thought of as goals for a self-analytic group: accommodation of a system to inflexible reality demands; mastery of a situation through instrumental activity; and emphases on realistic judgments, ideally on the prediction of social behavior and on the utilization of cognitive skills. As we have noted, adaptation is also associated with masculinity, universalism, and (group) analysis.

As an incidental note, it might be observed that in many respects all group action is anticipated in one form or another during the latency phase. Although the material anticipated is dealt with at more superficial levels during this phase, the very existence of it gives support to the Jungian notion that the contents of an entire analysis may be heard in the first session. In addition, latency anticipations provide a basis for the theoretical proposition that each phase contains materials of the other three phases.

The review of the AGIL system characteristics, coming as it does at the end of our discussion, allows us to see just how much one must manipulate theory and data in order to render them suitable for describing behavior in a self-analytic group.[55] The greatest theoretical adjustments have to be made in the integrative and goal attainment phases, but these are not serious problems for, as we have seen, each phase is characterized by the crises or group problems that must be resolved if the group is to "progress." Thus, for example, durable affective attachments, a component of the integrative system, is in fact the crisis met by members in the I-phase. When it is resolved, the group proceeds to the G-phase, where it depends upon these attachments in undertaking the work of expression. The slippage, therefore, between theory and data is surprisingly minimal.

Slippage, however, poses a far less serious problem than oversimplification. It goes without saying that both the theory of action *and* the data of self-analytic groups are far more complex and rich than we have presented them here. To reduce any utterance in a group to a single motivation or rationale is by definition going to be wrong. The complexity of one person, then several persons interacting over an extended period of time, is not easily comprehended nor honored sufficiently often. These are not merely the ritualized apologies appropriate for a theoretical chapter's concluding paragraphs, for any student of theory, like any student of groups, knows how profoundly complex is the reality they have chosen to examine.

In the present case, several ways of approaching the data of self-analytic groups may be employed for the purpose of developing theoretical formulations. First is the actual leading of groups over an extended period of time. Second is the observation of similar groups, watching in particular for systematic development. Third is the study of audio tapes and, if available, video tapes. That is, one must develop historical records of groups or, better, of several groups running simultaneously and led by different people. Fourth is the constant exchange of impressions and observations with people running groups in order to determine whether development does in fact show a certain constancy in the minds of those observing them. Naturally, in groups established as part of an academic course, there will be a tendency for all staff leaders to direct their respective groups to similar end points. Fifth, and a source of data not always available, is the content of student papers and group diaries.

The tension in many group endeavors exists between the individual's need for autonomy and a sense of uniqueness, on the one hand, and the recognition of the collective enterprise that other people in the past have experienced, on the other. Indeed, it is this tension that gives energy to the very material

self-analytic group instructors are proposing to teach. One of the many methodological dangers of this work, therefore, is to throw out individual or idiosyncratic behavior in one's conceptualization if it does not articulate closely enough with one's preconceived notions. While this is an ancient problem in the social sciences, having been discussed again and again, in the context of a self-analytic group the problem is central to the development of the identity of members and leaders alike. For how often do group practitioners hear members suggest to a leader, "You just said that because that's what you'll see even if it's not here."

In the present case, it goes without saying that phases are conceptual phenomena that do not exist as purely in reality as they do in theory. So much of what transpires in groups is poorly understood, misunderstood, or altogether incomprehensible. Nothing about the contents of the discussion or of the members present is simple. A myriad of acts are presented simultaneously which, if they even could be interpreted, would stop the group forever after its first twenty or thirty minutes of life.

Yet to describe behavior we must deal somehow in relational terms. The same act demonstrates highly different functions when we change the situational or phase aspect with which it is associated. So the complexity and richness need not discourage attempts at conceptualizing the processes and actions observed in groups, for these conceptualizations just might help group members, leaders, and observers understand a bit more of what happened that day in their group. A workable theoretical orientation, moreover, has ramifications and applications not easily seen at first glance. For example, despite the fact that self-analytic groups are described by instructors as being nontherapeutic or nontreatment oriented, there is, naturally, a therapeutic aspect to the group experience. Accordingly, the application of Parsons' theory elucidates, however minimally, therapeutic characteristics for the various phases. Thus, the LIGA phases, respectively, may be characterized by the following mental health criteria: the capacity to delay and prepare; the capacity to accept impulses; the capacity to express impulses, enjoy, and love; and the capacity for work and autonomy.[56]

An intriguing problem, and one to be explored more rigorously in future work, is the degree to which self-analytic groups are themselves experiences of a religious nature. The question to be posed is, how much would Parsons' scheme and the notions of developmental phases elucidate the universal rituals and ceremonies that one finds in these groups in the imagery of ascetism, immortality, mythology, moral purity and transcendental values?[57]

In the end, however, all theories, speculations, propositions, and inferences must be put to an empirical test. Nowhere is this fact more true than in group work. There seems to be so much group activity everywhere, and still so little data have been collected to confirm or disconfirm the types of notions we have been advancing. A simple and highly practical test of a theory is to take any set of propositions and see whether in fact they describe what one observes or feels in a self-analytic group. If reality is described, then the propositions might be retained. If they do not, then at least they represent the products of pure imagination rather than pure science, and thereby they might still manage to cling to a bit of dignity and truth.

NOTES

1. The texts serving as a foundation for the present work are Talcott Parsons and Robert F. Bales, *Family Socialization and Interaction Process* (Glencoe: The Free Press, 1955); Parsons, Bales, and Edward A. Shils, *Working Papers in the Theory of Action* (Glencoe: The Free Press, 1953); and Parsons and Shils (eds.), *Toward a General Theory of Action* (Cambridge: Harvard University Press, 1951). Also, Parsons, "An Approach to Psychological Theory in Terms of the Theory of Action," in S. Koch (ed.), *Psychology: The Study of a Science*, Volume III (New York: McGraw-Hill, 1959), pp. 612-711.

2. Parsons and Shils (eds.), *op. cit.*

3. See Robert F. Bales, *Personality and Interpersonal Behavior* (New York: Holt, Rinehart and Winston, 1970). Also, William G. Perry, "The Human Relations Course in the Curriculum of Liberal Arts," *The Journal of General Education*, 9 (1955), pp. 3-10.

4. On this point see Richard D. Mann with G. S. Gibbard and J. J. Hartman, *Interpersonal Styles and Group Development* (New York: John Wiley & Sons, 1967); and Theodore M. Mills, *Group Transformation: An Analysis of a Learning Group* (Englewood Cliffs: Prentice-Hall, 1964).

5. See Parsons, *Social Structure and Personality* (New York: The Free Press, 1964).

6. On this point see Parsons, "Evolutionary Universals in Society," *American Sociological Review*, 29 (1964), pp. 339-357.

7. For a theoretical discussion of this point see Emile Durkheim, *The Division of Labor in Society* (New York: The Free Press, 1964 [paperbound]). For its application in groups see Philip E. Slater, "Role Differentiation in Small Groups," *American Sociological Review*, 20 (1955), pp. 300-310.

8. See Parsons and Bales, *op. cit.*

9. Philip Slater, *Microcosm: Structural, Psychological and Religious Evolution in Groups* (New York: John Wiley and Sons, Inc. 1966).

10. For a description of these terms see Mircea Eliade, *The Sacred and the Profane* (New York: Harper and Row, 1961).

11. Parsons and Bales, *op. cit.* See also Parsons, "General Theory in Sociology," in Robert K. Merton, Leonard Broom and Leonard S. Cottrell, Jr. (ed.), *Sociology Today* (New York: Basic Books, 1959).

12. See Sigmund Freud, *The Interpretation of Dreams*, James Strachey (tr. and ed.) (New York: Basic Books, 1955).

13. See David Bakan, *The Duality of Human Existence* (Chicago: Rand McNally, 1966).

14. There is also a good discussion of this point in Herbert Marcuse, *Eros and Civilization* (Boston: Beacon Press, 1955).

15. For an important theoretical discussion of this point see Fred Weinstein and Gerald M. Platt, *The Wish to Be Free* (Berkeley: The University of California Press, 1969).

16. See Emile Durkheim, *The Elementary Forms of the Religious Life* (New York: The Free Press, 1965 [paperbound]).

17. See Parsons, *Social Structure and Personality*.

18. See Parsons, "Durkheim's Contribution to the Theory of Integration of Social Systems," in Kurt H. Wolff (ed.), *Emile Durkheim, 1858-1917: A Collection of Essays* (Columbus: Ohio State University Press, 1960).

19. Slater, *Microcosm*.

20. Bakan, *op. cit.*

21. See Sigmund Freud, *Totem and Taboo* (London: Kegan Paul, 1950); and *Group Psychology and the Analysis of the Ego* (New York: Liveright, 1951). Also, Parsons, *Social Structure and Personality*.

22. For a more theoretical discussion of this point see Bruno Bettelheim, *Symbolic Wounds* (London: Thames and Hudson, 1955).

23. The notion of phases in group development is not new. See, for example, Dexter Dunphy, "Social Change in Self Analytic Groups," unpublished Ph.D. dissertation, Harvard University, 1964; Robert F. Bales and Fred L. Strodtbeck, "Phases in Group Problem Solving," *Journal of Abnormal and Social Psychology*, 46 (1951), pp. 485-495; Mills, *op. cit.*; Warren Bennis and Herbert Shepard, "A Theory of Group Development," *Human Relations*, 9 (1956), pp. 415-437; and George Psathas, "Phase Movement and Equilibrium in Interaction Process in Psychotherapy Groups," *Sociometry*, 23 (1960), pp. 177-194.

24. In, "Youth in the Context of American Society," *Daedalus*, 91 (Winter 1962), pp. 97-123.

25. See Parsons and Shils (eds.), *op. cit.*

26. Not surprisingly, Parsons has referred to material in a totally different context which bears directly on these points. See his "Full Citizenship for the Negro American? A Sociological Problem," *The Negro American* (Boston: Houghton Mifflin Company, 1966) pp. 709-754.

27. See Weinstein and Platt, *op. cit.*; also Parsons and Gerald M. Platt, "Age, Social Structure, and Socialization in Higher Education," *Sociology of Education*, 43 (1970), pp. 1-37.

28. See S. Freud, *Beyond the Pleasure Principle* (New York: Liveright, 1950). Also, Marcuse, *op. cit.*

29. Slater, *Microcosm*.

30. In *Collected Papers*, Volume III (London: Hogarth, 1956).

31. See Bettelheim, *op. cit.*

32. *Microcosm*. See also his "Displacement in Groups," in W. G. Bennis, K. D. Benne, and R. Chin (eds.), *The Planning of Change* (New York: Holt, 1961), pp. 725-736.

33. Parsons and Bales, *op. cit.*

34. See Parsons, Bales, and Shils, *op. cit.*

35. On this point see Erik H. Erikson, *Identity and the Life Cycle*, Psychological Issues, No. 1 (New York: International Universities Press, 1959).

36. On this point see Parsons, "On the Concept of Value Commitments," *Sociological Inquiry*, 38 (1968), pp. 135-159.

37. As we have alluded frequently to the issue of social control, Parsons' own discussion on this topic should be cited. See his *The Social System* (Glencoe: The Free Press, 1951).

38. On this particular point see Parsons, "The Position of Identity in the General Theory of Action," in Chad Gordon and Kenneth J. Gergen (eds.), *The Self in Social Interaction*, Volume I (New York: Wiley, 1968).

39. See Philip E. Slater, *The Glory of Hera* (Boston: Beacon Press, 1968).

40. Parsons, *Social Structure and Personality*.

41. Parsons, Bales, and Shils, *op. cit.*

42. For a more theoretical discussion of this point see Parsons and Winston White, "The Link Between Character and Society," in Seymour Martin Lipset and Leo Lowenthal (eds.), *Culture and Social Character* (New York: The Free Press, 1961), pp. 89-135.

43. Slater, *Microcosm*.

44. Parsons, "Youth in the Context of American Society," *op. cit.*

45. Parsons, *Social Structure and Personality*.

46. Many of these ideas have been influenced by Anna Freud. See *The Ego and the Mechanisms of Defense* (New York: International Universities Press, 1946).

47. Parsons, Bales, and Shils, *op. cit.*

48. This term comes from Georges Gurvitch, *The Spectrum of Social Time* (Dordrecht, Holland: D. Reidel Publishing Company, 1964).

49. For an extended discussion of this point see Erik H. Erikson, *Childhood and Society* (New York: W. W. Norton, 1950).

50. For an empirical study of this and related points see Jack Sansolo, "Trainer Style and Group Reaction: An Analysis of Trainer Comments in T-Groups and Its Relation to the Learning and Satisfaction of Group Members." Unpublished Ph.D. Dissertation, Harvard University, 1969.

51. Much of this and the following discussion is derived from Cottle, "The Circles Test: An Investigation of Temporal Relatedness and Dominance," *Journal of Projective Techniques and Personality Assessment*, 31 (October, 1967), pp. 58-71. See also Cottle and Peter D. Howard, "Temporal Extension and Time Zone Bracketing in Indian Adolescents," *Journal of Perceptual and Motor Skills*, 28 (1969), pp. 599-612.

52. See Erik H. Erikson, *Identity, Youth and Crisis* (New York: W. W. Norton, 1968); and *Young Man Luther* (New York: W. W. Norton, 1958). See also Parsons, "The Position of Identity in the General Theory of Action," *op. cit.*

53. On this point see Philip E. Slater, "On Social Regression," *American Sociological Review*, 28 (1963), pp. 339-364.

54. On this point see Otto Rank, *The Myth of the Birth of the Hero* (New York: Vintage Books, 1964).

55. For a discussion of this problem see Parsons, "Some Problems of General Theory in Sociology," in John C. McKinney and Edward A. Tiryakian (eds.), *Theoretical Sociology: Perspectives and Developments* (New York: Appleton-Century-Crofts, 1970).

56. Parsons, Bales, and Shils, *op. cit.*

57. In some respects this task has already been undertaken, although not directly in terms of self-analytic groups. See for example, Robert N. Bellah, "Religious Evolution," *American Sociological Review*, 29 (1964), pp. 358-374.

14

NORMS AND BEHAVIOR

Francesca Cancian

One of the major theoretical perspectives in contemporary sociology is the general theory of the socialized actor. According to this theory, children are socialized to orient their actions to general values, and throughout their lives, individuals learn to select their actions according to shared norms. These norms and values are internalized into the personality, resulting in a correspondence between personal needs and social expectations. Individuals are motivated to conform to shared norms, which results in predictable and integrated patterns of social action.

This general viewpoint is taken for granted by many social scientists[1] and vigorously attacked by others.[2] But the discussions of this issue tend to be general and to lack clear implications for research.[3] As a result, the relation between norms and behavior is rarely the explicit focus of empirical studies, and the relevance of existing data is not perceived. Instead, the importance of norms or values tends to be accepted or rejected as an article of faith.

This essay shows that some of the basic assumptions of the theory of the socialized actor are not supported by previous research. The data suggest that norms are not stable attributes of individual personalities. Instead, norms seem to affect behavior only if they are shared by a group, and these shared norms can change rapidly.

An alternative theoretical framework is presented to explain these findings. This "social identity" framework defines norms as shared conceptions of what identities exist and how the claim to a particular identity can be validated. It assumes that norms affect behavior by specifying the actions that are required for different social positions or identities. The essay focuses on two areas where the theory of the socialized actor and the social identity perspectives have different implications: (1) the behavioral correlates of individual versus group norms and (2) the importance of evaluative normative beliefs versus reality-defining beliefs. Some consideration will also be given to the problem of normative change.

THE THEORY OF THE SOCIALIZED ACTOR

The theory of the socialized actor is closely identified with Talcott Parsons. The basic ideas of the theory were anticipated in the works of Sigmund Freud, Emile Durkheim, and others. However, it was Parsons who developed a comprehensive sociological theory of how individual actors are integrated into a social system through internalizing shared norms. Also, it was probably through Parsons' early works that most contemporary sociologists first encountered the theory of the socialized actor. For these reasons, I will quote extensively from Parsons' works in presenting the theory of the socialized actor. This is somewhat misleading because Parsons himself has criticized the theory to be presented here and has suggested qualifications and revisions, some of which will be presented later. However, many sociologists interpret Parsons as advocating the simplified model outlined here, and his early works still constitute the most convincing presentation of the theory of the socialized actor.

The cornerstone of Parsons' early work is his theory of how shared values account for social integration.[4] The theory grows out of Parsons' conception of social action, whereby actors are viewed as orienting themselves to a situation and selecting among alternative actions. A value is "an element of a shared symbolic system which serves as a criterion or standard for selection among the alternatives of orientation which

I am deeply indebted to John Meyer for many of my ideas on the nature of norms and institutionalization. I am also grateful for the thoughtful comments of Frank Cancian, Albert Bergesen, Jan Loubser, Stephen Olsen, Michelle Rosaldo and Renato Rosaldo.

are intrinsically open in a situation."[5] In specific situations, values are embodied in norms or moral standards, which define the mutual rights and obligations, or role expectations, of the relevant actors.[6]

According to Parsons, ego learns these evaluative standards by interacting with significant others and internalizing the common values of their interaction into his own personality.[7] As a result of internalization, ego develops a need or motive to conform to shared normative standards. Conformity is also maintained by sanctions, or the reactions of alter. That is, ego is dependent on alter's response, and getting what he wants from alter is generally dependent on conforming to the shared standards. However, the "basic type of integration of motivation with a normative pattern-structure of values" results from internalization, whereby acting in conformity with the standard "becomes a need-disposition in the actor's own personality structure, relatively independently of any instrumentally significant consequences of that conformity."[8] In this way, "the 'deeper' layers of motivation become harnessed to the fulfillment of role expectations."[9]

The process of learning shared standards of evaluation continues throughout a person's life, and the standards are maintained by the mechanisms of social control that are a part of everyday interaction.[10] However, the major value patterns tend to be established in childhood and "are not on a large scale subject to drastic alteration during adult life."[11] This is because "these patterns can only be acquired through the mechanism of identification, and because the basic identification patterns are developed in childhood."[12]

The theory of the socialized actor has been widely accepted because it seems possible to explain so many social patterns by the concepts of shared norms, socialization, and social control. However, the theory has also been criticized on a variety of grounds. Some have argued that the theory has a conservative bias and ignores dissensus, conflict, and the antisocial drives of individuals.[13] Others object to the vagueness of the theory and the subsequent difficulty of testing it.[14] Parsons himself has pointed out the necessity of specifying how values and norms influence action in particular situations, as "values cannot control action by mere 'emanation.'"[15] Of these criticisms, only the vagueness issue will be dealt with in this essay.

The discussion will focus on two of the basic features of the theory. First, the theory implies that standards of evaluation (hereafter called "ranking norms") are relatively stable attributes of individual personalities. The theory assumes that, in an integrated system, these norms become part of the actor's personality through socialization, that many crucial norms are learned in early childhood, and that early learning is difficult to change. These assumptions clearly imply that an individual's ranking norms will guide his behavior and that variation in ranking norms across individuals will correlate with variation in behavior.

The definition of norms as standards of evaluation is the second basic feature of the theory that will be critically examined. In the theory, norms are defined as rules that enable a person to select the best behavior pattern for himself and to evaluate the behavior of others; norms specify whether behavior is good or bad, conforming or deviant. The theory tends to ignore the cognitive, reality-defining aspect of normative beliefs, which will henceforth be labelled "reality assumptions."[16] Reality assumptions are common understandings about the good *and* bad meaningful behavior alternatives in a situation; they define meaningful as opposed to meaningless or "crazy" behavior.

The next section distinguishes different types of normative beliefs, including ranking norms and reality assumptions.[17] Then ranking norms are carefully defined to clarify the relevance of existing data. A review of some of this data shows that there is little empirical support for the theory of the socialized actor. The social identity perspective is then outlined, and some of the hypotheses suggested by this approach are considered.

SHARED BELIEFS ABOUT BEHAVIOR: RANKING NORMS, MEMBERSHIP NORMS, AND REALITY ASSUMPTIONS

The theory of the socialized actor focuses on norms as standards of evaluation. These types of norms will be called ranking norms. They are used differentially to evaluate actions or individuals, on the basis of how well they conform to some standard. They define the actions and attributes that distinguish a particular rank or status. For example, among professors, the belief that "good professors publish high-quality papers" is a ranking norm. There are two other types of normative beliefs. Membership norms are beliefs about the attributes and actions of a member-in-good-standing. They are the standards for including a person within a group or accepting him or her as a bona fide incumbent of a position, and they apply to all group members.[18] An example of a membership norm for professors is the belief that "professors are highly skilled at reading and writing." Reality assumptions are the most general type of normative belief. They define what social positions or identities exist and what actions are meaningful in a particular context. Thus, according to the reality assumptions of my culture, a professor who appears at his lecture course and sings for an hour is engaging in meaningless or crazy behavior. Insofar as rank and membership are dimensions of meaning, these two types of normative beliefs are included within reality assumptions. The types of beliefs are distinguished because they seem to have different relations to behavior.[19]

Ranking norms are shared beliefs that make it possible to evaluate behavior as good or bad, better or worse. Ranking norms differentiate people according to the degree to which they conform to a standard.[20] Therefore they must refer to behavior that varies within the community, because without variation, differential evaluation is logically impossible. These norms are the basis for the everyday process of evaluating behavior and selecting among alternative courses of action. They are constantly restated in daily gossip and in instructing children and others how to behave; therefore the members of a community tend to be fairly conscious of these normative beliefs.

Membership norms are shared beliefs about how all members of a group or community should behave, but they are not the basis for ranking.[21] Thus, the belief that a professor should be highly literate is not a ranking norm because there is not enough variance in literacy to differentiate among professors. Deviation from this norm is rare, and literacy tends to be taken for granted as a customary part of the professor role, much the same way as reality assumptions are taken for granted. Membership norms thus have some characteristics like reality assumptions and some like ranking norms.

Reality assumptions are common understandings about what types of behavior are meaningful, possible, or understandable. They define the meaning of alternative good and bad[22] actions in a situation, i.e., what motives or reasons justify these actions,[23] what types of person would perform them, and what consequences would be expected. These beliefs are labelled "reality assumptions" and not "reality norms" for two reasons. First, the word assumption conveys the idea that these beliefs are more general than ranking or membership norms. Second, the term norm is traditionally defined as a standard or rule that is applied to a (meaningful) act or object. However, reality beliefs constitute or define social reality; it seems misleading to conceive of them as standards applied to this reality.[24] The definition of norms presented in the last section is general enough to include reality beliefs; but the traditional conception of norms as standards is so deeply ingrained in sociology that it seems best to avoid the term "norm" in this context.

Reality assumptions define an action as possible or understandable, which has certain consequences for behavior. Possible actions are part of the shared universe of meaning; such actions will be noticed and taken seriously, and will elicit a response that is determined by the particular meaning of the act. Impossible actions are like a message in a private language. Such acts will either be ignored, or they will be treated as not serious (crazy, silly, mistaken) and will elicit responses appropriate for crazy behavior.

The definition and measurement of ranking norms will now be considered in more detail. This is followed by a presentation of past research on the relation between ranking norms and behavior, and the theoretical implications of these findings. A parallel discussion of reality assumptions will then be presented. Membership norms are not considered in detail because they share some characteristics of ranking norms and some of reality assumptions. In a preliminary analysis like this one, it is more fruitful to focus on the clearly contrasting types of normative beliefs.

Defining and Measuring Ranking Norms

Ranking norms can be precisely defined as shared beliefs about what behavior brings respect and approval from oneself and others, or what behavior validates high status. This definition meets three major criteria of an adequate definition of norms: (1) it clearly distinguishes norms from behavior, (2) it distinguishes between normative and other beliefs, and (3) it suggests methods of measuring norms.

It order to construct a testable theory of the relations between norms and behavior, it is clearly essential to define the two concepts independently from one another. Norms cannot be directly observed; therefore they must be inferred from some verbal or nonverbal behavior. However, they obviously should not be inferred from the same behavior that will be examined to assess the effects of norms.

The distinction between norms and behavior, or action, is far from clear in the writings of many sociologists. Parsons, for example, defines values as formulating "the directions of choice in the dilemmas of actions" and as "ways of organizing the totality of interests involved in the system of action."[25] Johnson defines a norm as "an abstract pattern, held in the mind, that sets certain limits for behavior."[26] Statements like these imply that norms and values, by definition, affect action. Other definitions of norms, and the closely related concept of role, equate norms with expectations or predictions of behavior. Expectations about how another will behave are based on information about the past behavior of that person, or others like him. Therefore, if norms are defined as expectations, there will obviously be a positive relation between norms (based on past behavior) and behavior.[27]

These problems are avoided in the preceding definition of ranking norms, which equates norms with shared beliefs.[28] This formulation follows the suggestion of Homans, who states that norms are "an idea in the minds of the members of a group, an idea that can be put in the form of a statement specifying what the members or other men should do, ought to do, are expected to do, under given circumstances. . . ." He stresses that norms "are not behavior itself, but what people think behavior ought to be."[29]

The definition of ranking norms deals with the problem of distinguishing between norms and other beliefs by referring to a particular type of sanction: respect and approval. The concept of sanctions is included in most sociological definitions of a norm. For example, Broom and Selznick's textbook, *Sociology*, introduces the concept as follows: "All societies have rules or norms specifying appropriate and inappropriate behavior, and individuals are rewarded or punished as they conform to or deviate from the rules."[30] And Homans qualifies his definition of norms, cited previously, as follows: "a statement of the kind described is a norm only if any departure of real behavior from the norm is followed by some punishment."[31]

The typical definition of norms is a combination of these two elements: (1) shared rules or beliefs about how people should behave, (2) that are backed by sanctions, or are the criteria for reward and punishment.[32] The core meaning of the concept seems to lie in the first element: shared beliefs about behavior. The purpose of adding the second element, sanctions, seems to be to eliminate from the category of "norms" those beliefs or rules that obviously are not taken seriously or that obviously do not affect behavior. It excludes rules like "automobile drivers should never exceed the exact speedlimit."

The relation between norms and sanctions is complex. On the one hand, if norms are identified with general sanctioning patterns, then the hypothesis of a positive relation between norms and behavior looks very much like a behaviorist learning theory. Norms become rules for predicting how to obtain reward and avoid punishment; the statement "people tend to behave in conformity with the norms" becomes equivalent to the statement "people tend to behave so as to maximize reward and minimize punishment." This statement can easily degenerate into a tautology, given the difficulty of defining punishment and reward for an individual independent of that individual's behavior.[33] On the other hand, if norms are completely separated from sanction patterns, then by what criteria will norms be distinguished from other beliefs?[34] The concept of ranking norms resolves this issue by focusing on a particular kind of sanction: approval-disapproval and respect-lack of respect.[35]

The definition of ranking norms also meets the criterion of suggesting methods for measuring norms. If norms are shared beliefs, then they can be measured by simply asking people to state them. My research in Zinacantan, Mexico, indicates that people are able to state their beliefs about what behavior elicits respect and approval and that an accurate description of these beliefs can be obtained by systematic interviewing and other techniques. The method that I developed in Zinacantan was based on previous work by anthropologists working on descriptions of cognitive domains from the actor's point of view.[36] The method consisted of eliciting a large corpus of normative statements through a sentence-completion procedure; the organization of these statements into categories was analyzed by a sorting technique, in which subjects grouped the statements on the basis of similarity.[37]

With this type of method, it is possible to obtain a reliable description of ranking norms, from the actor's point of view. The description of norms in Zinacantan was verified by several tests, and it also conforms to the results of other studies of Zinacantan and to the impressions of experienced field workers in the area. Somewhat similar methods have been used to study norms in the United States.[38] With further experimentation, it should be possible to develop a variety of methods of accurately measuring ranking norms.

Evidence on the Relation between Ranking Norms and Behavior

The results of three types of studies will now be reviewed. First the voluminous evidence on the relation between norms and behavior across individuals will be summarized. Then I will present the findings on norms and behavior across groups and describe some of the evidence on normative change.

Most of the evidence on the relation between norms and behavior comes from studies that examine variation in norms or attitudes within a community.[39] Norms are treated as attributes of individuals, and the studies analyze the consistency between an individual's norms and behavior.

This research has been done primarily by social psychologists, whose explicit concern was to examine attitudes, not norms. The concept of "attitude" is broader than "norms," according to most theoretical definitions; however, the operational definitions of the two concepts are often identical. Allport's definition is still accepted by many psychologists.[40] He defines an attitude as "a mental and neural state of readiness, organized through experience, exerting a directive or dynamic influence upon the individual's response to all objects and situations with which it is related."[41] Attitudes include norms, or shared beliefs about how people should behave or about what behavior deserves respect and approval. However, attitudes also include individual opinions, beliefs, and preferences.

Some theoretical definitions of attitude are very close to a definition of norms. For example, Harding *et al.*, define the conative or behavioral component of ethnic attitudes as "a pattern of beliefs about the way in which members of that group should be treated in specific contexts."[42] In general, the concept of attitudes is similar to norms conceived as attributes of individuals, and much less similar to norms conceived as attributes of groups.

The operational definitions of the two concepts are often identical; in these cases, the findings about "attitudes" obviously can be generalized to norms. For example, one of the questions in *The American Soldier* study was: "On the whole, do you think it is a good idea or a poor idea to have colored soldiers used as infantry troops?"[43] This question could be used to measure norms or attitudes; in this study it was interpreted as measuring attitudes. Many attitude scales contain normative items, such as "Fascists and Communists are entitled to preach their beliefs in this country"[44] or "I believe the Negro deserves the same social privileges as the white man."[45]

The main finding of more than four decades of research on attitudes and behavior is that there is no clear relation between them. Many studies have found virtually no relation between what an individual says he does, or likes to do, or should do, and what he actually does.[46] Some studies report a positive relation between attitudes and behavior[47] and others suggest that the relation may be negative.[48]

The most famous finding of no relation between verbal statements and behavior is LaPierre's early research on "Attitudes and Actions."[49] He travelled through the United States with a Chinese couple and stopped at 251 hotels, motels, and restaurants; they were refused service only once. Six months later, questionnaires were mailed to these establishments, and one of the questions was: "Will you accept members of the Chinese race as guests in your establishment?" Over 90% of the respondents answered "no." Inconsistency between attitudes and behavior has also been found in studies in which the measure of attitudes is closer to normative beliefs. Thus, Saenger and Gilbert[50] found virtually no relationship between attitudes toward Negro store clerks and making a purchase from a Negro clerk, using an attitude scale that included items like "What would you think if all New York department stores hired Negro sales personnel?"

Research in other areas besides attitudes has also failed to find a consistent relationship between an individual's verbal statements and his behavior. A review of psychological research on moral values reports that no one has been able to construct a test of moral attitudes or values that successfully predicts moral behavior.[51] Recent research on altruistic norms and behavior suggests that children's normative behavior is determined only by what others do.[52] A recent study of power in the family has found no relationship between the way family members say they behave and their observed interaction.[53]

These findings have been interpreted in various ways. A review by Deutscher[54] suggests that the relationship between "Words and Deeds" tends to be positive in laboratory research but not in field studies. On the other hand, a recent review of research on ethnic attitudes and behavior concludes that attitudes are most likely to determine behavior in intimate, long-lasting relationships and least likely to determine behavior in the specific and transitory situations that are usually measured in experimental studies.[55]

Some researchers believe that we now have sufficient evidence to conclude that attitudes, or verbal statements about behavior, usually have very little relationship with actual behavior,[56] while others remain convinced that attitudes and behavior are positively related and that the findings to the contrary can be explained as due to inadequate methods and poor theoretical distinctions.[57] According to the most detailed recent review,[58] the only empirical generalization that can be drawn from scores of studies is that attitudes and behavior are unrelated or have a slight positive correlation. Other reviewers conclude that we still know very little about the relationship between attitudes and behavior.[59]

There have been a few studies by sociologists that explicitly focus on norms; these studies also have failed to demonstrate a positive correlation between norms and behavior on the individual level. Kenkel[60] observed married couples as they made a series of decisions and measured their norms or attitudes on family roles. His results showed no consistent relation between norms and behavior. An early series of studies by Hartshorne and May on norms and behavior concerning honesty among school children also failed to find any consistent relationship.[67]

My own study of norms and behavior in Zinacantan came up with the same pattern of negative findings. Individual variation in normative orientation was measured by a series of paired comparison questions, in which the subject had to select which one of two norms was more important in determining respect and approval. For example, the respondent would be asked: "Which man is more respected, the one who speaks Spanish well or the one who takes many religious offices?" The content of these questions was determined by the results of the description of the normative system, and the data indicate that these questions accurately represent the major clusters of ranking norms in the community. Behavior was measured by self-reports, which were later checked for accuracy by informants who had first-hand information about most of the respondents. The behaviors constituted a series of action, that are highly significant to Zinacantecos and that are made over a period of several months or longer, such as participation in the system of religious offices or agricultural practices over the last three years. Finally, the perceived relevance of norm clusters to behavior alternatives was measured by asking respondents to associate particular normative statements with one of two behavior alternatives (e.g., taking religious offices versus not taking religious offices).

In spite of this careful attempt to obtain measures of norms and behavior that were accurate and that represented cognitive categories and behavioral alternatives that are significant to Zinacantecos, the results showed no consistent relation between an individual's norms and his behavior. An individual with a particular normative orientation did not behave as the community would expect him to. For example, almost all Zinacantecos say that norms about knowing Spanish and dealing with Mexican officials are associated with going to school. However, Zinacantecos that place a high importance on these norms are less likely to send their sons to school than individuals who place a low importance on these norms. The correlations between norms and behavior were not improved by taking into account an individual's own definition of what norms are consistent or associated with particular behaviors. Nor are the correlations strengthened by limiting the analysis to normative statements that specifically refer to the behavior in question.

Some critics might be tempted to reject all these findings on the grounds that they measure only conscious, stated beliefs as opposed to "real" norms. However, this criticism is invalid. If norms are defined as hidden, unconscious beliefs, then it will be impossible to measure norms independently of behavior and to investigate the relation between them.

The results of these studies, or any study, can also be rejected on sound methodological or substantive grounds. My results can be questioned on the grounds that I measured behavior patterns that are very important to the respondents and therefore are particularly dependent on nonnormative or instrumental factors; also one could argue that the behaviors occurred long before the measurement of norms, and the norms may have been different at the time that the behavioral decisions were made.

Other studies have been criticized for focusing on transitory and superficial behaviors. There will always be grounds for rejecting any finding. However, in my opinion there is now sufficient evidence to justify the following empirical generalization: variation in ranking norms among the individual members of a group is usually not consistent with variation in behavior.

There has been less research on the relation between norms and behavior across groups or communities; however, several studies have found that groups with different ranking norms show corresponding differences in behavior. Kohn[62] has found consistent relations between the values and socialization behavior of parents from different social classes. Strodtbeck[63] observed decision-making in married couples from three cultures and found that the observed authority structure corresponded to the norms of the culture, as measured by Florence Kluckhohn's value-orientation questionnaire. Her questionnaire has been used in a large number of societies[64] and it would be easy to draw up long lists of behaviors that varied across these societies consistently with the variation in values or norms.

The correlation between shared normative beliefs and behavior has also been demonstrated in a series of simulation studies by Alexander and his associates.[65] This research was designed to test Alexander's situated identity theory. It shows that if individuals agree on the relative evaluation of the different behavior alternatives in a psychological experiment, then most individuals will enact the behavior that brings the highest evaluation and will expect others to do so. A related study by Lauderdale[66] shows that if there is no consensus on the evaluation of different behaviors, then actual and expected behavior appears to be randomly distributed over the different behavior alternatives. In other words, if the members of a society share the belief that behaving in a particular way in an experiment will elicit a high evaluation or will validate their identity as "a good participant," then they will enact that behavior and will expect others to do the same. If there is no agreement on the identity implications of different actions, then there will be a high degree of variance in behavior and in expectations.

Many case studies of particular groups have also found that shared groups norms are consistent with behavior, for example, Homans' analysis of the Bank Wiring Room and the Norton Street Gang.[67] Finally, the importance of group norms as opposed to individual norms is indirectly supported by studies showing that individual perceptual judgments are much less stable in the face of opposition than shared group judgments.[68]

This evidence suggests the following generalization: Variation in the norms of different groups is usually consistent with variation in behavior across groups.

The last set of findings to be considered concerns normative change. One of the findings in this area that is especially relevant to the theory of the socialized actor is that norms can change very rapidly. Several studies have found that the greatest amount of normative change among students occurs before they have had the opportunity to form close interpersonal relationships, in the first few months of the freshman year. Wallace[69] found that the percentage of college freshman who reported that getting high grades was "highly important" to them changed from 75% to 40% between September and November. It then dropped to 31% by April (the percentage for nonfreshmen was 35%). Contrary to his expectations, the amount of change was much greater in the first 2½ months than the subsequent 5 months. A study of Philippine high school students by Benitez[70] also found that considerable normative change had occurred before the first four months of school.

These results suggest the following generalization: norms can change rapidly and the rate of change does not depend on the establishment of close interpersonal relationships.

THE "SOCIAL IDENTITY" THEORETICAL APPROACH

The research findings on norms and behavior seem to be best explained by a "social identity" theoretical perspective. This theoretical approach suggests that norms affect behavior insofar as they concern an individual's identity—his membership or rank within a group or category of people. The reality assumptions and norms of a community inform persons and collectivities about the social meaning or consequences of action. These beliefs state, in effect, that if an individual (or group) does certain things or has certain attributes, then he is a certain kind of person. Identity, membership, and rank must be given or validated by others. Therefore, norms define social identities only if they are shared with these others.

The social identity or reference group approach has a long history in the social sciences. It is closely related to the social construction of reality approach, to symbolic interactionism, role theory, and reference group theory, and to Parsons' recent formulation of social interaction.[71] However, the usefulness of this perspective as an alternative to the theory of the socialized actor has not been fully explored.[72]

Some of the assumptions of the social identity approach will now be discussed, followed by a presentation of hypotheses on norms and behavior, normative change, and reality assumptions. The dis-

cussion is intended to be a first step towards constructing a social identity theory of norms and behavior. Several crucial concepts are vaguely defined—in particular, the concepts of group, important identity, and behavior—and the direction of causation is often unspecified. However, I hope that this exploratory effort will clarify the empirical implications of the social identity perspective and will suggest fruitful problems for future research.

The basic assumption of a social identity approach to norms and behavior can be stated as follows: Normative beliefs are related to behavior insofar as these beliefs are shared with a group and define an important identity that is validated by this group.[73]

This assumption has important implications for two issues: (1) the behavioral consequences of individual versus group norms and (2) the behavioral consequences of ranking and membership norms as opposed to other shared beliefs. The assumption asserts that norms must be shared if they are to affect behavior. In order to define identities, norms must be shared, as the process of claiming, validating or assigning identities is necessarily a collective process. For example, if I am to be a successful professor or a dope addict, there must be some others who agree that I have these identities.

If norms must be shared in order to have behavioral consequences, then it is unlikely that the variance in norms across individuals will be closely related to behavior. If a study investigates the norms of individuals from the same group or community, and their norms vary, then the norms are obviously not shared and will not be closely related to behavior. If the individuals are from different groups, then the researcher usually will not know whether or not the norms are shared with significant others. On the other hand, studies that compare the norms of different groups are much more likely to find a consistent relationship between norms and behavior.

The assumption also states that only a certain class of shared beliefs will be related to behavior. The members of a group may agree on many beliefs, attitudes, and opinions, but only those that define their identities as members-in-good-standing with a particular rank will be consistent with behavior. For example, if the members of a group agree that children should go to summer camp but sending children to camp does not effect a member's position in the group, then the behavior of this group will not be consistent with the norm. In other words, only ranking and membership norms and reality assumptions will be related to behavior.

A second major assumption of the social identity approach can be tentatively stated as follows: If each member of a group believes that the others have changed their beliefs about membership and rank, then the group norms will have changed. This is essentially a definition of shared norms as shared perceptions of the norms of others. The assumption follows from the idea that individuals conform to norms because that is the way to validate a particular identity. Norms in effect are the rules for being a particular kind of person, and the rules often change. Thus, being a "patriotic American" may mean killing Japanese one year and entertaining them the next. The social identity approach suggests that individuals are not personally motivated or committed to the particular norms about an identity, although they may be committed to the identity itself.[74]

The theory of the socialized actor assumed that individuals conform to norms because, as a result of internalization, the individual needs, wants, or is disposed to conform. In this approach, shared norms are equivalent to common personalities, and changing norms requires reconstructing the personality through intensive interaction, identification, and finally internalization. The social identity perspective, in contrast, suggests that shared norms may change very rapidly and without intensive interaction.

The third major assumption of the social reality approach is: Shared reality assumptions delimit possible meaningful actions. If individuals or collectivities wish to validate some identity or obtain a response from others, they are limited to the meaningful alternatives that are defined by shared reality assumptions. For example, it is impossible to be a witch, a scientist, or a socialist state until the existence of these identities has been publicly accepted.

This assumption would probably be accepted by all social scientists with a phenomenological, actor-oriented approach, including Parsons. However, the theory of the socialized actor focuses on standards of evaluation or ranking norms, and tends to ignore reality assumptions. This is because interaction is viewed in terms of decision-making individuals who are maximizing personal gratification and whose goals and standards of choice have become socialized. If interaction is viewed as a process of claiming, validating, and attributing identities, then the importance of reality assumptions is highlighted.

This social identity perspective can explain much of the evidence on norms and behavior that was just reviewed: the correlation between behavior and group norms, but not individual norms, and the occurrence of extensive and rapid normative change in the absence of close interpersonal relationships. It is difficult to explain these findings in terms of a theory of the socialized actor that views norms as stable components of an individual's personality. This suggests that it would be useful to construct a new theory of norms and behavior that incorporates some of the assumptions of the social identity approach.

The remainder of this paper presents some hypotheses on norms and behavior that are implied by the social identity perspective. The first set of hypotheses concerns the behavioral consequences of individual and group norms; the second set focuses on reality assumptions. These hypotheses are extremely general. They are essentially guidelines for future research and theory construction, rather than precise, testable propositions.

Hypotheses on the Behavioral Consequences of Individual and Group Norms

The assumptions just discussed imply the following general hypotheses:

1. Ranking and membership norms will tend to be consistent with behavior, across groups. In other words, behavior will be consistent with shared normative beliefs that define important identities, i.e., beliefs that specify how to be a member-in-good-standing with a particular rank. This hypothesis is supported by the findings on group norms that were summarized earlier. The hypothesis refers only to ranking and membership norms. It does not refer to individual, personal beliefs.[75]

Group members may share many beliefs, attitudes, and opinions, but according to this hypothesis, their behavior will be influenced primarily by beliefs about what *behavior* determines rank and membership. For example, if the members of a neighborhood agree that racial integration is a good thing, this belief will be consistent with their behavior only if membership and rank in the neighborhood is contingent on supporting integration. Furthermore, the neighborhood may believe that membership and rank require making general statements in support of integration but not taking political action to integrate their neighborhood. In this case, the norms will be consistent with verbal behavior, but not with political action. This interpretation may explain some of the negative findings on group norms and behavior, such as the lack of relationship between voting norms and behavior that has been found in cross-national studies.[76]

The generalization that group norms will be consistent with behavior is qualified in the following two hypotheses. Each one concerns a situation in which there are several sets of ranking (or membership) norms, and the behavior of the group is not consistent with the official group norms.

2. Ranking and membership norms will not tend to be consistent with behavior, across groups, if the means for conforming to the norms are unavailable. Examples of this situation are: (1) American men who cannot secure stable employment and therefore cannot obtain prestige by being good husbands and fathers or (2) peasants without land who cannot gain

respect by being good farmers. The hypothesis is similar to Merton's ideas about deviance, anomie, and access to means[77]; the rationale for the hypothesis differs from Merton in that it stresses alternative systems of norms.

If the means for conformity are generally unavailable in a community, then a new system of ranking norms will develop or the group will disintegrate. This assertion is based on the assumption that all functioning groups will have shared beliefs that enable their members to discriminate between good and bad actions and to rank each other as better or worse. If it becomes impossible to be good, then the old ranking system will be replaced by a new one if the group persists. This process has been documented in studies of poor communities. Several researchers have found evidence that a set of "shadow values" or covert alternative norms has been developed, that allows the members of these communities to rank each other, given the absence of means to conform to good behavior as defined by the dominant system of ranking norms.[78]

3. Ranking and membership norms will not tend to be consistent with behavior, across groups, if rank and membership is controlled by some other group with different norms. This type of situation occurs when a community or group is controlled by outsiders, by a colonial or illegitimate government, or by a social class that is not highly evaluated by most of the community. For example, a group of radical professors may accept and evaluate each other on the basis of nontraditional beliefs about professional behavior. However, their behavior will be consistent with the traditional norms of their older colleagues, insofar as their professional identity is controlled by these colleagues. This hypothesis essentially points to the problem of system reference, and suggests that if different groups have conflicting ranking norms about the same identity, then behavior will be consistent with the norms of the group that has most control over rank and membership.

The previous hypotheses concerned the types of shared group beliefs that would and would not be consistent with behavior and specified some limiting conditions. The next hypothesis focuses on the normative beliefs of individuals.

4. The normative beliefs of an individual will be consistent with behavior insofar as the beliefs are ranking or membership norms that define an important identity and that are shared with others who validate that identity. An individual's behavior may be consistent with his or her norms, even if they are not shared with others in the immediate social environment. The significant others who validate the individual's identity may be located in a previous time or a distant place. Under certain (unknown) conditions,

some people maintain an identity without any apparent social support, even withstanding extended solitary confinement. A less extraordinary example of the importance of individual beliefs occurs when an individual with an identity that is validated by absent others finds or creates a group that shares his norms.

These situations suggest that, under some conditions, significant others can be internalized or can continue their influence after they have disappeared. Therefore, Parsons' concept of internalization should probably be included in a revised theory of norms and behavior, even though the evidence indicates that such internalization is infrequent.

Hypotheses on the Behavioral Consequences of Reality Assumptions

Reality assumptions have important consequences for behavior because they are taken for granted by the members of a community; behavior tends to fall within the boundaries of these assumptions because it is difficult to imagine a course of action that does not have an agreed-upon meaning for other members. Moreover, such behavior would be self-defeating, insofar as an individual wants to achieve a certain goal by means of his action. Finally, people probably tend to perceive even rather bizarre behavior in terms of familiar categories, thereby assimilating new actions into the old reality assumptions.

This theoretical perspective suggests the following general hypotheses:

5. People will rarely perform meaningless behavior (i.e., behavior not included in the reality assumptions). This is essentially a restatement of the classic definitions of social action[79] and asserts that most behavior is meaningful action. However, meaningless behavior may be caused by nonsocial factors, such as twitches caused by an individual's physiological state.

6. If meaningless behavior is performed, it will elicit no response from others, or it will lower the status of the actor or define him as an outsider, or it will elicit responses appropriate to incompetent (crazy, sick) actors. There is no systematic evidence to test these or any other hypotheses on the consequences of reality assumptions. This is probably because of the difficulty of conceptualizing and measuring reality assumptions independently of behavior. On the one hand, any public action that occurs frequently will be incorporated into the reality assumptions, if it is noticed at all. That is, it will be assigned a common meaning, including ideas about what motives would reasonably lead to such action and what consequences it might have. On the other hand, reality assumptions usually determine the definition of behavior or action. The behavior that is noticed by natives or measured by social

scientists is usually a socially significant act, whose boundaries and salient dimensions are defined by reality assumptions.[80] There are a variety of approaches to measuring reality assumptions that deserve careful exploration. For example, an informant could be presented with a variety of technically possible actions and asked to judge which ones are meaningful and which ones are crazy.[81] Or one could focus on areas where the reality assumptions are changing and are therefore relatively conscious and easy to elicit. However, until such measurement techniques have been developed, the hypotheses on reality assumptions can only be supported by illustrative examples.

Most general descriptions of communities include many examples that support hypotheses 5 and 6. In my own field work in Mexico, many such examples were forced on my attention when I unsuccessfully attempted to carry out behaviors that were taken for granted in the United States. For instance, in Zinacantan, Mexico, it is impossible to tell a guest to make himself at home and help himself to whatever food or other things he wants. Guests do not choose what they are to get. They do not ask for food but accept whatever they are offered, either to consume it at the moment or to take it home. Many Americans have tried to pass a bowl of fruit around to their Zinancanteco guests, only to have the first recipient take all the fruit, put it in his sack, and return the empty bowl to the host, with thanks. "Help yourself" is not part of the reality assumptions in Zinacantan, and to my knowledge, no Zinacantecos engage in this behavior, except a few informants who have been working for Americans for years.

One of the most interesting implications of the concept of reality assumptions is that major social changes will occur if these assumptions change and that, conversely, if they are not changed then many social patterns will remain stable. This idea is stated in the following hypothesis:

7. New behavior patterns that were not previously defined as meaningful (i.e., as part of some identity) will not be adopted by a community unless new reality assumptions that define the meaning of the behavior are first developed. This hypothesis is illustrated by the apparent effects of recent social movements in the United States. Consider, for example, the probable effects of the current Women's Liberation movement. Let us assume that at all periods of time, wives have occasionally refused to carry out their usual domestic tasks. In the past, this might have been interpreted as crazy behavior that should not be taken too seriously, indicating that the woman was sick or moody and she should be expected to "return to normal" soon and "be herself" again. If the same behavior occurred today, it might well be taken seriously as

a meaningful act, indicating that the woman intended to change the accepted behavior patterns of the family. In this hypothetical example, the frequency of the behavior may not have changed over time, but the consequences have drastically altered. It is essentially a different act, and accounting for this difference seems to call for a concept like reality assumptions.

Other examples are provided by the Black Power movement, which has created new meaningful action alternatives for interracial behavior, such as the possibility of a White person showing fearful respect to a Black person. In both of these examples, the critical feature is not standards of evaluation or the good-bad distinction. People may approve or disapprove of Women's Liberation or Black Power, but their behavior will nonetheless be affected by these shifts in the definition of meaningful behavior.

Finally, the consequences of reality assumptions can also be examined in situations of social stability. Reality assumptions limit the actions that are possible in a given setting. If different organizations or social institutions have different reality assumptions, this should result in different behavior patterns.

8. The behaviors that occur in different organizations or institutions will be consistent with the reality assumptions of those organizations. This hypothesis is supported by Meyer's analysis of the effects of different types of schools.[82] Meyer analyses the "charter" or reality assumptions of different educational institutions, e.g., some are defined as places that confer generalized elite status, while others are defined as places to learn specific skills. He then considers how these institutions have different effects on their members, e.g., schools that are expected to socialize students to an elite status have a broader range of effects on students.

CONCLUSION

The theory of the socialized actor assumes that shared norms are internalized to become stable elements of an individual's personality. However, the available evidence indicates that an individual's normative beliefs are not consistent with his behavior and that norms can change rapidly and without intensive resocialization. Therefore, the theory of the socialized actor needs to be substantially revised.

The social identity approach assumes that norms affect behavior by specifying the actions and attributes that will validate particular identities. This approach explains many of the findings on individual versus group norms and on normative change. It also clarifies the importance of reality assumptions.

Parsons' work on norms and values has defined a central issue in sociological theory. If we are to advance further in this area to which he has contributed so much, we need to develop a theory of norms and behavior that incorporates some of the assumptions of the social identity approach.

NOTES

1. The pervasiveness of this point of view can be seen by examining introductory textbooks in sociology, such as L. Broom and P. Selznick, *Sociology* (New York: Harper & Row, 1963). It was also evident in the sessions of the 1971 ASA Meetings that I informally observed; most participants attempted to explain part of their results by referring to the (unmeasured) norms and values of their subjects.

2. Many critics have strongly attacked Parsons' theory of values, but none of them seems to reject the idea that norms are sometimes an important determinant of behavior. These critics are reviewed in J. Blake and K. Davis, "Norms, Values and Sanctions" in R. Faris (ed.), *Handbook of Modern Sociology* (Chicago: Rand McNally, 1964), pp. 456-484.

3. For an exception, see Blake and Davis, *op. cit.*

4. This presentation of Parsons is based on his following works: *The Social System* (New York: The Free Press, 1951), Chapters 1-3 and 6-8; "The Superego and the Theory of Social Systems" in T. Parsons, R. F. Bales, and E. A. Shils, *Working Papers in the Theory of Action* (New York: The Free Press, 1953); "Values, Motives and Systems of Action" in T. Parsons and E.A. Shils (eds.), *Towards a General Theory of Action* (Cambridge, Harvard University Press, 1951); and "An Outline of the Social System," in T. Parsons *et al.* (eds.), *Theories of Society* (New York: The Free Press, 1961).

5. Parsons, *The Social System,* p. 12.

6. *Ibid.,* pp. 14 and 251.

7. *Ibid.,* p. 211.

8. *Ibid.,* p. 37.

9. *Ibid.,* p. 42.

10. *Ibid.,* Chapters 6 and 7.

11. *Ibid.,* p. 208.

12. *Ibid.,* p. 228.

13. See R. Dahrendorf, "Out of Utopia," *American Journal of Sociology,* 64 (1958), pp. 115-127; and D. Wrong, "The Oversocialized Conception of Man in Modern Sociology," *American Sociological Review,* 26 (1961), pp. 183-193.

14. See Blake and Davis, *op. cit.*

15. Parsons, "An Outline of the Social System," *op. cit.,* p. 55. Parsons makes a more fundamental criticism of the theory of the socialized actor when he points out the problem of explaining social regularities by childhood socialization, given the great variance in the socialization experiences of individuals, in *The Social System,* p. 229.

16. Parsons pointed out this aspect of shared beliefs in his early writings, *The Social System,* pp. 35 and 379, and *Working Papers,* p. 18. However, in this work shared cognitive standards are treated as a stable given, while evaluative standards are the focus of theoretical interest, the dependent variable of the mechanisms of social control and socialization.

17. The discussion considers only norms and ignores the more general concept of values because values seem more elusive and there is little evidence on their relation to behavior.

18. This phrase concerning "equal applicability" needs to be qualified to allow for different membership norms for different roles. Thus, the beliefs about being a member in good standing of a church are likely to be different for men and women.

19. In my own work, the distinction between ranking norms and other shared beliefs about behavior first emerged in the early stages of a study, *What are Norms?: A Study of Beliefs and Action in a Maya Community* (New York: Cambridge

University Press, 1974). The study attempted to elicit normative beliefs by asking people to complete sentences like, "He is good because . . . ." To my surprise, the three men who produced thousands of normative statements in completing the sentences never once mentioned a behavior pattern that did not vary in the community. This finding suggested the obvious logical principle that differential evaluation requires variation in behavior. The norms that are consciously used in daily decision making and evaluation (ranking norms) are those for which there is a high degree of variability in conformity. Ranking norms were originally labelled "active norms" because they were the most apparent types of norms in Zinacantan. Reality assumptions were first labelled "passive norms," then "customary norms," and then "reality norms" before the final draft of this paper.

20. For an interesting interpretation of norms in terms of ranking or stratification, see R. Dahrendorf's essay, "The Origin of Inequality," in his *Essays in the Theory of Society* (Stanford: Stanford University Press, 1968).

21. The distinction between ranking and membership norms is similar to J. C. Kimberly's distinction between task norms and nontask norms in "Relations among Status, Power and Economic Rewards," in J. Berger *et al.* (eds.), *Sociological Theories in Progress,* Vol. II (Boston: Houghton-Mifflin, 1972).

22. It is not clear whether all meaningful acts are good or bad. Evaluation may be a universal component of social meaning. This is suggested by Osgood's cross-cultural studies of semantic structure, which show that the good-bad dimension tends to be the major component of meaning in all societies (see Charles Osgood, "Semantic Differential Technique in the Comparative Study of Cultures," in A. Romney and R. D'Andrade (eds.), *Transcultural Studies in Cognition,* special issue of the *American Anthropologist,* 66 (1964), pp. 171-200. However, in some situations the meaningful action alternatives do not seem to be evaluated. Thus, I can get to work by the "possible" but unevaluated alternatives of walking, biking, or driving. It would be "impossible" or crazy if I crawled to work.

23. For an interesting discussion of how reality assumptions define reasonable motives for actions, see A. F. Blum and P. McHugh, "The Social Ascription of Motives," *American Sociological Review,* 36 (1971), pp. 98-109.

24. The issue of whether or not to conceive of reality assumptions as standards applied to (an independently defined) reality is complex. On the one hand, it seems difficult to imagine an actor as first perceiving reality independently of shared, meaningful categories and then selecting or deciding what meaning he will attribute to it. On the other hand, theorists like Howard S. Becker *Outsiders* (New York: The Free Press, 1963), present a convincing argument that social meanings and identities are often manipulated for personal or class interest. Labeling an event or assigning it a meaning often carries with it an evaluation, for example, calling an event a demonstration or a riot. Therefore assigning meaning is an essential part of justifying past and future behavior. This issue will have to be resolved in order to make it possible clearly to specify the relation between reality assumptions and the two types of norms.

25. Parsons, *The Social System,* pp. 379-380.

26. H. Johnson, *Sociology* (New York: Harcourt, Brace, 1960), p. 8.

27. N. Gross, W. Mason, and A. McEachern, *Explorations in Role Analysis* (New York: Wiley, 1958), pp. 58-59.

28. The definition of standards of evaluation as shared beliefs is clearly opposed by Parsons. He states that "patterns of value-orientation . . . are 'guided' by beliefs, but only partially determined by them. . ." (*The Social System,* p. 379).

29. G. Homans, *The Human Group* (New York: Harcourt, Brace, 1950), p. 124.

30. Broom and Selznick, *op. cit.*

31. Homans, *op. cit.*, p. 123.

32. Blake and Davis, *op. cit.*, p. 456.

33. Another problem with equating norms and sanction patterns is that it becomes difficult to deal with norms that persist for some time despite the lack of external support.

34. The distinctive attribute of normative beliefs seems to be the component of moral commitment that is operationally defined by using words like good, bad, should, or ought. However, on the theoretical level, this component is difficult to explicate. What theoretical guidelines can be used to decide whether to consider as "norms" statements like "girls have to act dumber than boys," "It's better to be respectful to policemen," or "you should get eight hours of sleep every night"?

35. It should be noted that ranking norms are defined as *beliefs* about the allocation of approval, and not as the criteria that determine the actual allocation of approval. If norms are defined as the criteria for approval, then people may not be aware of their norms; and the best way of measuring norms would be to observe the distribution of approval in gossip or daily interaction. With this approach the statement that norms determine behavior becomes equivalent to Homans' theory, which asserts that rewards determine behavior and that social approval is a very important reward. G. Homans, *Social Behavior*, (New York: Harcourt, Brace, 1961), pp. 34-35.

36. F. M. Cancian, "New Methods for Describing What People Think," *Sociological Inquiry*, 41 (1971), pp. 85-93.

37. For a detailed description of this method, see Cancian, *What Are Norms?*

38. W. A. Scott, "Empirical Assessment of Values and Ideologies," *American Sociological Review*, 24 (1959), pp. 229-310.

39. Most of the studies are not explicitly concerned with shared normative beliefs. Those that do focus on norms make no attempt to describe the normative system before formulating questions about beliefs. Therefore the questions have an unknown relation to the salient dimensions of the normative system, from the actor's point of view.

40. W. J. McGuire, "The Nature of Attitudes and Attitude Change," in G. Lindzey and E. Aronson (eds.), *The Handbook of Social Psychology* (Reading, Pa.: Addison-Wesley, 1969), Vol. III, pp. 136-314.

41. G. W. Allport, "Attitudes" in C. M. Murchison (ed.), *Handbook of Social Psychology* (Worcester, Mass.: Clark University Press, 1935), pp. 798-844.

42. J. Harding, B. Kutner, H. Proschansky, and I. Chein, "Prejudice and Ethnic Relations" in G. Lindzey (ed.), *Handbook of Social Psychology* (Cambridge, Mass.: Addison-Wesley, 1954), pp. 1021-1061, on p. 1027.

43. See S. A. Star, R. Williams, and S. Stouffer, "Negro Infantry Platoons in White Companies" in E. Maccoby *et al.* (eds.), *Readings in Social Psychology* (New York: Holt Rinehart, 1958), pp. 596-601.

44. S. W. Cook and C. Selltiz, "Attitude Measurement," *Psychological Bulletin*, 62 (1964), pp. 36-55, on p. 42.

45. S. Deri and D. Dinnerstein *et al.,* "Diagnosis and Measurement of Intergroup Attitudes," *Psychological Bulletin*, 45 (1948), pp. 248-271, on p. 262.

46. R. T. LaPierre, "Attitudes vs. Actions," *Social Forces*, 13 (1934) pp. 230-237; and B. Kutner, C. Wilkins and P. Yarrow, "Verbal Attitudes and Overt Behavior Involving Racial Prejudice," *Journal of Abnormal and Social Psychology*, 47 (1952), pp. 649-652.

47. M. DeFleur and F. Westie, "Verbal Attitudes and Overt Acts," *American Sociological Review*, 23 (1958), pp. 667-673.

48. I. Deutscher, "Words and Deeds," *Social Problems*, 13 (1966), pp. 235-254, on p. 250.

49. LaPierre, *op. cit.*

50. See G. Saenger and E. Gilbert, "Customer Reactions to the Integration of Negro Sales Personnel," *International Journal of Opinion and Attitude Research*, 4 (1950), pp. 57-76.

51. S. Pittel, and G. Mendelsohn, "Measurement of Moral Values," *Psychological Bulletin,* 66 (1966), pp. 22-35, on p. 25.

52. See J. H. Bryan, "Children's Reactions to Helpers" in J. Macauley and L. Berkowitz (eds.), *Altruism and Helping Behavior* (New York: Academic Press, 1970), pp. 61-73.

53. See D. H. Olson, "The Measurement of Family Power by Self-Report and Behavioral Methods," *Journal of Marriage and the Family*, 31 (1969), pp. 545-550; see also L. Weller and E. Luchterland, "Company Interview and Observations on Family Functioning," *Journal of Marriage and the Family*, 31 (1969), pp. 115-122.

54. Deutscher, *op. cit.*

55. Harding, *et. al., op. cit.*, p. 43, and C. R. Tittle and R. J. Hill, "Attitude Measurement and Prediction of Behavior," *Sociometry*, 30 (1967), pp. 199-213.

56. Deutscher, *op. cit.*

57. See D. T. Campbell, "Social attitudes and Other Acquired Behavioral Dispositions," in S. Koch (ed.), *Psychology: A Study of a Science,* Vol. VI (New York: McGraw-Hill, 1961), pp 94-172; and H. J. Ehrlich, "Attitudes, Behavior and the Intervening Variables," *The American Sociologist,* 4 (1969), pp. 29-34.

58. See A. W. Wicker, "Attitudes vs. Actions," *Journal of Social Issues*, 25 (1969), pp. 41-78.

59. McGuire, *op. cit.*, and M. Fishbein, "Attitudes and the Prediction of Behavior," in M. Fishbein (ed.), *Readings in Attitude Theory and Measurement* (New York: Wiley, 1967), pp. 477-492.

60. See W. F. Kenkel, "Observational Studies of Husband-Wife Interaction in Family Decision-Making" in M. Sussman (ed.), *Sourcebook in Marriage and the Family* (Boston: Houghton-Mifflin, 1963), pp. 144-156.

61. See H. Hartshorne and M. A. May, *Studies on the Nature of Character*, No. 1 (New York: Macmillan, 1928).

62. M. Kohn, *Class and Conformity* (Homewood, Ill.: Dorsey, 1969).

63. See F. L. Strodtbeck "Husband-Wife Interaction over Revealed Differences," *American Sociological Review*, 16 (1951), pp. 468-473.

64. See F. Kluckhohn and F. Strodtbeck, *Variations in Value Orientations* (New York: Row, Peterson, 1961).

65. See C. H. Alexander and G. W. Knight, "Situated Identities and Social Psychological Experimentation," *Sociometry*, 34 (1971), pp. 65-82.

66. See P. Lauderdale, "Social Reality and Social Psychological Experimentation," unpublished Master's Paper, Stanford University, n. d.

67. Homans, *op. cit.*

68. See C. Sherif, M. Sherif, and R. Nebergall, *Attitude and Attitude Change* (Philadelphia: W. B. Saunders, 1965).

69. See W. L. Wallace, *Student Culture* (Chicago: Aldine, 1966).

70. See J. C. Benitez, "Educational Institutionalization," unpublished Ph.D. dissertation, Stanford University, 1971.

71. See T. Parsons, "Interaction" in D. Sills (ed.), *International Encyclopedia of the Social Sciences* (New York: Crowell, Collier and MacMillan, 1968), Vol. 7, pp. 429-441. The "old masters" of this tradition include Emile Durkheim, G. H. Mead, and Alfred Schutz. Contemporary work includes H. S. Becker, *op. cit.*, E. Goffman, *Interaction Ritual* (Chicago: Aldine, 1967); R. K. Merton, *Social Theory and Social Structure* (New York: The Free Press, 1957); P. L. Berger and T. Luckmann, *The Social Construction of Reality* (Garden City, N.Y.: Anchor Books, 1967); A. Blum and P. McHugh, *op. cit.*

72. For significant advances in this direction, see Sherif *et al., op. cit.*

73. This assumption raises many problems that cannot be dealt with in this brief presentation. They include the effects of conflicting reference groups and role conflict, the degree of consensus implied by the term "shared," and the difference between perceived and actual consensus.

74. Explaining the relative commitment of individuals to

particular identities may introduce a motivational component into the social identity theory: the assumption that individuals internalize or become personally committed to an identity. This issue is complex, in part because of the difficulty of distinguishing between the norms relating to an identity (e.g., women are docile) and the identity itself (I am a woman). For a more extended discussion of this problem see Cancian, *What Are Norms?*

75. A correlation between personal beliefs and action might be found for a variety of reasons besides either socialization or the identity implications of the action. For example, the statement of belief may be a description of a recurrent behavior pattern, e.g., "I like chocolate ice cream better than vanilla" meaning "I always buy chocolate ice cream." Or the statement of belief may mean an intention to perform a particular act, e.g., "I like McGovern better than Nixon" meaning "I intend to vote for McGovern."

76. A. McClosky, "Political Participation" in D. Sills (ed.), *op. cit.*, Vol. 12, pp. 252-265, on p. 259.

77. See Merton, *op. cit.*

78. See E. Liebow, *Tally's Corner* (Boston: Little, Brown, 1967); and L. Rainwater, *Behind Ghetto Walls* (Chicago, Ill.: Aldine, 1970).

79. M. Weber, *The Theory of Social and Economic Organization*, A. M. Henderson and T. Parsons (trs.), edited and with an introduction by T. Parsons (New York: The Free Press, 1947), p. 88.

80. It is possible to define some behavior independently of social meaning, e.g., frequency of interaction or physical location; but all natives and most social scientists are primarily interested in meaningful behavior.

81. This is essentially a systematic version of the procedure developed by H. Garfinkel, *Studies in Ethnomethodology*, (Englewood Cliffs, Prentice-Hall, 1967), in which reactions to purposefully performed crazy behavior are elicited in order to define reality assumptions.

82. See J. W. Meyer, "The Charter: Conditions of Diffuse Socialization in Schools," in W. Scott (ed.), *Social Processes and Social Structure* (New York: Holt, Rinehart and Winston, 1970), pp. 564-578.

15

THE MILLENARIAN MOVEMENT ORGANIZATION AS A SOCIALIZATION AGENCY

Jesse R. Pitts

One of the major interests of action theory has been the relationship between the social system and the personality system. Breaking with the associationism of Miller and Dollard, Parsons uses a Freudian approach to the personality system as a way of restoring to the latter its own dynamics. On the other hand, he was immune to the reductionist attempts of the "Culture and Personality School" which saw in social structure essentially projections of the personality system.[1]

In *The Social System* Parsons had developed a theory of deviance and social control which led to the concept of the "secondary institution." The latter played a role parallel to the therapeutic role, which for Parsons found its prototype in the psychiatrist-patient relationship. The secondary institution was permissive within limits to deviance, yet it tied the deviant to the dominant institutions. Its mechanisms were comparable to those contained in the rituals of mourning. The two examples Parsons gave of secondary institutions were those of the youth culture and the gambling complex. In the youth culture, although adolescents find some permissiveness for deviance, they are at the same time securely tied to the institutions of learning, and the end of emotional dependency upon parents—dysfunctional to the assumption of adult roles—is encouraged.

Parsons described the radical sect as coming close to being a secondary institution. It was a pattern of deviance to which societies with universalistic value patterns are vulnerable, because of the generality and ambiguity of many of their value statements. The social control element that he saw in the existence of radical sects was precisely the "bridge" to the dominant society that the commitment to the same ultimate values provided. This was the basis for

the eventual incorporation of the radical sect, or of individual ex-members, to the dominant society through the process of "selling out," i.e., an acceptance of the dominant patterns of institutionalization as being the best possible under the circumstances.

The concept of the "fringe organization," first outlined in *Theories of Society,*[2] combines the therapeutic function of the secondary institution with the formal organization and the "bridge" function of the radical sect. It states that membership in the fringe organization, while it may grant the deviant the power of coalition, actually promotes "selling out," partly because of the common value bridges but above all through the socializing experience involved in membership. Thus the concept points to the function of social control played by groups the overt purposes of which are deviance and the partial or even complete subversion of the dominant society.

THE MILLENARIAN MOVEMENT ORGANIZATION

A variety of fringe organization is the millenarian movement organization,[3] which is an organization "aiming to restore, protect, modify or create values in the name of a generalized belief,"[4] through violent change divinely and/or humanly engineered.[5]

In its effort to create or alter values the movement organization will assume the following millenarian traits: it believes that it has (1) the secret of a perfect or near-perfect social order (2) which is certain to triumph over the forces of darkness (defined as the Devil, the Antichrist, Reaction, Communism, American imperialism (3) in the near future (4) through a conflagration (5) wherein the members of the movement organization will be victorious, saved, assume positions of leadership.[6]

One of the advantages of the concept millenarian movement organization (henceforth called MMO) is that it introduces more rigor in the analysis of collective behavior which, from the crowd orientation it inherited from Gustave Le Bon,[7] has often maintained a motivational orientation, leaving the social structural elements in an ambiguity which seemed to parallel the ambiguity of the street phenomena. The word movement was ideal in this respect. Eric Hoffer is among those who renewed the Le Bon approach, and he analyzed radical sects essentially in terms of their appeal to a certain type of personality which he named "the True Believer."[8]

Essentially, as Hoffer sees it, the motivation to join radical movements is a form of illness which, in sociological terms, would be defined as the involuntary incapacity of the personality to mobilize psychological facilities for the fulfillment of legitimate age, sex, and status roles. Such would be the incapacity to cathect collectivities such as family, marriage, work organizations, status groups, and difficulties in sustaining over time the activities necessary for the resolution of legitimate role tasks. These failures can be caused by a range of psychological problems ranging from depression or high anxiety states to schizoid and/or paranoid trends. They may be deep-seated problems or temporary disturbances caused by personality crises such as may occur in adolescence, or the feelings of despair and futility which sometimes overwhelm adults, whether men or women.[9]

An interesting aspect of membership in the MMO is the fact that members, far from being alienated from the broader society, actually claim to be more passionately committed to its welfare than nonmembers are. What the latter may see as rationalization for incapacity to participate in the roles and collectivities which are part of the total society is seen by members as the legitimate refusal to share in institutional patterns which threaten the welfare of the society and, even more important, degrade its moral standing. This is the regressive idealistic commitment.

It is regressive because it simplifies reality by reducing the number of relevant memberships to the situation that existed in early childhood when all authoritative pronouncements issued from the parental figure. The key to ethical behavior, praise, and feelings of self-worth came from parent-child interaction. All events were evaluated in terms of their immediate effects upon the self-parent figure dyad. The regressive idealistic commitment refuses the categorizations upon which universalistic criteria are based and performances measured; it rejects the segmentation of roles in favor of a total projection of self in each action sequence. Time, the holding back of commitment capacity, and the apportionment of commitment capacity become irrelevant.

Yet the regression does not lead to autism and solipsism because it is idealistic: it identifies the welfare of the self with the welfare of the millenarian group and its leader. It makes alienation and hostility to the institutionalized patterns a consequence of conformity to the ultimate values incarnated in the MMO. It resolves the ambivalence and conflicts inherent to multiple role behavior through a syncretic oneness with the source of all goodness.

Modally the process of socialization attempts to convert the cathexis and love of the parent-child dyad which is diffused to the church and the total society (fatherland and motherland) into a commitment to specified roles and limited collectivities. Concern for the total society is not supposed to become a primary motivational force except perhaps when there are serious conflicts and/or ambiguities in the obligations specified in role patterns and collectivity memberships. The constant and passionate concern for the welfare of the total collectivity puts into question the realism, the effectiveness of institutionalized patterns and introduces an uncertainty of conformity which, if generalized, would destroy the fabric of social order.

There are circumstances, however, where the society will encourage the "regression" of the citizen's commitment structures: there are rituals which, in processes first described by Durkheim,[10] "libidinize" the commitment to conformity by granting the individual a feeling of oneness with the omniscient and omnipotent group. There are the commitments to the national wars of the nineteenth and twentieth centuries, which have many aspects of a "legitimate" millenarian movement, rescuing the motherland from the forces of darkness and securing a peace worthy of the just and the brave. On a microcosmic level, another occasion for the legitimate regression of commitment structures is "romantic love," where the dyad of the elect becomes routinized into the marriage of the breadwinner and of the homekeeper.[11]

Indeed the process of joining an MMO before it is within reach of officialization and in a sense ceases to be a "fringe" organization resembles more often the process of falling in love than a self-conscious rational process which weighs pros and cons and determines that membership is the best possible expenditure of one's life energy. Certainly, in the early stages of the MMO the discrepancy between its effective power and its promises, the elements of uncertainty that are involved in the diagnosis of societal possibilities (revolution, European primacy, world dominance, a classless and prosperous society) preclude that the decision can be rational in the way that the choice of a place of employment, the purchase of a home, or even the decision to get married can be "rational." Joining means running the risks of negative sanctions, as the MMO is in a state of deviance toward the dominant society. Ridicule, separation from loved ones, the forsaking of opportunities in the legitimate economic, prestige, or power structure are the least of the negative sanctions one may incur. Certainly when an MMO is in a formative stage there are few rational justifications for the types of commitment most MMO's, at least theoretically, require. Joining the Nazi Party in 1920 had quite a different meaning than it had in 1931 when its victory seemed a realistic possibility even to its opponents. The level of "irrationality" involved in joining the Doomsday Cult[12] is greater in the U.S. than in the cult's native Korea, and certainly greater than that demonstrated by a German unemployed worker joining the German Communist Party in 1932.[13] Arthur Koestler describes his joining in 1931 the German Communist Party as following an intellectual conversion to the Leninist version of Marxism: "By the time I had finished with *Feuerbach* and *State and Revolution,* something had clicked in my brain which shook me like a mental explosion."[14] On the other hand, the Almond study shows that only 27% of a sample of ex-members "had been exposed to the classical writings of Communism before or at the time of joining."[15]

John Lofland[16] seems correct when he concludes that joining a cult (and his Doomsday Cult is a prototype of the MMO) is a conjuncture of "seekership" within a given intellectual tradition (religious, political) that includes the MMO's "theology" with the development of affective ties with members of the group. The combination of the two defines the most common form of conversion, which results in the member's belief that the MMO's doctrine is the source of life's meaning and the guide to moral behavior—which can now be called "outer millenarianism"—and that the membership is a community of human beings superior to all nonmembers, which can be called "inner millenarianism."

However, no organization and no pattern of deviance can be characterized by a specific type of motivational output. There are members who have followed a spouse or a loved one into the MMO without any special conviction. And in the same way as there are persons who will bring a millenarian motivation to a norm-oriented group such as the League of Women Voters, there are others who bring to the MMO a motivation that is at the level of what Smelser[17] calls the "hostile outburst." For them membership is above all a chance to act out an aggressive impulse toward a reference group in the dominant society, and they often drop out once their purpose has been accomplished.[18]

Members of MMO's will usually refuse to admit that their motivation for joining can be anything but a legitimate dissatisfaction with the institutionalized norms of the society and the desire for a higher level of value implementation than the society has demonstrated heretofore. A member may join on the basis of what he thinks—and what an observer of his action may think—is a relatively careful analysis of the social situation, evaluating realistically the capacity of the MMO to achieve its major objectives within a complex field of historical forces. This would be rational idealism. There is also a motivational pattern which can be called rational opportunism. All MMO's within reach of seizing power must cope with substantial influxes of both types.

In influencing the determination of the MMO's structure, the strategical motivational inputs are those of idealistic regressive commitment and rational idealism, with a clear dominance of the former. Most MMO's remain small, lasting only less than a decade or two. Of the few that reach mass movement size—as against the many that disappear or become encapsulated[19]—only a minute number succeed in creating legitimate institutions around their core values.[20] Hence rarely do they have to cope with the problems created by the massive inputs of rational idealistic and rational opportunistic motivational patterns. Few have to cope with the organizational problems created by social continuity across generations.

A major characteristic of the regressive idealistic commitment is the role that ambivalence and its resolution play in its structure. For Parsons[21] the MMO is a variety of delinquent subculture whereby the deviant is "enabled to act out *both* the conformative and alienative components of his ambivalent motivational structure . . . he can be compulsively conformative *within* the deviant sub-group at the same time that he is compulsively alienated from the main institutional structure."

Utilizing the active-passive dimension to analyze the structure of deviant motivation, Parsons also predicts that the conforming component in "active" members will be oriented in a dominating and norm-enforcing manner. Because in his opinion "delinquent subculture groups" (of which the MMO is a species) tend to attract people who have a need to dominate, the result will be a tendency for struggles for leadership with a tendency to splits, a tendency toward extraordinary risk taking, and the recruitment of persons who are "rather passively inclined and generally obedient types."

To this penetrating analysis could be added that motivational structures characterized by high ambivalence require constant reinforcements through ritual acts and the conversion of others. The only way that the member can take the role of the non-member is through martyrdom and/or proselytization, where he repeats all the reasons why he himself should be a member in the first place.

The "norm-enforcing direction" which Parsons perceived to be a consequence of the ambivalence of an "actively" oriented member can also be interpreted as the result of the member's projection upon others of his own doubts and temptations to betrayal. Hence the norm-enforcing direction will translate itself into a constant readiness to question other members' sincerity. Thus the member oscillates between inner millenarianism and the belief that members as a group are "saved" and a suspicion that some may be deviationists if not traitors.[22]

STRUCTURAL CHARACTERISTICS OF MILLENARIAN MOVEMENT ORGANIZATIONS

MMO's have six major structural characteristics, which we will now discuss.

1. They operate as "total institutions," or nearly so.[23] The Communist Party U.S.A. did not provide as close to a total experience as a boarding school or the U.S. Army might provide. On the other hand, outside of the preparation of food and shelter, or an occupational role to which the member gave only the minimum attention necessary for its retention, all other aspects of life came under the purview of the party. This is also true for all MMO's. The pressure is great upon the member to reduce his contacts with the outside world to those necessary for proselytizing or "witnessing."

Thus the organization isolates the member from competing world views. It depreciates all aspects of life which are not directly connected to the pursuit of the MMO's goals.

2. MMO's are authoritarian in structure. As the goals and the basic doctrine are accepted once and for all—either because they are "revealed" or because they define the very boundaries of the organization (one does not become a member of Progressive Labor unless one accepts the superiority of the Chinese variety of Marxism-Leninism)—the bulk of the policies are not elaborated through debate. Leadership is either charismatic or delegated from a charismatic center. Because, as shall soon be described, the bulk of the MMO's policies are rarely instrumental but most often in the nature of acts of faith, there is very little need for "reactive" information secured from the rank and file. As action flows from doctrine, failures are interpreted not as reflecting upon the doctrine but as the result of trials sent by God, or the results of interference by evil men, sometimes traitors in the MMO's ranks. Because it is assumed that

those longer in the MMO are better steeped in the doctrine, and as there is a constant danger of deviation and betrayal, there is a definite logic for the elitist manner in which decisions are made. These are typical rationalizations for the acceptance by members of authoritarian patterns in organizations that claim in their ideology to be completely democratic.

The degree of formal hierarchical structure can vary from the elaborate bureaucratic structure of Marxist-Leninist parties to the loose structure of the Hippie movement and its informal federation of communities (now "communes"). It might seem incongruous to speak of a Hippie community as being authoritarian, when the anti-authoritarian aspects of the doctrine[24] are so well known. Given the charisma of this doctrine, which is elaborated by gurus and underground media "intellectuals," the zone of freedom (more specifically, of dissent) of the member is not much greater than was found in a Communist party of the Trotskyist variety. It is anti-authoritarian as the militant Quaker church of the seventeenth and eighteenth centuries was anti-authoritarian.

3. MMO's are experienced by their members to be permissive. Because of their total institution aspects, MMO's imply relief from many of the role demands made by the dominant society. They insulate their members from many of the sanctions that would otherwise be meted out by the outside community. Because of the importance to the MMO of the very quality of membership,[25] the leadership is willing to disregard obvious personality failures that would otherwise not be tolerated. Thus in many religious MMO's (and this includes the Hippies), members who are "obviously" mentally ill are either carried or treated as if their illness were a special blessing.[26]

Furthermore, even in the apparently disciplined Communist Party, the MMO has many characteristics of the "near-group," i.e., there are many areas where the individual is free not to get involved and where his membership may be nominal. Beyond certain declarations of faith it is not difficult for a member to avoid many of the activities of the group. Thus even with its authoritarian structure, its "revealed" doctrine, the MMO is not as demanding an organization as its total-institution claims might make it seem. The member can move from near inactivity to great activity and back to inactivity pretty much as he wishes. This is largely due to the great value placed on proselytization and also to the high costs of coercion for any group that does not have legitimate access to force.[27]

The flexibility and *de facto* voluntarism is one of the major sources of the member's subjective feeling of support and acceptance. As long as the member does not question the outer millenarianism of the MMO, the range of acceptable behavior is broader than in the dominant society.

4. MMO's specialize in proselytization and expressive behavior. MMO's place themselves outside of the system, whether pursuing religious or politico-religious goals, by the very nature of their total and millenarian diagnosis of the problems of the society. The MMO cannot allow itself to become involved in reforming piecemeal a wicked world without exposing itself to becoming tainted with its sin.

Furthermore, the first concern of the MMO lies in the state of the members' motivation. If they keep the faith the organization is bound to triumph, because God or History is on its side. Both the fact that the organization is outside the political system (or the religio-educational system) and its emphasis upon maintaining and purifying commitments lead the MMO to stress expressive action, rather than instrumental action. Parades, demonstrations, confrontations with the police are the stock in trade of the MMO's involved in politico-religious salvation. They create Durkheimian opportunities for strengthening the MMO's collective consciousness. They symbolize and reinforce the boundaries of the MMO with the outside world. They reinforce inner millenarianism by adding to the community of the saved the "solidarity of the trenches." They bring the organization into the public eye and thus give opportunities for new conversions.

When MMO's engage in instrumental behavior it is usually to secure political control over other organizations through the placement of "sleeper" agents or Popular Front tactics, tactics largely imitated from the Nazi Party in the early 1930's. The Communist Party U.S.A. had done very successful work in organizing and staffing CIO trade unions, but most of it was undone by the changes in policies dictated by loyalty to the Soviet Union and its leader Stalin. Changes in the line handed down from the charismatic center led to the loss of many hard-won positions. What counted, more than immediate victories, was obedience to the party line, which eventually would lead to the triumph of the World Revolution. Those who thought differently were traitors who had to be purged relentlessly. Very often the successes of the MMO as a mass movement are due not so much to the shrewdness of its tactics as to the demoralization of its opposition. Historians, especially party historians, can always rationalize a contingent success into one due to historical forces which were judiciously exploited by an infallible leadership. True enough, if an MMO reaches mass movement size and can threaten the seat of power, it means that agencies of social control have been deficient. This may be the result not so much of their incapacity as their loss of self-confidence: A government well aware of the sins and errors of

power can be in a weak position when faced by a mass strong in moral righteousness. If the government and its supporters through their hesitations and guilt feelings allow an ambiguity of legitimacy to be created, it will be filled by the charismatic self-assurance of the MMO. In this sense the demonstration can indeed be as effective as the trumpets of Jericho.

5. The motivational primacy of the MMO, the high ambivalence of its members (the first largely a consequence of the second), and the belief in the infallibility of the organization qua organization lead to a constant search for traitors, police agents, and members who do not have the true faith (i.e., people who may be acting on the basis of error rather than the silent or the lazy). Members who have let error creep into their hearts must permanently be purged of it through some form of public confession or must be expelled.

6. A crucial characteristic of the MMO is its high turnover of members, especially in its active, proselytizing phase. An encapsulated MMO which is not engaged in proselytizing will not have a high turnover. The members will merely die out, the group getting its new members from the sons and daughters of old members. In 1934 the turnover of the Communist Party U.S.A. reached 90%.[28] Today, on the other hand, the party is largely encapsulated. So is the Socialist Labor Party, where the average age of members seems to be in the sixties.

The French Communist Party, which has become the established "Catholicism of the proletariat," has a much lower turnover. The present party is made up of a large stable core, probably 175,000-200,000,[29] the turnover being largely accounted for by some 50,000 new members yearly. Thus it must not be too different from the French Catholic Church, if we count as members those who are affiliated to some church-controlled organization.

The problem of the high turnover leads naturally to a discussion of the impact of membership upon the member.

THE FOUR STAGES OF MEMBERSHIP AND THEIR IMPACT UPON THE MEMBER

The regressive idealistic commitment is a way of resolving many of the strains of high ambivalence which bear upon the personalities of potential members, who are not usually at ease with the traditional delinquent subcultures. The majority of them are law-abiding citizens who because of sociological and/or psychological reasons (youth, marginality, downward mobility, illness) are unable to realize their value commitments through normative role participation. They are, as a result, anxious and frustrated. Their conformity to age, sex, and status roles is frequently compulsive, hiding a strong component of alienation which further reduces role effectiveness.

As long as ambivalence does not reach a high level, an ego of average strength can either repress or suppress those aspects of motivation that are not functional to the expression of the dominant cathexis. If ambivalence is very high, its psychic costs are such as frequently to decrease the capacity of the ego to cathect valued objects, whether persons, groups, or normative patterns. Ambivalence often results in apathy. It paralyzes the ego and threatens to split it. The act of regressive idealistic commitment is a reaction of ego defense: The ambivalence which cannot be successfully repressed is neutralized through regression and projection.

The First Phase of Membership

First there is regression in the sense that the MMO becomes the incarnation of all that is good and just. It takes on the attributes of the good parent, omnipotent and omniscient. The parental figure may be personalized through a form of charismatic leadership,[30] or the MMO as a whole may incarnate it. There is regression in that the member's identity is diffused into the organization. He is one with its power and righteousness.

At the beginning of membership there is a simplification of the perceptual and evaluative field. The MMO and the member's ultimate social values (his superego constituents) are seen as completely in tune with one another. Conformity is withdrawn from the major institutional patterns (or becomes a matter of pure expediency) in the name of a higher conformity to the MMO. Alienation becomes a corollary of value conformity rather than a contradiction to it. The ego is unified once more at the cost of splitting the world into two forces: one is the good MMO, the other is the evil unbelieving world.[31]

Outer millenarianism describes the resultant conviction of ultimate triumph in converting or controlling this world. Right is might. Belief will make it so. The MMO will recreate society around itself. The aggression and rage that members may have felt toward the dominant society are projected into the expectation of some Armageddon which will destroy that society, without the member having to assume responsibility for his aggression. Destruction of the society is part of the same order of things that assigns righteousness to the MMO.

Inner millenarianism describes the consequence of the fusion of ego and superego constituents for the self-image of the member and his conception of his co-members. By surrendering his will to the MMO (and/or its leader) the member partakes of its special dignity and infallibility. He sins no more, as the MMO and its leader are incapable of sin. All past role failures in the outside world become irrelevant, as well as all ascriptive disabilities (race, ethnic origin, exconvict or exmental patient stigma). To have failed in the past becomes a sign of election rather than a reason for guilt ("and the last shall be the first and the first shall be the last"). The member has found the company of the elect—the saved. The minority and deviant position of the MMO, rather than being seen as a disability, becomes a sign of its members' special honor, as the disinterested elite.

All demands of the outside world become transformed for the members into attempted intrusions upon the process of salvation, or are defined as confrontations with evil which, regardless of the immediate fluctuations of fortune (merely tests of the members' true dedication), must end with the triumph of the MMO.

The first phase of membership is regressive and de-differentiating. The second phase will see a new and more complex differentiation by the personality of the social field.

The Second Phase of Membership

In the second phase the member makes a difference between the ultimate value-total society complex and the MMO. In the act of joining it is often the contact with the MMO which determines belief in the doctrine: inner millenarianism precedes outer millenarianism. A personality made stronger by membership begins once more to segregate superego elements from ego elements. The very act of proselytism begins to make conditional what appeared at first to be unconditional: It is because the MMO has the right doctrine that the member joined. The MMO is no more its own justification. The perceptual and evaluative field is no more dyadic (the MMO and the wicked society) but tryadic: (1) the total society, which must be saved and from which all legitimacy eventually flows (it is also the world of potential members); (2) the MMO, which defends the true interests of the total society; and (3) the evil society trying to hamper the work of the MMO. Already a burden of proof has been reintroduced into the legitimacy of the MMO. Ambivalence reappears in the motivation of the member through a repressed conformity disposition toward the dominant society, which is neutralized by a compulsive alienative disposition. Proselytism is used to strengthen one's own convictions. Outer millenarianism has nevertheless begun to be corroded.

At the same time, the community of the saved—the core of inner millenarianism—becomes more differentiated. Freud[32] mentioned that the members of an organization identify with one another because they have put the same leader in their superego. This would describe the fraternity of the elect aspect of membership.

There is another aspect, the fraternity of the trenches, wherein the negative idiosyncrasies of each member become irrelevant compared to the utility of his presence in the good fight against the wickedness of the outside society. Again there is the splitting of the good member as against the bad (or ignorant or unfortunate) outsider.

In the second stage of membership the member is warned that some members may be insincere. There is fraternity but no genuine acceptance of the member as he truly is—no intimacy, no attachment to any one individual, save with the leader, with whom there is no real contact. What seemed at first to be unconditional support turns out to be very conditional indeed upon one's devotion to the MMO. This fraternity without intimacy, where the sibling rivalry of the members in relation to the beloved leader becomes projected into latent suspiciousness of betrayal, is the first step in the differentiation of inner millenarianism. For some members it is the maximum closeness they can bear; for others it becomes insufficient.[33]

The Third Phase of Membership

The third phase of membership involves the following steps, which imply further differentiation in the "cathectic system" made by the personality and the MMO.

1. Commitment to the MMO requires in turn commitment to role segregation and role discipline within the organization, which is facilitated by the increase in self-esteem and the decline in anxiety brought about by membership. Within the organization the member finds himself ready to accept limited objectives and partial success without either guilt feelings or paranoid rationalizations. The member receives sanctions according to the performance of his duties. Negative sanctions are mild except when heresy is involved. Positive sanctions involve greater closeness to the leader and the delegations of functions of responsibility. From the permissiveness and unconditional support of the first two stages of membership, the third stage brings in "refusal to reciprocate" and differential rewarding. There is a strengthening of ego processes and, within the basic assumptions of the organization, better reality perception on the part of the member.

2. A legitimated self has more ego demands which a more disciplined self is better able to pursue and realize. Relations with the outside world—family, job, random citizen contacts—are frequently more satisfactory because approached with more limited expectations (because they are "beyond the pale"), and the ego is better able to fulfill role tasks.

The paradox of the MMO is that, while it segregates the member from the outside world, it then throws him back upon it for proselytism and "acts of faith" and hopefully for those two types of action only. However, the MMO is only an imperfect total institution. Already the differentiation of outer millenarianism has given a new legitimacy and primacy to the total society (which must be saved), which the MMO serves best. Role relationships with the outside, if not too laden with MMO stigma, will often be more satisfactory than before.

3. The differentiation and attenuation of inner millenarianism proceeds further. The watch over heresy may not spot any heretics or police spies but it begins to spot the lazy, the ineffective, the mentally ill, as against the competent, the hard working, the self-controlled. If the leader is still perfect, his lieutenants are less so. Their rivalries do not exactly reek of the heavenly spirit. Better relations with the outside (or, often enough, more realistic and tolerant reconstructions of past relations with the outside) and more skeptical relations within the MMO weaken the psychological boundaries between the MMO and the outside world: some nonmembers are better people than some members. A stronger ego becomes capable of cathecting human beings without splitting them into the totally good or the totally bad. It becomes capable of dyadic friendships which increase the commitment to the MMO but also can operate as centers of resistance against the demands and the ideology of the MMO. Even if he cannot secure these friendships, the member begins to want them. Fraternity without intimacy is no more enough.

4. At the same time as there occurs a growing realism concerning the inner millenarian claims of the organization, there is more realistic evaluation of its outer millenarian claims. The members may question the effectiveness of some of the MMO policies. Once the MMO is no more coequal with the good society there is the possibility that the MMO might be in error. Outer millenarianism becomes corroded just as is inner millenarianism. Once the small size of the MMO was a "proof" that its members were among the elite of the elect. A stronger ego finds that the small size is even more the sign that there is much discrepancy between the MMO's claims and the objective possibilities. The obvious necessity to postpone the millennium, the likelihood that the fruits of victory will not be forthcoming for at least a generation, change the economics of

membership. A stronger ego finds itself capable of dissent without panic at the thought of expulsion.

Frequently this stage of disenchantment or greater realism, coming after the elation of the initial commitment, is manifested by a depressive phase, which occurs frequently toward the end of the first six months of membership. The member tries to escape his obligations, frequently by becoming busy with a hobby, or claims that the pressing demands of his occupation or school do not permit him as much activity as he had shown heretofore. For many this is the end of effective membership even if the formal break may not come until months afterwards.

The Fourth Phase of Membership

The fourth phase of membership involves surmounting the disenchantment and depression which comes at the end of the third phase. Unless the organization can accommodate greater ego demands through the granting of responsibilities which utilize the strengths of the member, he is likely to leave the MMO after a period of disengagement. For some the break will never take place because leadership positions and challenging tasks (putting out the MMO's paper, for instance) provide sufficient ego rewards to compensate for the decline of inner and outer millenarianism. Others are unable to do without the organization as a substitute for an integrated self and an autonomous ego. If he survives the first year the member is likely to become an "old member," and his dropping out will be the result of more complex forces than the psychological ones alone.

TYPES OF MEMBERSHIP DROPOUT

There are four basic types of "dropouts," three of which materialize relatively soon after joining.

The first type of dropout is a member who, in joining, is motivated mainly by a desire to aggress a reference group in the dominant society. He or she is really more committed to that reference group than to the MMO. Once the act of joining the latter is accomplished, there is at once relief and guilt, and dropping out will be delayed only by the need to save face. In this case, it is possible to argue that there was never any conversion in the first place, although the ex-member may believe that he actually had experienced it and will see in his dropping out an expression of legitimate disenchantment. This type of dropout might be called a "false member."

The second type is made up of the "true believers" (Hoffer) or the "seekers" (Lofland) who are constantly joining (or hanging on the periphery of) new MMO's without ever being able to make an effective commitment to any one. They do not survive the differentiation of the second phase of membership. They are to organizations what "love addicts" are to love—always in search of the regressive oneness and kept integrated by the conviction that around the next bend lies the MMO of their dream. They do not allow their personality structure to be affected by membership.

Both the "false members" and the "seekers" provide most of the realistic bases for the concern of the MMO about the sincerity of conversion among its members.[34]

The third type of dropout might be called "neophyte dropout." New members solidify their faith by great activity which results in experiences that challenge both inner- and outer millenarianism, as just described. The improvement (or the reinterpretation) of their relations with the outside world brings home the high costs of membership. The member has become aware that the MMO is not the warm fraternity it first appeared. On the other hand, continued membership will signify a relinquishing of many of the relationships that the member has with the outside, because of disuse and/or stigma. Yet it is obvious that the rewards of the millennium are further away than previously expected. If the balance of costs and potential losses and gains is felt to be unfavorable by the neophyte who has reached the third stage of membership, he is likely to drop out. The return to roles in the outside society is comparatively easy, as labeling and disuse have not had time to create any serious blocks.

The first three types of dropouts take place within the first year or so after joining, and they account for the majority of the membership turnover. Only MMO's that have elaborate screening devices and demanding rites of passage can hope to reduce these three types of "dropouts."

The fourth type of dropout is the "old-member dropout." He has survived the disappointments of the neophyte phase. In fact, his "sacrifices" have become, in a way familiar to students of "dissonance," an additional reason for greater dedication to the MMO. He uses his ego strengths for effective membership (often leadership) within the MMO. For the "old member" the major estrangements are likely to be with neophytes and the higher leadership.

The enthusiasm of the neophytes sharpens in the "old member's" mind the decline of inner and outer millenarianism. As he has survived the neophyte's disappointments, his expectations on those scores are already reduced. His idealism is less "regressive." Nevertheless, the "line" of the MMO is likely to be closer to the illusions of the neophyte than to his own sober appraisal of the effective possibilities. The organization may mitigate this dissonance by having several levels of knowledge to which higher initiates are privy and which reduce the "line" to a propaganda device for out-groupers. This will also be more effective if the MMO can institutionalize deference to the higher-level initiates, regardless of their instrumental functions. Otherwise the old members come to resent exposure to the neophytes whose enthusiasm is a secret accusation. They lose interest in the socialization of new members and in propagandizing. Unless the charismatic leadership is able to maintain the loyalty of old members who are themselves capable of leadership, the MMO is unlikely to grow to any substantial size.

The old members are also frequently much more conservative in their willingness to confront the outside world. Some of this reluctance may be due to their wish for a greater accommodation of the MMO to the outside world, so that they may maximize the rewards of membership while reducing the strains of stigma. They have a more realistic appraisal of the risks involved and, furthermore, they are unwilling to lose their monopoly of past prowess and the exclusiveness of their "veteran" status. The more risky they show the venture to be, the more they praise themselves for having undertaken it in the past. Thus, unless they can be accommodated in positions of higher leadership where their "cynicism" and greater detachment can be functional, the wisdom and experience of the old members become a burden for the MMO rather than an asset. Indeed, they often challenge the wisdom of the top leadership, if not directly because authoritarianism prevails, then by an attitude of reserve and casual familiarity which contrasts with the enthusiastic dedication and deference shown by the neophytes.[35]

Even with the turnover of neophytes there is likely to remain in the MMO an excess of "old members" who cannot all be accommodated in positions of leadership unless there is a rapid growth in the total membership. There is a structural pressure to push the surplus of "old members" out of the MMO, which complements the psychological processes described before. The ambivalence of the old members can sometimes be purged by "self-criticism" sessions, in which they can be made to shed their veteran status and begin membership all over again. Otherwise, purges and splits will accelerate the process whereby old members are pushed out of the MMO.

Even when the needs of a stronger ego combine with the structural pressures, the departure of the old member is often a serious strain for his personality. Only those who can stand it are likely to initiate the dropping-out process, for the MMO shows much antagonism toward the dropout or expellee, all the more if he was an old member. His friendships with members end immediately and, unlike the "neophyte dropout," his civilian roles are less likely to be waiting for him. Possibly hampered by a label gained from his lengthy attachment to the MMO, he must reintroduce himself into conforming society. The longer his membership, the more his perceptual pattern will be pervaded by the semantics and ideology of the MMO. His reintegration to the dominant society will be gradual and frequently will remain marginal.

CONCLUSION

The millenarian movement organization (MMO), which is dedicated to the transformation of the social order, in actuality functions most often as an agency of social control for the dominant society by molding the many types of deviant motivation in a predictable pattern that the society can cope with through standard measures.

Furthermore, the MMO acts as a resocializing agency for many of its members, acting as a therapeutic experience which permits them to perform better in their regular age, sex, and status roles. It resolves strong ambivalence which threatens the integration of the personality system by triggering a regressive idealistic commitment. Through various membership experiences this regressive idealistic commitment becomes differentiated into cathexes of increasing complexity, with lower normative expectations and greater tolerance for human error. A stronger ego is better able to handle the strains of ambivalence without recurring to simplified and unrealistic definitions of persons, groups, and institutionalized norms. Not only does the member "discharge" himself from the MMO, but structural pressures within the MMO also propel the member back to the dominant society, regardless even of his personal preference, through the practice of the "purge."

The type of analysis used in the case of the MMO could be fruitfully extended to the study of socialization into organizations which have strong millenarian components, for instance romantic love and therapeutic dyads, and to the commitments to professions which have a strong insulating and world-saving dimension: the ministry, medicine, and particularly psychiatry, where the scientific basis of practice is overshadowed by elements of faith.

NOTES

1. A. Kardiner, *Psychological Frontiers of Society* (New York: Columbia University Press, 1945); G. Gorer and John Rickman, *The People of Great Russia* (New York: Chanticleer Press, 1950).

2. T. Parsons, E. A. Shils, K. Naegele and J. R. Pitts, *Theories of Society* (New York: Free Press, 1961), Introduction to Part III, pp. 715-716.

3. The term "movement organization" is borrowed from Mayer N. Zald and Roberta Ash, "Social Movement Organizations," *Social Forces*, XLIV (1966), pp. 327-341. It describes

organizations that manifest social movements and makes some propositions as to changes brought to their structures by growth, decay, failure, or success.

4. Neil J. Smelser, *Theory of Collective Behavior* (New York: Free Press, 1963), Ch. X.

5. For a discussion of social movements, see Rudolf Heberle and Joseph Gusfield, "Social Movements" in D. Sills (ed.), *International Encyclopedia of the Social Sciences*, XIV (New York: Macmillan, 1968), pp. 438-452. A "movement" is more a cultural phenomenon than a concept of social structure. The Black Nationalist movement contains several movement organizations, such as the Black Muslims, the Black Panthers, the Republic of New Africa, and various splinter organizations. A movement organization may remain small or it may involve masses of people, and it also may become a "movement" which is propagated beyond the organization that was at the origin of the culture, for instance, the Nazi movement in Germany.

6. See Yonina Talmon, "Millenarianism," in Sills (ed.), *op. cit.*, X, pp. 349-362. Its frame of reference is somewhat different from the one offered here, but its analysis of the general traits of millenarian "movements" does not conflict with it in any significant way. Also Yonina Talmon, "Pursuit of the Millennium: The Relation between Religious and Social Change," *European Journal of Sociology*, III (1962), pp. 125-148; Norman Cohn, *The Pursuit of the Millennium* (New York: Harper, 1961); Sylvia Thrupp (ed.), *Millennial Dreams in Action* (The Hague: Mouton & Co., 1962); Bryan R. Wilson, "Millenarianism in Comparative Perspective," in *Comparative Studies in Society and History*, 6 (1963), pp. 93-114.

7. Gustave Le Bon, *The Crowd* (1895; reprinted New York: Macmillan, 1947).

8. Eric Hoffer, *The True Believer* (New York: Harper, 1951).

9. The specification of the motivation to join leaves open the question as to what causes its "illness" character: sociological factors such as low-status crystallization, failures of the socialization process which may reflect social strains in the wider society, genetic components, or more likely combinations of all three. Every society will have some schizophrenics, although whether they will join MMO's, or lead them, or simply languish within the protection of the local community or within hospital walls will depend on many factors, not the least important of which is luck.

10. The inter-psychological mechanisms used by Durkheim to describe the process of uplift and elation created by ritual may be dated but the phenomena he described are real and they have received little attention from social scientists. See E. Durkheim, *The Elementary Forms of Religious Life*, Joseph Ward Swain, tr. (New York: The Free Press, 1947).

11. In Romantic love the definitions of the forces of evil are more diffuse than they are in typical millenarian movements. Sometimes it may be the "uncomprehending society," the "vulgar society" or hostile parents. Sometimes it may be that part of the lovers which does not participate in the love dyad and makes the lovers feel that "he is not really worthy of her."

12. John Lofland, *The Doomsday Cult* (Englewood Cliffs: Prentice-Hall, 1966).

13. The "irrationality" of the German Communist Party during the period 1930-33, at the height of its millenarian delusions and hostility toward the Social Democrats, makes it resemble the Doomsday Cult more than might be expected.

14. R. Crossman (ed.), *The God That Failed* (New York: Harper & Bros., 1949). *State and Revolution* is probably Lenin's most utopian work.

15. Gabriel Almond, *The Appeals of Communism* (Princeton: Princeton University Press, 1954), p. 100.

16. Lofland, *op. cit.*, pp. 47-49.

17. Smelser, *op. cit.*, Ch. viii.

18. For a good analysis of the "motivational funnel" aspect of collective movements, see the analysis of the motivation of

the Hungarian Freedom Fighter in George Devereux, "Two Types of Modal Personality Models," in Bert Kaplan (ed.), *Studying Personality Cross-Culturally* (Elmsford, N.Y.: Row, Peterson & Co., 1961), pp. 227-241.

19. Encapsulation refers to the process whereby an MMO ceases to campaign actively and search for new members. It does not grow and its doctrines may remain the same; its membership is only replenished by occasional converts and the children of old members. An example of an encapsulated MMO (Zald and Ash, *op. cit.*, speak of a movement organization becoming "becalmed") is the Communist Party U.S.A. since the 1960's. Another example is the Socialist Labor Party, the average age of the members being in the sixties.

20. This does not mean that fleeting MMO's may not have lasting consequences for the social systems that have been subjected to their messianic fervor.

21. Parsons, *op. cit.*, p. 286.

22. In Hans Toch, *The Social Psychology of Social Movements* (Indianapolis: Bobbs-Merrill, 1965), the reader will find a good description of the psychological components which go into the membership of MMO's.

23. Egon Bittner, "Radicalism and Radical Movements," *American Sociological Review* 28 (December 1963), pp. 928-940. Lewis A. Coser, "Greedy Organizations," *European Journal of Sociology*, 8 (1967), pp. 196-215.

24. Jesse R. Pitts, "The Hippies as Contrameritocracy," *Dissent*, 16 (July-August 1969), pp. 326-337.

25. MMO's at their beginnings treat every new member as the prodigal son.

26. Lofland, *op. cit.*, pp. 143-150.

27. There are satanical cults on the West Coast that are said to be indulging in human sacrifice. The freedom of the member to quit is probably curtailed in this situation.

28. Figure communicated by Dr. F. X. Sutton in Harvard Lectures (1949). See also Irving Howe and Lewis Coser, *The American Communist Party* (New York: Praeger, 1962), pp. 527-530.

29. Annie Kriegel, *Les Communistes français* (Paris: Seuil, 1970), p. 17.

30. Although charismatic leaders tend to predominate in MMO's, they are not inevitable. The Communist Party U.S.A. was an MMO, but it would be difficult to speak of its early leaders as charismatic. (There were some attempts to make Earl Browder into a charismatic leader, but the raw material was not helpful. Maurice Thorez was somewhat more credible for the French Communist Party.) Ben Gitlow and Charles Ruthenberg were hardly charismatic in the sense that Lenin, Trotsky, or Stalin were charismatic. Yet they derived their leadership from their connection with the charismatic leaders of the Russian party. There are some MMO's which make great efforts to invest the total group with charisma rather than invest it in one leader. Leadership will reside *de facto* in a college of elders.

31. The ideology of the MMO may make the alienation from and hostility to the dominant society more or less explicit and rhetorically virulent. There are MMO's which have a pitying attitude toward the world rather than a remonstrating and aggressive one.

32. S. Freud, *Group Psychology and the Analysis of the Ego* (London: The International Psychoanalytical Press, 1922).

33. The development of suspicion of betrayal in the member marks the return of ambivalence and the latent attraction of the outside world and its institutionalized patterns upon the member.

34. This is true, given the fact that most MMO's never reach the stage where rational opportunists and police agents are likely to join.

35. Albert Speer, *Inside the Third Reich* (New York: Macmillan, 1970). Speer describes the strain that Hitler felt in meeting "old comrades" (p. 53).

16

THE HIPPIE MOVEMENT AS A SOCIALIZATION AGENCY

Jesse R. Pitts

The hippie movement is a social phenomenon which permits us to study the impact of social structure upon the personality. Adult social structure is comparatively well known through the standard structural-functional basis. The motivational "hook-ups" of the personality upon roles are still largely unknown. For instance, we know very little about the manner in which the adolescent personality interprets the demands of socialization systems or the role demands that flow from memberships in peer groups or social movements. In passing from role as element of the social system to role expectation as part of the personality system there are many unknowns, and often the researcher must use his intuition in assuming the meaning that a particular experience may have for a given class of persons. The output of the personality — as a need — is clearer than the way in which the social system fulfills that need.

In *Family, Socialization and Interaction Process*[1], Talcott Parsons proposed a conceptual scheme for the analysis of the relations between role participations and the differentiation of the adolescent personality system into sixteen basic "need dispositions." Not much work has proceeded along the lines indicated by Parsons. The description of the problems of adolescence by Erickson or Eisenstadt has been made in terms of their own categories and terminology. Recently, Parsons has analyzed the widespread prolongation of adolescence in terms of college "studentry," but he did not use the sixteen need dispositions of *Family, Socialization and Interaction Process* to explain the problems of adolescence and the way the university structures are either functional or dysfunctional to their resolution.[2] He used a variant of Freudian psychology, which today is still one of the most common languages of researchers in the field of socialization.

The first step in the analysis of the socializing impact of the hippie movement is to trace its cultural roots in the Bohemian subculture. The second step will be to describe the structure of the communities built on the basis of the movement as millenarian movement organizations, which make strong claims upon the loyalty and conformity of their members. Finally, some statements will be made—essentially based upon impressionistic data—as to the impact of the hippie community role structure and experience upon the personalities of adolescents and young adults who joined the movement in an experience of conversion.

The Bohemian subculture became an established fixture of the major Western capitals in the first half of the nineteenth century.[3] Bohemian ideology proclaims the supremacy of the writer, artist, and printer over the entrepreneur or the man of science. Through aesthetic sense and intuition the Bohemian can reach the world of beauty better than any practitioner of reason can ever hope to achieve. His poverty is a badge of his purity, of his total commitment to art, and a testimony that his art is so refined that it can only appeal to the happy few. Hence it cannot bring him prestige in bourgeois society, and even less bring him monetary rewards.

Bohemianism required for its existence a break-up of the patronage system and the dependence of the artist upon the market. Having lost a semi-ascriptive status, the artist has to accept the uncertainties of an achievement situation. Bohemianism thus springs from the ambivalence of the artist, usually sprung from a petty bourgeois milieu, to a market that at once gives him freedom from personal subordination, but also the opportunity to fail.

Bennett Burger[4] in his analysis of hippie morality cites Malcolm Cowley's summary of what he called the formal doctrine of Bohemia: the idea of salvation by the child, i.e., the denial of original sin, the idea of the primacy of self-expression, the idea of living for the moment, the idea of complete liberty, the idea of female equality, and the romantic love of the exotic.

This doctrine defines the aristocracy of the Bohemian: his immunity to the judgments of those who are by definition of a lower essence than himself, because they subordinate the inherent potential of the man-child to the social bondages of the economy, the family, the state. The Bohemian shares the aristocrat's scorn for trade, for the rationality of capital accounting, his preference for the charismatic over the democratic and the economic.

Bohemia resolved the problem of the artist dependent on the market by denying the legitimacy of the market. It provided a rationalization for the unsuccessful or not yet successful. In fact, it made the lack of success a sure sign of a deeper superiority. Bohemianism was a response to the pains of low status created by the opportunities afforded by industrialization and the development of the bureaucratic state. It provided a refuge for those who could not succeed and yet who would not accept their failure as a sign that their self-image was unrealistic.

In the United States of the 1950's the current expression of Bohemia was the beatnik movement, which derived many of its styles—the women's long hair, the black dress, the beards (especially the Mephistopheles-type)—from the Parisian existentialist movement of the late 1940's. The beatnik movement was essentially limited to some sections of the inner-city slums of major American cities, such as Greenwich Village in New York, Venice West in Los Angeles, North Beach in San Francisco, and Old Town in Chicago.[5]

The original contribution of America to the Western Bohemian subculture was the addition of a religious element sustained and symbolized by the experiences derived from peyote and other hallucinogens. Bohemianism had taken its basic patterns from Voltairean France and had developed in a climate where religious belief was felt to be an attribute of the hated bourgeoisie. Religious effusion is not in the Catholic tradition (even when all belief in God has been rejected) as it is in the Protestant tradition with its revivals and street preachers, or in the Hasidic tradition. True enough, Bohemianism had always had its fringe of Theosophists. Gurus like Gurdjieff had influence over some Paris intellectuals and Bloomsbury expatriates. But religiosity was a minor variety of the Bohemian experience rather than a central core as it frequently becomes for the beatniks.

From 1963-64 the numbers of college dropouts who joined the beat centers led to a qualitative change. Hipsters and beats retreated to other areas. In San Francisco they frequently moved to Sausolito while the new recruits occupied Haight-Ashbury. A new name, hippies, describes the transformation of Bohemia from an encapsulated phenomenon into a mass

movement of the young with its gurus, which systematize the creed, with its own press, which diffuses the creed all over the country, with its argot and its uniform.[6]

Eventually the hippie movement collapsed under the weight of its contradictions. Its belief in nonviolence made it the easy prey for various parasites who did not hesitate to use force to secure free board and room, free drugs, and free sex. Its ambivalence toward leadership made it very difficult to organize the necessary services its masses or devotees required when they arrived by the tens of thousands in its major urban centers.

Following the failure of the Convocation of the Tribes in San Francisco during the summer of 1967, when it had been announced that 200,000 hippies would congregate and only 20,000 or 30,000 showed up, a "burial of hippie" took place in Berkeley, declaring the formal end of the movement. Some of the hippies joined rural communes, and many faded into a youth society which, by then, had adopted many of its patterns of dress, hair style, drug intake, and language. A hippiefied New Left and Woodstock Nation took the relay from the defunct hippie movement.

The hippie movement can be described as a value-oriented movement in the Smelser classification, i.e., "a collective attempt to restore, protect, modify, or create values in the name of a generalized belief."[7]

Like all movements, it carries people whose motivation is at other levels, such as the craze, i.e., the fad. The enormous publicity that the hippie movement received from the mass media guaranteed the influx of people at that level. For some the hippie movement was in the nature of a "hostile outburst," fundamentally aimed at the WASP middle and upper class. Instead of aggression taking a violent channel (as it tended to do after the summer of 1967), it expresses itself through the put-down, the desecration of the symbols of consecrated authority and of middle-class morality. The interests in value change may be quite secondary. Many hippies were vacation hippies who returned in the fall to their studies. Many of the teenagers—or teenie-boppers, as they came to be known—used the movement as a convenient and prestigeful place to run away from home, where they met older, middle-class youth who took care of them.

To make an analysis of the impact of the hippie movement upon the personality of its members, it is necessary to concentrate upon those who have a strong commitment to its values. Those members believe that the movement, as incarnated by the organization to which they belong, possesses the secret of a perfect or near-perfect social order, that this order will triumph, in the near future, over the forces of darkness, probably through a conflagration. These beliefs define, for the members, the "outer millenarianism" of the millenarian movement organization (MMO).

Another aspect of the commitment of the "true believer" is a belief that the members of the MMO are superior to all nonmembers. They are the elite of the saved, "the beautiful people," and their example will lead those who are willing to be enlightened to be saved as well. This is the inner millenarianism of the MMO.

Both inner and outer millenarianism explain why the member is willing to change his way of life to conform to the values and norms of the MMO, and why he will undergo whatever frustration is implicit in the process of learning without flying from the field. Precisely, what are some of the demands made by the structure of the millenarian movement organization?[8]

THE HIPPIE COMMUNITY AS A TOTAL INSTITUTION

The hippie movement had several organizational dimensions. One was the local hippie community made up of one or several ecological clusters, usually located in a slum or decaying district closest to the local university.

The various hippie communities throughout the nation were linked by a constant stream of visitors and, thanks to this interaction, there developed regional and even national reputations for certain individuals, as well as a broad network of mutual acquaintances. The underground press also served as a link between the different communities and the unifiers of styles and rhetoric.

Finally there was the international hippie community with its connections to the jet set, largely dominated by American hippies both in numbers and influence. Participation in the international hippie community with its way stations on the way to Katmandhu (Tangiers, Torremolinos, Ibiza-Formentera, Istanbul) or in London was a source of prestige in the local and regional expressions of the movement.

Even though the boundaries of the movement were comparatively fluid—there was no formalization of membership or register of members, and people moved in and out of the movement relatively easily— the hippie movement shares with other MMO's the characteristics of being a total institution. Membership in the hippie movement, i.e., membership in one of its communities or traveling from one hippie community to the other, implied abandonment of occupational, school, and family commitments. This does not mean that odd jobs would not be taken once in a while in order to earn the money necessary for a trip across the states or overseas. Girls might do waitressing or take on Kelly Girl jobs or modelling.

Boys might take jobs house painting, landscaping, bartending, janitoring, record selling. However, these jobs must be temporary and not imply any ego involvement on the part of the hippie. Any contact between the hippie and the outside world must be through activities that are disvalued or which are exploitative. Frequently in a hippie couple it would be the girl who would take a job rather than the man. This is often the result of the fact that hippie girls can roll up their hair and borrow a dress to "pass" for the time the job requires more easily than the male hippies can change their appearance. It is also due to the fact that, although there is a rhetoric of female equality, the culture carriers in the hippie community are the males, especially with respect to the music. Hippie girls work for their man like the Schtetl women worked for their talmudic scholar.

The total institution aspect of the hippie movement is symbolized and reinforced by the change in language, dress, and hair style that is mandatory for continued participation in good standing. Relations with outsiders will only be episodic. Frequently dietary fads, such as vegetarianism or macrobiotic diets will make it difficult for hippies to eat in the company of nonmovement people.

Because the hippie community is a total institution[9] the reliability and range of rewards and punishment available to the organization for socialization of its members is very great, even though membership is completely voluntary. Isolation from competing ways of defining the situation is secured, and members reinforce in one another conformity to the fringe organization's views.

THE AUTHORITARIANISM OF THE HIPPIE COMMUNITY

At first glance the hippie movement as a whole seems to be in utter contradiction to the authoritarian characteristic of the fringe organization as a genus. The ideology commanded its members to do their own thing and not to "lay their thing" on others. The words "leader," "direct," "order" were taboo from the language, just as "thigh" and "belly" were banned from Victorian speech. The reality of course was more subtle. The authoritarianism of the millenarian movement is contingent upon the member granting legitimacy to the leader or to the organization as a charismatic center. MMO's have few effective means of coercion upon their members, although one hears once in a while of organizations like the Manson tribe[10] where some members have declared that potential defectors were threatened with death. Retaining members against their will is very difficult for an MMO unless it wishes to court sanctions from the dominant society that would be very detrimental to its continued existence. The expenditure of energy necessary to retain members against their will is likely to be too high to be worthwhile. Only in satanic cults is it possible to find members who are locked in through threats of blackmail and execution.

Within the limits set by voluntary membership, millenarian movement organizations are authoritarian in the sense that there is no patterned way for candidates to leadership to compete with one another and be chosen by ballot. The members, upon joining, find leaders who have been delegated by authority to control the local organization or leaders who have imposed themselves through their charisma and co-opt the talent they wish to recognize. The other aspect of authoritarianism is that the new member finds an ideology whose major components are beyond criticism. If he challenges them by his statements (much more than by his behavior), he must leave. Only tactics of implementation may be discussed, and even those are often determined by the local leaders.

Although the hippie movement denied the need and moral justification for leadership on the basis of its ideology of spontaneity and self-determination, the Bales-Parsons law of leadership differentiation[11] is nevertheless operating in the communities of relatively stable membership. The style of leadership is different, but leadership is present nevertheless. There will be a guru type, mystical, kind, giving, often with some talent in the less easily commercialized arts. This will be the expressive leader, and often enough it will be the only type of leader who is evident. There may be an instrumental leader whose word is decisive in the acceptance or rejection of strangers and who deals with the police in case of emergencies. Sometimes the two types of leadership are fused in a single charismatic role, but here charisma has to be self-deprecating rather than self-assertive.

During the 1963-67 period, before Black Power became a major theme in the black community, it was not rare to find in hippie communities an "angry black man," whose whims were catered to as atonement for the white man's sins against the black race. In certain cases, as described by Yablonsky,[12] the black man could become a tyrant, accepted by the more masochistic of the hippies on the basis of their white guilt. Hell's Angels types have always exercised a fascination for hippies, and time and again situations have occurred where hippie communities were exploited and the girls were gangraped,[13] while the hippies tried to explain away their fear and passivity under some ideological statements about "building bridges to the working class." Thus hippies who would be very prompt to rebel in front of suggestions or appeals to cooperation might be found completely cowed by

orders backed by the threat of force. Yet these were orders and leaders which required no identification; they were part of the violence present in a hostile world that one had to cope with as best one could.

Another form of leadership was sometimes seized by volunteers who would create Digger-type kitchens or organize free clinics. The latter were staffed by people who had straight jobs and who were usually well anchored in the dominant society, but for whom the hippies were a cause, a way to express their superiority over establishment types in their craft. Diggers would secure some prestige from their services, but they could count on no cooperation from their beneficiaries. It was part of the doctrine that people did what they wanted to do and were repaid by the pleasure it gave them. The recipient of a service owed nothing to the giver of the service.

On the national level there were admired figures who were sources of style and ideological elaborations. Alan Ginsberg, for instance, supported the policy of trying to build bridges to the Hell's Angels. Other pacesetters were the Beatles, Paul Krasner, the editor of the *Realist,* Alan Watts, and Ken Kesey. Rock band leaders and singers were also sources of style. The underground press presented the pronouncements of these style setters. One of the problems with Timothy Leary as a cultural leader was the fact that it was very obvious he considered and wished himself to be considered a leader. Very quickly the novitiates in the movement were warned that Leary was not really "in."

Once accepted into the hippie community the neophyte found himself pressured to do his own thing, but it was not expected that his own thing would be to get a crew cut, to hustle for good grades at school, or use traditional approaches to girls. He would be expected to "turn on" to drugs, learn the language of the group, its sex code, its attitudes toward the racial issue, the police, and so on. The pressure to learn was all the greater in that it was insisted at all times that one must do only what one wants to do. Hence whatever one was doing had better be a spontaneous expression of the self, unless one wanted to find himself under penalty of denying one's autonomy and identity.[14] It is possible that this learning situation promotes a greater commitment to what is being learned.

At the same time that the neophyte heard that he was to be doing his own thing, he was also warned against "ego trips." Thus, compliance to community pressures could be rationalized as reaching higher levels of individuality. When there was a failure of the "innate harmony of self-interests," the contradiction could be resolved by defining passivity, or giving in, or not demanding one's rights, as precisely the shedding of "ego." In many ways the hippie community was as demanding of conformity as any fraternity or sorority, but at the same time it denied that it was. Its sanctioning had to be much more subtle, as it had to accept a right to deviance as part of "doing one's own thing."

The taboo against "ego trips" was also a very strong restraint against obvious status-seeking. The egalitarianism of the hippie community was not indifference to status but rather a refusal to grant others more status than oneself. It was the egalitarianism of jealousy, rather than the egalitarianism of equal opportunity which characterizes the dominant society or the renunciation of status striving which comes from the contemplation of the infinite. All sorts of status games went on within the hippie community: name-dropping, entrance into the magic circle of some *guru,* friendship with a well-known musician or with a regional or national nonleader, or mention of one's name in the underground press. Yet at any one time the loser in the status game could call the game null and void as ego-tripping. The hippie could play to win and never lose. At all costs the appearance of subordination to a person had to be avoided.

Because the hippie communities engaged in minimal instrumental activities did not proselytize consciously, demands for style and value conformity need not be felt as a cramp on individual initiative. Members were free to come and go as they pleased, live with whomever they desired, and even engage in activities which, in the dominant society, might seem to have a disturbing valence to others, such as playing the drums, wearing outlandish costumes, and talking incessantly as people do when "high" under the influence of stimulants. In the hippie community they will be granted a tolerance that is usually not found in the "straight" world except in the mental hospital. Although the member had to conform to a rather rigid series of value judgments and style demands, trying to tune himself to invisible commands crucial to his good standing in the community, his consciousness was much more filled with the delights of the permissiveness and support which were granted to him in all areas which did not directly affect the hippie consensus.

THE HIPPIE COMMUNITY IN ITS EXPRESSIVE CONFRONTATIONS WITH THE DOMINANT SOCIETY

The hippie community could not engage in argumentative or exhortative proselytism without being in contradiction with its beliefs that the road to truth is through the spontaneous expression of the self. If the person could break through his "hangups," often

with the help of drugs, he would see the truth. The only role that a hippie could have in promoting the process was through "blowing people's minds," a concept derived from Zen Buddhism, where a certain action from the teacher at a propitious time can destroy negative psychic structures and force the "student" to question his past thought patterns and practices.

In the sense of "blowing people's minds," the hippies were constantly proselytizing. At once they maximized their separation from "straight" society and its awareness of them by their outlandish hair and dress style. Although there was a taboo against the systematic provocation of the police, the hippie communities held frequent revival meetings in the guise of "love-ins" or "be-ins," where there was some disrobing, public sexual intercourse, and widespread indulgence of drugs. These revival meetings, which drew hordes of spectators or rock music fans, often resulted in police sweeps and arrests. For the hippie it might mean a couple of days in jail, but it was proof of the outer millenarian message of his community, of its superiority to the outside world which knew only violence as the answer to the message of love carried by the movement.

The gurus of the movement, such as Timothy Leary and Alan Ginsberg, did engage in systematic proselytizing, as did the underground press. The major source of converts were (1) the rock bands who carried the message to the unaffiliated youth through their songs, words, and gestures endorsing the use of drugs, alienation from the establishment, and the orgiastic concept of sex; (2) the campus hippie subcultures protected and sponsored by the "hip" professors which promoted highbrow rock, drugs, and ideological justifications for the movement. The development of the hippie movement into a mass movement was considerably helped by friendly treatment by the mass media, especially between 1965 and 1967. From 1966 onward, many high school dropouts joined the movement.

POLICE PARANOIA AND THE HIPPIE COMMUNITY

All MMO's are concerned with the state of their members' motivation, as members are likely to be highly ambivalent and the pressures of the outside world for conformity are mediated by every encounter the member has with nonmembers. Hence the counter-pressure kept up by the movement to convert outsiders and to strengthen at the same time the faith of its own. Within the hippie community there was a constant concern as to whether individual members were truly dedicated or merely "plastic hippies." There was also a constant fear of police agents infiltrating the movement in order to make narcotics arrests or, from 1968 onward, to make political arrests. There were enough real instances to insure that the fear was not completely neurotic. Nevertheless, the number of hippies who believed that their phones were tapped or that the FBI or the CIA was following them was such that the movement itself tried to control this fear by labeling it "police paranoia." Constant "rap sessions," "scenes," and "meetings" permitted the movement to verbalize its doctrine and make sure its members knew "where it was at."

The relation of the dogma of tolerance to the concern for ideological purity resembled the relationship between the ideology of "doing your own thing" and the reality of leader-led relationships.

The problem that the hippie movement encountered is that the rewards of drugs and easy sex drew to the movement either working-class or lower-middle class youths for whom the hardships of hippie living were small compared to the exploitative opportunities.

Eventually the fear of police infiltrators and the presence of plastic hippies or parasites damaged considerably the "inner millenarium."[15] To prolong their belief in it, hippies had recourse to nomadism. They frequently moved from place to place. To explain the "bad vibrations" that emanated from various communities, the statement would be made that the "good people had just split."[16]

The hippie MMO had developed into a mass movement, and turnover of its members was high. Members dropped out of school and after a year or two or three most returned either to school or to some form of stable employment. All religious organizations which have special groups for adolescents know that the percentage of graduates who become adult militants is small. Even if the hippie movement did not have the turnover that is ascribed to its genus as an MMO (high ambivalence of motivation, therapeutic function of membership), it would have it as an organization composed mainly of adolescents and young adults. The process of aging pushes out the older members, who find it more and more difficult to identify with the younger members. Three years difference in adolescence and young adulthood make much more difference in self-image, whether objectively or because internalized norms tell the members that they are important. The hippie movement wanted to deny the relevance of sex and status categorizations and actually wound up reasserting them in the very process of denying them. The same result was obtained with age categorization. Age was said to be irrelevant, and yet it was reasserted as the key to the special sanctity of youth. The deprecation of the teenager was carried out through the put-down of the "teenie-bopper."

THE IMPACT OF THE MEMBERSHIP EXPERIENCE

Initiation

From the hippie subculture on campus the would-be hippie would eventually make contact with the local hippie community, which in 1963-67 was to be found near the city-located universities in the slums and near-slums that frequently surround them.

For many the initial experience was exhilarating (according to 12 out of 15 interviewed on this specific topic). "I sat there and those people knew how to make me feel totally accepted. For the first time in my life I felt completely at ease. It was as if a coat of anxiety I had been carrying all my life had finally slipped from my shoulders."

A typical "scene" would consist of people wandering in and out, dressed in all sorts of attire, and yet so easily assimilated into the group without anyone remarking on their oddity. A young man in his early twenties would walk into the room with a beanie on his head and sit on the floor, saying nothing, just smiling. A woman would nurse a child, others would smoke quietly. In a corner a boy with hair down to his shoulders would play the bongo drum, softly. Others by groups of two's and three's were talking. A couple would touch and then go into another room.

It was this capacity to move in and out of the group without its making any overt demands for admission or raising any questions about departure that appealed so strongly to the would-be hippie. It was also the lack of any evident leader, the feeling of noncompetition, the fact that the newcomer could be accepted without feeling that he was a second-class citizen, that appealed so much to the "candidate," for, whether he knew it or not, he was being observed as well as evaluated.

In 1964-66 it would be usual to find that those entering the community had never smoked marihuana and that they did not wear long hair. Smoking marihuana involved a certain technique, not only for smoking but also for the appreciation of the drug.[17] Quiet enjoyment was the norm in hippie groups. Giggling, evident sexual arousal were uncool.

Another must was the giving up of "bad-mouthing" parents. To become a hippie in good standing one should avoid recriminating parents because these recriminations gave a suspiciously egocentric and reactive basis to the protest embodied in the group. To become a hippie in good standing, one had to see that one's parents were victims of the system rather than evil in and of themselves. "Bad-mouthing parents" was typical of "teenie-boppers," the deprecating word that hippies reserved for the very young hippies or for those hippies who could not give up the more immature modes of acting and who affected a flamboyant attire.

Another test was the tolerance of interracial sex. The "angry black man" who was a fixture of many hippie communities was entitled to sexual favors from the white females of the community, and the burden of proof for refusing him was upon the white girl. Here again it would have been uncool for the black man to be constantly "hassling" white girls for sex under penalty of exposing himself as a racist. He had to act as if he did not care one way or the other, and the girls approached him often enough that he did not have to exert himself. White hippie boys of course has to show by their behavior that they approved of interracial sex, by studied indifference rather than by going out of their way to approve. Interestingly, there were practically never any black girls in the hippie communities.

These tests did not constitute an initiation rite, properly called, because the hippie group strove to avoid a formal structure. Although it had definite boundaries, it did not wish to recognize them. It often shunned the use of the word "hippie." Later on, in 1967-68, the word "flower-children" had some acceptance; but the hippie group, being antisociological in its ideology, found it very hard to accept any characterization of itself in return for segregation from the square world. It would, in its own thinking, segregate the square world, but it was very suspicious of the square world segregating it through the use of any vocable. The word "hippie"[18] became very quickly derogatory in square mouths, and the hippies found it hard to accept. The ideology decried being boxed into roles. Membership in any group was a moot question because membership implied constraints and the ideology was against any constraints.

Hence the group existed, and people would say they lived "on the street," meaning Haight, or in Old Town, or in the Castle. But no self-respecting hippie would say, "I am a member of the hippie community." He might say, "I am living in a commune," although that was comparatively rare before the loosely structured hippie movement disintegrated. Being a member implied obligations. "Living in a commune" implied geography without commitment. Thus membership (from an observer's point of view) stimulated the maximum of self-awareness. It promoted the discovery of what one is and what one wants. For adolescents whose identity is diffuse, it is hard to realize how much this self-direction can mean: it is like sight recovered for a blind man. It is not so much that they suffered from constraints of an especially demanding nature in their pre- and post-pubertal life spans. Rather, it is that a lack of commitment to the values of school, family, peer group, or community

made all role participation a constraint. It was as if they were victims of Durkheim's "suicide fatalists." Lack of meaningful memberships also robs self-direction of meaning. Where there are no claims and no directions, self-direction goes nowhere. The hippie movement first gives the direction of "no direction." Freedom is against; the individual can use what he wanted yesterday as ground for the figure of what he wants today, for surely it cannot be the same thing.

The world becomes a structured place where one chooses his way. For an individual who sees any obligations as a threat to his sense of self, the loose membership in the hippie movement, without "obligations or sanctions," helps to structure the self, helps in the task of relating to people without threatening it.

Regression in Service of the Ego

In the shelter of the primary group the member can now regress safely, all the more that the ego has been strengthened by the commitment to the group and the relief of some superego anxiety due to the legitimation process of the hippie ideology. This regression is evidenced by syncretic magical-type thinking, which in the hippie community is legitimated by the folklore of good and bad vibrations: the belief in telepathy, astrology, and the belief that under drugs the mind has access to truths denied to those who do not have the courage to take drugs.

In the hippie movement, besides their value as rituals of membership and solidarity, drugs such as marihuana and LSD had a sort of sacred character, especially the latter. The hippie movement did not treat them lightly.[19]

For boys troubled by their passive longings, drugs permitted the enjoyment of these longings without shame. For girls who feared passivity, drugs brought the first real pleasant experiences of passivity. "With pot I can relax, I let go, which I find very hard to do when having sex. In fact when I smoke with a guy I can get such good vibrations that it makes sex unnecessary."

Furthermore, for all tnose who had experienced feelings of depersonalization and odd sensations of lights and sounds, the drugs brought a welcome relief from the fears that they might be losing their minds. Depersonalization became a salutary experience, nay, a prestigeful experience. Contaminated perceptions became poetry.

This syncretism of perception, the tendency to think that reality is what you think it is, in the sense that the mind of youth creates the effective world, is a common enough occurrence among normal youth. But it is an occasional occurrence. Among would-be hippies the failure of the world to realize the mind's creation leads to a feeling of betrayal and withdrawal. For the hippie, however, the hippie community seems to be a realization of his fantasies. He is more willing to confront reality, as he has the feeling that he controls it more. Hence the beliefs that telepathy, "being in someone's mind," are proofs that the hippie is one with the cosmos, in tune with the universe. Here regression does not alienate him further from people, but somehow makes him more available to interaction. The regression serves the ego.

Another major source of anxiety for the would-be hippie is the uncertainty of sexual identification. He is rarely a homosexual, although it is not rare for the hippie community to have one or two homosexuals in its membership, although as marginals. These homosexuals, just like the angry black man with respect to issues of race, certify to the lack of prejudice against homosexuality. Yet their marginality gives the clue that the dominant form of sexual behavior is definitely heterosexual. In the hippie community homosexual sex is theoretically as good and desirable as is heterosexual sex. Guilt about homosexual longings is "unthinkable." The use of words like "love" in relation to same-sex individuals clues in the neophyte that he need feel no shame if his attitude toward a male becomes emotionally laden to the point of confusion and physical longing. Talking it out, verbalizing homosexual feelings, is highly supported. It may not result in any overt homosexual action, but it is proof enough that the neophyte is completely accepted.

At certain occasions like the "orgies," where there is always a surplus of males in relation to females, there will be occasion for homosexual contact that will be tension-reducing and will not require one to take responsibility for the act. It happens in the orgiastic exuberance rather than as a deliberate choice.

Of the three hippies (out of fifteen males interviewed extensively) who claimed to be bisexual, all made sure that the interviewer understood them to be predominantly heterosexual. In their verbalizations they would refuse the label of "predominantly heterosexual" because it might imply a rejection of homosexuality—which it does, of course—but this is part of hippie life: to disapprove of certain patterns but to deny that one is disapproving. It is the same with membership obligations, the existence of leadership, and the forms of hippie social control.

This type of latent conditioning is most effective because it minimizes the guilt and anxiety due to learning failure. It increases the gratitude and commitment of the socializee to the socializer and hence makes him more sensitive to the covert cues as to what is desirable. It supposes, of course, a strong commitment to begin with, which is given in the hippie community by the process of conversion. It supposes a powerful desire to learn on the part of the socializee, so that cues of low visibility and often of some ambiguity can be deciphered correctly. It also supposes that errors committed by the socializee do not threaten seriously the resources and standing of the socializer. Perhaps the prototype of such latent conditioning is the teaching by parents of sexual taboos and status taboos (at least in the liberal tradition). Whether the resonance of hippie training with Oedipal training is a reason for its special success must remain a moot question.

Girls who have problems of sexual identity often try to cope with them through promiscuity.[20] In the hippie community they can act out their promiscuity with no fear of disgrace; and, here again, it is more tolerance than approval, a nuance that will become more apparent to the hippie girl as she becomes "cooler" and more perceptive. She will become aware of the pressure for monogamy when she can bear to recognize it and control her behavior. Meanwhile she finds the relief from square pressure enthralling. Promiscuity becomes a symbol of liberation from bourgeois hang-ups. On the other hand, the sex ratio in the hippie community (between two to three boys for every girl) gives the girls an opportunity to secure a companion should they choose to become attached to any one man.

The girl will find in the hippie community an occasion to act out originating trends which in square society would give rise to sanctions for violations of the traditional sex role patterns. Often she will be the effective breadwinner for the group and/or for the man she lives with. She will work as a waitress, hospital attendant, she will panhandle with more success than her male counterpart. She can refuse the grooming responsibilities of the traditional female role, wear pants, be sloppy (American female hippies wash; it is the males who sometimes give up middle-class cleanliness), and no one will reproach her for it. If she likes to take care of men, treat them like dolls, and make sex into another form of nurturance, she is sure to find the type of passive, dependent man who will complement her needs. But even should men take advantage of her nurturance without giving much in return she knows that this implies no rejection of her as a woman, as the ideology approves of sex without emotional commitment and is hostile to people being "hung up" on anything. Nevertheless, the scarcity of women in the hippie community gives each one a high bargaining power, which reinforces her self-esteem independently of the support derived from the simple dignity of being a member of a superior group. She is needed for cooking, laundry, a minimum of household maintenance, but she cannot be pressured into the performance of these duties by invoking her traditional sex role. She must be coaxed into assuming these tasks. The line is thin between coaxing and exploitation: the hippie girl chooses to be exploited.

The hippie community provides an opportunity for the girl to develop her sense of self-directedness by making choices out of actions which in square life are conventional if not (in the family context) coerced. Promiscuous girls in high school and college are rapidly submitted to the crudest of exploitation. In the hippie world it appears to the neophyte that this self-degradation has ended.

The Differentiation of Membership Roles

1. The neophyte experiences a new legitimated identity which he has to practice. He rushes into activity, which involves ethnocentric behavior, drug taking, and "making the scene."

Ethnocentric behavior consists in action which is destined to symbolize one's commitment to the group, action which demonstrates one's rejection of square norms and values, action which discriminates against outsiders. The development of the hippie body image has an ethnocentric valence. Again the self chooses what it will wear: grooming becomes an easy terrain for self-directed and self-oriented action, especially for boys (for girls it is "not caring" that is self-direction). And here again self-expression, instead of creating disorder, creates a sign of recognition with like-minded youth, a sign of opposition to the square world, an occasion to suffer its jibes and insults with pride.

Drug taking has also an ethnocentric valence. It violates the moral and juridical norms of the square world and permits regression usually associated with pleasure. In the 1963-67 era, and especially after 1965, LSD was the drug that separated the hippies from the squares and also from the "plastic hippies." It was the second level of initiation for those who had come to the hippie community without marihuana experience, or the first level for those who, in increasing numbers from 1965 onward, had already some experience in marihuana prior to joining the community.

The taking of LSD required, at least for the first time, the company of a person who had already some experience with the drug but who would forsake taking it in order to be able to protect the neophyte from any imprudent or disturbed behavior. Subsequent trips were more casually undertaken, and how many LSD trips a person had taken became an element of prestige. In 1966 fifteen trips was a respectable number.

Drugs were a part of membership, the easy grounds of initial conversation when a hippie met another hippie. They constituted the sacrament whereby

action directed toward one's pleasure could be directed also to the strengthening of group ties. This was symbolized by the passing around of the "roach," similar to the passing around of the wine bottle on skid row. Although drug taking can "put you into your head," it also reinforced the commitment to the group. It was, like music, the incarnation of the utopian dream, of securing order and solidarity through everyone doing his own thing. Yet the neophyte learned the drugs that were approved and those that were merely tolerated, such as "speed." Methedrine was "put down," although a community would often carry one or two "meth heads" as marginals. "Meth heads" provided a negative focus of solidarity, symbolic of the tolerance and kindness of the group for these deluded meth heads who were "wasted" and should not be imitated. Heroin was definitely uncool, as was any drug that led to addiction and thus cut down on one's freedom. Nevertheless, drugs did give many new hippies a focus, a motivation, a source of interactional moments similar to the service heroin renders to the addict, i.e., providing him with a bare shred of identity. The advantage of the hippie "head" is that he was on the receiving line of cues which he was free to pick up as he became capable of following them (or attempting to follow them) and which encouraged drug taking as a group affair rather than as a private gratification. LSD also was encouraged as an expedition into one's psyche, rather than as a purely hedonistic adventure. As the hippie aged into the movement and drugs lost some of their appeal, both their novelty and his need for them as identity surrogates declined. They became the flag of the "teenie-boppers" who "did not know what they were doing." As in many other instances, the differentiation from the "teenie-boppers" will promote the alienation from the patterns of the neophyte and decrease the subjective distance to the "straight" world.

For a while, however, the neophyte rushes into ethnocentric behavior, which, besides his outlandish garb, require provocative behavior toward straights. Begging, which became a favored pattern from 1966 onward, was a way of blowing the square's mind.[21] It also took fortitude on the part of the ex-middle-class hippie: "Begging is probably the hardest thing I had to do. It went against my middle-class grain. But now I can do it without any guilt. I think I owe that to my trips on LSD."

Blowing the mind of straights requires the development of self-control and a good deal of perceptiveness of the social situation. It is to hippie life what smart crime is to "dumb crime." In order to blow people's minds, you must develop a keen sense of what they expect, in order to present them with the unexpected and shatter their composure. The hippie controls the situation without placing himself in jeopardy. And though a good deal of cruelty can be contained in the act of blowing someone's mind, it implies a differentiation of the social scene, a capacity to manipulate it, which will be useful in other contexts.

The new hippie "makes the scene." He goes to the innumerable parties which start spontaneously in the evening and go on to the wee hours of the morning. He was a Beatle fan and now escalates to the white blues singers like Paul Butterfield. He becomes an aficionado of blues and "acid rock," the latter being probably the only genuine contribution of the hippie movement to American art.[22]

As hard rock and acid rock were rapidly becoming the music of middle-class youth society, the hippie became an "in" expert. The music, soon integrated into the "love-in" and the "be-in," became acts of missionary zeal. This is not missionary activity of the soapbox variety but the seduction of the outsider by the promise of untrammeled pleasure. The group becomes a promise of unconditional, unlimited love and gratification.[23] At the love-in the enthusiastic neophyte takes off all his clothing (at once a protest and a claim for total acceptance) and copulates openly. He enjoys blowing people's minds and asserting his dedication to the cause.

It is likely that a strengthened ego has to cope with a greater ambivalence. A hippie identity is also one which activates superego components derived from parental socialization that conflict with hippie norms. If parents are to be forgiven, would this forgiveness strengthen the case for square values? In Parsons' terms we would expect that high ambivalence would result in a form of compulsive conformity to hippie norms, exemplified by a rush of activities which tend to overdo it. On the one hand, we have the "exercise of identity" hypothesis and, on the other, the resolution of ambivalence hypothesis, which are not altogether contradictory. This is the elated phase of the neophyte, the time when he feels he can do anything, nay, under drugs he feels that he really has the power to do anything.

2. Now comes the depressive phase, which is often related to a period of sexual quietness. Of fifteen hippies interviewed extensively, nine give a clear history of an elated phase followed by a depression. For instance, one said: "Well, after a while, I guess I had been around some four or five months, and I didn't feel like balling very much. The first months I was there, wow, every night, drugs, balling, both at the same times, and I got the clap. But hell, in three days, at the Free Clinic, I got rid of it. But now I was coming down. I had to do something else. Man, I began to think. Now when I took a trip I tried to find out where I was, and where I should be going. And I discovered that flower people or not flower people,

many were not beautiful people. I was robbed a couple of times, you know, blankets and things, my billfold also once. There were people around whom I definitely got bad vibrations, I mean real bad."

Some neophytes do not survive the depression. The girls start needing their parents, the boys think about school; there is a come-down, inevitable after the high hopes of the beginning. Many leave the community and return to a marginal straight life. Those who stay think of the quitters as vacation hippies, "plastic" hippies. Some of the more "premoral" cannot accept the discipline of the movement. They do not mind benefiting from the free food, the "crash pads." They do not like to give anything in return. They are impatient with the nonviolent ideology, the attempts to surmount the "hang-ups" of the self. Others cannot abide the dirt, the cockroaches. A girl, after having been raped twice, returned home and was back in college for the winter term. Some of those who drop out are not able to cathect the community once they are more familiar with it, and others are simply not capable of cathecting any group. They will return home to drift, to attempt psychotherapy under parental pressure.

Others struggle through their depression and stay on. Sometimes they stay because they have nowhere else to go and yet are not very capable of being socialized into the group. But those who stay on by conviction have now learned to accept the limitations of any group and the obligations of role behavior. These limitations and obligations are transmitted through the ideology of "keeping one's cool," which means, first, transforming one's longings for omnipotence into intellectual mastery. This has been fostered by the games destined to blow people's minds. The meaning of "keeping one's cool" means not being taken in, but also not expecting too much, understanding what is happening.

The second meaning of "keeping one's cool" is not getting overinvolved in any role context so that one can accept frustrations from that role context without flying from the field.[24] But it is through keeping one's cool that the hippie learns to measure his commitments and to differentiate his social space. From the commitment to the undifferentiated community he begins to differentiate preferred people, nonleaders, marginals as pets, and marginals as tolerated nuisances.

Although everyone is supposed to be equal, there are those who give better parties, those whose word on music is respected as taste leaders, those who do not lose their cool when someone is freaking out, those whose conversation is soothing and who seem to have an inner peace, and those who create constant hassles with the police, the landlords, or other people. There are the loudmouths, the two homosexuals always bickering in the apartment upstairs (marginals, tolerated), the sixteen-year-old girl who lays everyone (marginal as a pet).

There is the art of name dropping, whom you know— Ken Kesey, Paul Krasner, "Ginn," Allen Ginsberg—who never tries to lead anyone but who is really together. Travel ennobles one as in the Middle Ages, and the pilgrimage to Katmandhu makes one superior to those who have never left the East Village. There are those who write good poetry, play the bongo drums well, and are good at the guitar. It is not that one puts down the bad ones. One simply prefers the others. There are also those who write for the underground newspapers.

The opposition to the square world created the fraternity of the trenches. Members were valued because of their contribution to a struggle which appeared urgent, so that their idiosyncrasies, annoying in another context, became irrelevant. The neophyte hippie loved and found beautiful all hippies.

Now the feeling is different. "Police paranoia" is a little more self-conscious, and the experienced hippie knows, like the duck who lives in a pond with a crocodile, how to stay out of reach and not to panic unless the crocodile makes a specific lunge. He is more aware of what people cost and what they bring to the community. Life is still lived in an atemporal fashion, but the norms of reciprocity are being learned.

Another figure becomes salient in the life of the hippie: the wholesale drug dealer. Many people deal here and there in small quantities, making expenses, with a little bit left over once in a while. The "dealer" becomes an instrumental leader in a world which denies the need for his services. He sells, but he also gives it away, joining his client in turning on, by friendship, to prove the value of his merchandise. People come to him when they want some drugs. He becomes a specialist in the various varieties, a teller of stories, somewhat like an African witch doctor. Dealing always involves the chance of "getting burned," i.e., paying and not getting delivery. It sometimes involves adulterated merchandise. A dealer can become a wholesaler who deals in large quantities, in kilos of marihuana for instance. The wholesaler, especially in 1965-67, would often try to look as square as possible. He would be at once of the community and yet exploiting it, serving its culture and yet part of the square profit-making culture. Becoming a wholesaler is becoming a merchant, a marginal member of the hippie community.

Another aspect of the relationship to others, which becomes salient to the hippie beyond the neophyte stage, is the possible presence of the police agent. It is well known that when the police arrest a dealer, a relatively rare occurrence if one takes into account the commonness of the delict, or even when they arrest a wholesaler, they will frequently make a deal with him and introduce him into the stool-pigeon network. Detectives are also introduced as hippies into the community. Hence a factor of mistrust enters into the relations of brother to brother. Sisters are less likely to be introduced into the police network, and it increases their importance in the community. Ended is the bland form of forgiveness which characterized the neophyte's attitude to the deviant or the arrogant rejection of square norms of judgment ("if he is accused, he must be innocent"). The hippie learns suspicion but also forbearance. It is no more the neurotic or even the psychotic fear of the other, replaced by the unthinking love of the other. There is reality here, and the fear of reality displaces the fear of the unknown. People have to look out for themselves, and sometimes their self-interest conflicts with your own. Not that they are evil; it is the system again that forces them to do evil, and in particular the efforts of the square world to deny people their rights to have drugs.

Dealers, wholesalers, double agents, police agents, all force one to walk carefully and be careful in choosing one's friends. But precisely the great advantage of the hippie community resided in the lack of pressure upon the individual to make ties with people: he could take his time, send out his ultrasensitive tentacles, withdraw them, send them out again, at his own speed. Friends were needed: there was a premium on people you knew well, on people who could be trusted. By the back door of police fear, the concept of time, or of performance evaluated for its promise of the future, would reappear and become part of the life of the "mature" hippie.

Another factor which helped the hippie to make the time differentiation was his growing sense of estrangement from the "teenie-boppers." As he felt less need to prove himself a hippie in good standing, he often had little patience for their provocative behavior, their *nouveau* excesses. Often he would start wearing his hair shorter. His dress would become more similar to that of a student (while students' garb started more and more in the late sixties to resemble hippie garb). "I saw these kids parading around and I thought: now there is more to this life than hair, and 'making the scene' and turning on. So I started reading: Hesse, the Tibetan Book of the Dead, Sartre, Sade. And I got to know some of the students around college, and some of the professors too. Had quite nice talks with them. For them I was not a freak or a hippie, but another person who wanted to find out where it was at."

The older hippie finds himself cast into the role of the wise old man. They try to help the younger ones; they organize the kitchens, the love-ins; they cool the cops when the latter are ready to pounce on a sassy teenie bopper. The more desirable girls in looks and brains move toward the older members, who have more prestige. Even in the hippie world the girls gravitate toward the more prestigeful men.

Sex Roles in the Hippie World

We have mentioned how the neophyte hippie girl frequently goes through a period of promiscuity. Yet the pressures are real against her persevering in this pattern, for they are in line with the ideology that forbids the woman to make herself into an object which is the rationale (if not the reason) for the rejection of prostitution as a means of securing money. Although there is no overt rejection of prostitution—and reformed or retired (at an early age) prostitutes are sometimes found in hippie communities where they have relatively high standing ("how's that for tolerance!")—there is in this middle-class group an implicit understanding that prostitution is uncool.

Promiscuity also has a threatening impact upon the couples that do exist within the hippie community. As in every group, there is a premium on the young girls who have just arrived into the community. A girl may sleep around, but she should avoid the men that are committed to one woman. If she does not, the deprecating remarks will start to break through the surface acceptance and the tolerance ideology, and these remarks will begin to box the promiscuous girl into the sick role.

So here again we find a good deal of initial permissiveness and support combined with a subtle and relentless pressure to organize one's sexuality in ways which do not interfere with the group's stability and self-image. The high rewards the group makes available to the neophyte through the lifting of guilt make the neophyte eager to please. The redeemed self is better able to mobilize energy for complex role behavior.

Girls enjoy in the hippie man a type of man who does not require them to subordinate their shaky identity to his own. He is, in a sense, a "nonpenetrating man," with whom they can learn safely how to become passive. This is probably a common occurrence for "normal" girls in their early teens as they learn their heterosexual roles through fantasied reciprocity with entertainment figures who often strike the observer as obviously effeminate and/or with limited relationships with adolescents slightly older than themselves. The hippie girls are going through this process several years later.

In the hippie world sex has been "cooled off." Its connection with a lasting relationship has theoretically been broken, which means that girls do not have the obligation to maintain and develop a relationship in which they have been sexual partners.

They will have sex with the "nonpenetrating man," but the latter does not own them; they do not have to adjust and grant reciprocity in a situation which they heretofore have associated with danger.

In the same way the male does not have to conquer or seduce. Hippie sexual encounters take place through a sort of mutual "sniffing," where cues are at once more subtle (less verbal, there is no "line" in the hippie world) and yet more direct: "Let's fuck," or "let's ball," he will say (theoretically she could say it first, but it is rare). The burden of proof for saying "no" lies on the girl, so that a direct approach exposes the hippie to fewer chances of humiliation. Furthermore, there is less humiliation because sex is supposed to be separate from the person. The refusal of sex is not the refusal of the person. And the hippie male must never insist, as he is supposed to do in the *Playboy* world. He must not be "hung up" on sex.

Before becoming hippies both girl and boy had experience with fleeting encounters, but in the context of guilt. Now there is no guilt, and for the girl this is an important relief. The problem is still what happens afterwards: "I guess I cannot help hoping they will want to stay, and once in a while they do, and once in a while I don't let them stay. But it is not more seeing them get up and go away as fast as possible, because he really hates your guts now that he has had you. No one has me now. I do what I want to do."

And so boy and girl start groping for one another in the darkness of their mutual fear, and there is less fear. The group is closer, like an insurance policy in case the dyadic encounter should fizzle and leave one once more alone. The group is closer but more realistically appraised. The ego is stronger, ready for its own strategy, having withdrawn libido from the group and finding in the heterosexual venture an affirmation of self rather than a threat to the self, a certainty of pain and abandonment.

People start living together, and there is the presumption that they will be faithful to one another. The group must respect the boundaries of the dyad, although this rule is even less obeyed in the hippie world than it is in the straight world. As one person stated it:

> While Peter was away for a few days, John, the great nonleader, came down and balled with his woman. When he came back she told him and he was pissed at both she and John. Now it's allright, I guess. After all he does not own her and sex does not mean that much anyway. But John has to screw every woman who comes here. It is a hang-up of his.

The problem with the couple in the hippie community is that its legitimacy is not clear. On the one hand there has to be complete freedom for those who choose to live together. On the other hand the existence of the dyad threatens the group. A hippie couple must resist a much greater bombardment of sexual temptations than a square couple has to endure. As the community does not accept the idea that sex is conditioned on love, the burden of proof for refusing an occasional sexual encounter lies upon her. There is very little institutional pressure for the couple to stay together. The very tentativeness and escape clauses that made it easier for the hippies to try the interpersonal adventure make it more difficult for them to continue it, even while they wish to do so. They realize more or less clearly that if social structure can constrain the individual will, it can also strengthen it.

A pad where two people live together becomes an address. It has a tendency to become a free restaurant and laundry for unattached hippies. The rule of hospitality permits any outside hippie to crash the couple's pad. Under these conditions their social space is intruded upon, and the couple find it difficult to react as a couple. Property is bad, but property is symbolic of a couple's common living: the hippie's disregard for the privacy of the property is an attack upon the couple's intimacy. In the movie *Alice's Restaurant* (1969) the beautiful people are interested in Alice, rather than in her husband, who is the archetypal rival for the nurturance dispensed by Alice: She provides the food, the shelter, the sex, the bedding, the laundry.

To escape these pressures against their relationship the hippie couple will try traveling, thus presenting itself to new social surroundings as a unit. In the hippie community it is not rare to have the woman earning the couple's bread, as it is easier for her to secure employment. Theoretically this is of no importance, and the man could take over the care of the household. But it rarely happens that way. The man will do some household chores, but only some, and without much enthusiasm. So the girl ends up by working and keeping house. This is acceptable as long as the man is defined as "working" on something of spiritual value, such as writing poetry, painting, studying the wise men of the East, teaching at Rochdale College in Toronto.

Insofar as the hippie community has permitted both the man and the woman to differentiate a more stable sexual identification, it becomes more difficult for both to accept a role reversal that is in contradiction with the strengthened sexual identification. Co-operative managing of a head shop is one soultion, especially if the man has a manual skill that he can use to create articles to be sold — jewelry, sandals, pottery.

If the man is to do spiritual work, it must be legitimated as such, because by now the hippie woman has met dozens of poets and writers and mystics whose poetry and novels are nonexistent and whose mysticism is a nice name for schizophrenia. And legitimation is more valid if it comes from the intellectual establishment. Although hippies claim a special pipeline to truth and beauty, their cultural heroes — Ginsberg, Ferlinghetti, Corso, Kesey, Kerouac, Hesse, Tolkien — are all in good standing among the intellectuals of the establishment. Hippies are highbrow, and through their cultural and music commitments they keep a tie to the world of the mass media and of the university.

The woman wants to have a child. It would be the proof of her identity, and it is one more structural reinforcement to the couple she makes with her "old man." Because of the declining pull of the hippie community the hippie finds himself able to make contacts with straights. The hippie community ceases to provide for most of his needs.

Soon the hippie woman wants a nest she can keep outsiders away from. She wants it free of cockroaches. Hippies have given much to the rituals of atonement for white racism. Older hippies are usually free of any sentimentalism about blacks, and slum living has its drawbacks. There comes a time when it becomes obvious that if one is to have a home one has to have a stable source of income. It becomes also obvious that there are three ways of getting this income: a good job, a lousy job, and sponging off one's parents. A good job requires usually the completion of one's college degree. The hippie male is ready to return to college. The moratorium is over.[25]

It is not that the hippie couple will make a straight's adjustment to the straight world. There is no process of reverse conversion. It is rather a series of compromises, where one tries to safeguard as many of one's beliefs as is possible. An ego strong enough to participate is strong enough to preserve its identity. The hippie experience has done its share in making a working and loving relation to the dominant society possible.

NOTES

1. T. Parsons and R.F. Bales, *Family, Socialization and Interaction Process* (New York: The Free Press, 1955).
2. T. Parsons and G.M. Platt, "Age, Social Structure, and Socialization in Higher Education," *Sociology of Education,* 43 (1970), pp. 1-37.
3. Cesar Grana, *Modernity and Its Discontents* (New York: Harper & Row, 1967).
4. Bennett Burger, "Hippie Morality — More Old than New" in his *Looking for America* (Englewood Cliffs, N.J.: Prentice-Hall, 1971).
5. In 1959 Laurence Lipton, ex-communist sympathizer of the 1930's and 1940's, wrote a very successful book, *The Holy Barbarians,* which presented the beat life in a positive way. In 1961 Ned Polsky gave the first sociological analysis of the

beat movement in his article, "The Village Beat Scene: Summer 1960," *Dissent* (July 1961). In 1961 Basic Books published *The Real Bohemia* by F. Rigney and L. Douglass Smith, respectively a psychiatrist and a psychologist, who presented a friendly ethnographic report with an attempt at a serious diagnosis of the different personality types which made up a beat colony in San Francisco. The book also contained an anthology of beat poetry, some of which was remarkable.

6. For a description and analysis of the hippie creed, see Bennett Burger, "Hippie Morality," *op. cit.*; Lewis Yablonsky, *The Hippie Trip* (New York: Pegasus, 1968); Jesse Pits, "The Hippies as Contrameritocracy," *Dissent* (July-August 1969); Sherri Cavan, *Hippies of the Haight* (St Louis: New Critics Press, 1972).

The spread of the movement is reflected in its press. In 1955 a few people, among them Norman Mailer, started the *Village Voice*. It vegetated for many years. In 1964 the *Los Angeles Free Press* began publication, soon joined by the *Berkeley Barb* and the *East Village Other*. In 1964 the *Village Voice* had an audited circulation of 27,796, while the three other papers had a combined circulation of close to 50,000.

In 1969 the *Village Voice* had an audited circulation of 130,000. The *Berkeley Barb*, the *East Village Other*, and the *Los Angeles Free Press* had a combined circulation exceeding 200,000. See Robert J. Glenning. *The Underground Press in America* (Bloomington: Indiana University Press, 1970).

7. Neil Smelser, *Theory of Collective Behavior* (New York: The Free Press, 1963), p. 313.

8. Data on hippies were gathered between 1964 and 1968 in Chicago, Detroit, New York, Berkeley, San Francisco, Paris, London, and Ibiza-Formentera, through nonparticipant observation. Thanks to a grant from NIMH, questionnaires were administered to some 300 hippies in London and in Ibiza-Formentera. Interviews in depth were secured from 15 male hippies and 10 female hippies. The questionnaire data do not cover the hypotheses developed here because they were elaborated for the main after the questionnaires had been gathered.

9. Erving Goffman, *Asylums* (Garden City, N.Y.: Doubleday Anchor Books, 1961).

10. Ed Sanders, *The Family, The Story of Charles Manson's Dune Buggy Attack Battalion* (New York: E. P. Dutton, 1971).

11. T. Parsons, Robert F. Bales and Edward A. Shils, *Working Papers in the Theory of Action* (Glencoe: The Free Press, 1953). T. Parsons and Robert F. Bales, *op. cit.*

12. Yablonsky, *op. cit.,* Ch. X, describes the rule of a black man named Mystery over the Morningstar Commune, at least at the time he visited it.

13. A good example is given by Tom Wolfe, *The Electric Kool Aid Acid Test* (New York: Bantam Books, 1968), including the rationalizations. See also Yablonsky, *op. cit.*, pp. 203-205.

14. This mechanism sometimes worked to make hippies rationalize as personal choices acts into which they were actually coerced by fear.

15. In MMO's oriented to politics, their developments into mass movements bring necessarily either value-oriented people whose rejection of the dominant society is much more qualified and who argue for realistic tactics and compromise, or opportunists who flock to the movement for the advantages it may bring them. Success can destroy inner millenarianism much more effectively than defeat.

16. Yablonsky, *op. cit.,* p. 104.

17. Howard S. Becker, "Becoming a Marihuana User," *American Journal of Sociology,* 59 (November 1953), pp. 236-242.

18. It was actually derogatory in its origin within the beat communities.

19. The drugs have lost much of their sacred character now that they have become so vulgarized. The average candidate to a commune or to the freak life has now experimented with nearly everything, and for him drugs are no big thing. In 1965-66 LSD had the reputation of making its takers better humanitarians. There were projects of turning on the police or the Mafia so as to make good people out of them. Now everyone knows better.

20. Promiscuity is a female pattern of deviance that becomes a funnel for problems that have little to do with sexual identity.

21. "Square" was a typical teenie-bopper word. "Straight" was the expression used by the older hippies.

22. The hippie movement began with the cult of jazz inherited from the beats, but it quickly moved from the Coltrane, Albert Ayler, Archie Shepp type of jazz which was too "intellectual" to the acid rock of the Grateful Dead, the Fugs, the MC 5, the Canned Heat.

23. One of the problems was that the hippie communities became overloaded with demanding semi-psychopathic types, which overtaxed the organizing and socializing capacities of the principled types.

24. This is obviously not the way a hippie would put it, for the word "role" and its segmentation of behavior is something which he theoretically abhors.

25. In 1967 a list was made of 67 hippies who used to come to the Ibiza-Formentera islands every summer or lived there all year round but had not shown up that summer. They had been described by informants as hard-core hippies, whose period of activity in the movement ranged from one to four years. These hippies were mostly American and British. Out of 25 women, one was dead, 9 had married within the group, and another was living with a French sculptor. All but one of the husbands held relatively steady middle-class jobs. Of the 15 girls not known to be married, only 6 were involved in the type of employment that might permit the continuation of hippie life: 3 were photographer's models, 2 were night-club dancers, and 1 was a translator in Ibiza.

Of the 42 men, 1 was dead, and only 6 could be said to be still pursuing the hippie life. This does not mean that the teachers, the manager-owners of the macrobiotic restaurant in London, the published novelist, the American who became an interior decorator in Germany, the night-club manager in New York, have become entirely "straight." Some of these reconverted 35 are still "swinging" and living out patterns not too far removed from those of the hippie community. What is crucial here is the assumption of a full-time job, i.e., coming to terms with the dominant society in ways other than sponging or part-time low-skill employment. Nor will this adjustment be immune to relapse.

17

TOWARD A PSYCHOSOCIOLOGICAL THEORY OF ASPIRATIONS

Guy Rocher

The number of empirical studies on aspirations has greatly increased in recent years. They have mainly dealt with the educational and career aspirations of youth and with parental aspirations for their children. Others, although fewer, have been concerned with the individual and group aspirations of youth and adults for more promising life styles, better living and housing conditions, and so on. The field is broad in scope; it is diversified and complex.[1]

Two approaches dominate aspiration studies in sociology at the present time. One is concerned with the goal-orientation aspect of aspirations and accordingly centers attention on the identification of the goals toward which various aspirations are directed. The other deals with the identification of variables that account for the orientation and the intensity of aspirations.

The empirical emphasis on these approaches is responsible for a serious deficiency facing the field. Little attempt has been made to integrate existing knowledge about aspirations and about the processes whereby they change into a general conceptual and/or theoretical framework. There presently exists no general theory of aspiration to provide investigators with adequate hypotheses. The result is that too often the existence of aspirations is simply assumed, which at least partly explains the recurrence of the same indicator variables in study after study of aspirations, the piecemeal character of these studies, and their contradictory and often inconclusive findings.

The remedy for this state of affairs lies in a sociology with an analytical base in social action as the most fruitful approach to identifying the elements of a theoretical framework capable of guiding significant research in the field. Indeed, aspirations are a main component of directed social action; they provide human actors with goals (e.g., a profession, a life style, a place of residence) that are valued in given societies and that are potentially capable of bringing satisfaction to individuals.

As such the existence of aspirations is relative to at least two major systems, namely, personality and society. In the case of personality, the individual actor is seen as having within himself aspirations which he strives to elaborate and actualize. Analytically, this suggests that personality must serve as a reference system in the study of aspirations as it is from this system that aspirations gain much of their force and at least a part of their directional orientation. Aspirations, then, belong to the psychic realm of motivation because they contribute to the development of motivation and because they help sustain it, but also because in some respects they depend on that more encompassing phenomenon for their own existence.

The sociocultural environment, on the other hand, provides individual aspirations with what has been referred to as "the social context of ambition." This context includes the institutions in which aspirations originate, the media through which they are transmitted to individuals, the social structure in which they may be actualized, as well as the models, values, and symbols on which they are built and from which they partially derive their continuing existence. The social environment is also the basis for collective aspirations which, it will be noted later, help shape individual aspirations. They do this to a degree perhaps greater than current research findings would indicate.

Linked to both the personality and the socioculture systems, aspirations stand at the point of convergence of social forces and psychic energies. It follows that a suitable framework for the study of aspirations must look to both the fields of psychology and of sociology. More specifically, the study of aspirations—whether individual or collective—must be approached from the perspective of a social action theoretical framework having, as in the case of Parsons', enough scope to include the entire spectrum of psychosocial reality. Indeed, as we shall see, the concept of aspiration implies the existence of four social action subsystems such as suggested in the theory of action framework. From the analytic perspective of the general theory of action, aspirations are therefore to be seen as a choice field of investigation.

The aim of this essay is to suggest theoretically relevant elements serving as the basis for a sociological theory of aspirations consistent with the general theory of action. The first section will attempt to define aspiration and to give an indication of its complexity. In this we shall rely heavily on the work of Chombart de Lauwe. The second section will present an analysis of aspirations guided by the theory of action model of the structure of personality. Finally, in the third section, we shall attempt to analyze aspirations within the framework of the social system. Here again Parsons' analytical model will be our guide.

NATURE AND COMPLEXITY OF ASPIRATIONS

An aspiration may be thought of as an intended plan entertained by a social actor for whom it represents both a goal toward which to strive and a hope for the future; in many instances it provides a reason for engagement in social action. The term social actor, as used here, refers not only to an individual in a social role; it is extended also to include a group, a community, or an entire society. In Paul-Henry Chombart de Lauwe's words, an aspiration is a "desire directed toward an object." He holds to "this formulation even after having reviewed a large number of studies carried out by individual investigators."[2]

Despite the simplicity suggested by these definitions, an aspiration is highly complex. It is perhaps best thought of as an intricate network of tensions that can best be understood if analysed at both the theoretical level and at the level of concrete reality.

Needs and Aspirations

One of the few contemporary sociologists who have attempted the development of a theoretical base for the study of aspirations is Chombart de Lauwe. The central emphasis in both his theoretical[3] and his empirical[4] works is on the interplay between the complementary and the incompatible properties of needs and aspirations. Following the

model suggested in Maurice Halbwachs' research on the standard of living of working-class families,[5] Chombart de Lauwe has, in recent years, conducted a number of empirical studies in France. These have dealt primarily with the economic needs of individuals and families, with the manner in which these needs find satisfaction, and with the aspirations that develop when needs remain unsatisfied. An important outcome of these studies has been an increase in the awareness of various kinds of linkages, genetic as well as structural, that exist between needs and aspirations. These studies led Chombart de Lauwe to the conclusion that "it is impossible to understand the development of needs and the role they play in social change without reference to the individual and group aspirations that become needs or that originate in them; nor must these be examined in isolation, but in their relation to all elements of the environment and of the production system in each society."[6] Chombart de Lauwe therefore speaks of a "dialectic need-aspiration movement" to indicate the simultaneous existence of complementary and tension-producing elements between needs and aspirations. This dualism is held to be responsible for much of the observable relationships between the two. Carrying Chombart de Lauwe's argument one step further, it is possible to invert his formulation and state that it is impossible to study the development of aspirations and their roles without reference to the needs of the various systems involved in social action.

Sharpening his notions of need and aspiration, Chombart de Lauwe speaks of need as "the state of an organism, of a person, of a social group, or of a mechanical (cybernetic) system, seeking to regain an equilibrium disrupted by the occurrence of a deficiency."[7] The advantage of this definition lies in that it removes the concept of need from the exclusive realms of biology and psychology and broadens it sufficiently to permit its inclusion as an element of social and cybernetic systems. Chombart de Lauwe's extension of the concept of need brings it very close to Parsons' concept of "system needs."

Reference has already been made to Chombart de Lauwe's concept of aspiration as "a desire oriented toward an object." His following statement serves to distinguish aspiration from need:

Aspiration, as opposed to need, does not orient the individual toward the re-establishment of an equilibrium nor toward the fulfillment of an actual deficiency; rather, it orients him toward a yet non-existent state that is more desirable than the present one. This desire which orients the individual to more beyond his present state may either be a need-desire disposition aimed at the fulfillment of a deficiency, or a desire-aspiration disposition aimed at bringing about a state never yet attained.[8]

Chombart de Lauwe's distinction between need and aspiration, while useful, is not sufficient for our purposes. It suffers from some weaknesses. First, in his effort to draw a sharp distinction between need and aspiration, Chombart de Lauwe has thought it fit to look for exclusive properties in each. As we will try to make clear later on, there seems to be better ways to discriminate between need and aspiration. Second, Chombart de Lauwe has come to define need and aspiration as subcategories of a more general category, that he calls "desire." But desire is a very broad and vague concept, which brings no further clarification to the concepts of need and aspiration, which are fuzzy enough by themselves. Finally his definition leads us to believe that aspiration does not imply a feeling of deficiency or of disequilibrium between the present and the desired system state, but that aspiration assumes only a vague sort of desire extending into the future. Yet all research findings indicate that there are sharp and definite feelings of deficiency or of tension at the root of aspiration and that, indeed, these are its most important and visible indicators.

Our contention is that aspiration differs from need not so much because of mutually exclusive properties in each but, rather, because one is the expression of the other at a different level of reality. More specifically, aspiration is a disposition to act, but one of a symbolic nature, originating in a need and having the function of providing satisfaction for that need in future activity. Aspirations and needs therefore are situated at different levels of reality: need is the experience or awareness of a deficiency in a system, while aspiration is the translation or expression of that deficiency into a plan for the future which then serves as a goal to direct action. To distinguish even more clearly between these levels of reality we must note that, in the process whereby need is translated into aspiration, the plan for the future becomes the effective symbol of the need's anticipated gratification. Hence we can say that aspiration is the principal mode for the symbolic expression of need or, as has just been stated, that it is the principal mode of expression of a symbolic action orientation.

Aspiration, as an orientation to action, is but one of many possible expressions of a need. Indeed, within the context of a system of action, the experience of need can give rise to one of three action orientation responses. Inhibition is the first such response. It essentially consists in recognizing that a need will never be satisfied and that the most effective way to deal with the resulting frustration is to suppress the need as much as possible. Otherwise stated, it consists in minimizing the deprivation by developing appropriate attitudes, for example, of indifference or apathy. The second response is gratification.

Gratification consists in providing satisfaction for the need in the most expedient way possible, the need, in this case, being so strong and compelling that it requires at least a minimum degree of satisfaction even if it is not nearly adequate. Aspiration, of course, is the third possible response to an emerging need. It is appropriate when there is reason to believe that the need can be satisfied in a not too distant future.

At this point we rejoin Chombart de Lauwe's useful distinction between need-obligation and need-aspiration.[9] But we emphasize, maybe more than Chombart de Lauwe himself did, that the main distinguishing characteristic of aspiration—rendering it distinct from both gratification and inhibition—is not only that it constitutes a hope for the future. Rather, it is that, as a hope for the future, it produces—through images, representations, and even mythologies—a translation of the need into symbolic terms.

Symbolic Nature of Aspirations

In this perspective of symbolic social action the interdependence between need and aspiration takes on new meaning: the same kind of dialectic relationship found between a subject and its symbol is also found to exist between need and aspiration. It follows that a certain distance is always to be found between need and aspiration, a distance such that aspiration becomes a more or less adequate representation of the need. As the symbol of a need, aspiration can somewhat alter the true nature of that need. It may also represent need in a disproportionate, exaggerated, or extravagant manner. Utopias, myths, fantasies, and other products of overly fertile imaginations fall within this last category.

This distance between aspiration and need is at the root of the dynamic relationship between the two. In elaborating, entertaining, and making explicit the future state or event which is the object of his aspiration, the actor derives a certain anticipated satisfaction for his need. But at the same time, the aspiration perpetuates the existence of the need by maintaining a hope or an image of it. In this way there evolves a relationship between aspiration and need analogous to the relationship found between language and thought. Indeed, as thought produces language, so too does language contribute to the elaboration of thought. In much the same manner, needs give rise to aspirations which, in turn, contribute to the redefinition of the needs. It is because needs are manifested and expressed through aspirations that the latter are then able to help maintain and redefine needs.

Chombart de Lauwe has given an excellent

description of this need-aspiration-need cycle by printing out how needs engender aspiration and how these in turn—depending on the extent and mode of their realization provoke the emergence of new needs. These new needs, of course, bring about new aspirations, and the process goes on in a never-ending cycle.

It is this interaction cycle between aspirations (as a symbolic expression of needs) and needs (as objects symbolized) that is at the root of individual and social innovation and change. Aspirations commit the individual and/or society to the pursuit of what Alain Touraine has called a "cultural model of development" or a "model of creativity."[10] The term development is used here in its broadest meaning and not in its restricted economic sense, while the term "cultural" has the meaning of a symbolic system in the theory of action. The concept of "model of development" or of "creativity" is therefore taken to mean a project to be accomplished, a task (in the very broad sense of something to be done), or a *praxis* in the sense given this term in Marxian sociology. In theory of action terms, the cultural model corresponds to "goal-attainment."

It is in this "model of development" or project to be accomplished that the energy for the "dialectic need-aspiration movement" is to be found. The model of development is the symbolic expression of a hope or a dream perceived as attainable; it differs more or less from the reality situation that is the source of frustration. The dominant characteristic of the model of development, and of the aspiration derived from it, is therefore found in the strain produced by elaborating goals toward which to strive while having to remain in the existing unsatisfactory situation. There is here simultaneous affirmation and a negation: affirmation of a desired potential future state and the negation involved in an actual state of deprivation or frustration.

Because of this dialectic tension between need and aspiration as symbol of hope, aspiration brings about creative activity that involves the actor in goal-oriented behavior at both the levels of the imagination and of actual work. Aspiration calls for historical action, that is, for individual or community action aimed at bringing about change. But it does so only to the extent that it implies a consciousness of the distance between the valued norms or ideals and the actual existing realities, between the proposed models and the obstacles standing in the way of their realization.

Other Tensions Inherent to Aspiration

Apart from this basic tension between need and hope which is the essence of aspiration, there are others more peripheral, yet nonetheless inherent

to it. An aspiration is, first of all, a tension between a reality and a dream. Reality is the immediate environment in which—and in relation to which—personalities and social systems operate. The existence of any system assumes a sufficient knowledge of and an adequate adaptation to this reality. Dream, on the other hand, is a break from reality. It is a projection into another environment, one better suited to the satisfaction of given needs or, perhaps, one in which needs are in effect satisfied. Otherwise stated, a dream is the symbolic actualization of a yet unattained desired state. Aspiration lies between the two. Anchored in reality, it is directed toward the dream. It is a mental and an effective bridge between dream and reality.

Aspiration is also a tension between the possible and the ideal. As a bridge between dream and reality, aspiration causes the actor to hesitate between the goals that are realistically achievable and those that are ideal. In all intentional activity there exists a margin between what is a realistic outcome to expect and one that is ideal, what is desired but unattainable in practice. It is at this point between the possible and the ideal that the utopian can be distinguished from the ideological. The utopian belongs to an ideal realm known a priori to be never completely attainable; ideology, on the other hand, provides the basis for a real hope and for a concrete plan of action.

The third tension is found between institutionalized norms to which social actors look for guidance in actual conduct, on the one hand, and the desire to create new norms in order to bring about social change, on the other. From this vantage point, an aspiration may sometimes be a more or less complete rejection or disapproval of institutionalized norms, and even of the values on which they stand, in favor of other norms and other values. Aspirations are projections into the future; as such they may be inspired by the image and the hope of a different world from the existing one.

Finally, aspirations are the product of a tension between individual and social selves. In each instance the self is subjected to constraints from the environment. This frustrates attempts to act in a manner felt to be consistent with the realization of what the self perceives to be its true identity. Aspirations thus originate in the social environment even if they are in partial disagreement with that environment.

These various tensions may be seen as resulting from two main opposing forces built into all social aspirations. The first is that which opposes—or, at the very least, compares—the future with the present and/or the past. All aspirations represent a break in time expressed in a positive evaluation of a future state which will develop or which must be made to develop. This expression is made in comparison to a present and/or a past of which at least certain aspects are rejected or judged undesirable. Aspirations, hence, are tensions between points in time. They imply a fairly broad time perspective extending from the present or the past into the future. It is impossible for individuals or groups with severely limited views of the future to develop strong aspirations.

The second such set of opposing forces found in all social aspirations is much more subtle and has been little studied to date. It is made up of forces that provide linkages between different systems and between subsystems within larger systems. To illustrate this point, it need only be indicated that all aspirations originate in a disequilibrium, great or little, between systems and their environments or between internal subsystems.

The nature of this second set of forces can only be understood when analyzed within a systems framework like that elaborated in Parsons' general theory of action. The two following sections will deal with this analysis.

ASPIRATIONS AND THE PERSONALITY SYSTEM

Aspirations are driving forces behind action; they therefore imply activity in all four subsystems of the general system of action.[11] According to the theory of action framework, human social action always implies the contribution of four systems which can be analytically distinguished: the behavioral organism system, the personality system, the social system, and the cultural system. Human social action is comprehensive and must always be regarded as a whole, calling upon the four systems all at once. But at the same time, each of these four systems can be distinguished from the other on the basis of its unique contribution to an action system. It is so because, at the analytical level of the general system, each one of these four systems can be identified with one of the four functional dimensions of the action system. The organism corresponds to the adaptation function (A), which relates the action system to its environment; the personality system refers to the goal-attainment function (G), which is the definition of the objectives of the action system and the mobilization of its resources to attain the proposed goals; the social system is the integrative function (I) through the network of interrelationships and solidarities that it creates and maintains; culture corresponds to the latent pattern-maintenance function (L), which provides the motivational support of action through norms, values, ideals, and ideologies.

The four functional subsystems can be distinguished from each other, as each one enjoys some degree of relative autonomy. At the same time, they are interdependent because of their complementary contribution to the broader action system of which they are parts, with the resulting interrelationships that necessarily exist between them.

This interdependence of the four subsystems is especially clear in the case of aspirations, as each one provides a unique contribution to the action system relating to aspirations. There is, first, some biological energy provided by the organism and originating in certain impulses, or frustrations. Hunger and sex, for example, are impulses providing this kind of energy. The personality subsystem, on the other hand, is related to aspirations through the mechanism of motivation which it activates and, in so doing, brings the contribution of both cognitive and affective elements to bear on the development of aspirations. The social system for its part provokes the emergence of aspirations. It supports their continuing existence and diffusion and constitutes the environment in which aspirations may either be fulfilled or frustrated. Finally, the cultural system provides the universe of symbols and values through which aspirations are elaborated, expressed, and communicated to individuals and groups.

For the purposes of our analysis, it is necessary to begin with one of these subsystems and to make it our point of reference. We shall first adopt the personality as the system of reference and deal with it in this section. Then, in the following section we shall look at the social and cultural systems as they constitute the environments of the personality system and, therefore, the environments in which aspirations develop. For the purpose of this essay, we shall leave the part played by the organismic environment of the personality in aspirations aside. It would lead us too far away from the main theme to be developed here.

The Functional Tensions of Personality and Aspirations

According to Parsons' scheme, the AGIL divisions of the general system of action provide the analytical model for each of the four subsystems. Personality systems, as well as the other three types, are action systems that can be analyzed in terms of the four functional dimensions of the action system.

Using that framework, aspirations appear to be situated primarily in the goal-attainment function (G) of the personality system. In defining aspirations, we have emphasized that they are symbolic expressions of present needs in terms of future plans and goals. They contribute therefore to the identification and achievement of goals in the orientation of action. As a matter of fact, aspirations are both definitions of goals and pursuits of goals. They provide objectives, and they mobilize the energy and resources of the personality in pursuit of these objectives.

The place and role of aspirations in the personality structure can be fully understood, however, only within the complex network of interchange between G and the three other sub-systems. Goal-attainment is an open boundary subsystem within the personality system and is part of a network of interchange with the subsystems which constitute its environment. To understand the development of an aspiration in G, it is necessary to trace the pattern of interaction among G, A, L, and I.

As indicated in Figure 17-1, two approaches are possible. One is to begin with A, where the relationships between personality and environment are a source of dissatisfaction and frustration. Indeed, and for various reasons, the adaptation of the personality system to its environment is never entirely satisfactory. In certain cases frustrations stem from existing unsatisfactory physical and material conditions; in others, they result from inadequate adaptation to the sociocultural environment. These frustrations may be more or less severe. As stimuli they can elicit responses ranging from inhibition to gratification to aspiration. In one way or another, inadequate adaptation brings us back to the notion of need which, it will be remembered, is defined as a feeling of imbalance between certain system requirements, one source of which is found in L and another in environmental provisions for their satisfaction. One of the possible responses to this kind of frustration, as we have previously seen, is the projection into the future of certain definite tension-reducing provisions. These provisions then take the form of goals toward which to strive. It is in this manner that aspirations are formed.

The second possible approach is to begin with L. In this case the personality is exposed to norms or values from the sociocultural environment. These are presented as levels of accomplishment already achieved or as appropriate goals toward which to strive. Most often, however, a discrepancy is found to exist between the norms and values suggested to the personality and internalized in L and the level of their effective or possible realization in G. It is in this discrepancy that the personality's source of future projects is to be found. These future projects consist in projecting into the future such situations as would

establish an equilibrium between G and L. It is this process that generates goals which then become the objects of aspirations.

There is, however, another function that is fulfilled by the latency subsystem. In both the preceding approaches there occurs a tension build-up which is partially responsible for creating the motivation on which aspirations depend. This motivation in turn results from the frustration felt in A and from the future project created in G.

But what of the integration subsystem (I) in this pattern of inter-action? Its principal contribution is to the maintenance of cohesion required for the adequate functioning of the personality system faced with aspirations and the tensions they imply. Pursuing our analysis, we can then say that integration (I) serves two main functions. First, it serves to establish and maintain a balance between the future projects and the present requirements of the personality system. In other words, it may serve to prevent aspirations from being pursued when this would be detrimental to the satisfaction of actual requirements of the personality system. These requirements may be past traces in the personality, conscious or unconscious, or be related to present conditions or to actual constraints felt by the personality. Second, subsystem I provides controls in the form of the acceptance of delayed gratification. The existence of aspirations presupposes that present needs are frustrated, and this frustration requires the activation of controls to prevent the occurrence of other disturbances in the personality. On the whole, subsystem I seems to harmonize the aspirations with the other elements of the personality system, and the personality system with the aspirations.

It is clear, at this point, that the theory of action model provides an analytical framework for gaining a first insight into the nature of tensions and disequilibria between the subsystems of personality. It is these latter which explain the development and the role of aspirations in the human personality. At the very least, the theory of action enables us to sort out the various elements in the dynamics of aspirations: this has the advantage of clarifying the confusion too often present in empirical studies of aspiration.

Variable Time and the Theory of Action Model

It is through subsystem G that variable time is integrated into the system of action. An actor's goal-oriented behavior is an indication of the direction in which his future action will be oriented and in terms of which it will be guided. It is largely because of this subsystem that the theory of action model escapes the limitations inherent in behaviorism.

In order better to integrate all the aspects of the

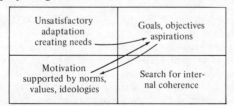

Figure 17-1. Paradigm of the system of interchanges, involving aspirations in the personality.

variable time into an analysis of aspiration, it becomes necessary, at this point, to extend the theory of action model somewhat. It is our contention that the projection into the future produced by subsystem G and by aspirations has the effect of superimposing a second set of subsystems—"future" subsystems—onto subsystems A, I, and L.

We already know through psychoanalytic theory how active the past is in the actual functioning of the personality system. Similarly, the image of the future is also part of the present in the personality system. The aspirations are largely responsible for the active presence of the future in the present. Parsons' notion of "situation" is broad enough to include together the past experience of the personality, its present conditions, and its projection into the future.

As illustrated in Figure 17-2, G is the function that serves mostly as a bridge between the present and the future. This is represented in the figure by the widely open boundary between G and G(f) (which stands for future G).

A(f) represents a projected adaptation at a future time, but one that also influences the orientation of action in the present. A(f) then is not merely a mental picture. Because of what is implied in aspiration, it is also an orientation to a quasi-reality, or perhaps more precisely, to a subjective reality which is very real to the actor. In this way a future adaptation subsystem is superimposed upon the present adaptation subsystem. The comparison that an actor makes between them becomes a constant source of tension in the dynamic system of interaction.

In similar fashion L(f) represents the symbolic universe of norms and values on which the actor draws in order to guide future action in the process of pursuing aspirations. Subsystem L(f), which is superimposed upon L, is therefore to be seen as a kind of anticipated motivation for future action that is perceived as such by the actor in the present and that is therefore capable of influencing the orientation of action in the present.

Finally, I(f) is the kind of integration that the actor presently foresees for the time when the goal he is now pursuing will be attained. As such, I(f) is already present in the mind of the actor; it is anticipated or

feared by him, depending on what he expects from the attainment or the nonattainment of his goal or goals.

This extension of the theory of action analytical framework brings us back to Chombart de Lauwe's notion of a need-aspiration cycle.

As illustrated in Figure 17-3, the personality system at TI is setting itself some goal in G to be achieved in the future. The whole system, as we have just seen, is influenced in its present functioning by the goal to be achieved and by the image of what the future will be when the goal is attained. The progressive achievement of the goal in T2 tends to reduce the distance between A(f) and A, between I(f) and I, and between L(f) and L. When these pairs become congruent or nearly so, a new tension develops between the new A and G or between the new L and G (exactly as in Figure 30-1), thus producing a new goal (Gf2), which has the effect of creating a new anticipated adaptation (Af2), a new anticipated integration (If2), and a new anticipated latency (Lf2).

Let us emphasize that T3 or T4 may sometimes be predicted and perceived well in advance by the actor in TI. This is the case where, for instance, the various stages of our action sequence are predictable. The influence of T3 or T4 on present behavior is then greater than it may be in cases when T3 is hardly predictable in TI. The impact of perceived future may therefore be variable, according to the degree of clarity with which it is perceived, the extent of change it presupposes, the level of gratification and frustration it is expected to bring with it.

Another important point must be brought up here. It has to do with clarifying the notion of the symbolic nature of aspiration stressed earlier. The nature of A(f), I(f), and L(f) is definitely symbolic as compared to A, I, and L. They are not fully expressive of the subsystems they symbolize, however, as they conform more closely to certain system requirements (needs) than the actual subsystems do. A(f), I(f) and L(f), then, are symbols of A, I, and L transformed into a "better world," into a situation or an environment deemed more favorable to the realization of the goals found in G.

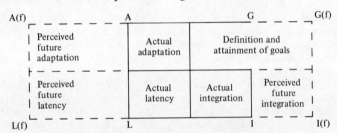

Figure 17-2. Present and future in the paradigm of the system of action.

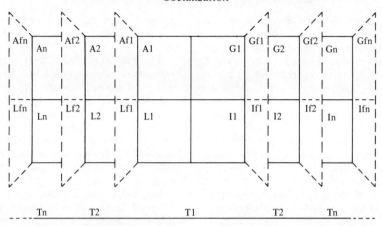

Figure 17-3. Paradigm of the personality system at different points of time.

Aspirations and Personality Types

The theory of action allows us to elaborate our thinking in another direction as well. To do so, however, we must make reference to a relatively unknown and little utilized portion of Parsons' work, namely, to his "Typology of Psychological Orientations."[12] More specifically, we refer to his classification of personalities into four basic types of psychological systems, each characterized by the primacy of one or another of the four subsystems of the general action system as it is observed in the overt behavior of individuals. Assuming that this classification is valid, it is then possible to state that an actor's aspirations are subject to influence from the psychological orientation of his personality system. The remainder of the present section is given to a brief outline of the usefulness of Parsons' typology of personality systems in the study of aspirations.

In cases where there is primacy of subsystems A or G, the personality is predisposed to direct its activity toward goals outside itself. The external situation, in these cases, is given more importance than the internal. This personality type is similar to the more widely known extrovert type. The difference found between instances of the primacy of A or of G lies in the orientation toward different objects in the external environment.

In personalities marked by the predominance of G, aspirations are pursued which require the subordination of demands from the other subsystems of the personality. There is a tendency for these aspirations to be idealistic and, at times, even utopian in nature. This type's tendency toward utopian aspirations can only be overcome when the need for success is sufficiently powerful to induce in the personality

system a motivation strong enough to assure the realization of aspirations and the attainment of goals in a limited period of time. If time is not seen as limited the goals sought may be very distant and therefore idealistic. In cases of this type, aspirations tend to have a relatively abstract character.

In personalities where A is predominant, aspirations are more short-term. They are of a kind to be realized rapidly by the manipulation of objects like wealth, knowledge, technical know-how, and power. There exists, in this case, a tendency for these objects to become transformed into aspirations, as success becomes a priority pursuit as an end in itself. This personality type is more pragmatic and utilitarian than idealistic and more oriented to tangible achievements than the former. It is also more ready to compromise on the choice of goals, motivated as it is to achieve as many as possible of the goals within reach. In comparison to the former, this type is characterized by a reality-orientation, by an orientation to the short-term achievement of goals that lie within easy reach, goals which would be looked upon as means by a G-type personality.

In personalities dominated by either I or L, the psychological orientation is most likely to be toward the inner psychological system, towards self-actualization, inner harmony, and self-respect. This psychological orientation corresponds to the introvert personality type.

When the integration function dominates, the main orientation is toward the maintenance of inner tranquility, of equilibrium, and of general internal harmony. The resulting disposition is to the selection of goals consistent with this dominant need, to the elimination of elements threatening inner peace, and to appropriate adjustments to the external reality. There is a certain flexibility about aspirations in this case. This personality type does not make strong commitments to specific goals. Instead, it has an array of goals from which to select on the basis of the requirements of inner coherence. The aspirations of this personality type are not always oriented in the same direction. They tend to change as the development of the personality system progresses.

Finally, in instances of personality systems where latency (L) dominates, the psychological orientation is to strong commitment to specific values and to a readiness to sacrifice much else in order to retain these values as dominant action guides. This type of personality generally tends toward strong idealism and is disposed to self-sacrifice to further the pursuit and the attainment of its important goals.

This classification leads us, at the level of microsociology, to expect the type of psychological orientation of the personality to condition both the content and the directional orientation of aspirations. This hypothesis has yet to be explored empirically, however. But it falls in line with Morris Rosenberg's conclusions on what he called "occupational values." Rosenberg tested the hypothesis that individuals may be classified in three classes according to the occupational values that are dominant in their behavior: extrinsic values, people-oriented values, intrinsic values. He also used the same categories to classify occupations, according to the type of occupational values they may be said to implement. Rosenberg could then measure the degree of congruence between the respondents' occupational values and the value profile of their occupational choices. The assumption was that respondents who displayed a greater degree of congruence had more chance than others for attaining academic and professional success.[13] Recently, Harvey and Harvey have used Rosenberg's scheme and found significant differences of congruence among Canadian students from higher and lower socioeconomic backgrounds and among male and female students.[14]

Following the same line of research, Chad Gordon has used Parsons' four functional dimensions and pattern variables to build a classification of personality types according to their self-conceptions.

> Each of the four functional problems is asserted to have a corresponding "sense of self" available to consciousness—the individual's interpretation of his standing with regard to that system problem. . . . I am suggesting the correspondence of the sense of *competence* to the problem of adaptation, the sense of *self-determination* to goal-attainment, the sense of *unity* to integration, and the sense of *moral worth* to pattern-maintenance.[15]

Gordon sees a possible interrelatedness between these four "senses of self" and what he calls the "super-senses" such as "self-esteem and the sense of personal autonomy."[16] As some relationships have been found to exist by Rosenberg between self-esteem and adolescents' orientations and aspirations,[17] Gordon's scheme might serve to relate aspirations to a typology of personalities. Thus, it might very well be that the level of aspirations will be higher in personalities with a high score of the sense of competence or of self-determination than in other types of personality; similarly, the content of aspirations might vary according to the type of self-conception to be found in a person.

Until now sociologists have been concerned with the collective features of aspirations, seeking to identify differences on the basis of grossly defined economic, social, or cultural variables. This approach is entirely acceptable at the macrosociological level, but there needs to be developed an awareness that similarity of aspirations at this level does not preclude the existence of differences at the level of individuals within given groups. Beside the variations at the societal level that have preoccupied researchers until now, there exists another universe of more subtle variations. These variations are related to the psychic structure of individual social actors, to the place of aspirations in that structure, and to the needs of the personality system to which these aspirations are linked and which they symbolize.

ASPIRATIONS AND THE SOCIAL AND CULTURAL ENVIRONMENT

One of the main tenets of the theory of action is that the development of the personality system cannot be understood independently of social and cultural systems that constitute its environments. In relation to aspirations, culture and society are environments in more ways than one. First of all, they present the individual with objectives, achievements, and levels of attainment. Society, for example, places a high value on given residential districts, on the possession of certain goods, on membership in certain professions and so on. Culture provides ideals, values, symbols that are incorporated in aspirations in various ways. Suffice it to say that this is the more obvious aspect of the influence of the social and cultural environment on aspirations.

At the same time as they are sources of aspiration goals, the social and cultural environments are also sources of impediments and obstacles to their realization; they create goals and then frustrate attempts to reach them, as it were. The effects of these obstacles and frustrations on aspirations vary. In certain cases they can discourage, inhibit, or completely destroy motivation. In others, they can provoke and thus bring about stronger motivation than previously existed. The latter case, in keeping with Atkinson's law,[18] exists when obstacles present a challenge that neither discourages by being too great nor disinterests by being too small. In other cases, constraints and frustrations can reduce the strength of aspirations without inhibiting them completely: they merely serve to render aspirations more "realistic."

Whatever the impact of the social and cultural environments on aspirations, their influence results in the development of a distance between these environments and the personality system. There ensue tensions of variable intensities. These two elements, distance and tension, are at the root of all aspirations. Otherwise stated, aspirations are to be found where there is imperfect congruence between the requirements of the personality and the properties of the social and cultural systems. This condition nearly always exists. To reiterate, we can go as far as to say that there exists a kind of dialectic relationship between the personality system and its social and cultural environments. This relationship is responsible for the development of an aspiration-need-dissatisfaction-aspiration cycle: The environments present personality with norms and values that stimulate the development of aspirations and needs. The environments do not, however, ensure the satisfaction of these aspirations and needs, at least not in any immediate or complete manner. The social system and culture then both develop and frustrate aspirations. In this latter role, they may also serve to reinforce the aspirations they helped create.

While still retaining the present analytic perspective, we will now turn to a consideration flowing from our preceding discussion, in which special emphasis was placed on the concept of aspiration as a projection of the self and of the self's activity into the future. We can now suggest, in the form of a hypothesis, that this projection must be accompanied by a more or less elaborate image of a future society to provide the context in which aspirations might be realized. In other words, this image becomes the environment for the personality system's A(f); indeed it is this A(f) personality subsystem that leads to the formulation of this hypothesis.

It is imperative that future research on aspirations consider the element A(f) in relation to G; that, in other words, it takes into account those future-society images that are entertained by social actors and in terms of which their aspirations are expressed. This implies two things: first, that an individual actor's aspirations must be viewed from the perspective of the collective aspirations of his group or society and, second, that they also be viewed from the perspective of the actor's attitudes toward the present and toward the anticipated future society.

We shall now consider some of the theoretical implications of these two requirements.

Individual and Collective Aspirations

Relative to aspirations, the image of a future society is probably the main link among the personal, social, and cultural subsystems of the general system of action. An actor's image of such a future society is seldom idiosyncratic, that is, it is seldom entirely original or unique. On the contrary, it can be assumed that individual aspirations are part of a larger context of aspirations held by a collectivity about its future. It is these latter aspirations, held by a group and oriented toward its future, that properly constitute collective aspirations. Hence collective aspirations are not merely shared aspirations; they are also collective in terms of the goal toward which they are oriented. Otherwise stated, they are collective aspirations because they deal with the future of a collectivity or of a society.

Without reifying the concepts of society or of collectivity, it seems possible to analyze the collective aspirations in a manner similar to that applied to individual aspirations. It can be argued, as it was in the case of the personality system, that collective aspirations are linked with an A(f) social system which, in relation to A, constitutes part of the image of the future society for the social system taken as a system of action. Assuming this to be the case, then, the manner in which collective aspirations are integrated into the social system varies with the nature of that system, as specified by the primacy of a subsystem.

This last point must be emphasized. Because little attention has been paid to the possible variation of aspirations in different types of societies, research on aspirations in the United States has not been evaluated in a comparative perspective. This explains why social scientists have not, until now, been concerned with the influence of collective aspirations on individual aspirations.

To overcome this deficiency, aspirations may be analyzed in terms of four broad types of societies. The existence of differences among these four types rests on the assumption that the relative influence of each of the four functional subsystems varies from society to society. It is indeed a fact of observation that there is primacy of the economic subsystem in some societies, of the political subsystem in others, and that, in still others, the function of integration or of latency is the central basis of the social structure.

Rainer Baum has shed some light on the typology of societies that can be evolved out of this observation, and he has demonstrated that this typology can be used in historical research. He described the "four major value systems" in the following terms:

> The first, the L-primacy system, is one in which major concerns lie with problems of meanings and ideals. The second, I-primacy, stresses above all the problems of social harmony or the ways making for maximal inter-unit adjustment. The third, G-primacy, places its focus on the problem of effective cooperativeness or how best to cooperate for the achievement of collective goals. The fourth, A-primacy, concentrates on the problem of how best to develop and make use of all possible means to the fullest extent. How very much simplified this scheme is should be apparent from the fact that it leaves the question of second or third order importance completely out of consideration.[19]

It is on the grounds of a similar typology that we hypothesize that the nature and the orientation of collective aspirations will vary with the type of society in which they are found. Societies basically structured around the economic subsystem are those least capable of fostering collective aspirations. Organized around the production, distribution, and consumption of goods, this type of society is characterized by a division of labor and by roles and groups that may be said to complement each other. To use Durkheim's terms, they are characterized by organic solidarity. In such societies there tends to exist a diversity of interests and a plurality of groups and communities. It is therefore not the type of society where the pursuit of common goals through the centralization of resources is apt to be found. As Baum puts it: "A society seems to be characterized by adaptation-primacy when its members' philosophy of life primarily orients them to the idea of practical success."[20] Its collective aspirations are essentially weak and generalized rather than specific. This allows for the existence of variations and a plurality of collective aspirations on the part of different social groups.

On the other hand, in societies where the primacy of the political subsystem is found, there tends to be a strong mobilization of human and material resources. These resources are directed toward societal goals that are determined by strong leadership having firmly established legitimacy and wide powers of intervention. Developing countries, especially those with a one-party system of government, exemplify this type. More generally, any society engaged in rapid and far-reaching change is to be included, as they engender relatively strong collective aspirations usually witnessed in formal ideologies.

In societies characterized by the primacy of societal community, the accent is on internal solidarity, on the need for harmony and order and, consequently, on societal control mechanisms that these needs require. This type of society, like the former, favors the development of collective aspirations. Contrary to the political type of society, however, the main concern here is with internal operations and not with the pursit of external goals. Strongly nationalistic societies having their own preservation as their dominant purpose are of this type. The romantic nationalism of late nineteenth-century Germany was a good example, where collective aspirations were aimed at social unity and at the development of a societal community spirit among the citizens.

Finally, there is the type of society where the latency function dominates and where, consequently, there is concern with safeguarding traditions and values and with maintaining loyalty to a history and to a self-image linked with this history. Here again aspirations are focussed on internal and community elements of the social system. Collective aspirations tend to be weaker than in the last two types but stronger than in the economic society.

As this brief sketch illustrates, collective aspirations have least chance of influencing individual aspirations in those societies dominated by the economic subsystems, as in this type of society collective aspirations are weakest. Furthermore, in the economic type of society, individual aspirations tend to center on the area of work and on one's chance for social mobility.

It is predominantly, not to say entirely, in this economic type of society — in North American society especially — that studies of aspirations have been carried out. This, undoubtedly, explains the preoccupation with the career aspirations of youth and/or of their parents and the lack of concern with the relationship between collective and individual aspirations.

The comparative approach set out in our analysis leads to the formulation of the following hypothesis: that in societies which are not predominantly economic, individual aspirations will have a different orientation from those found in North American society. One of the important reasons for this lies in the influence of the collective aspirations of the society as a whole. To verify whether such a process of influence does in fact occur, research guided by this hypothesis must be carried out in societies not having economic primacy.

Even in North American society, the aspirations of youth seem to be changing in a collective direction. Youth culture, especially at the secondary school and college levels, has become more political than it was even in the recent past. Rejecting the economic primacy in the industrial society, a subculture within the American youth culture is now characterized by collective aspirations that have a stronger influence on at least a portion of the youth population than was recently the case. Research must be undertaken in the direction of these developments.

Aspirations and Attitudes Toward Society

In order to study collective aspirations and the image of a future society as suggested in our outline, another item must be added to our framework. The social actor's image of a future society is to a large extent determined by that actor's perception of the existing society. Indeed, an actor's, a group's, or a society's image of a future society depends on the judgement made on the actual society and on the attitudes that develop as a result of this judgement. It must be added, however, that the image of the future society in some respects determines the judgement passed on the present. Between aspirations for the future and attitudes toward the present society there exists a complex and as yet unexplored set of relationships.

It is possible, by oversimplifying, to classify attitudes toward society having influence in the formation of aspirations and on the image of a future society into three principal categories: indifference, conservatism, progressiveness.

The first category contains attitudes of indifference toward society. It includes three main subtypes of attitudes of indifference toward society. The first is indifference toward society displayed by persons who are interested mainly in themselves, their personal and professional lives, and in persons close to them (friends, relatives). It is a form of withdrawal characteristic of the type of person we shall refer to as the egocentric-adaptive (A). On the other hand, an attitude of indifference can be the result of a radically negative view of society. This is the case, for example, of people who believe society to be irrevocably corrupt and who feel that nothing can be done to change it. To achieve the freedom necessary to pursue personal goals, this type of person feels that withdrawal from society is necessary. The psychological type characterized by the primacy of integration will be the most likely to adopt this attitude of rejection in favor of personal and individual accomplishment. We refer to this type as the fatalist-integrative (I). The third type of attitude is also one of withdrawal, but stemming from a different motivation. In this case, withdrawal from or rejection of society is inspired by some strong religious or quasi-religious ideas and feelings, that is, by very high or "pure" ideals, which put some form of isolated life—individual or collective—above any other part of life regarded as more "normal" by their society. From these persons' point of view, their lives may have an exemplary virtue for other men. This third type might be called the mystical retreatist (L). Finally,

as indifference is the general attitude here, there is no fourth type corresponding to (G).

The second category of attitude consists in accepting society as it is and in believing that it will not and/or should not change substantially in the future. This general attitude can be divided into four subtypes. First, there is the case of those who believe that it is always possible to get some good out of the present situation. This attitude is based on the deep-seated conviction that no change will or can occur and that the future can only be a continuation of a satisfactory present. This is the belief of the conservative-adaptive (A). The second attitude can be referred to as active-conservative (G). It expresses itself through the behavior of those who are actively engaged in the maintenance of the present state of affairs and who are fighting any suggestion of change. In their minds, the status quo is not only a fact, it must also be a policy. The third type of attitude is adopted by the participant-conservatives (I), that is, those who feel well-adjusted, or feel the need to be well-adjusted to the institutions as they are, who enjoy participating in their functioning and evolution, and who feel "at home" in the society as it works. Finally, the ideological-conservative (L) is a believer in the values and ideals implemented in the actual society. Upon seeing imminent or actual change, he would not have it and therefore opposes himself to all sources of such change.

The third category of attitudes toward the existing society contains those attitudes of belief in social changes that are aimed at substantially modifying the existing structure, whether it is through introducing appreciable discontinuities into it or not. Four subtypes can be distinguished.

The first one is the adaptive-reformer (A), which can be exemplified by the industrial entrepreneur, the research people, or those who want to bring changes through innovation in their professional fields. They believe in the impact of new techniques; they are fond of new methods of work and new ways of doing things, such as, the innovation brought by the entrepreneur or the engineer in an underdeveloped society is the type of achievement highly valued by the adaptive-reformer. They believe that involvement in economic activities, in scientific research, or in technological change is the best way to achieve social change.

The second type is the case of the political reformer (G). It is typified by the person who believes that it is necessary or desirable for political powers to intervene in order to bring about social change and who is willing to support and even to participate in political powers engaged in achieving change. The political reformer may be more or less radical, but he generally believes that society requires serious if not radical changes and that all necessary forces must be mobilized to this end.

The institutional reformer (I) exemplifies the third type of attitude by insisting on using influence more than power (in Parsons' terms) to achieve the desired change. It means that a person will work within a specific field of institutions and will have recourse to all possible means that the institutions provide in order to bring forth the objectives that are pursued. This might be the case, for example, of the bureaucrat reformer who is active in using his prestige, as well as others within the structure of his institution, in order to change the institution or to change things through the action of his institution.

Finally, the moral reformer (L) is rather interested in changing the normative foundations of individual and/or social life. It is the type of attitude that is identifiable with the prophet or the fundamentalist. Again, this attitude can be more or less radical, as in the case of the political reformer, ranging from purely individualistic moral reform to a complete

subcultures or of groups within the society as well. In fact, it is probably at this last level that attitudes are most easily seen. It is, at any rate, the level at which they are most meaningful to the sociologist.

If we wish to gain deeper insight into aspirations than we have until now and if we wish to explore new avenues of research, we must distinguish increasingly between subcultures and between the subgroups of attitudes and of aspirations that exist within the populations studied.

We must also make a determined effort to link the individual subjects in our studies to the subgroup(s) to which they belong. Until now, empirical research on youth educational and professional aspirations have generally proceeded on the assumption that there existed a homogeneity of attitudes toward society and toward the future within the populations studied. It is quite likely, however, that attitudes toward the present and the future society constitute an important line of cleavage along which subcultures and subgroups may be distinguished one from

Table 17-1. TYPOLOGY OF ATTITUDES TOWARD SOCIETY AND TYPES OF PERSONALITY ORIENTATION.

CATEGORIES OF GENERAL ATTITUDES TOWARD SOCIETY	TYPES OF SPECIFIC ATTITUDES TOWARD SOCIETY	TYPES OF PSYCHOLOGICAL ORIENTATION
Indifference	Egocentric-adaptive Fatalist-integrative Mystical retreatist	Adaptation Integration Latency Goal-Attainment
Conservatism	Conservative-adaptive Active-conservative Participant-conservative Ideological-conservative	Adaptation Goal-Attainment Integration Latency
Progressiveness	Adaptive-reformer Political-reformer Institutional-reformer Moral-reformer	Adaptation Goal-Attainment Integration Latency

"cultural revolution" for the whole society. This attitude may also be connected with political reform or be completely independent from it, as it is the case in many religious movements.

The typology of attitudes we have described is summarized in Table 17-1. Looking, for example, at the educational and career aspirations of students within the framework indicated in this figure, it is easily seen that career aspirations must vary with attitudes toward society because the image of the future society, being the locus in which and in relation to which these aspirations exist, varies from one category or type to the other.

Finally, it must be noted that this typology describes not only individual attitudes but attitudes of

the other, especially among the youth. These subcultures and subgroups may be of greater significance for research on individual aspirations than it has been assumed in the past.

Aspirations According to Personality Type and Society Type

We come finally to the last step, which consists in bringing together the typology of personality and the typology of society, in order to build a model of the various kinds of aspirations that are to be found when these two dimensions are taken into account at the same time.

The model can be summarized in the four-by-four

table in Figure 17-4. It is based on the postulate of a double primacy: the primacy of one psychological orientation within the personality and the primacy of one of the four functional dimensions within the society.

The table can be read horizontally or vertically. The rows describe the different aspirations that the same type of personality will have in different types of society. The columns tell us how the different types of personality will aspire in a given type of society.

It does not seem necessary to go into a detailed explanation of each cell. As it stands, the model is quite self-explanatory. It may just be said that this model is the outcome of another sort of "double contingency." Aspirations are contingent on both psychological and sociological conditions. They are psychosociological phenomena and must be taken as such in any piece of empirical research that intends to shed more light in this area.

CONCLUSION

One main conclusion stems from our proposed theoretical framework. Empirical studies of aspirations have traditionally been preoccupied with a limited number of explanatory variables that have tended not to differ from study to study. Generally these variables have dealt with past influences like social origin, level of parents' education and significant others, and with variables exerting influence in the present like patterns of interaction between individual and peers, teachers, parents, or guidance councellors.

Undoubtedly these factors do influence and ought to be ignored in future studies of aspirations. However, as Sewell's use of path analysis has demonstrated, these variables provide only a partial explanation of reality.[21] A more complete explanation is desirable.

It seems evident in the light of our analysis that two main groups of variables must be examined in future research. It must be emphasized that these are two groups and not two single variables. The first group consists of those variables having reference to the influence of collective aspirations on individual aspirations. In times of rapid change, a proliferation of collective aspirations expressed in ideologies, social movements, mass conversions, or renewed outbreaks of prophecy are observed. It is difficult to believe that this kind of ideological ferment has no serious impact on aspirations.

The second group of variables—not unrelated to the first—has to do with the image of the future society. For a social actor, an aspiration is the projection of the self and of the self's actions into a more or less distant future. Here again it is difficult, from our theoretical perspective, to imagine that this projection of self can be made without the support of an imaginary future social environment. This image of

Society

	A	G	I	L
A	Aspiration to achieve personal economic success	Aspiration to use economic needs for the purpose of the collective goals of the society	Aspiration to use economic goods to maintain the community ties	Aspiration to use economic goods to promote ideals and values
G	Aspiration to get economic power in order to share in the decision-making process	Aspiration to have a say in the definition of the collective goals of the society	Aspiration to bring support to those who have authority and are responsible for the maintenance of solidarity	Aspiration to mobilize all resources for the triumph or the maintenance of given values
I	Aspiration to order and stability through normative controls	Aspiration to maintain an ordered pattern of change	Aspiration to share in the controls to maintain the solidarity among institutions	Aspiration to see the values implemented in the concrete structure of the institutions
L	Aspiration to maintain or increase the "purity" of the motivation to follow patterns	Aspiration to maintain or enhance humanistic or spiritual purposes of collective goals	Aspiration to protect the established values against external threat and change	Aspiration to share in the transmission of established values

(left axis label: *Personality*)

Figure 17-4.   Aspirations according to personality type and society type.

the future can of course be more or less explicit and even more or less conscious depending on the individual. The actor who is engaged in political action or in a social movement will have a much clearer image of the desired society than will another who has only slight awareness of his total environment. But such an image exists even for the person who is unable to make explicit his image of the desired society. It may be unclear and more or less incoherent, but it is sufficient to influence the orientation of his individual aspirations.

That these two groups of variables have been neglected may be attributed to the culture-boundness of the very large majority of psychosociological research on aspirations. It is mostly in societies where the economy subsystem was predominant that research on aspirations has taken place. Most research on aspirations was also done before the emergence of an active anti-establishment youth culture. In industrial and advanced societies of that type, aspirations are polarized by economic achievement as the dominant model of achievement and by the emphasis on personal success through specific performance. It is not surprising therefore that the possible influence of political ideologies on youth aspirations has not been investigated.

In societies, groups, or subcultures, where polity or societal community are more predominant than economy, aspirations should theoretically have closer ties with political and social ideologies, because they get from the latter part of their inspiration and content. It is in cases of this sort that we should be able to test the relationships between individual aspirations and collective aspirations.

Until now, it has been taken for granted that there was practically no relationship between individual aspirations and political ideologies, because of the type of society where research was being conducted. But recent studies on youth culture in the more advanced countries, as well as on the aspirations of youth in developing countries, show that the links between individual aspirations and collective ideologies should be investigated more carefully than they have been in the past.[22] Thus, the degree of social consciousness and of social commitment, as well as the orientation of the commitment, should be tested as being possibly new explanatory factors in studies of school performance, dropping out, educational aspirations, and vocational choices.

This falls in line with the symbolic character of aspirations that we have emphasized. In translating present needs into symbolic forms through plans and goals for the future, the process of aspiration-building acts as a kind of language. The symbols and images to be found in ideologies or utopias can easily be translated into individual aspirations, or at least feed them. In highly politicized societies or groups, and in societies with strong collective goals like political and economic independence or revolutionary change, even such an economic decision as career choice can follow the inspiration of a political ideology.

Put in broader terms, the main purpose of this essay was to relativize the studies on youth aspirations by putting them in the light of the largest possible scheme of the general theory of action. In that perspective, we have emphasized that aspirations should be regarded as functions first of the personality type, second of the subcollectivity within the society to which the actor belongs or takes as reference group, and third the type of society, depending on which one of the four subsystems has primacy.[23]

Our purpose has been to open new vistas for research and to point out new research areas, in order to broaden our knowledge of the complex phenomenon of aspirations. The extent to which the research problems we have identified can be translated into operational proposals and used in empirical research remains to be seen.

NOTES

1. Our intention here is not to give a complete listing of research projects on aspirations. We will indicate only a few of the important and most recent titles of books and articles: James A. Davis, *Great Aspirations: The Graduate School Plans of America's College Seniors* (Chicago: NORC, Aldine Publishing Co., 1964); G. H. Elden, *Adolescent Achievement and Mobility Aspirations* (Chapel Hill, N.C.: Institute for Research in Social Science, 1962); Joseph A. Kahl, "Educational and Occupational Aspirations of 'Common Man' Boys," *Harvard Educational Review,* 23 (Summer 1953), pp. 186-203; I. Krouss, "Sources of Educational Aspirations among Working Class Youth," *American Sociological Review,* 29 (December 1964), pp. 867-879; M. L. Kohn, *Class and Conformity: A Study in Values* (Homewood, Ill.: The Dorsey Press, 1969); W. H. Sewell, A. O. Haller and M. A. Strauss, "Social Status and Educational and Occupational Aspirations," *American Sociological Review,* 22 (February 1957), pp. 67-73; W. H. Sewell and V. P. Shah, "Social Class, Parental Encouragement and Educational Aspirations," *American Journal of Sociology,* 73 (March 1968), pp. 559-572; Ralph H. Turner, *The Social Context of Ambition* (San Francisco: Chandler, 1964).

Few similar studies of social aspirations are to be found in France. The works of Chombart de Lauwe are a notable exception. See in particular, his *La vie quotidienne des familles ouvrières* (Paris: Centre national de la recherche scientifique, 1956).

2. Paul-Henry Chombart de Lauwe, "Convergences et controverse sur la genese des besoins," *Cahiers Internationaux de Sociologie,* XLVIII (1970), p. 32.

3. These essays are collected in: *Pour une sociologie des aspirations* (Paris: Editions Denoel, 1969).

4. Particularly in *La vie quotidienne des familles ouvrières* and in *Famille et Habitation,* 2 volumes (Paris: Centre national de la recherche scientifique, 1959 and 1960).

5. Maurice Halbwachs, *L'évolution des besoins dans les classes ouvrières* (Paris: Alcan, 1933).

6. "Convergences et controverse sur la genèse des besoins," *op. cit.,* p. 32.

7. *Ibid.,* p. 29.

8. *Ibid.,* p. 32.

9. Chombart de Lauwe, *Pour une sociologie des aspirations,* in particular, p. 24.

10. Alain Touraine, "Le Systeme d'action," *Sociologie et sociétés;* I (November 1969), pp. 221-247.

11. To simplify we make particular reference to Parsons' treatment of this paradigm in: *Working Papers in the Theory of Action* (with Robert F. Bales and Edward A. Shils) (New York: The Free Press, 1953), Chs. III and V; *Economy and Society* (with Neil J. Smelser) (New York: The Free Press, 1956), Chs. I and II; and *Societies: Evolutionary and Comparative Perspectives* (Englewood Cliffs, N. J.: Prentice-Hall, Inc., 1966), Ch. II.

12. Talcott Parsons, "An Approach to Psychological Theory in Terms of the Theory of Action," in Sigmund Koch (ed.), *Psychology: A Study of A Science* (New York: McGraw-Hill, 1959), Volume 3, pp. 612-711.

13. Morris Rosenberg, *Occupations and Values* (New York: The Free Press, 1957).

14. Edward and Lorna R. Harvey, "Adolescence, Social Class, and Occupational Expectations." *The Canadian Review of Sociology and Anthropology,* 7 (May 1970), pp. 138-147.

15. Chad Gordon, "Systemic Senses of Self," *Sociological Inquiry,* 38 (Spring 1968), p. 163.

16. *Ibid.,* p. 176.

17. Morris Rosenberg, *Society and the Adolescent Self-Image* (Princeton: Princeton University Press, 1965), especially Ch. 12.

18. J. W. Atkinson, "Motivational Determinants of Risk-Taking Behavior," *Psychological Review,* 64 (1957), pp. 359-372.

19. Rainer C. Baum, "Values and Democracy in Imperial Germany," *Sociological Inquiry,* 38 (Spring 1968), p. 180.

20. *Ibid.,* p. 181.

21. See in particular William H. Sewell and Vimal P. Shah, "Socioeconomic Status, Intelligence, and the Attainment of Higher Education," *Sociology of Education,* 40 (Winter 1967), pp. 1-23; William H. Sewell and Vimal P. Shah, "Social Class, Parental Encouragement and Educational Aspirations," *The American Journal of Sociology,* 73 (March 1968), pp. 559-572.

22. For instance, Kenneth Keniston, *The Uncommitted: Alienated Youth in American Society* (New York: Dell Publishing Co., Inc., 1960); Vera Rubin and Marisa Zavalloni, *We Wish to be Looked Upon: A Study of the Aspiration of Youth in a Developing Country* (New York: Teachers College Press, Columbia University, 1969).

23. After this article was written I read Paul-Henry Chombart de Lauwe (ed.), *Aspirations et transformations sociales* (Paris: Anthropos, 1970). Some contributions to this book come close to the general position taken here, especially Zdenee Strmiska. "Aspirations et orientations de valeur," pp. 97-128.

18

INADEQUACY, INSTRUMENTAL ACTIVISM, AND THE ADOLESCENT SUBCULTURE

Jackson Toby

The problem of insecurity is a commonplace. Every college freshman has at least a vague understanding of the Freudian notion that a stable relationship with a maternal figure is necessary for the personality development of the child. The problem of inadequacy is less well understood. Parsons clarified the implications for nonconformity of insecurity and inadequacy in his analysis of deviant motivation.[1] A role player can deviate from institutionalized expectations in either of two ways. He can fail to relate to the complementary role player in the prescribed manner; this is person-focussed deviance. Or he can fail to live up to the impersonal requirements of the norm; this is pattern-focussed deviance. A juvenile delinquent may (1) be hostile toward authority figures or (2) defy or evade societal rules. He can of course be both negativistic toward persons and rebellious toward rules, but these are the analytically distinct directions for deviance to take.

Let us ignore insecurity (on the grounds that the implications of insecurity for person-focussed deviance have been considered at length in the psychiatric and even the sociological literature) and focus on inadequacy. Parsons maintains that the feeling of inadequacy results from an inability on the part of the individual to live up to the normative standards of the expectation system—more specifically, to a belief on the part of the role player that attempts to conform to the pattern will not bring rewards. Either he will not be able to accomplish what he is supposed to accomplish or, if he does, other role players will not give him what he is thereby entitled to. Thus, Parsons links the motivation for pattern-focussed deviance to doubts about the worthwhileness of attempting to live up to social expectations. However, these feelings of inadequacy are often denied in an achievement-oriented society because normal socialization persuades modern man that he ought to accomplish great things, if at all possible. He wants to conform

to expectations by achieving, although he also needs to express his feeling of inadequacy by violating such expectations. In short, he is ambivalent, and his ambivalence produces compulsive motivation: either a tendency toward perfectionistic enforcement of the pattern on himself or others or a tendency toward its defiance or evasion. These tendencies are violently contradictory. But they spring from a similar mix of ambivalent motives. The tendency for perfectionistic enforcement arises from a marginal victory of the achievement motive over the motive to disregard expectations for achievement. The tendency for defiance-evasion arises from a marginal victory of the motivation for nonconformity over the motivation for achievement. It is the marginality of the victory in both cases that generates the compulsive tendency. Its compulsive character is also a clue to its instability. Despite outward appearances, Parsons would argue, the hippie and the hard-driving business executive are brothers under the skin. A small shift in motivational forces can change one into the other.

Parsons is concerned in this analysis mainly with deviant *motivation* rather than with deviant *behavior*. He says explicitly that whether or not the individual translates his deviant tendencies into deviant behavior—becomes a hippie or a hard-driving business executive—depends not only on the motivational mix within his personality but also on the social situation impinging on him, that is, on social controls. Parsons is less interested in manifestly different outward behavior than in motivational structures which he regards as fundamentally similar. Thus, Parsons approaches deviance in the sociological tradition that finds the motivation of deviant behavior in sources similar to those of conforming behavior, one source being achievement norms.

A critical question is: Why do achievement norms generate deeper feelings of inadequacy in some persons than in others? According to Parsons, feelings of inadequacy are inherent in role learning because roles require performances on the part of the social-izee, and performances are inevitably evaluated, first by the socializing agent and other members of the interactive system but ultimately by the social-izee himself. The evaluation of performance is most obvious when the role to be learned is entered upon through the competitive evaluation of performance or capacity to perform, as occupational roles are in contemporary societies. But even ascribed roles— sex and age roles, for example—involve living up to expectations of behavior, and therefore ascribed roles also are subject to judgments of adequacy of performance. To take an obvious example from American society, men are evaluated in terms of their masculinity; those who are judged effeminate by others and who internalize this social evaluation suffer serious psychic distress. But why do achieve-ment norms generate deeper feelings of inadequacy in some persons that in others? An obvious possibi-lity is differential socialization in the family of orien-tation. Indeed, research has shown idiosyncratic variation from family to family in the internalization of achievement norms and also systematic variation by social class and ethnic group.[2] A further factor is differential socialization in contexts occurring after childhood. Modern society does not merely capitalize on personality needs for achievement established in early childhood. It also reinforces and expands these needs by holding up a high stan-dard of performance as the main criterion of initial selection for many roles as well as a major basis for rewarding competence.

These variations in the need to perform well in a role are attributable to personality variations among societal members. It goes without saying that cultural values such as the Protestant Ethic indirectly con-tribute to such personality variations through social-ization experiences. But cultural values also produce feelings of inadequacy more directly: by an ideological emphasis in role definitions on invidious compari-sons among incumbents or potential incumbents. Thus, a teacher is implicitly (and sometimes explicitly) compared with other teachers. Is he below average in ability to stimulate his students? Is he the best teacher in the school? In the concept of the "achieved role" sociologists mirror the ideological desirability in modern societies of recruiting on the basis of competitive performance rather than ascription. An achieved role, by definition, is one in which per-formance or performance capacity is the main basis for allocation of the individual to the role. It is in-herently possible to define a role, such as that of teacher, so that training for performance occurs after allocation into the role, rather than selecting the best performers in advance. Instead of selecting

persons for the role of teacher who have above-average teaching ability, persons could be selected on other criteria and brought up to the performance norm through training. It can be argued that training cannot produce the requisite level of competence because of a scarcity of innate ability and that selection on the basis of past achievement is a social necessity. It seems more plausible that the preference for role selection on the basis of past achievement is ideo-logical in most cases and that some form of ascription is compatible with efficient social organization.[3]

Parsons alludes to the ideological stress on achieve-ment in Western industrial societies when he points out that "instrumental activism" is a central value[4], a conception of the desirable. He defines this value in terms of the individual's obligation to commit himself to accomplishment in those roles considered important in the society.[5] Thus, instrumental activ-ism impelled many nineteenth-century Americans toward business careers because economic produc-tivity was a major goal in that era. Quite consistently, Parsons argues that the internalization of instrumen-tal activism within the personalities of young people requires a lengthy socialization process; this process continues not only through adolescence but through a "studentry" phase of college and graduate school.[6] Because it involves training for high levels of com-petence, it inevitably arouses fears about incompe-tence. To put the same point in another way, Parsons is suggesting that one side of the coin is the inter-nalization of the Protestant Ethic and the other side is anxiety over adequacy. The same educational revolution that is pushing half of American high school graduates into higher education—and thereby upgrading the educational level of the future labor force—is increasing the number of hurdles students must jump.[7] The process of continuous evaluation that accompanies formal education has implications for the identity of the student.[8]

Parsons is aware that commitment to the value of instrumental activism varies within a population cohort. He suggests that a crude dichotomy exists between members of the cohort sufficiently commit-ted to instrumental activism to go on to college and those whose lesser commitment is reflected in the termination of their education with high school graduation or less. As with all operational defini-tions, this one classifies many cases incorrectly. Some college students are less committed to instru-mental activism than some terminal high school students. Parsons' assumption, however, is that the two groups can be crudely differentiated in terms of value commitments and capacities for achievement.[9] He also suggests that the peer group may reinforce the achievement orientation in youngsters with good academic potentialities but low-status family backgrounds—and discourage college aspirations in youngsters with poor academic abilities but high-status family backgrounds. Both groups need peer reinforcement because they are subject to cross-pressures, which give rise to ambivalence about academic achievement. This ambivalence may appear to the observer to be indifference or even alienation, but Parsons believes that the cross-pressured adolescent cannot be indifferent to academic achievement because achievement in one case or failure in the other disrupts the continuity of status between parents and offspring. Peer-group support helps resolve the identity crisis. In Parsons' analysis, only the academically marginal children of working-class parents can be genuinely indifferent to academic achievement—and only if the values of their peer group are congruent with this attitude. As will be seen in a later section of this paper, Parsons' concept of ambivalence toward achievement enables him to account for the seemingly anti-intellectual character of American youth culture without conceding that the appearance of indifference toward academic achievement should be taken at face value.

Musgrove, on the basis of data from the British educational system, concludes, as Parsons does, that youngsters not preparing for higher education have fewer inner conflicts over education and are on the whole happier in school than "grammar school" youngsters preparing for the university system.[10] Musgrove tries to explain what he regarded as a paradox: that there is greater subjective unhappiness and tension among youngsters in the objectively better schools—schools that promise those who pass through them a relatively high social status in British society.

> The grammar school and the technical college, which make extreme demands upon their pupils and emphasize their dependence and protracted exclusion from full involvement in adult affairs, may induce a deeper sense of conflict than the [secondary] modern school, with its more moderate demands and more intimate relationship, particularly for the 14- and 15-year-olds, with the adult world.[11]

Musgrove was speculating, admittedly. The point is not the correctness of his explanation but the similarity in the incidence of tensions in the British and American educational systems.

Feelings of inadequacy concerning academic achievement are predictable on the basis of Parsons' analysis, but so are reactions against them, collective defenses against the threat to self-worth. What are the consequences of this situation for social organization? Parsons has long considered the youth culture an integrative mechanism for the contemporary adolescent, a means of easing the strain of the transition from the particularism of the family of orientation to the universalism of the modern labor market. But the youth culture performs this support function largely for adolescents destined for occupations involving high levels of technical competence or responsibility, namely, middle-class occupations. Those destined for less universalistic occupations—say, inheritor of a family farm or business or a manual laborer from a working-class background—do not undergo such a strainful transition; they are less ambivalent about achievement and less dependent on peer-group support. For high school students who regard their futures as depending on their academic records, it might seem irrational to allow athletic or extracurricular activities to distract them from mobilizing their full intellectual potentialities toward attaining their goals for adulthood. This cold-blooded rationality does not take account of their emotional uncertainties.[12] Some students fear they are not performing well enough to get into college (or into the college of their choice); popularity seems more attainable. Other students, the intellectually able offspring of parents of low socioeconomic status, may be tempted by the occupational opportunities offered by higher education, yet be reluctant to repudiate parental and neighborhood values. Athletic interests enable them to keep a foot in both camps. In short, Parsons suggests that, far from being indifferent to the school's effect on their futures, many high school students are so deeply concerned with the competition that they cannot afford consciously to admit it. Surface preoccupation with sports and popularity in the student culture is necessary to ease the emotional strain. They hedge the bet for these students but are usually recognized as ephemeral forms of achievement.

Unlike Parsons, James Coleman takes the anti-intellectual character of the adolescent subculture at face value.[13] He was disheartened by student responses in ten Midwest high schools to the question, "How would you most like to be remembered in school: as an athletic star, a brilliant student, or most popular?" A majority of boys in all ten of the schools were more interested in being remembered as either athletic or popular than as a brilliant student. This reluctance to opt for intellectual achievement might be attributed to a peculiarity of question wording. Perhaps the word brilliant evokes the image of a solitary drudge, an oddball. Coleman's explanation of the response pattern, though much more sophisticated than this, is compatible with an interpretation of the brilliant student as antisocial. Coleman explained the emphasis on athletic values as reflecting the fact that an outstanding athlete represents his school and not himself alone when he plays on a varsity team. "The outstanding student, in contrast, has little or no way to bring glory to his school. His victories are always personal, often at the expense of his classmates, who are forced to work harder to keep up with him."[14] Coleman suggested that it might be possible to promote greater intellectual interests within the adolescent subculture by establishing interschool competition in academic matters and downgrading interschool athletic contests.[15] The brilliant student would thereby contribute to the glory of his school and make it possible for even unsuccessful students to identify with academic achievement. As far as I know, Coleman never pursued this speculation to the point of gathering systematic data. If Parsons is correct, such research would reveal little change in the values of the adolescent subculture because the character of the adolescent subculture does not derive primarily from the peculiarities of interschool athletic and academic competiton.

Coleman entitled his book *The Adolescent Society,* whereas Parsons speaks of the adolescent subculture. The issue is not mere terminology; it is the extent to which adolescence is functionally autonomous of the larger society or has to be understood as a subsystem of an achievement-oriented adult society, although more vulnerable to the strains of such an orientation. From the subsystem point of view, let us reanalyze the data from the ten schools studied by Coleman. Among the ten schools studied, the one in Executive Heights contained students who ought to have been the most oriented to intellectual interests. More than 70% of both boys and girls in the Executive Heights school intended to go to college, about twice the proportion in the nine other schools. So did virtually all the members of the "leading crowd." The field observer in the Coleman study described the value climate of Executive Heights in the following terms.

> There is too much pressure toward getting Executive Heights graduates into outstanding colleges. It is complained that the only thing that counts is grades, and that this has an adverse effect on the students, making them feel tempted to cheat at times—which is easy to do because of the quasi-honor system—and not really interested in knowledge for its own sake.[16]

The fathers of students in Executive Heights were largely high-income professionals and business executives, about 60% of whom had attended college. In eight of the other nine schools, less than 30% of the fathers had attended college and in Maple Grove slightly more than 30%. Thirty-one per cent of the students in Executive Heights were Jewish, and Jewish students were overrepresented in the leading crowd; none of the other schools approached this portion of Jews. In view of the importance of education in the Jewish cultural tradition, Coleman expected that the ethnic mix would reinforce other social factors making for an intellectual emphasis to the adolescent subculture. Despite the backgrounds and college intentions of students in Executive Heights,

students in this school were the least eager of all the students surveyed to wish to be remembered as a "brilliant student" (only 25% of the boys and 15% of the girls). Furthermore, members of the leading crowd at Executive Heights, although nearly all of them planned on going to college, were even less willing than their fellows to wish to be remembered as brilliant students.

Coleman had data on the college intentions of each student. He did not analyze his cases on the relationship between college intention and the tendency to want to be remembered as a brilliant student, but it seems reasonable to extrapolate from the attitudes expressed by the Executive Heights population that the relationship was negative: students planning to go to college were less likely to wish to be remembered as brilliant than students *not* planning to attend. How can this paradoxical finding be interpreted? Parsons' explanation, offered curiously enough in the same issue of the *Harvard Educational Review* in which Coleman published the first report on his study, was that indifference to school work, far from representing alienation from intellectual values, stems from the realization on the part of youngsters that their academic performance has implications for college attendance and ultimately for occupational opportunities.[17] In short, some students react to the threatening possibility of failure in academic competition by inflating their interest in consolation prizes. From an instrumental point of view, athletic or extracurricular activities may distract students from maximum academic effort, but such activities serve to stave off the anxiety of striving for an important goal in which success cannot be counted on.

This interpretation explains why among the ten schools the students from Executive Heights are least willing to want to be remembered as brilliant students. The stakes are higher for them than for students in communities where college attendance is not the general expectation or for students who don't intend to go to college anyway. It also accounts for a finding that puzzled Coleman and for which he gave an ad hoc explanation. He found that both boys and girls reported somewhat more frequently that their parents would be "very proud" of their athletic or extracurricular achievements than reported the same expectation about their academic achievements. In fact, three-quarters of the boys' parents preferred their sons to be "brilliant students" over being an "athletic star" (10%) or "most popular" (15%) and 55% of the girls' parents preferred their daughters to be "brilliant students" over being a "leader in activities" (35%) or "most popular" (10%). Coleman was troubled by the discrepancy between students' perception of parent values and actual parent responses and raised the question of honesty of response on the questionnaries. He finally decided that no one was lying but that the parents were expressing on the questionnaire their ideals but conveying to their children their operating values.

Are the parents' professed values and expressed values as greatly at variance as they seem—or do boys and girls see their parents' values as they want to see them? Perhaps neither is the case. It may be that most parents hold academic achievement as an ideal for their children in school, as their responses indicate. But parents also want their children to be successful in the things that "count" in the school, that is, the things that count in the eyes of the other adolescents. And parents know what things count. Being a biology assistant counts far less in the adolescent culture than does making the basketball team for boys, or making the cheerleading squad for girls.[18]

There is, it seems to me, a more convincing explanation. Parsons would hold that the achievement-oriented students misperceive their parents' values for precisely the same reason that they misperceive their own, namely, the anxiety aroused by staking everything on academic success. Athletics and extracurricular activities serve as an emotional hedge. This implies that students more committed to academic success (such as those in Executive Heights) would be more likely to misperceive their parents' values, a hypothesis testable by reanalysis of the Coleman data.

Coleman reported another anomaly in his data. He found[19] that having high grades was regarded by girls in all ten schools as more likely to win popularity with other girls than with boys. But the perceived differences in contribution to popularity of "high grades, honor roll" for girls and for boys was greater in the middle-class schools. This seemed surprising:

Why do the girls in the more middle-class schools feel that boys care nothing for their grades? The boys are themselves interested in grades, for many will need them for college entrance; one would suppose that they, far more than the boys from working-class backgrounds, would put a premium on a girl's scholastic achievement.[20]

Coleman tried to explain the puzzle by suggesting "greater role differentiation in the working-class milieu with respect to academic work." That is, he suggested that academic achievement is regarded as a female specialty in working-class schools, although he did not explain why greater role differentiation should occur in the working-class milieu. An explanation derived from Parsons' notion of ambivalence toward academic achievement helps clarify what is going on. Girls in all ten schools consider grades more prestigeful with other girls than with boys because their experience teaches them that some boys feel threatened by female academic competence. Why should they feel threatened? Because academic achievement has been culturally defined as a prerequisite to college entrance and ultimately to occupational success. Indeed, for many boys of middle-class origins academic achievement is a necessary component of male identity. The more inadequate the boy feels about his ability to compete academically and the more he regards such competence as symbolic of male competence, the likelier it is that he prefers to date girls with weak academic accomplishments.

I would like to suggest a theoretical model that embodies the assumptions made by Parsons, accounts for the findings of Coleman, and also predicts relationships not presently known to exist:

1. High school boys and girls prefer as friends youngsters with a similar orientation to academic achievement as they themselves have. If sociocentrism is defined as "the tendency to prefer members of one's own group or category for a social role even though such membership is functionally irrelevant to the performance of the obligations of the role,"[21] high school students are sociocentric with respect to academic performance. This means:

a. College-prep boys associate mainly with college-prep boys.
b. College-prep boys date mainly college-prep girls.
c. Boys not planning for college associate mainly with other boys not planning for college.
d. Boys not planning for college date mainly girls not planning for college.
e. College-prep girls associate mainly with college-prep girls.
f. College-prep girls date mainly college-prep boys.
g. Girls not planning for college associate mainly with other girls not planning for college.
h. Girls not planning for college date mainly boys not planning for college.

2. Certain categories of boys and girls are less sociocentric in their associations with members of the opposite sex than with members of the same sex. Specifically:

a. College-prep boys, although they are much more likely to date college-prep girls than are boys not going to college, are more likely to date girls not planning for college than they are to associate with boys not planning for college.
b. Girls not planning for college, although they are much more likely to date boys not planning for college than are college-prep girls, are more likely to date college-prep boys than they are to associate with college-prep girls.

Assumptions 2(a) and 2(b) complement each other in producing girls and boys who are less sociocentric than their classmates and who thereby become available to date one another. However, their motivations are different. The college-prep boys dating the noncollege girls are the less secure college-prep boys who are avoiding a threat to their masculine identities. The girls not planning for college dating college-prep boys are the more secure noncollege girls who are status-conscious enough to be willing to date high-prestige boys from an unfamiliar milieu. These ten assumptions are compatible with Coleman's data. The greater the proportion of middle-class youngsters in the school, the greater the proportion of students enrolled in the college-prep course. Under these conditions, "high grades, honor roll" will have a higher rank order of popularity with both boys and girls than in schools with a small percentage of middle-class students. Note that the rank order of popularity of academically competent boys with girls is likely to be higher than the rank order of such boys with boys and that this discrepancy will be greater the greater the proportion of working-class youngsters in the school. The reason for this reversal lies in the characteristics of the youngsters who are less sociocentric: the college-prep boys and the noncollege girls in their dating behavior.

Support for Parsons' explanation comes from another study of adolescents, this one of high school students in New York State that used an interesting variation of the Coleman question about preferred way of being remembered: "If you could be remembered here at school for one of six things below, which one would you like it to be?"

1. For being a good student
2. For being a good athlete
3. For being popular
4. For being a good student and popular
5. For being a good student and a good athlete
6. For being a good athlete and popular [22]

Note that the six alternatives gave respondents an opportunity to express an interest in academic suc-cess without forcing them to make it too exclusive an interest. Respondents could choose "a good student and popular" or "a good student and a good athlete" rather than "a good athlete and popular." If the adolescent subculture were actually as anti-intellectual as Coleman assumes, respondents would prefer "a good athlete and popular" over the other five. As Table 18-1 shows, this was not the case. Even among athletes not planning to go to college, 65% of the male and 82% of the female respondents chose an alternative including "good student"; as might be expected, somewhat more of them (78% of the male respondents) chose an alternative including "good athlete." However, among the male athletes planning on college, the percentage choosing an alternative including "good student" rose to 93% whereas only 80% chose an alternative including "good athlete." Among the male nonathletes — going to college or not — more than three-quarters chose an alternative including "good student" but only a third an alternative including "good athlete."

In short, these data suggest that the adolescent subculture is not fundamentally anti-intellectual. The culture has a double focus: on the future as represented by successful academic work and on current achievement in peer-group activities as represented by popularity and athletic prowess. Many students don't want to choose between the present and the future; they want the best of both worlds. If forced to choose by the format of the question, a majority may select one or another of the items reflecting the more fleeting peer-group value. This does not necessarily mean that they are more concerned with status in the peer group now than with status in adult society later. In fact, the distribution of responses suggests the opposite: that those most

Table 18-1. RESPONSES OF HIGH SCHOOL FRESHMEN TO QUESTION ON HOW THEY WOULD LIKE TO BE REMEMBERED* (per cent)

PREFER TO BE REMEMBERED AS:	SCHOLAR-ATHLETES		SCHOLAR-NONATHLETES		NONSCHOLAR-ATHLETES		NONSCHOLAR-NONATHLETES	
	Male	*Female*	*Male*	*Female*	*Male*	*Female*	*Male*	*Female*
Good Student	4.8	2.7	24.1	15.9	4.0	12.5	27.9	20.8
Good Athlete	4.8	0.0	2.2	0.5	7.5	3.5	6.7	1.1
Popular	0.6	0.0	4.7	2.5	5.1	5.0	10.2	9.6
Good Student and Athlete	62.8	32.0	28.0	7.1	47.0	21.2	20.5	5.4
Good student and Popular	14.9	61.3	36.2	72.1	12.6	48.7	27.6	61.0
Good Athlete and Popular	12.1	4.0	4.7	1.9	23.7	10.0	7.1	2.1
N	355	75	232	365	253	80	283	534

*Respondents were categorized as scholars or nonscholars on the basis of expressed plans for further education and as athletes or nonathletes on the basis of self-reported participation in interscholastic competition.
Source: Unpublished data from adolescent research being conducted by Richard A. Rehberg and analyzed independently by Harry Cotugno.

concerned with adult status (as reflected in their commitment to college attendance) are likely to hedge their bet by asserting a preference to be remembered also as an athlete or as popular. Interestingly enough, the double focus continues in college. Although some college students make a single-minded commitment to good times, drinking, and campus fun and other students to a purely intellectual life style, recent research shows a considerable constituency for "a balanced life style that combines a serious commitment to academic pursuits with an active involvement in the social and extracurricular realm of college."[23] Thus, almost a third of the students at the University of Oregon Honors College were also members of social fraternities. These "collegiate scholars" emphasized well-roundedness and training for elite career goals[24]; they did not feel forced to choose between social and academic values.

Parsons' notion that feelings of inadequacy are chronic in a society committed to instrumental activism can be explored further by examining various kinds of countercultures. Thus, the delinquent subculture has been considered a collective solution to the status problems of working-class adolescent boys.[25] Like the adolescent subculture, the delinquent subculture is a reaction to feelings of inadequacy aroused by emphasis on achievement, especially academic achievement. The difference between the adolescent subculture and the delinquent subculture is that the adolescent subculture does not repudiate adult society; it maintains its double focus except for minorities on the fringes. The delinquent subculture, on the other hand, breaks more radically with the educational and occupational values of urban industrial society.[26] Criminologists are in disagreement as to the degree of irrevocability of the break; one theory holds that delinquents rationalize their own misdeeds without repudiating the norms embodied in the criminal law.[27] But there is little doubt that members of a delinquent gang feel themselves more separated from conventional society than do high school athletes who don't wish to be remembered as brilliant students. Degree of estrangement (and of extrusion) is important because it influences the probability of reentry into conventional culture. The more radical the break, the less likely the return. To put it another way, it is harder to rehabilitate delinquents than it is to induce members of the adolescent subculture to attend college or to take a job.

Both the adolescent and the delinquent subcultures respond to the possibility of status degradation by emphasizing athletics and popularity or masculine toughness and daring as alternative forms of achievement. Other subcultures respond by retreating from achievement in any form and substituting quite different goals. The hippies, for instance, repudiate competitive achievement and attempt to find fulfillment in the expression of affect and in other forms of spontaneous behavior.[28] The close relationship between the drug scene and the flower-children movement makes sense in these terms. Drugs usually represent passive withdrawal rather than active mastery. Another counterculture, closely related to the hippie movement, is the cult of sexual freedom, both homosexual and heterosexual. Sexual hedonism places enjoyment in the center of life, not achievement.

The New Left, another counterculture in modern society, is very different from the hippies in its reaction to the problem of failure. Whereas the hippies define the material symbols of competitive achievement as not worth striving for, the New Left copes with the possibility of competitive failure by insisting that the competition is rigged by the power elite; success can be attained only by members of the in-group. But the New Left does not repudiate achievement. It merely values the achievement of disrupting an oppressive society instead of operating established institutions. Mark Rudd of the Weatherman faction of Students for a Democratic Society asked his draft board for a deferment on the grounds that he was working in an essential occupation, namely, that of revolutionary. Rudd was probably kidding but only because he knew that the draft board would not accept his evaluation of the importance of disrupting society. Rudd was committed to achieving his revolutionary goals—more committed perhaps than young executives who try to climb up to the presidential suite in the corporation. Parsons attributes the intensity with which radicals are preoccupied with ideological distinctions to an initial ambivalence about achievement and a compulsive commitment to one form of achievement. They must believe and convince others "that the aspects of the established society — such as 'capitalism' — against which they are in revolt, can be defined as illegitimate in terms of a common set of beliefs and values."[29] Parsons means more by this than that the radicals and the establishment types share a commitment to achievement; he is referring also to a shared commitment to freedom and equality. But the tendency on the part of radicals to justify themselves in strident terms is reinforced by the necessity of distinguishing their own activism from that of the ideological enemy. As he remarked in other connections, family quarrels are often more bitter than those of strangers.

The commune movement shares some of the characteristics of the hippies and some of the New Left. Some communes, especially urban communes, are permissive regarding drugs and sexual expression. Other communes, especially rural communes, are imbued with the pioneering spirit; they are building a new way of life in the wilderness. This is certainly an expression of achievement values. However, it is not the value of individual competitive achievement but of collective achievement. Parsons would, I think, regard this type of achievement orientation as different from instrumental activism. Commitment to communal achievement avoids much anxiety about personal inadequacy. However, such anxiety is avoided only as long as differentials of authority and reward are minimized. Equality of material reward is not so difficult to attain, as the kibbutzim of Israel have shown, but equality of prestige is more troublesome.[30] Equality of authority is the most troublesome and resolving conflicts.[31] In short, it is not clear that of all; leadership may be necessary for setting goals communes can embody collective achievement and completely repudiate individual achievement; but they certainly are reducing the emphasis on individual achievement and thereby on problems of personal adequacy.

CONCLUSION

David Riesman has spoken of the "nerve of failure,"[32] by which he means "the ability of a lonely thinker, or other minority-figure, to remain unimpressed by the judgments passed on his views, his personality, his system of values by the dominant authorities of his day." The feeling of inadequacy represents an inability to sustain the nerve of failure. Under what conditions is it less easy to sustain the nerve of failure? According to Parsons, one condition is the value emphasis of the society on instrumental activism, which tends to make men especially sensitive to the comparative adequacy of their performances in social roles. When this happens, individual and collective defenses develop against self-rejection. The individual defenses come to the attention of clinicians. The collective defenses are a factor in subcultural differentiation. Thus the adolescent subculture of the high school, the subculture of the delinquent gang, the hippie subculture, and the radical ideology of the New Left serve to protect their adherents from feelings of personal inadequacy. This is not to make any claim, one way or the other, about the cosmic validity of these subcultures, only on their ability to cope with an endemic psychic strain of industrial societies.

NOTES

1. See T. Parsons, *The Social System* (New York: The Free Press, 1951), pp. 261-264.

2. See Richard A. Rehberg, Judie Sinclair, and Walter E. Schafer, "Adolescent Achievement Behavior, Family Authority Structure, and Parental Socialization Practices," *American Journal of Sociology,* 75 (1970), pp. 1012-1034; Bernard C. Rosen, "Race, Ethnicity, and the Achievement Syndrome," *American Sociological Review,* 24 (1959), pp. 47-60; "Family Structure and Achievement Motivation," *American Sociological Review,* 26 (1961), pp. 574-85; Jackson Toby, "Orientation to Education as a Factor in the School Maladjustment of Lower-Class Children," *Social Forces,* 35 (1957), pp. 259-66; and Ralph H. Turner, "Some Family Determinants of Ambition," *Sociology and Social Research,* 46 (1962), pp. 397-411.

3. See Leon Mayhew, "Ascription in Modern Societies," *Sociological Inquiry,* 38 (Spring 1968), pp. 105-120.

4. See Parsons, *op. cit.,* pp. 182-191.

5. See T. Parsons and Winston White, "The Link Between Character and Society," in S.M. Lipset and Leo Lowenthal (ed.), *Culture and Social Character* (New York: The Free Press, 1961), pp. 89-135, at pp. 98-103.

6. See T. Parsons and Gerald M. Platt, "Age, Social Structure, and Socialization in Higher Education," *Sociology of Education,* 43 (1970), pp. 1-37.

7. See T. Parsons, *The System of Modern Societies* (Englewood Cliffs: Prentice-Hall, 1971), pp. 94-98.

8. See T. Parsons, "The Position of Identity in the General Theory of Action," in Chad Gordon and Kenneth J. Gergen (eds.), *The Self in Social Interaction* (New York: J. Wiley & Sons, 1968), pp. 11-23.

9. See T. Parsons, "The School Class as a Social System: Some of Its Functions in American Society," *Harvard Educational Review,* 29 (Fall 1959), pp. 297-318, at pp. 309-313.

10. See F. Musgrove, *Youth and the Social Order* (Bloomington, Indiana: Indiana University Press, 1964), pp. 106-124.

11. *Ibid.,* p. 121.

12. See Jackson Toby, *Contemporary Society: An Introduction to Sociology,* 2nd ed. (New York: J. Wiley & Sons, 1971), pp. 409-411.

13. See James S. Coleman, *The Adolescent Society: The Social Life of the Teenager and its Impact on Education* (New York: The Free Press, 1961).

14. See James S. Coleman, "The Adolescent Subculture and Academic Achievement," *American Journal of Sociology,* 65 (1960), pp. 337-347 at p. 347.

15. See James S. Coleman, "Academic Achievement and the Structure of Competition," *Harvard Educational Review,* 29 (Fall 1959), pp. 330-351.

16. Coleman, *The Adolescent Society,* p. 67.

17. See T. Parsons, "The School Class as a Social System," *op.cit.,* p. 312. See note 15 for Coleman's article.

18. Coleman, *The Adolescent Society,* p. 34.

19. *Ibid.,* p. 257.

20. *Ibid.,* p. 258.

21. Jackson Toby, "Universalistic and Particularistic Factors in Role Assignment," *American Sociological Review,* 18 (1953), pp. 134-141, at pp. 136-37.

22. See Rehberg *et al., op. cit.*

23. Robert A. Ellis, Robert J. Parelius, and Anne P. Parelius, "The Collegiate Scholar: Education for Elite Status," *Sociology of Education,* 44 (1971), pp. 27-58, at p. 29.

24. *Ibid.,* p. 55.

25. See Albert K. Cohen, *Delinquent Boys: The Culture of the Gang* (New York: The Free Press, 1955).

26. See Parsons, *The Social System,* pp. 305-318.

27. See David Matza, *Delinquency and Drift* (New York: J. Wiley & Sons, 1964).

28. See Jesse R. Pitts, "The Hippies as Contrameritocracy," *Dissent,* 16 (1969), pp. 326-27.

29. Parsons, *The Social System,* p. 355.

30. See Eva Rosenfeld, "Social Stratification in a 'Classless' Society," *American Sociological Review,* 16 (1959), pp. 766-74.

31. Jesse R. Pitts, "On Communes," *Contemporary Sociology,* 2 (July 1973), pp. 351-359.

32. David Riesman, *Individualism Reconsidered and Other Essays* (New York: The Free Press, 1954), p. 379.

19

FAMILY STRUCTURE AND SOCIALIZATION

Terrence S. Turner

INTRODUCTION

The Problem

The idea that the elementary structure of the family and the basic structures of the mind and personality might prove to be homologous, or at least intimately related, has exercised a great attraction for theorists in the social sciences. Much work on kinship and family structure has been motivated by the hope of discovering universal social patterns which would turn out to correspond to the basic structures of the mind or personality. The perennial effort to define the universal features of family structure has been the most common form taken by this interest. Parsons' writings on the incest taboo and family structure and their relationship to socialization and personality structure constitute the most comprehensive and suggestive attempt of this kind.[1]

There is, of course, abundant circumstantial evidence for the belief that a cross-culturally valid definition of the family would at the same time provide a model of the essential structure of the human personality. With few exceptions, the socialization of children is carried out by small, kinship-based groups in all human societies. A considerable body of psychological evidence has accumulated in support of the proposition that socialization, or the formation of the mature personality, consists, at least in its earlier stages, largely of the internalization of the social relations prevailing within the small groups in which primary socialization takes place. The doctrine of the psychic unity of mankind would seem to imply, granted the validity of these general propositions, that the social units in which socialization occurs have certain common structural properties. By the same token, the notion that at the most fundamental level all societies consist of units with identical structural properties leads easily (if not logically) to the

idea that the family, considered as the basic unit of socialization, can be regarded as the "elemental" unit or structural "core" of kinship systems in particular and social organization in general.

The goal of a viable universal definition of the family has, however, turned out to be an ethnographic chimera. With the partial exception of the mother-child bond, none of the role relationships most frequently cited as constituents of the family (i.e., the father-child, same-sexed sibling, cross-sexed sibling, or husband-wife bonds) has been found in cross-cultural perspective to have an invariant functional content or structural significance as components of family organization. Again with the exception of the mother-child dyad (and of course the sibling relationship between children while they are still members of the mother-child group), the role-composition of the domestic unit that serves as the effective socialization grouping seems to be flexible. Adult male roles are notoriously variable in this respect. In some societies, the husband/father is the exclusive adult male member of the domestic family; in others, there may in effect be no husband, the father may not be a resident member of the family, and the maternal uncle may play a prominent jural and domestic role. Beyond the level of the mother-child group, in other words, neither the specific role-composition of the family nor the functional content of the roles most frequently included in it seem to be constant in cross-cultural terms.[2]

Another obstacle to the notion of the family as a universal social unit is represented by the existence of societies in which the mother-child dyad is submerged within a much larger grouping, such as a lineage or extended family household, so that the "family," defined as a clearly bounded group focused around the socialization of a set of children who share at least one parent in common, and including only primary or at most secondary relations of those children, does not exist as an independent or distinctly bounded social unit.[3]

Cases such as these show that the attempt to identify the universal sociological concomitants

I am indebted to Professor David M. Schneider for his critical comments on an earlier draft of this paper.

of socialization, if such there be, in terms of a structurally and functionally uniform pattern of role differentiation in the primary socialization group is misconceived. Another unexplored alternative, however, remains open. This is the proposition that the locus of universal structural properties at both the psychological and sociological levels lies in the generic characteristics of the generative mechanisms that underlie the wide variety of empirically observed personality and family structures. The direct manifestations of these generative mechanisms should, in this view, be sought, not in the specific forms or "surface" structures of family roles or personality patterns, but in the organization of the processes of psychological and social (re-)production (e.g., the socialization process and the developmental cycles of the family and domestic group) by which those structures are produced.

It is this generative approach that I propose to explore in this essay. I shall seek, first, to develop a model of the general structural properties of the generative mechanisms that regulate the basic productive or reproductive processes at the personality and family levels. Second, I shall attempt to suggest the implications of this model for the nature of the relationship between socialization and personality structure, on the one hand, and family and domestic group structure, on the other.

A basic postulate of the generative approach as I have outlined it is that the fundamental generative mechanisms themselves are simultaneously abstract and concrete in character. They consist, on the one hand, of a set of symbolic categories and the formal principles by which they are ordered into systems and, on the other hand, of the practical social relations required to create, dissolve, and recreate the basic groupings on which both the social order itself and the process of socialization depend. The generative hypothesis presupposes no causal priority of either the symbolic or the concrete social aspect over the other: it rather assumes a reciprocal relation of interdependence between the symbolic and pragmatic aspects, which manifests itself in a structural correspondence of a certain kind between the two levels. The generative mechanism itself, in this view, is the focus of the relationship between the social and symbolic orders, because it must, to fulfill its practical functions, comprise a set of formal rules and symbolic categories capable of specifying the operations to be performed and, by the same token, correspond to a pattern of concrete social operations: the relations, as it were, of social and psychological production. This pattern of concrete social relations must in turn be closely adapted to the practical conditions of social reality in order to be effective. The productive function thus provides the structural focus for the correspondence between the formal structure of the symbolic order and the practical organization of the social order.

What, then, might constitute the practical functional aspect of such an elementary generative mechanism of family relations? All societies transform children into adults with sexually and generationally distinct role attributes. Of primary importance among these adult status and role attributes are the roles mature men and women play in the biological, psychological, and sociological propagation of the next generation of children. This set of adult roles, considered as a cultural pattern, is necessarily related to the roles and statuses ascribed by the culture to children by a set of regular transformational rules. The accomplishment of the transformations specified by these rules is, at the psychological level, more or less equivalent to the formation of the mature personality. At the level of the individual as social actor, it corresponds to the transition from the "family of orientation" to the "family of procreation" (employing these terms in a deliberately vague and provisional sense). Finally, at the level of the minimal social groups or subgroups which form the immediate context for these individual transitions, it corresponds to the developmental cycle of the group itself, i.e., of the family and domestic group, or the bigenerational subsegment of those groups that is renewed in each social generation.

This way of approaching the problem of the "universal structure of the family" has certain obvious differences from approaches of the usual kind, represented by the various formulations of the "nuclear family" hypothesis, which depend upon identifying a specific pattern of role structure as the locus of the universal structural and functional properties of family organization. It should be clear that focussing on the general structural properties of the generative mechanisms or social processes by which all family structures (whatever their specific role structures may be) are produced no more commits one to a specific role-model of the family than a similar interest in linguistics could commit the theorist to a particular phrase-structural model of the sentence. Our working hypothesis is not that the minimal bigenerational role complex to which we have referred necessarily corresponds to the role structure of the "family," as that group is defined in various societies ("families" may take extended forms which include more than two generations): it is rather that any family form must, at a minimum, include such a bigenerational pattern as its means of dispersion and renewal in each generation.

Another major point of difference is that the locus of this bigenerational transformational role complex is the passage between the families or domestic units of orientation and procreation, rather than the structure of a single family or domestic group *per se*. There must exist a formal correspondence between the interfamilial and intrafamilial levels of family structure, but the difference of levels has, as we shall see, important consequences for the nature of the dimensions and structural relations involved at each level. Here it need only be noted that the bigenerational transformational complex represents a higher level of the organization of family or domestic group relations than any pattern of roles within a single group, because it by definition establishes a connection between pairs of such groups (or subgroupings within more inclusive groups) on the basis of structural principles common to both.

What I am suggesting is that such a bigenerational, interfamily, transformational role-complex forms the basic generative mechanism of the developmental cycle of the family and the domestic group in all societies; that in spite of wide variations in role content and the specific forms of its transformational rules, it possesses, as a certain type of transformational structure, certain inherent general formal or structural properties; that these inherent formal properties constitute truly universal features of family structure, as well as (*mutatis mutandis*) of the structure of the domestic units within which socialization is carried out; that the bigenerational pattern of role transformations itself, rather than the structure of the individual family or domestic grouping *per se*, is the relevant context of the process of socialization through which the personality is formed; that its general structural features are also, formally speaking, the universal features of the structure of the human personality; that they furthermore turn out to be isomorphic with the general outlines of mental development as discovered and formulated by Piaget; that the process of socialization (i.e., the formation of the personality) must therefore be conceived as a progressive cognitive and affective accommodation (and to some extent "internalization") of the dynamic structural properties of this basic transformational structure of family relations; and finally that this process of accommodation, imitation, and internalization of the structure of the social relations of the family and domestic group cycles is made possible by the at least partially independent development of a formally isomorphic set of mental capacities at the level of the intelligence.

Parsons' formulation of the relationship between socialization and family structure is based squarely on the hypothesis of the universality of the nuclear family, which is taken as the relevant universal structure of family relations. This hypothesis must be rejected on ethnographic and, as I have argued, also on theoretical grounds. The sharply different formulation of the problem presented in this paper, however, may be taken as a defense of Parsons' general thesis that there does exist a fundamental and universal correspondence between the elementary structures of the psyche and society, albeit on the basis of a radically revised concept of structure at both levels.

The "Family" and the Primary Socialization Grouping as Universal Social Categories

A verbal distinction has been made in the foregoing discussion between the "family" and the group in which socialization is actually carried out, or "socialization grouping." The nature of the distinction between these two types of social groupings and their respective functions must be grasped as a prerequisite to any useful discussion of the universal properties of either.

All societies possess at least one standardized pattern of roles devoted to the socialization of children. With rare exceptions such as the Israeli kibbutz, this cluster of roles takes the form of a domestic group focused around the relation of the mother (or mother-substitute, e.g., a nurse) and her children. A male or males and in some cases other females (e.g., the maternal grandmother) are attached to this central dyad in various supportive capacities and participate to cross-culturally varying degrees in the actual socialization process. Such a role-cluster, focused upon the socialization of a single group of children (i.e., a set of children having at least one "natural," adoptive or foster parent in common), at least during the early years of the child's life, I call a "primary socialization grouping." The "primary socialization grouping," understood in these terms, appears, with the rare exceptions mentioned, to be an ethnographic universal (the term "grouping" is adopted to avoid the connotation of definite boundaries associated with "group").

Social anthropologists have for some time recognized a distinction analogous in many respects to that which we have proposed between the family and the primary socialization group. This is the distinction between the family, defined as a unit constituted of normative or jural relationships of kinship and marriage, and the domestic group, defined as the coresident, commensal household group. The latter forms the concrete arena of socialization as well as the locus of other basic biological and economic functions of production and consumption. It is, of course, not necessarily identical with the primary socialization group, as it may include individuals who are not directly involved in the socialization of a given set of children and also because its over-all structure may be largely determined by economic and residential criteria that have no direct connection with socialization.

Fortes, who is chiefly responsible for developing the family/domestic group distinction in anthropological theory, is actually something less than clear about the nature of the distinction between the two.[4] He correctly observes that the distinction is essentially analytical, as the two groups are often identical or overlapping in membership, but then leaves obscure the analytical grounds upon which the distinction should be made.

Fortes attempts to deal with the analytical problem by treating the domestic group and the family, considered as concrete and overlapping social groupings, as differing compounds of two more fundamental sets of factors, which he terms "the *domestic field* of social relations, institutions, and activities, viewed from within as an internal system, and the *politico-jural field*, regarded as an external system."[5] Fortes then defines both the structure and the dynamic, processual characteristics of the domestic group as the products of the interplay of these two "fields":

> A significant feature of the developmental cycle of the domestic group is that it is at one and the same time a process within the internal field and a movement governed by its relations to the external field.[6]

Although Fortes does not explicitly define what he means by "domestic field" and "politico-jural field," statements such as

> The differentials in [domestic group] structure are in part inherent in the procreative relationship and spring from the requirements of child-rearing. But their character is also decisively regulated by politico-jural norms.[7]

imply that his conception of the "domestic field" is substantially identical with what has been called in this paper the "primary socialization grouping." The "domestic field," in other words, is essentially the domain of relations directly related to the social, psychological, and biological requirements of child-rearing, exclusive of the explicitly "politico-jural" or normative aspects of group structure.

The implication of this formulation is that the latter aspects pertain, as we have suggested, to the family proper. Fortes, however, never provides an adequate definition of the family. He contrasts the family, as a jurally defined conjugal unit, to the domestic goup on the grounds that the family may form the nucleus of a more inclusive domestic group (the latter may, for example, comprise a range of three generations, form an extended family composed of distinct jural family units, or include domestic retainers).[8] In other cases, he notes, the family and domestic group may be identical. But these formulations only apply to instances in which the family as a jural unit is also a cohesive domestic unit, takes the form of a conjugal or "nuclear" family, and provides the normative structure of the domestic group. As has already been pointed out, there are abundant instances, both at the cross-cultural and intrasocietal levels, where these conditions do not hold. Fortes himself has dealt extensively with a society in which the "family" *per se* normally does not constitute a domestic unit,[9] which makes his inadequate formulation all the more puzzling. In sum, after introducing the concepts of the domestic and politico-jural fields in an attempt to clarify the distinction between the domestic group and the family, Fortes fails to relate either the domestic or jural-political field to any specific structural or functional feature of either the family or the domestic group and thus fails to make clear precisely how the latter two groups are related either to the two fields or to each other.

It seems clear that Fortes intended his concepts of the domestic and politico-jural "fields" to represent the "pure" form of the characteristic properties of the domestic group and the family, respectively. But if such pure properties can be clearly defined at a general level, then it should be equally possible directly to formulate general definitions of the family and domestic group themselves (taking full account of the range of ethnographic variation in both), considered as the social expressions of the pure "field" properties in question. This is doubtless the goal toward which Fortes' notion of the domestic and politico-jural fields is directed, but he somehow does not get beyond this preliminary step, and never, indeed, gets very far toward clarifying what he regards as the essential features of the two fields as they bear on family and domestic group structure. Once such general definitions of the essential features of the family and domestic socialization group have been arrived at, it is possible to deal with the prevalent instances of hybrid forms (i.e., families that are also domestic groups) of the kind that led Fortes to resort to his detour through the domestic and politico-jural "fields" by simple compound definitions, viz., the "domestic family" as suggested later.

Fortes' discussion of the differential functions of the family and domestic group is, if anything, more confusing than his remarks on the structural distinction between them. He begins by defining the domestic group as "the workshop of social reproduction," which he defines as including "all those institutional mechanisms and customary activities and norms which serve to maintain, replenish, and transmit the social capital from generation to generation"[10] When he comes to define the family, however, it is as the "reproductive nucleus" of the domestic group, the locus of "the strictly reproductive functions, in the sense given to our concept of social reproduction." These "family" functions are then contrasted to a residual category consisting of "the production of food and shelter and the nonmaterial means for ensuring continuity with society at large."[11]

Unfortunately, Fortes never defines what he means by "strictly reproductive functions" as he understands them to inhere in the family; and the vague definition he gives of his concept of "social reproduction" makes it impossible to divine what he has in mind, beyond the vague allusion to "institutional mechanisms" of a politico-jural character. Fortes' inadequately differentiated concept of "social reproduction" is actually the source of all the ambiguities in his discussion of the family and domestic group cycles. Taking this discussion as a whole, Fortes refers to at least four analytically distinct types or modes of social reproduction: the psychosocial maturation or socialization of the individual as an independent adult member of the community; the integration of the individual in a jural sense into the normative structure of social life through such *rites de passage* as initiation and marriage; the cyclical dissolution and reformation of the domestic group within which socialization takes place; and the parallel process of dissolution and reconstitution of the family, which serves as the point of reference for the placement and integration of the individual into the politico-jural aspects of community structure.

Fortes' scheme could be clarified by defining the term "family" to apply unambiguously to a group or segment of jurally or normatively defined kinship relations, whether or not its members form a domestic unit. The family, so defined, fulfills its *sui generis* functions of "social reproduction" at the level of the normative structure of the kinship system, with respect both to its own replacement with equivalent social units and the integration of new individuals in the kinship system. The reproductive role of the family *per se* is in these terms analytically independent of domestic relations and does not depend upon the family's functioning as a domestic unit. The term "domestic family" could be reserved for families (in the sense just defined), or parts of families, which also function as domestic groups or subdivisions thereof. The term "primary socialization grouping" could be retained to denote the domestic grouping primarily concerned with the socialization of a particular set of children. Primary socialization groupings may exist and fulfill their characteristic reproductive functions (biological nurturance and the production of psychologically mature, i.e., "socialized" individuals), independently of whether or not they constitute "domestic families" in the normative sense.

A further ambiguity in Fortes' discussion of the domestic and politico-jural fields is his equation of the former with the "internal" field ("viewed from within as an internal system") of domestic group relations and the latter with the "external system" of group relations.[12] Insofar as Fortes merely has in mind the locus of the *sources* of the characteristic features of the two domains, this is unexceptionable. Insofar as the statement also appears to apply to the extensions of the two fields, however, it is misleading. As Fortes himself points out, the internal structure of the domestic group is "decisively regulated by politico-jural norms."[13] Equally important are the external (i.e., extradomestic group) aspects of "domestic" relations (e.g., the prominent role played by extra-group relationships in the later phases of socialization and the reciprocal effect of these upon the internal structure of group relations). Both the domestic and the politico-jural fields, in other words, are organized on the basis of a dynamic interplay between "internal" and "external" factors of the social-psychological and politico-jural types respectively appropriate to the two fields. The question of the relation between the domestic and the politico-jural fields as such, and by the same token of the domestic group and family, is thus not identical with the problem of the relation between the "internal" and "external" fields of domestic group or family relations. The central role of the interaction of "internal" and "external" factors, considered as different levels of the same hierarchically integrated systems of group relations, in the structure and developmental cycles of both the family and the domestic (socialization) group will be a primary theme of the following analysis.

In conclusion, then, Fortes to some extent confuses three analytically distinct oppositions: that between the domestic and politico-jural fields, that between the domestic group and the family, and that between the internal and external fields of relations of both groups. His formulation, however, has the great merit of emphasizing the analytical and empirical distinction between the domestic and politico-jural domain, and thus between the domestic group and the family proper. This distinction forms the basis of the general definitions of the family and domestic (socialization) grouping put forward in this section. A second and even more important contribution of Fortes' formulation is his insight into the dynamic, processual character of family and domestic group structure: both groupings, he suggests, are essentially to be seen as mechanisms of "social reproduction"; their developmental cycles are themselves processes of social reproduction operating simultaneously at the level of the group and the individual; and in both cases these processes are "driven" and given form by the interaction of the "external" and "internal" fields of group relations. These two "fields," we have suggested, should be seen as different levels of group structure, considered as a hierarchically integrated system or code. These suggestions will be followed up in a later section. First, however, it is necessary to clarify the nature of the family as a normative or jural unit.

The Family, Kinship, Affinity, and Marriage

The family has been defined as a jural or normative (i.e., culturally institutionalized) unit or category of kinship relations whose primary function is to integrate children on a normative footing into the kinship system, and, in the process, to regenerate new family groups (and thus, indirectly, the kinship system as a whole). A family is further distinguished from other normative kinship groups or categories in that it is defined by reference to an affinal relationship linking the female parent to a male spouse or category of procreative partners. There are instances of affinal relations in which the jural spouse is not a male (e.g., Nuer woman and ghost marriage) but these exceptions are more apparent than real, as the spouse is symbolically defined as a male or as disposing of male procreative powers in relation to the female spouse. The family, therefore, cannot be defined without defining kinship and affinity, and the proposition that the family is a universal category of social organization entails the corollary proposition that some universal meaning can be attached to these two terms.

The affinal bond between the female and male consorts invariably presupposes sexual relations, in which the sexual roles of both partners are universally held to contribute in some essential respect to the reproductive process, i.e., to the formation and/or birth of children. "Kinship" can be universally defined as a cultural category of relationships derived from this symbolic procreative link within the framework of an affinal bond. This rough definition is universal in the sense that in all cultures the "full" or ideal definition of kinship involves some combination of these two factors. Most societies recognize auxiliary or variant forms of this ideal relationship, such as adoption (which lacks the procreative element and under some circumstances the affinal element, while retaining a basic reference to the concept of the family-centered relationship of filiation). Biological genitorship seems also to be generally regarded as establishing a special relationship, often with jural rights, privileges and obligations, between genitor or genetrix and offspring in the absence of an affinal bond between genitor and genetrix. This may be culturally regarded as a form of quasi-kinship, or as an "illegitimate" or "natural" relationship which nevertheless carries jurally recognized obligations, or as outside the culturally

defined domain of kinship relations altogether. The general point for our purposes is that the family, as distinct from the primary socialization group or domestic group, is the source and reference point for the definition of kinship relations and thus of the basic normative location of the individual with reference to the structure of society at large.

The affinal bond between the mother and her spouse or consorts serves to define the grouping formed by herself and her offspring as a family or segment of a family (depending on how the family is defined in the society in question). Affinity, as here defined, consists essentially of a socially procreative relationship operating at the level of inter-family, rather than inter-individual relations. It consists of a relationship between members of different families (usually, but not always, culturally defined as a "marriage," that is, a contractual relationship between individual affinal partners) which is socially defined as capable of giving rise to new families or descent group segments. The entrance of a member of a family into an affinal union has consequences for the over-all structure of relations within that family, if only because the family member's assumption of a different status within a new family unit (or subsegment of the larger extended family) reciprocally alters his or her relations with the members of the family of orientation and thus modifies its internal structure to a significant extent. It is because, in the case of affinal bonds, such global modifications in the internal structure of the family of orientation are caused by the creation of a new family unit through a relation of reciprocal exchange with a member of still another family unit that affinal relations must be seen in structural terms primarily as interfamily relations.

There are, of course, societies in which the groups involved in affinal relations are not culturally defined as bilateral family units but as unilineal descent groups or categories. In such cases the "spouse"—parent who does not stand toward the offspring of the affinally sanctioned union in the descent relationship may be conceived as an affine of his or her own offspring[14] and/or may not be regarded as a member of the family unit itself (e.g., the Ashanti and Nayar cases to be discussed). In such cases, however, the status of the children and the opposite, descent-linked parent as members of the cultural variant of the family (which will in this case take the form of a lineage segment or strip) is nevertheless defined by reference to their common affinal relationship to the "spouse"/parent who is excluded from the descent group and, as the case may be, family membership. Such cases, in short, do not alter the fundamental point that the family is invariably defined with reference to affinity, and that affinity is essentially an interfamilial rather than an inter-individual relationship.

There are societies in which affinity, as defined here, is clearly distinguished from marriage, defined as an affinal bond involving the specification of rights and obligations of specific individuals towards each other. The Ashanti of Ghana hold a female puberty ceremony which establishes a woman's ability to engage in sexual relations and the right of all her children to recognition as legitimate members and heirs of her minimal lineage segment, whether or not they are the offspring of a man to whom the woman is married. There is a separate marriage ceremony, which defines the husband as the exclusive sexual partner of the wife and the spon-sor of the children in certain ritual groupings deemed essential to a full social persona. It is nonetheless possible, and far from unheard-of, for a woman not to marry and for her children to go through life lack-ing the ritual "completeness" bestowable only by a husband/father. Such children are not considered illegitimate and are not disabled in law or civic status. [15]

The Northern Kayapó of Brazil hold ritual "mar-riage" rites for boys and girls as part of the initiation process, in which they are symbolically "married" to ritual spouses. These ritual "marriages" are not considered to constitute actual marriages and do not bind the partners to each other in any way be-yond the end of the ceremony itself. They are in-stead regarded as public enabling acts, establishing the boy's or girl's right to engage in courtship and to marry a spouse of his or her own choice. The ritual marriages of both sexes are replete with symbolism emphasizing the attenuation of the ritual bride's or groom's bonds as an offspring to his or her natal family and the acquisition of a set of obligations toward the symbolic "affines." These ceremonial marriages, in short, serve to assert the pattern of interfamilial affinal relationships which form the framework within which actual marriages may then take place. [16]

The Nayar of Kerala traditionally held a similar "ritual marriage" ceremony as a sort of girl's initia-tion rite. The marriage with the ritual husband was terminated by divorce at the close of the ceremony. The girl was thereafter allowed to take lovers, and the offspring of these affairs were treated as legiti-mate members of the matrilineage. They retained residual ceremonial ties with the ritual "husband/father," but the latter never formed part of the matri-lineal extended family. [17]

The Nayar "marriage" ritual closely resembles the Ashanti girls' puberty ceremony in its essential functions. In these two rather extreme matrilineal cases, the emphasis of the "intergroup" aspect of the affinal relationship is on the differentiation between a woman's families of orientation and procreation (or between the distinct clusters of rights and obliga-tions associated with her roles as offspring and as mother within the matrilineal extended family). The male consort is not (or, in the Ashanti case, not necessarily) included within the family at all, and the cultural counterpart of the family as we have defined it becomes a "uterine stirp" or shallow segment of a matrilineage).

Such cases demonstrate that "marriage", defined as an exclusive relationship between particular spouses, or as a bundle of sexual, economic, resi-dential, or jural rights and obligations of the spouses in each other as individuals, or as a means of legiti-mizing children, is not a universal feature of human family structure. [18] By the same token, they serve to emphasize that affinity, defined as a formally sanctioned exchange of procreative partners between jurally constituted families or descent groups for the purpose of constituting a new family or descent group or extended family segment, forms the basis of family structure even in societies which effectively dispense with marriage or treat it as a subordinate or optional supplement to the basic affinal relation-ship. It is affinity in this general sense, whether it is expressly separated from marriage as among the Ashanti or exists only as an analytically sep-arate component of marriage, as among modern Western societies, that establishes the normative place of the offspring of procreative unions in the kinship system, and hence their "legitimacy."

To put this point in somewhat different terms, what is essential (and therefore universal) from the point of view of kinship systems considered as normative structures, is a regular institutional means of regenerating the basic groupings through which the system itself is reproduced. The system must be reproduced through a grouping or cluster of roles, rather than by the simple addition of individual role-actors on the basis of serial dyadic attachments, because the key problem in the reproduction of the kinship system as a social system (as distinct from the reproduction of the biological and psychological aspects of the individual person) is the attachment and integration of the *relation* between the mother and child to the wider kinship system. The mother-child unit in and of itself is not, in other words, capable of constituting an element of a kinship system: to do this it must be linked to the system by some external tie of a normative character. The conjunction of these two essential relations is the minimal prerequisite for incorporating new members (i.e., children) into the kinship system and takes the form of a cluster or grouping of relations conforming to the definition of the family as previously formulated. An important point which emerges from this discussion is that the function of the family, and in particular of the affinal bond through which it is constituted, is to connect the offspring through at least one (and usually both) of the parents to a network of kinship relations transcending the family itself.

We are now in a position to distinguish more fully between the family and the primary socialization group on both structural and functional grounds. The primary socialization grouping does not necessarily constitute a normative set of kinship relations, as it does not presuppose that the parents or parent-surrogates who actually reside with and socialize the children are bound in any culturally recognized bond of marriage or affinity, or indeed that they are related to the children as parents or even kinsmen. The family, on the other hand, is not necessarily a coresident domestic unit and therefore does not necessarily serve as an effective socialization group. The essential structural unit of the primary socialization group is the mother-child (or mother surrogate-child) dyad; that of the family the affinal dyad of wife (or a woman whose reproductive capacity has been socially defined as fully integrated through an affinal bond into the ongoing system of family structure) and husband (or one or more members of a socially defined category of male affinal consorts).

As the preceding discussion has implied, the "primary socialization grouping," defined as the domestic nexus of the psychological functions of socialization, and the "family," considered as the basic cluster of kinship and marriage relations through which an individual is integrated into the normative order of society, are often not the same thing at all. Failure to recognize this simple fact has been the rock upon which numerous attempts to formulate "universal" models of the family have foundered. The assumption upon which many such models have been based is that the sociological structure of the family can be directly derived from (or reduced to) the psychological and other functions of the domestic socialization grouping. This assumption, which underlies the concept of the "nuclear" family and forms the basis of Parsons' analysis, must be rejected as both analytically unsound and ethnographically unfounded. It should be clear that if the relevant universe is defined in psychological-functional terms as that of all effective primary socialization groups, the "family," defined in cultural terms as a normatively established unit of kinship relations, cannot be considered a universal phenomenon. Conversely, the family, as it has been defined here, can be regarded as a universal social phenomenon in the more limited sense that all cultures possess forms of affinity and family structure; but a formulation of the minimal sociological and psychological requirements of

socialization, or an inductive generalization based on empirical regularities in the structures of all domestic units in which socialization is actually carried on, while it may have psychological and social-psychological value, cannot be directly relevant to the structure of the family, considered as a segment of a culturally defined system of kinship and marriage relations.

Clarification of the structural, functional, and analytical distinctions between the family and the primary socialization grouping is the prerequisite of being able to raise the empirical and theoretical question of the relationship between them. This problem, which is obviously central to the issue of the relationship between the basic structures of human society and the fundamental structure of the personality, is only obscured by the terms in which the question of the universal form of the family has usually been posed. This general question, as we have found, resolves itself into three distinct but related issues: (1) the universal structural and functional characteristics of the family, properly defined; (2) the universal structural and functional characteristics of the primary socialization grouping; and (3) the universal structural and functional properties of the relationship between the two.

ABSTRACTION, HIERARCHY AND DYNAMICS: TOWARD A TRANSFORMATIONAL MODEL OF FAMILY STRUCTURE

Misplaced Concreteness and the Absence of Generative and Dynamic Features as Related Aspects of the "Nuclear Family" Concept

These problems, however, cannot successfully be resolved without taking care to avoid two further basic errors of past attempts at universal definitions of the family. One of these is the attempt to conceptualize the universal properties of family structure at too concrete a level, i.e., the level of particular role patterns such as the "nuclear family." In such models, generic structural and functional attributes have been defined, in Aristotelian fashion, in terms of invariant associations between particular functions and particular roles. Virtually all of the purportedly universal structural and functional features and correlations claimed by such theories have been controverted by comparative ethnographic evidence, but objections to such formulations on ethnographic grounds alone do not get to the heart of the problem. It is not a matter of readjusting the models to fit additional data but of recognizing the fundamental limitations of the assumptions on which they are based. One of the most serious of these limitations is, I am suggesting, a fatal propensity toward fallacies of misplaced concreteness.

A closely related weakness of models of the "nuclear family" type is their static character, their lack of any built-in dynamic properties. This static quality is a direct corollary of the insufficiently abstract nature of the concept of structure upon which the model is based. The focus of this conceptual failure lies in the Aristotelian conception of norm which forms the basis of the notions of status and role, which in turn constitute the immediate constituents of the model of structure in question. The attempt to define the family in terms of a set of normative definitions of its constituent role-categories, supposed to represent its "essential" form or average state, produces a timeless, static paradigm. Such a model can be neither abstract enough nor concrete enough to express the social reality of the family as a dynamic system of relations, engaged in a continuous process of orderly change and development. The same can be said of attempts to conceptualize the primary socialization grouping in static terms, ignoring its sociological developmental cycle while the psychological development of the child within it is emphasized. The static "table of organization" conception of both family and primary socialization grouping, exemplified by the "nuclear family" concept, thus leads of necessity to a formulation that is at once too vague and general to correspond to the concrete configuration of role relations within the group at any specific stage of its developmental cycle, and too concrete to express the general principles governing the overall process of transformation in the structure and content of its role relationships in the course of the cycle. Yet the structure of any group characterized by a regular developmental cycle can be adequately defined only in terms of a dialectical interplay or feedback between these two levels (the particular state of the system at a given time and the general dynamic principles governing its over-all development). Static definitions of the "nuclear family" type thus fall between two analytical stools. Their inadequacy derives equally from their misconception of the nature of the family and their defective concept of structure.

Existing attempts to formulate universal definitions of the family have, in short, proved inadequate to deal with the observed variation of the phenomenon either in time (i.e., in the dynamic process of transformation of family structure in the developmental cycle) or in space (i.e., in the cross-cultural variation of family and domestic group configurations). The fundamental reasons for this failure, I have suggested, are that they have confused analytically and empirically distinct sets of structural and functional features (those pertaining to the family and to the socialization group, respectively), have sought to identify genotypic properties at the level of phenotypic features, and have attempted to define dynamic phenomena in terms of static models.

The universal, genotypic properties of family structure must be sought, if they are to be found at all, at a higher level of abstraction. These generic properties, furthermore, cannot be conceived as purely static role categories. They must include the rules governing the relationship between the dynamic and static aspects of the family, that is, between its cyclically changing and invariant aspects. Such a set of roles and parameters would of necessity comprise three categories or subsets: a set of transformational principles governing the developmental modifications of role relations in the family and domestic group cycles, a set of invariant principles coordinating the applications of the transformational rules, and of course a set of general substantive dimensions for defining the role categories themselves. The resulting model would constitute a self-regulating, hierarchically organized system, capable of maintaining a dynamic equilibrium. This over-all equilibrium would be conceived as the expression of invariant relationships, defined at a relatively abstract level, between the coordinated processes of transformation in the relations among lower-level relational categories of the system. The model would, in short, represent a simple "cybernetic" system, parallel in its basic organization to the structure of fundamental processes at the psychological and biological levels of behavior.

The Family as Developmental Cycle: The Contribution of Fortes

Fortes' conception of family and domestic group structure as the product of a dynamic interplay of forces emanating from the domestic and politico-jural or "external" fields led him to emphasize the central importance of the temporal aspect of domestic and family organization. Fortes more than anyone else has stressed that both families and domestic groups must be conceived less as static normative paradigms than as developmental processes and that these processes are simultaneously among the "nodal mechanisms" of "social reproduction."[19] Fortes further pointed out that these developmental processes have in all societies the character of cycles, that is, repetitive, self-regenerating processes with culturally patterned sequences of phases. He emphasized that these phases are closely related to, but not synonymous with, the major phases of the individual life cycle, as defined in terms of the transformations of jural, economic, ritual, and kinship status associated with changes in family and domestic relations.

Fortes suggests a simple paradigm of the developmental cycle which, he asserts, "applies *mutatis mutandis . . .* to all social systems."[20] Although he specifically states that his model applies to the domestic group, it seems clear from the terms in which it is stated that it is intended to apply equally to the family: as we have seen, Fortes is not clear on the analytical distinction between the two. According to the model, domestic groups (and families) pass through three main phases, which may overlap to widely varying degrees in different societies or in different households within the same society. First is the phase of expansion, lasting from marriage until the completion of the family of procreation. In this phase, all the children are completely dependent, economically, jurally, and politically, upon their parents. This is followed by the second major phase, that of dispersion or fission. This typically begins with the marriage of the oldest child and continues until all the children are married. The third and final phase is that of replacement, in which the married children and their families (specifically, the heirs of the jural family head) replace their parents in the control of the family estate, its domestic base, and the dominant social roles within it. This phase culminates with the death of the parents.[21]

Fortes points out that in "relatively homogeneous social systems" there exists a "close parallelism" between this sequence of phases at the domestic group and family level and the "stages of physiological growth" of the individual.[22] It is clear from Fortes' discussion that what he actually means by the latter phrase is not physiological growth *per se* but the progressive development of social status, rights, privileges, and obligations associated with it. He offers a paradigm of the phases of the individual life cycle between birth and "the attainment of jural adulthood." In the first phase, which may last for only a few days after birth, the infant is wholly a member of the "matricentral cell," that is, the subgroup formed by himself and his mother. There is no significant social or other differentiation between mother and infant. The second phase consists of the entry of the child into the "patricentral nuclear family unit": at this point the father assumes social and spiritual responsibility for the child, or rather for the mother and infant as a unit. The third phase, that of "childhood proper," comes when the child "enters the domain of the domestic group," i.e., is no longer confined to his mother's quarters but has the freedom of the whole dwelling house; this normally follows weaning and learning to walk. The final phase, admission to the politico-jural domain, often begins with an initiation rite and culminates with marriage and the fission of the natal domestic group.[23]

Fortes' paradigm of the early phases of the life cycle is obviously far from universally applicable as it stands; it seems to have been formulated with a particular type of society in mind (a patrilineal society with nuclear families forming sub-units of a larger household or compound, such as the Tallensi of Ghana studied by Fortes). It is nevertheless interesting as an attempt, however tentative and inadequate, to formulate a model of the socialization process that would take account not only of the growing child's passage into membership in progressively wider and more complex subdomains of family and domestic relations (in which respect it resembles Parsons' model of socialization) but of the correlation between this sequence of individual passages and the pattern of structural change occurring simultaneously in the social group which forms the setting or point of reference for these individual transformations. It is this type of structural and functional correlation Fortes has in mind when he speaks of the developmental cycle of the domestic group as "at one and the same time a process within the internal field and a movement governed by its relations to the external field."[24]

As in other respects, however, Fortes' attempt to formulate his insights in the form of a general model which will apply "*mutatis mutandis* to all social systems" falls far short of the mark, both on comparative ethnographic grounds (as we have already remarked) and because he does not systematically follow out the general implications of his ideas to the point where they might become part of a viable general analytical model. I shall try, in the remainder of this section, to explore further some of Fortes' insights along these lines.

To begin with, it is apparent that the idea of the parallelism between the culturally prescribed phases of the life cycle and the structure of the developmental cycle of the domestic group and family can be given a more comprehensive and structurally adequate formulation than Fortes' own. Such a formulation would start from the life cycle as a whole, rather than the segment from birth to the attainment of adulthood treated by Fortes, as its baseline. In Fortes' terms the first three phases of the life cycle correspond to the first phase (expansion) of the domestic group of orientation, while the fourth phase of the life cycle (the attainment of jural adulthood) corresponds to the second phase (dispersion) of that group. Considered from this point of view, the phase-structure of the life cycle as a whole would correspond to two consecutive but overlapping domestic group/family cycles: those of ego's groupings of orientation and procreation. Seen as part of a total system in these terms, the patterning of the early phases of the life cycle (e.g., those described by Fortes or their rough equivalents) would emerge as in part a reflection of the patterning of the later phases (i.e., those that the parents of the child are passing through at the same time in *their* life cycles), as both earlier and later phases would have to be coordinated within the identical, repeated framework of the domestic group/ family cycle. The impact of family and domestic group structure on the socialization process takes on, in these terms, a quite different set of structural and analytical properties than those ascribed to it in conventional models based on the notion that the patterning of the socialization process reflects the internal psychological requirements and family relations of that process considered alone as a distinct and analytically isolated stage of the life cycle. We shall be directly concerned with these properties and implications later in this paper.

Fortes' failure to distinguish clearly on analytical grounds between the family and the domestic group raises the question of whether his model of the developmental cycle properly applies to families that are not domestic groups, or, more generally, to the family *per se* as a jural structure rather than merely to the domestic corollaries of that structure. The answer is plainly that it does, as the transformations of "domestic group" relations to which he refers in his paradigms of the domestic group and life cycles pertain explicitly in many cases to jural familial relations (e.g., marriage). Both the jural structure of family relations and the concrete system of domestic relations, whether jural or simply ad hoc, have culturally prescribed developmental patterns of the type posited by Fortes. The important thing to bear in mind is that these patterns may be both distinct and dissimilar in societies in which the two types of grouping are not customarily congruent.

We come now to the general implications of the developmental cycle concept for the essential properties of family structure. The conception of the family (whether it corresponds to a domestic unit or not) and primary socialization grouping as developmental processes implies that transformation and change are not incidental or irrelevant to their basic structural patterns. They are, on the contrary, of the essence of those structures, conceived as dynamic, hierarchically organized processes. It follows that the structure of the family cannot adequately be defined in terms of a single "synchronic slice," representing the state of its component role relationships at a particular moment in time, or even of a single family in isolation. The Aristotelian concept of structure as a timeless, "essential" pattern of role relations or status categories that underlies the "nuclear" family and allied conceptions is similarly incapable of dealing with the temporal, developmental aspect of the family.

The regularity of the cyclical pattern of phases through which the developmental process is worked out nevertheless indicates that this temporal, transformational aspect conforms to certain invariant principles. It is these which account for the continuity of the identity and cohesion of the family or domestic group throughout the successive modifications of its internal and external relationships. But how are these structural constants, these invariant principles, to be conceived? Following Fortes' lead, let us suggest that they consist of rules regulating the interaction of the "external" and "internal" fields or levels of group relations, which provides the basic dynamic mechanism of the developmental cycle. The directly interacting segments of the internal and external fields of group relations fall into place, in terms of this model, as different levels of a single hierarchically organized code of structural rules. Now the question becomes, what generic elements or dimensions of family and domestic group relations constitute the relevant sets of internal and external structural components? What, in other words, is the essential structure of the internal and external fields, and precisely how are they related?

Family Structure as Interfamily Exchange: The Contribution of Lévi-Strauss

Lévi-Strauss came close to posing this question (though in somewhat different terms) in several early articles on kinship and the family. If his answers are not entirely satisfactory, he must nevertheless be credited with formulating the principle that the elementary structure of the family must be conceived in terms of a system of relations transcending the isolated family and directly linking it, through bonds of affinity, with other families.

Lévi-Strauss[25] took issue with the position of Radcliffe-Brown and Malinowski that the internal relations of the "elementary" or "nuclear" family are "primary" in a structural sense, while those lying outside it in the network of kinship and affinal relations are "secondary" (i.e., derivations of the primary, intrafamilial relations. Against this position, Lévi-Strauss proposed a counter-interpretation which amounts to an inversion of Radcliffe-Brown's thesis. Lévi-Strauss' counter-hypothesis is founded upon the assertion that affinal relations linking members of different families in relations of spouse-exchange (epitomized by the relationship of the wife's brother to the sister's husband, and the relation of the former, as mother's brother, to his sister's children) are "primary" in relation to intrafamily structure. The priority of affinal ties derives from the simple fact that every "elementary" or "nuclear" family presupposes a relationship of spouse exchange between two antecedent families. Intrafamily relations must accordingly be seen as "secondary" and derivative in relation to interfamily bonds. The "elemental" unit of kinship systems is not, therefore, the individual family but a group constituted by the juxtaposition of a "restricted" or "elementary" family with a brother-in-law/avuncular relationship, representing the affinal, interfamilial bond on the basis of which the restricted family was created.[26]

Lévi-Strauss' assertion of the structural priority of interfamily bonds in relation to intrafamily structure is in full accord with the thesis of this essay, which in this respect, indeed, derives directly from Lévi-Strauss' work. Several reservations must, however, be entered with regard to his formulation of the "element of kinship." He does not, for one thing, distinguish between the family and the domestic or primary socialization groups: his model, therefore, can be considered as applying only to the former, as defined here. It is arguable that the primary socialization group reverses the structural priorities of the family in the sense that the dynamics of its internal structure take precedence over its "external" relations with the wider household context or with other groups.

A second drawback of Lévi-Strauss' analysis is that he does not reject the "nuclear family" hypothesis *per se*: on the contrary, his formulation can be interpreted as an effort to save it by reformulating it in sounder analytical terms. The nuclear family continues to form the basic unit of Lévi-Strauss' "element of kinship," and his model retains the idea of a universal pattern of roles (father, mother, and so on) in which only the formal behavioral pattern varies. Lévi-Strauss, moreover, continues to conceive of his "elementary" role pattern in Radcliffe-Brownian terms as consisting exclusively of dyadic interpersonal relations, thus ignoring the significance of the character of affinity as an essentially intergroup relationship, and thus as a manifestation of a qualitatively distinct level of relationships. His use of the dyadic relationship between sister's husband and wife's brother to represent the affinal component of his model exemplifies his failure to grasp the essential structural significance of his own insight that intergroup relations are structurally prior to intragroup role patterns in the constitution of the family.

In his subsequent writings on kinship, Lévi-Strauss made the concept of affinity as an intergroup, rather than an interindividual relationship of exchange the cornerstone of his theory.[27] In an article on the family published in 1960,[28] he combined his insights into the nature and structural significance of affinity with a dynamic, cyclical formulation of the structure of the family that has obvious parallels with that of Fortes:

> The important conclusion to be kept in mind is that the restricted [i.e., "nuclear"] family can neither be said to be the element of the social group, nor can it be claimed to result from it. Rather, the social group can only become established in contradistinction, and to some extent in compliance, with the family, since in order to maintain the society through time, women should procreate children [and] benefit from male protection while they are engaged in confinement and nursing, and since precise sets of rules are needed to perpetuate throughout the generations the basic pattern of the social fabric. However, the primary social concern regarding the family is . . . a denial of its right to exist either in isolation or permanently; restricted families are only permitted to live for a limited period of time . . . under the strict condition that their component parts be ceaselessly displaced, loaned, borrowed, given away, or returned, so that new restricted families may be endlessly created. . . . Thus, the relation between the social group as a whole and the restricted families which seem to constitute it is not a static one, like that of a wall to the bricks it is built with. It is rather a dynamic process of tension and opposition with an equilibrium point extremely difficult to find. . . .[29]

The basic point of Lévi-Strauss' position is that the isolated family cannot be treated as the "nuclear" or "elementary" unit of social systems. It rather represents a relatively temporary and unstable combination of elements drawn from a structural field composed of pairs of families linked by bonds of affinal exchange. Affinal bonds between spouse-exchanging families, and the corollary interfamily relations arising from the creation of new families through marriage, such as the avuncular bond, must therefore be recognized as the "elementary" components of kinship and family organization.

The idea of interfamily relations as the fundamental components of family structure implies that the developmental cycle of the family cannot be adequately conceptualized in terms of a series of developments occurring within a single family in isolation from others. Fortes failed to develop the structural implications of his concept of the developmental cycle precisely because he attempted to define it as a process occurring within an individual family or domestic group, albeit under the vaguely defined catalytic influence of the "external field" of "jural-political relations." We are now in a position to recognize the crucial role played by interfamily relationships such as marriage in this "external field," and therefore to see that an adequate model of the cyclical process occurring within each family must also take into account the relations between this process and the parallel processes occurring within other, structurally equivalent groups. The consummation of the internal processes of each individual group, and the concrete expression of the relationship between them, is of course the exchange of spouses or legitimate procreative partners between the groups. The content and patterning of relationships within any single group, and the rate, duration, and nature of the changes that take place in this pattern during the course of the developmental cycle of the group, all depend directly upon the nature of this intergroup affinal exchange, which simultaneously marks the dispersion of the existing groups and the inception of a new one.

Process, Function, and Hierarchy in Family Structure: A Generative Model

The Dimensions of Family Structure

The question then becomes, how can the relation between the cyclical aspect of the family and the crucial role of interfamily relationships in its internal patterning be conceptualized in terms of an integral, formally adequate model? The focus of the problem is obviously the precise nature of the relationship of interfamily relations to intrafamily structure. Before this can be dealt with directly, however, the basic dimensions of the model must be identified and their structural properties specified.

In all families, roles are differentially assigned with reference to sex and age. Sex and age, however, cannot be said, in and of themselves, to constitute dimensions of family structure *per se*. They always occur as components of status-role categories whose position in the structure of the family is specified by a second pair of dimensions, which also form components of all statuses and role-categories belonging to the immediate family. This second pair of structural components comprises the dimensions of consanguinity/affinity and generation. This pair of dimensions may be said to pertain specifically to family structure in a sense that the former pair does not, and therefore to constitute the fundamental dimensions of family structure *per se*. The two pairs are, of course, closely connected. Consanguinity/affinity and generation refer to aspects of sex and age (respectively). They may be thought extrapolations of those aspects of sex and age which are directly relevant to the relationship between the interfamily and intrafamily levels of structure.

That consanguinity/affinity and generation are dimensions of the patterning of roles within all known forms of the family is well established. In some societies, families may not directly include affines (e.g., the husband/father in some matrilineal societies), but in these cases the mother's "affinal" relationship to a man or men occupying such a status in relation to her is nevertheless an essential criterion for her ability legitimately to fulfill the role of mother in the family and for it to be recognized as such.

A person's basic consanguineal connections are his or her relationships with (or linked through) members of his or her family of orientation. They are, in short, relations primarily determined by common memberships in or attachment to the family that represents ego's social point of origin. Affinal relations are the reverse of this: they are by definition between persons of different "points (families) of origin" and consist essentially in the creation of a new such "point" in social space. The consanguinity/affinity contrast thus pertains to that aspect of the structural continuum of interfamily and intrafamily relations concerned with the relative location of persons and families in social space.

"Generation," of course, refers to the complementary aspect of the family organization (including under this term both the interfamily and intrafamily levels of relations): namely, the relative placement of persons and families in social time. "Social time" is measured, for purposes of family and kinship relations, in terms of the revolutions of the family cycle. As a component of family and kinship relations, then, "generation" never denotes mere relative age. It refers essentially to the relative status of individuals (or families) with respect to the revolutions of the family cycle. Parents and children, for example, are considered to belong to adjacent (i.e., consecutive) generations relative to each other because the family of procreation of the former constitutes the family of orientation of the latter; siblings, on the other hand, are said to be of the same generation because they go through the same phase of the family cycle at the same time.

The point that emerges from a consideration of the nature of the two major dimensions of family structure, then, is that neither is primarily defined with reference to the internal structure for the family treated as an isolated unit. Both apply equally to the level of interfamily relations and are defined in terms of complementary aspects of the relationship between the interfamily and intrafamily levels of structure.

Let us go back now to our earlier remark that consanguinity/affinity and generation represent extrapolations of those aspects of the general role dimensions of sex and age specifically relevant to the relationship between the intergroup and intragroup levels of family structure. The dimension of consanguinity/affinity is related to sex in the sense that sexual relations are prohibited, or at least avoided, between close consanguines and prescribed between the partners to a marriage or a sanctioned procreative relationship of the type that constitutes the focus of the affinal bond. It is a common phenomenon that the range of permitted sexual partners does not coincide fully with that of permissible marital partners. There is in many societies an intermediate zone of relations, usually relatively distant consanguines, with whom sexual relations are permitted but with whom marriage is prohibited. This does not, however, contradict the general proposition that consanguinity and affinity represent the two poles of a continuum regulating the relations between the sexes in the crucial matter of the possibility, impossibility, or prescription of procreative, affinally sanctioned sexual intercourse, and that the universal limiting consideration in the organization of this continuum is that intercourse is prohibited (or, in the absence of a formal taboo, appears to be spontaneously avoided) between full co-members of the same family of orientation and permitted between members of different families of a sufficiently distant degree of relationship. It is in this sense, then, that the dimension of consanguinity/affinity represents an extrapolation of the generic feature of sex with specific reference to the contrast between interfamily and intrafamily relations. "Generation" bears a similar relation to the criterion of relative age. As we have seen, it focuses upon that aspect of age that is measured in the social terms of the revolutions of the family cycle, i.e., the temporal aspect of interfamily relations.

To sum up, although sex and age represent the basic biological and social variables out of which family organization is constructed, they do not, in and of themselves, constitute the basic dimensions of family structure. It is only when a second order of contrasts is superimposed upon them which reflects their differential relevance to the system of interfamily and intrafamily relations that they are transformed into dimensions of family structure *per se*, in the guise of the dimensions of consanguinity/affinity and generation, respectively. The hierarchical character of family structure, which our previous discussion of the relationship between the interfamilial and intrafamilial levels of relations has brought out in general terms, is thus inherent in the internal structure of the dimensions on the basis of which the continuum of family relations is organized.

Another issue related to the dimensions of family structure should perhaps be clarified at this point. The four dimensions to which we have referred (sex, age, consanguinity/affinity, and generation) are obviously related to biological characteristics (e.g., the nature of aging as a gradual and continuous process and the nature of sexuality as a bipolar, fixed, and unmediable attribute). This does not mean, however, that any of these dimensions is "biologically determined in its cultural significance," as Parsons claims for the generational distinction.[30] All four dimensions, like the over-all structure of the interfamily unit and the social division of labour with reference to which they are defined, constitute fully cultural or sociological structures, no less so because they relate biological attributes to the fundamental processes of social reproduction. The family and domestic group cycles are the simplest and most universal examples of such processes, being the

media through which new family and domestic group segments are produced out of relationships between similar existing groups by means of the cultural appropriation and transformation of the basic biological attributes of sexuality and the life cycle. The dimensions of generation and consanguinity/affinity, sex and age, define aspects of this process and derive their social significance from their role in it.

Hierarchy and Transformations in Family Structure; the Family Triangle as the Elementary Structure of Kinship Relations

We are now in a position to examine more closely the relationship between the intergroup and intragroup levels of structure. The conception of family structure as a hierarchical system, involving reciprocal interaction between different levels of organization, is the direct result of the genetic or generative analytical perspective developed out of our previous discussions of the ideas of Fortes and Lévi-Strauss. Among the most important of these ideas is Lévi-Strauss' point that the structure of any given family presupposes, and to some extent builds into itself, the affinal link between the two families of orientation of the spouses, and Fortes' point that the structure of a family must be seen as the product of an interplay between what he called the internal and external "fields" of family and domestic group organization (i.e., in our terms, the intrafamily and interfamily levels of structure, respectively).

These propositions may be brought together and slightly reformulated to bring them within the framework of the present discussion as the general thesis that the internal structure of any family (or bigenerational family segment) is an introjection of the triangular system of relations between the family in question and the families of orientation of the two adult affinal partners with reference to whose relationship the family or family segment is defined as such. The pattern of relations among these three families or subfamily groupings can be represented as an inverted triangle. The base of the triangle consists of the affinal relationship between the natal families of the two spouses or affinal partners: these two families are normally of the same generation or developmental stage. The sides of the triangle comprise the consanguinal and affinal bonds that link each of the basal pairs of spouse-exchanging families with the mutual family of procreation of their respective offspring, which forms the apex of the triangle of interfamily relations.

Within each of the families making up this minimal system, a similar pattern of relations prevails, which represents the introjection, at the level of intrafamily role relations, of the interfamily triangle we have just described. The base of this intrafamily triangle consists of the affinal relationships between the spouses or legitimate procreative partners with reference to which the family is defined. The sides comprise the ties of filiation (and/or affinity, depending on how the society in question defines the relationship) between the two affinal partners and their joint offspring. The children born to the latter within their joint family of procreation constitute the apex of the triangle. The apex thus represents a purely consanguineal relationship derived from common origin within the same family (i.e., the relation of siblingship among the offspring of the affinally linked couple): As such it is the structural opposite of the interfamily-derived affinal relationship represented by the base of the triangle. Just as the two spouse-exchanging families belong to a prior revolution of the family cycle with reference to the new family of procreation founded by their offspring and are thus associated with a different "generation," so the parents or affinal partners connected to a particular family are contrasted to their offspring within the family as belonging to an older or structurally prior generation. The whole triangular system of relations at both levels is thus generated by the intersection of a single pair of dimensions (consanguinity/affinity and generation, in the general sense in which these have been defined in this essay).

Although the two levels of the system are identical in terms of the substantive identity and formal pattern of relations of the two dimensions involved, there is a crucial difference in the structural and operational character of the two dimensions as they function on the intrafamily and interfamily levels. At the intrafamily level, the structure has the character of a static classificatory matrix, and the dimensions of generation and consanguinity function as normative components of this matrix. As we pass from this level to the interfamily level of the system, however, the nature of the dimensions is altered: from static definitional components they become dynamic logical operations (transformations). The combinatorial principle governing the relation between the dimensions is likewise transformed from a static definitional rule governing the paradigmatic relations of the dimensions as components of the matrix of intrafamily role categories to a dynamic principle embodying the invariant factors governing the coordination of the transformations of the two dimensions.

The transformational character of the dimensions of interfamily structure reflects the generative nature of interfamily relations, their capacity as relations of "social reproduction" (to use Fortes' phrase). This is consistent with the structural perspective of an individual within the system in terms of which interfamily relations are first and foremost relations of passage across family and status/role boundaries.

The individual passes from the status of son or daughter and sibling in his or her natal family to the status of father or mother and spouse or affinal partner in the family of procreation. In other words, the individual transforms his or her structural position at the intrafamily level by transforming his or her structural position at the interfamily level.

Paralleling the change in the character of the dimensions of the system from static definitional components of role categories at the intrafamily level to transformational rules regulating the permutation of individuals' status as defined in terms of those categories at the interfamily level is a change in the level of generality and abstraction of the dimensions. At the interfamily level, the dimensions of the structure apply, by definition, not to a single family with its fixed internal pattern of relationships, but to a group of families in different developmental phases and the modifications in the status of individuals as they pass from one family to another.

The transformations of the dimensions of family structure that occur in the ordinary course of the developmental cycle of the family do not take place in a random, uncoordinated manner, as is attested by the fact that the developmental cycle has in all societies a regularly prescribed form (or set of alternate forms). The regularity of the process is guaranteed by a principle (or set of principles) establishing an invariant form of correlation (or order of application, which comes to the same thing) between the transformations occurring on each dimension. Such a principle is the common norm that marriage, or in several terms the consummation of the transformation of an individual's status on the consanguineal affinal dimension from child/sibling in the family of orientation to parent/spouse in the family of procreation, is directly correlated with the consummation of the generational transformation (i.e., the transformation of the "child" into an "adult," as symbolized by a rite of initiation). Such invariance principles are an essential component of stable transformational systems: they express the fixed (untransformable) aspects of the structure with reference to which the transformations operate and thus regulate the application of the transformations in such a way that the equilibrium of the system is maintained.

The invariance principle governing the order and manner in which the transformations of the dimensions of family role structure are carried out is not a merely formal or arbitrary feature. Like the transformations themselves, it is merely the formal expression of a vital aspect of the concrete functioning of the system. We have been speaking of the set of relations and operations necessary to bring into being a single family. Any individual's system of kinship relations, however, includes more than the three families or bigenerational family segments necessary for this. By the time an individual completes his or her life cycle, he or she has built up a field of relationships covering several such "family triangles" and in many societies extending well beyond them to the collective categories or descent groups in which they are embedded.

From an objective analytical point of view, all of these "triangles" or subsystems of an individual's over-all system of kinship relations are structurally identical. From the individual's point of view, however, they are all different in the sense that he or she plays different roles in each, e.g., in relation to the primal triangle comprising his or her family of orientation and the families of orientation of his or her parents, ego plays the roles of son or daughter, grandson or granddaughter, nephew or niece, and so on. In relation to the family of procreation of his or her own child, however, ego will play the inverse roles of grandfather or grandmother; toward the family of procreation of a sibling, similarly, the roles of uncle or aunt. The point is that the over-all organization of an individual's field of kinship relations may be thought of as a set of projections of the same minimal triangular transformational structure, from the different positions within that structure successively occupied by an individual in the course of his or her life cycle. As this implies, a "kinship system" is a system in the strict sense of the word, consisting of an integrated set of subsections which constitute complementary projections or extensions of the same set of rules.

It is for this reason that kinship systems possess the inherent tendency toward self-regulation that is the chief functional attribute of systems: because each subsection of the system is a product of the same set of rules, the stabilization or reinforcement of one such subset of relations tends to reinforce all the rest. All societies have numerous institutionalized means of reinforcing the various major subsets of relations that comprise their kinship systems. Chief among these are the *rites de passage* surrounding the major transformations by which families are created or dispersed, like birth, initiation, and marriage. These rituals and other devices, by regulating and reinforcing the key transformations by which new "family triangles" are created (and therefore by which the subsystems of the kinship system are interconnected) promote the reciprocal balance or structural agreement between the different subsections of the system.

This balance and coherence of the system as a whole, conversely, becomes the functional basis and structural referent for the principle of invariant correlation regulating the transformations of the basic set of dimensions by which each part of the system is generated. The same aspect of the system as a whole that makes it greater than the sum of its parts, in short, makes it self-regulating with respect to the vital question of the order and correlation of the transformations which make up its highest level of formal structure.

We began this section by setting ourselves the task of integrating within the same model two fundamental aspects of family structure, the developmental cycle of the family and the set of interfamily relations involved in the "social reproduction" of new families. The model that we have outlined fulfills this task: the system of correlated transformations of the dimensions of family structure of which the upper level of the model is composed constitute both a formal description of interfamily relations and the framework within which and by reference to which the internal transformations of the family cycle take place. These will be treated in the following section.

The model we have proposed, then, takes the form of a hierarchically organized system of levels, the lower of which (intrafamily structure) consists of a classificatory matrix of role categories defined in terms of a static set of dimensions, while the upper consists of a set of transformations of these dimensions regulated by a principle of invariant correlation among them. Such a system, representing the minimal set of relations capable of generating a bigenerational unit or subsegment of family structure, comprises on its higher (intergroup) level of organization three families (or bigenerational family segments) related to one another in a system of three interlocking pairs along two dimensions (consanguinity/affinity and generation). The pattern of relations among these three groups is introjected as the model for the internal structure of each of the component groups. This formal structure, as we have emphasized, reflects the functional exigencies of a self-regulating and self-reproducing system. At the same time, the formal and functional aspects of the system are stated in sufficiently general terms to accommodate a wide variety of specific functional arrangements and forms of family structure.

The model we have outlined assumes neither that the bigenerational groupings which form the structural elements of the system correspond to free-standing, independent social units nor that they possess any particular pattern of role structure (e.g., the "nuclear" family pattern). The model thus applies equally well to societies where the nuclear family is the normative family unit, matrilineal systems like the Nayar or Ashanti, where the minimal family takes the form of a uterine stirp in which the husband/father role may be negligible or totally lacking and to systems in which the bigenerational grouping is absorbed within a larger extended family household. Each of these family forms makes use of the basic dimensions of consanguinity/affinity and generation, and each relies upon a regular pattern of transformations of the role relations defined by these dimensions in each new generation in order to integrate the generation that has come of age into the family system. Each, in short, in common with every other human society for which we possess ethnographic records, relies upon some form of the bigenerational role cluster which forms the basic component of our model as the "growing edge" of its form of family organization.

It is to this universal aspect of family structure that the model we have outlined directly applies, although it is also potentially applicable to extended families and domestic groups. On the basis of these considerations, then, we may assert that the model we have proposed represents the universal structural properties of the human family and, by the same token, the elementary structure of kinship relations, insofar as any meaning can be attached to this term.

The position represented by the model we have put forward is, in essence, that there is no universal form of "the family": there are only universal aspects of the process by which families are produced. Insofar as the model we have outlined adequately represents these aspects, it must constitute the central generative mechanism upon which all kinship systems depend. It therefore constitutes the "elementary structure of kinship," insofar as any meaning can be given to this phrase.

Our model, as far as we have developed it up to this point, deals with what might be called the external exigencies of family structure: its emphasis is on interfamily relations and their feedback upon intrafamily structure. It does not deal with the question to which most other models of family structure have principally (if not exclusively) addressed themselves, namely, what are the internal exigencies of the primary socialization group, and what bearing do they have, if any, on the structure of the family? It is time for us to take up these questions.

THE STRUCTURE OF THE PRIMARY SOCIALIZATION GROUPING

Parsons' Concept of the Family

A discussion of the structure of the primary socialization grouping is the appropriate place to consider Parsons' contribution to "family" theory, for as will become apparent Parsons treats the family only in the capacity of a domestic socialization group and ignores the criteria by which the family proper is distinguished from such groups, viz., the interfamily nature of the affinal bond and the jural character of family roles.

Parsons conceives of the family as a small group, whose basic functions are "not to be interpreted as functions directly on behalf of the society, but on behalf of the personality."[31] These functions essentially come down to two: the socialization of the child and the stabilization of the personalities of the adult members.[32] The major structural characteristics of the family are derived by Parsons from these functions. It must be a small group because it is necessary for children in the early stages of socialization to be able to stabilize their affective patterns in a cognitively simplified environment consisting of only a few social objects. It is internally differentiated into subsystems or "subcollectivities," consisting of discrete role-relations or combinations thereof, for essentially the same reasons: This socially compartmentalized structure means that the child need not interact at the same level of participation with all members of the family in the earlier stages of socialization. It can thus make a gradual transition from the dyadic mother-child subcollectivity to participation in the family system as a whole.[33]

The family, furthermore, must be a subsystem of a larger society, and never an independent society in its own right, because the adult members of the family must have sufficient external involvements to prevent their becoming so exclusively involved with their children that they cannot accept the partial dissolution of their ties to them when the time comes. The children, by the same token, must have opportunities to form alternative attachments outside the family in order to liberate themselves from it.[34]

The idea that the family is internally organized as a system of subcollectivities and that certain of these role clusters may exist as independent social units in some societies (or may have done so in the earlier stages of social evolution) is of course a familiar idea. Parsons' contribution was to emphasize the importance of the fact that even within the conjugal family, certain roles and role-clusters continue to function as semi-autonomous subcollectivities. The relationships within and between these subcollectivities, in Parsons' analysis, constitute a field with distinctive structural properties of its own. Parsons is emphatic that it is the structure of subcollectivity relations, rather than relations among individual family members *per se,* that is internalized as the structure of the personality. For example, Parsons' proposition that the "superego" essentially consists of the internalized structure of the family as an integrated system of subcollectivities rather than the paternal or, at the most, parental role in isolation constitutes his basic critique of Freud.[35]

The major structural property of the system of subcollectivities comprising the nuclear family as a whole is its internal stratification into two primary levels of organizational complexity. The lower of these two levels is represented by individual subcollectivities like the mother-child group. This unit is not necessarily identical with the "mother-child dyad" postulated by Adams as the basic structural unit of the family[36] except in the very earliest phases of socialization (oral-dependency and love-dependency in Parsons' terminology). As defined vis-à-vis the other major subcollectivities of the conjugal family, such as the father-child relationship or the husband-wife bond, the Oedipal and post-Oedipal mother-child subcollectivity may include not only the mother-child role relationship but sibling relationships as well. As this example shows, subcollectivities may include more than one individual role-relation. Parsons, it is true, tends to treat the subcollectivity as identical with the individual role relationship in his schematic analysis: the distinction is, however, implicit in the nature of the concept of the subcollectivity and is obviously important for certain aspects of the structure of family relations. Just as a subcollectivity may include more than one role-relationship, it may be internally stratified into further levels of subcollectivities. Relative to the primary distinction between the level of the individual subcollectivity and that of the integrated structure of subcollectivities making up the family as a whole, however, such distinctions have little significance in Parsons' analysis.

The higher of the two major levels of subcollectivity structure, then, is constituted by the family as a whole, considered as an integrated system of such units. In Parsons' analysis of socialization, these two basic levels of internal stratification in the social structure of the family constitute a sort of psychological "ladder" up which the developing child progresses.

The child's induction into participation in each successive level of family structure is accompanied by his internalization of the relational criteria and values of the subcollectivities involved as components of the structure of his personality. The resolution of the Oedipal crisis comes with the child's successful internalization of the second or upper level of the subcollectivity structure of the family as a whole. The family, in turn, comprises only the lowest of a hierarchy of progressively more complex social systems (peer group, school, family of procreation, and adult community), into which the individual becomes integrated and which he progressively internalizes in the later stages of socialization.

Parsons' conception of the organization of the family as an internally stratified system of subcollectivities forms the conceptual bridge by which he links his model of the family with the general theory of the dynamics of role-differentiation in small task-oriented groups. This aspect of Parsons' analysis constitutes his major contribution to the theory of the family (or, in the terms of this chapter, the domestic socialization grouping) and deserves a careful critical examination in its own right.[37]

The Domestic Family and Primary Socialization Grouping as Small Groups

Parsons, as we have seen, bases his entire theory of the family on the idea that the "nuclear" or conjugal family, conceived as a cohesive domestic unit, is the universal normative form of the family both within and across cultures. He attempts to account for this purportedly universal phenomenon by demonstrating that the nuclear family role-pattern is only a particular instance of a more general category, that of small, task-oriented groups. Following Bales and his associates at the Harvard Laboratory of Social Relations, Parsons argues that all such groups have similar structural properties and that the "nuclear" family pattern of role-structure is the direct result of these generic features.

Because, as I have argued, his concept of the family is both ethnographically inaccurate and theoretically inadequate, Parsons' "small group" model actually has no bearing on the nature of the "family," if the latter is defined in the terms put forward in the present paper. As a model of the structure of domestic groups, and in particular of what I have called the primary socialization grouping, however, Parsons' attempt to utilize the general theory of small group dynamics has much to recommend it. It is necessary to separate the useful aspects of Parsons' analysis from the unfortunate theoretical baggage of his ideas about the family *per se*, but this, fortunately, is easily done, for a close examination of Bales' small group research fails to support Parsons' interpretation of it in "nuclear family" terms and provides a basis for a more general theory of domestic and socialization group structure.

The major discovery of Bales' research was that two complementary types of role specialization regularly occurred in his experimental four-person groups. Bales and Slater[38] call the two emergent types of functional specialization the "task specialist" and the "social-emotional specialist." The "task specialist" takes the lead in organizing the efforts of the group as a whole in relation to the assigned task: he tends to introduce new ideas and, in general, "new elements in the common situation," thereby generating considerable frustration and hostility as well as performing the necessary function of leading the group toward successful completion of its task.[39] The "social-emotional specialist" tends to be rather less active than the task specialist. His activity consists chiefly in reciprocating and expressing the feelings of the other group members, including both the "positive," task-oriented values embodied by the "task leader" and the negative feelings of resentment and frustration he arouses.

Bales and Slater repeatedly emphasize that the "task leader" or innovative leader of the group is, like the "social-emotional" specialist, a focus of strong affective attachments and reactions. The difference is that feelings toward him tend to be more sharply polarized, more highly ambivalent, and consequently less freely expressed. It is the job of the "social-emotional specialist" in a smoothly functioning group to mediate these ambivalent feelings and as far as possible to resolve or divert the tension arising from them.[40] The functions of "task specialist" and "social-emotional specialist" are obviously of an opposite and complementary character and for this reason tend to be performed by different individuals. The groups that performed best in relation to their experimental tasks were those in which the two complementary functional specializations became allied in a mutually supportive coalition, with the "social-emotional specialist" acting to redirect or otherwise absorb the hostile feelings of the group toward the "task-values" and commitments in support of him and the performance of the collective task.[41]

In four-person groups the two specializations tended to be assumed by different individuals. It is worth noting that this was not always the case: the same individual sometimes developed both specialized roles, a relatively common phenomenon in groups with fewer than four members. Parsons' equation of the pattern of role differentiation in Bales' experimental groups with the structure of the nuclear family was obviously facilitated by the numerical coincidence that both happen to consist of four actors or role-types (respectively). It should be kept in mind, however, that the general properties of the pattern of differentiation observed by Bales are not restricted to groups of four members and do not depend upon the assumption of complementary role-specializations by different actors. They may even be present in collectivities consisting of two persons (e.g., a socialization group consisting only of a mother and child).

Bales and Slater recognize many of the differences between their experimental t-groups and families, e.g., the former are composed of sexually and generationally undifferentiated members, lack culturally pre-established patterns of role differentiation, and so on. They maintain, however, that precisely because of these dissimilarities the parallels between the pattern of spontaneous role differentiation and functional specialization in the experimental t-group and the internal structure of the nuclear family are all the more significant.[42] After developing the idea that the adaptation of a group to new tasks or needs is essentially a question of "extending the common culture of the group," they sum up their findings in the following statement:

> The appearance of a differentiation between a person who symbolizes the demands of task accomplishment and a person who symbolizes the demands of social and emotional needs is implicit in the very existence of a social system responsive to an environment. Any such system has both an "inside" and an "outside" aspect and a need to build a common culture which deals with both. The tendency toward this fundamental differentiation holds whether there are age and sex differences between members or not. In the small decision-making group it appears as the difference between the task specialist and the best-liked man, in spite of the absence of differences in age and sex. In the marital couple it appears as the difference between the role of husband and wife, according to the sex difference, with age usually about the same or irrelevant. In the parent-child relation it appears along the age or generation axis, and holds whatever the sex of the parent or child. Moreover, in none of these contexts is the difference simply one of activity or power. Power is a quite separate variable, and its allocation between specialists often presents a problem of integration of the system, once a specialization occurs. The difference is in maintaining the internal state of affairs of the system in a *steady state* (including existing emotional attachments to persons, objects, modes of gratification, and modes of symbolic control over behavior), versus responsibility for, or vested interest in *change,* usually for the sake of some improved adjustment *vis-à-vis* the environment.[43]

This statement makes admirably clear that the essential difference between the task leader and the social-emotional specialist lies in their association with different ranges of social space/time. The "social-emotional specialist" expresses the values of the immediate, intragroup range of relatively concrete, stable, and affectively toned face-to-face relationships (the "*internal* state of affairs of the system"). The "task specialist" is primarily concerned with relations across the boundary of this system with systems and goals more distant in structural and temporal terms. The essential point of Bales and Slater's formulation is that the functional and affective properties of the two role specializations are inseparably correlated with their structural involvements with the internal and external relational fields of the group.

Stated in structural terms, the general thesis of Bales and Slater's analysis is that small groups, like "any social system responsive to an environment" manifest a characteristic pattern of differentiation into two hierarchically ordered subsystems. The dominant subsystem is concerned with the relationship of the group as a whole to its external environment, while the less complex, subordinate subsystem is oriented toward the internal stability of the group. The internal role structure of the group is generated by the dynamic process of accommodating and mediating the requirements of the external and internal fields in relation to each other. In this process the generic pattern of functional bifurcation is counterbalanced by the tendency to develop specialized integrative mechanisms, such as the "coalition" between the leaders of the respective subsystems or, in more general terms, the building of a "common culture which deals with both."

As a general statement of the minimal internal structural properties and functional dynamics of the domestic group or domestic family, this formulation is strikingly similar to Fortes' conception of the domestic group cycle as the outcome of the dynamic interaction between the internal and external fields of group relations.[44] It is specifically compatible with the concept of the domestic group as an internally differentiated system of subcollectivities. At the same time, it is couched in sufficiently general terms to be adaptable to a wide variety of concrete patterns of role differentiation or subcollectivity structure.

It is precisely at the level of these striking general features, unfortunately, that it is necessary to part company with Parsons' use of Bales' small group model. Rather than draw the parallel between the small group and the "family" at the general level of the functional dynamics of the interaction of the "internal" and "external" fields, or the generic aspects of the structural pattern of differentiation and integration, Parsons attempts to identify the generic structural and functional properties of the small group model with specific dimensions of the role structure of the nuclear family. His starting point is the equation of the sexual dimension of role differentiation in the family with the dichotomy of the "task specialist" and the "social-emotional specialist" (or as he calls it, the "instrumental-expressive" dichotomy) in the small group. Females, in this view, play relatively "expressive" roles, primarily because

> . . . the bearing and early nursing of children establish a strong presumptive primacy of the relation of the mother to the small child, and this in turn establishes a pre-

sumption that the man, who is exempted from these biological functions, should specialize in the alternative instrumental direction.[45]

In sharp contrast to Bales and Slater themselves (in the passage just quoted), however, Parsons declines to consider the generational dimension, i.e., the relations between parents and children, as an axis of instrumental/expressive role specialization. He asserts, instead, that it is

> . . . in its social role-significance, biologically given, since the helplessness of the small child, particularly of course the infant, precludes anything approaching equality of "power" between the generations in the early stages of socialization. This biological "intrinsicness" does not, however, we feel apply in at all the same way to sex; both parents are adults and children of both sexes are equally powerless.[46]

Parsons thus winds up with a one-to-one identification of the two substantive dimensions of his model of nuclear family role structure, sex and generation, with the two general dimensions of structural differentiation and functional specialization in Bales' small group model, instrumentality/expressiveness and power. Parsons' exclusive identification of the sexual dimension of family role structure with the instrumental/expressive dimension of functional specialization in the small experimental group, together with his complementary equation of the generational and power dimensions, is the basis of his assertion that the role structure of the "nuclear family" is the sole form of family structure compatible with Bales' generic model of small group structure.[47] This claim becomes, in turn, the theoretical basis of Parsons' argument for the universality of the nuclear family. A proposition directly derived from this interpretation of the small group model is the explanation of the conjugal relationship between the adult male and female members of the family as an instance of the "coalition" of instrumental and expressive leaders. As Parsons interprets it within the framework of Bales' small group theory, the marriage relationship plays a vital role in the maintenance of the social and psychological stability of the family, considered as a coresident, interacting small group. The attempt to derive the relationship of marriage from the internal dynamics of the individual domestic group is, in terms of the analysis of family structure presented in the preceding section, perhaps the single most untenable point in Parsons' conception of "family" structure.

The major difficulty with Parsons' use of Bales' work in his model of nuclear family structure, however, is that it is manifestly inconsistent, not only with the ethnographic evidence but also with Bales' interpretation of his own research findings. Bales and Slater's clear statement that in their terms the parent-child relation is as much an instance of the instrumental/expressive dimension as the husband-wife relation, in direct contradiction to Parsons' attempt to identify this structural feature in an exclusive, one-to-one fashion with the sexual dimension of family structure, has already been cited. Parsons' exclusive identification of the "power" dimension with parent-child and not with male-female relations seems equally arbitrary in the light of Bales and Slater's statement, and is certainly unacceptable as an ethnographic generalization. Ethnographically speaking, "instrumental," "expressive," and "power" functions may be subdivided and distributed in a variety of ways among different "role types" within the family.

This is clearly a major area of cultural variability in family structure, rather than the essentially uniform pattern Parsons assumes. Examples of differing patterns of distribution of the basic functions of power and "instrumentality/expressiveness" between the sexes within the family-domestic group complex are actually rather common in the ethnographic literature, if one examines it with an eye to ascertaining variation.[48] True, male and adult roles tend, other things being equal, to be more "instrumental" and dominant in terms of power; female and children's roles tend to assume the complementary attributes of "expressiveness" and subordination. Ethnographic evidence, however, shows that the actual variability of sex roles in these respects renders such broad generalizations nugatory as bases for universal statements about particular family roles like "mother," "husband-father," and the like. That women not infrequently play instrumental and even dominant roles in the domestic group or family is ethnographically attested by a number of familiar cases. Among the Nuer of the Sudan, for example, a woman may set up her own household, keep cattle, marry wives, and become the pater of her children. A less exotic but more familiar case is that of the "matrifocal" household found in many Caribbean countries as well as in many urban areas of sub-Saharan Africa. In such households, the mother acts both as instrumental and expressive leader. This example, in common with a number of instances encountered by Bales and his associates in their experimental groups, makes clear that the "coalition" between instrumental and expressive leaders and the integration of the differentiated functions and structural levels they represent can be embodied by a single actor playing both complementary roles.

Even in many societies in which domestic families of the "nuclear" type are common, the wife/mother may play the instrumental roles related to the immediate domestic context (nuclear or even extended family household, gardening and collecting activities),

that is, all of the instrumental activities which have an immediate impact on children undergoing socialization. The father's role in the domestic context may in such societies take on relatively indulgent and "expressive" characteristics, while his "instrumental" functions are limited to relatively infrequent ceremonial, jural, and political situations, public contexts, and activities like hunting, all of which tend to be unrelated to the socialization process. I should say that this description applies to a number of Amerindian societies, such as the Central Brazilian people among whom I carried out field research, the Northern Kayapo. The Kayapo example, by the way, may also serve to illustrate the possibility that the function of stabilizing the personalities of the adult members of the family may be predominantly fulfilled by extrafamilial social groups, rather than by the marriage relationship within the family, as Parsons asserts. This is doubtless more commonly true for males than for females in cross-cultural terms. The Kayapo male, rather like the London working-class males described by Willmott and Young,[49] spends most of his free time in the men's house with his peers and remains relatively uninvolved in the affairs of his family. It would seem that in such cases, the family role contributes far less to the stability of the male personality than extrafamilial relations with male friends and associates.

This sort of variation in the structural differentiation of instrumental, expressive, and power functions is consistent with the analytical separation between the "power" and "instrumentality/expressiveness" dimensions emphasized by Bales and Slater (as in the passage previously quoted). It is, however, inconsistent with Parsons' representation of the two dimensions as essentially complementary and identified in a rigid, one-to-one manner with the crosscutting structural dimensions of sex and generation. The tendency in the relations between the two dimensions would seem, in fact, to be directly contrary to Parsons' formulation. It is improbable, on grounds of sheer common sense, that the position of paramount power within the family, or indeed in any group, should be located within the "expressive" subcollectivity, in situations where it is clearly differentiated from the "instrumental" level of subcollectivity structure. The leading "instrumental" role actor, representing as he does the higher of the two levels of intragroup structure (i.e., the group in its capacity as an integral unit vis-à-vis external situations and other social groups), must always tend to stand in a dominant relationship to the "expressive" leader or subcollectivity if the viability of the group in relation to its environment is to be maintained. This means that the leading instrumental figure of the family (in the case of the typical conjugal family, the father) will tend also to be the most powerful figure.

Ethnographic exceptions to this rule will tend to be of the sort already illustrated by the case of the Kayapo, where the father, as the ultimately more "powerful" parent, remains aloof from the day-to-day "instrumental" affairs of the household, leaving the mother to assume the role of "instrumental leader" for most practical purposes within this domain. Such exceptions, however, only prove the rule. Stated in general terms, the principle is that "power" and "instrumentality/expressiveness" are essentially parallel aspects of a single common axis of functional and structural differentiation, the central feature of which, as defined by Bales and Slater for their small group model, is the differentiation between "externally" and "internally" oriented subcollectivities or levels of group structure.

Parsons deserves great credit for calling attention to the relevance of small group research for the conceptualization of the generic properties of the structure of primary socialization groups and domestic groups in general. His application of the small group model as the basis of "nuclear family" structure, however, involves four interrelated analytical fallacies. In the first place, it rests on the confusion of the domestic group, to which the small group model properly applies, with the family, defined as a jurally or normatively sanctioned conjugal unit. In the second place, it purports to account for aspects of both domestic group and family structure (e.g., the conjugal bond) that are the direct products of intergroup relations solely on the basis of intragroup dynamics. In the third place, it is based on a distortion of the relationship of the dimensions of the original small group model. Finally, it depends on the identification of a set of highly general and abstract properties of small groups with the particular features of a single form of family structure. There is clearly no such necessary connection between the general structural and functional features of the Bales-Slater model and any particular form of family or domestic group structure. The potential applicability of the model in more general terms, e.g., to a model of the general properties of domestic or socialization group structure broad enough to encompass the known range of ethnographic variation, is, it goes without saying, by no means compromised by these strictures.

A Developmental Model of the Primary Socialization Grouping

The critique of Parsons and of Bales and Slater developed in the two preceding sections has put us in a position to reformulate their insights and findings into a new model of a more dynamic kind, consistent with the model of the family put forward in the earlier part of this paper.

A comprehensive analysis of any system of social action, as Parsons has emphasized, must proceed from two complementary perspectives: that of the categorization of social objects and that of the orientations of actors towards those objects. The model of family structure previously put forward is framed exclusively within the former of these two perspectives. Parsons' analysis of the domestic socialization group as a small group, as we summarized it here, stresses the complementary perspective. Parsons, of course, assumes a structure of role categories classified in terms of the "objective" dimensions of sex, age, and consanguinity/affinity, but he is primarily concerned with the relationships between role-actors and "subcollectivities" from the standpoint of the nature of the orientations of the actors involved towards each other. "Expressiveness" and "instrumentality," subordination and dominance (power), which form the primary structural components of Parsons' model of the domestic group as a system of subcollectivities, are modes of orientation of actors rather than of categorization of actors as social objects. In the preceding section, we proposed a simplified reformulation of Parsons' model, which followed Parsons in positing two hierarchically related levels of subcollectivity structure but differed from him in suggesting that the dimensions of power and instrumentality/expressiveness should be interpreted as essentially parallel aspects of the differentiation of the two structural levels. The lower level of the model consists of individual subcollectivities: in developmental terms, the mother-child subcollectivity, which at first represents the infant's total social universe, corresponds to this basic level. The higher level consists of the group as an integrated whole. The lower level is comprised of relatively "expressive" subcollectivities such as the mother-child and sibling groups, maintained in their proper relations to each other through the mediating role of the "power" and "instrumental" leader (or leaders) who represent the group as a whole.

In his analysis of socialization, Parsons introduces a further dimension of actor-orientation: autonomy/dependence. This he treats as parallel with the power dimension, which he considers as parallel to the generational dimension of object-categorization. The child, for example, has a basically dependent orientation to his parents, as dominant adults, and an essentially autonomous orientation toward his siblings, as peers of roughly equivalent "power." Parsons' analysis of socialization concentrates primarily on an account of the progressive transformation of the growing child's role-relationships, both within the family of orientation and outside it, along the dimensions of instrumentality/expressiveness and autonomy/dependency ("power" gets relatively little separate treatment).

It is characteristic of Parsons' approach to family structure that his entire discussion of socialization is couched in terms of an individual child moving through membership in successive subcollectivities and structural levels of the nuclear family (considered as the primary socialization grouping), without treating the structure of the family itself as changing at the same time. In the light of the foregoing discussion, it is clear that the development of the child through his successive stages of integration into the structure of the domestic group cannot be considered apart from the accompanying changes in the structural framework of those relationships themselves. When the relationships between the subcollectivities of family structure, defined according to Parsons' dimensions of actor-orientation, are considered from the developmental point of view, a pattern emerges that is strikingly similar to the model of the transformations of the objective dimensions of family role structure (i.e., generation and consanguinity/affinity) formulated in our earlier discussion.

Let us begin with the dimension of instrumentality/expressiveness. We have seen, following Bales and Slater, that the "expressive" orientation is essentially associated with maintaining the internal equilibrium of a relationship of collectivity against disturbances caused by demands for adaptation to external circumstances. "Instrumentality," on the other hand, consists in an adaptive orientation toward such demands, entailing the acceptance of the concomitant changes in the internal emotional and structural equilibrium of the group. For the Oedipal child in Parsons' model, the family is internally divided into relatively clearcut zones of expressive and instrumental relations. The former consists of the mother-child subcollectivity. The latter is constituted by the relationship of the instrumental leader of the family to the child and his mother, in her "nurturant," expressive capacity (as we have pointed out, this formulation is not cross-culturally valid, e.g., the mother may also play the leading instrumental role).

As the child develops toward maturity, however, this internally bifurcated, "Oedipal" structure shifts and is finally inverted. An initial development in this process in many families is the differentiation of a sibling play-group as a quasi-independent branch

of the mother-child subcollectivity. Within this group, the child is able to play relatively nondependent and pseudo-"instrumental" roles. Here he may practice, in his play behavior, conforming to the demands of the instrumental leader of the family. Peer-group relations outside the family continue this process, until, with adolescence, the growing child becomes capable of fully "instrumental" relationships with members of different families. At the same time, he ceases to orient himself toward the instrumental leader of his own family as a member of a dependent, subordinate subcollectivity of that family. He may, of course, continue to defer to the family head in his capacity as head of a superfamilial grouping such as a lineage. His entire family of orientation, including his relations with its "instrumental leader," instead progressively takes on the role of an "expressive" collectivity in relation to his new extrafamilial relations. The family as a whole, as the higher of the two levels of the structure of the individual family, now occupies a position in terms of the expressiveness/instrumentality dimension that is exactly the inverse of its position at the Oedipal crisis. What was "external" to the Oedipal mother-child collectivity has now become "internal" in relation to the wider systems of interfamily relations, whose culminating expression is the formation of a new family of procreation.

The inversion of the pattern of instrumental and expressive modes of orientation is accompanied by the reciprocal transformation of the pattern of dependent and autonomous orientations. Dependency can be functionally defined as a mode of orientation characterized by ego's inability to impose his wishes by direct action upon his environment, and his corresponding need to accommodate himself to the demands and requirements of that environment. Ego, in other words, acts as a dependent variable in relation to the object or environment, considered as an independent variable. Autonomy constitutes the complementary orientation, in which ego imposes his own desires and definition of the situation upon the object or environment. Here ego is the independent variable, and the objective environment the dependent variable. In early childhood, dependency is the primary mode of orientation toward the adult members of the family and, in a more general sense, toward the objective environment as a whole. Autonomous modes of interaction are developed at this stage, of course, but in considerable part this must take place through play, fantasy, and imitation. After the Oedipal phase, play with siblings and extrafamilial peers becomes increasingly important as an arena of development of autonomous relational capabilities. This development, however, does not take the form of the inversion or substitution of dependency by autonomy. It is rather a question of learning to balance dependent and autonomous elements within the same relationship, to arrive at an equilibrium characterized by reciprocal give-and-take. This equilibrium tends in many societies to be developed in relations with age mates drawn from different families within age-stratified peer groups. In these groups the age differentials characterizing the relations between intrafamilial role relations can be to a large extent avoided and their direct connotations of dependency and radical inequalities of power neutralized. This pattern is more widely followed for boys than for girls, partly because autonomous equilibrium and independence is more widely prized as a masculine than a feminine trait.

The climax of this development comes in adolescence, with the achievement of fully "reciprocal" relations, characterized by an equilibrium of autonomous and dependent orientations toward agemates from other families. The corollary of this development in the structure of intrafamilial role relationships is the achievement of a similar balance of dependency and autonomy in ego's relations with the "instrumental" and "expressive" leaders of his family of orientation. Dependency on the parents within the domain of the natal family is a function of the child's inability to have fully autonomous relations of his own, either within or outside of the family. Once the capacity for such relations is developed (a process which always involves extrafamilial relations), the individual no longer depends upon the imposition of ordered and protected intrafamilial relations by his parents. Structurally speaking, therefore, the passage out of the natal family and domestic field into the wider social sphere of communal relations is accompanied by the transformation of the intrafamilial relationship between the subcollectivities of the offspring-siblings, on the one hand, and the adult members of the family, on the other, from asymmetrical dependency and subordination to comparative equality and reciprocity.[50] The latter can be structurally defined as an equilibrium of dependency and autonomy orientations, accompanied by a weakening of the dominance of the parents in terms of domestic power and authority.

As in the case of the transformations of the structural dimensions of consanguinity/affinity and generation, the transformations of the orientational dimensions of expressiveness/instrumentality and dependency/autonomy are of complementary logical types (inverse and reciprocal, respectively). As such, they form mutually indispensable and supportive but essentially parallel aspects of the common process of developmental change in the subcollectivity structure of the family. Again, as in the former case, both transformations are directly correlated with the generalization of the normative patterns of role-orientation that accompanies the extension of the individual's network of role relations beyond the boundaries of the natal family.

Finally, the results of the transformations on both orientational dimensions are that ego becomes capable of combining complementary orientational modes within single role-relationships that were, in the initial phases of his life cycle within his family of orientation, polarized between structurally opposed subcollectivities. In adult relationships with peers and spouse, for example, an individual normally combines the autonomous and dependent modes of orientation in a more or less stable equilibrium. This adult situation stands in sharp contrast to the typical pattern of family relations of the young child, which is characterized by asymmetrical and unstable combinations of autonomy and dependence. Similarly, in the earlier phases of childhood the mother-child and sibling subcollectivities are characterized by an asymmetrical preponderance of "expressive" orientations. Relations to the instrumental leader of the family, meanwhile, have a relatively one-sided "instrumental" quality, since the behavioral demands and role-expectations this figure represents emanate from "outside" the relatively permissive and undemanding context of ego's "expressive" relations to the nurturing mother. Relations with siblings and playmates typically stand somewhere between these two extremes.

The successful "internalization" of these external demands, however, gradually alters ego's orientation to the instrumental leader of his own family, while providing him with the capacity for fully developed instrumental relations with others outside his family. These relationships, while instrumental from the standpoint of the individual's original position within the family of orientation, can now become new "expressive" relations. They may, in other words, become the focus of new sets of "internal" orientations from "within" which the individual may relate to other collectivities and subcollectivities (including his own natal family, for certain purposes) in an instrumental way. The result of the correlated transformations of both the dependency/autonomy and expressiveness/instrumentality dimensions, in short, is that they cease to be structural polarities anchored in distinct concrete role-collectivities and become instead reversible modes of relating to the same role relationships. The individual now has the capacity to shift (transform) his orientations, from context to context or moment to moment, from dependent to autonomous and back again, or from instrumental to expressive and the reverse.

This reversibility of orientational modes or attitudes, however, is achieved only within the framework of a process that is itself irreversible. The thrust of developmental change is always in the direction of instrumentality (adapting to wider relational fields and more demanding sets of behavioral expectations) and autonomy (developing the capacity to relate to the objective environment on its own terms, in order to maximize the effectiveness of one's own actions toward and within it). The "equilibrium" that is finally achieved between the autonomy and dependency orientations of the mature individual is thus one in which autonomy has the preponderant role. The equilibrium between instrumental and expressive subcollectivity orientations at the highest level of family structure is characterized by an analogous bias toward instrumental relations.

The implication of these "irreversible" aspects of the development of the orientational dimensions of the system of family subcollectivity relationships is that the transformations of these dimensions, like those of the dimensions of actor-categorization (generation and consanguinity/affinity) are correlated on the basis of an invariant principle of a skewed or asymmetrical character. In this case, the principle seems to be that the development of the capacity for reciprocal relationships (i.e., relations based on an equilibrium of autonomous and dependent orientations) is directly correlated with the attainment of a reversible equilibrium of instrumental and expressive relations, with the proviso that "equilibrium" must be based on the functional preponderance of autonomy in the former case and instrumentality in the latter.

A crucial point that emerges from this analysis is that the structural focus of the system of correlated transformations in role-orientations is the level of intergroup (or at least extragroup) relations. As in the case of the family, then, the generative structure of the developmental cycle of the primary domestic or socialization grouping is essentially a triadic hierarchy, in which the transformational ruler and invariance principles are institutionally coded at the highest or intergroup level.

A general formal model of the developmental cycle of the minimal socialization grouping has been developed on the basis of considerations which hold regardless of whether this unit takes the form of a "family" or merely an ad hoc domestic grouping. I have tried to show how Parsons' conception of the structure of the "family" as a "small group," composed of distinct "subcollectivities" related according to a set of elementary dimensions of actor orientation, can be integrated into this model. At the same time, it has become apparent that a virtually exact correspondence exists between the structure of this model and the model of the developmental cycle of the family previously worked out on the basis of the contributions of Fortes and Lévi-Strauss, which was formulated in terms of the cognitive dimensions of categorization of family roles, rather than the orientations of the actors playing such roles to each other in concrete face-to-face groups. A thorough treatment of both models in developmental terms has made it possible to see them for what they are: homologous structures for the fulfillment of discrete but complementary functions.

The modes of orientation in terms of which the subcollectivity structure of Parsons' family model is articulated are, as he has pointed out, directly bound up with the major types of psychological relations of a child undergoing socialization.[51] The pattern of development in the relationships among these subcollectivities that we have just outlined has, over and beyond the type of correspondence indicated by Parsons, a structural correspondence with the process of personality development. If, therefore, organization, including the correlated transformations and equilibration of the expressive, instrumental, dependent, and autonomous orientations that we have outlined, represents the universal parameters of the structure of primary socialization groups, it may be that this simple system of orientations and transformations represents a universal template for the psychological patterning of the socialization process. At a highly generalized level, it may thus be considered a basic paradigm of the cognitive, affective, and orientational structure of the human personality.

The Relationship between the Family and the Domestic Socialization Group

The recension of Parsons' analysis of the subcollectivity structure of the family provided in the preceding section does not presuppose the existence of a "family" in the normative sense defined in this paper, still less a "nuclear" family. It merely states the nature of the relationships among the constituent subcollectivities of the primary socialization grouping and the transformations that must tend to occur in these relations during the process of socialization, whether the grouping in question is a free-standing social unit or is inextricably embedded in a larger domestic group. What I have tried to show is that there is a homology between the developmental cycle of the family, considered as a unit or level of organization of normative systems of kinship relations, and that of the primary socialization grouping, considered as a domestic unit or portion thereof. This homology exists at the level of the formal parameters of the developmental processes of the two types of groups: It does not depend upon identical role structure or functional content. If the developmental cycle of the primary socialization grouping can be said to perform the functions of socializing individuals and replicating the domestic units within which this is done, the developmental cycle of the family could be said to fulfill the analogous functions of integrating individuals into the normative system of kinship relations and reproducing the basic units or segments of units through which the kinship system is perpetuated. The family and its developmental cycle represent, as it were, hypostatizations at the level of the symbolic categories of the kinship system of the cyclical, regenerative properties of the primary socialization group. The effect is the regeneration of the normative framework of the social order on the same plan as the reproduction of the concrete groupings of the domestic order and the psychological structure of the personality.

Let us summarize the common features of the structures of the family and the primary socialization group, together with their generative or cyclical properties. Both can be seen as hierarchical orders of relations. At the lowest level are individual role-relations or subcollectivity relations which cannot be said to possess, in and of themselves, a fully defined social character of meaning in terms of the categories of society at large. This social character is, properly speaking, the product of the next level of organization, at which the minimal units are set in relation to each other to form more complex units (e.g., families or domestic groups). It is only in terms of such combinatorial relationships that the lower-level units are defined in cultural terms. Finally, beyond the level of combinatorial sets or groupings, structures of the second level are dynamically related to each other in terms of a set of transformations. It is characteristic of such sets of transformations, as we have seen, that they tend to be correlated in determinate ways according to principles of invariance.

Two general points may be made about this organizational pattern. In the first place, the internal structural relations of the system constitute a template for the reproduction of the system itself. Stated from the opposite point of view, the regenerative capacity of the system becomes at the same time the basis of its internal organization and the template for its ability to adapt to new "inputs" and to adjust to losses and alterations of its components. In the second place, the hierarchical organization of the system has the basic property that relationships between the structure of its constituent units at a given level can always be expressed in terms of relationships between units of the adjacent lower level. This means that the structure of the system as a whole (i.e., at the highest level) can be continually recreated by the systematic recombination of lower-level units and is therefore best expressed by the rules governing this process.

This type of hierarchically integrated system of categories, transformations, and parameters represents, I have suggested, the universal form of the structure and developmental cycle of the primary socialization group and also of the "family" (or at least that segment of what is culturally defined as a family that is formed anew in every social generation). The point is not that the specific role structure of the two types of groupings need be identical in any given society. It is rather that, at the formal level, the patterning of their regenerative or developmental processes and the systematic properties of the resulting role structures will be homologous. The explanation of the homology is not far to seek. Both types of groupings perform similar functions. These are, at the individual level, the replacement and integration of individuals into the society as socially and psychologically mature adults, and, at the level of social organization, the regeneration of the social groupings within which these functions are accomplished. The two types of groupings are, in other words, broadly homologous in function as well as in structure, even though their functions remain analytically distinct and relate to different levels of social structure.

The explanation of the homologies between the two groupings has a great deal to do with the fact that both operate within the basic human parameters of birth, copulation, and death. At this level of analysis, in short, we approach the ultimate point of articulation between human cultural and social systems and the "brass tacks," as T. S. Eliot called them, of human biological and psychological existence. This is not to say that the elementary structures of human society can be reduced to emanations of human biology or personality structure. The point of the present analysis is that the former constitute collective cultural "appropriations" (in the Marxist sense) of these basic biopsychic factors. The decisive feature of this appropriation, I am suggesting, is the reformulation of the relationships of biological, psychological, and social reproduction as components of a systematically integrated symbolic code. This code, I have argued, functions both as an image of the crucial relations of social reproduction and a formula for their organization and replication at the collective level.

This essay has emphasized the formal correspondences between the family and the domestic socialization grouping, as well as their mutual variability in concrete role structure. The latter emphasis should not be allowed to obscure the constant substantive point of connection between the two species of groupings, to wit the mother-child subcollectivity. The latter forms an indispensable component of both groups, although its structural role, as we have seen, is rather different in each. It is the structural core of the socialization grouping, while the affinal tie through which it is connected to a wider framework of family and kinship relations forms the structural core of the family. As this implies, however, the mother-child dyad nevertheless constitutes one of the minimal structural references of the affinal tie (the other being the male genitor/spouse). The mother-child grouping therefore forms the common axis around which the remainder of the role structures of the family and domestic grouping vary more or less freely.

There is another substantive factor common to both the family and the domestic group: sex, as both a symbolic and presymbolic component of role structure. By the "symbolic" meaning of sex I refer primarily to the paradigm formed by the two basic modes of sexual connection, namely intercourse and procreation, and the manner in which these two meanings seem universally to be utilized to express the relationship between the intergroup and intragroup levels of family structure (affinity being universally associated with intercourse and filiation, which has its source within the family, being universally associated with procreative sexual connection). By "presymbolic" functions I refer to the apparently universal phenomenon of incest avoidance (that is, the spontaneous avoidance of sexual intercourse with members of one's domestic group of orientation). As recent primate studies have conclusively shown, incest avoidance does not depend on symbolic relations (incest taboos, which are cultural and therefore symbolic rules, are something else again, but are not universal cultural phenomena).[52] Incest avoidance properly refers to domestic group but not family structure *per se,* while the reverse is true of the symbolic paradigm of intercourse and procreation previously referred to. The two sets of sexual factors are associated, in a relatively loose and imprecise way, through the almost (but not quite) universal tendency for the set of relatives toward whom an individual ordinarily feels incest avoidance to form the core (but not necessarily the whole) of the category of prohibited marriage partners. In this way, the cultural and precultural meanings of sex provide another point of substantive connection between the family and the socialization grouping.

SOCIALIZATION, PERSONALITY, AND THE STRUCTURE OF INTELLIGENCE IN RELATION TO FAMILY AND DOMESTIC GROUP STRUCTURE

Parallelism between Social and Psychological Structures: Internalization or Analogy between Functionally Autonomous Levels?

We come now to the problem of the relation between the organization of the family and socialization grouping and the psychological structure of the mind and personality. Limitations of space allow only brief consideration of the two major questions bearing on this issue: first, what, if any, correspondences exist between the sociological structures we have outlined and the psychological structures that are the outcome of the socialization process (broadly defined as the formation of the mature personality and intelligence); and second, what evidence do such correspondences provide for the nature of the relationship between the social and the psychological levels of the socialization process?

The correspondences between the structures of the family, the primary socialization group, the personality, and the intelligence can be seen to best advantage by comparing the broad outlines of their developmental processes. There is obviously no space here to do more than sketch a few of these correspondences. The model of psychological development best suited to this purpose is, in my opinion, that of Piaget.[53]

Piaget conceives of the organization of the intelligence as a homeostatic system founded upon a pair of complementary "functional invariants," with their associated structural features and operations. These basic "functional invariants" are "adaptation" and "organization," which broadly correspond to Parsons' two primary categories of social action: the orientation of actors and the categorization of objects, respectively. The developmental processes of these two basic modes of mental functioning are conceived as parallel and mutually interdependent, although different in content.

The "adaptive" mode, which comprises the system of orientational schemata, is in turn subdivided into two broad types of orientation, assimilation and accommodation. These two orientational categories correspond closely to the categories of autonomy and dependency (respectively) in the Parsons-Freud model, as they have been defined and discussed in the preceding section. The development of mature adaptive capacity depends, for Piaget, upon arriving at a stable equilibrium between the two complementary orientations, in which assimilation nevertheless plays the primary role. The attainment of this equilibrium is in turn dependent upon a sufficiently complex "organization" of the system of cognitive and affective objects and schemata. Because of this interdependence, the mature development of both adaptive and organizational capacities tends to occur at roughly the same time (around puberty).

In the last section, I presented an account of the development of what in Piaget's terms would be called the basic "adaptive" schemata or orientational components of the personality. The correspondences between this set of psychological schemata and the social structure of the primary socialization group and its developmental cycle were emphasized. At the same time, a close parallelism between the structure and development of this system of "adaptive" orientations and the organization of the developmental cycle of the family, considered as a system of categories of social role-objects, was indicated. To complete the comparison with Piaget's model, then, it remains to explore the correspondences between the structure and developmental process of the family and the domestic socialization grouping and Piaget's model of the development of the "organizational" aspect of the mature intelligence.

The development of organizational capacity takes place, according to Piaget, in three broad stages. In the first or "sensory-motor" stage, the child acquires the fundamental sense of the "permanence of objects" in relation to himself. This sense becomes the basis for his advance to the next stage (at about one and one-half years of age). This stage, which Piaget calls "pre-operational," begins with the acquisition of the capacity for symbolic representation of particular objects and actions (one and one-half to two years), passes through a phase of proto-classificatory conceptual groupings of discrete objects, and culminates in the attainment of a capacity for simple logical manipulations of a relatively concrete and static nature, such as binary classification (e.g., of the members of one's family according to sex and age). This point, normally reached by five to six years of age, opens the way for the third major stage, that of "operations." "Operations" consist of logical procedures of a relatively dynamic type, capable of grasping a number of varying patterns of relations as permutations of a set of more general and powerful operations, i.e., transformations. In the first phase of the operational period, that of "concrete" operations, the child masters the two fundamental logical modes of transformation, the inverse and the reciprocal. He or she is, however, unable as yet to apply these in correlation with one another to the understanding of a single problem or situation. The capacity for abstract thought is, moreover, still relatively undeveloped so that mental operations tend to be limited to immediate concrete situations.

At about the age of puberty, the adolescent becomes capable of correlating sets of transformations of different types on the basis of principles of invariant correlation between them. The adolescent thus achieves the capacity to deal with more complex situations, for example, ones involving the interrelation of several sets or groups of objects separated in space and time, abstractly represented as logical permutations of each other. The individual sets or groups subsumed under such a permutational or transformational frame of reference are of the type

mastered at the second major ("pre-operational") stage of development, e.g., static classificatory matrices. Piaget's model for a fully functioning intelligence at the formal operational level is the "INRC group," that is, a group of four mutually commutative transformations (Inverse, Reciprocal, Correlative, and Identity), each of which is related to two others respectively. The logical relations constitute the principles of invariant correlation or "conservation" upon which the structure as a whole depends. This logical group is, in effect, a simple equilibrium system, capable of adjusting with perfect flexibility to modifications or transformations of its components in order to maintain its invariant parameters.

Piaget's model of the intelligence in its final (operational) stage of development thus comprises a hierarchical system closely analogous to the models of family and domestic group structure put forward previously. The levels of organization represented by the stages of the development of the intelligence according to Piaget, moreover, correspond closely to the structural levels of family and domestic group relations which the child typically enters at roughly the same time he or she develops the mental abilities in question. Piaget and several researchers influenced by his work have shown that important aspects of personality, such as moral attitudes and values and sex-role identification, develop along the same broad lines as the cognitive aspects of the system.[54] Piaget has claimed that affective patterns generally conform, in structural respects, to cognitive patterns.[55] The correspondence between the development of the orientational or "adaptive" components of personality and the transformational structure of domestic group relations outlined in the preceding section, which is, as we have just seen, itself formally parallel with the main lines of cognitive development and the structure of the mature intelligence, strongly reinforces this point. If Piaget and his followers are correct and the structure and development of the personality turn out to be homologous with that of the cognitive aspects of the mind, the systematic parallels between the psychological and sociological structures with which we have been concerned becomes, for the general purposes of this chapter, complete.

Family Structure, Mental Structure, and the Basis of Cultural Competence

Granted that the fundamental structure of the human mind is closely analogous to the elementary structures of social relations, as represented by the family and domestic grouping, and furthermore that the major developmental stages of the psychological and sociological levels of structure tend to coincide, does this finding allow us to reach any conclusions about the causal priority of either level in relation to the other? Specifically, does it afford us any basis for concluding that the structure of the mind is formed through a process of "internalization" of the social relations of the socialization group or the family? Alternatively, does it give grounds for the contention that the structures of the family and/or the socialization grouping are essentially projections of psychological factors or needs? Parsons, as we have seen, takes both of these positions in different phases of his analysis.

The analysis we have presented, it seems to me, gives no support for either of these contentions, while at the same time pointing to a more profound and thoroughgoing correspondence between the structural and developmental characteristics of both complementary manifestations of sociological and psychological levels (i.e., the family and socialization grouping and the intelligence and personality, respectively). The major conclusion that emerges from the generative model outlined in this paper is that the structural parallelisms between the two levels arise from the functional requirements of the organization of generative processes in terms of self-regulating symbolic codes. The intelligence and personality are, granted the validity of this analysis, to be interpreted as symbolic codes of a generative character, whose internal structure moreover preserves the template of the process by which they themselves were generated: the same holds for the family and the domestic group. The correspondences in the timing of the structurally analogous developmental stages are, from this point of view, to be accounted for as adaptations of the generative processes on the respective structural levels involved to the rate of development of the basic capacity for cognitive and emotional organization of the human child.

There is a further, profoundly significant piece of evidence that the features we have identified as universal properties of family and domestic group structure, on the one hand, and of the structure of the mind and personality, on the other, reflect the generic functional requirements of generative, self-regulating systems rather than derive directly from one another. This is that the same basic structural properties we have described appear to be shared by other fundamental cultural codes such as language and simple technological systems.

The example of language is the better known. The essence of the revolution in linguistic theory wrought by transformational grammar (which seems certain to survive the current ferment in linguistic theory) is the notion that the structure of language is most accurately represented by a hierarchical model in which the uppermost (most complex and descriptively powerful) level of organization consists of a set of transformational rules and a set of principles setting certain invariant limits on their order of application, while the level immediately "below" this comprises relatively static combinatorial or classificatory forms ("morphology" and "phrase-structure"). The latter level may be subdivided into a number of strata of varying degrees of inclusiveness and prescriptive rigidity: the number of such strata varies widely from language to language, much as the number of levels of complexity of "family" structure varies from cultures where the matrifocal or mother-child unit may be a normatively sanctioned form of "family" to societies in which extended families covering several generations and collateral degrees are normal. The point is that all such morphemic and phrase-structural strata of organization are of similar logical form by contrast to the level of transformation rules immediately above them, in that they all consist of combinatorial or substitution matrices of fixed structural parameters.

The structure of language rests, as is well known, upon an even more fundamental dichotomy between the level of meaningful units (including morphemes, words, and phrases) and the level of intrinsically meaningless sound patterns (i.e., phonemes and the articulatory units of which they are composed) which constitutes the medium of spoken language. This "duality of patterning," as Hockett has called it[56], is simply the linguistic form of the most basic feature of human culture, namely the symbolic function or its complementary and equally important technological analogue, which Holloway has called the "imposition of arbitrary form."[57] The latter capacity, as Holloway points out, is the fundamental basis of human technologies, which since the early Stone Age have relied upon fashioning raw materials into tools which bear no necessary resemblance to the initial shape of the raw material.[58]

A case could be made that simple technological processes (e.g., the manufacture of stone tools) are organized in terms of a hierarchy of levels analogous to that of linguistic structure, i.e., a fundamental "duality of patterning" consisting of the technical operations appropriate to working the particular material, which themselves have no intrinsic relationship to the shape or concept of the finished tool, on the one hand, and the aspects of the tool or manufactured object that are directly related to its finished form and functional "meaning" (e.g., edge, handle, blade-face), on the other. Within the latter domain of functionally "meaningful" elements there would seem to be a further dichotomy implicit in the existence of a repertoire of tool-types or "industry" (to use the archaeological term). This is the contrast between the particular combination of elements represented by a particular tool-form (e.g., a hand-axe) and the transformational rules regulating the recombination of the same functional elements (e.g., edge, blade-face, butt) in a different combinatorial matrix (e.g., a projectile point).[59] A technological industry or material culture would appear to depend, from this point of view, upon a hierarchical system of paradig-matic forms, combinatorial operations, and transfor-mation rules analogous to that of language.

The point of interest for our present purposes is that this elementary structural pattern of basic cultural codes, such as language and technology, appears to be identical, insofar as the basic structural aspects we have considered are concerned, with the structure of the family, the domestic group, the mind, and the personality.

The structure of the family, for example, has been described as a two-level hierarchy, the lower level of which consists of the paradigmatic matrix of role relations comprising the individual family unit (with the possibility of wide variation in the complexity of role organization and substratification within this level), and the upper level consists of the transfor-mational and invariance rules governing the develop-mental cycle of this unit and its structural relations to other such units (which latter two aspects, as we have seen, come to the same thing). These two levels of family structure are formally analogous with the morphological/phrase-structural and transforma-tional levels of language structure, respectively. Like language, moreover, family and domestic group organization rest upon a fundamental "duality of patterning."

CONCLUSION

The immediate structural constituents of the social groupings and relations we have discussed in this essay are not individual persons or groups as such but role categories. Role categories thus comprise the minimal units of sociological significance in much the same sense that morphemes constitute the minimal meaningful units of language. Individual human beings *per se* are not units of social systems, and in this sense they may be said to lack sociological significance; they rather constitute the medium of social interaction, in much the same sense that sound patterns constitute the medium of spoken language.

The transformational structure of the intelligence, considered in Piagetian terms as a symbolic system, is also founded upon an analogous duality of pat-terning. In the summary of Piaget's system just given, it was mentioned that before the appearance of the symbolic function (at about one and one-half years

of age) there is a presymbolic period of development. This "sensorimotor" stage culminates in the develop-ment of clear notions of the permanence and inde-pendent existence of objects. These conceptual ob-jects become in turn the foci of the imitation and play activities out of which come the child's first spontaneous symbols.[60] The fundamentally pre-symbolic level of object-concepts remains the basic medium of the mental operations of the higher (sym-bolic) levels of the intelligence. The symbolic and presymbolic levels of the mind thus complement one another in terms formally analogous to the hierarch-ical dual patterning of the cultural and social codes we have been considering.

This brief account suffices to indicate that the model of the universal features of social and psycho-logical structure developed earlier in this paper is merely a special instance (or rather, two sets of special instances) of an even broader and more fundamental phenomenon.

It appears, in effect, that we are dealing with the fundamental structure of cultural competence: a simple system of basic structural features common to all the major domains of human cultural behavior, including the personality and intelligence (which, as in part the products of socialization, must of course themselves be considered at least partly cultural phenomena). If we are correct that the same basic structure is shared in common by the family, the domestic or socialization grouping, the personality, the mind (intelligence), and the other major cultural phenomena that have been mentioned, the attempt to explain the existence of this structure in one domain (e.g., personality) by appealing to a special dependent relationship (such as "internalization") with another domain (e.g., the family or the domestic grouping) must be taken to imply a more extended argument of the same type to account for the existence of formally identical structural patterns in other domains such as language or technology.

Such an argument could logically take two forms: either that the domain judged to be dominant in the one case (e.g., family structure) is also dominant in relation to all the others (so that, for instance, the structure of language would also be claimed to be a reflection of family structure) or that the dominant domain in the first pair in turn plays the role of depen-dent domain in relation to another domain, and so on (e.g., the structure of the family is internalized as the structure of the personality, but is in turn a reflec-tion of the structure of language, and so on. Both of these possible forms of the argument are so radically untenable in terms of existing knowledge that they may be considered refutations by *reductio ad absur-dum* of all attempts to explain the relation between personality and family structure by unicausal propositions of the type "the structure of the personality is the product of the internalization of family structure" (or vice versa).

Not that such attempts do not continue to be made. Lévi-Strauss' attempt to reduce a wide range of cultural and social phenomena to permutations of "the fundamental structures of the human mind" stands as a contemporary example.[61] The trouble with Lévi-Strauss' attempt (and other similar attempts) is, as Piaget has pointed out, that it begs the question: If everything can be reduced to the structure of the mind, where does its structure come from, and what gives it the preeminence that permits the inference that in cases of parallelism between the structure of the mind and the structures of, say, language, the family, or myth, that the former is the independent and the latter are the dependent variables?[62]

It seems reasonable to conclude, then, that to try to account for the structure of any of the major categories of culture we have considered (e.g., the family, the personality) as the projection or introjection of the structure of one or more of the others is to put the question in the wrong terms. The fundamental problem posed by our findings is to rethink the problem of structure and what it represents, in terms that can become the basis for an alternative, viable explanation for the striking parallelism between the fundamental structures of the family, the socialization grouping, the mind, and the personality. We have outlined such an alternative conception in this paper; following the lead of Marx and Piaget, we have sought to account for structural features in terms of the organizational requirements of the basic, invariant functional tasks of generativity or production (including self-reproduction) and adaptation (including self-regulation). The family and domestic group share their fundamental structural properties with the mind, the personality, and cultural codes such as language and technology not because one serves as the model or causal principle of the others but because all constitute symbolic systems with analogous functional problems, each at its own level and within its own domain.

NOTES

1. See especially, T. Parsons, R. F. Bales, and E. A. Shils, *Working Papers in the Theory of Action* (New York: The Free Press, 1953); T. Parsons, "The Incest Taboo in Relation to Social Structure and the Socialization of the Child," *British Journal of Sociology*, 5 (1954), pp. 101-117; T. Parsons, Robert F. Bales, *et al.*, *Family, Socialization and Interaction Process* (New York: The Free Press, 1955); T. Parsons, "Part I: Theoretical Perspectives," in T. Parsons, *Social Structure and Personality* (New York: The Free Press, 1964); and T. Parsons, "Kinship and the Associational Aspect of Social Structure," in F. L. K. Hsu (ed.), *Kinship and Culture* (Chicago: Aldine, 1971).

2. See R. N. Adams, "An Inquiry into the Nature of the Family," in Gertrude Dole and Robert L. Carneiro (eds.), *Essays in the Science of Culture: In Honor of Leslie White* (New York: Thomas Y. Crowell, 1960); R. T. Smith, "The Nuclear Family in Afro-American Kinship," *Journal of Comparative Family Studies*, 1 (1970), pp. 55-70; and Marion J. Levy and Lloyd A. Fallers (eds.), *Aspects of the Analysis of Family Structure* (Princeton: Princeton University Press, 1965).

3. See Smith, *op. cit.*, and Levy and Fallers, *op. cit.*

4. See Meyer Fortes, "Introduction," in Jack Goody (ed.), *The Developmental Cycle in Domestic Groups* (Cambridge: Cambridge University Press, 1958).

5. *Ibid.*, p. 2, my italics.

6. *Loc. cit.*

7. *Ibid.*, p. 12.

8. *Ibid.*, p. 8.

9. The Ashanti of Ghana. See Meyer Fortes, "Time and Social Structure," in M. Fortes (ed.), *Social Structure: Studies Presented to A. R. Radcliffe-Brown* (Oxford: Russell and Russell, 1949); M. Fortes, "Kinship and Marriage Among the Ashanti," in A. R. Radcliffe-Brown and Daryll Forde (eds.), *African Systems of Kinship and Marriage* (London: International African Institute, 1950); and M. Fortes, *Kinship and the Social Order* (Chicago: Aldine, 1969).

10. Fortes, "Introduction," in Goody (ed.), *op. cit.*, p. 2.

11. *Ibid.*, p. 9.

12. *Ibid.*, p. 2.

13. *Ibid.*, p. 12.

14. See for example, Edmund R. Leach, *Rethinking Anthropology* (London: University of London, 1961).

15. Fortes, "Kinship and Marriage Among the Ashanti," *op. cit.*, p. 278f; and Fortes, *Kinship and the Social Order*, pp. 156n., 196n, 196f.

16. See T. Turner, "Northern Kayapo Structure," *Verhandlungen des XXXVIII. Internationalen Amerikanistenkongresses*, Komissionsverlag Klaus Renner, Munchen, Band III (1971), pp. 365-372.

17. See Kathleen Gough, "The Nayars and the Definition of Marriage," *Journal of the Royal Anthropological Institute*, 89 (1959), pp. 23-34.

18. Leach, *op cit.*, pp. 105-113. See also Gough, *op cit.*

19. Fortes, "Introduction," in Goody (ed.), *op. cit.*, p. 2.

20. *Ibid.*, p. 5.

21. *Ibid.*, pp. 4-5.

22. *Ibid.*, p. 10.

23. *Ibid.*, p. 9.

24. *Ibid.*, p. 2.

25. See Claude Lévi-Strauss, "L'Analyse structurale en linguistique et en anthropologie," *Word,* 1 (1945).

26. Claude Lévi-Strauss, *Anthropologie structurale* (Paris: Plon, 1958), pp. 61-62.

27. See Claude Lévi-Strauss, *Les structures élémentaires de la parenté* (Paris: Presses Universitaires de France, 1949).

28. Claude Lévi-Strauss, "The Family," in Harry L. Shapiro (ed.), *Man, Culture and Society* (New York: Oxford University Press, 1960).

29. *Ibid.*, p. 284.

30. Parsons, Bales, *et al., op cit.*, p. 22.

31. *Ibid.,* p. 16.

32. *Ibid.*, pp. 16-17.

33. *Ibid.*, p. 18.

34. *Ibid.*, pp. 18-19.

35. *Ibid.*, p. 55.

36. See Adams, *op. cit.*

37. It should be noted that Parsons, since the publication of his major works on the family and the incest taboo, has developed the concept of the "affinal collectivity," composed of families (or more precisely "sibling groups") linked by a bond of spouse exchange. He considers this unit the minimal group capable of carrying and transmitting a culture, in short, as the elementary

unit of social organization (Parsons, "Kinship and the Associational Aspect of Social Structure," *op. cit.*). This is obviously a long step in the direction of the conception I have proposed. Parsons, however, has nowhere developed the implications of this concept for his earlier ideas on family structure. He has not, for example, attempted to formulate the nature of the relationship between the level of interfamily affinal relations and the two lower (intrafamily) levels of which his previous model of family structure was composed. As a result, the essential structural principle of the transformational character of interfamily relations is lacking in Parsons' "affinal collectivity" concept. The latter nevertheless deserves recognition as a great improvement over the "nuclear" family model of the earlier works.

38. See R. F. Bales and P. E. Slater, "Role Differentiation in Small Decision-making Groups," in Parsons, Bales, *et al.*, *op. cit.*, pp. 259-306.

39. *Ibid.*, p. 297.

40. *Loc. cit.*

41. *Ibid.*, p. 298.

42. *Ibid.*, pp. 299, 300, 303.

43. *Ibid.*, pp. 303-304.

44. See Fortes, "Introduction," in Goody (ed.), *op. cit.*, p. 2.

45. Parsons, Bales, *et al.*, *op. cit.*, p. 23.

46. *Ibid.*, p. 22.

47. See *loc. cit.*, and Parsons, "The Incest Taboo in Relation to Social Structure and the Socialization of the Child," *op. cit.*, p. 100.

48. See Morris Zelditch, Jr., "Role Differentiation in the Nuclear Family: A Comparative Study," Chapter IV, in Parsons, Bales *et al.*, *op. cit.*

49. See P. Willmott and M. Young, *Family and Class in a London Suburb* (London: Routledge & Kegan Paul, 1960).

50. This does not preclude the possibility that the parents' authority may be rigidly maintained at a higher structural level, e.g., that of the extended family or linkage.

51. Parsons, Bales, *et al.*, *op. cit.*, Ch. II.

52. See Kinji Imanishi, "Social Behavior in Japanese Monkeys, Macaca fuscata," in C. H. Southwick (ed.), *Primate Social Behavior* (New York: Van Nostrand, 1963); and D. S. Sade, "Inhibitions of Son-Mother Mating among Free-Ranging Rhesus Monkeys," *Science and Psychoanalysis*, 12 (1968).

53. For convenient summary presentations of Piaget's systems, see Jean Piaget and Barbel Inhelder, *The Psychology of the Child* (New York: Basic Books, 1969); Jean Piaget, *The Psychology of Intelligence* (New York: Harcourt, Brace, 1950); and John H. Flavell, *The Developmental Psychology of Jean Piaget* (New York: Van Nostrand Reinhold and Co. 1963).

54. See J. Piaget, "Les Relations entre l'affectivité et l'intelligence dans le dévelopment mental de l'enfant," *Bulletin Psychologique*, Paris (1953-54), pp. 7, 143-150, 346-361, 522-535, 699-701; and L. Kohlberg, "A Cognitive Developmental Analysis of Children's Sex-Role Concepts and Attitudes," in E. E. Maccoby (ed.), *The Development of Sex Differences* (Stanford: Stanford University Press, 1966).

55. See J. Piaget, *Play, Dreams and Imitation in Childhood* (New York: Norton, 1951); and Piaget, "Les Relations . . . ," *op. cit.*

56. See C. F. Hockett, "The Origin of Speech," *Scientific American* (1960).

57. See Ralph L. Holloway, "Culture: A Human Domain," *Current Anthropology*, 10 (1969), Part II.

58. *Ibid.*

59. This account of the parallelism between the structures of linguistic and technological models was suggested by Holloway's formulation but departs radically from it in several respects. The most important of these is the transformational level of the model presented here: Holloway utilized a linguistic model of a more traditional, nontransformational type.

60. See Piaget, *The Psychology of Intelligence*.

61. See Lévi-Strauss, *Anthropologie structurale*.

62. See J. Piaget, *Structuralism* (New York: Basic Books, 1971).

INDEX

A

Abilities, 249
Abstraction, 3, 50, 63–65, 170, 423
Accommodation, 211–15, 221
Achievement norms, 407–409, 758, 774, 811
Action, 125, 152, 170, 202, 248, 290–91, 451–52, 510, 515–18, 523–27n., 536–37
    components of, 4–8, 241–42
    levels of, 8–9, 16, 22n.
    process, 117
    social, 4
    system of, 5, 183, 203, 241–43
Action theory
    criticisms of, 3–7, 10, 15–19, 35, 197, 258, 273, 297–300, 355, 642–48, 676, 802, 866–69
    epistemology, 3, 27, 39–44
    frame of reference, 4–5, 139, 278
    fundamental duality, 5, 91, 93, 108–109
    metaphysical foundations, 33, 39–44, 90–122
    methodology, 51–56, 296
Activities, 802, 861, 866–71
Actor, 4, 7, 33, 106, 130, 133
Actor-situation duality, 10, 13
Adams, R. N., 432
Adaptation, 210–12
Adaptive capacity, 669–71, 737
Adaptive function, 132–33, 471
Adaptive upgrading, 214, 456
Adolescence, 377, 407–14, 438, 442
Advertising, 618
Affect, 10, 131, 148, 154, 165, 201–202, 217, 343, 616–17, 899–902
Affinal bond, 420–21, 425–28
Age, 332, 900
AGIL scheme: *see* Four-function paradigm
Agrarian societies, 746, 764–66
Alexander, H. B., 285, 288, 359
Alienation, 19, 300, 303–306, 323, 346, 368, 372, 574, 634, 723, 746, 750
Allport, Gordon W., 357
Almond, Gabriel, 369, 454, 725
Altick, R. D., 631

Ambivalence, 372, 375
Analytical aspects, 3, 39–40, 49, 105, 280, 423
Analytical realism, 3, 27–28, 33, 39, 260
Anderson, A. R., 182
Angell, Robert C., 719–24
Anomie, 300, 303, 314, 762, 768–69, 884–86
Approval, 345
Apter, David, 762
Aquinas, T., 287
Archaic societies, 271, 513, 774, 780
Archimedes, 26
Arendt, Hannah, 288, 601
Aristotle, 32, 37, 102, 283, 288, 513
Art, 132, 152, 159, 168, 176, 228, 265, 267, 520
Ascetic, 305
Ashby, W. R., 508
Ascription, 465, 671–72, 744
Aspirations, 324–25, 391–406, 410
Assimilation, 211–15, 221
Associationism, 367
Atkinson, J. W., 400
Attitude, 357–59
Audiences, 741
Ault, P. M., 633
Authoritarianism, 370, 379–81
Authority, 322, 329, 332, 342, 810, 816, 830, 836, 848, 855, 863–64, 891–92

B

Bacon, Francis, 38, 41–42, 44, 298
Bales, R. F., 42, 122, 321–22, 332, 380, 432–37, 673
Banking, 254–55, 466, 645; *see also* Media of exchange
Barber, Elinor, 779
Barnard, Chester I., 822, 863
Barter, 9, 256, 457, 646–47
BASE model, 133
Baum, Rainer C., 26–34, 400–401, 448–69, 533–56, 579–608
Beatles, 380, 546
Behavior, 170
Behavioral organism, 7, 22n., 132, 155, 160, 195, 395

The editors gratefully acknowledge the assistance of Mr. Ed Herberg in the preparation of much of this index as well as the help of Ms. Sheila Nilsson and Ms. Eileen Swinton.

Behavioral system, 132–33, 147, 203–204, 213–15, 441–44

Behaviorism, 66–67, 198, 396–97

Beliefs, 126, 147

Bellah, Robert N., 212, 272, 535–37, 580, 674–76, 695, 706, 749, 758, 763, 774, 785

Ben-David, Joseph, 803, 874–88

Bendix, Reinhard, 745, 757

Beneviste, E., 543

Benitez, J. C., 360

Bentham, Jeremy, 300

Berelson, Bernard, 648–50

Berger, Bennett, 377

Berger, Gaston, 285, 290

Berle, A. A., 650

Bidwell, Charles E., 803–804, 889–909

Biehl, K., 453

Biological organism, 203

Blau, Peter, 863

Blumer, Herbert, 66, 515, 756

Body image, 385

Bohr, Niels, 36

Boorstin, D., 615

Bourricaud, François, 460, 557–78

Braithwaite, R. B., 47, 56

Brecht, B., 347

Broom, L., 357

Brown, Roger, 152

Buber, Martin, 290

Burckhardt, J., 304

Bureaucracy, 570, 573, 758, 803, 808, 858, 863

Burke, Kenneth, 152, 273–74, 295

C

Cancian, Francesca M., 47, 324–25, 354–66

Capital, 691

Capitalism, 296–97, 305–306, 483

Cartwright, Bliss C., 467, 639–60

Cassirer, Ernst, 152, 171, 266, 281

Cathexis, 42, 99–104, 130, 164, 373

Cazeneuve, Jean, 632

Center and periphery, 571, 575–76, 727, 739–41, 788–93

Centralization, 261

Change, 15–18, 29–30, 55, 69–71, 117, 126, 404, 450, 459–60, 541, 551, 563, 596–97, 604, 662–712, 795, 876; *see also* Differentiation, Evolution

Charisma, 372, 376n., 379, 466, 478, 500n., 706, 796, 882, 885

Chicago school, 79

China, 459

Chombart de Lauwe, P., 392–94, 397

Chomsky, N., 139, 155, 175

Church, 816, 833

Cicourel, Aaron V., 139

Class, 297, 299, 885

Code, 137, 140, 144, 252, 256, 444, 461, 475, 498n., 520, 589, 599–601, 640, 789–97

Cognitive rationality, 335, 345

Cognitive systems, 266

Coleman, J., 409–12, 647

Collective behavior, 368–69, 378, 382

Collective consciousness, 310, 371

Collective representations, 146, 148

Collectivities, 8–9, 451, 805–806

Collins, Randall, 757

Colonialism, 760

Commitments: *see* Value commitments

Commonsense, 26–28

Commune movement, 413

Communication, 137, 286, 511, 534, 540–56, 616, 724

Community, 298–99

Competition, 626, 677

Complexity, 262

Complexity (or contingency) reduction, 5, 11, 251–52, 508–24, 535, 539–50, 584, 592

Comte, Auguste, 84, 558, 681, 686

Concrete structures, 451

Conflation, 582, 587, 591–92, 601–606

Conflict, 4, 16–18, 129, 145, 297, 355, 671, 677, 747, 757, 765–69

Conflict theory, 558, 560, 684–85

Consciousness, 103

Consensus, 464, 576, 725, 739, 744, 815

Conservative bias, 18–19

Consummatory passivism, 323

Contract, 299, 301, 810, 860–62

Cooley, C. H., 510, 616–17

Coordinative standards, 14

Cottle, Thomas J., 321–23, 328–53

Cowley, M., 377

Creativity, 394

Crisis, 575

Cross, H. L., 628

Crozier, M., 573–74

Cultural system, 7, 22n., 119–20, 126–27, 147, 169, 284, 291, 395, 626

definition of, 182, 266

Cultural system *(Cont.):*
  evaluative, 264–65, 269
  expressive, 131, 264–65, 269
  functional subsystems, 183–85
  and intelligence, 233–34
  moral-evaluative subsystem, 223
  normative, 131
  science, 60–61, 184–94
  universals of, 227
Cybernetic hierarchy of control, 7, 15–16, 40, 43, 55,
  68–71, 120, 126–27, 192–93, 203, 213–15, 229,
  454, 475, 572, 738, 749
Cybernetics, 14, 43, 48, 94, 99, 126, 135, 183, 196,
  212, 242, 392, 423, 559, 663–70, 718, 744, 752,
  754n., 765

D

Dahl, Robert, 643, 645, 723
Dahrendorf, Rolf, 18, 454, 684, 756, 769
Death, 783–84
Decentering, 201–202
Decision, 535, 550
De-differentiation, 83, 334–37, 372, 671, 755n.
Deep structures, 172–75, 177, 251
Defense mechanisms, 315
Definition of the situation, 143–46, 148
Deflation, 11, 166, 254, 303, 492–95, 583, 587–91,
  599–601, 633, 644–45, 731–32
de Gaulle, C., 645
Degrees of freedom, 165, 631, 671–72
De Jouvenel, B., 721
Delinquent subculture, 369, 413
Demand, 483
Democratization, 723, 748–49
Denial of reciprocity, 344
Dependency, 347
Descartes, R., 37–38, 133, 138–39, 158, 198, 287,
  290, 509
Determinism, 28
de Tocqueville, A., 288, 570–72, 576
Deutsch, Karl, 573, 576, 585, 596, 722–24
Deutscher, I., 358
Development, 262, 690–94; *see also* Evolution
Devereux, George, 267
Deviance, 143, 146, 322–23, 367–69, 407, 773,
  890
Dialectic, 7, 133, 142, 247, 290, 392–94, 400, 423,
  673–76

Differentiation, 30, 73n., 78–80, 214, 261, 335, 450–
  51, 456–67, 459–60, 478, 512, 519, 539, 601, 639,
  670, 674, 715, 724–25, 759–64, 774–80, 789, 794,
  801, 803, 808, 840–41
Diffusion, 760
Dilthey, Wilhelm, 279–80, 286, 304
Disequilibrium, 7, 11, 217, 261, 395, 684–85, 694
Disorganization, 143
Division of labor, 558, 739, 840–45
Doctor-patient relationship, 610, 773, 776, 779, 784
Dollard, J., 200, 367
Dore, R. P., 702
Douglas, Mary, 724
Drama, 271, 288
Dramatistic model, 273–74
Dreams, 141, 152–53, 159, 177, 201, 343
Dreeben, Robert, 801–802, 857–73
Drives, 203, 217–18
Dropouts, 374
Drugs, 385
Duality, 108, 443–44
Dubos, René, 775
Duncan, Hugh D., 273–75
Durkheim, Emile, 1, 3, 7, 33, 68, 73n., 126–30, 138–
  39, 146, 148, 227, 234, 247, 273, 278, 289, 295–
  304, 310–13, 325, 334, 354, 371, 383, 401, 451–
  52, 466, 548–50, 558, 562, 591, 634, 639, 662,
  681, 686, 690, 694, 743, 759, 785, 884, 904
Dynamics, 7, 16, 93, 109, 121, 183, 423

E

Early modern societies, 271
Easton, David, 483
Eberhard, W., 764
Ecological fallacy, 453
Economic action, 451, 460–62, 539
Economics, 449, 452
Economy, 299, 480–86
Edelson, Marshall, 131, 141–42, 147–48, 151–181
Education, 626, 748, 800–801, 816–19
Effectiveness, 303, 459, 462, 813
Effrat, Andrew, 323, 662–80, 800–804
Ego, 160–61, 172, 311, 324, 332, 337, 343, 372–75,
  383, 386, 389, 438
Ego-alter paradigm, 29, 42
Egocentric, 205–206, 219
Ego-ideal, 160, 311, 344
Eibl-Eibesfeldt, I., 43

Einstein, Albert, 37, 233, 283, 594
Eisenstadt, S. N., 377, 666, 677, 785, 788
Eliade, Mircea, 285
Eliot, T. S., 440
Elites, 716, 725–28, 745, 748, 792–94
Ellul, Jacques, 87
Emancipation, 301–302
Emergence-constitution process, 283–93
Emerson, Alfred, 152
Empirical system, 5, 260, 829
Empirical theory, 260–63
Empiricism, 3, 36–41, 43, 158, 298
Enculturation, 313
Engels, Friedrich, 305, 693
Enlightenment, 300
Entrepreneurs, 705, 796
Entropy, 137, 541–43, 664, 674
Environment, 5, 6, 53, 67, 133, 216, 241, 248, 262,
    449, 664, 669–72, 806
Epistemology, 39, 302
Equilibrium, 7, 22n., 34, 42–43, 52, 254, 261, 301,
    392, 423, 439, 501n., 662–63, 676, 682–84, 689
Erasmus, 298
Erikson, Erik H., 322, 377, 673
Ethnic group, 723
Ethnomethodology, 147, 198, 231, 236
Etzioni, Amitai, 75, 84, 87–88, 718, 730, 863
Etzkowitz, H., 88
Evaluative standard, 169
Evaluative systems, 266
Evans-Pritchard, E., 780
Evolution, 7, 16, 44, 212, 225–26, 450, 459–60, 512–
    15, 519–21, 523, 525–27, 538–39, 552, 662, 668–
    72, 676, 739, 760, 773–87, 803, 878–79, 887n.;
    see also Change, Development, Modernization
  and assimilation, 214–15
  of culture, 227–28, 270–76n.
  and media, 232
  stages of, 262
Evolutionary universals, 225, 670, 723, 770n.
Exchange, 345
Existential beliefs, 804
Existential systems, 266
Expectations, 221–25, 313–14, 317–18, 320, 356, 510
Experience, 248–49, 251–52, 260–63, 284–86, 292–
    93, 510, 515–18, 523, 525–27, 536–37, 546, 607n.
Explanation, 30, 46
  teleological, 47–48, 51–52
Expressive action, 169, 331–32, 371
Expressive symbolism, 131–32, 154, 219–20, 264–
    76, 379

F

Fact, 27–28, 59, 77, 158
Factors of production, 452, 456, 476, 482–83
Factual order, 92
Fairbairn, W. R. D., 162
Faith, 277, 281
Fallacy of misplaced concreteness: *see* Reification
Family, 319–21, 328, 332, 339, 415–46, 675, 776–77,
    793
Fantasy, 168, 337, 344–45
Fararo, Thomas J., 32–34, 90–122, 127–28, 182–94
Fascism, 706–707
Fatalism, 782
Fénélon, 513
Fiduciary institutions, 314, 823–24
Fischer, G., 725
Flation, 254
Flavell, John, 204
Force, 464, 561–62
Formal-categorial sector, 225, 228–29
Formal operations, 218–21
Fortes, M., 418–31, 434, 439
Four-function paradigm, 6–7, 30, 33, 40, 53–55, 60,
    73–74n., 110–17, 126, 134–35, 149n., 198, 210–
    11, 243, 449, 455, 458, 540, 543, 687–88, 715–16,
    740
  and aspirations, 395–97, 401, 404
  and BASE paradigm, 291–93
  and behavioral system, 216–31
  and change, 459, 665, 692–93, 697–98
  criticisms of, 471–73
  and cultural level, 61
  and general action level, 395
  inherent tensions, 61–73
  and interchange paradigm, 255–60, 471
  and mass media, 622
  and media, 252
  and organizations, 801, 805–28, 866
  and pattern variables, 11–15
  and personality types, 404
  and phase movements, 322, 332–52, 673
  and Piaget, 210–11
  and sanctions paradigm, 10
  and school, 835–40
  scientific system, 61–74, 185–93
  and social problems, 19
  and societal types, 401–404
  and space/time, 349, 587
  and symbolization, 160
  and types of assimilation, 214–15

Four-function paradigm *(Cont.):*
   and value commitments, 401–404, 594–99
Fox, Renée C., 668, 675, 773–87
Frame of reference, 124
France, 570–75
Freud, Anna, 153
Freud, Sigmund, 1, 3, 42–43, 130–31, 151–76, 200–
   202, 218, 264, 267, 291, 303–17, 334, 340, 354,
   367, 373, 377, 407, 441–42, 451, 666
Fromm, Erich, 84
Frye, Northrop, 276
Function, 6, 30, 54, 210, 455, 538, 541, 682–83, 687,
   692, 832, 866
   and form, 270
   manifest and latent, 52
Functional analysis, 6, 8, 47, 73n., 196, 278, 683
   logic of explanation, 29, 46–58
   in Marx, 18
   methodology, 46–58
   popular, 29, 48–51
   technical, 29

G

Galbraith, John K., 304
Galileo, 283
Galtung, J., 719–22, 729
Gans, H. J., 614
Garfinkel, Harold, 139, 222, 231
Geertz, Clifford, 126, 737, 766
Gehlke, C. E., 453
Gemeinschaft, 300, 598, 601–604, 686, 759
General action level, 7, 125–26, 134, 272
   behavioral organism, 195, 203
   behavioral system, 215–36
   and experience, 248–49
   and language, 140
   media, 10
Generalization, process of, 16, 215, 520–23, 646–48,
   666, 672–73
Generalized media: *see* Media of exchange
Generation, 427
Generativity, 140–41, 416
Genetic epistemology, 199–201, 204
Germany, 601–604, 762, 769
Gesellschaft, 300, 598, 601–604, 686, 759
Gierke, O. v., 303
Gift exchange, 218
Ginsberg, Alan, 381, 387, 389

Gluckman, Max, 270
Goal, 4, 7, 497n., 812, 833, 845, 869–70
Goal attainment, 132, 806
   at general action level, 130–32
Goffman, Erving, 295, 584–85
Goods and services, 451–52
Gordon, C., 399
Gould, Mark, 258, 260, 456, 458, 466, 470–506, 548
Gouldner, Alvin W., 18, 75, 84, 88
Great Britain, 717
Greek tradition, 513
Group
   reality of, 71–72
   self-analytic, 328–53
Growth, 685, 691–92

H

Habermas, Jürgen, 139
Hagstrom, Warren O., 183, 884
Halbwachs, M., 392
Hanson, R. D., 730
Harding, J., 358
Hartmann, Heinz, 153, 159, 164, 166
Hartshorne, E. Y., 358
Harvey, E., and Harvey, L., 399
Hegel, G., 19, 296–305, 483, 507, 516
Heinemann, F. H., 287
Heisenberg, Werner, 35–39, 43, 283
Hemingway, E., 272
Hempel, C., 47, 56
Henderson, L. J., 158
Hermeneutics, 131
Hesse, H., 387, 389
Hierarchical structure, 261
Hierarchy of control: *see* Cybernetic hierarchy of
   control
Hills, R. Jean, 800, 802, 829–56
Hippies, 323–24, 370, 377–90, 413
Hirschman, A., 562–63, 567–68, 573
Historicism, 69, 133, 279–80, 296, 300
Hobbes, Thomas, 4, 41, 129, 261, 295–308, 507–509,
   520, 561, 651, 872
Hockett, C. F., 443
Hoffer, E., 368, 374
Holloway, R. L., 443
Holmberg, Allan, 88
Homans, George C., 26, 31, 357, 359, 453, 651
Homeostasis, 662–63

Humboldt, Wilhelm, 878
Hume, David, 101
Huntingdon, S., 725
Husserl, E., 280–81, 284, 286, 304, 526
Huygens, 27

I

Id, 43, 153, 160–61, 172, 217–18, 311, 332, 337, 342
Idealism, 3, 67–69, 198, 279, 296–97, 300
Ideal type, 3, 280, 286, 296–97
Identification, 315
Identity, 303, 321, 383, 385
    sex, 384, 388–89
Ideology, 63, 300, 405, 617, 630–35, 736–55, 786
Illich, Ivan, 87
Illness, 773–87, 891
Inadequacy, 407–14
Inclusion, 214, 335–39, 342, 346, 456, 672–73,
    716
Income, 481
Indeterminacy, 26, 28
Individualism, 297–305
Individualist fallacy, 453
Individuation, 331, 343
Industrialization, 685–86, 695–710
Inertia, 664, 689
Inflation, 11, 166, 253–54, 303, 492–95, 569, 582,
    588–91, 599–601, 643–45, 731–32, 817
Influence, 163, 464, 516, 549, 552–53, 590, 609–16,
    814–15
Information, 534, 547
Inhelder, B., 201–202
Instinct, 162–66
Institution, 68, 74n., 824, 841–45
Institutionalization, 127, 129, 144–45, 325, 667
Instrumental activism, 32, 321, 323, 408, 413–14,
    668, 677, 774, 778, 811
Instrumental-consummatory axis, 6–7, 13, 114, 136,
    169, 241–47, 305, 331–32, 434–49, 543
Integration, 136, 261, 354, 464–65, 639, 672, 722–23,
    747–52, 759, 765–68, 791, 810–11, 835; *see also*
        Solidarity
    at general action level, 128–29
Integrity, 465, 816, 837
Intellectuals, 565, 568
Intelligence, 133, 146, 148, 199–239, 441–44
    development of, 204–10, 213
Interaction, 4, 129, 142–46, 222, 234–36, 249–51, 313

Interchange paradigm, 7–11, 127, 134, 142, 184, 255–
    60, 303, 449, 456–59, 470–508, 521–33, 534,
    547–48, 581, 612, 616, 619, 645, 659n., 688–89,
    731–32, 807, 823, 830, 850–55
    and change, 697–710
    at cultural level, 191–93
    and personality system, 396
Interests, 41, 300–301, 304, 453–54, 457, 619
Internal dynamics, 117
Internal-external axis, 6, 13, 110, 241–47, 434, 475–
    76
Internalization, 127, 130–31, 313, 325, 354–55, 415,
    432
International relations, 713–35
Interpretation, 151–81, 219–21
Intrinsic satisfiers, 165, 462

J

Jackson, D. D., 43
Jackson, J., 852, 861–62
Jacobson, Edith, 137, 153
James, William, 157
Japan, 694–710, 756, 762, 790, 794
Jarvie, I., 47
Johnson, Harry M., 356, 465, 609–38
Jung, C. G., 350

K

Kaiser, Karl, 718, 724
Kant, Immanuel, 38, 287, 302, 332, 524, 553
Kaplan, Abraham, 35
Keats, John, 153
Kelly, George, 44n.
Kenkel, W. F., 358
Kerouac, J., 389
Kesey, K., 380, 387, 389
Keynes, J. M., 256, 303, 463, 480, 485, 551,
    694
Kinship: *see* Family
Klein, Melanie, 159
Kluckhohn, Florence, 359
Knowledge, 282, 297–98, 514
Koestler, A., 369
Kohlberg, Lawrence, 87, 225
Kohn, M., 359

Krasner, P., 380, 387
Kris, Ernst, 153, 159, 168
Kuhn, Thomas, 189, 276n., 282, 884
Kuznets, S., 496, 589

L

Labelling, 143
Labor, 474, 483, 691, 703
Land, 472, 474, 691
Landsberger, Henry, 866–68
Langer, Suzanne, 64, 152, 154, 159, 164, 168–69, 172, 175
Language, 137–42, 147–55, 166, 226, 252, 337, 204–207, 461, 511–14, 533, 583, 640, 654, 672–74
La Pierre, R. T., 358
Lauderdale, P., 359
Law, 298–99, 301, 334, 624–25, 674, 908n.
Lazarsfeld, P., 648
Leach, E., 140
Leadership, 380
Learning, 116, 200, 516
Leary, T., 380–81
Leavy, Stanley, 153
LeBon, Gustave, 368
Legitimacy, 68, 300, 303, 726
Legitimation, 129, 395, 302, 312, 465–66, 498n., 554, 619, 644, 788, 808–10, 818, 830, 835, 855
Lenin, V. I., 19, 571, 631
Levi-Strauss, C., 140, 152, 227, 425–26, 428, 439, 445, 780
Levy, Marion J., Jr., 744
Liberalism, 254, 297, 301
Libido, 130, 166, 170
Lidz, Charles W., 132–33, 146–47, 195–239, 448
Lidz, Victor M., 26–34, 124–50, 195–239, 448, 592, 778, 783
Life cycle, 423–25
Linder, S. B., 588
Lindsay, Robert, 634
Linguistics, 131, 141, 443, 543
Lipset, Seymour Martin, 717, 768
Locke, J., 297–304
Loewald, Hans, 153, 161
Loewenstein, Rudolph, 153
Lofgren, Lars Borje, 153
Lofland, John, 369
Lortie, Dan, 861, 864, 870

Loubser, Jan J., 1–23, 27, 30, 32, 51, 75–89, 134–36, 240–63, 465, 666, 673, 801
Love, 513–14, 516, 523
Luhmann, Niklas, 134, 290, 457, 507–32, 536–37, 540–41, 550–52, 554, 580, 582–83, 592
Lundberg, George, 66
Lustman, Seymour, 153
Luther, Martin, 305
Lynd, Robert S., 79

M

Machiavelli, 519
MacKay, D., 511
Macko, D., 193
MacRae, Duncan, Jr., 75
Magic, 777, 780
Malinowski, B., 273–78, 425, 777
Malthus, T., 557, 686
Managerial level, 822–23, 840–45
Mannheim, Karl, 282, 723, 742–43, 761
Marcuse, Herbert, 87, 304, 483
Marginality, 384
Market, 135, 457–58
Markov chain, 122
Marriage, 421
Marshall, Alfred, 278, 289, 313, 483
Marx, Karl, 18–19, 67, 84, 129–30, 281, 295–306, 394, 440, 445, 452–54, 480, 494, 499n., 501n., 505n., 507, 517, 557, 570, 588, 631, 634, 681–82, 686, 690, 695, 743, 752, 757
Mass media, 270, 609–38
Mass movements, 376n.
Materialism, 39, 68
Mathematical models, 32, 38–39, 90
Matza, D., 146
Mayhew, Leon, 27, 30, 59–74, 667–68
McCarthyism, 592, 601, 614, 634, 642, 645, 649, 685
McClelland, D. C., 599
McLuhan, Marshall, 270, 279, 295
McQuail, D., 625
Mead, George Herbert, 63, 66, 71–72, 130, 138–39, 206, 313, 315, 452, 510, 583, 587
Meaning, 4, 6, 27, 67, 125–26, 131–38, 144, 146, 154, 159, 163, 166, 169–76, 183, 198, 201, 206–207, 221, 266, 281, 285–91, 296–305, 369, 452, 536–39, 543, 774
Means-end scheme, 4–7, 29, 41, 47, 51–52

Media of exchange, 6–11, 138, 141–42, 147, 155, 159,
        165–66, 171, 174, 203, 252–55, 303, 448–79, 483,
        507–27, 533–56, 579–608, 639–60, 672, 753n.,
        791, 803, 848; *see also* Banking, Deflation,
        Inflation, Influence, Interchange paradigm,
        Money, Power, Value commitments
    analytical aspects, 545
    behavioral organism, 133, 195, 202
    and change, 16
    circulation of, 645
    flation of, 11
    general action level, 10, 14, 144–48, 255–60,
        448
    intelligence, 231–36
    and interchange paradigm, 255–60
    and psychoanalytic theory, 162–66
    security base, 252
    social system level, 448, 460–68
    societal level, 10
Medicine, 773–87, 815, 890–94
Memory, 201
Mendelsohn, H., 633
Merleau-Ponty, M., 285–86
Merton, Robert K., 29, 46–50, 53, 64, 182, 186–88,
        303, 362, 779, 884
Mesarovic, M. D., 193
Message, 140, 144
Meta-theory, 25–122
Methodological individualism, 296
Methodology, 37
    dilemmas, 59–74
    of functionalism, 46–58
Meyer, J. W., 363
Mill, J. S., 302
Millenarian movement, 322–24, 367–80
Miller, N. E., 200, 367
Mills, C. Wright, 75, 84, 557, 643, 649–
        50
Milton, John, 298
Mind, 139
Minsky, Marvin, 44n.
Mobilization, 487, 729–30, 768
Modalities, 11, 13, 33, 106, 109, 116–17, 120
Modelski, G., 714
Modernization, 564, 604, 674–75, 718, 725, 737, 741,
        744–52, 756–58, 774, 788–97
    partial, 756–72
Money, 10–11, 148, 152, 163, 453, 457, 461–62, 484–
        85, 501n., 516–17, 523, 533, 537, 552, 561, 589,
        604, 640–43
Moore, G. E., 62

Moore, O. K., 182
Moral authority, 129, 466, 816, 832–33
Moral judgment, 223–25
Morphemes, 444
Morris, Charles W., 154
Motivation, 22n., 130–32, 136, 202, 217, 219, 242–43,
        312, 317, 391, 395–96, 398
Musgrove, F., 409
Music, 73n., 386
Myrdal, Gunnar, 719
Myth, 140, 285–86, 535

N

Nader, Ralph, 631
Nagel, Ernest, 47–48
Nationalism, 601, 705–709, 721, 730, 747, 752, 761–
        62
Naziism, 649, 677, 685, 769
Needs, 392–400
Nettl, J. P., 725–26
Newman, Richard, 153
Newton, Isaac, 27–28, 829
Nietzsche, F., 296, 304
Nixon, Raymond B., 634
Nominalism, 3, 27–28, 39, 302
Non-functional variables, 260–63
Non-rational factors, 6
Normative upgrading, 456, 666
Norms, 8–9, 43, 68, 92, 113, 116, 129, 142–46, 169–
        70, 222, 242, 278, 311–12, 325–26, 333, 354–66,
        394, 510, 528n., 759, 849
    and behavior, 358–63
    change of, 361
    membership, 355–56, 361–62
    ranking, 355–62
    reality assumptions, 355–56, 361–63
    of science, 186–89, 235

O

Object representations, 162–65
Objectivity, 28, 77, 79
Occasions, 33, 103, 120
O'Dea, Thomas F., 133–34, 142, 277–94
Oedipus complex, 334, 340–41, 350, 432, 437, 668
Office, 464

Ogden, C. K., 152
Olds, James, 264
O'Neill, John, 129, 295–308
Ontology, 28, 71–72, 159, 297
Open system, 7, 30, 55, 71, 262, 664
Operationalization, 135
Opportunity, 484
Order: *see* Problem of order
Organism, 52, 58n.
Organization, 38, 68–69, 262, 691, 791, 800–73
    levels of, 819–28, 840–45, 867
Orientation, 5, 11, 13, 33, 42, 106, 109, 113, 120, 136,
    250, 268, 305
Oversocialized actor, 310–12, 325

P

Pareto, Vilfredo, 3, 44, 278, 289, 313, 451, 466, 652,
    686, 690
Parsons, Ann, 209
Parsons, Talcott, *passim.*, not indexed
Pattern, 93, 97, 100
Pattern maintenance, 136, 471–74, 542
    at general action level, 126–27
Pattern variables, 7, 11–15, 22n., 33, 85, 91–92, 106–
    19, 134–35, 160, 244, 250, 675, 725, 754n., 759,
    776, 804, 897, 900
    and four-function paradigm, 247
    and media, 10, 241–60
    and phase movements, 335
    and socialization, 316
Peacock, James L., 131–32, 264–76
Perceptual sector, 216–19
Performance capacity, 148
Perrow, Charles, 870
Personality system, 7, 22n., 130–32, 142, 148,
    151, 160–61, 169, 171, 200, 217–20, 311,
    315, 395
    and aspirations, 395–96
    and collective behavior, 368
    definition, 203
    development of, 315–19
    and expressive symbols, 267
    and family structure, 415
    identity subsystem, 230
    media, 163
    types, 398–99
Peru, 561–70
Peterson, T., 620

Phase movements, 17, 242, 322, 326–27n., 333–52,
    475–76, 673
Phenomenology, 125, 133, 137, 147–48, 198, 236,
    280, 285, 296, 305, 307n., 361
Philosophy of science, 47–48, 59
Piaget, Jean, 27–29, 132–33, 146–47, 152–58, 175,
    195–239, 321, 417, 441–45
Pious, William, 153, 177
Pitts, Jesse R., 322–24, 367–90
Plato, 288, 290, 296, 513
Play, 206
Pluralism, 261, 650
Policy decision, 502n.
Politics, 288, 295, 462–64, 557–78, 760
Polity, 486–92, 716–17, 721, 725–30, 759, 762–63,
    806–809; *see also* State
Popper, Karl, 47
Populism, 563–64
Positivism, 3, 28, 35, 41, 66–68, 158, 289, 296–98
Postmodern society, 783–85
Power, 152, 163, 448, 462–64, 486–95, 503n., 514,
    517, 523, 553, 557–78, 639–56, 768, 807, 824,
    831, 848, 858
Praxis, 298, 394
Prediction, 30
Prestige, 465
Price, 452
Primary group, 617
Primitive society, 270–71, 535, 674, 761–63, 766,
    774, 788, 791
Primordial ties, 768
Problem of meaning, 278
Problem of order, 4, 17, 55, 70, 129–30, 142, 145,
    295–308
Problem selection, 76–79, 85
Process, 30, 98, 103–104, 455, 663
Product, 479–80
Profession, 534, 627–28, 675, 723, 779, 794, 803, 810
    874–909
Protestant ethic, 408, 668, 795
Psychic reality, 155–67, 176
Psychoanalysis, 151–81, 311–13, 330, 332,
    397
Psychology, 199–201
Psychotherapy, 319, 367, 375, 777, 864

Q

Quantum physics, 36, 38

R

Racism, 19, 88
Radcliffe-Brown, A. R., 425–26
Radical movements, 368, 745
Radical sociology, 18–19, 75, 81–82, 84, 88
Rapaport, David, 153
Rational action, 6, 295–302, 304, 306, 378, 450–51,
    551, 599, 811, 889
  moral, 466
Rationalism, 38–40, 130, 297, 303, 305
Rationalization, 674–75, 693, 737, 758–60
Realism, 3, 27, 39, 69
Reality, structure of, 93–100, 155
Reductionism, 4–5, 18, 200, 203, 367, 454
Reference group approach, 360
Reflexivity, 524
Reform, 563–70
Reformation, 536
Regression, 337–39, 349–50, 368–72, 383–85
Reification, 3, 5, 17–18, 39, 422–23
Relativity, 26, 28, 36, 38
Relevance, 547
Religion, 228, 273, 277–80, 289, 674, 762–63, 771n.,
    780, 786
Religious conversion, 369
Religious symbolism, 285
Rescher, Nicholas, 30
Resistance, 246
Resources, 8–9, 11, 15–16, 162, 263, 460, 830
Revolution, 342, 565, 572
Ricardo, D., 686
Richards, I. A., 152
Rickert, H., 527n.
Riesman, D., 414
Rites, 270–71, 419, 778
Ritual, 535
Ritvo, Samuel, 153
Rivers, W. L., 614–15, 627–32
Robertson, Roland, 665, 670, 675, 713–35
Robinson, W. S., 453
Rocher, Guy, 324–25, 391–406
Rogers, D. I., 632
Rokkan, Stein, 726–27
Role, 8–9, 42, 71–72, 130–31, 331, 312–19, 315, 328,
    331, 333, 343–45, 360, 377, 444, 585
Role specialization, 334, 348, 432–33
Rosenberg, M., 399
Rosenthal, Alan, 858
Ross, Edward A., 768
Rostow, W. W., 690
Rudd, M., 413

Rudner, R., 47, 56
Rueschemeyer, Dietrich, 671, 675, 677, 736–72
Russell, B., 288
Russia, 790–93

S

Sacks, Harvey, 139
Saenger, G., 358
Saint-Simon, 557, 681, 686, 704
Samuelson, Paul, 452, 683, 690
Sanctions paradigm, 10–11, 134, 163–66, 200, 250–
    52, 314–18, 325, 355–57, 544–45, 549, 560, 653–
    55, 864
Sapir, Edward, 152
Sartori, G., 721
Sartre, J., 387
Saussure, F., 137, 206
Sauvy, A., 557, 559
Saving, 480
Scarcity, 263
Schafer, Roy, 153
Schemata, 132–33, 146, 196–217, 221, 227, 229, 441–
    42
Scheuch, E., 453–54, 588
Schizophrenia, 43, 389
School, 316–18, 409, 800–801, 816–19, 829–73, 899–
    902
Schramm, W., 614–15, 620, 627–32
Schumpeter, Joseph, 448, 455–56, 538, 549, 689
Schur, Max, 161, 173
Schütz, A., 286–87
Schwanenberg, Enno, 27–29, 34–45
Science, 30, 32, 35, 38, 59–74, 77–82, 84–85, 127–28,
    149n., 184–94, 306, 758, 774, 803, 874–88
Scott, J. F., 22n.
Scott, W. R., 863
Secondary institution, 367
Sect, 367
Security base, 462
Segmentation, 261, 671, 764–66
Self, 71–72, 130, 138, 149n., 164, 394, 400
Self-concept, 399
Selznick, P., 357
Sensori-motor behavior, 204–205
Sewell, W., 404
Sex, 332
  identity, 320
  roles, 331, 333–35, 338–42, 388–89, 434–35
Shakespeare, William, 453

Shils, Edward A., 264, 322, 649
Sibley, Elbridge, 75
Sick role, 388, 773–77, 892–93
Siebert, F. S., 620
Significance, 546
Signification, 138, 141, 176–77
Signs, 154–65, 175–76, 196, 206–207
Simmel, Georg, 292, 768
Singer, J. D., 714
Situation, 4, 7, 33, 107, 144–45, 160, 162, 248, 278, 868
Sjoberg, Gideon, 73n.
Slabbert, F. van Zyl, 27–30, 46–58
Slater, Philip, 332, 340, 432–37
Small group, 431–49
Smelser, Neil J., 11, 15–16, 54, 182–84, 193, 212, 369, 378, 450–60, 470–74, 550, 558, 579, 582, 592, 599, 645, 648, 665–69, 672, 676, 731
Smith, Adam, 295, 305
Social action, 260–63
Social contract, 41
Social control, 71–72, 318, 367, 890–91
Social identity approach, 354, 360–63
Social emotional specialist, 433
Social organization, 143
Social science, 30, 59–82
    boundaries, 124
Social structure, 129, 330
Social system, 7, 22n., 124, 128–29, 395, 663, 806
    components of, 8–9
Socialism, 303, 748, 752
Socialization, 44, 66, 130, 310–27, 368, 408, 415–46, 834, 864–65, 899
    generative approach, 416–17
    and hippie movement, 377–90
    resocializing agency, 375, 778
    theory of socialized actor, 354–63
Societal community, 473, 618, 716, 722, 747
Society, 713–15, 730, 824
    fiduciary subsystem, 229
    typology of, 595–99
Sociolinguistics, 147
Socrates, 298
Solidarity, 148, 218–19, 303–304, 464, 610, 740, 746, 779, 814–15, 893
    mechanical/organic, 7, 73n., 299, 302, 401, 549, 686
Solnit, Albert, 153
Sombart, Warner, 690
Sorokin, Pitirim A., 686
Space, 135, 263, 584–87
Specification processes, 16, 667

Spencer, Herbert, 302, 681, 686
Stability, 70, 261, 512
Stage, 672–76, 686
State, 300–301, 726–28
State variables, 135, 260–63
Status, 250, 335, 356, 381
Stevens, Wallace, 151–53, 155, 158–59, 168, 178
Stinchcombe, Arthur L., 643, 645
Stone, Leo, 153
Storer, Norman, 187, 193
Strain, 297, 459, 523, 664–65, 668, 678n., 723, 729, 742–43, 751, 759, 765–69, 890, 894, 898
Stratification, 720, 747–49, 767, 791–94
Strodtbeck, Fred L., 359
Structuralism, 140, 196–98, 870
Structure, 30, 36–38, 68–71, 116, 328, 423, 455, 496n., 682–84, 687, 691
    deep and surface, 140–45, 153, 174–75, 416, 251–52
    levels of, 8–9, 258–60
Studentry, 377, 408
Subculture
    bohemian, 377–78
Subjectivism, 65–67
Suicide, 383, 550
Superego, 131, 160–61, 172, 202, 222–25, 310–11, 332–37, 344, 372–73, 383, 431
Support, 493, 619
Suttles, Gerald, 145
Symbolic interactionism, 72, 125, 143, 147, 273, 360
Symbolization, 131–32, 152, 159–76, 201, 207, 272, 674
Symbols, 126, 147, 151–55, 163–65, 169–77, 196, 206–207, 264, 393, 654–55
System, 33, 94, 121, 198, 454, 497n., 510, 512, 538, 541, 683
    analytical, 17, 104–106
    concept of, 16
    concrete, 17, 104–106
    open, 124, 166
    reference, 54
Szymanski, Albert, 84

T

Takada, Yasuma, 690
Takahara, Y., 193
Task, 290
Task leader, 433

Tax, Sol, 88

Technical level, 820–22, 840–45

Technology, 690–91, 699, 802, 861, 869–70

Theory, 37, 61, 64, 498n.
  construction, 3, 10, 64–65, 77, 134–35, 451
  definition, 2
  framework, 77
  gnosiological approach, 27
  middle-range, 29, 49–50, 183, 753n.

Third World, 729

Thomas, W. I., 42, 143–44, 148, 231

Tiger, Lionel, 334

Tillich, Paul, 277, 281

Time, 135, 206, 347–50, 394–97, 586–87

Toby, Jackson, 321, 407–14

Toennies, F., 686

Tolstoi, Leo, 32, 306

Tominaga, Ken'ichi, 665, 681–712

Total institutions, 370, 373, 379–81

Touraine, A., 394

Toynbee, Arnold, 686

Transference, 167–68, 330, 345–46, 904

Transformational linguistics, 139–40, 151, 197, 226
  and model of family structure, 422–23, 427–45

Transformational processes, 141–46, 172, 175, 416–17

Troeltsch, E., 279–80, 283

True believer, 368, 379

Trust, 165–66, 252, 512, 550, 553, 583–84, 590–91, 635n., 644, 738–39, 753n., 803, 817, 890–909

Truth, 613–16, 523

Tumin, Melvin, 763

Turner, Terrence S., 320–21, 415–16, 535, 580

Turner, Victor, 266

U

Ultimate reality, 120–21, 774

Uncertainty, 536–37, 552

Underdevelopment, 558

Unit act, 13, 134, 241–47, 297

Universalism, 19, 63, 268, 882

Universities, 868, 876–78, 886

Utilitarianism, 4, 41, 296, 300–304, 314

Utility, 460, 813

Utopianism, 724

V

Value-added model, 16, 242, 246, 452, 478, 479, 499n., 545–47, 558, 665–70

Value freedom, 62–63, 76, 78

Value neutrality, 18–19, 62–63, 75, 77, 79

Value relevance, 62–63, 73n., 76, 78, 81

Values, 8–9, 14, 40–43, 66–67, 82–86, 302–303, 323, 354–56, 368, 459–60, 497n., 553, 592–601, 668, 737–38, 744, 749, 763, 801–802, 809–11, 816, 835–37, 845, 866, 872; *see also* Ideology
  change of, 666, 720
  commitments, 465, 474, 478, 832–33
  deflation-inflation, 82–83
  generalization of, 83–86, 456, 774
  innovation in, 82–83
  occupational, 399
  patterns of, 84–86
  primacy of, 262
  of science, 186–88
  in social science, 61–63, 75–89
  standards, 169

Veblen, Thorstein, 690

Verba, S., 454

Verification, 65–67

Verstehen, 31, 65, 133, 147, 280, 284, 286, 296, 306

Voluntarism, 3–7, 12–13, 19, 41, 51–52, 139, 146, 242, 278, 507, 663

von Weizsäcker, C. F., 26

Voting, 647, 650–51

W

Wallace, W. L., 360

Warner, R. Stephen, 467, 639–60

Watts, A., 380

Watzlawick, Paul, 43

Weber, Max, 1, 3, 18–19, 32–33, 42, 62–63, 73n., 75–79, 85, 125, 129, 152–53, 198, 202, 273, 278–90, 295–96, 299, 301, 304–306, 313, 450–52, 459–60, 466, 474, 478, 499n.–500n., 527n., 535, 554, 604, 641, 662, 705–706, 737, 757–61, 789, 858, 863, 882

Wexler, Henry, 153

White, Winston, 631

Whitehead, Alfred N., 2–3, 33, 38–40, 42–44, 93–105, 117–21, 157, 184–98

Whorf, B. L., 152

Williams, Robin M., 602

Willmott, P., 435
Wish, 173
World society, 525–27

Y

Yablonsky, Lewis, 380
Yippie, 303
Young, Michael, 435

Young, O. R., 730
Youth culture, 321, 323, 367, 401, 405, 409

Z

Zarate, A. O., 763
Zen Buddhism, 380
Zenger, J. P., 624
Zero-sum concept, 254–55, 466, 640, 643–44, 649–50